I0084435

Lucius R. Paige.

HISTORY

OF

HARDWICK

MASSACHUSETTS

WITH A

GENEALOGICAL REGISTER

Lucius R. Paige

HERITAGE BOOKS
2014

HERITAGE BOOKS

AN IMPRINT OF HERITAGE BOOKS, INC.

Books, CDs, and more—Worldwide

For our listing of thousands of titles see our website
at
www.HeritageBooks.com

A Facsimile Reprint
Published 2014 by
HERITAGE BOOKS, INC.
Publishing Division
5810 Ruatan Street
Berwyn Heights, Md. 20740

— Publisher's Notice —
In reprints such as this, it is often not possible to remove blemishes from the original. We feel the contents of this book warrant its reissue despite these blemishes and hope you will agree and read it with pleasure.

International Standard Book Numbers
Paperbound: 978-0-7884-5527-8
Clothbound: 978-0-7884-0021-6

To

THE MEMBERS OF THE

MASSACHUSETTS HISTORICAL SOCIETY,

AND OF THE

NEW ENGLAND HISTORIC GENEALOGICAL SOCIETY,

This Volume

IS DEDICATED BY ITS AUTHOR,

THEIR ASSOCIATE.

PREFACE.

FROM an early period I have been deeply interested in the history of Hardwick, and in the genealogy of its inhabitants; — the more deeply, doubtless, because my own ancestors were among the early pioneers, were actively engaged in the management of public affairs and by numerous intermarriages were connected with so many of its families. Although I have been a non-resident and comparative stranger for more than fifty-six years, my attachment to my native town has never grown cold; but its rocks and hills are still viewed with almost childish delight, whenever I visit them, and many of my old friends, though personally departed, are represented by worthy descendants, who are beloved for the fathers' sake. As I had opportunity, from time to time, I have gathered and preserved historical materials, intending to embody them in a permanent form. Other and imperative engagements intervened, and prevented the execution of my purpose until now: so that what I originally designed to be my first literary labor, of any considerable magnitude, has become absolutely the last; for at the age of eighty-one years it is altogether too late to commence another task requiring much time for its completion.

The materials embraced in this history were gathered from various sources; among the most important of which were the Records of the Proprietors, of the Church, and of the Town, of Hardwick, including the Registry of Births and Deaths by the Town Clerk, and of Baptisms from the beginning, and of Deaths since 1789, recorded by the several Pastors of the Church, and supplemented by inscriptions on monuments and head-stones in the several cemeteries. Besides these, I consulted such printed authorities as were within my reach, including files of newspapers; the manuscript records of the General Court; the vast collection of original papers in the Archives of Massachusetts; the Court Records, and Registries of Probate and of Deeds in several counties, — not only in Worcester, but in Bristol, Plymouth, and Barnstable, — and the records of many towns in those counties, from which came so many of the early inhabitants of Hardwick; and also the records of Bennington and Barnard in Vermont, which towns were originally settled by emigrants from Hardwick. Besides all this, I have thoroughly explored more ancient burial-places, both in Massachusetts and Vermont, than I can easily enumerate. Notwithstanding the expenditure of so much time and labor, however, I am conscious of many deficiencies, for which I am not wholly responsible; they are attributable rather to the neglect of parents to record the birth of their children, and of survivors to record the death, or to erect even the most humble memorial, of the departed.

It will be observed that, both in the History and in the Genealogical Register, some family names occur much more frequently than others, notably the names of Allen, Paige, Robinson, Ruggles, and Warner. The reason is twofold: first, the families bearing these names were among the very earliest in the town, and with the exception of the first named were from the beginning to the present time among the most numerous; and second, for the first hundred years they were more constantly and prominently than others engaged in the management of municipal affairs.

It will also be observed that my attention has been devoted chiefly to early events in the history of the town, and that comparatively few recent occurrences are mentioned. The reason is, that I desired to revive and perpetuate the memory of what might otherwise fade entirely from remembrance and pass into oblivion. The current events of the day are fresh in the minds of the living, and are not liable to be soon forgotten. In like manner, I have mentioned some organizations which formerly existed here, such as the Social Library and the Masonic Lodge, because they are wholly of the past, so far as this town is concerned, and have left no visible trace behind them (unless the painted device on the ceiling of the Ruggles Hall remains perceptible); and have omitted special notice of living organizations, such as the Library recently established under the patronage of the Ladies, which is already a treasure, and which gives promise of still greater usefulness; and of the High School, or a school equivalent to a High School, which is understood to be now in successful operation. I have not even ventured to prophesy the future establishment of a school of the highest grade, and of a Free Public Library, with funds for their perpetual maintenance, — a "consummation," not only "devoutly to be wished," but not impossible of accomplishment. One of the living organizations, however, deserves a conspicuous place in a history of the town, namely, the Grange. But I had no materials for an account in any degree adequate to this institution, representing, as it does, one of the most important branches of industry; and I considered it more proper to be silent than to speak without knowledge. The Grange is too well known, both at home and in all the region round about, to suffer from this omission of notice.

The "R. Map," or "Ruggles Map," sometimes mentioned in the History, and much more frequently in the Genealogical Register, is a Map of the Town drawn by Gardner Ruggles, Esq., and lithographed, about fifty years ago, indicating the position of the several houses and their distance from the Common.

I gratefully acknowledge the uniform kindness and courtesy of the gentlemen having custody of the records and archives which I have had occasion to consult, and of the Town Clerks and numerous individuals of whom I have sought information, not otherwise to be obtained. My special thanks are due to Albert E. Knight, Esq., the veteran Town Clerk of Hardwick, not only for the facilities granted to me, when making personal investigations, but for promptly and patiently answering my multitudinous inquiries, and performing much labor on my behalf. I also cherish a grateful remembrance of one of his predecessors in office, Dr. Joseph Stone, for his kindness, assistance, and encouragement, many years ago.

I should be unpardonable if I did not acknowledge the public spirit and generosity of the Town, which has caused this History to be published, and has placed a portion of the edition at my disposal, notwithstanding my willingness to furnish the manuscript without any compensation whatever. In justice to the Town, I here insert a certified copy of the vote authorizing the publication: —

"At a legal meeting of the inhabitants of Hardwick, Nov. 7, A. D. 1882, on motion of Hon. William Mixter, the following vote was unanimously passed: That the Town cause to be published four hundred copies of the History of Hardwick, written by Lucius R. Paige, D. D., of Cambridge, at an expense not exceeding sixteen hundred dollars, and that Mr. Paige retain fifty copies for his own use, for his labor of love in writing the History of his native town, and that the expense of publishing the above History be paid out of any money belonging to the Town. Voted, that the Selectmen be instructed to sell copies of this History, when published, to any who desire them, at four dollars per copy. A copy from the Records. Attest, ALBERT E. KNIGHT, Town Clerk."

A final word in regard to this work. I have spared no reasonable exertion to secure accuracy; yet the universal experience of authors admonishes me that undoubtedly some errors, perhaps many, have escaped correction, and I bespeak the forbearance of the reader. For the rest, I have not aimed at brilliancy, partly because it was beyond my reach, and partly because I consider it to be unsuited to sober history. If lack of vigor and sprightliness be regarded as a serious fault of style, I may plead in extenuation, as in the Preface to my History of Cambridge, and with additional force, that although many of my materials were gathered long ago, I was obliged by other engagements, literary as well as secular, to postpone their final arrangement for publication until impaired health and the infirmities of age became uncomfortably manifest.

LUCIUS R. PAIGE.

CAMBRIDGE, *March*, 1883.

CONTENTS.

CHAPTER V.

CHAPTER VI.

CHAPTER VII.

CHAPTER VIII.

CHAPTER IX.

CHAPTER X.

CHAPTER XI.

CHAPTER XII.

CHAPTER XIII.

CHAPTER XIV.

CHAPTER XV.

CHAPTER XVI.

HISTORY OF HARDWICK.

INTRODUCTORY.

Location. — Boundaries. — Soil. — Hills. — Ponds. — Rivers. — Brooks. — Climate. — Longevity of Inhabitants.

THE town of HARDWICK is situated very near the territorial centre of the Commonwealth of Massachusetts, on the western border of Worcester County, and midway between the States of New Hampshire and Connecticut. It is bounded on the south by Ware; on the west by Ware, Enfield, and Greenwich; on the northwest by Dana; on the northeast by Barre; and on the southeast by New Braintree, from which it is separated by Ware River, except at the southerly end of the line. Like many other towns, its boundaries have several times been changed, and its territory enlarged or diminished, as will hereafter be described. It now contains about 21,000 acres, of which, with the exception of a few ponds and a somewhat plentiful supply of rocks, almost every inch is improved or improvable.

The description given by Whitney in 1793 is substantially correct at the present time: "The town is of a good form and shape, being nearly square. The face of the town is rather rough, hilly, and uneven, although there are no very great and remarkable hills.[1] The soil is in general deep, loamy, and very fertile.

[1] There is one high hill at the south end of the town, called McDougal on the map, but generally known as Bugle Hill, which affords excellent pasturage. About three quarters of a mile north of the Common is Poverty Hill, so called, perhaps, on account of its unproductiveness. From the summit of this hill, though not greatly elevated above the surrounding highlands, a very extensive and magnificent landscape is visible, embracing Wachusett on the east, Monadnock on the north, and on the west the mountains beyond Connecticut River. In the early part of the century this was a favorite resort. On the very pinnacle a tower was erected, about twenty feet in height (whose stone foundation still remains in place), on which a choice company of young men and maidens were accustomed to assemble on summer afternoons and moonlight evenings, and make the air resound with music,

The lands produce all kinds of grain in sufficient plenty for the inhabitants; but they are best adapted to grass and pasturage. Here vast quantities of butter and cheese are made, and most excellent beef fatted for the market. All kinds of fruit-trees flourish here."[1]

With the exception of the manufacturing village at Gilbertville, Hardwick remains an almost exclusively agricultural town. A less quantity of grain, however, is raised now than formerly, and more attention is devoted to the production of hay, milk, butter, and cheese. The more general use of horses instead of oxen for farm-labor has also somewhat diminished the quantity of "beef fatted for the market."

The township is well watered. Near the southwest corner is Muddy Pond (through which Muddy Brook passes), formerly, and perhaps now famous for its abundance of fish; and on the northwest border, but now wholly included in Dana, was the even more productive Pottapaug Pond, fed and drained by Swift River. Though the pond is now severed from the town, Swift River still flows across its northwestern corner, furnishing water-power to Southworth's saw-mill and manufactory of powder-kegs, at the place marked "Wardwell's Mills" on the Ruggles map. On Ware River, which forms almost the entire easterly boundary of the town, there is a very valuable water-privilege at Gilbertville, and another, less powerful, at the paper mill near Barre, marked "N. W. Mills" on the Ruggles map. On that map are also delineated four brooks, all flowing in a southeasterly direction into Ware River, and on all of which, except perhaps the first named, are mill privileges of greater or less value: — namely, Board Meadow Brook, Moose Brook, Great Meadow Brook, and Muddy Brook. Besides these, there is another of considerable size, sometimes called Fish Brook, between Moose and Great Meadow brooks. Living springs abound throughout the town.

The climate of Hardwick is eminently favorable to health and long life. In the Registration Report for 1877, published under the supervision of the Secretary of State, is an abstract, exhibiting the number of deaths registered "for the thirteen years, 1865–1877," together with the proportion of deaths to the whole population. The ratio of "Deaths to 100 persons living" in the

both sacred and secular. They called the hill "Mount Pleasant," an appellation which it richly deserves, and which ought to be perpetuated. The few survivors of that company are widely scattered abroad; but they cherish a vivid remembrance of "auld lang syne."

[1] *Hist. Worcester County*, p. 175.

entire Commonwealth was 1.77; the same ratio in the town of Hardwick was 1.03, — less than three fifths of the general average. Only five towns in the State exhibited a less number of deaths in proportion to their living population. This result may be attributed partly to the skill of the physicians; but doubtless it is chiefly due to the clear air and the fresh breezes which sweep over the hills, dissipating and expelling the malaria, and purifying the atmosphere. Very seldom has any epidemic proved destructive in this favored place. The canker-rash, indeed, in 1803, made sad havoc among the children; and a malignant fever proved fatal to many adults in 1814; but generally the inhabitants have been preserved from "the pestilence that walketh in darkness," and from "the destruction that wasteth at noonday."

In very few towns has so large a proportion of the inhabitants attained the allotted age of threescore years and ten. Before the year 1789, the registry of deaths does not indicate the age of the deceased, with only two exceptions; but during that year a new system was adopted. If I have counted correctly, the whole number of deaths registered from

August 12, 1789, to December 31, 1881, is	2,222
The number under 70 years is	1,708
The number from 70 to 80 years is	253
The number from 80 to 90 years is	202
The number from 90 to 100 years is	58
The number over 100 years is	1

Hence it appears, that of the whole number who deceased in Hardwick during a period somewhat exceeding ninety-one years, nearly one fourth part (23⅛ in every 100) attained the age of 70 years; more than one ninth part (11¾ in every 100) reached 80 years; one in every 37⅔ survived 90 years; and one[1] completed the full century.

[1] The records and a headstone indicate a second centenarian; but the age is overrated.

CHAPTER I.

INDIAN HISTORY.

Indian Occupation. — Indian Fortress. — King Philip. — Indian Hostilities in Plymouth and Bristol Counties. — Sanguinary Conflict at Winnimisset. — Quabaog destroyed. — Report by Ephraim Curtis concerning the Nipmucks. — Captain Edward Hutchinson's Commission and Death. — Captain Thomas Wheeler's Narrative. — The Indians abandon their Stronghold at Winnimisset. — Personal Encounter between Captain Eleazar Warner and a Canada Indian.

THERE is no evidence within my knowledge, that the present township of Hardwick was ever occupied by the Indians as a place of residence; but that these hills furnished favorite hunting-grounds, there were manifest tokens in my younger days. Stone arrow-heads [1] were found so abundantly in the fields as to indicate their frequent and long-continued visitation in pursuit of game. Moreover, long before the settlement of the town by Englishmen the Indians had a military stronghold at Winnimisset, now in New Braintree, but for many years included in Hardwick. At this place occurred a sanguinary conflict between the two races, at the commencement of what is generally called King Philip's War. "From 1671 to 1674 we meet with no transaction of moment relative to the Indians, but it is affirmed that Philip was all this time using measures to engage the Indians in all parts of New England to unite against the English. . . . They did not expect to be prepared before the spring of 1676, but Philip precipitated his own nation and his allies into a war before they were prepared. . . . The war was hurried on by a

[1] Another vestige of Indian occupancy is in my possession. It is a stone implement, fashioned like a pestle, ten inches in length, with a groove at the smaller end for the purpose of attachment to a handle. The stone is different from the Hardwick rocks, and of much finer grain. It was given to me by Mr. William C. Wesson, the present owner of the field (formerly a part of my father's homestead), where it was found half a century ago. Very probably it passed unnoticed under my own hoe in my boyhood, when laboring in that field; and hence it has an additional value to me as a memento.

piece of revenge, which Philip caused to be taken on John Sausaman, a praying Indian."[1] Sausaman had exposed to the English some of the plots of Philip, who thereupon caused him to be murdered. The murderers were tried and executed at Plymouth in June, 1675. Philip was enraged, and commenced hostilities at once. "June 24th, in the morning, one of the inhabitants of Rehoboth was fired upon by a party of Indians, and the hilt of his sword shot off. The same day in the afternoon, being a fast, as Swanzey people were coming from public worship, the Indians attacked them, killed one and wounded others, and killed two men who were going for a surgeon, beset a house in another part of the town, and there murdered six more."[2] The English gathered troops, and in July attacked the Indians in a swamp at Pocasset, hoping to capture or destroy them; but the attempt was unsuccessful. "This disappointment encouraged the Indians in other parts of New England to follow Philip's example, and begin their hostilities against the English. Some few had begun before. The Nipnet or Nipmuck Indians had killed four or five people at Mendon, in the Massachusetts Colony, the 14th of July. The Governor and Council, in hopes of reclaiming the Nipnets, sent Captain Hutchinson with twenty horsemen to Quabaog (Brookfield), near which place there was to be a great rendezvous of those Indians. The inhabitants of Quabaog had been deluded with the promise of a treaty, at a place agreed upon, the 2d of August. Some of the principal of them accompanied Captain Hutchinson thither. Not finding the Indians there, they rode forward four or five miles towards the Nipnets' chief town. When they came to a place called Meminimisset,[3] a narrow passage between a steep hill and a thick swamp, they were ambushed by two or three hundred Indians, who shot down eight of the company, and mortally wounded three more, Captain Hutchinson being one of the number. The rest escaped through a by-path to Quabaog. The Indians flocked into the town; but the inhabitants, being alarmed, had all gathered together in the principal house. They had the mortification to see all their dwelling-houses, about twenty, with their barns and outhouses burnt."[4]

A more particular "narrative" of this sanguinary struggle,

[1] Hutchinson's *Hist. of Mass.*, i. 283-285.

[2] *Ibid.*, i. 286, 287.

[3] Now called Winnimisset, in New Braintree.

[4] Hutchinson's *Hist. of Mass.*, i. 291, 292.

written by Captain Thomas Wheeler, one of the actors therein, which Hutchinson seems not to have seen, was reprinted in the Collections of the New Hampshire Historical Society in 1827; and some manuscript details of preliminary proceedings have been preserved in the Massachusetts Archives, but I think have never been printed. From these sources it appears that in July, 1675, the Governor and Council employed Ephraim Curtis[1] to visit the Nipmuck Indians at Quabaog (Brookfield), and to ascertain their position in the controversy which had commenced. On his return he exhibited a report as follows: —

"To the honered Governer and Councle of the Massathusets Colony in New England.[2]

"Wheras your honors imployed your servant to conduct Uncheas his six men homwards as far as Wabaquesesue, and alsoe to make a perffet discovery of the motions of the Nepmug or Western Indians, your honors may be pleased here to see my return and relation. I conducted Unkeas his men safly while I com in sight of Wabquesesue new planting fielde; first to Natuck, from thenc to Marelborrow, from thenc to Esnemisco, from thenc to Mumchogg, from thenc to Chabanagonkomug, from thenc to Mayenecket, from thenc over the river to Seneksig, while wee cam nere to Wabaquasesu, wher they were very willing that wee should leve them, and returned thanks to Mr. Governer, and to all them that shewed them kindness, and alsoe to us for our company. And in my jorny my chefe indever was to inquire after the motions of the Indians. The first information which I had was at Marelborrow att the Indian fort, which was that my hous at Quansigamug[3] was robed; the Indians, to conferm it, shewed me som of the goods and alsoe som other goods which was non of mine. They told mee it was very daingerous for mee to goe into the woods, for that Mattounas, which they said was the leader of them that robed my house, was in company of fifty men of Phillips complices rainging between Chabanagonkamug and Quatesook and Mendam and Warwick, and they might

[1] Ephraim Curtis was of Sudbury (afterward of Worcester), and described himself as thirty-five years old in a deposition dated Sept. 11, 1675, now in the *Mass. Arch.*, lxvii. 254. He was an active scout and guide, and rendered very important service.

[2] I preserve the orthography, but supply the punctuation.

[3] Worcester. During the attack on Brookfield, "Ephraim Curtis, who may be considered as the first settler of Worcester, distinguished himself as a gallant soldier in repelling their attacks. Having actively engaged in military service, he received the commission of lieutenant." He left posterity in Worcester. Lincoln's *Hist. of Worcester*, pp. 19, 43.

hapen to mett mee; and if I mised them, yet it was daingerous to meet or see the other Nipmug Indians which wer gathered together, for they would be reddy to shoot mee as soon as they saw mee. With this newes, thos three Natuck Indians which wer with mee as vollenteres were discurriged and tould mee that if I did not provide mor company they wer not willing to goe with mee. Hearing this, I repaired to the Consable of Marelborrow and to the milletary officers and tould them my busnes, and they presed two men with horses and armes to goe along with mee. And soe as wee pased the forementioned place, wee could not find any Indians, neither in tents nor feldes; but after wee pased Senecksik som milds into the woods westwards, wee found an Indian path newly mad. There being with mee a vollenter Indian that cam from the Indians out of the wilderness but two or three days before, and hee tould mee hee would find them out. Soe in our travell wee followed this tract many milds, and found many tents built, wherin I supos they might keep their randivos for a day or two; and soe wee found three places wher they had piched, but found no Indians. And following still in pursut of the tract, wee com to the lead mynes by Springfield ould road, wher wee saw new footing of Indians: and soe looking out sharp, in about two milds riding wee saw two Indians, which when wee saw I sent the Indian that went with mee from Marrelborrow to speek with them. But soe soone as they had discovered us they ran away from us, but with fast riding and much calling two of our Indians stopped one of them; the other ran away. Wee asked the Indian wher the other Indians were; hee being supprised with feare could scarcely speak to us, but only tould us that the Indians were but a littel way from us. Soe then I sent the Marrelborrow Indian before us, to tell them that the Gouvner of the Massathusets messenger was a coming with peacable words; but when hee cam to them they would not beleve him; hee therfore cam riding back and meet us. Thes Indians have newly begun to settel themselves uppon an Iland conteinging about four acres of ground, being compased round with a brood miry swamp on the one sid and a mudy river with meaddow on both sids of it one the other sid, and but only one place that a hors could posably pas, and there with a great deal of difficulty by reson of the mier and dirt. Befor wee com to the river ther mett us att least forty Indians at a littell distance from the river, some with ther guns uppon ther shoulders, others with ther guns in ther hands reddy cocked and primed. As wee cam nere to the river most of them next to the river presented att us. All my aquantanc would not know mee, although I saw ner twenty of them together and asked ther wellfare, knowing that many of them could speek good Englesh. I speak to many of them in the Governor's name, which I called my master, the great Sachim of the Massathuset Englesh, requiring them to owne ther fidellyty and ingidgement to the Englesh, telling them that I cam not to fight with them or to hurt them, but as a messinger from the Governer to put them in mind of their ingaidgment to the English. I think some of them did beleve mee, but the most of them would not. Ther was a very great upror amonghst them: som of them would have had mee and my company presently kiled; but many others, as I understood afterwards, wer against it. I required ther Sachims to com over the river; but they refused, saying that I must com over to them. My comppany wer somthing unwilling, for they thought themselves in very great dainger wher wee wer; they said what shall wee bee when [wee] are over the river amongst all the vile rout? I tould them wee had better never have sen them, then not to speak with ther Sachims, and if wee run from them in the tim of this tumult they would shoot after us and kill som of us. Soe with much difficulty wee got over the river and meaddow to the Iland wher they stood to face us att our coming out of the mire, many Indians with ther guns presented att us, redy cocked and primed. Soe wee rushed between them and called for ther Sachim; they presently faced about and went to surround us, many of them with ther guns cocked and primed at us. We rushed between them onc or twice, and bid them stand in a body, and I would face them; but still the uprore continued with such noyes that the aire rang. I required them to lay down their armes, and they comanded us to put up our armes first, and com of our horses, which I refused to doe. Som of them which wer inclinable to beleve us, or wer our friends, som layd down ther armes, but the others continued the uprore for a while; and with much threattening and perswasion, at last the uprore ceased. Many of them sayd they would neyther beleve mee nor my master without hee would send them two or three bushells of powder. Att lingth I spok with ther Sachims, which wer five, and ther other grandes which I think wer about twelve more; our Natuck Indians semed to be very industrous all this tim to still the tumult and to persuad the Indians. And as soone as I cam to speek with the Sachims, we dismounted and put up our armes. I had a great deal of spech with them by an interpreter, being brought to ther court and sent out again three or four times. The nams of the Sachims are thes: 1, Muttaump; 2, Konkewasco; 3, Willymachen; 4, Upchattuck; 5, Keehood; 6, Nontatousoo. Muttaump I perceive is chosen to bee head over the other five, and was the chefe speaker. There company in number I judg may bee ner two hundred of men. They would fain have had mee to stay all night: I asked the reson of some that could speak Englesh; they sayd that they had som messengers at Cunnetequt and som southward, and that was the reson they would have mee stay. I asked them the reson of ther rud behavour toward us, and they sayd they heard that the Englesh had kiled a man of thyres about Merrymak River, and that they had an intent to destroy them all. I left them well apeased when I cam away. Mor might be added; but thus far is a true relation, p^{r} your honers most humbel servent. EPHRAIM CURTIS.

"July ye 16, 1675." [1]

Immediately afterwards Curtis was sent again with "a message to the Nipmug Indians." He reported, July 24, 1675, that he "found them att the same place wher they wer before;" that they manifested a better temper, and that "they promised that Keehoud and one mor of their principle men would come to the Massathusets Bay within foure or five days and speek with our Great Sachim." [2] This promise was not fulfilled, and the government organized a military expedition. A paper remains in the Archives, indorsed "Capt. Hutchinsons Instructions, 27 July, 1675," to wit:—

"Boston, 27 July, 1675. The Council, beeing informed that the Narraganset Indians are come downe with about one hundred armed men into the Nipmuck country,—Do order you, Capt. Edward Hutcheson, to take with you Capt. Thomas Wheler and his party of horse, with Ephraim Curtis for a guide, and a sufficient interpreter, and forthwith repaire into those parts, and ther laubour to get a right understanding of the motions of the Narraganset Indians, and of the Indians of Nipmuck; and for that end to demand of the leaders of the Narraganset Indians an account of the grounds of their marching in the country, and require an account of the Nipmuck Indians why they have not sent downe their Sagamore according to their promise unto our messenger Ephraim Curtis. And further let them know that we are

[1] *Mass. Arch.*, lxvii. 214-216. [2] *Ibid.*, lxvii. 222, 223.

informed that there are some among them that have actually joyned with our enimies in the murder and spoyle made upon the English by Philip, and that Matoones and his complices who have rob'd and murdered our people about Mendon are now among them; and that wee require them to deliver up to you, or forthwith bring in to us, those our enimies; otherwise wee must looke at them to bee no freinds to us, ayders and abbetors. . . . And in prosecution of this affayre, if you should meet with any Indians that stand in opposition to you or declare themselves to be your enimes, then you are ordered to ingage with them, if you see reson for it, and endeavor to reduce them by force of arms."[1]

The tragical result of this expedition was described by Captain Thomas Wheeler, in "A true Narrative of the Lord's Providences in various dispensations towards Captain Edward Hutchinson of Boston and myself, and those that went with us into the Nipmuck Country, and also to Quabaug, alias Brookfield." — "The said Captain Hutchinson and myself, with about twenty men or more, marched from Cambridge to Sudbury July 28, 1675, and from thence into the Nipmuck Country; and finding that the Indians had deserted their towns, and we having gone until we came within two miles of New Norwitch on July 31, . . . we then thought it not expedient to march any further that way, but set our march for Brookfield, whither we came on the Lord's day about noon. From thence the same day (being August 1), we understanding that the Indians were about ten miles northwest from us, we sent out four men[2] to acquaint the Indians that we were not come to harm them, but our business was only to deliver a message from our honoured Governour and Council to them, and to receive their answer, we desiring to come to a treaty of peace with them (though they had for several days fled from us), they having before professed friendship and promised fidelity to the English. When the messengers came to them they made an alarm, and gathered together about an hundred and fifty fighting men, as near as they could judge. The young men amongst them were stout in their speeches, and surly in their carriage. But at length some of the chief Sachems promised to meet us on the next morning about 8 of the clock upon a plain

[1] *Mass. Arch.*, lxvii. 227.

[2] One of these men was Ephraim Curtis, who says in his deposition: "The third time I was sent out with Cap. Hucheson, and by his order went and treated with the Nipmug Indians in a swamp about eight milds from Quabooge." *Mass. Arch.*, lxvii. 254.

within three miles of Brookfield; with which answer the messengers returned to us. . . . Accordingly we with our men, accompanied with three of the principal inhabitants of that town, marched to the plain appointed. . . . The Indians kept not promise there with us. But the three men who belonged to Brookfield were so strongly persuaded of their freedom from any ill intentions towards us . . . that the said Captain Hutchinson, who was principally intrusted with the matter of Treaty with them, was thereby encouraged to proceed and march forward towards a swampe where the Indians then were. When we came near the said swampe, the way was so very bad that we could march only in a single file, there being a very rocky hill on the right hand, and a thick swampe on the left, in which there were many of those cruel bloodthirsty heathen, who there waylaid us, waiting an opportunity to cut us off: there being also much brush on the side of the said hill, where they lay in ambush to surprise us. When we had marched there about sixty or seventy rods, the said perfidious Indians sent out their shot upon us as a showre of haile, they being (as was supposed) about two hundred men or more. We seeing ourselves so beset, and not having room to fight, endeavoured to fly for the safety of our lives. . . . There were then slain, to our great grief, eight men, viz., Zechariah Philips of Boston, Timothy Farlow of Billericay, Edward Coleborn of Chelmsford, Samuel Smedly of Concord, Sydrach Hopgood of Sudbury, Sergeant Eyres,[1] Serjeant Prichard,[2] and Corporal Coy,[3] the inhabitants of Brookfield, aforesaid. It being the good pleasure of God that they should all there fall by their hands of whose good intentions they were so confident, and whom they so little mistrusted. There were also then five persons wounded, viz., Captain Hutchinson,[4] myself, and my son Thomas, as aforesaid,[5] Corporal French of Billericay; . . . The fifth was John Waldoe of Chelmsford." [6]

The survivors fled to Brookfield, took possession of "one of the

[1] John Ayres.

[2] William Prichard.

[3] Richard Coye.

[4] Captain Hutchinson died of his wounds, August 19, 1675.

[5] Captain Wheeler's horse was killed, and himself sorely wounded. He bears this testimony to the good conduct of his son, who "had then received a dangerous wound in the reins: . . . he endeavoured to rescue me, shewing himself therein a loving and dutiful son, he adventuring himself into great peril of his life to help me in that distress; there being many of the enemies about me, my son set me on his own horse and so escaped a while on foot himself, until he caught an horse whose rider was slain, on which he mounted; and so through God's great mercy we both escaped."

[6] *Coll. N. H. Hist. Society*, ii. 5-10.

largest and strongest houses therein" (into which all the inhabitants were speedily gathered), and there defended themselves two days against the violent assaults of the Indians, until relieved by the force under Major Willard. On his approach, the Indians betook themselves to the wilderness. "But before they went away, they burnt all the town except the house we kept in, and another that was not then finished. They also made great spoyle of the cattel belonging to the inhabitants." [1]

After this, the Indians never returned to Brookfield as a place of residence; but for more than half a century they hovered around the town, occasionally destroying property and killing the inhabitants. It does not appear how long they retained their stronghold at Winnimisset; but it is certain that after a short time they returned and remained there until after the destruction of Lancaster on the 10th of the ensuing February. Mrs. Rowlandson says that on the second day after that disaster, "in the afternoon, about an hour by sun, we came to the place where they intended, viz. an Indian town called Wenimesset, northward of Quabaug," and remained there until after February 18, on which day her daughter, six years old, and wounded at Lancaster, died, and was buried on the hill east of the swamp.[2] Subsequently Muttaump, the chief Sachem of the Quabaogs, is said to have been hung at Boston, and the remnant of his tribe joined with the River Indians.

I have devoted much space to the narration of these events, partly because they occurred on territory which afterwards became our own, partly because they illustrate the labors and perils and sufferings to which the early settlers in the wilderness were exposed, and partly because at least one of the individual sufferers was represented by his posterity among the first English inhabit-

[1] Immediately after arriving at Brookfield, Ephraim Curtis and another started for Boston on horseback to report the disaster; but the Indians had already arrived, and they were obliged to return. "The next day," says Capt. Wheeler, "I spoke to Ephraim Curtis to adventure forth again on that service, and to attempt it on foot, as the way wherein there was most hope of getting away undiscovered; he readily assented and accordingly went out, but there were so many Indians everywhere thereabouts, that he could not pass without apparent hazard of life; so he came back again; but towards morning the said Ephraim adventured forth the third time, and was fain to creep on his hands and knees for some space of ground, that he might not be discerned by the enemy, who waited to prevent our sending, if they could have hindered it. But through God's mercy he escaped their hands, and got safely to Marlborough, though very much spent and ready to faint, . . . from whence he went to Boston. *Coll. N. H. Hist. Soc.*, ii. 11–13.

[2] *Indian Captivities*, pp. 25, 26.

ants of this town. With a brief notice of a single affair in which a prominent representative of that posterity was engaged, I shall dismiss what may be called the Indian History of Hardwick. One of the "principal inhabitants" of Brookfield, whose cattle, house, and household goods were destroyed by the Indians, was John Warner,[1] who fled for refuge to Hadley (where one or more of his sons then resided), and died there nearly twenty years later. His grandson, Eleazar Warner, who was born 27th January, 1686, very early entered the military service of his country, and was assigned to duty on the frontiers. Whether he enlisted in that company of his own choice, or was placed in it by authority, does not appear; but the fact is certain that he was for many years stationed at Brookfield (the scene of his grandfather's disasters), first as a private soldier, and afterwards, by gradual promotion, as sergeant, ensign, and lieutenant of the company commanded by Captain Samuel Wright of Rutland. Later in life, he was captain of militia in Hardwick and New Braintree, and retained that office until 1756, when he had attained the age of threescore years and ten. About 1730, while yet in the service of the government, he removed his family from his former residence near Ditch Meadow to a farm which included a part of the old Indian fortress at Winnimisset. Soon afterwards he went to Canada, to effect an exchange of prisoners. While there an Indian became offended, and followed him through the wilderness to his home. According to the family tradition, as I received it from his eldest daughter, my grandmother, after the Indian had lurked about the house for a few days, Captain Warner went into the forest with his musket. He soon discovered his enemy, who stepped behind a tree, and he dropped by the side of a log. He then adopted a common stratagem, placing his hat on a stick and cautiously elevating it above the log, as if to reconnoitre. Almost instantly a bullet passed through it, and he sprang upon his feet. The Indian was rushing forward with his scalping knife in hand; but his race was soon ended, and his body was consigned to a lily-pond between the road and the river, about half a mile east of the Old Furnace.

Except in the foregoing solitary case, I am not aware that the

[1] The Indian "deed of sale" was delivered by Thomas Cooper, December 19, 1673, to "John Warner, Richard Coye, and William Pritchard of Quabaog, alias Brookfield, for the use and as the proper right of the inhabitants of Brookfield, the said persons being betrusted by the town or present inhabitants of Brookfield for taking in and receiving this present deed." *Fiske's Centennial Sermon*, App. iii.

Indians ever molested the inhabitants of Hardwick, although in one respect it was a frontier town, when settled by the English. There was a settlement at Rutland on the east, and Brookfield on the south was again inhabited. A line of towns had also been established on Connecticut River; but otherwise the whole country, between Hardwick and Hudson River, was then a wilderness; and in a direct line to Quebec or Montreal there was not a single English settlement.

CHAPTER II.

CIVIL HISTORY.

Purchases of Indian Titles. — Indian Deed. — The Proprietors petition the General Court to confirm their Title. — The Representatives grant the Request, but the Council non-concur. — First Settlement at the "Elbows." — Title partially confirmed. — Purchase and Settlement of Leicester by the same Proprietors. — Associates admitted. — Claim by Hendrick Kekquoquau. — Answer by Proprietors.

AFTER the close of Philip's War some of the Nipmuck Indians returned to their former haunts; and both these, and others who dwelt elsewhere, asserted hereditary rights in the soil which the English recognized as valid, and extinguished by purchase.[1] Among these purchases was that which, about half a century later, resulted in the settlement of Hardwick. The deed of sale, executed by sundry Indians, was recorded in the county of Hampshire, in which this territory was then embraced, from which record it is here copied:[2] —

"Know all men by these presents, that we, John Magus, Lawrence Massowanno,[3] attorneys to Annogomok,[4] Sachem of the

[1] Such purchases became very frequent immediately after the abrogation of the Colony Charter in 1684. It was then assumed by the new representatives of royal authority that all titles to land derived from grants by the superseded government were utterly void and worthless; that the king was the absolute owner of the whole territory; and that he had an undoubted right to dispose of it at his own pleasure. Indeed the common and undivided lands of some towns, and the farms of several individuals, were seized and bestowed upon others. Apparently with the hope of securing themselves against the rapacity of their new rulers by obtaining another title which might be respected, many towns, which had peacefully existed under a grant by the General Court, now procured and placed on record deeds of release and warranty from the aboriginal owners of the soil. In like manner, individuals purchased large tracts of unoccupied territory, designing at some future time to organize new townships, or at least to have a place of refuge to which they might flee, if driven from their present habitations by arbitrary power.

[2] In this copy, the orthography is preserved, but the punctuation is revised. The deed was also entered on the Proprietors' Records, with slight variations which are designated in the following notes.

[3] In the Index of Deeds, this name appears as Lawrance Nesawanno, and on the Proprietors' Records as Lawrance Nassowanno.

[4] Anogomok. — *Prop. Rec.*

tract of land called Wombemesscook,[1] James and Simon, sons and heirs of Black James, Sachem of the Nipmug countrey, for divers good causes and considerations us thereunto moveing, and more especially for and in consideration of ye sum of twenty pounds, currant money of New England, to us in hand paid by Joshua Lambe, Nath. Paige,[2] Andrew Gardiner,[3] Benj^a^ Gamblin, Benjamin Tucker, John Curtis, Richard Draper, and Samuel Ruggles, of Roxberry in the county of Suffolk in New England, ye receipt whereof we do hereby acknowledge ourselves therewith to be fully satisfyed, contented, and paid, have given, granted, bargained, sold, aliened, enfeoffed, and confirmed, and by these presents do fully, freely, and absolutely give, grant, bargain, sell, aliene, enfeoffe, and confirm, unto the said Lambe, Paige, Gardiner, Gamblin, Tucker, Curtis, Draper, and Ruggles, their heirs and assignes, a certain tract or parcell of land, containing by estimation twelve miles long, north and south, and eight miles wide, east and west, scituate, lying and being near Quabaug, commonly known by the name of Wombemesiscook,[4] being butted and bounded southerly upon the land of Joseph Dudley, Esq., lately purchased of the Indians, easterly the southermost corner upon a pond called Sasagookapaug, and soe by a brook which runneth into the said pond, and soe up northerly unto a place called Nequaes,[5] and soe still northerly until it meets with a river Menamesick,[6] and westerly by the river untill it come against Quabaug bounds, and joynes unto their bounds, or however, or however,[7] otherwise butted and bounded; together with all and singular ye rights, commodities, liberties, privilidges, and appurtenances, whatsoever, to the same belonging, or however otherwise appertaining. To have and to hold the said tract or parcel of land, scituate, containing, and being, as aforesaid, to the said Lamb, Paige, Gardiner, Gamblin, Tucker, Curtis, Draper, and Ruggles, their heirs and assigns, in common tenancy, to their only propper use and behoofe[8] forever. And the said John Magus, Lawrence Nassowanno, attorneys as aforesaid, James and Simon, heirs of Black James, as aforesaid, do covenant, promise, and grant, for themselves, heirs, executors, and administrators, to and with the said Joshua Lamb, Nathaniel Paige, Andrew Gardiner, Benjamin Gamblin, Benjamin Tucker,[9] Richard Draper, and

[1] Wombemesisecook. — *Prop. Rec.*
[2] Nathanniell Paige. — *Prop. Rec.*
[3] Uniformly on the Proprietors' Records, this name is written Gardner.
[4] Wombemesisecook. — *Prop. Rec.*
[5] Ueques. — *Prop. Rec.*
[6] Nenameseck. — *Prop. Rec.*
[7] So in the record.
[8] Use, benefit, and behoofe. — *Prop. Rec.*
[9] John Curtis is here omitted in the record.

Samuel Ruggles, their heirs and assignes, that they will[1] the above granted and bargained land, and every part and parcel thereof, with their and every of their appurtenances, warrant and defend from all and every person and persons whatsoever, claiming any right or title thereto, or interest therein, from, by, or under us. In witness whereof, the said John Magus, Lawrence Nassowanno, attorneys as aforesaid, James and Simon, have hereunto set their hands and seales, this twenty-seventh day of December, Anno Domini one thousand six hundred eighty and six, annoq. R. R^{s} Jacobi Secundi Angliæ &c. Secundo.

Signed, sealed, and delivered in presence of us,	JOHN MAGUS, and seale.
	LAWRENCE NASOWANNO, his mark and seale.
	JAMES, his mark and seale.
JOHN GARDINER.	SIMON, his mark and seale.
SAMUEL ANAY.[2]	ANOGEMAG,[3] his mark and seale.[4]

"John Magus, James, and Simon, Indians, subscribers to this instrument, personally appeareing acknowledged the same to be their act and deed, June 25th 1687, before me,

WILLIAM STOUGHTON.

"On the 7th day of May 1723, this deed was received, and was then here registered from the original.

Pr JOHN PYNCHON, Reg^{r}"[5]

No immediate effort is known to have been made to derive any profit from the purchase of this territory in the wilderness.[6] Even the title-deed was not recorded until more than thirty-six years after its date. At this period all the original purchasers, except Deacon Richard Draper, had left all terrestrial possessions and departed to a better country, even a heavenly. At length, however, their heirs and assigns determined to take possession of the property, and to improve it for their "mutual advantage," for which purpose they adopted and placed on record the following agreement: —

"Whereas we, the subscribers, or our ancestors have fairly purchased of the native and original owners thereof a certain

1 This sentence is differently constructed on *Prop. Rec.*

2 Samuell May. — *Prop. Rec.*

3 Anogomog. — *Prop. Rec.*

4 The Indian marks are recorded, but here omitted.

5 Old *Hampshire Registry of Deeds* (now in the Hampden Registry at Springfield), Book D, page 237.

6 A similar delay occurred in the settlement of Leicester (including Spencer), which was purchased by the same persons, together with Ralph Bradhurst; the deed bears date 27th Jan. 1686–7, but no settlement of the territory was made until 1713.

tract of land lying near Quabaog or Brookfield, commonly then called by the name of Wombemesisecook for a valuable consideration, as per the deed thereof duly executed, acknowledged, and recorded, bearing date 1686, will be more plainly manifested: and whereas the bounds of said tract be not so certainly known, or the contents thereof: we, therefore, the persons concerned, viz., Joshua Lamb, for himself;[1] Nathaniel Paige and Christopher Paige, as heirs to Nathaniel Paige; Samuel Green and Edward Sumner, as assigns to Andrew Gardner's heirs; Caleb Seaver, one of the heirs of Benjamin Gamblin; Benjamin Tucker and Samuel Davis, as heirs to Benjamin Tucker; Benjamin Smith, on behalf of John Curtis' heirs; Richard Draper, for himself; and Joseph Ruggles, for the heirs of Samuel Ruggles: Do hereby authorize and empower the above-named Samuel Green to employ and improve a surveyor and two other persons suitable for that purpose to view and consider and mark out the said lands, as butted and bounded in said deed; to take an account of the waste land, ponds, as well as other land therein fit for settlements; and make report of their doings to ourselves the last Tuesday in April next: that so we may proceed therein for the mutual advantage of the purchasers;— the said meeting to be at the house of Simon Rogers in Boston on the said Tuesday. Witness our hands this 20th of February, 1726-7.

"RICHARD DRAPER.	BENJAMIN his B. mark SMITH.
JOSEPH RUGGLES.	
NATHANIEL PAIGE.	JOSHUA LAMB.
CHRISTOPHER PAIGE.	SAMUEL GREEN.
BENJAMIN TUCKER.	EDWARD SUMNER.
SAMUEL DAVIS.	CALEB SEAVER."

Subsequent proceedings are recorded as follows:—

"At a legal Proprietors' meeting at Simon Rogers in Boston on the 25th of April 1727; in the first place, by a major vote of the proprietors we chose Deacon Richard Draper Moderator of said meeting; in the next place, by a major vote of the proprietors, we chose Joseph Ruggles Proprietors' Clerk: in the next place, voted that Capt. Samuel Green should be allowed the charges in his account expended upon finding out the said land, to be paid the next meeting; and in the last place, voted that this meeting be adjourned to the same place the last Tuesday of May next, at one of the clock in the afternoon."

[1] Colonel Joshua Lamb was, probably, sole owner of the share purchased by his father, who died 23d September, 1690.

At the adjourned meeting, "Voted, on the 30th of May, 1727, by the Proprietors of a certain tract of land contained in a deed signed John Magus, Lawrence Nassawanno, &c., dated 27th of December, 1686, that Col. Joshua Lamb, Deacon Richard Draper and Capt. Samuel Green, be a committee to represent the whole proprietors, and to prefer such a petition to the honorable General Court as they in their prudence may think fit; the prayer of which to contain what may be most needful for the safe proceeding of said proprietors in settling the said propriety."

In the printed Journal of the House of Representatives, under date of June 10, 1727, we find this record: "A petition of Joshua Lamb, Richard Draper, and Samuel Green, as they are a committee of a number of proprietors and purchasers of a certain tract of land, lying near the town of Brookfield, formerly called Quabaug, shewing that the said Richard Draper and sundry others formerly purchased of some Indians a large tract of land called Wombemesiscook, butted and bounded as by said deed exhibited with the petition appears, being acknowledged and recorded, praying that this Court would confirm unto them and those they represent, and their associates, the said tract of land, that they may be encouraged to make a speedy settlement thereof, for the reasons mentioned. Read, and committed to the Committee appointed to take into consideration the several petitions for lands to be erected into townships." The Committee submitted a report June 23, 1727, and it was thereupon "Voted, that the contents of six miles square be allowed to the purchasers of the tract within mentioned, between the town of Brookfield and the Equivalent land in the county of Hampshire, to be laid out by a surveyor and chainmen upon oath; provided that within five years next after such survey and confirmation thereof by this Court, the grantees, their heirs and assigns, shall settle fifty families, that are now inhabitants of this Province, and have a meeting-house erected, a Minister settled, a lot for the ministry, and one for the school laid out; the houselots to be laid out as near as may be, and as regularly and defensibly as the land will allow of, provided the petitioners make no further claim to the said land within mentioned."[1] The General Court Records show that the Council non-concurred June 28, 1727.

[1] The tract here described includes substantially the town of Palmer, and the northerly part of Warren; it was then called "The Elbows," from the peculiar angles formed by the three rivers which there unite. On the revision of the line between the two States, in 1713, it was found that Massachusetts had granted some land for townships which properly belonged to Connecticut; and as a com-

It is evident that a settlement had already been commenced at the "Elbows"; for on the next day after the rejection of their petition by the Council, June 29, 1727, the Proprietors met at Boston, and "in the first place chose Deacon Draper Moderator; in the next place voted that Capt. Green should go upon the proprietors' land, and warn them off from making any further improvement thereon: again voted that Capt. Samuel Green should agree with those persons that have made a pitch upon the said land for the present year, as he and they shall agree, as our tenants."[1] It would seem that those who had "pitched upon the said land," without authority, were quieted in their possession, and that not long afterwards a colony of Scotch Presbyterians, sometimes called Scotch-Irish, were admitted.[2] The Rev. Simeon Colton, in a brief sketch of Palmer, published in the *Historical Magazine*, October, 1869, says: "The earliest date of the laying out of any lot of land is the 11th of June, 1728. . . . There are many lots laid out in 1728, most of which were laid out in December." Notwithstanding the Council had refused to concur with the House of Representatives in granting the authority which the proprietors desired, they asserted their just right to the territory, and determined to make it available by admitting settlers. At a meeting, July 25, 1728, after reciting the purchase, and the failure to obtain "the privileges of a township," they elected Joseph Ruggles to be their clerk, and directed that he should be sworn, and should "buy a good book of clean paper to record all our acts and votes in, from year to year." The record continues: "And we do also hereby appoint Capt. Samuel Green, and Mr. Nathaniel Paige, and the Rev. Mr. Timothy Ruggles, to be a Committee to procure a good and well approved of Surveyor and two Chainmen, who shall be under oath to the faithful discharge of their office and trust, and shall survey six miles square within our claim, and draw a fair platt thereof, and the same put on record; and any two of the committee to have full power to act; and also their power is to

pensation, or equivalent therefor, the former granted to the latter a large tract of land embracing the present towns of Belchertown and Pelham, and the greater part of Prescott and Ware. This tract was called the "Equivalent Land," which was sold by Connecticut for about six farthings per acre. See Palfrey's *Hist. N. Eng.*, iv. 363.

[1] Captain Samuel Green had then resided in Leicester more than ten years, of which town, as well as of Lambstown, or Hardwick, he was a proprietor.

[2] "As early as 1727, settlements were made in what is now Palmer, under grants or permits from the proprietors of Lambstown, by a colony of emigrants from the north of Ireland, among whom were Isaac Magoun and James Brakenridge." — Hyde's *Address* at Ware, 1847, p. 7.

extend to make an agreement with such persons as have settled upon the same as to the bounds of their farms, and what to give for their interests there, and to improve the money they shall gain thereby towards defraying the charge that the committee shall be at in the work they are empowered to do. . . . Then to proceed to make an allotment of forty or fifty lots, one for a minister, one for a ministry, and one for a school; and the other to be disposed of as the proprietors shall hereafter order and agree."[1]

During the next year another effort was made by the proprietors to have their claims recognized by the General Court. By the printed Journal of the House of Representatives, it appears that on the 24th of September, 1729, "A petition of Joshua Lamb, Esq. and Mr. Timothy Ruggles, a committee of a number of proprietors and purchasers of a certain tract of land lying near Brookfield, praying for confirmation of all or part thereof for a township, for reasons mentioned. Read, and the question was put whether the prayer of the petition should be granted. It passed in the negative."

Two months later the printed Journal describes a general scramble for this territory. November 25, 1729: "A petition of Josiah Edson and sundry others, inhabitants of Bridgewater, praying for a grant of a tract of land for a township between Ware River and Swift River. Read and referred to Thursday the 27th current, when other petitions for lands are to come under consideration." November 27, 1729: "A petition of Isaac Burr, John King,[2] and sundry others, shewing that they are settled upon a certain tract of land, bounded easterly by Brookfield, southerly and westerly by Brimfield, and northerly by Coldspring,[3] by ad-

[1] Both the trespassers, or squatters, and those who were regularly admitted, united in a petition to the General Court, November 24, 1732, for a grant of this land to themselves, alleging that "the reason why your petitioners entered on the said land was as follows: Some from the encouragement of Joshua Lamb Esq. and Company, that the said land belonged to them, and that they would give to such of your petitioners as entered under them a good right and title to such a part thereof as they respectively contracted for: . . . Others of your petitioners entered on from necessity, not having wherewith of their own to provide."

[2] On the fly-leaf of the first volume of the *Rochester Church Records* is this memorandum: "On the 18th May, 1729, then John King and Sarah his wife, who lived at a place called the Elbows in Hampshire County owned the covenant and their children were baptized, viz., William, Thomas, Joseph, Benjamin, Aaron, and Sarah, by me, who was sent by the proprietors of the lands to minister to them. Timothy Ruggles." Had the visit been six months later, the result might have been different.

[3] Now Belchertown.

mission of the Reverend Mr. Timothy Ruggles of Rochester and others, a committee of the proprietors of said tract of land (as they call themselves), praying that they may have the grant and authority of this Court for settling on said land, and be exempted from the conditions they have entered into with the said committee. Read. A petition of Robert Auchmuty, Esq., for and in behalf of Joshua Lamb, Esq., and Timothy Ruggles, Clerk, as they are a committee of the proprietors of a certain tract or parcel of land containing by estimation twelve miles long, north and south, and eight miles wide, east and west, lying near Quabaug, known by the name of Wombemsicunck, in which is concluded the land petitioned for by Isaac Burr, John King, and others, as also the land contained in the petition of Robert White, and John Stiles, Josiah Edson, Jr., and sundry others, as well as sundry other petitions for land within their propriety, praying that they may be heard by their counsel, to make out their right to the lands contained in their purchase from the Indian Sachems, before any grant on the said petitions be made, or that, if any grant should pass, that a saving of their right and claim may be inserted, for the reasons mentioned." December 2, 1729: All the parties were heard, and the petitions were rejected.

Similar petitions were presented in June, 1731, with this variation: that John King and others asked to "be confirmed in their possession of the said lands, saving to Col. Lamb and associates their right therein." June 16: "The House proceeded to the consideration of the several petitions of Joshua Lamb and others, Joseph Wright and others, and John King and others, entered on the 15th instant, which were severally read, and the papers referring to them; and after a long debate the questions were severally put, whether the prayers of the said petitions should be granted? and it passed in the negative." Apparently despairing of success in their effort to obtain confirmation of their title to the whole territory purchased by them, the committee, on the next day after the rejection of their petition, June 7, 1731, entered a new petition for "eight miles square, adjacent to the river called Nenemeseck, alias Ware River (in such form as the lands will admit of), for a township." This petition was rejected December 31, 1731; and on the next day "a petition of Joshua Lamb, Timothy Ruggles, Joseph Ruggles, and Ebenezer Pierpont, in behalf of themselves and associates," was presented for the grant of "a tract of land of the contents of *six* miles square." This petition was granted by the House January 13, 1732; the Council concurred; but the Governor withheld his consent.

The same committee renewed their petition, at the next session of the General Court, reciting the facts before stated, and praying for "a grant of land of the contents of six miles square on the northward of the river aforesaid, and adjacent thereto." "In the House of Representatives, June 17th, 1732. Read, and in answer to this petition ordered, that there be and hereby is granted unto the petitioners and their associates a tract of land of the contents of six miles square for a township, at the place petitioned for, to be laid out in a regular form by a surveyor and chainmen under oath, a plan thereof to be presented to this Court at their next session for confirmation:[1] the said land by them to be settled on the conditions following, viz., that they within the space of five years settle and have on the spot sixty families (the settlers to be none but such as are natives of New England),[2] each settler to build a good and convenient dwelling-house, of one story high, eighteen feet square at the least, and clear and bring to four acres fit for improvement, and three acres more, well stocked with English grass, and also lay out three shares throughout the town, each share to be one sixty-third part of the said town, one share for the first settled minister, one for the ministry, and the other for the school; and also build a convenient meeting-house, and settle a learned and orthodox minister, within the term aforesaid." The Council concurred June 20, and Governor Belcher consented June 30, 1732.

Thus, after a tedious and expensive delay of five years duration from the date of their first petition, the proprietors obtained legal recognition of their title to a little more than one third part of the territory which they claimed under their Indian deed; being the north end of the tract, instead of the south end for which they first sought confirmation. The question naturally arises, what occasioned such long delay? When the same proprietors desired to improve their property at Leicester in 1714, the General Court granted their first petition, and not only recognized their title, but established the territory at once as a township. Why was not their petition in the present case granted as readily?

[1] This plan was presented November 24, 1732, describing 23,043 acres, "north of Ware River and adjoining to it, near the mouth of Great Meadow Brook."

[2] In the order passed by the House, June 23, 1727, it was required that the grantees should "settle fifty families that are now inhabitants of this Province," under which provision the Scotch-Irish Colony was admissible; but this new restriction effectually excluded all except the native-born population. It is not improbable that this exclusion was made at the suggestion of the petitioners, who had already suffered so much annoyance and loss by the conduct of those who had settled at the Elbows.

Perhaps one reason was this: the "Equivalent Land," granted by the General Court in 1713, was so near to Brookfield and the "Braintree six thousand acres," that a tract of twelve miles in length and eight miles in width, bordering on Nenemeseck or Ware River, could not be found between the Elbows and Rutland, which then included Barre. Moreover, in this case the proprietors did not adopt the expensive method which had formerly proved so successful. The order of the General Court, confirming the title of Leicester to the nine persons who purchased the territory of the Indians, was passed February 25, 1713-4. "These proprietors had probably already associated others with them in the enterprise of settling the town and sharing in the speculation; for we find them executing a deed on the 23d of the same February, which was acknowledged before Penn Townsend, Esq., to thirteen other associates, dividing the same into twenty equal and undivided shares, of which two were equally divided, each between two, so as to make twenty-two proprietors of the twenty shares. The names of the persons who thus became interested with the original purchasers were Jeremiah Dummer, Paul Dudley, John Clark, Addington Davenport, Thomas Hutchinson, John White, William Hutchinson, Francis Wainwright, John Chandler and Thomas Howe as one, Daniel Allen and Samuel Sewall as one, and William Dudley. Every one of these were men of influence in the Province. . . . If it were proper, at this distance of time, to indulge in any conjectures in relation to the affairs of the proprietors, one would be led to remark upon the character and position of the men with whom the original purchasers shared the territory they had acquired. They embraced some of the most prominent and leading men of both political parties, some of them connected with the immediate government of the Province, and quite a proportion of them united by strong family ties; and if it could be supposed that by lapse of time, or defect in the original deed, or any other cause, it had become necessary to exert a combined influence over the government in order to obtain a confirmation of the title, it is pretty obvious that these were precisely the class of men through whose aid such a measure might be hoped to be accomplished."[1] No such lavish expenditure was made to secure the grant of Hardwick. But six months afterwards, December 27, 1732, Joseph Haskell of Rochester, Samuel Willis, Esq., of Dartmouth, and Ebenezer Pierpont and Colonel William Dudley of Roxbury were admitted

[1] Washburn's *Hist. of Leicester*, pp. 9, 10, 14.

as joint proprietors, "each of them for a whole share," making the shares "twelve in number and no more." If these persons did not purchase their shares by payment of money, Haskell and Willis probably rendered efficient aid in bringing forward the settlement by inducing their townsmen to emigrate to the wilderness; Pierpont was cousin to the Ruggles heirs, and was proprietors' clerk, and apparently legal adviser for several years; Dudley only can reasonably be suspected of having used official influence in obtaining the grant, but even of him it is recorded that his share was received in right of his brother Thomas, deceased.

Several years later, the title to this territory was challenged by a Stockbridge Indian. This subject is introduced here, somewhat out of the order of time, as a fit conclusion of this chapter. The original papers are still preserved: —

"To his Honor Spencer Phips, Esq., Lieut. Governor and Commander in Chief in and over his Majesty's Province of the Massachusetts Bay in New England, and to the Hon. his Majesty's Council and House of Representatives in General Court convened at Boston, September the 26th, 1750.

"The Memorial of Hendrick Kequoquau, now resident at Stockbridge, a native and claimer of the northern part of Brookfield, alias the land called Lambstown, lying on the northwest of the said Brookfield, humbly sheweth, That your memorialist, being born and brought up at said Brookfield, and by right of inheritance from his ancestors the proper owner of said land, your memorialist, not having yet sold the said land, or ever in any way or manner received any thing in consideration therefor, although your memorialist has had encouragement from Col. Stoddard that he should be paid for the same. Your memorialist has been long endeavouring to obtain justice respecting the premises, but has hitherto failed. Your memorialist being aged and necessitous, and standing in real need, having an honest and just right to the lands granted away by this Province, your memorialist prays that the honored Court would be pleased to consider the case, and agreeable to their invariable rule of justice and goodness be pleased to grant something by way of satisfaction for said lands. And your memorialist shall, as in duty bound, ever pray, &c.

"HENDRICK KEKQUOQUAU (mark).
ADAM MAHTAUNKAUMUT (mark).
MHTOCKAUMUNT (mark).

"N. B.— The reason of the two last signers is because they are partners by relation, and are agents for the memorialist."[1]

Instead of determining whether the Province should "grant something by way of satisfaction," as prayed for by the petitioner, an indorsement on the petition shows that the House of Representatives, October 10, 1750, "ordered that the proprietors of Hardwick make the within named Hendrick proper satisfaction in consideration of his right to the lands belonging to said Township; it appearing that he was one of the native owners of the same, and it not appearing that he has made sale thereof." The Council non-concurred; and an order of notice to the proprietors was issued, returnable at the next session, at which time they presented this answer:—

"To his Honor Spencer Phips, Esq., Lieut. Governor and Commander in Chief in and over his Majesty's Province of the Massachusetts Bay in New England, and to the honorable his Majesty's Council and House of Representatives in General Court convened, January 1750-1, the answer of the Proprietors of Hardwick to the memorial of Hendrick Kekquoquau, resident at Stockbridge, humbly sheweth:—That in order to set this affair in its proper light, we are obliged to recur to the year 1686, when our ancestors purchased a tract of land, twelve miles north and south, and eight miles east and west, of John Magus, Lawrance Nassawanno, James, Simon, and other Indian Sachems, to the northward of Brookfield, by the River Nenemeseck, now called Ware River; that your respondents, the said purchasers, were at many hundred pounds charge to bring forward a settlement of a plantation on the southerly part of their said purchase, about twenty years ago, at Kingston,[2] by the Elbows, which was quitted by the said purchasers without being reimbursed any of their expenses. And in the year 1732 your respondents, in consequence of their said purchase, obtained a grant of land, from the General Court, of the contents of six miles square, on the northward of Ware River and adjacent thereto for a township, subject to certain conditions of settling the same (being part of the premises purchased by our ancestors as aforesaid), which conditions of settling the said grantees many years since complied with, so as that in the year 1738[3] the General Court, in their wisdom saw cause to incorporate Lambstown into a Township by the name of Hardwick, wherein the bounds, in their act made for

[1] *Mass. Arch.*, xxxii. 68.

[2] Now Palmer.

[3] The Act of Incorporation was approved January 10, 1738-9.

that purpose, are expressed at large. So that they humbly apprehend, having in the first place obtained the native right, and afterward the General Court's grant, and complied with the conditions thereof, that they stand firm in their claim. More especially since they possess but little more than one third part of their purchase, having been obliged to surrender to the Secretary of this Province, for the public benefit, the remaining part of our said purchase,[1] with this proviso, that the said grantees should have, hold and enjoy the said grant of the contents of six miles square, to them, their heirs and assigns forever. And your respondents now want about one thousand acres of land to complete the said grant, besides the nine hundred acres in dispute with the proprietors of Quabin, which affair now lies before the Honorable Court. So that, upon the whole, when we call to mind that the Great and General Court, in their wisdom and goodness, have at all times encouraged industry and fidelity, we find our fears very much alleviated on account of the challenges made of our claims and right, one after the other; that we persuade ourselves that the premises in dispute, or any part thereof, will never be taken from those persons who have paid a dutiful regard to the Great and General Court, in complying with the conditions of their grant, and thereby promoted the public good, and be given to them who have neglected their duty in this respect; or that we shall be obliged to pay any sum or sums of money to a Native, upon his making any challenge without foundation. For though the memorialist, Hendrick Kekquoquau, was born and brought up at Brookfield, it does not necessarily follow that the lands to the northward thereof did belong to his ancestors, and so by right of inheritance descend to him; nor can we perceive that he ever made out any just claim that they or he had to the same. And as to any encouragement that Col. Stoddard might give the memorialist, we are wholly ignorant of it; but beg leave to represent that we have heard of, and some of us have seen, a large tract of land, lying northwest of Brookfield, at a place called Coyshill,[2] which we were informed that Col.

[1] Such surrender was required as a condition of the uncompleted grant, June 23, 1727; and though not expressly named in the valid grant of June, 1732, it was demanded by the government, and was actually made, at a meeting of the proprietors, February 21, 1732-3. This surrender was ratified and confirmed. Thus, under duress, the proprietors surrendered "for the public benefit" nearly two thirds of the territory rightfully belonging to them, in order to acquire peaceable possession of the remainder, rather than to give it to individuals as the price of their favorable influence.

[2] Coy's Hill is in the northerly part of Warren.

Stoddard claimed; so that it's highly probable that the memorialist has made a mistake as to the spot of land which he suggests he has a right to; for Col. Stoddard could not mean that the proprietors of Lambstown should pay him, the memorialist, for the lands which the General Court had granted to our propriety. Finally, we humbly leave the memorialist to the compassion and goodness of your Honor and Honorable Court, to relieve him, as to your wisdom shall seem meet, saving always our right to the lands purchased, granted, and settled by us, as aforesaid. And your respondents shall ever pray.

"January 29, 1750-1, being the 2d Tuesday of the setting of the General Court. } EBENEZER PIERPONT, in the name and at the desire of the Proprietors of Hardwick."[1]

This answer having been read, the petition was referred to a joint committee, and its further consideration assigned to "the first Friday of the next sitting of the General Court;" but no subsequent action thereon appears to have been had.

[1] *Mass. Arch.*, xxxii. 93, 94.

CHAPTER III.

CIVIL HISTORY.

Names of Proprietors. — Executive Committee. — Gratuities. — Arrangement of Lots. — Settlers to share the Expense of Surveying, and to aid in erecting a Meeting-House and maintaining a Minister. — Additional Grant of Land. — First Settler. — Other Settlers admitted. — Mill Lots. — Access of Inhabitants in 1736. — Incorporation as a District. — First Officers. — Rev. Timothy Ruggles. — Incorporation as a Town. — First Town Officers. — Act of Incorporation.

HAVING obtained confirmation of their title, the proprietors procured from John Chandler, Jr., Esq., a warrant, by virtue of which Joseph Ruggles gave notice of a legal meeting to be held at Roxbury on the 27th of December, 1732, "then and there to choose a Proprietors' Clerk, and to manage, improve, grant, dispose, and divide the said lands, more especially to admit our associates in due form, and to choose a committee to lay out convenient highways to accommodate a township, and to lot out so much of the said land to the proprietors and such as shall be hereafter admitted settlers in such ways as may most conduce to the promoting and settling thereof," etc.[1]

At this meeting, and the next succeeding which was held by adjournment, effective measures were adopted for the speedy fulfilment of the conditions imposed by the General Court. I shall quote freely: —

"Voted and chose Joshua Lamb, Esq. Moderator of said meeting; and chose Joseph Ruggles Proprietors' Clerk.

"Voted, That Nathaniel Paige's heirs, Andrew Gardner's as-

[1] To this notice is appended a certificate, dated Dec. 13, 1732: —

"The forewritten is a true copy of a notification which Abner Lee of Worcester this day made oath before me, the subscriber, that he set up on the house of William Thomas within the tract of land aforementioned, and which was done by eight o'clock in the forenoon of this day. Attest: John Chandler, Jr., Justice Peace." Very probably other persons may have already erected houses on this territory, but no proof of their identity is known to exist; and this William Thomas may therefore be regarded as the first known English resident in what is now Hardwick; though an ancient tradition gives the priority to Benjamin Smith.

signs, Benjamin Gamblin's heirs, Benjamin Tucker's heirs, John Curtis's heirs, Richard Draper's heirs, Samuel Ruggles's heirs, of Roxbury lately deceased, Joshua Lamb's heirs, and Joseph Haskell, Ebenezer Pierpont, Samuel Willis Esq., and Col. William Dudley Esq., are received as associates, according to said Court's grant, each of them for a whole share.[1]

"Voted, That five committee men are chosen to manage the affair of the settlement of the town according to the warrant, to wit: Col. William Dudley, Col. Joshua Lamb, Mr. Ebenezer Pierpont, Capt. Joseph Ruggles, and Mr. Samuel Davis; but three of the five to go at a time. Three men are chose a committee to audit all our accounts against the next meeting, to wit, Col. Dudley, Caleb Seaver, and Thomas Mayo. This meeting is adjourned or continued unto Wednesday the twenty-first of February next ensuing, at nine o'clock in the morning, at the Gray Hound Tavern in Roxbury.

"February 21, 1732-3, by continuation from Dec. 27th, at the Gray Hound, met and unanimously voted, in the first place, that two thousand acres of land in our new settlement or township hereby is given and granted to the petitioners and Committee, to be by them disposed of as a gratuity to such persons as have been serviceable to us in obtaining the grant of the same, as they shall think fit; all necessary highways needful for the same to be included. Voted, that we are adjourned for the space of one hour to the same place.

"And then met and voted that whereas in the Court's grant of our new township at Ware River, the Rev. Mr. Timothy Ruggles and Capt. Joseph Ruggles are two of the grantees, they have quitted to the proprietors the grant of Court to them as petitioners; they shall have, and hereby have granted them five hundred acres of land between them in said town, by allotment, over and above one share to the heirs of Capt. Samuel Ruggles, late of Roxbury deceased.

"Voted, That Benjamin Smith, who married one of the heirs of John Curtis deceased, since he has carried on his part of the charge with us, it is ordered that the said Benjamin Smith shall have recorded to him the ninth part of the said John Curtis's share.

"Unanimously voted, That whereas Joshua Lamb, Timothy Ruggles, Joseph Ruggles, and Ebenezer Pierpont, have given a general quitclaim to the Province of a Deed, signed by John

[1] At this date, it appears that all the original grantees had deceased.

Magus, Lawrence Nassawano, and other Indian Sachems, to Joshua Lamb and others; now we do declare we are contented and well satisfied, and do ratify and confirm said act, agreeable to said quitclaim. . . .

"Unanimously voted, That the whole township shall be lotted out as soon as may be by the committee as shall hereafter be determined by the Propriety; three convenient places, if they may be obtained, to seat mills on, reserved for the benefit of the proprietors, and the committee to make report of the same to the proprietors.

"Voted, That ten acres [1] of land be reserved near the centre of said tract, to set a meeting-house on, and for a burial-place and a training-field.

"Voted, That this meeting is adjourned to to-morrow morning at the same place.

"Roxbury, February 22, 1732-3. Met by continuation from the 21st of February, 1732-3.

"Unanimously voted, That the committee shall as soon as may be lay out one hundred and eleven lots for the proprietors and settlers, in one hundred acre lots, having respect to the quality of the land, viz., four lots to each proprietor's share, sixty settlers, and the lots for the minister, ministry, and school; the minister's lot to be laid out by the committee near the centre of the town, and the rest of the lots to be drawn for, both by the proprietors and settlers.

"Unanimously voted, That the remaining land belonging to the proprietors be all lotted out by the committee in such quantities as that each proprietor have three lots and so sorted as that in the draft each person may have a just and equal share.

"Unanimously voted, That each settler pay into the hands of the committee, upon his drawing his lot, the sum of five pounds towards the defraying the charges of surveying, &c.; and the further sum of ten pounds each, for the building a meeting-house and settling a minister, within the space of three years after his being admitted.

"Unanimously voted, That each proprietor have leave to offer

[1] This "ten acres" was near the old burial-place and training-field, or common; but that it did not include either is manifest from the fact that a different disposition of the whole tract was subsequently made: five acres, the easterly half, was sold to Rev. Timothy Ruggles, in February, 1758; half an acre, the northwesterly corner, was given to the "Separate Society," 10th March, 1761; and "four acres and an half remaining of the ten acres" was sold to Jonas Fay, 19th May, 1761. The ten acres was on the hill, northwesterly from the present common, which seems to have been substituted for the original grant.

for admission five settlers of such persons according to the Court's grant, and shall give bonds to the committee for the fulfilment of the order and conditions of Court within three years from their admission on forfeiture of their lots to be again disposed of; always provided that those who have paid their money and are already admitted be deducted out of the whole in proportion; and whereas the proprietors have each of them a draught of four lots, which makes nine lots including the settlers, five of any of the nine being settled by them shall be sufficient."

On a more careful survey, the proprietors found that they had interfered with other grants, and were curtailed in their territory. They petitioned the General Court for relief, June 15, 1733, representing that, "so it was, that the surveyor and chainmen, who were under oath, not knowing the bounds of a tract of land of six thousand acres granted heretofore by this Court to Braintree and adjoining to Rutland, and not thinking the said Braintree land or any part was on the northwest of Ware River, have included within that plat four hundred acres of good land,[1] fit for settlements; as also have included the quantity of three hundred acres more at the west end of the grant, being land formerly granted by this Court to the Government of Connecticut, called Equivalent lands, and belonging, as your petitioners are informed, to John Read, Esq.,[2] all which will appear by the plan herewith presented. Wherefore your petitioners being thus lessened in their grant, and having three large ponds of some hundred acres included, obliges us humbly to pray your Excellency and Honors that a strip or parcel of land belonging to this Province, between Braintree grant, Brookfield town, and Ware River, so far as the bend of the River is, may be added to the grant made your petitioners. . . . Our humble prayer is that the said land may be added to and accounted a part of the township granted as aforesaid, in full satisfaction of the land that is wanting of the contents of six miles square as aforesaid."

"In the House of Representatives, June 16th, 1733. Read, and ordered that the prayer of the petition be and hereby is granted, and the strip or parcel of land within mentioned is confirmed to the petitioners, and their associates, and their assigns,

1 This tract of "four hundred acres" was at the northeasterly corner of the town, and included the Robinson Farm. It was annexed to Hardwick, by act of the General Court, June 10, 1814. *Mass. Sp. Laws*, v. 10.

2 The angles at the west end of the line between Hardwick and Ware, on the map, indicate the locality of these "three hundred acres."

respectively, forever by the following bounds, viz., beginning at the east bank of Ware River, at the northwest [northeast?] corner of a tract of land laid out to James Hovey, and confirmed this present session; from thence running southerly, as that line runs, to Brookfield bounds; and from thence easterly, as Brookfield bounds run, to the southwesterly corner[1] of Braintree six thousand acres; and from thence extending northwesterly, bounding northeasterly on said six thousand acres, till the line comes to Ware River; and then bounding on Ware River to the first bounds: in lieu of the four hundred acres taken off by Braintree grant, and the three hundred acres taken off by land of John Read, Esq., and the ponds, etc., as aforesaid, provided it interferes with no former grant." The Council concurred three days afterwards, and the Governor gave his consent.

At the time of this grant, Lieutenant (afterwards captain) Eleazar Warner resided with his family on a farm, which was given to him and his wife by her father, Thomas Barns of Brookfield, in 1729, and included part of the Winnimisset swamp and upland. His house stood about a mile east of Ware River, at the corner of the old turnpike and the road leading to New Braintree meeting-house, and was afterwards long known as the Perez Cobb house. He was probably the first English settler on this territory.[2] At this time also very few settlers had become resident on the original grant. By the Proprietors' Records it appears that on the 12th of June, 1733, seventy-four of the one hundred and eleven proposed lots had been laid out; "and there is sixteen persons already settled and entered on them;" and it was "proposed that twenty-four persons[3] more shall at this time be admitted as settlers thereon, who, together with the proprietors, shall draw for the lots already laid out. . . . Then the

[1] This "corner" was not far southeasterly from the point where the road from New Braintree to West Brookfield passes the head of Ditch Meadow. The tract thus described became the westerly part of New Braintree when that town was incorporated.

[2] It is a family tradition, and it is so stated in the *Massachusetts Spy*, December 10, 1817, that his son Warham Warner, who was born November 1, 1730, and died December 4, 1817, "was the first [English] child born in New Braintree." At the date of this birth, probably no settlement had been commenced in what is now Hardwick.

[3] These "twenty-four" were not yet resident, as they had not drawn their lots, and some of them never personally occupied those lots. Several were delinquent for a full year, and it was voted, June 12, 1734, "that the Committee write forthwith to each settler that has not yet been at work on their lots, to come into the meeting on the adjournment to give bond to fulfil their settlements according to agreement; and provided they do not, others shall be admitted." Five such lots were declared forfeited July 21, 1736.

proprietors and the twenty-four proposed as settlers proceeded to draw their lots." And December 26, 1733, "The proprietors proceeded to draw for their two hundred acre lots, and drew the same as follows:" three lots of two hundred acres each to "Coll. Lamb, Gardner's heirs, Mr. Haskall, Mr. Paige, Ebenezer Pierpont, Mr. Tucker's heirs, Coll. William Dudley, Mr. Draper's heirs, Mr. Gamblin's heirs, Capt. Willis, Mr. Curtis's heirs, Capt. Ruggles' heirs." At the same meeting "the lots were drawn amongst the proprietors and settlers, viz.: the remaining thirty-two as follows." The list, however, was not entered on the Proprietors' Records until November 3, 1743, when it was "voted, that the list of the lots drawn by the proprietors and settlers, laid before the proprietors by their Committee, be and hereby is accepted, and that the Proprietors' Clerk be desired to record them forthwith in their Book of Records." Four one hundred acre lots are recorded, as drawn by each of the twelve proprietors. Then follows a record of the settlers' lots: "The following is a list of the persons' names and the lots drawn by them, with the number of acres belonging to each lot drawn by the persons admitted settlers in Lambstown, so called." I omit the numbers of the lots, as no plan of them is known to exist.

	Acres.
James Akins	100
Mr. James Allen	100
John Amadown	100
Thomas Bennett	100 and addition.
Lidel Buck	120, now R^{d} Church.
Roger Carary	100
Nathan Carpenter	110
Capt. Willm Chandler	94
Jonath^{n} Church	100, now Miricks.
Saml Church	100
Saml Cook	100
Ebenez^{r} Cuttler	120
Saml Davis	100
Samuel Duglass	104
Michal Gilson	100
David Goldthright	100
Stephen Griffen	100 Ezra Leonard.
Stephen Griffeth	100 and 50.
Griffen	98, now Pikes.
John Harwood	102
Joseph Haskal	125

	Acres.
Mr. Jos[h] Haskal	102
John Hunt	100, now Robinsons.
David Ingersole	100
Dudley Jordan	100
Edmund Jordan	100
John Jordan	116
Coll. Joshua Lamb	100
Ezra Leonard	100
William Maccoy	99, a mill lot, with 6 rodds allowed for a highway.
Sam[l] Marsh	104
Thomas Mayo	100, purchas'd.
Norcross	100
Christopher Page	100
Christop[r] Page	100
Ebenezer Pierpont	100
Elisha Pike	100, now Gillet.
Thomas Powers	100
Ramsdel	100
Sam[l] Robinson	103
Capt. Jos[h] Ruggles	100
Mr. Timo[y] Ruggles	112
Mr. Timo[y] Ruggles	100
Mr. Timothy Ruggles	100
Shaw	100
Sam[l] Shumway	100
Benjamin Smith	100
Jonath[n] Southwick	100
Moses Stockbridge	100 and 50.
Benj[n] Sumner	100, now Edw[d] Sumner.
Edw[d] Sumner	100
William Sumner	104, now Edw[d] Sumner.
William Thomas	104
John Tompson	100
Seth Twitchel	90, forfeited by him.
Wells	100
Andrew White	, now Hunt.
Mr. Will[m] Williams	100
Capt. Sam[l] Willis	100
Coll. Sam[l] Willis [1]	100

[1] After the lots were drawn in 1732, some were forfeited, and others changed owners, before the list was recorded in 1743, as indicated on the record; and Captain Willis was promoted to the office of colonel. Mr. James Allen, Mr. Timothy Ruggles, and Mr. William Williams were clergymen. Many of those who drew lots never became settlers.

	Acres.
The Common	10
Mill Lot	
Minister Lot	200
Ministry Lot	200
School Lot	200

On the East Side of Ware River.

George Abbot	100
Barr	100
Josiah Barrett	100
Blair	100
Robert Gatchell	100, now Haskal.
Nichols	50
Ebenezer Pierpont	50
Jeremiah Powers	100
Sam[1] Smith	100
Lt. Warner	50 and addition.

October 30, 1733. "Voted, That the Rev. Mr. Timothy Ruggles shall have the Mill Lot for one of his settlers' lots to the west side of the 69th lot."[1] "Voted, That Lieut. Leonard shall have the Mill lot adjoining to Ware River, at the southerly corner of the town,[2] provided he erects a good grist mill on the River in one year from the last day of June next, and that he keeps and maintains the said mill in good repair for the space of twenty years, so as to supply the inhabitants of the town with grinding from time to time, and for the usual toll; said lot to be accommodated as the Committee shall see cause, but not to include above one hundred and fifty acres of land."

Although never actually attacked by hostile troops, in its exposed situation on the frontiers the settlement of the town was retarded by fears of invasion. Hence the proprietors voted, December 27, 1733, "that if the inhabitants or settlers are mo-

[1] This lot was probably on Moose Brook at the Furnace Village, where a grist mill was very early in operation.

[2] At Gilbertville. Lieutenant Leonard failed to perform the conditions, and the lot was granted, September 10, 1735, to "William Jennison, Esq., and Thomas Stearns, both of Worcester, and Stephen Harrington of Lambstown in equal parts. . . . And it is to be understood that the said mill is to be set on either Ware River or the Brook running through said lot, as may best answer the end of the builders and inhabitants, both." The mill and lot subsequently became the property of John Wells, after whose death they were sold, 24th October, 1750, to Jonathan Warner. The water-power at this place is the most important within the town. Instead of a grist mill it now moves an extensive manufactory.

lested by a war with the Indian or French Enemy, it is agreed and allowed that if they, within two years after the expiration of the war, shall fulfil and bring forward their settlement according to the Court's grant, they shall enjoy their rights." And six months later, June 12, 1734, it was "represented to the proprietors, that Mr. Stephen Griffen[1] was desirous to build and settle on his brother Norcross's lot, that the neighborhood might be more complete and defensible in case of a war;" and liberty was granted accordingly.

A somewhat suspicious vote was adopted, December 27, 1733: "Voted, to Mr. Ebenezer Pierpont the quantity of three hundred acres of land, to be disposed of by him to two particular gentlemen, viz., one hundred acres to one of said gentlemen, and two hundred acres to the other gentleman." The mystery is partially solved by a memorandum made on the fourth Wednesday of September, 1734, that "whereas there was a grant of three hundred acres of land to Mr. Ebenezer Pierpont some time ago for two particular gentlemen: now the meaning is, that the Honorable Judge Dudley shall have two hundred acres, and one hundred acres to William Dudley, Esq." What service these gentlemen had rendered or were expected to render in consideration of this gift does not appear; nor is any reason obvious why their names were not mentioned in the original grant, like those of other recipients of land, whether by gift or purchase.

Until 1736, the settlement of the township made slow progress; but in that year there seems to have been a large accession of inhabitants. In the House of Representatives November 29, 1736, "a petition of Benjamin Smith and sundry other inhabitants of lands lately granted to Joshua Lamb, Esq. and others, at a place called Lambstown, setting forth that they have fulfilled the conditions of a settlement, being arrived to the number of sixty inhabitants,[2] and performed what was enjoined on them as to subduing and improving the lands, and have called and settled a minister, praying that they may be incorporated into a town-

[1] Stephen Griffith.

[2] If this mean sixty families, — the number required in the grant, — the greater part must have become inhabitants during this year. Deacon Joseph A en moved into the town in the early part of the year; and he says there were then only twenty-three families in the place.

"In thirty-six I came into
This then a wilderness:
Great hardships we did undergo,
Our wants did daily press.

ship, for the reasons mentioned. Read, and ordered that the prayer of the petition be granted."[1] The Council non-concurred; but two days afterwards proposed to incorporate the place as a district, to which the House assented, and it was enacted, "That the prayer of the petition be so far granted as that Mr. Benjamin Smith, one of the petitioners within named, be and is hereby authorized and empowered to notify and warn the inhabitants and residents on the tract of land within mentioned, qualified by law to vote in town affairs, to convene as soon as may be in some public place, then and there to choose town officers, and agree upon methods for the support of the ministry, and defraying other charges; the said officers to stand until the twenty-fifth day of March, one thousand seven hundred and thirty-eight. Provided, nevertheless, and it is hereby declared, that nothing herein contained shall extend or be construed to extend to the confirmation of the original grant of the said tract of land, but that the same remain as heretofore until this Court be fully satisfied that the grantees have fulfilled the conditions of the grant."[2] The meeting, thus authorized, was holden February 9, 1737; and its proceedings are here entered in full, as they show to a certain extent who were then inhabitants. It was voted:

"1. That Mr. Benjamin Smith be the Moderator of said meeting.

"2. That said meeting be adjourned to the house of Nathan Carpenter, on said day.

"3. That Samuel Robinson be Town Clerk.

"4. That Benjamin Smith, Joseph Allen, Samuel Robinson, Stephen Griffeth, and Benjamin Ruggles be Selectmen.

"5. That John Wells be Town Treasurer.

"6. That William Maccoye, Benjamin Ruggles, and Experience Johnson be chosen Assessors.

"7. That George Abbot and Ichabod Stratton be Constables.

"8. That all the remaining town officers be chosen by holding up of hands.

"9. That Thomas Perry and Benjamin Andrews be tiding men.

"10. That Josiah Barret and James Aikens be surveyors of highways.

"The families were twenty-three,
That then did here belong:
They all did hardships bear with me,
But now are dead and gone."

Last Advice and Farewell of Deacon Joseph Allen to the Church and Congregation of Hardwick. Printed at Brookfield, 1795, pp. 51, 8vo.

[1] Printed Journal of House of Representatives.

[2] General Court Records.

"11. That Dudley Jordan and John Hunt be fence-viewers.

"12. That Phineas Powers and Samuel Church be hog-reaves.

"13. That this meeting be adjourned to the 23d of this instant February, at the Meeting-house, at ten of the clock on said day."

Up to this time, the Rev. Timothy Ruggles was more active than any other person in carrying forward the settlement of the town. Although he sold, in 1736, his proportion of the share inherited from his father, Captain Samuel Ruggles, of Roxbury, he made frequent and extensive purchases from the heirs of other proprietors and from those who had received grants as settlers. His activity and the extent of his possessions by grant and purchase are partially indicated by votes passed June 29, 1737: "Whereas Mr. Timothy Ruggles of Rochester, one of the proprietors, was obliged to settle five lots, called settlers' lots, in said Lambstown, as granted to himself, each of them one hundred acres, and there was a vote passed, that if he did the duties of settling on the thousand acres, so called, that it should answer for the same, and he having performed his duty as such on said thousand acres, as appears by the view of the proprietors' committee, voted that those lots in said thousand acres which are No. 1, No. 2, No. 3, No. 4, No. 5, No. 6, No. 7, according to the plan of that part of the thousand acres, so called, which lies on the westerly side of Ware River [1] in Lambstown, containing in the whole eight hundred and seventy-three, signed William Chandler, Surveyor, and as entered on the original plan, &c., be and hereby are confirmed to the said Timothy Ruggles, and to be to him, his heirs and assigns forever." At the same time three other lots were confirmed to him, he having bought them of Samuel Willis, Esq., Samuel Shumway, and Samuel Douglass, and "having performed the like duties on the same."

During the two years between the grant of authority to elect

[1] This portion of the "thousand acres" was in the northeasterly part of the town, between the Moose Brook Road and the River. The farm marked "D. Billings" on the R. Map was the southwest corner of this tract, being described in the deed from Nathaniel Ruggles, of Roxbury, to Daniel Billings, May 8, 1765, as bounded west on the west line of the thousand acres, north on Caleb Nye (formerly Samuel Nye), east on Captain Benjamin Ruggles's homestead, and south on the mill lot, this line being "the line between the mill lot and the thousand acres." The proprietors voted, in September, 1734, "that the piece of land decyphered on the plat of one hundred and twenty-eight acres, lying eastward of Ware River, and on Braintree grant, and on Mr. Barnes's heirs, is allowed to make up the complement of one thousand acres on Ware River," etc.

certain officers and the full incorporation of the town, the inhabitants transacted very little business at their public meetings, except providing for the erection of a meeting-house and the maintenance of a minister, which will be noticed elsewhere. Heretofore the provision made by the proprietors for this purpose was inadequate; and the inhabitants manifested a strong desire for incorporation, that they might thus become able to raise a sufficient revenue by taxation of all the land, whether owned by residents or non-residents. Accordingly it was voted, June 30, 1737, "That Mr. Christopher Paige be the man to go to the General Court, to get the Town incorporated, or the land taxed." When this petition was under consideration in December, 1737, the proprietors asked the General Court to delay the act of incorporation for another year, and their request was granted.

At the election of officers, March 6, 1738, several new names appear: John Amadon, Matthew Barr, Samuel Gillett, Robert Gitchell, Roger Haskell, Stephen Herrington, Constant Merrick, Christopher Paige,[1] Eleazar Sanyer, Jonathan Warner, and Samuel West.

August 8, 1738, voted, "That Benjamin Smith's yard be a pound for the town this year."

October 19, 1738, voted, "That the town-meetings for the time be warned by posting at the meeting-house." Personal notice seems to have been given, heretofore, by two constables, each being directed "To warn all freeholders and other inhabitants in Lambstown, so called, in your district." The Great Meadow Brook was then the division between the two districts. At a later period, the county road, which afterwards became a turnpike, was established as the line between the north and south districts.

November 2, 1738, voted: "1. That Lieut. Eleazar Warner be the Moderator of this meeting. 2. That the town will send to the General Court, to pray for a tax of two pence per acre upon all the land lying within the limits of Lambstown. 3. That Deacon Christopher Paige be the man to go to the General Court, to pray for the laying of the aforesaid tax."[2]

This petition was presented in December, and an order of

[1] Deacon Christopher Paige was Moderator of the meeting April 4, 1737, and had then been here about two or three years.

[2] In anticipation of this movement, a petition was presented, December 2, 1738, by "Ebenezer Ayers, Eleazar Warner, and sundry others, proprietors and inhabitants of the southeasterly part of Lambstown, so called, on the southerly or southeasterly side of Ware River, showing that though they live on farm

notice was issued to the proprietors. December 15, 1738, in the House of Representatives, "The petition of Christopher Paige in behalf of Lambstown, so called, praying as entered the 9th current, read again, together with the answer of Joshua Lamb, Esq., and others, a committee of the proprietors and non-residents of Lambstown, and the matter being maturely considered, in answer to this petition, voted, That the Assessors of the plantation of Lambstown, so called, are hereby allowed and empowered to levy an assessment or tax of three half pence per acre per annum, for the space of five[1] years next coming, on all the lands therein and belonging either to resident or non-resident proprietors; the money arising hereby to be annually applied and paid, viz. one half thereof to the Reverend Minister there for his better encouragement and more comfortable support, the residue for building and finishing a handsome meeting-house for the better accommodating the inhabitants in attending the public worship of God. And the constables or collectors of said plantation for the time being during the said term are also hereby directed and required duly and seasonably to collect and pay in the sum of the said tax annually, for the uses and purposes aforesaid. And the petitioner is hereby further allowed and empowered to prepare and bring in a Bill for erecting the said plantation into a township, that so the inhabitants thereof may be vested with, hold, and enjoy, equal powers, privileges, and immunities, with the inhabitants of the other towns of the Province." The Bill or Act of Incorporation was duly enacted, and approved January 10, 1739.[2] It is inserted in full at the end of this chapter. On the following day it was "ordered, That Mr. Christopher Paige, a principal inhabitant of a new

land which they hold by purchase, and lately by this Court annexed to the said plantation of Lambstown, and are accounted to help make up the number of Lambstown settlers, yet they never received any of the propriety lands, that their habitations are so situated as renders it much more convenient for them to be annexed to Braintree new grant than to remain as they are; praying the order of the Court to annex them to Braintree new grant, for the reasons mentioned." This petition failed; but it was renewed several years later, and was then successful.

[1] Amended by substituting three years for five years.

[2] At this time the township received the name of Hardwicke, and it was thus written for many years. The final letter has since been omitted, and in conformity to the almost universal custom, I have written Hardwick, in this sketch. Hardwicke, however, is undoubtedly the original name. This name was probably given in compliment to Lord Hardwicke, an English nobleman. But if the whole vocabulary had been searched for the purpose, it would have been difficult to find a name more accurately descriptive of the character of this township; for it imports a place favorable for husbandry and the raising of cattle. See Rees's *Encyclopedia*.

Town, lately erected at a plantation called Lambstown, in the county of Worcester, by the name of Hardwicke, be and hereby is fully authorized and empowered to assemble the free-holders and other qualified voters there, on the first Monday in March next, at some convenient public place in said town, in order to their choosing a Town Clerk and other town officers for the year then next ensuing." A meeting was accordingly holden March 5, 1738-9, at which town officers were elected, to wit: Christopher Paige, Moderator; Cornelius Cannon, Town Clerk; Eleazar Warner, John Wells, Benjamin Smith, William Thomas, and Constant Merrick, Selectmen; John Wells, Treasurer; Samuel Robinson and Matthew Barr, Constables; Samuel Gillet and Josiah Barrett, Tythingmen; Ichabod Stratton, John Amadon, Roger Haskell, and Nathan Carpenter, Surveyors of Highways; Phineas Powers and Jeremiah Powers, Fence-viewers; Richard Church and Amos Thomas, Hog-reeves.

ACT OF INCORPORATION.

"*Anno Regni Regis Georgii 2d, &c.* 12 mo.

"An Act for erecting a plantation in the County of Worcester, called Lambstown, into a township by the name of

"Whereas the plantation of Lambstown, so called, in the County of Worcester is competently filled with inhabitants, who labour under divers inconveniences and difficulties for want of a power of enjoying and exercising town's privileges among them, and have addressed this Court setting forth the same, and praying for relief therein.

"Be it enacted by his Excellency the Governor, Council, and Representatives in General Court assembled, and by the authority of the same, that the said plantation of Lambstown inclusive of the additional grant, lying and being on both sides Weare River as the same is hereafter bounded and described, be and hereby is constituted and erected into a separate and distinct township, by the name of

"The bounds of said township being as follows; viz. Beginning at the East bank of Ware River at the northwest corner of a tract of land laid out to James Hovey; from thence extending southerly as that line runs to Brookfield bounds; and from thence easterly as Brookfield bounds run, to the southwesterly corner of Brantree six thousand acres; and from thence extending north-

[1] The name "Hardwicke" was inserted by the Governor, agreeably to the usual custom under the Provincial Charter.

westerly bounding northeasterly on said six thousand acres till the line comes to Ware River, and so over the River the same course till it comes to the corner of Brantree grant, and there strikes on Rutland Line. Then running N. 39° W. 1760 perch; then S. 40° W. 1800 perch; then S. 1° 30′ W. 1030 perch; then E. 2° 30′ N. 1005 perch to Ware River.

"And that the Inhabitants thereof be and hereby are vested and endowed with equal powers, privileges, and immunities which any of the Inhabitants of any of the other towns of this Province are or by law ought to be vested with.

"Provided nevertheless, that the Inhabitants of said Town do within three years from the publication of this Act erect and finish a suitable and convenient Meeting house for the public Worship of God among them, they having already an orthodox minister settled among them."

The foregoing is a copy of the original Bill, or act of Incorporation, on file in the office of the Secretary of State.

CHAPTER IV.

CIVIL HISTORY.

Early Arrangement concerning Meeting-house, Minister, Schools, Highways, and Pound. — Cattle. — Deer. — Destructive Birds and Beasts. — Squirrels. — Beaver-dam. — Land Bank Bills. — Province Tax. — Cartway across Great Meadow Brook. — Pauper. — Inhabitants on the East Side of Ware River desire to be set off. — Excise Bill — Proprietors' Meetings established at Hardwick. — Proprietors' Records. — Advent of Brigadier Ruggles. — Highways. — Lottery. — Fair.

For several years after the incorporation of the town, the records disclose no event of a remarkable character. Preparations for the erection of a new meeting-house and for the comfortable support of a minister were continued. A beginning was also made for a permanent establishment of schools. Highways were laid out, and made passable for man and beast, but scarcely for even carts; — pleasure-carriages were unknown here until long afterwards. Measures were adopted for the destruction of beasts of prey, and mischievous birds, for the protection of domestic animals, and for their restraint from doing damage. Attention was principally given to the construction of humble dwelling-houses and the conversion of the forest into fruitful fields. Those who now enjoy the fruits of their labor can scarcely conceive the toil, and hardship, and self-denial of the pioneers in accomplishing this work. A few extracts from the records may afford a glimpse of their primitive condition.

April 3, 1739, at the first meeting after the organization by choice of officers, it was voted, "That the town will build a pound, thirty feet square, and that it shall be set near the meeting-house, and that Samuel Robinson be the man to build said pound according to law." Voted, "That hogs shall run at large the year ensuing, being yoked and ringed." Voted, "That the former Records shall stand good."[1]

[1] A record of public transactions was commenced February 7, 1737, and continued regularly for the two years before the full incorporation of the town; and these "former records" were now duly authenticated.

April 23, 1739. Voted, "That droves of cattle shall not be brought into town, under the penalty of ten shillings per head, for the men to pay that taketh them in, or yardeth them, or salteth them, or is anywise instrumental in such affair." [This order was modified, a year afterwards, April 14, 1740, when it was voted, "That any person or persons belonging to this town, that shall keep, or salt, or yard, any cattle in this town belonging to any other town, except milch cows or working oxen, from the first day of May next, until the last day of July, shall pay the sum of fifteen shillings per head, one half to the use of the town, and the other half to any person that shall complain and sue for the same."[1]] Also voted, that fifty pounds be expended on the highways; "to be in work, at six shillings per day till the 10th day of September, and five shillings per day till the 1st of December; four shillings a day for a yoke of oxen, and two shillings a day for a cart."

December 10, 1739. "Samuel Robinson and Benjamin Ruggles were appointed to take care that the law be duly executed in respect to killing of deer to the first Monday of March."[2]

May 22, 1740. Voted, "To give three pence per head for old blackbirds, jays, and woodpeckers, and one penny per head for young ones; . . . that the Town Treasurer be ordered to receive the birds' heads as they shall be brought to him as abovesaid, and burn them or cut off their bills, and pay out of the Town's money to such persons as shall bring them in, according to the foregoing vote."

[1] This order was not quite so stringent as that which was adopted in Leicester, at about the same time, not only imposing the fine of ten shillings per head for entertaining cattle belonging elsewhere, but providing that "all rams, running at large, should be free plunder, and any one who should take such might have them for his own." *Worcester Magazine*, ii. 99.

[2] The limitation of time, probably, had reference to the next annual town-meeting. Not only were deer found in the forest, but the smaller wild game, such as squirrels, rabbits, foxes, etc., and various kinds of birds, were so abundant as to be troublesome, and rival parties were frequently organized for their destruction. In the days of my boyhood, the chattering of gray squirrels was a familiar sound; and I have heard my seniors relate marvellous stories of the size and abundance of wild turkeys at an earlier period. Whether the race of beavers had become extinct before the settlement of the town, I know not; but on my father's homestead, distinct traces of a beaver-dam were visible not many years ago, below a meadow on Great Meadow Brook, nearly opposite to the house of Mr. Forester B. Aiken. Perhaps bears, and certainly wolves, endangered the public safety. In December, 1738, the General Court granted "the petition of Stephen Herrington, of Lambstown, praying to be allowed the premium for killing two wolves, which he took in his trap, but by reason of the wolves carrying the trap away, so that he could not find it in a fortnight, the wolves' ears were eaten off, so that eh could not obtain a legal certificate."

May 18, 1741. "Voted, That Land Bank Bills shall pay all town debts in this town.[1] It was put to vote to see if the town will free the Governor's sons' land from land tax, and it passed in the negative."

May 19, 1746. On the question whether "the town will allow Mr. Benjamin Smith any thing for his service in going to Boston to get town privileges," &c.,[2] it was "voted, that the town will acquit Benjamin Smith of the rates that was committed to James Robinson and Samuel Church, to gather, provided Benjamin Smith will acquit the town of all demands from the beginning of the world to this day." . . . "Voted, That Mr. Jonathan Warner, our Treasurer, shall have ten pounds, old tenor, to employ a Deputy to use his best interest to prevent a Province tax from coming this year, provided he find a man that will effect the matter, or have nothing for his trouble."[3]

March 9, 1747. "Voted, that the town will free Joseph Ruggles from mending highways, so long as he will maintain a good cart-way over Great Meadow Brook in the highway against his house."[4]

October 5, 1747. "Voted, that Monday, Wednesday, and Friday, are sufficient for grinding at the mill Capt. Hammond now tends for one year."[5]

March 7, 1748. On the question, whether "the town will raise money to maintain Hannah Maccoye, sent to this town for that intent," it was "voted to raise fifty pounds, old tenor, to maintain Hannah Maccoye."[6]

1 "Land Bank Bills" were issued by a private banking company, and secured by mortgage of real estate; they were suppressed by the government after a sharp controversy.

2 This "service" was rendered in 1736. In September, 1739, the town had voted to pay fifteen pounds to Deacon Christopher Paige for similar service in 1738.

3 This vote indicates the rather excessive prudence which is elsewhere sometimes discoverable in the votes of the town. In this case a "deputy" was found; his effort was successful, and one pound was granted, February 23, 1747, "to Deac. Samuel Robinson, for preventing a Province tax being laid on our town."

4 The house stood at the place marked "O. Trow," on the R. Map. At an early day a grist-mill was erected here, and the dam was used as a road-way or bridge. It was voted, May 1, 1773, "to widen the bridge by Lieut. Joseph Ruggles' mill, as wide again as it now is, and to raise it some higher." Not many years ago, the grade of the road was again changed.

5 This mill was at Gilbertville. Its former owner, John Wells, had deceased, and his widow had married Captain Nathaniel Hammond, who took charge of the mill.

6 This is the first record which I find concerning pauperism in the town; but a petition presented to the General Court in 1754 indicates that this was not a solitary case. Hannah Maccoye remained chargeable until 1765.

March 6, 1749. Voted to oppose the "Petition[1] of the inhabitants of this town, living on the easterly side of Ware River, in which they pray to be set off to New Braintree and part of Brookfield, in order to be made a distinct township." August 11, 1749. "Chose Lieut. Constant Mirick to go to the General Court, to offer the reasons why the town is not willing the inhabitants living on the east side of Ware River should be set off with others as a town, or district, and there to do what he shall find necessary on that affair. William Andrewson appeared and entered his dissent against the proceedings of the meeting." October 8, 1749. "Voted, that the town be willing the inhabitants on the easterly side of Ware River be set off as a town or district."

September 30, 1754. "The question was put, whether the town be of the mind to have the Bill, published relating to an Excise by order of the Honble House of Representatives of the 18th of June, passed into a law; and it passed in the affirmative."[2]

The meetings of the proprietors were held in Roxbury until 1754, in which year their second Clerk, Ebenezer Pierpont, Esq., deceased. By this time the number of resident proprietors had greatly increased, by purchase from the original associates and their heirs, and Hardwick became a more convenient place for the transaction of business. Accordingly, by virtue of "a warrant issued by the honorable Jacob Wendell, Esq., one of his Majesty's Justices of the Peace through the Province," a meeting was held at the house of Mr. Joseph Ruggles, April 2, 1755, when Deacon Christopher Paige was elected Moderator, and Captain Paul Mandell, Proprietors' Clerk. Their subsequent meetings were in this town until May 19, 1761, when they had

[1] Among the petitioners were Eleazar Warner, Jonathan Cobleigh, Edward Ruggles, Beriah Hawes, Jonathan Higgins, James Robinson, Roger Haskell, Ebenezer Spooner, and Phineas Warner. This petition was unsuccessful; but incorporation was granted about two years later, January 31, 1751.

[2] "The taxes at this time had become heavy, and the House were desirous of relieving, so far as they could, the polls and estates from this burden; and, to do this, contrived a plan for laying an excise upon wines and spirituous liquors consumed by the people. The Council refused to approve of it. Governor Shirley sent for the House into the Council Chamber, and there stated his objection to the measure, that it would be inconsistent with the natural rights of every private family to be subjected to keep and render an account of the quantity of excise liquors which they consumed in their private houses. The House immediately ordered the objectionable part of the Bill to be printed, and sent to every town for consideration. . . . The towns voted, some, that it was contrary to their liberties, and some, that it was not. The measure, however, was dropped for a short time, but passed, with some amendments, in December, 1754." Washburn's *Hist. of Leicester*, pp. 65, 66.

apparently closed their business. Their transactions, during these years, were almost entirely limited to the sale of their hitherto ungranted lands, the settlement of a controvercy with Greenwich in regard to boundaries, and a general adjustment of their financial affairs.[1]

Until 1754 the town sent no representative to the General Court; but in that year Timothy Ruggles, Esq., was elected, and became at once a conspicuous member of the House. At that period representatives were paid by their several towns; and such towns as were not represented were subjected to fines. One of the first services demanded by this town of their representative, was to obtain a remission of a fine imposed for their former dereliction of duty. September 30, 1754. "Chose Timothy Ruggles, Esq., to petition the Great and General Court or Assembly of this Province, to get the Fine laid on our Town for not sending a Representative for the year 1752 remitted." He presented the petition, and urged these reasons: —

"That the Inhabitants of said Town less than twenty years before that time first began the settlement thereof, and in general went on said lands in poor and low circumstances, and by means of the exceeding roughness of said lands they are to this day obliged to expend yearly large sums in making and repairing their highways, and even this year are at the expense of a hundred pounds Lawful money for that purpose, and must be at the expense of some thousands of pounds upon their roads, before they will be brought to be as good as most of the roads in the Province are by nature, beside several large Bridges they are obliged to build and maintain; as also their crops of Indian corn having been for several years cut short to that degree that they have been obliged to buy and bring from the Towns upon Connecticut River near half the Corn necessary for their subsistence; as also at that time there were not much above eighty families in said Town, many of which were extremely poor; and before and ever since the Inhabitants of said Town are obliged to be at a

[1] It was voted by the town, May 19, 1773, "that the Proprietors' Records be lodged with the Town Clerk; but the Proprietors to have liberty to use them at their pleasure." Whether this vote was carried into effect, I know not. More than forty years ago I found the volume, much mutilated, in possession of the descendants of the last Proprietors' Clerk; I made a full copy of all the records which remained in it, and returned the original to its former possessor. Since that time the volume has disappeared, and the most persistent search for it has hitherto been unsuccessful. If it still exists, its present custodian should forthwith place it in the office of the Town Clerk, agreeably to the vote passed in 1773.

great expense for the support of several poor and indigent persons; for which reasons your memorialist in behalf of said Town, most humbly prays for the remission of the aforesaid fine, &c.

TIMOTHY RUGGLES."

Some of these reasons, I suspect were somewhat highly colored, especially in regard to the number of paupers, and the general poverty of the inhabitants; but they were effectual, and the fine was remitted December 17, 1754.[1]

During his residence here, from 1754 to 1774, Timothy Ruggles, Esq. (or, as he was generally styled, Brigadier Ruggles), was active in promoting the welfare of the town by introducing improved breeds of horses and neat cattle, and better methods for the cultivation of the soil. He also endeavored to promote its political importance by making it the shire town of a new county. Under his advice, doubtless, at a meeting held, May 16, 1763, "The town made choice of Timothy Ruggles, Esq., an agent to petition the Great and General Court, that the westerly part of the County of Worcester, and the easterly part of the County of Hampshire, be formed into a distinct County." This project failed. But in the previous year, through his influence, Hardwick was distinguished above other towns in the Province, by the establishment of a Fair,[2] after the English pattern. This Fair was considered so important, and of so great public interest,

[1] The construction of roads in Hardwick was very difficult and expensive, and their maintenance has always been burdensome. A quarter of a century after this date, a resort to a very popular method of relief was contemplated, but abandoned. At a town-meeting, January 25, 1779, "to see if the town shall think proper to apply to the General Court for liberty to make a lottery, to raise a sum of money for the purpose of repairing the public roads in said town," it was "voted that the article in the warrant, with respect to a lottery, should subside."

[2] "An Act for setting up a Fair in the Town of Hardwicke, in the County of Worcester.

"Be it enacted by the Governour, Council, and House of Representatives, that henceforth, there may be kept a Fair in said Hardwicke on the third Wednesday and Thursday of May, and on the third Wednesday and Thursday of October annually.

"And be it further enacted, that the said Town of Hardwicke be and hereby are enabled, at a meeting called for that purpose, to choose proper officers to regulate said Fair, until the annual meeting in March next, and to be chosen thereafter annually, in the month of March, during the continuance of this act.

"And be it further enacted, that no bargain and sale, made at any of the said Fairs, shall be deemed valid and effectual in the law, unless the same be made between sun-rising and sun-setting.

"This act to continue and be in force for the space of seven years from the first day of July next, and no longer."

This act was passed June 12, 1762. It seems to have been renewed after the expiration of seven years; the Fairs continued until 1775, when they ceased by special vote, not by limitation of time.

that its occurrence was duly predicted by the almanacs of the day, and "Hardwick Fair" had as conspicuous a notice as "General Election," or "Commencement at Cambridge." It attracted public attention and multitudes flocked to it from all the region round about.[1] It was holden twice a year, in May and October, when cattle and various articles of manufacture and merchandise were exhibited, bought, and sold. Wrestling, and other trials of strength and skill, were practised; and sometimes, it is said, pugilistic encounters were witnessed. It was uniformly under the direction of a superintendent, clerk, and from two to four constables, elected at the annual town meeting.[2] Drummers also were sometimes appointed. James Aiken was superintendent until 1771; after which, Thomas Robinson was elected until the Fair was discontinued, by vote of the town, in 1775. Its discontinuance was probably one of the effects of the intense political excitement which then prevailed. After the restoration of peace and quietness, the town twice petitioned, in 1785 and 1791, to have the Fair reëstablished, but the effort was unsuccessful.

[1] In anticipation of the great influx of strangers, ten persons obtained special license as innholders during the continuance of the Fair. The Records of the Court of Sessions, under date of September 23, 1762, contain this item: "The Court license the following persons to be innholders in the town of Hardwick during the times by law appointed for keeping the Fair in said town, viz., on the third Wednesday and Thursday in October next, and the third Wednesday and Thursday in May next, who recognized," etc. The persons named were Thomas Robinson, Challis Safford, Jonas Fay, Elisha Billings, Joel Carpenter, John Cooper, Daniel Wheeler, Jacob Fisk, Joseph Ruggles, and Joseph Warner. Although their expectations seem not to have been fully realized, half that number afterwards renewed their license.

[2] At a town-meeting, September 2, 1762, officers for the Fair were elected, to wit: James Aikens, Superintendent; Paul Mandell, Clerk; Thomas Robinson and Deacon John Cooper, Constables; (Deacon Cooper was excused and Jonathan Farr was elected in his place). "Appointed Capt. Paul Mandell to insert in the Public Prints when the Fair is to be holden in this town."

CHAPTER V.

CIVIL HISTORY.

Emigration to Bennington, Vt., with Personal Notices. — Emigration to Barnard, Vt., with Personal Notices. — Perils encountered by the Pioneer Emigrants.

BESIDES the ordinary removal of inhabitants to which all towns are subject, there have been two organized emigrations from Hardwick, each forming the nucleus of a new town in Vermont. The first occurred in 1761; it was less in numbers than the other, but even more important in its results.

"'The first settlement of Vermont, and the early struggles of its inhabitants not only in subduing a wilderness, but establishing an independent government,' says Sparks, in his 'American Biography,' 'afford some of the most remarkable incidents in American history.' If this is true of the State in general, it is especially true of Bennington, the cradle of its infancy; and no less true of Bennington's religious than of its secular life; for as it was the first town chartered, so its First Church was the first also in the territory afterwards Vermont. . . . On January 3, 1749, parties, many of them from Portsmouth, N. H., obtained a grant from the New Hampshire Governor, Benning Wentworth, Esq., in the name of King George II., of a township, six miles square, situated six miles north of the Massachusetts line and twenty miles east of the Hudson. According to the provisions of this charter these purchasers first divided off acre homesteads in the centre, to the number of sixty-four, for a village plot, and then divided the remainder into sixty-four equal parts, and cast lots for the same. Each original purchaser is believed to have sold his share without, perhaps, even seeing it, except upon paper, certainly to have never settled upon it, or improved it. . . . The township remained an unbroken wilderness for thirteen years, though men thus cast lots for it, and appropriated it to be some time a town under the name of Bennington, in honor of the Christian name of the New Hampshire Governor. Capt. Samuel Robinson, returning to his home in Massachusetts from one of the campaigns of the Continental army in the French War, mistaking his route, passed by accident this way; and, impressed by the attractiveness of the country, resolved to obtain others to join him and come up and settle here. His resolution was carried into effect. Others agreed to accompany him. They searched out the owners of the land; they purchased the rights of the original grantees, or of those to whom they had sold, and removed hither. . . . The first immigration had reached here June 18, 1761. It consisted of the families of Peter Harwood, Eleazar Harwood, Samuel Pratt and Timothy Pratt, from Amherst, Mass., Leonard Robinson and Samuel Robinson, Jr., from Hardwick, Mass. The party, including women and children, numbered twenty-two. During that summer and fall other families, to the number of twenty or thirty, came into town, among whom were those of Samuel Robinson, Sen., and John Fassett from Hardwick, Mass."[1]

It should be observed that the Harwoods and Pratts, here mentioned, were Hardwick families, who had resided a very short time in Amherst, and doubtless joined the emigrants under the influence of Captain Robinson. In addition to these, George Abbott and his son Timothy Abbott, John Pratt and his son Silas Pratt, John Roberts, and others, probably removed to Bennington at about the same time. The before mentioned persons, with Stephen Fay and his sons, who removed about five years later, were not only among the earliest inhabitants of the new town, but also among the most active and controlling spirits both in the town and in the State of which it became a portion; and their children were not degenerate scions of the parent stock. Some notice of them may be found in the Genealogical Register, at the end of this volume; but a brief and rapid sketch here also may be pardoned.

Samuel Robinson was apparently born to command. While he resided in Hardwick, for nearly thirty years, he was conspicuous for his activity in civil, military, and ecclesiastical affairs; he almost constantly held some important town office; commanded a company in the French War during five campaigns, from 1755 to 1759 inclusive; assisted in organizing the First Church, and was afterwards one of its deacons; and still later held the same office in the Separate Church, which also he assisted to organize. In Bennington, he "was the acknowledged leader in the band of pioneers;"[2] the first justice of the peace in what is now the State

[1] *Memorials of a Century*, by Reverend Isaac Jennings, pp. 19–22.

[2] *Ibid.*, p. 204.

of Vermont; an active participant in the bitter controversy between New Hampshire and New York in regard to jurisdiction; the agent of the settlers to represent them at New York and afterwards at London, where he died of small-pox, October 27, 1767, having partially accomplished the object of his mission. Of his children, *Leonard* fought bravely and effectively in the battle of Bennington, being a member of his brother Samuel's company; *Samuel* commanded a company in that battle, was afterwards colonel of militia, representative in the General Assembly, justice of the peace, and one of the judges of the Special Court which convicted Redding. He was one of the few persons who managed a correspondence with the British General Haldimand during the Revolutionary War, securing Vermont from invasion;[1] *Moses* was a deacon of the church, town clerk, colonel of the militia, a member of the famous Council of Safety, chief justice of the Supreme Court, governor of Vermont, and senator in Congress;[2] *Silas* was active and suffered nearly a year's imprisonment during the New York controversy, and bore arms in his brother Samuel's company at the Bennington battle; *David* fought in the same battle and in the same company, was afterwards major-general of militia, sheriff of the county twenty-two years, and United States marshal eight years; *Jonathan*, the youngest son of Samuel, Sen., was a lawyer, judge of the Supreme Court and of the Court of Probate, representative in the General Assembly, and senator in Congress. Such a family is not often found.

John Fassett was a deacon of the church, and captain of the first military company organized in Bennington; he was a representative in the first General Assembly of Vermont, and judge of probate. Of his children, *John* was captain of militia, representative in the General Assembly six years, a member of the Council fifteen years, judge of the Supreme Court, and chief justice of the County Court; *Jonathan* was representative two years; *Amos* was an assistant judge of the County Court; *Benjamin* was a commissary in the Revolutionary War, and afterwards colonel of militia. It is worthy of remark, that the father and his sons John and Jonathan held seats at the same time in the first General Assembly, in 1778.

Stephen Fay was a captain of militia, and landlord of the famous "Catamount Tavern" in Bennington. He was active

[1] See *Early Hist. of Vermont*, p. 408.

[2] John Staniford Robinson, who was Governor of Vermont in 1853, was a grandson of Governor Moses Robinson.

in the controversy with New York, and in 1772 was sent with his son, Dr. Jonas Fay, as special agents to make known to Governor Tryon "the grounds of their opposition to government."[1] When open hostilities with Great Britain commenced, he was active in a civil capacity, and his house was the headquarters of the Committee of Safety. He was then too old to perform military service; but he was represented by four or five of his sons: *John*, the eldest son, was killed in the Bennington battle, August 16, 1777; *Jonas* was surgeon in the army, member and secretary of many conventions, notably of that which met at Westminster in January, 1777, and adopted the Declaration of Independence, of which he was the author, member and vice-president of the Council of Safety, member of the State Council, judge of probate five years, judge of the Supreme Court in 1782, and delegate to the Congress of the United States, in 1777, 1779, 1781, 1782, and 1783. His public services are mentioned more fully in the Genealogical Register; *Benjamin* "was the first sheriff in the county and State;"[2] *Joseph* was secretary of the Council of Safety and of the State Council, and secretary of state. He was also one of the managers of the negotiation with General Haldimand; *David* was a lawyer, state attorney, United States attorney, judge of probate, and judge of the Supreme Court of Vermont.

The comparative influence of the Hardwick element in the affairs of Bennington and of Vermont is indicated by the activity of its representatives in the pioneer work of the town and church, and in the long and bitter territorial controversy with New York; moreover, when the civil government of the State was organized, John Fassett was the first representative of Bennington in the General Assembly (two of his sons representing other towns at the same session); Jonas Fay was a member of the first Council; Joseph Fay was the first secretary of state; and Moses Robinson was the second governor, and also was the first senator in Congress after the State was admitted into the Union, — all Hardwick men. In 1781, while Vermont was refused admission into the Union, and was contending single-handed with New York and New Hampshire for jurisdiction over its own territory, to avoid invasion by the common enemy, a plan was adopted by a few leading individuals to deceive the British officers "by feigning or endeavoring to make them believe

[1] *Vermont Hist. Mag.*, i. 171.

[2] Jennings' *Memorials of a Century*, p. 258.

that the State of Vermont had a desire to negotiate a treaty of peace with Great Britain;" the proceedings were necessarily concealed from the public; the managers, however, signed a "certificate for the protection of Colonel Ira Allen," their agent in the negotiation: "We are of the opinion that the critical circumstances this State is in, being out of the union with the United States and thereby unable to make that vigorous defence we could wish for, — think it to be a necessary political manœuvre to save the frontiers of this State. Jonas Fay, Samuel Safford, Samuel Robinson, Joseph Fay, Thomas Chittenden, Moses Robinson, Timothy Brownson, John Fassett."[1] Of these diplomatic leaders, all except Safford, Chittenden, and Brownson, were Hardwick men. One more case may be cited: "A special term of the Superior Court was held at Westminster, Sept. 11, 1782, for the trial of the prisoners. The court consisted of Moses Robinson, chief judge; and Dr. Jonas Fay, John Fassett, and Paul Spooner, side judges,"[2] — all Hardwick men.

A second emigration commenced in the spring of 1775, under the leadership of Asa Whitcomb, which laid the foundation of Barnard, Vermont. That town "was chartered July 17, 1761, to William Story, Francis Barnard, and their associates. James Call chopped the first timber here, in 1774, but left in the fall. The settlement was commenced in March 1775, by Thomas Freeman, his son William, and John Newton. The same season, Lot Whitcomb, Nathaniel Paige, William Cheedle, and Asa Whitcomb, moved their families into town. Thomas Freeman, Jr., came into town June 7, 1775."[3] All these were from Hardwick, with the possible exception of William Cheedle. They were very soon followed by many others. Asa Whitcomb had been appointed by the proprietors of the township as their agent to make sale of the land and bring forward the settlement. He first secured an energetic man, Thomas Freeman, as a leading pioneer, who removed in 1775 with at least four stalwart sons, (though yet in their minority), William, Thomas, Joshua, and Elisha, and his son-in-law, John Newton. He then induced many of his own relatives, both by blood and marriage, to em-

[1] *Coll. Vermont Hist. Soc.*, ii. 135.

[2] Hall's *History of Vermont*, p. 396. Paul Spooner was probably born in Hardwick, but was young when his father removed to Petersham. The "prisoners" were political adherents of New York, who resisted the authority of Vermont.

[3] Thompson's *Hist. of Vermont*, art. "Barnard."

bark in the enterprise of building a new town in the wilderness; among whom were his brother, Lot Whitcomb; his cousin, Joshua Whitcomb; his brother-in-law, Solomon Aiken, with his sons James, Nathaniel, Solomon, and Elijah; Steward Southgate, whose wife was sister to the wife of Whitcomb; his nephews Nathaniel, Asa, and George Paige, and his nephews Seth, Robert, and Nathaniel Dean. Besides these were Timothy and Gideon, brothers of John Newton, and Thomas Martin Wright, who married their sister; Joseph Byam; Captain Benjamin Cox, with his sons George, Benjamin, and Ebenezer; Prince Haskell, and his brother Nathaniel; Captain Edmund Hodges; Elkanah Steward and his son Samuel; and Thomas W. White. A few of these persons were then minors, but all were in Barnard very soon after the emigration commenced, and all remained and reared families. Within ten years after the town was organized, it received further accessions from Hardwick: James Byram; Shiverick Crowell, and his brother Nathaniel (their sister Salvina had married Nathaniel Paige); Aaron Fay, and his brothers Moses and Eliakim; Jacob Lawton; Sylvanus Washburn; and perhaps others. How much the population was increased by arrivals from other towns I know not; but the Hardwick men had almost all the important offices at the organization of the town. The first town meeting was held at the house of William Cheedle, April 9, 1778, by virtue of a warrant issued on the 4th of the same month, by "Thomas Freeman and Lot Whitcomb, Committee of Safety." The officers then elected were Thomas Freeman, Moderator; Thomas W. White, Town Clerk; Thomas Freeman, Asa Whitcomb, Solomon Aiken, Selectmen; Captain Edmund Hodges, Thomas W. White, Captain Benjamin Cox, Assessors; Thomas Freeman, Treasurer; William Cheedle, Grand Juror; Joseph Byam, Joseph Bowman, Constables; Henry Curtis, John Newton, Surveyors of Highways; Ebenezer Caul, Tythingman; and "at a meeting of this Town, July 7, 1778, chose Asa Whitcomb, Justice Peace."

Although this emigration was not, like that to Bennington, a distinctively religious movement,[1] the pioneers evinced their regard for religion by erecting a meeting-house at an early day. I quote from the Town Records: "July 5, 1779. "Met agreeable to adjournment, and made choice of Capt. Hodges, Moderator. Voted, to build a meeting-house at the spruce tree where the

[1] The emigrants to Bennington were connected with the Separate Church, and removed for the purpose of gaining greater freedom in ecclesiastical affairs.

town made the centre. Voted, to build a log meeting-house, and to meet at the centre the 15th of this month with axes, in order to peel bark and cut timber for the said house." When they had become more able to do so, they voted, March 18, 1782, to build a meeting-house, 40 × 30 feet, and 16 foot posts, with a convenient gallery.

In order to show the perils, as well as the hardships encountered by these emigrants, one fact is added: "On the 9th of August, 1780, this town was visited by a party of twenty-one Indians, who made prisoners of Thomas M. Wright, Prince Haskell, and John Newton, and carried them to Canada. Newton and Wright made their escape the spring following, and Haskell was exchanged in the fall. They suffered many hardships while prisoners and on their return; but they arrived safely at Barnard, and were all living in 1824 upon the farms from which they were taken." [1]

[1] Thompson's *Hist. of Vermont*, art. "Barnard." A more particular notice of the emigrants to Barnard may be found in the Genealogical Register at the end of this volume.

CHAPTER VI.

CIVIL HISTORY.

American Revolution. — Taxation without Representation. — Stamp Act. — Congress at New York. — Brigadier Ruggles, its President, refuses to sign its Petitions; his Reasons therefor unsatisfactory to the Representatives, who reprimand him, but satisfactory to his Townsmen. — Riot in Boston. — The Town refuses, but afterwards consents, that the Damage may be paid "out of the Province Treasury." — Brigadier Ruggles stands alone in Opposition to a Bill ostensibly designed to encourage Domestic Manufactures, and renders his Reasons publicly. — The Town instructs its Representative in 1773, to stand fast in Defence of its Chartered Rights and Privileges. — Final Departure of Brigadier Ruggles from Hardwick. — Form of Association prepared by him; his Letter of Explanation; he refuses to bear Arms against his Country, and retires to Nova Scotia. — Post of Honor assigned to him in an Act of Banishment. — His Death, Public Services, and Character.

In this history of a small town, it may not be expected that all the causes of the American Revolution should be enumerated and discussed, or the various events recounted, which occurred during its progress. Some of those causes and events, however, should be mentioned, in which this town was more or less actively engaged; especially because its most eminent citizen was among the foremost actors on one side of the controversy, in its early stages, while the town itself, though for a few years apparently following his leadership, stood manfully and almost unanimously on the other side, when the struggle came to a crisis.

One very prominent question at issue, in the commencement of this political and ultimately sanguinary controversy, was whether or not the British Parliament had a legal right to impose taxes on the American Provinces without their consent. In the exercise of this pretended right of supremacy, among other methods for raising a revenue from the provinces, Parliament enacted a law, styled the "Stamp Act," and directed that it should take effect November 1, 1765. It does not appear that the town took any action on this subject in town meeting; but the House of Representatives acted promptly and decisively. They sent a circular to the other Provinces, or Colonies, proposing concerted action: —

"Boston, June, 1765. Sir, the House of Representatives of this province, in the present session of the General Court, have unanimously agreed to propose a meeting, as soon as may be, of committees from the House of Representatives, or Burgesses of the several British colonies on this continent, to consult together on the present circumstances of the colonies, and the difficulties to which they are and must be reduced by the operation of the acts of parliament for levying duties and taxes on the colonies; and to consider of a general and united, dutiful, loyal, and humble representation of their condition to his majesty and to the parliament, and to implore relief. The house of representatives of this province have also voted to propose that such meeting be at the city of New York, in the province of New York, on the first Tuesday in October next, and have appointed, the committee of three of their members to attend that service, with such as the other houses of representatives or burgesses, in the several colonies, may think fit to appoint to meet them; and the committee of the house of representatives of this province are directed to repair to the said New York, on the first Tuesday in October next, accordingly; if, therefore, your honorable house should agree to this proposal, it would be acceptable that as early notice of it as possible might be transmitted to the speaker of the house of representatives of this province.

"SAMUEL WHITE, Speaker."[1]

Governor Hutchinson remarks, that "the delegates from Massachusetts Bay were James Otis, Oliver Partridge, and Timothy Ruggles. The two last named had the character of friends to government. Mr. Ruggles accepted the trust, expecting nothing would be required of him that was not expressed in the vote of the assembly, and left the house in order to prepare for his journey. He was afterwards informed that the house of representatives had passed a set of instructions to their delegates, in which they were required to insist upon an exclusive right in the colonies to all acts of taxation. He determined, thereupon, to excuse himself from serving; but, being urged by his friends, he changed his mind, and went on to New York."[2]

The several committees assembled in New York "on Monday the 7th of October, 1765," and exhibited their credentials. "Then

1 *Journal of the Continental Congress of* 1765, pp. 7, 8.

2 Hutchinson's *Hist. of Mass.*, iii. 118.

the said committees proceeded to choose a chairman by ballot; and Timothy Ruggles, Esq., on sorting and counting the votes, appeared to have a majority, and thereupon was placed in the chair." On the next day (the day fixed for the meeting), "the Congress took into consideration the rights and privileges of the British American colonists, with the several inconveniences and hardships to which they are and must be subjected by the operation of several late acts of parliament, particularly the act called the stamp act; and after some time spent therein, the same was postponed for further consideration."[1] The Congress met from day to day until October 24, 1765, when it adjourned without day. During this time a Declaration of Rights was adopted, together with an address "to the King's most excellent majesty," a memorial to the House of Lords, and a petition to the House of Commons, of Great Britain; in all which the Congress professed allegiance to the King, but protested against the recent enactments of Parliament. To the House of Commons it was said that "it is with the most ineffable and humiliating sorrow that we find ourselves of late deprived of the right of granting our own property for his majesty's service, to which our lives and fortunes are entirely devoted, and to which, on his royal requisitions, we have been ready to contribute to the utmost of our abilities. We have also the misfortune to find that all the penalties and forfeitures mentioned in the stamp act, and divers late acts of trade extending to the plantations, are, at the election of the informers, recoverable in any court of admiralty in America. This, as the newly erected court of admiralty has a general jurisdiction over all British America, renders his majesty's subjects in these colonies liable to be carried, at an immense expense, from one end of the continent to the other. . . . By this means we seem to be, in effect, unhappily deprived of two privileges essential to freedom, and which all Englishmen have ever considered as their best birthright, — that of being free from all taxes but such as they have consented to in person or by their representatives, and of trial by their peers."[2] For these and similar reasons an earnest appeal was made for the repeal of the objectionable and oppressive laws.

President Ruggles refused to affix his official signature to these documents, for reasons which he afterwards formally presented to the Massachusetts House of Representatives. By their printed

[1] *Journal of the Cont. Congress of* 1765, pp. 25, 26.

[2] *Ibid.*, p. 38.

journal it appears that on the 26th of January, 1766, the House then being in session, "the following letter was signed by the Speaker and directed to be forwarded to Brigadier Ruggles, viz., Sir, the House of Representatives have this day resolved to take into consideration the services of their committee at the late Congress at New York, and some things having been mentioned in general relating to your conduct which the House think proper to inquire into, — they direct your attendance on Thursday the 6th day of February ensuing." The subsequent proceedings were published in the printed journal as follows: February 6, 1766. "The House, according to the order of the day, entered into the conduct and services of the committee at the late Congress at New York; and after a debate, the question was put, whether the reasons offered by Brigadier Ruggles for his not signing the petitions prepared by the late Congress at New York be satisfactory to this House? It passed in the negative. Then the question was put, whether the reasons offered by Brigadier Ruggles for leaving the late Congress at New York before they had completed their business,[1] be satisfactory to this House? It passed in the negative. Resolved, unanimously, that the account given by James Otis and Oliver Partridge, Esquires, of their conduct at the late Congress at New York, is satisfactory to this House." February 12, 1766. "Resolved, that Brigadier Ruggles, with respect to his conduct at the Congress at New York, has been guilty of neglect of duty, and that he be reprimanded therefor by the Speaker." February 13, 1766. "Brigadier Ruggles appearing in the House, Mr. Speaker said to him as follows, viz., —

"Brigadier Ruggles, the House last evening voted, that with respect to your conduct at the late Congress at New York, you were guilty of neglect of duty, and thereupon ordered, that you should receive a reprimand from the Speaker of this House. Therefore

"Sir, in discharge of my duty as Speaker of this House, and in pursuance of their order, I do reprimand you accordingly. Sir, it gives me very sensible pain, that a gentleman who has been heretofore in such high estimation in this House, should fall under their publick censure.

"I hope, Sir, that by your future conduct, you will not only regain the good opinion this House have heretofore entertained of

[1] The only business which remained unfinished was the signing of the documents by the committees; as he would not sign, he did not choose to wait for his associates.

you, but also the good opinion of all those whose displeasure you may have fallen under on this occasion."

A vote was then passed by the House permitting the publication in their Journal of the reasons which he offered in justification of his conduct; but, February 19, 1766, "Brigadier Ruggles (according to order) laid upon the table his reasons for his conduct at the Congress at New York, which being read, after a debate, the question was put, whether the paper offered as containing his reasons be printed in the Journal of the House? It passed in the negative." Having thus been denied the privilege before promised to him, he caused his Reasons to be published in the "Boston Post Boy and Advertiser," May 5, 1766: —

"Brigadier Ruggles's Reasons for his dissent from the Resolutions of the Congress at New York, as given into the House, February 19, 1766.

"The Honourable House having on my motion been graciously pleased to indulge me with adjoining the Reasons in justification of my conduct to a publication of the Proceedings of said Congress, ordered by the House to be inserted at the end of the Journals of the present Sessions, first laying them before the House, — I beg leave to offer the following: —

"First. My instructions from this honorable house, conceived in the following words, viz., 'It is the expectation of the house that a most loyal and dutiful address to his Majesty and his Parliament will be prepared by the congress, praying as well for the removal of the grievances the colonies labor under at present, as for the preventing others for the future; which petitions, if drawn up as far *as you shall be able to judge* agreeable to the mind of this house, you are empowered to sign and forward.' The petition agreed upon by the congress to be presented to his majesty not being conceived in terms clearly enough expressive of that duty and loyalty which are due to the best of sovereigns, and consequently not agreeable to my above instructions from this house, left as a mere matter of judgment and discretion, if I had signed it I must have acted in direct opposition to those instructions, and thereby have exposed myself not only to the censures of this house, but to the reproaches of my own conscience, a tribunal more awful to me than this (however great) by which I have been condemned.

"2dly. That it is more regular, constitutional and conformable to the constant practice of the colonies to have their petitions and remonstrances to the King and Parliament of Great Britain signed by the Speaker of their House.

"3dly. That the signing said addresses by the committees of the several colonies which attended the congress, and who were empowered to sign the same, could by no construction come up to a general address from the colonies, as the committees from the colonies of South Carolina, Connecticut, and New York, were not empowered, and therefore could not sign, and the colonies of Nova Scotia, New Hampshire, Virginia, North Carolina, and Georgia, did not send committees to the congress, and some had no regular appointment, so that in this respect it was but a very partial signing; and therefore it was more agreeable to the instructions of this house to their committee, after having, conformable not only to the spirit but to the very words of their instructions, 'to unite in sentiments and agree upon such representations as may tend to preserve our rights and privileges,' to return the same to the house for their approbation; especially as we knew the house was then sitting, and as I then apprehended, and in fact would have been the case, little or no time would have been lost.

"4thly. A matter of so great importance to the colonies and of so delicate a nature as the open and avowed claim of an exclusive right of taxation (however true) to be asserted in addresses to the King and Parliament for relief from an Act made by this very Parliament was a measure I could not bring myself to adopt, as at my appointment to this service, upon motion made, I could not obtain an explanation on that point, nor did I think it was then the sense of this house; I therefore thought it my duty, and most respectful to the house to report the draughts agreed upon for their acceptance.

"5thly. In my apprehension those addresses would have had greater weight, and would have been more favorably received by the King and Parliament, had they been authenticated by the suffrages of the various houses of representatives and burgesses throughout the continent, and signed by their respective speakers.

"As to the charge of leaving the congress before the business was completed, I beg leave to say, that after the draughts were completed, and the petition to his Majesty was laid before me, such difficulties arose in my mind as that in its present form I could not bring myself to sign; and the reasons for reporting the draughts to the several assemblies operating so strongly on my mind I made some exceptions to the gentlemen of the congress on the address to his Majesty and offered some general reasons for the expediency of reporting the draughts to our respective assemblies, in which I was seconded by divers members, and which occasioned a long and warm debate; upon which it was determined by a vote that the address to his Majesty, which was at that time in a fair draught, together with those to the Lords and Commons, should be laid on the table the next morning, in the form they had before passed the congress and been entered upon the journal, to be signed by such of the members as thought proper. I then acquainted the congress that I proposed to go out of town early the next morning; and after the congress was adjourned to the next morning I took my leave of the members, which was on Thursday evening the 24th October, when I concluded all the business of the congress was entirely finished, except the bare signing, which, for the reasons given, I had refused.

"MR. SPEAKER, This honorable House have adjudged my reasons insufficient to support my conduct; and I feel the weight of their indignation. I have, Sir, more than once trembled under a sense of my own insufficiency to support the dignity of the high trust, with which my country unasked has honoured me; and to answer their just expectations in the discharge of them. Their candour has heretofore estimated my services rather by the integrity of my heart than the clearness of my head; this uprightness they have not only been pleased to accept, but bountifully to reward. When this house honoured me with this appointment, in undertaking it I promised myself the same indulgence. I have exercised the same freedom of judgment, I have attended the duty with the same diligence, I have been actuated with the same love to my country and its liberties, I have acted with the same singleness and uprightness of intention, and with the same ardent desire to serve the publick weal, which I have ever made the rule of my conduct: But alas! I meet with a very different reward."

Before printing these reasons, Brigadier Ruggles submitted them to his immediate constituents at a town meeting, March 3, 1766; and it is not surprising that "after Brigadier Ruggles' reading the reasons he exhibited to the General Court for not signing the petitions drew at the late Congress at New York to his Majesty &c. the town voted [that they were] in their opinion sufficient to vindicate his conduct." They did not lose their confidence in him as a patriot, and a true friend to his country as well as to his king; and for four years longer, continued to elect him as their representative in the General Court.

The publication of the Stamp Act produced great excitement in Boston, and some grossly violent deeds of the populace were the natural result. In August, 1765, by hanging him in effigy, breaking into his house, and destroying part of his furniture, some of the inhabitants had induced Mr. Secretary Oliver to promise that he would not act as Distributor of Stamps; and on the evening of the 26th of the same month they attacked the house of Lieutenant-governor Hutchinson, who had rendered himself extremely obnoxious by his subserviency to the British ministry, and "destroyed, carried away, or cast into the street, every thing that was in the house; demolished every part of it, except the walls, as far as lay in their power; and had begun to break away the brick-work. The damage was estimated at about twenty-five hundred pounds sterling, without any regard to a great collection of public as well as private papers in the possession and custody of the Lieutenant-governor."[1] The Governor recommended that the General Court should provide compensation to the sufferers, but the court declined to act. A year later, however, the odious Stamp Act was repealed, and a demand was made by the British government that the loss should be made good. The General Court, after long debate, enacted a resolve, granting compensation to the sufferers, and at the same time a free pardon to all "who had been guilty of any crimes or offences against law, occasioned by the late troubles." This act was disapproved by the King, but the money was paid and no prosecutions of offenders followed.[2]

Meanwhile, before the final settlement of this affair, this town expressed an opinion:—

"At a town-meeting in Hardwick duly warned the 15th day of August A. D. 1766, first chose Deac. Joseph Allen, Moderator. 2d, Voted to give the following instructions to Timothy Ruggles, Esq., the present representative of said [town], repecting the indemnification of the late sufferers by riots and tumults in the town of Boston.—First. We reflect upon the disorders that from time to time have been perpetrated to the great terror of the good people of that town, in evil example to others, and the great loss and damage that some of them have sustained, with the utmost abhorrence, hereby declaring our greatest readiness to do every thing in our power that justice be done to those unhappy sufferers, as well as the persons concerned in the perpetration of those horrid crimes.—Secondly. That at

[1] Hutchinson's *Hist. Mass.*, iii. 124. [2] *Ibid.*, iii. 158-160.

any sessions of the General Court, while you are a member thereof, you use your utmost endeavors that the persons concerned in those crimes be discovered and discountenanced by all proper and lawful means, that they and their accomplices be obliged to make good all damages to the sufferers. — Thirdly. In case of their inability, that you use your endeavors that those damages be made good by the town of Boston, as we have been informed that numbers of the inhabitants were spectators of these horrid scenes, without interposition to prevent them. — Fourthly. You are not to [consent to] the moneys being paid out of the Province Treasury, to make good those losses, unless at the same time it be resolved by the House that it shall be added to the taxes of the town of Boston, and collected accordingly. — Fifthly. That you take due care that the damages be justly stated and estimated, and no more be voted to any person [than] the loss he really sustained."

The town acted once more on this subject. At a town-meeting, November 28, 1766, under a warrant "to consider of a Bill pending in the House of Representatives of this Province, entitled 'An Act for granting compensation to the sufferers, and of free and general pardon, indemnity and oblivion, to the offenders, in the late riots,' — Voted, that, as it appears to the said town to be his Majesties most gracious intention that compensation should be made to the sufferers in said Bill mentioned, that Timothy Ruggles, Esq., the present Representative of said Hardwick do vote for the substance of said Bill, and that he use his influence to obtain an Act of the General Court, which [he] shall think has the most proper tendency to prevent future disturbances. As to the other parts of said Bill, we leave it to his discretion to act as he may think proper and best for the interest of the Province."

Among the measures adopted by the "Sons of Liberty," in this controversy with the British government, was substantially the non-consumption of foreign goods. This was designed to produce a twofold effect; it would prevent the government from obtaining any revenue under the form of duties, and would tend to create dissatisfaction among the English manufacturers, and enlist them against the oppressive acts of Parliament. For this purpose, a preamble and two resolutions, so carefully and guardedly drawn that they might not have attracted notice under other circumstances, were reported by a committee consisting of the

Speaker, Samuel Adams, Samuel Dexter, Ebenezer Thayer, and John Hancock, and adopted by the House of Representatives, February 26, 1768, by a vote of eighty-one in the affirmative against a single negative, to wit: "Whereas the happiness and well-being of civil communities depend upon industry, economy, and good morals, and this house taking into consideration the great decay of the trade of the province, the scarcity of money, the heavy debt contracted in the late war, which still remains on the people, and the great difficulties to which they are by these means reduced;

"Resolved, That this house will use their utmost endeavors, and enforce their endeavors by example, in suppressing extravagance, idleness, and vice, and promoting industry, economy, and good morals, in their respective towns.

"And in order to prevent the unnecessary exportation of money, of which this province has been of late so much drained, it is further Resolved, That this house will by all prudent means endeavor to discountenance the use of foreign superfluities, and to encourage the manufactures of this province."

Brigadier Ruggles requested liberty to enter upon the Journal of the House his reasons for dissent; but his request was refused. He therefore caused them to be printed in the "Boston Chronicle," March 7, 1768: —

"Province of Massachusetts Bay, Feb. 29, 1768. Mr. Speaker, The honorable house of representatives of this province, on the 26th instant, having resolved that they will use their utmost endeavors, and enforce the same by example, in suppressing extravagance, idleness, and vice, and promoting industry, economy, and good morals in their respective towns. And in order to prevent the unnecessary exportation of money, of which the province has of late been so much drained, they further resolved that they would by all prudent means endeavor to discountenance the use of foreign superfluities, and to encourage the manufactures of this province.

"The passing said resolutions being determined by yea and nay, the representative of the town of Hardwicke being the only one who answered nay to the question put for passing said resolutions, begs leave to explain himself upon his dissenting answer, and says, that he had no objection to the resolution of endeavoring to suppress extravagance, idleness, and vice, and promoting industry, economy, and good morals, but was pleased with the appearance of such necessary reformation; nor has he any objection to the encouraging any manufactures[1] which do not interfere with those of the mother country, but on the contrary might be beneficial to both that and this country. But as it is generally supposed that the true interest of this province consists in the cultivation of a good harmony with their mother country, the improvement of the land, and the encouragement of a legal trade, it is humbly apprehended it cannot be for the interest of this people to encourage manufactures in general, for the following reasons: —

"1. Because in all countries, manufactures are set up at the expense of husbandry, or other general employment of the people; and if they have not peculiar advantages over husbandry, they will, by discouraging the latter, do the country more harm than good.

"2. That in this country, manufactures are so far from having peculiar advantages that they lie under insurmountable difficulties, of which thinness of people, and the consequence of it, high price of labor, are the chief; and therefore they can never balance the mischief they will do by taking the hands off the husbandry and fishery.

"3. That at all times it behoves us to avoid setting up any business which may be detrimental to the mother country, as the preservation of a good understanding between Great Britain and her colonies is essential to the welfare of both.

"4. That at the time when we are petitioning for redress, to give particular encouragement to manufactures will look like a threat against and a defiance of Great Britain, and will bring a resentment against the province, as it is said the like proceedings have already done against the town of Boston.

"5. That if by these and other means, an actual breach should be made between Great Britain and her colonies in general, or this in particular, whoever gets the victory, we are undone. Wherefore he humbly begs leave to enter his dissent to the said resolution, and to pray that it may be entered in the Journal.

"TIMOTHY RUGGLES.

"In the House of Representatives 29th Feb. 1768. The honorable Timothy Ruggles, Esq., offered this paper to the house.

[1] Domestic manufactures were encouraged by the town; and it was voted, 17th November, 1774, "that the hatter's shop stand on the ground where it is now built, provided we have a good workman, and one that minds his business."

And the question being put whether the same shall be entered on the journals of the house, past in the negative.

"Attest SAMUEL ADAMS, Clerk."

The resolutions to which Brigadier Ruggles dissented were doubtless consistent with the intention cherished by many, though not yet openly avowed, — to dissolve all political connection with the mother country, and to become independent; but he was right in describing them as inconsistent with an honest desire for "the preservation of a good understanding between Great Britain and her colonies," and as tending to produce "an actual breach" between them. And although rich and abundant blessings in due time resulted from that "breach," his prediction of its immediate disastrous results was substantially accurate. The new-born nation came out of the conflict financially "ruined;" it was utterly bankrupt, and was compelled to repudiate its debt to its own citizens, and to refuse payment of its "bills of credit," which it had issued as money to defray the expense of the long war. The inability of the colonists to become successful rivals of Great Britain in general manufactures was also correctly stated. They might make and wear homespun cloth, if they chose to do so; but they could not manufacture the finer goods, except at a cost greatly exceeding that of the imported articles. The causes of this inability, assigned by Brigadier Ruggles, long remained operative. It was nearly half a century before general manufactures became prosperous in this country, and even then only because they were sustained by a subsidy, or artificial aid, called "protection," in the form of a high tariff of duties on foreign manufactured goods; indeed a full century elapsed before they could successfully compete in foreign markets with similar goods manufactured in Europe.

Up to this time, and for two years afterwards, the inhabitants of Hardwick evidently hoped for a peaceful solution of the controversy between the Province and the British Parliament, and manifested their approval of the method pursued by Brigadier Ruggles for the attainment of that result, as in 1770, for the fifteenth time, they again elected him as their representative in the General Court. They also associated with him, Daniel Oliver,[1] a

[1] Son of Andrew Oliver, who grad. H. C. 1724, was successively Secretary and Lieutenant-governor of the Province, and died in 1774. Daniel, the son, grad. H. C. 1762, became a refugee, and died in England in 1826.

young lawyer whom he had introduced into practice here, and who was known to agree with him in politics. About this time, however, they seem to have lost confidence in the measures heretofore adopted, though they still desired a reconciliation with Great Britain, rather than a separation. In 1771 and 1772 they sent no representative; but in 1773 they elected Paul Mandell, a man of less dignity than Brigadier Ruggles, but of different politics, and equally resolute in their maintenance.

May 19, 1773: At a town-meeting, it was "Voted, That relative to the Book[1] sent from Boston, that our rights and privileges are infringed upon.

"Chose a committee of seven men, viz., Capt. William Paige, Stephen Rice, Daniel Warner, Thomas Robinson, Asa Whitcomb, Ebenezer Washburn, and Ens. Edward Ruggles, to draw up instructions for our representative, and lay them before the town on the 14th day of June next, at one o'clock afternoon."

June 14, 1773. The committee reported instructions, which were adopted: —

"To Capt. Paul Mandell, Representative for the town of Hardwick. We esteem it of very great importance that our natural and constitutional rights, as men, as Christians, and as subjects, be preserved inviolate; so any alarm of their being unjustly arrested from us, — more especially as they are privileges that were purchased by the blood and treasure of our worthy and renowned ancestors, and handed down as a free and good right of inheritance to us, their posterity, — torn away by an oppressing hand, fills us not only with fear, concern and grief, but also warms our breasts, and will ever engage us to join with our aggrieved brethren, not only of this, but also with those of our neighboring colonies, in pursuing every lawful and prudent method whereby we may obtain redress, which we look upon to be our duty and interest at a time thus melancholy and distressing. Beholding innovations that have been already made on our natural and constitutional rights, the perplexities in which our public affairs are involved, the heavy burdens under which we together with by far the greatest part of these American Colonies are groaning on ac-

[1] This "Book" was issued by the Committee of Correspondence elected by the town of Boston, November 2, 1772, "to state the rights of the colonies, and of this province in particular, as men, as christians, and as subjects; to communicate and publish the same to the several towns in the province and to the world, as the sense of this town, with the infringements and violations thereof that have been, or from time to time may be made; also requesting of each town a free communication of their sentiments on this subject."

count hereof, and as yet unheard complaining of, give us great reason to look forward to that distressing day when the plan of Despotism which we fear the enemies of our invaluable rights have concerted shall be accomplished, which no sooner than it should take place must involve us and our posterity in a state of slavery, and we and they viewed in no other point of light than machines of mere arbitrary power and lawless ambition; the thought of which will not suffer us any longer to conceal our impatience, secrete our sentiments, or neglect using all lawful and constitutional measures to quiet our fears, redress our grievances, and prevent if possible that [which], should it take place, would of consequence, involve us and our posterity in a state of abject slavery. As, therefore, we, the inhabitants of the town of Hardwick, have made choice of you, Sir, to represent us in the Great and General Court of this Province, this present year, do repose confidence in you, and expect you will exert yourself in every proper and constitutional way for the securing and maintaining our rights and privileges, and for the supporting our ancient happy form of government. Although the situation of our affairs with respect to the state of the colonies, and this in particular, has of late and still does wear a dark and gloomy aspect, in our opinion threatening the ruin of our happy constitution, [we] however rejoice that we are not as yet denied the privilege of choosing some person from among us, to represent us in the Great and General Court of this Province; and although the representative body have not heretofore had that regard paid to them which we earnestly wished for, and had just reason to expect from the order of happy constitution (which has been greatly discouraging to us in choosing any person to represent us, fearing lest that the original purposes designed would fail of being answered hereby), yet having a respect to and looking upon ourselves under indispensable obligations to do all we can to maintain and defend that good and orderly government by which the people of this province have been long distinguished, — we send you forth, and recommend to your vigilance, wisdom, and integrity, the important concerns of this aggrieved and oppressed people; taking it for granted that a regard to your own honor and interest, as well as a regard to the honor and welfare of those who have chosen you to represent them, will make you truly attentive to every thing that shall tend to secure us in a free and full enjoyment of all our constitutional rights, carefully guarding against and vigorously opposing (as you would never betray your constituents nor prove unfaithful to your trust) every thing and every attempt that shall naturally tend to destroy our ancient privileges; and that you will never give up that right into the power of others, which the law of God, nature, and nations hath invested us with. And as we are of opinion that the most likely and effectual way to gain the Royal ear, and obtain a redress of our grievances, is by petitioning our most gracious Sovereign in all proper and constitutional ways, and at all times proving ourselves loyal and dutiful subjects, so we particularly recommend this to your serious consideration, hoping you will always be ready to join with others in this and all other measures that shall be likely to relieve us in the most easy and happy manner, and most effectually secure our invaluable rights and privileges, and restore that mutual harmony and confidence between the British nation and the American colonies, which we look upon to be of the utmost importance and necessity to secure the emolument and welfare of both; and in this way we hope (under the smiles of heaven) our natural rights as Christians and subjects will be fixed on such a sure basis as that all future attempts to invade or destroy them, will prove entirely fruitless and abortive."

These instructions, probably drawn up by Ebenezer Washburn the village school-master and poet (one of the committee), though not very concise, nor wholly grammatical, with some circumlocution and repetitions, clearly enough express two ideas, which were, probably, uppermost in the minds of the inhabitants: (1.) Loyalty to the King, notwithstanding their dissatisfaction with the proceedings of the Parliament, — even as American citizens now preserve sincere loyalty to the country, however much they may disapprove the proceedings of the dominant majority in Congress for the time being; and hence they still desired a reconciliation, and a permanent union with the mother country on just and honorable terms; and (2.) a determination to unite with the other towns in the Province in resisting the parliamentary encroachments on their rights and privileges, in the most effectual manner. Although no distinct reference is made to resistance by force of arms, it is clearly enough implied.

In August, 1774, Brigadier Ruggles took his final leave of this town, for whose material prosperity he had labored so earnestly and successfully during the last twenty years, and whose political guide and leader he had been acknowledged until recently.

Although he had now forfeited the favor of the Sons of Liberty, by opposing their revolutionary proceedings, he had secured and retained the approbation of the King by his loyalty. He was this year designated as one of the thirty-six members of the Council, appointed by mandamus, for the government of the Province (of whom twelve declined the office, and nine soon resigned), and was one of the fifteen who did not shrink from the responsibility of the difficult and hazardous position, and was sworn into office August 16, 1774.

It was the current tradition among his contemporaries, that when he left Hardwick to take his seat in the Mandamus Council, a multitude assembled at the bridge, near the old Furnace, to prevent him from crossing. His brother, Captain Benjamin Ruggles, was a leader and the chief speaker. After using other persuasions and expostulations in vain, Benjamin, with much solemnity, assured his brother, that if he persisted in proceeding to Boston, he would never be permitted to return. The Brigadier's warlike spirit was roused. "Brother Benjamin," said he, "I *shall* come back, — at the head of five hundred soldiers, if necessary." "Brother Timothy," was the reply, "if you cross that bridge, this morning, you will certainly never cross it again — alive." The General waved his hand, and proceeded at a deliberate pace; the crowd gave way, and he crossed the bridge, — and crossed it for the last time. He never returned; and the two brothers saw each other no more in this world.

I anticipate the order of events a few months, to close my account of Brigadier Ruggles' connection with the revolutionary contest, so far as it had any immediate reference to Hardwick. At the last session of the first Provincial Congress, in Cambridge, December 10, 1774, "the committee appointed to take into consideration the letter and papers enclosed, received from the committee of correspondence of the town of Hardwick, reported; which was read and accepted, and ordered to be published in the public papers, and also the papers on which the said report is founded. The report is as followeth, viz: — Whereas it appears to this Congress, that one or more members of the lately appointed unconstitutional council in this province, now residing in Boston, has sent to the town of Hardwick a paper, purporting [to be] an association to be entered into by those persons who falsely assume the name of friends to government, calculated to counteract the salutary designs of the Continental and Provincial Congresses, to deceive the people into agreements contrary to the welfare of this country, and tending in its consequences to hinder an amicable accommodation with our mother country, the sole end of these Congresses, and the ardent wish of every friend to America:[1] it is therefore recommended by this Congress, to the several committees of correspondence in this colony, that they give notice to the Provincial Congress, that shall meet in this province on the first day of February next, and the earliest notice to the public, of all such combinations, and of the persons signing the same, if any should be enticed thereto, that their names may be published to the world, their persons treated with that neglect, and their memories transmitted to posterity with that ignominy, which such unnatural conduct must deserve."[2]

The order of Congress, for the publication of these proceedings, not having been immediately carried into effect, Brigadier Ruggles caused the "Association" to be published in the "Boston Evening Post," December 26, 1774, with a prefatory letter: —

"To the Printer of the Boston News-Paper: As Messrs. Edes and Gill, in their paper of Monday the 12th instant, were pleased to acquaint the public that 'the Association sent by Brigadier Ruggles, &c., to the town of Hardwicke, &c., together with his Son's certificate thereof, and the resolves of the Provincial Congress thereon, must be referred till their next,' I was so credulous as to expect then to have seen their next paper adorned with the form of an Association which would have done honor to it, and if attended to and complied with by the good people of the province, might have put it in the power of any one very easily to have distinguished such loyal subjects to the King, as dare to assert their rights to freedom, in all respects consistent with the laws of the land, from such rebellious ones as, under the pretext of being friends to liberty, are frequently committing the most enormous outrages upon the persons and properties of such of his Majesty's peaceable subjects who, for want of knowing who to call upon (in these distracted times) for assistance, fall into the hands of a banditti, whose cruelties surpass those of savages: — But find-

[1] The members of the Congress professed a desire for a peaceful close of the existing controversy, notwithstanding they had made preparations for forcible resistance by recommending a new organization of the militia under trustworthy officers, the enlisting of minute-men, the procuring of arms and ammunition, the manufacture of saltpetre, gunpowder, and fire-arms, and the payment of all taxes to a treasurer appointed by themselves. See their *Journal*, pp. 45–64. The town of Hardwick expressed the same sentiments, and promptly adopted the measures recommended by the Congress.

[2] *Journals of each Provincial Congress*, pp. 68, 69.

ing my mistake, now take the liberty to send copies to your several offices, to be published in your next papers, that so the public may be made more acquainted therewith than at present, and be induced to associate for the above purposes. And as many of the people for some time past have been arming themselves, it may not be amiss to let them know that their numbers will not appear in the field so large as was imagined, before it was known that independency was the object in contemplation; since which, many have associated in divers parts of the province, to preserve their freedom and support Government; and as it may become necessary in a very short time to give convincing proof of our attachment to Government, we shall be much wanting to ourselves if we longer trample upon that patience which has already endured to long-suffering, and may, if this opportunity be neglected, have a tendency to ripen many for destruction who have not yet been guilty of an overt act of rebellion, which would be an event diametrically opposite to the humane and benevolent intention of him, whose abused patience cannot endure forever, and who hath already by his prudent conduct evidenced the most tender regard for a deluded people. TIMOTHY RUGGLES.

"Boston, 22[d] Dec. 1774."

"THE ASSOCIATION.

"We the subscribers being fully sensible of the blessings of good Government on the one hand, and convinced on the other hand of the evils and calamities attending on Tyranny in all shapes, whether exercised by one or many, and having of late seen with great grief and concern the distressing effects of a dissolution of all Government, whereby our Lives, Liberties, and Properties are rendered precarious, and no longer under the Protection of the Law; and apprehending it to be our indispensable duty, to use all Lawful means in our power, for the defence of our Persons and Property, against all riotous, and lawless violence, and to recover, and secure the advantages which we are intituled to, from the good and wholsome Laws of the Government; Do hereby associate and mutually covenant, and engage to and with each other as follows. Namely

"1st. That we will upon all occasions, with our Lives, and Fortunes, stand by and assist each other, in the defence of his Life, Liberty, and Property, whenever the same shall be attacked, or endangered by any Bodies of Men, riotously assembled, upon any pretence, or under any authority, not warranted by the Laws of the Land.

"2ndly. That we will upon all occasions, mutually support each other in the free exercise, and enjoyment of our undoubted right to Liberty, in eating, drinking, buying, selling, communing, and acting, what, and with whom, and as we please, consistent with the Laws of God, and the King.

"3dly. That we will not acknowledge, or submit to the pretended authority of any Congresses, Committees of Correspondence, or other unconstitutional Assemblies of Men; but will at the risque of our Lives, if need be, oppose the forceable exercise of all such authority.

"4thly. That we will to the utmost of our Power, promote, encourage, and when called to it, enforce obedience to the rightfull Authority of our most Gracious Sovereign King George the third, and of his Laws.

"5thly. That when the Person or Property of any one of us shall be invaded or threatened by any Committees, mobs, or unlawful Assemblies, the others of us will upon notice received forthwith repair, properly armed, to the Person on whom, or place where such invasion or threatening shall be, and will to the utmost of our Power, defend such Person and his Property, and if need be, will oppose and repel force with force.

"6thly. That if any one of us shall unjustly and unlawfully be injured in his Person or Property, by any such Assemblies as before-mentioned, the others of us will unitedly demand, and if in our Power compel the Offenders, if known, to make full reparation and satisfaction for such injury; and if all other Means of Security fail, we will have recourse to the natural Law of Retaliation.

"In witness of all which we hereto subscribe our Names this day of ."

In a letter written by Lord Percy, at Boston, in October, 1774, a copy of which is in possession of Rev. Edward G. Porter, of Lexington, it is stated that a body of "Loyal American Associates" had been organized for the defence of the Government, of which "Brig. Hon. Timothy Ruggles" was "Commandant," and Abijah Willard, James Putnam, and Francis Green were captains; but it does not appear that they were ever called into service. It has been said that after hostilities commenced, and the British army evacuated Boston, Brigadier Ruggles went to New York, and served in the army; but I have not seen any satisfactory proof that he ever bore arms against his country.

On the contrary, the uniform tradition among his relatives and townsmen, while his contemporaries were still living, was, that he utterly refused to take an active part in the conflict of arms, on the one side or the other. He had eaten the King's bread, and he would not lift up his heel against him ; he had repeatedly sworn allegiance, and he would not violate his oath. And just as firmly he refused to aid in the effort to crush his kindred and his fellow countrymen by brute force. He retired to Nova Scotia, and devoted himself to agriculture on a tract of land granted to him in consideration of his services and his losses.

It may be added, that he was highly distinguished in an act, passed in September 1778, forbidding the return of refugees, providing that if any such should return they should be forthwith sent out of the jurisdiction, and if they returned a second time without permission, they should "suffer the pains of death without benefit of clergy." The preamble of the act commences thus: "Whereas, Thomas Hutchinson, Esq., late governor of this state, Francis Bernard, Esq., formerly governor of this state; Thomas Oliver, Esq., late lieutenant-governor of this state, Timothy Ruggles, of Hardwick, in the county of Worcester, Esq." Then follow the names of more than three hundred persons, arranged alphabetically in the several counties and towns, including the late Secretary and Treasurer, the Chief Justice of the Supreme Court and other Judges, members of the Mandamus Council, and at least one Baronet, Sir William Pepperell. Brigadier Ruggles alone was selected from the mass of offenders, and associated with the former governors and lieutenant-governor, as the most conspicuous group. He deserved this distinction, for he was confessedly their most powerful supporter for several years before their government was overturned and terminated.[1]

[1] Even the most stalwart Sons of Liberty sometimes quailed before him, and shrunk from a contest in debate. Tudor mentions an instance of this kind, in his life of the younger Otis. At the session of the House, in Cambridge, May, 1769, by adjournment from Boston (where cannon had been placed in front of the State House), "on some question in dispute between the Legislature and the Governor, Brigadier Ruggles, the staunch friend of the latter, had delivered a very powerful and ingenious argument, which seemed to make a strong impression on the members. Otis rose after him, and with the fullest tone and most impassioned manner, that seemed to arrest the very breathing of the House, began: 'Mr. Speaker, the liberty of this country is gone forever! and I'll go after it!' He immediately turned around and walked out of the chamber." *Life of James Otis, Jr.*, p. 356.

In the same connection it may be added that the following paragraph in the *Boston Chronicle*, October 10, 1768, probably refers to Brigadier Ruggles. In reference to the report that Governor

While he remained in Hardwick, General Ruggles contributed more than any other person to the agricultural prosperity of the town, by improved methods of tillage, the introduction of choice breeds of cattle and horses, and the culture of engrafted fruits.[1] In the performance of his various public duties, he reflected honor on his constituents. As colonel and as brigadier-general in the French War, as representative and as speaker of the House, as president of the Congress at New York, and as chief justice of the Court of Common Pleas, he was equal to his position and adorned it.[2] He closed his long and eventful life at Wilmot, near Annapolis, N. S., August 4, 1795, aged nearly 84 years, leaving behind him the well-earned reputation of loyalty to his king, love of his country, and strict honor, faithfulness, skill, and energy in the performance of every duty incumbent on him.

To this estimate of his character I do not recollect to have seen any objection until recently. But a respectable writer in

Bernard might be appointed Governor of Virginia, the writer says: "If his Excellency accepts of the above offer, it is said his Honor the Lieut. Governor will be appointed to succeed him; and that a certain Honourable gentleman, a Brigadier of the Colony Troops in the late war, during which he distinguished himself, and who is equally esteemed for his probity and firmness, will succeed the Lieut. Governor."

[1] After his removal to Nova Scotia, he seems to have abandoned politics and to have devoted himself entirely to agriculture. In an obituary notice, published in a Halifax newspaper immediately after his death, it is said that "At the conclusion of the late war, General Ruggles came to this Province, and with a degree of philosophy rarely to be met with at the age of 74 [his age was 64 in 1775] sat himself down in the wilderness, and began to cultivate a new farm, which he carried on with wonderful perseverance and success. The idea that his advanced age would not admit him to reap the fruit of his labor never damped the spirit of improvement by which he was in a most eminent degree actuated; and the district of country in which he lived will long feel the benefits resulting from the liberal exertions he made to advance the agricultural interests of the Province. It may not be without its use to remark that for much the greatest part of his life General Ruggles ate no animal food, and drank no spirituous or fermented liquors, small beer excepted; and that he enjoyed to his advanced age almost uninterrupted health."

[2] In person, General Ruggles is said to have been somewhat more than six feet in height, and well proportioned. When arrayed in the costume then fashionable, surmounted by the formidable wig and cocked hat, his aspect must have been imposing and majestic. And in manner he was equally dignified. President Adams (who was his kinsman), in contrasting him with Gridley, the Attorney General, in 1759, says, "Ruggles' grandeur consists in the quickness of his apprehension, the steadiness of his attention, the boldness and strength of his thoughts and expressions, his strict honor, conscious superiority, contempt of meanness, &c. People approach him with dread and terror. Gridley's grandeur consists in his great learning, his great parts, and his majestic manner; but it is diminished by stiffness and affectation. Ruggles is as proud, as lordly as Gridley, but he is more popular; he conceals it more; he times it better; and it is easy and natural in him, but is stiff and affected in Gridley. It is an advantage to Ruggles' character, but a disadvantage to Gridley's." *Life and Works*, ii. 67.

the "History of Worcester County," published in 1879, while he bears frank testimony that "though living in style, he was temperate in his habits, prudent and sagacious in the management of his affairs, and capable of filling any position to which he might be raised," yet on the same page, speaking of the ill-fated daughter, Mrs. Spooner, he makes the astonishing statement, that "the father, with all his talents and public spirit, was a man of low moral principle, and it is believed that he set his children an example of conjugal infidelity."[1] I doubt not that this writer "believed" his statement to be true; but to me it is utterly incredible. I was born, and resided for the first twenty-four years of my life, within a few rods of Brigadier Ruggles' homestead; and during that period I often heard his character discussed by his townsmen who had personally known him, and had opposed him politically. I have also read much concerning him in contemporary newspapers, and in authentic history. I have heard and I have read most bitter denunciations of his political opinions and conduct. But never, until now, have I known him to be characterized as a "man of low moral principle." And as to his domestic relations, although an unhappy incompatibility of temper was notorious, and was the subject of free conversation among those who personally knew the parties, I do not remember to have heard the slightest suspicion of "conjugal infidelity" on the part of either husband or wife. On the contrary, there are unmistakable indications that his townsmen had full confidence in his high "moral principle," and in the general uprightness of his conduct.

Equally destitute of truth, I am confident, are the stories which have been current concerning the outrageous conduct of his townsmen. I have seen no evidence that they ever treated him with personal disrespect, or maimed his cattle, or wantonly destroyed his property. Mob law was never countenanced in Hardwick.

Before taking final leave of this eminent citizen, the insertion of a few anecdotes, illustrative of his grim humor and plainness of speech, may be pardoned.

It is related that while he was a young lawyer an old woman entered the court-house, at recess, and desired a seat. Ruggles gravely pointed to the judges' bench, which she gladly accepted. When the Court came in and sternly questioned him, he replied that he considered the seat to be very convenient for old women.

Under the Provincial Charter, "the General Sessions of the

[1] *Hist. Worcester County*, i. 56.

Peace was composed of all the justices within the county, who commonly attended and decided the matters presented for adjudication by vote. . . . General Ruggles, the Chief Justice, in stern derision of the constitution of this Court, on one occasion, reprimanded a dog who had taken his seat beside his master, for appearing on the bench before he had been qualified as a Justice of the Peace, and directed him to go and be sworn before he came to vote there." [1]

The famous bull story rests on a slight foundation. That a bull chased the Brigadier into his house, and was there shot after having demolished a valuable looking-glass, is probably true; but the remainder of this oft-told tale is so utterly inconsistent with the Brigadier's high sense of honor, that it may without hesitation be pronounced apocryphal and unworthy of repetition.

Other anecdotes have been preserved by tradition, which I do not recollect to have seen in print. Among these may be mentioned that which describes one of his boyish pranks while he was a student in Harvard College. A sign had been removed from some store or tavern, and conveyed to his room, by him or by some of his associates. Search was made for it in the evening, but the door was bolted, and the sign was placed on the fire. When the footsteps of the tutors were heard approaching, Ruggles began to pray, very audibly, and in his prayer repeated the language found in Matthew xvi. 4: "A wicked and adulterous generation seeketh after a sign; and there shall no sign be given unto it but the sign of the prophet Jonas." In due time the sign was consumed, the prayer ceased, and the door was opened to admit those who had scrupulously abstained from interrupting the devotions of the students.

The account of another youthful extravagance indicates that some of the son's facetiousness was inherited from the father. Having purchased a horse, and agreed to pay for it on the next Election day, he wrote a promissory note, in which, instead of Election day, he inserted the words Resurrection day. When Election day arrived and payment was demanded, he insisted that the note had not yet matured, and called for the reading of it; he would pay when it became due. The father, overhearing the conversation, exclaimed, "Timothy, if you owe that man anything, pay him. You will have enough else to attend to at the Resurrection, besides paying for old horses."

[1] Lincoln's *Hist. Worcester*, p. 59.

There is yet another horse story: The father, Rev. Timothy Ruggles, had a favorite horse which became sick. The son was requested to give his opinion in the case. After due examination, he said, "The difficulty is plain enough, father; the horse has the same disease which troubles the larger portion of your parish; he has been very severely priest-ridden."

Two military anecdotes must close this list, already perhaps too long.

Before the attack on Ticonderoga, in 1758, Brigadier Ruggles earnestly objected to the order of battle proposed by General Abercrombie, and suggested another, which involved much greater personal hazard to himself. Abercrombie, however, with true English obstinacy, persisted in his own plan, and was repulsed with disastrous loss. When they met, on the next morning, to the General's formal salutation the Brigadier responded, "Good-morning, General Abercrombie; I hope your terrible defeat yesterday may be sanctified to you."

"On the morning of the battle of Bunker Hill, General Gage said to him, that the rebels would disperse at the sight of his cannon; that he should not be under the necessity of discharging a gun; 'without discipline, without officers, and under the disadvantage of being engaged in an unjust cause,' continued he tauntingly, 'it is impossible for them to withstand our arms a moment.' Ruggles replied with warmth, 'Sir, you know not with whom you have to contend. These are the very men who conquered, Canada. I fought with them side by side; I know them well; they will fight bravely. My God! Sir, your folly has ruined your cause.'"[1]

[1] *Worcester Magazine*, ii. 59.

6

CHAPTER VII.

CIVIL HISTORY.

Committee of Correspondence. — County Convention. — Courts of Law obstructed. — New Organization of Militia, and Officers elected. — Minute Men. — Alarm List. — Provincial Congress. — Constables indemnified. — Contribution to Boston Sufferers. — Tories treated with Neglect, disarmed, confined, and advertised as Public Enemies. — Temporary State Government organized. — Few Tories in Hardwick. — Sharp Controversy with One of the Number; settled by Appeal to the General Court. — The Conflict succeeded by Peace. — Anecdote.

At a meeting, on the 22d of August, 1774, the town "Chose a committee of fifteen men for a Committee of Correspondence, nine of whom being met shall have power to act, to correspond with the Committees of other towns within this Province respecting the important matters relating to our civil and political rights and privileges, as may be necessary from time to time, and to agree to such measures as may be thought most proper to be taken in order to frustrate and disappoint the purposes of wicked and designing men to deprive us and our posterity of our just rights and privileges; and that said Committee shall have power from time to time, as they shall think necessary, to appoint some person or persons from among themselves to attend upon any Convention of members from the Committees of any other towns within this Province, to consult upon matters relating to our civil rights and privileges, and that said person or persons, so delegated, shall have power to agree with the majority of such Convention in any method that they may think proper to come into, to answer the above purposes; and that the town will pay the expenses of those persons, and their horses, that may attend upon such convention. And furthermore, the town chose a committee of three men, viz.: Capt. Paul Mandell, Mr. Stephen Rice, and Lieut. Jonathan Warner, as a Committee to meet the Committee of Correspondence at Worcester, on Tuesday the 30th instant."

The Committee of Correspondence, elected in Boston, November 2, 1772, was the first in the Province, and was a device of the sterling patriot, Samuel Adams. "This inaugurated the system of local committees of correspondence. They multiplied and widened under successive impulses, until they constituted the accredited organs of the party that founded the Republic of the United States."[1] The inhabitants of Hardwick did not so soon respond to the message from Boston, nor so promptly as some other towns elect their Committee of Correspondence; but in due time, and after careful deliberation, they heartily joined in the movement which induced Governor Hutchinson to say: "Thus, all on a sudden, from a state of peace, order, and general contentment, as some expressed themselves, the province, more or less from one end to the other, was brought into a state of contention, disorder, and general dissatisfaction; or, as others would have it, were roused from stupor and inaction to sensibility and activity."[2] The power exercised by this committee was not absolutely unlimited, because, from time to time, they reported their proceedings to the town, for approval. But in the general confusion which prevailed until the adoption of the Constitution in 1780, they exercised to a considerable extent both judicial and executive authority; and from their known character we may be certain that the individuals first elected did not perform their duty negligently. This committee consisted of "Capt. Benjamin Ruggles, Capt. Constant Merrick, Capt. Paul Mandell, Deac. Joseph Allen, Deac. William Paige, Deac. John Bradish, Lieut. Jonathan Warner, Mr. Daniel Warner, Mr. Stephen Rice, Ens. Ezra Leonard, Ens. Timothy Newton, Mr. Thomas Robinson, Mr. Seth Paddleford, Mr. Josiah Locke, and Lieut. Joseph Safford."[3]

The committee of three, namely, Paul Mandell, Stephen Rice,

[1] Frothingham's *Rise of the Republic*, p. 266.

[2] Hutchinson's *Hist. of Mass.*, iii. 370.

[3] The same persons were reëlected in 1775. Their successors were, — 1776: William Paige, Thomas Robinson, Samuel Dexter, Samuel Billings, John Bradish, Daniel Warner, David Allen, Abraham Knowlton, and Gamaliel Collins. — 1777: William Paige, John Bradish, Thomas Robinson, Stephen Rice, Timothy Paige, Barnabas Sears, Samuel Dexter, David Allen, Timothy Newton, Thomas Haskell, John Hastings, and Elisha Billings. — 1778: Daniel Warner, Elisha Billings, Thomas Wheeler, Isaac Fay, Denison Robinson, Timothy Newton, and Zebadiah Johnson. — 1779: David Allen, Samuel Dexter, Aaron Barlow, Ephraim Cleaveland, Jr., James Paige, Jr., Daniel Warner, Ezra Leonard, Elisha Billings, John Hastings, Timothy Paige, John Haskell, Thomas Robinson, Timothy Newton, Jonathan Warner, and Ephraim Pratt. — 1780: Daniel Egery, Oliver Allen, Isaac Fay, John Haskell, and James Wing. Further elections were rendered unnecessary by the establishment of a regular government.

and Jonathan Warner, elected August 22, 1774, and increased, September 22, 1774, by the election of John Bradish, to "meet the Committee of Correspondence at Worcester," faithfully performed their duty, and from time to time reported to the town the proceedings of the Convention. That Convention met at Worcester, August 9, 1774, organized, and adjourned to the thirtieth day of the same month, in order that, as "a considerable number of respectable towns in this county have not yet chosen committees, and by that means may not have received the letters notifying this Convention," such towns might receive notice and be duly represented. At the appointed time, the Convention reassembled. Rev. Ebenezer Chaplin, then of Sutton, and afterwards of Hardwick, one of the members, officiated as chaplain at its various sessions until its final dissolution, May 31, 1775. Under the form of recommendations, this body exercised substantial legislative authority; and their fellow citizens yielded a ready obedience to whatever was required. Among the earliest recommendations were the following, adopted August 31, 1774:—

"Resolved, that it is the indispensable duty of the inhabitants of this county, by the best ways and means, to prevent the sitting of the respective courts under such regulations as are set forth in a late act of parliament, entitled an act for regulating the civil government of the Massachusetts Bay.

"Resolved, that in order to prevent the execution of the late act of parliament, respecting the courts, that it be recommended to the inhabitants of this county to attend, in person, the next inferior court of common pleas and general sessions, to be holden at Worcester, in and for said county, on the sixth day of September next.

"Resolved, that it be recommended to the several towns that they choose proper and suitable officers, and a sufficient number, to regulate the movements of each town, and prevent any disorder which might otherwise happen; and that it be enjoined on the inhabitants of each respective town, that they adhere strictly to the orders and directions of such officers.

"And whereas, the courts of justice will necessarily be impeded by the opposition to the said acts of parliament, therefore, Resolved, that it be recommended to the inhabitants of this province in general, and to those of this county in particular, that they depute fit persons to represent them in one general provincial convention, to be convened at Concord, on the second Tuesday of October next, to devise proper ways and means to resume our original mode of government, whereby the most dignified servants were, as they ever ought to be, dependent on the people for their existence as such; or some other which may appear to them best calculated to regain and secure our violated rights. . . .

"Resolved, that it be recommended to the several towns that they indemnify their constables for neglecting to return lists of persons qualified to serve as jurors."

The convention then adjourned to September 6, when it again met and "voted, as the opinion of this convention, that the court should not sit on any terms," . . . and "that the body of the people in this county now in town assemble on the common." Not only were the courts prevented from sitting, but the judges and officers of the courts were required to promise that they would "stay all such judicial proceedings," and would not attempt to put the parliamentary "act into execution."[1] On the same day, the Convention "voted, that it be recommended to the military officers in this county that they resign their commissions to the colonels of the respective regiments:—voted, that the field officers resign their offices, and publish their resignations in all the Boston newspapers: — voted, that it be recommended to the several towns of the county, to choose proper officers for the military of the town, and a sufficient number."

At a subsequent session, September 20, 1774, it was "voted, as the opinion of this convention, that the sheriff adjourn the superior court appointed by law to be held this day, and that he retain such as are, or may be, committed as criminals, in his custody, until they have a trial." The Convention then recommended a more thorough reorganization of the militia: —

"As the several regiments in this county are large and inconvenient, by the increase of its inhabitants since the first settlement of said regiments, therefore, voted, that the county be divided into seven distinct regiments, in the following manner, to wit: — . . . Fourth. Brookfield, Western, Braintree, Hardwick, Oakham. . . .

"Voted, that it be recommended to the several towns in this

[1] In a note to these proceedings, it is stated that "on the invitation of the convention, the people of the county had assembled to the number of about six thousand. The companies of the several towns were under officers of their own election, and marched in military order. Having been formed in two lines, when the arrangements were completed, the royalist justices and officers were compelled to pass through the ranks, pausing, at intervals, to read their declarations of submission to the public will. At evening, finding that no troops were on their way to sustain the judicial tribunals, whose constitution had been corrupted by the act of parliament, the great assembly dispersed peacefully."

county, to choose proper military officers, and a sufficient number for each town, and that the captains, lieutenants, and ensigns, who are chosen by the people in each regiment, do convene on or before the tenth day of October next, at some convenient place in each regiment, and choose their field officers to command the militia until they be constitutionally appointed; and that it be recommended to the officers in each town of the county, to enlist one third of the men of their respective towns, between sixteen and sixty years of age, to be ready to act at a minute's warning; and that it be recommended to each town in the county, to choose a sufficient number of men as a committee to supply and support those troops that shall move on any emergency.

"Voted, that it be recommended to the company officers of the minute-men, to meet at Worcester, on the 17th of October next, at ten o'clock of the forenoon, to proportion their own regiments, and choose as many field officers as they shall think necessary."

On the same day the Convention made provision for a political emergency, by recommending a Provincial Congress, which exercised almost unlimited power for the next year: "Resolved, that it be recommended to the several towns and districts, that they instruct their representatives, who may be chosen to meet at Salem, in October next, absolutely to refuse to be sworn by any officer or officers, but such as are or may be appointed according to the constitution, or to act as one branch of the legislature in concert with any others, except such as are or may be appointed according to the charter of this province; and that they refuse to give their attendance at Boston, while the town is invested with troops and ships of war: And should there be any thing to prevent their acting with such a governor and council as is expressly set forth in the charter, that they immediately repair to the town of Concord, and there join in a provincial congress with such other members as are or may be chosen for that purpose, to act and determine on such measures as they shall judge to be proper to extricate this colony out of the present unhappy circumstances." [1]

How promptly and heartily the inhabitants of Hardwick responded to these recommendations may be seen in their recorded votes. At a town-meeting, September 16, 1774, — "The town made choice of officers to regulate the soldiers that went to

[1] The proceedings of this County Convention are printed with the *Journals of each Provincial Congress*, pp. 627–652.

Worcester. — Voted, to accept the Resolves of the Committee of Correspondence, which was laid before the town at that time.[1] — Chose Deac. Joseph Allen, Capt. Paul Mandell, Stephen Rice, Capt. William Paige, and Ebenezer Washburn, to draw up a covenant that may bind them to abide by whatever the majority of the town think proper to vote." Six days later, the town "voted to accept the covenant drawn up by a committee chosen for that purpose." [2]

September 22, 1774, only two days after the recommendation of the measure was adopted by the County Convention, a town meeting was held under a warrant, of which one article was, "to see if the town will make some consideration, as an encouragement to a certain number of persons, as the town may think proper, to serve as minute-men, upon any sudden invasion, for the defence of our country." At this meeting all the officers of the two militia companies having resigned, new officers were elected by the town, to wit: for the South Company, Captain, Jonathan Warner; Lieutenant, Elisha Billings; Ensign, Elijah Warner: for the North Company, Captain, Paul Mandell; Lieutenant, Stephen Rice; Ensign, Josiah Locke, who being transferred to the company of minute-men, Ensign Timothy Newton was elected in his stead: for the company of minute-men, Captain, Jonathan Warner; Lieutenant, Simeon Hazeltine; Ensign, Josiah Locke. And it was "voted, that if there should be an invasion, and the minute-men should march for our relief, they should be supported by the town." The minute-men were also offered pay for the time which they devoted to drilling and instruction. But this they were too patriotic to allow, while others were not paid. They proposed at a town meeting, January 2, 1775, "that if the town in general would provide themselves with arms, and be equipped as they be, and endeavor to acquaint themselves with the art military, it would be satisfactory to them, without any other pay." Whereupon the town voted, "that all between six-

[1] Probably the Resolves (already quoted) which were adopted, August 31, 1774, by the Worcester Convention of Committees of Correspondence.

[2] This covenant is not found on the records, nor among the files of the town. Perhaps it had reference to a recommendation of the County Convention, August 10, 1774: "We greatly approve of the agreement entered and entering into through this and the neighboring provinces, for the non-consumption of British goods. This, we apprehend, will have a tendency to convince our brethren in Britain that more is to be gained, in the way of justice, from our friendship and affection than by extortion and arbitrary power. . . . Such an agreement, if strictly adhered to, will greatly prevent extravagance, save our money, encourage our manufactures, and reform our manners."

teen and seventy years of age, be equipped with arms and ammunition equal to the minute men, by the first day of February next;" also voted, "that all above forty years of age meet at the training field on Monday next at nine o'clock in the forenoon, to choose their officers." When thus assembled, they organized two companies of "alarm men." Of one company, Deacon Joseph Allen, then sixty-seven years of age, was elected Captain; Lieutenant Joseph Safford, First Lieutenant; and Lieutenant Daniel Fay, Second Lieutenant; and of the other, Deacon William Paige, aged fifty-one years, who had been a captain in the French war, was elected Captain; Mr. Thomas Robinson, First Lieutenant; and Ensign Ezra Leonard, Second Lieutenant. Thus while this town contained not much more than twelve hundred inhabitants, five military companies, averaging about fifty men each, were prepared for service, before the first blood was shed in the contest; — one for action in any sudden emergency; two for more regular service, in such detachments as circumstances might require; and two of old men, to defend their hearthstones at the last extremity, and to sacrifice their lives, if necessary, in defence of their families.[1]

One more recommendation of the County Convention met a ready response at this town-meeting September 22, 1774: "Chose Mr. Stephen Rice to represent the town at the Provincial Congress to be held at Concord." The town had previously elected Paul Mandell as their representative for this year in the General Court. He was desired and empowered to act in the Provincial Congress, if the House of Representatives should be dissolved by the Governor. Instructions to him, drawn up by Captain William Paige, Lieutenant Stephen Rice, and Dr. John Paddleford, were reported and adopted at a town-meeting, September 30, 1774: "To Capt. Paul Mandell; Sir, As we have chosen you to represent us in the Great and General Court to be holden at Sa-

[1] "Hardwick Jan. 19. Such is the military spirit, and such the opposition to military tyranny, in this town, that, exclusive of the train-band companies and one company of minute-men, the alarm-men consisting of near one hundred and twenty, most of whom are able-bodied and good marksmen, met on Monday the sixteenth instant, and having formed themselves into two companies and made choice of their officers, did likewise enter into a covenant to attend military duty and equip themselves to a man, agreeable to the laws of the province in that case made and provided. So that we have reason to believe that the Tory Covenant or Association, sent into this town by Brigadier Ruggles, will have little or no effect amongst us, nor will any other means used by our enemies to divide or divert us from pursuing the measures which we think will have a tendency to recover and secure to us and our posterity our just rights and privileges." *Massachusetts Spy*, February 2, 1775.

lem, on Wednesday, the fifth day of October next ensuing, we do hereby instruct you to adhere firmly, in all your doings as a member of the House of Representatives, to the Charter of this Province granted by their Majesties King William and Queen Mary, and that you do no act that can possibly be construed into an acknowledgement of the validity of the British Parliament for altering the Government of the Massachusetts Bay; and that you acknowledge no other than the honorable Board of Councillors elected by the General Court in their sessions last May as the only constitutional and rightful Council; and that you pay no regard or act in any manner whatever with the Council appointed by Mandamus from his Majesty. And as we have reason to believe that a conscientious discharge of your duty will produce your dissolution as a house of representatives, we do hereby empower and direct you to join with the members who may be sent from this and the other towns in this province, and to meet with them at a time to be agreed on in a general Provincial Congress, to act upon such matters as shall then come before you in such a manner as may appear most conducive to preserve the liberties of North America."

The anticipated emergency occurred. The House of Representatives was dissolved by the Governor, and the Provincial Congress "convened at Salem on Friday the seventh day of October A. D. 1774," organized by electing Hon. John Hancock, chairman, and Benjamin Lincoln, Esq., clerk, and "adjourned to the court-house in Concord, there to meet on Tuesday next;" and on the next Friday "adjourned to the court-house in Cambridge, there to meet on Monday next, at ten o'clock in the forenoon." A recess was taken from October 29 to November 23, and the Congress was dissolved December 10, 1774. Among the recommendations by this Congress were these: —

October 21, 1774. "Resolved that this Congress do earnestly recommend to the people of this province an abhorrence and detestation of all kinds of East India teas, as the baneful article of a corrupt and venal administration for the purpose of introducing despotism and slavery into this once happy country; and that every individual in this province ought totally to disuse the same. And it is recommended, that every town and district appoint a committee to post up in some public place the names of all such in their respective towns and districts, who shall sell or consume so extravagant and unnecessary an article of luxury."

October 29, 1774. "Whereas, it has been recommended by this

Congress, that the moneys heretofore granted and ordered to be assessed by the general court of this province, and not paid into the province treasury should not be paid to the Hon. Harrison Gray, Esq., for reasons most obvious:—Therefore Resolved, that Henry Gardner, Esq., of Stow, be, and hereby is, appointed receiver general. . . . And it is hereby recommended to the several towns and districts within this province, that they immediately call town and district meetings, and give directions to all constables, collectors, and other persons who may have any part of the province tax of such town or district in their respective hands or possession, in consequence of any late order and directions of any town or district, that he or they immediately pay the same to the said Henry Gardner, Esq., for the purposes aforesaid. And it is also recommended that the several towns and districts, in said directions, signify and expressly engage to such constable, collector, or other persons as shall have their said moneys in their hands, that their paying the same to Henry Gardner, Esq., aforesaid, and producing his receipt therefor, shall ever hereafter operate as an effectual discharge to such persons for the same."[1]

At a legal meeting, November 17, 1774, the town, by vote, approved the proceedings of the Provincial Congress, generally; and in particular ordered the constables to pay the public moneys to the Receiver-General instead of the King's Treasurer, and agreed to indemnify them for so doing; appointed a committee "to post up in some public place the names of those persons who shall hereafer sell or consume Bohea or Indian Tea;" and "made choice of the following men as a committee to observe the conduct of all persons in this town, touching the observation of the determinations of the Provincial Congress, viz., Deac. Joseph Allen, Col. Jonathan Warner, Thomas Haskell, Deac. William Paige, Thomas Robinson, Col. Paul Mandell,[2] and John Paige."

Four days afterwards, "The town met according to adjournment, Nov. 21, 1774, and 1st, Voted to reconsider the former votes respecting officers for the south side of the town, and proceeded to an entire new choice. 2d, Voted, and chose Samuel Billings,

[1] *Journals of each Provincial Congress*, pp. 26, 45.

[2] Paul Mandell is styled Colonel here, and in the record of his election, January 2, 1775, as a delegate to the next Congress; and he bears that title in the official Roll of Delegates. Perhaps he was elected colonel of militia, and Jonathan Warner colonel of "minute-men," at their first organization. If so, he held the office only a short time. The "minute-men" were soon merged in the militia, and Jonathan Warner was elected colonel.

Jr., for their Captain; Elijah Warner, for their Lieutenant; and Isaiah Hatch, for their Ensign."[1]

January 2, 1775. Pursuant to a recommendation of the Provincial Congress, in regard to "the persons suffering in the towns of Boston and Charlestown, under the operation of certain acts of the British parliament," that the people generally should "contribute liberally to alleviate the burdens of those persons, who are the more immediate objects of ministerial resentment, and are suffering in the common cause of their country," the town ordered that collections should be made for that benevolent purpose. That Congress having voted to dissolve on the tenth day of December, 1774, and recommended the election of delegates to a second Provincial Congress, to sit from February 1, "until the Tuesday next preceding the last Wednesday of May next, and no longer,"[2] the town at this meeting, "chose Col. Paul Mandell to attend at the Provincial Congress at Cambridge, on the first day of February next, and sooner if occasion requires." Also, "Voted, to accept the resolve of the Committee, in having no dealings with the Tories, except grinding for them."[3]

After the commencement of actual hostilities, those who were regarded as Tories were subjected to a more strict discipline. Not only were they treated with neglect and contempt, and excluded from all social or commercial intercourse, but they were disarmed and subjected to confinement, more or less absolute, as circumstances might seem to require. One person, at least, was committed to prison; others confined to the limits of the town,

[1] The company had probably remained destitute of a captain after the promotion of Captain Jonathan Warner to the office of colonel. The new captain proved his fitness for the office by subsequently enlisting and commanding a company, composed almost entirely of Hardwick soldiers, in the Revolutionary army.

[2] *Journals of each Prov. Congress*, p. 73.

[3] Grinding was a work of necessity, as "bread is the staff of life." But in regard to all else, they seem to have been as exclusive as the blacksmiths of the county, who agreed, September 8, 1774, that they would not "do or perform any blacksmith's work, or business of any kind whatever, for any person or persons whom we esteem enemies to this country, commonly known by the name of tories" . . . and "Resolved, that all lawful ways and means ought to be adopted by the whole body of the people of this province, to discountenance all our inveterate political enemies in manner as aforesaid. — Therefore we earnestly recommend it to all denominations of artificers, that they call meetings of their respective craftsmen in their several counties, as soon as may be, and enter into associations and agreements for said purposes; and that all husbandmen, laborers, &c., do the like: and that whoever shall be guilty of any breach of any or either of the articles or agreements, be held by us in contempt as enemies to our common rights." *Journals of each Prov. Congress*, p. 640.

or of their own farms; others, again, were published as unfriendly to the patriotic cause, and the public were cautioned to regard them as enemies.[1]

April 24, 1775. "Voted, that the town are not satisfied with Jonathan Danforth's declaration of his being a friend to liberty. Voted, that Lieut. Timothy Ruggles[2] be put under guard, and also John Rion, until said Ruggles shall satisfy all the men that now live at Brigadier Ruggles' house for their labor, and see that they go out of town forthwith, and see that the arms and ammunition, now at Brigadier Ruggles' house, are delivered up; and then he is confined to his farm, and not to go out of it, excepting on Sabbath-days, fast days, or some other public days; and that he pays the guard for their trouble in taking care of him."

May 15, 1775. Voted, to take possession of the guns found at the house of Brigadier Ruggles, "and to return them when they think proper. Voted, that Lieut. Timothy Ruggles have liberty to go to Boston, and live there, if he pleases."

May 22, 1775. The town met "to elect one or more persons to serve for and represent them in a Provincial Congress, to be held at the meeting-house in Watertown, on Wednesday the

[1] "In Committee of Correspondence for the town of Hardwick, August 7th, 1775. Whereas Deacon James Fay, Jonathan Danforth, Abner Conant, Joseph Ruggles, Jr., Israel Conkey, and Jonathan Nye, all of Hardwick, in the County of Worcester, have, by their conduct in various instances, manifested a disposition inimical to the rights and privileges of their countrymen,—therefore Resolved, that their names be published to the world, agreeable to the association of the Continental Congress; and that it be earnestly recommended to the inhabitants of this town, county, and colony, not to have any commercial connection with the said Fay, Danforth, &c., but to shun their persons and causes, and treat them with that contempt and neglect they deserve. And whereas the said Committee have thought it necessary that the said Danforth, Fay, &c., be confined to this town, and that they assemble not together more than two of them at a time (except at public worship and at funerals), therefore further recommend it to the good people of this colony, that (if the said persons or any one of them should depart out of this town without a permit from said Committee) they take up and confine or send them back again. Per order of the said Committee. SETH PADELFORD, Clerk of said Committee." *New England Chronicle*, August 17, 1775.

[2] Timothy Ruggles was son of the Brigadier; his brother, John, had previously fled to Boston, though he escaped with some difficulty, as appears by the report of a committee of Congress, concerning a prisoner named John Jones: "We find by said Jones' account of himself, that he went to Boston soon after the memorable Lexington battle, of the 19th of April last, in company with John Ruggles of Hardwick, who was ordered by a committee to the said town of Hardwick; and that said Jones was knowing to the proceedings of said committee against said Ruggles, before they set out together from Weston to take refuge in Boston; and that they left the common road, and went in the woods and difficult places, to pass the town of Roxbury." *Journals of each Prov. Congress*, pp. 315, 316.

thirty-first day of May instant, and to be continued by adjournment, as they shall see cause, until the expiration of six months from their being first convened on the thirty-first day of this instant May, and no longer; and to consult, deliberate, and resolve upon such further measures as under God shall be effectual to save this people from impending ruin, and to secure those inestimable liberties derived to us from our ancestors, and which [it] is our duty to preserve for posterity." The town elected three delegates, to serve by turns, one at a time, namely: Captain William Paige, for June and July; Captain Stephen Rice, for August and September; and Colonel Jonathan Warner, for October and November; but as the Congress dissolved on the 19th of July, to give place to the newly elected General Court, only one of these delegates took his seat. At the same meeting it was "Voted, that the following persons be looked upon as unfriendly to the common cause of liberty, viz., Richard Ruggles,[1] Jonathan Nye, Deac. James Fay, Gardner Chandler, and Ebenezer Whipple. Voted, that as Gardner Chandler[2] has now made some acknowledgments, and says he is sorry for his past conduct, they will treat him as a friend and a neighbor as long as he shall behave himself well."

The second Provincial Congress, believing that "the sword should, in all free states be subservient to the civil powers," and that such powers were then exercised only on sufferance, without due form of law, appealed to the Continental Congress May 16, 1775, for "advice respecting the taking up and exercising the powers of civil government, which we think absolutely necessary for the salvation of our country; and we shall readily submit to such a general plan as you may direct for the colonies; or make it our great study to establish such a form of government here, as shall not only most promote our advantage, but the union and interest of all America." In answer to this appeal, the Continental Congress, June 9, 1775, "Resolved, that no obedience being due to the act of parliament for altering the charter of the colony of Massachusetts Bay, nor to a governor and lieutenant-governor who will not observe the directions of, but endeavor to subvert, that charter; the governor and lieutenant-governor are to be considered as absent, and their offices vacant. And as there is no council there, and the inconveniences arising from the sus-

[1] Son of Brigadier Ruggles. He became a refugee, and never returned.

[2] Mr. Chandler afterwards became a refugee, and his property was confiscated. Some years later he returned, and resided in peace at Brattleborough, Vt., and Hinsdale, N. H., where he died.

pension of the powers of government are intolerable, especially at a time when General Gage hath actually levied war, and is carrying on hostilities against his majesty's peaceful and loyal subjects of that colony; that in order to conform, as near as may be, to the spirit and substance of the charter, it be recommended to the Provincial Congress, to write letters to the inhabitants of the several places which are entitled to representation in assembly, requesting them to choose such representatives; and that the assembly, when chosen, should elect counsellors: which assembly and council should exercise the powers of government, until a governor of his majesty's appointment will consent to govern the colony according to its charter." Accordingly, the third Provincial Congress, now in session, issued letters, June 20, 1775, requesting the selectmen of the several towns to cause the inhabitants to assemble and "elect and depute one or more freeholders resident in the same town, according to the numbers set and limited by an act of the general assembly, entitled an act for ascertaining the number and regulating the house of representatives, to serve for and represent them in a great and general court or assembly, to be convened, held, and kept, for the service of the said colony until the end of the day next preceding the last Wednesday of May next, if necessary, and no longer, at the meeting house in Watertown, upon Wednesday the nineteenth day of July next ensuing the date hereof."[1] In accordance with this request, Capt. Stephen Rice was elected, July 15, 1775, a member of this House of Representatives, — the first which derived its authority directly and absolutely from the people.

October 10, 1775. "Voted, that Lieut. Timothy Ruggles be set at liberty. Voted, That the late proceedings of the Committee of Correspondence with respect to the Tories are satisfactory to the town." Precisely what these "proceedings" were does not appear on record; but it may safely be assumed that they were less "satisfactory" to the Tories than to the town. The number of Tories in Hardwick was not large. Indeed it is remarkable that Brigadier Ruggles, whose services to the colony had been so conspicuous, and to the town so important and beneficial, should have secured so few political adherents outside of his family circle. The more active and troublesome of them soon left the town. Those who remained, with a single exception, seem to have submitted unresistingly to the discipline adjudged necessary

[1] *Journals of each Prov. Congress*, p. 359.

by the Committee of Correspondence, and to have conformed to the new state of affairs so entirely as to secure the respect and confidence of the most ardent Sons of Liberty. And even Jonathan Danforth, the most unmanageable and pugnacious of the whole number, finally obtained the same boon, though he secured it "through much tribulation." Several documents relative to him are preserved in the records and archives of the Commonwealth, which have not heretofore been published, and from which I shall quote somewhat freely, as they perhaps include, and certainly illustrate, some of the "proceedings of the Committee of Correspondence with respect to the Tories" at that time and afterwards.

"Worcester, ss. To the Sheriff of the County of Worcester, or to the Keeper of the Common Goal in said County. Greeting. In the name of the Government and People of the Massachusetts Bay in New England: You are required to take into safe custody, and commit to said Goal, Jonathan Danforth of Hardwick, a person inimical and dangerous to the States of America, there to remain in safe keeping till he shall be liberated and discharged by due course of law. Given under my hand this 4th day of December Anno Domini 1776. WILLIAM PAIGE (by order), Chairman of the Committee of Correspondence for Hardwick." [1]

"To the Honorable Council of the State of the Massachusetts Bay: We, the Committee of Correspondence, Safety, and Inspection, for the Town of Hardwick do show, — That we have committed to the common goal in Worcester Jonathan Danforth of this town for the several crimes following, viz., (1.) That he, being collector for said Hardwick, refused to pay to the Treasurer of the State, Henry Gardner, Esq., the public monies he had in his hands, according to a resolve of Congress. (2.) But being compelled to answer for said money, he produced other men's security and took a receipt of the Committee, which receipt afterwards he gave to Harrison Gray, Esq., on the account of which one of the said Committee was seized by said Gray and contained [detained?] to his great loss and damage. 3. Afterwards he was published in the public papers, and confined to the town as an enemy to the United States; but notwithstanding, he broke through his confinement, and went to New York and other places, which we apprehend was to confer with and give information to our enemies. 4. Concealing the goods of Richard Ruggles, a fugitive, when sought for; and when part was found with him, sol-

[1] *Mass. Archives*, clxxxi. 369.

emnly declared there was all he knew of; but afterwards others were found in a certain wood, which he confessed he put there. 5. And also absconded from said town of Hardwick for many months, conferring with our enemies, to the great uneasiness and worry of the inhabitants of said town. — For these and many other reasons which we are ready to show, if called to it, I have committed the said Danforth, as above stated. By order of said Committee, WILLIAM PAIGE, Chairman. Worcester Dec. ye 5th 1776." [1]

"To the Honorable Council for the State of Massachusetts Bay, in Council assembled, Dec. ye 6th 1776: Jonathan Danforth of Hardwick, in the County of Worcester, now a prisoner in the common Goal in said county, humbly shows, — That, some time in the month of July last, he left the town of Hardwick aforesaid and went to North Yarmouth in the county of Cumberland, and let himself to the Hon. Jeremiah Powell, one of this Honorable Board, and lived with him until the sixth day of November last, when he returned home to Hardwick, bringing proper credentials with him from the said Mr. Powell that, during the time he had lived with him, he had behaved well: that, during his absence, the Committee of Correspondence &c., for said Hardwick seized upon the estate of your petitioner and leased the same out, although he had left a proper person on it, to take care of it and his family in his absence; that, some little time after your petitioner's arrival home, the Committee aforesaid seized him, and in a most ignominious manner put him under guard and charged him with having been, in his absence, with the British troops, and made out a mittimus, signed by one William Paige, their chairman, directed to the Sheriff of the County, ordering him to be committed to goal as a person inimical and dangerous to the States of America, and at the same time forbidding the Sheriff to take any bail, although your petitioner could have procured ample security for his good behavior, and he is confined in the goal aforesaid among prisoners of war, thieves, &c., and must remain there, unless your Honors interpose in his behalf. Since civil government has taken place among us, and civil magistrates are appointed for the due execution of the laws, your petitioner apprehends that Committees cannot lawfully grant mittimuses for the commitment of any person; but the late law of this State directs that if any person is supposed [suspected?] of being inimical to the States of the United Colonies, upon complaint made by Com-

[1] *Mass. Archives*, clxxxi. 370.

mittees, &c. to a Justice of the Peace, the Justice is to examine the matter of complaint, and upon due proof being made to bind the offender to the next Court, and to his good behavior in the meantime; which law your petitioner is willing to submit to. Therefore [he] prays your Honors to direct the Sheriff that, upon your petitioner's giving bond, &c. agreeable to the direction of the law, he may be liberated; and as in duty bound shall pray:

"JONATHAN DANFORTH."[1]

This petition was referred, December 7, to a committee, and no further notice of it is found on the records of the General Court; but it elsewhere appears that the petitioner "was set at liberty by the Judges of the Superior Court." Then followed a sharp and troublesome contest between him and the committee, the details of which, as well as the antecedent transactions, are set forth in the following petition:—

"To the Honorable the Council and House of Representatives for the State of the Massachusetts Bay: The petition of the Selectmen and Committee of Correspondence, Inspection, and Safety, for the town of Hardwick, humbly showeth,—That whereas Jonathan Danforth of said town has in many instances, in our opinion, been aiding and assisting the unnatural enemies of the United States of America, therefore we, the said Selectmen and Committee, shall endeavor to inform the Honorable Court of the said Danforth's conduct, from the time of the date of the Resolve of the Provincial Congress requiring every town in this State to appoint Committees to call their Constables to account for the outstanding monies in their hands, and also the transactions of the Town, Selectmen, and Committee, aforesaid, with the said Danforth.

"In the first place, with regard to the said Danforth, when the said town's committee, agreeable to a Resolve of the Provincial Congress of the State (the said Danforth being constable for said town), proceeded to call him to an account for said outstanding monies, the said Danforth then absolutely refused to give any account respecting said monies, when requested, till after being compelled thereto by said town, agreeable to said Resolve,—who thereupon gave his note for said monies, for which they gave him a receipt. And further, the said Danforth made a humble acknowledgment for his past conduct, and solemnly engaged for the future that he would not oppose, but assist all in his power the people of this Town and State in every thing that is not con-

[1] *Mass. Arch.*, clxxxi. 367, 368.

trary to the constitution of this state and the laws of the same; and that he would religiously stand to all the covenants of the town, which he had signed; and that he would stand or fall with the people. But instead of performing his engagement, he immediately returned said receipt to Harrison Gray, by which means the gentleman who gave his receipt on the back of the Province-Warrant, in behalf of the town, was arrested for said monies, to his damage; and also did his endeavor to discourage the people from taking up arms to fight against the King of Great Britain; and whenever the inhabitants of said town met together for the purpose of raising men for that purpose, he would appear to ridicule them in a contemptuous way and manner; and did actually conceal the household furniture of Richard Ruggles, who has actually joined our unnatural enemy, and, being suspected, he delivered up a part, and point-blank declared he knew nothing about any more; but on further evidence being obtained against him, he confessed in an open town-meeting that he had concealed some other articles in a certain hill, which was afterwards actually found on said hill. And also the said Danforth, notwithstanding the restrictions which were laid on him by the Committee, in obedience to a Resolve of the Provincial Congress requiring them to take effective measures to prevent suspected persons from executing their wicked designs, in open contempt of their authority went to New York, or elsewhere, and purchased a large quantity of Bohea Tea and brought [it] into town, and immediately absented himself; by which circumstances the Committee was led to suspect that he had actually gone and joined our cruel enemies, he having previously disposed of all his stock and part of his household furniture, and part thereof he conveyed away privately and concealed in the woods, as his wife afterwards informed us, and also carried away all his valuable writings; and when he returned back to town informed the Committee of his coming, and also gave hints that he was ready to give an account for his past conduct; the Committee soon after gave him an opportunity therefor; and when various questions were asked him by said Committee respecting his conduct, he refused giving any direct answer thereto. Furthermore, he endeavored to and actually did, in a clandestine manner, make conveyance of his real estate, in order as was supposed to secure it from being taken as a forfeited estate. Finally, his whole conduct, ever since the time first mentioned in this petition, has been to insult and act in contempt against the Resolves of the Continental Congress, the covenants and engagements entered into by the town, and the orders of said Committee agreeable to said Resolves and Acts of the Great and General Court of this State, unless compelled thereto.

"In the second place, we shall endeavor to inform the Honorable Court of the transactions of the Town, Selectmen, and Committee, with said Danforth, from time to time. Viewing him as an enemy to the rights and liberties of this country, they thought themselves in duty bound, — in pursuance of a Resolve of the Provincial Congress in the year 1775, recommending it to Selectmen and Committees in all and every town in this State to take effectual steps to put it out of the power of such persons to obstruct by any means whatever the measures that shall be taken for the common defence, — to publish his name to the world as an enemy, and lay him under restrictions not to pass over the bounds of the town without license first obtained from said Committee. They also proceeded, in the year 1776, to enter a complaint to a Justice of the Peace, viewing him, agreeable to a Resolve of the Continental Congress, as a person that ought to be withdrawn from, and have no commercial intercourse with, to grant a warrant to take the forementioned Tea, and to have it stored, which was accordingly done. They also proceeded, agreeable to an Act of the Great and General Court in April 1776, — requiring Committees to make returns of the names of all such persons who had in any manner acted against or opposed the rights and liberties of the United States of America, together with their respective crimes, and evidences or depositions, — to make return of said Danforth's name, with depositions accordingly. They also proceeded, — some time after the said Danforth had fled and left the town as before mentioned, in the opinion of said Committee and every true friend and well-wisher to [the] rights and liberties of America, to join our unnatural enemies, or elsewhere, for protection, agreeable to a Resolve of the Great and General Court of this State in 1776, empowering Committees to take immediate possession of all such persons' estates, and to lease out all such real estate for the space of one year, — to take possession of all such personal estate as could be found belonging to said Danforth, and to lease out said real estate, and returned an inventory thereof to Court, agreeable to said Act. They further proceeded, after said Danforth had returned to town (he being absent from the fore part of July till late in the Fall, the same year), to bring him under examination, as before mentioned, he giving no direct answers to questions asked him, it was our candid opinion, — referring to a Resolve of the Continental Congress, recommending it to Committees that the most bold, impudent, and dangerous, enemies of this kind ought to be confined, — that it was not for the safety and welfare of the good people for him to go at large; therefore the said Committee, with the advice of the principal men and Judges of the Inferior Court for the County of Worcester, having no particular Act at hand pointing out the method for commitment, proceeded to commit him to Worcester Goal, having first laid the case before the town at a full town meeting assembled, and having a very unanimous vote therefor. After said Danforth had remained in goal for some time, he was set at liberty by the Judges of the Superior Court, the Committee not knowing that he was to be brought upon trial at that time, and consequently had no opportunity to be heard. And on his returning home, the inhabitants of the town being very uneasy, thinking it not safe for the matter to remain in such a situation, — and in conformity to an Act of the Great and General Court, recommending it to Committees that any persons that were found to be enemies to the liberties of the people, that they enter complaint against such persons, and have them brought before proper authority for examination and trial, — thought it advisable to proceed with him agreeable to said act; and when coming to trial, and producing sufficient evidence against him, as we supposed, yet he was after all very unexpectedly set at liberty, without any punishment or paying damages; by which means he has taken encouragement to proceed against said Town and Committee by endeavoring to take advantage of law, and has interceded with some magistrate to grant him a writ, by which means he has recovered the tea before mentioned, and has summoned the officer, who served the warrant to take the tea, to make his appearance at the next Quarter Sessions to be holden at Worcester, to answer for his default; and is further endeavoring to take advantage of the Town and Committee, in an insulting and impudent manner, by threatening to commence divers law-suits against them for their proceedings against him and his estate as before expressed.

"And whereas this town in a particular manner has had the hard fortune to suffer greatly by being infested with villains of this kind, beyond what has been undergone by many towns in this State, it must give your petitioners great uneasiness to see one which we think in no case ought to have the advantage of law suffered to disturb the town, and, if it were in his power, involve the whole land in ruin and misery. Your petitioners therefore humbly pray the Honorable Court would take the matter into their wise consideration, and point out some effectual method to bring the matter to a speedy issue. And your petitioners, as in duty bound, shall ever pray. Dated at Hardwick, the 18th of February 1778.

"WILLIAM PAIGE,
THOMAS ROBINSON,
DAVID ALLEN, } *Selectmen.*
TIMOTHY PAIGE,
TIMOTHY NEWTON,

"Signed per order, WILLIAM PAIGE, Chairman" (of the Committee of Correspondence.) [1]

June 3, 1778. "In the House of Representatives, on a petition of the Selectmen and Committee of Correspondence of the town of Hardwick, setting forth that Jonathan Danforth of said Hardwick hath conducted in an inimical manner towards this and the other United States, &c., and has commenced two actions at law, one against Timothy Paige, the other against Thomas Robinson, both of said town, which actions are to be tried at the next Inferior Court of Common Pleas to be holden at Worcester on the second Tuesday of June instant: Resolved, that the petitioners serve Jonathan Danforth of Hardwick with a copy of their petition and the order thereon, that cause may be shewn, if any there be, on the second Tuesday of the next setting of the General Court, wherefore the prayer of said petition should not be granted; and notice be given to said Danforth fourteen days at least before the second Tuesday aforesaid; and that all processes brought against the inhabitants of said Hardwick by said Danforth be stayed in the meantime. In Council. Read and concurred. Consented to by fifteen of the Council." [2]

At the time appointed, the following depositions (and several others) were presented, and are still preserved; the first, here inserted, was dated September 26, 1778, and taken by Paul Mandell, Esq.; the others were taken at the house of Eliakim Spooner in Hardwick, September 14, 1778, by John Mason, Esq., of Barre.

"I, Uriah Higgins, of Hardwick, of lawful age, testify and say, that, in the month of December 1775, I was at Albany, and see Jonathan Danforth of said Hardwick purchase about half a barrel of Bohea Tea, which he brought to Hardwick for sale, as I took it. URIAH HIGGINS." [3]

[1] *Mass. Arch.*, ccxix. 440–443.

[2] *Gen. Court Records*, xxxviii. 538.

[3] *Mass. Arch.*, ccxix. 459.

"I, Gamaliel Collings, of Hardwick, yeoman, of lawful age, doth testify and saith, that at Worcester, in the year 1776, at the Inferior Court held there, I was in company with Deac. William Paige of Hardwick, one of the Committee of Correspondence, [who] had Jonathan Danforth of said town in possession as a suspected person of treason against these States. Deacon William Paige not knowing what method to commit said Danforth, and said Paige asking Judge Moses Gill in what manner he should proceed with said Danforth, the said Judge Gill replying that the Committee had authority to commit to goal any person that the Committee should think was an enemy to their country. Further saith not. GAMALIEL COLLINGS.

"Question put by the Committee to said Collings: Did Judge Baker give any advice respecting said Danforth? Answer: Yes; after said Danforth was committed to goal, I heard Judge Baker say that there had not been much law in the land, only the law of the Committees, and that the Committees had a right to commit any person for treason, till further order of the Court." [1]

"I, Jonathan Warner of Hardwick, being of lawful age, testify and say, that, agreeable to a Resolve of the Provincial Congress directing the several towns to call on their constables for the outstanding moneys in their hands, Jonathan Danforth being one of the constables, said Danforth being at my house, the question being asked him where he would pay the money he had in his hands, his answer was, he would not pay the money to Hardwick or their Committee; he was not accountable to them for said money; he either would see them damned first, or he would be damned before he would pay the money; and said, I swear, before I will pay the money to Henry Gardner, Esq., he would pay the money to Harrison Gray. In May 1775, after the Battle of Lexington, the people of Hardwick met for the purpose of raising men; said Danforth, instead of appearing with his arms like a good soldier, he rode his horse round the companies in an insulting manner. And further saith not. JONATHAN WARNER." [2]

"I, Thomas Robinson of Hardwick in the County of Worcester, of lawful age, testify and say, that in the month of November, 1774, being one of the Committee of the town of Hardwick appointed to examine the constables concerning what public monies they had not paid in, Jonathan Danforth, being one of the constables, refused to give any account to said Committee, which refusal he repeated in public town-meeting; upon which, being

[1] *Mass. Arch.*, ccxix. 458.

[2] *Ibid.*, ccxix. 445.

told by the deponent that he must account for the monies as required, or he should be given up to the people, he replied, 'damn you all.'[1] In the spring of the year 1775, the whole militia being together, consisting of divers companies, the said Danforth, instead of bearing arms, rode amongst us, to the no small disturbance of the companies. Further saith not.

"THOMAS ROBINSON.

"Quest. put by said Danforth to said Robinson, whether the riding of said Danforth in the spring of the year 1775, among the militia was before the Lexington Battle? Ans. Yea."[2]

"We, Elijah Warner and Denison Robinson, both of Hardwick, being of lawful age, testify and say, that in the month of February 1775, or thereabouts, being in Boston in company with Daniel Warner, each of us having a team, the above named Daniel Warner was arrested by Harrison Gray, Esq., and, as we understand, in consequence of Jonathan Danforth returning the Province Warrant after the said Daniel Warner had given his receipt thereon to said Danforth in behalf of the town; the said Danforth having been previously compelled by said town to pay the outstanding money in his hands to Henry Gardner, Esq., or give security to the town for the same, as directed by [the] Provincial Congress. And further saith not.

"ELIJAH WARNER,
DENISON ROBINSON.

"Quest. put by the Committee to the above named persons: How did you know that Daniel Warner was arrested on the receipt on the Province Warrant? Ans. Mr. McIntire first informed us of the matter; on which we went to the goal in Boston, and there we found the said Warner in custody of an officer; and we the said Robinson and Elijah Warner gave our bonds for said Daniel Warner, for his appearance at Court; and said Rob-

[1] Perhaps this was the time when some individuals attempted to seize Mr. Danforth as he left the meeting-house. Instead of then "giving him up to the people," Mr. Robinson caught him by the shoulder and conducted him to the pound, which then stood on the westerly side of the Common. He then addressed the multitude, endeavoring to persuade them to disperse quietly; and at length assured them, that however much he disapproved the offending individual's conduct, he would not see him abused, but would defend him to the last extremity. Being a man of giant form and strength, and known to be fearless and resolute, no one cared to attack him; and he succeeded at last in conveying his charge to a place of greater security, and finally to his home in safety. Mr. Danforth told me in his old age, that he verily believed he should have been killed at that time, if Mr. Robinson had not protected him. This was probably the nearest approach to the execution of "lynch-law," which occurred in this town during that period of high excitement.

[2] *Mass. Arch.*, ccxix. 453.

inson declares that he read the writ, and read thereon, 'Take no Rebels for bail.'"[1]

"I, Stephen Gorham, of Hardwick in the County of Worcester, of lawful age, testify and say, that, in the Fall of the year A. Dom. 1774, after Jonathan Danforth was dismissed from being a minute-man, he asked me if I was going to take up arms against King George. I told him, yea, if he was going to fight against me. Then said Danforth said, we should be all styled Rebels, and often repeated it. And further saith not. STEPHEN GORHAM."[2]

"I, Ebenezer Lawrence, Jr., of Hardwick in the County of Worcester, of lawful age, testify and say, in the year 1775, in conversation about Bunker Hill Fight, he told me they would have Cambridge within a month; and said Danforth told me, that if I was you, I would not stir one step to help; and said Danforth advised me to stay at home about my business. Furthermore saith not. EBENEZER LAWRENCE, JR."[3]

"I, Job Dexter, of Hardwick in the County of Worcester, being of lawful age, testify and say, that at a certain time, 1776, as I was in conversation with Jonathan Danforth of said Hardwick, and discoursing about secreting the estate of Richard Ruggles, he said he was a damned fool for discovering to the Committee where any thing of the said Richard Ruggles' estate was; for they had no more business with it than the Divil had. And further saith not. JOB DEXTER."[4]

"I, James Paige, of Hardwick, of lawful age, testify and say, having in May, 1776, a considerable discourse with Jonathan Danforth, he God-damned the Committee, and the Selectmen, and the whole town, repeatedly. And further saith not.

"JAMES PAIGE.

"Quest. put by said Danforth to said Paige: Did not you tell me that the Committee would have my estate, if I did not behave better? Ans. I do not remember it now. Quest. Was I in a passion when I discoursed with you? Ans. Yes. Quest. Did you ever hear me say any thing against any authority except in the town of Hardwick? Ans. No."[5]

After an examination of these and several other depositions of like tenor, and a full consideration of the question at issue, the

[1] *Mass. Arch.*, ccxix. 447.

[2] *Ibid.*, ccxix. 456.

[3] *Ibid.*, ccxix. 451.

[4] *Ibid.*, ccxix. 446.

[5] *Ibid.*, ccxix. 457. In justice to Mr. Danforth it should be said that he was not in the habit of using profane language (at least while I knew him), except when he was "in a passion," under strong provocation. He made very familiar use, however, of the word devil, always pronounced by him divil.

General Court, on the 9th of October, 1778, entered their decision on record: —

"In the House of Representatives. Whereas it appears to this Court that Jonathan Danforth, late of Hardwick (now of Barre), since September, 1774, from time to time hath behaved in a very insolent and abusive manner towards the said town of Hardwick, and especially towards the Committee of said town, in their executing the duties of office, particularly in his unreasonable turbulent obstinacy in accounting for public monies in his hands, when properly called thereto; his endeavoring to conceal the goods and effects of persons fled to the enemy; his discouraging and insulting speeches and behavior to and among the good people of said town, when pursuing the orders of government, &c.; which line of conduct he continued till about July, 1776, when he, in a sudden and secret manner absconded, having first secretly conveyed away his most valuable effects; all which gave the strongest presumptive evidence that he was actually fled to the enemy, with others, his friends, that was known to be gone thither. Under these circumstances the Committee of said town proceeded agreeable to the Resolves of the General Court, and in behalf of the Government took possession of his estates that could be found, as a Refugee's estate. That, in about four or five months after, said Danforth returned; and without applying to this Court for restoring his estates, taken as aforesaid, is harassing said Committee with expensive and perplexing law-suits, and is threatening to bring many more, not only to their damage, but also to the disturbance of the good and liege people of this State. Wherefore it is become absolutely necessary for this Court to interpose in this matter:

"Therefore, Resolved, that the two actions brought by the said Jonathan Danforth, one against Timothy Paige, for replevying a quantity of tea, the other against Thomas Robinson, for the recovering of a certain house, claimed by said Danforth, which are mentioned in the petition of the Selectmen and Committee of the said town of Hardwick, addressed to this Court, and are now pending in the Inferior Court of Common Pleas for the county of Worcester, shall be, and they are hereby, declared utterly null and void; and all further proceedings thereon shall cease forever; and that the said Danforth shall be, and he hereby is, utterly disqualified and disabled forever from bringing any other action or actions against said Committee, or either of them, or any other person, either in his own name, or in the name of any other in his behalf, for the recovery of damages done or supposed to be done in consequence of the proceedings of said Committee or town of Hardwick, dealing with him, the said Danforth, as a person inimical to the common cause, without leave first had and obtained from the General Court. And whereas it doth not appear to this Court that the said Danforth has been guilty of actually joining our unnatural enemies, or giving information to or supplying them, but rather the contrary is supposed: therefore, Resolved, that the said Committee be, and they hereby are, directed and ordered to acquit and release to the said Danforth all the estate by them taken as the estate of said Danforth, the inventory whereof is lodged in the Secretary's office. In Council, Read and concurred. Consented to by fifteen of the Council." [1]

This decision rendered substantial justice to both parties: it justified the Committee, and protected them from further annoyance or harm; on the other hand, while Mr. Danforth was held to have deserved what he had already suffered, in consequence of his intemperate and exasperating opposition to the patriotic movement, yet as he had not actually held correspondence with the enemy, nor been guilty of any treasonable act, his liberty and property were restored. He soon returned from Barre, and for nearly half a century resided here in quietness and tranquillity, performing faithfully the duties of a good and loyal citizen, and enjoying the confidence and esteem of his townsmen. Yet he never entirely forgot his early conflicts. A characteristic story was related of him by his pastor, the Rev. John Goldsbury. In 1831, when he was eighty-eight years old, Colonel Stephen Rice, a member of the Revolutionary Committee of Correspondence, died, at the age of ninety-five. Soon afterwards, Mr. Goldsbury called on Mr. Danforth, who recounted some of his early trials and sufferings. Among other grievances, he said the Committee of Correspondence prohibited him from leaving his own farm, except to go to meeting on Sundays, and to attend funerals. "One day," said he, "a member of the Committee informed me there was to be a funeral, and inquired whether I wished to be present; I told him I always liked to go to funerals, and I hoped I might live to attend the funerals of the whole Committee; and I have done it; I have seen every divil of them under ground; Rice was the last of them."

[1] *Gen. Court Records*, xxxviii. 673.

CHAPTER VIII.

CIVIL HISTORY.

Declaration of Independence recorded by the Town Clerk. — Paper Money. — Heavy Taxes. — Financial Distress. — Stay Law. — Scale of Prices. — Abortive Attempts to make Paper equal with Gold. — Protest against a proposed Bill for refunding the Public Debt. — Scale of Depreciation. — The Town approves the Articles of Confederation of the United States, and almost unanimously rejects a Form of Constitution proposed by the General Court. — Eccentricities of the Town Clerk. — Delegates elected to a Constitutional Convention. — The proposed Constitution accepted, but various Important Amendments suggested. — Subsequent Constitutional Conventions.

SOON after the Declaration of Independence was adopted on the memorable 4th of July, 1776, the Town Clerk entered a full copy on the Town Records, "to remain as a perpetual memorial thereof." Thenceforth all professions of loyalty to the King, and desire for an amicable agreement between Great Britain and her colonies disappear from the Records. The last recorded warrant, "in his Majesty's name," bears date February 25, 1775; no warrants for the town-meetings, held April 24, July 5, and September 28, of that year, are recorded. The warrants, dated May 15, 1775, and February 14, 1776, required the constable to warn the inhabitants "agreeable to the Constitution," that is, the charter, which was frequently so designated; and that which was dated September 26, 1776, demanded the same service "agreeable to the government and people of this State." This is the earliest instance of such use of the word "State," which I have discovered on the Town Records. From this time the town promptly and energetically bore its full share of the burdens assumed by the State, in the maintenance of national independence.

To defray the enormous expenses of the war, paper money was issued by the several States and by the United States, which soon depreciated in value, and which ultimately became valueless, and was utterly repudiated. Heavy taxes were imposed by the State, and burdensome debts assumed by the towns in addition to the large sums raised by local taxation. General distress followed, such as, a few years later, resulted in open rebellion. As early as 1776, "the people were so pressed with public claims, that they were unable to meet private demands. Laws were made for their relief by suspending legal processes for the collection of debts. The paper money depreciated; and the soldiers and their families suffered much by it. A committee was appointed to meet others from Connecticut, Rhode Island, and New Hampshire, to adopt measures for preventing the depreciation of the bills, and a spirit of monopoly and speculation which prevailed, the committees had two meetings, but it was found impossible to remedy the evil."[1] Again, in March, 1777, it is said, "the expenses and debts of the State were such, at this period, as to require another large emission of paper, and a tax of £100,000. The amount of bills was £125,000; but these depreciated as soon as issued, and the taxes were not easily collected. This was a time of very great distress and suffering."[2] Among the "measures for preventing the depreciation of the bills" was one which had many times before been unsuccessfully adopted; namely, definite prices were fixed for various kinds of labor and merchandise, with the hope that by such uniform prices the uniform purchasing value of the bills might be maintained. The scale of prices prescribed in Hardwick was very minute, and may seem tedious; yet it is not without interest, as exhibiting the various articles of traffic and consumption, at that period, and their relative value. It seems to have been adopted not long before March 17, 1777, on which day the town granted nine shillings each to Thomas Robinson and John Bradish, "for setting prices on articles in this town."

"At a meeting of the Selectmen and Committee of Correspondence for the town of Hardwick, agreeable to an Act of the Great and General Court respecting the stating and affixing prices upon labor, victualling, clothing, and other articles hereafter enumerated:

"Farming labor, from the 1st of June to the 1st of September, at 3*s.* per day; from the 1st of Sept. to the 15th of Nov., 2*s.* 4*d.*; from the 15th of Nov. to the 15th of Mar., 1*s.* 8*d.*; from the 15th of Mar. to the 1st of June, 2*s.* 4*d.* Carpenters' and house-joiners' work, from the 1st of April to the 1st of Oct., 3*s.* 4*d.*; from the 1st of Oct. to the 1st of April, 2*s.* 6*d.* Mill-wrights, from the 1st of April to the 1st of Oct., 4*s.*; from the 1st of Oct. to the 1st of

[1] Bradford's *Hist. of Mass.*, p. 273. [2] *Ibid.*, p. 275.

April, 3*s*. Masons' work, from the 1st of March to the 1st of Nov. [Oct. ?] 3*s*. 8; from the 1st of Oct. to the 1st of April [Mar. ?] 2*s*. 8*d*. For shoeing a horse round, steeled toe and heel, 5*s*. 4*d*.; for plain shoeing of a horse, 4*s*. For shoeing a pair of oxen, steeled toe and heel, 9*s*. For a falling axe, well steeled, 7*s*. 3*d*. For a grass scythe, well steeled, 7*s*. Good plough-shares, well steeled, 10*d*. per lb. For making good men's and women's shoes, 2*s*. 10*d*. per pair, and all other shoe-making in proportion. Men's good neat-leather shoes, 8*s*. a pair. Women's good neat-leather shoes, 6*s*. a pair. Men's Taylor's work at 2*s*. 2*d*. per day; women's do. 1*s*. per day. For tanning raw hides, 2*d*. a lb., and skins in proportion. Good merchantable wheat, 6*s*. per bushel. Good merchantable rye, 4*s*. per bushel. Good merchantable Indian corn, 3*s*. Good merchantable oats, 2*s*. Good merchantable barley, 4*s*. Good barley malt, 4*s*. Good merchantable beans and peas, 6*s*. Good merchantable Spanish potatoes, 1*s*. in the field, and 1*s*. 6*d*. in the cellar. Good merchantable turnips, 8*d*. Good onions, 4*s*. Good winter apples, 9*d*. Doctor's riding in their office, 7*d*. per mile. For weaving all-wool cloth, ell wide, 6*d*. per yard. For weaving tow cloth, yard wide, 4*d*. per yard; and all other weaving in proportion. For weaving coverlids of the best kind, 6*s*. each, and other coverlids in proportion thereto. Good fleece wool, 2*s*. per lb.; and wool of an inferior kind in proportion. Fresh pork, of the best kind, 4*d*. per lb. Grass-fed beef of the best kind, 2*d*. 3*qu*. per lb. Good well-fatted, stall-fed beef, 3*d*. 3*qu*. per lb. Salt pork, by the barrel, 220wt. in a barrel, £4. 7*s*. Good salt beef, by the barrel, 240wt., £3. 9*s*. 6*d*. Good salt pork, clear of bone, 7*d*. per lb. Raw hides, 3*d*. per lb. Raw calf skins, 6*d*. per lb. Good merchantable imported salt, 15*s*. per bushel. Good salt, manufactured in this State, 17*s*. per bushel. West India rum, by the hogshead, 7*s*. 3*d*. per gallon, including the hogshead. W. I. rum, by the barrel, 7*s*. 5*d*. per gallon, and by the single gallon, 8*s*. 3*d*.; do. by the quart, 2*s*. 1*d*.; do. by the pint, 1*s*. 1*d*. New England rum, by the hogshead or barrel, exclusive of the cask, 4*s*. 5*d*.; do. by the single gallon, 5*s*. 1*d*.; by the quart, 1*s*. 4*d*.; by the pint, 8*d*. Best Muscovado sugar, 9*d*. per lb., and 8*d*. 2*qu*. by the seven lb.; and other sugar of an inferior quality, in equal proportion. Best molasses, by the single gallon, 4*s*. 9*d*. Best chocolate, 1*s*. 10*d*. per lb. Best new-milk cheese, 6*d*. per lb. Best butter, by the single pound, 9*d*. Best men's yarn stockings, 6*s*. Best cotton-wool, 3*s*. 10*d*. per lb. Good, clean, well-dressed flax, 1*s*. Good coffee, 1*s*. 6*d*. Good tried tallow, 5*d.* per lb. Good yard-wide tow cloth, 2*s.* 3*d.* per yard, and all other tow cloth in proportion to its width and quality. Good yard-wide striped flannel, 3*s.* 6*d.*, and all other flannels in proportion. Good all-wool men's wear, wove ell, 9*s.* per yard, well fulled and sheared. Good charcoal, 2*d.* 2*qu.* per bushel. Good yard-wide cotton and linen cloth, 4*s.*, and other cotton and linen cloth of an inferior quality in proportion. Good lamb and mutton, 3*d.* per lb. Good veal, 2*d.* 2*qu.* per lb. Good merchantable wheat flour, £1. 1*s.* per hundred wt. For keeping a horse one night, or twelve hours, 10*d.*, on good English hay. For the best of English hay, 1*s.* 8*d.* per cwt. For keeping a pair of oxen one night, 1*s.* For turkeys, dung-hill fowls, and ducks, 4*d.* per lb. For geese, 3*d.* per lb. Good refined iron, 50*s.* per cwt. Good bloomery iron, 30*s.* per cwt., at the place of manufactory. Teaming work, 1*s.* 6*d.* for every ton weight per mile, excepting from Northampton to the Northern Army, for which may be taken 2*s.* per mile for each ton weight. Good new milk in the winter season, 2 coppers per quart; in the summer season, 2 coppers per quart.[1] A dinner of common meat-victuals, and proper sauce and other conveniences, 8*d.* For a dinner, two dishes, roast and boiled, 10*d.* For a supper of common meat-victuals, and a breakfast, 8*d.* For a supper or breakfast of milk, 4*d.* For a night's lodging, 3*d.* For a mug of good West India flip, 11*d.*; do. of N. E. rum, 9*d.* W. I. rum, by the half pint, 8*d.*; by the gill, 4*d.* For a mess of oats, 2 quarts in a mess, 3*d.* N. E. rum, by the half pint, 6*d.*, by the gill, 3*d.* Good cider, 2*d.* 2*qu.* by the mug. Good merchantable cider-barrels, 3*s.* 6*d.* each, with split ash hoops. Good merchantable pails, with locked hoops, 2*s.* each, and all other cooper-work in the same proportion. Ox-work in the summer season, 1*s.* 6*d.* per day; do. in the winter, 1*s.* Horse-hire, 2*d.* per mile. For pasturing a horse, 1*s.* 6*d.* per week. For pasturing a yoke of oxen, 2*s.* 4*d.* per week; do. for a cow, 10*d.* per week. For keeping a cow in winter, 1*s.* 8*d.* per week. For a man's day's work, with four oxen and cart, 7*s.* per day. For keeping a horse in the winter season 3*s.* per week. For keeping a yoke of oxen, in the winter season, 4*s.* per week. For a bushel of flax-seed, clear of foul seed, 6*s.* For a thousand of good merchantable bricks, 18*s.* per thousand. Good merchantable shingles, 12*s.* per thousand. Good merchantable men's saddles, £2. 14*s.* each. Good merchantable women's saddles, deer's-leather or plush seat, £3. 12*s.* Good bridles, made of neat's

[1] Probably one of these figures is an error.

leather, 6*s.* each Good broad hoes, 3*s.* 6*d.* Linen wheels, 16*s.* each. Woolen wheels, 7*s.* For boarding a common laboring man, 6*s.* per week. White pine boards of the best kind, £3. per thousand. Common yellow pine boards, £1. 6*s.* 8*d.* per thousand. For making a pair of good cart wheels, 33*s.* For boarding colliers and furnace-men, 7*s.* per week. For floor-boards of the best kind, £1. 12*s.* per thousand. For oak and chestnut boards, and common slit-work, £1. 4*s.* per thousand. Men's labor, by the year, £19. Bohea tea, 4*s.* 6*d.* per lb. Good shovels, 4*s.* each. Good sole leather, 1*s.* 3*d.* per lb. Curried leather, in usual proportion to tanned hides."

Notwithstanding this effort to sustain it, the value of paper money continued to depreciate, and larger sums were required in exchange for labor and for the necessaries of life.[1] A law was subsequently enacted, imposing a heavy penalty on any person who should demand or receive a higher price in bills of credit than in gold or silver for his merchandise; but this measure was equally unsuccessful. Before proceeding to this extremity, however, the General Court, on the 13th of October, 1777, passed "An Act for drawing in the bills of credit of the several denominations, not on interest, which have at any time been issued by this Government, and are still outstanding, and for prohibiting the currency of said bills and the bills of any one of the United States after a certain time.

"Whereas, many inconveniences have arisen from the frequent and large sums of money and the various kinds, emitted for carrying on the present war, and it has become necessary for the welfare of this State that the whole sum, not on interest, now outstanding in bills of credit emitted by this State, small change of less than a dollar only excepted, should be called in and sunk, by exchanging them for Treasurer's notes for sums not less than ten pounds, on interest, to be paid annually, at the rate of six per cent per annum.

"Be it therefore enacted by the Council and House of Representatives in General Court assembled, and by the authority of the same, That the Treasurer of the State be and hereby is authorized and empowered to receive into the public Treasury the whole and every part and parcel of the bills of public credit emitted by this State, not on interest, (small change, less than a

[1] During the recent civil war, a similar difficulty was experienced; far less severe, indeed, among those who were loyal to the Union, but strikingly parallel in the Confederate States.

dollar only excepted), and in lieu thereof to give to the possessor or possessors his note or obligation for any sum not less than ten pounds, until he shall have exchanged or redeemed the sum of two hundred and fifty thousand pounds, in the form following," [namely, a note, payable March 1, 1781], "and for the remaining sum now outstanding as aforesaid, his note or obligation, in the form following," [namely, a note payable March 1, 1782. Provision was made for the payment of these notes by taxes to be reasonably assessed.]

"And be it further enacted by the authority aforesaid, That the possessor and possessors of the bills of public credit of this State are hereby called upon and directed to bring the same to the Treasurer on or before the first day of January, 1778, from whom they shall be entitled to receive in exchange for all such bills, so delivered in, a Treasurer's note as aforesaid, for any sum not less than ten pounds, upon interest at the rate of six per cent per annum, which interest shall be paid annually.

"And for the more speedy accomplishing the good intentions of this Act, and preventing the evils arising from large emissions of various kinds of bills, — Be it further enacted by the authority aforesaid, That if the possessor or possessors of said bills shall neglect to offer the same to be exchanged by the said first day of January, 1778, all right or claim to the redemption or exchange of said bills shall cease and determine.

"And be it further enacted by the authority aforesaid, That if any person or persons within this State shall offer to pass, after the first day of December next, in any kind of payment whatsoever, any of the bills of public credit emitted by this or any of the United States, except bills on interest emitted by this State, and such as are under the denomination of one dollar, every person so offering or passing any such bill shall forfeit and pay for each offence the sum of five pounds," etc. Provision was made for extension of time to constables, or collectors of taxes, and to soldiers serving in the army.[1]

This method of funding the public debt, strongly resembling a forced loan, and withdrawing suddenly nearly the entire currency of the country, drew from the inhabitants of Hardwick almost the only protest to be found on their Records against the proceedings of the General Court, during the Revolutionary period. At a town-meeting, November 24, 1777, a committee, consisting

[1] *General Court Records*, xxxviii. 111. *Laws of Massachusetts from July*, 1775, *to October*, 1780, p. 142.

of Joseph Allen, William Paige, and David Allen, reported a remonstrance, which was adopted: —

"State of Massachusetts Bay. To the honorable the Council and House of Representatives in General Court assembled. A remonstrance and petition of the town of Hardwick, regularly assembled. Taking into consideration the late Act made for calling in all the bills of public credit of this State not on interest, so sudden, and putting them on interest (excepting those that are under a dollar), this town look upon said Act to be attended with many grievances, considering the circumstances of the public affairs at this day, which necessarily raises the public charges exceeding high, had there been no vile oppressors risen up, whose covetous and sordid measures have almost doubled the same, by which multitudes of the poorer sort of people have been and will be reduced to poverty. (1.) To us it appears the manner of calling in said bills puts another great advantage into the hands of men, who of all others should be guarded against; for these very men have taken advantage of the times, and engrossed by cruel oppression great estates, and many of them from little or nothing; and instead of suffering by this sore expensive war, rise upon the ruins of their fellow-men. (2.) It appears to us very extraordinary, when the bills are emitted for various sums, promising to receive them into the treasury for the sums specified, and now declare they will not receive them, unless to the amount of ten pounds. Where then is the public faith? (3.) We look upon it cruel and oppressive, when compared with former acts which made the money a lawful tender till the last instant, and the next day a fine to offer it; and the possessor who is then obliged to take it is exposed to have it die in his hands. Therefore, for these and other reasons which may be given, we see no way how the greater part of the poorer sort of people will ever be able to pay their public charges. We well remember what cruel and oppressive acts has been endeavored to be enforced on the good people of these United States, by the King and Parliament of Great Britain; but we hope and trust we never shall be oppressed in like kind by our own Legislature. Therefore we bear our testimony against said Act, and desire a speedy repeal thereof. As in duty bound shall ever pray."

Similar remonstrances from other towns were presented; and the General Court yielded so far to the public demand as to postpone the time at which bills of credit should be repudiated, if not offered in exchange for treasury notes, to April 1, and again to June 1, and a third time to December 1, 1778.[1] Still, the value of paper-money continued to depreciate. Once more an effort was made to check the evil, by a general establishment of prices. A convention for that purpose assembled at Concord in October, 1779, at which Timothy Paige was a delegate from Hardwick. A scale of prices was adopted, and the people were exhorted to conform to it in all their pecuniary transactions. But this experiment, like all others of the kind, proved ineffectual; all whose income was a fixed sum, like the clergy, and the officers and soldiers in the army, suffered severely; and the whole community shared in the suffering. No man knew, when he received paper-money, whether he could dispose of it at half its present rate. It depreciated so rapidly[2] that it was almost impossible for even the imagination to keep pace with it. Some idea of the magnitude of this evil may be formed from a vote of the town, July 28, 1780: "Voted, to give to each soldier, one thousand pounds, which is esteemed equal to twelve pounds in silver money." One dollar in silver was equal in value to eighty-three dollars and thirty-three cents in paper.

During this period of sore financial distress, in addition to the unavoidable anxieties and calamities of war, an attempt was made to establish a firm and stable government, in place of that which had been violently overturned. The delegates of the several colonies agreed on articles of confederation and union, the more effectually to protect themselves against the common enemy, and submitted the same to their constituents for approval. At

[1] *Laws of Mass.*, 1775 to 1780, pp. 149, 169, 183.

[2] The rate of depreciation is exhibited in Felt's *Massachusetts Currency*, p. 196.

"Massachusetts Scale of Depreciation agreeably to a Law of the State for the settling of contracts, both public and private, made on and since the first day of January, 1777; one hundred dollars in gold and silver in January, 1777, being equal to one hundred and five dollars in the bills of credit of the United States.

	1777.	1778.	1779.	1780.
January,	105	325	742	2,934
February,	107	350	868	3,322
March,	109	375	1,000	3,736
April,	112	400	1,104	4,000
May,	115	400	1,125	
June,	120	400	1,342	
July,	125	425	1,477	
August,	150	450	1,630	
September,	175	475	1,800	
October,	275	500	2,030	
November,	300	543	2,308	
December,	310	634	2,593	

"From April 1, 1780, to April 20, one Spanish milled dollar was equal to forty of the old emission.

April 25,	42	June 20,	69
April 30,	44	August 15,	70
May 5,	46	September 10,	71
May 10,	47	October 15,	72
May 15,	49	November 10,	73
May 20,	54	November 30,	74
May 27,	60		
May 30,	62	1781.	
June 10,	64	February 27,	75"
June 15,	68		

a town-meeting, January 12, 1778, "after reading the Articles of Confederation and perpetual Union of the United States of America, the town voted, unanimously, to give their Representatives of the Great and General Court instructions to vote to confirm the same."

At about the same time the General Court resolved itself into a Constitutional Convention, and prepared a Constitution for Massachusetts; this, however, did not meet the popular approval, but was rejected by a decisive vote. In this town, the inhabitants met, April 6, 1778, "to hear a Constitution and Form of Government read, for the State of Massachusetts Bay, agreed upon by the Convention of the State, Feb. 28, 1778, to be laid before the several towns and plantations in said State for their approbation or disapprobation." At an adjournment of this meeting, April 20, 1778, the proposed Constitution was referred to a committee, and it was "voted to adjourn this meeting to Monday the 11th day of May next at 2 o'clock afternoon, and met accordingly, and proceeded as follows. (1.) Accepted the report of the committee by a great majority. (2.) A motion was made to have the whole Constitution put to vote, all at a lump;[1] it was accordingly done, and passed in the negative. (3.) Voted, that the report of the Committee should be sent to the General Assembly by the Town Clerk. No. of voters at said meeting, 156; No. of voters for said Constitution, 16; No. of voters against it, 140."

This first effort having failed, the General Court passed a Resolve, February 19, 1779, requiring the several towns to determine "whether they choose, at this time, to have a new Constitution or form of Government made," and "whether they will empower their Representatives for the next year to vote for the calling a State Convention, for the sole purpose of forming a new Constitution." At a town-meeting, May 11, 1779, to act on these

[1] The town clerk, Sylvanus Washburn, often used great latitude of expression in his records, of which this is one instance. Another occurs under date of March 6, 1780, when the town met "to see in what manner the town will consider a request to us presented by a respectable number of the inhabitants of this town concerning a late Tax Act of the 13th of December, 1779." "Voted to choose a Committee to draught a petition to send to the General Court, praying that the time of payment might be lengthened, . . . and to make report to the town as soon as may be, for their acceptance." On the next day, "the above committee laid before the town a scandalous petition, and it was put to vote to see if the town would accept of said petition, and it passed in the negative." To this record the clerk added a marginal note: "a ridiculous article in the warrant, that cost the town a whole day to act upon it." Other specimens of Mr. Washburn's official humor may be found under dates of June 14, 1780, and March 5, 1787.

questions, the record is, "N°. of voters at said meeting 81, and all voted in the affirmative." A large majority of voters in the State expressed the same desire, and the General Court directed that delegates should be elected in the several towns to meet in Convention. This town elected William Paige, Jonathan Warner, and John Hastings. The Convention met at Cambridge, September 1, 1779, and continued in session, by several adjournments, until March 2, 1780, when having agreed on a Constitution, it was "Resolved that this Convention be adjourned to the first Wednesday in June next, to meet at Boston." It was ordered that printed "copies of the Form of Government" be sent to every town and plantation, and "if the major part of the inhabitants of the said towns and plantations disapprove of any particular part of the same, that they be desired to state their objections distinctly, and the reasons therefor." The selectmen were requested to make return of the result on the first Wednesday in June; and it was "Resolved, that the towns and plantations through this State have a right to choose other delegates, instead of the present members, to meet in Convention on the first Wednesday in June next, if they see fit."[1] The Convention reassembled June 7, 1780, and remained in session until the 16th of the same month, when it was finally dissolved.

The town held four meetings, May 1, 8, 22, and 25, 1780, to act on the proposed Constitution. At the second meeting, it was "voted that there be no Governor appointed, by a majority of 27 against 15." At the third meeting, it was "voted, that if there be a Governor, that he be of the Christian Protestant Religion," instead of "the Christian Religion." At the fourth meeting, a committee, consisting of Joseph Allen, William Paige, Aaron Barlow, Thomas Robinson, and John Sellon, submitted a report, embracing several amendments to objectionable articles, with the reasons therefor; which report, with the proposed amendments, was accepted by a vote of 40 against 2. Some of the objections and amendments were as follows:—

"In the Bill of Rights, Article I, page 7, objected to and amended: it reads thus,—'All men are born free and equal, &c., amended,—'All men, whites and blacks, are born free and equal,' &c.; Reason: lest it should be misconstrued hereafter, in such a manner as to exclude blacks."[2] Article III. "Voted, That a person that does not attend the public worship of God at any

[1] *Journal of Convention*, pp. 168, 169.

[2] This question was decided by 68 yeas against 10 nays.

place ought not to be taxed in the place where he lives. Every other article in the Declaration of Rights approved."

Article 1, page 15, objected to, because the two branches have a negative on each other; whereas it ought to be but for a given time, and at the expiration of said time, if non-agreed, that both houses meet, and by a majority decide the controversy."

"Article 2, objected to, because the majority of the court can't make a law, without being exposed to a negative by the Governor."

The qualification of voters was objected to, "because every male, being twenty-one years of age, must have an annual income of three pounds, or an estate worth sixty pounds, to be qualified to vote for a senator. Reason: That every male, being twenty-one years of age, ought to vote in all cases."

The mode of filling vacancies in the senate objected to: "Reason: The persons having the highest number of votes in the District ought to be the men."

The office of Governor was disapproved: "Provided, nevertheless, that if the inhabitants of this State shall see meet to choose a Governor, Lieutenant-Governor, and Council, they should by no means have power over the militia; but the militia shall be under the order and direction of the General Court; and that they or either of them shall not prorogue, adjourn, nor dissolve the General Court without their request; and that they by no means appoint any officers, either civil, judicial, or military."

It was further recommended by the committee, and the town voted its approval, to wit:—

"That the power of pardon always be in the hands of the Legislature:

"That the Justices of the Superior Court be appointed by the General Court:

"That the Justices of the Inferior Court be chosen by the people of their county, as the Registers now are:

"That all Justices of the Peace shall be chosen annually by the people in each town in which they dwell, by ballot:

"That the Register of Deeds for each town in this State be annually chosen by ballot:

"That the Judges of Probate for each town in this State be annually chosen by the people of each town, by ballot, to serve in that town only: [1]

[1] June 5, 1780. The town proposed a different amendment, "that each county should be divided into proper districts . . . because some counties are so large that by

"That the captains and subalterns of the militia shall be elected by written votes of the alarm list and training band of their respective companies, of twenty-one years of age and upwards:

"That the colonels and majors be chosen by their respective regiments, the brigadiers and brigade majors by their respective brigades, the adjutants and quarter-masters by their respective regiments, by ballot."

Acting upon the suggestion of the Convention before mentioned, the town now "voted to dismiss the former delegates to the Convention, and dismissed them accordingly; and voted to choose one man to attend said Convention on the first Wednesday in June next, to be held in Boston, and made choice of Deac. William Paige for said delegate." [1]

Some of these proposed amendments were subsequently adopted, — such as universal suffrage, and election by plurality of votes. In the Declaration of Rights, the first article was interpreted to secure the freedom of the "blacks" in this State, nearly a century before universal emancipation resulted from a desperate attempt to extend and perpetuate the institution of slavery; and the proposed amendment of the Third Article was adopted in 1833, since which time the maintenance of public worship has been voluntary, not compulsory. So far, the inhabitants of Hardwick were somewhat in advance of the age. In some other respects, they exhibited that excessive love of liberty which is unwilling to submit to any restraint, or to give the government sufficient power to execute its proper functions. The same spirit was manifested by a majority of the people here, as in almost all the towns in the western counties of the State, during the stormy period which followed; and in 1788 it nearly prevented the adoption by Massachusetts of the Constitution of the United States, because it was supposed to invest the general government with too much power.[2]

reason of time and cost in travelling and attendance in the settling of estates, widows and orphans are put to great expense which might be lessened by the proposed amendment."

[1] June 14, 1780. The town modified its action in regard to delegates, as quaintly expressed by the town clerk: "Voted, that the town does approve of Brig'r Jonathan Warner as their delegate at the Convention; also voted, that the Honble William Paige be considered as a member in full communion of said convention."

[2] The town voted, August 21, 1820, "that it was expedient that Delegates should be chosen to meet in Convention for the purpose of revising or altering the Constitution of government of this Commonwealth;" and on the 16th of the following October, Timothy Paige, Esq., and Dr. Joseph Stone were elected delegates. Four unsuccessful ballots were taken March 7, 1853, for the election of Delegates to the Constitutional Convention which met in that year, and the town was not represented therein.

CHAPTER IX.

CIVIL HISTORY.

The Shays Insurrection. — Public and Private Debts Excessive. — Debtors become Desperate, and forcibly resist Payment. — Demagogues stimulate the Popular Discontent, which results in Open Rebellion. — The Town proposes a Convention at Worcester in 1782, and elects Delegates. — Conventions in 1786. — Grievances. — General Warner discharges one of his Aids, on Suspicion of Disloyalty: he promptly responds to the Governor's Order for the Protection of the Courts at Worcester, but is unable to rally a Sufficient Force. — The Courts prevented from sitting at Worcester and Springfield in September and again in December. — Troops raised by Enlistment. — Hardwick Company. — Attack on the Arsenal at Springfield. — Defeat of Shays: he is pursued by Lincoln, in a Terrible Night's March from Hadley to Petersham, where the Insurgents are utterly routed. — Oath of Allegiance taken by many Hardwick Men. — Some of the More Active Partisans abscond. — One of the Most Prominent is arrested, convicted of Treason, and sentenced to be hung; but is fully pardoned, and receives Tokens of Public Approbation. — Other Pardons. — The Shays Cause Popular, having a Majority in Hardwick, and generally throughout the Western Counties; even in the House of Representatives a Majority favor it. — Its Advocates afterwards become Good Citizens, but never Friendly to a Strong Government.

THE Constitution was adopted by the requisite majority of citizens, but this did not relieve their financial distress; on the contrary, it was aggravated by the legal machinery thus provided to enforce the payment of public and private debts which had long been held in abeyance. The result was a forcible resistance to the constituted government, which, from the name of a prominent leader, was called the "Shays Insurrection," or "Rebellion." Its immediate cause is succinctly stated by its historian: —

"The citizens were then left free indeed, and in full possession of the valuable objects which they had fought to obtain. But the price of those objects was high, and could not but be attended with the usual consequences of great exertions, when founded on the anticipation of public resources. Their private state debt, when consolidated, amounted to upwards of 1,300,000£., besides 250,000£., due to the officers and soldiers in their line of the army. Their proportion of the federal debt was not less, by a moderate computation, than one million and a half of the same money.[1] And in addition to this, every town was embarrassed by advances which they had made, to comply with repeated requisitions for men and supplies to support the army, and which had been done upon their own particular credit. The weight of this burden must strike us in a strong point of view, if we compare it with the debt before the war, which fell short of 100,000£., and with still more force, perhaps, if we consider that by the customary mode of taxation, one third part of the whole was to be paid by the ratable polls alone, which but little exceeded ninety thousand.[2] True it is, that a recollection of the blessings which this debt had purchased must have operated, in the minds of a magnanimous people, to alleviate every inconvenience arising from such a cause; but embarrassments followed which no considerations of that nature could be expected to obviate."[3]

In this emergency, the people very naturally resorted to those agencies which proved so effectual in the Revolutionary period, — town-meetings, namely, and county conventions. These assemblies, like those of the former period, found more and more grievances as they sought relief from the principal burden. The government removed some of these alleged grievances by legislative enactment, and uniformly manifested a forbearing and forgiving spirit. The public discontent, nevertheless, increased, being fomented and stimulated by political demagogues, until it culminated in absolute rebellion and resort to arms. After the rebellion was overpowered by superior military force, some of the persons who had been actively engaged in the field became fugitives from justice, and fled from the State; the large majority of them received a full pardon, on surrendering their arms and taking the oath of allegiance; a small number were fined, or imprisoned, or both; and a few of the leaders were convicted of treason and sentenced to be hung, but not one of the number was executed for the crime of treason only. I do not propose to recite all the details of this unhappy conflict; but some of the

[1] Amounting, exclusive of town and private debts, to £3,050,000, equal to $10,166,666.

[2] The whole was more than a hundred and thirteen dollars for each tax-payer, and one third was almost forty dollars for each ratable poll. In addition to this enormous public debt, a large portion of the people were hopelessly indebted to their fellow-citizens, who were becoming clamorous for payment and attempting to enforce it by legal process, involving heavy costs.

[3] Minot's *Hist. of Insurrections*, etc., pp. 5, 6.

events, in which this town or its individual inhabitants had an active agency, should be mentioned.

The first trace of opposition to the due course of law, which appears on our records, is found under date of January 8, 1782, when, upon petition of sundry persons "with regard to the numerous law-suits that are or may be commenced,[1] — fearing that the dangerous consequences thereof, unless some measures be speedily adopted to prevent it, will reduce us to poverty and distress," the town "Voted to address the General Assembly on the subject," and chose William Paige, Ebenezer Washburn, and Daniel Warner, to prepare the address. Two months later, what seems to be the initial movement for a county convention had its origin here, to wit: The town met March 4, 1782, under a warrant "to take into consideration a petition which is as follows: the petitioners taking into consideration our public affairs, and the great demands from the public for money by taxation, and the multiplicity of law-suits, and a scarcity of money, which renders it entirely out of the power of the good people of this State to comply with the above demands, they therefore desire that a town-meeting be called, to consider the articles following: 1. To see if the town will choose a committee, to write circular letters to other towns in the county of Worcester, to meet in convention, in the town of Worcester, at the house of Mr. Brown, innholder in said Worcester, and choose a member or members for said convention. 2. To see if the town will petition the General Court for a redress of grievances." The town "voted to choose a committee to write circular letters to the other towns in this county, agreeable to the warrant, and made choice of Ichabod Dexter, Col. Winslow,[2] and David Allen, for said committee. Voted to adjourn to the 18th of March, at one o'clock afternoon, and then met and chose Capt. Ichabod Dexter, Capt. Daniel Egery, and Nathaniel Haskell, members to meet in convention at Worcester on the second Tuesday of April next."

Apparently in response to this invitation, "on the 14th of April of that year, the delegates of twenty-six towns of the county assembled in convention, and attributing the prevailing dissatisfaction of the people to want of confidence in the disburse-

[1] This grievance increased rapidly. "In 1784, more than 2,000 actions were entered in the County of Worcester, then having a population less than 50,000, and in 1785, about 1,700. Lands and goods were seized and sacrificed on sale, when the general difficulties drove away purchasers." Lincoln's *Hist. of Worcester*, p. 131.

[2] I am unable to identify this person satisfactorily.

ment of the great sums of money annually assessed, recommended instructions to the representatives to require immediate settlement with all public officers entrusted with the funds of the Commonwealth; and if the adjustment was delayed or refused, to withdraw from the General Court and return to their constituents; to reduce the compensation of the members of the House, and the fees of lawyers; to procure sessions of the Court of Probate in different places in the County; the revival of confessions of debt; enlargement of the jurisdiction of justices of the peace to £20; contribution to the support of the continental army in specific articles instead of money; and the settlement of accounts between the Commonwealth and Congress. At an adjourned session, May 14, they further recommended, that account of the public expenditures should be annually rendered to the towns; the removal of the General Court from Boston; separation of the business of the Common Pleas and Sessions, and inquiry into the grants of lands in Maine in favor of Alexander Shepherd and others."[1] The convention then adjourned until August; and July 1, 1782, on the question "whether the town will join any further in the county convention, which now stands adjourned in the town of Worcester," it was "voted that they look upon it expedient that they join further in the abovesaid county convention." At the appointed time, however, very few delegates assembled, and the convention was dissolved without further action.

The measures adopted by the General Court produced temporary quiet. No further disturbance occurred in this county for nearly four years, except that a convention met in 1784, at the request of the town of Sutton, in which, however, it does not appear that Hardwick was represented. This convention was comparatively orderly, but prepared a formidable list of grievances, in the form of a petition to the General Court. Early in 1786 the agitation was recommenced, with additional energy. The first concerted action of this town, which appears on the record, bears date January 25, 1786. Under a warrant "to see if the town will give their Representative some instructions with regard to the present difficulty that the inhabitants of the Commonwealth labor under, for the want of a circulating medium, that he use his influence in the General Court that some mode might be adopted for their relief," it was "Voted, to instruct their Representative to use his influence in the General Court to have a Bank of Paper

[1] Lincoln's *Hist. of Worcester*, p. 132.

emitted, and chose a committee for that purpose, viz., Capt. John Hastings, Capt. Ichabod Dexter, David Allen, Thomas Wheeler, and Deac. William Paige."

"The want of a circulating medium," or the lack of money, for the payment of debts and taxes, was the most pressing burden which then rested on the people; and how to remove it was the problem to be solved. Hardwick recommended the issue of paper money by the government. Other towns expressed the same desire. Resort was had to county conventions, by which the list of grievances was rapidly enlarged, and the measures proposed for relief were multiplied. The historian of the Insurrection selects one of those conventions, as presenting probably a more full statement of the whole difficulty than is elsewhere to be found: —

"At a meeting of delegates from fifty towns in the county of Hampshire, in convention held at Hatfield in said county, on Tuesday the 22^d day of August instant [1786], and continued by adjournments to the twenty-fifth, &c. Voted, that this meeting is constitutional. The convention from a thorough conviction of great uneasiness subsisting among the people of this county and Commonwealth, then went into an inquiry for the cause; and, upon mature consideration, deliberation, and debate, were of opinion that many grievances and unnecessary burdens, now lying upon the people, are the sources of that discontent so evidently discoverable throughout this Commonwealth. Among which the following articles were voted as such, viz. (1.) The existence of the Senate. (2.) The present mode of representation. (3.) The officers of government not being annually dependent on the representatives of the people, in General Court assembled, for their salaries. (4.) All the civil officers of government not being annually elected by the representatives of the people in General Court assembled. (5.) The existence of the Courts of Common Pleas and General Sessions of the Peace. (6.) The fee table, as it now stands. (7.) The present mode of appropriating the impost and excise. (8.) The unreasonable grants made to some of the officers of government. (9.) The supplementary aid. (10.) The present mode of paying the governmental securities. (11.) The present mode adopted for the payment and speedy collection of the last tax. (12.) The present mode of taxation, as it operates unequally between the polls and estates, and between landed and mercantile interests. (13.) The present method of practice of the attornies at law. (14.)

The want of a sufficient medium of trade, to remedy the mischiefs arising from the scarcity of money. (15.) The General Court sitting in the town of Boston. (16.) The present embarrassments on the press. (17.) The neglect of the settlement of important matters depending between the Commonwealth and Congress, relating to monies and averages. (18.) Voted, that this convention recommend to the several towns in this county, that they instruct their representatives to use their influence in the next General Court to have emitted a bank of paper money, subject to a depreciation ;[1] making it a tender in all payments, equal to silver and gold, to be issued in order to call in the Commonwealth's securities. (19.) Voted, that whereas several of the above articles of grievances arise from defects in the constitution, therefore a revision of the same ought to take place. (20.) Voted, that it be recommended by this convention to the several towns in this county, that they petition the Governor to call the General Court immediately together, in order that the other grievances complained of may by the legislature be redressed. (21.) Voted, that this convention recommend it to the inhabitants of this county, that they abstain from all mobs and unlawful assemblies until a constitutional method of redress can be obtained."[2] Votes were also passed directing the transmission of these proceedings to the county conventions of Worcester and Berkshire, and "to the press in Springfield for publication ;" and also directing the chairman to call another county convention, if he should consider it expedient.[3]

One week earlier, August 15, 1786, a similar convention met in Worcester, by adjournment from the previous May, which enumerated a similar list of grievances, and further adjourned to the last Tuesday in September. I find no record that Hardwick elected a delegate to this convention; but it seems evident that one of its members was Major Martin Kinsley, an aid-de-camp of Major-General Warner ; for, at a meeting, May 16, 1787, the town "voted to Mr. Kinsley for his attendance at the county

[1] "A more exact idea of this hopeful financial scheme will be found from the action of Conway, which, on the 24th of October, 'instructed its representative in the General Court to use his influence to have a bank of paper currency emitted that should sink one penny a pound per month!'" *Hist. of Pittsfield,* i. 398. The plan of paying honest debts by a "circulating medium" having no permanent value, is almost an hundred years old.

[2] Whether this recommendation was honest or deceptive, it was followed within a week by a "mob or unlawful assembly" at Northampton, which effectually prevented the regular action of the Courts of Common Pleas and Sessions.

[3] Minot's *Hist. of Insurrections,* pp. 33-36.

convention, last fall, the sum of £2. 17. 5." Probably this indication of disloyalty to the government induced General Warner to remove him from office,[1] and to appoint in his stead Captain Artemas Howe of New Braintree, who was commissioned aid-de-camp August 28, 1786. The change was not made too soon; for within a few days the General had need of aids in whose fidelity he could implicitly confide. In anticipation of the outbreak at Worcester, he received this official order: —

"Boston, September 2d, 1786. Sir, I have received information that the Court of Common Pleas and Court of General Sessions of the Peace have, by a large concourse of people, in a riotous and tumultuous manner, been prevented from setting at Northampton, in the county of Hampshire, on the day appointed by law for that purpose. It is possible some people, not considering the great criminality and dangerous consequences of such unwarrantable proceedings, may attempt to prevent the Court setting at Worcester on the fifth instant. It is of the utmost importance that every lawful exertion should be made by every friend to the present Constitution of Government to suppress all such riotous proceedings. You are therefore hereby directed to aid the Sheriff of the county of Worcester, if he should request it, by furnishing him with such a number of the militia belonging to your Division as he may judge sufficient to suppress any such

[1] Three months later, Major Kinsley published an appeal to the public, of which it does not appear that General Warner took any notice whatever: — "To the impartial public. As it is a matter of public notoriety that I have lately been superseded in the office of aid-de-camp to the Hon. General Warner, without a resignation of my commission on my part, or the usual (and heretofore indispensable) formality of a Court Martial on his; and as it is now a matter of popular conversation and public dispute, whether or not it is in the power of a Major General to remove any officer who has been duly commissioned; or whether every officer, so commissioned, must not by the militia law of this Commonwealth, and by the established military custom throughout the civilized world, be officially arrested and formally tried before a regular court martial, purposely appointed, and properly authorized and empowered for that special purpose: I say, as this has got to be a matter of public disputation within this county, and as I have not only *not* had the usual formality of a court martial, but have even been kept in the secret for (I suppose) some months since his son-in-law has been commissioned, and finally have come to the knowledge of it only by common report, I take the liberty in this public manner to call upon the worthy General, and desire him, or whoever it may concern, to inform me and the public with regard to the cause or propriety of the procedure. I do not wish to trouble the public with this appeal to their impartiality on account of any particular fondness I have for holding a commission of the worthy gentleman, or any other authority; but because I conceive that any man, who has been in commission and will peaceably suffer himself to be kicked out, discovers as great a meanness as the person who attempts to do it. I am with due respect, &c., M. Kinsley. Hardwick, Nov. 24, 1786." *Worcester Magazine*, December, 1787.

attempt; and from your well known attachment to justice, peace, and good order, I am persuaded you will exert yourself to the utmost to prevent all such riotous proceedings. You have herewith enclosed a copy of the instruction which was sent to Mr. Sheriff Greenleaf. By his Excellency's command, with the advice and consent of the Council. Major General Warner."[1]

The response was prompt and loyal: —

"Hardwick, September 3^{d}, 1786. May it please your Excellency. I have this instant had the honor to receive your express, by which I am required to give such aid and assistance to the High Sheriff of the county of Worcester as shall be necessary to suppress any riots, or tumultuous proceedings in the people at the sitting of the Courts to be holden at Worcester on the 5th instant. Your Excellency may rest assured that every effort in my power shall on all occasions be exerted for the due regulations and support of government; — particularly on this occasion I shall use all the influence in my power to prevent and suppress any riotous and unwarrantable proceedings in the people; and I have accordingly issued orders to several of the Colonels within my Division to hold themselves in readiness in case they should be wanted, which is more than probable will be the case, as the people in general are grown very clamorous, and have not patience to wait for a regular redress of their real or supposed grievances. I am, sir, with all due respect, your Excellency's most obedient and very humble servant. JONATHAN WARNER.

"His Excellency, J. Bowdoin, Esq."[2]

This letter was soon followed by another: —

"May it please your Excellency. Agreeably to what I wrote you in my last, I exerted myself to have the militia in as good a state of readiness as was possible, for the support of government. But notwithstanding the most pressing orders for them to turn out and to appear at Worcester, equipped as the law directs, there did appear universally that reluctance in the people to turn out for the support of government as amounted in many instances to a flat denial; in others, in an evasion or delay,[3] which amounted to the same thing; — that finally the insurrections of the people for the purpose of stopping the Court were not to be resisted by all the efforts of government. This statement of the

[1] *Mass. Archives*, cxc. 228.

[2] *Ibid.*, cxc. 229.

[3] Colonel Timothy Paige, Lieutenant Colonel John Cutler, Major Joseph Jones, and Adjutant James Lawton, of the regiment which included Hardwick, promptly responded to this and subsequent similar calls; but probably with a very small force of militia.

affair at Worcester, however painful and disagreeable to relate, is the plain truth; and I can only leave it with the superior wisdom and discretion of your Excellency and the honorable Council to determine what shall be most expedient to be done at this unhappy crisis. I have the honor to be, with all due respects, your Excellency's most humble servant.

"JONATHAN WARNER, M. G.

"His Excellency James Bowdoin, Esq." [1]

The anticipated resistance to legal transactions at Worcester occurred during the first week in September. "The Courts of Common Pleas and General Sessions of the Peace being by law to be holden at Worcester, a body of insurgents to the number of 300 and upwards posted themselves at the Court-house in that place. The judges were admitted to the door, where a line of bayonets prevented their entrance. The chief justice remonstrated with the rioters on the madness of their conduct; but the court were obliged to retire to an adjacent house, where they opened agreeably to law, and adjourned to the next morning. The violence of the mob, however, soon obliged the Court of Common Pleas to adjourn without day, and the Court of Sessions to adjourn to the 21st of November following." [2] The insurgents "were under the command of Capt. Adam Wheeler of Hubbardston, though, when charged with being their leader, he disclaimed both the office and the responsibility. His lieutenant was Benjamin Converse [3] of Hardwick. Other principal officers were Capt. Hazeltine of Hardwick, and a Capt. Smith of Shirley. Only 100 of the men were under arms. The remainder carried bludgeons." [4] Benjamin Convers acted not only as lieutenant, but also as adjutant. A demand for adjournment of the Court, signed by him, has been preserved: —

"To the Honble Court of Common Pleas and Court of General Sessions of the Peace for the county of Worcester, and to all the Justices of the Peace in said county. The Petition of the Body of People now collected for their own common good and the good of the Commonwealth, to your honors humbly showeth: That we

[1] *Mass. Arch.*, cxc. 230.

[2] Minot's *Hist. of Insurrections*, pp. 38, 39.

[3] Benjamin Convers was engaged in a similar affair, a week afterwards, as related in the *Hist. of Western Mass.*, i. 242: "On the 11th of September a hundred armed men assembled at Concord, under the command of Job Shattuck of Groton and the afore-mentioned Capt. Smith. . . . On the following day . . . they were reinforced by a company of ninety men from the counties of Hampshire and Worcester, under the command of Adam Wheeler and Benjamin Converse."

[4] *Hist. of Western Mass.*, i. 242.

are informed that the Body of People that were collected on the ground in Worcester yesterday did by their Committee prefer a petition to your honors, requesting the Court of Common Pleas and Court of General Sessions of the Peace to be adjourned or dissolved, and your honors by your answer to the people then collected agreed to adjourn the Court of Common Pleas; notwithstanding the people from different parts of the said county generally appearing and collected on the ground this day for the purpose aforesaid do not consent to the answer that the said Court have given, therefore by their committee of the body now collected request that your honors do adjourn the Court of General Sessions of the Peace. And as in duty bound will ever pray. Worcester, Sept. 6, 1786. The above petition signed in behalf of the Body of People now present, and request answer in 30 minutes from the time of preferring. Signed at the request of committee. BENJ.N CONVERS, Adjutant."[1]

The "Body of People," having compelled the courts to adjourn, dispersed at the close of the second day, without committing essential violence to the peaceable citizens of Worcester. Their next riotous assembly in this vicinity was at Springfield on the twenty-sixth day of the same month, when they succeeded in preventing the regular session of the Superior Court. This was selected by the government, in the subsequent trials, as the first overt act of treason on the part of the insurgents; the forcible interruption of the Courts of Common Pleas and of Sessions being apparently regarded as minor offences. As John Wheeler[2] was convicted of treason on proof of his participation in this affair, I insert an account of it by the historian of the insurrection: —

"It was determined by the insurgents to prevent their doing business at Springfield, if possible; and the Governor, on the other hand, took measures to obviate their designs. Accordingly he ordered the Court House to be taken into possession by 600 men, under the command of Major General William Shepard. This party were well officered and equipped, and contained the most respectable characters for abilities and interest in the county of Hampshire. On the day of the Court's sitting, the insurgents also appeared, equal if not superior in numbers, but vastly inferior in officers and arms. They were headed by one Daniel Shays, who had been a captain in the late continental army, but had resigned his command for reasons quite problematical. They were

[1] *Mass. Arch.*, cxc. 236.

[2] Whether any other inhabitant of Hardwick was present does not distinctly appear.

highly incensed at government's taking possession of the Court House previously to their arrival. They sent a request to the Judges, that none of the late rioters should be indicted; but received a very firm reply, purporting that the Judges should execute the laws of the country agreeably to their oaths. In the confusion, however, necessarily attending two such large bodies of armed men, who, before they retired, amounted to more than 2,000, the court could transact but little business. On Wednesday, the panel of jurors not being filled, those jurymen who appeared were dismissed. On the next day, which was the third of their sitting, the court adjourned, after resolving that it was not expedient to proceed to the county of Berkshire. The mortification which the insurgents suffered from the Court House being preoccupied by the militia, led them to several bold measures. At one time they marched down upon the militia with loaded musquets, and every preparation was made for an engagement; but they were dissuaded from an attack, as it was said, at the instance of their commander."[1] After thus confronting each other for four days, both parties retired, and Springfield once more had rest.

About two months later, another struggle was imminent at Worcester. "Orders were issued to Major General Warner, to call out the militia of his division, and five regiments were directed to hold themselves in instant readiness to march. Doubts however arose, how far reliance could be placed on the troops of an infected district. The sheriff reported that a sufficient force could not be collected. The first instructions were therefore countermanded, a plan having been settled to raise an army whose power might effectually crush resistance, and the Judges were advised to adjourn to the 23^d of January following, when the contemplated arrangements could be matured to terminate the unhappy troubles."[2] The following correspondence refers to this transaction: —

"Worcester Dec. 1st, 1786. May it please your Excellency. The Insurgents in this county, and a number from the county of Hampshire, under the command of Daniel Shays, not exceeding two hundred and fifty or three hundred men, proceeded on the 29th instant[3] as far as Shrewsbury" . . . most of whom "marched out of Shrewsbury, on their return home. By express

[1] Minot's *Hist. of Insurrections*, pp. 47, 48.

[2] Lincoln's *Hist. of Worcester*, p. 141.

[3] The writer uses the word *instant* twice erroneously.

received this day, I learn that Shays met a reinforcement from the county of Hampshire, and a number from this county, at which time Shays ordered his men to halt; and I have the greatest reason to believe, by the best intelligence I have been able to obtain, their intention now is, to prevent the setting of the Court of Common Pleas in this town next week. On the 29th instant the party from Hampshire marched through Hardwick; upon observing the movement, I issued orders to the Commanders[1] of the Regiments in the upper part of this county to march, and I proceeded on to this town, in order to obtain intelligence. On the Insurgents proceeding homeward, I issued orders to the militia that had marched, to return home, and hold themselves in readiness to march on the shortest notice to Worcester." General Warner adds that he had ordered all the regiments in the county to be ready in like manner, but expresses grave doubts how many would obey his orders, saying, "I believe not a number sufficient to repel the force of the Insurgents in this county, exclusive of those which will probably collect from the counties of Hampshire and Berkshire. If it should be the opinion of your Excellency, that the Court of Common Pleas in this county should be protected the week ensuing, I conceive it will be necessary to send on a formidable force from the lower counties, and perhaps some pieces of artillery, as I am credibly informed the Insurgents have obtained some. I shall wait your further commands, which will be executed without delay. In the mean time, I am, with esteem, your Excellency's most obedient and very humble servant, JONA WARNER, M. G. His Excellency James Bowdoin, Esq. N. B. I forward this by Major Asa Coburn, by express."[2]

To this report of proceedings, the Governor replied: —

"Dec. 3. Sir, You are hereby directed to issue your orders to the militia that you may have ordered to march to the town of Worcester for the support of the Court of Common Pleas and Court of Sessions that are to set there on Tuesday next, not to proceed upon that business, any former orders that you may have received to the contrary notwithstanding. The above orders are given from a suggestion in your letter, that the Court could not be supported without some aid from the counties this way; however, if, contrary to your expectation, your militia should have turned out in such numbers and with such spirit as fully to con-

[1] Colonel Paige and his field officers responded as before; but probably with scanty, if any, support.

[2] *Mass. Arch.*, clxxxix. 46, 47.

vince you that the Court can be effectually supported, you will not be influenced by them. By advice of Council. Sir, Your humble servant, J. B. Maj. Gen. Warner." [1]

The militia did not turn out in such numbers as to support the Court; but the insurgents held possession of the Court House and of the town for about a week. On Sunday evening, December 3, a party which had quartered at Grafton entered Worcester, "under the command of Abraham Gale of Princeton, Adam Wheeler of Hubbardston, Simeon Hazeltine of Hardwick, and John Williams, reported to be a deserter from the British army and once a serjeant of the continental line. They halted before the Court House, and, having obtained the keys, placed a strong guard around the building, and posted sentinels on all the streets and avenues of the town, to prevent surprise. Those who were off duty, rolling themselves in their blankets, rested on their arms on the floor of the court room." [2] The Court, being thus excluded from the Court House, was opened in a tavern, and adjourned to the 23d of January, as directed by the Governor. The insurgents, however, remained in Worcester through the whole week, suffering much from a severe snow-storm, which commenced on Monday evening, and were finally dismissed on Saturday, in the midst of another furious tempest, in which it is said that "some were frozen to death," and many others narrowly escaped the same fate. Separate companies from the towns of Ward, Holden, Spencer, Rutland, Barre, Hubbardston, Petersham, and Belchertown, are mentioned by historians; and, although not specially named, it can scarcely be doubted that several inhabitants of Hardwick accompanied Captain Hazeltine, who was one of the active leaders.

Three weeks later, December 26, the session of the court at Springfield was prevented; and it was understood that the Court of Common Pleas would not be permitted to hold its adjourned meeting at Worcester on the 23d of January. The government now adopted more vigorous measures to sustain its authority, and organized an army of 4,400 infantry, besides four companies of artillery, all under the command of Major-General Benjamin Lincoln. On the 4th of January, orders were issued to Major-General Warner to detach 1,200 men from the seventh division, and to organize them into two regiments, for this service.[3] He re-

[1] *Mass. Arch.*, clxxxix. 53.

[2] Lincoln's *Hist. of Worcester*, p 142.

[3] *Mass. Arch.*, clxxxix. 68. In the same volume, p. 67, is found "an estimate of what it may cost to supply 5,000 men, 30 days, with rations: —

ported that Colonel Timothy Newell had engaged to enlist one of these regiments, with authority to appoint his subordinate officers. Colonel Newell performed his engagement. Lieutenant-Colonel John Cutler, of Colonel Paige's regiment, was his associate: and one company was enlisted in Hardwick and New Braintree, under command of Captain Edward Ruggles of Hardwick. As this company served from January 22 until February 21, and shared the perils and sufferings of that terrible night march from Hadley to Petersham, which Minot styles "one of the most indefatigable marches that ever was performed in America," and which resulted in the utter and final dispersion of the rebel army, I copy the names borne on the Pay Roll, preserved in the "Massachusetts Archives," cxcii. 69: —

Edward Ruggles, Captain.
Sampson Whitherly 1st Lieut.
Wyman Hoit, 2^{d} Lieut.
Jeduthun Spooner, Clerk.
Samuel Shaw, Serg^{t}.
Elisha Matthews, do.
Joseph Hale, do.
Lemuel French, Fife-major.
John Stevenson, Drummer.
John Doty (orderly), Corporal.
John Thompson, do.
James Woods, do.
Daniel Billing, do.
Stephen Newton,
Moses Fay.
Samuel Clark.
Robert Voax.
Zenas Hanmer.
George Wightington.
Elijah Barns.
Abner Whipple.
William Tidd.
Persival Hall.
George Whetherell.
Benj^{a} Estabrooks.
Moses Paige.
William Davice.
Justice Warner.
Isaac Denny.
James Weston.
Lemuel Kenedy.

General Lincoln's force was concentrated at Worcester on the 22d of January, and the court held its session the next day without molestation. "Detachments of insurgents collected at Rutland, New Braintree, Princeton, Sterling, and Sutton, but, intimidated by the military, hovered at a distance, while the courts proceeded. On the 25th of January, General Lincoln hastened westward for the relief of Shepard, and of the arsenal at Springfield, invested by Shays and Day. Major-General War-

"1^{l} Bread, 2$\frac{3}{4}$^{d}
$\frac{1}{2}$p^{t} Rum, 1$\frac{1}{2}$
1$\frac{1}{2}$^{l} Beef, 5
—
9$\frac{1}{4}$ is nearest to £40 for 1000 men per day. 5000 men, 30 days, is £6000, specie: if paid in orders on collectors will be upwards of £15,000.
300 Barrels of Rum, @ 70^{s} per Bl. £1050
750 Barrels of Flour, 1500
225,000^{l} Beef, @ 3$\frac{1}{2}$^{d} 3124 = 5674."

ner was left in command at Worcester, with a regiment of infantry, a corps of artillery, including Capt. Treadwell's company, two field pieces, and a party from the legionary battalion of volunteer cavalry." [1] With this force General Warner protected Worcester, and dispersed large bodies of insurgents at New Braintree, and at the barracks in Rutland. Meanwhile, General Shepard, with about a thousand men, had taken post at Springfield, for the protection of the arsenal. On the 25th of January Shays approached with a still larger force. General Shepard "sent one of his aids with two other gentlemen, several times, to know the intention of the enemy, and to warn them of their danger. The purport of their answer was, that they would have possession of the barracks; and they immediately marched onwards to within 250 yards of the arsenal. A message was again sent to inform them, that the militia were posted there by order of the Governor, and of Congress, and that if they approached nearer they would be fired upon. To this, one of their leaders [2] replied, that *that* was all they wanted; and they advanced one hundred yards further. Necessity now compelled General Shepard to fire; but his humanity did not desert him. He ordered the two first shot to be directed over their heads; this, however, instead of retarding, quickened their approach; and the artillery was at last pointed at the centre of their column. This measure was not without its effect. A cry of murder arose from the rear of the insurgents, and their whole body was thrown into the utmost confusion. Shays attempted to display his column, but it was in vain. His troops retreated with precipitation to Ludlow, about ten miles from the place of action, leaving three of their men dead, and one wounded on the field." [3]

Two days later, General Lincoln arrived at Springfield, and immediately pursued the insurgents, who fled to Pelham, and he took post at Hadley. After vainly attempting to secure a cessation of hostilities, Shays withdrew from Pelham, and marched to Petersham, on the 3d of February. At eight o'clock in the evening of the same day, General Lincoln commenced that "indefatigable" march through Shutesbury and New Salem, which

[1] Lincoln's *Hist. of Worcester*, p. 149.

[2] This "leader" was John Wheeler, of Hardwick. In a letter from General Shepard to Governor Bowdoin, January 26, 1787, he says, "A Mr. Wheeler, who appeared to be one of Shays' Aids, met Mr. Lyman, after he had delivered my orders in the most peremptory manner, and made answer that *that* was all he wanted." *Independent Chronicle*, February 1, 1787.

[3] Minot's *History of Insurrections*, pp. 110, 111.

he described in his report dated at Petersham, February 4: — "We arrived here about nine o'clock, exceedingly fatigued by a march of thirty miles, part of it in a deep snow, and in a most violent storm. When this abated the cold increased, and a great part of our men were frozen in some part or other; but I hope none of them dangerously so, and that most of them will be able again to march in a short time."[1] The surprise was complete. The insurgents fled, without attempting any defence, some to their homes, and others through Athol, beyond the limits of the State. This was a crushing blow to the insurrection. Although a guerilla contest was carried on a few months longer in the western counties, no large number was ever again gathered in opposition to the government. The immediate effect was described by General Warner in a report to the Governor: "Worcester, Feb. 10th 1787. His Excellency J. Bowdoin, Esq. Sir, General Lincoln, on his leaving this county, left under my command the troops which were raised in my Division, with a request that I would discharge them as speedily as might be consistent with safety. I have hitherto conceived it expedient to keep the greater part of them in service, as many of the insurgents in this county retain an unsubdued and uncurbed spirit of rebellion and insolence. There has not, indeed, of late been any large collection of insurgents within this county; but small numbers have been collecting in diverse parts of the county, to the annoyance and terror of the friends to order and regularity. Thoroughly to subdue this spirit appears to me to be of the highest importance. For this purpose I have kept detachments in such parts of the county as I have conceived would best tend to the accomplishment of the design. Numbers have been captured; numbers have voluntarily submitted, and thrown themselves on the mercy of government; and numbers there are, which still remain to be reclaimed. I have, in my proceedings with them, endeavored to conform to the proposals offered by Major General Lincoln, and approved of by the General Court, not having received any particular directions upon the subject. . . . I have the honor to be, with the highest esteem, your Excellency's most obedient humble servant, JONA WARNER, M. G."[2]

It remained for the government to disperse the predatory bands which still infested various parts of the country, and to deal

1 *Independent Chronicle*, February 8, 1787.

2 *Mass. Arch.*, cxc. 366.

judiciously with the conquered insurgents. The first was accomplished with comparative ease, by means of an overpowering military force, but what disposition to make of the offenders was a problem difficult of solution. A previous offer of amnesty to non-commissioned officers and privates, who would lay down their arms and take the oath of allegiance, had been generally disregarded; but it was now renewed to such as would submit on or before the 21st day of March, and was accepted by large numbers, among whom were at least sixty inhabitants of Hardwick: — David Elwell, Frederick Wicker, Gideon Carpenter, Lemuel Willis, Ezra Winslow ("neither of the above three persons used any arms against the government, as they affirm"), David Pratt, Symonds Whipple, Samuel Sibley, Samuel Clifford, Thomas Elwell, James Paige, Jr. (p. 125); Ephraim Tucker, James Robinson, Adonijah Dennis, Samuel Dennis, Constant Mirick, James Pearce, Nathaniel Gleason, Silas Newton, Calvin Oakes, Isaac Robinson, Eleazar Dexter, John Dexter ("these took and subscribed the oath of allegiance before the Act of the General Court was received," p. 126); Nathaniel Haskell, Samuel Hopkins, Joseph Robinson, Job Dexter, Gideon Brimhall, Timothy Newton, George Haskell, Abner Weston, Ebenezer Childs, Eli Freeman, Robert Prout, Zephaniah Spooner, Israel Roach, Thomas Clark, Benjamin Carpenter, James Rogers, Samuel Haskins, Jr., Aaron Johnson (sworn "on or before the 21st day of March, A. D. 1787," p. 130); William Smith, Thomas Reed Smith (March 23, 1787, p. 161); Arthur Rawson ("physitian, declares he never took up arms against government, only acted as physitian"); Benony Shurtleff, Ebenezer Lawrence ("declare they never took up arms, but were only in some degree aiding and assisting," March 25, 1787; p. 169); Jonathan Parkhurst, David Whipple, David Warren, Caleb Bryant, Experience Luce, John Gorham, Stephen Gorham, Joseph Gorham, Barzillia Flagg, James Wing, Ichabod Dexter (September 10, 1787, p. 209); Seth Taylor, John Harris, Nathan Wheeler (September 29, 1787, p. 216).[1]

Several others in Hardwick, who had not taken up arms, were politically involved in this insurrectionary movement.[2] The Sheriff of Worcester County, in a letter to the Governor, says: "I take leave to transmit the names of a number of their principal leaders and commanders; their names are as followeth, viz.,

[1] *Mass. Arch.*, cxc. 125–216.

[2] Martin Kinsley, and other delegates to county conventions, have already been mentioned.

Adam Wheeler, Hubbardston, Benjamin Convers, Ichabod Dexter,[1] Samuel Dexter, Simeon Hayselton, and Seth Taylor, all of Hardwick, Oliver Watson, Spencer, Abraham Gale, Henry Gale, Norman Clark, all of Princeton, Abraham Holman of Templeton, all in the County of Worcester."[2] And on the 19th of January, 1787, the Governor issued his warrant for the arrest of sundry persons in Worcester County, "deeming the safety of the Commonwealth to be inconsistent with their personal liberty;" among these were Benjamin Convers and Captain Simeon Hazeltine. The sheriff made return that he had arrested some of the persons named, adding that the said Convers and Hazeltine "are not to be found within my jurisdiction."[3] They and some others had been so actively and prominently engaged under arms, that they were not entitled to the amnesty offered, and dared not take the hazard of a trial for treason.

A more sad fate was reserved for one of the Hardwick insurgents. John Wheeler, a Revolutionary soldier, who enlisted under Captain Daniel Shays, in 1778, serving as sergeant, and afterwards as quartermaster sergeant, was lieutenant of Captain Edward Ruggles' company at the outbreak of the insurrection. He attached himself to his former leader, and became his aide-de-camp. He was described to me by his contemporaries, many years ago, as a skilful, brave, and energetic officer, — much superior to his chief. He shared the excitements and perils of the contest until early in February, 1787, when he was taken prisoner.[4] The papers, descriptive of his trial, conviction, sentence, and pardon, are preserved, and are here inserted: —

"Hampshire ss. At the Supreme Judicial Court, begun and holden at Northampton, within and for the county of Hampshire,

[1] Ichabod Dexter and Seth Taylor had, perhaps, borne arms; they are included among those who were required to take the oath of allegiance.

[2] *Mass. Arch.*, cxc. 235.

[3] *Ibid.*, clxxxix. 75. I have not ascertained where Mr. Convers found refuge. Captain Hazeltine fled to Vermont; resided at Sandgate, and represented that town, 1794, in the General Assembly. Several others, not here named, are known to have absconded at about the same time, and for a similar reason.

[4] "Last Thursday evening, His Excellency the Governor received a letter from the Hon. General Lincoln, dated the 13th instant. He was then with his troops at Pittsfield, in the county of Berkshire. His Excellency has also received a letter, dated the 12th, from General Shepard, who, with a detachment of the army, by another route, was then marching into the same county. Several of the rebels, and some suspected of being their abettors, have been apprehended; the most noted are John Wheeler, late one of Shays's Aids, and Matthew Clarke, said to have been busy in organizing the rebel militia," &c. *Independent Chronicle*, February 22, 1787.

on the ninth day of April, in the year of our Lord seventeen hundred and eighty-seven, by adjournment to that time from the first Tuesday of the same, by Writ in virtue of an Act of the General Court, made and passed in February last past. The Jurors of the Commonwealth of Massachusetts upon their oath present that John Wheeler of Hardwick in the county of Worcester, gentleman, and Henry McCullock of Pelham in the county of Hampshire, gentleman, together with others named in the indictment, being members and subjects of the said Commonwealth, and owing allegiance to the same, not having the fear of God in their hearts, nor having any regard to the duty of their allegiance, but being moved and seduced by a lawless and rebellious spirit, and withdrawing from the said Commonwealth the cordial love and due obedience, fidelity, and allegiance, which every member of the same Commonwealth of right ought to bear to it, and also most wickedly and traitorously devising and conspiring to levy war against this Commonwealth, and thereby most wickedly and traitorously intending, as much as in them lay, to change and subvert the rule and government of this Commonwealth, duly and happily established under the good people the inhabitants and members of the same, according to the constitution and form of government of the same, and to reduce them to anarchy, confusion, and lawless power, upon the twenty-sixth day of September in the year of our Lord seventeen hundred and eighty-six, and on divers days and times, as well before that time as since, at Springfield within the county of Hampshire aforesaid, with a great number of rebels and traitors against the Commonwealth aforesaid, viz. the number of one thousand whose names are yet unknown to the jurors aforesaid, being armed and arrayed in a warlike and hostile manner, viz. with drums beating, fifes playing, and with guns, pistols, bayonets, swords, clubs, and divers other weapons, as well offensive as defensive, with force and arms did falsely and traitorously assemble and join themselves against this Commonwealth and the law and government of the same, as established by the constitution and form of government of the same, and then and there, with force and arms as aforesaid, did falsely and traitorously array and dispose themselves against the Commonwealth aforesaid and the due administration of justice in the same according to the law and authority of the same, and then and there with force and arms as aforesaid, in pursuance of such their wicked and traitorous purposes aforesaid, did falsely and traitorously prepare, order, wage, and levy, a public and cruel war against the Commonwealth aforesaid, and then and there with force and arms as aforesaid, wickedly and traitorously did assault, imprison, captivate, plunder, destroy, kill, and murder, divers of the liege subjects of the said Commonwealth in the peace of the said Commonwealth being, and lawfully and in the duty of their allegiance to the said Commonwealth defending the same from the traitorous attacks as aforesaid, all which is against the duty of their allegiance and the law of the Commonwealth aforesaid in such case made and provided and the dignity of the same.

"A true Bill. SETH MURRAY, Foreman. R. T. PAINE, Att[y] for Repub.

"Hampshire ss. April Term at Northampton, 1787. The said John Wheeler and Henry McCullock are arraigned at the bar, and have this indictment read to them, and they severally say that thereof they are not guilty, and thereof for trial put themselves on God and the country. JOHN TUCKER, Clerk.

"And now in this present term, before the Court here come the said John Wheeler and Henry McCullock, under custody of the Sheriff of said County, and being set to the bar here in their proper persons, and forthwith being demanded concerning the premises in the indictment above specified and charged upon them, how they will acquit themselves thereof, they severally say that thereof they are not guilty, and thereof for trial severally put themselves on God and the country (Simeon Strong and Caleb Strong Esquires, having been assigned by the Court as counsel for the prisoners): a jury is immediately impanelled, viz., William Stebbins, Foreman, and Fellows, namely, Amos Baldwin, Jonathan Parsons, Gideon Searl, Phineas Chapin, Jr., Jonathan Clark, Daniel Fowler, Aaron Fisher, Simeon Chapin, Joshua Phillips, Martin Clark, and Moses Kellogg, who, being sworn to speak the truth of and concerning the premises, upon their oath say that the said John Wheeler is guilty, and that the said Henry McCullock is guilty. And now the Attorney General moves that sentence of death might be given against the said John Wheeler and Henry McCullock, the prisoners at the bar; upon which it is demanded of them the said John Wheeler and Henry McCullock if they have or know aught to say wherefore the Justices here ought not, upon the premises and verdict aforesaid, to proceed to judgment against them, who nothing further say unless as they before had said. Whereupon, all and singular the premises being seen and by the said Justices here fully understood, it is considered by the Court here, that the said John Wheeler be taken to the goal of the Commonwealth from whence he came, and from thence to the place of execution, and there be hanged by the neck until he be dead: — that the said Henry McCullock be taken to the goal of the Commonwealth from whence he came, and from thence to the place of execution, and there be hanged by the neck until he be dead. A true copy of Record.

"Att. JNº TUCKER, Clerk."[1]

There were manifestly extenuating circumstances in favor of Mr. Wheeler, for within a few days a full and free pardon was granted to him, and to three others who were convicted at the same term of the Court:[2] —

"Commonwealth of Massachusetts. To the Sheriffs of our several Counties, and all others our loving and faithful subjects, to whom these presents shall come. Greeting.

"Whereas, John Wheeler of Hardwick, in the county of Worcester, gentleman; Daniel Luddington, of South Hampton, in the county of Hampshire, yeoman; James White, of Colerain, in the same county, yeoman; and Alpheus Colton, of Longmeadow, in the same county, laborer; were, at our Supreme Judicial Court, begun and holden at Northampton within and for the county of Hampshire on the ninth day of April, in the year of our Lord seventeen hundred and eighty-seven, by adjournment to that time from the first Tuesday of the same April, in virtue of an Act of the General Court made in February last past, convicted of Treason: — Whereupon the said John Wheeler, Daniel Luddington, James White, and Alpheus Colton, were by the Justices of our said Supreme Judicial Court adjudged to suffer the pains of death, as by the records of the said Supreme Judicial Court manifestly appears; — and whereas the said John Wheeler, Daniel Luddington, James White, and Alpheus Colton have humbly supplicated our grace and favor for remittance of the said sentence: —

"We, therefore, by and with the advice of the Council, of our special grace do hereby remit to the said John Wheeler, Daniel Luddington, James White, and Alpheus Colton, a full, free, and ample pardon of all the pains and penalties they were liable to suffer and undergo by virtue of the sentence and judgment aforesaid; of which the Sheriff of our said county of Hampshire is in an especial manner to take notice.

[1] *Mass. Arch.*, clxxxix. 262-264.

[2] Fourteen persons in all were convicted: six in Berkshire, six in Hampshire, one in Worcester, and one in Middlesex; but, at length, all were pardoned.

"In testimony whereof we have caused our public seal to be hereunto affixed. Witness, JAMES BOWDOIN, Esq., our Governor and Commander-in-chief, at Boston, this thirtieth day of April in the year of our Lord one thousand seven hundred and eighty-seven, and in the eleventh year of the Independence of the United States of America. By his Excellency's command, with the advice and consent of the Council." [1]

So "full, free, and ample" was this "pardon," that Mr. Wheeler was not degraded from the office of lieutenant which he had held for three years; and on the first day of September, 1789, he was commissioned by Governor Hancock as captain of the same company, and remained in office until the 8th of June, 1794, when he died at the early age of 37 years. The government exercised similar forbearance and clemency in regard to Captain James Paige, Jr., who was so far involved in the insurrectionary movement as to be required to take the oath of allegiance, yet was permitted to retain his military position, and was promoted to the office of major, receiving his commission 19 December, 1791. Indeed, a strong sympathy with this movement pervaded not only the community but the government itself. A large proportion of the representatives approved it, and resisted active measures for its suppression. In the spring of 1787, its friends and supporters obtained a substantial victory in the Commonwealth, by the defeat of Governor Bowdoin, and the election of Governor Hancock, with a still larger proportion of the representatives. The authority of the government was nominally maintained; but its administration was rendered difficult by this disturbing element. The same spirit was visible in the convention called in 1788 to consider the proposed Constitution of the United States, and nearly prevented its adoption on the ground that it granted too much power to the general government. So powerful and so persistent was the opposition, that even with the hope of certain amendments to render it less objectionable, approval of the Constitution was secured by the meagre majority of nineteen, there being, on the final question, 187 yeas and 168 nays.[2]

Both before and after the collapse of the insurrection, a majority of the voters in Hardwick seem to have sympathized with it. They were officially represented in the county conventions, many

[1] *Mass. Arch.*, clxxxix. 265.

[2] This opposition was especially manifest in the western counties: there were in Worcester, 7 yeas, 43 nays; in Hampshire, 19 yeas, 33 nays; in Berkshire, 7 yeas, 15 nays. Among the nays appears the name of Martin Kinsley, the delegate from Hardwick.

of them took up arms, and their votes in town-meeting indicate their political preferences. Under a warrant for a meeting, January 8, 1787, "to take into consideration a petition from a number of the inhabitants of the town of Hardwick, praying that Capt. Shattuck and others lately imprisoned at Boston may be liberated, and that the Courts of Common Pleas and General Sessions may be suspended till a new election, and sundry other articles, and for the town to act thereon as they shall think proper," it was "voted to choose a committee to petition the General Court for the purpose expressed in the warrant, &c., and made choice of Major Kinsley, John Raymond, Ichabod Dexter, Capt. Hazeltine, and Doctor Rawson, for said committee, and they to make report at the adjournment of this meeting." At the adjourned meeting, January 29th, "the petition that the aforesaid committee had prepared was publicly read before the town and accepted. Voted that the petition be signed by the Town Clerk as the doings of the town. Voted to choose a committee to repair to General Lincoln's and Shays' army, in order to accommodate matters, if possible to prevent the shedding of blood; and chose Capt. [Daniel] Wheeler and Capt. [Daniel] Egery." At the annual meeting, March 5, 1787, the same spirit was in the ascendant. The record is characteristic of the eccentric town clerk; but there is no reason to doubt its literal truthfulness: "The town met and proceeded as follows: (1.) Chose Gen. Jonathan Warner, Moderator; and then, after quarrelling the remainder of the day, voted to adjourn the meeting to Monday the 2^d^ day of April next, at nine o'clock in the morning. Met accordingly and proceeded as follows: chose Sylvanus Washburn, Town Clerk; Major Martin Kinsley, Town Treasurer; Capt. Daniel Egery, Capt. Seth Peirce, Seth Johnson, Deac. Nathaniel Paige, and Daniel Billing, Selectmen; Sylvanus Washburn, Daniel Ruggles, and David Allen, assessors." The personal popularity of General Warner secured his election as moderator; notwithstanding his active support of the government; but Major Kinsley, whose sympathy and influence were manifestly on the other side, was elected treasurer in place of Colonel Paige, whose loyalty was never doubted. An entire change was made in the board of selectmen; the loyal incumbents were superseded by new men, all of whom, except, perhaps, Mr. Billings, were of different politics. And in the next month Major Kinsley was elected representative.

In Hardwick, as elsewhere, there were doubtless some demagogues and political agitators, who took advantage of the general distress for selfish and sinister purposes; but most of this class soon left town. Of those who remained, the larger portion were, probably, as excusable in their resistance to the government now as they formerly were in resisting the authority of Great Britain. Goaded to desperation by the pressure of financial obligations which they could not cancel, they sought relief by the means which had previously been so effectual, namely, County Conventions, the obstruction of the Courts of Law, and at last an appeal to Arms. They made a sad mistake, not properly distinguishing between laws arbitrarily imposed on them by a foreign power, and laws enacted by their own representatives, and subject to amendment or repeal by the same authority. In subsequent years, they were peaceable, law-abiding citizens, trusted and honored by their townsmen, and steadfast upholders of government; yet, almost without exception, they maintained through life the political theory that the government should be clothed with no more power than is indispensable to its existence.

The proper "conclusion of the whole matter" seems to be this: Their financial distress furnished an excuse, approximating justification, to the insurgents. On the other hand, those who held fast their integrity in the midst of such wide-spread calamity, and supported the government in its terrible struggle to maintain the supremacy of law, deserve the highest honor for their loyalty and true patriotism.

CHAPTER X.

CIVIL HISTORY.

Boundaries. — Additions and Diminutions of Territory. — Incorporation of New Braintree, and of Dana. — Annexation of the Gore, now included in Gilbertville. — Four Bridges across Ware River. — Roads, hilly and difficult of Construction. — Sixth Massachusetts Turnpike. — Ware River Railroad. — Massachusetts Central Railroad. — Pounds. — Paupers. — Town Farm. — Proposal to maintain State Paupers. — Slavery. — Town House. — Bell. — Burial Places. — Epitaphs.

Boundaries. — It has already been mentioned[1] that the surveyor, in delineating the township, inadvertently included at the northeast corner four hundred acres[2] belonging to the "Braintree six thousand acres," and three hundred acres at the southwest corner, being a part of the "Equivalent Lands," which had been purchased by John Read, Esq.; in consideration of which, the General Court, in 1733, granted to the proprietors the tract of land between Ware River and the "Six Thousand Acres," which now constitutes about one half of New Braintree. This grant, however, was only of temporary value. The inhabitants of that tract soon became weary of climbing the long hill to attend public worship and transact town affairs, and for this and probably other reasons, desired a separation. After some unsuccessful efforts their object was accomplished January 31, 1751, when that part of Hardwick which was east of the river, together with the "Six Thousand Acres" and a part of Brookfield, was incorporated as a separate district, which subsequently became a town, by the name of New Braintree.

Half a century later, the town was again curtailed in its dimensions. The movement commenced as early as August 25, 1788, when the town "Voted, that they have not any objection to the prayer of a petition being granted, which was presented to the General Court of this Commonwealth, at their last session, by a

[1] Chapter iii., June, 1733.

[2] This tract was annexed to Hardwick June 10, 1814. *Mass. Special Laws*, v. 10.

number of inhabitants in the northwesterly part of this town, praying to be incorporated, with a part of Petersham and Greenwich, into a distinct town by the name of Tolland." This petition was not granted; but on the eighteenth day of February, 1801, substantially the same territory was incorporated into a town by the name of Dana.[1]

A small gore of unincorporated land was annexed to Hardwick, February 7, 1831, described as follows: "Beginning at the northwest corner of said Hardwick, and running N. 70° E., 5 rods, to the southerly corner of Petersham; thence S. 41¼° E., 184 rods, on the line of Petersham, to the southeast corner thereof; and thence N. 37½° W., 186 rods, on the line of Hardwick, to the bound first mentioned."[2]

This gore was included in the large tract of land annexed to Dana, February 4, 1842, and described as follows: "Beginning at the southwest corner of Silas N. Johnson's land, on the line of said Hardwick and Dana; thence running S. 49° E., 204 rods, to the corner of Stephen Hillman's land; thence N. 31½° E., 543 rods, to Barre, Hardwick, and Petersham corner,"[3] together with a part of Petersham. The portion of Hardwick thus annexed to Dana was estimated to be one seventy-fifth part of the whole town.

Many years ago, as indicated on the Ruggles map, several acres of land, measuring nearly seven-eighths of a mile in length, and about a quarter of a mile in width, were set off from Hardwick and annexed to Greenwich.

More important than any other, indeed more important than all others, was the last addition to the territory of Hardwick. On the east side of Ware River, between the towns of Hardwick, New Braintree, and Ware, was a tract of unincorporated land, called "Hardwick Gore." Though separated from Hardwick by the river, in many respects its inhabitants were more closely connected with this town than with the others; they voted here for state officers, their state tax was assessed here, and here they buried their dead. Attempts were made, from time to time, for the annexation of this Gore to the town. As early as March 2, 1807, the town "voted to postpone the taking of a vote upon the petition of the people in the Gore, so called, and choose a committee of three to see upon what terms the petitioners are willing to be annexed to the town of Hardwick." The desired

[1] *Mass. Special Laws*, ii. 416.
[2] *Ibid.*, vii. 26.
[3] *Ibid.*, viii. 239.

object was not accomplished until a quarter of a century later, when the General Court enacted, February 6, 1833, "that the gore of land lying at the southeasterly part of the town of Hardwick, and adjoining said town, called Hardwick Gore, containing about two hundred acres, and described as follows: beginning at a monument in the pond above Anderson's mill, at a place where the westerly line of New Braintree leaves Ware River, thence on the said westerly line of New Braintree, south, fourteen degrees east, one hundred and twenty-two rods, to a stone monument: thence south, thirty-seven degrees west, two hundred and eighty-nine rods, to another stone monument, at the southwest corner of New Braintree and northeast corner of Ware; thence north, eighty-seven degrees west, thirty-six rods, to said Ware River; thence on the said River, northerly, four hundred and twenty-one rods, to the southeast corner of Hardwick; thence sixty-one rods, to the place of beginning, — together with the inhabitants thereof, be and the same is hereby annexed to the town of Hardwick, in the county of Worcester; and said inhabitants shall be liable to the same duties and entitled to the same privileges as the other inhabitants of the same town." [1]

On this annexed territory, within the last twenty years, has grown up the larger part of the village of Gilbertville, now containing about half of the population of the whole town, and furnishing a convenient market for agricultural products. The annexation involved large disbursements by the town for schools, and for the construction of roads and a very expensive bridge; but the advantages derived from the increased value of taxable property, and the incidental stimulus given to farming and other industrial pursuits, appear to be fully equivalent to the outlay. The "George H. Gilbert Manufacturing Company" deserve high praise, not only for erecting one of the most beautiful meeting-houses in the Commonwealth, but also for the extraordinarily neat and substantial character of their tenements, and generally for their well-directed and constant efforts to beautify the village, and to make it a pleasant home for those whom they employ.

ROADS AND BRIDGES. One of the earliest tasks to be performed by pioneers is the construction of roads and bridges. This task in Hardwick was one of more than ordinary difficulty. The largest and most expensive bridges were those across Ware River; of which the earliest was that near the Old Furnace.

[1] *Mass. Special Laws*, vii. 291.

At a meeting of the proprietors, October 30, 1733, it was ordered that a committee should allot certain lands on the east side of the river, and "agree with the settlers for a price for the same; the produce of which to be laid out to build a good Cart Bridge over Ware River aforesaid against the highway lately laid out towards Brookfield; and the said committee to agree with persons to build the bridge, and take care that it be effected." This bridge has been several times renewed, and is a very important avenue. The present iron structure was erected in 1875. The "highway lately laid out towards Brookfield" was the road which, turning to the right, about a quarter of a mile east of the bridge, runs southeast to Ditch Meadow in New Braintree. It is referred to in the laying out of a highway, August 3, 1747, "from Eleazar Warner's,[1] through land of William Ayers and Josiah Barrett, to the road from Ditch Meadow to the Great Bridge, across the bridge, along the dug-way, across Moose Brook, in front of Nathan Carpenter's door, up the hill to land of Caleb Benjamin, through land of Zechariah Haskell, John Cooper, and John Roberts, to the highway[2] from Cornelius Cannon's to the Great Meadow Brook east of Joseph Ruggles's house."

Another bridge is here indicated. Cornelius Cannon resided on the east side of the river, opposite to the late residence of Mr. Reed S. Ruggles, marked "A. Rich" on the R. map. The town voted, May 14, 1744, "to build a horse-bridge over the River, near Cannon's." In my boyhood, vestiges of this bridge, and of a roadway leading to it, were visible; but the bridge itself had disappeared. A wooden structure was placed here in 1845, which was succeeded by the present substantial iron bridge in 1857.

Another bridge was early erected about half a mile above the crossing at Gilbertville. A reference to it is found under date of March 4, 1765, when the town "voted to Mr. Isaac Thomas the sum of £26. 13. 4., said Thomas having engaged to build a sufficient bridge over Ware River, near his iron-works, at the most convenient place, and to the acceptance of the town, and to be completed at or before the first day of September next." The

[1] Eleazar Warner resided about a mile east of the river, at the junction of the roads leading to Rutland and to the meeting-house in New Braintree. The highway described had for several years previously been a "country road," and was that which afterwards became a turnpike through the Furnace Village to its junction with the easterly road from the Common to Gilbertville, a few rods east of the present residence of Captain Orin Trow.

[2] This highway passed up the hill to the house of Mr. George Warner, marked "Mr. Bolster" on the R. map, and thence northerly to its junction with what afterwards became the turnpike, near Great Meadow Brook.

form of this vote indicates that no bridge had been previously erected at that place. Mr. Thomas did not fulfil his contract, but sold his "iron-works" to Abraham Savage and Joseph Blake. The town, May 19, 1766, "voted to Mr. Savage and Mr. Blake £40. 0. 0., to enable them to build a bridge over Ware River near their works, . . . to be completed at or before the first day of November next." The treasurer's account for the same year exhibits a payment "to Lot Whitcomb, for building the bridge over Ware River, at Messrs. Savage and Blake's works, £40. 0. 0." This bridge was rebuilt in 1814, and probably again rebuilt at a later date.

The bridge in Gilbertville was erected in 1871. It took the place of an ordinary structure, built a few years earlier, and was much more expensive than either of those before mentioned; but it was so thoroughly and firmly constructed that it may be expected to resist all the ordinary processes of decay and destruction for many years.

The construction and maintenance of highways in this town involved great expense from the beginning. Twenty years after the settlement commenced, it was represented in a petition to the General Court, heretofore quoted, that the inhabitants are "obliged to expend yearly large sums in making and repairing their highways, and even this year [1754] are at the expense of a hundred pounds, lawful money, for that purpose; and must be at the expense of some thousands of pounds upon their roads before they will be brought to be as good as most of the roads in the province are by nature." Not only was almost the whole township covered with a heavy growth of timber, but the surface of the ground was very uneven and hilly, thickly sprinkled with rocks and ledges. The hills and valleys run chiefly in a northerly and southerly direction; and the highways running across them from east to west are far from level. Between the Common and Muddy Brook, on the roads leading to Enfield and Greenwich, and on the old road to Greenwich Village, the hills are both long and steep. The old road from Mandell Hill to Ware River is yet visible, and affords a specimen of the difficulties originally encountered. Indeed a portion of it, near the Old Furnace, still open but disused, was said by teamsters, half a century ago, to be more difficult of ascent than any other hill between that point and Boston. This difficulty is now avoided by a comparatively new road, which, by a long detour to the north, ascends the hill more gradually. Relief has been obtained also on the old road (or turnpike) to Greenwich Village, by opening a new highway between Muddy Brook and the Common, which both diminishes the steepness of the ascent and shortens the distance. But notwithstanding these and other similar changes, the Hardwick roads generally remain hilly, and their maintenance requires much care and expense; and yet it should be said that in few if any towns, at the same distance from Boston, are the roads kept in so good condition. For more than a century a "highway tax" was annually assessed, which was "worked out" by the inhabitants and their teams, under the direction of "Surveyors of Highways;" but recently all the roads are placed under the supervision of a single person, who employs all necessary assistance. Thus far, the new system has given general satisfaction.

Shortly before the commencement of the present century, an effort was made to improve the great thoroughfares of public travel by the construction of turnpikes. The "First Massachusetts Turnpike," in the towns of Palmer and Western (now Warren), was chartered by the General Court, June 11, 1796, on petition of the veteran stage-driver Levi Pease and others. So popular did this movement speedily become, that at the end of nine years (June 15, 1805) there were sixty similar corporations in this Commonwealth. The corporators were required to construct and maintain good roads for the convenience and advantage of the public, and were empowered to erect gates thereon, and to receive toll from all who passed through them with vehicle or beast, for their individual emolument.[1] Among the earliest was the "Sixth Massachusetts Turnpike," which passed through Hardwick. The indications are unmistakable that General Warner[2] was the leading spirit in this enterprise; and sixteen of the twenty-nine petitioners for the charter were Hardwick men. The petition so vividly describes the condition of the roads at that period that I insert it in full:—

"To the Honorable the Senate and the Honorable House of Representatives in General Court assembled, May, 1798.[3] The

[1] The experiment proved to be more profitable to the public than to the corporators; and before the introduction of railroads, almost all the turnpikes in the Commonwealth were surrendered to the towns wherein they were located, and became public highways, by permission of the General Court.

[2] Although his name is the seventeenth on the petition, yet in the Court Records it is styled "the petition of Jonathan Warner and others:" he is the first person named in the charter, and was the first president of the corporation.

[3] Probably the petition was prepared too late for presentation at the summer

subscribers, inhabitants of the counties of Hampshire, Worcester, Middlesex, &c., humbly shew, that the road leading from Hadley, through Amherst, Pelham, Greenwich, Hardwick, New Braintree, Oakham, Rutland, Holden, and Worcester, to the great road in Shrewsbury, which leads from New York to Boston, are at present very bad, and almost impassable for carriages, not from the negligence and inattention of the said towns through which they pass, but from the roughness of the country which is in many places uneven, hilly, and very rocky, and that they can never be properly repaired by the aforesaid towns without distressing them with a very great and unreasonable burden ;[1] but that with sufficient labor and expense they are capable of being very much improved ; and that as the route from Albany to Boston is in a direct line through the aforesaid towns, by a proper improvement the travelling to the western part of the County [country ?] may be greatly facilitated, and the distance very considerably curtailed. Your petitioners, therefore, from the fullest conviction of the importance of the measure to the trade and agriculture of the County [country ?] pray that your Honors would grant to the subscribers and such as may associate with them an Act of Incorporation, empowering them to make a good Turnpike Road from the town of Hadley in the county of Hampshire to the town of Shrewsbury in the county of Worcester, through the aforesaid towns, with all such powers, rights, privileges, and tolls, as the subject matter and the situation of the County [country ?] may render necessary. And as in duty bound will ever pray,[2] Francis Blake, Moses White, Richard Kelly, Joseph Chaddock, Jesse Allen, Artemas Howe, Roger West, Robert T. Field, Moses Mandell,* James Paige, 2d,* Jason Mixter,* Samuel Beals,* Jonathan Warner, 2d,* Timothy Paige,* James Lawton,* Nathaniel Whitcomb, Jonathan Warner,* Stephen Rice,* Nehemiah Hinds, John Rinker,[3] Lemuel Willis,* Seth Hinkley,* William Cutler,* Seth Peirce,* Jonathan Danforth,* Abner Conant,* Joel Marsh,* Thomas Powers, Zebina Montague." On this petition an order of notice was issued February 25, 1799, returnable at "the first session of the next General Court."[4] The charter was granted

session of the General Court, as no action was had on it until the following winter.

[1] The preamble to the charter also sets forth that the present highway "is rocky and mountainous, and the expense of making and maintaining the same, so that it may be convenient for horses and carriages, is much greater than reasonably ought to be required of the inhabitants of said towns." *Mass. Special Laws*, ii. 327.

[2] The names marked with a star (*) indicate inhabitants of Hardwick.

[3] This name is spelled Rankin in the charter.

[4] *Mass. Spy*, April 3, 1799.

June 22, 1799, omitting the names of some of the petitioners and containing several additional names. The provisions of this charter may be interesting to the younger portion of the present generation, who do not remember the period of turnpikes. Among other things, and principally, the corporators were authorized to construct "a turnpike road from the east line of Amherst . . . to the great road in Shrewsbury, . . . which road or turnpike shall not be less than four rods wide, and the path for travelling not less than eighteen feet wide in any place; . . . the said corporation may and shall be authorized to erect five turnpike gates[1] on the same, . . . and shall be entitled to receive of each traveller or passenger, at each of said gates, the following rate of toll, viz., for every coach, phaeton, chariot, or other four wheel carriage, drawn by two horses, twenty-five cents, and if drawn by more than two horses, an additional sum of four cents for each horse; for every cart or waggon, drawn by two oxen or horses, twelve and a half cents, and if drawn by more than two oxen or horses, an additional sum of three cents for each horse or ox; for every curricle, sixteen cents; for every chaise, chair, or other carriage, drawn by one horse, twelve and a half cents; for every man and horse, five cents; for every sled or sleigh, drawn by two oxen or horses, nine cents, and if drawn by more than two oxen or horses, an additional sum of three cents for every horse or ox; for every sled or sleigh, drawn by one horse, six cents; for all horses, mules, oxen, or neat cattle, led or driven, besides those in teams or carriages, one cent each; for all sheep or swine, at the rate of three cents for one dozen. . . . Provided, that nothing within this act shall extend to entitle the said corporation to demand or receive toll of any person who shall be passing with his horse or carriage to or from public worship, or with his horse, team, or cattle, to or from his common labor, or to or from any mill, or on the common or ordinary business of family concerns within the said town, or from any person or persons passing on military duty."[2] And it was "further enacted, that the first meeting of said corporation shall be holden at the house of Jonathan Warner, in Hardwick aforesaid, on the tenth day of September next, at ten of the clock

[1] One of these gates was to be erected "near the house of Zephaniah Spooner in Hardwick" (near Muddy Brook); but it was soon afterwards placed near the Old Furnace, between Moose Brook and Ware River; where toll was gathered for many years by Mr. Ebenezer Cobb, a very honest though somewhat eccentric man.

[2] The town of Hardwick had previously (April 2, 1798) "voted, to let a Turnpike Road go through the town, if the inhabitants of the said town may pass and repass free of any expense in said town."

in the forenoon, for the purpose of choosing all such officers and establishing such rules as said corporation may think proper."[1]

The corporation, when organized, issued an "advertisement," describing in strong terms the advantages which would accrue both to the public and to the stockholders from the execution of their design, and soliciting subscriptions:—"The Public are informed that a Company has been incorporated by a late Act of the legislature of Massachusetts, for the purpose of making a TURNPIKE ROAD from Amherst in the County of Hampshire to Shrewsbury in the County of Worcester, and that agreeably to the act of incorporation the Company have proceeded to lay out the road and make an estimate of the probable expense. The object of this association is to establish a direct line of communication from Boston to Albany, and to facilitate the travelling from Connecticut River to the Capital of Massachusetts. It is a well-known fact that the trade of this wealthy and flourishing part of New England has for many years past (in consequence of the roughness of the roads and the difficulty of communication with the town of Boston) been gradually diverted from our metropolis to Hartford and New York. To the mercantile interest of Boston this has become a very serious injury, and with their brethren in the country a subject of very serious regret. It is presumed, therefore, that an enterprise, the object of which is to remedy this evil, as well as to promote the convenience of the public, cannot fail to meet the approbation and encouragement of the citizens of Boston in particular, and the inhabitants of Massachusetts in general, even without the prospect of private emolument. But the proprietors, feeling themselves authorized, from a due attention to the subject, to state to the public a rational prospect of individual emolument to be derived from an interest in this undertaking, calculate with confidence upon receiving such pecuniary aid from the patriotic and liberal citizens of New England as will enable them to carry into immediate effect the object of their association. They therefore inform the public that the proposed Turnpike comprehends a distance of about forty-three miles, beginning at Shrewsbury, on the great post road from Boston to New York, passing through a fertile and flourishing country in the counties of Worcester and Hampshire, and terminating at Amherst, on Connecticut River, where it will connect with a turnpike already established from Northampton to the line of the State of New York. It is well

[1] *Mass. Special Laws,* ii. 327–331.

ascertained that this is the most direct route from Boston to Albany, and will embrace the travelling from the western country and the most flourishing settlements on Connecticut River, within the States of Massachusetts and Vermont. From the best information, the proprietors of the turnpike from Northampton, with which this is to be immediately connected, have already realized from seven to nine per cent for their capital, and their income is rapidly increasing. From the difference in the face of the country, the proposed turnpike will be made with much less expense than the other, and the income of course proportionably greater. The expense has been estimated by a committee appointed for that purpose at twenty-five thousand five hundred and thirty dollars,[1] which sum is divided into ten hundred and twenty-one shares, at twenty-five dollars each. The first assessment is five dollars, which sum is to be paid on the delivery of the Certificate, and the future assessments made known by advertisements in the public papers. It is contemplated by the proprietors to engage in the business early in the ensuing spring, and if sufficient encouragement can be obtained to have the road completed in the course of the next season. Many wealthy and respectable inhabitants of the country are now earnestly engaged in the object, and solicit the co-operation of the commercial citizens of Boston, whose interest is so peculiarly concerned, and upon whose assistance the accomplishment of the work will perhaps ultimately depend. The shares are now offered for sale, and any person inclining to become interested in an enterprise which affords a fair prospect of private advantage and of great public utility may receive more particular information, and have an opportunity of purchasing until the 10th day of February next (at which time the sales will be closed), by applying to the following persons, viz.: Mr. John Marston, N. Patch, Boston; Nathaniel Paine, Esq., Worcester; Ebenezer Hunt, Esq., Northampton; John Dodds, Esq., or Mr. Lemuel Davis, Holden; Moses White, Esq., or Francis Blake, Esq., Rutland; Doctor Spencer Field, Oakham; Jonathan Warner, Esq., Hardwick; Thomas Powers, Esq., Greenwich; Major John Conkey, Pelham. Signed by order of the Corporation. JONATHAN WARNER, President."[2]

[1] As generally happens in similar cases, the expense far exceeded the estimate. The "Road was forty-three miles and one hundred and twelve rods long; was made in one summer; and cost about thirty-three thousand dollars." Reed's *Hist. of Rutland*, p. 44.

[2] *Mass. Spy*, January 1, 1800.

The corporators and stockholders were disappointed in their hope of individual profit. The construction of the road involved an expense of about eight thousand dollars beyond the estimate, the payment of which absorbed all or nearly all the net income. By a statement signed "Jonas Reed, late Proprietors' Clerk," it appears that "the road being made and accepted, the Corporation for a little time took considerable toll; but it was appropriated to the payment of outstanding debts. The proprietors were under the necessity of taking their own money to pay themselves. New roads were made, toll evaded, and the shares had the same destiny as the old Continental money. The Corporation relinquished its Franchise, and on August 11, 1828, held its last meeting. The turnpike became a County road or common Highway."[1] But though the proprietors thus suffered loss, the towns through which the turnpike passed were doubtless benefited by its construction. It became a more direct and practicable thoroughfare, and the tide of travel was attracted to it, with the usual profitable results. In Hardwick, the turnpike followed substantially the county road from the Old Furnace to Greenwich village, except between the Common and the house of Mr. John W. Paige (marked "J. Gorham" on the R. map). The old road from the southwesterly corner of the Common ran westerly up the steep hill[2] until it intersected the present road to Ware, and then more northerly to its junction with the turnpike. Both ends of this old road, which was discontinued in 1808, remain visible to the present day, and its whole course may be traced with little difficulty.[3] By the construction of the turnpike, the distance was shortened and the ascent of the hill rendered more easy.

About half a century later, May 24, 1851, a charter was granted to Charles A. Stevens, Jason Gorham, William Mixter, and their associates, to construct the Ware River Railroad from

[1] Reed's *Hist. of Rutland*, pp. 44, 45.

[2] From a point near the middle of this steep ascent, a road diverged at right angles, and passed southerly towards Gilbertville to its junction with the present road (which was laid out in 1808 as a county road), about a hundred rods north of the house of Mr. Forester B. Aiken.

[3] The northerly section of this old road was probably the westerly boundary of the "ten acres" which was granted by the proprietors, February 21, 1732-3, "to set a meeting house on, and for a burial place, and a training field." For this lot another was afterwards substituted, and half an acre in the northwest corner of the original "ten acres" was granted, March 10, 1761, to "those people called the Separate Society in Hardwick," who erected a meeting house thereon and occupied it a few years.

Palmer to the line of New Hampshire, to be constructed within two years.[1] Additional time for its construction was repeatedly granted by the General Court, but in vain. At length a new charter was granted, March 16, 1867, to George H. Gilbert, William Mixter, Orrin Sage, Charles A. Stevens, George S. Hill, and their associates, authorizing them, for the purpose of construction, to divide the road into four sections, viz.: 1. From Palmer to Gilbertville; 2. From Gilbertville to Barre; 3. From Barre to Templeton; and 4. From Templeton to the New Hampshire line; and also to "receive subscriptions for the building of each of said sections separately."[2] The time limited for its construction having expired, the charter was revived by the General Court, April 1, 1869, and the corporators were authorized, May 22, 1869, to mortgage the road to secure the payment of bonds to be issued to defray the expense of construction.[3] By an act passed March 15, 1870, the several towns through which this road was to pass were authorized to subscribe for stock, not exceeding in amount five per cent. of the assessed valuation of each town, by a majority of two thirds of the voters voting thereon by ballot.[4] Accordingly, at a town-meeting, June 27, 1870, it was voted, "That the town of Hardwick subscribe for thirty thousand dollars of the capital stock of the Ware River Railroad Company, under and pursuant to the authority given by an Act of the Legislature of Massachusetts, at the late session thereof; such amount to be applied to the construction of the second section of the said Ware River Railroad, from Gilbertville to Barre." On this question, the votes were, Yeas, 113; Nays, 43. The road was soon afterwards constructed and put in operation.[5] It proved unprofitable, however, to the proprietors, and the bondholders foreclosed the mortgage, and sold the property for a sum not exceeding the amount of the bonds. The General Court had already, April 21, 1873, authorized the purchasers at this sale to organize a new company under the old name, and to issue new bonds secured by mortgage.[6] The new company was duly organized, and it is understood that the property yields a satisfactory income to the present stockholders. To the original subscribers, towns as well as individuals, the amount invested was entirely lost; nevertheless, to the towns and to many individuals

[1] *Mass. Special Laws*, ix. 408.
[2] *Ibid.*, xii. 202.
[3] *Ibid.*, xii. 763.
[4] *Ibid.*, xii. 907.
[5] Cars commenced running to Gilbertville in 1870; to Barre about 1872.
[6] *Mass. Special Laws*, xiii. 582.

the loss was fully balanced by the incidental benefit derived from the construction of the road. Both the agricultural and manufacturing interests of the town were promoted by the increased facilities of transportation; and the town was enriched rather than impoverished by the expenditure.

In the year 1870 the railroad fever raged violently in Hardwick. Not content with one road, involving an expense of thirty thousand dollars, the town pledged its credit for almost as large a sum, to aid in the construction of another, which promised even greater advantages, and which, if it shall ever be completed, will probably redeem this promise, substantially, in spite of its failure to perform the stipulated conditions. On the 10th day of May, 1870, the General Court incorporated Edward Denny and others (among whom was Constant Southworth of Hardwick), as the "Massachusetts Central Railroad Company," and authorized them to "locate, construct, maintain, and operate a railroad, with one or more tracks, commencing at some convenient point in the town of Williamsburg, thence running by the most convenient route through the towns of Northampton, Easthampton, Westhampton, Hatfield, Hadley, South Hadley, Amherst, Granby, Ludlow, Belchertown, Enfield, Greenwich, Ware, Palmer, West Brookfield, New Braintree, Hardwick, Dana, Petersham, Barre, Phillipston, Oakham, Hubbardston, Rutland, Princeton, Holden, Sterling, Boylston, West Boylston, Clinton, Lancaster, Northborough, Berlin, Bolton, Hudson, Stow, and Marlborough, or any of them, to Mill Village, thence over the line of the Wayland and Sudbury Branch Railroad Company, incorporated in the year 1868, to its terminus near the Stony Brook Station on the Fitchburg Railroad," with authority to become consolidated with the said Wayland and Sudbury Railroad and the Williamsburg and North Adams Railroad, and to use the tracks of intersecting railroads."[1] An inspection of the map will show that as far as to the easterly line of the county of Worcester, this roving commission embraced almost the entire territory between the Fitchburg and the Boston and Albany railroads; and, at one time or another, a large portion of it has been surveyed, and selected as "the most convenient route." Hardwick had its full share of these surveys, selections, and changes. After many ineffectual attempts had been made to find a feasible route across or near the Common, it was determined to follow the valley of Ware River,

[1] *Mass. Special Laws*, xii. 736.

either upon or parallel with the Ware River Railroad, from the northeast corner of the town to a point near Gilbertville, and thence to sweep around westerly and northerly almost or quite to Southworth's Mills in the northwest part of the town, near Greenwich. Upon the westerly portion of this route large sums of money were expended, in deep excavations of rocky hills, high embankments across valleys, and abutments for bridges, which may hereafter be a study for antiquaries; but the work was at length abandoned, to the grievous disappointment of Mr. Southworth and others who had actively labored in behalf of the road, and a new route was adopted, extending down the River Valley to Ware Village, thus entirely avoiding the highlands in Hardwick. Whether this will be the permanent location of the road, and how soon the proposed work may be completed, are problems yet unsolved.

By the act of incorporation, the several towns on the line of the railroad were authorized to subscribe for its stock, to an amount not exceeding five per cent. of their respective taxable valuation. Encouraged by the hope that the several portions of the town would be benefited by accessible stations, at a town-meeting held November 8, 1870, it was "voted by one hundred and thirty-four (134) yes, to ninety (90) no, by ballot, that the Treasurer of the town of Hardwick be and he is hereby authorized and directed to subscribe immediately, in the name of the town of Hardwick for two hundred and eighty-one shares of one hundred dollars each, of the capital stock of the Massachusetts Central Railroad Company, agreeably to the terms of their charter, being 260 of the Acts of 1869. Provided, that this subscription be made upon the following conditions, to wit: that the said Road shall be located, and a contract be made with responsible parties to construct the Railroad of said Company from Northampton, through and by the way of Greenwich and Hardwick, north of the Dugal[1] Hill, so as to make a continuous line to Stony Brook Station on the Fitchburg Railroad; and further provided, that the town shall not be liable to any amount till not less than three millions of dollars, including this subscription, shall have been made to the capital stock of said company. And provided further, that a depot for freight and passengers be established in the vicinity of the Old Furnace, Hardwick, and another in the most convenient locality between Gilbertville and the centre of Hardwick. And provided further, that this subscription shall not be valid, unless the whole capital stock

[1] Or "McDougal," or "Bugle."

of three million dollars be subscribed by responsible parties within six months from the first day of January next." It is questionable whether any of these conditions have ever been fulfilled by the Railroad Company. It is certain that some of them have not been fulfilled, and have become impossible of performance, unless the strange doctrine be held, that a location of the road north of Bugle Hill, and the stating of a place for a depot between Gilbertville and the centre of the town, was a substantial fulfilment of the conditions, notwithstanding the road was never constructed, and the location was utterly abandoned. Nevertheless, on the presumption that the Company would comply with the conditions in good faith, the town paid forty per cent. of its subscription, amounting to $11,240 ; but on the 5th of November, 1872, it was "voted, that the money on the subscription of the town of Hardwick to the capital stock of the Massachusetts Central Railroad be withheld until the definite location of the depots of said Railroad in the vicinity of the Old Furnace Village, Hardwick, and between the Common in said Hardwick and Gilbertville, and until the depot in the vicinity of the Old Furnace Village be located within the limits of the town of Hardwick."[1] During the controversy which ensued, the Railroad Company proposed to sell the stock belonging to the town; whereupon at a town-meeting, August 3, 1878, "voted and chose Hon. William Mixter an agent of the town of Hardwick to agree with the Directors of the Massachusetts Central Railroad Company, that if the said Company will consent not to sell the shares of the town in the stock of said Company, as heretofore notified, the town will waive all benefit of the Statute of Limitations for six months from this date," without prejudice to the legal rights of either party. A similar vote was passed, February 6, 1879, extending the time two years. Whether the town will hereafter be compelled to pay the remaining sixty per cent. of its subscription, notwithstanding the non-performance of the conditions, or whether, in consequence of such non-performance the company will be required to refund the amount already paid, remains to be judicially determined. Meantime there is now an encouraging prospect that at least so much of the road as will shorten the distance between Hardwick and Boston twenty miles will be completed at no remote day, and that the town will thus obtain a great advantage, though less than it bargained for.

[1] The company had commenced grading the road on the east side of the river, passing the Furnace Village at a point not "within the limits of the town of Hardwick."

POUNDS. One of the earliest safeguards against the destruction of property in the infant settlement was the establishment of a pound for the confinement of cattle unlawfully running at large. At the third meeting, after partial town privileges had been obtained, holden June 30, 1737, it was "voted, that George Abbott provide a Pound and be the pound-keeper for this year;" the next year, August 8, 1738, it was "voted, that Benjamin Smith's yard be a Pound for the town this year;" and at the first meeting after the town was fully incorporated, holden April 3, 1739, it was "voted, that the town will build a Pound, thirty feet square, and that it shall be set near the meeting house,[1] and that Samuel Robinson be the man to build said Pound according to law." This inclosure served its purpose more than half a century; but on the 3d of March, 1794, it was "voted, that Jonathan Danforth finish the Pound before the first day of June next." This vote is supposed to refer to the pound on the westerly side of Great Meadow Brook, where it is crossed by the old turnpike, near the spot where Mr. Danforth then resided, now owned and occupied by Captain Orin Trow. The substantial stone walls remain standing, and fragments of the fence, composed of sawed chestnut posts and rails, are still visible, after so long exposure.[2]

PAUPERS. The first reference to that unfortunate class, dependent on public charity and support, which appears on record, is under date of March 7, 1747–8, when upon an article in the warrant, "to see if the town will raise money to maintain Hannah Maccoye, sent to this town for that intent," it was "voted to raise fifty pounds, old tenor, to maintain Hannah Maccoye;" she remained chargeable until 1765. Doubtless other persons had received public assistance at an earlier date; indeed, it is alleged by General Ruggles, in a petition dated in 1754 and heretofore quoted, that "the inhabitants of said town are obliged to be at a great expense for the support of several poor and indigent persons;" but the aid was probably rendered from the general fund raised for town expenses. From the annual accounts of the town treasurer, and from other sources, the following names are gathered of persons who received public aid up to the end of the last century; the figures denote the date when

[1] It was on the westerly side of the Common, near the late residence of Mr. Moses Smith.

[2] I am very confident that these are fragments of the same fence which excited my childish wonder three quarters of a century ago, and whose gradual decay I have since observed at short intervals of time.

such aid was first rendered: Edmund Jordan's wife and children, 1757;[1] Isaiah Glazier's children, 1761; Temperance Pratt, 1764;[2] Sarah Cummings, 1764; Widow Zerviah Pratt, 1765, died April 18, 1798, aged 89; Ephraim Rice's wife, 1765; Samuel Abbott, "a poor child," 1766; Charles Thomas, "a poor child," in care of Asa Hatch, 1768; James Harwood's wife, 1777; Mary Stratton, "a poor girl," 1783; Widow Mary Bradshaw, 1786; John Hedge, 1786; Thomas Shaw, 1786; Paul Morgan,[3] 1789; Widow Jemima Blackington, 1792, died May 18, 1796, aged 70; Isaac Pratt, 1793, died November 27, 1808, aged 83; Hannah Aiken, 1798, died December 9, 1814, aged 64; Anna Farr, 1799; Abraham Chamberlin and wife, 1799; John Hunt, and wife, and child, 1799; Edward Curtis, 1800, died October 17, 1800, aged 66; Roxa Elwell, 1800, temporarily.

What method was originally adopted for furnishing the necessary assistance to paupers, does not appear; but at the commencement of this century, and for many years afterwards, their maintenance was allotted to the lowest bidder, from year to year,[4] with this qualification, however, that a preference was given to relatives who were willing to assume the task.[5] But in 1837 a more humane plan was adopted; and at a town meeting, April 3, 1837, after appropriating the sum of $2,000 (a portion of the "Surplus Revenue" received by the town) to defray the expense of building a Town Hall, it was "voted, to apply the residue of said surplus to the purchase of a Farm, on which to support the paupers; voted, that the present Board of Selectmen be a committee to purchase a Farm for the purpose of making it a home for our paupers;" and on the 13th of the following November it was "voted, to instruct the selectmen to complete the purchase of the Farm of Mr. John Wheeler, on the terms they

[1] Edmund Jordan died in the army, 1756.

[2] Temperance Pratt was an idiotic daughter of Widow Zerviah Pratt, and remained a pauper for fifty years, until she died December 17, 1814, aged 64.

[3] Paul Morgan had the care of a gristmill which formerly stood near the present residence of Captain Orin Trow; he died in 1789; his widow Hannah, also a pauper near the close of her life, died January 17, 1824, at the supposed age of 95 years.

[4] On a loose paper among the archives in the town clerk's office is a memorandum of the disposition of the paupers in 1819, to wit: — Daniel Thomas and wife to Ephraim Ruggles; Molly Reed (who died January 22, 1822, aged 83) to Jedediah Dexter; Mrs. Hammon to Bassett Fay; Anna Farr to David Bond; Mrs. Hedge to Sally Hedge; Hannah Morgan (State pauper) to Deacon Joseph Allen; Dudley F. Lawrence to Ephraim Ruggles; Widow Freeman to Jedediah Dexter; Lucius Doolittle to Franklin Ruggles; Widow Newton and two children to Samuel Freeman.

[5] In 1811, and for several years earlier and later, Sally Hedge was paid for supporting her grandmother, Deliverance Hedge, who died June 4, 1819, aged 93.

have reported." On this farm suitable buildings were erected for the convenience and comfort of the poor, who were thenceforth protected against an annual flitting from one family to another, and from the constant peril of being committed to the charge of such persons as would have less regard for their welfare than for their own personal profit. Under the judicious and tender care of a warden and matron, the inmates are made more comfortable in their old age and helplessness, without material increase of the expenses of the town.

Before dismissing this subject, it may be mentioned that a speculation in the maintenance of State Paupers was once seriously proposed in town meeting. Who suggested the idea, or advocated the measure, does not appear; but the following vote was passed, May 9, 1791, and duly recorded: "Voted, that the town will receive one third part of the poor persons supported by the Commonwealth, and they hereby offer and agree, on their part, to support said poor persons, with suitable lodging and boarding, for the term of ten years from and after the time of contracting, provided the Commonwealth will pay them five shillings per week for adults, and two shillings and sixpence per week for children, and their proportion of one hundred pounds per annum for doctoring said poor, the money to be paid quarterly; and will remove said poor from Boston at their own expense." I find no evidence that their offer was accepted, or that any further action was had by the town in reference to this magnificent project.

SLAVERY. There are very faint traces of human bondage in Hardwick. Among the marriages solemnized by Rev. Mr. White was that of "Tack and Rose, Kenelm Winslow's man and maid servant, April ye 3^{d}, 1755." Mr. Winslow not long afterwards removed to Petersham, and in his will, dated April 5, 1775, gave to his wife, during her widowhood, his three negroes, Sarah, Rose, and Phillis, probably the offspring from this marriage. Rev. Mr. White also baptized, July 27, 1755, "Zebulon, the son of Philip and Bathsheba, man and maid servant to Capt. Joseph Warner," and a second Zebulon, son of the same parents, April 10, 1757. One more slave appears where we might least expect to find him, namely, in possession of a man who had served in the French war, on behalf of his country; who had already accepted office as captain of a company of minute-men, ready to march, at a moment's notice in defence of human rights against foreign domination, and did thus march, soon afterwards; and who, a dozen years later, again took up arms and put his life in peril, when he imagined the execution of law would be hurtful to the poorer class of the community. Moreover, he had never lived in luxury, but evidently suffered financial embarrassment, and seemed in no respect exposed to the temptation of holding a fellow-man in bondage. But the following advertisement shows that his practice was inconsistent with his avowed principles, and unsuited to his condition: "FIFTEEN DOLLARS REWARD. Ran away from me, the subscriber, on Thursday, the twentieth of October instant, a Negro Man, named Cæsar, about 26 years old, five feet four inches high; had on, when he went away, a green ratteen coat, red everlasting jacket, white linen breeches, blue yarn stockings; he has a mark or scar over one of his eyes, the little finger of his left hand is a little crooked by the cut of a sickle; it is suspected that some one assisted him, by changing cloaths, or gave him a pass; Whoever will take up said Negro and return him to me, or confine him to any of his Majesty's Goals, so that he may be returned to me, shall have the above reward and all necessary charges paid by SIMEON HAZELTINE. Hardwick, October 21, 1774."[1] Captain Hazeltine himself became a fugitive in 1787, to escape the consequences of his active participation in the "Shays Rebellion."

There is no evidence that many negroes, bond or free, ever resided here. A census of the inhabitants twenty-one years of age and upwards, was taken, January 31, 1777, by the Selectmen and Committee of Correspondence, who certified that "we have no Quakers, no Indians, and no Negroes." Probably, however, there were some negro inhabitants under twenty-one years old; for in May, 1781, a descriptive Roll of men, enlisted in the army for three years, contains the names of Cato Boston, aged 22, Jupiter Lee, aged 16, and Zebulon Bassett, aged 23, all described as "black." The last named patriotic soldier was probably the same Zebulon, son of Captain Joseph Warner's servants, who was baptized April 10, 1757. At a later day, a few negro families have resided here, but never many at any one period; and never at any time have they disturbed the peace of the community.

TOWN HOUSE. For nearly a century after its incorporation, the town held its public meetings in the Congregational meeting-house, which was the common property of the town, — the town

[1] *Boston Gazette*, October 24, 1774.

and parish being substantially the same. At length a portion of the old parish withdrew, organized a new society, and erected a meeting-house at the south end of the common. A Universalist Society had also been formed, which held its meetings in a hall, and no longer contributed towards the expenses of the old parish. Under such circumstances, it was unreasonable that the whole town should make free use of a meeting-house which belonged to a single parish, and was to be kept in repair or rebuilt without expense to the town in its corporate capacity. Better accommodations for the transaction of public business were also needed and generally desired. Accordingly, at a town meeting, April 4, 1836, "the Committee to whom was referred the subject of building a Town House made a report, accompanied by a plan, recommending to the town to build such a house, estimating the expense at $1,500." The report was accepted, and a committee was appointed to carry the recommendation into effect, and to "select a suitable spot for the erection of said house in the old burying-ground." The northwest corner of the burial-place was selected, August 22, 1836, on which a convenient edifice was constructed, two stories high, having on the lower floor rooms for the use of the various boards of town officers, and on the second floor a spacious hall for town-meetings and for other large assemblies. The cost of the building was defrayed without resort to taxation. Fortunately the revenue of the United States had exceeded the necessary disbursements, and a surplus had accumulated in the Treasury. This surplus was divided by Congress among the several States; and the General Court of Massachusetts distributed its share to the several towns, on certain conditions, one of which was that each town should refund its proportion, if it should afterwards be demanded. On the 3d of April, 1837, it was "voted, that the town consent to receive their proportion of the Surplus Revenue, under the conditions and limitations imposed by law. . . . Voted, that two thousand dollars of said Surplus be appropriated to the discharge of the debt to be incurred by building the Town House, and to discharge the other debts of the town."

Having completed the edifice and paid for it, the town manifested a willingness that it should be used for purposes other than strictly municipal affairs; and while it rightly demanded compensation from those who used it, was very moderate in its exactions. Moreover, in the use of the Hall a proper distinction was made between the common benefit of the public and the private advantage of a class, or of individuals. Having authorized the selectmen, November 13, 1837, "to take charge of the Town House, to keep it in order, to let it, &c.," the town gave some special directions concerning its use, May 8, 1838, when it was "voted that the Universalist Society shall be entitled to use the Town Hall as a place of worship, on the second Sabbath of each month, at one dollar per Sabbath, and oftener at the same rate, if the Hall be not otherwise engaged, and said Society can obtain preaching; also that said Society be entitled to the use of said Hall for evening Lectures, at the rate of fifty cents for each evening:[1] — voted, that the use of the Hall be granted to Mr. Goldsbury, for the purpose of keeping a High School, at the rate of five dollars per quarter; damages done to the Hall by the school to be repaired by the school: — voted, that the Hardwick Lyceum be entitled to the use of the Hall without paying anything to the town: — voted, that the use of the Hall be granted for the purpose of singing, without any charge therefor being made by the town." The High School was closed in 1839, and about two years later the Universalist Society, having erected a new meeting-house (under a mutual arrangement with the Congregational Society), ceased to occupy the Hall "as a place of worship"; but it continues to be used for all proper purposes, either gratuitously, or at a very reasonable charge. On the 24th of May, 1847, the town accepted a bell, as a gift from Jason Mixter, Esq., and ordered it to be placed on the Town House, bearing this appropriate inscription, — "Presented to the Town by Jason Mixter, Esq., A. D. 1847."

BURIAL-PLACES. In the "Massachusetts Spy," dated Friday, June 2, 1871, it was announced that, — "Last Friday, as the workmen on the Ware River Railroad were engaged in excavating for the road-bed in Hardwick, near Old Furnace Village, they came upon an old graveyard, where they have exhumed some ten or twelve skeletons. The Town Records have been searched, and nothing can be found that gives any information in regard to the matter. An old lady, eighty-five years of age, says that her grandfather used to tell of a public burying-ground somewhere in that locality. At present the whole affair is a mystery, and there seems to be no means of obtaining any clue in regard to the matter." Additional particulars were mentioned

[1] On the passage of this vote, which was sharply contested, there were 45 yeas and 34 nays.

in the "Springfield Republican" of the same date: "Twenty-eight skeletons had been exhumed, up to Tuesday night, in the old cemetery at Furnace Village, Hardwick, brought to light by the excavations for the Ware River Railroad, and there was a prospect of finding still more. These were all found in a space of fifty feet in length and twenty feet wide, being the square cut upon the centre line of the road-bed. It is very curious that no definite information in regard to so large a yard can be obtained. The remains that have been lately taken out have the hair more plainly defined than the first, and pieces of boards, used in making the coffins, have been found, — in fact were attached to coffin-nails, old fashioned, wrought, about such as blacksmiths use for horse-shoes, now-a-days. The pieces of boards were so plainly defined that one could tell that the boards were split from the logs instead of being sawed."

I visited the place[1] June 8, 1871, and found the skeletons described, then numbering thirty; some were of persons apparently well advanced in life, some of middle age, and others of young children. The number exceeded my expectations; but that several persons had been buried there, was a tradition, current in my boyhood, though strangely unfamiliar to the present generation. Indeed, the greatest "mystery" in regard to this matter is, that so few persons now living should have any knowledge or remembrance of that tradition; I could find none, except the "old lady,[2] eighty-five years old" in 1871, and her recollection was vague and indistinct. Among the very earliest pioneers, if not absolutely the first, was William Thomas, the owner and occupant of the farm where the skeletons were found. Nearly three quarters of a century ago I received from my elders the tradition that he and several members of his family were buried on his own farm, and that some of his neighbors had permission to bury their dead in the same place. The precise spot was never designated to me; but it was always described as on this farm, and there can be no reasonable doubt that it was where the skeletons were exhumed in 1871. Mr. Thomas died May 22, 1747, aged probably about 60; his wife Patience died October 27, 1746. In 1749 the farm passed out of the possession of the Thomas family, and gradually all traces of the ancient graves were obliterated.

[1] This spot is about a mile and a quarter southerly from the Furnace Village, and nearly three miles southeasterly from the Common; it is a gravelly knoll, about twenty rods southeasterly from the house marked "C. Paige" on the R. map.

[2] Daughter of Deacon James Paige, and mother of Deacon James N. Brown. She died June 16, 1880.

This was never a public burial-place, and no reference to it on the Town Records need be expected. Mr. Thomas had possession of this farm and occupied a house thereon as early as December 13, 1732, and how much earlier does not appear. Before the public burial-place was established, before any saw-mills were erected, as is indicated by some remnants of "boards, split from the logs instead of being sawed," and possibly before he had any neighbors nearer than Rutland and Brookfield, some member of his family may have deceased; and in such case it was natural that he should use a portion of his own land as a private cemetery; it was natural, also, that he and his family, as long as they retained possession of the farm, should bury their dead in the same place. It is a part of the tradition, and the large number of skeletons indicates the same fact, that some of the neighboring families were buried in this rural spot, so much more easy of access than the public burial-place on the highlands, even after it was prepared for use. There may have been a special reason for the clustering of graves in this spot, if there be substantial truth in another tradition, communicated to me in 1838, by a very intelligent lady,[1] then ninety years old, namely, that before the first meeting-house was erected on the Common, meetings for religious worship were for some time held in or near the house of Mr. Thomas. If this were so, it was natural that his neighbors should desire to bury their dead here rather than on their own farms.[2] Except the theory mentioned in the note, I am not aware that any other explanation has been offered concerning the bones, which having rested undisturbed for more than a century, until the memory of them had nearly perished from the

[1] The widow of Major-General Jonathan Warner.

[2] A theory gained temporary currency that these skeletons were "the relics of a portion of the Shays Rebellion;" that after the attack on the arsenal at Springfield in January, 1787, "the Shays party retreated to Hardwick where they encamped and kept quiet. That winter was severe, and many died, being buried in rough wooden boxes." But this theory is incredible for several reasons: — Whatever may have been the scarcity when the first deaths occurred in the families of Mr. Thomas and his neighbors, there was certainly no lack of saw-mills half a century later, in 1787, nor any necessity to construct coffins of boards "split from the logs instead of being sawed;" nor is it probable that so many women and children were camp-followers, and died in one winter, as the skeletons indicate. Moreover, there is no evidence that the Shays army ever entered Hardwick, after the retreat from Springfield. On the contrary, all the authorities agree that instead of encamping and keeping quiet, here or elsewhere, through the winter, the troops were utterly routed and scattered at Petersham, February 4, 1787, just ten days after their abortive attempt at Springfield. Indeed, they did not even pass through Hardwick on their retreat, but fled from Petersham in the opposite direction through Athol.

earth, were accidentally disinterred in 1871, to the great astonishment and bewilderment of the living inhabitants. After due examination, they were placed together in a box and again deposited in the earth, under the direction of the selectmen.

The oldest public burial-place in Hardwick is in the centre of the town, on the east side of the Common. It is not a part of the "ten acres," devoted by the proprietors, February 21, 1732–3, to public use; but it was probably substituted for the original grant, about 1741, when the second meeting-house was erected. How early this burial-place was used does not appear. The most ancient date now to be found on any head-stone, is on that of Hannah, wife of Thomas Haskell, who died, May 16, 1749, aged 25. Deacon John White, the father of Rev. David White, was born at an earlier date (1663) than any other person known to have been buried in that ground; he died November 13, 1750, in the eighty-eighth year of his age. Next to him in seniority of birth was Daniel Warner, the progenitor of almost all who now bear that name in Hardwick, who was born in 1666, and died March 12, 1754, in the eighty-eighth year of his age. Both of these patriarchs were born in Hatfield. Far exceeding them in age, and the oldest person ever buried in that ground, was Mercy, widow of Deacon William Paige, who was born at Brookfield January 3, 1720–1, and died here February 19, 1823, having completed more than one hundred and two years of life.

This burial-place has been sadly shorn of its original proportions. In 1768 the northerly line was 15½ rods in length; the easterly line, 14 rods; and the southerly line, 11 rods. The westerly line appears to have been a continuation of what is now the easterly line of the road running northerly from the Common towards Petersham.[1] The first mutilation was authorized by a vote passed May 9, 1791, when a committee consisting of sixteen prominent inhabitants, previously appointed "to view the Common and the lands adjoining, and see what alterations may be convenient and necessary to be made; also to inquire of the pro-

[1] These dimensions are gleaned from a deed of the meeting-house lot to the town, executed by John Rowe, May 30, 1768, and another deed of the adjoining premises to Daniel Ruggles, from the heirs of the same John Rowe, dated July 9, 1803. *Worc. Reg. Deeds*, lix. 113; cliv. 126. In my school-boy days there were several depressions in the surface of the ground on the easterly side of the present Common, which were then reputed to be indications of ancient graves; but whether their contents had been removed to the present contracted limits of the burial-place, is not certainly known.

prietors of the lands adjoining, to know of them on what conditions they will dispose of their lands, provided the committee shall think it expedient to enlarge the Common; also to examine respecting the expediency and propriety of removing the Burying-yard wall, and laying a part of the present Burying-yard common," submitted a report which was accepted; and the town thereupon voted to enlarge the Common by taking in a portion of the burying-ground on the easterly side of the Common, and a strip of land on the westerly side, given by General Warner on certain conditions to which the town assented. No further material encroachment seems to have been made until August 22, 1836, when the town instructed its committee to erect a Town House "on the northwest corner of the old Burying-ground." At this time a new cemetery had been established, and an inclination was exhibited by many, not only to discontinue their accustomed use of this place, hallowed for a century by the dust of the dead and the tears of the living, but to sell it outright, for "thirty pieces of silver," more or less, and permit it to be utterly perverted from its original destination.[1] It was thought to be a desirable location for dwelling-houses, and especially for stores and public buildings. The Town House had covered several

[1] While this spirit of vandalism was rife, the town celebrated its centennial anniversary. In the address on that occasion my fellow citizens were besought to refrain from the proposed alienation of this "God's acre" from the use to which it had been piously dedicated. I venture to republish the appeal in this note: —

"Of those who commenced the settlement here, not one remains. Most of those who were active, during the first fifty years of our history, have also departed. They sleep in the grave, — all that was mortal of them, — chiefly in the inclosure near this house, which was devoted as a burial-place, by the proprietors of the township. I exceedingly regret that a few individuals have manifested a disposition to appropriate it to other purposes entirely. I know not how some persons may feel on this subject. But my fathers sleep in that ground; and I would gladly preserve their remains from indignity. In regard to most of my fellow citizens, I may say your fathers sleep there, and it becomes you to watch over them. They who converted a howling wilderness into fruitful fields and pleasant gardens, sleep there. They sleep there, who labored, suffered privation, and freely perilled their lives in contests with savage beasts and more savage men, that we might enjoy plenty, and liberty, and peace. Of all which they once possessed, they withheld nothing from us, but that small spot of ground, where, with their fellow-laborers and fellow-sufferers, their wives and their children, they might rest in peace till the resurrection. Let us not grudge them this scanty pittance. They gave us their houses and lands; — do not deprive them of their graves. Let not their ashes be scattered to the four winds, nor their bones be thrown out, to be trampled under foot by the unthinking multitude. Let not that spot of ground, already shorn of its original proportions, be further desecrated. Let it rather be neatly and substantially inclosed, and planted with trees and shrubbery. It will then be a pleasant retreat for meditation, an ornament to your village, and a perpetual monument of your respect for the memory of your ancestors."

graves, without disturbing their contents; and this was regarded by some as a sufficient excuse for digging to any required depth for the construction of basements and cellars. After the project had been freely discussed for several months, it took definite form March 5, 1838, when an article was inserted in the warrant for the annual town meeting, "to see if the town will dispose of a portion of the old burying-ground to Joel S. Marsh, lying between the elm trees near the Town House, 44 feet in length, north and south, and 34 feet in width, for the purpose of erecting a store;" to the honor of the town, I glady copy the record that "a motion that the town consent to sell the land to Mr. Marsh, as requested by him, passed in the negative." It does not appear that a similar proposition was afterwards presented to the town by any individual; but an attempt was made December 30, 1840, to purchase a part of the burial-place for a very different purpose, which could be carried into effect without disturbing the bones of the dead. At that date, the second article in the warrant was "to see if the town will sell to the First Universalist Society, for a reasonable compensation, a spot of land in the old burying-ground, sixty feet deep and fifty feet front, lying directly back of two elm trees between the Town House and Mixter and Delano's store, for the purpose of erecting a church thereon. . . . The subject contained in the second article of the warrant was discussed at considerable length, and many objections having been made to granting the spot referred to in said article, it was voted to dissolve the meeting."[1] This was equivalent to an absolute refusal to grant the request. Such decisive action by the town, after full discussion, settled the question for one generation at least, and it may be hoped for all generations, that neither individuals nor societies should be permitted to disturb the ashes of "the rude forefathers of the hamlet." Up to this time, no further attempt has been made to diminish the size of this old grave-yard. It has long ceased to be used for the burial of the recent dead, partly because it would be difficult to find a spot not already occupied, and partly because a more commodious and more attractive cemetery has been provided; but it has not been unduly neglected, nor is its appearance, as a disused burial-place, discreditable to the town.

[1] A similar application had been rejected, May 5, 1828, when it was "voted not to grant the First Calvinistic Society a spot for a meeting-house lot, either on the northwest corner of the burying-ground, or on the southerly part of the Common."

As early as 1804 it was found that the burying ground had been made too small by its recent reduction in size, and a committee was appointed to select another place. At a town meeting, May 6, 1805, it was "voted that the committee chosen last year for the purpose of procuring a suitable spot for a burying-yard, be empowered to purchase one as central as they can find." No purchase was made, however, until January 11, 1815, when a committee reported in favor of buying one acre and a half [1] of the Rev. Thomas Holt, and were authorized to close the bargain on the proposed terms. This lot has been several times enlarged by the purchase of another acre on the north side, November 12, 1849, afterwards of an adjoining tract, on the east side, of Mr. John Paige, and April 3, 1876, of somewhat more than two acres on the south side, of Mr. Joseph C. Paige. No lack of care or attention in regard to this cemetery is chargeable to the town or to individuals. It is very substantially fenced and ornamented by trees. Many monuments have been erected, and the head-stones are generally of a good character, and preserved clean and erect. Altogether, it is one of the neatest, well-ordered cemeteries in that section of the country. The first person buried here was Mr. Lendall Whipple, who had a few days previously assisted in erecting the stone inclosure, and who died November 21, 1817, aged nearly twenty-two years. The oldest person was probably Mrs. Sibillah Dexter (successively the wife of Mr. Samuel Thurston, and of Captain Samuel Dexter, both of Hardwick), who died at New Braintree, July 13, 1849, at the age of one hundred years, as inscribed on her head-stone, and on the Town Record of New Braintree. The head-stone of Mr. Asahel Billings, who died July 16, 1838, represents him to have attained the age of one hundred years; and the Town Record calls him 99; both overrate his age, which probably did not exceed 97, and was equalled or exceeded by that of three others, at least: Mrs. Mary, widow of Daniel Billings, who died June 8, 1835, aged 97; Mrs. Hannah, widow of David Aiken, who died July 28, 1837, aged 97; and Mrs. Olive, widow of Ephraim Ruggles, who died August 3, 1858, aged 98.

About the commencement of the present century, a burial-place was established in the southwesterly part of the town, near the place where the Baptist meeting-house stood. It contains

[1] Situated about a quarter of a mile north of the Common, at the intersection of the roads leading to Petersham and to Barre.

many graves, a reasonable proportion of which are designated by suitable memorials. The earliest date which I observed is on the head-stone of Abel Burt, son of Rev. Ebenezer Burt, who died June 23, 1803, aged 9 months. The greatest age denoted on any head-stone is that of Mr. Samuel L. Robinson, who died January 18, 1863, aged 95 ; and nearly approaching this is the age of Mr. Henry Higgins, who died March 15, 1837, aged 94. It is highly probable that Mr. Jesse Snow, who died in June, 1825, aged 96, was buried here, but no head-stone is found where it might be expected to stand, near that of his wife, Mrs. Mary Snow, who died February 5, 1813, aged 77.[1] Much credit is due to those who have charge of this cemetery for keeping it in so good condition in all respects.

In the northerly part of the town, near Barre, is a very neat inclosure, apparently a private burial-place belonging to the Taylor family. The earliest date is on the head-stone of Seth Taylor, who died July 7, 1811, aged 66, and the greatest age is inscribed on that of Sylvanus Taylor, who died April 5, 1849, aged 75.

In the old cemetery, near the Common, in addition to the poetical inscriptions, common to others at the same date, a few are found which appear to be original: —

In memory of Capt.
Ebenezer Cox who died
March ye 2^{d} 1768 in y^{e}
42^{d} year of his age.

Beneath this stone a noble Captain's laid
Which for his King and Country was displayed
His courage that no terrors could disarm
Nor when he fac'd ye foe his fears alarm
But now he's conquer'd and ye silent grave
Can boast that power ye French could never have
Under his care his soldiers were secure
Equal with them all hardships he'd endure
In six campaigns intrepid trod ye field
Nor to ye Gallic Power would ever yield
At last he's gone we hope where Wars do cease
To spend a whole Eternity in Peace.

On a large head-stone, erected agreeably to a vote of the town, the following epitaphs are inscribed in parallel columns: —

[1] It is not unlikely that the Rev. Ebenezer Burt, who died at Athol, November 25, 1861, aged nearly 96, was buried here, by the side of his wife and two sons, and near the spot where he had faithfully preached the gospel for many years.

Sacred to the memory of the REV^D DAVID WHITE who died Jany ye 6th 1784 in ye 74th year of his age. He was the first minister settled in the Town and faithfully and conscientiously performed the sacred functions of his office for almost 50 years to the great edification and enlargement of his Church and the universal peace & tranquillity of the Town.

Adieu to sickness pain and death
Adieu to vanities and cares
Submissive I resign my breath
And rise to Bliss beyond the stars.

Almighty Father hear my prayer
And send salvation to this land
May this my people be thy care
And ever dwell at thy right hand.

Sacred to the memory of MRS. SUSANNA WHITE consort of the REV^D DAVID WHITE who died July ye 17th 1783, in the 69th year of her age. She lived a life of unexampled Piety and Virtue and of the greatest Patience and Resignation under her long continued bodily indisposition and died in the firm hope of a Glorious Immortality.

With heartfelt Joy I yield my breath
And quit a life of pain and woe
Rejoicing pass the scene of death
To live where Joys forever flow.

New transports now inspire my frame
With joys celestial and sublime
O may you catch the heavenly flame
And soar beyond the reach of time.

Hail kindred spirits of the etherial skie
We come to visit your divine abode
To spend a long Eternity on high
To love adore and bless our Saviour God.

A large stone of peculiar shape stands near the centre of the cemetery, denoting the grave of a "beloved physician," and bearing this inscription: —

SPE
SALUTIS
ETERNE

In memory of Doct^r
CHARLES DOOLITTLE who died
June 12th 1785 in the 37th
Year of his age.

Beneath this dust in ruin lies
A man once virtuous just and wise
He view'd his death approaching near
And gave his life without a tear
Now we commit with sacred trust
His body to the mould'ring dust
His soul we trust has wing'd its way
To realms of light and endless day.

At the grave of ROSAMOND WINSLOW, who died September 13, 1803, aged 18 (long commemorated by her contemporaries as a maiden of remarkable beauty and amiability), a head-stone bears a stanza which expresses the idea so frequently found in early grave-yard literature, but clothed in a form of simplicity and tenderness which I do not remember to have seen elsewhere: —

> Oh, my dear friend, I once like you
> Did stand such monuments to view;
> But with me here you soon must be
> And others stand and read of thee.

CHAPTER XI.

ECCLESIASTICAL HISTORY.

Meeting-house and Ministry. — Mr. Ephraim Keith. — Church organized. — Rev. David White ordained. — First Meeting-house. — Sharp Controversy concerning the Location of the Second Meeting-house. — Unwillingness to contract Debts. — People seated anew in the Meeting-house. — Deacon Paige absents himself from the Communion and is censured. — Ecclesiastical Council. — Deacon Paige resigns Office, and unites with the Church in Petersham. — Deacon Robinson resigns Office, and becomes a Deacon in the Separate Church. — Changes in the Manner of Singing and also in the Versions of the Psalms sung. — Deacon Allen absents himself from the Communion, alleging a lack of Discipline in the Church; but is afterwards pacified, and returns to his Official Duty. — Third Meeting-house, a Magnificent Structure. — Abortive Attempt to settle a Colleague Pastor. — Death and Character of Rev. David White, and of his Wife. — Deacon Allen elected Moderator of the Church. — Attempts to settle a Pastor. — Rev. Thomas Holt ordained. — Confession of Faith and Covenant. — Rev. Mr. Holt appeals in vain for an Increase of Salary; his Dismission and subsequent Labors. — Pastorate of Rev. William B. Wesson. — Division of the Original Parish. — The Congregational Society settle Rev. John M. Merrick and Rev. John Goldsbury; afterwards unite with the Universalist Society. — New Meeting-house. — Pastors. — The Calvinistic Society settle Rev. Martyn Tupper. — Confession of Faith. — Meeting-houses. — Pastors. — Deacons.

When the General Court, in June, 1732, granted to the proprietors of this township a little more than one third part of the territory which their ancestors had purchased from the Indians, the boon was conferred "on the conditions following, viz.: That they within the space of five years settle and have on the spot sixty families (the settlers to be none but such as are natives of New England), each settler to build a good and convenient dwelling-house of one story high, eighteen feet square, at the least, and clear and bring to four acres fit for improvement, and three acres more, well stocked with English grass, and also lay out three shares throughout the town, each share to be one sixty third part of the said town, one share for the first settled minister, one for the ministry, and the other for the school; and also build a convenient meeting-house, and settle a learned and orthodox minister within the term aforesaid."

In conformity with these conditions, the proprietors voted February 21, 1732–3, "that ten acres of land be reserved, near the centre of said tract, to set a meeting-house on, and for a burial-place, and a training-field." On the next day they directed a committee to "lay out one hundred and eleven lots, . . . viz., four lots to each proprietor's share, sixty settlers, and the lots for the ministry, and school;" also, "unanimously voted, that each settler pay into the hands of the committee, upon his drawing his lot, the sum of five pounds towards the defraying the charges of surveying, &c., and the further sum of ten pounds,[1] each for the building a meeting-house within the space of three years after his being admitted." It was also voted, December 27, 1733, "That the proprietors pay the sum of forty-eight pounds, which is to be raised equally out of each whole share, to help pay a minister for preaching the gospel amongst the inhabitants there, for one year next after the 2d day of May next. Also voted that the settlers, both resident and non-resident, pay fifteen shillings each, as their part and proportion of a further encouragement for a minister to preach; and that Mr. Timothy Ruggles be desired to procure some suitable person to serve them for the same."

The first person employed, under this arrangement, was apparently Mr. Ephraim Keith, who probably commenced his labors at the time specified, May 2, 1734, and continued through the year. At a meeting of the proprietors, September 10, 1735, it was "voted, that the parcel of land lying between Draper's lot, No. 1, and Esq. Willis's lot, No. 2, about fifty or sixty acres, be granted to the Rev. Mr. Ephraim Keith, for his preaching to the people at a place called Lambstown last year, in full discharge of his due from said proprietors, his accepting the same, and likewise a note of fifteen pounds ten shillings of Mr. Joseph Haskell, of Rochester, and he to have full power to receive the same." Whether he continued to preach here for a longer period does not appear. He was at Petersham a few Sabbaths in 1736,[2] but soon abandoned the ministry, having

[1] Ten pounds each for "sixty settlers," amounted to six hundred pounds, one half of which sum was expended before September 7, 1738, and the remainder, which was a fruitful source of difficulty between the settlers and the proprietors, was afterwards styled the "three hundred pounds," or the "ten pounds," until the matter was fully settled, March 7, 1747–8.

[2] "The first preaching in this place was probably in the month of May, 1736. On the 16th of June, of that year, Mr.

never been ordained. He was son of Joseph, and grandson of Rev. James Keith of Bridgewater, born in 1707, grad. H. C. 1729, and, after a brief service in the pulpit, returned to his native town, and devoted himself to agriculture. He was appointed justice of the peace in 1762, and died about 1781.

Rev. David White seems to have commenced preaching as a candidate for settlement about July, 1736. At a meeting April 4, 1737, it was "voted that the sum of twenty-eight pounds and sixteen shillings be raised, to pay Mr. David White for his service in the ministry, for his victualling and horse-keeping, for the quarter of a year before his ordination;" also "that the year wherein Mr. White's salary be paid begin the first of October." Also voted, "that the sum of fifty pounds be raised for the Rev. Mr. White, for his half year salary, beginning October the first Anno Dom. 1736." A permanent arrangement of the salary was made March 6, 1737–8, when it was voted "that the town give the Rev. Mr. David White for his yearly salary one hundred pounds per year, for five years successively, beginning at the first of Oct. Anno Domini 1736; and a further sum and sums from year to year for ten years next coming, namely, one hundred and five pounds to be paid at the expiration of the [[1]] year, from the aforesaid first of Oct. 1736; and to increase the said sum, five pounds a year, yearly, until his yearly and stated salary shall come to one hundred and fifty pounds: and that sum, namely, one hundred and fifty pounds to be paid him yearly during his continuance in the work of the Gospel ministry in this place; and the said sum of money to be paid in the common currency of this Province, at the rate and in the proportion that Bills of Credit are now valued with silver money, namely, reckoning twenty-seven [2] shillings in Bills equal to one ounce of silver."

Soon after the commencement of Mr. White's labors, a church was organized in Hardwick (then called Lambstown), and on the same day he was ordained to the work of the ministry. These solemnities, together with the preliminary proceedings, are duly entered upon "The Church Record;" to wit:—

"Lambstown, Oct. 20, 1736. The members of other churches, living in Lambstown, met together and concluded upon the following particulars respecting Church Government, viz:

Ephraim Keith was paid fifty shillings a day for three days preaching past." Willson's *Address at Petersham*, July 4, 1854, p. 29.

[1] Record mutilated.

[2] A modification was made September 22, 1746, when it was "voted to allow Mr. David White's salary to be at thirty-six shillings per ounce for the present year." At a later day the salary was reduced to one hundred pounds per annum, exclusive of the income of the ministerial land.

"1. That there should be no relation required of those that are received into the church.

"2. That after the minister has taken an account of the knowledge and faith of those that have a desire to come into the church, and is well satisfied therewith, that they shall be received into full communion in the church upon their making a public confession of their faith.

"3. That the power of calling church meetings lay in the power of the minister.

"4. That Messi. Christopher Paige and George Abbot should sign letters missive to the Pastor and Delegates of several churches, to gather a church in Lambstown and ordain Mr. David White Pastor thereof.

"November ye 17th 1736. A Church was gathered and imbodied in Lambstown, and the members of the church publicly invited and chose Mr. David White to be their pastor. Accordingly, the same day, the said Mr. David White was ordained Pastor of the Church of Christ in Lambstown [1] by prayer and laying on of hands of the Presbytery.

"The names of the men that solemnly entered into a church state in Lambstown, that before were members of other churches: — Christopher Paige, George Abbot, Thomas Perry, Joseph Allen, John Wells, John Kidder, Richard Church. The names of the men that entered into a church in Lambstown, which before were not members in full communion in other churches, but were then received into the church: — Eleazar Warner, Nathan Carpenter, Experience Johnson, Samuel Robinson, Samuel Gillet.[2]

"Dec. ye 3^{d} 1736. The Church of Christ in Lambstown met together, and after a unanimous vote to choose two men to the office of Deacons in said church, Mr. Christopher Paige and Mr. Joseph Allen were chosen to the office of Deacons, by a majority of the votes of the church.

[1] The names of the Ordaining Council are not recorded; but the moderator was Rev. William Williams, probably pastor of the church in Hatfield, where Mr. White was born. The Proprietors voted, June 29, 1737, "that the two hundred acres of land, laid out by Mr. Timothy Ruggles and Mr. Christopher Paige to the first settled minister, be settled on and recorded to the Reverend Mr. David White, now their settled minister (as appears by the moderator, Mr. William Williams), to him his heirs and assigns forever."

[2] Whether it were the usual custom, at that period, to exclude females from participating in the organization of a church, or not, it is certain that several women were here at this time, who did not become members until two or three months later, although they were members of other churches, in good standing.

"Oct. ye 9th 1737. The Church voted, that no person living in Lambstown, formerly belonging to another church, shall have liberty to partake of the sacrament of the Lord's Supper without a letter of recommendation, after they have had a sufficient time to get one, without a good and sufficient reason why they have not done it." [1]

Having organized a church, and settled a pastor with a fixed salary, it became necessary to devise ways and means for the regular payment of that salary. By a vote of the Proprietors, February 22, 1732–3, each settler was bound to pay fifteen shillings per year, "to help pay a minister for preaching the gospel," and each of the twelve proprietors was pledged to contribute four pounds for the same purpose. But these several sums, namely: forty-eight pounds by the proprietors, and forty-five pounds by the sixty settlers, amounted to no more than ninety-three pounds, while the salary promised was one hundred pounds, with a prospective increase to one hundred and fifty pounds. At the present time, such a small deficiency may seem scarcely worthy of notice; but in the "day of small things," it was a matter of great importance to the pioneers. The settlers, not yet fully incorporated as a town, had no power to tax the unimproved lands, and the proprietors did not impose such a tax. Indeed, it would seem that they discontinued their annual contribution of forty-eight pounds, after partial town privileges were granted to the inhabitants.[2] The burden was heavy, and an appeal was made to the General Court for authority to tax all the land in the township, whether improved or not, and whether owned by resident or non-resident proprietors; also for incorporation as a town, with full authority to raise money for all lawful purposes, by taxation. The Court records do not indicate whether the petition for liberty to impose a tax was granted, or rejected; but it is certain that the proprietors secured a delay of incorporation for one year. The inhabitants became impatient; and at two meetings, October 19, and November 2, 1738, resolved on another effort for incorporation, and liberty to tax the lands of all proprietors. Their agent, Mr. Christopher Paige, presented their petition December 8, 1738. A committee of the proprietors remonstrated. But on the 15th day of the same month the

[1] Thus far, I have copied the Church Record in full.

[2] The town appointed a committee, November 6, 1741, "to adjust accounts with the committee which was empowered to sell land for the payment of the three forty-eight pounds towards the support of the minister in this town."

petition was granted; a tax of three half pence per acre on all the land in the township was authorized to be assessed annually for three years, to be applied "one half thereof to the Reverend Minister there for his better encouragement and more comfortable support, the residue for building and finishing a handsome Meeting-house, for the better accommodating the inhabitants in attending the public worship of God;" and the agent was empowered to bring in a bill for the incorporation of the township. This bill, having passed both Houses, received the Governor's approval, January 10, 1739.

It does not appear from the Records when the first meeting-house was erected; but the inhabitants held a meeting in it February 9, 1736–7. It was probably not very large or elegant. The bills allowed for materials and labor appear to have been less than fifty pounds. It was not entirely finished until after August 8, 1738, when it was "voted that the town will finish shingling the old meeting-house, and finish the seats, and make forms as shall be needed, and build the minister's pew."[1] Its size and value may be estimated by the fact that the town voted, March 1, 1742–3, to dispose of it "at a vendue, and accordingly sold it to James Robinson for sixteen pounds, old tenor." This first meeting-house was erected on the "ten acres" originally devoted to public use, and probably stood on the easterly side of the old road, long ago discontinued, running southerly from the present residence of Mr. John W. Paige, nearly parallel with the turnpike, to the road to Ware. It is not unlikely that the precise spot was about midway between the two points last indicated, at the northwest corner of the "ten acres," the spot which was afterwards given by the proprietors, for a similar use, to "those people called the separate Society in Hardwick."[2]

Wherever this house stood, like those generally erected by

[1] The town had voted, January 16, 1737–8, to "build a new meeting-house;" but the controversy concerning its location was so sharp, that it was not erected until more than three years after that date.

[2] In my address at the Centennial Celebration in 1838, it was stated that this meeting-house "stood on the Common, about midway between the two present meeting-houses;" and that the new house, erected in 1741, was "placed within ten feet of the old one," pp. 19-21. From whom I received this tradition I do not remember. I consulted several of the "oldest inhabitants," more than forty years ago, and gathered from them much traditional lore; but in this case I was misinformed. The town voted July 29, 1740, to "set the meeting-house on the ten acres, on which the old meeting-house stands." But the present Common was not a part of the "ten acres" as has already been stated. The old meeting-house, therefore, did not stand on the present Common, but probably about half a mile northwesterly from it, near the summit of the hill.

pioneers it was small and inconvenient, designed only for temporary use; moreover its location was unsatisfactory. Accordingly it was voted, January 16, 1737-8, "that the town will build a new meeting-house: that said meeting-house be built fifty feet long, and forty feet wide, and twenty-two feet between joints, and set two feet from the ground: that Joseph Allen, John Wells, Christopher Paige, Benjamin Smith, and Benjamin Ruggles, be a committee to see to the building or letting out said frame, and finish the outside, and glaze the same with square glass set in wood, according to their discretion." A week later, under a warrant "to see whether the town will choose a man to go down to the Proprietors' Committee to see whether they have power to dispose of the three hundred pounds that was voted to build the meeting-house," and for other purposes, it was voted January 23, 1737-8, "that Deacon Christopher Paige be chosen to carry a letter to the Proprietors' Committee, and to bring an answer back: — that the new meeting-house be raised by the first of July next, provided the three hundred pounds come from the Proprietors: — that the meeting-house be set on "Gamblin's Lot,[1] on the east side of the Great Meadow Brook." At the next meeting of the Proprietors, September 7, 1738, it was "Voted, that the Proprietors are willing that a new meeting-house be built, provided it be set on the spot of land already agreed upon by the Proprietors and settlers:[2] and that a committee be chosen out of the Proprietors to join with the committee that the settlers shall choose, to agree upon the dimensions of the house, and other things necessary in order to effect the building a convenient house for the public worship of God there: and that the remaining part of the six hundred pounds, which is three hundred, formerly agreed upon by the Proprietors, to be for the building a meeting-house, be applied to that use and no other whatsoever." The town appointed a committee, October 2, 1738, "to join with the Proprietors' committee, to agree upon the dimensions of the meeting-house," etc., and another committee

[1] "Gamblin's Lot," on the easterly road to Gilbertville, about a mile southeasterly from the Common and marked "J. Marsh" on the R. map, was afterwards the homestead of Timothy Paige, Esq., and is now owned by Mr. E. L. B. Wesson. Like the northwesterly corner of the "ten acres," where the first meeting-house probably stood, on the brow of a hill, it commanded an extensive prospect in every direction, and was a more eligible site for a meeting-house than that which was finally selected, except that it was not so near the centre of the township.

[2] What action was had by the proprietors in the subsequent controversy does not appear, as their records from September 7, 1738, to April 6, 1743, have been destroyed.

November 2, 1738, "to agree with the Proprietors' committee upon things necessary in order to effect the building of a convenient meeting-house in Lambstown; and that the said committee may give to the Proprietors a discharge from building said meeting-house, upon their giving good security to the town of Lambstown for the payment of the three hundred pounds appropriated for the building of the aforesaid meeting-house."

The vote, adopted January 23, 1737-8, "that the meeting-house be set on Gamblin's Lot," occasioned a sharp controversy between the east and the west sections of the town, which continued two years and a half, until a compromise was effected by abandoning both the "ten acres" and the Gamblin Lot, and placing the house on the present Common. The violence of the contest, and the extreme measures adopted by one of the parties for the accomplishment of its favorite purpose, distinctly appears in the proceedings of a town-meeting, held in June 1739, under a warrant, "(1.) To see whether the town is willing and ready to set off the west part of the town, beginning at Rutland[1] Corner, and so to run a straight line to Muddy Brook, where the road runs over said Brook to go to Quoben;[2] — and then to run by said Brook to the south line of the town; and said land to be laid to Quoben. (2.) To see whether the town will choose a committee to go down to Boston, to treat with Quoben Committee on the affair," — it was "Voted, That the town is willing and ready to set off the land on the west side of Muddy Brook, and said land to be laid to Quoben: — that Benjamin Smith, Constant Merrick, Cornelius Cannon be a committee chosen to go down to Boston, to treat with Quoben Committee, or the Rev. Mr. Timothy Ruggles and John Foster Esq., on the affair: that the committee shall have but one man's pay for going to Boston aforesaid. Note. That Samuel Robinson hath entered his detest against the first and second articles in the warrant. Note. That David Sabin hath entered his detest against the first and second articles in the warrant. Note. That John Wells hath entered his detest against sending a committee to Boston. Note. That Experience Johnson hath entered his detest against sending a committee to Boston. Note. That Phinehas Powers hath entered his detest against sending down a committee to Boston." The proposition to "set off the west part of the town" to Quoben was persistently opposed and finally defeated. After wrangling for somewhat more than a year longer, the former decision

[1] Rutland West Wing, now Barre. [2] Or Quobbin, now Greenwich.

was reversed, and the majority voted, July 29, 1740, "that they will set the meeting-house on the ten acres on which the old meeting-house stands: — that whereas this town have stated a place to set the new meeting-house on, which will accommodate that part of the town next to Quoben as well as other parts of the town, that the vote that was passed in this town the last year, whereby they signified that they were ready and willing to have a part of this town set off to Quoben, be void and of none effect."

But this did not end the difficulty. The inhabitants of the east part of the town, though temporarily in the minority, made such a sturdy and formidable resistance, that it was not considered prudent to carry the last vote into execution. Accordingly another meeting was held, December 15, 1740, when it was voted "that they will choose a committee[1] to state a place where the meeting-house shall be set in this town, and that their judgement be a final determination of the affair: — Chose Capt. Josiah Convers, Mr. Elisha Rice, Mr. Noah Ashley, committee: — that all former committees about building the meeting-house in this town be dismissed: — chose Capt. Joseph Allen, Mr. Constant Merrick, John Foster, a committee: — that the committee last chosen shall have the care of building a meeting-house in this town, or to join with the original Proprietors' committee on the affair; and to purchase or otherwise provide land to set said meeting-house on; and that they forthwith proceed to get timber cut and lined, and proceed to have said house framed, and raised, and as far finished as the money will go that the settlers is to pay, and all the money raised or to be raised by the land tax, and to let it out if they shall think best: . . . Chose Mr. Eleazar Warner, Mr. John Wells,[2] to wait on the committee to state a place to set a meeting-house on, and to go or send to them, to desire them to come to state a place to set the meeting-house on." The committee seem to have selected a spot near the centre of the present Common, instead of the "ten acres" otherwise disposed of, by the sale of nine and a half acres, and the gift of half an acre to the "Separate Society." The erection of the long desired edifice during the ensuing year is indicated by a vote, November 23, 1741, to pay Samuel Robinson for rum and other refreshments, furnished at the "raising of the new meeting-house." The house was not finished, however, until several years later, though it was

[1] "Not belonging to this town," as expressed in the warrant.

[2] "Two men, one at each end of the town," as stated in the warrant.

made habitable. The proprietors did not promptly enforce the payment of the "three hundred pounds," and it was not easy to raise the funds necessary to complete the work.[1] When the town was ready to abandon and sell the old house, and did sell it, March 1, 1742–3, the third article in the warrant, "to see if the town will raise money . . . to build the pulpit and minister's pew, and body of seats," was passed over without action. The house seems to have been merely a shell at that time. Three years later, February 25, 1745–6, a settlement was made with the committee, by which it appeared that they had thus far expended £409. 9. 3. in the erection of the house; they had received of "money raised by the land-tax, £110. 1. 2.; and of the ten pounds they have received £243. 0. 0.;" in all £353. 1. 2. To meet the deficiency of £56. 8. 1., there was an uncollected balance of the land-tax £54. 18. 10., and of the ten pounds not yet gathered £57. 0. 0., in all £111. 18. 10. The account was not fully settled until December 23, 1747. Even then the house remained in an unfinished state; for two years later, December 25, 1749, it was "voted that the town will finish the meeting-house: — voted that they will finish it by plastering it;" and £300. 0. 0. was granted to Christopher Paige and Joseph Allen, to finish the inside of the house. This work seems to have been accomplished before August 29, 1750, when it was voted to seat the people anew, "the highest payers in the highest seats, having respect to age and other qualifications, except such as have pews in the meeting-house." The house contained a few pews; but the larger part of it, as was then customary, was occupied by long seats, called "the body of seats," for males on one side of the centre aisle, and for females on the other. Besides these, it seems several chairs were used; for it was voted, March 4, 1750–1, "that the chairs standing in the alleys be ordered into the place left behind the women seats, and to stand nowhere else." One more notice closes my account of this meeting-house: it was voted, March 4, 1754, "that the town refuse to let the young

[1] It had not yet become fashionable to contract enormous debts for the erection of meeting-houses, and the pioneers wisely avoided that folly. Indeed they submitted to great discomfort, occupying unfinished houses which furnished scant protection in inclement weather, in preference to assuming an indebtedness which might prove burdensome. Their perhaps extreme caution in this regard is manifest in their action at a town meeting August 14, 1741, "during Mr. White's indisposition," when it was "Voted, to hire a minister to preach in this town for two months, if the town shall need so long: — voted to choose a man to go to Mr. Frink, and see if he can hire him for a reasonable price: and if not, to hire another, — the best he can and cheapest."

men that have built a seat in the women's side galleries to have it there: voted, that the same persons have liberty to build their seat on the men's side gallery."

This long controversy in regard to the place of public worship must have grieved the heart of Rev. Mr. White, who was eminently a man of peace; but he probably lamented even more bitterly certain dissensions in the church itself, which sadly disturbed its harmony and prosperity, and which culminated in the resignation of two of its deacons in 1749. "The Church of Christ in Hardwick met together," September 9, 1747, "to hear and consider Deacon Christopher Paige's reasons for absenting himself from the public worship and ordinances of God." After due consideration, the church voted that his reasons did not furnish a satisfactory excuse, and accordingly laid him "under censure," and suspended him "from the sacrament of the Lord's Supper." Unwilling to cast off utterly a brother, who was not only their first elected deacon, but also one of the most active and honored citizens of the town, before proceeding to extremities the church voted, May 24, 1748, "that the Rev. Mr. Edwards, of Northampton, Mr. Billings, of Coldspring,[1] Mr. Abercrombie, of Pelham, Mr. Whitney, of Nitchawagg,[2] be applied to, to come to Hardwick and give their advice in the case that is between the church and Deacon Paige." The council assembled and gave advice; but the proceedings do not appear on record. "At a church meeting in Hardwick, December ye 20th, 1748, voted, that the church comply and fall in with the advice of the Rev. Ministers on the 29th day of June last, in the case depending between the church and Deacon Christopher Paige. Upon which it was proposed to Deacon Paige whether he would comply with the said advice, and he declared that he would not comply with the substance of it. Upon which declaration, the church voted, that Deacon Christopher Paige be proceeded with, by giving him the second admonition." Nothing further in regard to this case appears on record until April 13, 1749, when "Deacon Paige's desire of laying down the office of deacon was mentioned to the church, and the major part thereof complied with and gratified him in his desire, and dismissed him from said office of deacon."

The cause of this controversy between the church and its senior deacon does not appear on record, nor has it been preserved even by tradition. On the one hand, we cannot well suppose it to have been of a trivial character, as it involved such

[1] Now Belchertown. [2] Now Petersham.

serious results. On the other, there is no evidence of aggravated guilt on either side. The council which met June 29, 1748, either exonerated the church from blame, or administered so slight a rebuke and required so little concession, that it was voted, December 28, 1748, "that the church comply and fall in with the advice of the Rev. Ministers." And although Deacon Paige "declared that he would not comply with the substance of it," he evidently had not forfeited his good name as a Christian and as a trustworthy citizen: — at the first town-meeting after the decision of the council he was elected moderator, selectman, and assessor, to which offices he was reëlected the next year, after he had resigned the office of deacon; and the church in Petersham, whose pastor had been a member of the advising council and fully understood the merits or demerits of the whole case, admitted him to fellowship in full communion. Whereupon, "At a church meeting in Hardwick, May ye 20th, 1752, Voted (1.) To send to the church in Nichawaug, to signify to them that we look upon their conduct in receiving Deacon Christopher Paige into their church to be irregular, and matter of just offence, and to desire a brotherly conference with them, to make up the difference. (2.) Voted, that Mr. White, Deacon Freeman, Deacon Allen, Deacon Cooper, Nathaniel Whitcomb, Lieut. Merrick, and Ensign Warner, undertake this business as a committee. The said committee are empowered by the church to make up the whole difference with the church at Nichawaug respecting their receiving Deacon Paige, if they can agree; if not, to propose to them to join with us in the choice of a council to advise in the matter." What response was made by the Petersham church does not appear. So far as the Hardwick records show, the whole matter rested for nearly twenty years, until June 21, 1770, when it was voted "that this church do overlook what the church of Christ in Petersham formerly did relative to Deacon Christopher Paige, and are now in charity with said church." This was a substantial acknowledgment that no good reason existed why he should be debarred from Christian privileges.

Troubles seldom come singly. "At a church meeting in Hardwick March ye 2^d^, 1748 (1748–9) Deacon Samuel Robinson desired the church that he might lay down his office of deacon in said church; which desire the church complied with."[1] Like

[1] No record is found of any election to fill the vacancy occasioned by the resignation of two deacons; but the election of John Cooper is distinctly indicated by the fact that, on his admission to the church, March 1, 1746–7, he was called simply "John Cooper;" but when his wife was admitted, July 9, 1751, she was styled "wife of Deacon John Cooper."

his senior in office, Deacon Robinson was an active and energetic leader in public affairs, and his secession tended to weaken the church, through its effect on many of its members. He held office a short time. "April ye 30th, 1746. At a church meeting in Hardwick, Samuel Robinson was chosen to the office of a deacon in said church, by a majority of the members; which office he afterwards accepted." His delay, if not actual hesitancy, in accepting the office probably foreshadowed his reason for resigning it so soon. About this time an extraordinary wave of religious excitement passed over New England and engulfed many churches. The controversy waxed so sharp and bitter that many withdrew from the established churches, and were thenceforth styled "New Lights," or more generally "Separates," of whom more will be said in another place. In this movement Deacon Robinson was early interested, and became a prominent leader. He felt constrained, therefore, to "lay down his office." It does not appear that there was any other cause for his resignation. The church afterwards called him and several of his associates to account, and censured them for withdrawing "from the public worship of God at the meeting-house in Hardwick;" but there is no evidence that any of them were excommunicated from the church for that offence.[1]

For the next thirty years the records indicate almost uninterrupted peace and harmony in the church. Few cases of discipline are mentioned, and these of such a nature that the offenders were forgiven, and "admitted to former privileges."

A change was made in regard to the psalms and hymns proper to be sung, and to the manner of singing them. "March 10, 1765. It being moved to the church after public exercise on the Sabbath, whether Messieurs Tate and Brady's version of the Psalms should be sung in the public worship of God, — voted in the affirmative."[2] "At a church meeting held in Hardwick at the meeting-house, June 21, 1770, voted, with respect to the present method of singing in public worship, that one half of the portion that shall be sung shall be read, line by line, as has been the former practice in this Congregation, sung in some old tune; that

[1] There is no record of excommunication, for any cause whatever, during Mr. White's ministry.

[2] President Dunster's revision of the Bay Psalm Book had probably been in use up to this time. Tate and Brady's version was used, until the town voted, March 7, 1791, "that Doct. Watts' Psalms and Hymns be introduced to be sung in this town, in the room of Tate's and Brady's; and that they are to begin to be sung in the congregation within three months." Various changes have been made more recently.

the other half shall be sung without being thus read in some new tune; that the psalm or hymn that shall be appointed to be sung at the Communion Table shall be read, line by line, and sung in some old tune, so called." The change, thus partially made, became entire at a later period; but it was exceedingly disagreeable to many, and of some it is said they would leave the meeting-house while psalms or hymns were sung without having been read, line by line, and return after this offensive exercise was concluded.[1]

About this time two deacons were elected: November 9, 1769, "Capt. William Paige was chosen to the office of deacon, by a great majority of votes," probably in the place of Deacon John Cooper, who seems to have died, or removed a few months previously; and April 28, 1774, "Mr. John Bradish was chosen to be a deacon in said church, by a majority of votes." Soon afterwards, however, danger of losing an important officer appeared in an unexpected quarter. The senior surviving deacon was so much exercised in spirit by the shortcomings of his brethren, that he absented himself from the Lord's Supper, and in rendering reasons for so doing, preferred grave charges against the church in general, and one of its members in particular. The proceedings are recorded under date of February 1, 1779: "Deacon Joseph Allen having withdrew himself from the sacrament of the Lord's Supper, he gave in his reasons in writing to the Reverend Pastor, Mr. White, which are these: (1.) The young people walking disorderly on the Sabbath, both in time of public worship and in the intermission season. (2.) The youth frequently gathering in set frolics at a public house, and carrying them on with music and dancing, both males and females, and many of them using profane language. (3.) That he suspected that there were some in this town that had owned the baptismal covenant, and promised publicly that they would perform the duties of it, yet that they walked disorderly, and neglected family prayer. (4.) That there were some in full communion in this church, that absented themselves from the sacrament of the Lord's Supper,

[1] While I would not willingly return to the old method of alternate reading and singing of hymns, "line by line," yet I confess my deep sympathy with these old saints in what many will regard as their unreasonable prejudice as to the manner of conducting public worship. I have often been sorely tempted to leave the sanctuary during an exhibition of vocal gymnastics, when fashionable opera-music, dramatically rendered by professional artists, was substituted for the unostentatious singing of "psalms, and hymns, and spiritual songs," by a voluntary choir or by a Christian congregation.

and also neglected public worship, and yet were not called to give the reasons of their neglect of these ordinances. (5.) The special reason why he withdrew at that time was the conduct of a Brother, viz., Thomas Robinson, at the last church meeting and the town-meeting following, which appeared to him not of a piece, not in the simplicity of the gospel, not agreeable to the Scripture.

"The church were regularly called and assembled together to hear Deacon Allen's reasons, at the meeting-house in Hardwick, on Wednesday, Feb. 24, 1779, and after a consideration of the abovementioned matters of grievance, came into the following resolves : — *Article* 1. Young people walking disorderly on the Sabbath; resolved, that the March meeting being near at hand, when tyding-men[1] and wardens are to be chosen for the year, whose special business it is to inspect and prevent all disorder on the Sabbath, this affair is submitted to and left with them, as their proper business. *Article* 2. As to young people gathering together in set frolics, especially at a public house, resolved, that we will every one of us here present, that are heads of families, take all proper care that the youth under our care and charge, to prevent them from running into these frolics, and acting any part in them. *Article* 3. As to those persons that are called half-members[2] &c., resolved, that we will keep a watch over them, according to our solemn promise when we received [them] into their present standing in the church; that we will reprove them when we see them walk disorderly, and encourage them to the practice of virtue and piety by our counsels and our good practice. *Article* 4. That there were some persons in full communion in this church that absented themselves from the public worship of God and the sacrament of the Lord's Supper; two persons were named in particular; resolved, that (these persons not being present) the Rev. Mr. White shall send to them, to know their reasons of their neglect of these holy ordinances, and when obtained of them he lay them before the church to consider whether [the] reasons are a sufficient excuse or not. *Article* 5. The special reason given why he withdrew himself at that time was the conduct of a Brother, viz., Thomas Robinson, &c. The church having considered and weighed this matter, some few of the church voted that said Robinson his changing the side that he first held with was an evidence that he had changed his mind;

[1] Tything-men.

[2] Those who had taken the "half-way covenant," in order that their children might be baptized, but were not qualified to participate in the Lord's Supper; or such as the record describes as "received into the covenant, and under the watch and government of the church."

but the majority of the church thought that the matter did not belong to them to determine, and therefore declined voting any way; and thus the matter was left respecting Deacon Allen and Thomas Robinson, and no further determination or [illegible] upon it."[1]

It would seem that the meeting-house erected about 1741 proved unsatisfactory, and in little more than a quarter of a century, preparations were made for the erection of a new one, equal if not superior in size and magnificence to any church edifice in the county. September 7, 1767, "Voted that the town will build a meeting-house in Hardwick for public worship. Voted, that they will set said house (if they can purchase the land) in the field at the north end of the burying place, occupied by Mr. Asa Hatch." This field contained somewhat more than one acre and three quarters of land, and was owned by John Rowe, Esq., of Boston, who conveyed it to the town for £6. 13. 4. by deed dated May 30, 1768.[2] Without waiting for the execution of the deed, the town proceeded at once to make arrangements for the erection of the house, and on the 21st of October accepted the report of a committee previously appointed: "The committee have heard the proposals of Deac. Joseph Allen and Mr. Joseph Safford, who are willing and ready to undertake the building of said house, and finish it in a workmanlike manner, only for the benefit of the money they can raise by the sale of the pews agreeable to a plan herewith humbly laid before the town for their consideration. TIM° RUGGLES, in the name of the committee." "Voted that the town will choose a committee to contract with Deac. Joseph Allen and Mr. Joseph Safford to build a meeting-house, as mentioned in the report of the former committee.[3] Voted that Mr. Daniel Oliver, Brig^r. Ruggles, Capt. Mandell, Deac. Fay,[4] and Capt. Paige, be the committee. Voted, to build a steeple to said house, and that the town pay what said steeple shall cost more than a convenient porch for stairs into the galleries." May 16, 1768, "Voted the sum of £66. 13. 4. to the un-

[1] I have somewhat anticipated the regular succession of events, in order to group together all the recorded difficulties between the church and its deacons during Mr. White's pastorate.

[2] The description is "one acre, three quarters, and six rods of land, lying in said Hardwick, adjoining to the public burying-place there, bounded as followeth: beginning at the northerly corner of said burying-place, and from thence running northerly, by the road, 22 rods; then turning at right angles, and running easterly 13 rods; there turning at right angles, and running southerly 22 rods; there turning at right angles, and running westerly, by the burying-place, 13 rods to the bounds first mentioned." *Worcester Deeds*, lix. 113.

[3] The "undertakers" are said to have lost money.

[4] James Fay was deacon of the "Separate Church" until it removed bodily to Bennington, Vt., in 1761.

dertakers of the meeting-house, to enable them to proceed in building a steeple to said house." May 18, 1769, "Voted to raise £120 lawful money, to enable the undertakers to finish the steeple, besides what has already been voted," and "to choose a committee to treat with the undertakers, in order that they be obliged to finish the steeple for the above price." October 19, 1769, under a warrant "to see if the town will allow the undertakers of the meeting-house to build a pew in the steeple above the west gallery," it was "voted, to shut up the place in the steeple, over the west gallery, which was proposed for a pew." October 27, 1769, "Voted to grant the undertakers of the meeting-house the privilege of building a pew over the west gallery, providing they make it tight and close; and the town reserved the privilege of having an officer to set in the pew, to oversee the boys."[1] The house was finished probably not long before December 31, 1770, at which date it was "voted to choose a committee to seat the meeting-house [2] and that said committee consist of five persons; and made choice of Capt. William Paige, Lieut. Roland Sears, Deac. Joseph Allen, Capt. Constant Myrick, and Paul Mandell for said committee; and they to seat each person according to age and pay to the last year's valuation or invoice. Voted, that the front seats in the gallery be appropriated to the use of the men. The question was put, whether the town would grant the seats on the side galleries next the front gallery for the use of the men and women singers, and it passed in the negative.[3] Voted, that the town will purchase the pew, the west side the pulpit stairs, for the use of the minister's family for the time being, viz., to be kept by the town as a ministry

[1] The apprehensions expressed in this vote were not altogether unfounded. The pew was so high above the general level that its occupants were screened from observation. According to my recollection, seventy years ago, an officer to "oversee the boys" was more needed there than in any other part of the house.

[2] A "Body of Seats" was originally constructed, seven on each side of the centre aisle, for the use respectively of the men and women, who were not otherwise provided for, and who were "seated" by committees duly appointed.

[3] The "method of singing in public worship" had not then been changed. A convenient place was assigned February 1, 1779: "The committee appointed to consider what seats would be convenient for the singers, and what room necessary for that purpose, reported as follows: that they thought it would be proper to appropriate the west division of the front seat and the first and second seats in the division of the side gallery next adjoining, for said purpose; and the town accepted of the above report." Subsequently the east division of the front seat and the adjoining side gallery were substituted, and became a permanent location; and during the first quarter of the present century, it may be doubted whether better church music, both vocal and instrumental, was heard in the county, than that which was rendered by the voluntary choir who entered into that court with thanksgiving.

pew, at £26. 13. 4., being the sum set on the same by Deac. Joseph Allen and Joseph Safford, undertakers for building the meeting-house." August 19, 1771, under a warrant, "to see if the town would purchase the pew adjoining the pulpit, there not appearing persons as was proposed to purchase the same," it was voted, to buy the pew adjoining the pulpit,[1] and to keep it for their own use. "Voted, to give the undertakers of the meeting-house £20. lawful money, for said pew." As a proper adjunct to the temple for worship, the town voted, May 18, 1772, "to allow Deac. Joseph Allen 10^s 8^d for making the stocks."

Having completed the house, of which our ancestors were justly proud (for it was then one of the most elegant in the county), they took some measures for its preservation, which their less hardy descendants might not altogether approve. They voted, March 2, 1772, "that there be no stows carried into the new Meeting-house [2] with fire in them." How long this prohibition was enforced, I know not. It is certain, however, that foot-stoves were generally used in the house more than seventy years ago. But the larger stoves, designed to make the whole house comfortable, were not introduced until within the last fifty or sixty years. At the present day, it would be regarded as a painful sacrifice of bodily comfort, to sit in the midst of winter, without any fire in the house, to listen to a sermon one or two hours long, and other services of corresponding length; but the men who were preparing, and prepared, to march barefooted in the snow, and lodge on the cold ground, in defence of their liberties, could easily undergo such a slight inconvenience.

These were apparently the golden days of Mr. White; but they were soon overshadowed. The political excitement preceding and during the Revolutionary War so entirely engrossed public attention, that the church became comparatively inactive. For several years before 1779, scarcely any action directly affecting the interests of the church can be gleaned from the records of either the church or the town, in addition to what has already been mentioned. In 1779 the bodily infirmities of Mr.

[1] This pew was in front of the pulpit, and behind the deacon's seat. Several aged men occupied it, within my recollection, supposing they could hear the preacher more distinctly there than elsewhere; and hence probably it derived its amiliar name of "Deaf Pew." It was used by the pastor, during the celebration of the Lord's Supper. It was also occupied by the moderator, selectmen, and town clerk, at town-meetings, until the town house was erected.

[2] The old meeting-house was sold, March 2, 1772, at auction, for £44, to be removed within three months.

White, indicated by the employment of an assistant for two months, in 1741, before mentioned, seem to have increased to such an extent that the settlement of a colleague was considered desirable. Contrary to the usual custom, the town took the lead, and at a regular meeting, January 25, 1779, requested the church to unite with the town in giving a call to Mr. Joel Foster.[1] "Feb. 1, 1779. The church . . . being regularly called and assembled together at the meeting-house, to know the minds of the members of the church respecting giving a call to Mr. Joel Foster, to settle in the work of the ministry in said town, as a colleague with the Rev. Mr. White; the vote being put, there appeared thirteen members that were desirous of giving Mr. Joel Foster a call as above, and sixteen appeared against." The town was unwilling to yield the point entirely, and on the same day (February 1, 1779), voted, "to apply to Mr. Joel Foster, to preach the gospel in this town for a number of Sabbaths, and chose a committee for that purpose, viz., Jonathan Warner, Timothy Paige, Timothy Newton." The effort to obtain this manifestly favorite preacher was in vain, and he was soon ordained at New Salem. After this date, only two votes of the church appear on record during the ministry of Mr. White, the former of which, by the indefiniteness of its conclusion, indicates some failure of his mental energy: "July 5, 1781. The church regularly called and met at the meeting-house; this thing was proposed: (1) Whether it be the mind of the church that all baptized are visible members of the church, and under the special care and watch of it; voted in the affirmative: (2) If it be the mind of this church that the baptized persons under the care of this church, that are arrived to years of discretion, be called upon to see whether they own their baptismal vow or not; voted in the affirmative. Agreeable to the above vote, in a convenient time, it was moved in the congregation that all that was willing to comply with the above vote, by owning their baptismal vows, would show their consent by standing up; and a great number did, — too many to set down their names." The last

[1] Rev. Joel Foster, son of Nathan Foster, was born at Stafford, Conn., April 8, 1755, grad. D. C. 1777, was ordained at New Salem, June 9, 1779, dismissed for lack of competent support, January 21, 1802, and installed at East Sudbury (now Wayland), September 7, 1803, where he died in office, September 25, 1812. "He possessed excellent pulpit talents, and was specially gifted in prayer." 2 *Mass. Hist. Coll.*, iv. 62. He was brother to Rev. Daniel Foster, who was born at Stafford, in 1751, grad. D. C. 1777, was ordained at New Braintree, October 29, 1778, as colleague with Rev. Benjamin Ruggles, and died in office, September 4, 1795.

vote recorded by Mr. White had reference to the employment of an assistant in his labor: "May 13, 1782. At a church meeting regularly called and met in the meeting-house, it was put to vote whether they would invite Mr. Josiah Spaulden [1] to preach any more with us; and it passed in the affirmative by a very great majority." Although the ministry of Mr. Spalding did not result in his permanent settlement, it did produce a profound impression on the church and congregation. It does not appear at what precise date he commenced or ended his labor here; [2] but he was actively engaged May 13, 1782, and was then desired to continue; and the records show that during the eight months from December 30, 1781 to August 25, 1782, ninety-one persons were admitted to the church by profession, — a larger number than had been thus admitted during the preceding twenty years.[3]

Rev. David White, son of Deacon John and Mrs. Hannah (Wells) White, was born at Hatfield, July 1, 1710 (see Genealogies). He grad. Y. C. 1730, was ordained pastor of the first church in Hardwick on the day of its organization, November 17, 1736, and after a faithful ministry of more than forty-eight years died in office, January 6, 1784. His salary was small, and probably was never so much as three hundred dollars per annum, in silver money, though nominally more in paper currency. Yet on this sum, together with presents, and the fruits of his own industry, he managed to support his family, and to give both his sons a public education. His talents were respectable, but by no means brilliant. His success in giving satisfaction to his people depended not so much on the energy of his mind, as on the meekness, simplicity, and purity of his heart. He lived in a troublesome period, both political and ecclesiastical. Near the

[1] Rev. Josiah Spalding was born in Connecticut, grad. Y. C. 1778, was ordained at Uxbridge, September 11, 1783; dismissed October 23, 1787; installed at Worthington, August 21, 1788; dismissed in 1794; installed at Buckland, October 15, 1794; and died in office, May 8, 1823, aged 72. Of him and his predecessor at Uxbridge, Mr. Whitney says: they "were dismissed more on account of the peculiarity of their religious sentiments than anything beside." I suppose this "peculiarity" was what was denominated Hopkinsianism, or Hopkintonianism, about a hundred years ago. "He was one of the best men and one of the best ministers in the county." *Hist. of Worcester Co.*, p. 127; *Hist. of Western Mass.*, ii. 325.

[2] He was here June 15, 1782, when he preached "A Sermon on the Nature and Criminality of Man's Inability to serve the Lord," which was printed, and which forcibly exhibits the author's "peculiarity" of opinion, and his power as a revival preacher.

[3] During the pastorate of Mr. White there were added to the original twelve founders of the church, two hundred and eighty-six members by profession, and one hundred and thirteen by letter, in all, three hundred and ninety-nine, being an average of a fraction more than eight per annum. The baptisms were 1,275, including adults.

close of his life the Revolution occurred; and he shared the trials and distresses of his people. But he lived to witness the conclusion of hostilities, and the independence of his country. At a much earlier period, the elements of the ecclesiastical world were violently agitated. About the year 1740 a "new light," as it was called, was discovered. Parties were formed in various churches, who bitterly contended with each other, freely bandying the epithets of fanaticism, on the one hand, and formality, or legal righteousness, on the other. Some churches were rent asunder. And this church did not entirely escape the ravages of the storm which swept through the land. A portion of its members withdrew, and were styled "New Lights," or more generally "Separates." They erected a meeting-house, and established a regular meeting. Mr. White and his church manifested much forbearance, laboring with their dissatisfied, separating brethren, but never using the rod of excommunication. The effect of such measures was favorable. The separate party, as such, became extinct; some of its members removed from the town, and others were reconciled to the church; their meeting-house was demolished, and Mr. White had the happiness to behold again a state of harmony and peace in his parish. Thus, though he encountered storms during the journey of life, the evening of his days was calm and serene, and his sun went down in a clear sky. His wife (who was a niece of Thomas Wells, Esq., of Deerfield), had closed her pilgrimage about six months previously, July 17, 1783.[1] Their virtues are commemorated on their head-stone in the old burying-place, which was erected agreeably to a vote of the town, March 1, 1784, "to be at the cost of setting up grave-stones at Mr. White's grave, and also at Mrs. White's." A committee reported, May 8, 1786, that the grave-stones had been procured, at an expense of £7. 18. 0.; the bill of "Mr. Sikes," the stone-cutter, being £4. 10. 0., and bills for incidental expenses, paid to Captain Warner, David Allen, Benjamin Convers, Widow Doolittle, and Joseph Perry, amounting to £3. 8. 0.

The church met January 9, 1784, three days after the decease of Mr. White, "and made choice of Deac. Joseph Allen as their Moderator while destitute of a minister. Also voted to give the ministers who were bearers at the Rev. Mr. White's funeral,

[1] In the early part of this century, the uniform testimony of those who remembered Mrs. White was, that she was one of the excellent of the earth, and remarkable not only for her lady-like and Christian deportment, but also for her intellectual power, in which she was far superior to her husband.

each of them gloves." Prompt measures were taken to fill the vacancy occasioned by the death of Mr. White, but for a long time they were unsuccessful. The church appointed a meeting January 22, 1784, "in order to give Mr. Jedson[1] a call to settle in the work of the gospel ministry with us." The town concurred, February 10, 1784, by a vote of "45 for it, and 19 against it, the majority 26." At an adjourned meeting, February 16, 1784, it was proposed to reconsider this vote, "and there appeared 30 for it and 30 against it." The church then voted, June 3, 1784, "to give Mr. Medad Rogers a call to settle with us as a gospel minister in this place, by a number of fifty-three members present." The town concurred June 4, 1784 (12 aff. 1 neg.), and agreed to give Mr. Rogers £200 settlement, and £80 per annum while able to perform pastoral duty, and £40 per annum afterwards; or £100 per annum, and no settlement. At a church meeting, September 2, 1784, "then voted and appointed Wednesday the thirteenth day of October next to ordain Mr. Medad Rogers, Pastor over this church and congregation," and selected the members of the ordaining council. In this action of the church, the town also concurred on the next day, September 3, 1784. But for some reason, not stated in the record, the ordination was not accomplished. During these negotiations, the church met July 1, 1784, "to consult whether the practice of baptizing the children of those that own the covenant, as it is called, is warranted in scripture or not; after debating the matter calmly it was proposed to adjourn the meeting for further consideration. Then voted and adjourned said meeting to the 22^d day of July instant, having first voted that Mr. Rogers be desired to preach a sermon on said subject before the congregation. According to adjournment, the church met, and being opened by prayer, proceeded on the affair above named, and after further debating the matter, it was proposed to adjourn the meeting to Thursday the twelfth of August next,

[1] Rev. Adoniram Judson, born at Woodbury, Conn., June 25, 1751, grad. Y. C. 1775, was first settled in the ministry at Malden. "On the third of July, 1786, their call devolved on Rev. Adoniram Judson, on which occasion, Capt. John Dexter entered his protest upon the church records against 'settling a minister of the Bade Hopkintonian Principels.' After calling four councils he was ordained at last, amid a tempest of opposition, Jan. 23, 1787." He was dismissed in 1791; was installed at Wenham December 26, 1792; dismissed October 22, 1799; installed at Plymouth May 12, 1802; became a Baptist, and was dismissed in August, 1817. He died November 25, 1826. See *Bicentennial Book of Malden*, p. 166. The Hardwick church in 1784 was decidedly Hopkintonian in sentiment.

at three of clock afternoon: also voted, that those persons that have been heretofore admitted as half-way members,[1] as called, are desired to meet with the church at the same time, to hear their debates on the subject in hand. August twelfth: According to adjournment the church met, and opened by prayer; and after debating the case above named a suitable time it then was put to vote that the church would not admit any more to own the covenant, in order to baptize their children for the future." Thus, while destitute of a pastor, but with due deliberation, and probably under the lead of Deacon Allen, the church discontinued a custom which had existed in the New England churches for more than a century, and which had often been the cause of contention and heart-burnings. It continued in use, for the next half century, in some other churches, but has at last, it is supposed, been entirely abandoned.

At a church meeting, October, 1784, it was "put to vote to see if the church thinks it expedient to give Mr. Medad Rogers a call, a second time, to settle with us in the work of the gospel ministry in this place, and it passed in the affirmative by a number of voters, in favor 40, dissenters 7." The town concurred January 11, 1785, by a vote of 68 affirmative, 40 negative. This effort was fruitless, and the church voted, May 19, 1785, to give Mr. Judson a second call to become its pastor; the vote "passed in the affirmative by upwards of forty members." The town concurred, June 2, 1785, by a vote of 57 affirmative, 19 negative. This effort also failed, and a majority of the church, March 9, 1786, voted "to give Mr. Thomas Crafts a call to settle with us as a gospel minister;" but another meeting was held, March 23, 1786, "to reconsider the call given by this church, 9th in-

[1] "It was felt that the children of baptized persons should have a different position from Indians and other pagans who might hear the word of God. It was held by many, that if baptized parents, even if not regenerate, were willing to renew the baptismal covenant, and become subject to church discipline, their children could properly be baptized. This feeling and practice were growing up in the churches, when a synod of the elders and messengers of the churches was called. This was held in Boston in the spring of 1662. . . . In regard to the matter of baptism, the result was substantially that the members of the visible church are subjects of baptism, and that children are members of the same church with their parents, and when grown up are under the care of that church. But this does not of itself admit them to full communion. Yet when they understand and publicly profess the faith, and are upright in life, and own the covenant, and submit themselves to the government of the church, their children are to be baptized. . . . This decision in regard to baptism is known as the Half-way Covenant, inasmuch as it granted baptism to the children of certain persons who were not qualified for admission to the Lord's Table." McKenzie's *History of the First Church of Cambridge*, pp. 110, 111.

stant, to Mr. Thomas Crafts, to settle in this place as a gospel minister; then put to vote to recall as above, and it passed in the affirmative."[1] At a town-meeting, May 7, 1787, on the question of giving a call to Mr. Elijah Kellogg, probably in concurrence with the church, there were "one hundred in favor of it and none against it."

It would seem, from Mr. Holt's letter of acceptance and Dr. Trumbull's sermon at his ordination, that there was great disagreement and contention in both town and church, so that for almost two years they could not agree upon a candidate for the pastorship. The clouds, however, at last dispersed, and the town, April 6, 1789, unanimously concurred with the church in extending an invitation to Mr. Thomas Holt, of Wallingford, Conn., to become their pastor; which invitation he accepted in a letter so characteristic of his habit of amplification, that it is here inserted, as entered on the records of both the church and the town: —

"To the Church of Christ and other Inhabitants of the Town of Hardwick. — Friends and Brethren: The affection and respect which you have manifested towards me are highly worthy of my attention, gratitude, and warmest acknowledgments. The idea of a church destitute of a pastor, and a numerous people without a teacher, — the spirited altercations and unhappy divisions[2] which have appeared imminently to threaten the cause of religion and very existence of Christianity in this place, the present perfect unanimity and affection of this church and people, — and the unhappy consequences which would probably follow, should I manifest an excusing disposition, — are considerations very solemn and important. Your present respect and entire union among yourselves exhibits an event which by no means corresponds with my previous expectations, especially your choice of me for your Pastor and Teacher; this, doubtless, is the Lord's doing, and ought to be marvellous in our eyes. But 'who is sufficient for these things?' sufficient to stem the torrent of vice, mixed with delusion, which at the present day appears greatly to threaten the cause of religion. Who among men or angels is

[1] Probably, to reconsider, or to recall the invitation previously given. The continuation of the Church Records, after this date, until the settlement of Rev. Thomas Holt, more than three years later, are not known to exist; they disappeared more than forty years ago.

[2] "We have occasion of abundant joy and thanksgiving to God, that after this Zion hath been covered with a cloud, and experienced unhappy years of controversy and division, he hath visited you in mercy, healed your divisions, and given you uncommon unanimity and peace." *Ordination Sermon, at Hardwick*, June 25, 1789, by Benjamin Trumbull, A. M., of North Haven, pp. 34, 35.

sufficient against temptations, internal and external, against the infernal stratagems of the grand apostate, to watch for souls as one who must give an account? The office of a Bishop is a good, though a painful, trying, and laborious work. Since I received an invitation to assume the office and work of a Gospel Bishop or Minister in this place, I have attempted to consider your situation with mature deliberation. A reply to your unanimous invitation is considered as solemnly important to the church and people in this place and to myself. My Fathers and Brethren in the ministry have been consulted, as from experience they know the cares, the trials, and labors of a minister. A consciousness of my self-deficiency, and apparently inadequate ability, excites emotions not the most pleasing; and might I not depend upon divine support and assistance, self-diffidence, discouragement, and despondency, would appear formidable obstacles.

"But let us come to the important decision. My friends and brethren; the manifestations of your benevolence and affection towards me, in treating my character and youth with esteem, respect and tenderness, while I have labored among you in word and doctrine, must necessarily excite sensations of peculiar endearment towards you, and presage future exhibitions of the same if not increasing and reciprocal affection. I hope and trust that with humility, dependence, and prayerfulness, I have looked to the great Head of the Church, for his guidance and direction. Your respect, esteem, and affection, manifested as I have already observed, your unexpected, happy and perfect unanimity, in giving me an invitation to take the charge of this church and people, under Jesus Christ the Captain of our salvation, — the pleasing prospect arising from your union and affection of answering the great end of preaching the gospel, of being a happy instrument of building up the kingdom of the Great Redeemer in this place, and in promoting, if not the temporal, yet the highest, the immortal interests of this church and people, — these considerations are powerful arguments and inducements to excite and support a belief that yours is a CALL FROM GOD; that it is the design of the Great Head of the church that he whom you have unanimously chosen should be constituted Pastor of the church and Minister among the people in Hardwick. Trusting not by constraint, but of a ready mind, this public declaration is made, that I comply with your unanimous invitation. I consent, if it should be the divine pleasure, to spend my life and strength in this place, for the cause of Christ, and the interest and immortal happiness of this church and people. Since an inspired apostle hath said, 'If any provide not for his own, and especially for those of his own house, he hath denied the faith and is worse than an infidel,' it would doubtless be improper and sinful for any one to deny the faith or gospel, which he is to preach, by neglecting a decent support. Again he saith, 'No man that warreth entangleth himself with the affairs of this life, that he may please him who hath chosen him to be a soldier;' and 'even so hath the Lord ordained, that they which preach the gospel should live of the gospel.' While I may dispense to you the mysteries of the kingdom of God, and preach the unsearchable riches of Christ, — while I spend the remainder of my days, and wear out my life and strength in the cause of the Redeemer, for the purpose of promoting your highest interest, your everlasting peace, — while I sow unto you spiritual things, — is it a great thing if I should reap some of your carnal things? As it would doubtless contribute greatly to your advantage, and my own peace, happiness, and usefulness among you, could I give myself wholly to these things, or the work of the gospel ministry, with full confidence, under the disposal of a wise and beneficent Providence, I must rely upon your generosity and affection, to afford that comfortable and honorable support which I trust comports with your present intention.

"Permit me to acknowledge with thankfulness the peculiar affection, kindness, and generosity, of numbers, manifested by subscription, for the purpose of furnishing a great domestic convenience and defence against the uncomfortable effects of inclement seasons.

"Men, Brethren, and Fathers, I request an interest in your prayers, that I may be furnished abundantly to the great and important work of the evangelical ministry; that I may be made a faithful, zealous, and successful minister of the gospel; that I may be made an eminent and lasting blessing to this church and people; that I may be a son of consolation to the humble brokenhearted penitent, and a son of thunder to the careless impenitent sinner; that my ministration may become a savour of life unto life to immortal souls, and not a savour of death unto death; and that many souls may be given to me for my crown of rejoicing in the day of Jesus Christ. 'Let brotherly love continue. Let us therefore follow after the things which make for peace, and things wherewith one may edify another.' Let peace, harmony, unanimity, and affection, abound among you. 'Finally, brethren, be perfect, be of good comfort, be of one mind, live in peace, and the God of love and peace shall be with you.' I am, friends and brethren, yours in the Gospel of Christ. THOMAS HOLT, Hardwick, May 23^{d}, 1789."

Rev. Mr. Holt was ordained[1] June 25, 1789, and for several years the church had peace. Up to this time the records of the church had been kept on loose sheets of paper, so folded that each sheet would make sixteen pages, the larger part of which, though never bound, remain until the present time, but somewhat mutilated. Immediately after Mr. White's decease, the church met, January 15, 1784, and "chose a committee to search the Church Records, viz., Joseph Allen, William Paige, and Nathaniel Paige; also voted, to purchase a church bound book containing two quire of paper." The book was bought but not used until Mr. Holt became pastor of the church. From the old loose records he transferred into the new volume what related to the gathering of the church and the ordination of Mr. White, and entered at full length his own letter of acceptance of his call to the pastorship. Then he inserted, in his remarkably distinct and legible chirography, "The Church's Confession of Faith" and "Covenant." Whether these had been in use from the time when the church was organized, or whether they had been adopted at a more recent period, I am unable to determine; but as they exhibit the form of doctrine professed by the church in 1789, I insert them in full: —

"THE CHURCH'S CONFESSION OF FAITH.

"We believe that there is one true and living God, who is over all blessed forever, who is the Creator, Preserver, and Governor of the Universe. We believe that in the unity of the Godhead there are three distinct Persons, the Father, the Son, and the Holy Ghost, each possessed of all divine perfections. We believe that God made Adam, the first man, in his own holy image, consisting in knowledge and true holiness, giving him a law for a rule of his obedience, and entering into a covenant with him,

1 The services at Mr. Holt's ordination were as follows: Introductory prayer, Rev. Charles Backus, Somers, Conn.; sermon, Rev. Benjamin Trumbull, North Haven, Conn.; consecrating prayer, Rev. Josiah Dana, Barre, Mass.; charge, Rev. Nathan Fiske, Brookfield, Mass.; fellowship, Rev. Daniel Foster, New Braintree, Mass.; concluding prayer, Rev. Joseph Appleton, Brookfield, Mass.

Rev. Daniel Tomlinson, Oakham, Mass., Rev. John Willard, Jr., Meriden, Conn., and Rev. Joseph Blodgett, Greenwich, Mass., were also members of the ordaining council. Rev. Mr. Fiske was moderator, and Rev. Mr. Foster, scribe.

promising life to him and all his posterity in case of perfect obedience, but threatening death in case of disobedience; that Adam broke covenant with God by eating the forbidden fruit, and subjected himself and all his posterity to the wrath and curse of God; so that every man comes into the world in a state of entire alienation from God. We believe that from all eternity God designed to glorify the riches of his grace in the salvation of an elect number of the fallen children of Adam, through the mediation of Jesus Christ. To effect this purpose, we believe that the Lord Jesus Christ, the eternal Son of God, became man, and offered himself a sacrifice on the cross, to reconcile the Elect to God; and as he was delivered for their offences, so he was raised for their justification, and ascended into heaven to make intercession for them. We believe that it is the peculiar office of the Holy Spirit to apply the benefits of Christ's Redemption to the souls of men, and that he does this by working faith in them, and thereby uniting them to Christ in their effectual calling. We believe that fallen man has lost all power to do that which is spiritually good, and is not able to convert and turn himself to God; and therefore that effectual calling is the special and almighty work of the Spirit of God in and upon the hearts of sinners, whereby, if unwilling, they are made willing in the day of his power to go to Christ for life. We believe that those who are effectually called are justified through the righteousness of the Lord Jesus Christ, imputed to them, and received by faith alone. We believe that those who are justified are also sanctified; and that the work of sanctification will be carried on, and they will be enabled to persevere in grace and holiness to the end of their lives. We believe that the Scriptures of the Old and New Testaments are a Revelation from God, that they are a plain, perfect, and unerring rule of life, and that we ought to believe all their doctrines and obey all their precepts. We believe that God has appointed his ordinances for the spiritual good of his people, for the improvement of grace and holiness in them. We believe that at death the souls of the righteous are made perfect in holiness, and do immediately pass into glory and happiness, but the souls of the wicked into torment and misery. We believe that the Lord Jesus Christ will come a second time, to raise the dead and judge the world; then shall the wicked, in their raised bodies, go away into a state of endless misery; but the righteous into life eternal.

"THE COVENANT.

"And now, in a serious and humble sense of our indispensable duty to answer the call of Christ in the gospel, who, notwithstanding our miserable and lost condition by nature and practice, is still inviting us to partake of all the blessings of the Covenant of Grace, as we have obtained help, we do now, in the presence of God, angels, and this assembly, avouch the Lord Jehovah, the only true and living God, to be our God, giving up ourselves to God, the Father, as our Creator, to God, the Son, as our Redeemer, to God, the Holy Ghost, as our Sanctifier, in the way and on the terms of the Covenant of Grace, and in our place, we do engage to bear witness against sin, and, by the assistance of divine grace, to walk in a holy obedience to all the laws and ordinances of Christ, upholding the worship of God in this place, and submitting ourselves to the discipline of Christ, according to his word, contained in the Scriptures of the Old and New Testaments, which we receive as the only Rule of Faith and Manners."

In the interregnum preceding Mr. Holt's ordination, the church met, May 12, 1785, and elected two additional deacons,—Ebenezer Willis and Nathaniel Paige;[1] so that there were then four officers of that grade. But the number was soon diminished. Deacon Joseph Allen died August 18, 1793, aged 84, after active service as a church officer for the extraordinary period of more than fifty-six years; during the larger portion of which time, according to ancient tradition, he was the leading spirit in the church. He was also the last survivor of those who organized the church in 1736.[2] Some of his manuscripts, both in prose and rhyme, were published at Brookfield, 1795, in a pamphlet containing 51 pages, octavo, entitled, "The Last Advice and Farewell of Deacon Joseph Allen to the Church and Congregation of Hardwick."

The pastorate of Mr. Holt was uneventful. He zealously

[1] Nathaniel Paige was son of Christopher Paige, the first deacon of the church, and brother of William Paige, who was elected deacon November 9, 1769, and died February 14, 1790. The two brothers were colleagues in office nearly five years.

[2] "July, 1791. It may be remembered I mentioned in the year 1781, there were two males and three females living, who were members of the church when first gathered. I would now observe that since the beginning of 1789, there has none survived except myself." *Last Advice, etc.*, p. 19.

preached that form of Calvinism which was then styled Hopkinsianism, as set forth in the "System of Doctrines" arranged by Samuel Hopkins, D. D., and insisted on the most rigid observance of all the forms and ceremonies prescribed by the Puritan Church. Perhaps the same lack of variety in his discourses which afterwards caused dissatisfaction at Essex, may have prevented any signal success here. For some reason no extraordinary interest or activity was developed in the church or congregation. The additions to the church averaged only a fraction more than four per annum, namely, forty-six by profession, and nineteen by letter, sixty-five in all, during the sixteen years of his ministry; being less than half the average number admitted by his predecessor, the Rev. Mr. White. Few cases of discipline occurred in the church, at this period, and none which resulted in excommunication.[1] Gradually the tie which united the pastor and people was weakened, until at length it was sundered, apparently on account of his inability to subsist upon his salary and their unwillingness to increase it; but there must have been some other reason on their part; for immediately after his dismission, they readily granted a much larger salary to his successor. Mr. Holt's salary was three hundred dollars. Finding this sum, and the income of a small farm which he owned and cultivated, insufficient to supply his wants, after previous ineffectual appeals for relief, he presented to the town a characteristic address at a meeting held March 4, 1805, "to hear a statement or proposition from the Rev. Thomas Holt, and to act thereon as they in their wisdom shall think fit or proper." I quote the record in full:—

"The Rev. Mr. Holt attended and made the following communication.—The inhabitants of the town of Hardwick, assembled in town-meeting, March the 4th, A. D. 1805: Gentlemen, The committee appointed by the town, the last spring, to confer with the undersigned, appeared fully sensible, after conference, that his salary was by no means competent to meet his necessary annual expenditures. Through the medium of the same committee, by their advice, he made a communication to the town, May the 30th, A. D. 1804, respecting the incompetency

[1] The record of one such case exhibits the pastor's formality of speech and skill in amplification. The charge, entered on the church record, was that the offending member was guilty of "uttering a profane curse, in imprecating damnation in the name of God upon a fellow-creature." Probably the "profane curse" contained three short words. The culprit made a satisfactory explanation, and was forgiven.

of his salary. He has never been informed that the town, generally speaking, are not fully sensible that his salary was as inadequate as he represented ; yet no means of relief was granted. This inadequacy is not considered as arising from a defect in the sum stipulated in the original contract, but from a depreciation in the comparative value of the circulating medium with the necessaries of life, since : — which, for several years has been estimated, it is conceived, at one third. The following statement of the prices current of some of the principal articles of support about the year 1789, and the present prices current of the same articles, may show the justness of the estimation above suggested, and illustrate the great diminution of the present salary of the undersigned, and its consequent inadequacy for a support.

"12 Bushels	of Wheat,	at 6ˢ pr. B.	$12.00	
25 B.	of Rye,	at 4ˢ pr. B.	16.67	
50 B.	of Indian Corn,	at 3ˢ pr. B.	25.00	
600 wt.	of Beef,	at 20ˢ pr. Ct.	20.00	
500 wt.	of Pork,	at 25ˢ pr. Ct.	20.83	
300 wt.	of Cheese,	at 5ᵈ pr. lb.	20.83	
100 wt.	of Butter,	at 8ᵈ pr. lb.	11.11	
A man's labor 6 months,			40.00=	166.44
		Add one third,		83.22
				249.66

"Prices of the same articles current in the years 1804 and 1805 :

"12 Bushels	of Wheat,	at 10ˢ pr. B.	$20.00	
25 B.	of Rye,	at 6ˢ pr. B.	25.00	
50 B.	of Indian Corn,	at 5ˢ pr. B.	41.67	
600 wt.	of Beef,	at 30ˢ pr. Ct.	30.00	
500 wt.	of Pork,	at 36ˢ pr. Ct.	30.00	
300 wt.	of Cheese,	at 54ˢ pr. Ct.	27.00	
100 wt.	of Butter,	at 20 cents pr. lb.	20.00	
A man's labor 6 months,			74.00 =	267.67
	Compare the old prices, ⅓ added,			249.66
	Reduced $18.01 more than one third,			18.01

"The above statement is the result of consulting men of good information, and examining merchant's books, with reference to the different periods above stated ; and it is believed that the difference in the prices current of the articles above specified is not exaggerated. From this it appears that the sum stipulated as a salary for the undersigned will procure scarcely so much, by one third, of the articles essential to a support as it would in the year in which he was ordained. The estimate is made on the principal articles from which the inhabitants procure the means of paying their minister's salary. The consequence then appears to be that the nominal sum stipulated for a salary does not at present require hardly two thirds so much property in value as it did in the year 1789, when the contract was established; the whole of the depreciation in the value of the circulating medium must consequently fall on the undersigned, and render his salary greatly below a competency for a support. Hence he cannot suppose it beyond what was mutually expected from the contracting parties at the time of forming the contract, for the town to grant a pecuniary consideration sufficient to make his salary competent for a support.

"It is his request, therefore, that they would grant him a consideration adequate to this purpose. But if the town should judge it unreasonable to grant such pecuniary consideration, yet they surely will not suppose it reasonable that he should be confined to labor in their employment, the remainder of his life, for a stipend so materially inadequate to his necessary expenditures, and so much less in value than what his contract appears originally to have comprised; and it may be added so much less than what has universally been judged no more than adequate to a minister's support in all those towns in this vicinity, nay in the Commonwealth, where ministers have been ordained within six or eight years, and numbers of others where people have granted their ministers a consideration for the present depreciation in the value of their stipulated salaries. Although it is the heart's desire of the undersigned not to leave the town, but to live and die with the people of his charge, with whom he has been connected by a solemn and responsible relation for almost sixteen years, yet the inconveniences necessarily resulting from a salary so much diminished from its original value, and so incompetent to a decent support, compel him, if the town should not alleviate his burdens, to seek a degree of relief by a regular dismission. If the town then prefer a dissolution of the existing connection to a grant of a consideration for the present reduced state of his salary, then his request is that they would by vote give their consent that he may take a dismission in the common form, by the advice and consent of an Ecclesiastical Council to be called for that purpose by the Pastor and Church. — Gentlemen, with due consideration, yours in the Gospel of Christ, THOMAS HOLT. Hardwick, March 4th, 1805.

"The town took the foregoing communication into consideration, and on motion, — will the town grant any additional sum to the Rev. Thomas Holt for his support? it passed in the negative: on motion, — will the town consent that the church join with their Rev. Pastor in calling an Ecclesiastical Council, for his regular dismission? it passed in the affirmative."[1] The Council granted an honorable dismission March 27, 1805.

April 1, 1805. "Voted, to make a present of seventy-five dollars to the Rev. Thomas Holt. Voted, that the Rev. Mr. Holt be requested to preach to us on the approaching Fast-day; Mr. Holt consented to supply the pulpit on said day, by himself or another."

After his dismission, Mr. Holt preached occasionally, as opportunity offered, until January 25, 1809, when he was installed as pastor of the church in that part of Ipswich which afterwards became the town of Essex. This new home was not permanent. He "was esteemed a sound, scriptural preacher; but after hearing him two or three years, his parishioners began to complain of a sufficient variety in his discourses, which they first imputed to his not writing them. They therefore chose a committee to wait on him and request him to write his sermons. With this he complied; but as the evil, in their judgment, was not removed, they respectfully requested him to resign. With this also he complied, and on the 20th of April, 1813, he was honorably dismissed by a Council. The parish gave him a hundred dollars to defray the expense of his removal, and he returned to his farm in Hardwick."[2]

During the remainder of his life, Mr. Holt cultivated his farm and preached occasionally. He had no other pastorate, but performed some missionary labor, of which he preserved an exact account from day to day, and the sum total at the end of each engagement, in what he styled his "Missionary Journal." I have three of those Journals before me, describing labors at Paris, Me., from July 26, 1816, to February 26, 1817; at Lovell and Albany, Me., from March 5 to September 3, 1819; and at Springfield, Wendell, and Goshen, N. H., from November 25, 1819, to June 5, 1820. The summary of his services in the first

[1] It was a tradition in my younger days that both of these votes passed without opposition, so that Mr. Holt united the whole town twice, — both his call and his dismission being determined by unanimous vote. It was also said that this result was utterly unexpected by Mr. Holt, and that he subsequently expressed regret that he had presented the alternative to the town.

[2] Crowell's *History of Essex*, p. 269.

of these missions may serve as a fair specimen of the whole: — "During seven months of missionary labor, I have made 10 school-visits;[1] 18 visits to the sick and afflicted; attended one funeral; admitted, by vote of churches, 10 persons as members in full communion; baptized 20 adults and children; administered the Lord's Supper 4 times; preached 145 sermons; and made 434 family visits."

Rev. Thomas Holt, son of Daniel and Mary Holt, was born at Meriden, Conn., November 9, 1762, grad. Y. C. 1784, married Sarah, daughter of Rev. Ebenezer Chaplin of Sutton, May 5, 1796, had seven children, named in the Genealogies, and died February 21, 1836. He was buried in that part of the new cemetery which was formerly a portion of his homestead. During his ministry here, he admitted 65 persons into the church, baptized 191, including adults, and married 177 couples.

The successor of Mr. Holt was Rev. William Brigham Wesson, who was born in Hopkinton, May 29, 1777, but in early life was carried to Athol by his parents, William and Mary Wesson. Chiefly if not entirely by his own exertions, he defrayed the expense of a liberal education at Williams College, and graduated in 1802, thus early displaying that energy of character which distinguished him through life. The town concurred with the church, August 7, 1805, in calling him to become their pastor, and voted to fix his salary at five hundred dollars per annum; but added a proviso, apparently designed to guard against a repetition of embarrassments previously encountered: — "Provided, nevertheless, that if three fourths of the qualified voters in the Society should think proper, at any time, to dismiss the said Mr. Wesson, it shall be in their power; and also the said Mr. Wesson shall be at liberty to dismiss himself when he thinks proper. Either party is to give one year's previous notice. . . . Chose Capt. Daniel Warner, Doct. William Cutler, and Timothy Paige, Esq., a committee to wait on Mr. Wesson, and inform him of the doings of the town." Without unnecessary delay, Mr. Wesson gave an answer, characteristically different from that of his predecessor, before quoted: —

"To the church and congregation of the town of Hardwick. — Brethren and Friends: The time has come at which you have

[1] His "school-visits" were not a mere form, as is manifest from his Journal under date of December 31, 1816: "Visited a school; found it in decent order; heard the children and youth spell and read, inspected their writing and arithmetic, heard a grammar-class parse, addressed the school, and prayed."

reason to expect an answer to the call which you have presented me, to settle with you in the work of the gospel ministry. Having had the subject under serious and prayerful consideration I have come to the following conclusion, — to answer in the affirmative. Sincerely wishing grace, mercy, and peace, through our common Lord and Saviour Jesus Christ, may be multiplied, WILLIAM B. WESSON. — To Messrs. Warner, Cutler, and Paige, Committee in behalf of said church and congregation. Hardwick, Sep. 21, 1805."

Mr. Wesson was ordained October 20, 1805,[1] and for several years the harmony between the pastor and the flock was undisturbed. In the pulpit, his stately form and magnificent voice gave full effect to his discourses; while in private life, his affability of manners and buoyancy of spirit attracted a multitude of friends. In 1810, sixty-five persons became members of the church, precisely the same number which were admitted by his predecessor, during his entire pastorate; and in 1820 there was a further addition of one hundred and fourteen members; a larger number than were ever before or since admitted in any one year. So far, his ministry must be regarded as successful. But about the year 1815 the Trinitarian and Unitarian controversy became public, and it was prosecuted very vigorously, not to say furiously, until it resulted in a widespread breaking up of churches and parishes. Mr. Wesson did not become an active partisan on either side. Avoiding this exciting topic in his public discourses, and discussing chiefly such subjects as might promote peace and mutual edification, he preserved comparative harmony in the parish, and secured the rich harvest of 1820 to the church. Unfortunately for him, however, Hardwick was embraced within the limits of the Brookfield Association,[2] which was largely composed of stern and resolute champions of Trinitarianism, who could not endure opposition, or even neutrality, on the

[1] At Mr. Wesson's ordination the services were as follows: —

Introductory prayer, Rev. Daniel Tomlinson, Oakham, Mass.; sermon, Rev. Joseph Lee, Royalston, Mass.; consecrating prayer, Rev. Joseph Pope, Spencer, Mass.; charge, Rev. Ephraim Ward, Brookfield, Mass.; fellowship, Rev. Thomas Mason, Northfield, Mass.; concluding prayer, Rev. Joseph Blodgett, Greenwich, Mass.

Rev. Joshua Crosby, Greenwich, (now Enfield), Rev. Ezekiel L. Bascom, Gerry, (now Phillipston), Rev. John Fiske, New Braintree, and Rev. Thomas Snell, Brookfield, were also members of the ordaining council. Rev. Mr. Ward was moderator, and Rev. Mr. Snell, scribe.

[2] Had his lot been cast in the adjoining Association, which contained some of his most intimate clerical associates, such as Rev. Messrs. James Thompson, of Barre; Festus Foster, of Petersham; Ezekiel L. Bascom, of Phillipston; and Alpheus Harding, of New Salem; the result might have been very different.

part of their associates. Suspecting Mr. Wesson's soundness in the faith, after ineffectual attempts to enlist him under their own banner, they assumed a hostile attitude, and persevered until they succeeded in alienating from him the confidence and Christian sympathy of a majority of his church. A majority of the parish adhered to him, and at a meeting, May 26, 1823, "to see whether the Congregational Society in Hardwick are acquainted with any facts relating to the previous conduct of the Rev. William B. Wesson, which would induce them to desire his dismission," it was "voted, to choose a committee of three to request the Rev. William B. Wesson to come and read the communication from the Brookfield Association; Voted, and chose Elijah Amidon, Samuel Billings, and Stephen K. Wardwell, a committee for that purpose; Voted, to divide the house, and it was counted; there was one hundred and five in favor of the Rev. William B. Wesson, and none against him." During the next year, the condition of affairs "bettered nothing, but rather grew worse." Apparently despairing of a restoration of peace and harmony, Mr. Wesson at length addressed to the selectmen a communication which is preserved in the Hardwick Archives: "To the Selectmen of the town of Hardwick. — Gentlemen, Having had occasion to notice, within a few days, that the 'fire' of opposition 'is not quenched,' and having come to the conclusion that my continuance in the ministry will neither promote my own happiness, nor, under existing circumstances, be so useful to the people as I could wish, I have therefore thought proper to request you to issue your warrant to notify a legal meeting of the inhabitants of Hardwick, and especially those belonging to the Congregational Society in said town, to meet in town-meeting, to act on the following question, to wit: — whether they will consent that the contract existing between us be dissolved at my request. By complying with this request you will confer a favor on your friend and Pastor, WILLIAM B. WESSON. Hardwick, May 29, 1824." A meeting was accordingly held June 14, 1824, at which it was "voted unanimously, that the contract existing between the Rev. William B. Wesson and said Society be dissolved at his request." These proceedings were ratified and confirmed by an Ecclesiastical Council, June 30, 1824.[1] During his ministry Mr. Wesson admitted 232 persons

[1] It is indicated in the record of a town-meeting, May 26, 1823, that the Brookfield Association, or some of its active members, in their crusade against Mr. Wesson, not only pronounced him to be unsound in the faith, but impeached

into the church (an average of somewhat more than twelve per annum), baptized 395 adults and children, and attended 463 funerals. After his dismission he engaged temporarily in mercantile business, but chiefly devoted his attention to the cultivation of his farm, which is now in possession of his eldest son. He died May 9, 1836, aged nearly 59 years, and was buried in the new cemetery. Some account of his family is inserted in the Genealogical department.[1]

Several ineffectual attempts were made to fill the vacant pulpit. A large majority of the church were Trinitarians; a minority of the church and a decided majority of the congregation were Anti-Trinitarians, composed of Unitarians, Universalists, and others; and on this rock the original parish was wrecked. The church invited Rev. Wales Tileston, October 14, 1824, to become their pastor, by a vote of 33 aff. to 5 neg. The town non-concurred November 1, 1824, by a vote of 45 aff. against 79 neg. April 14, 1825, the church invited Rev. Henry H. F. Sweet by unanimous vote; the town concurred May 16, 1825, by a vote of 58 aff. to 44 neg., "on condition that he avow a willingness, on his part, to make exchanges and hold ministerial intercourse and fellowship with Unitarian clergymen as well as others." He was not ordained; probably he declined making the required avowal. By unanimous vote, December 12, 1825, the church extended a call to Rev. John Wilder, Jr.; the town concurred, 70 aff., 41 neg., in the invitation to this candidate, "who has avowed a willingness to hold ministerial intercourse with the denomination of Christians called Unitarians." This call was declined. August 28, 1826. The town refused to call Rev. Eliphalet P. Crafts, 42 aff., 49 neg. December 18, 1826. The church refused to invite Rev. Nathaniel Gage, 3 aff., 27 neg.; the town voted, January 1, 1827, to "concur with a minority of the church in giving Mr. Nathaniel Gage a call to settle," &c., 107 aff., 37 neg. This was the last joint effort of the two parties to agree upon a candidate

his moral character or "conduct." By advice of friends, he commenced a suit at law against some of the principal offenders; and although one of them is said to have insisted that he had always been particularly cautious to avoid saying anything "actionable," the jury pronounced them guilty, and assessed damages. Although more than half a century has elapsed, it seems proper to refrain from mentioning names or any further particulars in connection with this unhappy controversy.

[1] My personal recollections of Mr. Wesson are very pleasant. He gave me my first lessons in Latin, and encouraged me in my studies generally; and through the whole period of youth, from time to time, imparted very useful advice.

for the pastorate; and this also was unsuccessful. As a last resort, the town, or Congregational Society, as it had for some time been called, held a meeting, October 1, 1827, "to see if they will grant the orthodox party the privilege of drawing their proportionable part of the money already raised and not expended, for such preaching as they shall choose, and also the use of the meeting-house their proportion of the time." The meeting was adjourned to October 9, and was then dissolved, without any definite action upon the subject.

At length, in 1827, the "orthodox party," embracing a majority of the church and holding the church records, seceded from the original parish and organized a separate society; and thenceforth those who remained were styled the Congregational Society, embracing a minority of the church, and holding the church and parish property, as legal representatives of the original organization. In what follows I shall notice the two divisions separately, — the old society first, and the new society afterwards.

CONGREGATIONAL SOCIETY. In the official records, under date of February, 1828, it is stated that "The minority withdrew from said society, and formed a new religious society called The First Calvinistic Society in Hardwick." To induce the seceders to refrain from erecting a new meeting-house, and to return to their old home, the Congregational Society made a proposition, May 5, 1828, which certainly appears very generous, especially when it is considered as an offering from a majority to a minority: — "That the Calvinistic Society have the use of the meeting-house forty-six Sabbaths in a year, on condition their minister, Mr. Tupper, will exchange with Mr. Thompson, of Barre, Mr. Wilson, of Petersham, and Mr. Harding, of New Salem, as with other ministers, not less than once a year with each of them." This conciliatory offer was rejected by the Calvinistic Society, as involving at least the countenancing of Unitarianism. Thereupon the Congregational Society with a minority of the church, extended to Rev. John M. Merrick an invitation to become their pastor, and he was ordained August 27, 1828. On the first day of November, 1829, "at a regular meeting of the church the following resolution was passed: — Whereas, by the secession of a part of this church from the Congregational Society, the records and covenant of the church have passed into other hands, and are not now to be had by us, we agree to offer the following profession of faith to those who may present themselves for admission into this church: — Impressed with a sense of duty, you offer yourself for admission to this Christian church. You regard this transaction as a profession of your belief in the one only living and true God; as a testimony of your faith in Jesus Christ as the Son of God and the Saviour of the world; and as an acknowledgment of the sacred scriptures as containing a revelation from God to man and a perfect rule of faith and duty. You design to commemorate the Author and Finisher of our Faith in the way that he hath appointed, resolving, by the divine favor, to live in obedience to the divine commandments, and hoping, through the mercy of God to obtain everlasting life. In a humble and grateful reliance upon God for the pardon of sin and for assistance in duty, you now enter upon the Christian profession; and you intend to walk with this church in Christian ordinances and in the exercise of Christian affection." March 5, 1832. The society voted "to accede to the request of Rev. John M. Merrick, that his pastoral relation to said Society shall be dissolved." Mr. Merrick was subsequently for many years pastor of the Unitarian Church in Walpole, Mass., and was also a Senator in the General Court, 1857, 1858. On the first of April, 1869, he became pastor of the church in Charlestown, N. H., where he died March 20, 1871, aged nearly 67 years.

The successor of Mr. Merrick was Rev. John Goldsbury, who "was born in Warwick, Mass., Feb. 11, 1795; fitted for college at different schools, and academies, and under private instruction; graduated at Brown University in 1820; commenced the study of divinity at Harvard College in 1821, under Professors Ware, Norton, and Willard; taught in Taunton Academy several years; was ordained in North Bridgewater, Wednesday June 6, 1827, where he remained till Sept. 4, 1831."[1] He was unanimously invited, June 11, 1832, to become pastor of the Congregational Church and Society in Hardwick, and was installed July 4, 1832. In connection with his parish work, he established and instructed a High School. He labored faithfully, both as pastor and teacher, until June, 1839, when, at his own request, he was dismissed, removed to Cambridge, and was master of the High School there about five years. He afterwards returned to Warwick, where he still survives in a ripe old age, honored and respected.

For nearly three years afterwards, the society had no settled

[1] Kingman's *Hist. of North Bridgewater*, p. 48.

pastor, but hired occasional supplies. Their number had become small, by the formation of other societies, and it was difficult to pay a sufficient salary. At length an arrangement was made with the Universalist Society (then worshipping in the Town Hall, under the ministry of Rev. Rufus S. Pope), to build a new meeting-house, and unite their strength for the maintenance of public worship. The details of this arrangement are entered on the records of the Society. After other ineffectual negotiations, it was voted May 17, 1841, "That this Society will proceed to take down the old meeting-house, and will unite with the Universalist Society in rebuilding a meeting-house on the same ground. Voted, to choose a committee, to fix on terms of agreement between the Congregational and Universalist Societies, in relation to the rebuilding of the meeting-house." May 24, 1841. The committee submitted a report, recommending that the materials of the old house, so far as practicable, might be used in the construction of the new edifice, with certain reservations; and it was provided, that "The above recommendation take effect when the Universalist Society shall agree, as an offset or consideration for the use of the materials above specified, and for the benefit they are to receive by the joint occupancy of the spot on which the old meeting-house now stands, that they, the said Universalist Society, will furnish all the funds required to pay the expense of taking down the old meeting-house, and also funds to pay the owners of pews in said old meeting-house, the sums at which the respective pews shall be appraised;[1] and said Universalist Society also agree that said Congregational Society shall have the right to supply the desk in said new meeting-house, whenever it is not occupied by a minister procured by said Universalist Society. And said Universalist Society are further to agree that whenever the owners of pews in said new meeting-house, or any of them, shall express a desire to have the desk occupied a part of the time by a Unitarian preacher, such pew-owners shall be entitled to that privilege for such a portion of the time as the original cost of their pews bears to the original cost of the whole number of pews in the house." This report was accepted (aff. 17, neg. 10), and the agreement was confirmed by both societies. To prevent any possible doubt concerning its legality, a town-meeting was held June 15, 1841, "to see if the town will permit the First Universalist Society in Hardwick to erect a meeting-house on the site now occupied by the old meet-

[1] The sum total of the appraisal was $817.88.

ing-house, to be used as a union meeting-house by the Congregational and Universalist Societies in such proportion of time as said Societies shall agree." Permission was granted, by a vote of 92 aff., 44 neg.

No time was lost in carrying the foregoing agreement into effect; within twenty-four hours after permission was granted by the town, the work was commenced. On the parish records is this memorandum: "Note. The work of taking down the old meeting-house was commenced June 16th, 1841." The new house was erected with commendable dispatch, and was dedicated January 25, 1842. It was by no means equal to the former edifice in size and general magnificence; but sufficiently capacious to accommodate the congregation which remained after the Calvinistic Society was formed, together with the Universalists, who had hitherto worshipped in the Town Hall, but had now taken possession of the new house. Instead of claiming the use of the house a portion of the time, for the employment of a "Unitarian preacher," this society wisely preferred to make a temporary union with the Universalists, and to employ one pastor for both societies. They accordingly voted, April 4, 1842, that "preachers should be obtained as far as practicable, for terms not less than one year; and that we coincide in the propriety and expediency of endeavoring to retain the services of Rev. R. S. Pope for the ensuing year." They also voted to add the amount of their subscriptions to the funds of the Universalist Society, provided that the same should be repaid if the Congregational Society should be obliged to furnish a preacher for the United Society.

Upon the removal of Mr. Pope, at the close of his engagement, the Rev. Norwood Damon, a Unitarian preacher, was employed as acting pastor. At a meeting, November 27, 1843, it appeared that the Congregational Society had raised about $300, and yet lacked about $200 of enough to pay "Mr. Damon for his services one year." A communication from the clerk of the Universalist Society was read, stating that after repaying to this society the sum which it advanced last year, there remained in their treasury about $140, which they would loan "to this Society, to be replaced hereafter;" which offer was accepted. Mr. Damon remained here about two years, and was succeeded by Rev. Benton Smith, a Universalist, who was ordained July 2, 1845. The two societies acted together for a considerable length of time, as a united body, though I have found no record of a formal union. I do find, however, that this society voted, April 30, 1847, "that the sum we pay for the supply of the desk be paid to the treasurer of the Union Society for the present year;" and a similar vote was passed in 1848 and 1849. Mr. Smith remained pastor until 1850, when he removed to Shirley Village, and afterwards to South Reading, 1854; Chatham, 1859; and Waltham, 1865. He was the State Missionary for several years. In 1879 he removed to South Newmarket, N. H., but subsequently returned to Waltham.

For some years after the departure of Mr. Smith, the desk was supplied by occasional preaching. A formal union of the two societies seemed necessary to their mutual prosperity. The Universalists were more numerous and had more financial strength than the Unitarians; but as the Congregational Society had certain corporate rights which it was important to preserve, the Universalists allowed their own organization to slumber, and became members of the Congregational Society, which was thenceforth substantially a Universalist Society, in fellowship with the State Convention, though retaining the original name, and inheriting the rights and immunities of the original parish. In November, 1855, Rev. George J. Sanger, who was ordained at Sippican, September 8, 1847, and removed to Sandwich, 1849, and to Gloucester, 1851, was invited to take charge of this society, which invitation he accepted, and was installed May 7, 1856. His ministry was very acceptable, and continued for eight years, except a slight intermission in 1862, when he accepted a commission as lieutenant in the army of the Union (which was afterwards exchanged for another as chaplain), and offered a resignation of his pastorate. At a meeting, September 25, 1862, it was voted, "that the Society request Mr. Sanger to continue his connection with this Society as their pastor; and after leave of absence for the term of nine months in his Country's service, hope that he will be able to resume all the pastoral duties of said Society." He performed his military duty, was taken prisoner at Galveston, and "endured hardness as a good soldier." He resumed his labor after his return, but resigned June 1, 1864, and removed to Webster; he removed again, in 1869, to Danvers, where he still resides, devoting a portion of his time to secular affairs.

The successor of Mr. Sanger was Rev. John Harvey Moore, who was ordained at Warren May 23, 1844, removed to South Reading, 1849; Concord, N. H., 1855; and returned to Warren, 1862. He commenced preaching here in 1864, continuing to reside in Warren, where he preached in the afternoon, after supplying the desk here in the forenoon. This arrangement continued until 1874, after which he ceased preaching in Hardwick, and became pastor of the society in Webster. In 1878 he removed to Newark, N. Y., where he now resides.

Rev. Henry Jewell was ordained at Salem, N. H., August 24, 1836, and removed to South Reading, 1838; Lynn, 1840; Cincinnati, O., 1847; Stoneham, 1852; Lynn again, 1855; Canton, 1858; Terre Haute, Ind., 1866; Manchester, Iowa, 1868; Rome, N. Y., 1870; Bristol, N. Y., 1872. In 1875 he removed to Hardwick, and remained pastor of this society until April 1, 1878, when he resigned, and removed to Malden. In 1881 he removed to Merrimac, and became pastor of the society in that town.

Rev. Lucan S. Crosley of Waterloo, P. Q., graduated at the St. Lawrence Theological School in 1874, and preached at Plainfield, Vt., 1875, and Weymouth, 1876, 1877. He commenced his ministry here in September, 1878; was ordained November 13, 1879; resigned in September, 1880, and removed to Woodstock Vt.

The present pastor is Rev. Benjamin V. Stevenson, who was ordained in Boston, June, 1844, and preached in Barre six years, from April 1, 1844, to 1850; he was afterwards settled in Winchester, N. H., 1850; at South Hingham, 1851; at New Bedford, 1854; at Chicopee, eleven years, from 1857; at Shelburne Falls, six years, from 1868; and at Southbridge, seven years, from 1874. Having thus labored constantly for the long period of thirty-eight years, he took charge of this ancient parish, in connection with a society at Ware, April 1, 1882.

Calvinistic Society. A minority of the congregation, with a large majority of the church, withdrew from the original parish, and on the 13th of November, 1827, organized the first "Calvinistic Society in Hardwick." Rejecting an offer of a joint occupancy of the old meeting-house, although the "lion's share" was tendered to them, they proceeded without delay to erect a new house at the south end of the Common. The corner-stone was laid in September, 1828, when an address was delivered by Rev. Parsons Cooke of Ware, setting forth the reasons for separation from the parent stock. A year afterwards, September 9, 1829, the house was dedicated;[1] and the sermon on that occasion, by

[1] This meeting-house was taken down in 1860, and a more commodious edifice erected on the same place.

Rev. John Wilder, Jr., of Charlton, was devoted to a consideration of "the present prospects of evangelical religion," which was thus defined: "The doctrine of the Triune Deity; the doctrine of the divine inspiration of the Sacred Scriptures; the doctrine of the entire native sinfulness of the human heart; the doctrine of redemption by the Blood of Christ; the necessity of regeneration by the influences of the Holy Spirit, *i. e.*, repentance and faith in Christ in this life, essential to the obtaining of God's favor; the doctrine of the sovereign Purposes of God; the doctrine of the perseverance of the Saints unto eternal life; and the doctrine of an Endless Retributive State beyond the grave. These are, summarily, the Evangelical Faith." Both this sermon and the previous address were published.

Before the erection of the meeting-house a unanimous invitation was given to Rev. Martyn Tupper to become pastor of the church and new society, which he accepted, and was ordained April 16, 1828.[1] He was a diligent and zealous workman, and his labors were rewarded by forty-six admissions to his church in 1831, this being the last extraordinary harvest enjoyed by that body. Soon after this religious awakening, the church was for some reason induced to adopt a modified creed, or confession of faith, which is here inserted: —

"The Confession of Faith and Covenant adopted by the Congregational Church[2] in this place, March 2^d^, 1832. (1.) We believe that there is one God, the Creator and rightful disposer of all things, existing as Father, Son, and Holy Ghost; and that to these three persons, as the one God, all divine perfections are to be equally ascribed. (2.) We believe that the Bible was given by inspiration of God, as the only unerring rule of faith and practice. (3.) We believe that mankind are fallen from their original rectitude, and are, while in a state of nature, wholly destitute of that holiness which is required by the divine law. (4.) We believe that Jesus Christ, the eternal Word, became man, and by his obedience, sufferings and death, made an atonement for the sins of the world. (5.) We believe that they, and they only, will be saved, in consequence of the merits of Christ, who repent of sin, and believe in him. (6.) We believe that, although the invitations of the gospel are such that all, who will, may come and take of the water of life freely, yet the wickedness

[1] A further notice of Mr. Tupper is inserted at the close of his second pastorate here.

[2] Retaining the deacons, records, and a majority of the members, they claimed to be the "Congregational Church," the legitimate successors of the original founders.

of the human heart is such that none will come, unless drawn by the special influences of the Holy Spirit. (7.) We believe that the sacraments of the New Testament are Baptism and the Lord's Supper, — Baptism to be administered only to believers and their households, and the Supper only to believers in regular church standing. (8.) We believe that God has appointed a day in which he will judge the world, when there will be a resurrection of the dead, and when the righteous will enter on eternal happiness, and the wicked will be sentenced to eternal misery." [1]

The successor of Mr. Tupper, who resigned April 29, 1835, was Rev. Edward J. Fuller, who was born at Plainfield, Conn., January 5, 1806, grad. at A. C. 1828, and at Andover 1831, was ordained at Chelsea, January 11, 1832, and dismissed in 1835. He was installed in Hardwick November 3, 1835, and dismissed March 21, 1837. His ministry here was short and uneventful. For the next three years I do not trace him distinctly; but from 1840 to 1845, he was lecturer for the Western Anti-Slavery Society. In 1845, repeated attacks of epilepsy compelled him to retire from active mental labor. He died of apoplexy at Brighton, O., March 12, 1876. See "Obituary Record of Grad. of Amherst College," 1876.

Rev. William Eaton was the next pastor. He grad. at W. C. 1810, and at Andover 1813; was ordained at Fitchburg, August 30, 1815, and dismissed June 4, 1823; installed at Middleborough March 10, 1824, and dismissed April 10, 1834. He was at Charlotte, Vt., about two years, after which he was installed here September 6, 1837. The connection between pastor and people seems to have been very pleasant; but the failure of his health compelled him to cease from his labors. He resigned March 26, 1840, and before a council could assemble to dissolve the connection, he died at West Brookfield, April 15, 1840, aged 56 years.

The successor of Mr. Eaton was Rev. Barnabas M. Fay, who was born at Berlin, July 27, 1806, and grad. Y. C. 1833. He was a professor in the Deaf and Dumb Asylum, New York city, from 1833 to 1836; studied in the Union Theological Seminary, 1837 and 1838; was ordained in Hardwick May 20, 1840, and was dismissed August 23, 1843; was a teacher in Durham, Conn., 1843, 1844; pastor at Wilmington, 1845 to 1850; profes-

[1] Substantially the same confession is now in use by the church, with one additional article: "We believe in the necessity of a change of heart, and that this change is wrought by the Holy Spirit."

sor at the Blind Asylum, Indianapolis, Ind., 1850 to 1854; professor at the Deaf and Dumb Asylum, Flint, Mich., 1854 to 1864; a banker at Saginaw, Mich., 1864 to 1869; without charge, Saratoga Springs, 1869 —. See "Gen. Catalogue Union Theol. Sem. 1876."

Mr. Fay was succeeded by Rev. Asa Mann, who was born at Randolph, Vt., April 9, 1816, grad. at A. C. 1838, and at Andover, 1842. He was ordained in Hardwick June 19, 1844, and resigned October 14, 1851; after which he was pastor at Exeter, N. H., 1851 to 1858; stated supply at Wellfleet, 1862, at Granville, 1863, at Springfield, Vt., 1864, 1865, and Bath, N. H., 1866; pastor at Bath, 1867 to 1872; at Raynham, 1873, 1874; at Carlisle, 1875, 1876; stated supply at South Plymouth, 1878, 1879, and at Hardwick again, 1880 to 1881.

Rev. Martyn Tupper, the successor of Mr. Mann, was born in West Stafford, Conn., January 6, 1800, grad. Nassau Hall, 1826, was ordained here April 16, 1828, and resigned April 29, 1835, as before mentioned. He was next installed at East Longmeadow in October, 1835, dismissed in September, 1849, soon afterwards installed at Lanesboro, and dismissed May 19, 1852. He was reinstalled in Hardwick June 23, 1852, and after a peaceful ministry of more than eighteen years, resigned, September 1, 1870, and removed to Waverly, Ill. His wife died there July 27, 1871. About a year afterwards Mr. Tupper conveyed her remains to Hardwick, where two daughters had previously been buried. Having accomplished this pious task, he visited his friends at West Stafford, where he sickened and died July 31, 1872, and was buried in his family lot in the new cemetery.

Rev. Elbridge W. Merritt succeeded Mr. Tupper. He took a partial course at Union College, and also at the Union Theological Seminary (then in Connecticut, now in New York). He was ordained in 1866, preached at Stafford, Conn., 1867, at Charleston, S. C., 1868, at Williamsburg, 1869, 1870, and became a stated supply in Hardwick, October, 1870, acting pastor, April 1871, and was installed as pastor June 5, 1873. He resigned October 1, 1876, and after laboring for a time at the West, returned and settled in Dana, supplying also a parish in Petersham.

Rev. Augustus C. Swain was ordained in 1873, preached at Needham 1873, 1874, at West Warren 1875, and at Hardwick from February, 1877 to July, 1879, when he removed to Hyde Park. He was not installed here.

The present pastor of the church is the Rev. Gilbert B. Richardson, who graduated at A. C. 1853, and at the Bangor Theol. Seminary, 1856. He was first settled in Douglass, Mass.; afterwards at Bath, Me., from 1860 to 1874, and at Alstead, N. H., from 1874 to 1881. He commenced preaching here 17th July, 1881, and was installed 7th December, 1881.

DEACONS.

	Elected.		*Held Office until*	*Age.*
Christopher Paige . .	Dec. 3, 1736.	Resigned.	Apr. 13, 1749.	
Joseph Allen	Dec. 3, 1736.	Died.	Aug. 18, 1793.	84
Samuel Robinson . . .	Ap. 30, 1746.	Resigned.	Mar. 2, 1749.	
John Cooper	1749.	Removed.	1769.	
William Paige	Nov. 9, 1769.	Died.	Feb. 14, 1770.	66
John Bradish	Ap. 28, 1774.	Removed.	1778.	
Ebenezer Willis	May 12, 1785.	Died.	Feb. 5, 1813.	78
Nathaniel Paige . . .	May 12, 1785.	Removed.	About 1812.	
Joseph Allen	Aug. 16, 1810.	Died.	Nov. 11, 1822.	73
James Paige	Aug. 10, 1812.	Died.	Feb. 18, 1818.	70
Benjamin W. Childs .	Aug. 10, 1812.	Removed.	About 1819.	
Henry Fish	Ap. 18, 1819.	Resigned.	May 20, 1830.	
Josiah C. Chandler . .	Ap. 18, 1819.	Removed.	About 1816.	
Elijah Amidon	Mar. 10, 1824.	Removed.	About 1830.	
Anson Winchester . .	Mar. 10, 1824.	Removed.	About 1830.	

The portion of the church which remained with the Congregational Society, elected to the office of Deacon: —

	Elected.		*Held Office until*	*Age.*
Joseph Stone	Nov. 19, 1830.	Died.	June 27, 1849.	59
Ichabod Dexter	Nov. 19, 1830.	Died.	May 11, 1851.	76

The other branch of the church, in addition to Deacons Fish, Amidon, and Winchester, elected: —

	Elected.		*Held Office until*	*Age.*
Mark Haskell	May 20, 1830.	Resigned.	Mar. 5, 1841.	
Jason Carpenter	Sep. 2, 1836.	Resigned.	Ap. 4, 1851.	
Joseph Whipple . . .	Sep. 2, 1836.	Resigned.	Ap. 10, 1842.	
Emery B. Foster . . .	Ap. 30, 1841.	Resigned.	About 1849.	
Philander Chandler . .	Sep. 7, 1849.	Removed.	About 1864.	
Reuben Tyler	Sep. 7, 1849.	Died.	Nov. 21, 1859.	51
William A. Warner, Jr.	Dec. 31, 1864.			
James N. Brown . . .	Dec. 31, 1864.	Resigned.	1878.	
Charles L. Warner . .	Mar. 15, 1878.			
Henry G. Towne [1] . .	Mar. 15, 1878.	Term expired.	1882.	
Charles A. Wheeler .	Mar. 1881.			

[1] Agreeably to a recent arrangement, the deacons are elected for a limited term of years.

CHAPTER XII.

ECCLESIASTICAL HISTORY.

Separate Church. — Reasons for Separation. — Early Separatists. — Covenant. — List of Members. — Removal to Bennington. — The Original Separate Church in Hardwick becomes the First Congregational Church in Vermont. — Baptist Society. — Early Members. — Corporators. — Meeting-houses. — Pastors. — Deacons. — Universalist Society. — Petition for Incorporation. — Corporators. — Pastors. — Deacons. — Amalgamation with the Congregational Society. — Methodist Society. — Meeting-house. — Trinitarian Congregational Church. — Munificent Benefactors. — Pastors. — Deacons. — Meeting-house. — Catholic Church. — Meeting-house. — Priest.

SEPARATE CHURCH. About the year 1740 occurred what was then called the "Great Awakening," which extended throughout New England. It was occasioned, or at least greatly encouraged, by the labors of the celebrated Rev. George Whitefield.[1] One of its results was the rending asunder of many churches, those who seceded being styled "New Lights," and afterwards "Separatists" or "Separates." Terms of obloquy were freely interchanged between the two parties. The New Lights were denounced as enthusiastic and unscrupulous disorganizers, and they, in their turn, stigmatized the Old Lights, or established churches, both clergy and laity, as cold, lifeless, and dead, utterly unworthy the name of Christians. One of their preachers, Rev. Ebenezer Frothingham, of Weathersfield, Conn., published a Discourse, in 1750, entitled, "The Articles of Faith and Practice, with the Covenant, that is confessed by the Separate Churches of Christ in general in this Land. Also a DISCOURSE, holding forth the great privileges of the Church of Jesus Christ,

[1] Rev. Dr. Wigglesworth, in his Discourses, November 12 and 19, 1754, "after the Rev. Mr. Whitefield's preaching at Cambridge," in regard to itinerant preachers and laymen "thrusting themselves into other men's labors," says, "To the encouragement given to the same person (Mr. Whitefield) and those who followed him in this uninstituted and very disorderly and pernicious practice, twelve or thirteen years ago, we may ascribe all the separations from our churches, and most if not all the enthusiasm, error, contention, and confusion, with which we have been perplexed ever since." P. 34.

and the same privileges vindicated from the Sacred Scriptures; and some points of practice in the Church of Christ, that are in great dispute between the learned and unlearned, fairly settled in a line of Divine Truth. — Written by Ebenezer Frothingham." In this Discourse the author devotes one chapter "to answer some objections that is made against the present great and misterious work that God is a doing in New England." He mentions seven objections, which probably embody the most material: — "We cannot think that this is a good work in the land, or a work of God's Spirit, that inclines persons to separate and rend away from the churches of Christ that are established by the laws of this colony and land, and to leave the house of God, and set up a worship contrary to the gospel, as has been the practice of some of late in the land." pp. 338, 339. "We cannot believe that this is a work of God in the land, which the Separates hold to be God's work, because none of our learned and good ministers own it. They say it is delusions and a false religion." p. 344. "We cannot believe that the Separates are right; for God is a God of Order, and their practice is Disorder and Confusion. When they separate from us, they go off, one by one, and do not unite in a body, and then get a regular dismission; but they rend away, some at one time, and some at another. And when there are a number that is sufficient for to set up public worship, then they are all of them preachers, women as well as men; and this we know is contrary to the will of God." pp. 352, 353. "We cannot think that this present work is of God, which the Separates hold to be of God, for it makes divisions and disorders, and breaks the peace of churches and families; therefore it cannot be a work of God, for Christ's Kingdom is a peaceful Kingdom; and the promoters of this work are censorious, judging persons, who speak evil of our ministers and rulers, which is contrary to the word of God." p. 363. "We don't believe that the Separates are right, or that God is with them, because that there are such divisions and jars amongst themselves; for if God is with them, surely they would be agreed and have fellowship together, as they profess the saints of God have in a high degree; but they are contending one with another, as is manifest to all; and that religion and power amongst them, which they call the power of God, is a false religion, nothing but a mere noise and an empty sound." pp. 373, 374. "Notwithstanding all that the Separates pretend to, we think that they are them false prophets that Christ speaks of in the 24 of Matt. — 'that if it were possible they shall deceive the very elect.'" p. 392. "Notwithstanding all that the Separates say, or preach, or write, yet they do not convince us that they are right, or that God is with them; and surely if God was with them, as they contend, they would be able to convince us, either by scripture, or sound reason, or they would be able to work a miracle, to show some undeniable sign, that we might believe." p. 398.

To each of these objections Mr. Frothingham makes a formal reply; of which the first may serve as a fair specimen. He denies that the established churches from which so many had separated were true churches of Christ for the following reasons: "The Churches that we have separated from generally hold that external morality is the door into the church, and that the Lord's Supper is a converting ordinance; or that all have a right to join with the church, that will make an outward public profession of Christianity, although they be unconverted." p. 340. "In the churches that we have left, there are many that are hardened and believe not, but speak evil of the ways, work, and power of God, and are awful mockers at the Spirit of God and the saints that are under the influence of the same Spirit; and these persons are indulged in the churches; therefore we have a just right and warrant in the word of God to separate from them. Acts xix. 9." p. 341. "Again, the Churches that we have left, have dwindled away into a dead, dry, lifeless form of godliness, and have denyed the power and life of godliness, and from such we are to turn away. See 2 Timo. iii. 5." pp. 341, 342. "Again, the Churches that we have left, are stuffed full of hypocrites or dissemblers; for they professedly take in the unconverted, and when they are in the church, they profess themselves saints, and are counted and treated as such; which is manifest hypocrisy in the sight of God and his saints." p. 342. This language manifests the same spirit which was exhibited by Whitefield, as quoted by Dr. Wigglesworth, in his Discourses heretofore referred to: One "unretracted error of Mr. Whitefield" is "what we find in his Journal when at Boston, in the year 1740, Thursday October 9th, where, after he hath told us 'that he saw a great number of ministers sitting around and before him, and that the Lord enabled him to open his mouth boldly against unconverted ministers; for he was verily persuaded the generality of ministers talk of an unknown and unfelt Christ,' he adds, 'and the reason why congregations have been so dead is because they have had dead men preaching to them.' . . . I believe many a stupid sinner hath read with secret pleasure, and thanked him in his heart, for thus transferring the blame to his minister, and so far excusing him for his unprofitableness under the sound preaching of the gospel of Christ." p. 32.

One more specimen may be pardoned, in which the author manifests some keenness of thought, though expressed in his customary uncouth style. In reference to the third objection, he says, "The fourth and last thing held forth in the objection is, Women's speaking in the Church, 1 Cor. xiv. 34, 35. This text no ways forbideth a woman's speaking, or breathing forth the ardent desire of her soul after God; and when she is placed at Christ's feet with Mary, Luke x. 39, in true humility and brokenness of soul by faith, beholding the divine excellencies and glories of the Godhead shining forth in that spotless and innocent Lamb of God. When the case is thus with any woman or child, they have a just right from Christ, who gives them these discoveries, when sweetly constrained thereto by the Spirit of God, to speak openly in the Church of the beauties and excellencies they see in their beloved; Cant. iii. 4, 5; and chap. v. 10, 16. But to take the scripture aforementioned in this sense, — that a woman shall not speak at all in a public assembly, — will contradict the examples of the following scriptures: Luke xi. 27, 28. 'And it came to pass as he spake these things, a certain woman of the company lift up her voice and said unto him, Blessed is the womb that bare thee, and the paps which thou hast sucked. But he said, Yea, rather blessed are they which hear the word of God and keep it.' Here is an example one would think sufficient to stop the mouths of all creatures who oppose a woman's speaking in a public assembly, in a proper season; for if a woman ever ought to be silent in a public assembly, surely it should be when the Son of God was personally a preaching with his own blessed mouth; but yet at this very time 'a certain woman of the company lift up her voice,' &c. No doubt but the carping Pharisees, who love a smooth form of worship, were highly offended at this woman's speaking and especially because she lifted up her voice so loud, and broke in upon Christ in his discourse, like a disorderly woman; and had it been so that them Pharisee hearers, who stood much for an even form, had been acquainted with Paul's Epistles (which were not then written), no doubt they would have (as our Pharisees do now), pick out them texts that say a woman shall not speak in the church (not considering what speaking Paul had reference to), and so accused her therewith, and have told her that she had broken the commands of God, and gone contrary to his word, &c. But let us consider, — Doth Christ, who is the great Head of the Church, say, Woman, be silent, and not disturb the public worship of God, by speaking with such a loud voice whilst I am a preaching; you are disorderly; you have broken the commands of God and the civil law: Constable, take her out of the assembly, and let her be fined, or cast into prison, 'till she is more regular, and learns not to disturb the public worship? Was this Christ's reply to the woman? Surely no! but the contrary. Christ shows his approbation of her speaking by taking an occasion further to teach her and all the assembly, from what she said, that true blessedness did not lie merely in being in human relation to him, but rather in being united to his divinity by a divine principle of grace implanted in the soul, which will lead a person both to hear the word of God and keep it." pp. 357–360. Other scriptures are then quoted to the same effect.

The first notice found on record concerning this separate movement in Hardwick is under date of July 25, 1749, when it was "Voted, that the church make choice of, and send to the Rev. Mr. Edwards, Hall, and Eaton, to come and give their advice about the dissatisfied brethren in our church, viz., Samuel Robinson, James Fay, Benjamin Harwood, Silas Pratt, and George Abbott, jr., whether they will advise the church to dismiss them, or proceed to censure them as irregular, disorderly members: — which council also came and gave their advice, as may be seen under their hands." "Sept. 20, 1749. At a church meeting in Hardwick, voted, that the church comply and fall in with the advice that the Rev. council gave. Silas Pratt, one of the dissatisfied brethren, complied with the council's advice. James Fay, Benjamin Harwood, and John Roberts [1] declared their non-compliance." At a later period, December 18, 1751, Silas Pratt and Jacob Abbott [2] were called to account; and February 4, 1752, it was "voted, that the reasons that George Abbott and Silas Pratt gave for their absenting themselves from the public worship of God at the meeting-house in Hardwick are not sufficient to justify their conduct. Voted, that

[1] John Roberts was not before named as one of the "dissatisfied brethren"; but he was among the most prominent; and Samuel Robinson, who was named, is here omitted from the list.

[2] From what follows, it seems probable that this name should be George Abbott. Similar mistakes are not unfrequent in Mr. White's records.

George Abbott and Silas Pratt be suspended from the sacrament of the Lord's Supper until they acknowledge their fault and amend." Again: "At a church meeting in Hardwick, Nov. 14, 1753, voted that Experience Johnson, Ichabod Stratton, Ezekiel Pratt, Elisha Higgins and his wife, and Oliver Rice, be called to give the reasons why they absent themselves from the sacrament of the Lord's Supper in this place, and that Edward Allen be also called to give his reasons why he refuses to partake of the Lord's Supper in any church whatever." Also, "that a committee be chosen to meet with the members that have separated from this church, and to propose some reconciling methods to them: Deacon Allen, Deacon Cooper, Lieut. Mirick, John Bradish, Ichabod Stratton, Jr., and Benjamin Whipple, were chosen for this committee." The result of this labor does not appear on record, except that, March 3, 1757, Experience Johnson was "censured by the church for his absenting himself from the sacrament of the Lord's Supper for several years;" and, May 26, 1763, "Ichabod Stratton confessed his fault in separating from the Church of Christ in Hardwick, was forgiven by the church, and admitted to former privileges."[1]

Meanwhile, the Separates had organized a church, and had probably erected a meeting-house on the northwest corner of the "ten acres" devoted to a public use, which was subsequently confirmed to them by the proprietors. The original Covenant is still in existence, and was manifestly written by an uneducated scribe, of which the following is a literal copy, made in 1877, the spelling and punctuation only being revised:

"THE COVENANT.

"We whose names are under written, apprehending ourselves called of God into church state of the gospel, do first of all confess ourselves unworthy to be so highly favored of the Lord, and admire that rich and full grace of his, which triumphs over so great unworthiness; and then, with a humble reliance on the

[1] The only action of the town in regard to the Separates, which I find, is under date of May 9, 1754, and May 16, 1757; at the first date, when met "to see if the town will release a number of the inhabitants of the town from paying towards the support of the settled minister in said town, who assemble and meet together for religious worship by themselves, and are generally called Separates, after considering the matter respecting freeing the Separates, as expressed in the last article in the warrant, it being put to vote, it passed in the negative." The second trial had a similar result.

aids of grace therein promised for them, in a sense of their inability to do any good thing, do humbly wait on him for all; and we now thankfully lay hold on his covenant, and would choose the things that please him.

"We declare our serious belief of the Christian Religion, as contained in the Sacred Scriptures, and with such a view thereof as the Confession of Faith and Rule of Discipline in Cambridge Platform has exhibited, — heartily resolving to conform our lives unto the rules of that holy religion as long as we live in the world. We give ourselves unto the Lord Jehovah, who is the Father, and the Son, and the Holy Spirit, and avouch him this day to be our God, our Father, our Saviour, and our Leader; and receive him as our portion forever. We give up ourselves unto the blessed Jesus, who is the Lord Jehovah, and adhere to him as the head of his people in the covenant of grace, and rely on him as our Priest, and our Prophet, and our King, to bring us unto eternal blessedness. We acknowledge our everlasting and indispensable obligation to glorify our God in all the duties of a godly, a sober, and a righteous life, and very particularly in the duties of a church state, and a body of people associated together for an obedience to him in all the ordinances of the gospel; and we herein depend upon his gracious assistance for our faithful discharge of the duties thus incumbent on us. We desire, and intend (with dependence upon his powerful grace), we engage to walk together as a church of the Lord Jesus Christ, in the faith and order of the gospel, so far as we shall have the same revealed to us, conscientiously attending the public worship of God, the sacraments of his New Testament, the discipline of his kingdom, and all his holy institutions, in communion with one another, and watchfully avoiding all sinful stumbling-blocks and contention, as become a people whom the Lord hath bound up together in the bundle of life. At the same time also we do present our offspring with us to the Lord, purposing with his help to do our parts in the methods of a religious education, that they may be the Lord's. And all this we do, flying to the blood of the everlasting covenant for the pardon of our many errors, and praying that the glorious Lord, who is the great Shepherd, would prepare and strengthen us for every good work, to do his will, working in us that which will be well pleasing: — to whom be glory for ever and ever. Amen."

This original covenant was written on the first page of a folio sheet of paper, which is still preserved by the First Church in

Bennington, Vt. On the second page the earliest signatures are arranged in two columns, as follows: —

John Roberts,[1]
Samuel Robinson,[1]
James Fay,[2]
Benjamin Harwood,[2]
George Abbott,[1]
Jacob Fisk,[1]
George Abbott, Jr.,[2]
Jedediah Rice,[2]
James Breckenridge,[3]
Oliver Rice,[1]
James Fay, Jr.,[2]
David Doane,[1]
John Fassett,[1]
Daniel Fay,[2]
Ichabod Stratton, Jr.,[1]
William Breckenridge,[3]
Benjamin Whipple,[1]
Eleazar Harwood,[4]
Samuel Pratt.[4]

Jonathan Scott,
Elisha Field,
Samuel Montague,
Elizabeth Scott,
Experience Richardson.

Rebekah Abbott,
Lydia Fay,
Marcy Robinson,
Baty Pratt,
Bridget Harwood,
Elizabeth Roberts,
Elizabeth Fisk,
Elizabeth Pratt,
Peace Atwood,
Prudence Whipple,
Martha Abbott,
Mehitable Fay,
Hannah Rice,
Elizabeth Fay,
Marcy Newton,
Hepzibah Whipple.

Joseph Safford,
Ann Safford,
Stephen Story,
Bethia Burnham,
Eleanor Smith.

Aaron Leonard,
John Wood,
Zachariah Harwood,
Philippa Wood,
Margit Harwood.

This Separate Church was organized in Hardwick about the year 1750.[5] Its deacons were Samuel Robinson and James Fay; perhaps, also, John Fassett. There is no known evidence that it ever had a settled pastor while it remained here.[6] So many of

[1] Removed to Bennington, Vt., in or about 1761.

[2] Did not remove to Bennington.

[3] The Breckenridges were of Ware. James removed to Bennington, but William remained at Ware.

[4] Probably removed to Amherst about 1756, and thence to Bennington in 1761.

[5] It must have been formed as early as 1750, for one of its members, Mrs. Elizabeth Roberts, died before the end of that year.

[6] There was a tradition, half a century ago, that the church had a pastor, whose name was Roberts. Perhaps it had this foundation: Mr. John Roberts whose name heads the list of subscribers to the Covenant, may have ordinarily officiated as a lay-preacher, or exhorter, which would account for his taking precedence of Samuel Robinson in the list.

its members removed to Bennington in 1761, that the Church, as an organized body, together with its covenant and records, was transferred to that town. It formed a union, December 3, 1762, with a much smaller representation of a similar Church which had removed from Sunderland to Bennington, and on the same day admitted five persons who had formerly been members of a Separate Church in Newint (a parish in Norwich), Conn., and thus was organized the First Church in the territory now embraced in the State of Vermont.

The particular method of this union of churches is recited by Rev. Isaac Jennings, the present pastor of the united church, in his "Memorials of a Century," pp. 31–33. That the covenant under which the union was consummated was not originally prepared for that occasion, but was the old covenant adopted at Hardwick about twelve years previously, and already bearing thirty-five signatures, is manifest for several reasons: (1.) The only reference to a covenant to be found in the articles of union is this: "It is agreed upon and voted by the Church of Christ in Bennington, that they make an exception in the fourth paragraph in the eleventh chapter in Cambridge Platform, in respect of using the civil law to support the gospel; and also the ninth paragraph in the seventeenth chapter, in respect of the civil magistrate's coercive power." The Hardwick covenant accepted the Cambridge Platform without qualification. In renewing or re-adopting that, it was natural to make exceptions, if desirable; but altogether unnatural to make such exceptions to the provisions of a new covenant at that time prepared as a basis of ecclesiastical union. (2.) Of the first thirty-five signatures to this covenant, all are recognized as Hardwick names except the two Breckenridges, who resided in the adjoining town of Ware; but there is sufficient evidence on the town records, that four of them, to wit, Deacon James Fay and his sons James Jr. and Daniel, and William Breckenridge, never removed to Bennington. (3.) Another reason is of itself conclusive: The signatures of the first nineteen males are autographs; but at least three of them had deceased before the union of the churches; namely, Dr. Jedediah Rice, who died at Hardwick April 4, 1756; Benjamin Harwood, who removed to Amherst and died August 19, 1758; and George Abbott, Jr., who had died, and the inventory of his estate was rendered August 16, 1761. Also, of the sixteen females whose names stand first in the second column, three had died, and three had changed their names by marriage, before the date of the union; namely, Elizabeth, wife of John Roberts, who died November 4, 1750; Elizabeth Fay, who died November 24, 1756; and Lydia, wife of Deacon James Fay, who, died before September 13, 1760, when he was published to his second wife; Betty Pratt, who married Elisha Field of Sunderland, January 11, 1753; Prudence Whipple, who was published to Deacon James Fay, September 13, 1760; and Mehitable Fay, who married Benjamin Rogers September 10, 1760. There can be no possible doubt that all these names were subscribed to the covenant before the union was formed December 3, 1762; after which new names were added to the list of subscribers on the same paper. The signatures to the covenant may with perfect confidence be classed thus: the names in both columns, above the first cross lines, indicate the members of the Hardwick church; those below the line in the first column, the members of the Sunderland church; those between the cross lines in the second column, the Newint members admitted at the time of the union; and those below the second cross line, the new members afterwards admitted. The conclusion of the whole matter is, that this ancient document, providentially preserved, furnishes incontestable evidence that the Separate Church, formed in Hardwick about 1750, together with the associates admitted December 3, 1762, became not only the first Congregational Church in Bennington, but also the first Congregational Church in the State of Vermont, retaining its original Covenant, with a single modification.

BAPTIST SOCIETY. The earliest notice of Baptists in Hardwick, which I have seen, is under date of March 31, 1777, when Ephraim Pratt, Ebenezer Lawrence, Abiathar Babbitt, William Perkins, Nathaniel Haskell, Jeremiah Sibley, Ephraim Cleveland, Jr., and Zebadiah Johnson, were so named, and their tax for the support of the ministry was remitted. In the Hardwick Archives is preserved a certificate, to wit: "The names of those that formed a Baptist Society in the southwest part of Hardwick: Moses Winchester, Seth Tucker, Jeremiah Hathaway, Joshua Tucker, David Elwell, Samuel Bowen, Henry Higgins, Seth Willis, Samuel L. Robinson, Aaron Chamberlin, Jesse Snow, Apollos Snow. — APOLLOS SNOW, *Clerk.* Hardwick, April 12, 1799." It is observable that this list does not contain a single name which was mentioned twenty-two years earlier, and when the society was legally incorporated seventeen years later, February 3, 1816,[1] another almost total change appears: David Elwell and Seth Willis being the only names which occur in either of the former lists. Before its incorporation, this society erected a meeting-house in 1801. In 1832, a new and commodious edifice was constructed; but this was sold to Mr. Daniel S. Collins, and converted into a barn, in 1846, when the society established its place of worship at Ware. The society was organized November 16, 1797. The church in connection with it was instituted September 16, 1801. The first pastor was Rev. Ebenezer Burt, who was ordained June 20, 1798. After a faithful and devoted ministry of nearly thirty years, he was dismissed November 19, 1827.[2] He subsequently resided several years in Ware, and then removed to Athol, where he died November 25, 1861, aged nearly 96. He continued to preach, occasionally, until extreme old age disabled him.

The successor of Mr. Burt was Rev. Joseph Glazier, who was installed August 2, 1831. From the number gathered by him into the church,[3] his ministry seems to have been successful; but it continued somewhat less than four years, and ended in April 1835.

Rev. Nelson B. Jones became pastor of this church in May, 1837, and sustained that office about two years. I have not been able to trace his subsequent pastoral labors; but in 1881 he was

[1] The corporators were John Raymond, Elisha Sturtevant, Seth Willis, Enos Newland, Masa Newland, Benjamin Rider, Timothy Hathaway, John Croff, Lemuel Wheeler, David Elwell, Judah Simonds, Judah Marsh, Gamaliel Collins, Asa Sturtevant, John Wetherell, Jeremiah Newland, Daniel Barrows, Aquilla Collins, Jonah Collins, Cary Howard, Jeremiah Campbell, Jeremiah Campbell, Jr., Lemuel Gilbert, Aaron Marsh, Zenas Marsh, Cary Howard, Jr., Isaac Barlow. *Mass. Spec. Laws*, v. 87.

[2] Some of these facts and dates were communicated to me in 1838, by Rev. Nelson B. Jones, then pastor of the church, and are presumed to be correct. A somewhat different account is found in Clark's *History of Norton*, p. 503, which I insert on account of some details: Ebenezer Burt, "born Mar. 9, 1766, was the son of Deacon Ebenezer and Abigail (Bassett), grandson of Ebenezer and Naomi (Campbell), and great-grandson of Ebenezer and Lydia (Tippen) Burt, who were among the early inhabitants of Norton. When fourteen years old he joined the old Baptist church. Aug. 29, 1794, he was licensed to preach by the Baptist church of Dighton, and preached in this vicinity till Nov. 2, 1796, when he removed to Hardwick, and gathered a society in the southwest part of that town, where he was ordained as an evangelist (standing upon a great rock), June 20, 1797. A church was organized in 1806, and he was installed the pastor, which position he held till November, 1846, when he preached his half-century Sermon." He may have preached such a sermon; but he certainly was dismissed long before that date, and had had at least two successors.

[3] The whole number of baptisms in this church, up to November, 1838, was 214: viz., by Mr. Burt, 134; by Mr. Glazier, 42; by Mr. Jones, 7; by other persons, 31.

residing in Prescott, without official charge, but continuing to preach as opportunity offered.

After the dismission of Mr. Jones, the pulpit was supplied one year by Rev. William Brown. About 1840, Rev. Joseph Glazier was recalled, and remained pastor of the church until April 1, 1846, when he resigned, and the place of public worship was transferred to Ware. He was not again settled in the ministry, but resided in Ware until his death, which occurred September 1, 1860.

The deacons of this church, while it remained in Hardwick, were as follows: —

Daniel Lamson,	elected 1801, dismissed 1806.
Seth Willis,	elected 1801, dismissed 1811.
Benjamin Rider,	elected 1806, dismissed 1814.
Eseck Brown.	elected 1811, dismissed 1812.
Enos Newland,	elected 1812, dismissed 1814.
Henry Higgins,	elected 1817, dismissed 1833.
Joseph Metcalf,	elected 1817, dismissed 1829.
John Pepper,	elected 1829.
John Chamberlain,	elected 1833.

UNIVERSALIST SOCIETY. At a quite early date there were in Hardwick several believers in the doctrine of Universal Salvation. Before 1790, Rev. Caleb Rich, Rev. Zephaniah Lathe, and perhaps other itinerant ministers, had preached here, in private houses or elsewhere, as opportunity offered. In 1796, Rev. Hosea Ballou was engaged to preach, once a month, in that section of the town which was afterwards incorporated as a part of Dana. He resided there, doing the manifold work of a pastor at home, and of an itinerant or missionary abroad, until February, 1803, when he removed to Barnard, Vt.[1] He afterwards removed to Portsmouth, N. H., in 1809, to Salem in 1815, and to Boston in 1817, where he died June 7, 1852, aged 81, having accomplished a work such as has been allotted to few mortals. He was one of the most remarkable men of this age. He has been not inaptly described as "an uneducated man, but a born theologian, a man endowed with the simplicity of a child and the intellect of a

[1] During Mr. Ballou's ministry, the General Convention of Universalists held its annual session here in September, 1798. On his removal to Barnard, he found among his hearers several Hardwick emigrants, such as Nathaniel Haskell, Prince Haskell, George Paige, Robert Dean, Seth Dean, Elijah Aiken, Solomon Aiken, Jr., Aaron Fay, Eliakim Fay, and Moses Fay. They may have been instrumental in his removal, having heard him preach when visiting their friends in Hardwick.

giant." His biography, in four volumes, by his friend and disciple, Rev. Thomas Whittemore, was published not long after his decease.

Before Mr. Ballou removed to Barnard, the town of Dana was incorporated, including within its limits that portion of Hardwick in which he and many of his hearers resided. Those who dwelt in the present town of Hardwick did not, for several years, organize a legal society, or maintain constant preaching. Some continued to worship at Dana, where Rev. Joshua Flagg [1] had succeeded Mr. Ballou; and others employed such other preachers as could be had, generally meeting in the hall of the Ruggles Hotel until the Town House was erected. Among those who thus occasionally ministered at the altar, the most prominent in all respects was the Rev. John Bisbe, who was born at Plympton, grad. B. U. 1814, studied law for a considerable time with Hon. Marcus Morton, then prepared for the ministry, and was ordained at Brookfield, November 14, 1821. From Brookfield he removed to Hartford, Conn., where he was installed August 19, 1824, and thence to Portland, Me., was installed there in August, 1827, and died March 8, 1828, at the early age of 36 years. He was regarded as a remarkably eloquent and powerful preacher, and as an exemplary Christian. During his residence in Brookfield he preached frequently in Hardwick; and under his influence, as it would seem, a petition for the incorporation of a Universalist Society was presented to the General Court, which was granted June 12, 1824.[2] A copy of the petition remains on file in the Town Archives, sufficiently characteristic to justify its insertion: —

" To the Hon. the Senate, and the Hon. House of Representa-

[1] Mr. Flagg was settled in several towns in the course of his long life; but I am not able to construct an accurate list. His decease was mentioned in the *Universalist Register* for 1861, then edited by Rev. Aaron B. Grosh, with an appreciative obituary: "Rev. Joshua Flagg died in Dana, Nov. 10, 1859, aged 86 years, 6 months, and 20 days, — after a ministry of more than sixty years, and the oldest Universalist minister in the State. Though of rude vigor and controversial spirit in his early days, when persecution and violent opposition were met on every side, yet his devotional spirit and earnest sincerity in later years won general regard, and the clergy of his town generally attended his funeral and paid due tribute of respect to his memory."

[2] *Mass. Spec. Laws*, vi. 215. The corporators were Daniel Ruggles, Constant Ruggles, Ezra Ruggles, Samuel Weston, Ira Ruggles, Samuel Granger, Gardner Ruggles, Anson Ruggles, Franklin Ruggles, Crighton Ruggles, Moses Mandell, Ebenezer Cobb, Simeon Crosby, Daniel B. Hinkley, Nathan Perry, James Sturtevant, William P. Jordan, Seth Hinkley, Stephen W. Paige, Ebenezer Perry, and Noah Beach.

tives in General Court assembled. The petition of the subscribers, inhabitants of the town of Hardwick, humbly sheweth: That we, being deeply impressed with a sense of the duty as well as the privilege of worshipping the Supreme Being agreeable to the dictates of conscience, and as we believe in the restitution of all things spoken of by the mouth of all God's holy prophets since the world began, and that God will have all men to be saved and come to the knowledge of the truth, and believing that the knowledge of this truth will have the most powerful influence to produce order, morality, and rational happiness, and as faith comes by hearing, and as we cannot hear without a preacher, — the prayer of your petitioners therefore is that we, together with others that may join us, may be incorporated into a society by the name of the First Universalist Society in the Town of Hardwick, in order that we may be enabled to command our own resources for the purpose of procuring and supporting a preacher of this great and common salvation, and other necessary concerns of said Society. And your petitioners, as in duty bound, will ever pray."

Little use of the act of incorporation seems to have been made for several years. Occasional preaching [1] was had from time to time, but regular services were not established until 1837, when Rev. John Pierce, a young man who had recently entered the ministry, was employed, and was ordained September 27, 1837. He remained here about a year; and subsequently preached in Dana and Lunenburg in 1838, and in Lunenburg and Shirley Village, 1839, during which year he also gathered a society in Townsend. "In the spring of 1840, he engaged to labor with the two societies in Lunenburg and Townsend." But he was soon prostrated by disease of the lungs, and died at Lunenburg, his native place, August 31, 1840, at the immature age of 26 years. He was a young man of fair mental endowment, and of great earnestness and zeal. His interest in the cause which he had espoused was manifested by the legacy of all his earthly possessions to the society in Lunenburg, the income to be devoted to the maintenance of religious worship, on condition that the society should raise a prescribed amount annually, for the same purpose. [1]

The successor of Mr. Pierce was Rev. Gilman Noyes, who was

[1] One of the occasional preachers was Rev. John H. Willis, who labored faithfully in many fields, and died on College Hill, October 9, 1877, aged 70 years.

[2] *Memoir of Rev. John Pierce*, pp. 39, 68.

born at Atkinson, N. H., in 1804, and grad. D. C. 1830. He was settled at Charlton in June, 1831, having charge also of the parish in Brookfield. He removed to Spencer in 1838, and thence to Hyannis in 1839. While residing in Spencer, he preached in Hardwick regularly once a month. About 1843 he removed to Brimfield, where he devoted a portion of his time to agricultural pursuits, and where he died October 18, 1863, aged 59.

Rev. Rufus S. Pope, born in Stoughton, April 2, 1809, was ordained during the session of the Boston Association at Gloucester, December 4, 1833. He had commenced preaching in the previous August, at South Dedham (now Norwood), where he remained three years, dividing his services a portion of the time between that parish and Milford. In 1836 he removed to Sterling, and had charge of that parish until April, 1840, when he came to Hardwick. While here, his ministry was very successful. A church of twenty-seven members was organized. A new meeting-house was erected, under an arrangement with the Congregational Society, in 1841, and for the next year the two societies united in one congregation. In April, 1843, he removed to Hyannis, where he died June 5, 1882. He was a representative in the General Court, in 1855; register of probate in Barnstable County, from 1855 to 1857; and postmaster in Hyannis from 1862 to 1870.

The subsequent history of the Universalist Society, embracing its substantial consolidation with the Congregational Society, and its succession of pastors, — Rev. Messrs. Smith, Sanger, Moore, Jewell, Crosley, and Stevenson, — has already been narrated, and need not be repeated. The deacons elected by the Universalist Church, at its organization December 24, 1842, were:

Constant Ruggles, died April 28, 1846, aged 79.
Joseph Burgess, died July 20, 1879, aged 79.
Constant Southworth, died December 5, 1877, aged 63.

Methodist Society. Many years ago a Methodist Society was organized at the Furnace Village, and erected a neat and commodious meeting-house on the west side of Moose Brook about the year 1845. Though not lacking in zeal, it was never strong in membership and wealth. It has generally been classed with Barre by the Conference, the same preacher having charge of both societies. I would be glad to record the names of the several preachers from the beginning, but all my efforts to obtain an accurate list have been unavailing. And equally unsuccessful have I been in seeking from both preachers and laymen such information as would enable me to give a satisfactory account of the fortunes of this society, whether prosperous or adverse.

TRINITARIAN CONGREGATIONAL CHURCH. Almost all the facts here related concerning this church are gleaned from its Manual, and from a Decennial Sermon by its pastor, the Rev. Willard D. Brown. "The very first words in the records of the Church are these: 'From the commencement of the present manufacturing village of Gilbertville in 1860, the proprietors have felt much interest in the moral welfare of the place, and have spared no pains to secure the improvement of its population.'"[1] The princely munificence of Mr. George H. Gilbert, of his family, and of the manufacturing corporation bearing his name, richly deserves this recognition by the beneficiaries. "The Gilbertville Hall was dedicated December 27, 1863, and was used as a place of worship until the completion and dedication, on September 10, 1874, of the house of worship now occupied by the church and society. From December, 1863, until August, 1865 (except during a portion of the winter of 1864–65), there was preaching Sunday afternoons by Rev. Messrs. Perkins, Tuttle, Gordon, and Merrill, of Ware, Tupper, of Hardwick, and Gurney, of New Braintree. From that time till March, 1866, Rev. William H. Beecher, of North Brookfield, preached as a stated supply, and he was succeeded by Rev. R. P. Wells, from Tennessee, who became acting pastor of the church, and remained with it until January, 1869."[2] The Rev. Rufus P. Wells grad. A. C. 1842, and took a partial course at the Theol. Inst. in Connecticut in the class of 1845. After a successful ministry at Gilbertville, he preached at Southampton, 1869–1874, and at Mason, N. H., 1874–1877. He died at Norton, May 25, 1877, aged 59.

The successor of Mr. Wells was Rev. Willard D. Brown, who grad. at Middlebury Coll., 1868, and at Andover, 1869. He became acting pastor of the church in September, 1869, and was ordained and installed December 6, 1870. The church "was organized March 7, 1867, and was composed of thirty-eight members, twenty-three of whom were received by letter, and fifteen on profession of faith. There were connected with it,

[1] *Sermon*, p. 5. [2] *Manual.*

during its first year, forty-eight members. There have been connected with it, up to the present time (1878), one hundred and thirty-three members, forty of whom were males and ninety-three females; forty-four have been received by letter, and eighty-nine on confession of faith."[1]

DEACONS.

Isaac H. Hoyt, elected February 14, 1868, resigned 1868.
Warner H. Joslyn, elected February 14, 1868, resigned 1869.
Wales T. Wilder, elected March 10, 1869.
Melzar Lamberton, elected March 1, 1877.

The meeting-house occupied by this church and society deserves special notice. Constructed of granite, "from foundation to top of spire," it is a perfect gem of architecture, and is the crowning ornament of the most beautiful and neatly-kept manufacturing village in the Commonwealth. For its erection, Mr. George H. Gilbert, who died May 6, 1869, aged 63, devised by his will the sum of $20,000; the manufacturing corporation which bears his name contributed $20,000 in cash, and in addition gave a spacious lot of land suitably graded and inclosed, and also put in the foundation of the edifice; his widow gave an organ, and his children the furniture, together with a memorial window in memory of a deceased sister. The whole amount of this magnificent gift is estimated at not less than fifty thousand dollars.

CATHOLIC CHURCH. The building up of a large manufacturing establishment at Gilbertville naturally attracted a numerous foreign population, most of which consisted of Catholics. Having worshipped for several years at Ware, they are understood to have been organized into a separate parish at Gilbertville. A spacious brick church was erected in 1872, on the west side of the river, in the northerly part of the village. Mass is celebrated in the forenoon of every Sabbath, with Sunday-school exercises at two o'clock, and Vespers at three o'clock in the afternoon. The congregation is larger than any other in the whole town, embracing about eight hundred souls, including children. The pastor in 1883 is Rev. John T. Sheehan, who resides in Ware. I am unable to give a more particular account of the parish.

[1] *Manual.*

CHAPTER XIII.

LITERARY HISTORY.

Graduates. — Clergymen. — Lawyers. — Physicians. — Poets. — Poetry. — Schools. — Early Teachers. — Appropriations. — School-Houses. — High School. — Social Library. — Early Proprietors. — Catalogue of Books. — Mount Zion Lodge. — Original Members. — Removal to Barre. — Masters. — Post-Offices and Postmasters. — Post Riders and Mail Carriers. — Centennial Celebration.

GRADUATES. The number of native-born sons of Hardwick who have received a liberal education and collegiate honors is not large. The following list is probably imperfect, but it approximates the truth. Two graduates, Lemuel Hedge and Sanford Lawton, though born elsewhere, are included, because they were brought here in their infancy, were of Hardwick stock, and were trained in our schools. Further notice of all these graduates, and also of the lawyers and physicians named, may be found in the Genealogical Register contained in this volume.

Luther E. Barnes	A. C.	1871.
Andrew J. Bartholomew	Y. C.	1856.
Barnabas Billings	B. U.	1791.
Joseph Blake	H. C.	1786.
George Blake	H. C.	1789.
Charles E. Bruce	A. C.	1845.
Henry James Bruce	A. C.	1859.
John Field	W. C.	1807.
Horace Gleason	W. C.	1828.
Matthew W. Haskell	A. C.	1853.
Lemuel Hedge	H. C.	1759.
Abiathar Hopkins	D. C.	1806.
John Lawton	Mid. C.	1805.
Sanford Lawton	Y. C.	1825.
William A. Mandell	A. C.	1838.
Daniel W. Mandell	Mid. C.	1850.
William Mixter	H. C.	1829.
George Mixter	Y. C.	1836.

George Mixter	H. C.	1863.
Samuel J. Mixter[1]	H. C.	1879.
James Monroe	Y. C.	1845.
Christopher Paige	D. C.	1784.
Reed Paige	D. C.	1786.
John Keyes Paige	W. C.	1807.
Winslow Paige (honorary)	B. U.	1828.
Lucius R. Paige (honorary)	H. C.	1850.
Charles G. Pope	T. C.	1861.
Thomas Rice	Y. C.	1803.
Moses Robinson (honorary)	Y. C.	1789.
Jonathan Robinson (honorary)	D. C.	1790.
Alfred Stearns	W. C.	1812.
Squire Whipple	U. C.	1830.
Thomas Wells White	H. C.	1759.
John White	H. C.[2]	1765.

CLERGYMEN. The several clergymen who have had pastoral charge in Hardwick have already been mentioned under the ecclesiastical head, which may suffice.

LAWYERS. TIMOTHY RUGGLES, H. C. 1732, came here in 1754, and was soon appointed justice, and subsequently chief justice, of the Court of Common Pleas. He left Hardwick in 1774, at the commencement of the Revolution, and died at Wilmot, near Annapolis, N. S., August 4, 1795, aged nearly 84.

DANIEL OLIVER, H. C. 1762, commenced practice here early in 1767. He was one of the very few barristers at law in the Province, and apparently popular and successful. He left town with General Ruggles in 1774, and died at Ashstead, England, May 6, 1826, aged 82.

SETH PADDLEFORD, Y. C. 1770, soon commenced practice here. He removed to Taunton about 1778, was judge of probate for Bristol County, received the degree of LL.D. from B. U., 1798, and died January 7, 1810, aged 58.

PELATIAH HITCHCOCK, H. C. 1785, commenced practice here before 1791. He removed to West Brookfield, where he died April 25, 1851, aged 86.

LUKE BROWN, H. C. 1794, commenced practice here before

[1] Educated at the Mass. Inst. of Technology, and at the Harvard Medical School.

[2] CONTRACTIONS. A. C. — Amherst College. B. U. — Brown University. D. C. — Dartmouth College. H. C. — Harvard College. Mid. C. — Middlebury College. T. C. — Tufts College. U. C. — Union College. W. C. — Williams College. Y. C. — Yale College.

1799. He removed about 1807, and died at Enfield in 1835, aged about 60.

ELISHA P. CUTLER, W. C. 1798, commenced practice here. In 1805 "he removed to North Yarmouth, Me., and died there Aug. 29, 1813, aged 32. He was a man of much promise." "Williams Biog. Annals," p. 214.

SAMUEL EASTMAN, D. C. 1802, commenced practice here in 1807. He remained longer than any of his predecessors, but at length removed to Springfield. He died at Amherst, April 11, 1864, aged 81.

JOSEPH KNOX was here before 1831. He removed in 1837 to Rock Island, Ill., where he died August 6, 1881.

JOEL W. FLETCHER, A. C. 1838, came here in 1841, and removed to Leominster in 1843. About 1865 he removed to Cambridge, abandoned the practice of the law, and became an insurance agent. In 1879 he went to Chicago, where he died February 15, 1880, aged 62.

Since 1843, no lawyer has established himself in Hardwick. It is much to the credit of the town, as a peaceable and law-abiding community, that it has never required professional aid in its transaction of business, and its settlement of differences, to such an extent as to induce any lawyer to make this his permanent residence through life.

PHYSICIANS. No trace has been discovered of any physician in Hardwick earlier than 1749; since which time, however, the town has never been destitute of at least one medical adviser.

JEDEDIAH RICE was here as early as April 11, 1749. He had scarcely sufficient time to make full proof of his skill and usefulness, as he died April 4, 1756, before he was thirty years old. He was one of the earliest members of the Separate Church.

JOEL CARPENTER commenced practice here as early as March 25, 1752. He remained certainly until March 1, 1764; but how much longer does not appear.

CHALLIS SAFFORD was here in 1755. He died in 1771, aged 38, and left the reputation of a skilful physician.

JONAS FAY commenced practice soon after 1760. He ranked high as a physician, and still higher as a politician and a patriot. He removed to Bennington about 1768, and closed his active life March 6, 1818, aged 82.

ISAAC ROBINSON was born here in 1747. After a short practice here, he removed to Chesterfield about 1771, and later to Stamford, Vt.

JEDEDIAH FAY was born here in 1755. He is said by tradition to have practised in this town for many years; but precisely how long, and whether he died here, is not ascertained.

JOHN PADDLEFORD, Y. C. 1768, commenced practice here. He was authorized to establish an "inoculating hospital" in 1776. About 1778 he entered the navy as a surgeon, was taken prisoner, and died in 1779, aged about 31.

CHARLES DOOLITTLE was here as early as 1771. He was highly esteemed as a skilful physician and a useful citizen. He died June 12, 1785, aged 36.

LUCIUS DOOLITTLE was here in 1783, with his brother Charles, and succeeded him in practice. After a few years he removed to Lyndon, Vt., but afterwards returned, and died here December 1, 1831, aged 70.

ARTHUR RAWSON was here in 1785. Like several of his predecessors, he was cut off in early life. He died December 25, 1796, aged 38.

CYRUS WASHBURN was born here in 1774. After practising medicine in Hardwick a few years, he removed in 1803 to Vernon, Vt., where he died March 2, 1860, aged 85.

ELIAS PENNIMAN came here about 1793. He became insane, and died February 9, 1830, aged 81.

WILLIAM CUTLER came here in 1795. He was for many years the only apothecary in town, but refrained from medical practice. He died February 9, 1832, aged 78.

CONVERS CUTLER came here in 1796. He died November 1, 1831, aged 76.

JOSEPH WHITE bought the homestead of Martin Kinsley, January 7, 1796, and practised here for a few years. He was published, June 30, 1799, to Beersheba Jenney of New Bedford, to which place it is supposed he soon afterwards removed.

ELLIOTT BECKWITH probably commenced practice here in early life. When he died, March 6, 1814, aged 58, there was a general lamentation.

DAVID BILLINGS was born here in 1771. He practised through life, chiefly in the westerly section of the town and in Ware; he died October 15, 1833, aged 62.

JOSEPH STONE commenced practice here immediately after the death of Dr. Beckwith in 1814. He was skilful and successful as a physician, and rendered various important services to the town which are not yet forgotten. He died June 27, 1849, aged 59.

STEPHEN K. WARDWELL also commenced practice here immediately after the death of Dr. Beckwith in 1814. He was specially distinguished as a surgeon, and had an extensive practice in the neighboring towns. He died October 8, 1844, aged 55.

WILLIAM H. WILLIS was here in 1842, but removed to North Reading before November 14, 1843, when he was recommended to the church in that place.

LAFAYETTE RANNEY, D. C. 1842, and M. D. at the same College, 1845. He commenced practice here, but removed to New York city about 1852.

ISAAC G. CUTLER was here for a time after the death of Dr. Wardwell, but soon removed.

CHARLES FIELD also practised here for a short season after the death of Dr. Wardwell.

ALMON M. ORCUTT was the recognized successor of Dr. Stone, in 1849, and entered at once into a successful practice, which he still retains.

GEORGE CHAMBERLAIN was here about 1850, but soon removed to Brimfield.

JAMES P. LYNDE practised here a few years, but soon after 1855 removed to Athol, where he still resides.

JUBAL C. GLEASON was the first settled physician in Gilbertville. He came from Hubbardston to that village in 1867, and removed to Rockland in 1870.

WILLARD H. STOWE came from Vermont to Gilbertville about 1870, and removed to Palmer in 1876.

WILLARD C. HAVEN, son of Rev. John Haven of Charlton, commenced practice in Gilbertville in 1877, and removed to Brookfield in 1878.

WESLEY E. BROWN came from Paxton to Gilbertville about 1878, and is still a practising physician in that part of the town.

MRS. MARIA RUGGLES (wife of Moses Ruggles), though not a member of the Massachusetts Medical Society, has practised medicine in Hardwick for several years, and generally secured the confidence and approbation of her patients.

POETS. Many sons of Hardwick, whether residing here or elsewhere, have been eminently useful to the community in the various learned professions, as well as in the ordinary affairs of life; but very few have been publicly known as authors, either in prose or poetry. Of those few, in addition to brief notices in the Genealogies, I may be pardoned for mentioning two, — the one a permanent resident, and the other native-born.

Deacon Joseph Allen, who spent almost the whole of his active life here, and died August 18, 1793, aged 84, together with an absorbing interest in the straightest theology of his day, had also a passion for rhyming. During his life, especially in old age, he was accustomed to commit to writing his opinions and arguments on theological subjects, with exhortations to his brethren to stand fast in the faith, evidently with the hope that what he had written might at some time be published. He also expressed many of his thoughts in homely verses. After his decease, some friend caused at least a portion of his manuscripts to be printed in a pamphlet entitled "The Last Advice and Farewell of Deacon Joseph Allen to the Church and Congregation of Hardwick," pp. 51, octavo, Brookfield, 1795. The prose articles I omit entirely, but give space to two specimens of history "done into rhyme." The first[1] is entitled —

"SOME OBSERVATIONS ON THE TOWN OF HARDWICK, IN THE EARLY STAGES OF IT.

"When I look back, and take a view
Of that which now has been,
There then was found but very few
Which did this Town begin.

"In thirty-six I came into
This then a wilderness;
Great hardships we did undergo;
Our wants did daily press.

"Near thirty miles, without a road,
We were obliged to go,
Through woods, and streams, and depth of snow,
To fetch our daily food.

"The families were twenty-three
That then did here belong;
They all did hardships bear with me,
But now are dead and gone.

"My wife and I are left alone
Of all that married were;

[1] Written apparently in 1789.

And we remain their loss to mourn
Of whom we loved so dear.

"Of single men, there are but two,
And both advanced in age;
And all the rest, though but a few,
Are gone from off the stage.

"A Church was gathered the same year
A Minister ordained;
His call it was perfectly clear;
Great blessings he obtained.

"For more than forty-seven years
He did with us remain;
His doctrines were both sound and clear,
All of a gospel strain.

"Five years ago, he took his leave,
And bid us all farewell;
The loss, so great, we can't conceive,
'Tis hard for us to tell.

"So long we have been destitute;
How long we so must dwell;
For it is known without dispute
That none of us can tell.

"Yet must not do as some here say,
But constant use the means,
And wait for the appointed day
Till God shall change the scene.

"The greater part that here was born
Have early took their flight
Into a state that's most forlorn,
Or to a world of light."

. . . . . .

The next has reference to the extraordinarily cold winter of 1779-80,[1] during which, I have heard my elders say, for many

[1] The following article was republished in the *Boston Evening Transcript*, January 1, 1873:—

"COLD WEATHER IN OLD TIMES.

"NEW YORK, December 28, 1872.

"*To the Editors of the Evening Post:*— The present winter, thus far, has proved weeks the snow did not melt on the south side of the house-tops; the public roads became so blocked that locomotion was accomplished almost exclusively on snow-shoes, and burdens were moved on hand-sleds. It is entitled —

"ON THE SEVERE COLD WINTER IN 1779.

"Full seventy years I 've seen, and more,
Since I my breath did draw;
But never knew such cold before
As lately here I saw.

"From twenty-sixth of November,
Till ten weeks had an end,
A time we all shall well remember
How wood and hay did spend.

"The cold increased for seventy days,
With multitude of storms,
Till snow had clogged up all the ways,
For few of them were worn.

"The snow came down like fleecy wool
At times for forty days,

to be the most severe known for some years, and I thought the following extracts from an old journal might be of interest to some of your readers.

"The winter of 1779–80 was, in America, the severest that had been known since 1741. From November 25 to the middle of March the cold was severe and almost uninterrupted. The following was the state of the thermometer (Fahrenheit) at Hartford, Conn.:

January 1, 1780,	2	deg.	above.
" 2, "	7	"	below.
" 3, "	14	"	above.
" 4, "	16	"	"
" 5, "	6	"	"
" 6, "	10	"	"
" 7, "	9	"	"
" 8, "	1	"	below.
" 9, "	5	"	above.
" 10, "	19	"	"
" 11, "	26	"	"
" 12, "	11	"	"
" 13, "	8	"	"
" 14, "	9	"	"
" 15, "	15	"	"
" 16, "	10	"	"
January 17, 1780,	17	deg.	above.
" 18, "	12	"	"
" 19, "	13	"	below.
" 20, "	5	"	above.
" 21, "	6	"	below.
" 22, "	5	"	above.
" 23, "	9	"	below.
" 24, "	6	"	above.
" 25, "	16	"	below.
" 26, "	6	"	"
" 27, "	2	"	"
" 28, "	8	"	"
" 29, "	20	"	"
" 30, "	15	"	"
" 31, "	4	"	"
February 1, "	2	"	above.
" 2, "	3	"	"
" 3, "	3	"	"
" 4, "	15	"	"
" 5, "	8	"	below.

"Mean temperature for January at sunrise, 4 degrees; almost 20 degrees below the temperature of the same month in ordinary winters. . . .

"Very respectfully,
"Your obedient servant,
"COLEMAN BENEDICT."

Both at the change and at the full,
Which puts us to amaze.

"But little rain did then come down
To mix among the snow,
To wet the dry and thirsty ground,
Till springs were very low.

"But at the last, for thirty days,
No storm of any kind,
But only squalls, the wind did rise
And left keen cold behind.

"The freezing cold did waste the springs,
Till they were almost dry;
We hardly could, by any means,
Get ground our corn and rye.

"We could obtain but little meal,
To make for us our bread,
While we the keenest cold did feel,
Both up, and in our bed.

"The cattle too could hardly get,
From springs that used to burst,
The watery element, to wet,
To quench their daily thirst.

"This is thy hand, Oh mighty God,
Who orders seasons all,
And makes us feel thy smarting rod,
To make us prostrate fall.

"It is most fit that we endure
Thy sore chastising hand,
For our bold crimes they did procure
These judgments on our land.

. . . .

"Have mercy, Lord, for mercy's sake,
Give us thy sheltering wing;
And cause the winter soon to break,
And hasten on the spring."

. . . . .

Timothy Paige, Jr., Esq., native born, left town when young, and, after residing a few years in Georgia, settled in Southbridge, where he died November 14, 1822, aged 34. He published several poetical articles, generally with the signature of "JAQUES," in the "Massachusetts Spy" and other journals, which were well received, though most of them had a tinge of sadness, the result, perhaps, of a discouraging lack of health. I select the last verses which he prepared for publication (printed in the "Spy" December 25, 1822), together with editorial remarks: —

[With emotions which we cannot easily define, we publish, this week, the "Farewell to Summer," the "saddest and the latest lay" of one who (as is known to many of our readers),

"His finest chords by death unstrung,
Has yielded life's expiring sigh."

The "Farewell" derives additional interest from the fact that, although it has just reached us, it is altogether, even its superscription, in the handwriting of JAQUES. It comes to us like the breathings of a disembodied spirit, like a strain from the chambers of the dead. JAQUES was no stranger to us; in years long gone by we were inmates of the same dwelling. His spirit was too gentle, his chords too finely strung, to encounter the harsh realities of life; and he finally sunk under a sensibility too exquisite to endure the "ills which flesh is heir to." . . . . *Ed. Spy.*]

"FAREWELL TO SUMMER.

"Farewell, glowing Summer, thy last sun is beaming
His glow on thy cheek, and his light on thine eye;
To-morrow shall come, and his mellow beams, streaming,
Shall chequer the clouds of an autumnal sky.

"The foliage and flowers thou so fondly hast cherished,
The embryo hope and the wreck of the Spring,
Deprived of thy warm beams, ere long shall have perished
In the chill blast and shadow of Autumn's dark wing.

"Yet, welcome the change. — He who fashion'd creation
In wisdom such changes saw fit to ordain;
By contrast, life's joys have their just graduation;
Spring owes half its charms to stern Winter's dark reign.

"The sun, o'er his rising when gloomy clouds lower,
Like shadows that darken the light of the breast,

More brightly his beams sheds o'er streamlet and flower,
As in cloudless effulgence he sinks in the west.

"To the Spring let youth's jocund heart pay its devotion,
Contentment still revel on bright Summer cheer;
But misfortune's eye gazes, with deeper emotion,
On Autumn's dark landscape and foliage sere.

"And Winter, to warm hearts so chilling and cheerless,—
I remember the season when I too was gay;
When my heart was as light, and mine eyes were as tearless;—
But the flowers of that Summer have withered away.

"The cold blasts of Winter that sweep o'er the mountain,
His ice-fettered streams, and his wild waste of snow,
Add no chill to man's feelings, when pleasure's pure fountain
Has ceased in his bosom forever to flow.

"Man's Winter is death. In the cold grave shall slumber
The mortal; in mercy Heaven fixed the decree;
Pain, disease, disappointment, life's ills without number,
Return to the earth; yet his spirit is free.

"From that Winter of death, yet a bright Spring ensuing
Shall flourish thenceforth in perennial bloom;
Earth hath change, from the Spring-flower to Winter's dark ruin;
Existence unchangeable wakes from the tomb.

"*August* 31, 1822. JAQUES."

SCHOOLS.—For the first ten years after the settlement of the town I find no trace of public schools.[1] But at a town-meeting, April 2, 1744, it was "voted to get a school-master for the town, to begin in the first of September, and to continue eight months, and to remove four times." The first school-master was William Thomas.[2] At the close of his first engagement, under a warrant,

[1] The education of the young, however, was not wholly neglected, as is manifest from the fact that a large proportion of those who were then children appear to have been able, in mature life, both to read and to write.

[2] Father of Robert B. Thomas, the original "Author and Editor of the Farmers' Almanac," who, in a "Concise Memoir" of himself, published in the almanacs for 1833 and 1834, says his father, William Thomas, was born at Marlborough in 1725, and was educated in the common schools of that town, and of Shrewsbury. "Being of a studious turn of mind and fond of reading, he purchased many books and soon became quite a scholar for those days. In the year 1744 he commenced school-keeping at Brookfield, at the age of nineteen years, which he followed, winters, more or less, for upwards of forty years. The same year commenced in Hardwick, being the first school-master in that town."

"to see if the town will agree with the school-master for a longer time," the town, May 13, 1745, "agreed and voted to have Mr. William Thomas to be our school-master for the space of nine months; he is to begin to keep school the first of September, and keep nine months next ensuing; and for his so doing, he is to have eight pounds, old tenor, for each month he finds his own boarding." In the previous January, the town appointed a "Committee to divide the town into five parts for the school to be kept in"; and the teacher, probably, removed five times, instead of four times, as required by a former order. At a town-meeting, May 16, 1748, the town raised one hundred and fifty pounds, old tenor, for schools, to be divided equally between the five districts. This rule of division prevailed for several years; but it was voted, December 28, 1761, "that the Quarter in the middle of the town shall have three pounds out of the money raised to defray the necessary charges, for the use of the school, more than their equal part of the money raised before for the use of the school, by reason of other Quarters sending so many children into it."

The town voted, September 22, 1746, "that the Selectmen shall provide a school-master to keep school thirteen months." Under this vote, it appears that Thomas Ruggles,[1] of Rochester, was employed. Payments "for keeping the schoolmaster Thomas Ruggles" were made, October 19, 1747, to Captain Benjamin Ruggles (for "four weeks and a half"), £4 10*s*. 0*d*.; and to Constant Merrick (for four weeks), £4 0*s*. 0*d*.; also, March 6, 1748-9, to Matthew Barr (for four weeks), £4 0*s*. 0*d*. The names of several early school-masters are gleaned from the treasurer's accounts; but the materials for a perfect list have not been discovered. It may be observed that almost the whole number were inhabitants of the town, and that Lemuel Hedge, Thomas Wells White, John White, Reed Paige, and, probably, Alexander McDowell, were either students in college, or had already graduated.[2]

[1] Son of Rev. Timothy Ruggles. He subsequently returned to his native town, was a physician, and died before May 6, 1776.

[2] The earliest teachers were: William Thomas, 1745-6; Thomas Ruggles, 1747; Deacon John Freeman, 1748-57; Humphrey Peirce, 1749-50; Deacon John Cooper, 1751-9, 1766; Deacon Joseph Allen, 1751; Joseph Safford, 1753; Dr. Joel Carpenter, 1753; Stephen Fisk, 1756-7; John Bradish, 1757; Lemuel Hedge, 1757; Thomas Wells White, 1759-60, 1763, 1772, 1774; Dr. Jonas Fay, 1761-3; Alexander McDowell, 1765; Christopher Paige, Jr., 1766; William Oliver, 1766; Philip Jordan, 1766-7; John White, 1770, 1785; Ebenezer Washburn, 1771-2; Barnabas Sears, 1772; Nathan Wheeler, 1782; Reed Paige, 1785; Nathan Merrick, 1785, 1789; John Rice, 1787.

The Court of Sessions exercised a strict supervision over the towns in regard to schools. In February, 1746-7, apparently before Thomas Ruggles commenced his term of service, this town narrowly escaped presentment, or indictment, for neglect, and voted to pay ten shillings to "Lieut. Eleazar Warner for preventing the town from being presented for want of a school;" probably by showing that the town had already passed a vote to "provide a school-master, to keep school thirteen months." In August, 1758, Hardwick was presented for lack of a grammar school; but the record states that "the said town, being now provided with a school, plead that they would not contend with the king, but put themselves upon his grace; whereupon the said town was dismissed, paying costs."[1] In January, 1767, a fine of £8 6*s.* 8*d.* was actually imposed on Hardwick for delinquency in duty; whereupon it was voted, March 2, 1767, "to provide a grammar school-master for the year ensuing." At a later period, March 7, 1785, it was "voted to raise £80 for schooling, and to have the grammar school kept in four parts of the town so long as will clear the town of a fine, an equal proportion in each part, viz., at Edward Ruggles',[2] Colonel Timothy Paige's,[3] David Allen's,[4] and John Paige's,[5] on condition of their finding a suitable room and firewood for said school, free of cost from the town." If this vote seem to savor of parsimony, it should be remembered that it was passed at a time when the people, not only of this town, but throughout the Commonwealth, were groaning under the pressure of obligations, both public and private, so intolerable that a year later they were driven to utter desperation, and took up arms to prevent the collection of debts by process of law; so that the appropriation was as large as could be reasonably expected in such a state of financial distress. Generally, through the whole period of its corporate existence,

Among the more recent teachers were Colonel Samuel Mixter, of New Braintree, in the centre district, for five successive winters, before and after 1810, who was afterwards representative, senator, and councillor. Another was Hon. Henry O. Houghton, now of Cambridge (of which city he has been mayor), who graduated at the University of Vermont, 1846, taught in the northeasterly district during the succeeding winter, and has since acquired an enviable reputation as a publisher, printer, and manager of the "Riverside Press."

1 *Worcester County Records.*

2 On Ruggles Hill, at the place marked "A. Ruggles," on the R. Map.

3 On the easterly road to Gilbertville, at the place marked "A. Warner," on the R. Map.

4 On the road to Petersham, at the place marked "D. Allen," on the R. Map.

5 On the old road to Greenwich, at the place marked "Wid. Paige," on the R. Map.

this town has made a generous provision for the education of the young; but it has never been anxious to obtain notoriety by a competition with other towns in extravagant and unnecessary expenditures. Some of the early appropriations have been mentioned. From 1798 to 1821, the amount annually raised by taxation was five hundred dollars, each district receiving from the treasury the same sum which was assessed on its inhabitants. In 1821, it was ordered that seven of the districts should receive additional sums, amounting in all to eighty dollars; and thenceforth, until 1829, five hundred and eighty dollars was assessed. Since that time, in addition to voluntary subscriptions, and the amount received from the School Fund and from the Dog Tax, the sum annually raised by taxation is exhibited in the following table: —

1830, 1	$600.	1854,	$1,300.	1874, 5,	$3,000.
1832,	800.	1855–61,	1,500.	1876,	2,600.
1833,	700.	1862,	1,300.	1877,	2,000.
1834–6,	800.	1863, 4,	1,500.	1878,	2,500.
1837–44,	1,000.	1865, 6,	1,800.	1879,	2,000.
1845–50,	1,200.	1867, 8,	2,500.	1880,	2,300.
1851, 2,	1,300.	1869–71,	3,000.	1881,	2,500.
1853,	1,500.	1872, 3,	2,500.	1882,	3,500.

In 1745, the town was divided into five districts: the number was subsequently increased, from time to time, and has been as high as eleven; there are now ten districts, embracing fourteen schools. For many years each district managed its own financial affairs, and employed its own school-teachers, — subject, however, to their approval by the School Committee as competent and duly qualified to teach. This system has been abandoned, and the whole power is now vested in the School Committee, one of whom acts as the general Superintendent of Schools.

The first notice which I find on record concerning public school-houses is under date of April 5, 1790, when it was "voted to raise £500, for the purpose of building school-houses." The several districts were required to keep these houses in repair, and to rebuild in case of loss. Three quarters of a century later, the town assumed the whole charge and expense, and in a code of by-laws, adopted April 1, 1867, provided that all the school-houses be under the charge of one officer, to be styled Superintendent of School-houses.

Soon after his settlement as pastor of the Congregational Church, in 1832, Rev. John Goldsbury established a High School, which he conducted successfully until 1839, when he removed to Cambridge, to take charge of a similar institution. This school was attended chiefly by Hardwick students, and was maintained at private expense. After the erection of the Town House, the town voted, May 8, 1838, "that the use of the Hall be granted to Mr. Goldsbury for the purpose of keeping a High School."

LIBRARY. At the commencement of the present century two associations were organized in Hardwick, from both of which I derived so much personal benefit that I cannot forbear some notice of them. One of these was a Library Association. Under date of September 16, 1802, an agreement was made as follows: "That a Social Library may be purchased for our mutual benefit, we, the subscribers, do severally agree to the following articles, viz., 1. That as soon as a sufficient number of subscribers shall be obtained, we will each pay a sum not exceeding two dollars and fifty cents, and pay annually a sum not exceeding fifty cents for the term of seven years from the first payment. 2. That no person shall dispose of his right in said Library to any individual until he shall first give the proprietors an opportunity to purchase it at such a price as the proprietors shall annually agree upon. 3. We do further agree that when a sufficient number of subscribers shall be obtained, we will form ourselves into a Society agreeably to the laws of the Commonwealth."

The Society was duly organized at a meeting held in the "Centre School-house," December 13, 1802, when officers were elected, to wit: Thomas Holt, Moderator; Elisha P. Cutler, Clerk; Timothy Paige, Job Dexter, and Samuel Hinkley, Proprietors' Committee; Elisha P. Cutler, Librarian and Treasurer; Cyrus Washburn, Collector; and "It was voted to accept the rules and regulations drawn up by a committee appointed for that purpose, as the Constitution and Laws of the Library Proprietary. . . . It was voted that the subscription paper for said Library should be recorded in the Book containing the Laws and Constitution."

The subscription paper was recorded as directed; but the names of the subscribers are omitted. There is on record, however, "a list of the names of the Proprietors of the First Social Library in Hardwick, November the 12th, 1805, with the number of their shares," which probably corresponds very nearly with the list of subscribers: —

1. John Hastings, Esq.,
2. Timothy Paige, Esq.,
3. Col. Stephen Rice,
4. Seth Hinkley,
5. David Richards,
6. Samuel Hinkley,
7. Thomas Egery,
8. Livy Lawton,
9. Seth Peirce,
10. Job Dexter,
11. Israel Trow,
12. Nathaniel Paige,
13. Daniel Warner,
14. Ashbel Rice,
15. Timothy Fay,
16. Elijah Carpenter,
17. Josiah Newton,
18. Elliott Beckwith,
19. James Perkins,
20. John Gorham,
21. Lemuel Ruggles,
22. Prince Nye,
23. Silas Newton,
24. John Jenney,
25. Thomas Wheeler,
26. Elijah B. Harmon,
27. Josiah C. Chandler,
28. Jeduthun Spooner.

To these should be added the names of six original subscribers, whose shares had been assumed or purchased by the society before the date of this list, viz.: Samuel Beals, December 13, 1802; Cyrus Washburn, Ebenezer Ayer, and James Lawton, November 14, 1803; Elisha P. Cutler, August 1, 1805; and Thomas Holt, November 11, 1805.

At the meeting for organization, December 13, 1802, "it was voted, to receive certain Books formerly belonging to the old Library, to constitute a part of the new."[1]

Elisha P. Cutler remained in office as librarian until August 1, 1805, when being about to remove to Maine, he resigned, and Jeduthun Spooner succeeded him for the remainder of the year. At the annual meeting, in November, 1805, Elijah B. Harmon was elected librarian, and held the office for eight years. Samuel Eastman was elected in 1813, Timothy Fay in 1815, William B. Wesson in 1816, and Samuel Hinkley in 1817, who was re-elected from year to year until November 12, 1827, at which date the record abruptly ends. In the Book of Records a loose sheet is preserved, containing a memorandum of another annual meeting, without date, at which Joseph Stone was elected librarian; and it was "voted that the Librarian have permission to

[1] I have found no other trace whatever of this "old Library;" but of "the new" I made abundant use in my young days, and the general appearance of the books, as well as the fascinating character of their contents, remains vividly imprinted on my memory in my old age. Their perusal stimulated a taste for historical and biographical studies which has not yet entirely deserted me.

agree with Messrs. Hammond & Mixter to keep the Library at their Store." A "Catalogue of Books belonging to the Social Library Proprietary in Hardwick, and in possession of the Librarian, May 31st, 1831," was made, and Hammond & Mixter gave to the librarian a receipt for the same, which remains on file. An inspection of the Catalogue will afford proof that the books, though few in number, were of the most instructive and useful character; and it may surprise the readers of this generation, that among the whole number there was only one work of pure fiction, viz., the "Vicar of Wakefield."

CATALOGUE, ETC.

	Vols.
Belknap's History of New Hampshire	3
Hutchinson's History of Massachusetts	2
Biography of Naval Heroes	1
American Biography	2
Robertson's Charles V.	3
Buffon's Natural History	2
Ramsay's American Revolution	2
Hume's History of England	8
Park's Travels	1
History of Vermont	1
Apostolical Fathers	1
Spanish America	1
Life of Josiah Quincy, Jr.	1
Ramsay's United States	3
Adams' Defence of American Constitutions	3
Hubbard's History of New England	1
Millot's Elements of History	5
Historical Transactions	1
Marshall's Life of Washington	5
Flavius Josephus	3
Smellie's Philosophy	1
Robertson's Scotland	1
Minot's Continuation	1
Life of Charles XII.	1
Smith's Lectures	1
History of Greece	1
Bruce's Travels	1
Life of General Putnam	1
Hall's Journal	2
Life of Franklin	1
Jackson's Morocco	1
Clark's Travels	1

	Vols.
Discourse on Meekness	1
Plutarch's Lives	8
Rambler	4
Dodd on Death	1
Junius' Letters	1
Beauties of Spectators, etc.	2
Rollin's Ancient History	8
Forsyth's Italy	1
Life of Souvaroff	1
Watson's Apology	1
Vicar of Wakefield	1
Dodd's Thoughts in Prison	1
Paley's Evidences	1
Doddridge's Sermons	1
British Spy	1
Letter on the Genius, etc. of French Government	pamphlet.
Mr. Webster's Plymouth Discourse	pamphlet.

Unfortunately these books were scattered or lost, and the society ceased to exist. A new and much more extensive library has recently been established, under the patronage of the ladies. May the enterprise be crowned with abundant success and prosperity.

Mount Zion Lodge. The other association for intellectual and moral improvement, organized at the commencement of this century, was a society of Freemasons, bearing the name of Mount Zion Lodge. Its charter from the Grand Lodge bears date March 11, 1800, and its original members were Calvin Eaton, William Stone, James Lawton, John Shaw, 2d, Abijah Powers, Clark Powers, Asaph Newcomb, Rufus King, Roger West, Bradford Newcomb, James Stone, Thomas Powers, Jr., Seth Hinkley, Daniel Ruggles, Daniel Billings, Jr., Luke Brown, Nathan Freeman, Edward Ruggles, Peter Blackmer, Jr., Sylvanus Thompson, Samuel Beals, Daniel Thomas, 2d, Samuel French, Thomas Wheeler, Jr., and Elias Hall. About one half of these persons resided in Hardwick, and nearly all the others in Greenwich, including what is now Enfield. For the first quarter of the century the Lodge prospered, and embraced among its members many of the most eminent citizens of the before-named towns, and also of Brookfield (especially that portion which is now West Brookfield), New Braintree, Barre, and Dana. Its first place of meeting was in a spacious hall in the Willis Tavern, on the turnpike, marked "Dr. Wardwell" on the R. Map. In 1809, Daniel Ruggles erected a new tavern in the centre of the town, in which he fitted a hall for masonic purposes, and the Lodge was removed thither on the 18th day of October in that year. A procession was formed at the old hall at ten o'clock A. M., and proceeded to the meeting-house, where a discourse was delivered by Rev. James Thompson, of Barre, and the officers of the Lodge were publicly installed. The procession was then again formed and proceeded to the new hall, which was duly dedicated, and was thenceforth the masonic home of the Lodge, until, by permission of the Grand Lodge, it was removed to Barre, March 14, 1855.

In 1826, an anti-masonic tornado originated in Western New York, and rapidly gathering strength, swept furiously over the Northern States, carrying devastation and ruin in its path. Not only Masonic Lodges were destroyed, but the Churches of Christ were rent asunder, and many of them utterly ruined. Mount Zion Lodge was not seriously affected by this tempest until about 1832. It was not then absolutely destroyed, but for the next ten years was in a disorganized condition, and had scarcely more than a name to live. After its revival in 1842, its return to prosperity was very slow. Many of its former most active members had either deceased or had become disheartened, and retired from participation in its labors; and of those who had become of lawful age during the period of furious excitement, many had imbibed prejudices against the institution, which it was very difficult to overcome; and hence the accession of new members was hindered. Gradually, however, and notably since its removal to Barre, it has renewed its activity, and its prospect of permanent prosperity is highly encouraging.

I append a list of the successive Masters of the Lodge, with their respective residences, so far as ascertained.

1800–1802,[1]	Calvin Eaton,	Greenwich.
1803,	James Lawton,[2]	Hardwick.
1804 (Feb.),	Samuel Beals,	Hardwick.
1804,	Asaph Newcomb,	Greenwich.
1805,	Calvin Eaton,	Greenwich.
1806,	Asa Walker,	Barre.
1807–1809,	Argalus Thomas,	Brookfield.

[1] The annual meeting was in June until 1807; afterwards, in September.

[2] James Lawton died in office, and Major Beals was elected for the unexpired term.

1810,	Joseph W. Hamilton,	Brookfield.
1811,	Joseph W. Jenkins,	Barre.
1812,	Benjamin Jenkins,	Hardwick.
1813,	Argalus Thomas,[1]	Brookfield.
1814,	Peleg Aldrich,	Prescott.
1815, 1816,	Samuel Mixter,	New Braintree.
1817,	Warren P. Wing,	Greenwich.
1818,	Luther Spalding,	Greenwich.
1819, 1820,	Apollos Johnson,	Dana.
1821, 1822,	John Warner,	Greenwich.
1823, 1824,	Gardner Ruggles,	Barre.
1825,	Samuel Lee,	Barre.
1826,	Lucius R. Paige,	Hardwick.
1827,	Gardner Ruggles,	Barre.
1828,	James Thompson,	Barre.
1829,	Gardner Ruggles,	Barre.
1830, 1831,	Denison A. Robinson,	Barre.
1832–1841,	Few meetings held, and apparently no election of officers.	
1842, 1843,	Gardner Ruggles,[2]	Hardwick.
1844,	Denison A. Robinson,	Barre.
1845,	Gardner Ruggles,	Hardwick.
1846, 1847,	George Washburn.	
1848, 1849,	Gardner Ruggles,	Hardwick.
1850,	Joshua Flagg,	Dana.
1851–1853,	No record found.	
1854,	John Winslow,	Barre.
1855,	William A Fuller,	Barre.
1856–1858,	George J. Sanger,	Hardwick.
1859–1862,	James Holland,	Barre.
1863,	Chauncy C. Hemenway,	Barre.
1864,	James Holland,	Barre.
1865,	George M. Buttrick,	Barre.
1866–1868,	Joseph F. Snow,	Barre.
1869,	John W. Rice,	Barre.

[1] Captain Thomas afterwards removed to Worcester, and kept a popular hotel on Main Street, opposite to the Court House. In 1821, his name was changed to Samuel B. Thomas, by Act of the General Court.

[2] It was chiefly through the exertions of Major Ruggles (who had returned from Barre to Hardwick) that any vitality in the Lodge was preserved. For many years the Grand Lodge constituted him a "special agent" to conserve the interests of Freemasonry in Worcester County and all that part of the State lying west of it. On the first day of January, 1842, he reorganized Mount Zion Lodge, and, as its Master, nursed it judiciously for the next three years. This was the first-fruits of renewed masonic prosperity in Western Massachusetts.

1870,	Joseph F. Snow,	Barre.
1871, 1872,	Sewell Underwood,	Barre.
1873,	Charles E. Newton,	Barre.
1874,	John W. Rice,	Barre.
1875,	George L. Brown,	Barre.
1876,	Henry W. Hubbard,	Barre.
1877,	Joseph D. Wadsworth,	Barre.
1878, 1879,	Willie H. Osgood,	Barre.
1880, 1881,	William W. Stacey,	Barre.
1882,	I. T. Hinkley,	Barre.

POST-OFFICES, MAIL-CARRIERS, AND POST-RIDERS. At the commencement of the present century there was no post-office in Hardwick, nor indeed in this part of the county of Worcester. Letters addressed to our inhabitants were left at the post-office in Worcester, advertised occasionally, and at length obtained personally or by private conveyance. Some were probably conveyed by the post-riders, who distributed newspapers weekly through the county. The Worcester postmaster advertised letters remaining in his office, December 26, 1801, for persons residing in Gardner, Hardwick, Hubbardston, Oxford, Sutton, and Westborough; and the same towns are mentioned in an advertisement dated April 5, 1802, with the addition of New Salem and South Brimfield.

About the year 1805, a post-office was established here, and Dr. William Cutler was appointed postmaster, who was succeeded by his son, Samuel Fiske Cutler; together they held the office about thirty years, until 1836, when Frederick W. Delano was appointed, and the office was removed from its former location (where William Paige now resides) to the "Mixter Store." In 1850, Albert E. Knight was appointed, and is still in office after the lapse of more than thirty years. At a comparatively recent period, two more post-offices have been established here, one at Gilbertville, April 1, 1863, Lewis N. Gilbert, postmaster (Charles F. Hitchcock, assistant); and the other at the Furnace, April 1, 1875, Benjamin F. Paige, postmaster. The long-continued service of these several officers indicates faithfulness on their part and the approbation of their fellow-citizens.

For several years before the establishment of the post-office, newspapers, and very probably letters occasionally, had been brought into the town by post-riders, who resided here, and travelled, on horseback, once a week, to Worcester and back, and also to Northampton and back again,—each trip occupying two days. The earliest of these, whose name I have ascertained, was Eleazar Barrows, whose family resided in New Salem, though he died here, April 15, 1803, aged 58.[1] He announced his retirement from business, April 24, 1799, in the "Massachusetts Spy": "Eleazar Barrows informs his friends and customers that he has disposed of his route to Abraham White of Hardwick, who he is confident will be punctual in his business, and that the terms will be as usual. Said Barrows, sensible of the liberal support he has had from many of his customers, returns them his warmest thanks. And those who have been in arrears and still remain so, he flatters himself that this warning (being the last that will lay in his power to give them) will rouse them to a sense of their duty: for why will ye be sued? O, ye delinquent ones." I find no further trace of "Abraham White of Hardwick." But in January, 1803, George W. Webb, also of Hardwick, commenced his service in the same capacity, and six months later addressed to his customers a moving exhortation: "George W. Webb, news-carrier from Worcester to Northampton, informs his customers, that it is now six months since he began to supply them with news. He hopes he has given satisfaction to all, in the line of his business. He wishes those who are indebted to him to make an immediate settlement; they must remember that without the refreshing showers from heaven, the corn must wither on the stalk." [2]

Soon after this date the post-office was established; but whether Mr. Webb became the first mail-carrier, I know not. I do remember, however, that for several years the mail was carried by the post-rider, and that the service was performed on horseback. Afterwards, until 1818, a wagon, drawn by one horse, was used, affording opportunity to accommodate a single passenger. One of the latest professional post-riders was Nathan Reed, Jr., who left the service under a cloud, and who was the only one suspected of dishonesty, so far as my knowledge extends. He advertised, June 16, 1816, that he "will have rode six months as Post on the 26th instant, up to which time he requests payment." [3]

In 1818, Cyrus Stockwell made a vast improvement in the mail service. He had advertised, February 25, 1818,[4] that six months' service as post-rider would expire on the 11th of March;

1 "Died at Hardwick, Eleazar Barrows, formerly Post-rider from this office." *Mass. Spy*, April 27, 1803.

2 *Mass. Spy*, June 29, 1803.

3 *Ibid.*, June 26, 1816.

4 *Mass. Spy*.

and on the 26th of May he gave notice[1] that he would immediately commence running a MAIL STAGE from Worcester, through Hardwick, to Northampton, once a week; to leave Worcester every Wednesday, at 9 o'clock A. M., and arrive at Hardwick the same day and at Northampton every Thursday afternoon; to leave Northampton every Friday at 8 A. M., and arrive at Hardwick on the same day; and to leave Hardwick every Tuesday at 8 A. M., and arrive at Worcester on the same day. In other words, the mail stage was to run from Hardwick to Worcester every Tuesday, and return on Wednesday, and to Northampton every Thursday, and return on Friday.

The next material improvement was made after the present Boston and Albany Railroad was opened as far as West Brookfield. The mail was then carried for several years from West Brookfield to Hardwick by Mr. William C. Wesson, who ran a two-horse mail-coach between the two towns, daily, from July 1, 1845, to April 12, 1858. He was succeeded by others, until the cars commenced running on the Ware River Railroad, from Palmer to Gilbertville, in 1870. Since that time the mails have been brought into Hardwick by steam power, and each of the three post-offices receives at least a daily mail.

CENTENNIAL CELEBRATION. At a town meeting, April 2, 1838, it was "Voted to celebrate the Centennial Anniversary of the incorporation of the town; Voted, that the selectmen be a Board of Managers to conduct and manage said celebration; Voted, that the selectmen be requested to fix on a day for said celebration as near the date of said anniversary as can conveniently be done." The Board of Managers selected November 15, 1838, as the appropriate day for the celebration; but for what reason I know not. The anniversary of the incorporation did not occur until January 10 (or, allowing eleven days for change of style, January 21), 1839. Perhaps it was anticipated that the weather would be more propitious in November than in January; but the event proved otherwise. On the day of the celebration I think more rain fell than on any other day during that year. Despite this inclemency, however, a goodly number assembled, and, omitting the intended preliminary ceremonies, made their way, as best they could, to the old meeting-house, where for the next four hours they exhibited the most praiseworthy patience and forbearance. An account of the celebra-

[1] *Mass. Spy.*

tion, written by Dr. Joseph Stone, was published in the "Barre Gazette," November 23, 1838. A commendable local pride and a generous friendship to the orator of the day may have imparted a somewhat roseate tint to the picture; but I venture to insert it, as the only contemporaneous description of the Centennial Celebration which is known to exist: —

"CENTENNIAL CELEBRATION AT HARDWICK.

"The day assigned for this celebration, Thursday, the 15th instant, was peculiarly unfavorable. With the exception of a short period, from ten to eleven o'clock A. M., the rain fell copiously through the day. In consequence of this, many were prevented from attending, and many of the previous arrangements could not be carried into effect.

"A procession of citizens only was formed at the Brick Church, and, attended by a fine band of music, the members of which were mostly from Barre, proceeded to the old meeting-house, where the following exercises were attended to: —

"1st. Music; the 100th of Watts' Psalms. Tune, Denmark.

"2d. Introductory Prayer, and reading selections from the Scriptures, by Rev. John Goldsbury.

"3d. Music; the 408th Hymn of Greenwood's collection. Tune, St. Martin's. Read in beautiful style, line by line, by Deacon Josiah C. Chandler, and sung in that manner by the choir.

"4th. Prayer, by Rev. Mr. Goldsbury.

"5th. Music; Hymn by Flint, the 555th of Greenwood's collection.

"6th. Address, by Rev. Lucius R. Paige.

"7th. Concluding Prayer, by Rev. Nelson B. Jones, of the Baptist Church in Hardwick.

"8th. Music; Anthem, 'O, come, let us sing unto the Lord.'

"9th. Benediction.

"Notwithstanding the unpleasant state of the weather, the large meeting-house was well filled by an attentive and gratified auditory.

"After the services about one hundred citizens and ladies sat down to an excellent repast furnished by Mr. S. A. Smith. A gentleman from Hampden County, who was probably unused to the style in which such things are done in this vicinity, assured the writer of this article that he considered the entertainment superior to any he had ever before witnessed.

"The people of Hardwick are much indebted to the efforts of Mr. Moses Mandell, a native of that town, but now a resident in Barre, for the excellence of the musical performances by the choir.

"The devotional exercises, and especially the introductory prayer, were peculiarly appropriate and impressive.

"In delivering his address, Mr. Paige occupied two hours and fifty minutes. Perhaps higher praise cannot be given it than by saying that a large and promiscuous audience, going without their dinners to a late hour in the afternoon, and with a prospect, which was fully realized, of a dark and stormy night to travel home in, were nevertheless so highly entertained as to show no marks of impatience, but continued in rapt and undivided attention to the close. He described the purchase of the township from the Indians, and disclosed all that could now be known of the early history of the town, from the time when its northernmost inhabitant had no white settler between him and Canada to the time of the incorporation of the town, and gave a hasty sketch of the most prominent particulars in its history from that period to the present; and closed with an eloquent appeal to the inhabitants in behalf of their shorn and neglected centre burying ground. Arrangements have been made for printing the address; and its appearance from the press will be anxiously looked for by many, both of those who heard, as well as those who did not hear it.

"It is believed that the people separated with the conviction impressed on their minds, that the contemplation of the hardships and the sufferings, of the piety and the patriotism, of their excellent forefathers, was a much purer and nobler employment, and left much more pleasing emotion on the mind, than could result from either successful or unsuccessful electioneering efforts.

"S."

At the request of the hearers, the Address was published with an appendix, in a pamphlet of 76 pages, octavo. It was prepared under serious disadvantages, — a principal one of which was a lack of time to verify certain traditions received from the "oldest inhabitants," and to examine the original authorities for currently reported facts. For this and other reasons, several errors occurred in the printed copy, the more important of which are corrected in this volume.

CHAPTER XIV.

MILITARY HISTORY.

French War. — Brigadier Ruggles. — Muster Rolls. — Revolutionary War. — Minute-Men. — General Warner. — Lieutenant-Colonels Rice and Sears. — Muster Rolls. — Descriptive Rolls. — Petition of Shearjashub Goodspeed. — War of 1812. — Abortive Attempt to enlist Volunteers. — Political Celebration of Independence. — Oration. — Toasts. — War of the Rebellion. — Hardwick Soldiers. — Officers of Militia.

THE political action of the town in seasons of warfare has been described heretofore. It remains that the personal service of individuals should be mentioned. Except the sanguinary struggle at Winnimisset, in 1675, and the hand-to-hand conflict near the same spot, about half a century later, briefly related in Chapter I., the inhabitants of this territory were not engaged in actual hostilities until what is sometimes denominated the "old French War," commenced in 1744.[1] In this war, Hardwick contributed one victim, Samuel Abbott, who was killed at Fort Massachusetts, August 2, 1748. He was a member of Captain Ephraim Williams' company.

In the "French War" which followed, commencing in 1753, though not formally declared until 1756, Hardwick furnished its full quota of officers and privates. The most conspicuous officer hailing from this town was Timothy Ruggles,[2] who having already been commissioned colonel of the regiment of militia which embraced this town within its limits, entered the army as a colonel in 1755, was promoted to the office of brigadier-general,

[1] A military force, however, had been constantly employed, since "Queen Anne's War," to protect the frontiers against the incursions of the Indians, instigated and encouraged by the French.

[2] It is worthy of remark, that in the French War, the Revolutionary War, and the Shays Rebellion, the military commander, highest in rank in this county, resided in Hardwick, namely, Brigadier-Gen ral Ruggles and Major-General Warner. Moreover, the commander of the regiment to which Hardwick belonged resided here: Brigadier Ruggles, as the custom then was, retained the command of his regiment; Lieutenant-Colonel Stephen Rice, who was elected April 10, 1776, was the commander, after the resignation of Colonel Converse in 1778, until 1781, when Colonel Timothy Paige was elected, who remained in office during the Shays Insurrection.

and served faithfully until the close of the war.[1] Among his staff officers, inhabitants of Hardwick, were Samuel Robinson, Jr., adjutant, 1757; Challis Safford, surgeon, 1757; and Challis Safford and Joel Carpenter, surgeons' mates, 1759.

Next to Brigadier Ruggles in prominence among Hardwick officers was Captain Samuel Robinson, who commanded a company in every campaign from 1755 to 1759 inclusive, with perhaps a single exception. His muster-roll from March 27 to December 26, 1755, includes thirty-eight Hardwick names, to wit:—

Samuel Robinson, Captain.
William Paige, Lieutenant.
Eleazar Rice, Ensign.
John Blunt, Sergeant.
David Doane, Sergeant.
Ebenezer Whipple, Sergeant.
Richard Ellis, Clerk.
William Wood, Corporal.
Edward Blair, Corporal.
Isaac Gibbs, Corporal.
Thomas Barnes, Corporal.
Philip Safford, Drummer.[2]
David Aiken.
Simeon Bacon.
Jason Badcock.
Nathan Billings.
Oliver Cobleigh.
Jonas Fay.
Joseph Gilbert.[3]
John Green.
Larkin Green.
Thomas Johnson.
Edmund Jordan.
John Jordan.
Jacob Knowlton.
Phinehas Powers.
Moses Seaver.
Job Smith.
Nathaniel Sprout.
Daniel Stearns.[4]
Thomas Stevens.
Elkanah Stewart.
Seth Stewart.
William Stone.
Bartholomew Taylor.
James Taylor.
Pelatiah Ware.
James Whipple.

This company was engaged in the sanguinary battle near Lake George, on the 8th of September, 1755, and Sergeants Blunt and Whipple, Corporal Gibbs, and privates John Green and Bartholo-

[1] The value of his service was recognized both by the provincial and by the royal government. By an act of the General Court, January 6, 1764, a farm in Princeton was "granted to the Honourable Timothy Ruggles, Esq., his heirs and assigns forever, in testimony of the grateful sense this Court has of the important services the Grantee rendered his Country in the late war; more particularly while Commander-in-Chief of the Troops of this Province, furnished for the reduction of Canada." A few years later he received from the British government an office, probably designed in part as a reward for the same service. "We hear there are new appointments for Surveyors of his Majesty's Woods in North America. . . . Hon. Brigadier Ruggles for this Province and the northern parts of Nova Scotia, . . . with salaries of £300 sterling, per annum, each." *Boston News Letter*, October 11, 1770.

[2] Philip Safford was drum-major in 1757, and lieutenant in 1759.

[3] Died November 4, 1755.

[4] Daniel Stearns died in service, November 4, 1755.

mew Taylor, were killed; on the next day, Corporals Wood and Blair were promoted to the rank of sergeants, and Edmund Jordan, Jacob Knowlton, and James Whipple were made corporals, to supply vacancies caused by death and promotion.

In the campaign from February 18 to December 24, 1756, Captain Robinson commanded a company in which were Hardwick men (with their ages indicated by the figures in parentheses), as follows: —

Samuel Robinson, Captain (48).
Ezekiel Pratt, Ensign (37).
Jonas Fay, Clerk (20).
Philip Safford, Drummer (20).
Benjamin Whipple, Sergeant (30).
Jacob Knowlton, Sergeant (27).
David Gitchell, Sergeant (21).
Samuel Atwood (30).
Daniel Billings (28).
Samuel Church (40).[1]
Samuel Dexter (21).
James Doane (26).
Joshua Farr (21).[2]
Benjamin Goddard (19).
Dudley Jordan (20).[3]
Edmund Jordan (45).[4]
Amos Marsh (22).
Joseph Nichols (18).
Isaiah Pratt (35).[5]
Samuel Robinson, Jr. (17).
Samuel Stewart (18).[6]
Seth Stewart (20).[7]
Nathaniel Winslow (23).
Seth Winslow, Jr. (20).

It does not appear that Captain Robinson performed regular service in the field during the campaign of 1757; but he was not idle. The records of the Council show that provision was made to pay "to Captain Samuel Robinson the sum of £245, for ninety-eight men, and the sum of £9 15. 6. for his expenses in enlisting said men."[8] And in the pay-roll of Colonel Timothy Ruggles, in the expedition for the relief of Fort William Henry, is found the name of Samuel Robinson, captain.[9]

The regular muster-roll of Captain Robinson's company for the campaign from March 13 to December 1, 1758, is not found; but a descriptive roll, omitting the officers, contains eighteen Hardwick names: —

David Allen.
Oliver Cobleigh.
Samuel Dexter.
Daniel Fay.
James Fay.
Jonas Fay.
Watson Freeman.
David Gitchell.

[1] Died in service.
[2] Died October 2, 1756.
[3] Died December 6, 1756.
[4] Died November 18, 1756.
[5] Died October 26, 1756.
[6] Died November 18, 1756.
[7] Died November 6, 1756.
[8] *Council Records*, April 19, 1758. See next note.
[9] No allowance was made to Captain Robinson for travel, indicating that his service was rendered near home, probably in enlisting the "ninety-eight men" for the relief of Fort William Henry in August, 1757.

David Glazier.
Isaiah Glazier.
Stephen Gorham.
Daniel Hastings.
Jacob Hastings.
John Roberts.
James Robinson, Jr.
Samuel Robinson, Jr.
Philip Safford.
James Whipple.

For this military duty in 1758, the Council made provision to pay "to Capt. Samuel Robinson and Company the sum of £1422 3s. 7d., for their service on the intended expedition against Canada, under the command of General Abercromby, to discharge the Muster Roll, beginning the 13th day of March 1758, and ending the 1st day of December following."[1]

There is similar proof of similar service in 1759, but the Muster Roll has disappeared. The Council passed an order to pay "to Capt. Samuel Robinson and Company for their service in the expedition against Canada under General Amherst the sum of £908 10s. 6d., to discharge their Muster Roll beginning the 31st day of May 1759, and ending the 24th day of December following."[2]

Captain William Paige, who had served as lieutenant of Captain Robinson's company in 1755, commanded a company, from May 31 to December 24, 1759,[3] composed of officers and soldiers belonging to several towns. The commissioned officers were: —

William Paige, of Hardwick, Captain.
Cornelius Stowell, of Worcester, First Lieutenant.
James Henderson, of Rutland, Second Lieutenant.
William Ward, of Worcester, Ensign.

The following Hardwick names are found: —

Elisha Cobb, Corporal.
Samuel Billings.
Joseph Chamberlain.
John Cobb.
Lemuel Cobb.
Zurishaddai Doty.
Jonas Paige.
Shubael Winslow.

From March 11 to December 29, 1760, Captain Paige commanded a company, composed, like the other, of officers and men residing in several towns, and including seven Hardwick names: —

[1] *Council Records*, January 31, 1759.

[2] *Ibid.*, February 26, 1760.

[3] Captain Paige is supposed to have commanded a company at an earlier date; but no muster roll of such service is found.

William Paige, Captain.
Samuel Hedge, Corporal.[1]
Edward Foster.
David Glazier.
Isaiah Glazier.
Jonas Paige.
David Weeks.

Captain Ebenezer Cox, of Wrentham, commanded a company during the campaigns of 1758, 1759, 1760, and, probably, in 1761.[2] He then removed to Hardwick, and from March 4, to December 19, 1762, commanded a company, in which were Hardwick men, to wit: —

Ebenezer Cox, Captain.
Daniel Hastings, Corporal.
David Aiken.
Samuel Billings.
John Cobb.
Lemuel Cobb.
Thomas Freeman.
Stephen Gorham.
John Haskell.
John McSwain.
Caleb Nye.
Benjamin Raymond.
John Raymond.
Joel Simonds.
Nathaniel Whitcomb.
James Winslow.

To the foregoing persons should be added regimental staff-officers, namely: —

Samuel Robinson, Jr., Adjutant.
Elisha Hedge, Commissary.
Challis Safford, Surgeon.
Joel Carpenter, Surgeon's Mate.

Besides these were others who performed similar service under captains who did not reside in Hardwick, to wit: —

Stephen Fay, Sergeant.
Ebenezer Safford, Sergeant.
Samuel Winslow, Sergeant.
Isaac Clark, Corporal.
Ebenezer Lyscomb, Corporal.
Timothy Abbott.
Abel Benjamin.
Elisha Church.
Richard Church.
Dan (a negro).
Ichabod Dexter.
Joshua Elwell.
Caleb Green.
Zachariah Haskell.
Richard Hatch.
Simeon Hazeltine.
Samuel Hunt.
Ebenezer Lawrence.
Benjamin Mann.
William Merrick.
Peter Ott.
Joseph Petrell.
Timothy Sauge (or Sogg).
John Train.
Holland Weeks.
Paul Whipple.
James Whitcomb.[3]

[1] Samuel Hedge died September 11, 1760.

[2] Captain Cox, probably, rendered service before 1758, perhaps in a subordinate station. His epitaph asserts that he

"In *six* campaigns intrepid trod the field,
Nor to the Gallic Power would ever yield."

[3] James Whitcomb, aged 23, was in General Winslow's army, in the Eastern Expedition, and was killed in July, 1755,

All the persons before-mentioned are enrolled as officers and soldiers in the regular army for one or more campaigns. In addition to these, two whole companies were in the field, for shorter periods, on special occasions. One of these companies was in the Crown Point Expedition, from September 20 to December 5, 1756, namely: —

Paul Mandell, Captain.
Nathan Stone, Lieutenant.
Noah Mandell, Ensign.[1]
Timothy Newton, Clerk.
James Fay, Sergeant.
Solomon Aiken, Sergeant.
Silas Bowker, Sergeant.
Samuel Steele, Corporal.
Nathaniel Merrick, Corporal.
Joseph Higgins, Corporal.
Henry Chase, Corporal.
Eliphalet Ayers.
James Bacon.
David Barr.
Abel Benjamin.
Edward Blair.
Jotham Bruce.
Jonas Butterfield.
Isaiah Carpenter.
Lemuel Cobb.
Ebenezer Cummings.
Elijah Cummings.
Ebenezer Curtis.
John Fay.
Watson Freeman.
Solomon Gilbert.
Samuel Harrington.
Zachariah Haskell.
Jacob Hastings.
Elisha Hedge, Jr.
Joseph Hinds.
Seth Hinkley.
Sylvanus Howe.
David Marble.
Nathan Marble.
Benjamin Negus.
Daniel Parkhurst.
John Paige.
Jonas Paige.
Ephraim Rice.
Oliver Rice.
Whiting Ruggles.
Timothy Sauge.
James Whipple.
Asa Whitcomb.
Nathaniel Whitcomb, Jr.
Thomas White.

Another company marched, August 9, 1757, as far as Kinderhook, for the relief of Fort William Henry.

Joseph Warner, Captain.
Joseph Ruggles, Lieutenant.
Ezra Leonard, Ensign.
Silas Newton, Clerk.
Stephen Fay, Sergeant.
John Aiken, Sergeant.
Jonathan Farr, Sergeant.
Elisha Billings, Sergeant.
Solomon Aiken, Corporal.
Samuel Bridge.

as mentioned in the manuscript diary of Surgeon John Thomas: "July ye 25, A. D. 1775. I lodged at Fort Lawrance. Lieut. Willson came from Gauspereau, bringing an account that one of Capt. Cobb's men were killed, passing from ye foart to ye vilige on his hors; he and his hors ware both killed; his name was Whitcum; he came from Hardwicke. Colonel Munckton ordered Major Bourn out with 200 men to Gauspereau, to inquire into the affair."

[1] Noah Mandell was promoted to the office of lieutenant, October 29, 1756.

Joseph Chamberlin.
Richard Church.
Timothy Church.
Silas Dean.
Thomas Elwell.
John Fay.
Jonas Fay.
Aaron Forbush.
Joseph Higgins.
Thomas Johnson.
John Paige.
John Paige, Jr.
Timothy Pike.
Abraham Powers.
William Powers.
Oliver Rice.
Solomon Rice.
Leonard Robinson.
Daniel Warner.
Elijah Warner.
Thomas Weeks.
Asa Whitcomb.
Shubael Winslow.

During the Revolutionary War, Hardwick furnished its full quota of officers and soldiers. In anticipation of its commencement, as heretofore related, the whole military force was organized under officers elected by the town, including a company of "minute men," of whom the first captain was Jonathan Warner; he was immediately elected colonel, and became brigadier-general February 13, 1776, and major-general June 28, 1781, in which office he served his country faithfully until the end of the war, and during the Shays Insurrection. The company of "minute men," under a new captain, promptly reported for duty at Cambridge immediately after the memorable 19th day of April, 1775. The members of this company who responded to the call were: —

Simeon Hazeltine, Captain.
Josiah Locke, Lieutenant.
Ebenezer Washburn, Lieutenant.
Barnabas Sears, Sergeant.
Denison Robinson, Sergeant.
Stephen Gorham, Sergeant.
Moses Whitcomb, Sergeant.
John Raymond, Corporal.
Adnah Bangs.
Nathan Bangs.
John Butler.
Nathan Carpenter.
Edward Chaloner.
Isaac Clark.
Uriah Converse.
Jabez Cobb.
Paul Dean.
Samuel Dexter.
John Dunsmore.
Simon Fletcher.
Edmund Freeman.
Stephen Fuller.
Shearjashub Goodspeed.
Jonathan Hastings.
John Hedge.
Edmund Hodges.
Aaron Hudson.
Solomon Johnson.
Philip Jordan.
John Kinney.
Ebenezer Lawrence.
James Lawton.
Nathan Leonard.
Moses Mandell.
Caleb Nye.
Joseph Nye.

Prince Nye.
James Paige, 2d.
Jesse Paige.
Timothy Paige,
William Paige, Jr.
Josiah Perkins.
Elisha Pike.
Samuel Pike.
Edmund Rawson.
Isaac Rice.
Henry Rixford.
Josiah Roberts.
Joseph Robinson.
Thomas Robinson, Jr.
Benjamin Ruggles.
Edward Ruggles.
Nathaniel Ruggles.
Samuel Ruggles.
Thomas Ruggles.
Steward Southgate.
Daniel Thomas.
Ephraim Titus.
Joseph Washburn.
Joseph Weeks.
Judah Weeks.
John Wheeler.
Adam Willis.
David Witt.
James Wright.
Thomas Martin Wright.

Of these sixty-four persons, twenty-one immediately enlisted in the "Continental Army;" and of the forty-three others, at least thirty rendered service, sooner or later, in the same army. Captain Hazeltine was among the first to organize a company, consisting chiefly of Worcester County men, to serve three months from May 1, 1775. The roll, exhibited at Roxbury, June 10, containing fifty-nine names, included thirteen belonging to Hardwick, namely: —

Simeon Hazeltine, Captain.
John Raymond, Sergeant.
Prince Haskell, Drummer.
Seth Babbitt.
John Butler.
Edmund Freeman.
Ebenezer Luce.
Joseph Nye.
Josiah Perkins.
Daniel Rice.
Ebenezer Sprout.
Nathaniel Sprout.
Ephraim Titus.

It has already been mentioned that in reorganizing the militia with reference to the impending outbreak of hostilities, the town elected Samuel Billings, Jr., as captain "for the south side of the town," November 21, 1774. When the first blow was struck on the memorable nineteenth day of April, he immediately enlisted a company consisting of fifty-nine persons, fifty-seven of whom were Hardwick men, to serve eight months from May 4, 1775, to wit: —

Samuel Billings, Jr., Captain.
Barnabas Sears, Lieutenant.
Stephen Gorham, Ensign.
John Hanmer, Sergeant.
Steward Southgate, Sergeant.
Abraham Chamberlin, Sergeant.

Caleb Nye, Sergeant.
Adnah Bangs, Corporal.
Aaron Hudson, Corporal.
Joseph Weeks, Corporal.
Thomas M. Wright, Corporal.
Shubael Wilder, Drummer.
Moses Doty, Fifer.
Solomon Aiken.
Jedediah Bassett.
John Batchelder.
Joshua Boyden.
Nathan Carpenter.
Moses Chamberlin.
Edward Church.
James Crossman.
Daniel Evans.
Aaron Fay.
Simon Fletcher.
Philip Freiker.
John Giffin.
Benjamin Glazier.
Shearjashub Goodspeed.
Jonathan Hastings.
Elisha Hedge, Jr.
Henry Higgins.
Antipas Howe.
Philip Jordan.
Joseph Loring.
Marshall Miller.
William Merrick.
Reuben Ned.
Stephen Newton.
Timothy Newton.
Isaac Otis.
Joseph Pike.
John Plant.
Levi Pratt.
Stephen Pratt.
Moses Rice.
Josiah Roberts.
Jesse Safford.
Reuben Snow.
Thomas Spooner.
Zephaniah Spooner.
Robert Sprout.
Ephraim Thayer.
Daniel Thomas.
Ephraim Tucker.
David Weeks.
Edmund Willis.
Job Winslow.

Samuel Dexter, a member of the company of "minute-men," having enlisted a company at a later day, was commissioned captain December 10, 1775. "A Muster Roll of Capt. Samuel Dexter's Militia Company in Col. Learned's Regiment, from Hardwick, New Braintree, and Oakham, for their travel from and to home, at one penny a mile, — Roxbury Camp, January, A. D. 1776," contains the following Hardwick names: —

Samuel Dexter, Captain.
Thomas Robinson, Jr., Sergeant.
Samuel French, Corporal.
Atwood Aiken.
John Aiken.
Nathaniel Aiken.
Jonathan Childs.
Uriah Converse.
Nathan Crosby.
Paul Crowell.
Thomas Crowell.
Seth Dean.
Daniel Fay, Jr.
Alexander Forbush.
Jonathan Glazier.
Thomas Haskell.
Asa Hedge.
Moses Hunt.
Jesse Kenney.
Moses Mandell.

George Paige, Jr.
Jesse Paige.
Timothy Paige, Jr.
Lemuel Ruggles.
Thomas Ruggles.
John Wheeler.
Jacob Whipple.

Barnabas Sears, sergeant of minute-men, and lieutenant under Captain Billings, was captain in February, 1776, was elected major June 26, 1776,[1] and was styled Lieutenant-Colonel Commandant in a roll of field officers dated 1781. The roll of his company, at the Dorchester Camp, February 15, 1776, contained fourteen Hardwick names, to wit: —

Barnabas Sears, Captain.
Consider Eddy.
Nathan Foster, Jr.
John Gorham.
Andrew Haskell.
Moses Haskell.
Solomon Hedge.
Israel Lawton.
John Lawton.
William Merrick.
Reuben Ned.
Nathaniel Paige.
Daniel Ruggles.
Zephaniah Spooner.

In June, 1777, General Warner was appointed to command an expedition to St. John's River, N. S. His acceptance exhibits both his patriotism and his modesty: "May it please your Honors. By the direction of your Honors, the Secretary has acquainted me of my appointment as Brigadier General to command the Forces destined to St. Johns in Nova Scotia, and requires my immediate answer. I could wish a person of more experience had been made choice of, as your Honors must be sensible that military knowledge and experience is highly necessary in an undertaking of this importance, and the little opportunity I have had to qualify myself for so important an affair. But since it has pleased your Honors to appoint me to command in this Expedition, I will exert my poor abilities, and endeavor to deserve the honor conferred on your Honors' most obedient humble servant. JON^A. WARNER. Boston, June 25th, 1777. To the Honorable Board." [2]

[1] "The House made choice by ballot of the following Gentlemen as Field Officers for the Battalion to be raised in the County of Worcester for the continental service, agreeable to a Resolve which passed the House yesterday, viz:

"Jonathan Holman, Col^o.

"Paul Raymond, Lt. Col^o.

"Barnabas Sears, Major.

"In Council, Read and Concurred."

This battalion was destined to serve in New York; and the proportion allotted to Hardwick was thirty-eight. See *General Court Records*, June 26, 1776.

[2] *Mass. Archives*, cxcvii. 198.

Before this expedition was fully organized, however, the advance of General Burgoyne on the northern frontier created widespread alarm, and urgent appeals for aid were issued by the civil and military authorities. Among these was a letter from Colonel Seth Warner, still on file in the Mass. Archives, cxcvii., 321. On its receipt, General Warner forwarded it by express to the Council of this State: — "To the Honble Council of the State of the Massachusetts Bay: Gentlemen, I have this minute received an express from Col^{o}. Warner which I thought it my duty to forward to your Honors immediately. Accordingly I thought it expedient to issue out orders for every sixth man in my Brigade to march to the assistance of Col^{o}. Warner, by the way of Bennington, and desire your Honors would give direction in the matter as you shall think proper. As I have orders to march on an expedition to St. John's River, in Nova Scotia, your Honors will determine what is most expedient in the present distressing circumstances of affairs.[1] I am your Honors' most obedient humble servant, Jon^{a}. Warner. Hardwick, July 22, 1777, at 11 o'clock at night."

The detachment from General Warner's brigade marched within a few days, one company of which was commanded by Captain Edmund Hodges, one of the "minute-men," who had already become captain of militia. He was detached, with a portion of his company, to which were added officers and soldiers from other towns. The company, thus formed, was attached to the regiment of Colonel Job Cushing,[2] and served in the Northern Army from July 27 to August 29, 1777. The muster roll included twenty-nine Hardwick names: —

Edmund Hodges, Captain.	Atwood Aiken, Corporal.
Solomon Aiken, Sergeant.	Oliver Bailey, Corporal.
Ebenezer Lyscom, Sergeant.	Abraham Chamberlin.
Stephen Newton, Sergeant.	William Chamberlin.
Daniel Fay, Jr., Corporal.	Aaron Forbush.

[1] The Council directed General Warner, August 8, 1777, to disband the troops designed for the expedition to St. John's River, and on the next day appointed him to take command, as brigadier-general, of all the militia which had been fo r the reinforcement of the Northern Army.

[2] "A Pay Abstract of the Staff Officers of Col. Job Cushing's Regiment of Mass. Bay Militia in Gen. Warner's Brigade, on the Alarm to Bennington," contains the names of Colonel Job Cushing, of Shrewsbury; Lieutenant Colonel Stephen Rice, of Hardwick; Major John Rand, of Westminster; Major Joseph Bowman, of New Braintree. They continued in service from July 25 until November 30, and assisted in the capture of Burgoyne's entire army, November 19, 1777. See *Muster Rolls*, xxvi. 8, 10.

Nathan Freeman.
George Haskell.
Solomon Hedge.
Ephraim Hodges.
Moses Hunt.
Prince Jenney.
Philip Jordan.
Ezra Leonard, Jr.
Joslyn Munroe.
Timothy Newton.
Benjamin Ruggles.
Ephraim Ruggles.
Seth Ruggles.
Lewis Sweeting.
Gardner Wait.
Daniel Warner.
Elijah Washburn.
David Whipple.
Moses Whitcomb.

"A Pay Roll of Capt. Timothy Paige's Company, for going to Bennington in an Alarm," and remaining in service from August 21 to August 31, 1777.[1]

Timothy Paige, Captain.
John Dunsmore, First Lieutenant.
Job Dexter, Second Lieutenant.
Thomas Robinson, Sergeant.
John Raymond, Sergeant.
Samuel Beals, Sergeant.[2]
Jonathan Hastings, Corporal.
Thomas Ruggles, Corporal.
Ephraim Thayer, Corporal.
Prince Haskell, Drummer.
George Paige, Jr., Fifer.
Captain William Paige, Cadet.
Captain Simeon Hazeltine, Cadet.
Lieutenant Elisha Billings, Cadet.
Lieutenant Ebenezer Washburn, Cadet.
Seth Babbitt.
William Bassett.
Daniel Billings.
Elijah Carpenter.
Thomas Crowell.
Isaac Cummings.
Barnabas Cushman.
Silas Dean.
Jedediah Fay.
George Field.
John Giffin.
Lemuel Gilbert.
Shearjashub Goodspeed.
John Gorham.
Uriah Higgins.
John Jenney.
Lemuel Johnson.
Seth Johnson.
Gideon Newton.
Prince Nye.
William Nye.
Jesse Paige.
David Pratt.
Freeman Sears.
Abijah Sibley.
Elisha Sibley.
Jesse Snow.
Jeduthun Spooner.
Zephaniah Spooner.
Joel Stratton.
Nathaniel Swift.
Daniel Thomas.
Ephraim Tucker.
Robert Tucker.
Edmund Willis.
Silas Willis.

Before the arrival of this company at Bennington, the party

[1] *Muster Rolls*, xxii. 64.

[2] Samuel Beals was lieutenant in 1781, and deputy quartermaster general in 1787, with the rank of major.

detached by General Burgoyne had been defeated by the troops under General Stark, at the famous Bennington Battle, August 16, 1777, and the danger of serious disaster had been averted. But the main army of Burgoyne was still advancing. The volunteers had made no preparation for long service, and soon returned home. In this emergency, fresh levies of troops were necessary for the public defence. The order of General Warner to the commander of a regiment in his brigade has escaped destruction, and remains on file in the Massachusetts Archives, cxcviii. 127: —

"Bennington, August 25, 1777. Sir, With grateful acknowledgments of your forwardness in turning out men for the assistance of the Army in the late alarming crisis, wherein we have been favored with a surprising victory, but as the enemy are repulsed, and the men who came on the alarm cannot be prevailed with to tarry till the last of November, I am to direct you to see that every sixth man in your Regiment, agreeable to the Resolves of the General Court, be detailed and with all possible despatch marched to join my Brigade in the Northern Army, now stationed at this place, as those that turned out as volunteers are not prepared to tarry so long, and it is very necessary that the General Officers should know what number of men they have to depend on, in order to plan proper measures for the further repelling of the enemy. Therefore said Order of Court must be immediately complied with. I am, Sir, yours &c., JON^A WARNER, B. G. You will form the men detached from your Regiment into Companies, as near as may be to Order of Court, and appoint proper Officers to command the same, and order them to march with all possible despatch. To Col. Abijah Stearns."

Nathan Leonard, one of the "minute-men," commanded a company composed of Worcester County men, through the campaign from January 18, 1778 to January 1, 1779. The Hardwick names were: —

Nathan Leonard, Captain.
John Harris, Sergeant.
Josiah Green.
Andrew Haskell.
John Thayer.
Samuel Thayer.
Moses Winchester.

Daniel Shays, afterwards so conspicuous in the Insurrection in 1786, commanded a company during the campaign of 1778. Although he was not a resident in Hardwick,[1] I give him a place

[1] At this time Captain Shays resided in Shutesbury; he afterwards removed to Pelham.

here, as the influence which he gained over his men at this time may account for the adherence of some of them to him afterwards. His muster roll, dated Albany, February 9, 1778, contains eight Hardwick names: —

Daniel Shays, Captain.
Edward Chaloner, Ensign.
John Wheeler, Sergeant.[1]
John Plant, Corporal.
Shubael Wilder, Drummer.
Moses Doty, Fifer.
Joseph Hunt.
Elisha Pike.
Henry Rixford.

"A Pay Roll of Capt. Timothy Paige's Company, in Col^o John Rand's Regiment of Massachusetts Militia, raised for the defence of the United States, agreeable to a Resolve of the Great and General Court, bearing date June 22, 1780; raised for three months, and did duty at West Point in the State of New York." This company, which commenced service July 5, 1780, consisted of one hundred and two men, of whom thirty were residents in Hardwick: —

Timothy Paige, Captain.
Israel Lawton, Sergeant.
Israel Aiken.
John Aiken.
Ebenezer Barlow.
Joseph Barlow.
James Byram.
David Chamberlin.
Solomon Dennis.
John Earl.
John Gilbert.
Stephen Gorham.
Timothy Hathaway.
Job Hinkley.
John Hunt.
Elnathan Jenney.
Lemuel Johnson.
Gideon Newton.
Samuel Pike.
Peter Rice.
James Robinson.
Ephraim Ruggles.
Zephaniah Spooner.
James Sturtevant.
Jacob Terry.
John Thayer.
Samuel Thayer.
Isaiah Tower.
Abel Warner.
Silas Willis.

Many of the before-named soldiers served at other times, under other commanders; but I forbear the repetition of their names. Besides these were others, who performed one or more terms of service, under captains who were not resident in Hardwick, to wit: —

[1] John Wheeler was promoted to the office of quartermaster-sergeant before the close of the campaign, and in 1786 was aide-de-camp to General Shays.

Abraham Knowlton, Lieutenant.
Lemuel Leach, Ensign.
John Cobb, Sergeant.
Eli Freeman, Sergeant.
Silas Wright, Sergeant.
Jabez Elwell, Corporal.
Abisha Packard, Fifer.
Philip Amidon.
Jonathan Belding.
Phinehas Blood.
Joseph Boynton.
Joseph Byam.
Nathaniel Crowell.
Abijah Edson.
Thomas Edson.
Stephen Forbush.
Christopher Foreland.
Thomas Gilmore.
Bial Harrington.
John Hatch.
Samuel Hayford.
Samuel Hinkley.
Seth Hinkley.
Philemon Holden.
Sylvanus Hopkins.
David Hunt.
Samuel Huxford.
Stephen Johnson.
Thomas June.
Moses Lawrence.
Experience Luce.
Amos Mandell.
Calvin Marble.
Edward McMullen.
Constant Merrick.
Daniel Munden.
Ebenezer Nye.
Elias Nye.
Isaac Nye.
John Nye.
James Peirce.
William Raymond.
John Walker Robinson.
Cornelius Ryan.
Dennis Ryan.
John Ryan.
Roland Sears.
John Sellon.
Samuel Spooner.
Lemuel Swift.
Silas Town.
Thomas Tupper.
Jabez Upham.
Stephen Wait.
Ammiel Weeks.
Samuel Whipple.
Thomas W. White.
Thomas Winslow.

The following descriptive rolls, containing many names which have already been mentioned, and some which I have not found on the muster rolls, seem to be of sufficient interest to have place here. They are dated in 1778, 1779, 1780, and 1781: —

May and June, 1778.	Age.	Height.	Complexion.
Israel Aiken	18	5 feet, 9 inches.	Dark.
Gideon Billings . . .	19	5 " 6 "	Light.
Jonathan Childs . . .	22	6 " 0 "	Dark.
Aaron Fay	19	5 " 6 "	"
Jedediah Fay	23	5 " 6 "	Light.
Elnathan Jenney . . .	16	5 " 6 "	Dark.
Samuel Johnson . . .	22	5 " 6 "	Light.
Benjamin Ruggles . .	23	5 " 9 "	"
Levi Wellman . . .	19	5 " 9 "	"
Seth Winslow . . .	42	5 " 8 "	"

June, 1779.	Age.	Height.	Complexion.
Joseph Marapin . . .	17	5 feet, 5 inches.	Dark.
Gideon Newton . . .	19	5 " 9 "	Light.
Foster Paige	17	5 " 6 "	"
Nathan Paige	17	5 " 9 "	Dark.
Abner Perkins . . .	18	5 " 8 "	"
Stephen Pratt . . .	26	5 " 10 "	"
Charles Spooner . . .	16	5 " 0 "	Light.
Robert Sprout . . .	25	5 " 11 "	"
Jonathan Warner . .	16	5 " 3 "	Dark.
December, 1779.			
James Fay	45	6 " 0 "	Light.
John Gorham	20	5 " 9 "	"
Josiah Gorham . . .	18	5 " 6 "	"
July, 1780.			
Joseph Barnard . . .	30	5 " 5 "	Fresh.
Joseph Burgess . . .	19	5 " 11 "	Light.
David Chamberlin . .	19	5 " 5 "	"
Luther Conant . . .	22	5 " 7 "	"
Shiverick Crowell . .	18	5 " 10 "	"
Ezra Doty	19	5 " 8 "	"
Mark Elwell	17	5 " 9 "	Dark.
Solomon Farr . . .	17	5 " 5 "	Ruddy.
John Giffin	32	5 " 4 "	Light.
Nathaniel Haskell . .	18	5 " 8 "	"
Samuel Haskins . . .	21	5 " 9 "	Dark.
Noah Hatch	20	5 " 10 "	Ruddy.
Asa Hedge	24	5 " 7 "	Light.
John Hedge	28	5 " 9 "	Dark.
Ezra Hodges	18	5 " 4 "	Light.
Benjamin Lemoine . .	19	5 " 5 "	Dark.
Ezra Leonard, Jr. . .	22	5 " 8 "	"
John Marsh	19	5 " 6 "	Fresh.
Josiah Roberts . . .	26	5 " 10 "	Dark.
Nathan Sprout . . .	17	5 " 10 "	Light.
Samuel Sprout . . .	20	5 " 11 "	"
Jonathan Stanwood . .	39	5 " 7 "	Dark.
Heman Swift	19	5 " 10 "	Light.
Ebenezer Washburn .	46	6 " 1 "	"
May, 1781.			
James Bailey	18	5 " 2 "	Dark.
Zebulon Bassett . . .	23	5 " 5 "	Black.
Daniel Billings . . .	16	5 " 3 "	Light.

May, 1781.	Age.	Height.	Complexion.
Cato Boston	22	5 feet, 7 inches.	Black.
Luther Burgess	37	5 " 6 "	Dark.
Zimri Dean	18	5 " 5 "	Light.
Asa Doty	16	5 " 0 "	"
Moses Fay	18	5 " 7 "	"
Silas Gorham	17	5 " 8 "	"
Jupiter Lee	16	5 " 0 "	Black.
Jonathan Nye	22	5 " 11 "	Light.
Jacob Terry	30	5 " 8 "	"
Joseph Thomas	31	5 " 8 "	Dark.
Nathan Weeks	17	5 " 4 "	Light.

To these may not improperly be added the names of Sylvanus Brimhall, Jeremiah Campbell, Adonijah Dennis, Theophilus Hastings, and Captain Zenas Phinney, who rendered service while residing elsewhere, and afterwards removed to Hardwick, where, in their old age, they were enrolled as pensioners. Captain Daniel Egery, of Dartmouth, and Captain Israel Trow, of Norton, each commanded a company during one or more campaigns, but spent their last days here.

Among the large number of soldiers furnished by this town, it must be supposed that some were killed, and that others lost their health, or suffered other casualties. But the Muster Rolls, unlike those of the French War, are almost entirely destitute of information in this regard. There is preserved, however, in the Massachusetts Archives, clxxxiii. 405, a petition in regard to a minor casualty, which may deserve insertion, as it exhibits the character of a private soldier's outfit: —

"To the Hon. the Council and House of Representatives of the State of the Massachusetts Bay. The petition of the subscriber humbly sheweth, that your petitioner, being a soldier in Capt. Warner's Company in Col. Holman's Regiment, when our troops retreated out of New York, A. D. 1776, and being on guard when the retreat began, your petitioner lost his pack, containing the following articles, viz.: —

One knapsack, @ 4*s*. One straight bodied all wool coat, @ 60*s*.	£3.	4.	0.
One jacket of broadcloth, lined with shalloon, @ 40*s*.	2.	0.	0.
One pair of long woollen trowsers, @ 8*s*.	0.	8.	0.
One blanket, @ 20*s*. 2 pair stockings, @ 6*s*.	1.	12.	0.
One pair checked woollen shirts, @ 22*s*.	1.	2.	0.
Total,	£8.	6.	0.

These are, therefore, to pray the Honorable Court that the above account may be allowed, and your petitioner, as in duty bound, will ever pray. SHEARJASHUB GOODSPEED.

"Hardwicke, Feb. 9, 1778."

A large majority of the inhabitants of Hardwick were politically opposed to the War of 1812, and no action in its favor by the town is found on record. Personally, I remember that in consequence of a military requisition, there was an assembly of the militia in the spacious meeting-house, at which Major Thomas Wheeler presided. I was one of the excited group of boys who occupied the gallery, and witnessed the proceedings with intense interest. Although opposed to the war, Major Wheeler, as a good soldier, obeyed orders, and earnestly exhorted the soldiers to volunteer for the public service. At the close of his speech, he ordered a drummer to pass through the aisles, and invited volunteers to "fall in." But, according to the best of my recollection, only one soldier responded. Convers Cutler, Jr., followed the drummer on his noisy march round and round the house many times, but in vain. The attempt to procure volunteers was abandoned, and resort was had to the draft. Of those thus compelled to enter the army I remember only one, Jonathan Warner, Jr., son of my father's nearest neighbor. He returned safely after a short service, and subsequently removed to Hardwick, Vt., where he died in a good old age. Among the Hardwick soldiers in that war should be included Jacob D. Rand, a native of Charlestown, who resided here several years about the commencement of this century. Before the war, he enlisted as a soldier in the United States army, in which capacity he served until the surrender of General Hull, at Detroit, which act he always regarded as cowardly, if not treacherous, and could never speak of it except in language of indignation. After he was liberated, either by exchange or parole, he returned here, resumed business as a cabinet maker, and died October 8, 1840, aged 63.

A few weeks after the declaration of war, the Fourth of July was celebrated here by an oration in the densely-packed meeting-house, and a dinner and toasts under a bower on the Common. The orator was the Rev. Festus Foster, of Petersham, who sharply arraigned the Democratic party, represented by its great leader, Jefferson, and his successor, Madison, as responsible for the quarrel with England, which had resulted in war, — as he alleged under the influence and for the special interest of France. After extolling the administration of Washington and Adams, the orator proceeded to denounce the measures adopted by the opposing party : —

" Mr. Jefferson's accession to the Presidency formed a new era in our political history. . . . That system of policy under which our nation had enjoyed unparalleled prosperity was discarded for the abortive experiments of a visionary philosophy. The internal taxes, which were laid to augment our naval establishment, were suddenly repealed, and our ships dismantled and abandoned. For our new philosophers considered a navy worse than useless ; and a full treasury, lest it should tempt the cupidity of foreign nations, and involve us in war. . . . European nations smiled at our folly, and seized our defenceless commerce. Our merchants petitioned to government for protection ; our government remonstrated to the belligerents, who knew our weakness, and were insulted. Under the pretext of avenging our wrongs and insults, our whole commerce was suddenly annihilated ; many of our merchants made bankrupts ; our seamen made to beg their bread or flee their country ; and the whole community made poor in the midst of plenty. That a measure, which injured us more than all other nations, should be adopted and persevered in by our government, against the loud remonstrances of half the nation, is a mystery which yet remains to be explained, unless the hand of Napoleon was there. . . . The Embargo was not only approved by France after it was laid, but it was known in Paris that such a measure was about to be adopted, before Mr. Jefferson recommended it to Congress. Can any one who impartially views these facts doubt for a moment who originated and imposed upon us that destructive system ? Do you wish to know who has annihilated neutral commerce, and barred you from the ocean ? Ask France. Do you wish to know why the importation of British goods into these United States has been prohibited by law ? Ask France. Do you wish to know why and by whom you have been driven into a war with England ? Ask France. Her continental system has become the basis of our maritime law. The Embargo, under which we so long groaned and now groan, is her offspring. She dictates to us with whom we shall make peace, with whom war. We bow submissively to her imperious mandates, and yet contend that we are free."

The toasts, which followed the dinner, exhibit a similar partisan spirit : [1] —

[1] None of them, however, are quite so spicy as one which is said to have been

"The day we celebrate: It dissolved our union with Britain; may it never witness our alliance with France. — The memory of Washington: Had not our rulers set at nought his counsels, we had been at peace. — James Madison: It is not the most distinguishing trait in his character, that he does wrong by design, but that he should never do right by mistake. — His late Excellency Elbridge Gerry: Charity hopeth all things; we therefore say to the proscriptions and outrages of his last year's administration, his poverty, and not his will, consented. — His Excellency Caleb Strong: At the call of his countrymen, he comes like Cincinnatus, from the sweets of retirement to correct the abuses of a maladministration, and restore to the people their equal rights. — The Hon. Timothy Pickering: A real patriot, ever faithful in declaring those stubborn facts which Democrats dread to hear. — Massachusetts: The first to resist the encroachments of foreign despotism, — may she be the last to submit to the usurpation of a domestic faction. — Thomas Jefferson: He found our government 'in the full tide of successful experiment;' he left it ebbing to the common vortex of Republics. . . . The projected conquest of Canada: The feats of Don Quixote shall no longer excite laughter, nor his character want a parallel. . . . Modern Democracy: it has bruised our heel; let the next presidential election break its head. — The United States of America: may they remember from whence they have fallen, repent, and do their first works." One volunteer toast may properly be appended, concerning the "projected conquest of Canada," which, if not strictly decorous, was at least pointed and suggestive: President Madison: With both his feet in one stocking, and a Canada thistle in his small-clothes."

Such is only a faint reflection of the intense political heat which was manifested by both Federalists and Democrats, before and during the War of 1812. Within the next ten years it subsided entirely, and was succeeded by what was styled "The Era of Good Feeling."

Far different was the public sentiment at the commencement of the War of the Rebellion in 1861, and during its continuance until 1865. With scarcely any exceptions, the inhabitants of Hardwick, without distinction of party, rallied to the support of

offered by a zealous Democrat, in a neighboring town, on a similar occasion: —'The Federalists.' May they die and be buried, and sleep till the resurrection; and if God has n't a better opinion of them than I have, he won't call them up then."

the government, and promptly responded to all requisitions for men and money. Side by side, and with equal patriotic ardor, Republicans and Democrats marched to the frontiers, where they rendered faithful service, and some of them sacrificed their lives on their country's altar. The following list, gathered from the Adjutant General's official "Record of the Massachusetts Volunteers," probably embraces the names of nearly all the soldiers furnished by this town in the Massachusetts Line.

12th Regiment Infantry (three years), 1861.

Names.	*Age.*	*Date of Muster.*	*Date of Discharge.*
George H. Rolston	28	Sept. 22, 1862.	

15th Regiment Infantry (three years), 1861.

Names.	*Age.*	*Date of Muster.*	*Date of Discharge.*
Sanforth Botham	18	July 31, 1861.	Dec. 17, 1862.
George W. Davis	18	Aug. 5, 1862.	July 28, 1864.
Silas D. Marsh [1]	26	July 12, 1861.	Sept. 17, 1862.

18th Regiment Infantry (three years), 1861.

Names.	*Age.*	*Date of Muster.*	*Date of Discharge.*
George W. Campbell [2]	21	Aug. 24, 1861.	Jan. 25, 1862.

19th Regiment Infantry (three years), 1861.

Names.	*Age.*	*Date of Muster.*	*Date of Discharge.*
Edward Dunn [3]	18	Jan. 9, 1865.	Jan. 31, 1865.
August Ernst [4]	28	Jan. 9, 1865.	March 28, 1865.
Henry Lewis	24	March 22, 1864.	
John O'Brien	26	March 22, 1864.	
Joseph Patrick	21	March 22, 1864.	June 30, 1865.
Carl Rammelsburg	26	May 13, 1864.	June 30, 1865.
Thomas M. Stanton	27	March 22, 1864.	

20th Regiment Infantry (three years), 1861.

Names.	*Age.*	*Date of Muster.*	*Date of Discharge.*
Henry J. Coburn	20	July 5, 1864.	July 16, 1865.

21st Regiment Infantry (three years), 1861.

Names.	*Age.*	*Date of Muster.*	*Date of Discharge.*
George F. Lawrence [5]	21	July 19, 1861.	Aug. 30, 1864.
Augustus T. Barnes [6]	24	July 19, 1861.	July 12, 1865.
Lauriston Barnes [7]	22	Feb. 25, 1864.	May 15, 1864.

[1] Silas D. Marsh died at Antietam, Md., September 17, 1862.

[2] George W. Campbell died at Hall's Hill, Va., January 25, 1862.

[3] Edward Dunn died in the regimental hospital, January 31, 1865.

[4] August Ernst deserted, March 28, 1865.

[5] George F. Lawrence, promoted, second lieutenant, September 26, 1862; first lieutenant, March 6, 1863.

[6] Augustus T. Barnes, transferred to 36th Regiment Infantry, January 2, 1864.

[7] Lauriston Barnes, died of wounds, May 15, 1864, at Spottsylvania, Va.

Names.	*Age.*	*Date of Muster.*	*Date of Discharge.*
Barnes Brigham [1]	24	July 19, 1861.	Dec. 15, 1864.
William H. Cleveland [2]	21	July 19, 1861.	Aug. 19, 1863.
Marcus A. Emmons [3]	21	July 19, 1861.	June 2, 1864.
Clark Hill	31	Aug. 19, 1861.	Deserted.
Benjamin F. Pease	43	July 19, 1861.	May 8, 1862.
Henry M. Sherman	18	July 19, 1861.	Jan. 2, 1864.
Oramel F. Thresher [4]	18	July 19, 1861.	May 26, 1862.
Gilman E. Warner [5]	22	July 19, 1861.	Dec. 13, 1863.
Thomas Winn [6]	19	July 19, 1861.	July 12, 1865.
Hiram A. Wyman	22	July 19, 1861.	Aug. 30, 1864.

22d Regiment Infantry (three years), 1861.

John Banti	22	June 23, 1864.	
William Brown	29	June 23, 1864.	
Francis Kenna	23	June 27, 1864.	
Thomas McGinnis	22	June 27, 1864.	
Michael Muldoon [7]	42	June 27, 1864.	June 29, 1865.
David Pichitte	19	June 23, 1864.	
Philip Wagner	22	June 22, 1864.	

25th Regiment Infantry (three years), 1861.

Hiram V. Moulton	32	Oct. 12, 1861.	Jan. 2, 1864.
Adin P. Wetherbee	31	Sept. 21, 1861.	Nov. 28, 1864.

26th Regiment Infantry (three years), 1861.

Charles Edmands	22	Jan. 10, 1865.	

28th Regiment Infantry (three years), 1861.

Henry Bigelow	22	March 25, 1864.	June 30, 1865.
Thomas Hunt	22	March 25, 1864.	June 20, 1865.
Edward Lunt [8]	19	March 25, 1864.	April 23, 1864.
Malcolm McGregor	21	March 25, 1864.	June 22, 1865.
Thomas Shannon	23	March 25, 1864.	

30th Regiment Infantry (three years), 1861.

Edwin W. Hammond	25	Sept. 26, 1861.	July 5, 1866.

[1] Barnes Brigham transferred to 36th Regiment Infantry, January 2, 1864.

[2] William H. Cleveland died at Washington, D. C., August 19, 1863.

[3] Marcus A. Emmons killed in battle at Bethesda Church, Va., June 2, 1864.

[4] Oramel F. Thresher died May 26, 1862.

[5] Gilman E. Warner died at Camp Nelson, Ky., December 13, 1863.

[6] Thomas Winn transferred to 36th Regiment, January 2, 1864.

[7] Michael Muldoon transferred to 32d Regiment Infantry, October 26, 1864.

[8] Edward Lunt transferred to the Navy.

31*st Regiment Infantry (three years)*, 1862.

Names.	*Age.*	*Date of Muster.*	*Date of Discharge.*
Frank S. Knight, Sergeant [1] .	25	Nov. 20, 1861.	Jan. 10, 1863.
David D. Rogers, Corporal .	30	Feb. 9, 1864.	Sept. 9, 1865.
Newell A. Bacon	44	Dec. 15, 1861.	March 11, 1864.
Alonzo P. Brewer	18	Nov. 20, 1861.	July 22, 1865.
Charles H. Chandler . . .	21	Nov. 20, 1861.	Sept. 2, 1862.
John Devlin	25	Aug. 26, 1864.	Sept. 9, 1865.
Ebenezer W. Gleason [2] . .	43	Nov. 20, 1861.	Aug. 2, 1864.
James H. Gleason [3]	36	Dec. 2, 1861.	Feb. 8, 1864.
John L. Gore	26	Jan. 20, 1862.	Aug. 4, 1865.
Charles E. Mahar	18	Aug. 25, 1864.	Sept. 9, 1864.
John W. Parker [4]	18	Nov. 20, 1861.	Jan. 8, 1863.
Alden Rawson	18	Aug. 10, 1864.	Sept. 9, 1865.
George W. Richardson . . .	24	Nov. 20, 1861.	Aug. 27, 1863.
Joseph D. Richmond . . .	21	Nov. 20, 1861.	Sept. 9, 1865.
George W. Robinson [5] . . .	22	Dec. 10, 1861.	April 22, 1864.
Alfred D. Ruggles [6]	21	Nov. 20, 1861.	April 16, 1862.
Eugene Southworth . . .	21	Nov. 20, 1861.	Nov. 19, 1864.
Francis Spooner	18	Nov. 20, 1861.	Sept. 9, 1865.
James B. T. Tupper [7] . . .	22	Nov. 20, 1861.	June 30, 1863.

32*d Regiment Infantry (three years)*, 1862.

Frederick L. Taylor [8] . . .	20	July 18, 1863.	May 27, 1864.
Michael Muldoon	42	June 27, 1864.	June 29, 1865.

33*d Regiment Infantry (three years)*, 1862.

Calvin C. Deane, Sergeant [9] .	25	Jan. 7, 1865.	

34*th Regiment Infantry (three years)*, 1862.

William H. Tucker, Corporal	22	July 31, 1862.	June 16, 1865.
Dwight Cleveland	18	July 31, 1862.	July 16, 1865.
Samuel D. Peck [10]	25	July 31, 1862.	Feb. 11, 1864.

36*th Regiment Infantry (three years)*, 1862.

Barnes Brigham, Sergeant .	26	Jan. 2, 1864.	Dec. 15, 1864.

[1] Frank S. Knight died at New Orleans, January 10, 1863.

[2] Ebenezer W. Gleason died at Baton Rouge, La., August 2, 1863.

[3] James H. Gleason transferred to Veteran Reserve Corps.

[4] John W. Parker, died at Fort Jackson, La., January 8, 1863.

[5] George W. Robinson died at New Orleans, April 22, 1864.

[6] Alfred D. Ruggles died at Ship Island, Miss., April 16, 1862.

[7] James B. T. Tupper joined the Navy.

[8] Frederick L. Taylor died May 27, 1864.

[9] Calvin C. Deane "never joined Regiment."

[10] Samuel D. Peck transferred to Veteran Reserve Corps.

Names.	*Age.*	*Date of Muster.*	*Date of Discharge.*
Thomas Winn, Corporal[1] . .	21	Jan. 2, 1864.	June 8, 1865.
Augustus T. Barnes[2]	26	Jan. 2, 1864.	June 8, 1865.

42d Regiment Infantry (nine months), 1862.

George J. Sanger, 1st Lieut.[3]	36	Oct. 14, 1862.	Aug. 20, 1863.
William A. Perry, Sergeant .	41	Oct. 14, 1862.	Aug. 20, 1863.
Harmon C. Spooner, Sergeant	34	Oct. 14, 1862.	Aug. 20, 1863.
William F. Alden, Corporal .	32	Oct. 14, 1862.	Aug. 20, 1863.
Henry A. Spooner, Corporal .	24	Oct. 14, 1862.	Aug. 20, 1863.
Charles J. Wood, Hosp. Stew.	33	Oct. 14, 1862.	Aug. 20, 1863.
Lauriston Barnes	21	Oct. 14, 1862.	Aug. 20, 1863.
Warren J. Barnes	31	Oct. 14, 1862.	Aug. 20, 1863.
Wilder U. Barnes	22	Oct. 14, 1862.	Aug. 20, 1863.
Frederick W. Burgess . . .	20	Sept. 30, 1862.	Aug. 20, 1863.
Frederick A. Cobb	39	Oct. 14, 1862.	Aug. 20, 1863.
Samuel S. Dennis	29	Oct. 14, 1862.	Aug. 20, 1863.
Hiram B. Douglass	35	Oct. 14, 1862.	Aug. 20, 1863.
Chiron J. Elwell	19	Oct. 14, 1862.	Aug. 20, 1863.
Rodolphus W. Homer . . .	18	Oct. 14, 1862.	Aug. 20, 1863.
Samuel Johnson	29	Oct. 14, 1862.	Aug. 20, 1863.
Samuel King	44	Oct. 14, 1862.	Aug. 20, 1863.
Samuel W. Knight[4]	28	Oct. 14, 1862.	May 24, 1863.
Sardius J. Sibley	33	Oct. 14, 1862.	Aug. 20, 1863.
James M. Smith	28	Oct. 14, 1862.	Aug. 20, 1863.
Joseph P. Snow	34	Oct. 14, 1862.	Aug. 20, 1863.
Stuart M. Stafford	31	Oct. 14, 1862.	Aug. 20, 1863.
Albert S. Sturtevant	19	Oct. 14, 1862.	Aug. 20, 1863.
Andrew J. Thayer	29	Oct. 14, 1862.	Aug. 20, 1863.
Elmer M. Thayer	20	Oct. 14, 1862.	Aug. 20, 1863.
Samuel E. Thayer	22	Oct. 14, 1862.	Aug. 20, 1863.
Josiah W. Witt	20	Oct. 14, 1862.	Aug. 20, 1863.

42d Regiment Infantry (100 *days*), 1864.

Frederick A. Cobb, Sergeant	40	July 16, 1864.	Nov. 11, 1864.
Henry P. Aiken	19	July 22, 1864.	Nov. 11, 1864.
Frank H. Cleveland	19	July 22, 1864.	Nov. 11, 1864.
James B. Conkey	18	July 16, 1864.	Nov. 11, 1864.
John Harper	18	July 16, 1864.	Nov. 11, 1863.

51st Regiment Infantry (nine months), 1862.

Franklin Nye	22	Sept. 25, 1862.	July 27, 1863.

[1] Thomas Winn transferred to 56th Regiment Infantry, June 8, 1865.

[2] Augustus T. Barnes transferred to 56th Regiment Infantry, June 8, 1865.

[3] Rev. George J. Sanger was appointed chaplain, November 6, 1862.

[4] Samuel W. Knight died at Brashear City, La., May 24, 1863.

56th Regiment Infantry (three years), 1863.

Names.	*Age.*	*Date of Muster.*	*Date of Discharge.*
Thomas Winn, Corporal . .	21	Jan. 2, 1864.	July 12, 1865.
Augustus T. Barnes	26	Jan. 2, 1864.	July 12, 1865.
Thomas Penny	23	March 10, 1864.	June 27, 1865.

61st Regiment Infantry (one year), 1864.

George C. Howe, Musician .	17	Jan. 9, 1865.	June 16, 1865.
Bernard McHeough	22	Jan. 7, 1865.	July 16, 1865.
Richard Roland	21	Jan. 9, 1865.	June 19, 1865.

3d Battalion Riflemen (three months), 1861.

John Wheeler, 2d	31	May 19, 1861.	Aug. 3, 1861.

6th Battery Light Artillery (three years), 1862.

William H. Hunter[1]	25	Dec. 18, 1861.	Dec. 13, 1862.

8th Battery Light Artillery (six months), 1862.

Chas. G. Bartholomew, Corp.	19	June 3, 1862.	Nov. 29, 1862.

10th Battery Light Artillery (three years), 1862.

Henry H. Granger, 1st Lieut.[2]	47	Aug. 20, 1862.	Oct. 30, 1864.
Asa F. Richardson, Corporal .	28	Sept. 9, 1862.	June 9, 1865.
Norman H. Butterfield . . .	22	Sept. 9, 1862.	June 9, 1865.
Harmon Newton[3]	31	Sept. 9, 1862.	Sept. 18, 1864.
George W. Parks	18	Sept. 9, 1862.	June 9, 1865.
Leverett Pierce	26	Sept. 9, 1862.	June 9, 1865.
Waldo Pierce[4]	24	Sept. 9, 1862.	Jan. 1, 1865.
John M. Ramsdell	29	Sept. 9, 1862.	June 9, 1865.
Timothy G. Redfield[5] . . .	34	Sept. 9, 1862.	Aug. 25, 1864.
Alvah F. Southworth . . .	19	Sept. 9, 1862.	June 9, 1865.
James L. W. Thayer . . .	25	Sept. 9, 1862.	June 9, 1865.

14th Battery Light Artillery (three years), 1864.

Joseph Atwood	43	Feb. 27, 1864.	June 15, 1865.

[1] William H. Hunter died at New Orleans, December 13, 1862.

[2] Lieutenant Granger was wounded at Hatcher's Run, October 27, 1864, and died three days afterwards at City Point, Va. His body was brought home, and the town, November 8, 1864, adopted appropriate resolutions and ordered a public funeral. The Adjutant General's Record represents Lieutenant Granger to have been brevetted Lieutenant-Colonel.

[3] Harmon Newton died at Washington, D. C., September 18, 1864.

[4] Waldo Pierce transferred to Veteran Reserve Corps, January 1, 1865.

[5] Timothy G. Redfield "missing in action," August 25, 1864.

16th Battery Light Artillery (three years), 1864.

Names.	*Age.*	*Date of Muster.*	*Date of Discharge.*
Anson S. Comee, Sergeant[1]	21	March 11, 1864.	April 3, 1865.

2d Regiment Heavy Artillery (three years), 1863.

James Higgins	19	July 29, 1863.	Sept. 3, 1865.
William M. Smith	37	July 18, 1864.	Sept. 3, 1865.

2d Regiment Cavalry (three years), 1862.

Michael Cameron[2]	25	Jan. 26, 1863.	Feb. 6, 1863.

4th Regiment Cavalry (three years), 1863.

Robert W. Davis, Sergeant[3]	23	March 1, 1864.	
Peter Grib, Sergeant[4]	23	March 1, 1864.	May 14, 1864.
James B. Wade, Q. M. Serg.[5]	21	March 1, 1864.	Aug. 12, 1864.
Henry C. Hack, Corporal	34	March 1, 1864.	Nov. 14, 1865.
Robert Bailey	21	March 1, 1864.	Nov. 14, 1865.
William Hickey	21	March 1, 1864.	Nov. 14, 1865.
James O. Mahoney[6]	21	March 1, 1864.	May 1, 1865.

Regular Army.

Dennis Murphy	22	Sept. 10, 1864.	1st Artillery.
William H. Mayhugh	33	Aug. 26, 1864.	2d Artillery.
Albert S. Sturtevant	21	Jan. 31, 1865.	3d Artillery.
John Watts	23	Aug. 11, 1864.	11th Infantry.
Stephen Wickizen	21	Sept. 8, 1864.	11th Infantry.

Head-stones are erected in the cemetery in memory of other soldiers, namely: —

Edgar J. Cummings, aged 20, died at Newbern, N. C., Jan. 14, 1863.
Henry C. Granger, aged 22, killed at Williamsburg, Va., May 5, 1862.
Asa G. Sturtevant, aged 27, died at New York, October 28, 1862.
Dexter Z. Tinney, aged 33, killed at the Wilderness, May 6, 1864.

And the Town Records show that —

Orin C. Trow, aged 34, died at Washington, D. C., October 27, 1864.

There was an early organization of militia in Hardwick, first in a single company, afterwards in two, and during the Revolutionary period in three companies. About 1794 the number was

[1] Anson S. Comee deserted, April 3, 1865.

[2] Michael Cameron deserted, February 6, 1863.

[3] Robert W. Davis was commissioned second lieutenant August 6, 1864.

[4] Peter Grib deserted, May 14, 1864.

[5] James B. Wade died in hospital, August 12, 1864.

[6] James O. Mahoney deserted, May 1, 1865.

reduced to two, styled the South (or First) and North (or Second) Companies, divided by the road which afterwards became a turnpike. Before 1781 I have not found any record of election of officers, except by the town in 1774; but from other sources it is ascertained that the following persons held the office of captain as early as the dates affixed to their respective names: Joseph Allen, 1740; Benjamin Ruggles, 1747; Timothy Ruggles,[1] 1754; Constant Merrick, 1755; Samuel Robinson, 1755; Paul Mandell,[2] 1755; Joseph Warner, 1758; William Paige, 1759; Ebenezer Cox, 1762; John Ruggles, 1771; Daniel Wheeler, 1771; Jonathan Warner,[3] 1774; Samuel Billings,[4] 1774; Simeon Hazeltine, 1774; Stephen Rice,[5] 1775; Thomas Robinson, 1775; Timothy Paige,[6] 1776; Barnabas Sears,[7] 1776; Samuel Dexter, 1776; Daniel Warner, 1776; Josiah Locke, 1776; Edmund Hodges, 1777; Denison Robinson, 1778; Nathan Leonard, 1778.

In 1781, after the adoption of the Constitution of Massachusetts, the militia was reorganized, and a roster of officers was commenced; from which it appears that Jonathan Warner was commissioned as one of the three major-generals in the Commonwealth, June 28, 1781; and Timothy Paige as colonel of the Fourth Regiment in Worcester County, July 1, 1781; and, also, the following named officers of their respective companies: —

[1] Timothy Ruggles was a captain long before he removed to Hardwick in 1754. He enlisted a company in 1740 for service in the West Indies, consisting almost entirely of Indians, as appears by the muster roll still preserved in the Massachusetts Archives. He was duly commissioned captain; but his company was disbanded because a larger number of companies had been organized than the exigency required, and thus escaped the destruction which befel almost all who embarked on the expedition. It is not certainly known whether he commanded a company of militia in Hardwick; but it appears that he was not only colonel and brigadier-general in the army, but that he also commanded the regiment which embraced Hardwick, Rutland, Rutland District (Barre), Pequaog (Athol), Petersham, New Braintree, Western (Warren), and Brookfield. Under date of "Rutland, April 10, 1759," Lieutenant-Colonel John Murray certified that several soldiers of Colonel Ruggles' regiment, in each of these towns, had enlisted for service in the Invasion of Canada. *Mass. Arch.*, xcvii. 111.

[2] Brigade major, March 13, 1778; styled colonel, November 17, 1774.

[3] Colonel, 1774; brigadier-general, February 13, 1776; major-general, June 28, 1781.

[4] Afterwards major.

[5] Lieutenant-colonel, April 10, 1776.

[6] Colonel, July 1, 1781.

[7] Major and lieutenant-colonel in the regular army.

NAMES.	2d Lieutenant.	1st Lieutenant.	Captain.
James Paige . . .	–	–	July 1, 1781.
Isaac Fay . . .	–	July 1, 1781.	–
Samuel Beals[1] . .	July 1, 1781.	–	–
John Hastings . .	–	–	July 1, 1781.
Edward Ruggles .	–	July 1, 1781.	Jan. 17, 1784.
Benjamin Ruggles .	July 1, 1781.	–	–
Ephraim Pratt . .	–	–	July 1, 1781.
Joel Johnson . .	–	July 1, 1781.	–
Earl Flagg . . .	July 1, 1781.	–	–
Elijah Warner . .	–	–	May 23, 1783.
Antipas Rice . .	–	May 23, 1783.	–
James Paige, Jr.[2] .	May 23, 1783.	–	Jan. 17, 1784.
Jabez Cobb . . .	–	Jan. 17, 1784.	–
Timothy Paige, Jr.	Jan. 17, 1784.	–	May 30, 1788.[3]
John Wheeler . .	–	Jan. 17, 1784.	Sept. 1, 1789.
Samuel Whipple .	Jan. 17, 1784.	–	–
James Lawton . .	–	Oct. 15, 1786.[4]	–

NAMES.	Ensign.	Lieutenant.	Captain.
John Raymond . .	–	Sept. 16, 1788.	July 2, 1792.
John Jenney . . .	Sept. 16, 1788.	July 2, 1792.	–
Daniel Ruggles . .	–	Sept. 1, 1789.	–
Seth Hinkley, Jr.[5] .	Sept. 1, 1789.	Sept. 18, 1792.	July 24, 1794.
Moses Hunt . . .	–	July 2, 1792.	–
Isaac Stowell . .	July 2, 1792.	–	–
David Pratt . . .	July 2, 1792.	–	–
Nathan Freeman .	–	July 24, 1794.	June 14, 1800.
Francis Jenks . .	July 24, 1794.	–	–
John Campbell . .	–	–	Sept. 24, 1794.
Charles Paige . .	–	Sept. 24, 1794.	–
James Paige, 3d .	Sept. 24, 1794.	–	–
Timothy Billings[6] .	Aug. 20, 1795.	June 14, 1800.	May 5, 1801.
Daniel Billings, Jr. .	–	–	Sept. 25, 1795.
Jonathan Warner .	Sept. 25, 1795.	–	–
Samuel Dexter, Jr. .	June 14, 1800.	May 5, 1801.	Aug. 26, 1806.
Barnabas Hinkley .	May 5, 1801.	–	–
Thomas Wheeler, Jr.[7]	–	–	Aug. 3, 1801.
William Walker .	–	Aug. 3, 1801.	–

[1] Deputy quartermaster-general, with rank of major, November 2, 1787.

[2] Major, December 19, 1791.

[3] Captain of Cadets; see forward.

[4] Commissioned as adjutant.

[5] Adjutant, September 18, 1792; major, June 16, 1800.

[6] Major, August 13, 1806.

[7] Major, May 8, 1811; lieutenant-colonel commandant, July 12, 1813.

NAMES.	Ensign.	Lieutenant.	Captain.
Uel Thayer . . .	June 7, 1803.	–	–
Thomas Egery . .	–	Aug. 26, 1806.	April 4, 1809.
Moses Allen . . .	May 5, 1807.	April 4, 1809.	Jan. 7, 1813.
Benjamin Paige .	–	July 6, 1807.	June 3, 1811.
Daniel Mandell . .	Mar. 17, 1808.	June 3, 1811.	–
Luther Paige . .	April 4, 1809.	Jan. 7, 1813.	–
Samuel Billings [1] .	June 3, 1811.	–	May 4, 1813.
Ezra Ruggles . .	Jan. 7, 1813.	May 3, 1814.	May 18, 1815.
Benjamin Jenkins .	–	May 4, 1813.	–
Mason Mandell . .	May 4, 1813.	May 3, 1814.	–
Apollos Luce . .	May 3, 1814.	May 18, 1815.	–
Jonathan Webb . .	May 3, 1814.	–	Sept. 24, 1816.
Daniel Wheeler .	May 18, 1815.	–	–
Brigham Ruggles .	–	Aug. 21, 1815.[2]	–
Elbridge Cutler [3] .	–	Aug. 23, 1816.	Feb. 5, 1818.
Joseph Allen, 3d .	Sept. 16, 1816.	Feb. 26, 1817.	–
Nathan Perry . .	Sept. 16, 1816.	–	–
Zenas Phinney . .	Feb. 26, 1817.	–	–
James Danforth [4] .	–	Feb. 5, 1818.	Aug. 28, 1820.
Charles Lee . . .	May 15, 1818.	–	–
John Gilbert . .	May 4, 1819.	May 12, 1821.	July 10, 1824.
Moses Whipple, Jr. .	May 4, 1819.	Aug. 28, 1820.	–
Martin Mandell . .	–	–	Aug. 28, 1820.
Timothy Fay, Jr. .	Aug. 28, 1820.	–	–
Crighton Ruggles .	May 12, 1821.	July 26, 1824.	April 5, 1826.
Calvin Jenney . .	July 10, 1824.	April 5, 1826.	June 28, 1827.
John Raymond . .	April 5, 1826.	June 28, 1827.	Aug. 6, 1829.
Willard Allen . .	July 11, 1827.	Aug. 21, 1829.	April 5, 1833.
David Aiken, Jr. .	Aug. 8, 1829.	Apr. 5, 1833.	May 6, 1834.
Joseph Knox . .	–	Apr. 17, 1830.[5]	–
Benjamin J. Cobb .	April 5, 1833.	May 6, 1834.	May 5, 1835.
David C. Paige . .	May 6, 1834.	–	–
Sylvester Bowen .	–	May 5, 1835.	–
Thos. P. Anderson .	Aug. 13, 1835.	–	–
Elmer B. Miles . .	–	Mar. 6, 1837.[6]	–

The old North (or Second) Company was disbanded February 18, 1824, and a company of riflemen was organized. Officers were elected as follows:—

[1] Major, August 27, 1816; lieutenant-colonel commandant, April 9, 1817.

[2] Commissioned as adjutant.

[3] Major, May 30, 1820; lieutenant-colonel commandant, May 2, 1821.

[4] See Riflemen.

[5] Adjutant.

[6] Adjutant.

NAMES.	Ensign.	Lieutenant.	Captain.
James Danforth [1] .	–	–	May 15, 1824.
Walter Mandell .	–	May 15, 1824.	Aug. 11, 1825.
Luke Earl . . .	May 15, 1824.	Aug. 11, 1825.	May 5, 1829.
Joseph Burgess, 2d.	Aug. 11, 1825.	May 5, 1829.	–
Joseph Whipple [2] .	May 5, 1829.	–	Feb. 24, 1830.
Apollos Rich [3] . .	Feb. 24, 1830.	May 4, 1830.	June 29, 1833.
Jason Haskins . .	May 4, 1830.	–	–
Orin Trow . . .	Aug. 24, 1831.	June 29, 1833.	Sep. 20, 1833.
Z. F. Shumway .	June 29, 1833.	Sep. 20, 1833.	May 2, 1837.
William C. Wesson	Sep. 20, 1833.	May 2, 1837.	–
Rufus P. Chase .	May 2, 1837.	–	–

Soon after the reorganization of militia in 1781, a company of cavalry was formed in the regiment, which then included the present towns of Hardwick, New Braintree, Oakham, North Brookfield, Brookfield, West Brookfield, and Warren. Its Hardwick officers were as follows: —

NAMES.	Cornet.	Lieutenant.	Captain.
Joseph Bruce . .	Aug. 26, 1806.	May 5, 1807.	–
Joshua Lawrence .	–	June 12, 1809.	–
Stephen W. Paige .	–	–	Aug. 22, 1812.
John Lawton . .	Feb. 19, 1816.	–	Jan. 23, 1819.
Joseph Robinson [4] .	May 11, 1819.	Sep. 20, 1819.	July 12, 1823.
Warren Smith . .	–	Aug. 16, 1825.	May 1, 1828.

After the suppression of the Shays Insurrection in 1787 (in which the Hardwick militia were sadly divided in opinion and action), the staunch friends of government seem to have felt the necessity of organizing an independent company, which could be relied upon to act unanimously, in case of emergency, and which might be a body-guard to the major-general. The Council Records, under date of May 30, 1788, show that "His Excellency communicated to the Council a letter from Major General Warner, recommending the establishment of a Company of Cadets in

[1] Major, June 10, 1825.

[2] Colonel, May 24, 1833.

[3] Major, August 26, 1833; lieutenant-colonel, August 14, 1835.

[4] Lieutenant-colonel, June 13, 1825; colonel, June 27, 1827.

the Seventh Division under his command, and asked the advice of Council. The Council advised that His Excellency issue his orders for the establishment of said Company." On the same day the necessary orders were issued, the company established, and officers commissioned, to wit: —

Timothy Paige, Jr., of Hardwick,		Captain, . .	May 30, 1788.
Samuel French,	" "	First Lieutenant,	May 30, 1788.
Jeduthun Spooner,	" "	Ensign, . .	May 30, 1788.
Wyman Hoyt, of New Braintree,		Second Lieutenant,	June 25, 1788.

To this company, and to the company of cavalry before mentioned, a complimentary reference was made in the "Massachusetts Spy," October 14, 1790: "On Tuesday, the fifth instant, the Fifth [Fourth ?] Regiment of the First Brigade, under Colonel Paige, with Captain Felton's Cavalry, and Captain Paige's Cadets, paraded at Brookfield. They were favored with fine weather, and every officer and soldier was fired with extraordinary military ardor, and the troops exhibited a variety of military movements greatly to their honor."

CHAPTER XV.

STATISTICS.

Population. — Tax in 1776. — Valuation. — Manufactures and Agricultural Products. — George H. Gilbert Manufacturing Company. — Furnaces. — Forge. — Paper Mills.

POPULATION. The General Court, on the 9th of December, 1776, passed a Resolve, requiring a census to be taken of all males, sixteen years old and upwards, distinguishing such as were Quakers, Indians, Negroes, or Mulattoes. The following return was made on the back of the broadside upon which the resolve was printed: "In obedience to the within Order, we have numbered the male inhabitants of the town of Hardwick, as within directed, and find the number to be three hundred and forty-six white or English inhabitants, and one mulatto man. We have no Quakers, no Indians, and no Negroes.

"HARDWICK, Jan. 31, 1777.

"THOMAS ROBINSON, *Selectman.*
SAMUEL DEXTER, } *Committee of*
DAVID ALLEN, } *Correspondence.*

"Worcester, ss. Jan. 31, 1777. Capt. Thomas Robinson, Capt. Samuel Dexter, and Ensign David Allen, made oath, that in executing the within order of the Great and General Court, they have acted uprightly, faithfully, and impartially, according to the best of their knowledge. Before me, PAUL MANDELL, Justice of the Peace."[1]

The special object of this census manifestly was to ascertain the military strength of the State, and to furnish a basis for requiring a fair proportion of soldiers from each town during the war of the Revolution. Other enumerations have been made periodically for more general purposes. The population of this town gradually increased during the first century after its settlement, then decreased until manufacturing was established at Gilbertville; since which time, although the agricultural com-

[1] *Mass. Archives,* clxi. 132, 133.

munity has probably diminished, the manufacturers have more than supplied the deficiency; so that the sum total, as exhibited by the last census, exceeds that at any former period.

1765,	1,010.	1830,	1,888.	1860,	1,521.
1776,	1,393.	1837,	1,818.	1865,	1,967.
1790,	1,725.	1840,	1,789.	1870,	2,219.
1800,	1,727.	1850,	1,631.	1875,	1,992.
1810,	1,657.[1]	1855,	1,523.	1880,	2,237.[2]
1820,	1,836.				

TAX IN 1776.—The original assessment of a tax dated January 30, 1776, is preserved in the archives of the town. The polls were rated at 2*s.* 6*d.* each. The rate of taxation on property is not mentioned; but the sum total of the tax, after deducting the amount assessed on the polls, exhibits the relative liability of the tax-payers to bear the public burdens at the commencement of the Revolutionary War. The "North Side" and the "South Side" were separated by the county road (afterwards a turnpike) from the Old Furnace to Greenwich Village.

NORTH SIDE.

	Polls.	£	s.	d.	qr.		Polls.	£	s.	d.	qr.
Joseph Allen	2	0	10	8	3	Gideon Carpenter	2	0	10	1	1
David Allen	2	0	17	9	3	Nathan Carpenter	1	0	3	7	3
Joseph Allen, Jr.	1	0	9	5	3	Ephraim Cleaveland, Jr.	1	0	8	4	0
John Ammidown[3]	2	0	10	11	1	Edward Chaloner	1	0	2	6	0
Philip Ammidown	1	0	7	11	0	Ebenezer Chipman	0	0	2	7	1
Zaccheus Atwood	1	0	5	5	0	Gardner Chandler	0	0	7	6	0
John Bradish	1	0	8	4	0	Uriah Convers	1	0	3	4	0
Seth Bangs	1	0	5	6	1	John Canady	1	0	2	6	0
Daniel Billing	3	0	15	10	0	Samuel Dexter	1	0	14	5	3
Abiathar Babbit	2	0	12	2	1	Wid^{w} Mary Dean	0	0	1	3	0
John Bradish, Jr.	1	0	8	10	1	Paul Dean	2	0	9	5	3
William Bassett	1	0	3	11	2	Charles Doolittle	1	0	7	2	2
Adna Bangs	1	0	3	9	0	Job Dexter	1	0	8	6	2
Jedediah Bassett	1	0	3	4	0	Zurishaddai Doty	3	0	12	2	1
Seth Blanchard	1	0	2	8	2	Jonathan Danforth	1	0	17	3	2
Joseph Bowman	1	0	2	6	0	Stephen Forbes	3	0	14	8	1
John Bachelor	1	0	2	6	0	Daniel Fay	3	0	15	11	1
Edward Clark	2	0	11	4	1	John Freeman	1	0	2	6	0
Benjamin Cox	1	0	6	3	0	Eli Freeman	1	0	4	8	1

[1] In 1801, the town parted with a considerable portion of its territory and inhabitants, at the incorporation of Dana.

[2] In consequence of the great increase of business at Gilbertville since 1880, the population of the whole town is probably now about 3,000. Gilbertville alone is supposed to contain about 1,500 inhabitants.

[3] The mode of spelling the names is preserved: also the order in which they are inserted.

	Polls.	£	s.	d.	qr.
Watson Freeman	1	0	4	9	2
Reuben Fay	1	0	6	4	1
Earl Flagg	1	0	5	10	0
Daniel Fay, Jr.	1	0	2	6	0
Stephen Gorham	2	0	7	7	1
Jonathan Glazier	1	0	2	8	2
Shearjashub Goodspeed	1	0	2	8	2
Simeon Hazeltine	1	0	6	11	3
Andrew Haskell	1	0	7	8	2
Elisha Hedge	1	0	3	2	3
Edmund Hodges	2	0	14	9	2
Nehemiah Howard	2	0	8	7	3
John Hastings	2	0	11	5	2
Jonathan Hastings	1	0	2	8	2
Thomas Haskell	3	0	15	5	0
Moses Haskell	2	0	9	5	3
John Haskell	1	0	10	5	0
Nathaniel Haskell	2	0	12	7	1
Seth Hinkley	3	0	16	3	0
John Haskell, Jr.	1	0	3	6	2
Ephraim Haskell	1	0	9	0	3
Stephen Hastings	1	0	2	8	2
John Hedge	1	0	2	6	0
Nathaniel Johnson	1	0	12	8	2
Zebadiah Johnson	2	0	13	9	0
Dudley Jordan	1	0	3	11	2
Philip Jordan	1	0	6	5	2
Solomon Johnson	1	0	4	9	2
Joel Johnson	1	0	5	10	0
Silas Johnson	1	0	5	5	0
Stephen Johnson	1	0	3	5	1
Abraham Knowlton	1	0	7	2	1
Jesse Kinney	1	0	2	6	0
John Keith	1	0	9	0	3
Clark Lawton	1	0	6	4	1
Lemuel Leach	1	0	5	8	3
Ebenezer Lawrence	1	0	3	1	2
Joshua Lawrence	1	0	11	10	2
Ebenezer Lawrence, Jr.	1	0	14	3	1
Experience Luce	1	0	4	9	2
Josiah Lock	1	0	10	0	0
Constant Myrick	2	0	13	2	3
Nathaniel Myrick	1	0	8	0	1
Robert McIntyre's Est.	0	0	8	0	0
Timothy Newton	2	0	14	8	1
Joseph Nye	1	0	8	0	1
Joseph Nye, Jr.	1	0	2	8	2
Jonathan Nye	2	0	7	3	2
Prince Nye	1	0	9	4	2
Joshua Nye	1	0	5	0	0
John Paddleford	1	0	5	1	1
Seth Paddleford	1	0	2	8	2
Ephraim Pratt	2	0	8	0	1
James Paige	2	0	13	2	3
Samuel Pike	1	0	2	8	2
Elisha Pike	1	0	2	6	0

	Polls.	£	s.	d.	qr.
William Perkins	1	0	4	10	3
Capt. Benjamin Ruggles	2	0	16	5	2
James Robinson	0	0	9	7	0
James Rogers	1	0	5	2	2
Benjamin Ruggles, Jr.	2	0	13	6	2
Benjamin Ruggles, 3d	1	0	6	6	3
Thomas Ruggles	1	0	3	9	0
Joseph Ruggles	1	0	6	9	1
Edward Ruggles	2	0	13	9	0
Joseph Ruggles, Jr.	1	0	2	8	2
Nathaniel Ruggles	1	0	2	6	0
Edward Ruggles, Jr.	1	0	7	4	3
Whiting Ruggles	1	0	8	1	2
Denison Robinson	1	0	7	9	3
Widw. Susanna Rice	0	0	5	1	1
Stephen Rice	1	0	12	3	2
Joseph Robinson	1	0	8	9	0
William Shaw	1	0	6	6	3
Roland Sears	1	0	9	7	0
Freeman Sears	1	0	9	3	1
Barnabas Sears	1	0	9	2	1
Steward Southgate	1	0	2	6	0
Joseph Safford	2	0	7	3	2
Jeremiah Sibley	3	0	13	6	2
Samuel Sibley	1	0	3	4	0
Amaziah Spooner	1	0	8	1	2
Thomas Spooner	1	0	2	6	0
Zephaniah Spooner	1	0	2	6	0
Elkanah Steward	1	0	7	7	1
Edward Smith	1	0	9	4	2
John Sellon	2	0	10	7	2
Reuben Snow	1	0	7	4	3
Nathaniel Sprout	2	0	5	0	0
Nathaniel Sprout, Jr.	1	0	8	1	2
Jonathan Stanwood	1	0	2	6	0
Ephraim Tucker	1	0	2	6	0
Edward Taylor	1	0	2	6	0
Ephraim Titus	1	0	2	8	2
Seth Taylor	1	0	5	0	3
Thomas Wells White	1	0	5	0	0
Wareham Warner	0	0	1	0	2
Thomas Winchester	2	0	13	7	3
Widw. Sarah Winchester	0	0	5	7	2
Lemuel Willis	2	0	12	6	0
Daniel Wheeler	2	0	18	10	1
Nathan Wheeler	1	0	11	4	1
Joseph Washburn	0	0	1	2	0
Eliphalet Washburn	1	0	6	3	0
Ammiel Weeks	1	0	5	5	0
Thomas Weeks	0	0	2	9	3
Asahel Warren	1	0	5	2	2
Ebenezer Washburn	1	0	2	8	2
Samuel Whipple	1	0	8	11	2
James Wicker	1	0	3	6	2
Total, North Side		53	17	1	0

SOUTH SIDE.

	Polls.	£	s.	d.	qr.		Polls.	£	s.	d.	qr.
Solomon Aikens	2	0	17	3	2	James Lawton	2	0	12	11	0
David Aikens	1	0	8	7	3	Nathan Leonard	1	0	9	8	1
Gamaliel Arnold	1	0	3	0	1	James Lawton, Jr.	1	0	6	5	2
Atwood Aiken's Guardn.	1	0	2	6	0	Jacob Lawton	1	0	2	8	2
Samuel Billing	1	0	5	0	0	Joseph Loring	1	0	2	6	0
Elisha Billing	1	0	11	5	2	William Lyon	1	0	2	8	2
Samuel Billing, Jr.	2	0	18	11	2	John Lawton	1	0	2	6	0
Asahel Billing	1	0	8	1	2	Paul Mandell	3	1	5	2	2
Samuel Bridge	1	0	5	2	2	Amos Mandell	1	0	2	6	0
Samuel Beals	1	0	6	2	1	Lemuel Newton	1	0	10	2	2
Nathan Bangs	1	0	4	7	3	Stephen Newton	1	0	2	6	0
Joseph Biam	1	0	6	3	0	Caleb Nye, Jr.	1	0	2	8	2
Isaac Bowman	1	0	2	6	0	Andrew Nelson	1	0	6	3	0
Gamaliel Collins	1	0	11	9	1	Daniel Oliver, Esq.	1	0	13	11	2
Joshua Crowell	2	0	15	7	0	William Oaks	1	0	4	2	0
Paul Crowell	1	0	2	6	0	William Paige	2	0	16	0	2
Edward Curtis	1	0	5	1	1	George Paige	3	0	18	11	2
Isaac Clark	1	0	2	6	0	Timothy Paige	1	1	2	4	3
Isaac Clark, Jr.	1	0	6	11	3	Nathaniel Paige	1	0	11	9	1
Isaac Cummings, Jr.	1	0	6	10	2	John Paige	1	0	14	7	0
Ephraim Cleaveland	2	0	10	3	3	John Paige, Jr.	1	0	9	3	1
Abraham Chamberlain	2	0	8	2	3	William Paige, Jr.	1	0	7	1	0
Moses Chamberlain	1	0	2	6	0	James Paige, Jr.	1	0	11	4	1
Lemuel Cobb	1	0	6	9	1	Jesse Paige	1	0	2	6	0
Jabez Cobb	1	0	8	9	0	Phineas Powers	1	0	9	0	3
Elijah Cleaveland	1	0	2	7	1	Stephen Pratt	1	0	2	6	0
Benjamin Cleaveland	1	0	2	7	1	William Perkins, Jr.	1	0	2	6	0
Abner Conant	1	0	5	0	0	Capt. Jeremiah Powers	0	0	2	1	0
Derby Dwire	1	0	2	8	2	Samuel Robinson	1	0	9	3	1
Silas Dean	2	0	7	9	3	Solomon Rice	1	0	2	6	0
Thomas Elwell	1	0	9	0	3	Thomas Robinson	1	1	1	7	3
Jabez Elwell	1	0	2	6	0	Benjamin Raymond	1	0	8	4	0
James Fay	1	0	11	3	0	John Raymond	1	0	2	8	2
Aaron Furbush	2	0	10	7	2	Thomas Robinson, Jr.	1	0	2	11	0
Isaac Fay	1	0	9	10	2	Edmund Rawson	1	0	4	5	3
John Fay	1	0	9	10	3	Isaac Rice	1	0	7	6	0
George Field	1	0	8	2	3	Antipas Rice	1	0	10	2	2
Samuel French	1	0	2	6	0	Moses Rice	1	0	2	6	0
Philip Fraker	1	0	2	6	0	Aaron Rice	1	0	2	8	2
Paul Fay's Guardian	1	0	2	6	0	Samuel Rawson	1	0	2	6	0
Aaron Furbush, Jr.	1	0	2	7	1	Timothy Ruggles, Esq.	0	1	12	3	2
Causimai Fletcher	1	0	2	6	0	Timothy Ruggles, Jr.	2	0	13	4	0
John Giffin	1	0	5	10	0	Josiah Roberts	1	0	2	6	0
Timothy Gilbert	1	0	5	1	1	John Rich	1	0	2	6	0
John Hunt	1	0	17	1	0	Henry Rixford	1	0	2	6	0
John Hunt, Jr.	1	0	11	1	3	Robert Stetson	1	0	5	0	0
Uriah Higgins	1	0	8	10	1	Jesse Snow	1	0	3	11	2
John Hanmore	1	0	2	6	0	Robert Sprout	1	0	2	6	0
Aaron Hunt	1	0	8	1	2	Jabez Stratton	1	0	6	3	0
Isaiah Hatch	1	0	10	10	0	Daniel Thomas	1	0	4	9	2
Aaron Hudson	1	0	2	6	0	Joseph Thomas	1	0	3	1	2
Henry Higgins	1	0	4	0	3	Robert Tucker	1	0	4	4	2
Silvanus Hopkins	1	0	4	4	2	Joseph Warner	0	0	3	1	2
Samuel Jenny	1	0	3	8	0	Daniel Warner	1	0	19	1	2
William Johnson	1	0	4	8	1	Elijah Warner	1	0	14	3	1
Seth Johnson	1	0	10	0	0	Jonathan Warner	1	1	3	11	2
Jacob Knowlton	1	0	8	6	2	David Wheelock	0	0	6	4	1
Ezra Leonard	2	0	13	7	3	Gideon Wheelock	1	0	2	11	0
Ebenezer Liscomb	1	0	6	9	1	Thomas Weeks, Jr.	2	0	5	11	1

	Polls.	£ s. d. qr.		Polls.	£ s. d. qr.
Silas Willis	1	0 8 3 2	Elias Walker	1	0 6 0 2
Silas Willis, Jr.	1	0 2 6 0	David Weeks	1	0 2 6 0
Adam Willis	1	0 3 7 2	William Wicker	1	0 7 2 1
James Wing	1	0 5 8 3	Ephraim Wheeler	1	0 3 9 0
William Washburn	1	0 2 8 2	Moses Whitcomb	2	0 8 11 2
Silvanus Washburn	1	0 4 7 0	Edmund Willis	1	0 2 6 0
Judah Weeks	1	0 2 6 0	John Whipple	1	0 3 11 2
Seth Winslow	1	0 7 4 3	Thomas Martin Wright	1	0 2 6 0
Job Winslow	1	0 2 6 0			
Joseph Weeks	1	0 2 11 0	Total, South Side		48 11 5 3
Samuel Wait	1	0 5 6 5			

VALUATION. In 1781, a general valuation was taken of the property in the Commonwealth, as the basis of a State tax. The Hardwick List follows: [1] —

			Property.			Income.		
			£	s.	d.	£	s.	d.
363	Polls							
230	Houses	50s.				575		
200	Barns	18s.				180		
30	Stores, shops, &c.	6s.				9		
12	Distill-houses, mills, &c.	60s.				36		
2,500	Acres of English mowing	12s.				1,500		
1,000	Barrels of Cyder	2s. 6d.				125		
1,500	Acres of Tillage-land	9s.				675		
1,200	Acres of Salt and Fresh meadow	6s.				360		
2,500	Acres of Pasturing	3s.				375		
17,737	Acres of Wood and unimproved land	20s.	2 per cent.			354	14	
£298	Money on interest and on hand		298					
£600	Amount of goods, wares and merchandise		600					
200	Horses	£6	1,200					
300	Oxen	£7	2,100					
750	Cows	£4	3,000					
4,000	Sheep and Goats	6s.	1,200					
400	Swine	12s.	240					
£100	Coaches, Chaise, &c.		100					
10	Ounces of gold, coined or not coined		50	13	4			
470	Ounces of silver, coined or not coined		136	13	4	536	18	
	Deducted £500					4,726	12	0

In 1798, a valuation was taken by order of Congress, for the purpose of a direct tax. The principal assessor for the district embracing this town was General Jonathan Warner; his assistants here were Captain Daniel Warner and Colonel Stephen Rice. Each house and farm was valued separately. The general recapitulation, dated April 10, 1799, exhibits the following results: [2] —

[1] *Mass. Arch.*, clxii. 63.

[2] Valuation of the whole State, deposited in the library of the New England Historic Genealogical Society.

Houses over $100 in value	176	
Houses under $100 in value	56	232
Acres of land, with houses over $100	87½	
Acres of land, not included as above	23,543½	23,631
Value of houses and lots over $100, not including ministerial property	$43,534	
Value of houses under $100	2,575	$46,109
Value of land		248,123
Total valuation		$294,232

A very thorough valuation of property in the Commonwealth was made in 1875, with the following result as to Hardwick:—

Property.		Number.	Value.
FARMS.			
From 3 to 5 acres		1	
From 5 to 10 acres		4	
Above 10 acres		196	
		201	$630,169
BUILDINGS.			
Houses		210	
Barns		249	
Sheds		35	
Shops		11	
Carriage-houses		9	
Cider mills		4	
Out-buildings		15	
		533	$229,100
LAND.			
Land under crops	acres	4,801	$164,215
Orchards (the land)	acres	101½	4,662
Unimproved land	acres	12,334	145,240
Unimprovable land	acres	192	130
Woodland	acres	3,237½	86,822
		20,666	$401,069
FRUIT TREES AND VINES.			
Apple trees		13,898	$16,305
Cherry trees		144	64
Crab-apple trees		2	2
Peach trees		190	175
Pear trees		460	658
Plum trees		36	12
Grape vines		1,949	1,177
			$18,393
DOMESTIC ANIMALS.			
Bees (swarms of)		28	$149

PROPERTY.	Number.	Value.
Bulls	85	$2,593
Calves	491	4,622
Colts	31	2,825
Dogs	80	386
Ducks	16	14
Geese	23	33
Guinea fowls	11	9
Heifers	291	7,033
Hens and chickens	3,892	1,799
Hogs	350	4,824
Horses	231	18,670
Lambs	45	156
Milch cows	1,337	61,517
Oxen	144	12,850
Pigeons	50	6
Pigs	353	1,704
Sheep, merino	4	22
Sheep, Saxony	2	16
Sheep	46	227
Steers	68	2,765
Turkeys	304	325
		$122,545
AGGREGATES.		
Land		$401,069
Buildings		229,100
Fruit trees and vines		18,393
Domestic animals		122,545
Agricultural implements in use		21,985
		$793,092

MANUFACTURES AND AGRICULTURAL PRODUCTS.

From time to time the General Court has required from assessors, or other authorized agents, information concerning certain branches of industry. The earliest statistical tables on this subject exhibited a very scanty summary for the year ending April 1, 1837. This was confined almost exclusively to manufactured articles, and consequently Hardwick ranked very low in the list: —

"Saxony sheep, 2; merino sheep, 100; other kinds of sheep, 810; Saxony wool produced, 12 lbs.; merino wool, 250 lbs.; other kinds of wool, 1,600 lbs.; average weight of fleece, 2½ lbs.; value of wool, $1,000; capital invested, $1,820.

"Boots manufactured, 5,000 pairs; shoes, 5,000 pairs; value of boots and shoes, $14,500; males employed, 20; females, 8.

"Tanneries, 2; hides tanned, 1,500; value of leather tanned and curried, $5,250; hands employed, 6; capital invested, $4,500.

"Paper mills, 2; stock manufactured, 55 tons; value of paper, $5,600; males employed, 6; females, 2; capital invested, $3,000.

"Manufactory of chairs and cabinet ware, 1; value of chairs and cabinet ware, $1,000; hands employed, 2.

"Plough manufactory, 1; ploughs manufactured, 150; value of the same, $900; employing one person.

"Straw bonnets manufactured, 300; value of same, $500.

"Palm-leaf hats manufactured, 75,000; value of same, $15,500."

Twenty years later, Hardwick appears to better advantage in the Statistical Tables for the year ending June 1, 1855.

Property.		Number.	Value.
Ploughs and agricultural tools manufactured		12	$100
Saddles manufactured			1,000
Wagons and other vehicles manufactured			3,700
Hides of all kinds tanned		1,700	7,000
Boots and shoes of all kinds			1,600
Palm-leaf hats manufactured			3,000
Casks manufactured			200
Boxes for packing, etc., manufactured			9,000
Lumber, prepared for market	feet	65,000	9,800
Fire-wood, prepared for market	cords	1,548	2,812
Horses		282	18,080
Oxen, 360; steers, 92		452	25,951
Cows, 1,389; heifers, 256		1,645	41,926
Swine raised		412	3,435
Sheep of all kinds		217	776
Wool produced	lbs.	712	
Butter	lbs.	33,725	6,745
Cheese	lbs.	310,540	31,054
Honey	lbs.	80	14
Beeswax	lbs.	9	3
Indian corn	bush.	18,543	15,373
Wheat	bush.	255	496
Rye	bush.	1,825	1,844
Barley	bush.	1,171	953
Oats	bush.	8,211	4,129
Potatoes	bush.	24,892	12,516
Turnips	bush.	450	40
Carrots	bush.	840	210
English hay	tons	3,139	37,468
Meadow hay	tons	1,000	5,000
Apple trees		4,878	3,467
Pear trees		336	52

The result of the very comprehensive census in 1875 is even more favorable to Hardwick in all respects, except in regard to manufactures, wherein it is very unsatisfactory. The quantity and value of land, buildings, trees, and animals have already been stated. The domestic and agricultural products enumerated are as follows: —

Products.		Quantity.	Value.
DOMESTIC PRODUCTS. — FOR SALE.			
Butter	lbs.	35,003	$12,419
Cheese	lbs.	124,493	14,358
Cider	gals.	29,165	2,662
Dried fruit	lbs.	569	63
Firewood	cords	1,107	3,653
Maple molasses	gals.	143	224
Palm-leaf hats (work on)		784	100
Quilts		4	12
Railroad sleepers		3,777	1,294
Shingles		100,000	300
Straw hats (work on)		144	18
Wine	gals.	774	432
FOR USE.			
Blankets	pairs	3	15
Boots	pairs	4	10
Butter	lbs.	17,303	5,902
Carpets	yds.	25	25
Cheese	lbs.	6,248	794
Cider	gals.	14,686	1,247
Dried fruit	lbs.	2,015	221
Firewood	cords	2,100	7,025
Maple sugar	lbs.	150	15
Maple molasses	gals.	103	138
Mittens	pairs	14	10
Quilts		3	9
Shoes	pairs	25	40
Socks	pairs	41	27
Wine	gals.	77	95
Yarn	lbs.	10	11
AGRICULTURAL PRODUCTS.			
Apples	bush.	24,364	7,921
Barley	bush.	285	292
Beans	bush.	170	384
Beans, string and shell	bush.	52	88
Beef	lbs.	133,162	11,087
Beeswax	lbs.	8	2

Products.		Quantity.	Value.
Beets	bush.	430	$271
Blackberries	qts.	700	71
Blueberries	qts.	302	30
Buckwheat	bush.	22	26
Butternuts	bush.	36	16
Cabbage	heads	11,502	928
Carrots	bush.	704	349
Cherries	bush.	20	37
Chestnuts	bush.	27	50
Chickens, dressed	lbs.	4,962	958
Corn, green	bush.	140	152
Corn, Indian	bush.	7,066	6,925
Corn, pop	bush.	25	42
Crab-apples	bush.	27	30
Cranberries	bush.	22	88
Cucumbers	bush.	91	88
Currants	qts.	775	65
Eggs	doz.	8,362	2,165
Feathers	lbs.	63	15
Fodder, corn	tons	101	1,088
Game, wild		–	30
Geese, dressed	lbs.	168	34
Gooseberries	qts.	40	4
Grapes	bush.	478	398
Hay, English	tons	4,093	60,939
Hay, meadow	tons	818	6,904
Hay, clover	tons	1	15
Hay, millet	tons	7	100
Hides		62	252
Honey	lbs.	160	44
Hop-poles		1,108	339
Huckleberries	qts.	3,403	235
Ice	tons	37	50
Lettuce	heads	800	36
Mangoes	bush.	100	50
Manure	cords	3,545	10,572
Melons		50	5
Milk	gals.	172,582	19,208
Millet	bush.	6	14
Mutton	lbs.	400	32
Oats	bush.	3,522	2,416
Onions	bush.	475	615
Parsnips	bush.	36	29
Peaches	bush.	166	281
Pears	bush.	59	125
Pease	bush.	4	6
Pease, green	bush.	134	205
Peppers	bush.	2	4
Plums	bush.	4	15

PRODUCTS.		Quantity.	Value.
Pork	lbs.	90,894	$8,873
Potatoes, Irish	bush.	19,811	10,938
Poultry, other than chickens, geese, and turkeys,	lbs.	150	26
Pumpkins	lbs.	26,300	153
Rye	bush.	634	653
Seeds, grass	bush.	2	6
Shellbarks	bush.	20	45
Squashes	lbs.	17,000	331
Straw	tons	40	567
Strawberries	qts.	800	175
Tobacco	lbs.	11,600	1,160
Tomatoes	bush.	315	244
Trees, fruit, in nurseries		120	65
Turkeys, dressed	lbs.	2,855	576
Turnips	bush.	4,157	1,125
Veal	lbs.	60,865	7,062
Wool, Saxony	lbs.	15	5
Wool, other than Saxony	lbs.	191	61
AGGREGATES.			
Domestic Products, for sale		–	$35,535
Domestic Products, for use		–	15,584
Hay, 4,919 tons		–	67,958
Other Agricultural Products		–	100,232
			$219,309

This exhibition is creditable to a town whose entire population was only 1,992; especially when it is considered that one fifth part of the adult inhabitants were engaged in manufacturing establishments. But the account of manufactures and the results of mechanical labor is very unsatisfactory. Excluding the value of butter and cheese manufactured, the sum total assigned to Hardwick is as follows:—

INDUSTRIES.	Number of Establishments.	Value of Products.
Blacksmithing	3	$3,000
Cheese-box making	1	1,250
Carpentry and joinery	1	5,000
Lumber, planed, and boxes . . .	1	2,000
Lumber, sawed	2	2,355
Machinist's work	1	10
Powder-keg making	1	1,500
Wheelwrighting	1	100
	11	$15,215

The same census represents that 310 inhabitants of Hardwick were then employed in "manufactures and mechanical industries;" of whom 193 were woollen factory operatives, and 24 were paper makers; yet I can find no evidence in the census that a yard of cloth or a pound of paper was manufactured in the town. Indeed, I cannot trace the manufacture of paper to any other town; it is certain, however, that a manufactory was then in operation here. The manufacture of woollens is easily traced to the town of Ware, which has credit in the census for all the woollen goods manufactured here. The occasion of this transfer is indicated in an article published in the Boston "Daily Advertiser," October 7, 1880, concerning the several manufacturing establishments in Ware: —

"After the dissolution of Gilbert & Stevens, the firm of George H. Gilbert & Co. was established, from which has sprung the George H. Gilbert Manufacturing Company, incorporated in 1867, with a paid-up capital of $250,000. The first president was George H. Gilbert; but his death occurring one year later, the present officers of the company were chosen, as follows: Lewis N. Gilbert, president; Charles D. Gilbert, treasurer; and J. H. Grenville Gilbert, secretary. In 1860 was erected, in addition to the granite mill in Ware, a brick mill, 130 by 56 feet, five stories high, on the site of the old paper mill in Hardwick, four and a half miles north of Ware, to increase the manufacture of flannel goods. In the immediate vicinity of the new mill were built many tenements for the operatives; thus was formed Gilbertville, named in honor of its founder. Three other brick mills have been built there, — one, 125 by 60 feet, three stories high; another, 84 by 60 feet, four stories high; and a third, 230 by 68 feet, five stories high. The two hundred tenement-houses owned by the company, on its 325 acres, constitute the entire settlement of what is probably the prettiest strictly manufacturing village in Massachusetts. It is on the line of the Ware River and Massachusetts Central Railroads. The greater part of the manufactures of the company are now produced at Gilbertville; and as a large part of the dress goods and blankets woven at Gilbertville are finished at Ware, the few statistics given below refer to the total products at all these mills."

Being unwilling that Hardwick should be shorn of one of its chief glories, as it is by the census of 1875, and desiring to state the precise facts in the case, I addressed an inquiry to the president of the corporation, who gave me the desired information, to wit: The foregoing statement in the "Daily Advertiser" was correct when it was written; but since that time the business at Gilbertville has been greatly enlarged. To the mill erected in 1860 an addition has been made, 154 feet in length by 82 feet in width, and nine sets of machinery have been added; so that, in 1883, the following statistics are substantially accurate: —

Capital	$250,000
Sets of machinery	47
Wool consumed, per day	17,000 pounds.
Operatives employed	1,000
Goods manufactured, per year	3,500,000 yards.
Value of goods manufactured	$2,500,000.

Of these forty-seven sets of machinery, forty sets are operated in Hardwick and seven in Ware; and these numbers may be supposed to indicate with sufficient accuracy the proportion of goods manufactured in the respective towns. Hardwick may therefore claim much the largest share of this immense business. Although the owners, who furnish the capital and control the operations, reside in Ware, the water-power and almost all the mills are within our limits; most of the operatives both dwell here and perform their daily tasks here; the stock is brought here in the form of raw materials, and is here converted into manufactured goods.

The beautiful village of Gilbertville, where this business is transacted, has been elsewhere described. It may suffice to add here, that the land was purchased and the first mill erected in 1860, and that the business of manufacturing was commenced in

1862. George H. Gilbert, the first president of the company which bears his name, was born at Brooklyn, Conn., and died at Ware, May 6, 1869. The present president, Hon. Lewis N. Gilbert, is the nephew, and Charles D. Gilbert, treasurer, and J. H. Grenville Gilbert, secretary, are the sons of George H. Gilbert. His youngest son, Edward H. Gilbert, has also recently become a member of the company.

FURNACES AND FORGE. The subject of manufactures should not be dismissed without a brief notice of what was formerly a very important branch of industry. At the original division of lands by the proprietors, a mill lot, sometimes called "saw-mill lot," was laid out, which included a part of what is now called "Furnace Village." Moose Brook furnished the water-power, which remains in constant use, even to the present day. Besides the saw-mill and grist-mill, which were erected very early, and a cloth-dressing establishment of a later date, a Furnace for the manufacture of iron hollow-ware was erected about the middle of the last century,[1] which, for sixty or seventy years, furnished employment to many persons. The larger part, if not the whole, of the iron ore was procured in West Brookfield; but, notwithstanding the expense of transporting this principal material, the business yielded a satisfactory profit. A general assortment of hollow-ware was manufactured, from the ponderous and capacious potash-kettles,[2] then in use, to tea-kettles, pans, spiders, skillets, and even smaller culinary vessels; for all which articles a ready market was obtained.

In the Revolutionary War, this furnace rendered important public service, which is mentioned in a petition which is still preserved: "To the Hon. Council and the Hon. House of Representatives of the State of Massachusetts Bay in New England, humbly show Stephen Rice and James Woods, in behalf of themselves and partners, owners of a Furnace at Hardwick, in the County of Worcester, that your petitioners have agreed to furnish the Commissary General of this State with a large quantity of Cannon Ball and other warlike stores, a part of which we have already supplied, which are allowed to be of the very best kind.

[1] The precise date of its erection I have not ascertained; but, as early as 1763, Deacon Joseph Allen became one of the joint-owners, which he afterwards lamented in a poetical account of "the time and place of the author's birth, and some things that happened in the course of his life."

[2] In the days of my boyhood there were two manufactories of potash in Hardwick, — one owned by Jason Mixter, Esq., and the other by Dr. William Cutler.

We have with great difficulty, by reason of the scarcity of labor, procured stock for making another blast, which has been attended with considerable additional expense, by reason of the large draughts of men which have been made from among us. We are at this present time just entering on said blast, and understanding that this Honored Court have just ordered one half of the militia of said County of Worcester to march to Ticonderoga on an alarm, it will be impossible to proceed in carrying on our blast should one half of the militia of Hardwick and New Braintree be ordered to march. Wherefore your petitioners pray that thirty persons, which is the number employed in carrying on the business of said Furnace, may be excused from the present or a future requisition of men, during our present blast, from said towns of Hardwick and New Braintree. And your petitioners, as in duty bound, shall ever pray. STEPHEN RICE. JAMES WOODS. Dated at Watertown, Oct. 25, 1776."[1]

During the continuance of a "blast," — generally a period of five or six months, — the fire was not quenched nor the labor intermitted. As on shipboard, relays of hands wrought day and night, not resting even on the Sabbath. After such continuous labor for several months, the workmen gladly hailed the day when the fire was extinguished for the purpose of constructing a new crucible and making general repairs. This was technically called "blowing out," and the day was devoted to unlimited fun and jollity. Some of the jovial frolics and wild pranks of the laborers are still remembered by the elderly inhabitants; but, perhaps, it may not be well to record them as matters of history.[2] It should be added, that many who were gay and merry "furnace-men" in their younger days were afterwards among our most respected citizens, and attained honorable and official position, both in town and in commonwealth. For several years before the manufacturing of iron was discontinued, this furnace was owned and managed by Colonel Samuel Billings and Mr. Harmon Chamberlain.

[1] *Mass. Arch.*, clxxxi. 288.

[2] Take one specimen: A mock-trial was had, and the alleged culprit sentenced to be hung. As his chin was unnaturally short, the attempt to execute him was unsuccessful. A piece of slag, resembling an auger, was then found, and an effort made to bore a hole through his neck, so that a pin might be inserted to prevent the rope from slipping over his head. The victim required nursing several days, being kept quiet, meanwhile, by a plentiful supply of his favorite beverage.

It is related of one who became intoxicated early in the morning and slept in his bunk until evening, that he afterwards lamented that "he lost all his sport at the 'blowing out,' by getting drunk *too soon.*"

Early in the present century another furnace was erected on Ware River, about a quarter of a mile above the dam at Gilbertville. The spot is marked "New Furnace" on the R. Map, and this name was applied to the whole neighborhood until it was superseded by the present name of Gilbertville. The projectors of this enterprise were Colonel Thomas Wheeler,[1] a blacksmith and very skillful worker of iron, and Mr. Lemuel Harrington, formerly a tanner, but retired from that business and willing to invest capital in a new adventure. In the "Massachusetts Spy," July 12, 1815, Jesse Bliss advertised that "The new Furnace, lately erected by Harrington, Wheeler & Co., on Ware River in Hardwick, is now in blast." I know not who were the other members of the company. The business was probably not very successful, and it was not long continued. Colonel Wheeler removed to Ticonderoga in 1818 or 1819, and those who were left behind had not his skill or energy as iron-workers.

Before the erection of this new furnace, Colonel Wheeler carried on business at a Forge which stood near the spot now occupied by the large mill of the George H. Gilbert Manufacturing Company on the west side of the River. This forge seems to have been erected by Isaac Thomas, who bought seven acres of land, July 18, 1763, of Captain Daniel Warner, with certain rights in Ware River; said Warner reserving the privilege to build "one half of a saw-mill on the ditch said Thomas is cutting or may hereafter cut for conveying the water out of said River to carry a saw-mill and other mills." In March, 1765, the town "voted to Mr. Isaac Thomas the sum of £26. 13. 4., said Thomas having engaged to build a sufficient bridge over Ware River near his Iron-works." Mr. Thomas sold one third part of this estate to Joseph Blake, October 20, 1763, and Blake sold his share to Lot Whitcomb, January 18, 1770, which then embraced one third part of a dwelling-house, one third of a corn-mill, one sixth of a saw-mill, and one third of a forge and coal-house. In October, 1772, this forge is described as the property of Samuel Beals and Amos Thomas. I have not further traced the change of ownership. While the forge was in possession of Colonel Wheeler, a sad event occurred. As I remember the story, Nathan Bonney, aged 17 years, in a competitive trial of strength, lifted one of the trip-hammers, weighing six hundred pounds; he very

[1] Colonel Wheeler's son, William A. Wheeler, as manager of a furnace in Brookfield and an extensive iron-foundry in Worcester, acquired a wide reputation and a large estate.

soon became sick, and died April 13, 1811, as it was reported, "of spotted fever, after an illness of 34 hours;" [1] but his death was generally supposed to have been occasioned by his foolhardy rashness.

PAPER MILLS. About the year 1832 a paper mill was erected by Joseph S. and Moses Smith on Ware River, on the spot now occupied by one of the mills of the George H. Gilbert Manufacturing Company. The easterly end, with two engines, was rented to Thornton K. Merrick and William Dickinson for the manufacture of wrapping paper. The westerly end, fitted for four engines, was occupied by William Mixter and Moses Smith, about two years, for the manufacture of printing paper, and afterwards by Moses Smith alone. In 1842 the building was leased to Laflin and Clark, who manufactured writing paper; at the expiration of their lease it was again rented to George Maynard for the same purpose; while in his hands, the building was burned, and the business was abandoned.

In 1866, Dr. Almon M. Orcutt of Hardwick, and Dr. D. W. Miner and Mr. George Robinson of Ware, purchased the water-privilege on Ware River, near Barre, long known as "White's Mills," designated on the R. Map by the letters "N. W.," and organized the "Ware River Paper Co." They immediately commenced the erection of a mill, which was completed in 1867, at the cost of $75,000. About this time Mr. Robinson withdrew from the company, and the business was carried on by Drs. Orcutt and Miner about three years. The principal article manufactured was white wall paper. In 1870, Fred. A. Mellen, who had been superintendent for Drs. Orcutt and Miner, purchased the mill, and manufactured book paper until the following year, when he died, and the business seems to have been discontinued. It was afterwards resumed, and prosecuted with more or less regularity and success, and with occasional interruptions.

About 1880 a new company was organized, understood to consist of Henry Page of Fitchburg, George W. Wheelwright and D. S. Greenough of Boston, and Andrew J. Bartholomew of Southbridge, with a capital of $80,000. The mill is well supplied with all the modern improvements for paper-making, and its capacity is about to be increased by additional machinery. The following facts in regard to its present condition were kindly

[1] *Massachusetts Spy*, April 24, 1811.

furnished by the superintendent, J. W. Plowman, under date of February 13, 1882: "Page Paper Co. is the title of this corporation. Number of hands, — male 23, female 14. We manufacture a No. 1 News, and Book Papers of various kinds, of which we produce about 800 tons per annum. The present company commenced business a little more than a year ago."

CHAPTER XVI.

CIVIL OFFICERS.

Councillors. — Senators. — Representatives. — Delegates to Congresses and Conventions. — Justices of the Court of Common Pleas. — Justices of the Peace. — Moderators. — Selectmen. — Assessors. — Town Clerks. — Town Treasurers.

THE following list of Civil Officers, resident in Hardwick, is compiled chiefly from official records of the State and of the Town: —

COUNCILLORS.

General Timothy Ruggles was elected Councillor in 1764, but declined the service. He was appointed Mandamus Councillor in 1774, and was sworn into office.

General Jonathan Warner, being one of the Senators of the County, was elected Councillor in 1795 and 1796.

SENATORS.

Jonathan Warner, 1781 - 1785, 1791-1796.
Samuel Eastman, 1819, 1820.
Joseph Stone, 1845, 1846.
John Raymond, 1850.
William Mixter, 1857.

REPRESENTATIVES.

Timothy Ruggles, 1754, 1755, 1757-1759, 1761-1770.
Daniel Oliver, 1770.
Paul Mandell, 1773, 1774.
Stephen Rice, 1775, 1777, 1784.
William Paige, 1776, 1778-1780.
Jonathan Warner, 1777, 1780, 1785, 1798, 1799.
Timothy Paige (Colonel), 1781.
Ichabod Dexter, 1782, 1783.
John Hastings, 1786, 1800-1804, 1809.
Martin Kinsley, 1787, 1788, 1790-1792, 1794-1796.[1]
Timothy Paige (Esq.), 1805-1821.[2]
Seth Peirce, 1806.
Jason Mixter, 1810, 1815, 1816, 1837.

[1] Major Kinsley removed to Hampden, Me., in 1798, and was afterwards representative, senator, councillor, representative in Congress, Judge of Common Pleas, and Judge of Probate. He died at Roxbury, June 20, 1835.

[2] Timothy Paige died in office, October 29, 1821, having served for seventeen successive years.

Jeduthun Spooner, 1811–1814.
Joseph Stone, 1823.
Samuel Billings, 1826, 1827, 1829.
Moses Allen, 1830, 1832, 1838.
Scotto Berry, 1833.
Samuel F. Cutler, 1835.
Gardner Ruggles, 1838, 1839.
John Raymond, 1840.
William Anderson, 1841, 1842.
Stephen W. Paige, 1843, 1844.
Constant Southworth, 1847, 1857.
Franklin Ruggles, 1850.
Alvan Southworth, 1851.
Forester B. Aiken, 1852, 1860.
William Mixter, 1854, 1856, 1868.
James P. Lynde, 1855.
Orin Trow, 1861.
Albert E. Knight, 1864.
Samuel S. Dennis, 1866.
Jubal C. Gleason, 1870.
Almon M. Orcutt, 1874.
James H. Walker, 1882.

DELEGATES TO PROVINCIAL CONGRESSES.

Paul Mandell, Stephen Rice, (1st) at Concord, October, 1774.
Paul Mandell, (2d) at Cambridge, February, 1775.
William Paige, Stephen Rice, Jonathan Warner, (3d) at Watertown, May, 1775.

DELEGATES TO CONVENTIONS.

Paul Mandell, Stephen Rice, Jonathan Warner, John Bradish, At Worcester, August, 1774, County Convention for the Public Safety.
William Paige, Jonathan Warner, John Hastings, At Cambridge, September, 1779, to frame a Constitution for the State.
Timothy Paige (Colonel), at Concord, October, 1779, to affix prices.
Martin Kinsley, at Boston, February, 1788, to act on Federal Constitution.
Timothy Paige (Esq.), Joseph Stone, At Boston, November, 1820, to revise the Constitution of Massachusetts.

JUSTICES OF THE COURT OF COMMON PLEAS.

Timothy Ruggles, April 19, 1757, Chief Justice January 21, 1762–1774.
Jonathan Warner, May 27, 1799, died January 7, 1803.

JUSTICES OF THE PEACE.

Timothy Ruggles, April 19, 1754; also of the Quorum.
Daniel Oliver, January 13, 1768; died in England, May 6, 1826.
Paul Mandell, September 26, 1775; died September 16, 1809.
Jonathan Warner, April 26, 1787; also of the Quorum.
Martin Kinsley, October 14, 1789; died at Roxbury, 1835.
Seth Paddleford, July 2, 1796.[1]
John Hastings, February 4, 1802; died May 29, 1829.

[1] Removed to Taunton, and was Judge of Probate; he died January 7, 1810.

Timothy Paige, May 9, 1803; Quorum, August 29, 1816; died October 29, 1821.

William Cutler, February 20, 1808; died February 9, 1832.

Daniel Ruggles, March 9, 1811; died February 26, 1838.

Samuel Eastman, November 18, 1812; Quorum, January 20, 1820.[1]

Thomas Wheeler, February 21, 1814.[2]

Samuel Hinkley, January 22, 1819; died January 19, 1849.

Jason Mixter, June 16, 1821; died January 31, 1850.

Samuel F. Cutler, February 17, 1824.[3]

Samuel Billings, January 22, 1828.[4]

Joseph Stone, January 29, 1828; died June 27, 1849.

Ebenezer Perry, January 26, 1829; died June 27, 1845.

Joseph Knox, May 14, 1831.[5]

Gardner Ruggles, December 13, 1839; died August 5, 1853.

John Raymond, February 17, 1841; died June 6, 1854.

Joel W. Fletcher, May 22, 1841.[6]

Stephen W. Paige, March 1, 1843; died February 24, 1871.

William Mixter, March 1, 1845.

William Anderson, February 17, 1848; died April 21, 1867.

Constant Southworth, April 15, 1850; died December 5, 1877.

Dwight Billings, April 30, 1851.[7]

Almon M. Orcutt, March 22, 1854.

James P. Lynde, May 23, 1855.[8]

John G. Dennis, July 15, 1856; died July 31, 1858.

Daniel S. Collins, September 2, 1858.

Andrew J. Bartholomew, November 18, 1858. Removed to Southbridge.

Albert E Knight, May 27, 1861.

James P. Fay, April 27, 1864; Trial Justice, April 27, 1869.

William H. Tucker, January 16, 1867.

John F. Rich, August 24, 1871.

G. Albert Williams, Trial Justice, April 22, 1873.

Alfred H. Richardson, December 21, 1875.

Moderators of Annual Town Meetings.

Benjamin Smith, 1737.[9]

Joseph Allen, 1738, 1740–1742, 1745, 1766–1769, 1771, 1773, 1775.

Christopher Paige, 1739,[10] 1744, 1747, 1749, 1750, 1754, 1758.

Eleazar Warner, 1743, 1746, 1748.

Constant Merrick, 1751.

Benjamin Ruggles, 1752, 1753, 1755, 1759, 1762, 1765, 1770.

Paul Mandell, 1756, 1757, 1760, 1761.

Timothy Ruggles, 1763, 1764.

William Paige, 1772, 1774, 1776–1778, 1781.

Jonathan Warner, 1779, 1780,

[1] Removed to Springfield; died at Amherst, April 11, 1865.

[2] Removed to Ticonderoga, N. Y.; died at Worcester, April 26, 1851.

[3] Removed to Amherst, and died there, September 9, 1863.

[4] Removed to Greenfield; died at Worcester, May 13, 1868.

[5] Removed to Rock Island, Ill.; died August 6, 1881.

[6] Removed to Leominster and Cambridge; died at Chicago, February 15, 1880.

[7] Removed to Connecticut; died November 23, 1881.

[8] Removed to Athol.

[9] District meeting.

[10] First March meeting after incorporation of the town.

1782, 1787, 1788, 1790, 1791, 1795, 1798, 1799, 1801.
David Allen, 1783–1786, 1793.
Martin Kinsley, 1789, 1794, 1796.
Daniel Warner, 1792.
John Hastings, 1797.
Daniel Ruggles, 1800.
Timothy Paige, 1802–1821, except 1807.
James Paige, 1807.
Samuel Eastman, 1822, 1823.
William Cutler, 1824.
Samuel Billings, 1825–1827, 1833.
Moses Allen, 1828–1830.
Ebenezer Perry, 1831, 1832, 1836, 1841.
Joseph Knox, 1834, 1835, 1837.
John Raymond, 1838–1840, 1842–1850, 1852.
Constant Southworth, 1851, 1853, 1855, 1857–1860, 1863, 1866, 1867, 1873.
Almon M. Orcutt, 1854, 1856.
William Mixter, 1861, 1862, 1865.
Joseph W. Powers, 1864, 1868–1871.
Samuel S. Dennis, 1872, 1874–1882.

Selectmen.

Benjamin Smith, 1737, 1739.
Joseph Allen, 1737, 1738, 1740–1742, 1745–1748, 1750, 1751, 1756, 1757, 1766–1769, 1771–1773.
Samuel Robinson, 1737, 1741, 1742, 1748, 1752–1757.
Stephen Griffith, 1737.
Benjamin Ruggles, 1737, 1738, 1743, 1744, 1746, 1749, 1750, 1752–1755, 1758, 1759, 1761, 1765, 1770.
Jonathan Warner, 1738, 1740–1742, 1745, 1751.
John Wells, 1738–1741.
Constant Merrick, 1738, 1739, 1742, 1747, 1749, 1756, 1760, 1762–1764, 1770.
Eleazar Warner, 1739, 1743, 1744, 1746–1748.
William Thomas, 1739.
Christopher Paige, 1740, 1741, 1743, 1744, 1749–1751.
John Foster, 1740, 1741.
George Abbott, 1742.
Nathaniel Whitcomb, 1745, 1752, 1753, 1758, 1759.
Timothy Ruggles, 1754.
Elisha Hedge, 1755, 1758, 1759, 1762–1764.
Paul Mandell, 1756, 1757, 1760, 1761, 1765, 1766, 1770, 1772–1775.
Ezra Leonard, 1760, 1767, 1768, 1776.
John Cooper, 1761.
Stephen Fay, 1762–1764.
William Paige, 1765, 1769–1773, 1775–1778.
Roland Sears, 1767–1769, 1771.
Joseph Warner, 1770.
Thomas Robinson, 1771–1773, 1776, 1777.
Daniel Warner, 1771–1773, 1776, 1784, 1786.
Timothy Newton, 1774, 1777, 1786.
Stephen Rice, 1774, 1775, 1779, 1780.
Jonathan Warner (General), 1774, 1775, 1779.
Elisha Billings, 1774.
John Bradish, 1775.
Abraham Knowlton, 1776, 1780.
David Allen, 1777, 1781–1785, 1792–1798.
Timothy Paige (Colonel), 1777–1780.
Gamaliel Collins, 1778.
Daniel Billings, 1778, 1782, 1784, 1787–1790.

Elijah Warner, 1779, 1780, 1782, 1793-1795.
John Hastings, 1778–1780, 1795.
Aaron Barlow, 1781.
Ichabod Dexter, 1781, 1782, 1785.
Ephraim Pratt, 1781.
Isaiah Hatch, 1781, 1782.
Daniel Egery, 1783, 1787–1792.
James Paige, Jr. (Major), 1783–1786, 1791–1794, 1803–1805.
Charles Doolittle, 1783.
John Paige, 1783–1785.
Moses Mandell, 1785, 1786, 1800–1802, 1817.
James Lawton, 1786.
Seth Peirce, 1787–1791, 1803–1805.
Nathaniel Paige, 1787.
Seth Johnson, 1787–1790.
Job Dexter, 1788–1794, 1796–1799, 1803–1805.
Lemuel Willis, 1791, 1792.
Prince Nye, 1793–1799, 1806–1810.
Seth Hinkley, Jr., 1795, 1796.
Jeduthun Spooner, 1796–1800, 1811, 1812.
Jonathan Danforth, 1797.
Timothy Paige (Esq.), 1798–1810, 1817–1821.
Daniel Ruggles, 1799-1802.
Samuel Hinkley, 1800–1810.
Samuel Beals, 1801, 1802.
Jason Mixter, 1806–1810, 1817–1819, 1835–1839.
Lemuel Newton, 1806.
Elijah B. Harmon, 1807, 1811.
Henry Fish, 1808–1812.
Jonathan Warner, 1811–1813.
Samuel Dexter, Jr., 1811–1813, 1829.
Moses Allen, 1812–1815, 1817–1825, 1829–1831, 1835, 1836.
Lewis Howe, 1813, 1814.
Samuel Eastman, 1813–1816.
Thomas Egery, 1814–1816.
Thomas R. Smith, 1814–1816, 1836, 1837.
Moses Wheeler, 1815, 1816.
Samuel Billings, 1816, 1818–1825.
Joseph Stone, 1817–1822, 1826.
Ezra Ruggles, 1820.
Samuel F. Cutler, 1821–1825, 1836.
William Walker, 1822–1824.
David Paige, 1823.
Scotto Berry, 1824, 1826–1829, 1835.
Martin Mandell, 1825.
Ebenezer Perry, 1825–1828.
Charles Paige, 1826.
William Sumner, 1826.
Stephen Morton, 1827.
John Gilbert, 1827, 1828.
Joseph Robinson (Colonel), 1827, 1828, 1830.
Joseph Robinson, 2d, 1828–1830.
Haffield Gould, 1829–1832, 1836–1845.
Warren Smith, 1830.
John Dean, 1831–1833, 1847, 1848.
Beals Thomas, 1831.
Marshall Nye, 1831, 1832.
Joseph Knox, 1832.
Walter Mandell, 1832–1834.
Timothy P. Anderson, 1833, 1834.
Joseph Whipple, 1833.
Ebenezer Burt, Jr., 1833.
Anson F. Allen, 1834.
James Browning, 1834, 1838, 1839.
John Raymond, 1834, 1837–1840, 1842–1850, 1852–1854.
Elbridge Cutler, 1835.
Mark Haskell, 1835.
Charles C. Spooner, 1837–1839, 1846–1848, 1852, 1865–1868.
Sardius Sibley, 1840.
William Anderson, 1840–1846, 1854, 1856.
Adolphus Bartholomew, 1840.
Gardner Bartholomew, 1841, 1847.
William Mixter, 1841–1843.

Erastus W. Paige, 1841–1846.
Asa Sturtevant, 1844–1846.
Constant Southworth, 1847–1849, 1851, 1854, 1855, 1863, 1864.
Timothy Fay, 1848.
Lilly S. Manly, 1849, 1850, 1856.
Dwight Billings, 1850, 1851, 1853.
Moses Lawrence, 1851, 1855.
Forester B. Aiken, 1851.
Orin Trow, 1851, 1863, 1865–1868.
James H. Walker, 1852, 1856, 1857, 1872–1874.
Joseph W. Powers, 1853, 1854, 1856–1862.
Adonijah Dennis, 1855.
Alvin Cleveland, 1855.
H. G. Otis Monroe, 1855.
Henry B. Gould, 1856–1862.
George Manly, 1857–1862, 1869–1882.
William P. Ruggles, 1857.
Elbridge Mandell, 1863.
Nathan W. Sargent, 1864.
Samuel S. Dennis, 1864–1882.
Calvin W. Mann, 1869-1871.
Alfred H. Richardson, 1875.
George Warner, 1876–1882.

Assessors.

William Maccoye, 1737.
Benjamin Ruggles, 1737, 1738, 1741, 1743, 1744, 1746, 1749, 1750, 1758, 1759, 1761.
Experience Johnson, 1737.
Joseph Allen, 1738, 1740–1742, 1745–1748, 1750–1757, 1765–1767, 1773.
Jonathan Warner, 1738, 1745.
John Wells, 1738, 1739.
Constant Merrick, 1738, 1739, 1742, 1747, 1749, 1760, 1762–1764.
Eleazar Warner, 1739, 1743, 1744, 1746–1748.
Benjamin Smith, 1739.
William Thomas, 1739.
Christopher Paige, 1740, 1743, 1744, 1749, 1750.
John Foster, 1740, 1741.
Samuel Robinson, 1742, 1748, 1757.
Nathaniel Whitcomb, 1745, 1758, 1759.
Paul Mandell, 1751, 1752, 1754–1757, 1760, 1761, 1769, 1770, 1772, 1774, 1775.
Stephen Fay, 1751, 1753, 1762–1766.
John Cooper, 1752–1756, 1761, 1765, 1766, 1768, 1769.
Elisha Hedge, 1758, 1759, 1762–1764.
Ezra Leonard, 1760.
Jonas Fay, 1766, 1767.
Thomas Wells White, 1767–1769, 1771, 1776, 1777.
Challis Safford, 1769.
Joseph Warner, 1770.
William Paige, 1770, 1772, 1773, 1776.
Daniel Wheeler, 1771, 1783.
David Allen, 1771, 1777, 1778, 1780, 1783–1787, 1795, 1796.
Daniel Warner, 1772, 1773, 1776–1780, 1784–1786.
Stephen Rice, 1774, 1775.
Josiah Lock, 1774.
Barnabas Sears, 1775.
Thomas Wheeler, 1777, 1782.
John Hastings, 1777, 1779, 1782, 1793, 1794.
Silvanus Washburn, 1778–1780, 1782–1787.
Ephraim Cleveland, 1781.
Seth Johnson, 1781.
James Paige, Jr. (Major), 1781, 1787–1794, 1796, 1803–1805, 1809–1811, 1813.
Daniel Ruggles, 1787–1792, 1801, 1802, 1823–1825.

Lemuel Willis, 1788-1800, 1802, 1806, 1807.
Jonathan Danforth, 1795, 1797.
Seth Hinkley, 1797-1800.
Timothy Paige, 1798-1821.
Moses Mandell, 1801, 1806-1808, 1817-1819.
Jeduthun Spooner, 1803-1805, 1814-1816.
Timothy Billings, 1808-1811.
Samuel Hinkley, 1812, 1813.
Thomas Wheeler (Colonel), 1812.
Ebenezer Perry, 1814-1816, 1826-1830, 1835, 1837, 1841.
Samuel Billings, 1817-1828, 1833, 1834.
Moses Allen, 1820, 1822-1825, 1828-1831, 1835, 1836.
Lemuel Harrington, 1821, 1822.
Samuel F. Cutler, 1826, 1827, 1835, 1836.
Franklin Ruggles, 1829.
Walter Mandell, 1830-1834, 1837-1840.
Scotto Berry, 1831, 1832.
Joseph Whipple, 1831-1834, 1841.
David Billings, 1831.
Ebenezer Burt, Jr., 1836-1838.
Gardner Ruggles, 1838-1840, 1844, 1850.
Sardius Sibley, 1839.
Anson F. Allen, 1840-1843, 1850, 1851, 1857-1860.
Adolphus Bartholomew, 1842, 1843.
John Raymond, 1842-1849, 1852-1854.
William Anderson, 1844-1846, 1850-1852, 1854, 1856.
Dwight Billings, 1845-1849.
Lilly S. Manly, 1847-1849.
Moses Ruggles, 1851, 1866.
Constant Southworth, 1852-1854, 1865.
Edward Dean, 1853.
Timothy Fay, 1855.
Lysander Powers, 1855.
Emory B. Foster, 1855, 1863.
Forester B. Aiken, 1856-1860.
William Browning, 1856, 1857.
William P. Ruggles, 1858, 1859, 1861.
Moses Smith, 1860.
Orin Trow, 1861, 1862.
Joel D. Mandell, 1861-1863.
Leander Sibley, 1862-1864, 1866-1873.
James W. Powers, 1864, 1867-1870.
George Manly, 1864, 1867, 1868.
Nathan W. Sargent, 1865.
John B. Aiken, 1865.
George Warner, 1866, 1869-1874.
John J. Newcomb, 1871-1877.
Samuel D. Kendall, 1874-1878.
Joel L. Powers, 1875-1882.
James P. Fay, 1878-1882.
Calvin W. Mann, 1879-1882.

Town Clerks.

Samuel Robinson, 1737, 1738, 1741,[1] 1742.
Cornelius Cannon, 1739.
John Foster, 1740, 1741.
Experience Johnson, 1743-1746.
Joseph Allen, 1747-1764.
John Cooper, 1765-1769.
Thomas Wells White, 1769,[2] 1771, 1777.
Paul Mandell, 1770.
David Allen, 1777.[3]
Silvanus Washburn, 1778-1787.
Lemuel Willis, 1787[4]-1800, 1806-1808, 1810, 1811.

[1] Elected in place of John Foster.
[2] Elected in place of John Cooper.
[3] Elected in place of Thomas Wells White.
[4] Elected in place of Silvanus Washburn.

Jeduthun Spooner, 1801–1805.
Samuel Eastman, 1809.
Samuel Hinkley, 1812–1828.
Joseph Stone, 1829–1848.
William Mixter, 1849–1857.
Almon M. Orcutt, 1858, 1860.
George Ruggles, 1859, 1860.[1]
Albert E. Knight, 1861–1882.

Town Treasurers.

John Wells, 1737–1740.
Joseph Allen, 1741, 1742, 1763–1769.
Benjamin Ruggles, 1743.
Jonathan Warner, 1744–1762.
Jonathan Warner (General), 1770–1777, 1779, 1780.
David Allen, 1778.
Timothy Paige, 1781–1786.
Martin Kinsley, 1787–1792.
Daniel Ruggles, 1793–1798.
Joseph Allen (2d), 1799–1807.
Elijah B. Harmon, 1808–1810, 1812–1825.
Moses Mandell, 1811.
Elbridge Cutler, 1826–1831.
Jason Mixter, 1832–1835, 1840–1845.
Walter Mandell, 1836, 1837.
Gardner Ruggles, 1838, 1839.
William Mixter, 1846–1849, 1851–1862.
Dwight Billings, 1850.
Frazier Paige, 1863–1866.
Albert E. Knight, 1867–1877.
Lucien D. Trow, 1878.
Almon M. Orcutt, 1879–1882.

[1] Died January 7, 1861, and A. M. Orcutt served for remainder of his term.

GENEALOGICAL REGISTER.[1]

ABBOTT, GEORGE, "with three sons, *George*, *Nehemiah*, and *Thomas*, emigrated from England. He d. in Rowley, A. D. 1647." *Abbott Genealogy*, p. 147.

2. GEORGE, s. of George (1), "settled in Andover 1655, where he m., May 1658, Sarah Farnum, and lived near the North meeting-house, served as sexton, and was respected; he d. 22 Mar. 1689; she d. 1728, a. 90, the widow of Henry Ingalls, who d. 1719, a. 92. Their chil. were *George*, b. 28 Jan. 1659, d. 24 Jan. 1724; *Sarah*, b. 6 Sep. 1660; *John*, b. 26 Aug. 1662; *Mary*, b. 29 Mar. 1664; *Nehemiah*, b. 20 July 1667; d. 8 Oct. 1750; *Hannah*, b. 20 Sep. 1668; *Mehetabel*, b. 17 Feb. 1671, d. young; *Lydia*, b. 29 Sep. 1675; *Samuel*, b. 30 May 1678; *Mehetabel*, b. 4 Ap. 1680." *Abbott Gen.* p. 147.

3. GEORGE, s. of George (2), "m., 1689, Elizabeth Ballard, who d. May 1706, and he m. Hannah Easty." His chil. were "*George*, b. 17 July 1691; *Uriah*, b. 26 Nov. 1692, d. 7 Ap. 1770; *Jacob*, b. 19 Mar. 1694, m., 1722, Ruth Foster, settled in Brookfield, Mass.; *Elizabeth*, b. 6 Nov. 1695, m., 1714, Deac. David Foster, Boxford, who d. June 1759; *Obed*, b. 6 Mar. 1697, d. 11 May 1772; *Moses*, b. 4 Feb. 1699; *Peter*; *Sarah*, m. Comfort Barns, Brookfield; *Hannah*, m., 1727, David Gilbert, Brookfield." *Abbott Gen.* pp. 147, 148.

4. GEORGE, s. of George (3), of "Hardwick, d. at Bennington, Vt., about 1771. His chil. were *Isaac*; *Jacob*; *Sarah*, m. —— Roberts, Morristown, Vt.; *Timothy*, d. 3 Nov. 1807, a. 69; *Ruth*, m. —— Pratt, Shaftsbury, Vt." *Abbott Gen.* p. 158. This GEORGE was the first of his family who resided in Hardwick. According to the Church Record, his chil. born here, by w. Rebecca, were *Ruth*, bap. 8 May 1737, m. Timothy Pratt 14 Oct. 1756, prob. rem. to Bennington, and perhaps afterwards to Shaftsbury, Vt.; *Timothy*, bap. 10 June 1739, prob. the same who assisted in rescuing Remember Baker from his captors at Bennington, 22 Mar. 1772. See *Records of the Council of Safety*, etc., *Vermont*, i. 150; *Mary*, bap. 7 June 1741, d. 5 May 1753. Of the chil. b. before the removal to Hk., *Sarah* m. John Roberts 1 Ap. 1752, and prob. rem. to Morristown. Besides these there was a s. *George* (named below) who was b. about 1720. GEORGE the f. was a blacksmith, one of the earliest white

[1] This plan of a Genealogical Register is adopted because it is less complicated than others, yet sufficiently particular for all practical purposes. The system is too plain and obvious to require any explanation. The ordinary abbreviations are used, such as a., for aged; b., for born; bap., for baptized; chil., for children; d., for died; d. s. p., for died without issue; m., for married; f., for father; w., for wife or widow; s., for son; dau., for daughter; rem., for removed; res., for resides or resided; ret., for returned, etc. The names of towns are also frequently abbreviated, as Amh., for Amherst; Bel., for Belchertown· Brk., for Brookfield; Dart., for Dartmouth; Enf., for Enfield; Gr., for Greenwich; Hk., for Hardwick; N. Br., for New Braintree; N. Brk., for North Brookfield; N. Sal., for New Salem; Pelh., for Pelham; Pet., for Petersham; Presc., for Prescott; Roch., for Rochester; Shutes., for Shutesbury; Springf., for Springfield; W. Brk., for West Brookfield; Worc., for Worcester; and if there be any other, the reference will be easily perceived. As already stated in the Preface, the contraction, "R. Map," which so often occurs, indicates the Ruggles Map, or a map of Hardwick drawn by Gardner Ruggles, Esq., about fifty years ago, showing the position of each dwelling-house and its distance from the Common.

inhabitants of Hk., an original member of the First Church, afterwards joined the Separate Church, and prob. rem., with most of its members, to Bennington, Vt., where he is said to have d. "about 1771."

5. GEORGE, s. of George (4), m. Martha Ayers of Brookfield 5 Dec. 1745, and had in Hk. *Nathan*, bap. 1746; *Lydia*, b. 16 Sep. 1747; *Samuel*, b. 24 Aug. 1750; *Nathaniel*, b. 8 Nov. 1753. GEORGE the f. d. prob. 1761, as the inventory of his estate was presented, 16 Aug. 1761, by his w. Martha, who m. Benjamin Roberts 29 Feb. 1764. In the settlement of his estate, 9 Sep. 1762, provision was made for "fulfilling the obligation the deceased gave unto his father George Abbott for paying him a yearly annuity of eight pounds, and maintaining his mother if she should outlive his father." *Worcester Prob. Rec.*

6. ISAAC, s. of George (4), m. Elizabeth Goodnow 14 Aug. 1760, and had *David*, b. 17 July 1762. ISAAC the f. was a simple inoffensive man, who in his old age afforded much amusement to children by a peculiarly shrill whistle, produced, according to my recollection, by placing his fingers in his mouth. He became a pauper, and d. 25 Ap. 1814, a. 82.

7. JACOB, s. of George (4), was adm. to the ch. 4 Ap. 1742. No further trace of him is found on the records.

8. SAMUEL, perhaps s. of GEORGE (4), was a soldier in the old French War, and was killed at Fort Massachusetts 2 Aug. 1748. His service is described in a muster roll among Col. I. Williams' papers, preserved in the Library of the Massachusetts Historical Society.

ADAMS, JAMES, had dau. *Mary*, bap. 16 Dec. 1750; nothing more is ascertained concerning him.

2. OLIVER, by w. Elizabeth, had *Enoch*, *Elizabeth*, and *Mary Parkhurst*, all bap. 20 June 1810.

AIKEN, JAMES (otherwise written Aikens, Aitkens, Ekens, Ekins, and Eakins), is said to have been an emigrant from Scotland. He res. several years in Brookfield, where he m. Mercy Gibbs, 15 Oct. 1718, and where all his chil. were prob. born, though only one of the births appears on record, namely, "*Marcy Ekens*, daughter of James and Marcy, born January y^{e} 3^{d} 17$\frac{20}{21}$." She m. William Paige of Hk. 12 Jan. 1743-4, and d. 19 Feb. 1823, at the great age of one hundred and two years, having been a member of the church more than eighty-six years. Of the chil. whose births are not found on record, were *John*, *Solomon*, and perhaps *Abigail*, who m. James Bacon, 5 June 1755, and also *Margaret*, who m. Nathaniel Whitcomb, Jr., 19 June 1755. JAMES the f. was one of the pioneers in the settlement of Hk., and res. on the easterly side of Great Meadow Brook, about a mile and a half south of the meeting-house, on or near the spot marked "Z. Phinney" on Ruggles's Map of Hardwick. It was currently reported by his contemporaries, that, before he rem. his family, and while he was preparing a shelter for them in the wilderness, his dau. *Mercy*, then about twelve or thirteen years old, many times rode through the pathless forest between Brk. and Hk. on horseback, guided by marked trees, to convey his weekly rations of food, — thus displaying that energy which characterized her whole life. He was Superintendent of the Hardwick Fair from its establishment in 1762 until 1771, and d. 10 Aug. 1775, a. 82. His w. Mercy united with the church 29 May 1737; the date of her death does not appear.

2. JOHN, s. of James (1), came to Hk. with his father about 1733. He m. Jerusha Atwood 19 Oct. 1749, and had *Hannah*, b. 6 Aug. 1750, d. unm. 9 Dec. 1814; *Jerusha*, b. 17 Ap. 1752, d. 24 Aug. 1753; *Sarah*, b. 16 Jan. 1754, m. Elias Walker 27 Feb. 1772; *John*, b. 17 Mar. 1755; *Atwood*, b. 6 Sep. 1756; *Solomon*, b. 15 July 1758, grad. D. C. 1784, ordained pastor of the church in Dracut, 4 June 1788, dismissed 4 June 1812, and entered the U. S. Army as chaplain. He had served two years in the Revolutionary Army before entering college, He m. Mary, dau. of Capt. Daniel Warner, pub. 12 Oct. 1788, and had four sons and five daughters, all living in 1853. He rem. in 1818 to Hardwick, Vt., was representative in 1821 and 1822, and d. 1 June 1833. He was chiefly distinguished as a politician. See *History of Mendon Association*,

pp. 227–229; *Israel*, b. 6 June 1760, m. Susanna Smith 23 Sep. 1784, at which time he res. at Windsor; *Jerusha*, b. 26 Ap. 1762, m. Jedediah Fay 12 Nov. 1778; *Samuel*, b. 2 Feb. 1764, d. young; *Bathsheba*, bap. 17 Mar. 1765, d. unm. 27 Dec. 1797; *Samuel*, b. 4 July 1768, m. Raby Pettingell 30 July 1797. JOHN the f. was a housewright, and res. on part of the homestead. He d. not long before 18 July 1768, when his Inventory was presented; his w. Jerusha m. Benjamin Ruggles, Jr., 11 Feb. 1773, and d. 28 Oct. 1787, a. 57.

3. SOLOMON, s. of James (1), came to Hk. with his father, m. Dorcas, dau. of Nathaniel Whitcomb, 8 Feb. 1749–50, and had *Mercy*, b. 16 Nov. 1750, m. Benjamin Stebbins 24 Sep. 1772; *James*, b. 8 Oct. 1752, m. Abigail ——, who d. at Barnard, Vt., 10 July 1789, a. 29, and he there m. Gratis Graves 25 Mar. 1790; *Anne*, b. 31 Mar. 1754, m. Beriah Green, at Barnard, 26 Dec. 1781; *Margaret*, b. 27 June 1755; *Jerusha*, b. 3 Oct. 1757; *Nathaniel*, b. 9 Oct. 1759, m. Mary Tupper at B. 27 Dec. 1784; *Dorcas*, bap. (with Solomon) 13 Mar. 1763, m. Nathan Parmenter at B. 19 June 1781; *Solomon*, b. 3 Mar. (bap. 13 Mar.) 1763, m. Betsey ——, and had two chil. at Barnard; *Susanna*, b. 3 Feb. 1765, m. Shiverick Crowell 15 Sep. 1785 at B.; *Levina*, b. 25 Aug. 1769; *Elijah*, b. 11 Feb. 1772, m. Rebecca Tupper at B. 23 Ap. 1797. SOLOMON the f. was a farmer and res. on a part of the homestead. He rem. with the early emigrants from Hardwick to Barnard, Vt., and was one of the first board of selectmen elected in that town at its organization, 9 Ap. 1778. He was a very active and useful citizen, and d. 10 Dec. 1805, a. 79; his w. Dorcas d. 10 Dec. 1803, a. 73. This family is still represented in Barnard.

4. JOHN, s. of John (2), m. Sarah, dau. of Benjamin Ruggles, Jr., 10 Oct. 1782, and had *John*, b. —— 1783; *Benjamin*, b. ——; *Sarah*, b. ——, m. Joseph Allen 3d, 12 May, 1814; *Harriet*, bap. 24 July 1791, d. unm. 3 Sep. 1869; *Lucia*, bap. 13 Ap. 1794, m. Jonas Winter of Shutesbury 6 Dec. 1826; *Clarissa*, bap. 10 July 1796, d. 3 Sep. 1797; *Bathsheba*, bap. 27 May 1798, d. 25 May 1803; a child d. 20 June 1802, a. three weeks; *Samuel Ruggles*, bap. 1 Jan. 1804, m. Nancy M. Smith of N. Sal., pub. 24 Ap. 1826, and soon rem. from Hk. JOHN the f. was a farmer and res. on the southerly part of the homestead, at the place marked "L. Bartlett" on the Ruggles Map, where vestiges of the cellar and garden still remain. He d. 10 Sep. 1810; his w. Sarah d. 17 Jan. 1822, a. 62.

5. ATWOOD, s. of John (2), m. Hannah Willis 9 Dec. 1779, and had *Betsey*, b. 15 Jan. 1782; *Calvin*, b. 31 May 1783; *Polly*, bap. 8 Nov. 1789; *Solomon*, bap. 31 July 1791. ATWOOD the f. rem. to Richfield, N. Y.

6. JOHN, s. of John (4), m. Celia Brown of Ware, pub. 17 Jan. 1814, and had *H. Almeda*, b. about 1819, m. George P. Wheeler of Pet. 13 June 1848; *John Brown*, b. about 1823, m. Fidelia F., wid. of David A. Dean, 25 Feb. 1858, is a farmer and res. on his father's homestead; *Moses B.* b. about 1825, d. unm. 30 Oct. 1851, a. 26. JOHN the f. was a farmer, res. at the place marked "J. Aiken" on the Ruggles Map, and d. 13 Nov. 1854, a. 71; his w. Celia d. 9 Oct. 1851, a. 67.

7. DAVID, nephew of James (1), m. Hannah Simons of Ware 15 July 1765, and had *Joseph*, b. 16 Ap. 1766, m. Hannah Gibbs of N. Sal., pub. 5 March 1792, rem. early; *Lucy*, b. 27 Nov. 1767, m. Moses Paige 27 Aug. 1789, and d. 27 Mar. 1800; *Mary*, b. 17 Jan. 1769, m. Moses Paige, pub. 17 May 1801; he d. 5 Dec. 1818, and she m. Jonathan Marsh of Ware 1 Dec. 1824; *Sila*, b. 28 Dec. 1771, m. Paul Dean 8 Dec. 1811; he d. 23 Sep. 1828, and she m. Nathaniel Fish of Presc. 30 Dec. 1835, and d. 7 Mar. 1844; *Hannah*, b. 26 Nov. 1773, d. unm. 24 Ap. 1800; *David*, b. 3 Oct. 1778; *Annas*, b. 9 June 1782, d. unm. 4 Feb. 1802. DAVID the f. was a farmer and resided on the road to Gilbertville, at the place marked "D. Aiken" on the Ruggles Map. It is understood that he was left an orphan at an early age, and was admitted to the family of his uncle, James Aiken. He d. 27 Feb. 1805, a. 70; his w. *Hannah* d. 28 July 1837, a. 97, as inscribed on her gravestone.

8. DAVID, s. of David (7), m. Patty, dau. of Capt. Zenas Phinney, 24 Ap. 1805, and had *David*, b. 10 Feb. 1806, m. Fanny Upton of Boston 17 Sep.

1851 (she d. 29 Mar. 1878, a. 70); *Forester Berry*, b. 1 Mar. 1808; *Annas*, b. 9 Dec. 1811, d. 4 Ap. 1813; *Brigham*, b. 20 Feb. 1813, m. Sarah Pepper of Warren 16 Ap. 1846, and d. s. p. 23 Feb. 1864; his w. d. 11 Nov. 1859, a. 47; *Lewis*, b. 6 Nov. 1816, res. several years in Boston where he m. Sarah J. Sherman 1 Oct. 1844, ret. to Hk. and d. s. p. 29 Sep. 1875; a child b. ——, d. 29 June 1818; *Charles P.*, b. 20 Jan. 1821, m. Louisa, dau. of Dr. Joseph Stone, 27 Sep. 1846. DAVID the f. was a farmer, res. on the homestead, and d. 18 Feb. 1852; his w. Patty d. 16 or 17 Ap. 1877, a. 92.

9. FORESTER BERRY, s. of David (8), m. Fanny, dau. of Daniel Wheeler, 10 May 1837, and had *Martha M.*, b. 2 Feb. 1839, d. 1 Feb. 1840; *Mary Ann*, b. 23 Feb. 1841, m. George Manly 23 Feb. 1864; *Charles W.*, b. 23 Feb. 1843, pub. to Salome McKenney 25 May 1868, and had Charles E., b. 22 Nov. 1881; *Henry P.* b. 16 Nov. 1844, m. Carrie L. Gilmore of Southbridge 22 Nov. 1869; *Ellen F.*, b. 25 May 1847, m. Benjamin Manly 23 May 1874; *Sarah E.*, b. 2 Feb. 1859; *David*, b. 20 Sep. 1862. FORESTER BERRY the f. is a farmer and res. on the homestead; he has been representative, selectman, and assessor; his w. Fanny d. 23 Dec. 1872, a. 55.

ALDEN, JOHN, m. the celebrated Priscilla Mullins, and had *John*; *Elizabeth*, m. William Paybody, and d. at Little Compton, 31 May 1717, in her 94th year, as inscribed on her head-stone; *Joseph*; *Jonathan*; *Sarah*; *Ruth*; *Mary*; *David*; and three others, whose names are not ascertained. JOHN the f. was one of the Mayflower Pilgrims, and the last survivor of those who signed the original compact of government. He res. in Duxbury, was one of the Assistants, and d. 12 Sep. 1687, a. 84 or 88, as Savage says (*Gen. Dict.*), or, according to Winsor (*Hist. Duxbury*), 12 Sep. 1686, a. 87.

2. JOSEPH, s. of John (1), res. in Bridgewater, m. Mary Simmons, and had *Isaac*; *Joseph*; *John*; *Elizabeth*; and *Mary*. He d. 8 Feb. 1697, a. 73.

3. DAVID, s. of John (1), m. Mercy, dau. of Constant Southworth, and had *Ruth*; *Alice*, m. Judah Paddock of Yarmouth, and d. ——, a. 93 (her dau. Rebecca m. Thomas Spooner 10 June 1742); *Benjamin*; *Samuel*, b. 1689.

4. JOSEPH, s. of Joseph (2), m. Hannah Dunham, and had *Daniel*; *Joseph*, d. young; *Eleazar*, b. 27 Sep. 1694; *Hannah*; *Mary*; *Joseph*; *Jonathan*; *Samuel*; *Mehetabel*; *Seth.*, JOSEPH the f. res. in Bridgew. was a deacon, and d. 22 Dec. 1747, a. 80.

5. ELEAZAR, s. of Joseph (4), m. Martha Shaw, and had *Jonathan*; *Eleazar*; *Absalom*; *David*; *Joshua*; *Caleb*; *Ezra*; *Timothy*, b. 1736, grad. H. C. 1762, pastor of the church in Yarmouth, and d. 13 Nov. 1828, a. 92. ELEAZAR the f. res. in Bridgew. and d. 30 Jan. 1773, a. 79.

6. EZRA, s. of Eleazar (5), m. Miriam Richardson of Stafford, Conn., where he had *Sarah*; *Judith*; *Eunice*; *Ezra*, b. 25 July 1769. His w. Miriam d. and he m. Sarah, widow of Abel Harwood and dau. of Capt. Benjamin Ruggles, 2 Jan. 1772, by whom he had *Miriam*, d. young; *Dorothy*; *Anna*; *Abel*; *Alice*; *Miriam*. EZRA the f. rem. from Stafford to Greenwich in 1770, was elected deacon in 1775, and d. in 1818, a. 84.

7. EZRA, s. of Ezra (6), m. Achsah Stebbins, and had *Pliny*, b. 1 Ap. 1792; *Samuel*, b. 25 Aug. 1793; *Alma*, b. 26 Aug. 1795; *Jason*, b. 26 June 1797, d. young; *Abel*, b. 23 July 1799; *Emery*, b. 2 July 1801; *James*, b. 10 Mar. 1804, d. young; *Sally Colburn*, b. 30 July 1806, d. young; *Festus*, b. 5 May 1808; *James Milton*, b. 20 June 1810; *Lyman*, b. 31 Aug. 1812; *Sarah*, b. 13 Ap. 1818. EZRA the f. res. in Gr. and d. 23 Nov. 1846.

8. PLINY, s. of Ezra (7), m. Elizabeth Works at Shutesbury 11 Sep. 1828, and had *Cornelia*, b. 10 Oct. 1830, for many years a school-teacher, m. Albert E. Knight, Esq., 25 Oct. 1870; *Mary E.*, b. 23 July 1831, m. Lorenzo West of Pet. 15 June 1853; *John Pliny*, twin, b. 20 Dec. 1834, d. at Wyandotte, Kansas, 2 June 1879; *Julia A.*, twin, b. 20 Dec. 1834, m. Alden B. Spooner 7 Jan. 1873. PLINY the f. was a carpenter, and captain of militia; he rem. from Gr. to Hk. about 1832, res. at the north end of the Common, and d. 11 Mar. 1877; his w. Elizabeth d. 17 Jan. 1878, a. 73.

9. FESTUS, s. of Ezra (7), m. Fanny N. Gibbs 28 Ap. 1831; she d. 19 Oct. 1838, and he m. Sylvia Terry 10 Sep. 1840. His chil. were *Angeline*, b. 20

Nov. 1832, m. Lathrop C. Spicer 28 Nov. 1850; *Theodore L.*, b. 17 May 1841; *George A.*, b. 11 Feb. 1846, d. 9 Sep. 1846; *Harrison F.*, b. 20 Ap. 1848, d. 2 Dec. 1849; *Ezra P. S.*, b. 27 Oct. 1851; *Fanny L.*, b. 12 May 1854. FESTUS the f. rem. from Gr. to Hk. before 27 Oct. 1851.

10. LYMAN, s. of Ezra (7), by w. Dorcas, had *Alonzo Lyman*, b. 15 July 1845; *Henrietta Augusta*, b. 23 Sep. 1848; *Loren* (or *Lona*) *Howard*, b. 21 Sep. 1850.

11. THEODORE L., s. of Festus (9), m. Emily Legrow 30 Ap. 1863, and had *Adin Royal*, b. 20 Aug. 1873; *Charles E.*, b. 3 May 1877.

12. *Alonzo L.*, s. of Lyman (10), m. Henrietta M. Frost 15 Ap. 1868, and had *Lilian Maria*, b. 6 Nov. 1870.

ALEXANDER, ISAAC, by w. Elizabeth, had *Lurana*, b. 25 May 1866; and by w. Alice, had *Elizabeth*, b. 22 Sep. 1875.

2. SAMUEL, by w. Mary, had *Henry*, b. 6 Aug. 1870.

3. PETER, m. Ellen Kennedy of Ware, 7 Feb. 1867, and had *John*, b. 27 Aug. 1870; *David Kennedy*, b. 23 Sep. 1873; *Joseph Nelson*, b. 29 May 1875.

CHARLES, of Winchester, N. H., m. Eliza Anderson 21 Sep. 1834. JEANETTE m. Alexander Kennedy, pub. 31 Aug. 1868. ELIZABETH, m. Charles Nelson of Warren 28 Mar. 1814. JEANETTE, d. 27 May 1880, a. 71.

ALLEN, WALTER, res. in Newbury 1640, rem. to Watertown before Ap. 1662. By deed of gift, 1 Oct. 1603, he conveyed land in Wat. to his sons *Daniel* and *Joseph*, and soon afterwards rem. to Charlestown, where he m. Abigail Rogers 29 Nov. 1678, and d. 8 July 1681, naming in his will, dated 19 Feb. 1679–80, w. Abigail and chil. *John* of Sudbury, *Daniel*, and *Joseph*.

2. JOSEPH, s. of Walter (1), res. in Weston, where he m. Anna Brazier 11 Oct. 1667, and had *Abigail*, b. and d. Dec. 1668; *Rebecca*, b. 8 Ap. 1670, d. 30 Jan. 1674–5; *Anna*, b. 22 Aug. 1674, d. 26 Jan. 1697–8; *Joseph*, b. 16 June 1677; *Nathaniel*, b. 8 Dec. 1687, a deacon in Weston; *Sarah*, b. ——, d. 15 Feb. 1698–9; *Deborah*, b. ——, m. John Moore of Sudbury 24 Dec. 1714; *Rachael*, b. ——, m. Joseph Adams of Cambridge 26 June 1718; *Patience*, b. ——. JOSEPH the f. d. 9 Sep. 1721; his w. Anna d. in Dec. 1720.

3. JOSEPH, s. of Joseph (2), res. in Weston, where he d. 1 Nov. 1729; his first w. Elizabeth d. in Nov. 1712, and he soon m. Abigail ——. His chil. were *Isaac*, b. 10 Nov. 1701; *Prudence*, b. 18 May 1703, m. Isaac Hagar 16 July, 1724; *Ame*, b. 21 Sep. 1706; *Rebecca*, b. 25 Feb. 1707–8; *Joseph*, b. —— 1709; *Elizabeth*, bap. 8 Ap. 1711; *Ann*, bap. 8 Ap. 1711, pub. to Daniel Mason (?) of Lexington 14 Mar. 1726–27; *Silence*, bap. 23 Nov. 1712; *David*, b. 26 Sep. 1714; *Abigail* b. 14 May 1716; *Elijah*, b. 11 Sep. 1718; *Sarah*, b. 10 Aug. 1720; *Tabitha*, b. 26 Oct. 1722, m. Abraham Whitney 20 Jan. 1742–3; *Daniel*, b. 31 Aug. 1724; *Timothy*, b. 8 Ap. 1727. Thus far I have followed the account of this family, given by Bond in his Watertown Genealogies, except in regard to *Joseph*, whom he omits, *David*, whom he calls *Daniel*, and *Ame* (or Amy), whom he calls *Ann*, and says she " d. soon." There are other inaccuracies in his list, as appears by the variations between it and the names subscribed to an agreement by the children and heirs at law of Joseph Allen of Weston deceased, dated 30 Sep. 1731, which is preserved in the Middlesex Probate Office, to wit: *Isaac* Allen; *Joseph* Allen; Isaac Hagar and w. *Prudence; Ame* Allen; *Rebecca* Allen; Ebenezer Goodnow and w. *Elizabeth*; Joseph Goodnow and w. *Anna; David* Allen and *Abigail* Allen, by their guardian Nathaniel Allen; *Elijah* Allen, *Tabitha* Allen and *Daniel* Allen, by their guardian Jonas Allen. A final settlement of the estate was made 16 June 1753 (the elder children, *Joseph*, *Prudence*, *Elizabeth*, *Anne*, *Amy*, and *Rebecca*, having previously released their reversionary interest), when receipts for that part of the estate " which was allowed to our mother Abigail Allen, the widow of the said Joseph as her dowry," were given by *Daniel* Allen of Sheffield, housewright, for himself and as attorney for his brother *David* Allen of Claverack, N. Y., blacksmith; *Elijah* Allen of Sutton, housewright, by his attorney Joseph Coolidge; Abraham Whitney of Weston and his w. *Tabitha*.

4. JOSEPH, s. of Joseph (3), m. Mercy Livermore of Grafton 16 Aug. 1733, and had *Sarah*, b. 25 July 1734, m. Benjamin Winchester 19 Feb. 1761; in

1736 he rem. to Hardwick, where he had *David*, b. 18 Aug. 1738; *Lydia*, b. 19 Sep. 1743, m. Lemuel Cobb 10 Oct. 1765; *Mercy*, b. 19 Ap. 1746, m. John Amidon 4 Feb. 1771; *Joseph*, b. 21 Dec. 1748. His w. Mercy d. 1 Mar. 1789, a. 76, and he m. widow Sarah Knowlton 6 Aug. 1789. JOSEPH the f. was b. in Weston 1709, res. in Grafton from about 1730 to 1736, when he rem. to Hk. and for seven years res. near the Old Furnace; in 1743 he rem. to the place marked "Mr. Holt" on the Ruggles Map, where he remained thirty-one years, during which time his house was destroyed by fire and he erected that which now stands on the same spot; on the 20th day of May 1774 he removed once more to the place on the road to Petersham marked "Seth Winslow" on the same map, where he d. 18 Aug. 1793, aged, according to the church record, 84 years, 4 months, and 16 days. He was not only one of the earliest but also one of the most active and energetic of the pioneers in Hardwick. He was a joiner, or housewright, a captain of militia, selectman, assessor, clerk and treasurer of the town, and a deacon of the church nearly fifty-seven years. After his death, a pamphlet was published containing several articles written by him, chiefly on religious subjects. In one of these is a scrap of autobiography which fixes the date of his birth and, in connection with the records heretofore quoted, sufficiently identifies him as one of the sons of Joseph (3): —

"My native place where born was I,
In seventeen hundred nine,
Does sixteen miles from Boston lie,
In Westown, called mine.

"Between my third year and my fourth
My mother left this life;
Which was to me affliction sore,
My father lost his wife.

. . . .

"In all my father's family
Once sixteen did survive;
Before my father two did die,
Then fourteen left alive."

5. DAVID, s. of Joseph (4), m. Elizabeth Fisk 12 Nov. 1761; she d. 22 Oct. 1791, a. 48, and he m. Lydia Woods of N. Bra. 22 Jan. 1794. His chil. were *Rhoda*, b. 27 Sep. 1763, m. David Barnard of Shelburne 4 Mar. 1783; *Eunice*, b. 22 Aug. 1765, m. John Earl 2 Oct. 1785; *Daniel*, b. 20 Sep. 1767; *Elizabeth*, b. 27 Oct. 1768, m. Isaac Wing of Rochester, Vt., 24 Jan. 1793; *David*, b. 12 May 1771; *Mercy*, b. 11 May 1773, d. unm. 6 Jan. 1857; *Moses*, b. 9 Mar. 1776, d. 15 Sep. 1777; *Moses*, b. 11 Mar. 1779; *Lydia*, b. 18 Oct. 1784, m. Daniel Matthews of N. Bra. 21 Jan. 1800. DAVID the f. was a very active citizen, selectman, and assessor, and d. 5 Aug. 1799.

6. JOSEPH, s. of Joseph (4), m. Greele Singleterry of Sutton 15 Jan. 1772; she d. 8 Feb. 1800, a. 56, and he m. Polly Gray of Worcester, pub. 21 Sep. 1800; she d. 3 June 1816, a. 50, and he m. Mary Gray of Ware, pub. 3 Mar. 1817. His chil. were *Lucy*, b. 20 May 1773, d. 3 Oct. 1785; *Joseph*, b. 14 July, 1777, m. Hannah Gould 14 Oct. 1800; *Azubah*, b. 30 Mar. 1780, d. 19 Feb. 1781; *Mary Singleterry*, b. 23 May 1818, d. unm. 23 Nov. 1834. JOSEPH the f. res. on the homestead, was a deacon, town treasurer nine years, and d. 11 Nov. 1822; his w. Mary m. Seth Winslow of Barre, pub. 22 Oct. 1826, continued to res. here, and d. 15 Jan. 1842, a. 64.

7. DANIEL, s. of David (5), m. Kezia, dau. of James Wing 20 Jan. 1791, and had *Betsey*, bap. 29 July 1792; *Justus*, bap. 6 Dec. 1795. DANIEL the f. d. 1 Dec. 1796, a. 29; his w. Kezia was pub. to David Barnard of Shelburne 1 May 1815.

8. DAVID, s. of David (5), m. Ruth, dau. of Job Dexter, 27 Ap. 1794, and had *Luthera*, b. 12 Ap. 1796, m. John Gleason 18 Nov. 1813, and d. at Dana 3 Oct. 1875; *Clarissa*, b. 7 Oct. 1796, m. Amaziah Spooner of Amh. 27 Ap. 1825; *Anna*, b. —— 1797, d. 14 Nov. 1803; *Willard*, b. 8 Feb. 1801, m. Mercy dau. of Maj. Gardner Ruggles, pub. 8 Oct. 1826, and rem. to Westminster,

where he d. 24 Sep. 1852; *Mary*, b. —— Ap. 1803, d. 24 Nov. 1803; *Mary*, b. 18 Nov. 1804, d. 3 Aug. 1818; *Sarah*, b. 5 Oct. 1808; *Anna*, b. 21 Nov. 1811. DAVID the f. res. on the Petersham road, at the place marked "D. Allen" on the R. Map, and d. 20 Jan. 1835; his w. Ruth d. 26 Mar. 1847, a. 74.

9. MOSES, s. of David (5), m. Anna, dau. of James Paige, 26 June 1802; she d. 7 June 1824, a. 45, and he m. her sister Fanny, wid. of Stephen Rice, Jr., pub. 7 May 1825. His chil. were *Almira Warner*, b. 20 Feb. 1803, m. William A. Wheeler of Worcester 13 Jan. 1825; *Anson Fisk*, b. 31 Jan. 1805; *Daniel Freeman*, b. 6 Feb. 1807, d. 17 Nov. 1816; *James Franklin*, b. 26 Feb. 1809, res. in Worcester; *Calvin Paige*, b. 30 June 1811. MOSES the f. res. on the Petersham Road, at the place marked "Capt. Allen" on the R. Map, was a farmer, assessor, selectman, and representative in the General Court. He d. 22 Ap. 1843; his w. Fanny d. in Boston 15 Feb. 1873, a. 88.

10. JUSTUS, son of Daniel (7), m. Betsey F., dau. of Nathan Robinson, 21 Nov. 1831, and had *Mary*, b. 14 Jan. 1835, d. unm. 12 Nov. 1860; *Frederick Warner*, b. 11 Ap. 1847, d. 9 June 1847; and perhaps others. JUSTUS the f. d. 24 Aug. 1869; his w. Betsey F. d. 4 Dec. 1876, a. 69.

11. ANSON FISK, s. of Moses (9), m. Ruth Randall 14 June 1846, and had *Philinda*, b. 3 Aug. 1846; *Almira R.*, b. 12 Aug. 1848, d. 3 Nov. 1848. ANSON FISK the f. was a farmer and inherited the homestead, which he sold soon after his father's death. He was early crippled by the loss of a leg, after which he was an assessor for several years. He d. at the Old Gentlemen's Home in Boston 2 Sep. 1876; his w. Ruth d. 28 Aug. 1848, a. 27.

12. JONAS, prob. s. of Elijah of Sutton, who was named in the settlement of the estate of his father Joseph (3), 1758, m. Prudence, dau. of Benjamin Winchester, 15 Feb. 1781; she d. 19 Dec. 1797, a. 35, and he m. her sister, Sarah Winchester, 29 Aug. 1798. His chil. were *Joseph*, b. —— 1784, a carpenter and for many years lieutenant of militia, m. Sally, dau. of John Aiken, 12 May, 1814, and d. 22 Dec. 1833, a. 49 (his w. Sally prob. m. John Sherman of Barre 3 Dec. 1835); *Jonas*, b. —— 1786 (prob. the same who m. Abigail Thayer 10 May 1809); *Benjamin*, b. —— 1788, d. unm. 14 Sep. 1815, a. 27; *Elijah*, b. 7 Mar. 1791; *Polly*, b. 28 Nov. 1793; *Cyrus*, b. 8 Aug. 1796; *Increase Sumner*, b. 31 Dec. 1798, d. 6 Sep. 1800. The first three of these chil. were prob. b. at Sutton. JONAS the f. rem. from Sutton to Hk. before 1791, was a carpenter, honest and harmless, and res. between the road to Gilbertville and the road to Ware, at the place marked "J. Aiken" on the R. Map; he d. 13 July 1817, a. 65; his w. Sarah d. 10 May 1802, a. nearly 35.

13. ELIJAH, prob. brother of Jonas (12), by w. Anna had, in Sutton, *Polly*, b. 24 May 1787; *Timothy*, b. 30 Mar. 1789; *Sally*, b. 31 Aug. 1795; and in Petersham, *David*, b. 19 Feb. 1798; *Artemas*, b. 27 Sep. 1800; *Cyrus*, b. 24 Dec. 1802. ELIJAH the f. was a carpenter, would swallow a quart of cider without visible motion of his throat and without apparent harm, rem. from Sutton to Pet. about 1797, and thence to Hk. soon after 1802. He d. 22 Jan. 1817, a. 54.

14. JONAS, prob. s. of Jonas (12), m. Abigail Thayer 10 May 1809, and had *Balara Thayer*, b. 28 Feb. 1810; *Jonas*, b. —— 1812. JONAS the f. d. 4 Mar. 1812, a. 26.

15. ELIJAH, prob. son of Jonas (12), m. Olive Chapin 8 Mar. 1816, and had a child which d. 12 Jan. 1817, a. 3 months.

16. JONAS, s. of Jonas (14), m. Anna F. Richardson, pub. 8 Nov. 1833, and had *Mary Matilda*, b. 28 June 1848. JONAS the f. d. 19 Jan. 1864, a. 51; his w. Anna F. d. 9 Jan. 1864, a. 51.

17. NATHAN, parentage not ascertained, m. Esther Haskins 17 Dec. 1789, and had *Lucy*, b. 25 Nov. 1790, m. Philip Grant, Jr., 2 Nov. 1809; *Josiah*, b. 10 June 1792, d. 25 Jan. 1810; *Artemas*, b. 12 Jan. 1795; *George*, b. ——, d. at Gardner 4 Sep. 1855; prob. *Nathan*, b. ——, pub. to Betsey Juckett 16 Feb. 1823. NATHAN the f. d. before 25 Jan. 1810; his w. Esther d. 16 Feb. 1835, a. 79.

EDWARD, adm. to the ch. 29 Ap. 1744. OLIVER (from Rochester), res. here from 1777 to 1784. ABIA, m. Ezra Leonard, Jr., 23 Oct. 1781. ABIGAIL, pub. to Reuel Keith 11 Ap. 1784. REUBEN, m. Betsey Ellis 24 Dec. 1812, and d. 4 Jan. 1823, a. 38.

AMES, SAMSON, had w. Elizabeth, who d. 10 Aug. 1842, a. 42, and he m. Elizabeth S. Allen of Barre, pub. 2 Ap. 1843; she d. 14 Mar. 1865, a. 62, and he m. Mrs. M. Minerva Hastings 1 Dec. 1865. His chil. were a child d. 13 July 1833, a. 6 months; *Eugene A.*, b. 29 Aug. 1844; *Orville Adelbert*, b. 6 Nov. 1866; *Marcia P.*, b. 12 Sep. 1868.

BETSEY P., of Barre, m. Theophilus Hastings 22 Dec. 1785. ANNA, of Barre, m. Lemuel Wheeler 2 May 1793. MARIA P., m. E. Warren Combs of W. Brk., pub. 25 Aug. 1845. LOUISA S., m. Martin Swift, Jr., of Bridgewater 11 Dec. 1845.

AMIDON, PHILIP, of Oxford, s. of Roger, and b. 26 Jan. 1669, in his will dated 16 Dec. 1743 and proved 12 May 1747, mentions wife Ithamar, chil. *Ephraim*, *Henry*, *Roger*, *Ichabod*, *Philip*, *John*, *Mary* Chamberlin, *Hannah* Wheelock, and the heirs of son *Ithamar* deceased.

2. JOHN, s. of Philip (1), b. 19 May 1713, m. Sarah, dau. of Daniel Hastings then of Oxford, 14 July 1737, and had *Sarah*, b. 3 Ap. 1738, d. young; *Abigail*, b. 25 Ap. 1740, d. young; *Sarah*, b. 7 July 1742, m. Jonathan Gilbert of N. Brk. 5 Jan. 1779; *John*, bap. 6 Jan. 1744–5; *Abigail*, bap. 31 May 1747, m. Lemuel Cobb 27 Mar. 1777; *Philip*, b. 16 Jan. 1749–50; *Hannah*, b. 25 Oct. 1752, m. Seth Ruggles 25 Nov. 1790. JOHN the f. settled in Hk. before his marriage, and res. on or near the place marked "J. A." on the R. Map, near the line of Barre. He d. between 15 Mar. and 12 May 1755.

3. JOHN, s. of John (2), m. Mercy, dau. of Deac. Joseph Allen, 4 Feb. 1771, and had *Chloe*, b. 17 Jan. 1772, d. unm. 11 Sep. 1842; *Lydia*, b. 26 Aug. 1774, d. unm. 23 Ap. 1828; *John*, b. 1 June 1782; *Elijah*, b. 27 Sep. 1787. JOHN the f. was a farmer, res. on the homestead, and was noted for his remarkably strict economy. His w. Mercy d. 9 Feb. 1808, a. nearly 62, and he m. Anna, wid. of Edward Ruggles, 14 Dec. 1809; after a few years, they preferred to live apart, and mutually agreed on a separation. He d. 25 Oct. 1825; she d. 9 Jan. 1842, a. nearly 89.

4. PHILIP, s. of John (2), m. Rhoda, dau. of Shearjashub Goodspeed, 27 Nov. 1788, and d. 11 Aug. 1796; she d. 16 June 1841, a. 71. No record is found of the birth of children; but prob. the following were of this family: *Sarah*, b. about 1789, d. unm. 13 Sep. 1828, a. 39; *Alice*, b. ——, m. Ichabod Dexter 26 Mar. 1822, and d. 26 June 1830, a. 39; *Hannah*, b. ——, m. Elijah Bangs, Jr., 19 Dec. 1814, d. 2 Sep. 1844, a. 51; *Sophronia*, b. ——, m. Stillman Clark 9 Sep. 1819, d. 12 Oct. 1840, a. 47.

5. JOHN, s. of John (3), m. Sally Hutchinson of Ware, pub. 19 May 1821, had son *Philip*, was a farmer, and res. on the homestead. He d. 10 Jan. 1862; his w. Sally d. 15 Oct. 1877, a. 94.

6. ELIJAH, s. of John (3), m. Martha P. Nye of Barre, pub. 18 May 1818, and had *Mercy*, b. 12 Mar. 1819; *Martha*, b. 30 Oct. 1820; *John Allen*, b. 13 Feb. 1822, d. at Springfield 17 Jan. 1860; *Augustus B.*, bap. 26 Feb. 1827, d. at Boston 5 Nov. 1870. ELIJAH the f. was a farmer and deacon; he res. near the homestead, at the place marked "Dea. Amidon" on the R. Map, rem. to Belchertown about 1830, and d. 7 June 1857; his w. Martha P. d. 29 Mar. 1878, a. 86.

7. PHILIP, s. of John (5), m. Sarah A. Warner of N. Br., pub. 14 Nov. 1848, and had *John Edwin*, b. 1 Nov. 1850.

8. JOHN EDWIN, s. of Philip (7), m. Lucy Jane Lamb of Phillipston 19 Oct. 1875, and had *Elmer Warner*, b. 15 Mar. 1877; *Carrie May*, b. 8 Ap. 1880.

AMSDEN, EPHRAIM, JR., of Greenwich m. Relief Thayer 15 Oct. 1816, and had *Sophia Thayer*, b. here 19 Jan. 1817; *Almira Marilla*, b. 30 July 1820, m. —— Allen, and d. at W. Brk. 15 Sep. 1873; *Ansel White*, b. 21 Feb. 1822; *Benjamin Franklin*, b. 12 Aug. 1823, d. at Ware 28 May 1878. EPHRAIM the f. was a shoemaker, and res. on the lot now occupied by Mr. Joseph R. Robinson. His w. Relief d. at Ware 27 May 1868, a. 70.

2. NELSON, s. of David and nephew of Ephraim (1), m. Sarah F., dau. of

John Gleason of Dana, and had *Ella J.*, b. in N. Sal. 24 Oct. 1856, m. Joseph A. Manning of Worc. 27 Dec. 1876; *Nelson Willis*, b. here 19 Nov. 1862. NELSON the f., a blacksmith, res. at the north end of the Common.

ANDERSON, WILLIAM, of Blandford, a weaver, bought a farm on the east side of the river, 30 Dec. 1741; he m. Margaret Crooks of Medway 18 Oct. 1744, and had *Ann*, b. 1 Aug. 1745; *Jane* and *Mary*, twins, b. 30 Dec. 1748; *William*, b. 23 Oct. 1750; *Jeremiah*, bap. 6 Feb. 1753; prob. *John*, b. about 1755, and perhaps others.

2. TIMOTHY PAIGE, s. of John of N. Br., and probably grandson of William (1), m. Betsey Hastings, 17 Oct. 1811, and d. 8 Ap. 1842, a. 50; she d. 25 Nov. 1868, a. 82. Among their chil. (no births recorded) were *Elvira*, b. about 1813, m. Charles Alexander of Winchester, N. H. 21 Sep. 1834, and (2d) John Severance of Win. 24 Nov. 1844; a child b. ——, d. 10 Jan. 1818; *Eliza*, b. —— 1820, d. unm. 24 May 1841, a. 21; *Almeda*, b. about 1825, m. Joseph D. Dexter, Jr., 8 Mar. 1846; and perhaps also *Maria*, b. ——, m. Festus Spooner of Jericho, Vt., 25 May 1836. TIMOTHY P. the f. res. near Gilbertville at the place marked with his name on the R. Map; he was a selectman two years, and a worthy citizen.

3. WILLIAM, brother of Timothy P. (2), m. ——, and d. s. p. 21 Ap. 1867, a. 72. He res. on the road to Gilbertville, near the place marked "P. Lawton" on the R. Map, and was assessor eight years, selectman nine years, representative two years, and justice of the peace.

4. ALPHONSO L., by w. Mary C., had *Almon Alphonso*, b. 19 Oct. 1851, d. 7 May 1852.

ANN, m. William Whitager of Rut. 10 Oct. 1745. ALMIRA, d. unm. 19 July 1880, a. 65.

ANDREWS, BENJAMIM, by w. Joanna, had *Joanna*, b. 20 May 1737; *Elizabeth*, bap. 22 Ap. 1739; *Mary*, bap. 10 May 1741. BENJAMIN the f. prob. rem. to Pet. about 1739; his dau. *Elizabeth* was bap. there.

ARNOLD, GAMALIEL, by w. Hannah, had *Mary*, b. 7 July 1766, m. Joseph Harvey 2 Feb. 1786; *Henry*, b. 8 Dec. 1768, m. Sylvia Cobb, pub. 17 Ap. 1791; *Francis*, b. 21 Sep. 1770; *Calvin*, b. 29 June 1772; *Waite*, b. 24 Mar. 1775; *Louisa*, b. 3 Ap. 1777, m. Joseph Cole 29 Nov. 1792; *Sprague*, b. 26 Aug. 1779; *Andrew*, b. 31 Dec. 1781; *Gamaliel*, b. 9 Aug. 1785. GAMALIEL the f., with six sons, rem. to Randolph, Vt., in 1791, his eldest son *Henry* having rem. thither in the preceding year. See *Vermont Hist. Mag.* ii. 1045. Mr. Arnold was lieutenant of militia.

ATWOOD, ISAAC, a cooper, b. in Plymouth about 1783, m. Kezia, dau. of Simeon Nye, and died in Hk. 11 Dec. 1860, a. 77; she d. 2 Oct. 1861, a. 77. No record is found of children.

2. ZACCHEUS, by w. Chloe, had a child, b. ——, d. 6 Aug. 1791; and, by w. Hannah, *Elijah Gregory*, b. in Pet. 30 Aug. 1799; *Charles*, b. here 28 Ap. 1801; *Abiathar*, b. here 9 Mar. 1803.

3. *Simeon Nye*, prob. s. of Isaac (1), m. Prudence Haskins of Shutes. 6 June 1835, and had *Susan*, b. ——, d. 2 Sep. 1840, a. 3; *Hannah Amelia*, b. 10 June 1843; m. William C. Peck 11 Mar. 1862; *Susan Arletta*, b. 17 Ap. 1849, d. 10 Ap. 1850; *John Allen*, b. 13 July 1853; *Effie Cecilia*, b. 13 Oct. 1854.

4. JOSEPH, by w. Harriet S., had *Benjamin Smith*, b. 3 Oct. 1859; *Ada Lizzie*, b. 15 July 1862; *Amy Marshall*, b. 23 July 1867; *George Halsey*, b. 26 Feb. 1876.

KEZIA, was pub. to Abraham Gibbs of Quobbin 10 Mar. 1743–4, but refused to "proseed in marrige" 24 Nov. 1744. JERUSHA, m. John Aiken 19 Oct. 1749. SAMUEL, m. Peace Stewart 30 Aug. 1753. LYDIA, m. Phina Cole 6 Dec. 1795. MARY, of Brewster, m. Ebenezer Perry, pub. 3 May 1807. SUSAN, d. unm. 18 Aug. 1874, a. 18.

AYERS, EBENEZER, prob. from Brk., m. Mary Ballard 28 Feb. 1739–40, and had *Joseph*, b. 8 Sep. 1741. He had other chil. by a former wife, and d. before Aug. 1748.

2. DAVID, s. of Ebenezer (1), m. Ginnet Shaw 21 Dec. 1742, and had *Ebenezer*, b. 12 Ap. 1743; *David*, b. 8 Nov. 1745; *Mary*, b. 16 Ap. 1748; *Dorcas*, b. 2 May 1750; *Sarah* and *Abigail*, prob. twins, bap. 23 Aug. 1752.

Capt. WILLIAM is named in 1747 as the owner of land on the Rutland road, about half a mile east of Ware River, then in Hardwick. JENNY, m. Calvin Fairbanks 24 June 1776. RUTH, m. Seth Woodward of Pet. 25 Aug. 1778.

BABBITT, SAMUEL, by w. Polly, had *Samuel*, b. 11 Feb. 1786; *Elkanah*, b. 10 Sep. 1787; *Dwight*, b. 12 Feb. 1789; *Rhoda*, b. 20 Feb. 1791.

ABIGAIL, m. Seth Blanchard 19 July 1775. SETH, m. Betty Blanchard 22 Ap. 1779. LEVI, of Norton, m. Betty Babbitt 21 Dec. 1779, and had s. *Levi*, who d. in Athol 9 May 1863, a. 82.

BALLOU, HOSEA, m. Ruth Washburn of Williamsburg 15 Sep. 1796, and had (born here) *Fanny*, b. 13 Oct. 1797, m. Leonard Holmes of Boston 7 Oct. 1827, and d. 28 Mar. 1846; *Hosea Faxon*, b. 4 Ap. 1799, a Universalist clergyman, m. Mary Ballou, and res. in Wilmington, Vt., d. 20 May 1881; *Massena Berthier*, b. 28 Nov. 1800, a Universalist clergyman, m. Mary S. Jacobs of Scituate 21 Dec. 1825, and res. in Stoughton; *Cassendana*, b. 9 Jan. 1803, m. Joseph Wing of Boston 25 Ap. 1822, and d. ——; after his removal from Hk. he had *Mandana*, b. 17 Sep. 1804, m. Rev. Benjamin Whittemore of Boston 4 June 1823; *Elmina Ruth*, b. 3 Ap. 1810, m. Rev. Josiah C. Waldo 26 Oct. 1831, and d. at New London 29 June 1856; *Clementina*, b. 10 July 1812, m. Col. Isaac Hull Wright of Boston 4 June 1837; *Fiducia*, b. 1 May 1814, m. Abijah W. Farrar of Boston 22 Ap. 1838; *Maturin Murray*, b. 14 Ap. 1820, a publisher, m. Mary A. Roberts 15 Sep. 1839, and res. in Boston. HOSEA the f. was s. of Rev. Maturin Ballou, and was b. in Richmond, N. H., 30 Ap. 1771. He was a very eminent Universalist clergyman, and wrought a marvellous change in the theological opinions of the world. He res. for several years in that part of Hk. which was included in Dana when that town was incorporated 18 Feb. 1801; in 1803 he rem. to Barnard, Vt., and thence to Portsmouth, N. H., in 1809, to Salem in 1815, and to Boston in 1817, where he d. 7 June 1852, full of years and of honors.

BANGS, SETH, res. in Harwich, and, by w. Deborah, had *Chipman*, b. 20 June 1727, d. 4 Ap. 1750; *Solomon*, b. 23 May 1729; *Elijah*, b. 3 June 1731; *Samuel*, b. 9 Ap. 1733; *Perez*, b. 20 Feb. 1735–6; *Seth*, 14 July 1738; *John*, b. 17 Feb. 1742; *Deborah*, b. 5 Feb. 1744, m. Edward Foster in Hardwick 13 Jan. 1762; *Chipman*, b. 8 Aug. 1750.

2. DAVID, prob. brother of Seth (1), by w. Eunice, had *Nathaniel*, b. 18 Ap. 1733; *Enoch*, b. 2 Oct. 1734; *Nathan*, b. 2 May 1736; *Reliance*, b. 29 Aug. 1738, m. Nathan Billings in Hardwick 26 Dec. 1769; *Azariah*, b. 8 Ap. 1740; *Huldah*, b. 27 Feb. 1741–2. DAVID the f. rem. from Harwich to Hardwick in 1768.

3. SOLOMON, s. of Seth (1), by w. Experience, had in Harwich *Temperance*, b. 13 Jan. 1753; *Elijah*, b. 18 May 1757; *Perez*, b. 4 Jan. 1763; *Experience*, b. 15 Sep. 1766.

4. ENOCH, s. of David (2), with his w. Hannah was dismissed from the church in Harwich 21 Nov. 1762, and admitted to the ch. in Hardwick 4 Sep. 1763. Their chil. were bap. as follows: *Watson*, 10 Ap. 1763; *Hannah*, 1 Sep. 1765, d. young; *Hannah*, 28 June 1767; *Enoch*, 21 Jan. 1770; *Reuben*, 7 May 1775; *William Freeman*, 11 Ap. 1779; he had also son *Nathaniel*, named in his will. ENOCH the f., then styled of Barre, d. 12 Ap. 1798.

5. NATHAN, s. of David (2), rem. early to Hk., and had *Bethia*, b. 19 July 1761; *Huldah*, b. 26 June 1762; *John*, b. 21 June 1764; *Joshua*, b. 14 Oct. 1766; *Mary*, b. 28 Nov. 1768; *Mark*, b. 10 Sep. 1771; *Nathan*, b. 1 Sep. 1773, d. 7 Mar. 1774; *Abigail*, b. 21 Mar. 1775.

6. AZARIAH, s. of David (2), rem. with his f. to Hk. in 1768, m. Huldah Stow of Southborough, pub. 2 Mar. 1769, and had *Nathaniel*, bap. 6 May 1770; *Judith Fox*, bap. 13 Mar. 1774; *Azariah*, bap. 10 Nov. 1776.

7. ELIJAH, s. of Solomon (3), rem. early to Hk. His w. Sally d. 7 May 1790, a. 34, and he m. Sally, dau. of Abraham Knowlton, 21 Ap. 1791. His chil. were *Sally*, b. 28 Ap. 1782, m. Luther Paige 22 Aug. 1802; *Bela*, b. 10 Ap. 1784; *Solomon*, b. 8 Ap. 1786, d. 4 Feb. 1811; *Alba*, b. 10 Feb. 1788; *Elijah* b. ——; *Martin*, b. —— 1792, d. at Cambridge 8 Mar. 1865; *Luthera*, b. ——, m. Charles Wheeler 2 Mar. 1814 or 1815, and (2) Joseph Adams of

Shutes, 1 Ap. 1824; *Lucy*, b. ——, m. Robert Fitts, Jr., of Ward, 1 Nov. 1819. ELIJAH the f. was a farmer, res. on the Pet. road, at the place marked with his name on the R. Map, and d. 28 Sep. 1818; his w. Sally d. 1 Feb. 1835, a. 69.

8. ELIJAH, s. of Elijah (7), was a farmer, res. on the homestead, and m. Hannah Amidon 19 Dec. 1814; she d. 2 Sep. 1844, a. 51, and he m. Mrs. Lucy Elwell of Brk., pub. 10 May 1845. He d. s. p. 28 Jan. 1855, a. 64.

9. JAMES, parentage not ascertained, by w. Susanna, had *Samuel*, b. 20 Aug. 1771.

ADNAH, with his wife, rem. to Hk. in 1768, from "Falmouth, Casco Bay." MARY, m. Jacob Hastings 22 July 1762. EUNICE, m. Amos Thomas 20 Dec. 1770.

BARLOW, WYATT, m. Susanna Hammond in Rochester, pub. 21 Jan. 1772, and had *Susannah*, b. —— 1772, d. here unm. 12 June 1857; *Ann*, b. —— 1773, d. here unm. 5 Aug. 1846; *John*, b. 1 Dec. 1778. Besides these, six others are named in their father's will, 28 Jan. 1819: *Ebenezer*, *Wyatt*, *Betsey* Heywood, *Nancy* Cooley, *Mary* Harris, and *Harriet* Demmon. WYATT the f. was styled Captain, rem. here early, and res. in the Gore, now embraced in Gilbertville, where he d. 19 June 1827, a. 85, his w. Susannah d. 5 Oct. 1830, a. 83.

2. JOHN, s. of Wyatt (1), m. Roxana, dau. of James Sprout, pub. 12 Jan. 1808, and had *James Madison*, b. 3 July 1809, d. unm. 6 or 7 Aug. 1867; *Cynthia*, b. 18 Ap. 1811, m. Selah Barrett of Worc. 30 Nov. 1831; *Lewis*, b. 12 May 1812, res. at Rock Island, Ill.; *Alanson*, b. 10 Nov. 1813, m. Elizabeth Demond 2 Oct. 1839, res. in the State of New York; *Roxana*, b. 28 Sep. 1815, m. Harrison G. O. Monroe 18 May 1843; *Wyatt*, b. 22 Dec. 1819; *John H.*, b. 25 Ap. 1827, res. in Fitchburg. JOHN the f. was drowned 1 July 1850; his w. Roxana d. 20 July 1876, a. nearly 91.

3. WYATT, s. of John (2), m. Mary G. Flint of Athol, pub. 27 Dec. 1847, and had *Charles Flint*, b. 19 Jan. 1849; a son, b. 5 Nov. 1850; *John Hammond*, b. 18 June 1852. WYATT the f. d. 23 Ap. 1856.

4. MOSES, perhaps brother of Capt. Wyatt (1), by w. Elizabeth, had *Moses*, *Jonathan*, *Lemuel*, *Nabby*, *Deborah*, and *Betsey*, all bap. 29 Sep. 1782.

5. AARON, perhaps brother of Capt. Wyatt (1), m. Priscilla Andrews 6 July 1780, and had *Aaron*, bap. 14 July 1784. He was dism. to the church in Barnard, Vt., 22 Aug. 1784.

6. THOMAS, parentage not ascertained, m. Mercy (or Mary) Nelson 26 Sep. 1793, and had *Thomas*, bap. 12 July 1797.

7. EBENEZER m. Betsey Smalley of Truro, pub. 10 Aug. 1787, and had *Sophronia*, bap. 1 July 1792. EBENEZER the f. rem. to Plainfield.

8. IRA G., m. Clarissa Haskins 25 Sep. 1842, and had *Clara Louisa*, b. 23 Jan. 1845. His w. Clarissa d. 7 July 1847, a. 26.

Mrs. ABIGAIL, prob. mother of Wyatt (1), d. 29 Jan. 1793, a. 85. Deacon JOSEPH and his wife were adm. to the church 9 Sep. 1781; also WILLIAM, 23 Mar. 1783. WILLIAM WYATT, m. Ruth Rice of Gr., pub. 7 Sep. 1790. TIMOTHY, m. Betsey Smith of Ware, pub. 6 June 1791. NABBY, m. John Campbell 26 Aug. 1793. EBENEZER, m. Jane Graham 26 Oct. 1831.

BARNARD, JOSEPH, by w. Betty, had *Joseph*, b. ——, m. Prudence Marsh, pub. 28 Nov. 1796, and perhaps m. (2d) Abi Presho 17 Oct. 1819; *Benjamin*, b. 19 Oct. 1776; *Edward*, b. 15 Aug. 1778; *William*, b. 30 Aug. 1781; *Henry*, b. 4 Oct. 1790; *Sarah*, b. 3 Aug. 1792; *Anna*, b. 14 Sep. 1794, d. 13 Mar. 1797.

BARNES, JESSE (otherwise written Barns), was the sixth of the fourteen children of Moses and Hannah (Olds) Barnes, and was b. at Brookfield 7 Nov. 1744. He m. Patience Gilbert 8 Dec. 1763, and had in Brk. *Jonas*, b. 26 June 1764; *Miriam*, b. 29 Sep. 1766, m. Ebenezer Sprout in Hk. 3 June 1790; *Eli*, b. 26 June 1768; *Lydia*, b. 2 May 1770, m. Phineas Wetherbee of Brk. 6 Jan. 1795; *Adonijah*, b. 12 Oct. 1772; *Betsey*, b. 20 Nov. 1774 (or 1777), d. unm. 10 Mar. 1859; and in Hk. *Lucy*, b. 22 Ap. 1781. JESSE the f. rem. from Brk. to Hk. about 1780, was a farmer, res. in the westerly part of the town, and d. 18 Nov. 1823; his w. Patience d. 4 July 1821. For many years the record of births in this family is so imperfect that I am unable to trace its several lines of descent with desirable accuracy.

2. ELIJAH, prob. brother of Jesse (1), and the tenth child of Moses and Hannah, b. in Brk. 12 Feb. 1753, became a member of the church in Hk. 24 Feb. 1782, and his chil., *Elijah*, *John*, and *Polly*, were bap. 30 June 1782, after which I find no trace of this family on record.

3. JONAS, s. of Jesse (1), m. Abiel Sprout 20 Mar. 1791; she d. 17 June 1805, and he was pub. to Joanna Thomas 24 Mar. 1806. No record is found of the birth of his chil.; but by record of deaths it appears that he had by first wife, *Patience*, who d. unm. 24 Jan. 1869, a. 78, according to the record, but prob. 77; and by 2d w., *Jonas*, who d. 14 May 1812, a. nearly 2 years. JONAS the f. d. 1 Nov. 1830; his w. Joanna d. 30 Nov. 1837, a. 63.

4. ELI, son of Jesse (1), m. Polly Merritt 21 July 1789. No record is found of the birth of his chil.; but he had *Polly*, who d. 17 May 1811, a. 16, and prob. *Eli* and *Harvey*, named below. ELI the f. d. 30 Ap. 1845; his w. Polly d. 29 Mar. 1848, a. 77. His house was consumed by fire 12 Mar. 1810.

5. ADONIJAH, s. of Jesse (1), m. Chloe Knights 9 Ap. 1793. Four of his chil. were *Clarinda*, d. unm. 19 Dec. 1876, a. 83; *Jonas*; *Ruth*, d. 27 July, 1815, a. 13; and *Chloe*, m. Stephen Hillman 7 Mar. 1820, d. 28 June 1881; but their birth is not recorded. ADONIJAH the f. d. 21 Aug. 1841; his w. Chloe d. 26 Sep. 1851, a 77.

6. JONAS, s. of Adonijah (5), m. Olean (or Oleyine) Fry 30 Nov. 1830, and had *Harrison F.*, b. about 1834; *Henry*, b. 21 Jan. 1844; *Adelbert Forester*, b. 19 Ap. 1846, m. C. Elizabeth Hunt 20 Oct. 1881; *Emeline*, b. 9 Aug. 1849; *Evelyn*, b. about 1852, m. W. Frank Carruth of Barre 7 Sep. 1873; *Clariette*, b. 28 Nov. 1853; *Alla Velorous* (called *A. Deforest* in the record of his death), b. 1 Aug. 1856, d. 1 or 7 July 1857; and perhaps others. JONAS the f. d. 26 July 1878, a. 78.

7. ELI, prob. s. of Eli (4), m. Vinsa Baker 19 June 1823, and had a child b. ——, d. 6 Dec. 1830, a. 3 days; *George Danforth*; and perhaps others. ELI the f. d. 15 Oct. 1851, a. 52.

8. HARVEY, prob. s. of Eli (4), by w. Harriet, had a child b. ——, d. 18 Mar. 1830; *Sarah A.*, b. about 1833, m. Augustus M. Graves of Dana, pub. 1 Ap. 1852; *Wilder U.*, b. about 1839; *Adeline*, b. about 1841, m. Wells Stacy of Bel. 11 Nov. 1869; *Joseph Loring*, b. 11 Nov. 1843; *Abigail*, b. 25 July 1845, m. Latham Avery of Syracuse, N. Y. 13 Nov. 1871; a son b. 25 Nov. 1847; a daughter b. 27 Feb. 1850; d. next day; *Caroline*, b. 23 May 1852; *Frederick*, b. 21 Jan. 1858.

9. RUFUS, parentage not ascertained, m. Polly Cleveland 31 Dec. 1818, and had a child b. — Mar. 1821, d. 19 Dec. 1822; *Elbridge*, b. about 1823, m. Catherine Bakely 22 Dec. 1852, and d. at N. Br. 31 Mar. 1870; *Calvin*, b. about 1826, m. Nancy R. Kelmer 6 Mar. 1851, and d. at Pet. 9 Feb. 1866 (his w. Nancy R. d. 12 Aug. 1852, a. 19). RUFUS the f. d. in May 1828, a. 30; his w. Polly d. at Gr. 1 May 1854.

10. AMOS, m. Mary Barnes, pub. 26 Dec. 1825, and had *Huldah M.*, b. —— 1830, m. Jesse W. King 21 Oct. 1848; he d. 3 Dec. 1855, and she m. Billings Cummings 22 Nov. 1859, and d. 10 Dec. 1868, a. 38; *Lucy Jane*, b. ——, m. George H. King 7 May 1846; MARY the mother d. 23 Feb. 1865, a. 62.

11. LUCIUS, m. Nancy Cole of Milbury, pub. 6 May 1838, and had *Elmer L.*, b. about 1841, m. Huldah H. Sturtevant 8 Jan. 1864; *Luther Emerson*, b. 19 Nov. 1843, a lawyer, m. Maria L. Sheldon of Leominster 8 Ap. 1874; and perhaps others.

12. CUTLER, m. Arminda S. Rogers 20 Dec. 1837, and had *Martin Luther*, b. about 1841, m. Frances M. Goodwin 4 July 1860; a daughter b. 2 Ap. 1845; *Loring*, b. 17 Dec. 1847; *Luthera S.*, b. 14 Ap. 1850; a son, b. — June 1852.

13. WILLIAM S., m. Lucinda H. Cummings 24 May 1842 (who d. 11 Ap. 1881, a. 58), and had *Helen J.*, b. ——, 1843, m. Frederick M. Cleveland 4 May 1864; *Delia M.*, b. 19 Jan. 1845, m. Ezra B. Glazier, 13 Ap. 1880; *Julia Ann*, b. 14 Aug. 1846; a son and dau., twins, b. 6 Aug. 1849; *Lura Luthera*, b.

27 Oct. 1851; *William*, b. 3 Mar. 1854; d. 14 Jan. 1858; a son, b. 14 May 1856.

14. WARREN W., m. Harriet A. Robinson of Barre, pub. 10 May 1854, and had *Albert Warren*, b. 27 Aug. 1855; *Mary Augusta*, b. 24 Oct. 1856, m. George F. Bacon of Gr. 1 Sep. 1874; *Emma Luella*, b. 9 May 1858, d. 26 May 1861; *Emma*, b. 26 Aug. 1859, d. 23 Sep. 1862; *George Amos*, b. 28 July 1861; *Flora*, b. about 1863, d. 21 May 1866; *Atheda Fiducia*, b. 14 June 1865; *Cora Eliza*, b. 28 Aug. 1867; *Lucy Mabel*, b. 8 Dec. 1869, d. 15 Ap. 1880; *Orcutt Mitchell*, b. 28 Feb. 1873.

15. WARREN J. (or JONAS W.), perhaps s. of Jonas (6), by w. Emily A., had *Harrison Almon*, b. 31 Dec. 1860; *Albertine Augustine*, b. 29 May 1863; *Jennie Estelle*, b. 21 June 1868; *Hiram Ellis*, bap. 2 Sep. 1870; *Clara Louise*, b. 23 Dec. 1871; *Emily Warren*, bap. 4 July 1875.

16. HARRISON F., s. of Jonas (6), m. Mary A. Swift of Bridgewater 12 June 1861, and had *Harry Francis*, b. 30 Mar. 1862.

17. GEORGE D., s. of Eli (7), by w. Maria, had *George Herbert*, b. 22 June 1863; *Jenny Cornelia*, b. 8 July 1866, d. 30 Nov. 1869. GEORGE D. the f. d. 25 Aug. 1867, a. 37; his w. Maria d. 29 June, 1870.

18. WILDER U., s. of Harvey (10), m. Rhoda J. Fay 20 Ap. 1864, and had *Frederick*, b. 26 Feb. 1865; *Jane Maria*, b. 26 Sep. 1866; *George Hammond*, b. 5 Aug. 1868; *Herbert Wells*, b. 24 June 1870; *Adda Larrisa*, b. 20 Aug. 1872.

19. ASA, by w. Caroline, had *Myron Eugene*, b. 8 Nov. 1847.

20. LUCIUS E., by w. Sarah H., had *Willard Eliot*, b. 15 June, 1864.

BARR, MATTHEW, by w. Margaret, had *David*, bap. 20 May 1739; *James*, bap. — Dec. 1740; *George*, bap. 31 Mar. 1743; *Samuel* and *Margaret*, bap. 18 Oct. 1745; *Hugh*, bap. 7 May 1749, d. 4 Nov. 1750. MATTHEW the f. res. on the east side of Ware River, in what is now New Braintree.

JENNY, m. Samuel Fantan of Rut. 21 Nov. 1745. JOHN, pub. to Damaris Wheeler of Shrewsbury 21 Sep. 1751. JOHN, Jr., m. Mary Bridges 15 Sep. 1789.

BARRETT, JOSIAH, by w. Catherine, had *Sarah*, bap. 17 July 1737; *Joseph*, bap. 28 Mar. 1742; *Miriah (Maria?)*, bap. 16 Feb. 1745-6.

2. JOSEPH, by w. ——, had *Sarah*, bap. 15 Mar. 1752; *Oliver*, bap. 25 May 1755; *Moses*, bap. 1 May 1757.

BARTHOLOMEW, SAMUEL, formerly of Woodstock, Conn., d. in Hk. 16 Ap. 1832, a. 81; his w. Susanna d. 2 Aug. 1836, a. 72. Their chil. who res. in Hk. were *Persis*, b. about 1784, d. unm. 13 Feb. 1869, a. 85; *Susan*, b. about 1789, m. —— Wiswall, and d. 11 Feb. 1869, a. 80; *Adolphus*, b. about 1793; probably *Nancy*, who d. 5 Feb. 1829, a. 36; *Gardner*, b. about 1796.

2. ADOLPHUS, s. of SAMUEL (1), by w. Lydia, had *Harriet Nye* and *Elizabeth*, twins, b. 21 Aug. 1827; *Nancy*, b. 6 Nov. 1828; *Andrew Jackson*, b. 1 Oct. 1832, a lawyer, res. in Southbridge, and has been representative and senator; *Nelson*, b. 27 Dec. 1834; a soldier in the Civil War, d. at Philadelphia in Nov. 1861, and was buried here; and perhaps others. ADOLPHUS the f. was an assessor and selectman. Late in life he rem. to Barre, where he d. 4 Nov. 1870, a. 77, and was buried here.

3. GARDNER, s. of Samuel (1), m. Abigail S., dau. of John Jenney, pub. 17 Feb. 1831, and had *Abbie Jane*, b. 6 Aug. 1834, m. Charles L. Trow, 10 Sep. 1855, and (2d) Joseph N. Lincoln 12 May, 1870; *Susan Victoria*, b. 10 Feb. 1837, m. Rev. George J. Sanger 31 May 1859; *Martha Ann*, b. 28 Jan. 1839, d. unm. 2 or 3 May 1869; *Hannah Josephine*, b. 10 Dec. 1840, m. George F. Lawrence of Corn Planter, Pa., 1 Oct. 1870; *Charles Gardner*, b. 30 Ap. 1843; *John Jenney*, b. 11 Nov. 1845, d. 23 June 1847; *John Calvin*, b. 8 Mar. 1848, res. in Barre. GARDNER the f. res. near the Old Furnace, was a trader, insurance agent, and also engaged in the express business between Hk. and Worcester. He was selectman two years. He d. 26 Feb. 1874, a. 77. His w. Abigail d. at Danvers, Feb. 2, 1881, a. 72, and was buried here.

4. CHARLES GARDNER, s. of Gardner (3), m. Jennie E. Finch 22 Feb. 1867, and had *Martha Finch*, b. 13 July 1869.

BARTLETT, BENJAMIN, by w. Thanks, had *Philip*, bap. 14 May 1745.

2. BETHUEL m. Betsey Story 3 Feb. 1794, and had *Luke*, b. —— 1794; *Avery*, b. —— 1796; *Almira*, b. —— 1800, m. —— Patrick, and d. at Warren 29 Mar. 1864, a. 64; *Adeline*, b. —— 1803, m. Simeon Williams of Pres. 23 Nov. 1823, and (2d) —— Clark, and d. at Ware 28 Nov. 1874, a. 71; *Lewis Howe*, b. —— 1809, d. 26 Feb. 1811, a. 15 months; *Lewis*, b. —— 1813, d. 12 Mar. 1873, a. 60; *William*, b. —— 1818. BETHUEL the f. res. near Gilbertville, was a blacksmith and a famous fifer, and d. 28 Feb. 1821, a. 48.

3. LUKE, s. of Bethuel (2), m. Lucy, dau. of Capt. Zenas Phinney, 7 Dec. 1817, and had a child d. 7 May 1821, a. 3 weeks; *Zenas P.*, b. —— 1822, d. 16 Aug. 1838, a. 16; *Elbridge*, b. —— 1827, d. 6 Sep. 1838, a. 11; and prob. others. LUKE the f. was a farmer, res. on the road to Gilbertville, at the place marked with his name on the R. Map, and d. 24 Aug. 1838.

4. AVERY, s. of Bethuel (2), m. Mary Clifford of Enf. 20 Ap. 1818, and had *Bethuel*, b. 29 Nov. 1818; a child b. —— 1820, and d. 27 Sep. 1821, a. 11 months. AVERY the f. d. 21 Feb. 1825, a. 29; his w. prob. m. Freeman Pepper of Ware 19 Ap. 1832.

5. WILLIAM, s. of Bethuel (2), by w. Clarissa M., had *Emily*, b. about 1844, d. 26 Ap. 1846; *Maria*, b. 24 Nov. 1846. He rem. to Ware, where he d. 12 Nov. 1874, a. 56.

6. FRANKLIN, by w. Harriet, had *Edward*, b. 22 May 1871; *Delia*, b. 6 Aug. 1873; *Agnes*, b. 28 June 1879.

DOROTHY, m. Joseph Parks of Norwich 11 Dec. 1783. ELIZA, of N. Br., m. Harmon Clark, pub. 19 Jan. 1818. SOPHIA, m. Stillman Elwell, 28 Jan. 1821. MARY, a widow, dau. of Marcus Marsh, d. 24 Jan. 1873, a. 71.

BASSETT, WILLIAM, by w. Anna, had *William*, b. (prob. in Norton) about 1772; *Anna*, b. here 13 Oct. 1774; *Polly*, b. 9 Dec. 1776, m. Robert Morton of Gr. 6 Mar. 1800; *Ephraim*, b. 7 Feb. 1779; *Masa*, b. 7 Ap. 1781; *Lydia*, b. 3 May 1783, d. unm. 1 Mar. 1816. WILLIAM the f. rem. to Hk. from Norton about 1773, was a farmer, res. in the southwest part of the town, and closed a long and exemplary life 23 Dec. 1838, a. 89; his w. Anna d. 26 Nov. 1822, a. 69.

2. WILLIAM, s. of William (1), m. Lavina Wicker 28 Nov. 1799, and had *William Erastus*, b. 23 July 1801, prob. m. Mrs. Sarah Bassett of Ware 4 Ap. 1844; *Mary*, b. 3 July 1803, m. Calvin Jenney 19 Sep. 1824; *Fidelia*, b. 4 Mar. 1805, m. Seth Peirce 21 Sep. 1831; *Alvan*, b. 16 Ap. 1807; *Melinda*, b. 11 July, 1809, m. William Ward of Ware 10 Mar. 1831; *Franklin*, b. 18 Sep. 1811, d. 24 Feb. 1839; *Lavina*, b. 29 Aug. 1814, m. Oziel Shaw, Ware, 10 May 1836, and d. at Amh. 9 Feb. 1872. WILLIAM the f. was a farmer, res. at the place marked with his name on the R. Map, and d. 22 Sep. 1847, a. 75; his w. Lavina d. 26 Feb. 1856, a. 77.

3. EPHRAIM, s. of William (1), m. Tabitha, dau. of Lemuel Newton, 19 Jan. 1804, and had *Lemuel Newton*, b. 10 Oct. 1804, d. at Enfield 12 Aug. 1857; *Chloe Lane*, b. 4 June 1807; *Calvin Harvey*, b. 15 Aug. 1809, m. (then res. at Enf.) Susan Newton 6 Dec. 1854; *William Watson*, b. 25 July 1811; *Tabitha Gilson*, b. 22 Nov. 1813; *Ephraim Lane*, b. 3 May 1816; *Masa Newland*, b. 27 Oct. 1818; *Lydia*, bap. 24 June 1821; *Ralph Harmon*, bap. 28 Jan. 1824, d. at Enf. 13 Mar. 1861. EPHRAIM the f. res. in the southwest part of Hk. and afterwards in Enf., where he d. 12 Mar. 1867, a. 88; his w. Tabitha d. at Enf. 24 Ap. 1865, a. nearly 85.

4. MASA, s. of William (1), m. Susanna Utley 10 May 1814, res. at the place marked with his name on the R. Map, and d. 31 Oct. 1833, a. 52; his w. Susanna d. 17 July 1820, a. 30. No record is found of children.

5. ALVAN, s. of William (2), m. Nancy Richardson, pub. 22 Sep. 1828, and (2d) Sarah Ward 28 Nov. 1848. His chil. were *Jennie*, b. ——, m. Asa F. Richardson 26 May 1858; *Abbie A.*, b. ——, m. Waldo Peirce 15 Sep. 1861; *Alanson S.*, b. about 1845, m. Abbie E. Sturtevant 13 Oct. 1874; *Francis Luther*, b. 25 June 1851; *Sarah Emma*, b. 2 Mar. 1859. ALVAN the f. d. 30 Aug. 1879, a. 72.

6. BENJAMIN, m. Nancy Johnson 20 Ap. 1837; she d. 4 Feb. 1847, and he

m. Catherine W. Richmond 29 June 1847, who d. at Dana 1 May 1874, a. 70. He had *William F.*, b. ——, d. 10 May 1854, a. 6 years and 10 months; *William Benjamin*, born 31 Oct. 1848.

PETER, m. Hannah Lindsey of Providence, pub. 24 Oct. 1779; he d. ——, and she m. Timothy Fay 7 Dec. 1780. DAVID, m. Phebe Terry 11 Dec. 1783, rem. to Ware. NANCY, m. Masa Newland 31 Oct. 1802. WILLIAM S., m. Ruth E. Tucker 1 Dec. 1836; PHILIP and Bathsheba Gunn, negro servants of Capt. Joseph Warner, were m. 2 Oct. 1754.

BATES, DAVID, a Baptist clergyman, res. near Gilbertville, at the place marked "Mr. May" on the R. Map, preached statedly at Dana, was very corpulent, and d. of apoplexy 20 May 1813, a. 52. He had no children. His w. Prudence d. at Windsor, Conn., 1840, a. 78.

BAXTER, WILLIAM, by w. Joanna, had *Jonathan*, b. 29 August 1743; *Mary*, b. 27 May, 1746 (called dau. of Richard and Mary in the record of baptisms); *William*, bap. 9 Ap. 1749; *Francis*, bap. 3 Feb. 1750–1.

BEACH, NOAH, of Rutland, was pub. to Phebe Johnson 9 July 1780. No record of chil. He may have d. before 29 Oct. 1789, when Phebe Beach, perhaps his widow, m. Nathan Lothrop of Easton.

2. NOAH, prob. s. of Noah (1), m. Priscilla, dau. of John Webb, 8 Jan. 1805, and had a child, d. 1 Nov. 1810, a. 10 months. The family remained in Hk. several years, and resided in the westerly part of the town, but no further trace appears on record.

BEALS, SAMUEL, a farmer, m. Abigail, dau. of Amos Thomas, 31 July 1767; she d. 6 May 1813 a. 72, and he m. Huldah Bowker 30 Jan. 1814. He was appointed deputy quartermaster-general in General Warner's Division, 2 Nov. 1787, with the rank of major, by which title he was ever afterwards known. He res. on the easterly road to Gilbertville, at the place marked "B. Thomas" on the R. Map, until late in life, when he rem. to the place marked "Mr. Cobb," on the same road, where he d. 21 Nov. 1827, a. 81; his w. Huldah d. 31 Jan. 1833, a. 55. No chil. by either wife.

BEAMAN, PHINEAS, came here from New Salem in 1832, and m. Eliza Atherton of that town in 1837. He had *Edwin P.*, b. —— 1838; *Elizabeth M.*, b. —— 1841, m. John Harvey 23 Feb. 1860. PHINEAS the f., a farmer, res. nearly forty years at the place near Gilbertville marked "P. Lawton" on the R. Map, and in 1874 erected a new house a few rods nearer to the village.

2. EDWIN P., s. of Phineas (1), m. Mary A. Wallace of Barre 7 Dec. 1859; she d. in childbed 22 Jan. 1865, a. 27, and he m. Hattie E. Webber of Pittsfield, 24 June 1872. He had *Mary Wallace*, b. 20 Jan. 1865; *Susan Medella*, b. 14 Aug. 1873.

BECKWITH, ELLIOTT, the "beloved physician," res. on the road to Barre, at the place marked "W. Sturtevant" on the R. Map, and had a very extensive practice both in Hardwick and in the westerly part of Barre. Though destitute of such thorough instruction as may now be obtained, he was very skilful and successful. During the prevalence of the "spotted fever" in 1810, which was so fatal in the adjoining towns, he lost only two patients out of more than sixty who were under his care in Hardwick. His w. Rebecca d. 18 Feb. 1806, a. 32, and he m. Sally, dau. of Lieut. Job Dexter, pub. 9 Nov. 1806; she d. 18 July 1811, a. 27, and he was pub. to Hannah Willis 2 Mar. 1812. No record is found of children. He d. much lamented 6 Mar. 1814, a. 53, or 58 according to the *Columbian Centinel.*

MARY, prob. mother of Dr. Elliott, d. 2 Ap. 1812, a. 89.

BELDING, SILAS, s. of John Belding of Hatfield, m. Hannah, dau. of Samuel Billings, 2 Jan. 1745–6, and prob. became a resident here immediately afterwards. He d. 1 Oct. 1756, a. 39, as inscribed on his head-stone still standing in the old burial-ground. In his will, proved 2 Nov. 1756, he names wife Hannah, father John, brother Reuben, sisters Eunice Porter, Dorothy Billings, Submit, and Martha; also Samuel and Mary, chil. of brother John deceased. His w. Hannah m. Deac. Samuel Ware of N. Br. 3 Nov. 1757.

DOROTHY, of Hatfield, sister of Silas (1), was pub. to Elisha Billings 24 June 1749. STEPHEN, of Northfield, m. Martha Jackson 7 Nov. 1764.

BENJAMIN, JOHN, constable of Cambridge in 1633, afterwards res. in Watertown, where he d. 14 June 1645. He had w. Abigail, and chil. *Mary*, b. ——, d. 10 Ap. 1646 ; *Abigail*, b. ——, m. Joshua Stubbs ; *John*, b. about 1620, d. 22 Dec. 1706, a. 86 ; *Richard*, b. ——, rem. to Connecticut ; *Joshua ; Samuel*, b. 1628, rem. to Connecticut ; *Caleb*, b. ——, rem. to Connecticut ; *Abel*, b. ——, res. in Charlestown, and d. about 1710.

2. JOHN, s. of John (1), res. in Watertown, and by w. Lydia had *John*, b. 10 Sep. 1651, d. 18 Nov. 1708 ; *Lydia*. b. 3 Ap. 1653, m. Thomas Batt ; *Abigail*, b. 14 July, 1655 ; *Mary*, b. 2 Aug. 1658 ; *Daniel*, b. 12 Sep. 1660 ; *Ann*, b. 4 Aug. 1662 ; *Sarah*, b. 1663, m. William Hagar, Jr. ; *Abel*, b. 20 May 1668. See Bond's *Hist. Watertown.*

3. ABEL, s. of John (2), res. in Watertown, and by w. Abigail had eleven chil., of whom the fifth was *Caleb*, b. 28 Jan. 1702.

4. CALEB, s. of Abel (3), m. Abigail Livermore 16 Aug. 1726, and had *Abigail*, b. 3 Jan. 1726-7 ; *Caleb*, b. 26 May 1729 ; *Keziah*, b. 18 Ap. 1731. See Bond, *ut sup.* I suppose this Caleb to be the same who rem. to Hardwick, res. near the Old Furnace, at the place marked "E. Trow" on the R. Map, and by w. Abigail had *Mary*, b. 1 Sep. 1743 ; *Anna*, b. 5 June 1746, m. Eliphalet Washburn 19 Sep. 1769 ; *Keziah*, b. 16 May 1749. His w. Abigail d. 24 June 1756, and he m. Elizabeth, widow of Aaron Rice, of Rut. 18 Nov. 1760.

5. CALEB, prob. s. of Caleb (4), had dau. *Rhoda*, bap. 17 May 1767, and perhaps others.

6. ABEL, prob. s. of Caleb (4), m. Susanna Carpenter 22 Mar. 1759, and had *Abigail*, b. 30 Mar. 1760 ; *Levi*, b. 9 Oct. 1762; and perhaps others. ABEL the f. prob. rem. to Montague about 1782, when his w. Susanna was dism. to the church there.

ABIGAIL, prob. dau. of Caleb (4), m. Joseph Powers of Gr. 25 Dec. 1751.

ABIGAIL, a widow, prob. mother of Caleb (4), d. 30 Mar. 1755.

BERRY, JUDAH (s. of John, who d. 1745, a. 93, and grandson of Richard, who was in Barnstable 1643, and d. in Yarmouth 1681), res. in Harwich, now Brewster ; he m. Mary, dau. of John Freeman, 1713, and had *Lemuel*, b. 21 Feb. 1713-14 ; *Theophilus*, b. 12 Oct. 1715 ; *Mary*, b. 15 Dec. 1717. His w. Mary d. 19 Aug. 1719, a. "about 26," and he m. Rebecca Hamlin 11 Aug. 1720, by whom he had seven children. JUDAH the f. d. between 21 Nov. 1769 and 11 May 1773.

2. LEMUEL, s. of Judah (1), by w. Lydia, had *Mary*, b. 1 Nov. 1741, m. —— Snow ; *Judah*, b. 24 Dec. 1743 ; *Scotto*, b. 20 Oct. 1745 ; *Rebecca*, b. 20 Jan. 1747-8, m. Lemuel Willis 27 May 1771, d. 16 Ap. 1826 ; *Mehetabel*, b. 12 Feb. 1749-50, m. John Hastings 11 Ap. 1779, and d. 15 Dec. 1836 ; *Lemuel*, bap. 12 Ap. 1752 ; *Lydia*, bap. 28 July, 1754, d. young ; *Sarah*, bap. 3 Oct. 1756, m. Zenas Phinney, and d. 20 Dec. 1833 ; *Reliance*, bap. 13 Aug. 1758 ; *Lydia*, bap. 27 July 1760, m. Seth Hinkley, Jr., 12 May 1782, d. 27 Aug. 1805. He also had dau. *Elizabeth*, to whom was assigned a share of his estate 6 Feb. 1770. LEMUEL the f. res. in Brewster; but his daus. *Rebecca*, *Mehetabel*, *Sarah*, and *Lydia* res. and d. in Hardwick.

3. SCOTTO, s. of Lemuel (2), res. in Brewster, and, by w. Hannah, had eleven children. His w. Hannah d. 12 Dec. 1806, a. 55; his second w. Bethia d. 9 Mar. 1846, a. 85; and he d. 12 June 1832, a. 87.

4. SCOTTO, the third s. of Scotto (3), b. Feb. 1779, rem. early to Hk., was pub. to Polly Baker of Harwich 20 Jan. 1805, and had *Barnabas*, b. 20 Mar. 1809, d. 12 June 1829; *Harriet*, b. 22 Oct. 1813, m. Perley Hammond 1 Ap. 1832; *Mary Ann*, b. 17 Dec. 1815, d. 3 Nov. 1831; *Scotto*, b. 14 Oct. 1817; *Caroline*, b. 21 Sep. 1819, d. 21 July 1820. His w. Polly d. 24 July 1825, and he m. Mrs. Lucy Powers of Gr., pub. 22 May 1826, who survived him and d. 21 Nov. 1872, a. nearly 90. SCOTTO the f. was a tanner, and res. at the place, between the Pet. road and the Turnpike, marked with his name on the R. Map. Late in life he retired from the tanning business and removed into a new house which he had erected on the opposite side of the road, a few rods westerly from his former homestead. He was an assessor two years, selectman six years, and representative one year. He d. 7 Nov. 1864, a. nearly 86.

BILLINGS, RICHARD, of Hartford 1640, rem. to Hatfield 1661, and d. 13 Mar. 1679; his w. Margery d. 5 Dec. 1679.

2. SAMUEL, s. of Richard (1), res. in Hatfield, and by w. Sarah had *Samuel*, b. 8 Jan. 1665; *Ebenezer*, b. 29 Oct. 1669; *Sarah*, b. ——, d. 15 July 1674; *Richard*, b. 7 Ap. 1672; *John*, b. 11 Oct. 1674, slain 15 July 1698; *Sarah*, b. 18 Oct. 1676, m. Samuel Dickinson. SAMUEL the f. d. 1 Feb. 1678, and his w. Sarah m. Samuel Belding, Jr., 9 Oct. 1678, and d. 5 Feb. 1713.

3. SAMUEL, s. of Samuel (2), res. in Hatfield, m. Hannah Wright 18 Nov. 1686; she d. 18 Nov. 1687, and he m. widow Rebecca Miller. His chil. were *Samuel*, b. ——; *Sarah*, b. 15 Mar. 1697, m. Deac. Samuel Smith; *Joseph*, b. 15 Nov. 1700; *Zechariah*, b. 29 Nov. 1702; *Benjamin*, b. 18 Jan. 1705. Thus far I have relied on Judd's *Hist. of Hadley*.

4. SAMUEL, s. of Samuel (3), res. several years in Sunderland, where, by w. Hannah, he had *Hannah*, b. 23 Sep. 1724, m. Silas Belding 2 Jan. 1745-6, and (2d) Deac. Samuel Ware of N. Br., 3 Nov. 1757; *Elisha*, b. 1 Dec. 1726; *Sarah*, b. 29 May 1729, m. William Merrick 7 Sep. 1749; *Daniel*, b. 21 Nov. 1731; *Nathan*, b. 23 May 1734; *Rebecca*, b. 3 Jan. 1737, m. Leonard Robinson 31 Aug. 1758; *Samuel*, b. 19 Aug. 1739; *Asahel*, b. about 1741. Soon after the birth of his youngest son, SAMUEL the f. rem. to Hardwick, where he subsequently res., at the place marked "Dr. Billings" on the Ware road, and where his eight chil. were married. His w. Hannah d. 5 Mar. 1767, and he m. Mrs. Sarah Crosby 26 Nov. 1767. He d. between 21 Jan. and 4 May 1778, a. prob. about 83; his w. Sarah and all his chil. except *Sarah* and *Rebecca* survived him.

5. ELISHA, s. of Samuel (4), m. Dorothy Belding of Hatfield, pub. 24 June 1749, and had *Jonathan*, b. 19 Sep. 1750, d. 22 Dec. 1753; *Sarah*, b. 7 Jan. 1753, living unm. in 1802; *Mary*, b. 1 Oct. 1754, m. Joseph Thomas 17 Mar. 1774; *Hannah*, b. 21 Sep. 1756, d. — Sep. 1758; *Hannah*, b. 22 Nov. 1758, m. Stephen Pratt 3 Feb. 1780, and d. at Bennington 16 Feb. 1839; *Martha*, b. 2 Ap. 1761, m. Jedediah Barrett (or Bassett) of Wilmington, Vt., 26 Aug. 1787; *Dolly*, b. 8 Jan. 1764, m. Israel Lawton 26 Aug. 1784; *Jonathan*, b. 14 Aug. 1768, d. 3 Oct. 1775. ELISHA the f. res. on the Ware road, at the place marked "Keyes Tyler" on the R. Map, was a farmer, lieutenant of militia, selectman one year, and d. 29 Sep. 1803; his w. Dorothy d. 8 May 1787, a. 58, and his second w. Mrs. Prudence Gilbert of Monson, to whom he was pub. 15 Sep. 1788, survived him.

6. DANIEL, s. of Samuel (4), m. Mary, dau. of Capt. Benjamin Ruggles, 23 Feb. 1758, and had *Gideon*, b. 9 Jan. 1759, settled in Barnard, Vt. (where, by w. Polly, he had Daniel, b. 7 Mar. 1794, d. 15 July 1867; Nancy, b. 28 Aug. 1796; and prob. Gideon, who d. 30 Mar. 1852, a 46); *Mary*, bap. 12 Ap. 1761, d. young; *Eunice*, b. 7 July 1763, m. Robert Dean of Barnard, Vt., 23 Dec. 1784, had ten children, and d. — Mar. 1843; *Daniel*, b. 9 July 1765, a merchant and captain of militia in Hk., d. unm. at Trinidad, W. I., shortly before 6 July 1808; *Barnabas*, bap. 16 Ap. 1769; *Mary*, b. 25 Sep. 1771, m. Barnabas Hinkley 8 Oct. 1797, and (2d) Luther Paige 4 Sep. 1816, and d. at Bangor, Me., 11 Mar. 1849; *Timothy*, b. 3 July 1774; *Samuel*, b. 4 June 1779. DANIEL the f. was a farmer, and res. near the Old Furnace, at the place marked "D. Billings" on the R. Map; he was lieutenant of militia and selectman seven years. He d. 23 Dec. 1778; his w. *Mary* d. 8 June 1835, a. nearly 97.

7. NATHAN, s. of Samuel (4), m. Lydia, dau. of John Wells, 24 Feb. 1757; she d. 1 July 1769, a. about 31, and he m. Reliance, dau. of David Bangs, 26 Dec. 1769. His chil. were *Silas*, b. 14 Jan. 1758, d. 7 Jan. 1759; *Silas*, b. 30 Jan. 1760; *Anna*, b. 10 Aug. 1761, d. young; *Moses*, b. 15 Mar. 1765; *Persis*, b. 29 Jan. 1767; *Lydia*, b. 28 Nov. 1770; *Anna*, bap. 11 Feb. 1776; *Hannah*, bap. 1 Mar. 1778. Some of these dates (wrongly entered in the Town Record) are corrected by the registry of baptisms.

8. SAMUEL, s. of Samuel (4), m. Beulah, dau. of Stephen Fay 28 June 1764, and had *Lydia*, b. 28 Feb. 1765; *Susannah*, b. 1 Jan. 1767; *Beulah*, b. 14 Nov. 1768; *Samuel*, 23 May 1771; *Polly*, b. 6 July 1773. SAMUEL the f. res. on the Ware road, according to a tradition, opposite to the place marked

22

"C. Ruggles" on the R. Map. He was elected, by the town, captain of the South Military Company 21 Nov. 1774, and was commissioned 23 May 1775 as captain in Colonel Learned's regiment in the Revolutionary Army. At some subsequent period, either in Massachusetts or Vermont, he seems to have attained the rank of major. He rem. to Bennington, Vt., where he d. 23 June 1789; his w. Beulah d. 18 Sep. 1833, a. nearly 88; a monumental slab denotes their graves in the Bennington Centre Cemetery.

9. ASAHEL, s. of Samuel (4), m. Elizabeth, dau. of James Robinson, pub. 29 Ap. 1765, and had *Elijah*, b. 30 Ap. 1766; *Stephen*, b. 18 Nov. 1767; *Asahel*, b. 25 Nov. 1769, m. Tamasen Gilbert 9 June 1796, had two dau., and d. 6 Oct. 1803; his w. m. Jedediah Foster of Wilmington, Vt., 12 Nov. 1804; *David*, b. 6 May 1771; *Joseph*, bap. 5 Sep. 1773, d. 3 Ap. 1806; *Betsey*, bap. 7 May 1775, m. Gamaliel Collins 29 Nov. 1804, and d. 10 Dec. 1805; *Polly*, bap. 13 Ap. 1777, m. Silas Flagg of Pet., pub. 18 Dec. 1808; *Samuel*, bap. 10 Oct. 1779; *Jonathan*, bap. 9 Sep. 1781, d. unm. 5 Dec. 1820; *Silas*, b. 25 Sep. 1783; *Sally*, b. ——, d. 22 July 1804, a. 18. ASAHEL the f. was a farmer, res. on the homestead, and d. 16 July 1838, a. prob. about 97. His age is erroneously written 99 on the Town Records, and 100 on his gravestone in the new cemetery. See *family of Samuel* (4). His w. Elizabeth d. 13 (or 14) Dec. 1826, a. nearly 84. Her age, like that of her husband, is overrated on the records as 85, and on her gravestone as 86.

10. BARNABAS, s. of Daniel (6), m. Martha, dau. of Doct. Medad Pomeroy of Northfield, —— 1793, and had *Mary Ann*, b. 30 Jan. 1795, m. Martin Paige of Hk. 20 Aug. 1817, and d. at Providence, R. I., 27 Jan. 1875; *Frederick A.*, b. 12 Mar. 1798, m. Lucy Bent, and res. in Framingham; *Martha*, b. 16 Ap. 1800, m. Russell Hayes of Brattleboro', Vt., 13 June 1837, and d. — Aug. 1872; *Daniel*, b. 7 Mar. 1802, m. Sally Tillottson of Northampton; *Julia*, b. 13 Aug. 1804, m. Doct. George Wright of Montague; *Medad Pomeroy*, b. 30 Jan. 1809, d. at New Bedford. BARNABAS the f. grad. B. U. 1791, was a merchant, and town treasurer in Northfield many years until about 1805, when he rem. to North Hampton and afterwards to Chesterfield, where he d. 14 Nov. 1824; his w. Martha d. 16 May 1845.

11. TIMOTHY, s. of Daniel (6), m. Alinda, dau. of Samuel Hopkins, pub. 10 Nov. 1805, and had *Dwight*, b. 31 Jan. 1806; *Adeline*, b. 10 Aug. 1807, m. James S. Davis of Warren, pub. 3 Jan. 1840, and d. 8 Jan. 1883; *Samuel*, b. 24 May 1809, d. at Auburn, N. Y., — Jan. 1873; *Timothy Ruggles*, b. 16 Ap. 1811, rem. to California. TIMOTHY the f. was a farmer and res. on the homestead; he was an assessor four years, and major of militia. He d. 19 May 1812; his w. Alinda d. 5 or 6 Aug. 1832, a. 48.

12. SAMUEL, s. of Daniel (6), m. Rebecca, dau. of Doct. W. Cutler, 7 Sep. 1811. He res. near the Old Furnace, at the place marked with his name on the R. Map. In company with Harmon Chamberlain he was for many years engaged in the manufacture of iron-ware at the Furnace, and also managed a store of English and West India goods. Being possessed of a competent estate, however, he did not apply himself very closely to business, but he was a laborious, and persistent fox-hunter; partly, as some supposed, for pleasure, and partly to prevent excessive corpulency. He was much engaged in public affairs, being a selectman nine years, assessor fourteen years, and representative three years; he was also justice of the peace, and colonel of militia. Some of his later years were spent in Greenfield, and afterwards in Worcester, where he d. s. p. 13 May 1868, a. nearly 89; his w. Rebecca d. at Greenfield 30 July 1864, a. 76; both were buried in the new cemetery in Hardwick.

13. ELIJAH, s. of Asahel (9), m. Abigail, dau. of John Jenney, 24 Ap. 1796 and had *Martha Eddy*, *Daniel* (d. at Ware, 31 July 1873, a. 71), *Lewis*, *James Robinson*, and *Sarah Robinson*, all bap. 12 Sep. 1810. They had also *Lucius*, b. —— 1797, d. 8 Oct. 1803.

14. STEPHEN, s. of Asahel (9), m. Elsa ——; no record of children. He d. (of a cancer in the face) 11 Feb. 1817; his w. Elsa d. 11 Oct. 1822, a. 50.

15. DAVID, s. of Asahel (9), m. Betsey, dau. of Capt. Seth Peirce, pub. 6 Ap. 1806, and had *Elizabeth Peirce*, b. 19 May 1807, m. David Ellis of Ware

19 Dec. 1849, d. 30 May 1877; *Hannah Robinson*, b. 9 Oct. 1808, m. Hiram P. Lee of Palmer, 15 Sep. 1841; *David Paige*, b. 30 June 1810, res. in Ware; *Seth Peirce*, b. 1 Aug. 1812; *Huldah Sampson*, b. 28 Aug. 1814, m. Hiram W. Leonard 23 Feb. 1834; *Mary Ann*, bap. 18 June 1820; d. unm. 21 May 1842; *William Robinson*, bap. 18 May 1821, and d. same day; *Lucius Flagg*, bap. 19 Dec. 1822, a physician in Barre; and perhaps others. DAVID the f. was a physician, with a considerably large practice in Hk. and Ware. He res. on the homestead, and d. 15 Oct. 1833; his w. Betsey, d. 1 Feb. 1857, a. 75.

16. SILAS, s. of Asahel (9), m. Roxana Parkhurst of Pet. 3 Dec. 1809, and had *Elizabeth F.*, b. 2 Dec. 1812, m. Wm. Augustus Warner 24 May 1832, and d. 11 May 1878. SILAS the f. res. about three miles north of the meeting-house, at the place marked with his name on the R. Map, but spent his last years with Mr. and Mrs. Warner. He d. 3 Feb. 1876, a. 92 years, four months, and nine days, being then the oldest person in the town; his w. Roxana d. 11 Nov. 1870, a. 82.

17. DWIGHT, s. of Timothy (11), m. Ann J., dau. of Franklin Ruggles, 31 Dec. 1834, and had *Mary Ann*, b. 31 Oct. 1835, m. William D. Cummings of Waterbury, Conn., 18 Sep. 1855, and d. at Brooklyn, N. Y., 8 Feb. 1882. DWIGHT the f. was a farmer, res. a few years on the homestead, and afterwards near the meeting-house. He was an assessor five years, selectman three years, and a justice of the peace. He d. at Brooklyn, N. Y., 23 Nov. 1881, and was buried here; his w. Ann J. d. 11 Jan. 1864, a. 50.

18. SETH PEIRCE, s. of David (15), a farmer, res. on the homestead, by w. Rebecca F., had *Henry Peirce*, b. 13 Nov. 1852; *Lizzie Ella*, b. 25 Dec. 1856, m. Herbert J. Felton 15 Oct. 1879; *Willie F.*, b. 27 Aug. 1860, d. same day.

MARY, m. John Jackson of Paris, Me., pub. 5 Jan. 1806; MARY, m. John Goodspeed 31 Dec. 1807. ELIZABETH, m. Reuben Tyler 3 Ap. 1831. MARY, m. Andrew Wood, Jr., 2 Feb. 1873. STEPHEN R., b. in Hk., d. at Springf. 27 Jan. 1848, a. 30.

BLACKMER, WILLIAM H., by w. Harriet, had *Mary A.*, b. —— 1848, d. unm. 24 Dec. 1869, a. 21; *Charles H.*, b. —— 1852, d. 7 Dec. 1869, a. 17; *Emory W.*, b. —— 1854, d. 24 Dec. 1869, a. 15; *Frederick Willie*, b. 10 Ap. 1858; *George Albert*, b. 26 Mar. 1860; *Herbert*, b. 11 Feb. 1862. WILLIAM H. the f., a farmer, res. on the Pet. road, at the place marked "D. Allen" on the R. Map.

2. AUGUSTUS D., by w. Rachel Jane, had a son b. 3 Sep. 1859; *Charles Sumner*, b. 12 Aug. 1864. His w. Rachel Jane d. 30 Oct. 1864, and he m. Ellen Patrill, pub. 3 May 1867.

DAVID, m. Mrs. Abigail Cobb, 13 Oct. 1823.

BLAIR, JOHN, by w. Ann, had *James*, bap. 23 Oct. 1748; *Lucy*, bap. 6 Feb. 1750-1.

JAMES, of Western, m. Mrs. Sarah Robinson 26 Mar. 1805.

BLAKE, JOSEPH, formerly a merchant in Boston and Hingham, rem. to Hk. in or soon after 1763, and was one of the owners of a forge and saw-mill at the place now known as Gilbertville. He rem. to Rutland about 1770, and in 1779 returned to Hingham. While at Hardwick he had *Joseph*, bap. 13 Sep. 1767, grad. H. C. 1786, lawyer in Boston, d. in Jamaica 10 July 1802; *George*, bap. 16 Ap. 1769, grad. H. C. 1789, was an eminent lawyer in Boston, where he d. 8 Oct. 1841; and at Rutland, *Francis*, said to have been born 14 Oct. 1774; he grad. H. C. 1789, at the remarkably early age of fifteen years, if the reputed date of his birth be correct, and became one of the most eloquent advocates at the bar of the county; he died at Worcester 23 Feb. 1817.

BOLSTER, EASTMAN, by w. Miriam, had *Charles*, b. about 1806, d. at Boston 2 Mar. 1851, a. 45; *Salome*, b. about 1813, m. Edmund Vokes of Barre 3 May 1832, and d. 10 Sep. 1858, a. 45; *Moses L.*, b. about 1818, m. Rebecca Rich of Barre 26 June 1836, d. at Worc. 23 July 1864, a. 45 years 8 months; a child b. — Jan. 1822, d. 15 Feb. 1822; *Joel H.*, b. about 1827, d. at Worc. 18 Ap. 1849, a. 22; a child b. ——, d. — Feb. 1828. The following chil. were prob. of the same family: *Sally*, m. Hervey Brown of Ware 27 Sep.

1826; *Aurilla*, m. Hervey Thresher of N. Br. 5 Dec. 1826; *Mary Eliza*, m. Lewis Shumway of Barre 17 Aug. 1834; *William A.*, m. Mary Bigelow of Oxford, pub. 7 Ap. 1842. EASTMAN the f. came to Hk. before 1822, was a laborer, and res. on the east road to Gilbertville, at the place marked with his name on the R. Map. His w. Miriam d. in 1841 a. 59.

BOND, DAVID, d. 13 Feb. 1847, a. 68; his w. Susanna d. 30 Sep. 1833, a. 58. The following may have been their chil.: *David P.*, m. Mary R. Freeman 24 Mar. 1831; *Susanna C.*, m. Dorice D. Rogers 1 Dec. 1831.

JOHN B., of Worcester, m. Eliza Hathaway 13 Nov. 1834. BENJAMIN of Ware, m. Arathusa Bowen 5 Oct. 1837.

BONNEY, WILLIAM, m. Fanny Crowell of Brk., pub. 17 Feb. 1817, and had *Melita*, b. —— 1818, m. Isaac H. Hoyt of Brk. 27 May 1846; *Isaac S.*, b. —— 1824; *Christina*, b. —— 1833, m. George L. Watkins of Washington, D. C. 11 Mar. 1858. WILLIAM the f. d. 10 Sep. 1852, a. 65; his w. Fanny d. 8 Nov. 1863, a. 73.

2. ISAAC S., s. of William (1), m. Olive Eaton of Ware, pub. 7 Nov. 1846; she d. 16 Sep. 1857, a. 33, and he m. Mrs. Paulina Fish 10 Mar. 1864. His chil. were *Mary*, b. 26 Nov. 1847; *Clarissa* (or *Mary*) *Ella*, b. 26 Nov. 1849, d. 5 Jan. 1850; *Mary E.*, b. 2 Mar. 1851, d. 8 June 1851; *Fanny Maria*, b. 16 June 1852.

RUTH, m. Abiel Stetson of Chesterfield 24 Feb. 1767. LUKE, m. Mercy Thomas 5 Nov. 1772. POLLY, m. John Kent of Brk. 24 Feb. 1801. HANNAH D. of Chesterfield m. Ruggles Smith, pub. 16 Mar. 1838.

BOWEN, SYLVESTER, m. Abigail Rich of Ware 19 Aug. 1804, and had *Sylvester*, b. ——; prob. *Eliza*, b. ——, m. Anson Warren of Tewksbury 23 Dec. 1829; prob. *Arathusa*, b. ——, m. Benjamin Bond of Ware 5 Oct. 1837.

2. SYLVESTER, s. of Sylvester (1), m. Mary Eaton of Ware, pub. 27 Feb. 1830, and had *Henry*, b. 11 Ap. 1844.

MOSES, d. 6 June 1830, a. 79.

BRADISH, ROBERT, was of Cambridge as early as 1635. By his w. Mary he had *Joseph*, b. —— May 1638; his w. d. —— Sep. 1638, and he m. Vashti ——, by whom he had several chil. and d. 1659.

2. JOSEPH, s. of Robert (1), was in Sudbury, 1662, Framingham, 1672, and returned to Cambridge about 1678. By w. Mary he had *Mary*, b. 10 Ap. 1665, m. John Green, 22 Nov. 1684; *Sarah*, b. 6 May 1667, prob. d. young; *Hannah*, b. 14 Jan. 1669–70, m. Edward Marrett, and d. 9 Ap. 1754; *Joseph*, b. 28 Nov. 1672, supposed to be the pirate who was sent to London, 1699, and executed; *Ruth*, m. Thomas Ford of Marshfield 5 Ap. 1711; *John*, b. 18 Sep. 1678; *James*, b. about 1680. JOSEPH the f. d. before 2 Ap. 1725, when part of his estate in Cambridge was sold by *Mary*, *Hannah*, and *John*, of Camb., *James* of Westborough, and *Ruth* of Marshfield, described as "children of Joseph Bradish, late of Cambr. yeoman, deceased."

3. JAMES, s. of Joseph (2), rem. to Marlborough, m. Damaris Rice, 16 June 1708, and had *Hepzibah*, b. —— 1709; *Sarah*, b. —— 1711; *Robert*, b. —— 1712; *Mary*, b. 1715; *James*, b. —— 1717; *John*, b. 30 Aug. 1719; *Jonas*, b. 7 Aug. 1724; *Sarah*, b. about 1727, d. 27 Aug. 1740; *Anna*, b. 6 June 1729, prob. m. John Green of Hk. 7 Nov. (or 7 Dec.) 1751; *Joseph*, b. 26 Feb. 1731–2, d. 28 Aug. 1740. JAMES the f. seems to have res. a short time in Westborough, and d. 13 Feb. 1768, a. 87; his w. Damaris d. 25 Dec. 1769, a. 81.

4. JOHN, s. of James (3), purchased a farm in the northerly part of Hk. 19 Nov. 1742, being then a resident in Grafton. He m. Mary Green of Southborough, pub. 12 May 1746, and had *Sarah*, b. 21 June 1747, m. Joseph Nye 27 Dec. 1764; *Hannah*, b. 4 Sep. 1748; *John*, b 25 Sep. 1750; *James*, b. 21 Oct. 1752; *Mary*, b. 13 Aug. 1754; *Dinah*, b. 8 Nov. 1757; *Ruth*, b. 13 June 1760; *Joseph*, b. 15 Dec. 1762. JOHN the f. was a cordwainer, and deacon of the church; traditionally distinguished for the plainness of his apparel;[1] rem. with his family to Cummington in 1778.

[1] It was related by those who knew him, that Deacon Bradish often wore his leather apron to church on Sunday, and kept his great-coat in its place with a leather strap instead of buttons.

5. John, s. of John (4), m. Hannah, dau. of Capt. Joseph Warner, 4 Mar. 1773, and had *Calvin*, b. 26 Dec. 1773; *Chloe*, b. 29 Ap. 1775; *Charles*, b. 20 Ap. 1778; and in Cummington, *Sarah*, b. 25 Sep. 1781; *Luther*, b. 15 Ap. or Sep. 1783, grad. W. C. 1804, a lawyer, Lieut.-Governor of New York four years from 1839, and President of the N. Y. Historical Society, d. 30 Sep. 1863; *Rowena*, b. 30 Sep. 1786. John the f. rem. to Cummington, soon after the birth of his son *Charles*, and was subsequently a colonel.

Brady, Michael, m. Rosanna Devlin, pub. 5 Nov. 1856, and had *Michael John*, b. 7 Oct. 1857; *Mary Jane*, b. 15 May 1860; Peter, b. 12 May 1862; *Margaret*, b. 19 Feb. 1864; *James*, b. 2 May 1867; *Fanny Lucretia*, b. 15 Aug. 1869, d. 13 Aug. 1871. Michael the f. d. 26 Aug. 1873, a. 52.

Breen, Daniel, m. Bridget Wrin, pub. 9 July, 1862, and had *Margaret*, b. 28 Feb. 1863; *Mary*, b. 19 Nov. 1864; *Henry*, b. 2 June 1867; *John*, b. 22 Oct. 1868; *Daniel Andrew*, b. 26 July 1871; *David Humphrey*, b. 15 June, 1874.

Brennan, Philip, m. Ellen Carroll 25 June 1871, and had *Philip*, b. 28 Dec. 1877; *John*, b. 11 Sep. 1880.

Bridge, Samuel (s. of Matthew, who d. in Lexington 29 May, 1738, gr. s. of Matthew, who d. in Lex. 28 Ap. 1700, and great-grandson of Deac. John, who d. in Cambridge about 1665), m. Susanna, dau. of Nathaniel Paige of Bedford, 9 Ap. 1734, and had *Samuel*, b. 6 Jan. 1735; his w. Susanna d. 16 Jan. 1735, and he m. Martha Bowman 27 Ap. 1738, by whom he had eleven chil., and d. 8 June 1791, a. 86.

2. Samuel, s. of Samuel (1), m. Hannah Johnson of Gr., pub. 19 Aug. 1760, and had *Joshua*, b. 20 Dec. 1761; *Susanna*, b. 24 Feb. 1763; *Bezaleel* (called *Barzilla* on the Record of Baptisms), b. 21 Nov. 1764; *Hannah*, b. 11 Jan. 1766; d. 22 Jan. 1767; *Hannah*, b. 26 Ap. 1767 (perhaps the same as Anna, who m. Daniel Robinson of Monson 28 Ap. 1788); *Samuel*, b. 1 May, 1768. Samuel the f. inherited land in Hk. under the will of his grandfather Paige, who died 2 Mar. 1755, and res. here as early as 1760. He prob. rem. to Wilmington, Vt., about 1779.

Sarah, m. Aaron Woods of Gr. in 1786.

Bridges, Isaac, Jr., m. Deborah, dau. of Sylvanus Cobb, 27 Jan. 1795, and had *Eliza Augusta*, b. 29 May, 1795, d. unm., at the town farm, 12 Aug. 1877; *Benjamin Franklin*, b. 14 Ap. 1797; *Willard Moors*, b. 26 July, 1798; *Martin Kinsley*, b. 1 Aug. 1800; *Jonathan Fletcher*, b. 20 Aug. 1802. Isaac the f. prob. rem. from Hk.; his w. Deborah d. at Deerfield 3 May 1860, a. 86.

2. Elijah, m. Cornelia K. Hervey 1 Aug. 1861, and had *Nettie Cornelia*, b. 27 Oct. 1866.

Mary, m. John Barr, Jr., of N. Br., 15 Sep. 1789. *Eunice*, m. Sylvanus Taylor 19 Nov. 1801. Betsey, m. William Lawrence 25 Mar. 1804. Jonas m. Hannah Ross 16 Feb. 1806. Josiah, d. 26 Nov. 1793, a. 20.

Brimhall, Sylvanus, m. Triphena Johnson 14 Sep. 1783, and (2d) Lucy Lincoln 3 July 1810; he res. in Barre at the time of his first marriage, and perhaps had chil. there; by his second w. he had *Lucy Lincoln*, *Elbridge Farr*, *Susan Ann*, all bap. 8 Oct. 1820; *Mary King*, bap. 29 Sep. 1822. Besides these he names in his will, dated 10 Sep. 1839, *Nathaniel*, *Joel Johnson*, and "in distant parts of the United States," *Sylvanus*, *Joseph*, and *Triphena*, wife of Elijah Hartwell, also sons *Aaron* and *Caleb*, deceased. Sylvanus the f. res. on the turnpike, at the place marked "S. Brimhall" on the R. Map, and d. 18 Sep. 1839, a. 82; his w. Lucy d. 27 Feb. 1847, a. 59.

Caroline J., m. David Fish of Worc. 6 Jan. 1853.

Brown, Luke (s. of Luke, an innholder in Worcester, who d. 6 Nov. 1776, a. 30, and gr. s. of Luke, also an innholder in Worcester, who d. of small-pox 14 Ap. 1772, a. 58), m. Bathsheba, dau. of Gen. Jonathan Warner, 8 June 1798, and had *Mary Brimmer*, b. 6 July 1799, d. unm. at Chicago, —— 1863; *Bathsheba Warner*, b. 9 Sep. 1801, m. Luman Scott, res. at Amh.; *Harriet Warner*, b. 21 Nov. 1803, unm. res. (1878) at Belchertown; *Elizabeth Follett*, b. 5 June 1806, m. James Hill, res. at Worthington; *Luke*, b. ——, res. at Chicago, d. 23 Oct. 1871, on board a steamer as he was ascending the

Mississippi River on his return from New Orleans. He left wife and chil. LUKE the f. grad. H. C. 1794, was a lawyer, settled in Hk. before his marriage, and rem. soon after 1806. After a checkered life, he d. at Enf. about 1835; his w. Bathsheba d. at Springf. —— 1855.

2. MOSES, of Ware, m. Mercy, dau. of Maj. James Paige 10 Dec. 1807, and res. in Ware. One of his chil. was *James N.*, who res. in Hk. a deacon of the church, and warden of the almshouse.

3. ESECK, m. Anna Waters, pub. 2 Ap. 1809, and had *Julia Ann*, b. 10 Mar. 1810.

4. SELLECK OSBORN, of Fitchburg, m. Harriet K. Whipple 1 May 1845, and had *Charles A.*, b. —— 1847, d. 9 Ap. 1849, a. 1 yr. 9 mo. His w. d. 18 Sep. 1847, a. 23, and he m. Mary Maria Whipple 5 June 1850, at which time he res. in Hartford, Conn.

BETSEY, m. Vincent Newland 6 Sep. 1820. SABRINA, m. Daniel J. Converse, pub. 23 Jan. 1826. SARAH, m. Alex. Brown, Ashford, pub. 24 Ap. 1826. LUCY, m Hiram Newland 30 Mar. 1831. IRENE, m. Nathaniel Topliff 23 Jan. 1833. HULDAH, d. 20 Dec. 1854, a. 72.

BROWNING, JAMES, rem. from Rutland to Hardwick about 1827, with w. Alice, and chil. *Fidelia F.*, b. —— 1818, m. David A. Dean 22 June 1842, and (2d) John B. Aiken 25 Feb. 1858; *Adeline S.*, b. —— 1820, m. William E. Prouty, of N. Brk. 17 Oct. 1855; *Daniel*, b. —— 1822, d. 8 June 1851, a. 29; *William*, b. —— 1824; *Franklin*, b. —— 1826, d. 17 July 1852, a. 26; he had in Hk. *Charles*, twin, b. 24 June 1828, d. 1 May 1830; *Frederick*, twin, b. 24 June 1828. His w. Alice d. 22 July 1829, a. 35, and he m. Lucy P., widow of Orin Trow, 26 Nov. 1829, by whom he had *Lucy*, b. 16 Oct. 1830, m. William A. Perry 13 Nov. 1850; *Charles A.*, b. 8 June 1832; *Harriet E.*, b. 21 Nov. 1834, m. Harmon C. Spooner 14 Nov. 1855, and d. 11 July 1860; *James E.*, b. ——. JAMES the f. was a farmer, res. several years on the old turnpike, at the place marked with his name on the R. Map, and afterwards a few rods northwesterly from the Common. He was a selectman three years, and d. 4 Nov. 1871, a. 82 years and 9 months.

2. WILLIAM, s. of James (1), m. Harriet J., dau. of Joseph Robinson, 5 Ap. 1849, and had *Franklin Joseph*, b. 11 Nov. 1852, m. Fannie, dau. of Frazier Paige, 15 June 1876; *Ellen Maria*, b. 18 Feb. 1856, m. Timothy Paige 11 Nov. 1874. WILLIAM the f. was a farmer, an assessor two years, and d. 16 Mar. 1858, a. nearly 34; his w. Harriet J. m. Albert E. Knight, 5 Ap. 1866, and d. 16 Sep. 1869, a. 39.

3. FREDERICK, s. of James (1), m. Mary Ann Witt 29 Mar. 1859, and had *Harriet Smith*, b. 7 Nov. 1860. FREDERICK the f. d. 2 Ap. 1861, a. 32; his w. Mary Ann d. 27 Jan. 1862, a. 25.

BRUCE, JOHN, with his w. Temperance (Packard), from Rutland, was admitted to the church here 1 Oct. 1789. They had *Charles*, d. 10 Mar. 1791, a. nearly 5 years; *Chester*, d. 13 Mar. 1791, a. 2 years and 6 months; also (named in the father's will, dated 19 May 1811, and proved 7 Dec. 1824) *Joseph*, *John*, *Levi*, *Winslow*, *Timothy*, and *Packard*. JOHN the f. was a farmer, and res. near Barre, at the place marked "T. Bruce" on the R. Map, where he d. 13 Oct. 1824, a. 78; his w. Temperance d. 30 Sept, 1834, a. 85.

2. JOSEPH, s. of John (1), m. Mary Trow 28 Ap. 1799, and had a child who d. 26 May 1803, a. 9 months and 23 days.

3. JOHN, s. of John (1), res. in Springfield, and m. Mrs. Betsey Nye 19 May 1813.

4. TIMOTHY, s. of John (1), m. Sally Kimball, pub. 10 Sep. 1812, and had *Elmira*, b. 12 June 1813, m. J. Rhodes Mayo of New York (one of the jury which convicted "Boss Tweed"); *Timothy Packard*, b. 30 June 1815, m. Maria Richmond 3 Mar. 1836; *Asa Kimball*, b. 7 Feb. 1817, m. Elizabeth C. Hammond of Pet., pub. 14 Mar. 1839; *Charles Emerson*, b. 4 Feb. 1819, grad. A. C. 1845; *John Augustus*, b. 22 Feb. 1822; *Sally Louisa*, b. 18 Mar. 1826, m. Chester R. Chaffee, and d. at Springfield — Ap. 1860; *Mercy Williams*, b. 20 Nov. 1827, m. Rev. Asa Mann, pub. 31 Mar. 1848, and d. 27 Aug. 1882; *Mary Ann*, b. 27 Feb. 1829, m. Benjamin Merriam of Ashtabula,

and (2d) —— Prosser of Windsor, Conn.; *Julia*, b. ——, m. Dr. J. M. Foster of Springfield; *Henry James*, b. ——, grad. A. C. 1859, missionary in India. TIMOTHY the f. late in life rem. to Springfield.

BUCKLEY, THOMAS, m. Mary Mack, pub. 8 Jan. 1862, and had *John*, b. 30 Oct. 1862; *Cornelius*, b. 10 July 1865; *Mary Anastasia*, b. 27 July, 1867; *Catherine Johanna*, b. 27 May 1870. *William Thomas*, b. 1 June 1864; *Timothy Edward*, b. 4 Sep. 1876.

BURGESS, LUTHER (a descendant from Thomas, who was in Sandwich 1637, and d. there 13 Feb. 1685, a. 82), m. Alice Southworth, and had *Luther*, b. about 1776; *Joseph*, b. ——, a mariner, impressed into the English navy, wounded in the Battle of the Nile, and after a long absence returned to Hk., where he was with some difficulty recognized; he was pub. to Achsah Thayer of Gr. 24 May 1819, had a dau. Alice, and d. at Fairhaven, Mass.; *Mary*, b. in Hk. 3 Ap. 1780, m. Jacob Earl 4 Oct. 1798, and d. 24 May 1850; prob. *Abigail*, b. about 1784, d. 27 Sep. 1791, a. nearly 7 years. LUTHER the f. was a shipmaster, sailing from New Bedford, but rem. his family to Hk. before 1780; he d. at sea about 1786; his w. Alice m. Benjamin Estabrook 12 Oct. 1787, and d. 3 May 1807, a. 57.

2. LUTHER, s. of Luther (1), m. Bathsheba Turner 24 Dec. 1797; she d. 16 May 1802, a. 26, and he m. Sarah Carpenter 21 July 1805. His chil. were *Luther*, b. 19 Mar. 1798, a farmer, m. Prudence Earl of N. Br., pub. 25 Mar. 1822, rem. to Sturbridge, and d. 25 Mar. 1871; *Joseph*, b. 18 Nov. 1799; *Nathaniel S.*, d. 6 June 1802, a. 7 mo.; *Bathsheba*, b. 14 Jan. 1806, m. Joseph Cleveland, pub. 12 Sep. 1825, and d. 5 Nov. 1881; infant, b. ——, d. 26 Feb. 1808; infant, b. 28 Mar. 1809, d. 4 Ap. 1809; infant, b. — Feb. 1810, d. 31 May 1810; *Samantha*, b. 28 Nov. 1811, d. unm. 11 Sep. 1852, having exhibited extraordinary patience and cheerfulness under long-continued suffering and disability; *Daniel Southworth*, b. 9 Nov. 1814, a mason and builder, res. in Worc.; *Alice Southworth*, b. 5 May 1817, d. unm. 2 May 1838; *Alvin Terry*, b. 31 July 1819, a mason and builder, res. in Worc.; *Martha Howe*, b. 10 Oct. 1821; *Elizabeth Ann*, b. 12 Feb. 1824; child b. ——, 1826, d. 14 Ap. 1827, a. 1 year. *Henry Mortimer*, b. 5 Feb. 1828; *Edwin Kilburn*, b. 3 Oct. 1830. LUTHER the f. res. many years at the place marked with his name on the R. Map, and d. 12 Ap. 1843, a 67; his w. Sarah d. 6 Oct. 1848, a. 65.

3. JOSEPH, s. of Luther (2), m. Thankful Taber of Providence, pub. 29 Jan. 1831; she d. 2 Ap. 1840, a. 41, and he m. Hannah, dau. of Capt. Peter Mayo, 5 Sep. 1841. His chil. were *Joseph A.*, b. 25 Sep. 1833; *Samuel T.*, b. 25 Sep. 1835, d. 23 Mar. 1836; *Frederick W.*, b. 25 June 1842, m. in Uxbridge, Sarah Washburn — Nov. 1866; *Alice A.*, b. 18 Sep. 1843, m. Frank W. Millett of Portland, Me., 30 May 1874; *Sarah Elizabeth*, b. 19 Jan. 1845, d. 10 Jan. 1846; *Elizabeth*, b. 20 May 1846; *William M.*, b. 25 Dec. 1847, m. Nelly Nevens — Jan. 1873, res. in Worc.; *Daniel S.*, b. 19 Sep. 1850, d. 21 July 1851; *Sarah S.*, b. 25 April 1852, m. Lewis Peckham of Pet. 7 Aug. 1870. JOSEPH the f., a shoemaker and deacon, res. near the Common on the Pet. road, and for more than forty years was bell-ringer for the town; he d. 20 July 1879, a. 79.

BURSLEY, MARY, d. unm. 9 Oct. 1791, a 28. HANNAH, m. Seth Ruggles 22 Nov. 1792.

BURT, ISAAC, by w. Lydia, had *Lydia*, b. 29 Jan. 1797; *Isaac*, b. — 1798, d. 11 Ap. 1877, a. 78 years and 6 months; *Mary B.*, b. about 1806, d. unm. 12 Oct. 1880, a. 74. Lydia, wid. of ISAAC, d. 12 Ap. 1857, a. 84.

2. EBENEZER, s. of Ebenezer, was b. at Norton 9 Mar. 1766. He m. Lucy Stacy of Taunton, 19 Nov. 1789, and had, in Norton, *Lucy*, b. ——, m. John Ellis 15 Ap. 1817, and d. 19 Sep. 1832, a. 42; *Nabby*, b. ——, m. Thomas Ellis, 11 Ap. 1820; *Eunice*, b. ——, m. Marshall Durkee; and in Hardwick, *Nancy*, b. 19 Ap. 1797, m. Jacob Thomas of Shutes. 5 Nov. 1837, and d. at N. Sal. 2 Ap. 1852; *Ebenezer*, b. 19 May 1799; *Abel*, b. 10 Oct. 1802, d. 23 July 1803. EBENEZER the f. rem. from Norton to Hardwick in 1796, and was pastor of the Baptist Church and Society until 19 Nov. 1827. While here he res. in the southwest part of the town, at the place marked "Mr. Burt" on the R. Map. He rem. to Ware, and thence to Athol where he d. 25 Nov. 1861. His w. Lucy d. 26 or 27 Feb. 1828, a. 67.

3. Ebenezer, s. of Ebenezer (2), m. Luthera, dau. of Joseph Robinson of Stamford, Vt., pub. 13 Mar. 1825, and had *Luthera R.*, b. 6 Ap. 1826, d. 23 Oct. 1834. Ebenezer the f. d. at Ware 20 May 1850; his w. Luthera m. Job Fry of Athol 15 Ap. 1851.

John, of Springf., m. Bathsheba, wid. of Jonathan Warner, 4 June 1765. Leonard, of Westminster, Vt., m. Susanna Fay 19 Dec. 1790. Polly, m. Solomon Ruggles 8 Mar. 1803.

Butterfield, Abel, m. Susanna Forbush 7 Ap. 1785.

2. Aaron, by w. Mary, had *Hosea*, b. —— 1796, m. Almira Town 11 Ap. 1820, and d. at Gr. 5 Mar. 1851, a. 54 y. 5 mo.; *Mandell*, b. —— 1798, d. at Gr. 6 Feb. 1856, a. 57 y. 7 mo.; and perhaps *Benjamin*, b. about 1814, d. at Brighton 7 Feb. 1856, a. 42.

Byam, Joseph, by w. Sarah, had *Sally*, b. 3 Sep. 1775. He sold his homestead in the southwest part of the town, 6 Nov. 1775, and rem. to Barnard, Vt., where he was constable in 1778.

Byram, James, m. Elizabeth Cox 8 Feb. 1781, and had *Jonathan*, b. 3 Aug. 1781; *Nabby*, b. 7 Mar. 1783, d. young; *Wight*, b. 14 Mar. 1785; he rem. to Barnard, Vt., where he had *Sally*, b. 21 Nov. 1786; *Nabby*, b. 9 July 1788; *Lyman*, b. 17 Feb. 1790.

Campbell, Jeremiah, by w. Peggy, had *Peggy*, b. — June 1784, d. 28 Aug. 1803, a. 19 years and 2 mo.; *Susanna*, b. ——, m. Daniel Barrows 12 Aug. 1813; *Jeremiah*, b. 5 Dec. 1790; *Nancy*, b. — Oct. 1795, d. 31 Aug. 1803, a. 7 years and 10 mo.; *Sally*, b. —— 1801, d. 1 Sep. 1803, a. 2. Jeremiah the f. res. near Gr., at the place marked with his name on the R. Map, and d. 18 Sep. 1841, a. 90; his w. Peggy d. 19 Feb. 1841, a. 83.

2. Jeremiah, s. of Jeremiah (1), had *Nancy N.*, b. 1820, m. — Knight, d. at Templeton 5 Aug. 1878, a. 57; a child b. —— 1828, d. 25 June 1829, a. 1; *Caroline*, b. —— 1835, d. 4 May 1840, a. 5. Jeremiah the f. d. — Jan. 1850.

John, m. Nabby Barlow, 26 Aug. 1793. William A., m. Wilhelmina Payton, pub. 8 Aug. 1853. Philena, m. Robert Carr, 3 Dec. 1855. George D., m. Ellen A. Pierce, 19 Nov. 1862.

Cannon, John, of Dartmouth, m. Sarah, dau. of John Hathaway, 11 Oct. 1709, and had *Cornelius*, b. 18 July 1711; *John*, b. 11 Aug. 1714, d. 11 Sep. 1726; *Elizabeth*, b. 20 Mar. 1716–17; *Mary*, b. 3 Ap. 1719; *Philip*, b. 11 Sep. 1721; *Joanna*, b. 27 Mar. 728. John the f. bought a farm in Hk., on the east side of the river, opposite to the estate of Mr. Reed S. Ruggles (marked "A. Rich" on the R. Map), 14 Mar. 1736–7, upon which his son Cornelius immediately settled; but he himself remained at Dartmouth, where he d. 28 Mar. 1750.

2. Cornelius, s. of John (1), m. Mehetabel ——, and had at Dart. *Sarah*, b. 7 Nov. 1733, d. at Hk. 18 May 1750; *Susanna*, b. 4 Aug. 1735; and at Hk., *Temperance*, b. 3 Aug. 1737; *John*, b. 17 Nov. 1739; *Kezia*, b. 27 Feb. 1741–2; *Seth*, b. 15 Ap. 1744; *Mehetabel*, b. 25 Ap. 1745; *Jesse*, b. 17 Ap. 1746; *Cornelius*, b. 31 May 1748; *Simeon*, b. 8 Feb. 1749–50; *Thomas*, bap. 26 Jan. 1752; *Philip* (posthumous), bap. 20 May 1753. Cornelius the f. rem. from Dart. to Hk. in 1737, was town clerk 1739, and d. before 12 Dec. 1752, when the inventory of his estate was presented; his w. Mehetabel m. Samuel Nye 16 Nov. 1756. Of their twelve chil. seven were living in 1761: — *Susanna* (then wife of Joseph Barns), *Kezia*, *Mehetabel*, *Jesse*, *Cornelius*, *Simeon*, and *Philip*.

James, m. Sally Putnam, pub. 28 Oct. 1793.

Carpenter, Nathan, of Dudley, bought land in Hk. 29 June 1733, and prob. rem. here about that time, being one of the earliest inhabitants. By his first w. Patience, he had *Gideon*, b. —— 1725; *Freelove*, b. ——, m. Josiah Chandler; *Nathan*, b. 9 Oct. 1731, d. —— 1748; by 2d w. Abigail, he had *Abigail*, b. 9 Ap. 1733, m. —— Searl; *Isaiah*,[1] b. 18 Mar. 1735, pub. to Hannah Robinson, 24 Feb. 1762; *Benjamin*, b. 8 Ap. 1737; his w. Abigail d. and he m. Sarah Powers, 8 June 1738, by whom he had *Susanna*, b. 29 Feb. 1739–40, m. Abel Benjamin 22 Mar. 1759; *Patience*, b. 14 Ap. 1744, m. Silas Nye 27 Nov. 1766; *Sarah*, b. 10 Aug. 1746, d. young; *Sarah*, b. — Aug. 1747, m.

[1] See note under David Gitchell.

Philip Washburn 8 Jan. 1767; *Joseph*, b. 7 Sep. 1748; *Lydia*, b. 16 Oct. 1750, m. Daniel Clark of Springf., pub. 21 Ap. 1771; *Dinah*, b. 15 Ap. 1754, m. David Nutting of Brimfield, pub. 6 June 1773; *Hepzibah*, b. 21 Nov. 1757. Of these chil. *Gideon* and *Freelove* are named in their father's will, 1769; the births of all the others are recorded in Hk. NATHAN the f. res. near the Old Furnace, at the place marked "D. Granger" on the R. Map, and owned a part of the saw-mill then standing on Moose Brook; he d. 12 Aug. 1770, a. 69.

2. GIDEON, s. of Nathan (1), by w. Mary, had *Nathan*, b. 6 Feb. 1748; his w. Mary d. and he m. Jemima Jenney 31 May 1753, had *Mary*, b. 1 Ap. 1754, m. James Nutting of Brimf. 29 June 1774; *Elijah*, bap. 16 Ap. 1758; *Rhoda*, bap. 6 Ap. 1760; *Jahazael*, bap. 12 Sep. 1762, d. unm. about 1820; *Benjamin*, bap. 21 July 1765; *Elizabeth*, bap. 19 June 1768, m. Oliver Chapin 25 Nov. 1790. GIDEON the f. d. 28 Nov. 1805, a. 80; his w. Jemima d. 3 Oct. 1804, a. 77.

3. NATHAN, s. of Gideon (2), m. Anna, dau. of Capt. Ebenezer Cox, 15 Mar. 1773, and had *Ebenezer*, b. 10 Nov. 1773, *Mary*, b. 2 Ap. 1775. NATHAN the f. rem. to Royalton, Vt., before 28 Oct. 1783, and m. Hannah Andros in Barnard 8 May 1788.

4. ELIJAH, s. of Gideon (2), m. Sarah, dau. of James Wing, 1 Feb. 1784, and had *Dulcinea*, b. 27 Dec. 1784, m. Elijah Stetson, 17 Ap. 1808; *Rhoda*, b. 15 June 1788; *Harriet*, b. 12 Sep. 1791, m. Anson Winchester 2 Sep. 1812; *Jason*, b. 8 Sep. 1793; *Hannah*, b. — Sep. 1797, m. Lewis Foster of Palmyra, N. Y., pub. 24 Sep. 1827. ELIJAH the f. was a farmer, res. on the Ware road (formerly called Turkey Street), at the place marked "J. Carpenter" on the R. Map, and d. 28 Aug. 1814; his w. Sarah d. 10 Jan. 1842, a. nearly 81.

5. JASON, s. of Elijah (4), m. Sarah Gray of Pel., pub. 5 May 1821, and had *Elijah Stetson*, bap. 21 July 1822; *William Gray*, b. —— 1824, d. 6 Oct. 1830, a. 6; *Hannah Foster*, bap. 31 Aug. 1830; *Susan Huntington*, bap. 4 Nov. 1831; *Benjamin Wisner*, bap. 2 May 1835. JASON the f. inherited the homestead, was a farmer, and deacon of the church. He rem. to Ware about 1851, where he d. 17 Aug. 1864, and was bur. at Hk. in the new cemetery.

6. JOEL, parentage unknown, was here as early as 25 Mar. 1752, m. Mary, dau. of Rev. Benjamin Ruggles of N. Br., 9 Dec. 1755, and had *Eli*, b. 12 Dec. 1756; *Mary*, bap. 6 May 1759; *Lucy*, bap. 3 May 1761. JOEL the f. was a physician, and res. at the place marked "Mr. Wesson" on the R. Map, which he purchased 1 May 1760; and part of which he sold 1 Mar. 1764; how long he remained in Hk. does not appear.

RACHEL, of Coventry, m. Abraham Powers, pub. 1 Dec. 1759. RUFUS, of Woodstock, m. Olive Whitcomb 27 Feb. 1777. SARAH, m. Luther Burgess 21 July 1805. JOSEPH HENRY, s. of Joseph and Adeline, b. 2 Feb. 1849. MARY, w. of Charles W., d. 29 Nov. 1865, a. 55.

CARTER, EDWIN, by w. Sarah P., had *Porter*, b. 9 Nov. 1848; *Cutler*, b. 2 Jan. 1853; *Nellie Augusta*, b. 15 Aug. 1866. SILAS J., d. 29 Jan. 1842, a. 46. RUTH, d. 23 May 1880, a. 83.

CHAMBERLAIN, JOSEPH, m. Sarah Cook of Douglass, pub. 16 Feb. 1753, and had *Molly*, b. 21 Oct. 1756; *John*, b. 6 Dec. 1757; *Sarah*, b. 22 Dec. 1759, m. Jesse Byam of Williamstown 30 Jan. 1777; *Asahel*, b. 11 Feb. 1762.

2. ABRAHAM, by w. Kezia, had *Thomas*, b. 9 Aug. 1766.

3. WILLIAM, by w. Elizabeth, had *Polly*, b. 20 Jan. 1779.

4. MOSES, b. in Natick about 1753, m. Hannah, dau. of Charles Church of Bristol, and a lineal descendant from Col. Benjamin Church, a famous leader in King Philip's War, 12 Aug. 1781, and had *Charles Church*, b. 24 Nov. 1781; *Harmon*, b. 24 Oct. 1784. MOSES the f. res. near the Old Furnace, was an innholder, and d. 13 May 1813, a. 59; his w. Hannah d. at Worc. 28 Aug. 1826, a. 63.

5. CHARLES CHURCH, s. of Moses (4), m. Sophia Orcutt of Templeton, pub. 21 Aug. 1808, and had *Humphrey*, b. 5 Aug. 1809, d. young; *Mary*, b. ——, m. —— Hutchinson, and d. ——; *Sophia*, b. ——, m. William A. Parker of Roxbury; *Charles C.*, b. —— 1813, d. 2 Jan. 1815. CHARLES C. the f. d. 16 May 1814.

6. HARMON, s. of Moses (4), m. Arathusa, dau. of Maj. Seth Hinkley, pub. 27 Ap. 1806, and had *Caroline*, b. 8 Mar. 1807, m. Joseph Pratt of Worc.; *Hannah Church*, b. 23 Jan. 1809, m. George Perrin 13 Oct. 1828; he d. 26 May 1834, and she m. Clarendon Wheelock 18 Sep. 1848, and d. 9 May 1853; *Rebecca Willis*, b. 14 Feb. 1811, d. 8 Sep. 1814; *Henry Harmon*, b. 7 Jan. 1813, a merchant in Worc., m. Charlotte Clark of Princeton; *Charles Church*, b. 26 or 30 June 1815, a watchmaker and jeweller, m. Cordelia M. Felton 15 Sep. 1836, and d. 24 Dec. 1851; *Arathusa Hinkley*, b. 20 Dec. 1817, res. unm. at Worc.; *Moses Bradford*, b. 14 Mar. 1820, d. 13 May 1825. HARMON the f. was an innholder and manufacturer of iron ware at the Old Furnace; he res. at the place marked "Tavern" on the R. Map, until 1822, when he rem. to Worc., where he kept a hotel a few years, was afterwards a grocer, and d. 12 Ap. 1838; his w. Arathusa d. 20 Dec. 1872, a. 86.

REBECCA, bap. 19 July 1772. ELIZABETH, of Grafton, m. Silas Pratt, pub. 21 Feb. 1746–7. JOSEPH, of Pet., m. Deborah Nye 18 Ap. 1776. KEZIA, m. John Shaw of Brk. 12 June 1780. KATY, m. James Faxon of Worthington 24 Jan. 1792. AARON, m. Rachel Herod of Ware 19 Nov. 1795. SAMUEL, of Pet., m. Chloe Newton 15 Jan. 1804. LEVI, m. Amittai Barnes 27 Oct. 1841.

CHANDLER, WILLIAM, was one of the earliest English inhabitants of Roxbury. A very full genealogy of his descendants was published by Dr. George Chandler of Worc. in 1872, but unfortunately almost the whole edition was destroyed by the great Boston fire in that year, while in the hands of the binder; less than fifty copies were preserved. Much of what follows is gathered from that work, which, it is expected, will soon be republished.

2. JOHN, s. of William (1), rem. to Woodstock, Conn. (formerly a part of Massachusetts), m. Elizabeth Douglass, was a deacon, and d. 15 Ap. 1703, a. about 68; his w. Elizabeth d. at New London 23 Sep. 1705.

3. JOHN, s. of John (2), b. at Roxbury 16 Ap. 1665, rem. to Woodstock with his father, res. a few years in New London but returned to Woodstock, was colonel of militia and judge of the Court of Common Pleas and of Probate for the county of Worc., from its organization in 1731 until his death in 1743, and member of the Council from and after 1727. His w. was Mary Raymond of New London.

4. JOHN, s. of John (3), rem. to Worc. in 1731, was clerk of the courts, register of deeds and of probate, sheriff, and succeeded his father as colonel, judge of the C. C. P. and of Probate, also as member of the Council. His w. was Hannah, "dau. of John Gardner, Lord of the Isle of Wight in the Province of New York." He d. at Worc. in 1763.

5. JOHN, s. of John (4), b. 26 Feb. 1720, was a merchant in Worc., lieutenant-colonel (under Colonel Ruggles) and afterwards colonel of militia. He m. Dorothy Paine, who had four chil. and d. 5 Oct. 1745; he then m. Mary, dau. of Colonel Charles Church of Bristol, R. I., who had thirteen chil. and d. 18 Sep. 1783. JOHN the f. was a loyalist and refugee; he d. in London 26 Sep. 1800.

6. GARDNER (or GARDINER), the sixth child of John (5), was b. 27 Jan. 1749, m. Elizabeth, dau. of Brigadier-General Ruggles, pub. 18 May 1772. He was a merchant in Hk., but left his home during the Revolution, and his property was confiscated. He subsequently returned, and "purchased the Dummer farm in Brattleboro', Vt., and resided there, and was justice of the peace from 1789 to 1795." He d. in Hinsdale, N. H. His will was dated 7 June 1811. By his w. Elizabeth, he had *Sarah*, m. George Hall (by whom she had five chil.) and (2d) Richardson Bigelow, and d. before 7 June 1811; *Elizabeth Augusta*, m. Francis Blake, an eminent lawyer in Worc.; *Charles*, clerk in a Brattleborough store, d. unm. and his estate was distributed 20 Ap. 1820.

7. JOSIAH, s. of Joseph of Pomfret, Conn., and grandson of John (2), b. 2 Oct. 1724, res. at Barre, m. Freelove, dau. of Nathan Carpenter of Hk; she d. 5 Sep. 1758, and he m. Lydia Richardson; she d. 2 May 1776, and he m. Mary Blanchard.

8. JOSIAH COTTON, s. of Josiah (7), b. at Barre 22 May 1774, m. Olive, dau. of Timothy Fay, 24 Nov. 1799; she d. at Enf. 17 Nov. 1837, and he m.

Abigail Manly. His chil. were, *John*, b. 29 Aug. 1800, fell from a scaffold and fractured his skull when a boy, after which he was feeble-minded, and d. at the House of Industry, Boston, 16 Sep. 1832; twin children b. 1 and d. 2 and 3 June 1802; *Philander*, bap. 18 Mar. 1804, d. 3 Nov. 1804; *Philander*, b. 1 June 1805, a carpenter and deacon, m. Myra Keith of Pres. 29 Nov. 1833, and res. in Hk., Pres., and Bel. (his son, Charles Henry, b. 25 Aug. 1840, grad. A. C. 1866, and has been a very successful teacher and author); *Elizabeth Lindsey*, b. 15 Oct. 1808, m. Frederick W. Shaw of Enf. 6 Feb. 1833; *Hannah Fay*, bap. 20 Jan. 1811; *Mary Ann*, bap. 2 May 1813; *Samuel Nowell*, b. 3 Sep. 1815; *William Fay*, b. 17 Dec. 1817; *Hannah Maria*, b. 31 May 1820, m. Warren Chapin 1 Mar. 1848; *Josiah Henry*, b. 26 May 1822; *Rebecca Ann*, b. ——, m. Edwin Merrick, and d. — Aug. 1857; *Pliny Fisk*, b. 18 Aug. 1829. JOSIAH COTTON the f. was a carpenter and for several years deacon of the church; he res. on the old turnpike, at the place marked "B. Fay" on the R. Map; he rem. to N. Br. about 1816, and thence to Enf. about 1823, and d. 12 Mar. 1849.

CHAPLIN, EBENEZER, Y. C. 1763, was ordained pastor of the church in the second parish of Sutton (now Millbury), 14 Nov. 1764; and was dismissed 22 Mar. 1792. His dau. *Sarah* m. Rev. Thomas Holt of Hk. 5 May 1796, with whom he made his home in his old age, and in whose house he d. 13 Dec. 1822, a. 89. He was a staunch supporter of the established Theology, and a rigid disciplinarian, both in the church and in the family. His intellect was clear, strong, and logical, and he had an ample fund of grim humor. Both of these characteristics were manifest, not only in his sermons and familiar conversation, but in a volume published by him in 1802, entitled "A Treatise on the Nature and Importance of the Sacraments." He was tall, well-formed, and athletic; and his favorite mode of travelling was on horseback. He was among the last, if not the very last in Hk., to wear the full-bottomed wig, cocked hat, breeches, and white-topped boots, — which costume gave him a strikingly venerable appearance.

CHASE, LYMAN, m. Lorinda Oakes of N. Sal., pub. 27 Ap. 1854, and had *Lillian Adella*, b. 20 Aug. 1858, d. 24 Mar. 1880; *Nellie Gray*, b. 14 Aug. 1863; *George Lyman*, b. 23 Sep. 1865.

2. HORACE, m. Eunice J. Haskell 4 July 1864, and had *William Horace*, b. 4 May 1865; *Mary Winona*, b. 22 Sep. 1866; *Frank Haskell*, b. 22 Feb. 1869; *Helen M.*, b. 6 Dec. 1870; *Joseph Harmon*, b. 7 Dec. 1872; *Nathan P.*, b. 22 Aug. 1875; *John H.*, b. 4 Oct. 1877.

3. JOSEPH, by w. Caroline, had *Joseph Herbert*, b. 15 Aug. 1868.

LYDIA, m. Lewis Thresher of Pres. — Dec. 1842. NATHAN P., m. Mehetabel Mayo 17 May 1854. REBECCA, w. of James, d. 31 May 1853, a. 67.

CHILDS, EBENEZER, s. of Deac. Ebenezer of Barnstable, b. 10 Ap. 1723, m. Hannah Crocker 15 Jan. 1745, and had *Ebenezer*, b. about 1745, and perhaps others; he m. (2d) Abigail, dau. of Hatsuld Freeman of Harwich, now Brewster, 1 July 1756, and had *Jonathan*, b. 13 May 1757, m. Deliverance, dau. of Nathan Freeman of Hk., 13 Jan. 1778, and prob. m. (2d) Rebecca Hinkley of Hk. 3 Feb. 1785; *Abigail*, b. 26 Dec. 1758, m. Dr. Arthur Rawson of Hk. 23 June 1785; *Hope*, b. 21 Jan. 1761; *Mary*, bap. 10 Ap. 1763. EBENEZER the f. settled in Barre as early as 1776.

2. EBENEZER, of N. Sal., s. of Ebenezer (1), m. Abigail, dau. of Capt. Benjamin Willis of Hk., 26 Dec. 1769, and had *Betsey*, b. 27 May 1772, m. Gideon Tenney of Barre 8 Mar. 1792, and d. 15 Mar. 1870; *Moses*, b. 6 July 1777; *Eben*, b. 21 Mar. 1784, d. 7 Mar. 1786; *Ebenezer*, b. 2 July 1787; *Tyler*, b. — Aug. 1772, d. 8 Nov. 1800. Of these chil. the first was b. at N. Sal., the next three at Barre, and the last two were bap. at Hk. 2 July 1797. Besides these, was prob. *Benjamin Willis*, b. about 1775. EBENEZER the f. rem. to Hk. about 1785, and d. 7 Mar. 1 809, a. 65; his w. Abigail d. 26 Dec. 1810.

3. BENJAMIN WILLIS, prob. s. of Ebenezer (2), m. Anna, dau. of Eliphalet Washburn, 25 Nov. 1798, and had *Benjamin Willis*, b. 6 Nov. 1799, d. at Oxford 31 Dec. 1866; *Triphena Washburn*, b. 13 Aug. 1801; *Aurelia*, b. 28 June 1803; *Elvira*, b. 28 May 1805; *Franklin*, b. 10 Sep. 1807; *Tyler*, b. 18

June 1809; *Martin Luther*, b. 2 June 1811; *Anna*, bap. 11 July 1813; *Julia Ann*, bap. 25 June 1814; *Alexander Hamilton*, bap. 1 June 1817. BENJAMIN W. the f. res. in the northeasterly part of the town, was elected deacon 10 Aug. 1812, rem. to Barre, and d. in 1838. A sad calamity befell him 2 Oct. 1811, at a military training. During the excitement of a sham-fight, he neglected to remove the ramrod from his musket; the fatal missile struck John Warner (a young soldier twenty years old) in the forehead, and broke, leaving exposed about an inch of its length in front, and a part of the screw protruding through the skull at the back of the head. Death ensued in a few hours.

ELIPHAZ, m. Ruth Gibbs of Gr., pub. 14 Ap. 1788. MERCY, of Barre, m. Apollos Luce, pub. 30 Oct. 1808. HORACE S., of Brandon, Vt., m. Mary P. Rice 15 Oct. 1817.

CHURCH, SAMUEL, an early settler, by w. Damaris, had *Abigail*, b. 16 Oct. 1735; *Martha*, b. 23 Sep. 1737; *Elisha*, b. 1 Dec. 1739; *Sarah*, b. 28 Ap. 1741; *Damaris*, b. 29 Aug. 1742; *Susanna*, bap. 14 July 1745; *Hannah*, b. 1 Sep. 1747; *Samuel*, b. 10 Oct. 1749; *Ursula*, b. 14 Oct. 1751. SAMUEL the f. d. before 13 Nov. 1771, when his w. Damaris m. Stephen Warner of Granby. For many reasons it seems probable that this family descended from Richard Church, who was of Hartford 1637, rem. to Hadley 1659, with sons Edward and Samuel, and d. 16 Dec. 1667. See *Judd's Hist. Hadley*, p. 460.

2. RICHARD, prob. brother of Samuel (1), by w. Hannah, had *Richard*, b. 23 Jan. 1741-2; *Samuel*, b. 6 Aug. 1743; *Simeon*, 13 Aug. 1745; *Mary*, b. 18 Feb. 1747-8, m. Seth Winslow, pub. 23 Nov. 1775; *Susanna*, b. 11 Mar. 1749-50; *Edward*, b. 3 Nov. 1752; *John*, bap. 15 Aug. 1756. RICHARD the f. was one of the earliest inhabitants of Hk. and an original member of the church organized in 1736. He prob. rem. to Gr. before 15 Aug. 1756, when his sons *Edward* and *John* were bap. there.

3. TIMOTHY, possibly bro. of Samuel (1), by w. Abigail, had *Reuben*, b. 21 Mar. 1757; *Eleanor*, b. 21 Oct. 1759; *Samuel*, bap. 16 Aug. 1761; *Calvin*, bap. 19 June 1763.

CHARLES, of Bristol, Mass., bought land in Hk. (then Lambstown) 26 Nov. 1735, of William Dudley, and sold the same to THOMAS CHURCH of Little Compton, R. I., 26 Dec. 1735, but no evidence appears that either of them ever res. here. ABIGAIL, of Hadley, m. Ichabod Stratton, Jr., 14 Oct. 1743. HANNAH, m. Moses Chamberlin 12 Aug. 1781. SARAH, m. Zephaniah Spooner 5 Nov. 1789. [Hannah and Sarah before named were daughters of Charles Church of Bristol, and lineal descendants from the famous Colonel Benjamin Church of Little Compton, R. I. They seem also to be descended from John Alden and Governor Bradford; but the line of descent is not traced.]

CLAPP, WILLIAM, had *William*, bap. 27 July 1817; *Samuel Emerson*, bap. 30 Sep. 1821.

CEPHAS, of N. Br., m. Hannah Spooner 21 Mar. 1821. REBECCA and SARAH, adults, were bap. 14 May 1820.

CLARK, JOSEPH, res. in Rochester, and by w. Thankful had *Isaac*, b. 6 Sep. 1721; Katherine, b. 17 Oct. 1723, m. Thomas Weeks of Hk. 3 Ap. 1743; *Joseph*, b. 30 Nov. 1724; *Thankful*, b. — Aug. 1727; *Nathaniel*, b. 7 Feb. 1729-30; *Willard*, b. 21 Mar. 1731-2.

2. ISAAC, s. of Joseph (1), m. Content Weeks of Hk. 29 Oct. 1742, and had *Bethia*, b. 2 July 1744; *Isaac*, b. 24 Nov. 1746; *Catherine*, b. 29 May 1749; *Thankful*, b. 18 May 1752, m. Jabez Elwell 21 Dec. 1769; *Content*, b. 21 Aug. 1754, m. Jabez Cobb, 8 Dec. 1776; *Sarah*, b. 3 July 1757, m. Joseph Robinson, 30 Sep. 1773, and (2d) James Blair of Western (now Warren), 26 Mar. 1805, whom she survived, and d. 16 Dec. 1844; *Thomas*, bap. 10 Feb. 1760, d. young; *Rhoda*, b. 27 Jan. 1762, m. Timothy Hathaway 23 Sep. 1784; *Thomas*, b. 10 July 1764; *Asa*, bap. 18 Ap. 1767; *Susanna*, b. 29 Jan. 1768, m. Simeon Clark 1 Dec. 1791. ISAAC the f. rem. to Hk. about 1747, was a farmer, and d. 24 Dec. 1804; his w. Content d. 22 Feb. 1809, a. 85.

3. ISAAC, s. of Isaac (2), m. Patience Stearns of Worc. 6 Jan. 1774, and had *Polly*, b. 3 Mar. 1774, m. John White 19 Nov. 1795; *Alinda*, b. 19 July

1775, m. Asa Witherell ——; *Ira*, b. 5 June 1777; *Ezra*, b. 26 Aug. 1779; *Patience*, b. 21 July 1781, m. George W. Webb 16 Oct. 1803; *Bethia*, b. 14 Nov. 1782; *Fanny*, b. 25 Ap. 1785, m. Samuel Hathaway 17 Oct. 1805; *Willard*, b. ——, m. Fanny Giffin 25 Mar. 1810; *Harmon*, b. ——, m. Eliza Bartlett of N. Br., pub. 19 Jan. 1818. ISAAC the f. was a farmer, res. on the Ware road, at the place marked "C. Ruggles" on the R. Map, and d. 19 Aug. 1814; his w. Patience survived.

4. EZRA, s. of Isaac (3), m. Elizabeth Webb, 17 Nov. 1803, and had *Alma*, b. 27 Aug. 1806, m. Willard Sloan; *Luthera*, b. 21 Feb. 1810, m. Levi Whipple Warner 10 Ap. 1832; *Elisha Winslow*, b. 22 Nov. 1811, d. unm. 6 Feb. 1848; *Susan*, b. 22 May 1813, m. Lucius Lawton 3 Ap. 1834. *Elizabeth* (posthumous), b. 19 Jan. 1815, m. —— Chilson. EZRA the f. was a farmer, rem. to Danville, Vt., but returned in 1807, and res. on the Ware road next northerly from his father's farm, and d. 11 Aug. 1814; his w. Elizabeth m. Capt. Benjamin Paige, 6 June, 1819, and d. 16 Mar. 1856, a. 73.

5. EDWARD, b. at Bellingham, m. Anna Jennison, and had *Simeon*, b. ——; prob. *Polly*, b. ——, d. 26 Feb. 1789, a. 26; *Anna*, b. ——, m. John Paige, pub. 15 Sep. 1788, d. 27 Mar. 1845, a. 77; *Samuel*, b. ——; *Philena*, b. ——, d. 16 Aug. 1790, a. 17 or 18; *Edward*, b. ——; *Nathaniel*, b. ——, m. Sally Curtis 14 July 1793; *Sophia*, b. ——, m. Samuel King, pub. 11 Oct. 1801, d. at Barre 27 Mar. 1877, a. 93. EDWARD the f. came here from Pet. and d. 2 Jan. 1820, a. 88, according to the records of the town and church; but his head-stone is inscribed 5 Dec. 1819, a. 85; his w. Anna d. 16 Oct. 1802, a. 62.

6. SIMEON, s. of Edward (5), m. Susanna, dau. of Isaac Clark, 1 Dec. 1791, and had *Stillman*, b. 6 Feb. 1793; *Cyrus*, b. 8 Mar. 1795; *Asa*, b. 12 June 1797; *Caroline*, bap. 3 Aug. 1800; *Livy*, bap. 3 Mar. 1805. SIMEON the f. d. in 1809; his w. Susanna d. in 1811.

7. SAMUEL, s. of Edward (5), m. Mehetabel Ingerson of Ashford, Conn., pub. 30 Oct. 1791, and had *Philena*, b. ——, d. 11 Mar. 1809, a. 15; *Clarissa*, b. ——, d. 5 Feb. 1809, a. 12; *Horace*, b. ——, d. 21 Nov. 1811, a. 12; *Almond Ingerson*, b. ——, d. 18 Aug. 1807, a. 21 months; and perhaps others.

8. EDWARD, s. of Edward (5), m. Betsey Paige 23 Feb. 1800, and had *Eliza*, m. Abraham Stevens; *Maria B.*, m. Barnes Green; *John Paige*, d. in Oakham 20 July 1869, a. 63; *Charles Safford; Joseph Cutler; Henry Harrison; Benjamin Paige*, m. Julia Ann Emerson of Waltham, pub. 9 Ap. 1841, a confectioner, res. in Cambridge, and owns a hotel and large estate at Coldbrook.

9. STILLMAN, s. of Simeon (6), m. Sophronia Amidon, 9 Sep. 1819; she d. 12 Oct. 1840, a. 47, and he m. Charlotte Howe of Barre, pub. 23 Ap. 1842. His chil. were *Charles Stillman*, b. 19 June, 1823; *Rhoda Ann*, b. 20 Mar. 1825, m. Bela B. Paige 28 Nov. 1844; *Susan Sophronia*, b. 16 Aug. 1826; *Sarah Amidon*, b. 17 July 1829, m. Oren Gould 25 Nov. 1851, and d. 25 Feb. 1878; *Alice*, b. ——, d. 8 June 1855, a. 19; *Henry*, b. 25 Ap. 1844, d. 9 Jan. 1845. STILLMAN the f. was a farmer, res. on the Barre road, at the place marked with his name on the R. Map, and d. 7 Feb. 1881, a. 88; his w. Charlotte d. 25 July 1877, a. 75.

10. ASA, s. of Simeon (6), m. Patience Dennis 5 June 1823, and had *Elizabeth Eunice*, b. in Barre 26 Mar. 1824, m. Elijah Warner Robinson 20 Oct. 1855, and d. 19 Mar. 1881; *Lucy Henry*, b. in Barre, 1 June 1826, m. Willard Broad, 18 July 1854; he d., and she m. Alpheus Harding of Barre, 24 June 1874. ASA the f. res. at different times in Pet., Barre, and Hardwick; he d. here 16 Mar. 1881, a. nearly 84; his w. Patience d. in Barre 1 Oct. 1868, a. 67.

11. CHARLES STILLMAN, s. of Stillman (9), m. Sarah W. Newcomb 14 Dec. 1856, and had *Charles Laman*, b. 4 Nov. 1857, d. 6 May 1858; *George Stillman*, b. 30 June 1859; *Frederick Williams*, b. 13 Oct. 1862; *Frank Dexter*, b. 11 Oct. 1868; *Carrie Maria S.*, b. 15 Nov. 1871. CHARLES STILLMAN the f., a farmer, res. on the Barre road, at the place marked "Mr. Haven" on the R. Map.

12. NATHAN, by w. Anna, had *Relief*, b. 8 Sep. 1801.

13. HENRY H., by w. Freelove, had *Henry R.*, b. ——, d. 31 July, 1838, a. 3; a daughter b. 7 Sep. 1848; and perhaps others. His w. Freelove d. 23 Sep. 1850, a. 39.

14. KENAS, by w. Jane Ann, had *Julia Maria*, b. 4 Mar. 1849; *Martha Maria*, b. 27 Mar. 1851.

SALLY, d. 3 Mar. 1813, a. 23. PHILENA, d. 20 Oct. 1840, a. 37. LYDIA, of Rochester, m. Moses Haskell, pub. 18 May 1751. HANNAH, of Barre, m. Samuel Robinson, Jr., 15 May 1758. EDWARD, of Hubbardston, m. Mrs. Susanna Rice, 22 Ap. 1779. SETH, m. Ede Love, pub. 15 Oct. 1780. HANNAH, m. Samuel Haskins 3d, 19 Jan. 1804.

CLEVELAND, EPHRAIM, "m. Hannah Hayward, 1747, and settled in W. B., and had *Joseph* 1749, *Benjamin* 1751, *Elijah* 1753, *Lucy* and *Ebenezer* 1755, *Olive* 1758, *Persis* 1760." (Mitchell's *Hist. Bridgewater*, p. 137.) Besides these there was prob. *Ephraim*, b. in 1747 or 1748. All the chil. except *Benjamin* were m. in Hk.: — *Ephraim*, m. Lydia Whipple 15 Nov. 1770; *Joseph*, m. Elizabeth Wheeler 4 May 1772; *Elijah*, m. Sally Marsh, pub. 14 May, 1789, and d. 15 July 1812, a. 60; *Lucy*, m. Ichabod Eddy, pub. 24 Dec. 1780; *Ebenezer*, m. Betsey Barnard 28 Nov. 1790; *Olive*, m. Silas Whitaker of Pet. 7 Ap. 1785; *Persis*, m. Aaron Cooley of Athol, 9 Oct. 1783. EPHRAIM the f. was a saddler, bought a farm in the westerly part of Hk. 27 Mar. 1761, to which he prob. rem. immediately, and d. 9 Ap. 1822, a. 96;[1] his w. Hannah d. 21 Nov. 1810, a. 81. Their posterity in Hk. was numerous; but as only one of their sons caused the birth of his children to be entered on the town records, and the later generations were alike neglectful until 1843, I have no means to trace the family genealogy with exactness. I can only gather a few fragments, chiefly from the records of marriages and deaths.

2. EBENEZER, s. of Ephraim (1), m. Betsey Barnard 28 Nov. 1790, and had *Polly*, b. 6 Dec. 1791, m. Rufus Barnes 31 Dec. 1818; *Asa* (or *Asaph*), b. 6 Nov. 1795, m. Nancy Freeman, pub. 20 Dec. 1824, d. 25 Sep. 1880; *William*, b. 1 Sep. 1798; *Newcomb*, b. 18 Feb. 1800, m. Sophronia Gilbert 17 Feb. 1824. EBENEZER the f. d. 7 Dec. 1800, a. 45.

3. JOSEPH, prob. s. of Joseph and Elizabeth (Wheeler), m. Anna Barnes, and had *Jason*, who m. Lucy H. Smith 3 Jan. 1845; his w. Anna, d. 17 Mar. 1823, a. 16, and he m. Bathsheba, dau. of Luther Burgess, pub. 12 Sep. 1825, and had *Joseph*; *Andrew*; *Henry*; *Cutler*; *Charlotte*, d. 14 Aug. 1835, a. 20 months; *Frederick M.*, b. —— 1836; *William H.*, b. —— 1840, m. Mary A. Atwood 17 July 1861, two days afterwards joined the Union Army, and d. in the service 19 Aug. 1863; *Dwight*, b. 23 Nov. 1843; *Franklin H.*, b. 11 Dec. 1846; *Alpheus*, b. 3 June 1852; a son b. 29 Dec. 1854, d. 31 Dec. 1854.

4. ELIJAH, prob. s. of Elijah and Sally (Marsh), m. Lucy Barnes 14 Dec. 1819; some of their chil. were *Henry E.*, b. —— 1820, m. Abigail B. Holden of N. Sal. 26 Aug. 1846; *Albert A.*, b. —— 1822, m. Mary J. Dart 28 Mar. 1847; *Ephraim*, b. —— 1823, m. Angeline C. Holden of N. Sal., pub. 5 Ap. 1848; *Lucia C.*, b. —— 1825, m. Eli Warner of N. Br. 1 Ap. 1845; *William Warren*, b. 1831. ELIJAH the f. d. 28 Oct. 1856, a. 66; his w. Lucy d. 31 Jan. 1858, a. 61.

5. ROYAL, s. of Elijah and Sally (Marsh), m. Sally Smith of Pet., pub. 3 Ap. 1820; some of their chil. were *Porter C.*, b. —— 1823; *Edward S.*, b. —— 1829, m. Nancy G. Turner of Alna, Me., 4 May 1869; *Almira N.*, b. —— 1835, m. William W. Cleveland 20 Jan. 1853. ROYAL the f. d. 26 Feb. 1875, a. nearly 82; his w. Sally d. 23 Nov. 1873, a. nearly 78.

6. NEWCOMB, s. of Ebenezer (2), m. Sophronia Gilbert 17 Feb. 1824, and had *William Orson*, b. 21 Oct. 1827; *Sarah Gilbert*, b. 29 Aug. 1829; *Sophronia Jane*, b. 25 June 1831; *Alpheus Angel*, b. 25 Aug. 1834.

7. JOSEPH A., s. of Joseph (3), by w. Mary E., had *Joseph Anson*, b. 30 Jan. 1847.

8. FREDERICK M., s. of Joseph (3), m. Helen J. Barnes 4 May 1864, and

[1] The Town Record gives 86 as the age, but the date of marriage and other facts plainly indicate a mistake.

had *Eugene Sumner*, b. 31 Mar. 1865; *Leslie Linwood*, b. 10 Mar. 1871; *Heber Howe*, b. 3 Sep. 1872; *Ernest Elgin*, b. 23 July 1876. FREDERICK M. the f. d. 19 Dec. 1876, a. nearly 41.

9. DWIGHT, s. of Joseph (3), by w. Sarah J., had *Arletta Rowena*, b. 25 Nov. 1862, d. 4 Mar. 1863; *Leverett Dwight*, b. 16 July 1866.

10. WILLIAM WARREN, s. of Elijah (4), m. Almira M. Cleveland 20 Jan. 1853, and had *Mason Webster* (or *Warren Webster*), b. 9 Sep. 1853, d. 10 Dec. 1853; *Julia Eva*, b. 1 Jan. 1861. WILLIAM WARREN the f. d. 5 Jan. 1862, a. 31.

11. PORTER C., s. of Royal (5), m. Armanilla M. Hinkley of Barre, pub. 10 Oct. 1845; she d. 15 Mar. 1866, a. 45, and he m. Mrs. Ellen M. Howe of Barre, 1 Nov. 1866, and had *Julian P.*, b. 23 Sep. 1868.

12. *Joseph A.*, s. of Joseph A. (7), by w. Abbie J., had *Etta Bell*, b. 23 Sep. 1868.

13. ALVIN, parentage not ascertained, by w. Ruth, had *Sylvester S.*, b. —— 1838, m. Nettie A. Sears of Gr. 2 Dec. 1863; and prob. the same ALVIN, by w. Rosetta, had *Leora Elmina*, b. 27 June 1849.

14. ANDREW, by w. Mary E., had *George La Fayette*, b. 27 Sept. 1848; *Charles Laforest*, b. 28 Feb. 1850.

15. WILLARD, m. Mary L. Cook of Warwick, pub. 20 May 1857, and had *Elliott Edwards*, b. 17 June 1861; *Mary A.*, b. 13 Mar. 1865; *Carrie Maria*, b. 2 Ap. 1867; *Royal Cook*, b. 17 Aug. 1871.

CHARLES R., m. Eunice S. Thayer of Athol, pub. 24 Aug. 1842. L. ANGELINE, m. Emerson Warner of N. Br., pub. 18 Jan. 1851. SARAH M. J., m. William N. Gore, pub. 11 Feb. 1851. R. ALICE, m. Walter W. Warner of N. Br., pub. 2 Dec. 1852. CALVIN, s. of Elijah, d. at Fitchburg 4 June 1878, a. 74.

CLIFFORD, EDWARD, m. Abigail Winslow 30 Nov. 1761, and had *Samuel*, b. 25 Mar. 1762; *Anna*, b. 7 Jan. 1769; *Amelia*, b. 6 Feb. 1775; *Fanny*, b. 6 Sep. 1778.

2. SAMUEL, prob. s. of Edward (1), by w. Ruth, had *Daniel Pratt*, b. 12 Aug. 1786.

PLINY, m. Elvira Leonard of N. Sal., pub. 11 June 1825.

CLINTON, HENRY. See JONATHAN S. SLOAN.

COBB, ELISHA, by w. Priscilla, had *Lemuel*, b. 9 Jan. 1735; a dau. b. 26 Sep. 1737 (prob. the *Lydia* who m. Elkanah Stewart 7 Sep. 1761); *John*, b. 6 Sep. 1741; *Elisha*, b. 22 June 1744, m. Elizabeth Barnet 8 Nov. 1770; *Sylvanus*, b. 13 Aug. 1747; m. Elizabeth Warren of Westborough 9 Mar. 1772; *Hannah*, b. 1 Feb. 1749, m. Ephraim Titus 20 Dec. 1770; *Jabez*, b. 3 Ap. 1752. ELISHA the f. was styled a "mariner" in 1754, and is supposed to have been one of the very numerous posterity of Elder Henry Cobb, who d. in Barnstable, 1679.

2. LEMUEL, s. of ELISHA (1), m. Lydia, dau. of Joseph Allen, 10 Oct. 1765; she d. 11 July 1776, a. 32, and he m. Abigail, dau. of John Amidon 27 Mar. 1777. His chil. were *Anna*, b. 19 Feb. 1766, m. Samuel Dennis 3 May 1788; *Lydia*, b. 4 Jan. 1769, m. Alpha Warner 14 Jan. 1796; *Hannah*, b. 24 Nov. 1771; *Elizabeth*, b. 18 Mar. 1774, d. young; *John*, bap. 26 July 1778; *Lemuel*, b. 17 July 1780, m. Loesena (Lucina ?) Newton 2 June 1803; *Elizabeth*, b. 7 Mar. 1782, m. Micah Haskell 8 May 1797; *Nabby*, bap. 26 July 1789. LEMUEL the f. rem. to Hardwick, Vt.

3. JOHN, s. of Elisha (1), m. Thankful Sears 19 July 1764, and had *Molly*, b. 18 Mar. 1765.

4. JABEZ, s. of Elisha (1), m. Content Clark 8 Dec. 1776, and had *Isaac*, b. 3 Sep. 1777; *Elnathan*, b. 16 Nov. 1779.

5. SHEREBIAH, parentage not ascertained, by w. Charity, had *Hannah*, b. ——, m. Nathan Paige 25 Ap. 1784; *Sally*, b. ——, d. unm. 17 Aug. 1855, a. 86; *Cynthia*, b. ——, d. unm. 5 May 1826, a. 50; *Zenas*, b. 31 Mar. 1779, m. Cinderilla, dau. of Joseph Robinson, 1 Dec. 1803; she d. 9 May 1804, a. 24, and he m. Eleanor Smith, 2 June 1805. SHEREBIAH the f. was a farmer, rem. from Raynham to Hk. before 1779, res. on the westerly side of Muddy

Brook, at the place marked "S. Cobb" on the R. Map, and d. 3 July 1811, a. 72; his w. Charity d. 20 or 22 Oct. 1817, a. 78.

6. GERSHOM, m. Meletiah, dau. of John Smith, 19 Jan. 1726–7, and had, at Middleborough, *Hope*, b. 10 Nov. 1727; *Jonathan*, b. 14 Nov. 1729; *Perez*, b. 5 Aug. 1731; *Andrew*, b. 13 Oct. 1733; *Joseph*, b. 23 Jan. 1735–6; *Lydia*, b. 31 May, 1739; *Sylvanus*, b. 13 June, 1741; *Ebenezer*, b. 27 May 1744. GERSHOM the f. is supposed to have been son of Deac. Jonathan and Hope (Huckins) Cobb (who rem. from Barnstable to Mid. about 1695, and d. 15 Aug. 1728, a. 68), and grandson of Elder Henry and Sarah (Hinkley) Cobb (who was of Plymouth about 1629, of Scituate 1633, one of the founders and a deacon of the church there 1635, rem. with the church to Barnstable 1639, was subsequently ruling elder, and d. in 1679). GERSHOM was not the "*first* deacon" of the Middleborough church, as inscribed on his head-stone, but was elected in 1745 to that office. Late in life he rem. to Hk., where he d. 28 Aug. 1781, a. 86; his w. Meletiah, d. 26 Mar. 1788, a. 83. A large head-stone near the gate of the old cemetery denotes the place where their bodies were deposited.

7. PEREZ, s. of Gershom (6), was a farmer, and res. in N. Br., about a mile easterly from the Old Furnace, on the farm bought by him of Capt. Eleazar Warner 4 May 1764, and afterwards owned by his son *Perez*. I have not seen any record of his children. He d. 17 or 18 Nov. 1819, a. 88; his w. Abiel d. 27 Dec. 1819, a. 79.

8. ANDREW, s. of Gershom (6), res. in Mid., where, by w. Experience, he had *Gershom*, b. 2 May 1762; *Andrew*, b. 16 June 1764, m. Hannah F. Oliver; *Lewis*, b. 9 Dec. 1766, m. Abigail Cushman 1798.

9. SYLVANUS, s. of Gershom (6), m. Molly Ellis 13 Oct. 1765 at Mid., and rem. to Hk. about 1777. His chil. were *Joseph*, b. 15 May 1767; *Hope*, b. 20 June 1769, m. Elias White of Barre 2 Oct. 1789; *Sarah*, b. 1 Nov. 1770, d. 29 July 1772; *Polly*, b. 25 July 1772, m. Jonathan Fletcher of Barre 21 Dec. 1794; *Betsey* (twin), b. 12 June 1774; *Deborah* (twin), b. 12 June 1774, m. Isaac Bridges, Jr., 27 Jan. 1795; *Salome*, b. 12 Aug. 1776; *Benjamin*, b. 10 May 1778, m. Sally Jenkins of Barre, pub. 17 June 1801; *Ellis*, b. 11 Mar. 1780; *Daniel*, b. 15 Dec. 1782, m. Mrs. Hannah Clark of Ware, pub. 14 July 1817, d. at Deerfield 22 May 1856; *Clarissa*, b. 27 Dec. 1784, d. unm. 16 Jan. 1867; *Mivina*, b. 8 June 1786, m. Noah White of Barre 8 Feb. 1807; *Ammadulce*, b. 12 June 1788, m. Alanson Gilbert, pub. 18 Sep. 1825, and had one child, Alanson A., b. 6 Mar. 1827; she d. at Charlestown 18 May 1831. SYLVANUS the f. was a farmer, and res. near Barre, at the place marked "B. J. Cobb" on the R. Map, and d. 9 June 1834, a. 93; his w. Molly d. 16 Aug. 1830, a. 86.

10. EBENEZER, s. of Gershom (6), m. Martha, dau. of Walter Hastings, 5 Oct. 1780, and had *Otis*, b. ——, m. Daphne Fay, pub. 18 July 1802; *Ebenezer*, b. about 1784; and perhaps others. EBENEZER the f. was a cordwainer, res. for a time in Barre and afterwards in Hk. During the latter part of his life, for several years, he was toll-gatherer at the turnpike gate near the Old Furnace. He d. 15 Jan. 1816, a. 71; his w. Martha d. 2 June 1827, a. 81.

11. GERSHOM, s. of Andrew (8), m. Lydia Besse at Mid. in 1791, and the same year rem. to Hk., where she d. 14 Ap. 1808, a. 43, and he m. Abigail Thomas 2 Mar. 1811. His chil. were an infant, d. 29 Feb. 1792; *Lydia*. b. —— 1793, d. 5 July 1803, a. 10; *Gershom*, b. —— 1795, d. 24 Aug. 1833, a. 38; *Aretas*, b. —— 1797, d. 13 July 1803, a. 6; *Miles*, b. 25 Nov. 1798; *Experience*, b. —— 1800, d. 4 July 1803, a. 2 years 8 mo.; *Prior*, b. ——, d. ——. GERSHOM the f. was a cordwainer, res. on the easterly road to Gilbertville, at the place marked "Mr. Bolster" on the R. Map, and d. 15 Ap. 1812, a. nearly 50; his w. Abigail m. David Blackmer 13 Oct. 1823, and d. 22 Mar. 1832.

12. EBENEZER, s. of Ebenezer (10) by w. Joanna had *Lydia*, b.—— 1809, d. unm. 6 Oct. 1840, a. 31; *Clark Hastings*, b. —— 1813, d. 8 May, 1814, a. 14 months; a child b. —— 1818, d. 17 Sep. 1820, a. 2; *Frederick A.*, b. about 1823; and perhaps others. EBENEZER the f. res. on the old turnpike, about half a mile westerly from the Old Furnace, at the place marked with his name

on the R. Map, and d. 16 Nov. 1835, a. 51; his w. Joanna d. 30 Dec. 1845, a. 60.

13. MILES, s. of Gershom (11), m. Lucretia Tolman, pub. 30 Dec. 1826, and had *Amory B.*; *Lydia*, m. Luther Marsh of Holden 23 Ap. 1849, and d. 13 Nov. 1863, a. 35; *Aretas*, d. 13 Mar. 1851, a. 19; *Andrew*, d. 27 Ap. 1855, a. 22; *Prior*, d. 25 Feb. 1857, a. 21. MILES the f., a farmer, res. at Gilbertville, and d. 5 Feb. 1882; his w. Lucretia d. 1 Feb. 1879, a. 81.

14. FREDERICK A., s. of Ebenezer (12), m. Elizabeth S. Conkey 11 Dec. 1845, and had *William Frederick*, b. 21 Mar. 1850; *Carrie Frances*, b. 22 Sep. 1853, m. Charles E. Trumbull of N. Brk. 12 July 1879, and d. 2 June 1882.

15. *Amory B.*, s. of Miles (13), by w. Fanny (who d. 16 July 1859, a. 32), had *Crilla Acrora*, b. 22 Aug. 1857, d. 3 Nov. 1857; *Fanny Alline*, b. 10 July 1859, d. 12 Aug. 1859; and by w. Marietta, a daughter, b. 18 Sep. 1863, d. 18 Oct. 1863; *Fanny Louisa*, b. 10 June 1865; *Emma Jane*, b. 6 Sep. 1867. AMORY B. the f. res. at Gilbertville; rem. to Thetford, Vt., but soon returned.

SYLVIA, m. Henry Arnold, pub. 17 Ap. 1791. ALLEN, m. Olive Sampson 1 Jan. 1795. GRATIA, m. Israel Thomas, pub. 22 Jan. 1827.

COBLEIGH, JONATHAN (otherwise written Coble, Cobley, Cobleich, and Cobling), prob. the same who was in Concord 1737, by w. Elizabeth, had in Hk. *Reuben*, b. 6 July 1743; *Jonathan*, bap. 21 Sep. 1746; *John*, bap. 1 July 1753. JONATHAN the f. was a cordwainer, and res. in that part of the town which is now included in New Braintree.

2. ELEAZAR, prob. brother of Jonathan (1), by w. Phebe, had *Bathsheba*, bap. 12 June 1743; *Dan*, bap. 9 Feb. 1745-6; *Hannah*, bap. 21 Sep. 1746. It is not unlikely that *Simon*, b. 18 Aug. 1741, was son of the same parents, though their names are recorded "Eleazar and Phebe Ablich."

OLIVER, aged 23, was a soldier in the French War, 1758.

COLLINS, GAMALIEL, m. Rachel Rich, and had *Jonah Stevens*, b. ——; *Rachel*, b. ——, m. Elisha Newcomb of Gr. 23 Feb. 1790; *Gamaliel*, b. 20 Feb. 1776; *Ebenezer*, b. 2 Mar. 1777; *Jerusha*, b. 5 Aug. 1778, m. Judah Marsh of Ware 20 Feb. 1800; *Priscilla*, b. 24 Ap. 1780, m. John Wicker 15 Nov. 1803; *Aquilla*, b. 29 Jan. 1782 (it is understood by some members of the family that he never married; but the town records show that a person of the same name, and apparently the same individual, married Mary Smith of Gr. 18 Oct. 1807); *James*, b. 1 Sep. 1785. GAMALIEL the f. was born at Truro, was a shipmaster, and the "first adventurer in whale fisheries at Falkland Islands."[1] He rem. his family, about the commencement of the Revolutionary War, to the southwesterly part of Hk., a few rods northerly from the place marked "Mr. Collins" on the R. Map. He d. at Plymouth, apparently on his return from a voyage, as in his will, dated 27 Mar. 1786 and proved 13 June 1786, he mentions among his children the youngest son (b. in the previous September), "that was not named when I left home." Capt. Collins was evidently a man of mark; he was a member of the Committee of Correspondence in 1776, and selectman in 1778.

2. GAMALIEL, s. of Gamaliel (1), m. Patty Gilbert 21 June 1798; she d. 21 Aug. 1804, a. 28, and he m. Betsey Billings 29 Nov. 1804; she d. 10 Dec. 1805, a. 30, and he m. Ann Snow[2] of Truro. His chil. were *Jonathan*, b. ——, d. 3 Mar. 1831, a. 31 (leaving a dau. Mary Ann, who d. 10 Mar. 1831, a. 6 months); *Fanny*, b. ——, m. Foster Newcomb of Ware 18 Feb. 1819, and d. 19 Nov. 1878; *William Gilbert*, b. ——, a soldier in the Mexican War, and all further trace of him lost; *Gamaliel*, b. —— 1809, a lawyer, res. in Palmer, m. Martha Smith 13 Oct. 1834, and d. 8 Nov. 1869, a. 60; *Betsey B.*, b. ——, m. Daniel W. Hooker of Rut. 20 Sep. 1831; *Mary Ann*, b. —— 1811, d. 2 Oct. 1825, a. 14; *Daniel S.*, b. 28 Dec. 1812; *Martha G.*, b. ——, m. Charles Whitney of Watertown 29 Dec. 1840; *Anthony S.*, b. ——, m. Mary E. ——, and had dau.

[1] *Newcomb Genealogy*, p. 381.

[2] The descendants have a tradition that the mother of this Ann Snow attained the extraordinary age of one hundred and ten years.

Mary Emily, b. 12 Ap. 1849. GAMALIEL the f. was a farmer, res. on the homestead, and d. 28 Sep. 1825; his w. Ann d. at Wat. 24 Feb. 1861, a. 81.

3. EBENEZER, s. of Gamaliel (1), m. Polly, dau. of Timothy Gilbert, pub. 28 Sep. 1800, and had *Julia Ann*, b. ——, m. Adonijah Dennis, Jr., 11 Sep. 1827; *Ebenezer*, b. ——, d. in Iowa; *Lemuel G.*, b. ——, d. in Iowa; *Elbridge; Timothy*, res. in Iowa.

4. DANIEL S., s. of Gamaliel (2), m. Thirza Chaffee of Pal., pub. 11 Aug. 1840, and had *Mary Ann G.*, b. ——, d. 29 Ap. 1860, a. 17; *Fanny Maria*, b. 9 Ap. 1845, m. Oscar S. Southworth, 15 Ap. 1869; *Daniel C.*, b. 6 Ap. 1847, m. Eva J. Knight of Ware 18 Oct. 1871; *Francis C.*, b. ——, d. unm. 15 Nov. 1873, a. 25. DANIEL S. the f., a farmer, res. near the homestead.

ABIEL, m. William Thomas, 23 Sep. 1765. POLLY, m. Thomas Boyd of Shelburne 26 May 1816. CHARLES, d. 2 Jan. 1830, a. 78. JOHN, m. Mrs. Johanna Highland 3 Aug. 1871.

CONANT, TIMOTHY, s. of Lot, and a descendant from Roger, the governor of the first plantation at Cape Ann, was b. at Bridgewater in 1732, m. Hannah Blackman in 1754, and had, at Bridgewater, *James*, b. 1755; *Luther*, b. 1758; *Susanna*, b. 1760; *Lucy*, b. 1762; *Deborah*, b. 1764; *Timothy*, b. 20 Feb. 1770; and at Oakham, *Sylvanus*, b. 23 Ap. 1773; *Abigail* and *Sarah*, twins, b. 26 Oct. 1774; *Hannah*, b. 4 Mar. 1777. The births of the five children last named are entered on the Hk. records, indicating that the family rem. to this place.

2. ABNER, s. of Thomas, another descendant from the famous Roger, was born at Bridgewater in 1746, but spent a large portion of his life in Hk. He was a bachelor and a cordwainer. For several years he boarded in the family of Timothy Paige, Esq., plying his trade in a shop fitted up for his use. He d. 29 Oct. 1807, a. 61; but my memory of his kindness to me in my childhood is yet green.

CONKEY, NEHEMIAH, prob. s. of James and grandson of Alexander, named below, m. Marietta Lincoln 28 Nov. 1844, and had *James Burt*, b. 4 Sep. 1845; *Mary Louisa*, b. 27 July 1847, m. Lauriston Giffin of Barre 9 Ap. 1867; *Julia Elizabeth*, b. 17 Dec. 1851; *George Lincoln*, b. 6 June 1854, d. 17 May 1857; *Frederick Lincoln*, b. 24 Aug. 1857, d. 20 Ap. 1868; *Willard Alanson*, b. 5 Ap. 1861; *Frank Nehemiah*, b. 15 May 1863; *Frances Maria*, b. 7 Mar. 1866.

2. JAMES BURT, s. of Nehemiah (1), m. Charlotte Foster of Ware 1 Mar. 1870, and had *Louis Nehemiah*, b. 6 Dec. 1870; *Annie Louise*, b. 8 Ap. 1872, d. 12 Feb. 1878; *Harold E.*, b. 29 Sep. 1878.

ALEXANDER, a Revolutionary pensioner, b. in Pelham, d. 17 Jan. 1847, a. 93. JAMES, d. 15 Mar. 1842, a. 65; ELIZABETH, w. of James, d. 11 July 1859, a. 77. ELIZABETH, dau. of James and Elizabeth, m. Frederick A. Cobb 11 Dec. 1845.

CONVERS, BENJAMIN (otherwise written Converse), by w. Hannah, had *Asa Wright*, bap. 18 Mar. 1781; *Royal*, bap. 12 May 1782; an elder son *Royal*, d. 5 Feb. 1781, a. 4. His w. Hannah d. 25 July 1785, a. 34, and he m. Esther Grosvener of Windsor, pub. 17 May 1786. BENJAMIN the f., then of Windsor, bought the estate of Thomas Robinson, at and near the Old Furnace, 19 Oct. 1780 (for twenty thousand pounds in the depreciated currency of that period), and probably rem. immediately to Hk. He was licensed as a retailer in 1781 and 1782, and for a few years seems to have been prosperous. But in the troublous time which followed, he became an active military partisan of Shays, appearing as adjutant at Worcester on the 6th of September 1786; and on the collapse of the Rebellion found it necessary to abscond in order to avoid arrest. His subsequent history is unknown to me.

2. DANIEL J., m. Sabrina Brown, pub. 23 Jan. 1826. Their only child whose name appears on the record of births was *Emily Elvira*, b. 13 Sep. 1843. DANIEL J. the f. d. 16 May 1852, a. 49.

SARAH, d. 10 Ap. 1845, a. 19.

COOK, JOHN, by w. ——, had *Esther*, bap. 29 Oct. 1764; *Lucy*, bap. 5 Ap. 1767.

COOPER, JOHN, m. Mary Sherman of Grafton 15 Mar. 1748-9, and had

Sarah, b. 18 Feb. 1749–50, d. 8 Jan. 1767; *Nathaniel*, b. 8 Nov. 1751; *Mary*, b. 20 July 1753; *John*, b. 15 June 1755; *Joel*, b. 13 Ap. 1757; *Huldah*, b. 1 May 1759; *Sherman*, b. 8 Ap. 1761; *Matilda*, b. 16 Ap. 1762; *Barnabas*, b. 28 July 1764; *Chloe*, b. 20 Dec. 1766. JOHN, the f. was prob. s. of Samuel, who rem. from Cambridge to Grafton in the summer of 1730, and was elected deacon 21 Jan. 1732; if so, he was bap. 7 Mar. 1724–5, and was grandson of Deacon Samuel Cooper, and great-grandson of Deacon John Cooper, both of Cambridge. See *Hist. Cambridge*, pp. 516, 517. While residing in Grafton, 30 July 1746, he bought 100 acres of land in Hk., and was admitted to the church here on the first day of the succeeding March. He was elected deacon before 9 July 1751, when his name appears with that title on the church record; very probably the election soon followed the resignation of Deacon Paige and Deacon Robinson in 1749. He was selectman one year, assessor ten years, town clerk five years, and frequently school-teacher between 1751 and 1766. He prob. rem. or died in 1769, as in March of that year he was elected town clerk and assessor, and in the following May a successor in each office was elected; also the office of deacon in the church was filled by the election of Capt. William Paige (son of the former Deac. Paige) 9 Nov. 1769.

COVELL, ROYAL, m. Emeline Goss, of Winchester, N. H., 9 Aug. 1853. HARRIET E. C., m. John J. Johnson 11 Mar. 1852.

COX, EBENEZER, by w. Elizabeth, had *Anna*, b. ——, m. Nathan Carpenter 15 Mar. 1773; (prob.) *Sally*, b. —— 1759, d. unm. 2 Sep. 1808, a. 49; *Jemima*, b. 10 Nov. 1761, m. Noah Hatch 4 Feb. 1783; *Thankful*, b. 27 Aug. 1763; *John Davenport*, b. 24 Mar. 1765; *Hannah*, b. 2 Ap. 1767, m. Eliakim Fay of Barnard 5 Sep. 1790; *Elizabeth*, bap. 15 May 1768. EBENEZER the f. was born in Dorchester, rem. early to Wrentham, and thence to Hk. about 1760; he res. on a road leading from the turnpike to Ruggles Hill, at a place marked "L. Burgess" on the R. Map. He was a distinguished officer during the French War; his name is borne on the Muster Rolls as a lieutenant in 1757, and captain from 1758 to 1762. He d. 2 Mar. 1768, a. 41, and his patriotism, valor, and good conduct are commemorated on his head-stone, which remains standing in the old cemetery.

2. BENJAMIN, prob. brother of Ebenezer (1), by w. Jerusha, had *George*, b. 1 July 1762; *Jerusha*, b. 16 Feb. 1764, m. Holland Blackmer in Barnard 7 Nov. 1782; *Benjamin*, b. 13 Aug. 1766; *Ebenezer*, b. 28 Nov. 1768; *Philena*, b. 1 June 1771, m. Josiah Newton of Hk., pub. 29 Nov. 1792; *Charles*, b. 18 Oct. 1773; *Lucinda*, b. 7 Sep. 1776 (as recorded in Hk., or 26 Jan. 1776, according to the Barnard record); and in Barnard, *Thomas*, b. 20 Aug. 1778; *Fanny*, b. 30 Nov. 1783. BENJAMIN the f. also rem. from Wrentham to Hk. about 1760, and was actively engaged in the French War; his name is enrolled as a private in the company of Capt. Ebenezer Cox in 1758, as sergeant in 1759, and as ensign in 1760. He rem. to Barnard, Vt., about 1777, where he was one of the most active citizens, a captain of militia during the Revolutionary War, assessor, justice of the peace, and representative. He d. 25 Sep. 1788, a. 48.

3. JOHN DAVENPORT, s. of Ebenezer (1), m. Anna Powers of Brimfield, pub. 17 July 1786, and had *Stephen*, b. —— 1789, d. 2 Ap. 1791, a. 2; *Ebenezer*, b. — May 1791, d. at Worc. 14 Dec. 1863, a. 72; *Pamela*; and *Maria*; perhaps one of the dau. was b. before *Stephen*. JOHN D. the f. d. 26 Ap. 1795; his w. Anna survived.

ELIZABETH, perhaps dau. of Benjamin (2), and b. at Wrentham, m. James Byram 8 Feb. 1781, and rem. to Barnard about 1786.

CROWELL, JOSHUA, m. Mary Shiverick at Falmouth 5 Dec. 1745, and had *Bathsheba*, b. 25 May 1747, m. David Waite 23 Nov. 1769; *Joshua*, b. 8 Ap. 1749, m. Mary Field of Brk. 12 Jan. 1775; *Paul*, b. 20 May 1751, res. in Brk., m. Jerusha ——, and d. 28 Sep. 1830; *Salvina*, b. 17 Ap. 1753, m. Nathaniel Paige of Barnard, Vt., 1 Feb. 1781; *Hannah*, b. 14 July 1755, m. Jeduthun Spooner 27 Ap. 1781; *Thomas*, b. 1 July 1757, d. 22 Jan. 1812; *Mary*, b. 10 June 1759, m. Isaac Davis 28 June 1789; *Shiverick*, b. 24 Mar. 1762, m. Susanna Aiken 15 Sep. 1785, at Barnard, and d. there 19 May 1826; *Nathaniel*,

b. 4 Sep. 1764, d. unm. at Barnard 8 Aug. 1785; *Joseph*, b. 9 Oct. 1770. All these chil. except *Joseph* were b. and bap. at Falmouth. JOSHUA the f. rem. to Hk. as early as 1769, and caused the births of his chil. to be entered on record. He was prob. a descendant of John Crowell (formerly written Crow and Croel), who came to N. E. in 1635, "and was early in Yarmouth with w. Elishua." He was a farmer and res. on the easterly road to Gilbertville (with his son-in-law Mr. Spooner), at the place marked "Wid. Marsh" on the R. Map. His Christian character was severely tested by domestic affliction. His dau. *Hannah* (Mrs. Spooner) was insane for several years, and at length, on the 27th of January 1807, destroyed the life of her aged mother by stealthily approaching behind her chair, as she sat near the fire, and crushing her skull with an axe. After this Mrs. Spooner was more closely watched; but on the 16th of the following December she eluded the watchfulness of her keepers and destroyed her own life by cutting her throat. Mr. Crowell's son *Thomas* was also insane for many years; he was harmless and inoffensive, would seldom speak to any one, but would walk abroad in whatever weather, bareheaded and barefooted, and very thinly clad. I do not remember ever to have seen him with a hat or overcoat. In an unusually cold night, 22 Jan. 1812, he kindled a fire which consumed the house of his brother *Joseph* (who had the care of him), and perished in the flames.[1] The venerable father found rest from his earthly labors and trials 11 Sep. 1813, a. 91; his w. Mary, as before mentioned, met her tragical fate 27 Jan. 1807, a. 82.

2. JOSEPH, s. of Joshua (1), m. Perthenia Thomas 24 Oct. 1793, and had *Paulina*, b. 3 Dec. 1794, m. Jesse Shaw 19 Dec. 1813; *Adolphus*, b. 3 Feb. 1797; *Maria*, b. 25 Mar. 1798; *Erastus*, b. 10 May 1799, m. Rebecca Botherel, pub. 10 Ap. 1820; *Sophronia*, b. 14 Ap. 1801; *Jerusha*, b. 16 Ap. 1803; *Harvey*, b. 15 Dec. 1804; *Pliny Thomas*, bap. 16 Sep. 1810. JOSEPH the f. was not insane, but was thriftless and imprudent in his habits. He res. on the easterly road to Gilbertville, at the place marked "Mr. Cobb" on the R. Map; but several years after the destruction of his house by fire, as before related, and the erection of a new one on the same spot, he rem. to Broome, N. Y.

CUMMINGS, JACOB, by w. Ruth, had *Nathan*, bap. 25 July 1742, and no more is known of him.

2. ISAAC, by w. Susanna, had prob. *Isaac; Olive*, b. 11 Dec. 1755, m. Joseph Mixter of Templeton 25 May 1777.

3. ISAAC, prob. s. of Isaac (2), as he is styled Isaac, Jr., in the record of his first marriage, m. Catherine Ramsdell 11 May 1774, and (2d) Lydia Washburn, pub. 4 Sep. 1785. His chil. were *Catherine*, b. 7 Nov. 1779, m. Amos Larned of N. Sal. 1 Dec. 1803; *Isaac*, b. 6 Sep. 1784, m. Susanna Burden, pub. 12 Feb. 1809, and d. 4 Oct. 1835; *Joseph*, b. 25 Nov. 1786; *Lydia*, b. 28 Ap. 1788; *Zenas*, b. 12 July 1789; *Noah*, b. 5 May 1791, d. 17 Aug. 1847 (his son Henry King, d. 27 July 1829, a. 3); *Asa*, b. 11 Feb. 1793; *Polly*, b. 16 Ap. 1795, d. unm. 20 Nov. 1814; and perhaps *Loruhamah*, b. —— 1796, d. unm. 16 Oct. 1814, a. 18. His w. Lydia d. 13 Oct. 1814, a. 48.

4. JOSEPH, s. of Isaac (3), m. Polly Sprout of Gr., pub. 19 Sep. 1812, and d. 23 Oct. 1814. *Mary*, who d. 8 Nov. 1814, a. about 2, was prob. his daughter.

5. HOSEA, parentage not ascertained, m. Sarah, dau. of Marshall Johnson, 25 Feb. 1831, and had *Balarah*, b. —— 1837, d. 8 Ap. 1840, a. 2 years and 9 mos.; *Edgar*, b. 1842, a soldier in the Union Army, d. at New Berne, N. C., 14 Jan. 1863, a. 20; *Theresa* (or *Theolotia*) *Louisa*, b. 6 Jan. 1845, d. 18 Feb. 1847; *Almeda*, b. 6 May 1856, d. 15 May 1872; and perhaps others. HOSEA the f. d. 31 May 1877, a. 69; his w. Sally, d. 5 Nov. 1873, a. 59.

[1] Insanity appeared in the next generation. Among others, David Crowell of Brk., s. of Joshua, and grandson of Joshua (1), is well remembered as "King David." Sometimes on horseback, but generally on foot, with drum and fife, a feather on his hat, and a small flag whose staff rested in his side-pocket, he traveled the streets of Brk. and the adjoining towns, calling attention to his imperial commands by the sound of drum or fife, and enforcing them by waving his flag. Unlike his uncle Thomas, he was generally willing to converse with adults, and even with children; but pressure of important business compelled him to grant only brief audiences. The cares of his kingdom were so engrossing and oppressive that, as I remember, he was seldom seen to smile.

6. WILLIAM D., of Waterbury, Conn., m. Mary Ann, dau. of Dwight Billings, 18 Sep. 1855, and had *Hattie G.*, b. 19 July 1858. He now res. in Connecticut.

7. BILLINGS, m. Caroline Robinson, pub. 24 Dec. 1855; she d. 8 Sep. 1857, a. 27, and he m. Melissa Robinson, pub. 21 Dec. 1857; she d. ——, and he m. Mrs. Huldah King 22 Nov. 1859, who d. 10 Dec. 1868, a. 38. I find on record the name of only one child, *Herbert B.*, b. 12 May 1857.

8. AUGUSTUS H., m. Mary A. Pierce of Ware, pub. 13 Feb. 1871, and had *Freddie A.*, b. ——, d. 6 July 1872.

MRS. HANNAH (b. in Stafford, Conn.), d. 4 Jan. 1862, a. 71. AZUBAH, m. Nathaniel Sprout, Jr., 28 Dec. 1775. FANNY, m. John Gilbert 26 May 1815. BETSEY, m. Samuel Johnson 29 June 1829. CAROLINE R., m. Lauriston F. Crawford of Oakham, 8 Oct. 1829. CATHERINE R., m. Sumner Latham 22 Nov. 1831. LUCINDA H., m. William S. Barnes 24 May 1842. LUTHERA, m. George Betts of Waterbury, Conn., 5 Nov. 1844. ANGELINA C., m. James W. Sturtevant 27 Nov. 1850. I have no means to indicate the several families to which these persons belonged.

CUTLER, JAMES (prob. s. of Thomas, who d. in Lexington 13 July 1722, a. about 72, and grandson of James, who d. in Cambridge 17 May 1694, a. about 88), was bap. in Watertown 9 Jan. 1687, and by w. Alice had *James*, b. 13 Ap. 1715; *William*, b. 3 Ap. 1717; *Thankful*, bap. 24 Mar. 1719; *Robert*, b. 3 Ap. 1721; *Alice*, b. 27 Nov. 1729, m. Ephraim Jones, Jr., of Concord, 16 Nov. 1752. JAMES the f. d. in Cambridge (Menotomy) 16 Sep. 1756; his w. Alice d. 22 Sep. 1756, a. 67.

2. WILLIAM, s. of James (1), was an innholder, at Menotomy, m. Elizabeth Whittemore 15 Sep. 1743. She d. 29 Dec. 1770, and he m. Rebecca, wid. of Thomas Hall, pub. 2 Jan. 1773. Of the first wife, the "Boston News Letter," dated Jan. 10, 1771, says "she was the mother of 36 children; but the 35th was the only one that survived to follow her to the grave." The survivor was *William*, b. 23 Dec. 1764, grad. H. C. 1786, was a physician in Virginia, and d. in Dinwiddie Co. 17 May 1836. The second wife had *James*, b. 12 May 1774, a printer in Boston; *Rebecca*, b. — Jan. 1777, d. 6 Aug. 1778; *Rebecca*, b. 22 Dec. 1779. WILLIAM the f. d. 1 Ap. 1781. His w. Rebecca was living in 1817.

3. ROBERT, s. of James (1), grad. H. C. 1741, was ordained at Epping, N. H., in 1747, dismissed in 1755, installed at Greenwich, Mass., 13 Feb. 1760, where he d. 24 Feb. 1786, a. 65. He m. Hannah Crosby of Billerica; she d. and he m. Elizabeth Fiske of Lexington 3 Sep. 1751. His chil. were *Hannah*, b. 22 July 1745, m. John Haskell of Hardwick, and d. 4 Sep. 1831; *Millecent*, b. 20 Jan. 1747, m. Denison Robinson of Hardwick, and d. at Windsor, Mass., 5 July 1798; *Robert*, b. 2 Oct. 1748, a physician in Amherst, m. wid. Esther Guernsey, and d. 10 Mar. 1835; *Prudence*, b. 18 Feb. 1750, m. Joshua Clark, and d. 17 Aug. 1782; *Dudley*, b. 1 July 1752, m. Lydia Howard, and d. in 1838; *William*, b. 23 Dec. 1753; *James*, b. 24 Sep. 1756, d. 8 Oct. 1756; *Elizabeth*, b. 2 June 1758, d. 4 Nov. 1758; *Ebenezer*, b. 17 July 1759, d. unm. 26 June 1839; *James*, b. 5 Sep. 1761, d. 27 Mar. 1768; *Amos*, b. 11 Oct. 1763, d. 15 Ap. 1764; *Elizabeth*, b. 2 May 1766, m. Benjamin Harwood, and d. in Nov. 1849; *Alice*, b. 23 Nov. 1768, m. Jairus Howard, and d. 29 June 1811; *Samuel*, b. 16 Ap. 1771, d. 7 May 1771; *James*, b. 23 May 1772, d. 3 Oct. 1773.

4. WILLIAM, s. of Robert (3), m. Rebecca, dau. of Joseph Cutler of Western (now Warren) and had *William*, b. about 1782, d. unm. 18 Feb. 1811, a. 28; *Rebecca*, b. about 1788, m. Col. Samuel Billings 9 Sep. 1811, d. at Greenfield 30 July 1864, a. 76; *Harriet*, b. about 1790, m. Nathan Ruggles of Hartford, Conn., 23 Ap. 1813, and d. 1878; *Samuel Fiske*, b. —— 1792; *Elbridge*, b. about 1795, m. Huldah, dau. of David Paige, 20 Sep. 1817, had dau. Rebecca (who d. 4 Aug. 1820, a. 2), and other chil. whose names are not found on record; he was a merchant in company with his father and brother, res. at the place marked "E. Cutler" on the R. Map, rem. to Hartford about 1835, and d. there; *Caroline*, bap. 19 Aug. 1798, d. 18 Sep. 1798; an infant d. 8 Sep.

1803. WILLIAM the f. was a physician for several years in Western, but rem. to Hk. in 1795, retired from active practice, and established himself as an apothecary and dealer in English and West India goods; he was also postmaster[1] and justice of the peace. He res. on the old Parsonage Lot, half a mile north from the Common, at the place marked "E. Cutler" on the R. Map, until about 1810, when he erected the spacious mansion, on the easterly part of the same farm, marked "S. F. Cutler." He d. 9 Feb. 1832, a. 78; his w. Rebecca d. 27 Nov. 1820, a. 60.

5. SAMUEL FISKE, s. of William (4), m. Luthera, dau. of Daniel Ruggles, Esq., 24 May 1819; she d. 17 Aug. 1823, a. 25, and he m. Irene Cowles of Amherst, pub. 24 Ap. 1825. His chil., b. in Hk., were *Caroline*, b. 14 May 1819, m. Calvin C. Foster of Worc., and d. there; *Luthera*, b. 12 July 1823, d. 8 Mar. 1824; *Luthera*, b. 15 Jan. 1826, m. Ithamar F. Conkey of Amherst; *Samuel Porter*, b. 11 Dec. 1829, d. young; and at Amh., *William*, b. about 1843, d. unm. at Boston 8 Oct. 1875, a. 32. SAMUEL FISKE the f. was a merchant in partnership with his father and brother, succeeded his father as postmaster, was selectman five years, assessor two years, representative one year, and justice of the peace. He res. on the easterly part of the homestead (his brother having the westerly part), at the place marked "S. F. Cutler" on the R. Map. After 1835 he rem. to Amherst, where he d. 9 Sep. 1863, a. 71; his w. Irene d. 3 Oct. 1876, a. 71.

6. DAVID (s. of Thomas who was b. 15 Dec. 1677, grandson of James who d. 31 July 1685, a. 50, and great-grandson of James who d. in Camb. 17 May 1694, a. about 88), was b. at Lexington 28 Aug. 1705, m. Mary, dau. of Joseph Tidd, and had *Abigail*, b. 1 May, 1728, m. Samuel Hodgman of Western (now Warren) 7 May 1755; *David*, b. 15 July 1730, m. Dorcas Reed of Lex. and rem. to Western; *Joseph*, b. 31 May 1733; *Isaac*, b. — June 1736, d. — Jan. 1737; *Mary*, b. 12 Aug. 1738, m. John Paige of Hk. 15 Sep. 1757; *Solomon*, b. 15 May 1740, m. Rebecca Paige of Bedford; *Thomas*, b. 5 May 1742, m. Abigail Reed of Western; *Elizabeth*, b. 5 Aug. 1745, m. Benjamin Moore of Lex. 3 May 1768; *Amittai*, b. 15 July 1748, m. Nathan Leonard of Hk. 26 Nov. 1766. DAVID the f. res. at Lexington, was selectman three years, accumulated a large estate, and d. of small-pox 5 Dec. 1760; his w. Mary d. 25 May 1797, a. 93.

7. JOSEPH, s. of David (6), "settled at Western (now Warren) about 1755, m. May 6, 1775, Rebecca Hoar of Lincoln, and (2d) Sep. 20 1759, Mary Read of Western. Had *Converse*, and *Joseph*, a farmer, by his first wife; *Reuben*, b. 1775, twin brother to *Nathan*, A. M., Esq. Also 6 daughters, by second wife." — *Cutler Genealogy*, p. 59. *Reuben* taught school in Hk. one or more terms about the year 1800. One of the "six daughters" was *Rebecca*, b. about 1760, m. Dr. William Cutler (4) before named, and d. 27 Nov. 1820, a. 60.

8. CONVERS, s. of Joseph (7), m. Eunice —— (prob. Woodward); she d. 24 May 1821, a. 54, and he m. Mrs. Ruth Gorham of Barre, pub. 9 July 1824. His chil. were *Pamelia*, b. ——, m. David Trask of Leicester, pub. 21 July 1816; *Convers Franklin*, b. 22 Dec. 1791, d. unm. 16 May 1813 (styled *Convers, Jr.*, in the record of his death, and on his head-stone); *Eunice Woodward*, b. 19 July 1794, m. Reed Paige, at Barnard, Vt., 31 Mar. 1819, and d. s. p. at Bakersfield, Vt., 3 Aug. 1871; *Aaron Woodward*, b. 26 Dec. 1797, d. unm. at the almshouse, 26 Mar. 1865. CONVERS the f. was a physician, chiefly distinguished for his skill in obstetric cases and in managing chronic ailments; he was powerless where heroic treatment was necessary. In April, 1796, then residing in Wilbraham, he bought the place marked "J. Gorham," about three quarters of a mile northwesterly from the Common in Hk., where he spent the remainder of his days. He d. suddenly 1 Nov. 1831, a. 76; his w. Ruth survived.

DANFORTH, NICHOLAS, res. in Cambridge as early as 1635, was selectman and representative; he d. in Ap. 1638; his w. Elizabeth d. in England in 1629. His chil. were *Elizabeth*, b. 1619, m. Andrew Belcher, and d. 26 Oct. 1680, a.

[1] The first who held that office in Hardwick.

61 (she was grandmother of Governor Jonathan Belcher); *Thomas*, b. 1622, d. 5 Nov. 1699, a. 71, deputy governor of the Colony, for many years one of the foremost men in the government, and the acknowledged leader of the party in opposition to arbitrary power; *Anna*, b. about 1624, m. Matthew Bridge, and d. 2 Dec. 1704; *Samuel*, b. —— 1626, grad. H. C. 1643, ordained pastor of the church at Roxbury 24 Sep. 1650, and d. 19 Nov. 1674; *Jonathan*, b. 29 Feb. 1627-8.

2. JONATHAN, s. of Nicholas (1), m. Elizabeth Poulter 22 Nov. 1654; she d. 7 Oct. 1689, and he m. Esther, wid. of Josiah Convers of Woburn, and dau. of Elder Richard Champney of Cambridge. He "was the first captain of Billerica, was chosen representative in 1684, town clerk twenty years, and one of the most eminent land surveyors of his time." *Farmer*. By his first wife he had eleven chil., of whom the seventh was *Samuel*, b. 5 Feb. 1665-6. JONATHAN the f. d. 7 Sep. 1712.

3. SAMUEL, s. of Jonathan (2), m. Hannah Crosby, 8 Jan. 1694-5, and had seven chil., of whom the third was *Samuel*, b. 15 May 1701. SAMUEL the f. d. 19 Ap. 1742.

4. SAMUEL, s. of Samuel (3), m. Elizabeth Hosley, and had *James*, b. 10 Jan. 1729-30; *Isaac*, b. 9 Jan. 1731-2; *Samuel* and *Nicholas*, twins, b. 8 Dec. 1734; *Elizabeth*, b. 10 May 1736; *Jonathan*, b. 26 Feb. 1741-2. SAMUEL the f. d. 28 June 1750; his w. Elizabeth d. 3 July 1756.

5. JONATHAN, s. of Samuel (4), m. in Hk. Susanna, dau. of Rev. David White, 19 Ap. 1770; she d. 14 Nov. 1779, and he m. Anna, dau. of Joseph Ruggles, 1 Oct. 1780. His chil. were *Samuel*, b. 9 Mar. 1771, res. at Rupert and Pawlet, Vt., but d. at Ithaca, N. Y., 17 Dec. 1824, leaving son Charles, b. 23 Aug. 1800, grad. W. C. 1826, a clergyman, chiefly engaged as a missionary in the Western States, d. at Oberlin, O., in 1867; *Jonathan*, b. 25 Feb. 1773, d. unm. 3 Ap. 1797; *David White*, b. 10 Nov. 1774, d. 16 Dec. 1774; *Pamela*, b. 8 Nov. 1777, d. unm. at Rupert, 16 Dec. 1802; *Susanna W.*, b. 28 Dec. 1781, m. Capt. Moses Gray of Pres. 22 May 1828; *Joseph Ruggles*, b. 20 Mar. 1784, d. unm. 23 Ap. 1803; *Hannah*, b. 8 June 1786, d. unm. 13 June 1811; *Lyman*, b. 22 Oct. 1788, rem. to Pownall, Vt.; *Ann R.*, b. 2 Mar. 1791, d. unm. 29 Nov. 1873; *Cyrus*, b. 29 Sep. 1793; *James*, b. ——, was major of militia, m. Nancy R. Smith of Barre, pub. 11 Sep. 1830, and about that time rem. from Hk. JONATHAN the f., in early life, was a merchant, or keeper of a country store in Hk., and incurred public disapprobation by dealing in tea while it was contraband in 1776. After his second marriage he res. less than half a mile south of the Common, at the place marked "O. Trow" on the R. Map, which was the homestead of Mrs. Danforth's father. During the Revolution he was regarded as a Tory, and was subjected to confinement, which he resented and expressed his opinions in language more forcible than elegant. The breach was afterwards healed, however; he dwelt among his townsmen in peace, and served them as selectman, assessor, and collector of taxes. He d. 15 Sep. 1833, a. 90; his w. Anna d. 4 Mar. 1824, a. 69.

4. CYRUS, s. of Jonathan (3), m. Hannah P., dau. of John Jenney, 16 Mar. 1817, and had *Joseph R.*, b. 19 July 1818, res. in Worcester and d. 4 Sep. 1880; *Hannah*, b. 19 Jan. 1821, m. Waterville (or Walter) Sibley of Brk. 29 Mar. 1843; *Mary R.*, b. 16 Jan. 1823, m. Chester Hubbard of Templeton, pub. 3 Feb. 1844 (they rem. to Keokuk, Iowa, where he d. 29 June 1861, a. 45, and his monument stands near the northerly gate of the new cemetery in Hk.); *George E.*, b. 3 Feb. 1825, rem. to California; *Pamela W.*, b. 15 Sep. 1827, m. Benjamin F. Paige 31 Dec. 1848. Mrs. Danforth m. (2d) Clark Stone of Enf. 30 Sep. 1858, and d. 31 Oct. 1873, a. 73.

DAVENPORT, JOHN, by w. Martha, had *Ruth Jamerson*, b. 15 Oct. 1845; *Lunette Rowena*, b. 12 June, 1852.

DAY, ISRAEL, had *Jacob*, bap. 29 Mar. 1752.

2. WARREN, of N. Sal., m. Lucinda Robinson, pub. 7 Nov. 1829, and had in Hk. *Maria*, b. 17 Sep. 1830; *Hannah*, b. 7 Aug. 1832.

DILLY, m. Aaron Nazro, 21 Mar. 1808. RUFUS, of N. Sal., m. Fanny Dexter 22 Nov. 1830.

DEAN, WALTER, at Dorchester 1636, and at Taunton 1640, m. Eleanor, dau. of Richard Strong of Taunton, England, and had *Joseph, Ezra, Benjamin,* and three chil. whose names do not appear. He is said to have come from Chard, Eng., and was a tanner; he was deputy or representative 1640, and selectman 1679–1686. He and his wife were both living in 1693, affording an example of that longevity which distinguished so many of their descendants.

2. EZRA, s. of Walter (1), m. Bethia, dau. of Samuel Edson of Bridgewater, 17 Dec. 1676, and had *Bethia*, b. 14 Oct. 1677, d. 27 Nov. 1779; *Ezra* b. 14 Oct. 1680, had sixteen chil., of whom thirteen attained the age of 80 years and upwards (and of this extraordinary number, seven reached the age of 90, and one completed a full century); *Samuel*, b. 11 Ap. 1681, d. 16 Feb. 1683; *Seth*, b. 3 June 1683; *Margaret*, b.——, m.—— Shaw; *Ephraim*, b. ——. EZRA the f. d. about 1732.

3. SETH, s. of Ezra (2), res. in Taunton, and had *Ichabod, Jacob, Edward, Paul, Silas,* and *Sarah.*

4. PAUL, s. of Seth (3), m. Mary, dau. of Nathaniel Whitcomb, 4 Dec. 1745, and immediately rem. from Taunton to Hk., where he had *Paul*, b. 20 Oct. 1746; *Rosilla*, b. 13 Ap. 1751, m. —— Cheedle of Barnard, Vt.; *Anna*, b. 24 Mar. 1753, m. Edward Ruggles, Jr., pub. 12 Jan. 1772, and (2d) John Amidon 14 Dec. 1809, and d. 9 Jan. 1842; *Seth*, b. 3 Oct. 1755; *Robert*, b. 20 Oct. 1757; *Sarah*, b. 4 Feb. 1759; *Molly*, b. 26 Feb. 1762; *Asa*, b. 19 June 1764; *Nathaniel* and *Phebe*, twins, posthumous, b. 11 Ap. 1767. PAUL the f. was a carpenter and farmer; he res. on Ruggles Hill, at the place marked "J. Dean" on the R. Map; he d. before 8 Ap. 1767, when the inventory of his estate was presented; his w. Mary with remarkable energy kept her numerous brood of chil. together until they could provide for themselves; she m. Deac. Daniel Spooner of Pet. 16 Oct. 1780, and after his death ret. to Hk. where she d. 9 May 1822, a. 94 years and 7 months.

5. SILAS, s. of Seth (3), bought a farm here 29 Sep. 1740 (then res. in Rehoboth); he m. Joanna, dau. of Robert Whitcomb of Rochester 13 Sep. 1744; she d. about 1764, and he m. Elizabeth Ramsdell of Gr. 30 Nov. 1768. His chil. were *Thankful*, b. 18 June 1745; *Phebe*, b. 14 July 1748; *Mary*, b. 20 Oct. 1750; *Joanna*, b. 18 Jan. 1753, m. Timothy Nichols, 13 Jan. 1774; *Silas*, b. 6 May 1755, m. Azubah Washburn of Stafford, pub. 23 Feb. 1783, rem. from Hk. and is said to have d. in 1844; *Lot*, b. 9 Oct. 1757, rem. to Ware, and d. about 1819; *John*, b. 30 Mar. 1761; *Zimri*, b. 1 May, 1763.

6. PAUL, s. of Paul (4), m. Elizabeth, dau. of Edward Ruggles, 19 Sep. 1773; she d. 21 Dec. 1810, a. 58, and he m. Sila, dau. of David Aiken 8 Dec. 1811. His chil. were *Joel*, b. 27 Ap. 1774; *Lucy*, b. 16 May 1776, m. James Bell of Hardwick, Vt., 1801; *Edward*, b. 1 Nov. 1778, a physician; *Betsey*, b. 26 Ap. 1781, d. unm. 15 July 1803; *Paul*, b. 5 Feb. 1783; *Eunice*, b. 17 Jan. 1785, d. unm. 2 Oct. 1811; *John*, b. 19 Mar. 1787; *Joseph*, b. 25 Jan. 1790; *Justus*, b. 16 Feb. 1792, d. 25 Mar. 1804; *Seth*, b. 10 Mar. 1795; *David Aiken*, b. 18 Oct. 1812. PAUL the f. was a farmer, res. on the homestead, and d. 23 Sep. 1828; his w. Sila m. Nathaniel Fish of Pres. 30 Dec. 1835, and d. 7 Mar. 1844.

7. SETH, s. of Paul (4), rem. to Barnard, Vt., 1778, and there m. Molly Bicknell 3 June 1782; she d. 9 Sep. 1802, a. 39, and he m. Ruth Wright, 12 Mar. 1805. His chil. were *Paul*, b. 28 Mar. 1783, an eminent Universalist clergyman for many years in Boston, afterwards affiliated with the Unitarians, a steadfast friend and advocate through life of Freemasonry, and an officer in many of its highest grades, d. at Framingham 1 Oct. 1860; *Amos*, b. 5 Aug. 1784, d.—— 1802; *Seth*, b. 19 Feb. 1786, m. Patty French 25 Feb. 1813, and d. 22 Ap. 1833; *Asa*, b. 26 Sep. 1787, and d. in Barnard 3 May 1861. SETH the f. was a Revolutionary soldier, and closed his long and useful life at Barnard 22 Nov. 1851, a. 96; his w. Ruth d. 17 Mar. 1858, a. 92.

8. ROBERT, s. of Paul (4.), rem. to Barnard, Vt., before 23 Dec. 1784, when he m. Eunice, dau. of Daniel Billings of Hk., and had in B. *Daniel*, b. 19 Feb. 1786, m. Delphia, dau. of Eliakim Fay, had nine children, rem. to Bakersfield, Vt., where he d. 6 Feb. 1872; *Asa*, b. 7 Feb. 1788, d. in Bakers-

field 18 Jan. 1879; *Myra*, b. 23 Dec. 1789, m. —— Newton, and d. in Barnard 30 Jan. 1861; *Paul*, b. 20 Aug. 1791, d. 30 Dec. 1791; *Eunice*, b. 14 or 15 Dec. 1793, m. —— Parker, and is still living (1883) in Bakersfield; *Robert*, b. 20 Jan. 1796, d. in Fairfield, Vt., 22 Mar. 1864; *Polly*, b. 4 Oct. 1797, m. —— Boutelle, and d. in Bakersfield since 1873; *Paul*, b. 26 Ap. 1800, d. in Cabot, Vt., 16 Oct. 1880; *Sarah*, b. 11 Dec. 1801, m. —— Reed, and d. in Burke, N. Y., 12 Oct. 1863; *Timothy*, b. 20 Dec. 1803, d. 28 Dec. 1831; *Betsey M.*, b. 31 Dec. 1806, m. —— Webster, and d. in Johnson, Vt., since 1873. ROBERT the f. d. 28 Feb. 1828; his w. Eunice d. in Cabot — Mar. 1843, a. nearly 80.

9. NATHANIEL, s. of Paul (4), by w. Rhoda, had in Barnard *Amos*, b. 16 Jan. 1803; *Mary*, b. 30 Dec. 1804; *Minerva*, b. 17 June 1806. NATHANIEL the f. is said to have been living at Albany in 1850, at which date his son *Amos* is styled a lawyer and historian, and another son, *Nathaniel*, is mentioned.

10. JOHN, s. of Paul (6), m. Mary Penniman, pub. 15 Sep. 1822, and had *Mary Elizabeth*, b. 9 Oct. 1823, m. Joel D. Mandell 2 Ap. 1846, and d. 17 Ap. 1847; *Edward*, b. 19 Jan. 1826; *Lucy Ann*, b. 5 Mar. 1833, d. 22 May 1853; *Luthera*, b. 4 Nov. 1834, d. 8 Sep. 1839. JOHN the f. was a farmer, selectman five years, res. on the homestead, and d. 18 Ap. 1863; his w. Mary d. 23 Ap. 1859, a. 60.

11. DAVID AIKEN, s. of Paul (6), m. Fidelia F., dau. of James Browning, 22 June 1842, and had *Charles Browning*, b. 15 July 1846, d. unm. 17 June 1880. DAVID A. the f. was a farmer, and d. 6 July 1848; his w. Fidelia F. m. John B. Aiken 25 Feb. 1858.

12. EDWARD, s. of John (10), m. Luthera A., dau. of Daniel Wheeler, 19 June 1851, and had *Mary Elizabeth*. b. 6 Oct. 1852, d. unm. 17 Sep. 1877; *William Edward*, b. 12 Jan. 1854; *John Adams*, b. 31 Oct. 1856; *Joseph*, b. 27 Mar. 1859, d. 15 Sep. 1877; *Adelia Jenney*, b. 16 July 1861, d. 27 Mar. 1878; *Anna Maria*, b. 22 Aug. 1863. EDWARD the f. was assessor 1853, member of school committee four years, and rem. to Worcester after 1859; his three chil. who d. in Worc. were buried in Hardwick.

KEZIA, m. Isaac Fay 22 Nov. 1764. LUCY, widow of Stephen (b. at Raynham), d. 11 Jan. 1851, a. 77.

DEMMON, EDWARD, by w. Elizabeth, had *Lydia*, bap. 20 Aug. 1749; *Mary*, bap. 3 Nov. 1751.

DENNIS, SAMUEL, was a Baptist minister; he was born in Sutton, but removed to Petersham, where he preached several years; from Pet. he rem. to Barre, and soon afterwards to Hk., where he bought the Sears farm in 1777, and died in 1784.[1] He had chil. *Adonijah*, b. 12 July, 1759; *Patience*, b. ——, m. Thomas Winchester 23 Dec. 1787; *Samuel*, b. ——, m. Anna Cobb 3 May 1788; *Polly*, b. ——, m. Roger Wing 24 May 1790; and perhaps others. SAMUEL the f. was prob. of the Ipswich family, but I am unable to trace the connection, step by step.

2. ADONIJAH, s. of Samuel (1), m. Eunice Sibley of N. Salem, pub. 1 May 1780, and had *Royal*, b. —— 1781; *Samuel*, b. —— 1784, m. Cynthia Barrett of Carlisle, and d. at Concord 21 Jan. 1864, a. 79; *Lucy*, b. —— 1786, m. John Dexter 1 Dec. 1803, and d. 15 Dec. 1817, a. 31; *Betsey*, b. about 1788, m. John P. Colburn of Fairhaven, Vt., 9 Mar. 1818; *Polly*, b. —— 1791, d. 31 Jan. 1793, a. 1 year, 10 months; *Adonijah*, b. —— 1793, d. 13 Aug. 1803, a. 10; an infant b. ——, d. 20 Ap. 1795; *Eunice*, b. 21 May 1796, d. unm. 9 Dec. 1874; *Louis*, b. 8 Feb. 1799, m. Lucy Henry of Boston, d. in Boston 8 Feb. 1860; *Patience*, b. —— 1801, m. Asa Clark 5 June 1823, d. 1 Oct. 1868, a. 67; *Adonijah*, b. 4 Oct. 1803. ADONIJAH the f. was b. in Sutton, whence he rem. with his father. He served in the Revolutionary Army, and was engaged in the Battle of Stillwater. He was a farmer, and inherited the homestead near Barre, at the place marked "A. Dennis" on the R. Map, where he d. 30 Sep. 1844, a. 85; his w. Eunice d. 15 Sep. 1842, a. 82.

3. ROYAL, s. of Adonijah (2), m. Sankey Watson, pub. 6 Oct. 1802, and

[1] For these facts and dates I am indebted to Samuel S. Dennis, Esq.

had a child b. — July 1803, d. 29 Mar. 1805; *Bowman W.*, b. 4 July 1805, and d. in Byron, Mich.; *William W.*, res. in Cambridge; *Polly*, m. William Barker of Pontiac, Mich.; *Elizabeth*, m. Stephen G. Hidden of Concord, 30 July 1838, and d. in 1869; *George R.*, res. in Fentonville, Mich.; *James Y.*, res. in Rochester, N. Y.; *Selah Gridley*, res. in Hallowell, Me. (see Adams' *Hist. Fairhaven, Vt.*, 1870). ROYAL the f. rem. in 1807 to Fairhaven, Vt., and was captain of militia. In 1823 he rem. to Hartford, N. Y., where he d. in 1830.

4. ADONIJAH, s. of Adonijah (2), m. Julia Ann, dau. of Ebenezer Collins, 11 Sep. 1827, and had *John G.*, b. 5 Aug. 1828, a lawyer, d. 31 July 1858; *Samuel S.*, b. 18 Dec. 1829, d. 15 Nov. 1832; *Samuel S.*, b. 12 Mar. 1833; *Ebenezer C.*, b. 26 July 1834; *Julia Ann E.*, b. 6 Aug. 1839, m. S. Williams Newcomb, 23 Ap. 1863; *Louis H.*, b. 5 May 1841; *Dahliette M.*, b. 9 June 1842, m. William H. Tucker 30 Ap. 1867, and d. 12 Aug. 1874; *Julius A.*, b. 1 Dec. 1844; *Charles P.*, b. 18 Nov. 1846, d. 9 Ap. 1851; *Frederick C.*, b. 8 Oct. 1848, m. Julia M. Williams, pub. 29 June 1869. ADONIJAH the f. was a farmer, selectman in 1855, res. on the homestead, and d. 24 Mar. 1881; his w. Julia Ann d. 18 Feb. 1858, a. 51.

5. SAMUEL S., s. of Adonijah (4), m. Julia Maria, dau. of Sardius Sibley, 26 Nov. 1863, and had *Jennie Maria*, b. 9 Nov. 1867; *Samuel S.*, b. 24 June 1877. SAMUEL S. the f., a farmer, res. on the homestead, representative in 1866, selectman from 1864 to the present time, and for many years member of the school committee, overseer of the poor, and legal agent of the town.

6. JULIUS A., s. of Adonijah (4), m. Elizabeth H., dau. of Albert E. Knight, 8 Oct. 1868, and had *Gracie Cornelia*, b. 9 Sep. 1871, d. at Spencer 9 Jan. 1872; *Gracie Cornelia*, b. at Spencer 1 Jan. 1873; *Dahlietta Maria*, b. here 11 Mar. 1875; *Nellie Bruce*, b. 13 June 1876; *Jennie Powers*, b. 25 Dec. 1877; *Annie Louise*, twin, b. 20 Sep. 1879; her mate, a boy, d. on the day of his birth.

MRS. ABIGAIL, prob. mother of Samuel (1), d. 28 Dec. 1798, a. 90.

DEXTER, BENJAMIN, of Rochester (son of William of Barnstable), who rem. to Roch. and d. there 1694, and grandson of Thomas who came to N. E. in 1630, res. at Lynn, Sandwich, and Barnstable, and d. in Boston 1677), was b. in Barn. — Feb. 1670, rem. to Roch. and had *Noah*, b. 26 Mar. 1697; *James*, b. 22 July 1698; *Benjamin*, b. 4 Mar. 1700; *Sarah*, b. 1 July 1702; *Josiah*, b. 12 Nov. 1704; *Constant*, b. 27 Nov. 1706; *Samuel*, 14 Dec. 1708; *Ephraim*, b. 27 May 1711; *Daniel*, b. 29 July, 1713; *Joanna*, b. 12 Dec. 1715; *Seth*, b. 3 Oct. 1718.

2. SAMUEL, s. of Benjamin (1), m. Mary Clark 18 May 1732, and had in Roch. *Joseph*, b. 2 May 1733, res. in Hk. 1753, and in Athol 1761; *Samuel*, b. 13 Oct. 1734; prob. *Ichabod*, b. —— 1736; and in Hk. *Job*, b. 3 Mar. 1740-1; *Mary*, b. 11 July 1743; *Sarah*, b. 8 May 1745, m. Solomon Johnson of Gr. 28 Dec. 1762; *Benjamin*, b. 17 Nov. 1747. SAMUEL the f. rem. from Roch. to Hk. between 1734 and 1741, and prob. again rem. to Athol before 31 Jan. 1754.

3. SAMUEL, s. of Samuel (2), m. Thankful, dau. of Deac. John Freeman, 25 Nov. 1759; she d. 20 May 1811, a. 69, and he m. Sibbelah (or Sybil), wid. of Samuel Thurston, 26 Sep. 1811. His chil. were: *Benjamin*, b. 17 March 1760; *Mary*, b. 18 Jan. 1763, m. John Gorham 3 June 1784; *Eleazar*, b. 5 July 1765; *Mercy*, b. 16 July 1767, d. 14 Mar. 1774; *Ichabod*, b. 23 Ap. 1770, d. 5 Mar. 1774; *Samuel*, b. 9 May, 1773; *Seth*, b. 5 Mar. 1775; *Jedediah*, bap. 26 Oct. 1777; *Susanna*, bap. 26 Sep. 1779; *Thomas*, bap. 19 May 1782; *Jonathan*, b. about 1786. SAMUEL the f. res. near Barre, at the place marked "J. Richmond" on the R. Map, was one of the "minute men" who marched from Hk. to Cambridge in 1775, and in January 1776 was captain of a company stationed at the "Roxbury Camp." He was afterwards involved (politically) in the Shays Rebellion, but was forgiven. He d. 3 May 1824, a. nearly 90; his w. Sybil, who had previously to his death departed from him, d. in N. Br. 13 July 1849, a. 100 years, according to the inscription on her headstone in the new cemetery in Hk.

4. ICHABOD, prob. s. of Samuel (2), was a captain, and perhaps was the

same who led a company from Athol to Cambridge in April 1775. If he res. temporarily in Athol, he returned to Hk. before 1781, in which year and also in 1782 and 1785 he was a selectman, and representative in 1782 and 1783. He was an active promoter of the Shays Rebellion in 1786, but afterwards made his peace with the government. He d. of apoplexy 13 Feb. 1797, a. 59 years, 7 months, and 19 days, as entered on the church record of deaths; his w. Abigail, d. 7 Ap. 1797, a. 54 years, 8 months, and 16 days. On the settlement of his estate, 17 Ap. 1798, shares were allotted to seven chil., namely, *Clark*, who m. Alice, dau. of Ezra Winslow, 16 Oct. 1796, and rem. to Barnard, Vt.; *Miriam*, who m. Asa Hedge 31 May 1780; *Benjamin W.*; *Lucy*, who m. Moses Cheney of Warwick 4 July, 1782; *Rhoda*, who m. Phineas Battle of Orange 7 Nov. 1793, and d. 9 Aug. 1845, a. 76; *Lydia*; *Betty*.

5. JOB, s. of Samuel (2), m. Mercy Hinkley 17 July 1766; she d. 28 July 1810, a. 66, and he m. Mary Walker of Barre, pub. 1 Nov. 1811. His chil. were: *John*, b. 3 Jan. 1769; *Anna*, b. 22 July 1770, m. Thomas Wheeler, Jr., 3 June, 1790, and d. 20 Mar. 1804; *Ruth*, b. 20 Mar. 1773, m. David Allen, Jr., 27 Ap. 1794, and d. 26 Mar. 1847; *Ichabod*, b. 19 Dec. 1775; *Mercy*, b. 28 Ap. 1777, d. unm. 24 July 1801; *Joseph*, b. 1 Mar. 1779; *Jonathan*, bap. 9 Sep. 1781; *Sally*, b. 16 Oct. 1783, m. Dr. Elliot Beckwith, pub. 9 Nov. 1806, and d. 18 July 1811; *Zenas*, b. 26 June, 1785; *Alma*, b. 27 May 1787, d. 7 Oct. 1790. JOB the f. was a farmer, and res. about a mile and a half northerly from the Common; he was a lieutenant in the Revolutionary War, and retained the title through life. He served the town very acceptably as a selectman fifteen years, between 1789 and 1805. He d. 10 July 1827. His w. Mary d. — Oct. 1824, a. 69.

6. BENJAMIN, s. of Samuel (3), m. Anna Mayo, of Rut. 10 Oct. 1784, and had *Judah*, b. —— 1788, d. 31 Mar. 1790; prob. *John Freeman*, b. ——; and perhaps others. BENJAMIN the f. d. 16 Aug. 1792.

7. ELEAZAR, s. of Samuel (3), m. Abigail Dexter 8 Ap. 1784; she d. ——, and he m. Charity Williams, pub. 18 June 1786. His chil. were: *Abigail*, b. 14 Mar. 1787, m. Martin Ruggles 27 Feb. 1816, and d. 5 July 1860; *Bathsheba Carver*, b. 22 Feb. 1789, m. Silas Newton 2d, 21 June 1810, and d. 29 Sep. 1855; *Alma*, b. —— 1791, d. 26 Jan. 1803; *Arathusa*, b. —— 1793, d. 18 Jan. 1803; *Charity Williams*, b. 5 Aug. 1795, m. Gardner Newton, pub. 17 Sep. 1827; *Joseph Dean*, b. 31 Aug. 1797; *Seth*, b. —— 1800, d. 2 Aug. 1803; *Willard*, b. 13 Sep. 1802; *Arathusa*, b. 7 Jan. 1805, m. John Johnson 5 Oct. 1828; *Thankful Freeman*, bap. 1 Sep. 1811; *Eleazar*, b. 7 July 1813, a famous musician and showman, res. in Reading, Vt. ELEAZAR the f. d. —— 1813; his w. Charity d. 3 June 1838, a. 70.

8. SAMUEL, s. of Samuel (3), m. Sally, dau. of Jacob Williams, 15 Dec. 1796, and had *Benjamin*, b. 6 July 1798, d. 8 May 1816; *Williams*, b. 7 Ap. 1800; *Alma*, b. 11 Nov. 1804, m. Joseph Newcomb, pub. 11 Feb. 1828. SAMUEL the f. res. on the homestead, was a captain of militia, selectman four years, and d. 24 Mar. 1861, a. nearly 88; his w. Sally (b. at Middleborough) d. 10 Jan. 1867, a. 92.

9. JEDEDIAH, s. of Samuel (3), m. Abigail Eager 29 Dec. 1798, and had *Jane*, b. —— 1800, d. 20 Feb. 1802; *Horace*, b. 26 Nov. 1802, d. 22 Oct. 1826; *Mary*, b. 11 June 1805, m. Milton Peck, pub. 13 Oct. 1823; *Thirza* bap. 18 Sep. 1808, d. 19 Feb. 1809; *Elliot Beckwith*, b. —— 1810, d. 27 Aug. 1813; *Sally Beckwith*, b. 6 May 1812, d. unm. 18 July 1830; *Crighton*, bap. 7 May 1816, d. same day; *Samuel*, bap. 24 Nov. 1817; *Luthera Gorham*, bap. 27 Jan. 1820, m. Ebenezer P. Staples of Taunton 26 Ap. 1841. JEDEDIAH the f. d. 1 Jan. 1827; his w. Abigail d. 23 Aug. 1828.

10. JONATHAN, s. of Samuel (3), m. Roxana Dean of Raynham, pub. 29 June 1812, and had *Cassandra*, b. 1 Sep. 1813, m. Samuel F. Taylor 9 Ap. 1835; *Jonathan*, b. 23 Oct. 1815; *Benjamin*, b. 28 Dec. 1187; *Samuel B.*, b. 10 May 1825, d. 15 Feb. 1827; an infant b. ——, d. — Oct. 1827. JONATHAN the f. d. at Hubbardston 14 March 1856, a. 70; his w. Roxana d. 5 Sep. 1872.

11. JOHN, s. of Job (5), m. Lucy Dennis 1 Dec. 1803; she d. 15 Dec.

1817, a. 31, and he m. Persis Gilbert 29 July 1821. His chil. were: *Anna Wheeler*, b. 17 Oct. 1804, m. Amos K. Smith of Wendell 12 June 1826; *Foster Dennis*, b. 19 July 1806, d. at N. Sal. 3 Mar. 1865; *Fanny Beckwith*, b. 13 Feb. 1809, m. Rufus Day of N. Sal. 22 Nov. 1830; *Job*, b. 28 Nov. 1811, d. at Barre 1 Ap. 1849; *Mercy Hinkley*, b. 20 May 1815, m. David L. Winslow of Barre 22 Mar. 1837, and d. 8 May 1847; *Henry Walker*, b. 22 Oct. 1821; *Horace*, b. 26 Sep. 1825. JOHN the f. was a farmer, res. on a part of the homestead marked "J. Dexter" on the R. Map, and d. 7 May 1836.

12. ICHABOD, s. of Job (5), m. Sally Eager 5 May 1803; she d. 25 July 1821, a. 40, and he m. Alice Amidon 26 Mar. 1822. He had a child, d. 17 Ap. 1804, a. three weeks; *Zenas Hinkley*, b. 9 May 1806; *Harriet Jane*, b. 15 Ap. 1810, d. unm. 26 Aug. 1835; *Edward*, b. 3 Nov. 1811; *Philena*, b. 23 May 1815, d. unm. 5 Sep. 1839; *Hannah*, b. 26 March 1823, m. Lysander Powers, pub. 21 May 1842; *Sally*, b. 6 May 1825, m. James P. Fay 8 Ap. 1845; *Ruth*, b. 30 May 1827, m. Zenas D. Tinney of Newburg, Me., 6 Nov. 1856; *John Bangs*, b. 30 July 1829: his mother died while he was an infant, and he was adopted by his uncle, Elijah Bangs; in early life he was a clerk in several stores, and rem. to Springfield, Missouri, of which city he was at one time mayor; he served in the Civil War as quartermaster, after which he was postal agent, with headquarters, first at Portland, Oregon, and subsequently at Springfield, Missouri. ICHABOD the f. was a farmer and res. on a part of the homestead, marked "Dea. Dexter" on the R. Map; he was deacon of the church, and d. 11 May 1851; his wife Alice d. 26 June 1830, a. 39.

13. JOSEPH, s. of Job (3), m. Sophia Hunt 13 July 1800, rem. to Westford, Vt., had two chil., who d. in Hk. (names not recorded); one 6 Feb. 1803, a. 2 years and 4 months, the other two days afterwards, a. 4 months.

14. JOHN FREEMAN, prob. s. of Benjamin (6), m. Comfort Haskell 14 Jan. 1812, had *Mary Melisse*, bap. 6 June 1813, and rem. to St. Albans, Vt.

15. JOSEPH DEAN, s. of Eleazar (7), m. Olive Gould 15 Nov. 1818, and had *Joseph Dean*, bap. 18 June 1820, m. Almeda Anderson 8 Mar. 1846; *Alma*, bap. 14 Aug. 1821, d. 4 Feb. 1823; *William Alfred*, bap. 25 Sep. 1823; *Nancy M.*, b. —— 1825, m. Henry B. Gould 6 May 1847, and (2d) Joseph C. Paige 2 Nov. 1865. JOSEPH D. the f. res. on the Pet. road, at the place marked "D. Dexter" on the R. Map. In early life, a serious accident befell him, while blasting rocks, resulting in the loss of one arm and of the sight of both eyes. In utter darkness himself, he became a successful showman to others, and secured a comfortable maintenance for his family.

16. WILLIAMS, s. of Samuel (8), m. Maria, dau. of Israel Knowlton 3 June 1828, and had *Samuel W.*, b. ——, d. 18 Aug. 1830, a. 18 months; *Lucy M.*, b. ——, m. James B. Wiggin, and res. in Cambridge. WILLIAMS the f. d. 12 May 1836; his w. Maria res. in Cambridge.

17. ZENAS H., s. of Ichabod (12), m. Sarah F. Penniman 19 May 1831; she d. 9 Mar. 1837, and he m. Lucinda Wood, 28 Aug, 1837. His chil. were *Zenas H.*, b. 14 Ap. 1832; *George Turell*, b. 20 June 1833; *Harriet J.*, b. —— 1836, m. Pliny Fisk Chandler 5 Mar. 1853, and d. at Warren 5 Ap. 1866, a. 30. ZENAS H. the f. d. 11 Oct. 1851.

18. EDWARD, s. of Ichabod (12), m. Louisa Powers 6 June 1842, and had *Charles E.*, b. —— 1843, d. at Springfield 29 July 1872, a. 29; *Frederick*, b. —— 1845, d. 29 July 1854, a. 9; *Albert H.*, b. ——; *Clara L.*, b. ——; *Willie H.*, b. ——. EDWARD the f. d. 24 Dec. 1862.

ABIGAIL, m. Isaiah Demmon of N. Sal., pub. 24 Dec. 1781. ANNA, m. Jacob Gilbert of N. Br. 7 Oct. 1794. MERCY, m. Paul Ruggles, pub. 28 Nov. 1796. HANNAH, of Royalston, m. Oren Utley, pub. 22 Sep. 1811. AMELIA, m. Marcus J. Marsh 29 June 1823. Mrs. THANKFUL, m. Levi Stevens 18 Oct. 1830. Mrs. LUCINDA, m. Z. F. Shumway 1 Oct. 1856.

DICKINSON, NATHANIEL, m. Elizabeth Fisk 1 Nov. 1764, and had *Lydia*, b. 20 Jan. 1765.

DINSMORE, JOHN (otherwise written Densmore and Dunsmoor), m. Elizabeth Amos 15 Ap. 1765, and had *Amos*, b. 4 Mar. 1766; *John*, b. 9 Feb. 1769; *Eliphalet*, b. 9 Ap. 1771; *Triphosa*, b. 29 July 1774; *Susan*, b. 20 Jan. 1777.

JANE, of Ware, m. Theodorus Doty 30 May 1759. KATHERINE, m. Enoch Badcock of Voluntown, Conn., 15 Dec. 1763. RACHEL, of Ware, d. here 27 Mar. 1814, a. 17.

DOANE, DAVID, by w. Lydia, had *David*, b. 19 Aug. 1752; *Bethiah*, b. 28 June 1754; *Nathan*, b. 15 Aug. 1756; *Molly*, b. 2 June 1759. DAVID the f. prob. came here from Eastham, and perhaps rem. to Bennington about 1761. He was a member of the Separate Church.

DOOLITTLE, BENJAMIN, s. of John of Wallingford (who was b. 14 June 1655, and m. Mary, dau. of John Peck of New Haven, 13 Feb. 1682), and grandson of Abraham (who was b. —— 1619, of New Haven 1640, of Wallingford 1670, and d. 11 Aug. 1690), was b. at Wallingford, Conn., 10 July 1695, grad. Y. C. 1716, first pastor of the church in Northfield 1718, m. Lydia, dau. of Samuel Todd of New Haven, 14 Oct. 1717, and d. 9 Jan. 1748-9. See *Hist. Northfield*, p. 433.

2. LUCIUS, s. of Benjamin (1), b. 16 May 1718, m. Sarah, dau. of Dea. Samuel Smith, and had *Oliver*, b. 3 Dec. 1746; *Charles*, b. 4 Sep. 1748; *Benjamin*, b. 6 Nov. 1751, d. 16 Ap. 1762; *Lydia*, b. 25 Dec. 1753; *Sarah*, b. 25 Dec. 1756, d. 20 Ap. 1773; *Lucius*, b. 11 Nov. 1761; *Benjamin*, b. 12 Jan. 1764; *Jesse*, b. 2 Feb. 1766; *Calvin*, b. — July 1768; *Adrastus*, b. 10 Aug. 1771; *Sarah*, b. 6 July 1773. LUCIUS the f. was an innholder in Northfield.

3. CHARLES, s. of Lucius (2), m. Tabitha, dau. of Daniel Morton of Whateley, 3 Oct. 1771, but had no children. He was a physician in Hk. as early as 1771, and res. at the northerly end of the Common, in a house still standing, marked "S. Hinkley" on the R. Map. To the sad disappointment of his townsmen, who respected him as a man, and had full confidence in his skill as a physician, he d. 12 June 1785, and a large head-stone, of a peculiar pattern, marks the place of his burial in the old cemetery; his w. Tabitha m. Samuel Hinkley, pub. 27 May 1787, and d. 26 Dec. 1816, a. 69.

4. LUCIUS, s. of Lucius (2), m. Esther, dau. of Daniel Morton of Whateley, 12 May 1783, and had *Esther*, b. —— 1785, m. Jacob D. Rand 21 Oct. 1813, and d. 1 or 2 Sep. 1815, a. 30. LUCIUS the f. was also a physician, but very unlike his brother. After an unsuccessful practice in Hk., he rem. to Lyndon, Vt., where he was res. in 1801; before 1819, however, he returned to Hk. utterly bankrupt in fortune and fame. His long-continued habit of intemperance had ruined him; and he, who in early life was too proud to permit his daughter to marry a mechanic,[1] was maintained by the town, for the last dozen years of his life, as a pauper. He d. 1 Dec. 1831.

DOTY, EDWARD (s. of Ellis by w. Eleanor, grandson of Joseph, Jr., and a descendant from that Edward Doty who came in the Mayflower, 1620, and was a party to the first duel fought by Englishmen in N. E.), was b. in Rochester 7 May 1705, m. Mary Andrews 17 Nov. 1726, and had in Roch. *Thomas*, b. 25 Oct. 1727; *Edward*, b. 25 Aug. 1729; *Zurishaddai*, b. 19 Nov. 1731; *John*, b. 7 Aug. 1734; *Theodorus*, b. 25 Dec. 1736; *Betty*, b. 14 Aug. 1739; *Abigail*, b. 30 June 1741, m. Samuel Robinson, Jr., pub. 10 Ap. 1762; *Eleanor*, b. 22 Mar. 1743-4.

2. ZURISHADDAI, s. of Edward (1), m. Mary, dau. of Jonathan Warner, 4 Dec. 1755, and had *John*, b. 12 Sep. 1756; *Moses*, b. 2 July 1758, m. Betsey Webster 20 Sep. 1781; *Ezra*, b. 28 Sep. 1760; *Ellis*, b. 20 Oct. 1762; *Asa*, b. 9 Sep. 1765; *Jonathan*, b. 27 July 1767; *Molly*, b. 10 July 1769; *Betsey*, b. 23 May 1773; *Horatio Gates*, b. 28 Aug. 1779. ZURISHADDAI the f. (ordinarily called Zu) was a blacksmith, whose shop stood near the southwest corner of the old burial-ground. He rem. from Rochester to Hk. before his marriage, and from Hk. to Wilmington, Vt., before 1 Nov. 1785, when he sold his shop to his son *John*.

3. THEODORUS, s. of Edward (1), m. Jane Dinsmore of Ware 30 May 1759. He was a housewright, and resided in New Braintree 1 Aug. 1767.

4. JOHN, s. of Zurishaddai (2), m. Mary, dau. of Paul Mandell, Esq., 19

[1] Jacob D. Rand and Esther Doolittle were published 12 Dec. 1801; but their marriage at that time was prevented by her parents, and they waited the event nearly twelve years.

Sep. 1779, and had *Chauncy*, b. 16 Feb. 1781; *Sukey*, b. 14 Jan. 1783; *Philotheta*, b. 28 Dec. 1784, m. —— Peirce; *Timothy*, b. 26 July 1788; *Patty Woodbridge*, b. 26 Oct. 1789, m. Abraham Wood at Westminster 16 Dec. 1836, and d. 18 Dec. 1837; *Lucia*, b. 14 Feb. 1793, d. 17 Mar. 1803; *Mary Warner*, b. 26 Jan. 1797, m. —— Wood. JOHN the f. was a blacksmith, and res. several years about half a mile eastward from the Common, at the place marked "Mr. Stimpson" on the R. Map; in 1791 he bought two and a quarter acres of land and erected the house now standing near the Common, marked "Mr. Wesson" on the R. Map; this estate he sold 28 Mar. 1805, and rem. to Westminster, where he d. 27 Feb. 1830; his w. Mary d. 26 May 1841, a. 81.

5. CHAUNCY, s. of John (4), m. Isabella, dau. of Seth Hinkley, 4 Mar. 1804, and had *Henry*, b. 25 June 1804. CHAUNCY the f. d. 2 Sep. 1804; his w. Isabella m. Josiah Stockwell, and d. at Vineland, N. J., 9 Aug. 1879, a. nearly 95.

6. TIMOTHY, s. of John (4), m. Susan Cowee 3 Jan. 1833, and had *Person*, b. 15 Oct. 1833. TIMOTHY the f. res. at Westminster, and d. 9 Mar. 1835; his w. Susan m. Milton Joslyn 6 July 1841.

DOW, PLINY, by w. Viah, had *Martha S.*, b. about 1830, m. E. L. B. Wesson 8 Ap. 1853; *William B.*, b. about 1837, m. Abby Root of Enf. 2 Sep. 1873; prob. *Pliny A.* (or *Augustus P.*), b. ——.

DOYLE, DENNIS, m. Julia Dunn, 9 Feb. 1868, and had *Mary Ann*, b. 4 Dec. 1868; *Michael*, b. 24 July 1870, d. 9 Mar. 1871; *Catherine Elizabeth*, b. 2 Jan. 1872.

EAGER, EBENEZER, by w. ——, had *Nancy*, bap. 29 Sep. 1793; his w. d. ——, and he m. Polly Brocklebank of Rindge, N. H., pub. 30 May 1801.

2. PAUL, m. Thankful Watson of N. Br., pub. 22 Oct. 1797, his former w. Joanna having d. 9 Feb. 1797, a. 48.

ABIGAIL, m. Jedediah Dexter 29 Dec. 1798. SALLY, m. Ichabod Dexter 5 May 1805.

EARL, JOHN (otherwise written Earle), m. Eunice, dau. of David Allen, 2 Oct. 1785, and had *Apollos*, b. —— 1786, d. 9 June 1794, a. 8; *Lucius*, b. —— 1788, d. 17 June 1794, a. 6; *Arathusa*, b. —— 1790, d. 9 Feb. 1792, a. 2; *Lewis*, b. about 1793; an infant b. ——, d. 10 Oct. 1795, a. eleven days; an infant b. ——, d. 20 Oct. 1796; an infant b. ——, d. 8 July 1798; *Arathusa*, b. —— 1799, m. Bradford Spooner 30 Nov. 1821, d. 7 Ap. 1872, a. 72 years and 9 months; *Luke*, b. —— 1802; *John F.*, b. —— 1803, m. Chloe Keith of Ward, pub. 12 May 1828, d. at Gr. 8 Aug. 1860, a. nearly 57. JOHN the f. was a farmer, and devoted much attention to the breeding of mules for the Southern market; he res. on the old turnpike, a mile and a half northerly from the Common, at the place marked "L. Earle" on the R. Map, and d. 17 Dec. 1832, a. 70; his w. Eunice d. 10 Sep. 1850, a. 85.

2. JACOB, b. in Berlin, m. Mary, dau. of Luther Burgess, 4 Oct. 1798, and had *Abigail*, b. 18 June 1799; *Ira*, b. 28 Mar. 1801, a carpenter, res. in Leicester and Worcester, d. by accident 30 Ap. 1881; an infant b. ——, d. 11 Aug. 1803, a. 1 month; *Eliza*, b. 29 May 1805, m. Henry Clinton 18 Ap. 1844; *Franklin*, b. about 1808, d. 7 Jan. 1813, a. 5; *Daniel*, b. —— 1810, d. 13 Aug. 1813, a. 3; *Apollos*, b. 22 Aug. 1812; *Benjamin Franklin*, b. 7 Sep. 1814; *James Perkins*, b. 23 Jan. 1817; *Ralph*, b. 10 Sep. 1819; *Mary*, b. 6 July 1823. JACOB the f. was a wheelwright, res. on the turnpike, half a mile easterly from the Common, at the place marked "Mr. Stimpson" on the R. Map, and d. 23 Oct. 1843, a. 72; his w. Mary d. 24 May 1850, a. 70.

3. LUKE, s. of John (1), m. Hannah B., dau. of Elijah Lane, 2 Feb. 1826, and had *Marietta*, b. 23 June 1827; *Harriet Elizabeth*, b. 1 Jan. 1834. LUKE the f. was a farmer and captain of militia; he res. on the homestead several years, but afterwards rem. to Greenwich, where he kept a tavern, and d. 12 Feb. 1865.

EASTMAN, SAMUEL, s. of Ebenezer, b. in Amherst 18 Mar. 1783, m. Sarah Pynchon of Springfield, pub. 25 Nov. 1809, and had, in Hk., *Harriet*, b. 14 Nov. 1810, m. Simeon Newell; *Henry Lyman*, b. 24 May 1812; *John Pynchon*, b. 20 Nov. 1813, d. 30 Oct. 1822; *Sarah*, b. 11 Oct. 1815; *Lucia*, b. 30 May

1817, a teacher, d. unm. in Springf. 22 May 1852; *Charlotte*, b. 15 July 1821, d. unm. in Springf. 29 Mar. 1855; *James Pynchon*, b. 15 Oct. 1825. SAMUEL the f. grad. D. C. 1802, commenced the practice of the law in Hk. in 1807, and after his marriage res. near the Common, at the place marked "Mr. Tupper" on the R. Map, now the res. of Mr. E. L. B. Wesson. Besides a creditable performance of his professional duties, he rendered important service to the town as a teacher of sacred music, and as the leader of the choir in the public sanctuary. He took a lively interest in the education of the young, and was for many years a member of the School Committee.[1] He was town clerk, 1809, selectman four years, 1813–1816, and senator in the General Court, 1819, 1820. The evening of his life was clouded, and was spent chiefly at Springf. He d. at Amherst, while on a visit, 11 Ap. 1864; his w. Sarah d. at Springf.

EDDY, ICHABOD, m. Lucy Cleveland, pub. 24 Dec. 1780. MARTHA, of Shrewsbury, m. Dr. Zephaniah Jenney, 28 Nov. 1799.

EDSON, ABIJAH, of Springf., m. Hannah, dau. of Joseph Ruggles, 10 June 1762, and had *Cushman*, b. 11 Dec. 1762, d. at Charleston, S. C., in 1797 (called "Colonel" in the notice of his death); *Nathaniel*, b. 1 Ap. 1765; *Susanna*, b. 10 Mar. 1767; *Timothy Alden*, b. 7 or 17 Aug. 1769.

EGERY, DANIEL, of Dartmouth, m. Mary Perry of Rochester 21 Nov. 1771; she d. 16 Sep. 1795, a. 52, and he m. Martha —— of Taunton, who d. 15 Feb. 1826, a. 81. His chil., all prob. b. before he rem. to Hk., were *Daniel; Samuel; Sarah*, m. Samuel Steward of Barnard, Vt., 22 Oct. 1789; *Bathsheba*, m. Silas Burbank of Royalton, Vt., 23 Jan. 1792; *William; Thomas*, b. about 1773; *Nathan; Job*, d. 10 Jan. 1796, a. 17 years and 9 months; *Mary; Deborah*, m. Stephen Putnam of Townsend 11 Jan. 1801. DANIEL the f. was a captain in the Revolutionary War, and an adherent of Shays in 1787. About 1777 he rem. from Dart. to Hk., was selectman seven years, and d. 23 Oct. 1801, a. 67, or 69 as inscribed on his head-stone. In his will, dated 22 Oct. 1801, all the before-named chil., except *Job*, are mentioned.

2. *Thomas*, s. of Daniel (1), m. Clarissa, dau. of Ebenezer Washburn, 28 Ap. 1796, and had *Ebenezer Hollis*, b. 22 Feb. 1798; *William Alexis*, b. 12 Ap. 1801, m. Susanna M. ——, and d. at Boston 29 Sep. 1874; *Dolly Washburn*, b. 27 May 1803, m. Beals Thomas 11 Ap. 1824; *Cyrus Washburn*, b. 16 Ap. 1805; *Samuel Perry*, b. 11 May 1807; *Thomas Newhall*, b. 10 Ap. 1809; *Clarissa Electa*, b. — Nov. 1811, d. 12 Dec. 1812; *Mary Perry*, b. 14 Ap. 1813; *Artemas Job*, b. 4 Feb. 1815; *Edwin R.*, b. 10 Sep. 1821. THOMAS the f. was a farmer and res. in the northerly part of the town, at or near the place marked "Capt. Whipple" on the R. Map. He was captain of militia, and a selectman three years. He d. at Dover, N. H., when on a journey, 12 Sep. 1827, a. 54.

3. EBENEZER HOLLIS, s. of Thomas (2), m. Mary Johnson 26 Feb. 1828, and had in Hk. *Ruth Hathaway*, b. 27 Feb. 1829; *Marshall Johnson*, b. 23 Feb. 1831; *Emeline Slade*, b. 9 Feb. 1833; *Mary Lettice*, b. 11 Feb. 1835, d. unm. at Barre 29 Jan. 1873; *Clarissa Washburn*, b. at Barre —— 1845, where she d. unm. 31 Jan. 1873, a. 27 years and 7 months; and perhaps others. EBENEZER H. the f. rem. to Barre, and d. 2 Mar. 1878.

ELDREDGE, DANIEL, m. Prudence, dau. of Capt. Eleazar Warner, 10 Feb. 1767, and had *Silas Warner*, b. 4 Jan. 1768. He rem. to the State of New York.

ELLIS, SETH, had w. Elizabeth and chil., *John*, b. —— 1789; *Elizabeth*, b. —— 1791, m. —— Fay, and d. 18 Nov. 1879, a. 88; *David*, b. —— 1795; and perhaps others. SETH the f. d. 1 Nov. 1842, a. nearly 89; his w. Elizabeth (b. at Bridgewater) d. 7 May 1858, a. 92.

2. JOHN, s. of Seth (1), m. Lucy Burt 15 Ap. 1817; she d. 19 Sep. 1832, a. 42; and he m. Mercy E. Peckham, pub. 4 May 1833; she d. 15 Feb. 1835, a. 35, and he m. Mrs. Sally Peeso of Enf., pub. 31 Oct. 1835; she d. —— and

[1] Personally, I remember with gratitude not only his words of encouragement in my school-boy days, but his substantial aid in the loan of books, and advice in regard to their proper and advantageous use.

he m. Lettice ——, who d. ("accidental") 10 Ap. 1864, a. 62; he d. (apparently in consequence of the same "accident") 9 Ap. 1864, a. 75. No record is found of chil., except one, not named, who d. 17 Mar. 1834, a. 6 months.

3. DAVID, s. of Seth (1), m. Lucy ——, who d. ——, and he m. Elizabeth P. Billings 19 Dec. 1849, who d. at Ware 30 May 1877. He had *Mary Luthera*, b. 25 June 1844. DAVID the f. d. at Ware 28 Mar. 1882.

4. EMORY B., by w. Mary Ann, had *Albert*, b. ——, 1842, d. 22 Sep. 1843; *Frederick E.*, b. 4 Jan. 1846, m. Persis R. Putnam 30 June 1870; *Franklin S.*, b. 6 Mar. 1848, d. 1 Oct. 1849.

5. ABIATHAR P., m. Rebecca A. Rice of Ware, pub. 24 Feb. 1844; she d. ——, and he m. Mary P. ——. His chil. were: *Mary E.*, b. —— 1854, m. Jay W. Powell 14 Mar. 1873; *Stella B.*, b. —— 1860, d. 25 June 1869; *John H.*, b. —— 1862, d. 22 May 1869; *Emma E.*, b. —— 1867, d. 27 May 1869; *Arwin P.*, b. 15 May 1874, d. 25 Oct. 1874.

GAMALIEL, m. Jemima Nye 21 Feb. 1782. BETSEY, m. Reuben Allen 24 Dec. 1812. THOMAS, m. Nabby Burt 11 Ap. 1820. MARY G., m. Claudius B. Orcutt of Amh. 5 Nov. 1839. EBENEZER B., m. Mary W. Stiles of Rindge, N. H., pub. 13 May 1841. SUSAN S., m. James H. Clements of Ware, pub. 24 Nov. 1847. EMERY B., d. 13 June 1882, a. 77.

ELLSWORTH, JOHN, b. at Pownall, Vt., m. Lucretia Thayer, pub. 31 May 1807, and had *Sabrina*, b. 14 Mar. 1808, m. —— Andrews, and d. at Pet. 24 Aug. 1871; *Henry*, b. —— 1813, m. Caroline Augusta, dau. of Jesse Paige, 2 June 1846, and d. at Barre 10 Oct. 1865, a. 52; *John T.*, b. about 1821; *Mary C.*, b. 17 Jan. 1825, m. —— Jameson, and d. at Barre 11 June 1858; *Alexander*, b. 27 Aug. 1827; *Hannah Gardner*, b. 17 Ap. 1830, d. 19 July 1833; and perhaps others. JOHN the f. rem. to Barre.

2. JOHN T., s. of John (1), m. Hannah Maria, dau. of Moses Lawrence, Jr., 1 May 1849, and had *Emory Alexander*, b. 3 Aug. 1852; *John Emerson*, b. 22 June 1854; *Maria L.*, b. 5 Sep. 1856, d. 22 Dec. 1856. JOHN T. the f. rem. to Barre; his w. Hannah M. d. in child-bed 15 Sep. 1856, a. 27.

ELWELL, THOMAS, had w. Lucy, who d. 15 Jan. 1762, and he m. Elizabeth Stratton, pub. 25 Ap. 1762. His chil. b. here were: *John*, bap. 8 Oct. 1758; *Jonas*, b. 16 July 1759; *Mark*, b. 2 Feb. 1763; *Anna*, b. 14 Aug. 1764, m. Noah Moody of S. Hadley 20 June 1787; *David*, b. 1 June 1766. Besides these, *Joshua*, *Moses*, *Thomas*, *Jabez*, *Abigail* (deceased), w. of Moses Olmstead, and *Lucy* Rice, deceased, are named in their father's will, dated 12 July 1790, and proved 6 Feb. 1798. THOMAS the f. was prob. of the Gloucester stock, bought a farm in Hk. 2 May 1758, prob. at or near the place on the west side of Muddy Pond, marked "Mr. Elwell" on the R. Map. He d. 27 Jan. 1798.

2. JABEZ, m. Thankful Clark, 21 Dec. 1769, and had *Jabez Pierce*, b. 28 Feb. 1772; *Asa*, b. 28 May 1774; *Amasa*, b. 27 Jan. 1776; *Stephen*, b. 27 Jan. 1778.

3. MARK, s. of Thomas (1), m. ——, and had *Polly*, b. 8 Ap. 1784; *Lucy*, b. 22 Sep. 1785; *Ruth*, b. 16 Oct. 1788, d. unm. at Barre, 11 Feb. 1871; *Roxana*, b. 26 May 1790. The two younger daughters were sorely afflicted by a cutaneous disease, being covered with minute scales like those of a fish; yet both lived to a good old age. MARK the f. prob. res. on part of the homestead, and d. before 12 July 1790.

4. DAVID, s. of Thomas (1), m. Eunice ——, and had *Betsey*, b. 19 Jan. 1792, d. unm. 15 Aug. 1822; a child b. ——, d. 29 Aug. 1793, a. 6 days; *Thomas*, b. 24 Sep. 1794; *David* (twin), b. 14 May 1797, accidentally killed by the bursting of a gun 17 Oct. 1817; *Noah* (twin), b. 14 May 1797; *Chester*, b. 29 Jan. 1802; *Eunice M.*, b. ——, m. Chauncy R. Shaw of Bel. 24 May 1831. DAVID the f. prob. res. on part of the homestead. He d. 15 Dec. 1848, a. 82; his w. Eunice d. 29 Dec. 1858, a. 91.

5. THOMAS, s. of David (4), m. Susanna N., dau. of Samuel L. Robinson, 25 Ap. 1819; she d. 15 or 16 Nov. 1822, a. 28, and he m. her sister, Adeline Robinson, 19 Oct. 1823; she d. 9 Dec. 1837, a. 34, and he m. Lucy Gilbert of Brk., pub. 15 Feb. 1838. No record is found of children. He d. 27 Sep. 1840, and his w. Lucy m. Elijah Bangs, pub. 10 May 1845.

6. NOAH, s. of David (4), m. Martha Berry 11 July 1819; she d. 15 Oct. 1821, a. 22, and he m. Louisa Bliss of Ludlow, pub. 20 Aug. 1822. No record is found of the birth of his chil., but the following imperfect account is gathered from the records of marriages and deaths: *Charlotte*, b. —— 1823, d. unm. 19 Aug. 1833, a. 10; *Hannah M.*, b. —— 1824, m. —— Willis, d. in Ware 24 Aug. 1877, a. 54; *Chester*, b. —— 1828, d. 2 Nov. 1855, a. 27; *Lucy A.*, b. —— 1830, m. Charles E. Smith of W. Brk. 25 Dec. 1850; *Charlotte F.*, b. —— 1834, d. unm. 16 Aug. 1851, a. 17; *Henry B.*, b. —— 1836, d. 6 Ap. 1859, a. 23; *Albert H.*, b. —— 1839, d. 25 Ap. 1858, a. 19. LOUISA B. the mother d. 15 Nov. 1845, a. 45.

7. DAVID (2d), m. Clara Paige Jenney 7 Sep. 1842, and had *Chiron Jenney*, b. 16 Jan. 1845; *William Y.*, b. 30 Nov. 1846, d. 27 Nov. 1847.

JOSHUA, m. Abigail Jones of Killingly, Conn., 2 Oct. 1765. REBECCA, m. Jabez Pike 7 Mar. 1791. STILLMAN, m. Sophia Bartlett 28 Jan. 1821.

EMMONS, ALONZO, m. Abigail, dau. of Moses Lawrence, 3 Dec. 1838; she d. 7 Mar. 1864, a. 64. Perhaps the two following were their chil.: *Marcus A.*, b. —— 1840, a soldier, d. near Bethesda Church, 2 June 1864, a. 24; *Edward Robert*, b. about 1842.

2. EDWARD ROBERT, perhaps s. of Alonzo (1), m. Caroline J. Towne of Gr. 30 Ap. 1863, and had *Leora*, b. 19 Jan. 1864; *Marcus Edwin*, b. 19 Sep. 1865; *Charles Frederick*, b. 4 Sep. 1867; *Herbert Elmer*, b. 18 Sep. 1869; *Mabel Maria*, b. 6 May 1871.

LOIS, m. Andrew Powers 27 Oct. 1740. THOMAS, m. Sarah Wheeler 30 Ap. 1741. SOLOMON, of Gr., m. Mary Marsh 31 Jan. 1754. NOAH, of Gr., m. Mary Farr 25 May 1758. ROBERT, m. Annis Hair, pub. 8 Nov. 1790.

ESTABROOK, BENJAMIN (generally called "Brooks"), m. Alice, widow of Luther Burgess, 12 Oct. 1787; she d. 3 May 1807, a. 57, and he m. Mrs. Patty Howe of Rut., pub. 14 Jan. 1817. His chil. were *Hannah*, b. 14 Jan. 1788, d. unm. 24 May 1811; *Arathusa*, b. 25 Oct. 1789, m. David Whipple 1 Dec. 1836. BENJAMIN the f. was a farmer, b. in Rutland 1750, res. on the old turnpike, at the place marked "Mr. Browning" on the R. Map, and d. 14 Nov. 1828, a. 80, according to the town record, or 76, as inscribed on his head-stone,—but both wrong, if date of birth be correctly stated in Reed's *Hist. Rutland*, p. 159.

ASA, m. Sally Hinds of Brk., pub. 1 Aug. 1801.

EVANS, LAERTES, m. Lydia Totman 2 June 1833; she d. 23 Oct. 1838, a. 25.

FAIRBANKS, CALVIN, m. Jenny Ayers 24 June 1776, and had *Patty*, b. 11 Ap. 1777; *Calvin*, bap. 21 Feb. 1779, d. young; *Calvin*, bap. 23 Ap. 1780. CALVIN the f. rem. to Barnard, Vt.

LYMAN (adult), bap. 25 June 1820. MARY, m. Joel Hagar 27 Ap. 1824. CAROLINE, m. Winthrop Jamerson, pub. 27 Mar. 1826.

FARR, THOMAS, prob. from Stow or Littleton, rem. to Hk. before Sep. 1742, where his w. Elizabeth was admitted to the church, but no further trace of him is found.

2. THOMAS, JR., prob. s. of Thomas (1) and w. Hannah, were adm. to the church 19 Dec. 1742. Their chil. were: *Ruhamah*, bap. 19 Dec. 1742; *Lydia*, bap. 16 June 1745; *Hannah*, bap. 29 May 1748; *Thomas*, bap. 5 Nov. 1752; *Samuel*, bap. 1 June 1755. THOMAS the f. res. near Gilbertville, his farm being bounded on the east by Ware River.

3. JONATHAN, prob. s. of Thomas (1), m. Mary, dau. of John Wells, 5 June 1751; she d. ——, and he m. Mercy, prob. dau. of Thomas Winslow, 19 Jan. 1757. His chil. were: *William*, b. 5 Mar. 1752; *Jonathan*, bap. 14 Ap. 1754; *Joshua*, b. 23 Sep. 1757; *Amos*, b. 9 Mar. 1759; *Mary*, b. 18 Oct. 1760; *Moses*, b. 18 May 1762; *Mercy*, bap. 1 Jan. 1764; *Asahel*, bap. 23 Mar. 1766. His homestead, which he sold to Isaac Thomas 27 Ap. 1763, was bounded east on Ware River, south on land of Thomas Farr, and west on the highway.

4. JONATHAN, JR., parentage not ascertained, m. Lucy, dau. of Deac. James Fay, 27 Oct. 1763, and had *Solomon*, b. 3 Mar. 1764; *Anna*, b. 27 Jan.

1766, d. unm. 31 July 1844, having been a pauper nearly or quite half a century.

KEZIA, m. John Wells 14 Dec. 1748. MARY, m. Noah Emmons of Gr. 25 May 1758. THOMAS, m. Hannah Powers of Littleton, pub. 5 Aug. 1758. JOSHUA, b. at Littleton, d. in the army, 1756, a. 21.

FASSETT, JOHN (of Bedford in 1753), s. of Josiah, was b. at Billerica 1 Ap. 1720, bought a farm in Hk., near Barre, 7 Mar. 1753, and prob. took immediate possession; this estate he sold to Jonathan Nye, Jr., 30 Ap. 1762, describing himself in the deed as of Hk., but he had prob. rem. previously[1] to Bennington, Vt., of which town he was one of the earliest and most energetic inhabitants. He was prob. elected deacon of the Separate Church in Hk.; he was also elected captain of the first military company organized in Bennington, 1764. He was a representative in the first General Assembly in Vermont, 1778, and in the same year was elected judge of probate for Bennington District. It is stated by Rev. Mr. Jennings, in his *Memorials of a Century*, that he had nine children: *Sarah* (who m. Dr. Jonas Fay in Hk. 1 May 1760), *John*, *Jonathan*, *David*, *Nathan*, *Amos*, *Mary* (who m. Hon. Jonathan Robinson), *Benjamin*, and *Hannah*. Of these I find the birth of only two recorded in Hk.: *Mary*, b. 19 Nov. 1754; *Benjamin*, b. 21 Mar. 1757. JOHN the f. d. at Bennington, 12 Aug. 1794.

2. JOHN, s. of John (1), rem. with his father to Bennington 1761, thence to Arlington 1777, and again to Cambridge 1784, in all which towns he held a conspicuous rank. "Few men were more constantly in public service than John Fassett, Jr. He was lieutenant in Warner's first regiment in 1775, and captain in Warner's second in 1776. In 1777 he was one of the commissioners of sequestration, and with Gov. Chittenden and Matthew Lyon successful in subduing the Tories of Arlington. He was elected representative of Arlington in the General Assembly for 1778 and 1779, and for Cambridge in 1787, 1788, 1790, and 1791, though in 1779, 1787, 1788, 1790, and 1791 he was also elected councillor. He served in each office portions of the time. He was a member of the council in 1779 and until 1795 (with the exception of 1786), fifteen years. He was judge of the Superior Court from its organization in 1778 until 1786, eight years, and chief judge of Chittenden county court from 1787 until 1794, seven years."[2]

3. JONATHAN, s. of John (1), rem. to Ben. with his father in 1761, and was representative of that town in 1782; he also represented Pittsford in the General Assembly 1778.[3] It is worthy of note that the father and two sons held seats together in the first General Assembly of Vermont.

4. AMOS, s. of John (1), rem. to Ben. with his father in 1761, and thence to Cambridge in 1784; he "was assistant judge for several years."[4]

5. BENJAMIN, s. of John (1), rem. to Ben. with his father in 1761, and was colonel of militia. "He was a commissary in the war of the Revolution, and served in other capacities in civil and military life."[5]

FAY, JOHN, b. in England about 1648, came to N. E. in the Speedwell, which arrived at Boston 27 June 1656; he became an inhabitant of Marlborough, where he m. Mary, dau. of Thomas Brigham of Cambridge, by whom he had four chil.; and, 5 July 1678, m. Susanna, wid. of Joseph Morse, by whom he had four chil., and d. 5 Dec. 1690.

2. JOHN, s. and eldest child of John (1), b. 30 Nov. 1669, m. Elizabeth Wellington; she d. and he m. Levinah Brigham 16 Dec. 1729. His chil. were: *Bathsheba*, b. 1 Jan. 1693; m. John Pratt 4 Jan. 1715–16; *Eunice*, b. 2 June 1696, m. Isaac Pratt 17 Ap. 1721; *Mary*, b. 29 Sep. 1698, d. 20 Nov. 1704; *John*, b. 5 Dec. 1700, m. Hannah Child 17 Ap. 1721; *Lydia*, b. —— 1702;

[1] "Deacon John Fassett was born April 1, 1720. He was one of the second company of settlers in Bennington in 1761. At his house the first town-meeting was held in March, 1762." Jennings' *Memorials of a Century*, p. 224.

[2] *Records of Governor and Council of Vermont*, ii. 1.

[3] Deming's *Catalogue of the Principal Officers of Vermont*.

[4] *Records of Governor and Council of Vermont*, ii. 132.

[5] Jennings' *Memorials of a Century*, p. 225.

Dinah, b. 5 Sep. 1705, m. David Goodnow —— 1722; *James*, b. 27 Dec. 1707; *Mehetabel*, b. 18 June 1710; *Benjamin*, b. 15 Aug. 1712, m. Martha ——; *Stephen*, b. 5 May 1715. JOHN the f. res. in that part of Marlborough which was incorporated as Westborough, in which town he held the principal offices, and d. 5 Jan. 1747.

3. JAMES, s. of John (2), m. Lydia Child of Watertown 9 Dec. 1727; she d. at Hk., and he m. Prudence, wid. of Ebenezer Whipple, pub. 13 Sep. 1760. His chil. were: *Daniel*, b. —— 1728; *Lydia*, b. —— 1730, m. Amaziah Spooner 22 Feb. 1749-50, d. 10 Aug. 1817, a. 87; *James*, b. ——; *Lucy*, b. ——, m. Jonathan Farr, Jr., 27 Oct. 1763; *Mehetabel*, b. ——, m. Benjamin Rogers 10 Sep. 1760; *Reuben*, b. 29 Nov. 1739; *Isaac*, b. ——; *Elizabeth*, b. ——, perhaps m. Benjamin Ruggles 3d, 26 Nov. 1766; *Hannah*, b. 23 Feb. 1749, at Hk., m. James Rogers 23 Nov. 1768, d. 18 Oct. 1835, a. 86. JAMES the f. owned land in Hk. as early as 1735, but prob. remained in Westboro' until after 1739, when his s. *Reuben* was b. there; he then rem. to Grafton, and was there 25 Sep. 1746, when he bought of Benjamin Smith the farm in Hk., which became his homestead; and came here before 23 Feb. 1749, when his dau. *Hannah* was born. In his will, 13 July 1774, he names all his chil. except *Lucy*, to whose son Solomon Farr and dau. Lydia Farr legacies are given. He resided on the old River road, at the place marked "A. Rice" on the R. Map. He was a farmer, a bone-setter, and a deacon of the Separate Church. He was denounced as a Tory, but forgiven, and died in peace 12 June 1777, a. nearly 70.

4. STEPHEN, s. of John (2), was the father of a very remarkable family, and was himself a man of mark. He m. Ruth Child 7 Mar. 1734, and had *John*, b. 23 Dec. 1734; *Jonas*, b. 28 Jan. 1736-7; *Stephen*, b. 19 Feb. 1738-9; *Ruth*, b. 12 May 1741; *Mary*, b. 16 Oct. 1743, m. Moses Robinson (judge, U. S. senator, and governor), pub. 25 July 1762, d. 12 Feb. 1801; *Beulah*, b. 29 Jan. 1745-6, m. Samuel Billings (major) 28 June 1764, d. 18 Sep. 1833; *Elijah*, b. 5 Mar. 1747-8; *Benjamin*, b. 22 Nov. 1750; *Joseph*, b. 11 Sep. 1753; *Sarah*, b. 4 July 1757, m. David Robinson (general, sheriff, and U. S. marshal), d. 25 Jan. 1801; *David*, b. about 1762. STEPHEN the f. bought a farm of 300 acres, bordering on the west side of Muddy Pond, 6 Dec. 1749, but soon rem. to the place afterwards owned and occupied by Col. Stephen Rice, on the old turnpike, marked "C. Paige" on the R. Map. He was selectman four years, assessor five years, innholder from 1754 to 1763, and retailer (perhaps innholder also) in 1764 and 1765. He was also prob. captain of militia, as he was known by that title during his residence in Vermont, and was so described on his headstone. In 1766 he rem. to Bennington and became landlord of the Green Mountain Tavern, afterwards so celebrated as the "Catamount Tavern."[5] This house was the general headquarters of the controlling spirits during the long contest with New York, and also during the Revolutionary War, and among those spirits Capt. Fay was not the least active. When it was determined in 1772, during the New York controversy, to send special messengers to confer with Governor Tryon, Capt. Fay and his son, Dr. Jonas Fay, were selected as the messengers. During the Revolution he was constantly active, and rendered efficient service in a civil capacity; and in the clash of arms he was represented by his sons. It is said that five of his sons were engaged in the Bennington Battle, 16 Aug. 1777, the eldest of whom was killed. It is matter of authentic history, that when the father was informed that he had been unfortunate in respect to one of his sons, he exclaimed: "What! has he misbehaved? did he desert his post, or run from the charge?" On being told that his son was dead, he bowed his head, saying: "I thank God that I had a son who was willing to give his life for his country." Capt. Fay lived to see the arms of his country triumphant, but did not witness the establishment of peace. He d. 17 May 1781; his w. Ruth attained the age of 88 years.

5. DANIEL, s. of James (3), m. Elizabeth, dau. of Deac. Daniel Spooner, 18

1 "The place where, in Bennington, the councils of the leaders were held — the Council of Safety — was the Green Mountain Tavern, kept by Capt. Stephen Fay. It had for its sign the stuffed skin of a catamount, with teeth grinning toward New York, and hence came to be called the Catamount Tavern." Jennings' *Memorials of a Century*, p. 143.

May 1749; she d. 24 Nov. 1756, a. 25, and he m. Mary Crosby 10 Mar. 1757. He had seventeen children: *Timothy*, b. 9 July 1750; *Daniel*, b. 14 Dec. 1752; *Jedediah*, b. 4 June 1755, m. Jerusha Aiken 12 Nov. 1778, was a physician several years in Hk., but no record is found of chil. or of his death; *Moses*, b. 5 Jan. 1758, d. young; *Aaron*, b. 1 Aug. 1759, m. Molly Hatch 19 Dec. 1782, rem. to Barnard, Vt.; *Elizabeth*, b. 2 Aug. 1761, m. Joseph Hunt 16 May 1779; *Moses*, b. 30 June 1763, m. Sally Hedge 24 Feb. 1788, rem. to Barnard; *Sarah*, b. 28 Mar. 1765, m. John Hunt 1 Oct. 1784; *Eliakim*, b. 1 Mar. 1767, m. Hannah, dau. of Capt. Ebenezer Cox, 5 Sep. 1790, rem. to Barnard; *David*, b. 25 July 1769; *Jonathan*, b. 22 Mar. 1771, d. young; *Mary*, b. 2 May 1772; *Jonathan*, b. 28 Ap. 1774; *Joseph*, b. 26 Dec. 1775, rem. to Rutland, Vt., d. in Hk. 15 Mar. 1814; *Florina*, b. 30 Nov. 1777; *Benjamin*, b. 28 Aug. 1779, rem. to Rutland, Vt.; *Hannah*, b. 28 Feb. 1782, m. Samuel Parker 29 Jan. 1801, and d. at Milford 17 June 1869. DANIEL the f. d. 28 Feb. 1815.

6. JAMES, s. of James (3), m. Mary, prob. dau. of Seth Winslow, 18 Mar. 1756, and had *Paul*, b. 30 Dec. 1756; *Barnabas*, b. 30 Oct. 1758; *Lydia*, b. 14 July 1761; *Mehetable*, b. 12 July 1763; *Mary*, b. 21 Jan. 1766, d. young; *Hannah*, b. 17 May 1768; *Mary*, b. 12 Ap. 1770.

7. REUBEN, s. of James (3), m. Elizabeth, dau. of William Perkins, 11 June 1767, and had *Susanna*, b. 14 Oct. 1767, m. Leonard Burt of Westminster, Vt., 19 Dec. 1790; *Jonas*, b. 14 Nov. 1768; *Jonathan*, b. 4 Dec. 1769; *William*, b. 17 July 1771; *Moses*, b. 13 Feb. 1773; *Betty*, b. 13 Oct. 1774, m. James Babbitt of Gr., 27 Nov. 1800; *Josiah*, b. 26 Feb. 1776. REUBEN the f. d. 26 Oct. 1800; his w. Elizabeth d. 15 Jan. 1803, a. 53.

8. ISAAC, s. of James (3), m. Kezia Doane 22 Nov. 1764, and had *Charles*, b. 18 Aug. 1765; *Lydia*, b. 7 June 1769; *John*, b. 9 Feb. 1773; *Cyrus*, b. 20 Feb. 1776; *Asa*, b. 5 Oct. 1777; *Cynthia*, b. 23 Oct. 1779. He bought the homestead 1774, but res. on the adjoining farm, marked "E. Trow" on the R. Map.

9. JOHN, s. of Stephen (4), m. Mary Fisk of Sturbridge, pub. 22 Oct. 1757, and had *Susanna*, b. 4 Dec. 1758; *Nathan*, b. 15 Nov. 1760; *Caleb*, b. 20 Oct. 1762; *Helena*, b. 7 May 1766; *John*, b. 1 May 1768; *Henry Fisk*, b. 26 Aug. 1770; *Joseph*, b. —— 1772, d. 14 Sep. 1777, a. 5; *Hiram*, b. —— 1775, d. 24 Aug. 1777, a. 2. JOHN the f. rem. to Bennington about 1772, and was killed in battle 16 Aug. 1777;[1] his w. Mary survived him only fifteen days, dying 31 Aug. 1777, a. 38; their two younger chil. also d. within a month after the father's death.

10. JONAS, s. of Stephen (4), m. Sarah, dau. of John Fassett, 1 May 1760; she d. after he rem. to Bennington, and he m. in Hk. Lydia, widow of Dr. Challis Safford, and dau. of Jonathan Warner, 20 Nov. 1777. His chil., b. in Hk., were *Josiah*, b. 1 May 1761; *Ruth*, b. 2 May 1763; *Polly*, b. 12 Jan. 1765. He had also in Bennington *Lydia*, who m. Uriah Edgerton, Esq.; *Sarah*, m. Henry Hopkins; and twin sons, *Ethan Allen* and *Heman Allen*. JONAS the f. was a man of extraordinary energy and versatility of talent. In 1756 he was clerk of the company commanded by Capt. Samuel Robinson in the French War, and was then styled "cordwinder." In 1761 he was called "ensign" on the town records. His taste, however, was rather civil than martial, and political than mechanical. He studied medicine, and practised the healing art for several years here, and also taught school, res. at the place marked "Mr. Wesson" on the R. Map. On his removal to Bennington about 1768, he at once became conspicuous both as a physician and as a leading politician. The following is a brief summary of his public services: "In 1772,

[1] At the Bennington Battle. "He was fighting behind a tree. His last words, as he raised his musket to fire once more at the enemy, were, 'I feel that I am fighting in a good cause.' And as his eye ran along the barrel, taking aim, his head just exposed from behind the tree, a ball struck him in the very centre of his forehead, and he fell with his gun undischarged. Quick as lightning ran the cry over the ranks of his townsmen, 'John Fay is shot!' Maddened to fury, they sprang from behind the trees, fired their guns in the very faces of the foe, and, clubbing the breeches, leaped over the breastwork with an impulse of onset nothing mortal could resist." Jennings' *Memorials of a Century*, p. 255.

when Gov. Tryon invited the people of Bennington to send agents to New York to inform him of the grounds of their complaint, he, with his father, was appointed for that purpose. He was clerk to the convention of settlers that met in 1774, and resolved to defend by force Allen, Warner, and others, who were threatened with outlawry and death by the New York Assembly, and as such clerk certified their proceedings for publication. At the age of nineteen he had served in the French War during the campaign of 1756 at Fort Edward and Lake George, as clerk of Capt. Samuel Robinson's company of Massachusetts troops, and he served as surgeon in the expedition under Allen at the capture of Ticonderoga. He was continued in that position by the Committee of the Massachusetts Congress who were sent to the Lake in July 1775, and also appointed by them to muster the troops as they arrived for the defence of that post. He was also surgeon for a time to Col. Warner's regiment. In January, 1776, he was clerk to the convention at Dorset, that petitioned Congress to be allowed to serve in the common cause of the country as inhabitants of the New Hampshire Grants, and not under New York, and also of that held at the same place in July following. He was a member of the convention which met at Westminster in January, 1777, and declared Vermont to be an independent State, and was appointed chairman of a committee to draw up a declaration and petition announcing the fact, and their reasons for it, to Congress, of which declaration and petition he was the draughtsman and author. He was secretary to the convention that formed the Constitution of the State in July, 1777, and was one of the Council of Safety[1] then appointed to administer the affairs of the State, until the Assembly, provided for by the constitution, should meet; was a member of the State Council for seven years from 1778; a judge of the Supreme Court in 1782; judge of probate from 1782 to 1787; and he attended the Continental Congress at Philadelphia as the agent of the State, under appointments made in Jan. 1777, Oct. 1779, June 1781, and Feb. 1782. Dr. Fay was a man of extensive general information, decided in his opinions, and bold and determined in maintaining them. His education was such as to enable him to draw with skill and ability the public papers of the day, of many of which, besides the Declaration of Independence before mentioned, he was the reputed author. In 1780, he, in conjunction with Ethan Allen, prepared and published, in their joint names, a pamphlet of thirty pages, on the New Hampshire and New York controversy, which was printed at Hartford, Conn. . . . Dr. Fay resided in Bennington, in a house that stood on the Blue Hill, a mile south of the meeting-house, until after the year 1800, when he removed to Charlotte for a few years, and afterwards to Pawlet, but returned again to Bennington, where he died March 6, 1818, aged 82."[2]

11. Stephen, s. of Stephen (4), m. Susan Fisk of Sturbridge, pub. 18 Ap. 1762, but no record is found of children. His life seems to have been less eventful than that of his brothers. It is said that he d. at Hk. about 1804.

12. Elijah, s. of Stephen (4), rem. to Bennington with his father, m. Deborah Lawrence, and d. 5 July 1835. He was engaged, with three of his brothers, in the Bennington Battle.

13. Benjamin, s. of Stephen (4), rem. to Bennington with his father, and "was the first sheriff in the county and State." He served in that office "from March 26, 1778, until Oct. 1781."[3] He m. Sarah, dau. of Capt. Samuel Robinson, and d. 19 June, 1786, at the early age of 35 years. His son *Samuel*, b. 16 Aug. 1772, and d. 25 Dec. 1863, res. in the old homestead, the "Catamount Tavern," was deputy sheriff sixteen years, and sheriff twelve years, up to the year 1823.

[1] It was this Council of Safety, assembled in the "Catamount Tavern" a month later, on the day of the Bennington battle, to which Professor Bartlett alluded in his centennial oration, August 16, 1877: "There was a noted tavern in the town, and there were gathered there Ira Allen, Thomas Chittenden, Jonas Fay, and their staunch comrades. There was one catamount on the sign-post, and twelve catamounts within." Gov. Hall, in his *History of Vermont* says: "The most active members of the council, as shewn by such minutes of its proceedings as have been preserved, were Thomas Chittenden, president of the body; Jonas Fay, vice president; Ira Allen, secretary; and Nathan Clark, Paul Spooner, and Moses Robinson." Fay, Spooner, and Robinson, it may be added, were Hardwick men.

[2] *Vermont Hist. Mag.*, i. 171, 172.

[3] Jennings' *Memorials of a Century*, p. 258.

14. Joseph, s. of Stephen (4), went "to Bennington, a member of his father's family in 1766. He was secretary to the Council of Safety and of the State Council from Sep. 1777 to 1784, and Secretary of State from 1778 to 1781. He was the associate of Ira Allen in conducting the famous negotiation with Gen. Haldimand, by which the operations of the enemy were paralyzed, and the northern frontier protected from invasion during the three last years of the Revolutionary struggle. He was a man of very respectable talents and acquirements, of fine personal appearance and agreeable manners, and well calculated to manage such a diplomatic adventure with adroitness and ability." [1] He m. Margaret, dau. of Rev. Jedediah Dewey, rem. to the city of New York in 1794, and d. there in October 1803, leaving posterity, of whom Theodore S. Fay, the author, was a representative.

15. David, s. of Stephen (4), was a "fifer" in the Battle of Bennington, then about fifteen years old. He was afterwards a lawyer, admitted to the bar in June 1794, was State attorney four years before 1801, United States attorney under President Jefferson, judge of the Supreme Court 1809 to 1813, and judge of probate 1819, 1820. He m. Mary, dau. of John Staniford of Windham, Conn., and d. 5 June 1827.

16. Timothy, s. of Daniel (5), m. Olive Leonard 23 Mar. 1775; she d. ——, and he m. Hannah, widow of Peter Bassett, and dau. of —— Lindsey, 7 Dec. 1780. His chil. were: *Leonard*, b. 21 Nov. 1775; *Olive*, b. 25 Mar. 1782, m. Josiah C. Chandler 24 Nov. 1799; *Bassett*, b. 3 Dec. 1783; *Lindsey*, b. 28 Sep. 1786; *Apollos*, b. 30 May 1789; *Hannah*, b. 12 Jan. 1792, m. James Perkins 23 Mar. 1837, d. s. p. 24 Mar. 1855; *Timothy*, b. 18 June 1794; *Daniel*, b. 22 Feb. 1797, d. unm. 22 June 1847. Timothy the f. was a farmer, res. on the old turnpike, at the place marked "A. Fay" on the R. Map, and d. 17 June 1831; his w. Hannah d. 2 June 1820, a. 63.

17. Daniel, s. of Daniel (5), m. Mary, d. of Col. Timothy Paige, 23 Aug. 1778, and had (born here), *Mary*, b. 10 Mar. 1779, m. Rev. Philander Chase, Bishop, successively, of Ohio and of Illinois, was mother of Rev. Philander Chase, Jr., and Rev. Dudley Chase, and d. at Worthington, O., 5 May 1818; *Nancy*, b. 25 Mar. 1781, m. Nathaniel Evans, d. at Middlebury, O., 12 July 1825; *Elizabeth*, b. 3 Sep. 1783, m. B. Batchelder, res. in Bethel, Vt., where she d. 4 May 1831 (her dau., Mary C., m. Rev. Henry Caswall, D. D., an English clergyman of the Episcopal Church, was several years in England, returned, and, since the death of her husband, has res. at Franklin, Pa., and Welland, Canada; *Jedediah*, b. 30 Jan. 1786, a physician in Owego, N. Y., m. Caroline Roberts, 1812, and d. 23 Ap. 1848, leaving several children; his w. Caroline d. 1 Mar. 1879, a. 84; *Timothy Paige*, b. 9 May 1788, a physician in Stockbridge, Vt., m. Eunice Denison 16 Dec. 1811, had seven chil., and d. 29 Aug. 1865 (his second dau., Mary, m. Rev. T. S. Hubbard of Stockbridge, and the third, Emily, m. H. D. Morgan, Esq.); *Almira*, b. 28 July 1790, d. unm. at Steubenville, O., 29 Oct. 1824; *Daniel*, b. 26 Oct. 1792, d. 16 Mar. 1796; (also in Bethel) *Cyrus Paige*, b. 17 Feb. 1796, a merchant in Columbus, O., d. 2 Oct. 1872, leaving posterity; *Oren*, b. 17 Dec. 1798, d. at New Madrid, Mo. — Sep. 1834. Daniel the f. was a mason, rem. about 1795 to Bethel, Vt., and thence to Randolph, Vt., where he d. 21 June 1810; his w. Mary d. at the house of her son, Dr. Fay, in Stockbridge, 27 Mar. 1834, a. 74.

18. Bassett, s. of Timothy (16), m. Nancy, dau. of Jesse Paige, 22 Jan. 1811, and had *Francis Paige*, b. 28 Nov. 1811, d. 27 Sep. 1816; *William* b. 17 Jan. 1814, d. 6 June 1816; *Mary Alathea*, b. 22 Ap. 1816; *Henry*, b. 9 Mar. 1818; *Eliza Jane*, b. 14 Aug. 1820; *William Bassett*, b. 9 Aug. 1824; *Sarah Ruggles*, b. — Nov. 1827, d. 20 Feb. 1828, a. 11 weeks; *George Breckenridge*, bap. 27 Dec. 1829. Bassett the f. was a carpenter, and resided on Mandell Hill, at the place marked "B. Fay" on the R. Map. He rem. to Indiana about 1838.

19. Lindsey, s. of Timothy (16), m. Esther Jenney Hunt 20 Mar. 1810, and had *Hiram*, b. 19 Oct. 1811; *Horace*, b. 21 Oct. 1813; *John Hunt*, b. 26 July 1815. Lindsey the f. rem. with his family many years ago.

[1] *Vermont Hist. Mag.*, i. 172.

20. APOLLOS, s. of Timothy (16), m. Celia, dau. of Eli Hudson, 7 July 1817, and had a child b. ——, d. 25 Feb. 1819 ; *Harriet*, b. 12 Ap. 1822, m. Joseph W. Powers 23 May 1844 ; *Sarah Perkins*, b. 27 Dec. 1826, m. Marshall P. Nye 16 Nov. 1848, d. 13 Sep. 1851. APOLLOS the f. was a farmer, res. on the homestead, and d. 24 Jan. 1864 ; his w. Celia d. 4 Sep. 1858, a. 68.

21. TIMOTHY, s. of Timothy (16), m. Mary H. Hammond 7 Nov. 1822 ; she d. 12 July 1841, and he m. Mrs. Mary J. Richmond 20 Ap. 1842. His chil. were: *James Perkins*, b. 2 Dec. 1823 ; *Rhoda Paige*, b. 9 Sept. 1825, d. 7 Jan. 1832; *Stephen Hammond*, b. 22 Dec. 1827, d. 5 Sep. 1846; *Mary Maria*, b. 6 Oct. 1829, d. unm. 19 Dec. 1856; *John Lindsey*, b. 4 Mar. 1832, d. 5 Ap. 1832; *Rhoda Jane*, b. 26 July, 1833, m. Wilder U. Barnes 20 Ap. 1864 ; *Larrissa Lomira*, b. 10 Aug. 1837 ; *Emily Augusta*, b. 16 July 1839, m. George Woods 6 Feb. 1862 ; *Mercy Ann*, b. 29 May 1843, m. Charles Pepper 7 Aug. 1862 ; *Franklin Hammond*, b. 2 Sep. 1848, m. Della A. Wheeler 6 Nov. 1873 ; *Sarah Eliza*, b. 24 June 1851, m. Charles E. Wilson 28 June 1876. TIMOTHY the f. was a farmer, selectman one year, member of the school committee six years, taught school many years, res. on the Barre road, at the place erroneously marked " F. Fay " on the R. Map, and d. 14 Ap. 1872 ; his w. Mary J. d. 11 Aug. 1855, a. 46 or 47.

22. JAMES P., s. of Timothy (21), m. Sally, dau. of Ichabod Dexter, 8 Ap. 1845, and had *George Elmer*, b. 21 Ap. 1852, d. 20 Oct. 1864; *John Hammond*, b. 28 Feb. 1854. JAMES P. the f. is a farmer, res. on the homestead, and has rendered public service as teacher of schools, member of the school committee, assessor, justice of the peace, and trial justice.

23. JOHN H., s. of James P. (22), m. Mary R. Slaney 15 Aug. 1877, and had *George John*, b. 8 Jan. 1879 ; *James*, b. 23 Sep. 1881, d. 24 Sep. 1881.

24. DANIEL H., of Southborough, m. Sarah R. Smith 1 Ap. 1841, and had (born here) *Sarah Elizabeth*, b. 20 Jan. 1842, d. unm. 23 Sep. 1874.

TABITHA, of Sturbridge, m. William Maccoye at Brk. 22 Nov. 1744. DAPHNE, m. Otis Cobb, pub. 18 July 1802. Rev. BARNABAS M., m. Louisa M. Mills of Morristown, N. J., pub. 27 Aug. 1842. JAMES, m. Sarah Horr of Pel., pub. 10 Mar. 1843. NATHAN, s. of Thomas, b. in Brimfield, d. 26 Dec. 1873, a. 88.

FIELD, PATRICK, by w. Abigail, had *Thomas*, bap. 28 Feb. 1768.

2. GEORGE, m. Prudence, dau. of Ebenezer Whipple, 13 Ap. 1775, and had *Robert*, b. 5 Jan. 1777 ; *Polly*, b. 18 Ap. 1778, m. Pliny Lawton 22 Feb. 1801 ; *John*, b. 5 Jan. 1780, grad. W. C. 1807, studied divinity ; with the exception of a pastorate at North Wrentham from 1 May 1816 to 15 June 1819, he was generally engaged as a missionary in Ohio ; the latter part of his life was spent at the South, where he preached and taught school ; he d. near Natchez, Miss., 7 Aug. 1827 ; *Ebenezer*, b. 9 Aug. 1783, prob. d. young ; *Fanny*, b. 13 July 1785, m. Carey Howard 26 Nov. 1813 ; *Joseph*, b. about 1788 ; *Elutheria*, b. — June 1791, d. 20 Sep. 1794 ; *Sophia*, b. — Ap. 1793, d. 25 Sep. 1794. GEORGE the f. was a clothier, and res. near Gilbertville, at the place marked " R. Field " on the R. Map, where he d. 2 or 4 May 1826, a. 80 ; his w. Prudence d. 15 Dec. 1838, a. 82.[1]

3. ROBERT, s. of George (2), m. Sally Tyler of Western (now Warren), pub. 20 Feb. 1802, and had Sophia, b. about 1805, d. unm. at Warren 24 July 1870, a. 65; *George*, b. about 1809, d. 16 Mar. 1813, a. 4. ROBERT the f. inherited the homestead, and d. 23 Aug. 1843; his w. Sally d. 28 Sep. 1859, a. 80.

FISH, HENRY, s. of Rev. Elisha Fish of Upton, b. about 1765, m. Elizabeth Holmes (b. at Worcester), and had *Henry*, b. —— 1790 ; *Hannah*, b. ——

[1] Mr. Field had good judgment in the affairs of life, and was highly respected for his strict honesty and integrity ; yet he created much amusement by the oddity of his language. For example, he said to his son, "Go up to the house, and fetch them down here." "Fetch what, sir ?" said the son. "Why, my shoes." In payment of wages to a laborer, he drew an order on a store-keeper, thus : "Mr. Bowman — Let him have it. George Field." On being told that this was a very unusual form of an order, he replied : "Just as well ; short way." Mr. Bowman knew his customer so well that he duly honored his order.

1792, m. Uriel Spooner of Brk., pub. 26 Ap. 1843, and d. 10 Nov. 1857, a. 65; *Elizabeth*, b. —— 1794, m. Wyman Spooner 10 Nov. 1818, and d. at Elkhorn, Wis., in 1867; *Nancy*, b. —— 1797, m. Daniel Warner 29 May 1821, and d. 2 Feb. 1875, a. 77; these four were prob. b. at Upton, and were baptized at Hk. 22 May 1803; *Catherine Holmes*, bap. 30 Ap. 1809, m. Foster Marsh of Ware 17 June 1846, and d. 18 Oct. 1873, a. nearly 64; *Elvira*, bap. 26 Ap. 1812, m. Rev. Rufus Case of St. Johnsbury, Vt., 2 June 1842. HENRY the f. was a farmer, and prob. rem. from Upton to Hk. about the year 1798, when he was styled lieutenant; he was elected deacon of the church 18 Ap. 1819, which office he resigned 20 May 1830; he was selectman five years, and d. 23 Ap. 1850, a. 85; his w. Elizabeth d. 30 June 1854, a. 84.

2. HENRY, s. of Henry (1), m. Sarah Ross of Brk., pub. 21 Sep. 1823; she d. 18 Aug. 1850, a. 51, and he m. Hannah Davis, pub. 11 Feb. 1851; his chil. were: *Sarah Jane*, b. —— 1825, m. Rev. Amos Holbrook of Sturbridge, 26 Mar. 1851; *John R.*, b. —— 1827; *Henry Dwight*, b. —— 1829; a child d. 31 Aug. 1831, a. 7 days; *Holloway*, b. —— 1833; d. 24 Aug. 1835. HENRY the f. was a farmer, res. on the homestead, and d. 19 Dec. 1864, a. nearly 75.

3. JOHN R., s. of Henry (2), m. Pauline M. Ruggles 27 May 1855, and had *Mary Elizabeth*, b. 9 July 1856, d. 15 June 1858; *Laura Elvira*, b. 1 Oct. 1857. JOHN R. the f. d. 3 Mar. 1857, a. 30; his w. Pauline M. m. Isaac S. Bonney 10 Mar. 1864.

4. HENRY DWIGHT, s. of Henry (2), m. Abby B. Mann 10 Mar. 1853; she d. 26 Oct. 1859, and he m. Almira C. Brown, 1861. His chil. were: *Abbie Carrie*, b. 18 Feb. 1854; *Sarah Isabel*, b. 29 Mar. 1856, d. 19 July 1858; *Harry*, b. —— 1859, d. 9 Sep. 1877, a. 18; *John Dwight*, b. 14 Oct. 1861; *Freddie Thomas*, b. 29 Ap. 1863; *Bertha*, b. —— 1865; *Gertrude*, b. —— 1873.

MARTHA, m. Deac. Nathaniel Paige, pub. —— Aug. 1783. NATHANIEL, of Prescott, m. Mrs. Sila Dean 30 Dec. 1835.

FISK, JACOB, came from Wenham, and by w. Elizabeth had *Elizabeth*, b. 4 Mar. 1745; *Jonathan*, b. 17 May 1748; *Abigail*, b. 17 Aug. 1750; *Sarah*, b. 28 Dec. 1752; a daughter b. 24 Sep. 1758.

2. EBENEZER, by w. Dorcas, had *Simeon*, b. 15 July 1762.

3. SAMUEL, by w. Sabrina, had *Lydia*, b. —— Feb. 1791, d. 3 Nov. 1791. SAMUEL the f. d. 6 Sep. 1818, a. 55.

4. CHARLES W., m. Sarah Lawrence 17 Mar. 1818, and had *Sarah Ann*, b. 18 Jan. 1820, m. Ebenezer Briggs 8 July 1840, d. at Amherst 16 Nov. 1858; *Charles W.*, b. 17 Ap. 1823. SARAH the mother d. 4 Ap. 1840, a. 43.

MARY, of Sturbridge, m. John Fay, pub. 22 Oct. 1757. STEPHEN, of Greenwich, m. Anna Green 29 June 1758. ELIZABETH, m. David Allen 12 Nov. 1761. DORCAS, m. Watson Freeman 26 Feb. 1761. SUSAN, of Sturbridge, m. Stephen Fay, Jr., pub. 18 Ap. 1762. ELIZABETH, m. Nathaniel Dickinson 1 Nov. 1764. MARY, m. Henry Higgins 9 Nov. 1768. ANNA, m. Ezra Conant of Warwick 21 Mar. 1770. NANCY, m. Daniel Wilson of Lynn, pub. 8 Nov. 1807. FANNY, m. Alvah Packard 4 Dec. 1820.

FITZGERALD, JOHN, by w. Margaret, had *Edward*, b. 22 Mar. 1871; *Gerald Dean* (or *Geraldine*), b. 27 Mar. 1874; *John*, b. 13 Oct. 1877.

2. WILLIAM, by w. Margaret, had *Mary Ann*, b. 28 Nov. 1872.

FITZPATRICK, MICHAEL, by w. Margaret, had *Mercy W.*, b. 7 May, 1851.

2. WILLIAM, m. Margaret Buckley 25 Feb. 1865, and had *Catherine*, b. 29 May 1866; *John*, b. 18 July 1868; a child b. and d. 9 Feb. 1871; *William*, b. 19 Ap. 1876; *Francis Cornelius*, b. 23 June 1879.

FLETCHER, BENJAMIN, by w. Lucy, had *Marjory*, b. 8 Dec. 1759.

Capt. JONATHAN, of Barre, m. Mary Sears 1 May 1760. ALPHEUS, m. Ruth Heywood 26 Feb. 1797. POLLY, m. Caleb Nurse of Barre, pub. 12 Feb. 1809. JOEL W., m. Mary Ann Marsh 28 Ap. 1845.

FORBES, THEODORE (prob. s. of Stephen Forbush, named below), by w. Elizabeth, had *Lancy*, b. 3 Aug. 1781; *Luther*, b. 10 Mar. 1787.

2. DANIEL, by w. Mary Ann, had *Jane R.*, b. about 1834, m. Samuel W. Knight of Barre 3 Sep. 1861; *Olean Augusta*, b. —— 1836, m. Joseph Dudley, Jr., 31 Dec. 1856; *Mary Ellen*, b. about 1841, m. Elmer M. Thayer 10 July 1861; *Mary*, b. 8 Aug. 1844, d. 24 Feb. 1846; *Charles*, b. 12 June, 1848.

FORBUSH, AARON, otherwise written Furrowbush,[1] perhaps s. of Aaron of Brk., m. Sarah Lamson of Ipswich, pub. 1 Dec. 1746, and had here *Sarah*, b. 25 Feb. 1747–8, m. Gideon Wheelock 14 Jan. 1771; *Margery*, b. 28 Nov. 1749, m. Moses Winchester 9 Mar. 1780; *Lucy*, b. 20 Sep. 1751, m. Paul Knowlton of Shrews. 8 Nov. 1769; *Aaron*, b. 29 May 1753; *Martha*, b. 14 Dec. 1754, m. Asa Hull of Montague 12 Oct. 1778; *Edna*, b. 21 Nov. 1756, m. Jacob Whipple 30 Dec. 1777; *Moses*, b. 15 July 1759; *Rhoda*, b. 26 Feb. 1761, m. Ephraim Hunt, Jr., of Gr. 5 Ap. 1781, and d. here 15 Aug. 1855, a. 94; *Lydia*, b. 25 Aug. 1762, m. Noah Marble 17 Nov. 1785; *Susanna*, b. 15 Ap. 1764, m. Abel Butterfield 13 Ap. 1785. AARON the f. d. 10 Aug. 1811, a. 89 or 90; his w. Sarah d. 21 Nov. 1808, a. 87 or 88.

2. STEPHEN, by w. Mary, had *Alexander*, b. 20 Feb. 1755; *Theodore*, b. 21 Dec. 1756 (probably the same who is named above as Theodore Forbes); *Rebecca*, b. 4 July 1759; *Asa*, b. 25 Dec. 1761; *Eunice*, b. 23 May 1764; *Sally*, b. 2 Nov. 1766; *John*, b. 1 Ap. 1769; *Polly*, b. 25 Sep. 1771; *Kate*, b. 20 Mar. 1774; *Stephen*, b. 12 Oct. 1776. STEPHEN the f. was a cordwainer, and rem. from Brk. to Hk. about 1754, and prob. to Wilmington, Vt., about 1779.

3. AARON, s. of Aaron (1), m. Catherine Rice, 27 Ap. 1774, and had *Luke*, b. 9 May 1775; *Huldah*, b. 25 June 1778; *Aaron*, b. 28 Aug. 1780; *Chloe*, b. 6 Mar. 1782.

4. MOSES, s. of Aaron (1), m. Patty Marble of Pet. 9 Jan. 1785, and had *Moses Wiley*, b. 5 Sep. 1785, d. 4 July 1786; *Zebina*, b. 7 Mar. 1788; *Patty*, b. 21 June 1792; *Burt*, b. 11 July 1800, d. 11 Feb. 1801. MOSES the f. d. 28 June 1810; his w. Patty d. 6 July 1830, a. 64.

5. ZEBINA, s. of Moses (4), m. Zeby, dau. of Josiah Manly, 24 Ap. 1811; she d. 27 or 28 July 1849, a. 59, and he m. Hannah Mills of Orange, pub. 1 Feb. 1851. His chil. were: a son, b. ——, d. 18 Jan. 1813; *Cynthia*, b. 26 June 1814, m. Chester Gore 12 Nov. 1845; *Patty*, b. about 1817, d. 27 Jan. 1830, a. 12; *Polly*, b. 16 Feb. 1818; *Susan*, b. 15 Jan. 1828, m. Charles P. Clark of Barre 11 Nov. 1853; *Elizabeth M.*, b. 8 July 1831; and perhaps others. ZEBINA the f. d. at Brk. 23 Feb. 1873, a. 85.

KATHERINE, m. Moses Whipple 25 May 1758. PATTY, m. Micajah Johnson of Shrewsbury, Vt., 31 Dec. 1811. MRS. LOIS, d. 22 Feb. 1867, a. 67.

FOSTER, THOMAS, by w. Elizabeth, had *Thomas*, b. 18 Aug. 1640, a physician in Cambridge; *John*, b. 7 Oct. 1642; prob. *Increase*, b. ——; *Elizabeth*, b. ——, m. Deac. James Frost of Billerica, 22 Jan. 1666–7; *Hopestill*, b. 26 Mar. 1648, a blacksmith in Woburn, d. 26 May 1679; *Joseph*, b. 28 Mar. 1650, a farmer and deacon in Billerica, d. 12 Dec. 1721. THOMAS the f. res. in Weymouth as early as 1640, and subsequently in Braintree and Billerica. He was a blacksmith and the progenitor of a long line of similar artisans. He was one of the early Anabaptists; but his posterity, for several generations, were steadfast adherents to the established church. He was selectman six years, and d. in Billerica 20 Ap. 1682; his w. Elizabeth d. 29 Jan. 1694–5.

2. JOHN, s. of Thomas (1), m. Mary, dau. of Thomas Chillingsworth[2] of Marshfield; she d. 25 Sep. 1702, and he m. Sarah Thomas 30 Dec. 1702. His chil. were: *Elizabeth*, b. 24 Sep. 1664, m. William Carver of Marshfield 18 Jan. 1682–3 (he d. 1 Oct. 1760, a. 102, as it is said; she d. — June 1715); *John*, b. 12 Oct. 1666, a blacksmith and deacon in Plymouth, d. 24 Dec. 1741;

[1] This name underwent many transformations. In 1660 it was written Farrabas, at Cambridge; at Marlborough it was written Farrowbush, in 1688, and Forbush in 1693; at Westborough, Forbes, at a latter date. At Hardwick it certainly had the two forms, Furrowbush and Forbush, applied to the same person, and probably Forbes as the name of another.

[2] Mr. Chillingsworth was probably the only male bearing this name in New England in the seventeenth century. After a short residence in Lynn and Sandwich, he settled in Marshfield, and was representative in 1648 and 1652. He had no son to perpetuate his name, yet it appears even to this day as a Christian name in the posterity of some of his daughters, who were *Elizabeth*, d. unm. 28 Sep. 1685; *Mehetabel*, m. Justus Eames of Marshfield; *Mary*, m. Deacon John Foster; *Sarah*, m. Samuel Sprague, the last secretary of Plymouth Colony. THOMAS the f. d. prob. about March 1652–3, when administration on his estate was granted to his w. Joanna, who m. Thomas Doggett of Marshfield 17 May, 1654 and was buried 4 Sep. 1684.

Josiah, b. 7 June 1669, a farmer in Pembroke, d. about 1757; *Mary*, b. 13 Sep. 1671, m. John Hatch of Marshfield 30 Dec. 1696, and d. 3 Ap. 1750; *Joseph*, b. about 1674, res. in Barnstable and Sandwich, d. — Ap. 1750; *Sarah*, b. about 1677, d. unm. 7 Ap. 1702; *Chillingsworth*, b. 11 June 1680; *James*, b. 22 May 1683, d. 21 July 1683; *Thomas*, b. about 1685, a farmer, town clerk, and deacon in Marshfield, d. 6 Feb. 1758, a. 72; *Deborah*, b. about 1691, d. unm. 4 Nov. 1732, a. 41. JOHN the f. was a blacksmith, selectman, and deacon in Marshfield, where he d. 13 June 1732, a. nearly 90; his w. Sarah d. 26 May 1731.

3. CHILLINGSWORTH, s. of John (2), m. Mercy, dau. of John Freeman[1] of Harwich (now Brewster); she d. 7 July 1720, a. 33, and he m. Susanna, wid. of Nathaniel Sears, dau. of John Gray; she d. 7 Dec. 1730, and he m. Ruth, wid. of Samuel Sears, dau. of William Merrick, 7 Dec. 1731. His chil. were: *James*, b. 6 Jan. 1705–6; *Chillingsworth*, b. 25 Dec. 1707, a blacksmith, selectman, representative ten years, justice of the peace, and special justice of the Court of Common Pleas; he d. in Harwich about 1779; *Mary*, b. 5 Jan. 1709–10, m. David Paddock of Yarmouth 12 Oct. 1727; *Thomas*, b. 15 Mar. 1711–12, m. Mary Hopkins, 11 July 1734; *Nathan*, b. 10 June 1715, m. Sarah Lincoln 14 June 1739; *Isaac*, b. 17 June 1718, a blacksmith, res. on the homestead, m. Hannah Sears, dau. of his stepmother, 2 Nov. 1738, and d. 10 Sep. 1777; *Mercy*, b. 30 Mar. 1720, d. 28 Aug. 1720; *Mercy*, b. 29 July 1722, m. Isaac Crosby 7 Oct. 1742; *Nathaniel*, b. 17 Ap. 1725; *Jerusha*, b. 9 Dec. 1727. CHILLINGSWORTH the f. settled early in that part of Harwich which is now Brewster. Like his father and grandfather, he was a blacksmith, and transmitted the mysteries of that craft to at least three sons. Like his father also, he was deacon of the church from 4 July 1731 until he died. He was selectman nine years, treasurer twenty-five years, town clerk twenty-eight years, and representative eight years. He d. 22 Dec. 1764; his w. Ruth d. 13 Feb. 1766, a. 82.

4. JAMES, s. of Chillingsworth (3), m. Lydia, dau. of Major Edward Winslow of Rochester, 10 July 1729; she d. 7 Jan. 1770, a. 60, and he m. Phebe Actil of Berkley, pub. 11 May 1771. His chil. were *Mercy*, b. 4 July 1730, m. Seth Rider of Roch., pub. 2 May 1747; *Mary*, b. 11 Ap. 1732, m. Col. Timothy Paige of Hardwick, 24 Oct. 1754, and d. 21 July 1825, a. 93; *Chillingsworth*, b. 8 Dec. 1733, m. Margaret Pope of Dartmouth, pub. 29 June 1754, and (2d) Mrs. Sarah Freeman of Roch., pub. 3 Aug. 1794, and d. 3 Mar. 1807; *James*, b. 17 Ap. 1735, d. 29 May 1735; *Lydia*, b. 13 Ap. 1736, m. Nathaniel Haskell of Hk., pub. 3 Ap. 1757; *James*, b. 12 Ap. 1737, a blacksmith and deacon in Roch., m. Mary Lewis, pub. 30 Nov. 1755, and d. — Nov. 1829, a. 92; *Edward*, b. 3 July 1738; *Nathan*, b. 4 Ap. 1740, d. 28 Oct. 1742; *John*, b. 5 Aug. 1742, d. 9 Sep. 1742; *Nathan*, b. 26 Jan. 1743–4, m. Hannah Haskell of Hk., 14 Mar. 1765, res. in N. Sal. and afterwards in Wilmington, Vt.; *John*, b. 30 July 1745. JAMES the f., like many of his ancestors, was a blacksmith and deacon; he was also selectman, town clerk, and treasurer. He res. in Roch. until 1774, when he rem. to Athol with his son *John*, and d. about 1788.

5. EDWARD, s. of James (4), m. Deborah Bangs of Hk., 13 Jan. 1762, and had *Seth*, b. 19 Feb. 1764; *Deborah*, b. 16 Oct. 1766; *Edward*, b. 6 Ap. 1769; *James*, b. 18 Jan. 1771. EDWARD the f. rem. from Hk. to that part of Pelham which is now Prescott.

6. JOHN, s. of James (4), m. Rebecca, dau. of Deacon William Paige of Hk. 6 Oct. 1768, and had *William*, b. 17 Oct. 1769; *Lydia*, b. 10 Feb. 1772; *John*, b. 3 Sep. 1776; *James*, b. 22 Sep. 1778, a Universalist clergyman in Onondaga County, N. Y., and d. at Bridgeport in the winter of 1854–5, a. 76; *Ebenezer*, b. 19 Oct. 1780; *Shadrach*, b. 20 Mar. 1783; *Aikens*, b. 7 Feb. 1788; *Rebecca*, b. 24 Feb. 1791. JOHN the f. rem. from Roch. to Athol in 1774, and after 1791 to Barnard, Vt.

[1] John Freeman (b. Dec. 1651, d. 27 July, 1721), father of Mrs. Mercy Foster, was son of Major John Freeman of Eastham (d. 28 Oct. 1719, a. 97), by his w. Mercy (d. 28 Sep. 1711, a. 80), who was daughter of Governor Thomas Prence (d. 29 Mar. 1673, a. 73), by his w. Patience (d. 1634), who was dau. of Elder William Brewster, of blessed memory.

[For a more full account of the descendants of THOMAS FOSTER (1), see *N. E. Hist. and Gen. Register*, xxvi. 394.]

7. JOHN, parentage not ascertained, by w. Eunice, had *Jonathan*, b. 18 Aug. 1740. He apparently rem. to Hk. from Grafton, and was selectman and town clerk in 1740 and 1741; he seems to have returned to Grafton, and the vacancies in office were filled 23 Nov. 1741; but he bought land again in Hk. 9 Sep. 1742, and is described as of Hk. in the inventory of his estate 27 Feb. 1745–6, which estate was divided, 4 Aug. 1751, between his chil. *Joseph*, *John*, *Jacob*, *Jonathan*, *Abigail*, and *Lydia*.

8. EMORY B., by w. Adeline, had *George Emory*, b. 27 Oct. 1842; *Frederick*, b. 21 Aug. 1844, d. unm. 16 July 1877; *William Alfred*, b. 1 Mar. 1849. EMORY B. the f., assessor 1858, and deacon 1841, formerly res. in Petersham.

JOSEPH, prob. s. of John (7), m. Susanna Roberts of Brk., pub. 9 Feb. 1751–2. ABIGAIL, prob. dau. of John (7), m. Jacob Pepper of N. Br. 28 Feb. 1754. SUSANNA, of Ware, m. Jacob Lawton, pub. 16 Nov. 1777. WILLIAM, of Barnard, Vt., prob. s. of John (6), m. Polly Paige, pub. 10 Oct. 1793. JEDEDIAH, of Wilmington, Vt., m. Mrs. Tamasen Billings 12 Nov. 1804. LEWIS, of Palmyra, N. Y., m. Hannah Carpenter, pub. 24 Sep. 1827.

FREEMAN, EDMUND, of Lynn in 1635, was one of the grantees of Sandwich 3 Ap. 1637, where he d. in 1682, at the supposed age of 92. By w. Elizabeth he had *Alice*, m. Deac. William Paddy 24 Nov. 1639; *Edmund*; *Elizabeth*, m. John Ellis; *John*; *Mary*, m. Edward Perry. EDMUND the f. was one of the assistants in the Plymouth Colony from 1640 to 1645, inclusive. See *Freeman Genealogy*, pp. 12–24.

2. EDMUND, s. of Edmund (1), m. Rebecca, dau. of Gov. Thomas Prence 22 Ap. 1646; she d. and he m. Margaret Perry 18 July 1651. His chil. were *Rebecca*, b. ——, m. Ezra Perry; *Margaret*, b. 2 Oct. 1652; *Edmund*, b. 5 Oct. 1655; *Alice*, b. 29 Mar. 1658; *Rachel*, b. 4 Sep. 1659, m. John Landers; *Sarah*, b. 6 Feb. 1662, m. Richard Landers; *Deborah*, b. 9 Aug. 1665, m. Thomas Landers. EDMUND the f. res. in Sandwich, and was deputy at the General Court of Plymouth seven years.

3. JOHN, s. of Edmund (1), m. Mercy, dau. of Gov. Thomas Prence, and gr. dau. of Elder William Brewster, 13 or 14 Feb. 1649–50, and had *John*, b. 2 Feb. 1650–1, d. young; *John*, b. — Dec. 1651; *Thomas*, b. — Sep. 1653, deacon, selectman, town clerk, and treasurer of Harwich; *Patience*, b. ——, m. Lieut. Samuel Paine 31 Jan. 1682–3; *Hannah*, b. ——, m. John Mayo 14 Ap. 1681; *Edmund*, b. — June 1657; *Mercy*, b. — July 1659, m. Samuel Knowles — Dec. 1679; *William*, b. ——; *Prince*, b. 3 Feb. 1665–6, d. young; *Nathaniel*, b. 20 Mar. 1669, selectman and town clerk of Eastham, justice of the peace and judge of the County Court, d. 4 Jan. 1760; *Bennett*, b. 7 Mar. 1670–1, m. Deac. John Paine 14 Mar. 1689. JOHN the f. early rem. to Eastham; he was a captain in 1675, actively engaged in King Philip's War, and major in 1685; he was also deacon of the church, selectman ten years, deputy at the General Court seven years, and assistant twenty-four years; sheriff of the county, under the Andros administration, and the first named judge of the Court of Common Pleas after the union of Plymouth and Massachusetts. His grave-stone in Eastham bears this inscription: "Here lies the body of MAJOR JOHN FREEMAN, died October ye 28th 1719, in ye 98th year of his age."[1] His w. Mercy d. 28 Sep. 1711, a. 80.

4. EDMUND, s. of Edmund (2), by w. Sarah, had nine chil., res. at Sandwich, and d. 18 May 1720, a. 65.

5. JOHN, s. of John (3), m. Sarah, dau. of William Merrick, 18 Dec. 1672; she d. 21 Ap. 1696, and he m. Mercy, wid. of Capt. Elkanah Watson of Plymouth. His chil., prob. all by his first w., were: *John*, b. 3 Sep. 1674, d. young; *Sarah*, b. — Sep. 1676, m. Edward Snow; *John*, b. — July 1678; *Rebecca*, b. 28 Jan. 1680–1, prob. d. young; *Nathaniel*, b. 17 Mar. 1682–3; *Benjamin*, b. —

1 Some writers have supposed that "98th" should be 93d. As Major Freeman was a deputy in 1654, when he was only 27 years old, if born in 1627, I am of opinion that he was born in 1622, and that the figures in the inscription are right. At that day, it was very unusual to elect a man as deputy before he was thirty years old.

July 1685; *Mercy*, b. 3 Aug. 1687, m. Deac. Chillingsworth Foster; *Patience*, b. ——, m. Eleazar Crosby 24 Oct. 1706; *Susannah*, b. ——, m. John Mayo, Jr., 22 Oct. 1712; *Elizabeth*, b. ——, m. John Bacon, Jr., 2 May 1726; *Mary*, b. ——, m. Judah Berry 1713. JOHN the f. res. near the line between Eastham (now Orleans) and Harwich (now Brewster), and his death, 27 July 1721, was recorded in both towns; his head-stone remains in Brewster; his w. Mary d. 27 Sep. 1721, a. 62.

6. WILLIAM, s. of Edmund (4), m. Mary Bodfish 6 Dec. 1726, and had *Hannah*, b. 13 Sep. 1728, m. Silas Tupper 2 June 1757; *Thomas*, b. 4 Mar. 1729–30; *Rebecca*, b. 2 Mar. 1731–2, m. Jonathan Nye, Jr., 18 Mar. 1756, and rem. to Hk.; *William*, b. 3 June 1734; *Joanna*, b. 21 Mar. 1736–7, m. Deac. Nathaniel Paige of Hk. 13 Sep. 1759; *Sarah*, b. 26 July 1739, m. Levi Nye 9 June 1767; *Elisha*, b. 21 Nov. 1741; *Joshua*, b. 6 Ap. 1744; *Mary*, b. 20 July 1746, d. unm. "at a great age." WILLIAM the f. res. in Sandwich, and d. 13 Mar. 1786.

7. ISAAC, s. of Edmund (4), m. Deborah Foster of Barnstable 22 Nov. 1733, and had *Ebenezer*, b. 19 Aug. 1734; *Nathan*, b. 19 Nov. 1735; *Deborah*, b. 2 Feb. 1738–9; *Isaac*, b. 11 Feb. 1741–2. ISAAC the f. res. at Sandwich, and d. 16 Sep. 1766.

8. JOHN, s. of John (5), m. Mercy, dau. of Capt. Elkanah Watson of Plymouth about 1701, and had in Harwich *Elkanah*, b. 28 Oct. 1702, d. 21 Jan. 1713–14; *Sarah*, b. 26 Jan. 1704, m. Constant Merrick, pub. 17 Feb. 1726–7, and rem. to Hk.; *Mercy*, b. 24 Ap. 1707; *John*, b. 13 Aug. 1709, rem. to Hk.; *Phebe*, b. 28 Nov. 1711; *Thankful*, b. 6 Oct. 1714, m. Barnabas Sears 25 Sep. 1732, rem. to Hk., *Elkanah*, b. 6 Feb. 1716–7; *Mary*, b. 13 Oct. 1719, m. Roland Sears, pub. 11 Nov. 1738, rem. to Hk.; *Eli*, b. 27 Ap. 1722; *Elisha*, b. 21 May 1724; *Hannah*, bap. 17 Jan. 1728. JOHN the f. rem. from Harwich (Brewster) to Rochester about 1723, and was styled "deacon" about 1729.

9. THOMAS, s. of William (6), m. Phebe Hall 9 Oct. 1752, and had *Lydia*, b. about 1754, m. John Newton of Hk. 15 Jan. 1778; *William*, b. 12 or 22 July 1757; *Mary*, bap. 16 Sep. 1759; *Thomas*, b. 1 Ap. 1762; *Joshua*, b. 10 Ap. 1764; *Elisha*, b. 3 Oct. 1766; *Stephen*, b. 16 Dec. 1768. THOMAS the f. res. in Sandwich until 1757, when he bought a farm in Hk., and prob. removed immediately, as all his children born after that year were bap. in Hk., when infants, though their births are recorded in Sandwich as well as in Hardwick. In March, 1775, he rem. to Barnard, Vt.,[1] of which town he was one of the first settlers, and both himself and his sons were among the most energetic and distinguished inhabitants. He d. 29 May 1811, a. 81 (the date on his head-stone is 1812); his w. Phebe d. 1 Feb. 1806, a. 76.

10. NATHAN, s. of Isaac (7), by w. Mary, had in Hk. *Jane*, bap. 19 July 1761; *Deliverance*, bap. 19 July 1761, m. Jonathan Childs 13 Jan. 1778; *Nathan*, b. 30 May 1762; *Joseph*, b. 1 May 1764, d. —— 1767; *Sarah Pope*, bap. 14 Sep. 1766; *Joseph*, bap. 13 May 1770, prob. m. Hannah Howard 26 Sep. 1796. NATHAN the f. d. 8 Nov. 1769, a. 34, and his w. Mary prob. m. Nathaniel Whitcomb, Jr., of Gr. 17 Oct. 1779.

11. JOHN, s. of John (8), m. Joanna Rickett of Plympton, pub. 29 Jan. 1730–1, and had *Mercy*, b. 15 July 1732, m. Silas Newton of Hk. 9 Nov. 1749 (he d. 7 Dec. 1763, and she m. Leonard Robinson of Bennington 13 Mar. 1766, by whom she became the mother of Samuel L. Robinson, who d. in Hk. 18 Jan. 1863, a. nearly 96); *Watson*, b. 25 Oct. 1734; *John*, b. 17 Sep. 1736; *Sarah*, b. 15 Oct. 1737, m. Stephen Gorham 16 Mar. or Ap. 1757; *Thankful*, b. 13 Nov. 1741, m. Samuel Dexter 25 Nov. 1759; *Susanna*, bap. 9 Sep. 1744; *Mary*, bap. 8 Jan. 1746; *Eli*, b. 3 July 1749. JOHN the f. accompanied his father to Rochester about 1723, and thence rem. to Hk. before 16 Oct. 1748, when he was dism. from the ch. in Roch. to the ch. in Hk., being then described as "deacon." He was a farmer, res. on a farm adjoining the Barre line, on the

[1] In a description of Barnard, the extraordinary tale is told that, "At the time of the battle of Bunker's Hill — on the 17th of June, 1775 — the firing was distinctly heard in this town by Thomas Freeman and others, a distance of more than one hundred miles." Thompson's *Vermont*, part iii. p. 7.

easterly side of Moose Brook, and taught the school in that part of the town eight years between 1748 and 1757. He d. 24 Jan. 1804, a. 94; his w. Joanna d. 29 Mar. 1797, a. 87.

12. NATHAN, s. of Nathan (10), m. Polly, dau. of Col. Stephen Rice, 1 Ap. 1790, and had *Hollis*, b. ——; *Nathan*, b. —— 1798, d. 14 Nov. 1800, a. 2; and perhaps others.

13. WATSON, s. of John (11), m. Dorcas Fisk 26 Feb. 1761, and had *Alpheus*, b. 23 Nov. 1767; *John*, b. 10 Aug. 1769; *Elijah*, b. 7 Oct. 1770; *Watson*, b. 2 May 1772; *Mercy*, b. 14 Mar. 1774; *Abigail*, b. 8 Mar. 1777; *Edmund*, bap. 11 July 1779; *Eunice*, bap. 24 Feb. 1782; and perhaps others before 1767. WATSON the f. and his w. were dism. from the ch. in Hk. to the ch. in Wilmington, Vt., 24 July 1785.

14. JOHN, s. of John (11), by w. Mary, had *Chloe*, bap. 15 Feb. 1767, prob. the same who m. Andrew Haskell of Wilmington, Vt., 12 Oct. 1780. Nothing further ascertained.

15. ELI, s. of John (11), m. Mary Rice of Barre 26 Mar. 1767; she d. 9 July 1812, a. 60, and he m. Lucy, dau. of Amaziah Spooner, 22 July 1813. His chil. were *Rachel*, b. 10 Sep. 1769, m. Abel Stowell of Pet. 5 July 1792; *Samuel*, bap. 2 Oct. 1774, d. young; *Hannah*, bap. 5 May 1776, d. young; *Hannah*, b. 14 Nov. 1778, m. Reuben Newton of Pet. 18 Feb. 1800; *Mary*, bap. 24 Feb. 1782, d. unm. 27 Jan. 1800; *Samuel*, b. 7 Ap. 1786; *Luther*, b. 19 Mar. 1790, m. Hannah King of Barre, pub. 24 Nov. 1810. ELI the f. d. 10 May 1816; his w. Lucy d. 4 Jan. 1849, a. 93.

16. HOLLIS, s. of Nathan (12), m. Margaret Gray 20 Feb. 1822, and had *Joseph Allen*, bap. 2 Feb. 1823; *Sapphira*, bap. 31 Oct. 1824; *Henry Deven*, bap. 20 May 1827. Removed from Hk. early.

17. SAMUEL, s. of Eli (15), m. Abigail Rice 23 Ap. 1807; and had *Washington Rice*, bap. 17 Nov. 1813, m. Sarah Fobes of Oakham, pub. 31 Jan. 1830; *Mary Rice*, bap. 17 Nov. 1813, m. David P. Bond 22 Mar. 1831; *John Philander*, bap. 17 Nov. 1813; *Samuel Henry*, bap. 21 Sep 1817, d. 11 Aug. 1818; *Rebecca*, b. —— 1825, d. 18 June 1830, a. 5. SAMUEL the f. d. — July 1825.

18. DAN, Jr., parentage not ascertained, m. Sally Mason, pub. 10 Sep. 1812, and had a child b. ——, d. 27 Jan. 1813.

NANCY, m. Asaph Cleveland, pub. 20 Dec. 1824. JULIA ANN A., of Oakham, m. Walter Mandell, pub. 15 Dec. 1828. HIRAM, m. Olive Chamberlin of Ware 11 Dec. 1834. SUSAN, m. Daniel W. Fairbanks of Cincinnati 25 June 1832. Dr. NATHANIEL, of N. Sal., m. Sarah E. Hemenway, pub. 6 May 1843. HANNAH, d. 22 Aug. 1826.

FRENCH, SAMUEL, m. Lydia, dau. of Capt. Daniel Warner, 23 Feb. 1775, and had *Lydia*, b. 12 July, 1775, m. Charles Paige 20 Sep. 1795; *Samuel*, b. 5 Mar. 1779, m. Tabitha, sister of Lorenzo Dow, erected at his own expense a Free Church at Hardwick, Vt., and d. in 1848; see *Vt. Hist. Mag.* i. 325; *Daniel*, b. 18 Jan. 1781; *Polly*, b. 5 Oct. 1784; *Jonathan Warner*, b. 28 June 1787; *Justus Warner*, b. 20 Ap. 1793; *Fordyce*, b. 13 Ap. 1795. SAMUEL the f. rem. with his family, in March 1799, to Hardwick, Vt., of which town he and his sons were active and useful inhabitants. He d. 17 June 1832, a. 78; his w. Lydia d. 28 Aug. 1814, a. 54.

2. LEMUEL, m. Sally P. Luce, pub. 30 Mar. 1789, and had *Lemuel*, *Sally*, *Timothy*, all bap. 20 Aug. 1794; *Haskell*, bap. 5 June 1796; *Bartlett Luce*, bap. 10 June 1798; a child b. ——, d. 16 March 1800; *William*, bap. 7 June 1801; *Jotham*, bap. 12 Aug. 1804. LEMUEL the f. rem. to Westford, Vt., about 1809.

3. TIMOTHY, s. of Lemuel (2), by w. Betsey had *Orin Ruggles*, bap. 1 June 1820, d. 15 Aug. 1822, a. 6; *Almond*, bap. 1 June 1820.

SAMUEL, of Craftsbury, Vt., m. Polly Ruggles 17 July 1796.

FRINK, PETER, by w. ——, had *Patty*, bap. 20 Ap. 1777.

FROST, WILLIAM, m. Harriet, dau. of Theophilus Hastings, 5 Feb. 1843; she d. 29 June 1845, a. 40, and he m. her sister, Henrietta Hastings, 22 Sep. 1846. The birth of only one child is found on record in Hk.: *Henrietta*, b. 15 Dec. 1843, m. Alonzo L. Alden 15 Ap. 1868. WILLIAM the f. was b. in Hubbardston, and d. 21 Ap. 1867, a. 66.

2. ORIN D., by w. Sophia, had *Benjamin Franklin*, b. 19 Nov. 1869.

FRYE, NATHANIEL, by w. ——, had a child d. 9 Oct. 1831, a. 6 days; a dau. d. 25 Sep. 1838, a. 3. NATHANIEL the f. d. 12 Mar. 1838, a. 38.

BENJAMIN, d. 30 Dec. 1851, a. 88. OLIVE, w. of Jedediah, d. 20 June 1843, a. 72. AURILIA, m. Ira Miller 27 Mar. 1824; and MARTHA, m. Ira Miller 12 May 1830.

FULLER, THOMAS, m. Lydia, dau. of Col. Timothy Paige, 26 Nov. 1778, and had *Martin*, b. 6 June 1780, m. Letitia Duncan of Hancock, N. H., and d. at Hardwick, Vt., 18 Oct. 1816 (his son, Thomas James Duncan, was several years a member of Congress, and d. at Washington, D. C., in 1876); *Thomas*, b. 24 Mar. 1782, m. Sally House, was a merchant in Enosburg, Vt., deacon, and representative in the General Court, d. 23 Feb. 1860 (his dau., Cordelia H. L., m. Dr. Horace Eaton, Governor of Vermont); *Lydia*, b. 6 June 1784, m. Daniel Weld; *Malinda*, b. 3 Feb. 1787, m. Charles Stevens, and d. —— Feb. 1857; a son b. 7 Mar. 1789, lived five days; *Timothy Paige*, b. 30 Mar. 1790, m. Rebecca Duncan of Hancock, N. H., was a farmer in Hardwick, Vt., representative, justice of the peace, judge of the County Court, and d. s. p. 21 July 1854; *Austin*, b. 13 Ap. 1792, m. Betsey Maynard, the first white child born in Bakersfield, Vt., was a merchant and manufacturer, representative, justice of the peace, and judge of the County Court. He rem. from Hardwick, Vt., to Bakersfield about 1815, to Enosburg in 1822, and to Saratoga, N. Y., in 1866, where he d. s. p. 24 Sep. 1870; FRANCIS ENOS, b. 20 Mar. 1794, a farmer in Hardwick, Vt., m. Martha Worcester of Hollis, N. H., who d. 9 Sep. 1824, and he m. Hannah Worcester of Hollis. He d. 24 Feb. 1869; *Rebecca Paige*, b. 29 Ap. 1796, m. Alvin House of Enosburg, and d. — Sep. 1872; *John Washington*, b. 4 Jan. 1799, d. 15 Aug. 1803. THOMAS the f. rem. to Westminster, Vt., about 1786, and thence to Hardwick, Vt., in 1798. The first church in that town was organized in his house, and he was its first deacon. He endured his share of privation in the infancy of the town,[1] and afterwards shared bountifully in its prosperity. He d. 1 Dec. 1823; his w. Lydia d. 8 July 1810, a. 55.

2. EDWARD J., was pastor of the Calvinistic Church from 3 Nov. 1835 to 22 Mar. 1837. By w. Anna C. he had *Edward Francis*, bap. 8 Jan. 1837.

MRS. TEMPERANCE, of Barre, mother of Thomas (1), m. James Lawton, pub. 14 June 1772. WILLIAM, of N. Br., m. Mercy Powers 3 Dec. 1767. SARAH, of Middleborough, m. William Oliver, pub. 25 Feb. 1770. MERCY, of Oakham, was pub. to Edmund Willis 26 Feb. 1775, and again pub. 23 Feb. 1777. MRS. LUCRETIA, d. 5 Feb. 1873, a. 81.

GALE, ELISHA, by w. Mary, had *Elisha*, b. 21 Nov. 1767; *Rhoda*, b. 4 June 1769.

GARDNER, BENJAMIN, by w. Nancy, had *Walter R.*, b. 28 Aug. 1843.

SARAH, m. Lemuel Gilbert 3 Nov. 1816. ROXANA, m. Anson Ramsdell, 28 Ap. 1820. MARTIN, m. Clarissa Ruggles 7 Feb. 1821. SARAH JANE, m. Harvey Gage of Ware 9 Feb. 1852. BENJAMIN O., m. Sarah P. Peck 7 Dec. 1853.

GIBBEN, PETER, m. Sarah Green 7 Dec. 1751, and had *Elizabeth*, b. 7 Nov. 1752; *Peter*, b. 1 Aug. 1754; *Lemuel*, bap. 22 Oct. 1758.

GIBBS, JACOB, of Quobbin, m. Bethiah Bacon 13 Mar. 1753, and had in Hk. *Daniel*, bap. 3 Sep. 1755.

ABRAHAM, of Quobbin, m. Kezia Atwood, pub. 10 Mar. 1743-4. ISAAC, killed in the army, 8 Sep. 1755. URIAH, m. Lucy Townsend of Gr. 3 Mar. 1766.

GIFFIN, SIMON, m. Abigail Higgins 24 Mar. 1761, and had *Edward*, b. 3 Dec. 1761; *James*, b. 22 Feb. 1764; *David Dodge*, b. 8 Sep. 1766, d. at Ogdensburg, N. Y., in Mar. or Ap. 1840.

[1] "In 1798 Thomas Fuller came to settle in Hardwick with his wife and children. For six months, he, with a family of eleven, occupied a log-house, 24 feet square, with Mr. William Cheever, whose family also numbered eleven. There was a stone fireplace in the centre of the house, and a hollow log for a chimney." *Vt. Hist. Mag.*, i. 325.

2. JOHN, a drummer from the beginning to the end of the Revolutionary War, m. Mary Weeks 7 Sep. 1769, and perhaps m. (2d) Kezia Smith 22 July 1783. His chil. were: *Calvin*, b. 11 Mar. 1770; *Janet*, b. 4 Sep. 1773; *Luther*, b. 23 Mar. 1775; *Abner*, b. —— Sep. 1777; *Anson*, b. —— 1787, a painter and a famous drummer, m. Anna, dau. of Paul Paige, 30 May 1809, rem. to Hardwick, Vt., and afterwards to N. Brk., where he d. 9 Aug. 1870, a. 83; and perhaps *Fanny*, b. ——, who m. Willard Clark 25 Mar. 1810.

3. ABNER, s. of John (2), m. Polly Stratton of Gr., pub. 3 May 1801; she d. 4 Sep. 1811, a. 29, and he m. Mary (or Mercy) Wicker, pub. 20 Dec. 1813, who d. at Ware 29 Jan. 1865, a. 80. His chil. were: *Alma*, b. —— 1802, d. 26 Nov. 1809, a. 7; *John W.*, b. —— 1804; a child b. —— 1810, d. 12 Nov. 1815, a. 5; *James F.*, b. about 1823. ABNER the f. d. 4 Nov. 1836.

4. JOHN W., s. of Abner (3), m. Achsah Berry 25 Dec. 1834, and had WILLIAM H., b. about 1852. JOHN W. the f. d. in Barre 20 May 1874, a. 69 years and 9 months.

5. JAMES F., of Ware, s. of Abner (3), m. Elvira A. Newton 12 Dec. 1848, and had *Eliza Augusta*, b. 3 Aug. 1856, m. William A. Newton of Dana 8 Dec. 1875.

6. WILLIAM H., son of John W. (4), m. Eliza J. Stevens 29 June 1875, and had *Grace Elizabeth*, b. 7 Mar. 1877.

MARY S., m. Erastus P. Giffen of N. Brk., 12 Ap. 1842. LAURISTON, of Barre, m. Mary L. Conkey 9 Ap. 1867.

GILBERT, JOHN, by w. ——, had *Jemima*, bap. 23 May 1756.

2. DAVID, Jr., of N. Br., m. Esther Jenney 23 Mar. 1758, and had in Hk. *Esther*, b. 1 Ap. 1763; *Cornelius*, b. 10 Mar. 1765; *Susanna*, b. 16 Feb. 1767.

3. TIMOTHY, b. 25 Jan. 1747, m. Martha Rogers, pub. 13 Oct. 1771, and had *Timothy*, b. 13 Mar. 1772; *Charles*, b. 5 Ap. 1773, m. Lydia Warner 25 Feb. 1796; *Joseph*, b. 1 May 1774; *Patty*, b. 20 Feb. 1776, m. Gamaliel Collins 21 June 1798; *Rhoda*, b. 12 Ap. 1778, m. Seth Pebbles of Gr. 25 Sep. 1803; *Polly*, b. 13 Feb. 1780, m. Ebenezer Collins, pub. 28 Sep. 1800; *Mehetabel*, b. 7 Aug. 1781; *Lemuel*, b. 1 Aug. 1783, m. Sarah Gardner 3 Nov. 1816; *Abner*, b. 20 Mar. 1785; *William*, b. 14 Jan. 1787; *Jason*, b. 19 Jan. 1789; *John*, b. 11 Ap. 1792, m. Fanny Cummings 26 May 1816, selectman two years, rem. to Prescott, and d. 4 Feb. 1862. MARTHA, the mother of this large family, d. 30 Jan. 1824, a. 77.

4. LEMUEL, prob. brother of Timothy (3), d. 9 Mar. 1817, a. 68; his w. Bethiah d. 28 May 1816, a. 70, and he m. Sarah Gardner, 3 Nov. 1816.

5. JOSEPH, s. of Timothy (3), m. Sally Wheeler of Gr., pub. 21 June 1801, and had *Loring*, b. —— 1802, m. Rachel Warner, 5 May 1831, and d. at Ware 15 Aug. 1868, a. 66; *Hiram*, b. —— 1808, d. at Southampton 26 Oct. 1874, a. 66.

6. ALANSON, m. Ammadulce, dau. of Sylvanus Cobb, pub. 18 Sep. 1825, and had *Alanson A.*, b. 6 Mar. 1827. ALANSON the f. d. 3 Ap. 1827, a. 31; his w. Ammadulce d. at Charlestown 18 May 1881, a. 93.

JOSEPH, died in the army 4 Nov. 1755. JONATHAN, of N. Br., m. Sarah Amidon 5 Jan. 1779. JACOB, of N. Br., m. Anna Dexter 7 Oct. 1794. PERSIS, m. John Dexter 29 July 1821. SOPHRONIA, m. Newcomb Cleveland 17 Feb. 1824. TILLY, m. Sarah Holmes of N. Br., pub. 7 Nov. 1825. MARY E., dau. of Theron H., b. about 1840, m. Charles H. Barnes of Westminster, pub. 18 Nov. 1861.

GITCHELL, DAVID (otherwise written Getchell), by w. ——, had *David*, bap. here 26 May 1735, by Rev. Timothy Ruggles of Rochester,[1] before Mr. White was settled.

2. ROBERT, by w. ——, had *Esther*, b. 19 July 1737.

GLAZIER, ISAIAH, m. Hannah, dau. of William Thomas, 8 Nov. 1738, and had *Thankful* (twin), b. 8 Aug. 1739, d. young; *Submit* (twin), b. 8 Aug.

[1] On the fly-leaf of his Church Record, Rev. Mr. Ruggles entered the following memorandum: "26 May 1735. I baptized *Hannah*, daughter of Stephen Griffith, also *Isaiah* son of Nathan Carpenter, and *David*, son of David Getchell; all of Lambstown, *now Hardwick*." The last two words were added at a later time.

1739, m. Elisha Gilbert of Oakham 26 Nov. 1768; *David*, b. 1 Mar. 1741-2; *Olive*, b. 16 Mar. 1744; *Joseph* and *Benjamin* (twins), b. 31 Jan. 1745-6; *Thankful*, b. 10 Mar. 1747-8, m. Stephen Rice 23 Oct. 1770; *Jonathan*, b. 13 May 1751, m. Azubah Nye 23 June 1774; *William*, b. 1 Sep. 1753; *Benjamin*, b. 20 June 1757. ISAIAH the f. was living in 1761; his w. Hannah d. 20 June 1759.

2. DAVID, s. of Isaiah (1), m. Sarah, dau. of Ezekiel Pratt, 6 Feb. 1766, and had *Hannah*, b. 20 Sep. 1766; *Ezekiel*, b. 12 Ap. 1769.

Rev. JOSEPH, m. Hannah W. Wilson of Southbridge, pub. 11 Ap. 1834.

GLEASON, NATHANIEL, m. Sarah Johnson 14 Jan. 1771, and had *Nathaniel*, b. ——; *Sally*, b. ——, m. John Gallond of Pet. 11 June 1804; *John*, b. 25 Feb. 1783; *Joel*, b. 15 July 1785; *Alexander*, b. 31 Oct. 1787. NATHANIEL the f. d. 19 June 1806, a. 62; his w. Sarah d. 28 May 1807, a. 59.

2. NATHANIEL, s. of Nathaniel (1), m. Lucinda Gleason of Pet., pub. 5 May 1800, and had *Horace*, b. 30 Aug. 1801, grad. W. C. 1828, lawyer and justice of the peace many years in Boston, d. at Malden 18 May 1877. NATHANIEL the f. rem. to Pet., where he perhaps had other children.

3. JOHN, s. of Nathaniel (1), m. Luthera, dau. of David Allen, 18 Nov. 1813, and had *Charlotte Eliza*, b. 3 Sep. 1814, m. Rev. John H. Willis 24 Nov. 1833; *Charles Allen*, b. 6 Jan. 1817; *Mary Ann*, b. 13 Dec. 1819 or 1820; *Henry*, b. 25 Feb. 1823; *Louisa L.*, b. 9 Feb. 1831; *Sarah F.*, b. 1 Mar. 1833, m. Nelson Amsden, res. in Hk.; *Helen R.*, b. 3 Feb. 1835. JOHN the f. rem. to Dana about 1825, and d. 17 Mar. 1845; his w. Luthera d. 3 Oct. 1875, a. 80.

4. JOEL, s. of Nathaniel (1), m. Sarah Whipple, pub. 24 June 1811, and had *Alexander W.*, b. about 1814, and perhaps others. JOEL the f. d. 26 Sep. 1823.

5. ALEXANDER W., s. of Joel (4), m. Mary Williams of Dana, pub. 9 Jan. 1835; she d. ——, and he m. Mrs. Mary Ryan 4 Feb. 1867, and had *Daniel Willard*, b. 18 Aug. 1867. ALEXANDER W. the f. d. in Ware 17 Ap. 1869, a. 55.

6. JAMES H., parentage not ascertained, by w. Charlotte, had *James Henry*, b. 15 Sep. 1849; *Frederick Wilson*, b. 6 Ap. 1853; a daughter b. 19 Mar. 1856; *Frank Leslie*, b. 16 June 1862.

HENRY F., b. in Lee, d. 18 Ap. 1867, a. 43. EBENEZER W., m. Bethia Richardson, pub. 10 Mar. 1849 she d. 14 Jan. 1854, a. 55. CHARLES A., of N. Br., m. Lizzie, dau. of Joel Dwight Mandell, 17 Nov. 1875.

GOODALE, JOSEPH, m. Abigail Warden of Pet. 15 Aug. 1780, and prob. d. not long before 23 Jan. 1801, when Mrs. Abigail Goodale's child d. a. 3 months and 14 days.

AARON, of Salem, N. Y., m. Betsey, dau. of Benjamin and Elizabeth Ruggles, 9 Feb. 1802.

GOODENOW, JONATHAN, by w. Hannah, had *Hannah*, b. 8 Sep. 1744, m. Aaron Powers 10 Mar. 1768; *Elizabeth*, b. 20 July 1746. JONATHAN the f. d. 12 Ap. 1750, and his w. Hannah m. Ichabod Stratton, Jr., 1 July 1755.

2. BENJAMIN, m. Ruth Sanderson of Sudbury 23 Mar. 1762, and had *Lydia*, b. 11 July 1763; *Benjamin*, b. 11 Feb. 1765; *Ruth*, b. 4 Ap. 1767, m. John Carter of Gr., pub. 15 Mar. 1790; *Luke*, b. 11 Sep. 1768; *Anna*, bap. 8 July 1770.

ELIZABETH, m. Isaac Abbott 14 Aug. 1760.

GOODSPEED, EDWARD, prob. from Barnstable, m. Judith, dau. of Thomas Winslow, 19 Oct. 1764, and had *Elizabeth*, bap. 24 Nov. 1765. No further trace found.

2. SHEARJASHUB, perhaps brother of Edward (1), m. Elizabeth, dau. of Capt. Benjamin Ruggles, 20 Nov. 1766, and had *Alice*, b. 20 Feb. 1767; *Rhoda*, b. 19 Nov. 1769, m. Philip Amidon 27 Nov. 1788; *Anna*, b. 31 Aug. 1775; *Jocktan*, b. 13 Mar. 1778; *Seth*, b. 11 May 1780. SHEARJASHUB the f. was a Revolutionary soldier, and prob. rem. fr. Hk. before 1800.

MARTHA, of Barnstable, m. Samuel Winslow 12 June 1760. ABIGAIL, of Barnstable, m. Caleb Nye, Jr., pub. 24 Mar. 1771. NANCY, m. Cyrus Perry, pub. 28 June 1795. JOHN, m. Mary Billings 31 Dec. 1807.

GORE, WILLIAM N., m. Sarah M. J. Cleveland, pub. 11 Feb. 1851, and had a dau. b. 14 Nov. 1852; *Almon Cleveland*, b. 5 May 1858; *Evert Edward*, b. 28 May 1860; *Charles Clarence*, b. 22 Nov. 1862.

CHESTER, m. Cynthia M. Forbush 12 Nov. 1845.

GORHAM, STEPHEN, prob. of the Barnstable family, m. Sarah, dau. of Dea. John Freeman, 16 Mar. 1757, and had *John*, b. 4 Jan. 1759; *Josiah*, b. 12 June 1760; *Stephen*, b. 19 July 1762; *Silas*, b. 19 Ap. 1764, m. Cynthia Hanmer, pub. 24 Oct. 1784, and had a child, who d. (infant) 26 Jan. 1797; *Joseph*, b. 13 Feb. 1766; *David*, b. 17 June 1768, m. Jane Luce 8 Aug. 1791, res. in Barre; *Challis*, b. 23 Feb. 1770; *Joanna*, b. 6 June 1771, m. Mayo Luce of Pet. 1 July 1793; *Priscilla*, b. 26 — 1773; *Eli*, b. 10 May 1775.

2. JOHN, s. of Stephen (1), m. Mary, dau. of Capt. Samuel Dexter, 3 June 1784, and had *Thomas*, b. —— 1784, m. Hannah Utley 12 Dec. 1811, and d. in Barre 15 Dec. 1867, a. 83; *Susan*, b. ——, m. Nathan Taylor, pub. 27 Nov. 1806; *John*, bap. 10 Feb. 1805; *Sally* and *De La Fayette*, both bap. 24 Mar. 1805. JOHN the f. d. in Barre 24 Ap. 1847, a. 88.

3. STEPHEN, s. of Stephen (1), m. Lettice, dau. of Samuel Thurston, 6 Nov. 1798, and had *Hiram*, b. 30 Aug. 1799, m. Mary M., dau. of Sylvanus Taylor, 26 Nov. 1829, and d. at Worcester 15 Ap. 1880; *Lewis*, b. 15 Mar. 1801, d. at Springfield 26 Jan. 1868; *Sally Weston*, b. 20 Ap. 1803, m. Beals Thomas, pub. 21 Oct. 1837, d. 19 Dec. 1857; *Lucinda*, b. 15 Mar. 1805; *Chester Field*, b. 16 Mar. 1807; *Joseph Warren*, b. 21 Mar. 1809, d. at Springf. 18 July, 1855; *William Osman*, b. 10 Oct. 1811, d. 29 June 1812; *William Osman*, b. 19 Sep. 1814, d. at Athol 7 Nov. 1869; a child b. ——, d. 27 Jan. 1817, a. 3 days; *Elbridge*, b. 8 Ap. 1818, d. at Worcester 19 Nov. 1858. STEPHEN the f. d. 7 Jan. 1825, a. 62; his w. Lettice d. 22 Ap. 1831, a. 55.

ANTIS, m. Seth Hinkley, pub. 25 Aug. 1822. MRS. RUTH, m. Dr. Convers Cutler, pub. 9 July 1824. JASON, m. Anna Newcomb 12 July 1827, and d. at Barre 23 May 1881, a. 84. MARY ANN, m. Daniel B. Hinkley of Bucksport, Me., pub. 8 Ap. 1830.

GOULD, SAMUEL, by w. Alice, had *Levi*, b. 22 Ap. 1763.

2. HAFFIELD, b. in Milbury, res. in Worc., where his w. Judith d. 1808, a. 25, and in Pelham, where his w. Betsey d. 8 July 1815, a. 35; he then rem. to Hk., and m. Lydia, dau. of Lemuel Ruggles, 26 Oct. 1817. His chil. were: *Ira P.*, b. about 1814; *Henry Brigham*, b. 7 Sep. 1818; *Austin*, b. 21 Dec. 1819, m. Arathusa C. Powers 16 Oct. 1851, and d. 31 Aug. 1864; *Jonathan Lewis*, b. 21 Sep. 1821, d. 27 Feb. 1823; *Orin*, b. 9 Dec. 1823; *Cordelia*, b. 20 Nov. 1827, m. John J. Newcomb, pub. 13 Mar. 1857. HAFFIELD the f. was a farmer, res. on Ruggles Hill, at the place marked "H. Gould" on the R. Map, was selectman fourteen years, and d. 21 Sep. 1856, a. 78; his w. Lydia d. 10 Mar. 1850, a. 67.

3. IRA P., s. of Haffield (2), was a school-teacher, member of the school committee nine years, rem. to Ware, where he d. 15 Nov. 1861, a. 47; Mrs. Martha M. Gould, prob. his w., and dau. of Arba Hastings, d. at Ware 19 Ap. 1850, a. 31.

4. HENRY B., s. of Haffield (2), m. Nancy M., dau. of Joseph D. Dexter, 6 May 1847, and had *Ella Maria*, b. 9 Sep. 1851, d. 13 Mar. 1858; *Nancy Maria*, b. 18 June 1859, d. 26 June 1859; *Henry Brigham*, b. 23 July 1860, d. 30 July 1860. HENRY B. the f. was a selectman seven years, and d. 8 July 1863; his w. Nancy M. m. Joseph C. Paige 2 Nov. 1865.

5. OREN, s. of Haffield (2), m. Sarah A., dau. of Stillman Clark, 25 Nov. 1851, and had *Sarah Alice*, b. 13 Oct. 1858, m. Joseph S. Hillman 3 May 1882; *Anna Emma*, b. 31 May 1861; *Lura Adelia*, b. 8 Feb. 1865. OREN the f., a farmer, res. on the turnpike, at the place marked "Mr. Browning" on the R. Map; his w. Sarah A. d. 25 Feb. 1878, a. 48, and he m. Mrs. Sarah H. Jones of Prescott, dau. of Benjamin Aiken, 16 Sep. 1879.

OLIVE, m. Joseph D. Dexter 15 Nov. 1818. JOSEPH A., m. Relief Shumway of Pet. pub. 18 Jan. 1839.

GRANGER, DANIEL, had w. Catherine, who d. 25 Mar. 1825, a. 38, and he m. ——, dau. of Jonathan Mead. His chil. were: *William F.*, b. about 1806;

John H., b. about 1808, d. at Boston 20 Jan. 1859, a. 50; a child b. —— 1814, d. 20 Oct. 1815, a. 10 months; *Henry H.*, b. about 1817; *Timothy D.*, b. —— 1819; *Catherine*, b. about 1822, d. 31 Oct. 1831, a. 9; and perhaps others. DANIEL the f. was a painter, and res. at the Furnace Village.

2. WILLIAM F., s. of Daniel (1), m. Elizabeth K. Mead, sister of his father's second wife, 26 Nov. 1829, and had *Helen J.*, b. about 1841, m. Josiah White 26 May 1863; and prob. others. WILLIAM F. the f. d. 12 Feb. 1864, a. 57; his w. Elizabeth K. d. 14 June 1879, a. 68.

3. HENRY H., s. of Daniel (1), m. Lucy M. Woodward 30 Mar. 1837, and had *Henry C.*, b. about 1840, a soldier in the war of the Rebellion, killed in battle at Williamsburg, Va., 5 May 1862; *Katie*, b. ——, m. John King; *Francis Wilson*, b. 24 Mar. 1845, d. 23 Mar. 1846; *Louis E.*, b. ——; *Carrie Louisa*, b. 22 Mar. 1853; *Leslie Manson*, b. 30 July 1855; and perhaps others. HENRY H. the f. was a painter, and res. in the Hinkley house, at the north end of the Common. He performed faithful and honorable service as a lieutenant in the war of the Rebellion, was wounded in the battle at Hatcher's Run, Va., 27 Oct. 1864, and d. three days later (30 Oct.), at City Point, a. 47. He was buried in the new cemetery, with public ceremonies.

4. TIMOTHY D., s. of Daniel (1), m. Ruth Carter 4 June 1844, and had *Lydia Jane Josephine*, b. 20 Ap. 1845; *George W.*, b. 22 Nov. 1850; *Louisa Lilian*, 20 June 1852. TIMOTHY D. the f. d. at N. Brk. 20 June 1867, a. 48.

5. DANIEL (2d), m. Emily Moulton 16 June 1837, and had *Emily Ann*, b. 10 July 1838; *Rebecca Bardwell*, b. 2 Sep. 1840, d. unm. 12 Mar. 1858; *Ella Charlotte*, b. 13 Jan. 1843; *Susan Elizabeth*, b. 1 Aug. 1846; *Daniel Franklin*, b. 9 Dec. 1848, d. 4 Oct. 1857; *Sarah Robinson*, b. 19 Feb. 1851. EMILY the mother d. 11 Dec. 1855, a. 40.

6. WILLIAM P., m. Samantha M. Stone 28 Oct. 1852, and had *Lizzie Josephine*, b. 3 Mar. 1856; *Nellie M.*, b. — Feb. 1859, d. 31 Oct. 1865; *Cora Louisa*, b. 28 Nov. 1861, d. 13 June 1865. SAMANTHA M. the mother d. 9 Feb. 1865, a. 29.

ANN MARIA, m. Joseph Robbins, pub. 23 Nov. 1851.

GRANT, PHILIP ROSAN, by w. Susan, had *Susan*, b. about 1783, d. unm. 25 Mar. 1813, a. 30; prob. *Hannah*, b. ——, m. Nathan Robinson 16 Oct. 1804; *Philip*, b. about 1787; *Joseph*, b. —— 1790, d. 6 July 1791, a. 1 year, 4 months; prob. *Susanna*, b. ——, m. Samson Presho, pub. 4 Nov. 1808; *Lucinda*, b. —— 1792, d. 8 Aug. 1795, a. 3; and perhaps others. PHILIP the f. is understood to have been a Hessian soldier, captured with Burgoyne's army. He d. 2 Jan. 1812, a. 52.

2. PHILIP, s. of Philip (1), m. Lucy Allen, 2 Nov. 1809; she d. 2 Feb. 1837, and he m. Lucy, dau. of Eli Barnes, 28 Feb. 1839; she d. 26 Jan. 1846, a. 60, according to the record. His chil. were: *Electa*, b. 20 July 1811; *Lucy*, b. 15 June 1813, d. unm. 10 Aug. 1835; *Lewis*, b. 31 Mar. 1815, m. Susan M. Davis of Falmouth, pub. 16 Sep. 1845; *George*, b. 20 June 1817; *Hannah Robinson*, b. 15 Mar. 1820, d. unm. 15 Dec. 1838; *Susanna*, b. 21 Sep. 1822; *Philip*, b. 9 Feb. 1825; *Esther Elizabeth*, b. 14 May 1827, m. Luther Smith 21 July 1847; *Harriet*, b. 16 Sep. 1830, m. —— Cowles, and d. at Chicopee, 12 July 1870; *Joseph*, b. 9 Oct. 1832.

ABIGAIL, m. Horace Stone, 14 Ap. 1822.

GREEN, JOHN, prob. s. of Thomas, and b. in Shrewsbury 2 Mar. 1726, m. Anna Bradish 7 Dec. 1751, and had *William*, b. 21 Sep. 1752; *John*, b. 3 May 1754. JOHN the f. was a tanner and a soldier. He was killed in battle 8 Sep. 1755. In his will he made provision for his wife and two children, and also for his mother Mary. His w. Anna prob. m. Stephen Fisk of Gr. 29 June 1758. MARY, of Southborough, who m. John Bradish, pub. 12 May 1746, and SARAH, who m. Peter Gibben 7 Dec. 1751, were prob. his sisters.

2. LARKIN, m. Elizabeth Rose, pub. 15 Feb. 1756, and had *Thomas*, b. 16 Ap. 1757; *Josiah*, b. 26 Sep. 1758.

DR. JOHN, of Worcester, m. Mary, dau. of General Timothy Ruggles, pub. 19 Mar. 1762. SOLOMON, of Leicester, brother of Dr. John, m. Elizabeth, dau. of Colonel Timothy Paige, 29 Dec. 1763; she d. 1 Ap. 1802, a. 59. BEN-

JAMIN, m. Hannah, dau. of James Robinson, 31 Aug. 1764. EBENEZER, m. Elizabeth Doane of Brk., pub. 5 Nov. 1798. JOHN, m. Asenath Burden 29 Jan. 1801. BENJAMIN, m. Eliza Barrows, pub. 29 May 1813. THOMAS R., of Bel., m. Persis M. Nye 9 May 1844. LUCRETIA, m. James Jackson 2 Ap. 1848. MRS. HANNAH, d. 25 May 1750.

GRIFFITH, STEPHEN, by w. Hannah, had *Stephen*, b. 20 Mar. 1720-1; *Nathaniel*, b. 24 Feb. 1722-3; *Elnathan*, b. 9 Feb. 1724-5; *Hannah*, bap. in Hk. by Rev. Timothy Ruggles 26 May 1735 (see note under *David Gitchell*); *Seth*, bap. 23 Oct. 1737. STEPHEN the f. was prob. b. at Harwich; he res. in Rochester, where his first three chil. were born, but rem. to Hk. as early as 1735, and was selectman in 1737. He is styled "Gent." in a deed of land, having been ensign of militia.

2. DAVID, s. of William, b. in Rochester 21 Dec. 1717, by w. Eleanor, had *Abraham*, b. 29 Dec. 1745; *Susanna*, b. 17 Mar. 1748; *Mehetabel*, b. 5 Mar. 1752. DAVID the f. settled in Hk. as early as 1745.

HAGAR, JOEL, for many years managed the farm formerly owned by Maj. Timothy Billings, was a jolly "trooper" in the cavalry, m. Mary Fairbanks 27 Ap. 1824, and rem. from the town.

HALE, JOSEPH, m. Nabby Hanmer, pub. 3 Dec. 1786, and had *Melinda*, b. 18 July 1787; *Nabby*, b. 4 Ap. 1791; *Patty*, b. 29 Sep. 1796; *Zenas Hanmer*, b. 11 Nov. 1798; *Mordecai*, b. 8 May 1800. JOSEPH the f. was a blacksmith, and res. in what is now Gilbertville. He prob. rem. from the town about 1802.

ALMIRA, m. Hiram Lawrence, pub. 26 Nov. 1827. THOMAS, m. Harriet Nye of Springf., pub. 12 Sep. 1848.

HALL, THOMAS, by w. Harriet M., had *Electa Luella*, b. 27 May 1851.

2. HOUGHTON, had w. Joanna F., who d. 13 Aug. 1862, a. 42, and he m. Priscilla McClintock 25 Dec. 1862. His chil. were: *George*, b. —— 1855, d. 14 Jan. 1860, a. 4 years and 8 months; *Josephine Augusta*, b. 20 Nov. 1858, d. 29 Sep. 1860; *Joanna Louisa*, b. 30 July 1861, d. 6 Feb. 1862; *Charles Herbert*, b. 7 July 1865; *Franklin Putnam*, b. 19 Ap. 1868; *Alfred Houghton*, b. 8 Feb. 1870.

DANIEL, m. Alma Spooner, pub. 9 Feb. 1806. SARAH, m. Joseph Lee 21 June 1851. SARAH E., m. Alfred C. King 1 Oct. 1873.

HAMILTON, JOSEPH N., m. Clara D. Prouty 16 June 1866, and had *Lulu Hannah*, b. 28 Oct. 1868.

2. JOHN, by w. Harriet E., had *John Lucius*, b. 25 Sep. 1868; and by w. Ellen, *James Frederick*, b. 6 Jan. 1871.

WIDOW MARGARET, d. 7 Dec. 1819, a. 91.

HAMMOND, THOMAS, by w. Abiah, had *Nathaniel*, b. 3 Oct. 1746; *Isaac*, b. 25 Oct. 1748; *Bridget*, b. 11 Sep. 1750.

2. NATHANIEL, m. Martha, widow of John Wells, 6 Aug. 1746, and had *Timothy*, b. 13 May 1748. At the time of his marriage, NATHANIEL the f. was styled captain. He had previously res. at Lower Ashuelot, now Swansea, N. H., which was that year abandoned by the English to the fury of the Indians. He d. before 19 July 1758, when his w. Martha m. Nathaniel Kellogg of Hadley.

3. GIDEON, had w. Abigail, who d. 31 Aug. 1795, a. 51, and he m. Lucy Jackson 15 May 1796. His chil. were: *Elisha*; *Nabby*, m. Nathaniel Perry of Pittsford, Vt., 17 Oct. 1793; *Molly Nye*; *Sylvina*; *Sally*, b. 3 Feb. 1780; all bap. 15 Sep. 1782. GIDEON the f. was a blacksmith, and res. near the Old Furnace. He rem. to Plainfield.

LOIS, of Rochester, m. Nathaniel Merrick 29 May 1764. HANNAH, of Pet., m. David Pratt 12 Oct. 1780. MARY, m. Timothy Fay, Jr., 7 Nov. 1822. PERLEY, m. Harriet, dau. of Scotto Berry, 1 Ap. 1832. TIMOTHY W., m. Mary A. Houghton of Pet., pub. 25 Ap. 1835. JOSEPH W., of Pet., m. Abigail Paige, pub. 26 Ap. 1844, and rem. to Cambridge.

HANMER, JOHN, son of John (who rem. from Halifax to Bridgewater in 1739), m. Martha, dau. of Joseph Prior, —— 1760, and had *Nabby*, b. 1 Sep. 1761, m. Joseph Hale, pub. 3 Dec. 1786; *Lucinda*, b. —— 1763; *Cynthia*,

b. 16 July 1765, m. Silas Gorham, pub. 24 Oct. 1784; *Zenas*, b. 5 Nov. 1767; *Perninah*, b. 8 May 1770, m. Paul Paige 15 July 1790; *Salmon*, b. 15 Feb. 1773, d. 20 Mar. 1791. JOHN the f. rem. to Hk. in 1770; all his chil. except the last were born in Bridgewater, though recorded here; his wid. Martha d. 1 Feb. 1823, a. 86.

POLLY, m. Ishmael Bowker of Ware 16 Sep. 1792.

HARMON, ELIJAH B., by w. Nancy, had Henry, b. 14 May 1791; *Celia*, b. 1 Dec. 1793, m. Francis Slason of Rutland, Vt., pub. 11 Aug. 1822; *Charles*, b. 26 Aug. 1795; *Ralph*, b. 3 Nov. 1797, d. 30 Ap. 1803; *William*, b. 1 July 1802, d. 12 May 1803. *Elijah B.* the f. was a hatter, selectman two years, treasurer seventeen years, res. on the turnpike, at the place marked "Mr. Stimpson" on the R. Map, until 1798, and afterwards at the place marked "W. Mandell," adjoining the estate of Hon. William Mixter. After 1825 he rem. to Rutland, Vt., where both he and his w. attained a good old age.

HARRINGTON, STEPHEN, was here in 1735, and, by w. Elizabeth, had *Daniel*, b. 16 Dec. 1737.

2. LEMUEL, with w. Eleanor, dau. of Capt. John McClenathan, came to Hk. from Rutland; he was a tanner, and res. at the place marked "S. Berry" on the R. Map, and afterwards, in connection with Col. Thomas Wheeler, erected the New Furnace near Gilbertville, and engaged in the manufacture of iron-ware, residing at the place marked "L. Harrington." He was an assessor two years, and d. s. p. 1 Feb. 1833, a. 69; his w. Eleanor d. 23 Nov. 1846, a. 90.

LAWSON, m. Elizabeth McClenathan of Brk., pub. 13 Aug. 1821.

HARRIS, GEORGE, by w. Hannah, had *William*, b. 24 Feb. 1764.

2. STEPHEN, by w. Arathusa, had *Sarah Abigail*, b. 6 Feb. 1841; *Harriet Alzina*, b. 4 Jan. 1843.

OLIVER, m. Mehetabel Shaw 4 Sep. 1781. MARGARET, m. Solomon Mason, Jr., of Gr. 30 Jan. 1783. JOHN, m. Abigail Ware of N. Br. 2 July 1787. SUSANNA, m. Calvin Bryant, pub. 25 Jan. 1789. OLIVER, Jr., of Dana, m. Mary Barlow, pub. 24 June 1811.

HARVEY, JOHN, m. Elizabeth M., dau. of Phineas Beaman, 28 Feb. 1860, and had *John Bernard*, b. 24 Dec. 1860; *Herman J.*, b. —— 1861, d. 6 Sep. 1863; *Eddie B.*, b. 26 Nov. 1864, d. 10 Aug. 1865; *Elmer Phineas*, b. 4 Oct. 1868.

MARY W., m. F. La Fayette Tibbetts of Charlestown 12 Jan. 1853. CHARLES A., m. Abbie H. Flint of Athol, pub. 17 Dec. 1855, and rem. to Boston. CORNELIA K., m. Elijah Bridges 1 Aug. 1861. JANE A., m. Horace Knight, pub. 20 Feb. 1866. HIRAM W., s. of Charles M., d. 21 Dec. 1852, a. 16. HANNAH R., wid. of Charles M. and dau. of Phineas Bond, d. 27 Jan. 1879, a. 77.

HARWOOD, PETER (otherwise written Harrard and Harrod), res. at Concord, and had *Nathaniel, John, Benjamin* (b. 30 Ap. 1713), *Joseph, Ebenezer, Mary*, and *Hannah*. See *Harwood Gen.*, by Mrs. Sarah Robinson.

2. JOHN, prob. s. of Peter (1), by w. Mary, had (all recorded here, though two or three were prob. b. elsewhere) *Sarah*, b. 26 Feb. 1729-30; *Lydia*, b. 22 Jan. 1731-2; *Mary*, b. 3 Mar. 1734; *John*, b. 25 June 1736; *James*, b. 3 Aug. 1737; *Andrew*, bap. 20 Sep. 1743, m. Rachel Higgins, pub. 3 Feb. 1771.

3. BENJAMIN, s. of Peter (1), m. Bridget Brown — May, 1733, and had at Concord *Peter*, b. 14 July 1735; he then rem. to Hardwick, where he had *Eleazar*, b. 28 Sep. 1737; *Benjamin*, b. 20 Ap. 1739, m. Catherine Chauncy, and d. at Amherst in 1760; *Zechariah*, b. 11 Mar. 1742, m. Lovina, dau. of Oliver Rice, 30 Ap. 1767; *Mary*, b. 10 June 1745; *Ebenezer*, b. 2 Feb. 1749, d. about 1753; *Stephen*, b. 25 June 1751; *Abigail*, b. 4 Nov. 1753; and *Hepzibah*, b. at Amherst 26 Nov. 1756. BENJAMIN the f. was a zealous Separatist, rem. to Amherst about 1756, and d. 19 Aug. 1758; his w. Bridget went with the first company of emigrants to Bennington, Vt., in June 1761, and d. there 8 Nov. 1762, a. 47; her chil. accompanied her to Ben., and Benjamin, son of her son *Peter*, was the first white child born in that town, 12 Jan. 1762. See *Harwood Gen., ut supra*.

4. ABEL, parentage not ascertained, m. Sarah, dau. of Capt. Benjamin Ruggles, 27 Nov. 1765, and had *Benjamin*, b. 13 Nov. 1766, m. Elizabeth, dau. of Rev. Robert Cutler, and d. in Enfield 24 Dec. 1852; *Sarah*, b. 21 Feb. 1769. ABEL the f. was a blacksmith, bought five acres of land here 1 Mar. 1762, and d. 2 Mar. 1770, a. 28; his w. Sarah m. Ezra Alden of Gr. 2 Jan. 1772.

5. ANDREW J., by w. Harriet, had *Albert L.*, b. 10 Sep. 1847.

6. DAUPHIN, by w. Sylvia, had *Mary M.*, b.——, d. 10 Feb. 1856, a. 14; *Ellen*, b. about 1850, m. Thomas F. Boyle of W. Dover, Vt., 22 Jan. 1873; *Mary Amelia*, b. 18 May 1851.

SARAH S., m. William W. Parks of Pal., pub. 10 Feb. 1866.

HASKELL, ROGER, b. in England, 1713, m. Elizabeth Hardy, and had *John* (settled in Middleborough), *William*, *Mark*, *Elizabeth*, *Hannah*, *Josiah*, *Roger*, *Samuel*, and *Sarah*. ROGER the f. was a fisherman, res. at Salem in 1636, and afterwards at Beverly, where he d. in 1667. He had brothers William and Mark.

2. MARK, s. of Roger (1), m. Mary, dau. of John Smith, 20 Mar. 1677–8, and had *Roger*, b. 17 Oct. 1680; *John*, b. 14 Feb. 1681–2; *Mark*, b. 5 Feb. 1683–4; *Elizabeth*, b. 10 Nov. 1686; *Mary*, b. 23 Ap. 1689; *Joseph*, b. 3 Nov. 1692. MARK the f. was a carpenter, and res. in Beverly until 3 Ap. 1693, when he bought a large tract of land in Rochester, to which place he rem. soon, was town clerk in 1697, and d. 17 May 1699; his w. Mary survived.

3. ROGER, s. of Mark (2), m. Joanna Swift of Sandwich 25 Jan. 1707–8, and had *Mark*, b. 28 Mar. 1709; *Ephraim*, b. 9 Feb. 1711–12; *Hannah*, b. 9 Sep. 1714; *Ebenezer*, b. 20 Feb. 1716–17; *Elizabeth*, b. 11 June 1720; *Joanna*, b. 26 May 1725; *Susanna*, b. 18 Oct. 1730. *Roger* the f. res. in Rochester.

4. JOHN, s. of Mark (2), by w. Mehetabel, had *Sarah*, b. 24 Sep. 1706; *Rebecca*, b. 14 Dec. 1707; *John*, b. 13 May 1709, perhaps m. Elizabeth Lawrence of Hk. 4 Mar. 1753; *Roger* and *Andrew*, twins, b. 8 Mar. 1710–11; *Mehetabel*, b. 3 Jan. 1712–13, m. Cornelius Cannon 5 Jan. 1732–3; *Mary*, b. 23 Ap. 1714, m. Dudley Jordan 23 Dec. 1739; *Thomas*, b. 27 Jan. 1715–16; *Zechariah*, b. 11 Ap. 1718; *Moses*, b. 18 Sep. 1719. JOHN the f. res. in Rochester; administration on his estate was granted to his w. Mehetabel 21 June 1728. The larger part of his children rem. to Hardwick.

5. MARK, s. of Mark (2), by w. Rebecca, had in Rochester *Joanna*, b. 29 Jan. 1710–11; *Mary*, b. 3 Jan. 1712–13; *Thomas*, b. 11 Sep. 1714; *Mark*, b. 22 Sep. 1716.

6. JOSEPH, s. of Mark (2), by w. Bethia, had *Nathaniel*, b. 26 July 1717, d. 27 May 1729; *Jane*, b. 17 May 1719, m. Joshua Lawrence 13 July 1743, and res. in Hk.; *Sarah*, b. 4 Oct. 1720; *Joseph*, b. 5 Mar. 1721–2; *Mary*, b. 22 Mar. 1723–4; *Elnathan*, b. 29 Dec. 1725, m. Dorothy, wid. of David Peckham and dau. of James Robinson, 26 Nov. 1749; *John*, b. 1 Mar. 1727–8; *Bethia*, b. 25 Jan. 1729–30; *Abigail*, b. 6 Feb. 1731–2; *Hannah*, b. 16 Aug. 1734. JOSEPH the f. was a carpenter, and one of the early proprietors of Hardwick, but res. in Rochester.

7. MARK, s. of Roger (3), m. Mary Spooner of Dartmouth 21 Dec. 1730, and had *Nathaniel*, b. 26 Feb. 1731–2, rem. to Hk.; *Samuel*, b. 6 Feb. 1733–4; *Micah*, b. 20 Nov. 1735; *Joanna*, b. 11 Dec. 1737; by second w. Abiah, he had *Mary*, b. 24 May 1741; *Roger*, b. 31 May 1742 (settled in Middleborough and had s. Simeon, who was father of Mark Haskell of Oakham); *Elisha*, b. 22 Feb. 1743–4. MARK the f. res. in Rochester.

8. EPHRAIM, s. of Roger (3), by w. Mehetabel, had *Joanna*, b. 13 May 1740; *Elizabeth*, b. 2 July 1741, prob. m. Nathaniel Merrick 26 June 1775; *Deborah*, b. 15 July 1743; *Ephraim*, b. 25 Feb. 1744–5; *Jabez*, b. 15 Nov. 1746; *Barnabas*, b. 25 Sep. 1748; *Elias*, b. 24 Mar. 1750–1; *Ebenezer*, b. 1 Ap. 1754. EPHRAIM the f. res. in Rochester; he bought a farm here 23 Feb. 1773, but d. before 25 Feb. 1774, and his son *Ephraim* had the farm.

9. ROGER, s. of John (4), m. Alice Spooner of Rochester, 13 Mar. 1736–7, and had *Rebecca*, b. 20 Nov. 1738, d. young; *Mehetabel*, b. 17 Jan. 1740–1; *Rebecca*, b. 29 Mar. 1743; *Roger*, b. 11 July 1746, m. Joanna, dau. of Thomas

Haskell, 28 May 1772; *Hannah*, b. 15 May 1750. ROGER the f. rem. to Hk. before his marriage and res. on the east side of the river (now New Braintree), near Ditch Meadow. He d. 21 Dec. 1750; the inventory of his w. Alice was filed 31 May 1759.

10. ANDREW, s. of John (4), m. Jane Clark 25 Nov. 1733; she d. and he m. Susanna Paine of Shutes. 10 July 1777. His chil., all b. in Rochester, were *Mehetabel*, b. 22 Dec. 1735, d. young; *Mary*, b. 26 Mar. 1738, m. —— Whitcomb; *John*, b. 28 July 1741, m. Hannah, dau. of Rev. Robert Cutler of Gr., 28 Ap. 1763; *Mehetabel*, b. 9 July 1744, m. Freeman Sears 22 Oct. 1761. ANDREW the f. was a housewright; he rem. from Roch. to Dartmouth after 1744, and thence to Hk. about 1761, when he bought a farm in the north part of the town, which he exchanged in 1779 for the parsonage formerly owned by Rev. David White. His son was joint owner of the estate, and it was sold, 27 May 1795, to Dr. William Cutler. Mr. Haskell's will was proved 21 Ap. 1796, about which time he d., and his son rem. from the town; his w. Susanna was living in 1795.

11. THOMAS, s. of John (4), m. Hannah Goss of Brk. 12 Nov. 1742; she d. 15 May 1749, a. 25, and he m. Joanna Hunt of Gr., pub. 13 Jan. 1749–50. His chil., all recorded here, were: *Hannah*, b. 12 May 1744, m. Nathan Foster 14 Mar. 1765; *Alice*, b. 17 Ap. 1746, d. 25 June 1746; *Lois*, b. 15 Sep. 1747, m. Asa Curtis of N. Sal. 27 Nov. 1766; *Joanna*, b. 19 Jan. 1750–1, m. Roger Haskell 28 May 1772; *Rhoda*, b. 20 Dec. 1753; *Thomas*, b. 14 Mar. 1755; *Andrew*, bap. 10 Ap. 1757, perhaps the same who (then of Wilmington, Vt.) m. Chloe Freeman 12 Oct. 1780. THOMAS the f. was a farmer, and res. on the Barre road, at or near the place marked "W. Sturtevant" on the R. Map. He prob. rem. to Wilmington, Vt., about 1779.

12. ZECHARIAH, s. of John (4), m. Kezia Goss of Brk. 20 Aug. 1745, and had *Sarah*, b. 8 Ap. 1747; *John*, b. 17 July 1749; *Kezia*, b. 19 May 1751; *Roger*, b. 2 Ap. 1753; *Philip*, bap. 13 July 1755; *Simeon*, bap. 21 May 1758. ZECHARIAH the f. was a tailor, and res. about a hundred rods northerly from the turnpike on the road from Mandell Hill to Ruggles Hill.

13. MOSES, s. of John (4), m. Lydia Clark of Roch., pub. 18 May 1751, and had *Mary*, b. 22 June 1752, m. John Hedge 7 Sep. 1777; *Lydia*, b. 4 July 1753, m. Edward Taylor 23 Nov. 1775; *Thankful*, b. 10 Aug. 1754; *Mehetabel*, b. 17 Mar. 1756, d. young; *Moses*, b. 20 Dec. 1757, m. Priscilla Hinkley 12 Jan. 1780; *Mehetabel*, b. 15 Oct. 1760; *Alice*, b. 13 July 1762; *Rebecca*, b. 6 Mar. 1765. MOSES the f. was a blacksmith, and res. on the Barre road at the place marked "S. Clark" on the R. Map.

14. NATHANIEL, s. of Mark (7), m. Lydia, dau. of Dea. James Foster of Roch., pub. 3 Ap. 1757; she d. and he m. Sarah Carter of Gr., pub. 25 May 1790. His chil. were: *Prince*, b. 26 Ap. 1758; *George*, b. 23 Ap. 1761; *Nathaniel*, b. 15 July 1762, settled in Barnard, Vt.; *Mary*, b. 1 July 1765; and perhaps *David*, who d. at Shutes. 22 Feb. 1850, a. 81, and *Lydia*, who m. Jeremiah Powers 3d, of Gr., pub. 24 Dec. 1788. NATHANIEL the f. was a farmer and cordwainer, and res. in the northwesterly part of the town, at the place erroneously marked "Dea. Haskins" on the R. Map; he d. 16 July 1821; his w. Sarah d. 15 Sep. 1809, a. 69.

15. EPHRAIM, s. of Ephraim (8), m. Eunice Nye of Roch. 22 Jan. 1769; she d. 11 Sep. 1796, a. 48, and he m. Mary Hammond of N. Sal., pub. 26 Feb. 1797. His chil. were: *Nathan*, b. about 1770, m. (then of Wendell) Lucy Knowlton 2 June 1795; *Micah*, b. about 1772, m. Betsey Cobb 8 May 1797; *Stephen*, b. 23 Sep. 1775, m. Phebe Robinson 27 Dec. 1801; *Ephraim*, b. 14 Mar. 1778 (these four were bap. 1 Oct. 1780); *Eunice*, b. 4 July 1781, m. Chester Powers of Western, (now Warren), 15 Oct. 1805; *Joanna*, b. 27 Ap. 1784, m. the same Chester Powers 1 Sep. 1830; *Lucy*, b. 27 Aug. 1786, m. Seth Clark of Conway 17 Feb. 1808; *Elizabeth*, b. 17 July 1789. EPHRAIM the f. was a farmer, rem. from Roch. to Hk. in 1774, and res. in the northerly part of the town, on a farm bought by his father the previous year, at the place marked "Mr. Haskell" on the R. Map. He attained old age but the date of his death is not recorded.

16. PRINCE, s. of Nathaniel (14), m. Leah Wilder of Hingham 4 Oct. 1780, and had *Edward Wilder*, b. 5 June 1782, d. young; *Deborah*, b. 18 Mar. 1784; and, at Barnard, *Harriet*, b. 9 June 1786; *Prince*, b. 2 May 1788; *Edward Wilder*, b. 29 Sep. 1789; *Nathaniel*, b. 30 Oct. 1791; *Polly*, b. 6 Feb. 1798; *Adeline*, b. 29 Aug. 1801. PRINCE the f. settled early in Barnard, Vt., and was there captured by the Indians, 9 Aug. 1780, and carried to Canada. His captivity, however, was short; for he was exchanged in season to be married in the succeeding October, having been pub. in February. It would seem that he did not expose his family to the dangers of a frontier life until after the birth of his second child. He rem. his family to Barnard, was an active citizen, and was living in 1824 on the same farm from which he was taken captive.

17. GEORGE, s. of Nathaniel (14), m. Comfort Knowlton 25 Ap. 1782, and had *Charles Holman*, b. 19 Jan. 1783; *Abraham*, b. 3 July 1784; *Lydia*, b. 11 Mar. 1786; *Comfort*, b. 22 Ap. 1789, m. Freeman Dexter, 14 Jan. 1812; *Sarah*, b. 23 Dec. 1791, m. Lemuel Wicker 5 Oct. 1813; *Mary*, b. 22 Dec. 1793, m. Ira Wicker of Bridport, Vt., 1 Oct. 1812; *Abigail*, b. 8 Sep. 1795, m. William Haskell of Pet. 16 May 1821; *Mark*, b. 6 Mar. 1798; *Benjamin Franklin*, b. 9 Mar. 1801; *Deborah*, b. 30 Sep. 1802, m. Joseph Whipple 2d, 15 Ap. 1824. GEORGE the f. was a farmer and cordwainer; he inherited the homestead, and d. at Waldoboro', Me., 25 May 1837, a. 76; his w. Comfort d. 14 or 16 Mar. 1837, a. 76. Both have head-stones in the new cemetery.

18. EPHRAIM, s. of Ephraim (15), m. Thankful, dau. of Capt. Zenas Phinney, 24 Oct. 1805; she d. 15 Nov. 1841, a. 60, and he m. Maria Ayers of N. Br., pub. 5 Mar. 1842. His chil. were: *Mary Clark*, b. ——, prob. d. unm. 3 Oct. 1838, a. 28; *Thankful*, b. 8 June 1813, prob. d. young; *Sarah Berry*, b. ——, d. unm. 2 Sep. 1836, a. 23; *William Nye*, b. 12 Mar. 1817, m. Susan B. Johnson of Pet., pub. 29 Mar. 1841 (*Mary C.*, *Sarah B.*, and *William N.* were bap. 16 June 1820); *Martha Phinney*, bap. 7 June 1821, d. unm. 5 May 1837. EPHRAIM the f. was a farmer and inherited the homestead. He erected a new house at the northwest corner of his farm, on the Petersham road, at the place marked "E. Haskell" on the R. Map. He d. at Pet. 5 or 6 Mar. 1863, but was buried here by the side of his first wife.

19. MARK, s. of George (17), m. Sarah Haskell of N. Brk., pub. 6 Jan. 1823; she d. 22 Mar. 1824, a. 25, and he m. Charlotte C. Holt of Brk., pub. 13 Mar. 1826. Some of his chil. were: *Sarah Carter*, b. —— 1824, bap. 29 Jan. 1829; *Matthew Wood*, b. —— 1827, bap. 29 Jan. 1829, grad. A. C. 1853, d. at Amherst 25 Nov. 1856, a. 29; *Charlotte Cordelia*, bap. 2 July 1830; *Abby M.*, b. —— 1831, d. unm. at Amh. 19 Ap. 1851, a. 19 years and 6 months; *William W.*, bap. 22 June 1834, d. at Amh. 7 May 1854; *Caroline Eliza*, bap. 1 July 1836. MARK the f. was a farmer and deacon, res. on the homestead, and rem. to Amherst about 1841.

20. JONATHAN R., m. Eliza H. Hunt 3 Dec. 1829, and had *Eunice J.*, who m. Horace Chase 4 July 1864. JONATHAN R. the f. d. 16 Jan. 1879, a. 76.

JOHN, m. Hannah Rice of Rutland District, pub. 22 July 1765. PAUL, of Brk., m. Sally Carter, pub. 10 Jan. 1796.

HASKINS, SAMUEL, JR., had w. Elizabeth, who d. 23 Feb. 1806, a. 81 (82 on grave-stone), and he m. Sarah Stetson, pub. 16 Nov. 1806. His chil. were: *Esther*, b. about 1755, m. Nathan Allen 17 Dec. 1789, and d. 16 Feb. 1835, a. 79; *Samuel*, b. 2 Feb. 1759; *Shiverick*, b. 18 Aug. 1763; *Bethia*, b. about 1765, d. — Sep. 1825, a. 60; and prob. *William*, who m. Polly Ide 29 Sep. 1788, and *Rebecca*, who m. Darius Rice of Gr. 17 Dec. 1789. SAMUEL the f. res. in Rochester when his s. *Shiverick* was bap., 12 Aug. 1764, but prob. rem. to Hk. soon afterwards. He res. in the northerly part of the town, and d. 4 Feb. 1819, a. 86; his w. Sarah d. 16 Aug. 1814, a. 79.

2. SAMUEL, s. of Samuel (1), by w. Persis, had *Betsey*, b. 31 Oct. 1783 (she seems to have been published to Isaac Lasell of Needham, 30 Nov. 1806, and also to Thomas Walton, 19 Aug. 1810, but to which she was married, if either, does not appear); *Samuel*, b. 22 Jan. 1785; *Aaron*, b. 21 Aug. 1786; *David*,

b. 14 July 1788, m. Nancy Mason of Dana, pub. 20 Jan. 1811; *Nathaniel*, b. 4 Feb. 1791; *Persis*, b. 3 Jan. 1793, m. Luther Mason 20 June 1813; *Thomas*, b. 15 Sep. 1795; *Joseph*, b. 19 Jan. 1797, m. Caroline Marsh of Dana, pub. 10 Jan. 1820; *Seth*, b. 26 Ap. 1801, d. 24 Nov. 1816. SAMUEL the f. was chiefly remarkable for his immense size; after his death, 25 Feb. 1818, it was ascertained that his body weighed four hundred and fifty pounds.

3. SHIVERICK, s. of Samuel (1), m. Anna Lincoln, and had *Shiverick*, b. 29 Mar. 1789, d. in Roxbury 2 Feb. 1861; *Josiah*, b. — Oct. 1790, d. 8 Nov. 1790; *Martin*, b. 8 Oct. 1791, d. 3 Nov. 1813; *Anna*, b. 5 Oct. 1793; *Rufus*, b. 2 Oct. 1795; *Amos*, b. 13 Oct. 1797; *Joel*, b. 17 July 1799; *Jason*, b. 3 May 1801, m. Susan A. C. Fales 28 Dec. 1834, and d. in Worc. 23 Oct. 1848; *Daniel* (or *David*), b. 18 Mar. 1803, prob. d. at Boston (drowned) 19 Mar. 1829; *Mary*, b. 14 Jan. 1805, m. Cyrus Chipman, pub. 14 Nov. 1825, and d. at Barre 9 May 1864; *Hosea*, b. 27 Nov. 1806, d. 1 Feb. 1808; *Melinda*, b. 7 Nov. 1809, m. John Newland 31 July 1831. SHIVERICK the f. d. 5 June 1836.

4. SAMUEL, s. of Samuel (2), m. Hannah Clark 19 Jan. 1804, and had *Philena Clark*, b. 8 Ap. 1801; *Mary Clark*, b. 26 May 1804; *Hiram Kinsley*, b. 25 Oct. 1805; *Lucinda Johnson*, b. 23 Ap. 1807, m. Hiram Castle 29 Nov. 1832; *Elvira Washburn*, b. 1 Jan. 1809; *Benjamin Clark*, b. 2 May 1811, d. at Barre 1 May 1843; *Sarah Ann*, b. 23 July 1813; *Henry*, b. 19 Ap. 1815; *Samuel*, b. 25 Mar. 1817, d. at Barre 6 Nov. 1844; *Seth*, b. 15 May 1819; *Clarissa*, twin, b. 30 Ap. 1821, m. Ira A. Barlow 25 Sep. 1842; *Clarinda*, twin, b. 30 Ap. 1821, m. Hiram Joyal 1 Dec. 1842; *David*, b. 21 Jan. 1823; *Joseph*, b. 20 Jan. 1824, d. 26 Jan. 1844; *Hosea*, b. 11 Aug. 1825, d. 28 Ap. 1846; *Caroline Elizabeth*, b. 24 Aug. 1828, d. 24 July 1830. There is apparent confusion in the early dates, indicating precocity; but I copy the record as I find it. SAMUEL the f. d. at Barre 14 Ap. 1864; his w. Hannah d. here 7 Feb. 1846, a. 63.

5. AARON, s. of Samuel (2), m. Nancy Barton 27 Jan. 1811, and had *William*, b. 16 Oct. 1812; *Lemira*, b. 9 May 1814.

6. THOMAS, s. of Samuel (2), m. Susanna Stone of Dana, pub. 25 Mar. 1818, and had *Sophia Stone*, b. 22 Ap. 1819; *Thomas Alonzo*, b. 23 June 1820; *John Stone*, b. 19 Feb. 1822; *Marcus Houghton*, b. 14 Feb. 1824; *Eleanor Adams*, b. 10 Sep. 1825; *Horatio Dwight*, b. 17 Aug. 1827, d. young; *Persis Malvina*, b. 23 July 1829, m. Reuben A. Snow, pub. 16 Nov. 1849; *Horatio Dwight*, b. 3 July 1831; *Susanna Jane*, b. 26 Feb. 1833; *Julia Ann*, b. 19 Oct. 1834; *Sarah Orinda*, b. 2 Aug. 1836; *Henry Harrison*, b. 10 Feb. 1840. THOMAS the f. d. at Orange 25 Ap. 1868.

7. JOEL, s. of Shiverick (3), m. Maria Williams 31 Dec. 1826, and had *Frederick*, b. 6 July 1827; *Daniel*, b. 19 Jan. 1829; *Irene*, b. 21 June 1830, d. 3 Feb. 1833; *Emily Maria*, b. 30 June 1832; *Rufus Chase*, b. 7 June 1834, d. 16 June 1837; *Alfred L.*, b. about 1835, a physician, d. at Boston 3 Ap. 1876, a. 40; *Lydia P.*, b. about 1837, m. Richard C. Noyes, and d. at Worc. 17 Ap. 1853, a. 16; *Jason A.*, b. about 1844, a hairdresser, d. at Boston 19 Nov. 1874, a. 30; *Joel J.*, b. 4 May 1846. JOEL the f. d. 15 Feb. 1848.

8. THOMAS ALONZO, s. of Thomas (6), m. Almira M. Andrews 25 Sep. 1844, and had *George A.*, b. —— 1845, d. 25 Jan. 1846, a. 4 months; a daughter, b. 27 Mar. 1847; *Lucy Ann*, b. 22 June 1852, m. Daniel Crossman of Athol, 2 Sep. 1873; *Frederick Alonzo*, b. 2 Mar. 1855; *Mary Almira*, b. 28 July 1857; *Lizzie Jane*, b. 23 Aug. 1860, m. Frederick W. Ward 18 Dec. 1879.

9. JOHN STONE, s. of Thomas (6), by w. Sarah, had *Elizabeth Field*, b. 25 Sep. 1848.

BETHIA, pub. to John Howard of Gr. 2 Feb. 1812. LYSANDER F., of Pres., m. Mary Ann A. Paige, 20 May 1833. PRUDENCE, of Shutes., m. Simeon Nye Atwood 6 June 1835. CELIA, m. William Fay of Barre 19 Mar. 1842.

HASTINGS, JOHN, freeman 1643, rem. from Braintree to Cambridge about 1654. His first wife d. at Braintree and he m. Ann, wid. of John Meane of

Camb. His chil., all by first w., were *Walter* and *Samuel*, bap. in England, and *John* and *Elizabeth*, bap. in Braintree. JOHN the f. was a tanner, and d. in Camb. 2 Dec. 1657; his w. Ann d. 25 Mar. 1666.

2. JOHN, s. of John (1), m. Hannah Moore 1 Mar. 1655–6; she d. 10 June 1667, a. 24, and he m. Lydia, dau. of Elder Richard Champney, 20 May 1668; she d. 23 Jan. 1690–91, a. about 47, and he m. Rebecca, wid. of Benoni Eaton, 28 Sep. 1691. His chil. were: *John*, b. 17 Ap. 1667; *Joseph*, b. 6 May 1669; *Lydia*, b. 30 Sep. 1671, m. Ebenezer Allen; *Hannah*, b. 13 Mar. 1672–3, d. 16 Ap. 1691; *Elizabeth*, b. 11 Ap. 1675, d. unm. — May 1727; *Daniel*, b. 3 Feb. 1676–7. JOHN the f. res. in Cambridge, was a tanner, and d. about 1720.

3. DANIEL, s. of John (2), m. Abigail Cooksey 13 Nov. 1701, and had *Abigail*, b. 9 and d. 27 Aug. 1702; *Walter*, b. 24 Mar. 1703–4; *Abigail*, bap. 19 May 1706; *Daniel*, b. 8 Jan. 1708–9; *Sarah*, bap. 9 May 1714, m. John Amidon 14 July 1737. DANIEL the f. was a blacksmith, rem. from Cambridge to Marlborough before 6 June 1722; he was in Sudbury 1727, in Oxford 1732, after which he rem. to Hk. with his son *Walter*, and d. 25 Jan. 1755.

4. WALTER, s. of Daniel (3), m. Mary Thompson 1 Nov. 1733, and had in Oxford *Daniel*, b. 23 Aug. 1734; *Jacob*, b. 9 Aug. 1737, m. Mary Bangs 22 July 1762; *Lydia*, b. 31 July 1739, d. unm. 5 Jan. 1757; *Martha*, b. 19 Sep. 1741, d. young; and in Hardwick, *John*, b. — Sep. 1743; *Martha*, b. 9 Dec. 1745, m. Ebenezer Cobb 5 Oct. 1780; *Elizabeth*, b. 11 Aug. 1748, m. Samuel Hopkins 17 Dec. 1778; *Joseph*, b. 27 Feb. 1750–1, d. 17 Aug. 1753; *Jonathan*, b. 23 Oct. 1752; *Joseph*, b. 4 June 1755, d. 21 Sep. 1756. Besides these, there is a tradition that there were two daughters by a former wife, one of whom m. —— Partridge, and the other —— Peacock. WALTER the f. was a farmer, rem. from Oxford to Hardwick before 21 June 1743, res. near Barre, at the place marked "S. Jamerson" on the R. Map, and d. 6 July 1792, a. 88; his w. Mary d. 25 June 1799, a. 87.

5. DANIEL, s. of Walter (4), m. Submit Jordan of Rutland District (Barre), pub. 22 July 1746, and had *Theophilus*, b. 25 Dec. 1764; *Jacob*, b. 17 July 1767; *Stephen*, b. 7 Feb. 1771; *Lucinda*, b. 19 May 1773; and perhaps others.

6. JOHN, s. of Walter (4), m. Mehetabel Berry 11 Ap. 1779, and had *Lemuel*, b. 13 Dec. 1779, d. at Saratoga Springs 23 Sep. 1801; *Joseph*, b. 16 Oct. 1781, manufacturer of ink in Cambridge, where he died; *Sophia*, b. 27 Sep. 1783, m. Moses Lawrence, pub. 18 Sep. 1814; *Anson*, b. 6 Aug. 1785, d. at Boston 14 Oct. 1815; *John*, b. 24 Sep. 1787, m. Ruth W. Newcomb 18 Sep. 1821; *Lydia*, b. 22 Ap. 1790, m. Seth Jamerson 3 Oct. 1814; *Mary*, b. 20 June 1792, m. Daniel Cutter of Gr. 31 Oct. 1839, and d. at Gardner 18 Aug. 1874; *Clark*, b. 6 July 1794, d. 10 Sep. 1812. JOHN the f. was a farmer, and res. on the homestead. He was captain of militia, selectman four years, assessor four years representative seven years, and justice of the peace. He d. 29 May 1829; his w. Mehetabel d. 15 Dec. 1836, a. 87.

7. JONATHAN, s. of Walter (3), m. Hannah Shaw of N. Sal. in 1778, and had in Hk., *Barnabas*, b. 22 July 1780; *Betsey*, b. 3 Feb. 1782; a child b. 26 Mar. 1787; and at Wilmington, Vt., *Polly*, b. 3 Feb. 1789; *Chauncy*, b. 2 Jan. 1791; *Hannah*, b. 3 Oct. 1793; *Francis*, b. 12 Feb. 1798. JONATHAN the f. was so deeply involved in the Shays Insurrection that he fled in 1787 to Wilmington, Vt., where he d. 3 Oct. 1822.[1]

8. THEOPHILUS, s. of Daniel (5), m. Betsey Prince Ames of Barre 22 Dec. 1785. Some of his chil., gathered from various records, were: *Betsey*, b. —— 1786, m. Timothy P. Anderson 17 Oct. 1811, and d. 25 Nov. 1868, a. 82; prob. *Anna*, b. ——, m. Sewell Marsh of Ware 11 May 1815; *Arba;* prob. *Walter*, b. ——, m. Mary Babbitt of Barre, pub. 27 May 1822; *John Ames*, b. —— 1798, d. 29 June 1801, a. 3; prob. *Hiram*, b. —— 1801, d. 27 Dec. 1831, a. 30; *Harriet*, b. —— 1805, m. William Frost 5 Feb. 1843, and d. 29 June 1845, a. 40; *Barnabas*, b. —— 1807, d. 9 May 1807, a. 3 months; *Henrietta*, b. ——

[1] This account of Jonathan Hastings was furnished to me by James P. Richardson of Portland, a young man of great promise, who grad. H. C. 1872, but d. of overwork the same year.

1810, m. William Frost 22 Sep. 1846. THEOPHILUS the f. was a carpenter, and res. on the Barre road, at the place erroneously marked "S. Hastings" on the R. Map. Although by no means one of fortune's favorites, he had an exuberance of animal spirits, and met the trials of life with cheerfulness; constantly full of fun and frolic, he would keep his company in a roar with his flashes of merry wit. He d. 31 Oct. 1842, a. 81; his w. Betsey d. 14 Aug. 1844, a. 76.

9. ARBA, s. of Theophilus (8), m. Laura Hunt of Barre, pub. 15 June 1818, and had *Martha M.*, b. about 1819, m. —— Gould, and d. at Ware 19 Ap. 1850, a. 31; *Henry*, b. about 1828, d. 31 Jan. 1833, a. 4; and prob. others.

MRS. M. MINERVA, m. Samson Ames 1 Dec. 1865.

HATCH, THOMAS, s. of Thomas of Scituate, "m. Sarah, dau. of Rhodolphus Ellms, 1662, and had eleven children born from 1664 to 1684." Deane's *Hist. of Scituate*, p. 280. THOMAS the f. d. 1686.

2. RHODOLPHUS, s. of Thomas (1), b. 26 Dec. 1674, by w. Elizabeth, had *John*, b. 16 Dec. 1703, resided in Truro; *Joseph*, b. 19 May 1705, res. in Falmouth; *Ezekiel* (or *Nathaniel*), b. —— 1707, res. in Plymouth; *Mary*, b. 24 July 1710, m. —— Mayo; *Sarah*, b. 12 May 1713, m. Joshua Atwood; *Asa*, b. 15 Aug. 1716. RHODOLPHUS the f. res. in Rochester, where his chil. were born, but is described as of Plymouth in the appointment of his administratrix, 28 Mar. 1744.

3. ASA, s. of Rhodolphus (2), by w. Mary, had *Asa*, b. ——; *Richard*, b. ——. ASA the f. was a mariner, res. in Plymouth, and d. before 8 Mar. 1745–6, when his w. Mary was appointed administratrix; she m. Isaac Thomas 12 May 1747, and rem. with her chil. to Hardwick, and d. between 22 Oct. 1765 and 28 Feb. 1766.

4. ASA, s. of Asa (3), described as a mariner, res. in Hk., discharged his late guardian, Edward Thomas of Pembroke, 28 May 1764; he m. Lucy, dau. of Jonathan Warner, 23 Jan. 1766, and res. on the lot next north of the Universalist meeting-house. No record of children.

5. RICHARD, s. of Asa (3), a miller in Hk., discharged his late guardian, Edward Thomas of Pembroke, 10 May 1766.

6. SAMUEL, s. of Walter and grandson of Elder William Hatch, all of Scituate, b. 22 Dec. 1653, in his will dated 13 June 1728, and proved 7 July 1735, mentions sons *Ebenezer* and *Josiah*, deceased, and *Samuel*, *Isaac*, *Elisha*, and *Ezekiel*; also dau. *Desire*, *Hannah* Tinkham, and *Elizabeth* Bonney.

7. EZEKIEL, s. of Samuel (6), by w. Ruth, had *Ruth*, b. 23 June 1719, m. Ebenezer Hathaway of Dartmouth 10 Sep. 1741, and d. in Hk. 31 May 1789; *Mary*, b. 29 Nov. 1721; *Hannah*, b. 29 Mar. 1724; *Isaiah*, b. 11 Sep. 1729; *Lucy*, b. 10 Sep. 1732; *Sarah*, b. 6 June 1736. EZEKIEL the f. res. in Rochester, and d. between 19 June 1765 and 14 July 1768, as appears by the date and proof of his will.

8. ISAIAH, s. of Ezekiel (7), m. Joanna, dau. of Nathaniel Whitcomb, 31 Jan. 1756, and prob. had in Rochester, before he rem. to Hk., *Lois*, b. ——, m. Jesse Dunham 7 Oct. 1779; *Molly*, b. ——, m. Aaron Fay 19 Dec. 1782; *Noah*, b. about 1760; *Olive*, b. ——, m. Lot Jenney of Hartland 4 Aug. 1784; and in Hk., *Lucy*, b. 27 May 1774; *Sarah*, bap. 21 Mar. 1779. ISAIAH the f. was a farmer, and res. near the brook, on the southerly side of the road running easterly from the present residence of Mr. George Warner, marked "Mr. Bolster" on the R. Map. He was selectman, 1781 and 1782, and removed to Westminster, prob. about 18 Ap. 1786, when he sold his farm to Maj. Martin Kinsley.

9. NOAH, s. of Isaiah (8), m. Jemima Cox 4 Feb. 1783, and had *Ira*, b. 13 Mar. 1784, d. 16 Oct. 1786; *Molly*, b. 3 July 1785; *Isaiah*, b. 28 Oct. 1786. NOAH the f. was a Revolutionary soldier, and was described as 20 years old, and of a ruddy complexion, in a descriptive roll dated in July 1780. He d. at Westminster about Feb. 1791, a. 31.

HATHAWAY, ARTHUR, "Marshfield 1643, m., 20 Nov. 1652, Sarah Cook, perhaps dau. of Rev. John, had *John*, b. 17 Sep. 1653, and *Sarah*, b. 28 Feb. 1656; ten years later was at Dartmouth, and took oath of fidelity 1684 there."

Savage's *Gen. Dict.* In his will, 9 Feb. 1709–10, proved 6 Feb. 1711–12, he names w. Sarah, and chil. *John*, *Thomas*, *Mary* Hammond, *Lydia* Sisson, and *Hannah* Codman. *Bristol Reg. Probate.*

2. JOHN, s. of Arthur (1), m. Joanna Pope 5 Mar. 1682–3; she d. 25 Dec. 1695, and he m. Patience —— 29 Sep. 1696. His chil. were: *Sarah*, b. 24 Feb. 1683–4, m. John Cannon 11 Oct. 1709; *Joanna*, b. 28 Jan. 1685–6, m. —— Blackwell; *John*, b. 18 Mar. 1687–8; *Arthur*, b. 3 Ap. 1690; *Hannah*, b. 16 Feb. 1692, m. —— Prower; *Mary*, b. 4 June 1694, m. —— Douglass; *Jonathan*, b. 23 June 1697; *Richard*, b. 21 May 1699; *Thomas*, b. 5 Feb. 1700–1; *Hunnewell*, b 21 Ap. 1703; *Abiah* (son), b. 21 Oct. 1705; *Elizabeth*, b. 6 May 1708; *Patience*, b. 27 Ap. 1710, m. —— Peckham; *Benjamin*, b. 10 Jan. 1712; *James*, b. 24 Jan. 1713–14; *Ebenezer*, b. 12 May 1717. JOHN the f. res. in Dartmouth and d. between 11 July and 15 Aug. 1732, when his w. Patience and all his children, except Thomas, were living and named in his will.

3. EBENEZER, s. of John (2), m. Ruth Hatch 10 Sep. 1741, and had *Lucy*, b. 17 Ap. 1742; *Samuel*, b. 9 Dec. 1744; *James*, b. 9 July 1747; *Ebenezer*, b. 6 Sep. 1749; *Abiah*, b. 7 July 1751; *Ruth*, b. 13 Ap. 1754; *Timothy*, b. 24 Mar. 1756. EBENEZER the f. res. in Dartmouth, and d. prob. not long before 10 Sep. 1759, when the inventory of his estate was filed in the Probate Office. His w. Ruth rem. to Hk. with her son *Timothy*, and d. 31 May 1789.

4. TIMOTHY, s. of Ebenezer (3), m. Rhoda, dau. of Isaac Clark, 23 Sep. 1784, and had *Lucy*,[1] b. 7 Aug. 1785, taught school many years, m. Dr. Cyrus Washburn of Vernon, Vt., pub. 24 Sep. 1827, and d. about 1850; *Ebenezer*, b. 13 Aug. 1787, d. — 1822, leaving a daughter Ann; *Susan*, b. 16 May 1790; m. Ira Ruggles 18 Jan. 1825, and d. in Iowa; *Timothy*, b. 27 Mar. 1794, m. Harriet —— (who d. 1850, a. 55), was an auctioneer in Boston, but returned to Hk., and d. 19 Mar. 1836, leaving one son, James E., who d. at West Townsend, Vt., 10 Jan. 1882, a. 57 years, 9 months, and 10 days; *Alvah*, b. 1 Sep. 1796, m. Susan A. Parker 13 Sep. 1824, res. here and in Barre, and afterwards several years in Boston, where he d. 19 Nov. 1877, leaving widow and sons and daughters: *Ruth*, b. 5 June 1800, m. Grover Spooner 28 May 1829 and res. in Barre; *Rhoda*, b. 9 Nov. 1802, m. Crighton Ruggles 30 Ap. 1820, rem. to Barre, where she d. 2 Nov. 1879. TIMOTHY the f. was a shoemaker and farmer, rem. about 1777 from Dartmouth to Hardwick, resided on the Petersham road, at the place marked "T. Hathaway" on the R. Map, and closed his long life 31 Aug. 1849, a. 93; his w. Rhoda d. 27 Oct. 1838, a. 76. All the sons in this family taught music; and all the daughters (especially the eldest) were famous singers in the church.

5. JEREMIAH, lineage not ascertained, by w. Lettice, had several chil. whose birth is not found on record, but other traces of them appear; among them were *Samuel*, b. about 1784; *Lettice*, b. about 1786, m. Marshall Johnson 1 Jan. 1811, and d. 3 Mar. 1859, a. 72; *Jeremiah*, b. —— 1788; prob. *Sally*, b. ——, m. William Eaton 5 Dec. 1811; *Celia W.*, b. ——, m. Shiverick Weeks 26 Nov. 1821; *William*, b. —— 1794, d. 20 Mar. 1795, a. 1 year; *John*, b. 22 May 1797; and *Eliza*, b. ——, m. John B. Bond of Worc. 13 Nov. 1834. JEREMIAH the f. res. near Enfield, at the place marked "J. Hathaway" on the R. Map; his w. Lettice d. 20 Aug. 1830, a. 66, and he m. Mrs. Sarah Gilbert of Ware, pub. 28 Dec. 1831. He d. 29 Mar. 1835, a. 78.

6. SAMUEL, s. of Jeremiah (5), m. Fanny, dau. of Isaac Clark, 17 Oct. 1805; she d. 6 Nov. 1809, and he m. Ruth, dau. of Maj. Seth Hinkley, 15 Mar. 1810. His chil. were: *Henry*, b. ——, d. 28 Ap. 1809, a. 1 year and 5 months; *Fanny Clark*, b. 19 Oct. 1810; *Henry*, b. 21 Ap. 1813; *Isabella*, b. 6 May 1815; and others born in Worcester. SAMUEL the f. was a shoemaker, and res. at the northerly end of the Common, at the place marked "Wid. Paige" on the R. Map; he rem. to Worc. about 1815, and erected a hotel on Washington Square, which he successfully conducted several years; He d. between 14 Dec. 1830 and 5 Sep. 1831; his w. Ruth d. 8 Mar. 1859, a. 68.

[1] Miss Lucy Hathaway is affectionately remembered by me as my first teacher at school, by whom for several years my early love of books was fostered and encouraged.

7. JEREMIAH, s. of Jeremiah (5), m. Sarah Gilbert of Ware, and had *Abby*, b. ——, d. 10 Aug. 1815, a. 3 years and 4 months; *Charles*, b. ——; and perhaps others. JEREMIAH the f. d. 29 Nov. 1836, a. 48; his w. Sarah d. at Ware 9 June 1874, a. 80.

8. JOHN, s. of Jeremiah (5), m. Claramond Winslow, pub. 10 Nov. 1823; she d. 27 Ap. 1834, and he m. Mary A. Howes of Boston 30 May 1837. His chil. by first wife were: a child b. ——, d. 14 Ap. 1828; *Francis Ebenezer*, b. 9 Mar. 1829; *Catherine Elizabeth*, b. 18 Feb. 1833. JOHN the f. rem. to Enf. and afterwards to East Hampton, where he died 4 Ap. 1873.

9. CHARLES, s. of Jeremiah (7), m. Mary A., dau. of Giles Warner, 24 Ap. 1845; she d. 28 Nov. 1847, a. 23.

CAROLINE, m. Tilly Mead, pub. 30 Ap. 1822. RICHARD L., m. Alma Ruggles, pub. 29 Mar. 1846. GARDNER, m. Levina Taylor, pub. 25 Aug. 1855.

HAYFORD, SAMUEL, of Hk., m. Bathsheba Tinkham of Halifax 1 Mar. 1776. He d. and she m. Samuel Work of Leicester, 3 May 1783.

MERCY, m. Silas Wright 15 Feb. 1781.

HAZELTINE, SIMEON, prob. s. of Daniel (who d. in Uxbridge between 25 May and 18 Aug. 1747), was here as early as 1758, when he was a soldier in the French War, at the age of twenty years. He shared largely in the vicissitudes of life. The town voted, 5 Mar. 1764, "to release to Paul Dean Simeon Hazeltine's rate, committed to him to collect, if he never comes in his reach again." He returned, however, bought a farm 9 Dec. 1771, and in 1774 was elected captain of the minute-men, whom he led to the field on the memorable 19th of April 1775. In 1787 he was so deeply involved in the Shays Rebellion that he left Hardwick permanently, and retired to Sandgate, Vt., which town he represented in the General Assembly in 1794. Nothing is found on record concerning his family.

HEDGE, ELISHA, of Shrewsbury, "m. Martha, dau. of Daniel Johnson of Marlboro', Dec. 30, 1728, admitted to the church here [Shrewsbury] in 1736 from the New North Church in Boston. . . . Chil.: *Josiah*, bap. July 12, 1730, and d. in 1733; *Samuel*, bap. May 14, 1732; *Lemuel*, bap. July 7, 1734." Ward's *Hist. of Shrewsbury*, p. 325. Besides these were *Elisha*, b. ——, and *Martha*, b. ——, m. Joseph Robinson of New Rutland (now Barre), pub. 7 July 1753. His w. Martha d. ——, and he m. Mrs. Elizabeth Stratton of Marlb., pub. 4 Nov. 1765, who appears to have left him, before his death, and returned to her former home. ELISHA the f. did not confine himself to a single place of residence or a single branch of business. He was dismissed from the ch. in Shrewsbury in 1740 to the ch. in Worcester; he bought 280 acres of land in Hk. 1745, and a year afterwards 300 acres more adjoining Rutland (now Barre), "lying on both sides of Moose Brook," and not long afterwards became a resident; he was in Marlborough from 1766 to 1769, but returned to Hk. In various documents he is styled taylor, 1745; shop-keeper, 1761; trader, 1765, and gentleman, 1767. He served also as commissary in the French War, 1755. He d. in Barre; Samuel H. Robinson was appointed administrator, and presented an inventory 20 Jan. 1789.

2. ELISHA, s. of Elisha (1), by w. Deliverance, had *John*, b. 12 Oct. 1751; *Mary*, b. 4 Mar. 1753; *Solomon*, b. 3 Mar. 1755, m. Dorcas Smith 8 Mar. 1781; *Asa*, b. 9 June 1756, m. Miriam Dexter 31 May 1780; *Daniel*, b. 7 Feb. 1758; *Samuel*, b. 19 Dec. 1760. ELISHA the f., it is said, was not a brilliant man; yet he rendered good service to his country, for he was a soldier in the French War; and in the War of the Revolution he served in the army, with three of his sons, *John*, *Solomon*, and *Asa*. The date of his death does not appear; his w. Deliverance d. 4 June 1819, a. 93, having for many years received aid from the public.

3. SAMUEL, s. of Elisha (1), gave his life for his country, in the French War; he was a corporal in the company commanded by Capt. William Paige, from 1 Ap. to 11 Sep. 1760, on which day he probably died, as the word "dyed" was attached to his name; his pay-roll was made up to that date, and his successor in office was appointed the next day afterwards.

4. LEMUEL, s. of Elisha (1), m. Sarah, dau. of Rev. David White, 5 Nov. 1761, and had *Lemuel*, b. ——, grad. H. C. 1784, devoted himself to the business of school-teaching; *Levi*, b. 19 Ap. 1766, grad. H. C. 1792, in which he was tutor 15 years, and professor 22 years; he d. at Cambridge 3 Jan. 1844; *Abraham*, b. ——, a physician in Windsor, Vt., d. 26 Ap. 1809, a. 38; *Samuel*, b. ——, also res. in Windsor; he had also daughters *Sarah*; *Susan*, m. Josiah Dunham; *Luthera*, m. Prof. Daniel Chipman; and perhaps others. LEMUEL the f. grad. H. C. 1759, was ordained pastor of the church in Warwick 3 Dec. 1760. "After a ministry of nearly 17 years, Mr. Hedge died at Hardwick, Oct. 17, 1777, in the 44th year of his age. Mr. Hedge was a Tory in the Revolution, or strongly suspected to be such. On the 6th of March, 1775, the inhabitants voted to disarm him and confine him to the town. He was persecuted most remorselessly." *Hist. of Western Mass.*, ii. 447. I find no record of his death in Hardwick; and it seems probable that he was buried in Warwick, where a monument was erected to his memory, bearing an inscription which was copied for me by Rev. John Goldsbury, formerly pastor of the church in Hardwick: "In private life he was cheerful, exemplary, and benevolent. In his ministerial character, faithful, solemn, and instructive. In full belief of the truths he preached to others, he fell asleep in Jesus, with the Christian hope of rising again to eternal life." His w. Sarah survived him, and is said to have d. in Middlebury, Vt., in 1808.

5. JOHN, s. of Elisha (2), m. Mary Haskell 7 Sep. 1777, and was prob. father of *Sally*, who long had the care of her aged "grandmother Deliverance Hedge," and who died unm. 15 Ap. 1841; her age was probably 62 years, although the town record indicates 72.

SALLY, m. Moses Fay 24 Feb. 1788.

HIGGINS, ELISHA, by w. Hannah, had *Joseph*, b. ——; *Uriah*, b. 24 May 1742; he prob. had also *Edward*, b. ——; *Abiel*, b. ——, m. Ebenezer Safford 24 Nov. 1759; *Abigail*, b. ——, m. Simon Giffin 24 Mar. 1761; and perhaps others. ELISHA the f. rem. prob. from Palmer to Hardwick, and became a member of the church 16 Jan. 1742-3.

2. JONATHAN, perhaps brother of Elisha (1), by w. Rachel, had *Jonathan*, b. 20 Ap. 1736; *Lurania*, b. 9 June 1738; *Henry*, b. 27 Dec. 1740, d. young; *Henry*, b. 24 July 1743; *Bethiah*, b. 26 Mar. 1746; *Joshua*, bap. 18 Sep. 1748; *Rachel*, bap. 19 May 1751, m. Andrew Harwood of Ware, pub. 3 Feb. 1771; *Philip*, bap. 13 Jan. 1754.

3. JOSEPH, s. of Elisha (1), m. Anna Hooker, pub. 6 Mar. 1756, and had *Joseph*, b. 6 Sep. 1760; *Charles*, b. 29 Aug. 1762; *Anna*, b. 5 July 1764; *Palatine*, b. 18 May 1766.

4. URIAH, s. of Elisha (1), m. Esther Cooley of Gr., pub. 7 Ap. 1763, and had *Sybil*, b. 30 Dec. 1763; *Abigail*, b. 21 Dec. 1765; *David*, b. 24 Sep. 1767; *Caleb*, b. 2 June 1770; *Uriah*, b. 10 Ap. 1772; *Frederick* (or *Shadrach*, as in the record of baptisms), b. 31 July 1774; *Alpheus*, b. 14 Sep. 1776; *Hadassah*, b. 6 Nov. 1778; *Lewis* (*Zenas* in rec. of baptism), b. 9 Sep. 1780; *Shady* (*Shadrach ?*), b. 17 Feb. 1783.

5. EDWARD, prob. s. of Elisha (1), m. Thankful Rice, 17 Oct. 1764, and had *Solomon*, b. 1 Mar. 1765; *Anna*, b. 1 May 1779; *Mercy*, b. 26 June 1781; and prob. others. EDWARD the f. joined the Hk. church 10 Aug. 1752, res. in Palmer at the time of his marriage, but returned very soon to Hk.

6. HENRY, s. of Jonathan (2), m. Mary Fisk 9 Nov. 1768, and had *Mary*, b. about 1771, m. Enoch Thayer, and d. at Amh. 15 Ap. 1860, a. 89; *Henry*, b. 27 July 1779; *Rachel*, b. about 1782, d. unm. 30 Mar. 1858, a. nearly 76; and prob. others. HENRY the f. was a deacon of the Baptist church, res. near the line between Hk. and Enfield, at the place marked "Dea. Higgins" on the R. Map, and d. 16 Mar. 1837, a. 94; his w. Mary d. 7 Feb. 1821, a. 71; they and their dau. *Rachel* were buried in the cemetery near the place where the Baptist meeting-house formerly stood.

7. HENRY, s. of Henry (6), m. Olla (Olive?) Metcalf of Royalston (b. 9 June 1789), pub. 19 Sep. 1813, and had *Henry Melville*, b. 22 Oct. 1814; *Olla Metcalf*, b. 8 Ap. 1816; *Sarah Luthera*, b. 11 Jan. 1818; *Whitman Fisk*, b. 26

Feb. 1821; *Lurania Maria*, b. 12 Dec. 1822; *Elon Galusha*, b. 11 May 1825, m. Lucy M. Graves of Worcester, pub. 31 Jan. 1845. HENRY the f. rem. to Ware, where he d. 21 Feb. 1860; his w. d. also at Ware 19 Aug. 1866.

8. ALVAH M., parentage not ascertained, by w. Sarah J., had *Mary*, b. 25 Aug. 1845; *Henry A.*, b. —— 1847, d. 19 Nov. 1850, a. 3; *Abby A.*, b. 13 Nov. 1854, d. 16 Jan. 1855.

9. WILLIAM, by w. Ellen, had *John*, b. 14 Sep. 1853, m. Catherine Connor of Ware 3 Aug. 1872; *Lucy*, b. 30 Jan. 1855; *Jeremiah*, b. 13 July 1856, d. 27 Oct. 1856; *William*, b. 4 Feb. 1859, d. 14 Aug. 1859; *Bridget*, b. 29 Dec. 1861, d. 18 Mar. 1863. His w. Ellen d. 29 Jan. 1871, and he m. Mary Sullivan 9 Feb. 1873.

10. MICHAEL, by w. Ann, had *Michael*, b. 16 June 1857.

11. THOMAS, by w. Winifred, had *Patrick*, b. 29 Mar. 1858; *Dominick*, b. 12 Oct. 1861; *Michael*, b. 19 Feb. 1864.

12. TIMOTHY, by w. Mary, had *John*, b. 31 Aug. 1858.

HILDRETH, ISAAC, JR., by w. Esther, had *Isaac*, b. 5 Dec. 1750.

HILLMAN, STEPHEN, of Dana, m. Chloe Barnes 7 Mar. 1820, and rem. to Hardwick, where his w. Chloe d. 28 June 1881, a. 82. No record found of children.

2. STEPHEN P., prob. s. of Stephen (1), m. Alma Maria Newcomb 4 Dec. 1851, and had *Joseph*, b. 17 Ap. 1855, m. S. Alice Gould 3 May 1882; a dau. b. 25 Nov. 1858; *Charles Dexter*, b. 9 May 1860; *John Newcomb*, b. 12 May 1864.

HINDS, ENOCH, by w. Elizabeth, had *Abner*, *Solomon*, and a dau., all bap. in Oct. 1742; *Enoch*, bap. 5 June 1743.

2. NEHEMIAH, by w. Sarah, had *Sarah*, bap. 25 July 1747; *Abigail*, bap. 1 Aug. 1756; *Moses*, bap. 27 Mar. 1757.

HINKLEY, THOMAS, prob. grandson of Governor Thomas Hinkley, m. Ruth, dau. of Nathaniel Merrick, 31 Mar. 1730, and had *Seth*, b. 2 Sep. 1730; *Thomas*, b. 22 July 1731; *Nathaniel*, b. 25 June 1738; prob. *Mercy*, b. about 1744, m. Job Dexter 17 July 1766; and perhaps others. THOMAS the f. res. in Harwich, and was living in 1747.

2. SETH, s. of Thomas (1), m. Sarah, dau. of Judah Berry of Harwich, 2 Feb. 1755, and had *Samuel*, b. 16 May 1757; *Seth*, b. 21 June 1759; *Judah*, b. 15 Dec. 1761; *Rebecca*, b. 15 Feb. 1764, m. Jonathan Childs of Barre 3 Feb. 1785; *Mark*, b. 14 Ap. 1766; *Ruth*, b. 22 Ap. 1768; *Scottoway*, b. 10 Ap. 1771, a physician, res. in Vernon, Conn.; *Barnabas*, b. 23 Jan. 1773. SETH the f. was a cordwainer, and prob. rem. here immediately after his marriage; he res. on the Barre road, at the place marked "S. Hinkley" on the R. Map, and d. 21 Ap. 1797, when all his chil. were living, except *Mark* and *Ruth*; his w. Sarah d. at the house of her son *Samuel*, 18 Ap. 1813, a. 81, after enduring the "shaking palsy" many years.

3. SAMUEL, s. of Seth (2), m. Tabitha, wid. of Dr. Charles Doolittle, pub. 27 May 1787; she d. s. p. Sep. 26 Dec. 1816, a. 69, and he m. Ann, wid. of Robert M. Peck, and dau. of Hon. Joseph Allen of Worcester, 18 Mar. 1817, by whom he had *Samuel Allen*, b. 4 Sep. 1820. SAMUEL the f. was a cordwainer, and res. at the north end of the Common, at the place marked "S. Hinkley" on the R. Map. After middle life he devoted most of his time to official duties; for many years he was a deputy sheriff and a famous detective; he was also selectman eleven years, assessor two years, and town clerk seventeen years. He was a useful and honored citizen, and d. in a good old age, 19 Jan. 1849, a. nearly 92; his w. Ann d. 29 June 1828, a. 49.

4. SETH, s. of Seth (2), m. his cousin Lydia, dau. of Lemuel Berry of Brewster, 12 May 1782, and had *Zenas*, b. 3 Feb. 1783, d. 17 Mar. 1786; *Isabella*, b. 3 Dec. 1784, m. Chauncy Doty 4 Mar. 1804; he d. 2 Sep. 1804, and she m. Josiah Stockwell; she d. at Vineland, N. J., 9 Aug. 1879; *Arathusa*, b. 5 Nov. 1786, m. Harmon Chamberlain, pub. 27 Ap. 1806, and d. 20 Dec. 1872; *Lydia*, b. 7 Sep. 1788, m. Otis Shurtleff 14 Feb. 1810, and d. at Worc. 17 Oct. 1858; *Ruth*, b. 16 July 1790, m. Samuel Hathaway 15 Mar. 1810, and d. 8 Mar. 1859; *Abigail*, b. —— 1792, d. 19 June 1796, a. 4; *Rebecca Berry*, b.

—— 1794, d. 3 Jan. 1796, a. 1 year and 7 months; *Hiram*, b. 13 Oct. 1798, res. and d. in Bucksport, Me.; *Harrington*, b. 7 Sep. 1804, res. in Bucksport, Me., and in Boston. SETH the f. was a mason, but much engaged in public affairs; he was major of militia, coroner, selectman two years, and assessor four years; his w. Lydia d. 27 Aug. 1805, a. 45, not long after which he rem. from Hardwick, and d. at Worc. 30 Ap. 1851, a. nearly 92.

5. JUDAH, s. of Seth (2), m. Sally, dau. of Timothy Ruggles, Jr., and gr. dau. of Gen. Timothy Ruggles, 15 Dec. 1785. He res. in Barre, where he d. between 7 Jan. and 6 Ap. 1819; in his will are mentioned his w. Sally, and chil. *Harriet*, w. of Moses Boyden, *Mark*, *Melatiah Bourne*, *Judah*, *Samuel*, *Simeon Dwight*, *Barnabas*, *Rufus*, *Fanny*, *Sally*, *Timothy Ruggles*.

6. BARNABAS, s. of Seth (2), m. Mary, dau. of Daniel Billings, 8 Oct. 1797, and had *Seth*, b. 24 June 1798; *Daniel B.*, b. 13 Sep. 1800, m. Mary Ann Gorham, pub. 8 Ap. 1830, extensively and successfully engaged in the manufacture of iron in Maine; *Mary*, b. 24 Jan. 1803, m. Daniel Wheeler 2d, pub. 5 Nov. 1826; *Sally*, b. —— 1806, d. 11 Dec. 1810, a. 4. BARNABAS the f. res. on the homestead, was an ensign of militia, and d. 2 Mar. 1807; his w. Mary m. Luther Paige 4 Sep. 1816, and d. at Bangor, Me., 11 Mar. 1849, a. 77.

7. SAMUEL ALLEN, s. of Samuel (3), by w. Cordelia, had *Rosilla Adeline*, b. 15 May 1843; *Ellen M.*, b. at Hartford about 1846, d. here 3 Aug. 1848, a. 1 year and 6 months. SAMUEL A. the f. rem. to Rockingham, Vt.

8. SETH, s. of Barnabas (6), m. Antis Gorham of Barre, pub. 25 Aug. 1822, and had several chil., whose names are not found on record. He res. on the homestead, and d. 30 Dec. 1836; his w. Antis d. 5 Nov. 1851, a. 49; their chil. (or most of them) res. in California.

PRISCILLA, m. Moses Haskell, Jr., 12 Jan. 1780. ABIGAIL, of Brk., m. Capt. Seth Peirce 19 Jan. 1797.

HITCHCOCK, PELATIAH, m. Hannah, dau. of Gen. Jonathan Warner 17 July 1791, and had *George Augustus*, b. 28 Ap. 1792; *Henry*, b. 7 May 1800, an upright and successful merchant in Boston, resided at Jamaica Plain, where he d. 30 Oct. 1880. PELATIAH the f. was b. at Brookfield, grad. H. C. 1785, and soon after commenced the practice of law in Hardwick. His brilliant talents gave promise of success, and his flashes of wit, as well as his words of wisdom, still survive in tradition.[1] His ardent hopes, however, were not realized, and he returned to his native town, where, after experiencing his full share of the trials and troubles of life, he d. 28 Ap. 1851, a. 86.

2. CHARLES F., a merchant, and assistant postmaster at Gilbertville, by w. Hannah, had *William King*, b. 26 July 1865; *Anna Minerva*, b. 6 June 1870, d. 25 Jan. 1879.

CLARENCE, of Springf., m. Laura G. Wetherell 23 May 1872.

HODGES, EPHRAIM, m. Catherine Johnson 25 Nov. 1779, and had *Ephraim*, b. 5 June 1780.

2. EDMUND, was a captain of militia, and went with a part of his company to the northern frontier in July 1777, when Bennington was threatened; he was also a lieutenant in a previous campaign. No record is found of his family. He rem. to Barnard, Vt., and was one of the assessors elected at the organization of that town 9 Ap. 1778, and representative the same year.

ABRAHAM, JR., m. Triphena Smith of Dana, pub. 25 Dec. 1815.

HOLDEN, THOMAS, m. Ruth Baker 21 Mar. 1751; and, on the same day, ABIGAIL, m. Josiah Bacon.

[1] Under the provisions of the old law, he was at Worcester, confined to the "jail limits," for debt. A stranger, entering the apartment where he was sitting, inquired if he was the jailor: "No sir," he replied, "I am the jailee." At another time, in Brookfield, he had a chance interview with the Rev. Dr. Griffin. Though entire strangers to each other, they became deeply interested in conversation on literary and scientific subjects. At length, in the heat of argument, Mr. Hitchcock uttered some expression bordering on profanity. Instantly perceiving that his language was offensive, he gravely addressed Dr. Griffin, whose noble stature towered, head and shoulders, above his own: "I ought not to have used such words; I ask your pardon; and if I need pardon from a higher source, I beg you to ask it for me, as you are much nearer heaven than I am."

HOLMES, PHILIP, m. Ann Powers of Gr., pub. 22 Nov. 1772. JAMES, m. Prudence Gibbs of Gr. 31 Oct. 1784.

HOLT, THOMAS, m. Sarah, dau. of Rev. Ebenezer Chaplin of Sutton, 5 May 1796, and had *Mary Chaplin*, twin, b. 19 Sep. 1797, m. Dwight Marsh 4 Nov. 1817, and d. 20 Ap. 1866; *Sarah Chaplin*, twin, b. 19 Sep. 1797, d. unm. 13 July 1848; *Thomas Russell*, b. 30 June 1799, studied law, settled in Connecticut, but soon disappeared, and his subsequent history is unknown; *Ann Tyler*, b. 15 Feb. 1801, d. unm. at Athol, 11 Jan. 1869; *Daniel Leander*, b. 4 Nov. 1802, m. Sophronia Briggs of Athol, pub. 11 June 1840; through lack of skill and energy he became a public charge, and d. at Athol 28 Ap. 1876; *Fidelia Morse*, b. 9 Sep. 1804, d. 3 Jan. 1805; *John Jay*, b. 2 Nov. 1805, d. unm. 10 Jan. 1832; he was the flower of the family, and many bright hopes were blasted by his early death. THOMAS the f., son of Daniel and Mary, was b. at Meriden, Conn., 9 Nov. 1762, grad. Y. C. 1784, ordained at Hardwick 25 June 1789, dismissed 27 Mar. 1805, installed at Chebacco (a parish in Ipswich, now the town of Essex) 25 Jan. 1809, dismissed 20 Ap. 1813, returned to Hardwick labored in various places as a missionary, and cultivated his farm; he d. 21 Feb. 1836; his w. Sarah d. 4 July 1854, a. 84.

HOPKINS, SAMUEL, m. Elizabeth, dau. of Walter Hastings, 17 Dec. 1778, and had *Moses*, b. 4 Sep. 1779; *Abiathar*, b. 14 July 1781, grad. D. C. 1806, a lawyer in Harrisburg, Pa., d. unm., while on a visit at Petersham, 27 Sep. 1821; *Alinda*, b. 8 Feb. 1784, m. Timothy Billings, pub. 10 Nov. 1805, d. 6 Aug. 1832; *Thirza*, b. 4 May 1786, m. James Paige of Boston 8 July 1810, d. at Medford 17 Feb. 1870; *Henrietta*, b. 16 July 1788, d. unm. at Boston 3 May 1854; *Betsey*, b. 22 July 1790, m. Thomas Hapgood of Petersham 3 Feb. 1818; he d. and she m. Hon. William Gates of Lunenburg, Vt., 28 Jan. 1829. SAMUEL the f. rem. fr. Hk. to Pet. soon after 1781, where he subsequently resided.

SARAH, m. Constant Merrick, Jr., 18 Mar. 1781.

HOWARD, NEHEMIAH (otherwise written Hayward and Heywood), m. Hannah Wilder of Hingham — Dec. 1772, and had *Hannah*, b. 4 Mar. 1775, m. Joseph Freeman of Ware 26 Sep. 1796; *Ruth*, b. 5 Jan. 1777; *Celia*, b. 20 Sep. 1778, m. Silas Johnson 24 Feb. 1799; *Nancy*, b. 6 Nov. 1780, d. unm. 30 May 1859; *Tamazine*, b. 20 Ap. 1782; *Pyam*, b. 4 Feb. 1784; *Emma*, b. 22 Dec. 1785; *Nehemiah*, b. 8 Feb. 1788; *Roxana*, b. 1 Jan. 1790; *Calista*, b. 12 Oct. 1791; *Edward Wilder*, b. 1 Nov. 1793; *Rowena*, b. 22 Sep. 1796. NEHEMIAH the f. rem. to Enfield.

2. CAREY, s. of Carey, m. Fanny, dau. of George Field, 26 Nov. 1813, and had *Eleuthera Field*, b. 11 Nov. 1814, m. Zeba Howard of Easton 21 June 1836; *Charlotte*, b. ——, d. 5 June 1816, a. 4 months; *Prudence Whipple*, b. —— 1817, bap. 30 Nov. 1819, m. Rev. Dana Goodsell of East Haven, Conn., 12 Jan. 1841, d. 6 or 8 Sep. 1847, a. 30, and was buried here in the new cemetery; *Catherine*, bap. 30 Nov. 1819, m. Martin L. Brett of Easton 12 Jan. 1841; *George C.*, b. —— 1823. CAREY the f. res. on the road to Gilbertville, at the place marked "Wid. Howard" on the R. Map; he d. 8 Ap. 1823, a. 35; his w. Fanny d. in Easton — Nov. 1865, a. 80.

3. GEORGE C., s. of Carey (2), m. Eliza J., dau. of Capt. John Lawton, 16 May 1850, and had *Mary Catherine*, b. 6 Mar. 1851, m. John A. Nutter of Montreal 2 Mar. 1876; *Eliza Jane*, b. 28 Feb. 1853, m. Frank M. Rice 6 Feb. 1879; *Dwight Field*, b. 3 Jan. 1856, m. Harriet J. Newton 15 Jan. 1883; *George C.*, b. 21 Sep. 1858; *Anna*, b. 28 Feb. 1862; *William Henry*, b. 25 Aug. 1864, d. 26 Aug. 1866; *Mattie Sanford*, b. 28 Aug. 1867; *Prudence Goodsell*, b. 29 June 1871. GEORGE C. the f. res. on the homestead.

4. CLINTON, of Sturbridge, m. Maria, dau. of Lemuel Ruggles, 20 June 1858, and had *Marion Lucretia*, b. 28 May 1859; *Arthur Clinton*, b. 26 Oct. 1861; *Franklin S.*, b. 10 Jan. 1864, d. 19 May 1865. CLINTON the f. rem. to Hk. about the time of his marriage, was a farmer, res. on the Moose Brook road near the Old Furnace, at the place marked "D. Billings" on the R. Map, and d. 8 Feb. 1876, a. 60; his w. Maria d. 13 May 1877, a. 51.

BENJAMIN, bro. of Carey (2), m. Barbara Baker 19 Mar. 1809. THOMPSON, bro. of Carey (2), m. Irene Sumner 25 July 1816. JOHN HEYWOOD, a State pauper, d. 30 July 1812, a. 65.

HOWE, THOMAS, m. Sarah Corlie — Feb. 1737–8, and had *Joseph*, b. 22 July 1739; *Mary*, b. 15 Sep. 1743; *Hannah*, b. 15 Sep. 1745; *Martha*, b. 9 June 1748.

2. SAMUEL, of Rutland, m. Hannah Smith 29 May 1739, and had *Benjamin*, bap. 29 Aug. 1742; *Sylvanus*, bap. — Mar. 1743; *Elizabeth*, bap. 1 June 1746; *Estes*, bap. 27 Sep. 1747; and in Rut. *Sarah*, *Moses*, and *Hannah*. SAMUEL the f. was s. of Moses and Eunice, and was the first male white child born in Rutland, 23 Sep. 1719; his parents had previously rem. to Rut. from Brk. He "was an active and useful citizen while at Rut., went into the war in 1755, and in 1759 was one of the committee to build the meeting-house, after which he moved to Belchertown, and was respectable and wealthy." Reed's *Hist. of Rutland*, p. 127. The author of this *Hist. of Rut.* represents all the chil. in this family to have been born there; but the first four were baptized here, and were prob. born here.

3. ARTEMAS, of N. Br., m. (his second wife) Susanna, dau. of Gen. Jonathan Warner, 16 Feb. 1786, and in October of the same year was appointed as his aid-de-camp, thus superseding Major Martin Kinsley.

4. LEWIS, s. of Artemas (3), by first wife, m. Sarah, dau. of Joseph Robinson, pub. 21 Aug. 1808, and had an infant, b. ——, d. 16 Aug. 1809; an infant, b. ——, d. 11 Nov. 1811; *Lucy Ruggles*, b. 28 May 1813 (or 20 May 1814), d. unm. 4 Mar. 1835. LEWIS the f. res. on the old Warner homestead (now owned by Mr. Frazier Paige), in the centre of the town, and managed both the farm and the tavern; he d. 23 May 1814, a. 37, and his w. Sarah m. Hon. John M. Niles of Hartford 17 June 1824.

JONAH, m. Betsey White 21 Sep. 1812. GEORGE L., m. Ann M. Rutledge of Worc., pub. 18 June 1846.

HOYT, ISAAC H., of Brookfield, m. Melita Bonney 27 May 1846, and had, in Hk., *Isaac Harvey*, b. 23 Aug. 1848, d. 25 Jan. 1850; *Emily Jane*, b. 12 June 1852.

HUBBARD, CHESTER, of Templeton, m. Mary R., dau. of Cyrus Danforth, pub. 3 Feb. 1844, and had, in Hk., *Joseph Reuben*, b. 23 Nov. 1846. CHESTER the f. d. at Keokuk, Iowa, 29 June 1861, a. 45; his monument stands very near the northerly gate of the new cemetery in Hardwick.

HUDSON, SARAH, of Ware, m. Nathaniel Perry, Jr., pub. 22 Nov. 1807. CELIA, dau. of Eli, m. Apollos Fay 7 July 1817. OLIVE, m. William Winter 5 June 1831. SARAH, wid. of Eli, d. 2 Mar. 1845, a. 92.

HUNT, JOHN, s. of Isaac of Sudbury, grandson of Isaac of Concord, and great-grandson of William of Concord, the emigrant ancestor, b. 12 Feb. 1711, was one of the earliest inhabitants of Hk. (having previously res. a few years in Grafton), and by w. Mary had *Samuel*, b. 27 Sep. 1736; *Moses*, b. 18 Dec. 1738, d. 20 June 1747; *Hannah*, b. 22 Ap. 1741, m. Nathan Wheeler 1 July 1762; *Aaron*, b. 18 Mar. 1744; *Mary*, b. 13 Oct. 1746, m. James Wright 18 June 1766; *John*, b. 31 Jan. 1749–50; *Moses*, b. 28 Oct. 1756; *Joseph*, b. 8 Dec. 1759, m. Elizabeth, dau. of Daniel Fay, 16 May 1779, and rem. to Bennington. His w. Mary d. 2 Ap. 1765, a. 45, and he m. Patience Wright 25 Dec. 1765. JOHN the f. res. three quarters of a mile northerly from the Common, at the place marked "Dr. Wardwell" on the R. Map, long famous as the Willis tavern-stand; here he kept a tavern and cultivated a farm. During the Revolutionary War, his house was frequented by soldiers on their march to and from the army; the small-pox was prevalent; and through fear of becoming infected, he went to a pest-house in New Braintree, was vaccinated, died 14 Feb. 1778, and was buried in an orchard at the angle of the N. Br. road, a few rods south of the former residence of Col. Stephen Fay.

2. SAMUEL, s. of John (1), m. Sarah Osgood of Rut. Dist., pub. 20 Sep. 1758; she d. and he m. Abigail Fisk 20 Feb. 1766. His chil. were: *Anna*, b. 17 Jan. 1761; *Samuel*, b. 3 Ap. 1763, d. at Shoreham, Vt., 15 Feb. 1825. SAMUEL the f. rem. to Pawlet, Vt., in 1762, as appears by the town records, and thence to Shoreham, where he d. in 1799. Goodhue's *Hist. of Shoreham*, p. 31.

3. AARON, s. of John (1), m. Sarah Robinson 24 Oct. 1765, and had *David*,

b. 15 Oct. 1766; *Polly Palmer*, b. — July 1770; *Aaron*, bap. 4 Oct. 1772; *Sally*, bap. 19 June 1774, d. young; *Sally*, b. 1 Ap. 1777; *John*, b. 26 Mar. 1779; *Betsey*, b. 28 July 1781.

4. JOHN, s. of John (1), m. Elizabeth Webster 23 Dec. 1772; she d. 2 Oct. 1779, and he m. Sarah Fay 1 Oct. 1784; res. in Ware.

5. MOSES, s. of John (1), m. Esther, dau. of John Jenney, 10 Dec. 1778, and had *Sophia*, b. 2 Oct. 1779, m. Joseph Dexter 13 July 1800; *Moses*, b. 27 Aug. 1781; *Abigail*, b. 23 Sep. 1786; *John*, b. 26 June 1788, m. Mabel Hopkins 4 Jan. 1816, res. at Hadley; *Mary Palmer*, b. 19 Ap. 1790, m. Lemuel Wicker 15 Jan. 1811; *Esther Jenney*, b. 10 Feb. 1792, m. Lindsey Fay 20 Mar. 1810; *Zephaniah*, b. 4 Aug. 1793, m. Mary Howland 19 Nov. 1821, res. Barre, d. 1 Sep. 1856; *Orsamus*, b. 16 Feb. 1797; *Horace* (or *Hiram*), b. 15 Ap. 1799, d. 15 Jan. 1803; *William*, b. 27 June 1800, d. 11 Jan. 1803; *Hammond*, b. 8 July 1802, d. 20 May 1803; *William*, b. 6 Sep. 1804, m. Patty, dau. of Capt. Edmund Mayo, pub. 3 Dec. 1827, d. at Sturbridge 17 June 1877. MOSES the f. was a farmer, res. in the northerly part of the town, and d. 10 July 1822.

6. MOSES, s. of Moses (5), m. Rebecca Winslow of Barre, pub. 20 Oct. 1805, and had *Elisha Winslow*, b. —— 1806, d. 14 May 1807, a. 5 months; *Eliza*, b. 9 Mar. 1808, m. Jonathan R. Haskell 3 Dec. 1829; *Elisha Winslow*, b. 9 July 1810; *Hammond*, b. 15 Ap. 1812; *Abel Herod*, bap. 16 Oct. 1814, d. 19 Dec. 1814; *Henry*, b. 14 Jan. 1816; *John Winslow*, b. 30 Nov. 1818, res. in Springfield; *Moses*, b. 12 Aug. 1821; *William*, b. 14 Dec. 1824, d. at Springfield 29 July 1849. MOSES the f. d. 8 Oct. (or 15, as on grave-stone) 1833.

7. ORSAMUS, s. of Moses (5), m. Laura, dau. of Silas Newton, 7 Jan. 1821; she d. at Granby, 14 Jan. 1851, a. 56, and he m. her sister, Caroline Newton. His chil. were: *Addison*, b. here 20 Jan. 1822, m. Clarissa E. Thomas, 16 Mar. 1852, and rem. to Worc.; and at Granby, *Calvin Newton*, b. 8 June, 1825, d. 21 May 1830; *Charles Edward*, b. 21 May 1830; *Edwin Newton*, b. 14 Dec. 1834. ORSAMUS the f. d. at Shrewsbury 25 May 1864.

8. ELISHA WINSLOW, s. of Moses (6), m. Louisa Vineca, pub. 20 Aug. 1841, and had *Edwin*, b. ——; *Newell*, b. 1 Oct. 1843; *William Sprague*, b. here 28 Feb. 1846, d. 24 Sep. 1852; *William N.*, b. ——. ELISHA W. the f. rem. to Springfield and d. 12 Dec. 1858.

9. HAMMOND, s. of Moses (6), m. Susan Walker 30 Ap. 1839, and had *Eunice Mary Ann*, b. 12 Ap. 1840, d. 15 Nov. 1841; *Mercy Ann*, b. 17 Nov. 1841, d. 23 Sep. 1842; *Susan Elvira*, b. 28 Jan. 1845. HAMMOND the f. d. 28 Aug. 1845, and his w. Susan m. Joshua Conkey of Rochester, N. Y., 3 Jan. 1848.

10. HENRY, s. of Moses (6), m. Eliza P. Sexton 12 June 1844, and had *Emily F.*, b. 20 Sep. 1845; *Eliza A.*, b. 12 Sep. 1847; *Daniel Sexton*, b. 4 Nov. 1850, d. 30 Nov. 1850; *Daniel*, b. 25 Dec. 1851; *William Henry*, b. 20 Jan. 1855; *George*, b. 20 May 1857; *Fanny*, b. 8 Aug. 1859; *John*, b. 12 Dec. 1861; *Mary Walker*, b. 29 June 1864; a son, b. 19 Nov. 1866. HENRY the f. was killed by lightning 22 Ap. 1867.

11. MOSES, s. of Moses (6), m. Jane Grier 31 Dec. 1856, and had *Hammond*, b. 31 July 1858, d. 3 Aug. 1858. MOSES the f. rem. to Springf., and d. 6 Feb. 1873.

12. CHARLES EDWARD, s. of Orsamus (7), m. Laura Warner 4 Sep. 1855, and had *Hattie Maria*, b. 21 Mar. 1858. CHARLES EDWARD the f. rem. to Greenfield.

13. EPHRAIM of Gr., s. of Ephraim of Dartmouth and grandson of Rev. Samuel of Dartmouth, m. Rhoda Forbush 5 Ap. 1781. It does not appear whether they had children. He d. 5 Sep. 1831, a. 72; his w. Rhoda d. 15 Aug. 1855, a. 94. There are indications that Ephraim of Dartm. rem. to Hardwick; and his sister Joanna, then of Gr., was pub. to Thomas Haskell 13 Jan. 1749–50.

14. JOHN, a merchant in Boston, not known to be of near kin to either of the foregoing, was an early and extensive land-owner in Hardwick. After his death, his real estate was divided between his three sons, *John*, *Shrimpton*,

and *Thomas*, and his dau., the w. *Elizabeth* Wendell, 10 Jan. 1754. One lot extended from the present southeasterly line of Mr. William C. Wesson's homestead along the northerly side of the street to the Common, and thence up the hill where the old road is still visible, nearly or quite to the Ware road, being 180 rods deep, at the easterly end; 174 rods, at the southeasterly corner of the Common; and 207 rods, at the westerly end; the northerly line was straight, and measured 125 rods. This lot included the present Common and burial-ground.

JACKSON, NATHANIEL, of Gr., m. Lucy Seaver, pub. 10 Jan. 1794. He was prob. the same who resided on the road connecting the Gilbertville and Ware roads, at the place marked "Mr. Warner" on the R. Map. No record found of children.

2. OTIS, of Woodstock, Conn., m. Ruth Jamerson 3 Jan. 1854, and had *Mary Jane*, b. 15 Nov. 1854, m. Henry W. Ayers of N. Br. 19 Jan. 1880; *William Otis*, b. 6 Oct. 1861; both b. in Hk.

SALOME, m. Luther Seaver, pub. 4 Nov. 1808, d. 13 Ap. 1809, a. 22. REBECCA, d. unm. 23 Sep. 1814, a. 30.

JAMERSON, SETH, m. Lydia, dau. of John Hastings, Esq., 3 Oct. 1814, and had *Clark Hastings*, b. — March 1815, d. 6 May 1816; *Rebecca*, b. 9 June 1818, m. Hiram Barrows of Dana, 26 May 1847; *Clark*, b. 20 Dec. 1819; *Ruth*, b. 26 Dec. 1821, m. Otis Jackson 3 Jan. 1854; an infant d. 8 Sep. 1828. SETH the f. was b. in Barre, a farmer, and resided at the place marked with his name on the R. Map (the Hastings homestead on the Moose Brook road, near Barre); he was a jovial and fearless rider in the troop of cavalry, and with his companion, Joel Hagar, was accustomed to keep the company wide awake. He d. 30 May 1858, a 67; his w Lydia d. 9 May 1872, a. 82.

2. WINTHROP, m. Caroline Fairbanks, pub. 27 Mar. 1826; he rem. to Barre.

JAMES, HUMPHREY, m. Mary Ann Newland, pub. 30 May 1855, and had *Sarah Jane*, b. 12 Feb. 1856; *Mary Abby*, b. 24 Feb. 1857; *John Dean*, b. 24 Ap. 1861, d. 5 Oct. 1863.

JENKINS, SOUTHWORTH, m. Huldah Wright 15 Nov. 1770, res. in Barre, where he had *Southworth*, b. ——, established himself in business as a clothier, at the Furnace Village in 1803, but ret. to Barre; *James Wright*, b. —— 1780; *Joseph*, b. —— 1781, res. in Boston, was a builder, Grand Master of the Grand Lodge of Masons, and d. 11 Oct. 1851; *Benjamin*, b. about 1784; *Charles*, b. about 1786, grad. W. C. 1813, pastor of a church in Portland, where he d. in 1831, a. 45; and prob. others. SOUTHWORTH the f. (if not his son of the same name) d. in Barre about the beginning of the year 1821; his w. Huldah d. — Nov. 1810, a. 62.

2. JAMES WRIGHT, s. of Southworth (1), m. Betsey Whipple of Grafton, pub. 1 Jan. 1804, and had *Josiah Whipple*, b. here 6 Oct. 1805; and others (among whom was *James W.*), after his removal to Barre. JAMES W. the f. kept a tavern in the Furnace Village 1807 and 1808, was Master of Mount Zion Lodge in 1811, returned to Barre, was captain of militia, and d. 19 Sep. 1866, a. 86.

3. BENJAMIN, s. of Southworth (1), m. Hannah Atwood of Barre, pub. 21 Aug. 1808, and had *Benjamin Franklin*, bap. 11 Aug. 1811, d. at Barre 19 May 1877, a. nearly 68; *Jason*, bap. 11 Aug. 1811; *Benjamin Atwood*, bap. 8 Ap. 1814; d. at La Crosse, Wis., 19 Jan. 1880. BENJAMIN the f. was a clothier, succeeded his brother Southworth in business at the Old Furnace, and his brother James W., as Master of Mount Zion Lodge in 1812; he was also lieutenant of militia, and d. 12 March 1814.

JENKS, FRANCIS, m Alice Nye 28 July 1793. SUKEY, m. Seth Ruggles, pub. 18 May 1794. Mrs. SALLY, m. John Ruggles 26 Ap. 1801.

JENNEY, JOHN, of "Plymouth, who was a brewer of Norwich, went to Holland in his youth, lived at Rotterdam, came in the James, a little vessel of 44 tons, built for the Pilgrims of Leyden, arrived Aug. 1623, with w. Sarah (whom he m. at Leyden 1 Nov. 1614, by the name of Carey), and chil. *Samuel*, *Abigail*, and *Sarah*, at the same time with the Ann, therefore with her passengers reckoned among 'old comers,' had born here *John* and *Susanna;* was an assistant 1637–39, and representative 1641." Savage's *Gen. Dict.* ii. 546. He d. between 28 Dec. 1643 and 5 June 1644.

2. JOHN, s. of Samuel or John, and grandson of John (2), settled in Dartmouth, where by w. —— he had *Sarah*, b. 21 May 1672, m. —— Sherman; *Mehetabel*, b. 26 Sep. 1673, m. —— Gifford; *Elizabeth*, b. 5 Feb. 1676–7; *Samuel*, b. 4 Feb. 1678–9; *Lydia*, b. — Aug. 1682, m. —— Benson; *John*, b. 18 Ap. 1684. JOHN the f. d. between 21 Mar. and 26 Ap. 1727.

3. JOHN, s. of John (2), m. Abigail, dau. of Isaac Pope, and had *Joanna*, b. 8 Dec. 1714; *Ephraim*, b. 20 Feb. 1716–17; *Alice*, b. 1 Oct. 1718; *Margaret*, b. 25 Mar. 1722; *Elizabeth*, b. 28 Jan. 1724–5; *John*, b. 2 Nov. 1730. JOHN the f. res. in Dartmouth. His will, dated 7 Nov. 1749, was proved 6 May 1755.

4. JOHN, s. of John (3), m. Abigail, dau. of Samuel Spooner, 23 Nov. 1752, and had *Zephaniah*, b. 2 Aug. 1753, was a physician, took the name of Jennings, m. Martha Eddy of Shrews. 28 Nov. 1799, and prob. soon rem. from Hk.; *John*, b. 16 Mar. 1755; *Joanna*, b. —— 1757, d. unm. 10 Mar. 1835, a. 78; *Esther*, b. about 1759, m. Moses Hunt 10 Dec. 1778; *Elnathan*, b. about 1762, was living in 1796; *Abigail*, b. ——, m. Elijah Billings 24 Ap. 1796.. JOHN the f. rem. from Dartmouth to Hk. with his family, probably soon after the birth of his son *John* in 1755; he was a farmer, and d. 31 May 1796; his w. Abigail d. 10 Dec. 1829, a. 97.

5. JOHN, s. of John (4), m. Hannah Perry of Barre 10 Ap. 1788, and had *Justus*, b. 25 Nov. 1788; *Esther Gates*, b. 6 May 1790, m. Benjamin Gates of Barre 18 Nov. 1817; *John*, b. 16 Feb. 1792; *Chiron*, b. 26 Ap. 1794; *Calvin*, b. 3 July 1796; *Seth*, b. 21 July 1798; *Hannah Perry*, b. 19 Nov. 1800, m. Cyrus Danforth 6 Mar. 1817, and (2d) Clark Stone of Enfield 30 Sep. 1858, and d. 31 Oct. 1873; *Hiram*, b. 23 Aug. 1803, d. 5 Jan. 1805; *Lucretia Perry*, b. 21 Aug. 1805, m. —— Cary, and d. at Enf. 19 Sep. 1870; *Abigail Spooner*, b. 27 July 1808, m. Gardner Bartholomew, pub. 3 Feb. 1831. JOHN the f. was a farmer, res. on the Ware road, at the place marked "J. Robinson" on the R. Map (probably the homestead of his father), and d. 23 Aug. 1814; his w. Hannah m. Dr. William Stone of Enf., 23 Nov. 1819.

6. JUSTUS, s. of John (5), m. Lucy Wicker 19 Feb. 1811, and had *Jane Parsons*, b. 25 Sep. 1811; *Charles Austin*, b. 20 Nov. 1813; *Sophronia*, b. 8 Dec. 1815; *John*, b. 18 Aug. 1818; *Susan*, bap. 19 Aug. 1821. JUSTUS the f. res. on the homestead, but rem. from the town soon after 1821.

7. JOHN, s. of John (5), was a blacksmith, and rem. from Hk. prob. about 1828. I find no record of marriage or children.

8. CHIRON, s. of John (5), m. Sophronia, dau. of Charles Paige, 28 Sep. 1817; she d. 25 Feb. 1854, and he m. Mary C. Bowker 23 Mar. 1865. His chil. were: *Clarissa Paige*, b. 25 Sep. 1818, m. David Elwell 2d, 7 Sep. 1842; *Algernon Sidney*, b. 6 Sep. 1821; *Hattie Bell* (a child of her father's old age), b. 5 July 1869, d. 11 Aug. 1870. CHIRON the f. was a tanner, res. at the old Furnace Village, and d. 29 June 1874.

9. CALVIN, s. of John (5), m. Mary Bassett 19 Sep. 1824, and had *Mary E.*, b. 19 June 1825; *Louisa*, b. 2 July 1827, d. 21 Oct. 1831; *Fidelia*, b. 9 Aug. 1829, m. —— Wheeler, and d. at Ware 20 Jan. 1861; *Clarissa*, b. 11 Aug. 1831, and d. at Ware 3 May 1853. CALVIN the f. was a farmer and captain of militia, res. on the Ware road for some years, at the place marked "C. Ruggles" on the R. Map, but rem. from the town.

10. ALGERNON SIDNEY, s. of Chiron (8), m. Mary J. Brigham of Pres., pub. 14 Feb. 1846, and had *Mary Jane Frances*, b. 3 Mar. 1851.

JEMIMA, m. Gideon Carpenter 31 May 1753. ESTHER, m. David Gilbert, Jr., of N. Br. 23 Mar. 1758.

JOHNSON, EXPERIENCE, m. Mary Hamlin, at Rochester, 18 Ap. 1728, and had *William*, b. 26 Aug. 1729; *Thomas*, b. 13 Nov. 1733, pub. to Hannah Chelson 10 Mar. 1759; he soon rem. from Roch. to Hk., and both his sons were bap. here 5 Dec. 1736.

2. ZEBADIAH, prob. s. of Zebadiah and Esther of Shrewsbury, and, if so, bap. 1 Ap. 1733, came here about 1753, m. Alice, dau. of Capt. Constant

Merrick, 25 Nov. 1756, and had *Samuel*, b. 23 May 1758; *Mary*, b. 10 Mar. 1760, d. unm. 5 Oct. 1837; *Constant*, b. 9 Jan. 1762; *Joab*, b. 9 Mar. 1765; *Zebadiah*, b. 16 June 1767, m. Sally Powers 9 Feb. 1791; *John*, b. 4 June 1769.

3. SETH, prob. brother of Zebadiah (2), and b. at Shrews. 15 Feb. 1736. pub. to Kezia Cooley of Gr. 2 Aug. 1760, and had *Jonah*, b. 19 Mar. 1761; *Catherine*, b. 3 Aug. 1763, m. Ephraim Hodges 25 Nov. 1779; *Phebe*, b. 29 Sep. 1764, m. Noah Beach of Rut., pub. 9 July 1780; *Electa*, b. 31 Jan. 1767, m. James Whipple 21 Ap. 1785. Widow KEZIA JOHNSON, the mother, d. 15 Feb. 1822, a. 85.

4. ISRAEL, prob. brother of Zebadiah (2), and b. at Shrews. 11 Sep. 1737, m. Abiel, wid. of Ebenezer Safford, 29 Dec. 1761, and had *Challis*, b. 1 Oct. 1762.

5. NATHANIEL, by w. Sarah, had prob. *Nathaniel*, b. ——; *Triphena*, b. 15 Sep. 1764, m. Sylvanus Brimhall 14 Sep. 1783. NATHANIEL the f. d. 3 Nov. 1790, a. 71.

6. SILAS, m. Patience Walker of Pet., 27 Nov. 1766, and had *Silas*, b. 27 Nov. 1767; *Susanna*, b. 15 Ap. 1770. SILAS the f. d. 12 July 1822, a. 76; his w. Patience d. 18 Oct. 1813, a. 69.

7. NATHANIEL, prob. s. of Nathaniel (5), m. Mary Nye 5 Sep. 1783, and had *Otis*, b. 5 May 1784.

8. STEPHEN, m. Abigail Rice of Barre 31 May 1774; she d. 22 Ap. 1777; and he m. Elizabeth Witt of Paxton, pub. 16 May 1779. His chil. were: *Abigail*, b. 19 Ap. 1776; m. Wyatt Richardson, pub. 6 May 1795; *Elizabeth*, b. 17 June 1780; *Stephen*, b. 14 Dec. 1781.

9. AARON, m. Susanna Bridgeman of Gr. — June 1787, and had *Aaron*, b. 22 May 1788.

10. DANIEL, m. Lucy Briggs of Orange — May 1797, and had *Samuel*, b. 29 Jan. 1798, m. Polly Sprout, pub. 15 May 1825, and d. 14 Aug. 1847; she d. 22 Jan. 1829, a. 37; *Ezra*, b. 22 Oct. 1799, m. Abigail Sprout, pub. 6 Nov. 1830, and d. at Presc. 1 Ap. 1878; *Philip*, b. 3 May 1802, m. Civilla R. Thayer, pub. 20 Mar. 1830; she d. 19 Dec. 1861, a. 58, and he m. Mrs. Elizabeth C. Stevens 21 Aug. 1862; his dau. Mary E. d. unm. 30 Nov. 1867, a. 36; and he d. 24 Mar. 1875; *Lucy*, b. 6 July 1804, m. Orville Lathrop of Shrews., pub. 31 Jan. 1825. LUCY the mother d. 3 Feb. 1814, a. 41.

11. SILAS, s. of Silas (6), m. Hannah Nye 15 Dec. 1785; she d. and he m. Celia Howard, or Haywood, 24 Feb. 1799, and had *Silas Nye*, b. 3 Sep. 1799, d. at Dana 1 Ap. 1879; *Alanson*, b. 9 Nov. 1800; *Hiram*, b. 3 Sep. 1802; *Gardner*, b. 25 Oct. 1804; *Nehemiah Haywood*, b. 26 May 1807, res. in Illinois 21 Sep. 1841, when he m. Eunice Randall; *Karylan*, b. 15 July 1809. SILAS the f. d. 19 Mar. 1840, and his w. Celia m. John Peckham of Pet. 20 Ap. 1841.

12. AARON, m. Celia Richardson of Gr., 11 Sep. 1800, and had *Alice*, b. 21 Mar. 1801, m. Seth Richardson, pub. 3 Ap. 1820; *William*, b. 1 Nov. 1803, m. Eliza Whipple 15 Aug. 1822, and d. 16 Aug. 1871. AARON, the f. d. 1 May 1813, a. 41; his w. Celia d. 2 Sep. 1846, a. 66.

13. JOHN, prob. s. of Zebadiah (2), by w. Mary, had *Chester*, b. about 1801; *John*, b. about 1805, m. Arathusa Dexter 5 Oct. 1828 (she d. 6 Ap. 1862, a. 56; he d. 2 May 1876, a. 71); their son, William W., m. Eunice C. Sturtevant 18 Aug. 1880; *Samuel*, b. about 1810, d. 31 May 1848, a. 38. JOHN the f. d. 25 Ap. 1828.

14. MARSHALL, m. Lettice Hathaway 1 Jan. 1811, and had *Balarah*, b. 19 Oct. 1811; *Mary*, b. 9 Dec. 1812, m. Ebenezer H. Egery 26 Feb. 1828; *Sarah*, b. 25 Dec. 1814, m. Hosea Cummings 22 Feb. 1831; *Justus*, b. 31 Aug. 1816. MARSHALL the f. d. 28 Oct. 1857, a. 81; his w. Lettice d. 3 Mar. 1859, a. 72.

15. ALANSON, s. of Silas (11), m. Amanda Wheeler, pub. 8 May 1826, and had *Henry A.*, b. 7 Ap. 1827; *William W.*, b. 4 Nov. 1835.

16. WILLIAM, by w. Ellen, had *Halsea Hurlburt*, b. —— 1843.

17. JUSTUS, s. of Marshall (14), m. Sylvia S. Smith of Gr., pub. 28 Feb. 1840, and had *George Franklin*, b. 3 Jan. 1845.

18. CHESTER, s. of John (13), by w. Rebecca had *George*, b. 11 Jan. 1847. CHESTER the f. d. 31 Aug. 1848, a. 38; his w. Rebecca d. 24 July 1851, a. 46.

19. PHILANDER, by w. Susan, had *William Warren*, b. 7 Aug. 1848.

20. DAVID W., by w. Clarissa A., had *Frederick D.*, b. 29 July 1850; *Oren Alpheus*, b. 9 July 1852.

21. GARDNER N., by w. Eliza, had *Joseph French*, b. 24 Aug. 1853.

22. JOHN J., m. Harriet E. Covell, 11 Mar. 1852, and had *Lestella*, b. 26 Oct. 1853; a son b. 27 Ap. 1861, d. 19 May 1861; *Cleola A.*, b. 4 Mar. 1863, m. Rollin D. Newton, 3 Mar. 1881.

23. JOHN, by w. Julia, had *Thomas Francis*, b. 21 Jan. 1857.

24. ALPHEUS, m. Frances M. Turner, pub. 28 Ap. 1853, and had *Fanny Adella*, b. 24 Feb. 1861.

25. AARON F., by w. Adeline, had *William Harvey*, b. 1 June 1861.

26. HALSEA H., s. of William (16), m. Mary E. Kendall 20 Oct. 1863, and had *Samuel Hurlburt*, b. 30 May 1864.

27. ENOS T., m. Emma C. Bacon of Gr. 16 Mar. 1864, and had *Charles Albert*, b. 23 Ap. 1873; *Rupert E.*, b. 20 Oct. 1881.

SOLOMON, of Gr. (prob. bro. of Zebadiah (2)), m. Sarah Dexter 28 Dec. 1762. JOEL, m. Eleanor Parks 27 Sep. 1768. WILLIAM, m. Hannah Johnson 26 Jan. 1775 or 1776. JOHN, m. Nancy Thayer, pub. 10 Nov. 1797. JOSHUA, m. Rachel Whipple 12 Aug. 1798. SETH, m. Sally Hillman, pub. 27 Nov. 1800. STEPHEN N., m. Susanna Whipple 3 Feb. 1823. SAMUEL, m. Betsey Cummings 29 June 1829. PEEBLES, m. Eliza Ellen Whipple 21 May 1861. JOEL, d. 10 Oct. 1813, a. 70. MILO, d. 31 Aug. 1845, a. 21.

The registration of births was so much neglected by the parents for many years, that I am unable to give a satisfactory account of the numerous families bearing the name of Johnson, and of their relationship to each other.

JORDAN, EDMUND, a nephew of Benjamin Smith and one of the pioneers, m. Temperance, dau. of William Thomas (at Brk.), 12 Mar. 1734, and had *Elizabeth*, b. 27 Ap. 1735, m. John Mellard, pub. 19 Ap. 1761; *William*, b. 13 Dec. 1737; *Submit*, b. 19 Ap. 1740, m. Daniel Hastings, pub. 22 July 1764; *Mary*, b. 23 Dec. 1743; *Sarah*, b. 13 Aug. 1746, d. 25 Oct. 1746; *Sarah*, b. 24 July 1748, d. unm. 24 Mar. 1771; *Eleazar*, b. 2 Mar. 1750; *Meits* (a son), b. 1 May 1752. EDMUND the f. was b. in Taunton, and was a carpenter; he was a corporal in Capt. Samuel Robinson's company 1755, in the French War; also in 1756, during which campaign he died, a. 45.

2. JOHN, prob. brother of Edmund (1), was here in 1735, in Nitchewaug (Petersham) 1738, returned to Hk., was a soldier in Captain Robinson's company 1755, and d. 14 Dec. 1755. His son *Dudley* was bap. in Nitchewaug by Rev. Mr. White, 30 July 1738, was a soldier in Captain Robinson's company 1756, and d. during that campaign, a. 20.

3. DUDLEY, prob. brother of Edmund (1), m. Mary, dau. of John Haskell, 23 Dec. 1739, and had *Susanna*, b. 20 Mar. 1740–1, m. Abraham Knowlton 12 Mar. 1764; *Philip*, b. 17 Mar. 1742–3; *Mercy*, b. 10 (or 14) June 1745, m. John Raymond 7 Mar. 1771; *Sarah*, b. 22 July 1747; *Dudley*, b. 8 Mar. 1749. DUDLEY the f. res. on Ruggles Hill, at or near the place marked "A. Ruggles" on the R. Map; he was a remarkably expert gunner, and is said to have alarmed the town by discharging his gun at a catamount three times in such rapid succession that it was supposed to be the "alarm," or established signal of danger. He d. 26 Ap. 1750; his w. Mary d. 27 May 1750.

4. DUDLEY, s. of Dudley (3), m. Bathsheba Rice 8 Aug. 1776, and had *Hannah*, b. 29 Ap. 1777; *Bathsheba*, b. 11 Jan. 1779; *Polly*, b. 19 Jan. 1781; *Prudence*, b. 11 Nov. 1782, d. unm. at Gr. 16 Dec. 1869; *Mercy*, b. 6 Jan. 1785, m. William Morton of Gr. 20 Mar. 1813; *William Pitt*, b. about 1786; *Cynthia*, b. ——, m. Seth B. Manly 12 May 1824; *Alma* (or *Almira*), b. about 1793, d. unm. 21 Mar. 1814, a. 21; *John Tyler*, b. 3 Sep. 1799, res. in Gr., d. 17 Sep. 1879, a. 80 years and 14 days; *George Anson*, b. about 1805, d. 11 July 1814, a. 9. DUDLEY the f. was a tanner, res. several years near Gilbertville, on the old road, now little used, a few rods below the place marked "R. Field" on the R. Map, in a house apparently one of the earliest erected in the town; he d. at Ware 5 July 1820; his w. Bathsheba d. 5 Dec. 1813, a. 53.

5. WILLIAM PITT, s. of Dudley (4), m. Sophia Bliss of Jamaica, Vt., pub.

19 Ap. 1813; she d. and he m. Mary Presho, 25 Mar. 1818; she d. 25 May 1834, a. 37, and he m. Electa Grant, who d. 4 Jan. 1838, a. 26, and he m. Mrs. Sophia King 26 June 1838. His chil. were: *Anson*, b. —— 1818, d. 24 Mar. 1820, a. 2; *Cynthia*, b. 3 Nov. 1821, m. James Davis, Jr., 11 Aug. 1836; *Mary Nye*, b. 9 Jan. 1823; *William P.*, b. 1828, d. 31 Dec. 1860, a. 32; and perhaps others. WILLIAM PITT the f. was a tanner, res. on the road to Barre, at the place marked "P. Jordan" on the R. Map, and d. 24 Ap. 1869.

JOSLIN, DINAH, m. Prince Nye 15 Dec. 1774. ELIZABETH, m. Abraham Bell of N. Br. 29 Dec. 1785. PETER A., m. Hannah T. Newcomb, pub. 31 Oct. 1829. MATTHEWS, m. Mrs. Margaret Holdridge 12 Dec. 1830, and d. 20 Mar. 1840, a. 73. A child of MATTHEWS, JR., d. 26 Oct. 1834, a. 6 mos.

KEITH, EPHRAIM, s. of Joseph, and grandson of Rev. James, b. at Bridgewater in 1707, grad. H. C. 1729, preached here about a year, commencing 2 May 1734, but was probably never ordained; he returned to Bridgewater, was justice of the peace, m. Sarah, dau. of Israel Washburn, had seven chil., and d. in 1781.

2. JOHN, prob. b. in Bridgewater, m. Ann Belcher of Bridgew., pub. 10 Ap. 1774; she d. and he m. Zerviah Willis 21 Oct. 1782. His chil. were: *John*, bap. 9 July 1775; *Joseph*, b. 5 Oct. 1783; *Benjamin*, b. 17 Feb. 1785; *Seth*, b. 17 Feb. 1788.

REUEL, m. Abigail Allen, pub. 11 Ap. 1784.

KELLY, WILLIAM, m. Annis Thayer, pub. 25 Dec. 1820, and had *Merrick Thayer*, b. 14 Feb. 1822; *James Harvey*, b. 20 Sep. 1824.

MARGARET, m. Cornelius Wrin, pub. 8 Nov. 1856.

KENNEDY, DANIEL, by w. Margaret, had *Nancy*, b. 24 Aug. 1856; *Daniel*, b. 24 Sep. 1858; *Timothy*, b. 24 Jan. 1861; *Jeremiah*, b. 5 Mar. 1864.

2. RICHARD, by w. Margaret, had *Michael*, b. 23 Sep. 1856.

3. DAVID, m. Catherine Cronan, pub. 12 Jan. 1855, and had *Thomas*, b. 1 Ap. 1861; *Dennis*, b. 26 July 1863; *Cornelius* (posthumous), b. 6 June 1867. DAVID the f. was b. in Ireland, and d. 20 Oct. 1866, a. 45.

4. ALEXANDER, m. Jane ——, who d. ——, and he m. Jeannette Alexander, pub. 31 Aug. 1868. His chil. were: *William*, b. 30 Oct. 1862; *Mary*, b. 11 Jan. 1869.

ELLEN, of Ware, m. Peter Alexander 7 Feb. 1867. CATHERINE, m. Timothy Daley 7 Sep. 1868. JESSIE, m. Samuel Ross 23 Dec. 1876.

KENNEY, JESSE, m. Hannah Stearns, 11 Aug. 1776.

KERLEY, ANNA, m. Elisha Pike 29 Nov. 1744.

KIMBALL, JUDE, m. Joanna, dau. of James Lawton, 25 Aug. 1793, rem. to Lyndon, Vt., where he had *James Lawton*, b. 25 Ap. 1799, grad. D. C. 1824, and at And. Seminary 1828, became secretary of the Amer. Tract Soc. at Boston 1831, and d. unm. at Lyndon 8 Sep. 1833.

KING, SAMUEL, of Barre, m. Sybil Raymond 5 May 1840, res. here, and had *Samuel Sumner*, b. 6 Mar. 1845, d. 2 Feb. 1876; *John*, b. 1 Mar. 1847, d. 4 Ap. 1862.

2. JOHN, m. Mary J. Richardson 3 Oct. 1844, and had a son, b. 13 Nov. 1849; *Harvey Walker*, b. 16 Aug. 1852; *Elizabeth Adella*, b. 8 Feb. 1857; *Marshall Johnson*, b. 20 Feb. 1859; *Albert*, b. 30 Sep. 1862.

3. JESSE W., m. Huldah M. Barnes 21 Oct. 1848, and had *Charles Walter*, b. 12 Nov. 1849. JESSE W. the f. d. 3 Dec. 1855, a. 30; his w. Huldah M. m. Billings Cummings 22 Nov. 1859, and d. 10 Dec. 1868, a. 38.

4. THOMAS, by w. Catherine, had *Edward Norbert*, b. 5 June 1855; *Mary Jane*, b. 27 Oct. 1856; *Caroline*, b. 25 June 1859, d. unm. at Ware 16 Sep. 1879; *William Wallace*, b. 20 May 1868.

5 EDWARD T., by w. Mary J., had *Nellie May*, b. 2 May 1872.

JOEL (b. Enfield, Conn.), d. 29 July 1861, a. 81. WARREN M., m. Louisa Cummings of Barre, pub. 17 Sep. 1821. GEORGE H., m. Lucy J. Barnes 7 May 1846. ALFRED C., m. Sarah E. Hall 1 Oct. 1873. Wid. ELIZABETH F., d. 23 Ap. 1880, a. 78.

KINSLEY, MARTIN, s. of Samuel, was born at Bridgewater in 1754, grad. H. C. 1778, settled immediately in Hardwick, m. Polly Bellows of Walpole,

N. H., pub. 3 Oct. 1784, and had *Polly Hubbard*, b. 26 May 1787, d. 28 Aug. 1791; *Sophia W.*, b. 17 July 1797, d. 12 Jan. 1800; and, after his removal from Hk., *Mary*, b. 6 July 1801, m. Samuel Gardner, Esq., of Roxbury, and d. in 1839; *Martin*, b. 23 Sep. 1808, d. 31 May 1811. MARTIN the f., soon after he rem. here, engaged in the sale of English and West India goods, and res. at the place marked "J. Mixter" on the R. Map. About 1780 he was commissioned as one of the aids of Maj. Gen. Warner, and was thenceforth known as Major Kinsley; from this office, however, he was removed in 1786, probably on account of his sympathy with the Shays Rebellion, against which removal he published a protest in the "Worcester Magazine" for December, p. 450, under date of 24 Nov. 1786. The Shays party, then a majority of the town, rewarded him for his services and mortification by electing him town treasurer six years, from 1787 to 1792, and representative eight years, from 1787 to 1796, except 1789 and 1793, when no representative was chosen. Between 4 Ap. 1797 and 16 Feb. 1798, he removed to Hampden, in the province of Maine, where he was actively engaged, on the Democratic side, in the fierce political contest which marked the commencement of the present century. He was justice of the peace, while at Hardwick, in 1789, recommissioned in 1802, representative of Hampden in the General Court 1801 to 1806 (except 1805), senator from Hancock County 1814, member of the executive council 1810, 1811, and member of Congress in 1819 and 1820. He was appointed justice of the Court of Sessions 3 Sep. 1811, and on the eighth day of the following October, judge of the Court of Common Pleas for the Eastern Circuit; he was afterwards, for several years, judge of Probate. In his old age he retired from public office, and removed to Roxbury, where he died, at the house of his daughter, 20 June 1835.

KNAPP, CHARLES, by w. Hannah, had *Caroline Wiswell*, b. about 1807, d. 22 Sep. 1811, a. 4; *Mary Jane*, b. 21 June 1809; *Charles William*, b. 9 Oct. 1811; *Daniel Field*, b. 7 Sep. 1813; *Amasa Mason*, bap. 17 Sep. 1816, d. 16 Aug. 1818, a 2; *Catherine Wiswell*, bap. 25 Dec. 1818.

2. GEORGE W., of Franklin, m. Clarissa Snow 21 Sep. 1823, and had twin chil., who d. 20 and 22 Oct. 1830.

KNIGHT, THEOPHILUS, b. at Plainfield, Conn., 2 June 1788, m. Theodotia Bliss, who was b. at Western (now Warren), 1 Feb. 1792, and had in Warren *Mary E.*, b. 20 Ap. 1814, d. 25 Oct. 1821; *Albert E.*, b. 2 Nov. 1816; *Lucy P.*, b. 1 Dec. 1818, d. unm. 24 Feb. 1872; *Wealthy S.*, b. 1 Jan. 1821, m. Frazier Paige 11 Mar. 1844; *Royal*, b. 7 Mar. 1824, d. 3 May 1838; *Aaron B.*, b. 15 June 1826, d. 13 May 1861; *Mary Ann*, b. 10 Nov. 1829, m. Dr. Almon M. Orcutt 16 Oct. 1850; *Samuel H.*, b. 3 Dec. 1831, res. in St. Louis; *Franklin S.*, b. 9 May 1835, was a member (clerk) of the 31st Regt. Mass. Vols. in the Union Army, and d. unm. in St. Charles Hospital, New Orleans, 10 Jan. 1863. THEOPHILUS the f. was a farmer, rem. to Hardwick, with his family, 1 Ap. 1837, res. at the south end of the Common, and d. 14 Mar. 1844; his w. Theodotia d. 2 Feb. 1875.

2. ALBERT E., s. of Theophilus (1), came here 1 Ap. 1837, and m. E. Augusta Phelps of Ware 12 May 1841; she d. 20 Feb. 1864, a. 46, and he m. Harriet J., dau. of Joseph Robinson and wid. of William Browning, 5 Ap. 1866; she d. 16 Sep. 1869, a. 39, and he m. Cornelia E., dau. of Capt. Pliny Alden, 25 Oct. 1870. His chil. were: *Jane E.*, b. 21 Dec. 1842, m. Joel L. Powers 1 Jan. 1866; *Elizabeth H.*, b. 29 May 1846, m. Julius A. Dennis 8 Oct. 1868; *Samuel H. P.*, b. 8 May 1852, d. 25 Sep. 1853; *William H.*, b. 26 Ap. 1855, d. 9 June 1857; *Harry Phelps*, b. 26 Nov. 1856. ALBERT E. was for several years a clerk in the store of Mixter & Delano and Delano & Co.; afterwards a merchant, on his own account, at the south end of the Common; postmaster since 1850; town clerk since 1861; town treasurer eleven years from 1867 to 1878; justice of the peace since 1861; and representative in 1864.

KNOWLES, SIMEON, by w. Eunice, had *Simeon*, b. about 1766; *Elisha*, b. about 1779, d. 14 Aug. 1858, a. 79; *Phebe*, b. about 1783, d. unm. 7 Ap. 1824, a. 41; and prob. others. SIMEON the f. res. in Eastham until after the birth of his son *Simeon;* and perhaps all his chil. were born there. His w. Eunice d. here 5 Ap. 1819, a. 79.

2. SIMEON, s. of Simeon (1), by w. Priscilla, had *Bangs*, b. about 1789, d. 17 Sep. 1806, a. 17; *Simeon*, b. about 1791; *Leonard*, b. about 1795, d. 7 Feb. 1811, a. 16; *Edward*, b. about 1799, d. at Leicester 29 Oct. 1876, a. 77; *Harriet*, b. about 1805, m. Calvin A. Burnett of Oxford 29 June 1830, and d. at Leicester 20 Ap. 1865, a. 60; and perhaps others. SIMEON the f. d. 22 Aug. 1823, a. 57; his w. Priscilla d. 5 Feb. 1839, a. 75.

3. SIMEON, s. of Simeon (2), m. Lucetta, dau. of Silas Newton, 14 Mar. 1814, and had *Laura Loraine*, b. 10 Oct. 1816, m. Rufus Washburn, Jr., of Johnstown, N. Y., 21 Feb. 1837; *Lucius James*, b. 2 July 1819, an eminent inventor and manufacturer in Warren and Worcester;[1] *Harriet Eveline*, b. 24 July 1821, m. Lorin Brown of Fitchburg 1 Oct. 1844; *Francis B.*, b. 29 Nov. 1823, a successful manufacturer in Worcester. SIMEON the f. res. about three miles northerly from the Common. His w. Lucetta d. at Warren 23 Aug. 1868, a. 76.

ABIA, m. Elisha T. Mason, pub. 3 June 1816. EUNICE, m. Moses Whipple, Jr., 6 Ap. 1823.

KNOWLTON, JOSEPH, said to have been son of Thomas and Margery (Goodhue), was b. in Ipswich and res. there until about 1733, when he rem. to Shrewsbury. He m. Abigail Bird and had, in Ipswich, *Joseph*, b. prob. about 1720; *Abigail*, b. about 1722, d. in Hardwick unm. 4 Mar. 1807, a. 84; *Jacob*, b. about 1729; *Abraham*, b. about 1731; and in Shrews., *Nathan*, b. 28 Jan. 1733; *Samuel* and *Nathaniel*, twins, b. 21 Jan. 1737; *Israel*, b. 28 Jan. 1740. These eight children are named in their father's will, dated 17 Mar. 1756; and besides these, Ward says (*Hist. Shrewsbury*, p. 348), there were *Margery*, who d. at Shrews. 5 Feb. 1740, and "*Thomas*, who was killed by the French and Indians at Hoosac Fort, Aug. 17, 1745." JOSEPH the f. d. at Shrews., between 17 Mar. 1756 and 2 Sep. 1760. His w. Abigail d. 3 July 1748, and he m. Ann ——, who survived him.

2. JACOB, s. of Joseph (1), settled in Hardwick as early as 1752, m. Sarah Pratt of Shrews. 21 Nov. 1759; she d. and he m. Sarah Smith, pub. 1 Nov. 1762. His chil. were: *Joseph*, b. 20 Nov. 1760; *Sarah*, b. 29 Sep. 1763, m. Ebenezer Rich, Jr., of Gr., pub. 14 Dec. 1786; *Elizabeth*, bap. 23 June 1765; *Elijah*, b. 2 Mar. 1767, d. 2 Dec. 1790; *Anna*, b. 17 July 1769; *Abigail*, b. 26 June 1771; *Jacob*, b. 16 June 1774, d. 22 Sep. 1775; *Jacob*, b. 6 Oct. 1776. JACOB the f. was a blacksmith, and owned a farm bounded north by Muddy Pond and south by Ware. He served two campaigns in the French War, as a corporal in Capt. Samuel Robinson's company. He d. before 6 Aug. 1789, when his w. Sarah m. Deac. Joseph Allen.

3. ABRAHAM, s. of Joseph (1), was in Templeton as early as 1756, and m. Comfort Holman; she d. about 1761, when he rem. to Hk. and m. Susanna Jordan 12 Mar. 1764. His chil. were: *Comfort*, b. —— 1761 at Templeton, m. George Haskell 25 Ap. 1782; *Sarah*, b. 13 June 1765, m. Elijah Bangs 21 Ap. 1791; *Israel*, b. 11 Jan. 1767; *Thomas*, b. 23 Jan. 1769, d. 8 Sep. 1777; *Lucy*, b. 21 Dec. 1770, m. Nathan Haskell of Wendell 2 June 1795; *Abraham*, b. 6 May 1774, d. —— 1777; *Philip*, b. 30 July 1776, d. —— 1777; *Thomas*, b. 9 Feb. 1782, settled in Winchendon. ABRAHAM the f. was a tanner, and res. on the Petersham road, at or near the place marked "Mr. Woods" on the R.

[1] "Lucius J. Knowles, a native of Hardwick, engaged in the manufacture of looms at Warren, with his brother, F. B. Knowles. In 1866 this branch of his business was removed to Worcester, where it has since been conducted. The looms first made by the firm were constructed to weave narrow fabrics, which still constitute an important part of the product of the firm. In 1863, Mr. L. J. Knowles took out his first patent for an open-shed fancy cassimere loom, which he has recently adapted to the weaving of many new fabrics, and he has devised mechanisms by which almost every kind of fancy textile fabrics, whether of cotton, wool, or silk, can be readily produced. Mr. Knowles has an inventive genius, which has produced other important inventions besides his looms. He has been engaged in the manufacture of cotton and woollen; and the Knowles' steam-pumps, which he manufactures in large quantities at Warren, have a world-wide reputation. He has been state senator, alderman, president of the Board of Trade, and is now (1879) president of the People's Savings Bank, and a trustee of the Free Institute." *Hist. of Worcester County*, ii. 665. While Mr. Knowles resided in Warren, he was a representative in the General Court 1865, and senator in 1869.

Map. He was a lieutenant in the Revolutionary War. In his old age his long white locks gave him a venerable aspect. He d. 9 June 1812, a. 81; his w. Susanna d. 27 Ap. 1816, a. 75.

4. ISRAEL, s. of Abraham (3), m. Abigail Carter 2 May 1793, and had *Israel*, b. 12 Mar. 1795, d. 28 Mar. 1795; *Calvin*, b. 2 Sep. 1797, m. Abigail Powers of Rye, N. H., 20 Sep. 1822, and d. there 30 Jan. 1878; *Israel*, b. 22 Dec. 1799, d. —— Ap. 1800; a son, b. and d. —— 1802; *Maria*, b. 8 June 1804, m. Williams Dexter 3 June 1828; *Abraham*, b. 12 Jan. 1807, a mason, res. unm. in Cambridge; *Timothy Carter*, b. 14 Aug. 1810, m. Susan Locke of Rye 18 Feb. 1836; she d. 17 July 1842, and he m. Augusta Locke of Rye 8 Sep. 1843; he d. 9 July 1869; *Lucy*, b. 28 July 1816, d. unm. in Cambridge 1 Sep. 1878. ISRAEL the f. rem. to Brighton, where he d. 12 Oct. 1842; his w. Abigail d. in Cambridge 9 Oct. 1851, a. 77.

PAUL, of Shrewsbury, m. Lucy Forbush 3 Nov. 1769.

KNOX, JOSEPH, m. Susan, dau. of Jason Mixter, 7 Sep. 1831, and had *Charles Mixter*, b. 19 Jan. 1835. JOSEPH the f. was a lawyer, and after a short residence here rem. in 1837 to Rock Island, Ill., where he d. 6 Aug. 1881.

LAMB, JONATHAN, by w. Rebecca, had *Martha*, b. 3 Aug. 1765; *Jonathan*, b. 26 Nov. 1767; *Armilla*, b. 16 Aug. 1769; *Eunice*, b. 14 June 1771.

LANE, ELIJAH, by w. Hannah, had *Elijah*, b. 29 July 1798; *Dan Wilmarth*, b. 7 May 1800; *Justus*, b. 19 Mar. 1802; *Hannah Brown*, b. 24 Mar. 1804, m. Luke Earl 2 Feb. 1826; *Nancy*, b. 15 Feb. 1807; *Rebecca Snow*, b. 15 Mar. 1809; *Elbridge*, b. 6 Dec. 1813; *Elizabeth Copeland*, b. 30 Nov. 1815, *Calvin*, b. 15 Mar. 1818; *Charles Foster*, b. 20 Ap. 1821, d. at Enfield 27 Jan. 1861. ELIJAH the f. was a farmer, and rem. from Norton to Hk. about 1799; his w. Hannah d. 18 June 1824, a. 46; and he was dism. to the church in Enfield 24 Jan. 1830.

2. EPHRAIM, brother of Elijah (1), m. Rebecca Snow 13 Nov. 1803; she d. 20 Mar. 1835, and he m. Mrs. Nancy Hemenway, pub. 29 Sep. 1837. No record found of children.

3. DAN WILMARTH, s. of Elijah (1), m. Alma, dau. of Orin Trow, 6 Jan. 1824, and had *Clarissa T.*, b. 24 Aug. 1825, d. the same year; *Joanna Maria*, b. 1 Nov. 1826; *Orin Trow*, b. 12 Ap. 1828; *Charles E.*, b. —— 1830, d. at Orange 11 Oct. 1854, a. 24.

OBED, m. Abigail Smith 16 Feb. 1802. REBECCA, of Gr., m. Deac. Ebenezer Willis, pub. 13 May 1811.

LAWRENCE, JOSHUA, by w. Elizabeth, had *Sarah*, b. 2 July 1704; *Joanna*, b. 14 Oct. 1706, m. Robert Whitcomb 13 Jan. 1731–32; *Ebenezer*, b. 10 Oct. 1708; *Experience*, b. 18 May 1711, d. unm. in Hk. 3 Dec. 1796; *Elizabeth*, b. 3 Jan. 1713–14, perhaps m. John Haskell of Roch. 4 Mar. 1753; *Joshua*, b. 7 Ap. 1719; *Benjamin* and *Deliverance*, twins, b. 21 Dec. 1727. JOSHUA the f. res. in Rochester, where all his chil. were born.

2. EBENEZER, s. of Joshua (1), m. Sarah Hammond 6 Feb. 1733, and had *Susanna*, b. 24 May 1735, m. Nathaniel Merrick 13 Feb. 1755; *Joseph*, b. 12 Jan. 1736–37; *Ebenezer*, b. 16 Ap. 1739; *Sarah*, b. 10 Ap. 1741. EBENEZER the f. was a farmer, rem. from Roch. to Hk. before 28 Dec. 1748, res. on the road from the Old Furnace to Taylor's Mills, at the place marked "Wid. Lawrence" on the R. Map, and d. 29 Nov. 1797, a. 89.

3. JOSHUA, s. of Joshua (1), m. Jane Haskell 13 July 1743, and had *Joshua*, b. 24 July 1744, d. here 16 Dec. 1835; *Joanna*, b. 18 Oct. 1746, prob. m. Antipas Howe of Swansey 20 Jan. 1782; *Elizabeth*, b. prob. 1748, m. Nathaniel Rice of Rut. Dist. 24 Nov. 1768; *Anna*, b. prob. 1750, m. *Experience Luce* 30 Nov. 1769; *Deliverance*, b. 25 Mar. 1753, m. Barnabas Cushman of Wilmington, Vt., 15 Feb. 1781; *Bethia*, bap. 13 May 1758; *Moses*, bap. 16 Nov. 1760. JOSHUA the f. was a farmer, rem. from Roch. to Hk. soon after 1 Ap. 1751, res. on the Barre road, near Taylor's Mills, marked "M. Lawrence" on the R. Map, and d. between 9 Ap. and 4 June 1777; his w. Jane d. 15 Nov. 1795, a. 77.

4. EBENEZER, s. of Ebenezer (2), m. Lydia Richmond of N. Br. 18 Dec. 1763, and had *Noah*, b. 22 Jan. 1765, d. unm. at the town farm 22 Jan.

1847; *Susanna*, b. 6 Dec. 1766; *Rachel*, b. 18 May 1769; *Lydia*, b. 26 June 1771, d. unm. 21 July 1817; *Elizabeth*, b. 1 Ap. 1773, m. William Newell, pub. 3 May 1797; *Joshua*, b. 27 June, 1777; *Wilder*, b. 16 Dec. 1779; *Sally*, b. 31 Oct. 1783, m. Charles W. Fisk 17 Mar. 1818. EBENEZER the f. was a farmer, res. on the homestead, and d. 2 Aug. 1811; his w. Lydia d. 21 June 1811, a. 68.

5. MOSES, s. of Joshua (3), m. Abigail Johnson of Barre 15 Feb. 1781; she d. (killed by falling upon the handle of a fire-shovel, which pierced her body) 16 July 1811, a. 51, and he m. Sophia, dau. of John Hastings, Esq., pub. 18 Sep. 1814. His chil were: *William*, b. 8 Ap. 1782, m. Betsey Bridges 25 Mar. 1804, who d. 16 May 1818, a. 38; *Elnathan*, b. 21 Oct. 1783; *Lucinda*, b. 6 June 1785, m. Joshua Lawrence 15 Oct. 1812; *Ira*, b. 9 May 1787; *Harlow*, b. 18 Sep. 1788; infant b. ——, d. 2 Dec. 1791; *Reuel*, b. 12 Mar. 1792; *Moses*, b. 1 May 1793; infant, twin with *Moses*, d. 17 Aug. 1793; *Aaron*, b. 22 Dec. 1794, d. 2 May 1819; *Sally*, b. 30 May 1797; *Abigail*, b. 28 Oct. 1799, prob. m. Alonzo Emmons 3 Dec. 1838; *Hiram*, b. 20 Feb. 1801; *Anna*, b. 5 Oct. 1802, m. Noah W. White 5 Nov. 1826, and d. at Brk. 24 Jan. 1868; *Abiathar*, b. 14 Aug. 1804, m. Harriet Hapgood of Barre, pub. 5 Nov. 1831, and d. at Barre 6 May 1877; *Mary*, b. 17 Ap. 1816; *Henry H.*, b. 5 Oct. 1817; and prob. three more by first wife, who was said to be the mother of eighteen children. MOSES the f. was a farmer, res. on the homestead, and d. 12 Oct. 1836; his w. Sophia d. in 1848.

6. JOSHUA, s. of Ebenezer (4), m. Lucinda, dau. of Moses Lawrence, 15 Oct. 1812, and had *Lucinda*, b. —— 1813, m. Erastus W. Paige 2 May, 1833, and d. 18 Mar. 1849. JOSHUA the f. was a farmer and lieutenant of cavalry; res. on the homestead, and d. 22 Mar. 1814; his w. Lucinda d. 30 Mar. 1856, a. 70.

7. MOSES, s. of Moses (5), m. Maria Howe of Barre, pub. 8 Feb. 1819, and had *Aaron*, b. 14 Feb. 1820; *Charles Emory*, b. 13 July 1824, d. (drowned) 9 Aug. 1845; *Hannah Maria*, b. 11 Ap. 1827, m. John Y. Ellsworth 1 May 1849, and d. 15 Sep. 1856. MOSES the f. res. near the Barre line, at the place marked "M. Lawrence, Jr.," on the R. Map.

8. HIRAM, s. of Moses (5), m. Almira Hale, pub. 26 Nov. 1827; she d. 10 Sep. 1850, a. 44, and he m. Emily Whitney of Clinton, pub. 17 June 1851. His chil. were: *Samuel Edmunds*, b. 15 July 1829; *Charles Elnathan*, b. 15 Oct. 1830; *Perley Hale*, b. 12 July 1832; *Hiram Henry*, b. 24 Sep. 1834; *Elvira Lucretia*, b. 28 May 1837, d. 3 Feb. 1838; *Lucius W.*, b. —— 1842, d. 14 May 1848, a. 6; *Moses Johnson*, b. 8 Nov. 1844, d. 8 Sep. 1845; *Emory J.*, b. 26 Jan. 1848, d. 16 Feb. 1848.

9. AARON, s. of Moses (7), m. Mary A. Perry 27 Dec. 1843, and had *George Howe*, b. 24 Dec. 1844. AARON the f. d. at Worcester 9 Mar. 1859.

10. FRANCIS, by w. Sophia, had *Mary*, b. 15 Oct. 1865.

EBENEZER, perhaps Ebenezer (2), was pub. to Jemima Shurtleff of Plympton 30 Sep. 1776. GEORGE F., of Cornplanter, Pa., m. Josephine H. Bartholomew 1 Oct. 1870.

LAWTON, JOHN, of "Suffield, had *James*, *Benedicta*, *Mary*, and perhaps others, d. 19 Dec. 1690, and his wid. Benedicta d. 18 Nov. 1692." Savage's *Gen. Dict.*

2. JAMES, s. of John (1), of Suffield, "had *Jacob*, who was several years representative, and, from caprice, adopted in his business as a lawyer the name of *Christopher Jacob*." Savage's *Gen. Dict.* He had also a son *James*. Both the sons rem. to Leicester in 1735.

3. JAMES, s. of James (2), had son *James*, and perhaps others. He was a saddler, and after 1735 res. in Leicester. No record is found of births or deaths of his family.

4. JAMES, s. of James (3), prob. b. in Suffield about 1714, went with his father to Leicester, where he m. Mary Earl 1 July 1741; she d. and he m. Joanna, dau. of Richard Clark of Watertown, 16 Nov. 1746; she d. at Hk. 31 July 1759, a. 41, and he m. Mrs. Temperance Fuller, of Rut. Dist. (Barre), pub. 14 June 1772. His chil. were: *James*, b. 22 Sep. 1747; *Clark*, b. about 1749; *Ja-*

cob, b. about 1752; *John*, bap. 28 July 1754; *Israel*, bap. 12 Feb. 1758. JAMES the f. was a saddler, rem. from Leicester to Hk. about 1752, bought the farm of Experience Johnson on the easterly road to Gilbertville, marked "J. Lawton" on the R. Map, and d. there 24 Sep. 1787, a. 73; a head-stone of peculiar appearance, in the southerly part of the old cemetery, marks the spot where he and his wife Joanna, the mother of his children, were buried.

5. JAMES, s. of James (4), m. Mary Raymond 3 Jan. 1771, and had *Pliny*, b. 29 July 1771; *James*, b. 24 Ap. 1773, d. young; *Joanna*, b. 7 Feb. 1775, m. Jude Kimball 25 Aug. 1793; *Relief*, b. 30 June 1777, m. Abijah Lathrop of Rutland, Vt., 22 Feb. 1801; *James*, b. 18 Aug. 1781; *Mary*, b. 18 Oct. 1783, m. Nathan Weeks 12 Ap. 1807; *Livy*, b. about 1785; *Almira*, b. — Nov. 1788, bap. 28 June 1789, d. 18 Feb. 1790; *Franklin*, bap. 22 Aug. 1790; *Dwight Foster*, bap. 16 June 1793, res. in the State of New York. JAMES the f. was a farmer and res. on the homestead; he marched with the "minute-men" in April 1775, was adjutant to Col. Timothy Paige, in opposition to the Shays Insurrection, a licensed retailer in 1778, innholder 1779, a deputy sheriff several years, coroner 1803, and d. 1 Jan. 1804;[1] his w. Mary m. Major James Paige 22 Mar. 1807.

6. CLARK, s. of James (4), m. Joanna Cook of Amherst, pub. 20 Sep. 1774, and had *Martin*, b. 19 Jan. 1776; *Hannah*, bap. 27 Mar. 1782; and in Amh., *Chester*, bap. 15 Aug. 1784; *James*, bap. 14 June 1789; *Joanna*, bap. 1 May 1790. CLARK the f. was a saddler, res. a few rods south of the Common, at the place marked "W. Mandell" on the R. Map, but rem. to Amherst before the 15th of August 1784. His subsequent history is not ascertained.

7. JACOB, s. of James (4), m. Susanna Foster of Ware, pub. 16 Nov. 1777; she d. at Barnard, Vt., 27 Nov. 1819, a. 64, and he m. Mrs. Anna Sabin 14 Dec. 1820. His chil. were: *Christopher Jacob*, b. 2 Oct. 1778, m. Polly Sabin at Barnard, Vt., 20 Sep. 1802; *John*, b. 14 Aug. 1780, grad. Mid. Coll. 1805, was a teacher at Poughkeepsie and Salem, N. Y., pastor of the church at Windham, Vt., 1809–19, and at Hillsborough, N. H., 1819–34, afterwards missionary in Illinois, and d. at Newport, N. H., 17 Ap. 1842; *Joseph*, b. 5 Feb. 1784, d. at Bar. 15 Oct. 1807; *Cyrus*, b. 10 Ap. 1786, m. at Bar., Deborah, dau. of Prince Haskell, 6 Sep. 1807, and d. there 16 Jan. 1817; and in Barnard, *Susanna*, b. 5 Aug. 1788; *Joanna*, b. 4 Jan. 1793; *Lydia*, b. 14 June 1795. JACOB the f. rem. to Barnard, Vt., about 1787, and d. there 23 Aug. 1836, a. 84; his w. Anna d. 2 Aug. 1831, a, 76. The graves of Mr. Lawton and his two wives are in the southeasterly part of the central burial-place in Barnard.

8. JOHN, s. of James (4), m. Sarah Healy of Dudley, and had *Lucinda*, b. about 1791, d. unm. 22 Dec. 1819, a. 28; *John*, b. about 1792; *Theolotia*, b. about 1794, m. Crighton Ruggles 21 Nov. 1816, and d. s. p. 27 June 1817, a. 23; *Sarah*, b. about 1796, d. unm. 5 May 1821, a. 24; *Sanford* and *Danforth*, twins, b. 11 Dec. 1798. JOHN the f. was a farmer, and lieutenant of cavalry; he res. in Dudley and Charlton from the time of his marriage until about 1807, when he rem. to Hk. with his whole family, and bought the homestead formerly occupied by his father and by his brother James. Late in life he rem. to Monson, where he d. 4 Ap. 1842, a. 88; his w. Sarah d. "near the same time," a. 76, "and was buried with him in the same grave." *MS. Letter.*

9. ISRAEL, s. of James (4), by w. Catherine, had *Polly*, b. 13 Ap. 1782. So says the record. He then m. Dolly, dau. of Elisha Billings, 26 Aug. 1784, and rem. to Wilmington, Vt., where he had *Charlotte*, b. 28 Nov. 1784; *Mersiloa*, b. 25 May 1788; *Harriet*, b. 22 Ap. 1790; *Dency*, b. 14 Jan. 1792; *Dulcena*, b. 4 Feb. 1796; *Israel*, b. 10 Feb. 1798; *James*, b. 30 Nov. 1799. ISRAEL the f. was a sergeant in the Revolutionary Army 1780, and a representative of Wilmington in the General Assembly of Vermont in 1801 and 1802. He d. at Wilm. 26 Sep. 1844, a. about 87; his w. Dolly d. 12 Feb. 1816, a. 52.

[1] At the time of his decease, Mr. Lawton was Master of Mount Zion Lodge, and his funeral was conducted with public Masonic ceremonies, at which Isaiah Thomas, the Grand Master of Masons in Massachusetts, and other representatives of the Grand Lodge were present.

10. PLINY, s. of James (5), m. Polly, dau. of George Field, 22 Feb. 1801, and had *Eluthera Field*, b. 10 July 1802, m. Rev. George Stone of Sandgate, Vt., 10 July 1831; *Pliny*, b. 29 Dec. 1804; *James*, b. 1 Oct. 1807, m. Mary L. Nichols of Brimfield, pub. 26 Feb. 1835; *Lucius*, b. 2 Jan. 1812, m. Susan Clark 3 Ap. 1834; *Laura Loraine*, b. 10 July 1816, d. unm. 5 June 1837. PLINY the f. was a farmer, for several years a member of the school committee, and res. near Gilbertville, at the place marked "P. Lawton" on the R. Map. About 1838 he rem. to Patterson, N. J.

11. JAMES, s. of James (5), m. Patty Wilson 12 Ap. 1804, and had *James Clark*, b. 20 Sep. 1805. JAMES the f. res. on the homestead, but early rem. from the town.

12. LIVY, s. of James (5), m. Mary, dau. of Maj. Moses Mandell, 5 Feb. 1810, and had *Algernon Sidney*, b. about 1811, d. 11 Mar. 1828, a. 17. LIVY the f. was a merchant in Rutland, Vt., at the time of his marriage; afterwards kept a hotel at Saratoga; he d. at Keene, N. H., when on a journey, in June 1824; his w. returned here and d. 5 Aug. 1874, a. nearly 88.

13. JOHN, s. of John (8), m. Mary Dwight of Warren, pub. 24 Jan. 1820, and had *William B.*, b. 29 Ap. 1821; *Mary Ann*, b. 1 Sep. 1823, m. Brainnard T. Brewer of Wilbraham 11 Sep. 1844; *Martha M.*, b. 25 Aug. 1825, m. William P. Ruggles 22 Feb. 1846; *Emily P.*, b. 12 Aug. 1829; *Eliza Jane*, b. 14 Nov. 1832, m. George C. Howard 16 May 1850; *Ellen Frances*, bap. 28 Dec. 1838. JOHN the f. was a farmer, and captain of cavalry; he res. on the homestead, rem. to Wilbraham about 1851, and d. 16 Nov. 1854, a. 62.

14. SANFORD, s. of John (8), grad. Y. C. 1825, studied for the ministry, and appears to have been ordained, but devoted himself to teaching in schools of high grade at Dudley, Monson, Springfield, and Long Meadow. He m. ——, and had *Mary Ann*, who d. unm. 22 Nov. 1870, a. 40; *Sanford*, grad. Y. C. 1852, a physician in Springf., where he d. 23 July 1882, a. 50; *John William*, a physician in Syracuse, N. Y. SANFORD the f. rem. from Long Meadow to Springf. in 1874, and d. 7 Nov. 1882. In the notice of his death it is stated that "his wife died in 1878, and his four children are all dead." My efforts to obtain a more full account of this family have been unsuccessful.

15. DANFORTH, s. of John (8), entered Williams College, but did not complete his course. He res. in Wilbraham, and was living unm. in 1882.

LEACH, LEMUEL, m. Rebecca Washburn 12 Oct. 1767, and had *Oliver*, b. at Bridgewater 3 June 1768, and bap. at Hk. 1 Nov. 1772; *Matilda*, b. at Hk. 2 Mar. 1770; *Rebecca*, b. 25 Mar. 1773; *Lemuel*, b. 2 July 1775, d. at Shutesbury 26 Ap. 1860; *Stephen*, b. 13 Nov. 1777; and at Wendell, *Gardner*, *Barnabas*, *Lewis*, and *Artemas*. LEMUEL the f. was s. of Stephen, and b. at Bridgewater in 1745, rem. to Hk. in 1769, and thence to Wendell about 1778, having served, in 1776, as an ensign in the Revolutionary War.

LEGATE, CHARLES, by w. Maria, had *Charles F.*, b. — Mar. 1840, d. 29 Nov. 1840; a son, b. 19 Feb. 1844; a son, b. 3 Ap. 1847; *Edwin Orlando*, b. 10 July 1849.

2. FRANCIS, s. of Charles and Abigail, and prob. brother of Charles (1), b. in 1817, m. Jane R. Peck 2 June 1847, and had *Francis Augustus*, b. 14 Feb. 1854; *Lizzie Jane*, b. 23 Dec. 1856, d. 30 Nov. 1858.

3. AUGUSTUS F. (called Francis Augustus in the record of birth), s. of Francis (2), m. Ida F. Eldridge 26 Oct. 1876, and had *Theron F.*, b. 4 June 1878.

HENRY A., s. of Charles and Martha, d. at Rowe, 14 Jan. 1878, a. 56.

LEONARD, MOSES, m. Mercy, dau. of Moses Newton (and sister of Deac. Josiah Newton), by whom he had *Moses*, b. 1 Nov. 1706; *Ezra*, b. 19 Sep. 1711; *Mercy*, b. 1 Dec. 1714, m. Samuel Robinson 29 May, 1732; and by second wife Hannah he had *Jonas*, b. 19 Oct. 1717; MOSES the f. res. in Marlborough (where his chil. were born), Southborough, Brookfield, Rutland, Barre, and for a short period in Hardwick. He d. in extreme old age.

2. EZRA, s. of Moses (1), m. Olive, dau. of Benjamin Smith, 1 June 1737, and had *Sarah*, b. 7 Mar. 1739, d. 15 Sep. 1746; *Benjamin*, b. 5 Aug. 1741, d. 7 Sep. 1746; *Nathan*, b. 25 Sep. 1743; *Mercy*, b. 3 Feb. 1746, d. 19 Sep. 1746; *David*, b. 30 July, 1747, res. at Cummington, m. Hannah Whipple 15

Feb. 1773; *Levi*, b. 10 Oct. 1749; *Sarah*, twin, b. 8 Sep. 1751, m. Samuel Whipple 30 Mar. 1775; *Mercy*, twin, b. 8 Sep. 1751, m. Jonathan Flynt of Western (Warren) 18 June 1772; *Olive*, b. 1 Nov. 1753, m. Timothy Fay 23 Mar. 1775; *Ezra*, b. 2 Nov. 1757. EZRA the f. was in Brk. 1735, but rem. to Hk. before June 1737, and res. in the westerly part of the town, at the place marked "D. Utley" on the R. Map. He was a farmer, selectman four years, and assessor in 1760. In 1757 he was ensign of Capt. Joseph Warner's company, which marched for the relief of Fort William Henry. In his old age he rem. to Wilbraham, with his son-in-law Flynt, and d. 29 June 1798; his w. Olive d. 16 Feb. 1798, a. 83.

3. NATHAN, s. of Ezra (2), m. Amittai, dau. of David Cutler of Lexington, 26 Nov. 1766, and had *Joseph*, b. 24 Oct. 1767; *Molly*, b. 7 Feb. 1770; *Nathan*, b. 17 July 1772; *Benjamin*, b. 23 Oct. 1774; *Luther*, b. 20 Ap. 1777. NATHAN the f. was a cordwainer, and captain of militia. He was a member of the company of "minute-men" which promptly responded to the summons on the 19th of April, 1775, and served his country in the year 1778 as captain in Col. Nathaniel Wade's regiment.

4. EZRA, s. of Ezra (2), m. Abia Allen 23 Oct. 1781; and prob. m. (2d) Lucy Seaver, pub. 5 July 1807. He had dau. *Joanna*, b. 9 Aug. 1783; and perhaps others.

5. HIRAM W., parentage not ascertained, m. Huldah S. Billings 23 Feb. 1834, and had *William Henry*, b. 29 Jan. 1844; a daughter, b. 3 Oct. 1851; and perhaps also *Carrie R.*, who m. Warren T. Tolman of Dana 18 Ap. 1866.

BEULAH, of Rut., m. Amos Marsh, pub. 16 July 1757. PRUDENCE, of Taunton, m. Capt. Israel Trow, pub. 1 Ap. 1811. ALVIRA, of N. Sal., m. Pliny Clifford, pub. 11 June 1825. HOPE C., m. Samuel Pike of Tolland, Conn., 3 Nov. 1831. ELIZA, m. Orestes S. Thayer of Dana 22 Dec. 1867. Widow PERSIS, d. 28 Mar. 1845, a. 73.

LINCOLN, SAMUEL, by w. Mehetabel, had *Roxana*, b. 27 Feb. 1788; *Emerson*, b. 2 Nov. 1789; *Obed*, b. 15 Ap. 1792.

2. BURT, by wife Mary, had *George Burt*, b. 25 Aug. 1817; *Marietta*, b. 17 Sep. 1820, m. Nehemiah Conkey 28 Nov. 1844. BURT the f. was a cooper, rem. here from Pet. in 1817, res. on the Barre road at the place marked "Mr. Lincoln" on the R. Map, and d. 14 Dec. 1866, a. 81; his w. Mary d. 2 May 1857, a. 66.

3. JOSEPH N., m. Abbie Jane, dau. of Gardner Bartholomew, and formerly w. of Charles L. Trow, 12 May 1870, and had *Mabel Caroline*, b. 11 Feb. 1871; *Joseph Gardner*, b. 18 Oct. 1876; *Waldo Chandler*, b. 1 Sep. 1878. JOSEPH N. the f., a carpenter and insurance agent, res. in the Old Furnace village.

SETH, of Western, m. Lucy, dau. of Deac. Christopher Paige, 10 Oct. 1751. CHLOE, m. Perez Rice 8 Ap. 1779. BETSEY, m. Robert Sprout, 17 Sep. 1781. LUCY, late of Abington, m. Sylvanus Brimhall 3 July 1810. FANNY, of Western (Warren), m. Joseph Paige 23 Ap. 1816. Mrs. HANNAH C., dau. of Stephen Chandler, Rochester, Vt., d. 24 Mar. 1873, a. 81.

LOCKE, JOSIAH, by w. Persis, had in Westborough, *Catherine*, b. 31 Aug. 1760, m. Amos Wheeler; *John*, b. 11 Nov. 1763, m. Phebe Matthews; in Leicester, *Persis*, b. 13 July 1766, m. George Jenkins, and d. s. p. 1844; *Josiah*, b. 14 Feb. 1768, m. Elizabeth Hartwell —— 1791; and in Hardwick, *Hannah*, b. 26 Aug. 1770, m. Elijah Easton 1793; *Hepzibah*, b. 16 Aug. 1772, m. Oliver Perry; *Fanny*, b. 4 Sep. 1775, m. Silas Hamilton 3 Ap. 1803; *Ira*, b. 14 Nov. 1777, m. Persis Hamilton — Nov. 1800. JOSIAH the f. was b. at Westborough 6 Feb. 1735, and was s. of Joshua, and a descendant from Deac. William Locke of Woburn. He m. Persis Matthews of New Braintree, who d. at Litchfield, N. Y., 21 Ap. 1839, reputed to have attained the extraordinary age of 103 years, 5 months, and 7 days, having had 8 chil., 67 gr. chil., 147 gr. gr. chil., and 32 of the fourth generation. Captain Locke rem. from Westborough to Leicester about 1765, to Hardwick about 1768, to Wilmington, Vt., about 1779, where he was a justice of the peace, and finally to Litchfield, N. Y., where he d. 18 Ap. 1819, a. 84. This sketch is condensed from a more full account in the "Book of the Lockes," which represents Captain Locke as a storekeeper in Hardwick. It may be added, that he was an assessor in 1774, lieutenant of the "minute-men," and marched with them to Cambridge on the memorable 19th of April, 1775, but did not enter the regular service. He was commissioned as captain of a company of militia in Hk. 31 May 1776.

LUCE, EXPERIENCE, res. near Barre, at the place marked "N. Richmond" on the R. Map, m. Anna Lawrence 30 Nov. 1769, and had *Anna Drusilla* (d. 3 Feb. 1803, a. 17), *Apollos*, and *Patty*, all bap. 29 Aug. 1794. Of these, *Apollos* was lieutenant of militia, and m. Mercy Childs of Barre, pub. 30 Oct. 1808; and *Anna*, prob. m. Benjamin Padden of Kingsboro, N. Y., 28 Dec. 1806. As no other record is found of births or deaths in this family, my account is necessarily very imperfect.

2. MAYO, prob. s. of Experience (1), m. Joanna, dau. of Stephen Gorham, 1 July 1793, then res. in Pet., but soon rem. to Barre, where he had ten chil., all baptized here, to wit: *Artemas, Gamaliel, Calvin, Anson, Horace*, all bap. 25 Jan. 1803; *Drusilla*, bap. 4 Sep. 1803; *Anna*, bap. 22 June 1806; *Elnathan Gorham*, and *Lyndon*, both bap. 10 Oct. 1811; and a dau. named *Emera*, bap. 11 June 1815.

PRUDENCE, m. Noah Rice of Barre, 30 Aug. 1781. SALLY, m. Lemuel French, pub. 30 Mar. 1789. JANE, m. David Gorham 8 Aug. 1791. RHODA, m. Moses Ruggles, 25 Jan. 1798. JEMIMA, m. Ira Draper, pub. 28 July 1822.

LYSCOM, EBENEZER, m. Mary Hooker 8 Oct. 1764, and had *Samuel*, b. 30 Nov 1765; *Persis*, b. 19 Mar. 1772. MARY the mother d. 16 May 1797, a. 57.

MACCOYE, WILLIAM, by w. Mary, had *Hannah*, bap. 4 June 1738; *Beulah*, bap. 24 May 1741. WILLIAM the f. was perhaps the same who m. Tabitha Fay of Sturbridge, pub. 20 Oct. 1744. He was prob. a carpenter, an assessor in 1737, and seems to have rem. and d. before 7 Mar. 1747–8, when it was voted to raise fifty pounds old tenor, "to maintain Hannah Maccoye sent to this town for that intent." She was the first pauper named on the records, remained chargeable until 1765, and is supposed to have been dau. of WILLIAM.

MARY, m. Benjamin Warren 29 May 1744.

MCEVOY, PATRICK, m. Ann Fehan 12 Feb. 1872.

MAHAN, MICHAEL, m. Ellen Carney 3 Mar. 1867, and had *Daniel*, b. 19 Sep. 1870; *John Patrick*, b. 22 Dec. 1876.

MANDELL, JOHN (or Mendall, as the name was formerly written, and still is written in Bristol and Plymouth counties), res. in Marshfield, was a ropemaker, and executed a will 10 May 1711, being then "aged and weak in body," which was proved 8 Feb. 1720. He devised to his son *John*, one shilling, having previously provided for him; to "grandson Francis Crooker all my rope-making tools that I do use in or about the making of ropes after I have done using them myself;" and the remainder of his estate to his daughters, *Mercy* Tinkum, *Sarah* Torry, *Hannah* Tilden, and *Ruth* Doty.

2. JOHN, s. of John (1), m. Joanna, dau. of Richard Standlake of Scituate, and had in Rochester, *John*, b. 15 Dec. 1688; *Joanna*, b. 13 May 1690; *Moses*, b. 24 Mar. 1695. JOHN the f. was a farmer, res. in Rochester, and executed his will 6 June 1738, proved 14 July 1743, directing his "body to be decently buried by my executor after named, and my son *John* to be at the charge of it, in consideration of what I have given him by deed;" specific legacies of personal estate are bequeathed to dau. *Joanna*, and son *Moses*, who is named as executor.

3. MOSES, s. of John (2), res. in Rochester, 1715, in Falmouth 1725, and in that part of Dartmouth now Acushnet, 1740; he was successively styled "house carpenter," "drover," "innholder," "dealer," and "gentleman"; he d. at Dartm. 18 May 1746, and his sons *Lemuel* and *Paul* were appointed administrators 27 July 1746. His real estate, valued at 1200 pounds, was divided in 1748 between his widow Susanna, and children *Lemuel* (or *Lamuel*, as he seems generally to have written his name), *Noah*[1] (who was here in 1756,

[1] "We hear that on the 20th ult. a daughter of Mr. Noah Mandell, of Rutland District, about 13 years of age, intending to take a dose of brimstone (her parents being from

and d. in Barre in 1800 or 1801), *Paul*, *Susanna* Bailey, *Hannah* Weaver, *Joanna* Nichols, and *Mary*, unmarried.

4. PAUL, s. of Moses (3), m. Susanna, dau. of Rev. Timothy Ruggles of Rochester, 8 Feb. 1746–7, and had *Hannah*, b. at Dartmouth 10 or 20 Jan. 1747–8, m. Gen. Jonathan Warner 5 Feb. 1766; *Susanna*, b. here 16 Nov. 1749, m. John Stone 12 May 1768, and d. at Dana 28 July 1844; *Moses*, b. 16 Dec. 1751; *Paul*, b. 31 Oct. 1753, m. Mary Briggs of Pet. 28 Nov. 1776, res. in Athol; his inventory was presented by his son Barnabas 25 Mar. 1807; *Barnabas*, b. 1 Dec. 1755, d. 2 May 1758; *Mary*, b. 3 Oct. 1759, m. John Doty 19 Sep. 1779. PAUL the f. changed the orthography of his name from Mendall to Mandell, was a "shopkeeper" in Dartm. until the spring of 1749, when he rem. to Hk., having purchased the valuable farm notable for its immense extent of stone wall, which still remains in possession of his posterity; his house stood on the old turnpike, at the place marked "M. Mandell" on the R. Map. He was a very active, energetic, and useful citizen. He was captain of militia, and led his company in the expedition against Crown Point from 20 Sep. to 12 Nov. 1756 (his brother Noah being promoted from the office of ensign to that of lieutenant on the 29th of October), and a second campaign in 1758, after the surrender of "Fort William Henry." At the commencement of the Revolution, when the militia was reorganized, as recommended by the Convention at Worcester,[1] he was again elected captain 22 Sep. 1774, and was commissioned as brigade major 13 Mar. 1778. He was a selectman eleven years, between 1756 and 1775, assessor thirteen years, between 1751 and 1775, town clerk 1770, representative 1773, 1774, delegate to the first and second Provincial Congress 1774, 1775, was appointed justice of the peace by the revolutionary government 25 Sep. 1775, and held that office many years, being generally designated "Squire Mandell." He d. 16 Sep. 1809, a. 86; his w. Susanna d. 16 Dec. 1813, a. nearly 92.

5. MOSES, s. of Paul (4), m. Mary, dau. of Capt. Daniel Wheeler, 28 May 1777; she d. 20 Ap. 1782, and he m. Abigail, dau. of John Mason, Esq., of Barre, pub. 22 Dec. 1782. His chil. were: *Daniel*, b. 27 Oct. 1783; *Martin*, b. 20 July 1785; *Mary*, b. 20 Nov. 1786, m. Livy Lawton 5 Feb. 1810; and d. here 5 Aug. 1874; *Sidney*, b. 4 July 1788, m. Eliza, dau. of David Jones of Boston, 27 Dec. 1812, res. in Boston, had chil., among whom was David J. of Athol, in early life a clergyman; *Mason*, b. 4 Mar. 1790, res. in Barre, where he m. ——, had chil., and d. 4 July 1825; *Abigail*, b. 13 Mar. 1792, m. Elijah Utley of Boston, 25 Sep. 1820, and d. 13 Mar. 1834; *Moses*, b. 1 Dec. 1793, res. at Dorchester and afterwards at Barre, where he d. 3 Sep. 1866, leaving posterity: *Walter*, b. 16 Dec. 1796; *Clara*, b. 3 Oct. 1799, m. Ebenezer Jones, of Augusta, Me., pub. 11 Ap. 1825, and is still living, a widow, in 1883. MOSES the f. was a farmer, and inherited the homestead. He was aid-de-camp to his brother-in-law, Maj. Gen. Warner, before Dec. 1782, probably in 1781, and was thenceforth known as "Major Mandell." He was selectman six years, between 1785 and 1817, and assessor seven years, between 1801 and 1819. He d. 18 June 1826; his w. Abigail d. 6 (or 7) Aug. 1840, a. 82.

6. DANIEL, s. of Moses (5), m. Eliza Patrick 30 Ap. 1807, and had *Martha Eliza*, b. 10 June 1808; *Delphia Maria*, b. 23 Feb. 1810, m. A. W. Seaver of Northborough; *William Andrew*, b. 13 July 1811, grad. A. C. 1838, pastor of the church in Lunenburg, and elsewhere, now res. in Cambridge; *Moses Johnson*, b. 14 Ap. 1813; infant b. ——, d. 22 Ap. 1815; *Mary Ann*, b. 29 Mar. 1816, d. unm. 10 Aug. 1839; *Thaddeus Sobieski*, b. 15 Feb. 1820, a merchant in Boston, d. 23 June 1882; *George*, b. about 1822, d. unm. at Lunenburg 23 May 1861, a. 39. DANIEL the f. was a farmer, and lieutenant of militia; he res. on the road to Barre, at the place marked "Mr. Haven" on the R. Map, and d. 26 June 1822.

home), through a mistake took from a shelf some copperas, and took about a spoonful in milk; soon after complaining, a physician being sent for, and an emetic immediately given, she was thought to be in a fair way of recovery; but was again taken between four and five o'clock in the morning and expired in about five minutes." *Mass. Spy*, 6 Feb. 1772.

[1] *Journal of Each Provincial Congress*, p. 643.

7. MARTIN, s. of Moses (5), m. Phila, dau. of Joel Marsh, pub. 18 Sep. 1808, and had *Delphia*, b. 25 Dec. 1810, d. unm. 19 May 1832; *Elbridge*, b. 8 Ap. 1812; *Henry*, b. 12 Jan. 1814, rem. to Ohio; *Charles*, b. 7 Jan. 1816; *Harriet*, b. 24 Oct. 1818, d. 27 Feb. 1821; *Joel Dwight*, b. 6 Nov. 1820; *Phila*, b. 5 Ap. 1824, m. Dr. Jason B. Thomas of Palmer (now Thorndike) 17 Ap. 1850. MARTIN the f. was a farmer, a captain of militia, and inherited the homestead; he was selectman in 1825, and d. 12 Sep. 1855; his w. Phila d. 14 Feb. 1879, a. 91.

8. WALTER, s. of Moses (5), m. Julia Ann Freeman of Oakham, pub. 15 Dec. 1828; she d. 29 Sep. 1833, a. 29, and he m. Olive P. Whiting 30 Nov. 1837; she d. 29 July 1838, a. 31, and he m. Adeline, dau. of Capt. Stephen W. Paige, 31 Jan. 1842; she d. 3 Oct. 1842, a. 31, and he m. a fourth wife. His chil. were *Henry E.*, b. ——; *Daniel Webster*, b. 19 Nov. 1831, grad. Mid. Coll. 1850, a teacher at Brandon, Vt., and Flushing, L. I.; *Walter Grenville*, b. 1 Oct. 1848. WALTER the f. was a farmer, and captain of militia; he res. on the farm formerly occupied by his brother Daniel, and afterwards near the Common. He was selectman three years, assessor nine years, member of school committee sixteen years, and d. 25 June 1853.

9. ELBRIDGE, s. of Martin (7), m. Lucy R., dau. of Capt. Stephen W. Paige, 18 June 1844, and had *Martin Elbridge*, b. 16 Feb. 1849, d. 14 Dec. 1852; *William Dwight*, b. 25 Ap. 1853, m. Emma F. Clapp 10 May 1882, and res. in Springfield; *Caroline Lucy*, b. 11 Mar. 1856; *West Paige*, b. 3 Nov. 1859, d. 18 Aug. 1861; *Mabel Reed*, b. 16 Jan. 1862. ELBRIDGE the f., a farmer, res. near the old homestead, at the place marked "B. Fay" on the R. Map. He was selectman in 1863.

10. CHARLES, s. of Martin (7), m. Martha, dau. of Dr. Joseph Stone, 3 Mar. 1846, and had *Joseph Stone*, b. 25 Aug. 1847; *Charles Martin*, b. 29 Nov. 1852; *Calvin*, b. 8 Mar. 1855, d. 29 Sep. 1863; *George*, b. 8 June 1858. CHARLES the f., a farmer, res. on the former homestead of Brigadier Ruggles, on the easterly road to Gilbertville, at the place marked "J. Mann" on the R. Map.

11. JOEL DWIGHT, s. of Martin (7), m. Mary Elizabeth, dau. of John Dean, 2 Ap. 1846; she d. 17 Ap. 1847, and he m. Malinda H. Winter of Ware, pub. 28 June 1851; she d. 27 Nov. 1863, a. 39. His chil. were *Dwight Dean*, b. 8 Ap. 1847, d. 23 Ap. 1849; *Frank*, b. 14 Ap. 1852; *Elizabeth*, b. 22 Oct. 1853, m. Charles A. Gleason of N. Br., 17 Nov. 1875; *Elliott*, b. 28 June 1855, d. 31 Aug. 1859; *Louis*, b. 2 Dec. 1858; *Arthur*, b. 27 Oct. 1860. JOEL DWIGHT the f., a farmer, assessor three years, 1861–3, res. on the homestead, rem. to Minnesota about 1880.

12. ALGERNON S., by w. Marietta, had *Eliza Marietta*, b. 3 May, 1852.

Widow SARAH, m. Ammiel Weeks 26 Feb. 1778.

MANLY, ICHABOD, m. Experience Phillips in Easton, —— 1739, and had *Josiah*, b. 21 Ap. 1740, prob. d. young; *Mary*, b. —— 1742; *Nathaniel*, b. —— 1744; *Freelove*, b. —— 1746; *Reuben*, b. —— 1757, res. in Enfield; prob. *Josiah*, b. about 1761. ICHABOD the f. res. in Easton, but in his old age (prob. in 1794, with his son *Josiah*) rem. to Hardwick, where he d. 11 Jan. 1799, a. 89; his w. Experience d. in 1805, a. 82.

2. JOSIAH, in all probability son of Ichabod (1), though the birth is not found on record, m. Elizabeth, dau. of Seth Bryant of Bridgewater, in 1789, and had *Zeby*, b. 24 Feb. 1790, m. Zebina Forbush 24 Ap. 1811; *Ichabod*, b. 2 July 1791, m. Lucinda Reed at Brookfield, Conn., 25 Ap. 1817; *Lillia Stafford*, b. 12 Mar. 1794, d. 13 Feb. 1795; *Lilly Stafford*, b. 16 Sep. 1796; *Seth Bryant*, b. 14 June 1798, m. Cynthia Jordan 12 May 1824; *Benjamin Paige*, b. 10 Aug. 1803, m. Sarah E. Barker. JOSIAH the f. rem. from Easton to Hk. in the autumn of 1794, and d. 6 Feb. 1844, a. 82; his w. Elizabeth d. 17 Mar. 1846, a. 80; she was cousin to Dr. Peter Bryant of Cummington, the father of the poet William Cullen Bryant.

3. LILLY STAFFORD, s. of Josiah (2), m. Susanna Horr, pub. 20 Feb. 1826, and had *Adeline*, b. 10 Mar. 1827; *Dwight*, b. 11 Nov. 1828, d. 11 Oct. 1829; *George*, b. 17 Oct. 1830; *Carlena*, b. 29 Jan. 1833; *Elutheria*, b. 13 Feb. 1835,

m. Charles Baker of Worcester 1 Sep. 1863; *Fanny*, b. 5 Nov. 1836, m. William Paige 26 June 1861; *Clara*, b. 11 Jan. 1839; *Dwight*, b. 13 May 1841, d. 27 Ap. 1842; *Benjamin*, b. 8 Mar. 1843, m. Nellie F., dau. of Forester B. Aiken, 23 May 1874; *Jane*, b. 16 Sep. 1845; *Charles*, twin, b. 25 Dec. 1849, d. unm. 20 June 1878 (drowned at Portland, Oregon); *Ellen*, twin, b. 25 Dec. 1849. Lilly S., the f. was an iron-founder, res. on the road to Gilbertville, at the place marked "L. Manly" on the R. Map, was selectman three years, and assessor three years; he d. 16 Sep. 1863.

4. George, s. of Lilly S. (3), m. Mary Ann, dau. of Forester B. Aiken, 23 Feb. 1864, and had *George Forester*, b. 14 Nov. 1865; *Susan Bryant*, b. 24 Jan. 1868; *Fanny Maria*, b. 20 June 1872; *May*, b. 1 May 1877, d. 19 Aug. 1877; *Charles*, b. 18, and d. 19 Aug. 1879. George the f., a farmer, res. on the homestead, was assessor three years, and has been selectman twenty years, up to the present time.

Mann, widow Sarah, had *Joseph* and *Sarah*, both bap. 24 Sep. 1820.

2. Southworth Jenkins, m. Isabella Whiting, pub. 19 Nov. 1827, and had *Abigail B.*, b. 22 Aug. 1828, m. Henry D. Fish 10 Mar. 1853; *Calvin Whiting*, b. 2 Ap. 1831; *Sarah Jenkins*, b. 15 June 1834, d. 9 May 1845; *Mary Morton*, b. 31 Oct. 1837. Southworth J. the f. was a farmer, res. on the easterly road to Gilbertville, at the place marked "J. Mann" on the R. Map, and d. 10 Ap. 1863, a. 64; his w. Isabella d. 31 May (1 June on the head-stone), 1869, a. 70.

3. Calvin Whiting, s. Southworth J. (2), m. Delphia M., dau. of Moses M. Warner, 2 Ap. 1856, at Lee Centre, Illinois, and had *Jennie Eliza*, b. 15 Jan. 1857; *Lucius Calvin Jenkins*, b. 17 Ap. 1870. Calvin W. the f., a farmer, was selectman 1869, 1870, 1871, assessor from 1879 to the present time, and res. on the easterly road to Gilbertville, at the place marked "Wid. Marsh" on the R. Map.

4. Asa, was pastor of the Calvinistic Church from 19 June 1844 to 14 Oct. 1851, and acting pastor in 1880 and 1881. He m. Mercy W., dau. of Timothy Bruce, pub. 31 Mar. 1848, and had *Ellen Louisa*, b. 11 June 1849; *Grace*, b. 22 Sep. 1869. He rem. to Exeter, N. H., in 1851.

Sarah Ann, m. Reuben Edward 28 Ap. 1828. Sarah, m. William Cushman of Tolland, Conn., 11 May 1831.

Marsh, John, of Hartford 1639, rem. to Hadley, thence to Northampton, and ret. to Hartford, where he d. in 1688. He m. Anne, dau. of Gov. John Webster; she d. 9 June 1662, and he m. widow Hepzibah Lyman, who d. 11 Ap. 1683. His chil. were *John; Samuel*, b. about 1645; *Joseph*, bap. 24 Jan. 1647; *Joseph*, bap. 15 July 1649; *Jonathan*, b. about 1650; *Daniel*, b. about 1653; *Hannah*, b. ——, m. Joseph Loomis; *Grace*, b. ——, m. Timothy Baker; *Lydia*, b. ——, m. David Loomis.

2. Samuel, s. of John (1), res. in Hatfield and was representative in 1705, 1706. He m. Mary Allison 6 May 1667, and had *Mary*, b. 27 Feb. 1668; *Samuel*, b. 11 Feb. 1670; *John*, b. 6 Nov. 1672; *Rachel*, b. 15 Oct. 1674, m. John Wells; *Grace*, b. 7 Jan. 1677, m. Thomas Goodman; *Mary*, b. 24 May 1678, m. Joseph Morton; *Thomas*, b. 10 Jan. 1680; *Hannah*, b. 18 Sep. 1681, m. Richard Billings; *Elizabeth*, b. 31 July 1683, m. Maynard Day of Hartford; *Ruth*, b. 16 June 1685; *Ebenezer*, b. 1 May 1687. Samuel the f. d. 7 Sep. 1728, a. 83; his w. Mary d. 13 Oct. 1726, a. 78.

3. Thomas, s. of Samuel (2), m. Mary Trumbull of Suffield, Conn., 1702, and had *Thomas*, b. 1 May 1703, d. unm. —— 1728; *Mary*, b. 27 Oct. 1704, m. Moses Smith —— 1726; *Samuel*, b. —— 1706; *Rachel*, b. —— 1708; *Ruth*, b. 15 Feb. 1710; *Judah*, b. 25 July 1712; *Joseph*, b. 14 Ap. 1714, perhaps m. Abigail Simons 17 May 1750; *Ephraim*, b. 5 Jan. 1717; *Daniel*, b. 12 June 1719; *Martha*, b. 12 Ap. 1721, prob. m. Ebenezer Marsh 17 Nov. 1741. Thomas the f. res. in Hatfield, and afterwards in Ware; he d. in 1759.[1]

4. Samuel, s. of Thomas (3), m. Zerviah, dau. of William Thomas, 18 Jan. 1731-2, and had *Eunice*, b. 15 Jan. 1733, d. young; *Amos*, b. 15 Nov. 1733;

[1] Thus far I have followed the genealogy of this family as published in Judd's *History of Hadley*, pp. 532, 533.

Mary, b. 13 June 1735, m. Solomon Emmons of Quobbin, 31 Jan. 1754; *Eunice*, b. 20 Nov. 1737; *Patience*, b. 20 July 1740, m. Henry Gilbert of Brk. 5 Ap. 1764; *Thankful* and *Submit*, twins, b. 1 Feb. 1741–2; *Miriam*, b. 18 Jan. 1743; *Samuel*, b. 18 Feb. 1744–5. SAMUEL the f. d. about 1745, and his w. Zerviah m. Isaiah Pratt 2 Mar. 1746–7.

5. JUDAH, s. of Thomas (3), m. Hannah, dau. of Jabez Olmstead 4 Nov. 1736, and had *Elijah*, bap. 1 Jan. 1737–8; *Joel*, bap. 8 Ap. 1739, d. young; *Rachel*, bap. 28 Aug. 1743; *Dorothy*, bap. 28 Ap. 1751; *Jonathan*, bap. 31 May 1752; *Mary*, bap. 7 July 1754; *Joel*, b. 18 July 1759. Besides these were *Thomas* and *Judah*.[1] JUDAH the f. res. at Ware, near the mills still known as Marsh's Mills, but his chil. were bap. at Hk.; he d. 7 May 1801, a. nearly 89.

6. EPHRAIM, s. of Thomas (3), m. Sarah, dau. of Jabez Olmstead, 8 Oct. 1741, and had *Noah*, bap. 17 Ap. 1743; *Huldah*, bap. 14 Sep. 1746; *Sarah*, bap. 28 Ap. 1751; *Mary*, bap. 5 Oct. 1755. EPHRAIM the f. res. at Ware, but his chil. were bap. here.

7. AMOS, s. of Samuel (4), m. Beulah Leonard of Rut., pub. 16 July 1757, and had *Samuel*, bap. 24 Sep. 1758; *Mercy*, bap. 5 Oct. 1760.

8. JOEL, s. of Judah (5), m. Annis Smith 20 Sep. 1785, and had *Phila*, b. 17 Feb. 1788, m. Martin Mandell 18 Sep. 1808, and d. 14 Feb. 1879; *Delphia*, b. 12 June 1790, d. unm. of spotted fever 25 Mar. 1810; *Dwight*, b. 19 Aug. 1793; *Joel Smith*, b. 21 Oct. 1803. JOEL the f. rem. from Ware to Hk. about the year 1800, was a farmer, and res. on the easterly road to Gilbertville, at the place marked "A. Warner" on the R. Map. He d. 12 Ap. 1804; his w. Annis m. Jonathan Warner 18 Oct. 1807, and d., his widow, 17 May 1859, a. nearly 94.

9. DWIGHT, s. of Joel (8), m. Mary C., dau. of Rev. Thomas Holt, 4 Nov. 1817, and had *Mary Ann*, b. 1 Mar. 1819, m. Joel W. Fletcher of Leominster 28 Ap. 1845, and d. 25 Ap. 1850. DWIGHT the f. was a farmer, and res. on the easterly road to Gilbertville, at the place marked "Wid. Marsh" on the R. Map; he was a member of the school committee, 1821–2, and d. 25 Jan. 1823; his w. Mary d. 20 Ap. 1866, a. 68.

10. JOEL SMITH, s. of Joel (8), m. Abigail Drury, dau. of Josiah Gleason, N. Br., 6 June 1837, and had *Joel Dwight*, b. 10 May 1838, d. 18 Ap. 1845; *Josiah Gleason*, b. 1 June 1839, d. 5 Feb. 1844; *Charles Smith*, b. 15 May 1842, res. in Springfield, a partner in business with his father; *Abby Maria*, b. 4 Dec. 1843, d. 9 Sep. 1863; *Henry Mandell*, b. 15 Sep. 1845, d. 24 June 1847; *George Parsons*, b. 16 Jan. 1848, d. 13 Ap. 1866. JOEL S. the f. owned the farm on the easterly road to Gilbertville, marked "J. Marsh" on the R. Map, but after his marriage generally resided near the Common, and managed a store of English and W. I. goods until about 1850, when he rem. to Springf., where he has since transacted an extensive business as a grocer.

11. MARCUS, parentage not ascertained, by w. Tamar, had prob. *Zenas*, b. about 1793; prob. *Triphena*, b. about 1798, d. unm. 7 Jan. 1843, a. 44; *Marcus J.*, b. about 1800; *Mary*, b. about 1801, m. —— Bartlett, and d. 24 Jan. 1873, a. 71; *Tyler*, b. about 1802, d. 8 Jan. 1875, a. 73; *Sally*, b. about 1813, d. unm. 2 Dec. 1873, a. 60. These, and perhaps others, were probably born before their parents rem. to Hk. MARCUS the f. prob. resided on the road to Ware, at the place marked "M. J. Marsh" on the R. Map; he d. 10 May 1823, a. 52; his w. Tamar d. 11 Sep. 1864, a. 93.

12. ZENAS, prob. s. of Marcus (11), by w. Fanny, had *Samuel Clifford*, b. 10 Dec. 1819. ZENAS the f. d. 2 July 1834, a. 41.

13. MARCUS J., s. of Marcus (11), m. Amelia Dexter 29 June 1823, and had *Marcus*, b. about 1825, d. 3 Ap. 1855, a. 29 years and 9 months; *Moses T.*, b. ——; *Addison Jefferson*, b. 28 July 1843; and prob. several others; but their birth is not found on record. MARCUS J. the f., a farmer, res. on the road to Ware, at the place marked "M. J. Marsh" on the R. Map. He d. 9 Mar. 1880, a. 80; his w. Amelia d. 10 Mar. 1880, a. 81.

14. MOSES T., s. of Marcus J. (13), m. Sarah B. Newcomb, pub. 30 Mar. 1854, and had *Carrie L.*, b. 1 Jan. 1857; a son b. 5 Ap. 1859; *Jennie L.*, b. 27 Nov. 1872.

[1] See Hyde's *Hist. Address* at Ware, 1847, p. 50.

15. Erastus, formerly of Townsend, Vt., by w. Sarah J., had *Ellen Maria*, b. 9 Nov. 1869. Erastus the f. d. 18 Aug. 1880, a. 57.

Sally, m. Elijah Cleveland, pub. 14 May 1789. Polly, m. John Oakes, pub. 14 July 1793. Prudence, m. Joseph Barnard, Jr., pub. 28 Nov. 1796; Judah, of Ware, m. Jerusha Collins 20 Feb. 1800. Jonathan, of Ware, m. Mary, wid. of Moses Paige, 1 Dec. 1824. Foster, of Ware, m. Catherine S. Fish 17 June 1846. Mary E., m. Dimick Willis, Jr., pub. 2 Nov. 1851. Martha, m. Alonzo Richardson, pub. 4 Feb. 1863. William A., m. Anna A. Marsh of Ware, pub. 7 Ap. 1863. Joel B., m. Julia E. Babbitt, pub. 28 Feb. 1865. Lucretia, m. Alfred H. Richardson 21 Nov. 1870.

Martin, Daniel, by w. Fanny, had *Fanny*, *Mary Ann*, *Louisa Maria*, *James Freeman*, *Lorenzo*, *Rachel*, *Thomas*, *Dwight Manly*, allbap. here 10 Sep. 1820, and *Sarah Wilde*, bap. 17 June 1821. Daniel the f. rem. to N. Br. about 1835.

Mason, Elizabeth (wid. of John, Esq., of Barre), d. 2 Feb. 1822, a. 95.

May, Samuel B., by w. Maria, had *Clinton*, b. at Hadley 6 Dec. 1827; *Franklin*, b. here 15 Jan. 1831, res. at Southbridge, and d. at New York 12 Oct. 1869. Samuel B. the f. d. 4 Oct. 1834, a. 32.

Maynard, George C., m. Adeline E. Perry of Worc., pub. 4 June 1849, and had *Hester Newton*, b. 26 Feb. 1851; *Cornelia*, b. 9 Ap. 1852; and the family soon afterwards left the town.

Patty, of Shrews., m. Dr. Joseph Stone, pub. 11 Mar. 1816.

Mayo, John (son of John, who d. at Eastham about 1706, and grandson of Rev. John, who was ordained colleague with Rev. John Lothrop at Barnstable 15 Ap. 1640, rem. to Eastham 1646, and thence to Boston, where he was installed first minister of the North Church 9 Nov. 1655, was dismissed in 1673, and after short residence in Barnstable and Eastham d. at Yarmouth in May 1676), was b. at Eastham 15 Dec. 1652, m. Hannah, dau. of Major John Freeman of Eastham, 14 Ap. 1681, and had *Hannah*, b. 8 Jan. 1682; *Samuel*, b. 16 July 1684; *John*, b. ——; *Mercy*, b. 23 Ap. 1688; *Rebecca*, b. ——; *Mary*, b. 26 Oct. 1694; *Joseph*, b. 22 Dec. 1696; *Elizabeth*, b. —— 1706. John the f. res. in Hingham until about 1700, when he rem. to Harwich, was representative six years, and d. 1 Feb. 1726. Savage's *Geneal. Dict.*, iii. 187.

2. Joseph, s. of John (1), m. Abigail Merrick 20 Feb. 1717–18, and had *Joseph*, b. 11 Nov. 1718; *Moses*, b. 1 Feb. 1720–1; *Lydia*, b. 23 Mar. 1721–2; *Thomas*, b. 1 Ap. 1725; *Abigail*, b. 1 Dec. 1727 or 1728; *Elizabeth*, b. 28 Mar. 1731, d. young; *Isaac* and *Elizabeth*, twins, b. 28 Mar. 1733; *Nathan*, b. 5 Ap. 1735 or 1736; *Eunice*, b. 7 Ap. 1738. Joseph the f. res. in that part of Harwich which is now Brewster, was elected deacon of the church 9 Mar. 1739, was selectman eleven years, and d. in 1772.

3. Moses, s. of Joseph (2), m. Phebe Freeman 10 Mar. 1742–3, and had *Phebe*, *Moses*, *Mary*, *Hannah*, *Issachar*, *Elkanah*, *Edmund*, all bap. 3 Sep. 1758; *Phebe*, bap. 30 Dec. 1759; *Watson*, bap. 7 Feb. 1762; *Katherine*, bap. 7 Sep. 1766; *Benjamin*, bap. 28 Aug. 1768. Moses the f. res. in Harwich (Brewster); but in his old age rem. here, prob. with his son *Edmund*, and d. 7 Mar. 1812, a. 94, according to the record of his death; but actually 91.

4. Nathan, s. of Joseph (2), by w. Anna, had *Mehetabel*, bap. 15 Aug. 1762; and prob. by 2d w. Mary,[1] had *Nathan*, bap. 16 Feb. 1766; *Anna*, bap. 10 July 1768; *Daniel*, bap. 3 Dec. 1769; *William*, bap. 28 Ap. 1771; *Peter*, bap. 3 July 1714; *Joshua*, bap. 24 Jan. 1779. Nathan the f. res. in Harwich.

5. Edmund, s. of Moses (3), m. Martha ——, who d. 20 Feb. 1797, and he m. Abigail ——. His chil. were *Martha*, bap. 19 Nov. 1786, d. young; *Edmund* and *Ezekiel*, twins, bap. 22 Feb. 1789 (*Ezekiel* was bap. privately, being supposed near death); *Ezekiel*, bap. 4 Sep. 1791; *George*, b. 24 Oct. 1801; *Patty*, b. 9 Jan. 1807, m. Wm. Hunt of Northampton, pub. 3 Dec. 1827. Edmund the f., styled captain, was prob. a master mariner, and res. in Brewster

[1] The Church Record calls *Mehetabel*, bap. 15 Aug. 1762, dau. of Nathan and Anna, yet says that Mary, w. of Nathan, was adm. to full communion 3 June 1764. The name of the mother of the other children is not mentioned in the record of baptisms.

until about 1800, when he rem. here and lived on the Barre road, between the places marked "Dr. Stone" and "Mr. Lincoln" on the R. Map, on which his name was accidentally omitted. He d. 9 Dec. 1841, a. 85; his w. Abigail d. 10 Nov. 1831, a. 64.

6. PETER, s. of Nathan (4), m. Bethia, dau. of John Smith, and had *Mehetabel*, b. 4 Dec. 1799, m. Nathan P. Chase of Hk. 17 May 1854; *Peter*, b. 24 May 1802; *William*, b. 30 Nov. 1804; *Bethia*, b. 30 Oct. 1806; *John S.*, b. 13 Dec. 1808; *Elizabeth S.*, twin, b. 24 Oct. 1810, m. Leonard Mellen of Hk.; *Hannah*, twin, b. 24 Oct. 1810, m. Joseph Burgess of Hk. 5 Sep. 1841; *Nathan*, b. 13 May 1812, d. 10 Ap. 1816; *Joseph*, b. 8 or 18 July 1814; *Isaac*, b. 22 Aug. 1816; *Harriet*, b. 16 May 1818, m. Rev. Martin J. Steere of Rhode Island, who afterwards rem. to Hk., and d. 18 Jan. 1877; *Warren*, b. 26 Sep. 1820. PETER the f., styled captain, was prob. a master mariner, and res. in Harwich until after 1810; his later years were spent in Hk., and he d. here 27 Jan. 1857, a. 82; his w. Bethia d. 12 Oct. 1870, a. 94; they were buried near the front of the new cemetery, and in the same lot were deposited, in 1877, the remains of his cousin Capt. Edmund Mayo, and his wife Abigail, which had long rested in a tomb.

7. EDMUND, s. of Edmund (5), was a merchant in West Brookfield and Warren; he d. in Newark, N. J., in 1865; but I have no record of his family.

VIRGINIA, m. John Young 27 Dec. 1865.

MCINTYRE, ROBERT, m. Rhoda, dau. of Jonathan Warner, 26 Nov. 1772, and had *Fanny*, b. 13 July 1773; *William Little*, b. 3 July 1775. ROBERT the f. d. 29 Aug. 1775, a. 25, and his w. Rhoda m. Jonathan Lynds of Petersham 26 Ap. 1778.

MEAD, JONATHAN, rem. from Pet. to Hk., was for many years the grave-digger, and d. 24 Mar. 1814, a. 50. I have not seen a record of his family; but he had son *Tilly* and dau. *Elizabeth K.*, who m. William F. Granger 26 Nov. 1829; another dau. who m. Daniel Granger, f. of William F.; prob. *Mary Ann*, who m. Benjamin Cummings, Jr., of Ware 25 Oct. 1830; and perhaps others.

2. TILLY, s. of Jonathan (1), b. in Pet., m. Caroline Hathaway, pub. 30 Ap. 1822, and had *Abner Alden*, b. 14 Feb. 1823, d. 29 Aug. 1846; *Caroline Hathaway*, b. 15 Sep. 1825, d. 3 May 1843; *Rebecca J.*, b. 8 Jan. 1832, m. William Adams, Jr., of W. Brk. 3 Oct. 1854; *John B.*, b. about 1834. TILLY the f. was a cabinet-maker, res. less than half a mile northerly from the Common, and d. 28 Mar. 1849, a. 54.

3. JOHN B., s. of Tilly (2), m. Sarah Carter 24 Feb. 1863, and had *Lucy C.*, b. 11 Ap. 1864; *John A.*, b. 22 Jan. 1866, d. 12 Feb. 1866; *Charles L.*, b. 22 Feb. 1867, d. 26 Oct. 1875. JOHN B. the f. was a cabinet-maker, res. on the homestead, and d. 10 May 1868, a. 34.

MELLEN, LEONARD (b. in Mendon), m. Elizabeth S., dau. of Capt. Peter Mayo, and had *Mary*, b. ——; *Hannah*, b. ——; *James Franklin*, b. 31 Jan. 1845; and perhaps others. LEONARD the f. d. 20 Jan. 1873, a. nearly 67.

2. EDWARD D., by w. Julia M., had *Lauretta Elizabeth*, b. 27 Oct. 1853.

DAVID (b. in Prescott), d. 20 May 1854, a. 70.

MERRICK, WILLIAM (otherwise written Mirick and Myrick), by w. Rebecca, had *William*, b. 15 Sep. 1643; *Stephen*, b. 12 May 1646, m. Mercy Bangs 28 Dec. 1670; *Rebecca*, b. 28 July 1648; *Mary*, b. 4 Nov. 1650, m. Stephen Hopkins 23 May 1667; *Ruth*, b. 15 May 1652; *Sarah*, b. 1 Aug. 1654, m. John Freeman, Jr., 18 Dec. 1672; *John*, b. 15 Jan. 1656–7; *Isaac*, b. 6 Jan. 1660–1; *Joseph*, b. 1 June 1662, m. Elizabeth Howes 1 or 8 May 1684; *Benjamin*, b. 1 Feb. 1664–5. WILLIAM the f. was a lieutenant, res. in Eastham. In his will, dated 3 Dec. 1686, and proved 6 Mar. 1688–9, he is described as "about eighty-six years of age;" by which it would seem that he was forty-three years old when the first of his ten children was born, and he might be supposed the grandfather of this family, rather than their father, were it not that he names his wife Rebecca and chil. William and Stephen in his will.

2. WILLIAM, s. of William (1), m. Abigail Hopkins 23 May 1667, and had

Rebecca, b. 28 Nov. 1668; *William*, b. 1 Aug. 1670. WILLIAM the f. res. in Eastham, where he d. 20 Mar. 1670-1, at the early age of 27 years and 6 months.

3. WILLIAM, s. of William (2), an ensign, res. in Harwich (now Brewster). I have not seen a record of his family; but in his will, dated 5 May 1723, and proved 9 Nov. 1732, he names w. Elizabeth (apparently not his first wife), children *Benjamin, Nathaniel, Stephen, Joshua, John, Ruth* Sears (wife of Samuel Sears, and subsequently the third wife of Deac. Chillingsworth Foster), and the children of daughter *Rebecca* Sparrow, deceased. He d. 30 Oct. 1732.

4. NATHANIEL, s. of William (3), by w. Alice, had nine children, named in his will, dated 18 Oct. 1743, to wit: *William* (deceased, leaving chil. William and Gideon), *Constant, Benjamin, Hannah* Snow, *Mercy* King, *Ruth* (w. of Thomas), Hinkley, *Priscilla* Cobb, *Alice* (w. of Capt. Benjamin) Ruggles, and *Sarah*, who m. Abner Lee of New Rutland (Barre) in Oct. 1744. Of this family, *Constant* was b. about 1701; *Benjamin*, 20 Mar. 1717-18, and *Sarah*, 5 July 1720. NATHANIEL the f. res. in Harwich (Brewster), was a captain, and d. 13 Nov. 1743; his w. Alice was prob. the "widow Merrick" who d. here 24 Dec. 1756.

5. CONSTANT, s. of Nathaniel (4), m. Sarah, dau. of John Freeman of Rochester (and sister of Deac. John Freeman of Hk.), pub. 17 Feb. 1726-7, and had *William*, b. 22 Ap. 1728; *Nathaniel*, b. 22 May 1730; *Sarah*, b. 30 Sep. 1732, m. Timothy Newton 5 July 1751; *Constant*, b. 21 Feb. 1734-5, d. young; *Alice*, b. 29 Aug. 1737, m. Zebadiah Johnson 25 Nov. 1756; *Constant*, b. 13 Sep. 1740. CONSTANT the f. rem. from Rochester to Hk. about 1735, and res. on the road to Barre, at the place marked "F. Fay" on the R. Map. He was captain of militia, selectman eleven years, assessor nine years, and d. 17 Mar. 1792, a. 91.

6. WILLIAM (s. of Constant (5), m. Sarah, dau. of Samuel Billings, 7 Sep. 1749, and had *Gideon*, b. 22 Aug. 1750; *William*, b. 7 July 1752, m. Hannah, dau. of Joseph Nye, 15 Nov. 1798, and d. about 1803; his wid. Hannah m. Aldrich Worley of Boston, pub. 8 July 1805; *Sarah*, b. 9 Ap. 1754. SARAH the mother d. before 1778, as noted in her father's will of that date.

7. NATHANIEL, s. of Constant (5), m. Susanna, dau. of Ebenezer Lawrence 13 Feb. 1755; she d. and he m. Lois Hammond of Rochester, 29 May 1764; she d. and he m. Elizabeth Haskell of Roch., 26 June 1775; she d. 4 Sep. 1796, a. 54 or 55, and he m. Susanna Taylor of Athol 23 Oct. 1797. His chil. were *Elizabeth*, b. 13 Jan. 1756, m. John Pratt 19 Jan. 1775; *Susanna*, b. 16 Feb. 1758, d. young; *Constant*, b. 7 Jan. 1760; *Nathaniel*, bap. 4 July 1762, prob. d. young; *Nathan*, b. 12 Mar. 1763; *Susanna*, b. 24 Sep. 1766, m. James Peirce 20 Nov. 1785; *Phebe*, b. 20 Aug. 1768; *Sarah*, b. 19 Dec. 1769, m. Heman Shurtleff 30 Nov. 1788; *Lois*, bap. 1 May 1773, m. Stephen Nye 10 Jan. 1802; *William* and *Elmira*, named in their father's will, of whom the former prob. m. Hannah Nye 15 Nov. 1798. NATHANIEL the f. d. 5 Feb. 1799.

8. CONSTANT, s. of Nathaniel (7), m. Sarah Hopkins 18 Mar. 1781, and had *Prince*, b. 14 Dec. 1781; *Barna*, b. 2 Jan. 1783; *Polly*, b. 3 May 1787; *Nathan*, b. 13 July 1789. No further trace found.

Rev. JOHN M. (pastor of the Congregational Church), m. Harriet L. Underwood of Portsmouth, N. H., pub. 1 Dec. 1828.

MERRITT, ELBRIDGE W., acting pastor and pastor of the Calvinistic Church from October 1870 to October 1876, by w. Eliza Jane, had *Lucy Sophia*, bap. 2 July 1871; *Mary Catherine*, bap. 5 July 1874. He rem. to Dana.

POLLY, m. Eli Barnes 21 July 1789. BENJAMIN, of Ware, m. Sarah Wheelock 8 Jan. 1797.

MILES, ELMER B., m. Elizabeth A. Bacon of Barre, pub. 19 Aug. 1842, and had *Frederick Brooks*, b. 16 Dec. 1845. He soon afterwards removed.

MILLER, WILLIAM R., by w. Mary Jane, had *William Hernando*, b. 12 Sep. 1866.

IRA, m. Aurelia Frye 27 Mar. 1824. IRA, m. Martha Frye 12 May 1830 JOHN F., m. Amanda Drury of Shutes., pub. 6 Aug. 1835.

MIXTER, SAMUEL, m. Elizabeth, dau. of Jason Bigelow of Brk., and had *Elizabeth*, b. 18 Nov. 1768, m. Ebenezer Tidd; *Jason*, b. 27 July 1772; *Sarah*, b. 22 Mar. 1774, m. Samuel Pope; *Mary*, b. 9 Sep. 1776, m. Gen. Samuel Lee of Barre; *Lucy*, b. 13 Nov. 1778, d. unm. 28 Oct. 1823; *Asenath*, b. 14 Mar. 1782, m. Joseph Green; *Samuel*, b. 15 Oct. 1784. All res. and d. in N. Br., except *Jason* and *Mary*. SAMUEL the f. was s. of Josiah, and a descendant in the fourth generation from Isaac Mixer of Watertown, where he was born 7 Aug. 1743. He was a farmer, lieutenant of militia, res. a short time after marriage at Brk. and thence rem. in 1776 to New Braintree, where he d. 17 Jan. 1821; his w. Elizabeth d. 2 July 1834.

2. JASON, s. of Samuel (1), m. Susan, dau. of Dr. Robert Cutler of Amherst, pub. 30 Mar. 1808, and had *William*, b. 5 Ap. 1809; *Charles*, b. 18 Mar. 1811; *Susan*, b. 7 Sep. 1813, m. Joseph Knox, Esq., 7 Sep. 1831, and rem. to Rock Island, Ill.; *George*, b. 28 Ap. 1815, Y. C. 1836, settled in Rock Island; *Mary Ann*, b. 19 May 1818, d. 8 Feb. 1830. JASON the f. was b. in Brk., went early with his f. to N. Br., and on the 15th of November, 1788, became a resident here for the remainder of his life. He was at first a clerk in the store of Gen. Jonathan Warner, then a partner, and afterwards, for many years, sole manager of the business, justice of the peace, member of the school committee, 1807, selectman thirteen years, town treasurer six years, and representative three years. He res. near the Common, at the place marked with his name on the R. Map, and d. 31 Jan. 1850; his w. Susan d. 30 Oct. 1861, a. 84. He bequeathed to the First Calvinistic Society five thousand dollars, as a fund for the maintenance of the ministry.

3. SAMUEL, s. of Samuel (1), m. Clarissa Moore, and had *William*, b. ——, d. unm. 17 Feb. 1869, a. 44; *James*, b. ——, d. young. SAMUEL the f. taught school in Hk. five winters, res. in N. Br., was much employed in public life, colonel of militia, justice of the peace, member of the school committee, selectman, assessor, representative, senator, and councillor. He d. 30 Mar. 1862.

4. WILLIAM, s. of Jason (2), m. Mary, dau. of Anson Ruggles, 7 July, 1840, and had *George*, b. 10 Sep. 1842, grad. H. C. 1863, a banker in Boston; *Mary Ann*, b. 24 Jan. 1845; *Fanny Louisa*, b. 29 Sep. 1850, m. Daniel Waldo Howard of Philadelphia 15 Feb. 1881; *Samuel Jason*, b. 10 May 1855, a graduate of the Technological School and of the Harvard Medical School, a physician in Boston, m. Wilhelmina Galloupe 12 Aug. 1879; *William Anson*, b. 24 Oct. 1856, d. 5 Jan. 1859. WILLIAM the f. entered Harvard College, in the famous class of 1829, but by the failure of his health was prevented from completing the prescribed course; he received the customary degree, however, from his Alma Mater in 1876, and his name was assigned to its proper place in his class. He was a merchant for several years, in the store formerly occupied by his father, from which he retired with a plentiful estate. He purchased a house in Beacon Street, Boston, where he spends his winters, but retains his homestead and his legal residence in Hardwick. He was a member of the school committee, 1831 and 1832; selectman, 1841 to 1843; town clerk, 1849 to 1857; town treasurer, 1846 to 1862, except in 1850; representative, 1854, 1856, 1858; and senator, 1857. He has been a justice of the peace since 1845; and in 1866 was appointed to the office of harbor commissioner.

5. CHARLES, s. of Jason (3), m. Frances Louisa, dau. of Nathaniel Curtis, Esq., of Boston, 30 Mar. 1848, and had *Emily Louisa*, b. in Roxbury 9 Sep. 1841, d. in Newport, R. I., 2 Oct. 1853; *Madeleine Curtis*, b. in Newport 27 May 1856; *Charles Cutler*, b. in Boston 15 Nov. 1857, d. in New York 22 Feb. 1861; *Helen Kortright*, b. in Boston 27 Ap. 1864. CHARLES the f. was a member of the mercantile house of Jabez C. Howe & Co. of Boston; he prospered abundantly, and retired in comparatively early life, fully satisfied with his accumulations. He had a pleasant summer residence in Newport, R. I., but spent much time in other cities, both here and abroad, at Paris and elsewhere. He embarked with his family for Europe on board the steamer Ville du Havre, and was wrecked and drowned, together with his

wife and her father, 22 Nov. 1873. His two daughters were also engulfed in the sea, but were providentially rescued; they now reside in Boston.

MONROE, JONAS, b. in Plainfield 15 Dec. 1773, m. Alice Butler in Oakham, 13 Sep. 1801; she was b. in Oak. 9 June 1775. Their chil., all b. in Oak., were *Lucretia Butler*, b. 26 Ap. 1803, d. 10 Ap. 1871; *Sally*, b. 11 Nov. 1804, d. 8 Feb. 1843; *Nelson*, b. 5 May 1806, d. 9 Ap. 1856; *Ruth Prouty*, b. 26 Oct. 1807, d. 28 Dec. 1874; *John*, b. 30 Mar. 1809, d. 26 May 1848; *Jonas*, b. 22 Sep. 1810; *Harrison Gray Otis*, b. 29 June 1812; *Alice*, b. 28 Nov. 1813; *James*, b. 25 Jan. 1818, grad. Y. C. 1845, d. in California 20 Nov. 1861. JONAS the f. rem. to Hk. late in life, res. at the place marked "J. Monroe" on the R. Map, and d. 12 Jan. 1849; his w. Alice d. 2 Sep. 1857.

2. HARRISON GRAY OTIS, s. of Jonas (1), m. Roxana, dau. of John Barlow, 18 May 1843, and had *Ellen M.*, b. 1 Ap. 1844, m. Albert L. Wiley of Boston 2 June 1865; *Mary E.*, b. 24 Mar. 1846, d. 5 July 1862; *Louisa Roxana*, b. 2 May 1848, m. Marshall Richards of Springf. 28 Jan. 1869; *Martha Lucretia*, b. 15 Oct. 1850, m. John B. Stebbins 11 Ap. 1877. HARRISON G. O. the f. came here before his marriage, was a farmer, res. on the homestead, about a mile and three quarters southerly from the Common (long ago known as the Winslow farm), and d. 26 May 1880.

MOORE, TIMOTHY (otherwise written More and Mores), m. Mary Warner 26 May 1768, and had *Thomas*, bap. 17 Sep. 1769; *Jonathan*, bap. 29 Dec. 1769 (*Jonathan* is styled in the record son of Timothy and Lois Mores).

MORGAN, PAUL, res. on the northerly side of the turnpike in a small house which formerly stood at the foot of the hill on the westerly side of Great Meadow Brook, and had the care of a grist-mill then standing on the southerly side of the road, but demolished long ago. He was simple and shiftless, and became a state pauper. He seems to have died in 1789, when an account was allowed for the expense of his last sickness and funeral. His w. Hannah d. 17 Jan. 1824, in extreme old age, — estimated on the town record at 95, though it is doubtful whether any one knew with certainty. In her day, most of the spinning and weaving was done in families; she could neither spin nor weave, when I knew her, but she would card wool, or comb worsted, for spinning, from morning until night. She thus made herself useful, going from house to house, as her services were required, until she was disabled by the infirmities of age, when she also became a public charge.

MARY, m. Simon Oliver of Barre 24 July 1785.

MORSE, WILLIAM, by w. Philadelphia, had *Levi*, b. 1 Oct. 1820.

2. RANSOM M., by w. Francina, had *Charles Willard*, b. 19 Mar. 1869.

3. FRANKLIN, by w. Catherine, had *Rosanna*, b. 27 May 1869; *Napoleon*, b. 18 Jan. 1871.

CAROLINE, of Southbridge, m. Albert E. Rice, pub. 13 Nov. 1835.

MORTON, STEPHEN, m. Abigail Whiting, 15 Ap. 1805, and had *Phinehas*, b. 12 Oct. 1805; *Eleanor*, b. 14 Oct. 1807, m. William M. Yerrington 19 May 1836, and d. 16 May 1855; *Mary*, b. 8 Oct. 1809, d. 1 Mar. 1833; *Lucia*, b. 16 Mar. 1812; *Abigail*, b. 19 Feb. 1814, m. Nelson Robinson of Norwich, Vt., 12 Jan. 1841, and d. here 3 Sep. 1877; *Stephen*, b. 22 Dec. 1816, d. 5 Ap. 1834. STEPHEN the f. was a blacksmith, noteworthy for his unflagging industry, thorough workmanship, and punctuality; his shop was on the easterly corner of the turnpike, and the way leading to the Petersham road; his house remains on the same lot, at the place marked "S. Morton" on the R. Map. He d. 26 Ap. 1835, a. 56; his w. Abigail d. 24 May 1845, a. 63.

2. PHINEHAS, s. of Stephen (1), m. Mary A. ——; she d. 2 Aug. 1840, a. 28, and he m. Sarah S. Brimhall of Worc., pub. 14 Feb. 1846. His chil. were *Sarah A.*, b. about 1835, m. Alden B. Spooner 26 Jan. 1858, and d. 2 (or 3) Dec. 1864; *Stephen P.*, b. about 1838, d. 19 Sep. 1860, a. 22; *George Lyman*, b. 18 July 1849; *Frank Allen*, b. 14 Oct. 1850.

TABITHA, of Whateley, m. Dr. Charles Doolittle 3 Oct. 1771. ESTHER, of Whateley, m. Dr. Lucius Doolittle 12 May 1783.

MOULTON, Rev. HORACE, by w. Julia Ann, had *Julia Ann*, b. 29 Oct. 1852.

2. MACE, by w. Mary A., had *Orson*, b. 1 Nov. 1861.

JULIA, m. Daniel Briggs, Jr., of Windsor, pub. 25 Oct. 1834. SALLY S., m. Samuel L. Robinson, Jr., 19 Ap. 1835. DAVID, m. Mary Seagrave of Uxbridge, pub. 7 Mar. 1840. SAMUEL, s. of Nathan, d. 26 Dec. 1833, a. 11.

MUNDEN, DANIEL, m. Rebecca Wheeler 8 Ap. 1771. No record of children. He survived to old age.

CHARLES, s. of Oliver, d. 17 Nov. 1832, a. 1 year.

MUZZEY, JOSEPH, m. Lucinda Paige 25 Ap. 1799.

MYER, JOHN L., m. Abigail Ramsdell, pub. 18 Nov. 1782.

NAZRO, AARON, m. Dilley Day, 21 Mar. 1808.

NELSON, MARY, m. Thomas Barlow 26 Sep. 1793. CHARLES, of Warren, m. Elizabeth Alexander, 28 Mar. 1874.

NEWCOMB, ANNAS, s. of Joseph (and a descendant from Francis Newcomb, who came to Boston 1635, rem. to Mount Wollaston 1638, and d. in 1692, reputed to be one hundred years old), m. Abigail, dau. of Nathan Babbitt, 18 Dec. 1783, and had *Annas*, b. 28 Oct. 1784; *Abigail*, b. 22 Oct. 1787, m. Edward Babbitt of Savoy 11 June 1812; *Sarah Wild*, b. 14 May 1792, d. unm. 9 Jan. 1871; *Ruth Washburn*, b. 2 Feb. 1796, m. John Hastings, Jr., 18 Sep. 1821, and d. in So. Shaftsbury, Vt., 20 Ap. 1861; *Mary*, b. 14 Mar. 1798, m. Alvan Dunham of Savoy, 23 Jan. 1827; *Joseph*, b. 16 Dec. 1800; *Anna*, b. 13 Jan. 1804, m. Jason Gorham 12 July 1827; *Nathan Babbitt*, b. 18 May 1806. ANNAS the f. was b. in Norton 25 Mar. 1762, and rem. to Hk. in 1791; he was a clothier and farmer, res. on the Petersham road, at the place marked "J. Newcomb" on the R. Map, and d. 5 Aug. 1823; his w. Abigail d. 11 (or 16) Mar. 1847, a. 83.

2. JOSEPH, s. of Annas (1), m. Alma, dau. of Capt. Samuel Dexter, pub. 11 Feb. 1828, and had *Alma Maria*, b. 29 Mar. 1830, m. Stephen P. Hillman 4 Dec. 1851; *John Joseph*, b. 29 June 1832; *Sarah W.*, b. 15 Oct. 1834, m. Charles S. Clark 14 Dec. 1856; *Samuel Williams*, b. 9 Oct. 1836. JOSEPH the f. was a farmer, res. on the homestead, and d. 21 (or 22) Sep. 1840.

3. JOHN JOSEPH, s. of Joseph (2), m. Cordelia Gould, pub. 13 Mar. 1857; no record of children. He res. on the Petersham road, opposite the homestead, and afterwards on the turnpike at the place marked "A. Fay" on the R. Map; he served the town as an assessor seven years, from 1871 to 1877.

4. SAMUEL WILLIAMS, s. of Joseph (2), m. Julia Ann, dau. of Adonijah Dennis, 23 Ap. 1863, and had *William Adonijah*, b. 6 Mar. 1865; *Julia Alma*, b. 25 Ap. 1869. SAMUEL W. the f. res. on the homestead.

5. ELISHA, s. of David (and a descendant from Andrew Newcomb, who was in Boston as early as 1664), was b. in Wellfleet 15 Jan. 1765, rem. with his father to Oxford 1772, and to Greenwich 1782, m. Rachel, dau. of Capt. Gamaliel Collins, 23 Feb. 1790, had twelve children, of whom the first two were b. in Hk. (but not found on record), and the other ten in Enfield; his third child, *Rachel Collins*, m. Levi Jones of Shutesbury, and their dau. Elizabeth, b. 18 Mar. 1817, m. William Cutler Wesson, pub. 29 May 1840. See *Genealogy of the Newcomb Family*, pp. 203, 204.

6. FOSTER, s. of Nehemiah, and grandson of David, named in the preceding paragraph, was b. at Gr. 26 Jan. 1789, m. Hannah Latham 1 May 1816; she d. 12 May 1817, and he m. Fanny, dau. of Gamaliel Collins, 18 Feb. 1819. Two of his eight chil. were *Anson Foster*, b. 15 Feb. 1821, and *John Holmes*, b. 28 Oct. 1838, m. Alice E. Powell 1 Oct. 1863, was a sergeant, and was wounded in the war of the Rebellion, and afterwards a wool-sorter at Gilbertville. FOSTER the f. was b. at Greenwich (now Enfield) 26 Jan. 1789, was a farmer, and res. principally in Enf., but owned grist and saw-mills in Hk. He d. 12 Feb. 1869. See *Gen. of Newcomb Fam.*, pp. 181, 182. His w. Fanny d. 19 Nov. 1878.

7. MOSES, s. of Nehemiah, as above, was b. at Gr. 31 Aug. 1790, m. Susanna Thayer 2 Dec. 1819, res. at Ware, and d. 3 Mar. 1832; his w. Susanna d. 2 Oct. 1868; and both were buried in Hk.

8. ISAIAH, s. of Nehemiah, as above, m. Betsey Fuller of Enf. 4 Dec. 1822; she d. 13 Feb. 1831, and he m. Lucina Carey of Ware, pub. 9 Aug. 1831. His

chil. were *Hannah Dorinda*, b. 22 Sep. 1823, d. 3 Oct. 1823; *Alanson La Fayette*, b. 15 Oct. 1824, d. 11 Aug. 1830; *John Fuller*, b. 20 June 1826, rem. to Michigan, where he m. Bethany Bettis in 1858; *Anna Fuller*, b. 19 May 1828, m. Sylvanus M. Danforth of Springf. 5 Feb. 1851; *William*, b. 31 Oct. 1829, d. unm. 27 Mar. 1881; *Sarah Blair*, b. 12 Nov. 1832, m. Moses T. Marsh, pub. 30 Mar. 1854; *Augusta Maria*, b. 20 May 1835, m. Sardius J. Sibley 13 Nov. 1856; *Abby Jane*, b. 23 June 1838, m. Elijah F. Tucker of Ware, pub. 19 Feb. 1856. ISAIAH the f. was b. at Gr. 26 July 1799, was a farmer, res. on the Ware road, at the place erroneously marked "T. Newcomb" on the R. Map, and d. 23 July 1868, a. 69; his w. Lucina d. 25 Oct. 1873, a. 72.

9. ANSON FOSTER, s. of Foster (6), m. Maria F. Richards, and had *Charles Anson*, b. 2 Oct. 1864.

HANNAH T., m. Peter A. Joslyn, pub. 31 Oct. 1829. BETHANY, of Enf., m. Bradford Newland, pub. 21 Nov. 1834.

NEWELL, LUCY, of Danvers, m. Jedediah Shurtleff 7 July 1785. WILLIAM, m. Betsey Lawrence, pub. 3 May 1797.

NEWLAND, JEREMIAH, res. in the southwesterly part of the town, and d. 18 Jan. 1821, a. 90. Susanna his wife d. 7 Ap. 1815. No record is found of the birth of his children; but he named in his will, 23 Jan. 1808, five sons: *John*, *Ziba*, *Enos*, *David*, *Masa*, and three daughters, *Experience*, *Lucy* (who d. unm. 10 Dec. 1818, a. 54), and *Matilda* (who d. unm. 9 Jan. 1824, a. 56). The record of their descendants is very defective.

2. ENOS, s. of Jeremiah (1), m. Lucy ——, and had *Enos*, b. about 1799; perhaps *Rachel H.*, b. about 1800, d. unm. 10 Feb. 1822, a. 22; *Lorenzo*, b. about 1810; and prob. others. ENOS the f. was a deacon of the Baptist Church, and d. 9 Oct. 1830, a. 60; his w. Lucy d. 26 Nov. 1840, a. 67.

3. MASA, s. of Jeremiah (1), m. Nancy Bassett 31 Oct. 1802, and had *Nancy W.*, b. about 1804, d. unm. 28 July 1857, a. 53; and prob. others. MASA the f. d. 7 Aug. 1851, a. 78; his w. Nancy d. 28 July 1854, a. 79.

4. ENOS, s. of Enos (2), m. Sophia Cutler 29 Dec. 1818, and had *Jason*, b. —— 1834, d. 18 Jan. 1835, a. 6 months; and probably others. ENOS the f. d. 26 June 1835, a. 35.

5. VINCENT, m. Betsey Brown 6 Sep. 1820, and had a child who d. 26 Feb. 1823.

6. ARBE D., m. Mary Borden of Belchertown, pub. 7 Sep. 1833, and had *Benjamin D.*, b. —— 1834, d. 6 (or 11) Ap. 1836, a. about a year and a half; *Mary Ann*, b. 31 May 1836, m. Humphrey James, pub. 30 May 1855; *George Masa*, b. 13 Aug. 1837; *Franklin Bassett*, b. 28 Feb. 1839, m. Fanny M. Snow, pub. 31 Jan. 1862; *Phebe Caroline Augusta*, b. 17 Dec. 1843, m. Franklin E. Rogers of Gr. 16 Sep. 1865; *Nancy Ardelia*, b. 2 Sep. 1845; *Lorenzo D.*, b. 28 July 1852.

7. LORENZO, prob. s. of Enos (2), m. Prolexana Sturtevant 22 Ap. 1835, and had *Mary*, b. 26 Sep. 1840; *Elvira*, b. 4 Ap. 1842; *Maria Louisa*, b. 2 Aug. 1844; *Ella*, b. 10 Ap. 1850.

DENCY, m. Ezra Sprout of Gr. 3 Dec. 1818. HIRAM, m. Lucy Brown 30 Mar. 1831. JOHN, m. Melinda Haskins, 31 July 1831. BRADFORD, m. Bethany Newcomb of Enf., pub. 21 Nov. 1834. ANNA D., m. Charles W. Kendall of Athol, pub. 18 Oct. 1867. Mrs. PEDA, d. 2 Mar. 1825, a. 65.

NEWTON, JOSIAH (s. of Moses, who d. at Marlborough 23 May 1736, a. 90, and grandson of Richard, who d. at Marl. 24 Aug. 1701, "almost a hundred years old"), m. *Elizabeth* ——, who d. and he m. Ruhamah ——, about 1730. His chil. were *Elizabeth*,[1] prob. b. about 1716, m. Silas Warren; *Paul*, b. 24 Sep. 1718, d. at Northborough 18 May 1797; *Thankful*, b. —— 1720, m. Stephen Maynard; *Tabitha*, b. 8 Feb. 1721-2, d. 23 Sep. 1728; *Silas*, b. —— 1724; *Mary*, b. —— 1726, said to have d. the same year; but in the division of her father's estate, 12 May 1755, a share was assigned to daughter *Mary*, wife of Asa Brigham; *Timothy*, b. 23 Feb. 1728; *Sarah*, b. 4 Oct. 1731; *Barnabas*, b. 18 Sep. 1733; *Stephen*, b. 3 Sep. 1735, d. 11 Aug. 1751; *Hannah*, b. 17 Feb.

[1] In the division of Deacon Newton's estate, 1755, a share was assigned to *Elizabeth*, wife of Silas Warren, apparently the eldest daughter.

1737, d. young; *John*, b. 15 Feb. 1739, d. young; *Rachel*, b. 21 Feb. 1741; *Lydia*, b. 22 May 1743; *Peter*, b. 9 Oct. 1745, d. 29 July 1751; *Josiah*, b. 9 May 1748. JOSIAH the f., born in Marl., was a tanner, and was elected deacon of the church 8 June 1738. In 1737 he bought for £377, "six tenths of one whole share that is already lotted out, or to be lotted out; there being twelve shares or whole proprietors," in Lambstown, now Hk.; out of which property he gave farms to his sons *Silas* and *Timothy*. He d. 9 Feb. 1755, a. about 67, leaving what was then a large estate, valued at £1,282. 4*s*. 7*d*.; his w. Ruhamah survived.

2. SILAS, s. of Josiah (1), m. Mercy, dau. of Deac. John Freeman, 9 Nov. 1749, and had *Lemuel*, b. 16 Feb. 1750–1; *Stephen*, b. 28 June 1754; *Susanna*, b. 7 Aug. 1761, m. Frederick Wicker 24 June 1784. SILAS the f. was a farmer, and prob. res. near the road to Enfield, about three and a half miles from the Common, at the place marked "S. Newton" on the R. Map. He was clerk of a company in the French War, 1757. He d. 7 Dec. 1763, at the early age of 39; his w. Mercy m. Leonard Robinson of Bennington 13 Mar. 1766 (and had son Samuel Leonard Robinson, b. 1767, d. here 18 Jan. 1863, a. nearly 96); she found her second marriage relation unpleasant, and ret. to Hk., res. with her s. *Lemuel*, and d. 24 Nov. 1814, a. 82.

3. TIMOTHY, s. of Josiah (1), m. Sarah, dau. of Capt. Constant Merrick, 5 July 1751, and had *John*, b. 12 Aug. 1753; *Timothy*, b. 1 Sep. 1755; *Elizabeth*, b. 26 Nov. 1757, m. Thomas Martin Wright 19 Dec. 1776; *Gideon*, b. 6 June 1760; *Sarah*, b. 11 Mar. 1763, m. Asa Brigham of Barnard, Vt., 25 Dec. 1783 (these five chil. rem. to Barnard); *Silas*, b. 11 Feb. 1766; *Josiah*, b. 21 Sep. 1768; *Chloe*, b. 15 Nov. 1771, m. Samuel Chamberlin of Pet. 15 Jan. 1804. TIMOTHY the f. was a farmer, and res. on the road to Barre, at the place marked "Mr. Lincoln" on the R. Map. He was clerk of Capt. Mandell's company in the French War, 1756, and afterwards ensign; he was also selectman three years, and d. 10 July 1811, a. 83; his w. Sarah d. 23 Nov. 1803, a. 71.

4. LEMUEL, s. of Silas (2), m. Chloe Hitchcock 12 June 1777; no record is found of the birth of his children; but some of their names are gleaned from other sources; *Betsey*, b. about 1778, d. unm. 23 Ap. 1854, a. 76; *Tabitha*, b. about 1780, m. Ephraim Bassett 19 Jan. 1804, d. at Enf. 24 Ap. 1865, a. nearly 85; prob. *Prudence*, b. ——, m. Aaron Day of Sutton, 19 Jan. 1797; prob. *Loesena* (*Lucina?*), b. ——, m. Lemuel Cobb, Jr., 2 June 1803; *Chloe*, b. —— 1785, d. 7 Feb. 1796, a. 10 years and 2 months; *Silas*, b. about 1788; *Anson*, b. —— 1793, d. 10 Feb. 1796, a. nearly 3. LEMUEL the f. was a farmer, res. on the supposed homestead, and d. 22 Oct. 1837, a. 86; his w. Chloe d. 26 Nov. 1843, a. 92.

5. JOHN, s. of Timothy (3), m. Lydia, dau. of Thomas Freeman, 15 Jan. 1778, rem. with him to Barnard, Vt., at the commencement of the settlement of that town, was taken prisoner, 9 Aug. 1780, by the Indians, and carried to Canada, where he was detained until the next spring, when he escaped and returned to his family, after suffering great hardship. His chil. were *Polly*, b. 9 Oct. 1778, d. 19 Oct. 1790; *Timothy*, b. 26 Jan. 1780; *Sally*, b. 14 Nov. 1781; *John*, b. 18 Aug. 1783; *Asa*, b. 27 Aug. 1785; *Nancy*, b. 5 July 1788; *Phebe*, b. 18 Feb. 1790; *Hannah*, prob. b. —— 1792, d. 29 Aug. 1795; *Polly*, b. 12 Ap. 1794; *Lydia*, b. 6 June 1796. JOHN the f. prob. m. for second wife widow Hannah Kenney 25 Nov. 1813, and was living in 1824.

6. TIMOTHY, s. of Timothy (3), settled in Barnard, where, by w. Nabby, he had *Josiah*, b. 5 Mar. 1784; *Earl*, b. 6 Mar. 1787; *Luthera*, b. 27 Oct. 1791.

7. GIDEON, s. of Timothy (3), settled in Barnard, where he m. Betsey Spooner 11 Oct. 1787, and had *Fanny*, b. 28 Oct. 1788; *Anson*, b. 9 Nov. 1790.

8. SILAS, s. of Timothy (3), m. Naomi, dau. of Eliphalet Washburn, 9 Ap. 1789, and had *Gardner*, b. 9 Oct. 1789; *Lucetta*, b. 2 Jan. 1792, m. Simeon Knowles 14 Mar. 1814; *Clarinda*, b. 11 Sep. 1794, d. unm. 9 Feb. 1865; *Laura*, b. 3 Feb. 1796, m. Orsamus Hunt 7 Jan. 1821; *Rufus Washburn*, b. 27 Mar. 1798, a carpenter, d. in Worc. 18 Sep. 1861; *Merrick*, b. 21 May 1801; *Caro-*

line, b. 23 Oct. 1803; *Silas Wesson*, b. 29 Dec. 1805; *John Calvin*, b. 19 Aug. 1810, and settled in Worcester. SILAS the f. was a farmer, and for some years after the death of Mr. Mead was the principal grave-digger. He res. on the homestead until 1817, and afterwards about a hundred rods farther eastward, at the place marked "S. Newton" on the R. Map. He d. 19 or 21 Oct. 1847, a. 81; his w. Naomi d. 15 Mar. 1850, a. 79.

9. JOSIAH, s. of Timothy (3), m. Philena, dau. of Capt. Benjamin Cox of Barnard, pub. 29 Nov. 1792, and had *Franklin*, b. 19 Oct. 1796; *Lurenza*, b. 20 Feb. 1799; *Warren*, b. 3 Oct. 1801, d. at Petersham 2 July 1878; *Philena*, b. 9 Jan. 1809. JOSIAH the f. res. on the easterly part of the homestead, at the place marked "J. Knowlton" on the R. Map; but at some time after 1809 rem. to Petersham, where he d. 5 May 1858, a. nearly 90.

10. SILAS, s. of Lemuel (4), m. Bathsheba C., dau. of Eleazar Dexter, 21 June 1810, and had *Elvira Augusta*, bap. 27 Oct. 1811, d. 28 Dec. 1812; *Stephen Dexter*, bap. 14 Ap. 1814, d. 12 Sep. 1837; *Benjamin D.*, b. about 1816, d. 7 Nov. 1837, a. 21; *Susanna Freeman*, bap. 29 Oct. 1819, m. Calvin H. Bassett of Enf. 6 Dec. 1854; *Elivira A.*, bap. 12 May 1822, m. James F. Giffin of Ware, 12 Dec. 1848; *Stephen E.*, b. about 1826. SILAS the f. res. on the homestead, and d. 22 Feb 1873, a. nearly 85; his w. Bathsheba d. 29 Sep. 1855, a. 66.

11. GARDNER, s. of Silas (8), m. Charity W., dau. of Eleazer Dexter, pub. 17 Sep. 1827, and had *Luke*, b. 12 Sep. 1829, d. 3 Sep. 1858; *John*, b. 28 Mar. 1833, d. 5 Mar. 1866; *Charles*, b. 28 Mar. 1837, m. Mary D. Sturtevant 14 Mar. 1861, d. in Pelh. 9 Ap. 1862, and was buried in Hk.; his w. Mary D. m. John S. Kelmer, pub. 5 Oct. 1863. GARDNER the f. d. 23 Mar. 1864.

12. STEPHEN E., s. of Silas (10), m. Thirza L. Peirce 27 Dec. 1849, and had *Amy Levina*, b. 6 June 1851, m. —— Richardson, and d. 20 July 1881; *Rollin D.*, b. —— 1857, m. Leora A. Johnson 3 Mar. 1881; still-born child, 25 Sep. 1854; *William Arthur*, b. 14 July 1859; *Lewis Edgar*, b. 25 Aug. 1867.

13. WILLIAM ARTHUR, s. of Stephen E. (12), m. Eliza A. Giffin 8 Dec. 1875, and had *Ethelle Elvira*, b. 18 June 1876. If the dates be correct, he was married before he was seventeen years old.

14. OLIVER, parentage not ascertained, by w. Elizabeth, had *Electa*, bap. 12 Nov. 1775.

15. REUBEN (then of Pet.), m. Hannah Freeman 18 Feb. 1800; she d. 17 Jan. 1812, a. 33, and he m. Prudence ——; his chil. b. here were a child who d. 25 Sep. 1802; *William*, b. about 1812. d. 9 Aug. 1818, a. 6; *Elijah C.*, b. about 1815. REUBEN the f. d. 12 Aug. 1817, a. 38.

16. ELIJAH C., s. of Reuben (15), m. Harriet Stedman 16 Nov. 1848, and had *Albert Eastman*, b. 20 Nov. 1851; *Samuel Elijah*, b. 3 June 1856, d. 18 May 1857; *Freddie Lincoln*, b. 25 July 1860, d. 17 Aug. 1862; *Harriet Jane*, b. 19 June 1863, m. Dwight F. Howard 15 Jan. 1883.

17. EPHRAIM, by w. Polly, had *Mary S.*, b. about 1821, m. Almon Snow 31 Dec. 1845; *Harmon*, b. about 1831, a soldier in the War of the Rebellion, d. at Washington, D. C., 18 Sep. 1864, a. 33.

ZACHARIAH, m. Hannah Goodnow, pub. 25 Nov. 1766. HANNAH E., m. Ebenezer T. Fox, 29 June 1834. POLLY M., m. Horace Barnes of Gr., pub. 7 Mar. 1837. ELIZABETH, widow of Davis Newton, d. 1 Jan. 1837, a. 81.

NEYLON, MICHAEL, m. Johanna Carney, pub. 3 Ap. 1864, and had *Margaret*, b. 22 Dec. 1866; *John D.*, b. 7 Dec. 1868; *William*, b. 5 Feb. 1871; *Joseph*, b. 18 Jan. 1873; *Francis Martin*, b. 22 Jan, 1877; *Michael Edward*, b. 23 June 1880.

2. JOHN, m. Catherine Hogan of Springf., pub. 27 Dec. 1867, and had *Michael Joseph*, b. 12 Dec. 1868.

NICHOLS, JACOB, by w. Elizabeth, had *Joseph*, bap. 23 Mar. 1739–40; *Benjamin*, bap. 20 Dec. 1741; *Jesse*, bap. 27 Nov. 1743; *Elijah*, bap. 5 Mar. 1748–9.

2. JACOB, by w. Almira, had *Eda Bell*, b. — Mar. 1872; *Walter J.*, b. 2 Jan. 1876, d. 16 Ap. 1876.

TIMOTHY, m. Joanna Dean 13 Jan. 1774. SUSANNA, w. of John, d. 9 Oct. 1796, a. 19. STEPHEN, d. 24 Sep. 1879, a. nearly 90.

NORRIS, RICHARD, by w. ——, had *John*, b. ——; *Patrick*, b. ——. RICHARD the f. d. 28 Aug. 1879, a. 70.

2. JOHN, s. of Richard (1), m. Mary Flynn, pub. 17 Dec. 1864, and had *Richard*, b. 8 Jan. 1866; *Mary S.*, b. 24 Jan. 1867.

3. PATRICK, s. of Richard (1), m. Bridget Sullivan 1 Jan. 1876, and had *Richard E.*, b. 20 Jan. 1880.

NURSE, CALEB, of Barre, m. Polly Fletcher, pub. 12 Feb. 1809.

BENJAMIN, d. 5 Nov. 1812, a. 81; and his w. LUCY, d. 14 Oct. 1809, a. 70.

NYE, BENJAMIN, was in Sandwich as early as 1637, m. Catherine Tupper 19 Oct. 1640, and had *John*; *Ebenezer*; *Jonathan*, b. 29 Nov. 1649; *Mercy*, b. —— 1652; *Caleb*; *Mary*; *Benjamin*; *Timothy*.

2. JONATHAN, s. of Benjamin (1), m. Hannah ——, by whom he had two chil., and (2d) Patience Burgess, by whom he had nine chil., one of whom was *Jonathan*, b. — Nov. 1691.

3. CALEB, s. of Benjamin (1), by w. Elizabeth, had *Elizabeth* and *Hannah*, twins, b. —— 1697; and prob. *Caleb*.

4. JONATHAN, s. of Jonathan (2), m. Deborah Blackwell 7 Feb. 1723; she d. ——, and he m. Remember or Remembrance ——, who survived him. His chil. were *Thomas*, b. —— 1726; *Hannah*, b. —— 1728; *Jonathan*, b. 23 Ap. 1731; *Joshua*, b. —— 1733.[1] JONATHAN the f. rem. to Hardwick about 1762. He prob. d. in 1770, as his will, dated 1 June 1761, at Sandwich, was proved as the last will of Jonathan Nye of Hardwick, 18 Sep. 1770.

5. CALEB, prob. s. of Caleb (3), m. Hannah Bodfish and had, at Sandwich, *Silas*, b. 27 Dec. 1732; *Joseph* and *Benjamin*, twins, b. 18 Ap. 1735. He had also *Simeon*, *Caleb*, *Ebenezer*, *Hannah* (who m. Benjamin Robinson 3 Nov. 1768), *Azubah* (who m. Jonathan Glazier 23 June 1774), and *Prince*, b. about 1752. CALEB the f. rem. from Sandwich to Hardwick, and prob. res. about a mile northerly from the Old Furnace, at the place marked "M. Nye" on the R. Map. His will, dated at Hk. 13 Dec. 1775, and proved 5 June 1787, names w. Hannah (who d. 7 Mar. 1779, a. 68), and the nine children before mentioned; and the homestead was bequeathed to his son *Prince*. His w. Hannah d. 7 Mar. 1779, a. 68, and he added a codicil to his will, 7 June 1781, distributing several articles of furniture inherited from his "honored mother-in-law, Lydia Bodfish of Sandwich."

6. JONATHAN, s. of Jonathan (4), m. Rebecca, dau. of William Freeman of Sandwich, 18 Mar. 1756 (she was sister of Thomas Freeman and of Joanna, w. of Nathaniel Paige, both of whom res. in Hk.). His chil. born here were *Oliver*, bap. 4 Ap. 1762; *Mary*, bap. 5 Aug. 1764, m. Nathaniel Johnson, Jr., 5 Sep. 1783; *Hannah*, bap. 12 Oct. 1766, m. Silas Johnson, Jr., 15 Dec. 1785; *Rebecca*, bap. 28 Jan. 1770; *Jonathan*, b. 12 Feb. 1773; *Thomas*, b. 13 Aug. 1776; and perhaps he had one or more others before he left Sandwich, about 1762.

7. JOSHUA, s. of Jonathan (4), by w. ——, had *Lydia*, bap. 18 May 1766; *Sarah*, bap. 17 Ap. 1768; *Joshua*, bap. 26 Jan. 1770.

8. SILAS, s. of Caleb (5), m. Patience, dau. of Nathan Carpenter, 27 Nov. 1766, and had *Sarah*, b. 13 Jan. 1768; *Hannah*, b. 22 Nov. 1769. No further trace found.

9. JOSEPH, s. of Caleb (5), m. Thankful ——, who d. 19 Feb. 1768, in childbed, and he m. Patience, dau. of James Robinson, pub. 14 Ap. 1771. His chil. were *Caleb*, b. 27 Sep. 1758, d. 8 Oct. 1758; *Jemima*, b. 28 Sep. 1759, m. Gamaliel Ellis 21 Feb. 1782; *Meribah*, b. 27 Oct. 1761, m. Stephen Chandler 23 May 1782; *Thankful*, b. 10 Feb. 1764, m. William Davis 5 July 1787; *Mary*, b. 18 Jan. 1766, d. 21 Feb. 1767; *Joseph*, b. 5 Feb. 1768; also, by second wife, and named in his will, dated 14 May 1806, *Elizabeth*, b. ——, m. Levi Robinson of Barre 20 Sep. 1798; *Mary*, b. about 1773, m. William Woods 15 Nov.

[1] The early residence of this family was in Sandwich, and, thus far, for most of the names and dates, I am indebted to the Rev. Frederick Freeman of that town.

1798, and d. at Pelham 19 Feb. 1855, a. 81; *Hannah*, m. William Merrick 15 Nov. 1798, who d. early in 1803, and she m. Aldrich Worley of Boston, pub. 8 July 1805; *Stephen*, b. about 1778; *Lucinda*, b. ——, m. Delano Witherell 10 July 1804, and d. before the date of her father's will, 14 May 1806; *Zenas*, b. ——. JOSEPH the f. d. 21 May 1806, a. 71.

10. SIMEON, s. of Caleb (5), by w. Alice, had *Bathsheba*, b. 10 Dec. 1769, m. Elijah Robinson of Barre, pub. 31 May 1786, and d. 21 Oct. 1843; *Alice*, b. 11 Oct. 1771, m. Francis Jenks 28 July 1793; *John Ruggles*, b. 27 June 1776; *Hannah*, b. 10 July 1779; *Keziah*, b. 27 May 1784, m. Isaac Atwood, and d. 9 Oct. 1861.

11. CALEB, s. of Caleb (5), m. Abigail Goodspeed of Barnstable, pub. 24 Mar. 1771. No record of children. They res. in a house which formerly stood on the easterly road to Gilbertville, about half a mile southerly from the Common, between the places marked "O. Trow" and "J. Mann" on the R. Map. I suppose he lacked energy, as he and his wife in their old age were dependent; but I never heard aught against their moral character; on the contrary, they were "Uncle Caleb" and "Aunt Nabby" to all the neighborhood. Personally, I cherish an affectionate memory of them for their kindness to me in my childhood, when I so often resorted to their fireside to warm myself, being chilled and nearly frozen on my way to and from school. Mr. Nye d. 15 Oct. 1811, a. 69.

12. EBENEZER, s. of Caleb (5), res. in Oakham, and executed a will 5 July 1793, which was proved 3 Sep. 1793; legacies were devised to his wife, and to chil. *Crocker; Temperance*, w. of Jonathan Richardson; *Lucretia*, w. of Alpheus Stone; *Mary*, w. of Bowman Chaddock; *Timothy; Meletiah*, w. of Calvin Chaddock; *Achsah; Salmon; John*.

13. PRINCE, s. of Caleb (5), m. Dinah Joslyn 15 Dec. 1774. No record is found of the birth of their children; but from other records and from his will the following names and dates are gleaned: *Anna*, b. ——, m. Jonathan Makepeace 10 July 1799; *Rufus*, b. about 1778; *Joseph*, b. ——; *Martin*, b. ——; *Marshall*, b. about 1787; *Frances*, b. about 1790, d. unm. 14 Ap. 1820, a. 30; *Sewall*, b. about 1792, d. 13 Nov. 1816, a. 24; *Francis*. PRINCE the f. was a farmer, and inherited the homestead. He was selectman twelve years, between 1793 and 1810. He was very corpulent, and d. suddenly 24 July 1812, a. 59; his w. Dinah d. 9 July 1842, a. 87.

14. STEPHEN, s. of Joseph (9), m. Lois, dau. of Nathaniel Merrick, 10 Jan. 1802, and had *Sarah Ellis Howe*, b. 13 Jan. 1803, m. —— Holbrook, and d. at Holden 23 Dec. 1870; *Elmira Mary Blackmore*, b. 4 Dec. 1805. STEPHEN the f. d. 28 Jan. 1807, a. nearly 29; his w. Lois survived.

15. JOHN RUGGLES, s. of Simeon (10), m. ——, and had a child b. ——, 1802, d. 11 June 1803, a. 1 year and 3 months. He prob. rem. early to Barre, where he d. 12 Ap. 1852.

16. RUFUS, s. of Prince (13), m. Betsey Edson of Oakham, pub. 4 Jan. 1801, and had *Calvin Edson*, b. ——; *Hosea W.*, b. 1804; *Lydia*. RUFUS the f. d. 15 May 1806, a 28; his w. Betsey m. John Bruce of Springf. 19 May 1813.

17. JOSEPH, prob. s. of Prince (13), m. Mary Robinson, pub. 10 Mar. 1805, and had a child d. 2 Feb. 1806, a. 3 months; a child d. 7 Feb. 1807, a. 2 weeks.

18. MARSHALL, s. of Prince (13), m. Polly Whittemore, pub. 29 Nov. 1813, and had *Persis Maria*, b. 10 Nov. 1816, m. Thomas R. Greene of Bel. 9 May 1844, and d. 16 Mar. 1848; *Susan*, b. 1 Mar. 1818, m. William W. Dunbar of Rochester, N. Y., 26 May 1846; *Ann Makepeace*, b. 22 May 1820, m. John D. Dunbar of W. Brk. 26 Dec. 1844; *Marshall Prince*, b. 6 Nov. 1822, m. Sarah P., dau. of Apollos Fay, 16 Nov. 1848; she d. 13 Sep. 1851, a. 24, and he m. Emily Ann, dau. of Hosea W. Nye, 9 Nov. 1852; he res. in Boston; *Sewall*, b. 5 Jan. 1832, m. Mary A. Pike of Pet., pub. 6 Ap. 1855, and res. in Boston. MARSHALL the f. was a farmer and inherited the homestead; he was selectman in 1832, and d. 2 Mar. 1860; his w. Polly rem. to Boston.

19. HOSEA W., s. of Rufus (16), by w. Emily ——, had *Emily Ann*, b.

about 1829, m. Marshall P. Nye, as above, 9 Nov. 1852; *Sarah Elizabeth*, b. about 1838, m. Rufus J. Peirce of N. Br. 16 Ap. 1860; *Charles Bartlett*, b. 3 Aug. 1844; a dau. b. 23 Feb. 1846; *Henry H.*, b. 1 Ap. 1848, d. at Auburn 3 Sep. 1865; *Lisette Frances*, b. 23 May 1850. HOSEA W. the f. d. at Worc. 14 Aug. 1874.

20. SAMUEL, parentage not ascertained, m. Lydia ——; she d. 30 June 1756, and he m. Mehetabel, widow of Cornelius Cannon, 16 Nov. 1756. His chil. were *Ebenezer; Susanna; Ann;* all bap. 16 Sep. 1750; *Lydia*, bap. 16 Sep. 1750, m. Lot Whitcomb 9 Dec. 1762; *Deborah*, bap. 16 Sep. 1750, m. Joseph Chamberlin of Pet. 18 Ap. 1776; *Jabez*, b. 13 June 1749, prob. d. young; *Ichabod*, b. 28 Mar. 1753; *Joseph*, b. 28 Mar. 1755.

21. SPENCER, parentage not ascertained, by w. Sarah B., had *Harry Spencer*, b. 11 Ap. 1870.

JOSEPH, m. Sarah Bradish, 27 Dec. 1764; ISAAC, m. Hannah Walker 29 Nov. 1770; MARY, m. Jonathan Orcutt of Shutes. 17 Aug. 1779. WILLIAM, m. Molly Purington 26 Dec. 1782. MARTHA P., of Barre, m. Elijah Amidon, pub. 18 May 1818. HARRIET, of Springf., m. Thomas Hale, pub. 12 Sep. 1848. ALPHEUS S., of Dana, m. Evelyn Sturtevant, pub. 3 Ap. 1854. CHARLES, d. 14 June 1803, a. 16. HARRIET, d. 5 Oct. 1810, a. 15. BATHSHEBA, widow of Benjamin of Barre, d. 26 July 1865, a. 96.

OAKES, ELEANOR, m. John Jenkins of Ware, pub. 4 Dec. 1785. CALVIN, m. Polly Carey of Ware 26 July 1787. NABBY, m. Levi Town of Gr. 8 Mar. 1790. JOHN, m. Polly Marsh, pub. 14 July 1793. LORINDA, of N. Sal., m. Luman Chase, pub. 27 Ap. 1854.

OLIVER, DANIEL, s. of Lieutenant-Governor Andrew Oliver, b. about 1744, grad. H. C. 1762, rem. from Boston to Hk. soon after 19 May 1767, when he bought of Caleb Benjamin, for £600, a farm of 177 acres, near the Old Furnace, at the place marked "E. Trow" on the R. Map, together with five acres in N. Br., five eighths of a saw-mill and utensils, and a pew in the meeting-house "between the pew of Timothy Ruggles, Esq., and Nathaniel Whitcomb." He was a barrister at law, and probably established himself here under the auspices of General Ruggles, to whose fortunes he constantly adhered. He was active in town affairs, and was representative in 1770. At the commencement of hostilities in the Revolution, he left town, and his estate was confiscated. He d. at Ashstead, Warwickshire, Eng., 6 May 1826, a. 82. No record is found of wife or chil. here.

2. WILLIAM, of Middleborough, "gentleman," perhaps s. of Chief Justice Peter Oliver, and, if so, cousin of Daniel (1), bought of Thomas Freeman 68 acres of land, formerly the homestead of Doctor Jedediah Rice, about midway between the places marked "M. Mandell" and "A. Ruggles," on the R. Map. This estate, which he purchased 12 Sep. 1767, he sold to Joseph Washburn 3 July 1770. He m. Sarah Fuller of Middleborough, pub. 25 Feb. 1770, and prob. left town before the end of that year.

3. THOMAS, a negro, perhaps brought here by Daniel (1), or William (2), as a hired servant, or possibly as a slave, d. 15 Oct. 1820, a. 71. No further trace of him appears on record.

4. NATHANIEL, prob. s. of Thomas (3), m. Lucia Bridges of N. Br., pub. 28 Dec. 1812; m. (2d) Esther Green of N. Br., pub. 24 July 1830; m. (3d) Mrs. Mary Freeman, "colored," 26 Ap. 1843; and d. 12 Feb. 1851, a. 74. He res. many years on the Petersham road, at the place marked "L. P." on the R. Map. *Nathaniel* 2d, who m. Mary H. Saunders of Boston, pub. 18 Dec. 1846, was perhaps his son.

ELIZABETH, m. Peter Newport of Hatfield, pub. 23 May 1779. SIMON, of Barre, m. Mary Morgan 24 July 1785. SUSANNA, m. Timothy Paine, "colored," of Boston, pub. 24 Ap. 1822. JUDITH, m. Luther Barber of Hartford, Conn., 25 Ap. 1824.

OLMSTEAD, JABEZ, of Brookfield, m. Thankful, dau. of Thomas Barnes, and had *Thankful*, b. 15 Feb, 1712-13, perhaps the same who m. Joseph Macmitchell 21 Jan. 1756; *Jeremiah*, b. 6 Jan. 1714-15; *Israel*, b. 24 Mar. 1716; *Hannah*, b. 22 Ap. 1718, m. Judah Marsh 4 Nov. 1736; *Martha*, b. 16 Sep.

1721, m. Thomas Hammond 21 Aug. 1741; *Dorcas*, b. 15 Ap. 1724, m. Benoni Walcott 13 Oct. 1741; *Sarah*, b. 24 May 1726, m. Ephraim Marsh 8 Oct. 1741; *Silence*, b. 30 Oct. 1728; *Abigail*, b. 24 Mar. 1731; *Prudence*, b. 28 Oct. 1733; *Moses*, b. 29 Jan. 1736. All these births and marriages are recorded in Brookfield. JABEZ the f. is supposed to have removed into the territory which afterwards became a part of Ware about 1729, "and to have made the first permanent settlement" there, and erected a house in the village, near the present location of the Bank, which was standing in 1821. "Tradition represents Capt. Olmstead to have been a man of great shrewdness and energy, and that Indian blood ran in his veins. He was a mighty hunter, and is said to have been an officer in the expedition against Louisbourg, upon the island of Cape Breton, in 1745."[1]

2. ISRAEL, s. of Jabez (1), m. Sarah Banister 12 May 1737; she d. ——, and he m. Anna Safford 25 Nov. 1756. Two of his chil. were bap. here, — *Joseph*, 28 Ap. 1751; *Israel*, 4 June 1758. ISRAEL the f. was a soldier in the French War, and prob. rem. to Warwick about 1761.

3. MOSES, s. of Jabez (1), by w. Abigail, had *Jabez*, b. 4 June 1760; *Moses*, b. 20 June 1762.

ORCUTT, ALMON M., m. Mary Ann, dau. of Theophilus Knight, 16 Oct. 1850, and had *Lucretia W.*, b. 31 Dec. 1851, m. Charles J. Kellogg of Orange 20 Jan. 1874; *Effie Miner*, b. 11 Dec. 1853, d. 24 May 1857; *Robert Bliss*, b. 27 Mar. 1861, d. 31 July 1862; *Emeline Babcock*, b. 9 Jan. 1863; *May Mitchell*, b. 25 Nov. 1870. ALMON M. the f. was b. in Cummington, and established himself here, as a physician, soon after the death of Dr. Joseph Stone in 1849; he still continues in a very successful practice. He was town clerk in 1858, representative in 1874, and has served the town several years as treasurer, collector, and a member of the school committee. He res. near the south end of the Common.

JONATHAN, of Shutesbury, m. Mary Nye 17 Aug. 1779. SOPHIA, of Templeton, m. Charles C. Chamberlain, pub. 21 Aug. 1808. CLAUDIUS B., of Amh., m. Mary G. Ellis 5 Nov. 1839. Widow ALICE, of Athol, d. 8 Aug. 1842, a. 70.

OSBORN, LEVI G., m. Candace Rawson of Orange, pub. 4 Feb. 1847, and had *Levi Arthur*, b. 31 Aug. 1859.

POLLY, m. Benjamin Sumner 10 Oct. 1816.

PACKARD, ELEAZAR, had w. Mercy, who was adm. to the church, by letter, 3 July 1768; she d. ——, and he m. Mary Woodbury 9 June 1769. Two of his chil. were *Daniel*, bap. 28 July 1765; *Mercy*, bap. 31 Oct. 1768.

LEAH, of Bel., m. Apollos Snow, pub. 14 July 1794. ALVAH, m. Fanny Fisk 4 Dec. 1820.

PADDLEFORD, JONATHAN (otherwise written Paddlefoot, Padlefoote, Padlfoote, and recently Padelford), m. Mary Blanford 5 Oct. 1652, and had *Jonathan*, b. 6 July, and d. 29 Oct. 1653; *Mary*, b. 22 Aug. 1654; *Jonathan*, b. 13 Aug. 1656; *Zechariah*, b. 16 Dec. 1657, d. in Framingham 7 July 1737; *Edward*, b. 14 June 1660, "slayn in the wars." JONATHAN the f. res. in Cambridge, and d. in 1661; his w. Mary m. Thomas Eames, rem. to Sudbury, and thence to Framingham, where she had five chil., and was killed by the Indians 1 Feb. 1675-6.

2. JONATHAN, s. of Jonathan (1), m. Hannah Flint of Braintree, had only child *Jonathan*, b. at Br. 1679; he afterwards rem. to Taunton, and d. there in 1710.

3. JONATHAN, s. of Jonathan (2), res. in Taunton, where, by w. Hannah, he had *Jonathan*, b. —— 1708, d. —— 1750; *Zechariah*, b. —— 1710, d. —— 1765; *Edward*, b. —— 1712, d. —— 1800; *Hannah*, b. —— 1715; *John*, b. —— 1720, d. —— 1758; *Philip*, b. —— 1722; *Peleg*, b. —— 1728, d. —— 1812; *Judith*, b. —— 1730; *Sarah*, b. —— 1732; *Abigail*, b. —— 1734.

4. JOHN, s. of Jonathan (3), res. in Taunton, and by w. Jemima had *John*, b. —— 1748; *Seth*, b. —— 1751; *Jemima*, b. —— 1755, m. —— Hewitt.

[1] Hyde's *Address, delivered at the Opening of the New Town Hall, Ware, Mass., March* 31, 1847, pp. 46, 47.

5. JOHN, s. of John (4), m. Bathsheba, dau. of Dr. Tobey of New Bedford, and had *Sophia*, b. 22 Feb. 1770, m. Benjamin Cooper; *John*, b. 6 Aug. 1771 (by w. Mary had six sons, of whom the youngest, Seth, b. —— 1807, was a merchant in Providence, Governor of Rhode Island, and d. 26 Aug. 1878; *Elisha*, b. 19 Dec. 1772, "left his widowed mother, a poor boy, to seek his living; shipped as cabin boy, and went to France; worked his way, by studious and honorable habits, up to a lieutenancy in the French navy, and d. in that service;" *Harriet*, b. 13 Oct. 1774, m. Capt. Nathaniel Crane; *William*, b. 28 May 1776; *Joseph*, b. —— 1778. JOHN the f., b. —— 1748, grad. Y. C. 1768, studied medicine with Dr. Tobey of New Bedford, and commenced practice in Hk., where all his chil. were born, except *Joseph*, and where he was an active patriot at the commencement of the Revolutionary War. He res. at the place marked "Mr. Wesson" on the R. Map. He "was skilful in his profession, entered the navy as a surgeon, was taken prisoner, and d. at St. Eustasie, 1779, when about to be exchanged. . . . He was a man of vigorous intellect, upright morals, and profound patriotism." [1]

6. SETH, s. of John (4), b. —— 1751, grad. Y. C. 1770, and received the degree of LL. D. from B. U. 1798. He commenced the practice of the law in Hk., where he was a member of the Committee of Correspondence in 1774 and 1775, and generally active in the Revolutionary struggle. He rem. to Taunton about 1778, was judge of probate, and, though not eminent as an advocate, was confessedly at the head of the bar as a counsellor. He m. Rebecca Dennis, had four sons and seven daughters, and d. of apoplexy 7 Jan. 1810.

PAIGE, NATHANIEL, m. Joanna ——, and had *Nathaniel*, b. about 1679; *Elizabeth*, b. prob. about 1681, m. John Simpkins of Boston 28 Dec. 1698, had three children, and prob. d. before 1735, when her husband sold her paternal inheritance, and her concurrence in the sale does not appear in the deed; *Sarah*, b. prob. about 1683, m. Samuel Hill, Jr., of Billerica, 7 Jan. 1698–9, had six children, and d. 30 Ap. 1758 (her only son, Samuel, m. widow Abigail Dunton, dau. of Thomas Richardson, and d. 26 Jan. 1748–9, leaving only one child, Abiel or Abigail, who m. Samuel Kidder); *James*, bap. at Roxbury 28 Nov. 1686, d. 31 July 1687; *Christopher*, b. at Billerica (now Bedford), 6 Feb. 1690–1. NATHANIEL the f. is supposed to have come from England to Roxbury about 1685, with w. and three children. The earliest trace which I have found of his presence in New England is contained in his deposition recorded with Suffolk Deeds (xiii. 470), that on the 10th of March 1685–6 he saw Joseph Dudley, Esq., take peaceable possession of certain real estate in Billerica on behalf of "Daniel Cox of Aldersgate Street, London." On the organization of the government, 2 June 1686, after the abrogation of the first Charter, he was appointed by President Joseph Dudley one of the two marshals (equivalent to sheriffs) of Suffolk County; and it was "ordered that the President have an honorable maintenance when 'tis known how the revenue will arise, and that Mr. Paige have five pounds a quarter for his attendance on the President." [2] He was also licensed by the County Court of Suffolk, 2 Aug. 1686, as an innholder in Roxbury. He was one of the eight original purchasers [3] from the Indian sachems 27 Dec. 1686, of the territory now embraced in the town of Hardwick. See chap. ii. pp. 15–17. A month afterwards, 27 Jan. 1686–7, the same persons, together with Ralph Bradhurst, in like manner bought the territory which is now embraced in the towns of Leicester and Spencer. These purchases, however, were merely speculative, from which no pecuniary benefit resulted for many years. For immediate use, Mr. Paige bought of George Grimes, 1 Mar. 1687–8, a farm of 250 acres in that part of Billerica which is now the easterly portion of Bedford, where he resided during the remainder of his life. His inventory in-

[1] See chart of the "Descendants of Jonathan Padelford" by S. C. Newman, 1859, in the library of the N. Eng. Hist. Gen. Society, from which the foregoing quotations are made.

[2] Council Records.

[3] The eight purchasers were Joshua Lamb, Nathaniel Paige, Andrew Gardner, Benjamin Gamblin, Benjamin Tucker, John Curtis, Richard Draper, and Samuel Ruggles, all of Roxbury.

dicates that he was a prosperous farmer, as the value of his farm had more than doubled during the four years of his ownership, and it was abundantly stocked with horses, neat cattle, sheep, swine, and farming tools; and among his possessions was also a "servant man" valued at fifteen pounds. His real estate at Billerica and the wild lands near Quabaog and Worcester he devised to his two sons (a double portion to the elder, as was then customary), and 200 acres of land in Dedham, near Neponset Bridge, which he bought of the Indians in 1687, to his two daughters, in equal shares. Whether he was in Boston on business, on a visit, or for medical aid, does not appear; but he died there on the 12th of April 1692, as the Billerica records show. His last will, dated on the day next preceding his decease, and describing him as "of Bilrekey in the County of Middlesex, New England, yeoman, being sick and weak of body," is signed "Natt Paige;" and the signature is unusually plain and distinct, indicating a remarkable steadiness of nerve so near the close of life. His w. Joanna probably died in 1724, as on the fourth day of July in that year her sons divided the real estate in which she had dower under the provisions of their father's will.

2. NATHANIEL, s. of Nathaniel (1), m. Susanna, dau. of Maj. John Lane of Billerica, and grand-daughter of Job Lane of Malden, 6 Nov. 1701; she d. 2 Sep. 1746, a. 63, and he m. Mrs. Mary Grimes, who long survived him. His chil. were *Nathaniel*, b. 4 Sep. 1702; *John*, b. 11 Oct. 1704; *Christopher*, b. 16 July 1707; *Susanna*, b. 29 Ap. 1711, m. Samuel Bridge of Lexington 9 Ap. 1734, and had son Samuel, b. 6 Jan. 1735; she d. 16 Jan. 1735; *Joanna*, b. 29 Oct. 1714, m. Josiah Fassett 14 Ap. 1747. NATHANIEL the f. was a farmer, cornet of a company of cavalry, selectman, and a prominent manager of affairs in Billerica, and in Bedford after the incorporation of that town, where he d. 2 Mar. 1755, a. 75; his head-stone, on which his name is erroneously spelled PAGE, is still standing in the cemetery near the Common. In his will, dated 1 June 1748, he devised his homestead to his son Christopher, 200 acres of land in Hardwick to his grandson Samuel Bridge, £350, old tenor, to his dau. Joanna Fassett, and the remainder to his three sons; and he directed that his chil. *John*, *Christopher*, and *Joanna*, and his grandson *Samuel Bridge*, on penalty of forfeiting £60 each, should release to his eldest son *Nathaniel*, all "right to the estate in Old England, which belonged to their mother Susanna Paige late of Bedford, deceased."[1] He appointed his three sons as executors of his will, who wrote their name PAIGE on their bond of administration in 1755; later in life they changed the orthography, and wrote it PAGE, and the larger portion of their descendants have perpetuated the error.

3. CHRISTOPHER, s. of Nathaniel (1), m. Joanna ——; she d. 27 Oct. 1719, and he m. Elizabeth, dau. of Deac. George Reed[2] of Woburn, 23 May 1720. His chil. were *Joanna*, b. 10 Aug. 1717, m. Benjamin Farley of Bedford, and

[1] This estate was probably in Yorkshire. Job Lane of Malden, in his will dated 28 Dec. 1696, devised to his son John "all the land I have in England, in Yorkshire, to him and his heirs forever." When the estate of Maj. John Lane of Billerica was divided, 26 Mar. 1718, it was agreed that the English estate should be shared by all his children, namely, *Job*, *John*, *James*, *Susanna*, w. of Nathaniel Paige; *Mary*, w. of John Whitmore; and *Martha*, w. of James Minott; the eldest son to take a double portion. Nathaniel Paige, son of Susanna, devised to his son Thomas, in 1772, "my estate in Old England." The same property is mentioned in the settlement of estates for a few years afterwards, and then disappears. There is a tradition, in various forms, and in several branches of the family, that the change of name from PAIGE to PAGE prevented the heirs from obtaining possession of the estate.

[2] Deacon George Reed, of that part of Woburn which is now Burlington, b. 14 Sep. 1660, and d. 20 Jan. 1756, was son of George Reed, who was b. in England about 1629, and d. at Woburn 21 Feb. 1705–6, and grandson of William Reed who m. Mabel Kendall and came from England in 1635, with wife and three children; res. successively at Dorchester, Scituate, Boston, and Woburn; returned to England, leaving his three elder children here, and d. at Newcastle-upon-Tyne, in 1656, a. about 69. His w. Mabel, with her younger children, again crossed the ocean, m. Henry Summers of Woburn 21 Nov. 1660, and after his death res. with her son George until 15 June 1690, when she d. a. 85. For a more full account, see *History of the Reed Family*, by Jacob W. Reed, pp. 61–150.

was living in 1770 (her dau. Joanna was b. at Bedford 22 Ap. 1733; and her son Benjamin was drowned in returning from Crown Point, during the French War); *Christopher*, b. 11 June 1721; *William*, b. 2 May 1723; *George*, b. 17 June 1725; *Timothy*, b. 24 May 1727; *Jonas*, b. 19 Sep. 1729 (he was early crossed in love, which partially unsettled his mind; he served in at least five campaigns during the French War, and was living, unm., in 1792); *Elizabeth*, b. 3 Oct. 1731, d. young; *Lucy*, b. 22 Feb. 1733–4, m. Seth Lincoln of Western (now Warren) 10 Oct. 1751 (he died in 1793, and she m. —— Tyler, and d. 1 Sep. 1821); *Nathaniel*, b. 12 May 1736; *John*, b. 6 July 1738; *Elizabeth*, b. 7 June 1743, m. Solomon Green, 29 Dec. 1763 (one of her eight children was Rev. Archelaus Green, a Universalist clergyman, who was b. 16 July 1770, and d. at Virgil, N. Y., 25 Dec. 1843). CHRISTOPHER the f. was a farmer and joiner, and res. on the easterly road to Gilbertville, at the place marked "A. Warner" on the R. Map. He came here from Bedford prob. early in 1735, and was very active in the management of the common property of the "Proprietors," and in the organization of the township and of the church. He was frequently the agent of the inhabitants or "settlers" to transact their business with the proprietors, while their meetings were held at Roxbury, and with the General Court at Boston, notably in their final and successful effort to obtain incorporation as a town. He was moderator of the first town-meeting in 1739, selectman seven years, and assessor five years. He was also moderator of all the meetings of the proprietors held in Hardwick until 1761; and compensation was granted to him 16 May 1757, "for service done the proprietors as their agent to the General Court." At the organization of the church, 17 Nov. 1736, his name stands first on the list of members; and he was elected, 3 Dec. 1736, as its first deacon. This office he resigned, 13 April 1749 (and prob. his membership also), and became a member of the church in Nitchawaug, now Petersham. This caused a breach between the two churches, which was not healed for about twenty years. He d. 10 Mar. 1774; his w. Elizabeth d. in 1786, a. 86. A numerous posterity survived, as appears by an obituary, published in the *Massachusetts Gazette*, 31 Mar. 1774: "At Hardwick, Deacon Christopher Paige, aged 83 years and 21 days, in a comfortable hope of a better life; he left a widow, and has had 12 [1] children, 9 now living and 3 dead, 81 grand-children, 66 living and 15 dead. A funeral sermon was preached by the Rev. Mr. Hutchinson at his funeral, on the Monday following."

4. NATHANIEL, s. of Nathaniel (2), m. Hannah Blanchard, and had *Nathaniel*, b. 22 May 1729, d. unm. 26 Mar. 1751; *Thomas*, b. 5 May 1733, m. Anna Merriam 4 Jan. 1756, and d. s. p. 21 July 1809 (his w. Anna d. in 1810); *Hannah*, b. 15 May 1736, m. Jonas French 5 Jan. 1758; *William*, b. 19 Feb. 1737–8, m. ——, and d. s. p. 10 Feb. 1812; *David*, b. 4 Ap. 1740; *Susanna*, b. 22 Jan. 1742, d. unm. 26 Jan. 1772; *Abigail*, b. 5 Sep. 1745, m. Bowman Brown of Lexington. NATHANIEL the f. res. in Bedford, and d. 6 Ap. 1779; his w. Hannah d. 7 Sep. 1763, a. 59.

5. JOHN, s. of Nathaniel (2), m. Rebecca Wheeler of Concord; she d. 12 July 1755, a. 43, and he m. Amittai, w. of Joseph Fassett of Lex., 15 Jan. 1756; she d. 25 Dec. 1771, and he m. Rachel Fitch 3 June 1773. His chil. were *John*, b. 2 Sep. 1733, *James*, b. 12 May 1735; *Ebenezer*, b. 3 June 1737; *Susanna*, b. 21 Oct. 1739, d. 26 Feb. 1750; *Timothy*, b. 11 June 1741; *Nathaniel*, b. 20 June 1742; *Rebecca*, b. 23 Aug. 1743, m. Solomon Cutler of Lex., and rem. to Rindge, N. H.; *Mary*, b. 5 July 1745, d. 13 Oct. 1745; *Joanna*, b. 15 June 1746, m. Samuel Reed of Woburn 25 July 1771; *Sarah*, b. 8 June 1747, m. Josiah Beard of Billerica; *Elizabeth*, b. 3 Aug. 1748, m. Micah Reed of Woburn 30 April 1772; *Susanna*, b. 12 June 1750, m. Amos Haggett of Concord; *Samuel*, b. 1 Aug. 1751; *Mary*, b. 9 Oct. 1753, d. 21 Oct. 1753. JOHN the f. res. in Bedford, where he d. 18 Feb. 1782; his third w. Rachel d. 16 Jan. 1801, a. 88.

[1] I find the names of only eleven children recorded, — six in Billerica, two in Bedford, after the incorporation of that town, and three in Hardwick; perhaps the first wife, shortly before her death, may have given birth to a child which died before receiving a name.

6. CHRISTOPHER, s. of Nathaniel (2), m. Susanna Webber of Medford, and had *Christopher*, b. 29 Oct. 1743, a captain, res. on the homestead, m. Lydia ——, and d. s. p. about 1828; *Susanna*, b. 17 May 1745, and d. 8 Sep. 1746; *Mary*, b. 20 Feb. 1746–7, m. Deac. Nathan Reed of Lex. 30 Ap. 1772, and d. 17 May 1831; *Job*, b. 31 May 1748, d. 7 Ap. 1754; *Susanna*, b. 7 Ap. 1750, d. 28 Mar. 1754; *Lucy*, b. 26 Mar. 1752, d. 26 Mar. 1754. CHRISTOPHER the f. res. on the homestead in Bedford, and d. 11 Nov. 1786; his w. Susanna d. 20 July 1792, a. 82.

7. CHRISTOPHER, s. of Christopher (3), came to Hk. with his father in 1735, m. Rebecca Haskell of Rochester, pub. 3 Mar. 1738–9, and had one son, *Christopher*, who rem. to Swanzey, N. H., and had many children; this numerous posterity, however, I have not been able to trace. CHRISTOPHER the f. was a precocious youth, being married before he was eighteen years old; but he manifestly lacked discretion or energy in the general affairs of life. He res. for a time on the northerly border of the homestead, about midway between the Gilbertville road and the house of his brother William; afterwards at Petersham and at Ware, where he d. 3 Dec. 1772.

8. WILLIAM, s. of Christopher (3), m. Mercy, dau. of James Aiken, 12 Jan. 1743–4, and had *William*, b. 1 May 1745; *James*, b. 19 Sep. 1747; *Rebecca*, b. 8 Oct. 1749, m. John Foster of Rochester 6 Oct. 1768;[1] *Jesse*, b. 4 Mar. 1752; *Mercy*, b. 18 May 1754, m. Nathaniel Graves, Jr., of Athol 29 May, 1777; *Lucy*, b. 19 Mar. 1757, m. Daniel Ruggles 31 Dec. 1779; *Christopher*, b. 12 June 1762. WILLIAM the f. was a farmer, and one of the foremost actors in public affairs. In the French War he served his country in at least four campaigns, — as lieutenant in 1755, and as captain in 1758, 1759, and 1760. In the Revolutionary period he was a member and chairman of the Committee of Correspondence, and of other important committees, representative in 1778, 1779, and 1780, and a delegate in the Convention at Cambridge in 1779 for framing a Constitution. His military spirit long survived; he accepted office 9 Jan. 1775 as captain of an "Alarm List;" and when the company commanded by his brother, Capt. Timothy Paige, marched "to Bennington in an alarm," 21 Aug. 1777, he volunteered his service as a "cadet." He was one of the committee appointed by the General Court for the sale of confiscated estates in the county of Worcester. He served the town as selectman ten years, and assessor three years; he was also a pillar in the church, of which he was elected deacon 9 Nov. 1769. He res. on the northerly side of a road which formerly extended easterly from a point about thirty rods northerly from the place on the easterly road to Gilbertville, marked "J. Marsh" on the R. Map, to the place marked "D. Warner." Traces of the old road are still visible, on the southerly border of the present homestead of Mr. Charles Mandell, and also on the side hill easterly from the brook. The house remained standing on the westerly side of the brook seventy years ago, and vestiges of the cellar and garden may probably yet be seen. This estate adjoined the homestead of his father, and here he dwelt until late in life, when he rem. to a house standing at or near the place marked "Moulton," not far from the present central bridge over Ware River, where he d. 14 Feb. 1790; his w. Mercy d. 19 Feb. 1823, at the great age of one hundred and two years and thirty-six days,[2] allowing eleven days for change of style. See JAMES AIKEN.

9. GEORGE, s. of Christopher (3), m. Rosilla, dau. of Nathaniel Whitcomb, 4 June 1752, and had *Nathaniel*, b. 11 Jan. 1754; *Asa*, b. 25 Jan. 1756; *George*, b. 9 Mar. 1758; *Rhoda*, b. 5 Oct. 1760, m. James Perkins 7 Ap. 1791, d. s. p. 8 Sep. 1835; *Nathan*, b. 7 Aug. 1762; *Paul*, b. 12 Feb. 1765; *Peirce* b. 16 July 1768; *Anna*, b. 23 July 1771, d. unm. GEORGE the f. was a farmer, and res. on a farm adjoining the homesteads of his father and his brother

[1] It is worthy of remark, that Rebecca Paige and her two elder brothers were all married on the same day.

[2] On the one hundredth anniversary of her birth, an appropriate sermon was delivered by Rev. Mr. Wesson, in the old church in Hardwick. The venerable lady walked up the pulpit stairs, leaning on the arm of her grandson, Mr. Charles Paige. Her ears having become dull of hearing, she stood by the side of the preacher during almost the entire service.

William, at the place marked "D. Warner" on the R. Map. He d. 8 May 1781; his w. Rosilla m. Capt. William Breckenridge of Ware 17 Mar. 1790, and after his death returned to Hk., res. on the homestead with her son *Paul*, and d. 29 Oct. 1807. Like her sister Mary (who m. Paul Dean before mentioned), she is said to have been noted for her industry and energy.

10. TIMOTHY, s. of Christopher (3), m. Mary,[1] dau. of Deacon James Foster of Rochester, 24 Oct. 1754, and had *Lydia*, b. 15 Sep. 1755, m. Thomas Fuller 26 Nov. 1778; *Timothy*, b. 16 Feb. 1757; *Mary*, b. 18 Oct. 1759, m. Daniel Fay, Jr., 23 Aug. 1778; *Foster*, b. 29 Aug. 1761; *Reed*, b. 30 Aug. 1764; *Moses*, b. 12 Dec. 1765, d. 28 Dec. 1765; *Moses*, b. 9 Feb. 1767; *Rebecca*, b. 28 Nov. 1768, m. Capt. Seth Peirce 22 Dec. 1793, had one child (which died in infancy), and d. 2 Aug. 1795; *Thomas*, b. 7 Nov. 1770, d. 21 Nov. 1770; *Thomas*, b. 12 Ap. 1772; *George Washington*, b. 24 Aug. 1775, an eminent physician and an elder of the Presbyterian church in Colchester, Delaware Co., N. Y., where he d. s. p. 10 Sep. 1834, having late in life m. Mrs. —— Cunningham, who survived him. TIMOTHY, the f. was a farmer, and much employed in the public service. He was selectman three years, 1778–1780; treasurer six years, 1781–1786; representative 1781; member of the Committee of Correspondence and other important committees during the Revolutionary period; as captain of militia, led his company to Bennington, at the alarm in August 1777, and to West Point in 1780, through a campaign of three months. On the organization of the militia after the adoption of the Constitution, he was commissioned colonel, which office he held during the remainder of his life. He was a staunch supporter of the government, and rendered service, 1786, in the suppression of the Shays rebellion. He res. on the homestead, where he d. 26 Aug. 1791; his w. Mary d. in New Braintree, 21 July, 1825, a. 93, and was buried by the side of her husband in Hardwick.[2] The following obituary notice appeared in the *Columbian Centinel*, Sep. 10, 1791: "In Hardwick, on the 26th ult., Col. Timothy Paige, aged 64 years, after a distressing sickness of upwards of twenty days, which he sustained with Christian patience and fortitude, and died in the firm faith and hope of a future resurrection and a happy immortality. He was a gentleman of abilities, and filled a number of important stations, both in the civil and military departments, with fidelity and honor. A number of gentlemen in the military line attended the interment of his remains, among a numerous concourse of mourning friends and relatives; and a company of infantry, dressed in uniform, attended the solemnity and performed military honors.[3] A pathetic and well adapted discourse was delivered on the occasion by the Rev. Thomas Holt, from these words, — 'O Death, where is thy sting? O Grave, where is thy victory?' "

11. NATHANIEL, s. of Christopher (3), m. Joanna, dau. of William Freeman of Sandwich, 13 Sep. 1759; she d. s. p. 30 Mar. 1783, and he m. Martha, sister of Rev. Elisha Fish of Upton, pub. — Aug. 1783, and had *Freeman*, b. 21 May 1786, a clothier; *Elizabeth*, b. 27 Ap. 1788; *Nathaniel F.*, b. 11 Aug. 1790; *Jason*, b. 18 Dec. 1792, a merchant in New York. NATHANIEL the f. was a farmer, and res. near the central bridge over Ware River, at the place marked "A. Rich" on the R. Map; his farm being separated from that of his brother George by the highway. He was elected deacon of the church 12 May 1785, was colleague about five years with his brother William in that office, and performed its duties with singular propriety and dignity until about 1812, when he rem. to Athol, where he d. 6 Jan. 1816, a. nearly 80; his w. Martha d. 15 Feb. 1816, a. 63. Deacon Paige was a true gentleman in his demeanor;

[1] Mary Foster was a lineal descendant from Elder William Brewster, Governor Thomas Prence, and Major John Freeman. See CHILLINGSWORTH FOSTER (3), note.

[2] Deacon Christopher Paige and four of his sons, — *Christopher*, *William*, *George*, and *Timothy*, were buried near each other, in the southwesterly corner of the old burial-place.

[3] This was probably the first military funeral in the town, and the only one until October 1811, when similar honors were rendered at the burial of John Warner, who was accidentally killed during a "sham fight," at a military parade on the second day of that month.

affable and polite; quiet and inoffensive; and remarkable for the purity of his character, adorning the office which he held and the doctrine which he professed. His white full-bottomed wig gave him a venerable appearance in the "deacon's-seat."

12. John, s. of Christopher (3), m. Hannah, dau. of Capt. Edward Winslow of Rochester, pub. 24 Dec. 1764. They had only one child, *Winslow*, b. 28 Feb. 1767. John the f. was a farmer, and is said to have resided for several years in the northeasterly part of the town, at the place marked "T. Bruce" on the R. Map. In 1786 he bought the estate at the junction of the Pet. and Barre roads, about a hundred rods north of the Common, marked "Mr. Holt," which he transferred a year afterwards to his son *Winslow*, who sold it, 2 Ap. 1790, to Rev. Thomas Holt, when both father and son rem. to Stephentown, N. Y. In 1794, the father rem. to Schaghticoke, N. Y., where he d. 14 or 15 Ap. 1812. His grandson wrote to me, "he attended the funeral of my grandmother on Saturday [Ap. 13], went to the grave; on his return, to his bed, died, and was buried in the same grave three days afterwards." He had served two campaigns during the French War, "was at Quebec at its capture, and was with and very near Wolfe when he fell; in this campaign he received a wound, and carried the ball in his leg to his grave." (*MS. Letter from John K. Paige, Esq.*, 20 Jan. 1840.)

13. David, s. of Nathaniel (4), m. Abigail Jones of Concord, 10 Oct. 1764, and had *David*, b. 7 Feb. 1767; *Hannah*, b. 11 Mar. 1773, m. Rev. Reed Paige of Hancock, N. H., 25 Dec. 1794. David the f. res. in Bedford, was a farmer, and for many years carried milk to the Boston market. He was a man of large frame and rather haughty manners, insomuch that he was familiarly known as "King David." Late in life he rem. to Middlebury, Vt. (where his son *David* then resided), and d. 11 Jan. 1819, a. nearly 79.

14. John, s. of John (5), m. Mary, dau. of David Cutler of Lexington, 15 Sep. 1757, and had *Rebecca*, b. 18 Nov. 1757, m. Thomas Robinson 11 Ap. 1776, d. at Onondaga — Oct. 1828; *Mary*, b. 10 Sep. 1760, m. John Wheeler 18 Nov. 1779; *Amittai*, b. 25 Sep. 1763, m. Foster Paige 6 Jan. 1785, d. 5 Nov. 1860; *John*, b. 19 Oct. 1766; *Sally*, b. 9 Oct. 1768, m. Jonathan Warner 25 Feb. 1789, d. 11 June 1807; *David*, b. 15 May 1771; *Joseph*, twin, b. 6 Aug. 1774, d. young; *Benjamin*, twin, b. 6 Aug. 1774; *Betsey*, b. 26 Sep. 1777, m. Edward Clark, Jr., 23 Feb. 1800, d. 9 Jan. 1862; *Joseph*, b. 19 Mar. 1780; *Hannah*, b. —— Sep. 1782, m. Zadok Dimond of Springfield, 15 June 1819, d. 25 Feb. 1859. John the f. was a farmer, rem. from Bedford to Hardwick in 1757, and res. two miles westerly from the Common, on the Greenwich road, at the place marked "Wid. Paige" on the R. Map. He d. 31 Oct. 1789 (wrongly inscribed 1790 on his head-stone); his w. Mary d. 31 May 1812, a. 74.

15. James, s. of John (5), m. Mary Stone 25 Oct. 1764; she d. in childbed 6 Jan. 1770, and he m. Anna, dau. of Capt. Joseph Warner, 25 Oct. 1770. His chil. were *Polly*, b. 8 Aug. 1766, m. Lemuel Page[1] of Rindge, N. H., 26 June 1798, and d. 26 Nov. 1853; an infant d. 6 Jan. 1770; *Luther*, b. 5 Nov. 1772; *Anna*, b. 1 Ap. 1775, d. 11 Aug. 1777; *James*, b. 13 Jan. 1777, d. 4 Oct. 1777; *Anna*, b. 18 Oct. 1778, m. Capt. Moses Allen 26 June 1802, d. 7 June 1824; *James*, b. 2 Jan. 1781; *Calvin*, twin, b. 8 May 1784; *Fanny*, twin, b. 8 May 1784, m. Stephen Rice, Jr., 4 Sep. 1811; he d. 16 Aug. 1821, and she m. Capt. Moses Allen, pub. 7 May 1825; after his death she rem. to Boston, and d. 15 Feb. 1873. James the f. was a cordwainer, and rem. from Bedford to Framingham before 21 Oct. 1762, at which date he bought a farm in Hardwick, and prob. rem. here immediately. He res. on the Petersham road, at the place marked "L. Paige" on the R. Map, and d. 18 Jan. 1817; his w. Anna d. 5 Jan. 1814.

16. Ebenezer, s. of John (5), m. Dorothy, widow of Joseph Fassett, Jr., of Lexington, 21 Feb. 1760; she d. 6 Feb. 1779, a. 41, and he m. Susanna ——, who survived him. His chil. were *Anna*, b. 29 Sep. 1760, m. Benjamin Lane

[1] He generally wrote his name "Lemma Page," and it so appears on the record. He descended from John Page of Watertown, who d. 18 Dec. 1676, a. "about 90."

9 Dec. 1779; *Rebecca*, b. 9 June 1763, m. Jonathan Wilson 22 July 1784; *Ebenezer*, b. 30 Mar. 1765; *John*, b. 18 Feb. 1767; *Dolly*, b. 11 Dec. 1768, d. 23 Ap. 1772; *Moses*, b. 11 Sep. 1770, d. 9 Aug. 1775; *Lucy*, b. 11 July 1772, d. 14 Aug. 1775; *Mary*, b. 24 July 1774; *Joshua*, b. 18 Jan. 1779; *William*, b. 19 Mar. 1783; *Moses* (posthumous), b. 9 Oct. 1784. EBENEZER the f. res. in Bedford, and d. 9 June 1784, a. 47.

17. TIMOTHY, s. of John (5), m. Margaret Wellington of Cambridge 12 May 1766, and had *Joseph*, b. 16 May 1767; *Dorcas*, b. 22 Ap. 1775, m. James Wright 16 Mar. 1797. TIMOTHY the f. res. in Bedford, was a soldier in the Revolutionary Army, and was killed in battle at White Plains, 25 Oct. 1776; his w. Margaret m. Asa Fassett.

18. NATHANIEL, s. of John (5), m. Sarah Brown of Lex. 10 Dec. 1774, and had *Nathaniel*, b. 25 Oct. 1775, m. Lydia Fitch, and d. in Bedford 30 Aug. 1858; *Sarah*, b. 22 May 1777, m. Samuel Randall, and d. in Boston 24 Mar. 1821; *Timothy*, b. 29 Jan. 1779, m. Isanna Harrington of Lex. 11 Jan. 1801, and d. at Bedford 26 Dec. 1860; *John*, twin, b. 3 Mar. 1781, m. Lucy Fitch, and d. in Woburn (now Winchester) 22 Feb. 1861; his w. Lucy d. 19 Feb. 1861, a. 75; *Benjamin*, twin, b. 3 Mar. 1781, m. Mary Penniman 9 Sep. 1804; she d. 25 July 1805, and he m. —— Newcomb of Quincy, where he d. 8 Ap. 1855; *Christopher*, twin, b. 10 Dec. 1783 or 1784, m. Lydia Wetherbee of Boxboro, and d. 4 May 1840; *Thomas*, twin, b. 10 Dec. 1783 or 1784, m. ——, and d. in Carlisle 22 Aug. 1860; *Thaddeus*, twin, b. 5 May 1788, a colonel and custom-house officer, m. Dolly Richardson of Leominster, and d. in Boston 27 Jan. 1837; his w. Dolly was living in 1882; *Ruhamah*, twin, b. 5 May 1788, m. Jonathan Lane of Bedford, where she died 19 June 1882. All these children, except *Thaddeus*, left posterity. NATHANIEL the f. was a farmer, res. in Bedford, and d. 31 July 1819; his w. Sarah d. in consequence of an accidental fracture of her thigh-bone, 2 Aug. 1839, a. 92.

19. SAMUEL, s. of John (5), m. Molly Hutchinson of Bedford 23 Nov. 1775, and had *Rebecca*, b. 4 Jan. 1778; *Benjamin*, b. 7 June 1780, a captain, res. in Ludlow, Vt.; *Samuel*, bap. 25 July 1784, a colonel, res. in Plymouth, Vt. SAMUEL the f., before his marriage, rem. to Rindge, N. H., where his children were born; later in life he rem. to Plymouth, Vt.

20. WILLIAM, s. of William (8), m. Mercy, dau. of Benjamin Raymond, 6 Oct. 1768, and had *Mercy*, b. 7 Oct. 1769; *Leonora*, b. 5 Ap. 1771, d. young; *Plethinia*, b. 5 Mar. 1773; *William*, b. 11 Dec. 1774; *Leonora*, b. 2 Feb. 1777; and others after he rem. to Ware. It is said that "he had a son, William, who died without issue, and eight daughters."[1] WILLIAM the f. rem. to Ware, was for many years deacon of the church there, and d. 23 June 1826, a. 81; his w. Mercy d. at Barnard, Vt., 23 Jan. 1795, a. 48.[2]

21. JAMES, s. of William (8), m. Thankful, dau. of Benjamin Raymond, 6 Oct. 1768 (the same day on which his brother William and sister Rebecca were married); she d. 31 Aug. 1806, a. 58, and he m. her sister Mary, widow of James Lawton, 22 Mar. 1807. His chil. were *Ralph*, b. 21 Aug. 1769, m. Sally Thomas at Brk. 1 Aug. 1793, and rem. to Rutland, Vt., where he d. 20 Aug. 1857; *Charles*, b. 16 Oct. 1771; *James*, b. 14 Oct. 1773, rem. to Lafayette, Ind., and d. 24 July 1831; *Nathaniel*, b. 14 Ap. 1776, rem. to Granville, Ohio; *Benjamin*, b. 24 July 1778, m. Mary Ann Magoun of Ware, pub. 13 Nov. 1803, and rem. to Richmond, Ind.; *Lucinda*, b. 28 July 1780, m. Joseph Muzzey 25 Ap. 1799, and after his death m. —— Armstrong; *Thankful*, b. 13 Aug. 1782, d. 24 Oct. 1795; *William*, b. 15 Nov. 1784, rem. prob. to Granville, Ohio; *Mercy*, b. 12 Nov. 1786, m. Moses Brown of Ware 10 Dec. 1807, and (2d) —— Pepper; she d. at Ware 16 June 1880; *Ira*, b. 17 June 1789, rem. to Springfield, Ohio. All these children, except *Thankful*, survived their father. JAMES the f. was a farmer, and res. near Ware River, at the place marked "C. Paige" on the R. Map. He was politically involved in the "Shays" delusion, but made his peace, and throughout his life was one of the most respected and

[1] Hyde's *Historical Address at Ware*, 1847, p. 51.

[2] She was probably at Barnard on a visit to her sisters, — Joanna, wife of Asa Whitcomb, Esq., and Deborah, wife of Steward Southgate, — who then resided there.

trusted citizens of the town. He was selectman eleven years, and assessor seventeen years; he was also major of militia, by which title he was generally known. He was elected deacon of the church 10 Aug. 1812, an office which had previously been filled by his grandfather, his father, and one of his uncles; and in which he was afterwards succeeded by his grandson, Deacon James N. Brown. He d. 18 Feb. 1818.

22. JESSE, s. of William (8), m. Mary, dau. of Capt. William Breckenridge of Ware, pub. 16 Jan. 1780; she d. 28 Feb. 1810, and he m. Mrs. Abigail Whiting 20 May 1812. His chil. were *Francis*, b. 12 Aug. 1780, d. unm. about 1800; *Mary*, b. 13 Ap. 1783, d. 21 Nov. 1795; *Christopher*, b. 11 Sep. 1785; *Nancy* (sometimes called *Agnes*), b. 31 Mar. 1789, m. Bassett Fay 22 Jan. 1811; a child b. ——, d. 17 Feb. 1792; *Sally*, bap. 23 Mar. 1794, m. George Briggs of Lenox 19 Nov. 1816; *Mary*, bap. 11 June 1797, d. 30 Aug. 1798; *Jesse*, bap. 19 May 1799; *Hadassah*, bap. 2 May 1802, m. Chauncy Dewey of Lenox, pub. 18 Feb. 1828. JESSE the f. was a farmer, and res. on the easterly road to Gilbertville, at the place marked "J. Mann," formerly the homestead of Brig.-Gen. Ruggles. He was one of the "minute-men" who marched to Cambridge in April 1775, upon the "Lexington alarm," and twice afterwards rendered service in the army. He had little culture, but a full share of sound common sense; and he is remembered as a good neighbor and an honest man. He d. 3 July 1818. His w. Abigail d. 29 Aug. 1856, a. 79.

23. CHRISTOPHER, s. of William (8), m. Rebecca,[1] widow of Rev. Elijah Fletcher of Hopkinton, N. H., and had *Elijah Fletcher*, b. ——, grad. H. C. 1810, and d. in Virginia in 1817; *James W.*, b. about 1793, an eminent merchant in Boston, where he d. 19 May 1868, a. 75; *Christopher*, b. ——, res. in Nashua, N. H.; and perhaps others. CHRISTOPHER the f. grad. D. C. 1784, was the first pastor of the Congregational Church at Pittsfield, N. H., 1789; was dismissed 1796, and after preaching for several years at Deering and Washington, N. H., was installed as the first pastor of the church at Roxbury, N. H., 21 Nov. 1816, from which charge he was dismissed 2 Mar. 1819, rem. to Salisbury, N. H., and d. 12 Oct. 1822.

24. NATHANIEL, s. of George (9), m. Salvina, dau. of Joshua Crowell, 1 Feb. 1781, rem. to Barnard, Vt., and had *Nathaniel*, b. 26 Oct. 1788, m. Nancy Gifford 21 June 1813; *Salvina*, b. 15 May 1794, m. Alpheus Howe of Royalton 20 Mar. 1817; *Polly*, b. ——, d. 30 Oct. 1795; *Polly*, b. 16 Dec. 1795. NATHANIEL the f. was a colonel, and d. 22 Aug. 1824; his w. Salvina d. 28 Aug. 1826.

25. ASA, s. of George (9), rem. to Barnard, Vt., where he m. Lydia, dau. of Elkanah Steward, 19 Feb. 1789, and had *Rosilla*, b. 25 Feb. 1790, m. Harris Pike of Waitsfield 26 Feb. 1824, and was living at Barnard in 1874; *Martin*, b. 8 Dec. 1791, d. — Mar. 1861; *Anna*, b. 19 Dec. 1793, d. 8 Sep. 1794; *Asa*, b. 18 Aug. 1795, d. 23 Jan. 1862; *Lydia*, b. 22 Oct. 1797, d. 3 Mar. 1798; *Cyrus*, b. 19 Jan. 1799, a farmer and deacon in Barnard, m. Laura Burke of Westminster, Vt., 19 Feb. 1826, and (2d) Elizabeth Rix of Royalton, Vt., 11 Feb. 1852, had posterity by both wives, and d. 28 Nov. 1875; *Leonard*, b. 7 Ap. 1801, was living at Oberlin, Ohio, in 1874; *Louisa*, b. 5 Sep. 1803; *Hiram*, b. 3 Dec. 1805, d. 18 Ap. 1835; *Luthera*, b. 20 July 1809. ASA the f. was a farmer, and d. 20 Dec. 1819; his w. Lydia d. 25 June 1847, a. nearly 80.

26. GEORGE, s. of George (9), rem. to Barnard, Vt., where he m. Betsey Bicknell 28 Oct. 1782, and had *Sally*, b. 8 Jan. 1784, m. David Lewis, 2 Nov. 1812; *George*, b. 28 Aug. 1786, m. Mary Walker 29 Nov. 1810; *Naomi*, b. 1 Mar. 1789, m. Elisha Richmond 21 Dec. 1815; *Gardner*, b. 6 Jan. 1791, m. Pluma McKinstry 20 June 1816; *Ira*, b. 2 Jan. 1789 (error in record, perhaps should be 1792), m. Sarah Eaton 19 Mar. 1818; *Betsey*, b. 1 Mar. 1793; *Bicknell*, b. 8 Ap. 1795; *Anson*, b. 12 June 1797; *Anna*, b. 14 Mar. 1799.

27. NATHAN, s. of George (9), m. Hannah Cobb 25 Ap. 1784, and rem. to Royalton, Vt., where he had *Alfred*, a physician in Bethel, recently deceased; *William*, *Otis*, *Nathan*, *Lucius*, *Edward*, *Betsey*, and *Hannah*; it is said there were two more daughters, who prob. d. young.

[1] Her dau. *Grace*, by first husband, m. Hon. Daniel Webster.

28. PAUL, s. of George (9), m. Perninah Hanmer 15 July 1790, and had *Erastus*, b. —— 1791, d. 14 Sep. 1792; *Anna*, bap. 15 May 1803, m. Anson Giffin 30 May 1809, d. at W. Brk. 20 Dec. 1868; *Judson; Laurinda; Lucinda; Rhoda*, d. at Hardwick, Vt., unm., a. 21; *Arminda;* these six bap. 15 May 1803; *Caroline*, bap. 24 July 1803; *George Hanmer*, bap. — June 1805; *Paul Whitcomb*, bap. 21 June 1807, deacon in Brimfield, where he d. 14 Ap. 1876; *Dwight*, bap. 10 June 1810, m. Sally Rice of Brk. 5 Mar. 1835, and (2d) Abigail Brown 28 Sep. 1843; d. at Springf. 17 Feb. 1881; *William*, twin, bap. 5 May 1811; *Willard*, twin, bap. 5 May 1811, m. Rebecca Rice 21 Oct. 1834, d. at W. Brk. 10 Oct. 1846. PAUL the f. was a farmer, and res. on the homestead. After the death of his w. Perninah, 16 Oct. 1814, he rem. to Hardwick, Vt.

29. PEIRCE, s. of George (9), m. Anna Durfee, res. in Royalton, Vt., and had chil.: *Roswell, David, Elijah, Calvin, Riley, Phila, Laura, Mary*, and *Elvira*.

30. TIMOTHY, s. of Timothy (10), m. Mary, dau. of Thomas Robinson,[1] 20 Jan. 1780, and had *Mary*, b. 28 Oct. 1780, m. Col. Thomas Wheeler 14 Feb. 1805, and d. at Ticonderoga, N. Y., 18 Sep. 1828; *Sophia*, b. 31 Oct. 1782, d. unm. 23 Oct. 1861; *Stephen West*, b. 3 May 1785; *Timothy*, b. 6 Mar. 1788; *Martin*, b. 27 Sep. 1791; *Cyrus*, b. 7 Ap. 1794, d. 16 Jan. 1796; *Rebecca*, b. 27 Aug. 1796, d. unm. 30 Mar. 1821; *Cyrus*, b. 16 Sep. 1799, d. 28 June 1803; *Lucius Robinson*,[2] b. 8 Mar. 1802. TIMOTHY the f. was a farmer, but during a large portion of his life was much engaged in public affairs. He was a member of the company of "minute-men," and marched to Cambridge upon the Lexington alarm; he afterwards served, for short periods, several times during the Revolution, but did not enlist in the regular army. He was lieutenant of militia in 1784, and on the 30th of May, 1788, was commissioned Captain of the "Cadet Company," then organized by special order of the Governor. He was selectman from 1798 to 1810, and from 1817 to 1821, eighteen years; assessor from 1798 to 1821, twenty-four years; also moderator of every March meeting, with a single exception (and nearly all the other town-meetings), from 1802 to 1821, representative in the General Court seventeen years successively, from 1805 to 1821 inclusive; and a delegate to the Constitutional Convention in 1820. He was commissioned justice of the peace 9 May 1803, and of the quorum 29 Aug. 1816; and from his first appointment until his death almost every "Justice Court" in the town was held by him. He res. about five or six years after his marriage on the homestead, with his father, and then erected the house which still remains on the place marked "J. Marsh" on the R. Map, about forty rods northerly from his former residence, and there d. 29 Oct. 1821; his w. Mary soon removed to the house marked "Wid. Paige," at the northerly end of the Common, and d. 29 Mar. 1836, a. 77. An obituary in the *New England Palladium*, 9 Nov. 1821, described him as "one of the oldest members of the House of Representatives; a man who united very many excellent and useful qualities, and who was universally esteemed among his acquaintances for his intelligence und unbending integrity;" and on the next day (10 Nov.) the *Columbian Centinel* referred to him as "one of the oldest members of the House of Representatives of this State; an undeviating patriot, and an intelligent man."[3]

31. FOSTER, s. of Timothy (10), m. Amittai, dau. of John Paige, 6 Jan. 1785, and had *Gardner*, b. 16 Oct. 1785; *Seneca*, b. 15 Feb. 1788, m. ——,

[1] Mary Robinson was a lineal descendant from Gov. Thomas Dudley[1] (who d. at Roxbury 31 July 1653), through his daughter Mercy,[2] who m. Rev. John Woodbridge of Newbury; their dau. Martha[3] m. Capt. Samuel Ruggles of Roxbury 8 July 1680; their dau. Patience[4] m. James Robinson of Boston 3 July 1711; their son Thomas,[5] b. 20 Ap. 1718, m. Mary, dau. of Capt. Eleazar Warner 23 Nov. 1744; and their dau. Mary,[6] b. 3 Dec. 1758, m. Timothy Paige, Esq., as in the text.

[2] The original name was *Lucius; Robinson* was added by an act of the General Court.

[3] He was one of the "first three" who, for a period of about twenty years each, held undisputed prominence in the management of public affairs in the town; namely, Brig.-Gen. Timothy Ruggles, from 1754 to 1774; Maj.-Gen. Jonathan Warner, from 1780 to 1802; and Timothy Paige, Esq., from 1802 to 1821.

res. in Bakersfield, Vt., and afterwards in Dunham, Canada East; he was a member of the Provincial Parliament, and d. s. p. 11 Oct. 1856; *Reed*, b. 28 Mar. 1790, m. (at Barnard, Vt.) Eunice, dau. of Dr. Convers Cutler of Hk., 31 Mar. 1819, was a farmer, res. in Bakersfield, Vt., and d. s. p. 22 Feb. 1867; *Mary*, b. 18 July 1792, m. Jesse Paige and d. here 19 Jan. 1823; *Rebecca Peirce*, b. 17 Mar. 1797, m. David Smith, and after his death m. Asahel Deming of West Berkshire, Vt., 5 Oct. 1828 (they celebrated their "golden wedding" 5 Oct. 1878, and both are living in 1883); *Foster*, b. 25 Oct. 1801; *Amittai Cutler*, b. 16 Nov. 1804, m. Lyman Hurlburt, and after his death m. Elijah Barnes, of Bakersfield, Vt., whom she survived and is living in 1883; *Sally Warner*, b. 5 Aug. 1808, m. Josiah Fay Brigham of Bakersfield, and d. 11 Mar. 1829. FOSTER the f. was a farmer, rem. to Hardwick, Vt., before 1800, and thence to Bakersfield, where he d. 22 June 1843; his w. Amittai d. at the house of her dau. in W. Berkshire, 5 Nov. 1860, a. 97.

32. REED, s. of Timothy (10), m. Hannah, dau. of David Paige of Bedford, 25 Dec. 1794, and had *Abigail*, b. 23 Jan. 1796, m. Jacob Flint 14 Nov. 1815; *Mary*, b. 2 Oct. 1799, m. Moses Whitney 2 Dec. 1817; *David*, b. 11 Mar. 1802, a physician at Belvidere, Ill., d. in 1868; *Timothy*, b. 31 Aug. 1805, was educated at West Point, a captain in the U. S. Army, resigned, and d. at St. Louis 14 June 1867; *Nathaniel George Reed*, b. 17 Aug. 1807, a farmer in Marengo, Ill., d. in 1853; *William*, b. 18 Ap. 1811, "went south about 1830, and no tidings were ever received from him; it is supposed that he was murdered on the overland route to California;"[1] *Lewellyn*, b. 18 July 1816, d. 26 July 1816. REED the f. grad. D. C. 1786, studied divinity with Dr. Emmons of Franklin, was a Hopkinsian after the straightest sect, and, what was then very unusual among the orthodox clergy, was an ardent Democrat in politics. He was ordained the first pastor of the church in Hancock, N. H., 21 Sep. 1791, which office he retained through life. He published two ordination sermons, an election sermon, 1805, and several others on different occasions. In the "Gazetteer" of New Hampshire, art. *Hancock*, he is described as "a learned, pious, able, and faithful minister; a good citizen; an honest and upright man; a firm patriot, and zealous and able advocate of his country's rights, which very much endeared him to the people of his charge, who frequently elected him to represent the town in the State Legislature of which he was a member at the time of his death." He d. of fever 22 July, 1816, in the midst of his usefulness, a. about 52; his w. Hannah d. 7 Oct. 1847, a. 74.

33. MOSES, s. of Timothy (10), m. Lucy, dau. of David Aiken, 27 Aug. 1789; she d. 27 Mar. 1800, and he m. her sister, Mary Aiken, pub. 17 May, 1801. His chil. were, twins, b. ——, d. 1 May 1790; *Mary Aiken*, b. ——, d. young; *Joel Simonds*, b. 25 Jan. 1793; a child, b. ——, d. 1 Feb. 1795; *Lucy*, b. 13 Ap. 1796, m. Anson Ruggles 14 June 1812, and d. 29 July, 1874; *Mary Ann Aiken*, b. 8 Mar. 1798, m. Lysander F. Haskins of Prescott 20 May 1833, and d. 29 or 30 Mar. 1862; *Moses*, b. 6 Feb. 1800; *Asa*, b. 9 Dec. 1801, m. Cordelia, dau. of Maj. Gardner Ruggles, was a physician and apothecary in Troy, N. Y., where he d. s. p. 19 Jan. 1836; *Hannah*, b. 11 May 1804, m. Horace H. Hayward of Ware 12 Dec. 1826, rem. to Marathon, N. Y., and d. 16 Jan. 1845; *Clarissa*, b. 24 Dec. 1807, m. William Breckenridge of Ware 6 Nov. 1827, d. 9 Dec. 1867. MOSES the f. was a farmer, and res. in several houses at different times; his last residence was on the turnpike, about three quarters of a mile north from the Common, at the place marked "S. Weston" on the R. Map, where he d. 5 Dec. 1818; his w. Mary m. Jonathan Marsh of Ware 1 Dec. 1824, and d. in 1845.

34. THOMAS, s. of Timothy (10), m. Susanna, dau. of Warham Warner of N. Br. 17 June 1798, and had *Susan Warner*, b. 10 Aug. 1800; d. unm. at Worc. 6 June 1880; *Hannah Ware*, b. 22 June 1802, m. Samuel Wood of Farnham, C. E., 9 Feb. 1843 (he d. 24 Jan. 1848); *Daniel Waldo*, b. 18 Feb. 1804, m. Sarah Smith 1836, res. in Lenoxville, C. E., and d. 7 Feb. 1877; *George Washington*, b. 18 May 1806, m. Elvira Waters of Barre, Vt., 24 Aug.

1 *Winslow Memorial*, p. 154; from which the last name in this family and some of the dates are taken.

1835, res. Chicago; *Almira Clark*, b. 7 Feb. 1808, d. unm. 11 Mar. 1838; *Prudence Maria*, b. 15 May 1811, m. Samuel A. Porter of Worc. 5 Ap. 1831; *Sophia Foster*, b. 4 Mar. 1815, m. Austin Bixby of Worc. 15 Mar. 1836; *Letitia Duncan*, b. 2 May 1817; *Thomas Reed*, b. 1 June 1821, killed by the kick of a horse 25 May 1836; *Harriet Antoinette*, b. 2 July 1825, d. 5 May 1827. THOMAS the f. was a farmer, and res. in Hancock, N. H., from about 1799 until about 1816, when he rem. to New Braintree; in 1836, when stricken in years, he rem. to Lenoxville, C. E., and subsequently to Compton, C. E., where he d. 16 June 1855; his w. Susanna d. 8 Dec. 1863, a. 87.

35. WINSLOW, s. of John (12), m. Clarissa, dau. of Gen. John Keyes of Windham, Conn., pub. 13 Aug. 1787, and had *John Keyes*, b. here 2 Aug. 1788; *Hannah Winslow*, b. — Aug. 1791, m. Archibald Croswell of Broome, N. Y., 1822; *Maria C.*, b. —— 1794, m. David Cady of Florida, N. Y., 1815; *Alonzo Christopher*, b. 31 July 1796; *Diana C.*, b. — Feb. 1799, m. Allen H. Jackson of Florida N. Y., 1820; *Antoinette A. L.*, b. — Aug. 1804, m. George Smith of Florida 1825; he d. 1828, and she m. Hon. Platt Potter of Schenectady 1836. WINSLOW the f. was a clergyman, and received the honorary degree of A. M. from B. U. in 1828. He res. on the homestead in Hk. until 1790, when he rem. to the State of New York, and was settled at Stephentown, 1790, at Schaghticoke, 1793, at Florida, 1808, and at Broome, 1820, where he d. 15 Mar. 1838.

36. JOHN, s. of John (14), m. Anna, dau. of Edward Clark, pub. 15 Sep. 1788; and had *Clark*, b. about 1789. JOHN the f. was a farmer, and res. on the Petersham road near the town line. He was very industrious, and remarkably successful in the accumulation of property, transmitting a very large estate to his grandchildren. He d. 21 Sep. 1836; his w. Anna d. 27 Mar. 1845, a. 77.

37. DAVID, s. of John (14), m. Martha, dau. of Capt. Seth Peirce, 23 Aug. 1792, and had *Cutler*, b. 5 Oct. 1792; *John*, b. 5 Mar. 1794, d. unm. 13 Dec. 1819; *Huldah*, b. 16 Sep. 1796, m. Col. Elbridge Cutler 20 Sep. 1817, rem. to Hartford, Conn., and d. — Mar. 1879; *Mary*, b. 13 Dec. 1799, m. Capt. Jonathan Webb 14 June 1819, and d. 2 Aug. 1869; *Martha Ann*, b. 23 July 1808, m. Dr. James M. Smith of New Haven, Conn., 25 Nov. 1829, and d. before 1845. DAVID the f. was a very successful farmer, and res. on the turnpike, about a mile northerly from the Common, at the place marked "D. Paige" on the R. Map. He d. 22 Jan. 1854; his w. Martha d. 31 July 1844, a. 74. His second w. Fanny, wid. of Sampson Peirce of N. Br., to whom he was pub. 15 Aug. 1845, ret. to N. Br. after his death, and d. 24 Ap. 1866, a. 84.

38. BENJAMIN, s. of John (14), m. Elizabeth, wid. of Ezra Clark and dau. of John Webb, 6 June 1819, and had *Benjamin Franklin*, b. 24 Mar. 1820; *Joseph*, b. 3 Sep. 1821, d. 3 July 1831; *John*, b. 11 Dec. 1822, d. 19 or 20 Dec. 1822; *Mary Cutler*, b. 18 Dec. 1823, m. Henry Bassett of Ware 9 Ap. 1845; *John W.*, b. 15 Aug. 1825. BENJAMIN the f. was a farmer and captain of militia; he res. on the homestead, and d. 14 Aug. 1827; his w. Elizabeth d. 16 Mar. 1856, a. 73.

39. JOSEPH, s. of John (14), m. Fanny, dau. of Seth Lincoln of Warren 23 Ap. 1816, and had *Emeline M.*, b. about 1819, m. Erastus W. Paige 7 Mar. 1850; *Seth Lincoln*, b. about 1821, m. ——, res. in Boston, and d. s. p. 28 Mar. 1879, a. 57; *Mary C.*, b. about 1823, m. Amasa W. Lincoln 10 June 1845; *Joseph*, b. prob. about 1825, rem. to the West, and d. several years ago; *Martha Ann*, b. ——; *Charlotte F.*, b. about 1828, m. Stewart Chase of Holyoke, 5 Feb. 1852; *Harriet M.*, b. about 1830, m. Dr. H. A. Harriman of Gardner 20 June 1853. JOSEPH the f. was a farmer; after his marriage he res. in Barre, where he d. 16 Ap. 1852, a. 72; his w. Fanny d. at Springfield 21 July 1878, a. 80.

40. LUTHER, s. of James (15), m. Sarah, dau. of Elijah Bangs, 22 Aug. 1802; she d. 21 Ap. 1816, a. 34, and he m. Mary, wid. of Barnabas Hinkley, 4 Sep. 1816. His chil. were *Erastus Warner*, b. 1 July 1803; *John Adams*, b. 12 Feb. 1805, a mason, res. in Boston, d. 5 Jan. 1864; *Bela Bangs*,

b. 13 July 1807, m. Rhoda Ann, dau. of Stillman Clark, 28 Nov. 1844, res. in Boston a few years, and afterwards on the homestead in Hk.; *Rosamond*, b. 6 July, 1809, d. 8 Mar. 1816; *Sarah Ann*, b. 16 Mar. 1813, m. Capt. John Raymond 31 Mar. 1833, d. 23 Sep. 1861; *Fanny*, b. 3 Ap. 1814, d. — July 1814. LUTHER the f. was a farmer, and res. on the homestead; he d. 18 Jan. 1843; his w. Mary d. at Bangor, Me., 11 Mar. 1849.

41. JAMES, s. of James (15), m. Thirza Hopkins of Petersham, 8 July 1810, and had *Henry A.*, b. 20 July 1811; *Elizabeth*, b. 5 Nov. 1821, m. Andrew J. Richardson, 5 July 1843. JAMES the f. was a mason, resided in Boston, wrote his name PAGE, and d. 2 Nov. 1846; his w. Thirza d. 17 Feb. 1870, a. nearly 84.

42. CALVIN, s. of James (15), m. Martha Ruggles 12 Nov. 1815; she d. 5 Aug. 1816, and he m. Philinda Gates 19 Sep. 1819. His chil. were *Silvanus Gates*, b. 13 June 1820, d. 1 May 1821; *Calvin Gates*, b. 3 July 1829. CALVIN the f. was a mason, res. in Boston, wrote his name PAGE, and d. 7 July 1850; his w. Philinda d. 23 Oct. 1867, a. 74.

43. CHARLES, s. of James (21), m. Lydia, dau. of Samuel French, 20 Sep. 1795; she d. 4 Oct. 1808, a. 33, and he m. Eliza Sargent 22 Mar. 1810. His chil. were *Sophronia*, b. 31 Mar. 1796, m. Chiron Jenney 28 Sep. 1817, d. 25 Feb. 1854; *Lucius*, b. 4 Jan. 1798, d. 4 Jan. 1800; *Charles*, b. 8 Dec. 1799, rem. to Fort Wayne, Ind.; *Thankful R.*, b. 4 Aug. 1801, m. Col. Abialbon Carter of Pet. (afterwards of Ware) 27 Feb. 1822, and d., his widow, at Whitehall, N. Y., 13 Ap. 1878; *Lucinda*, b. 1 Ap. 1803, d. the same month; *James*, b. 27 May 1804, rem. to W. Brk.; *Lydia W.*, b. 17 May 1806, d. unm. at Ware 21 Oct. 1881; a child b. ——, d. 11 Oct. 1808, a. two weeks; *Adelaide*, b. 27 Jan. 1811, m. Moses Smith 25 Dec. 1834; *Elbridge G.*, b. 5 Ap. 1813, a very prolific writer, under the assumed name of "Dow, Jr.," and author of the popular series of "Patent Sermons," which first appeared in the "New York Sunday Mercury," of which he was editor and publisher, and were afterwards published in three volumes; meeting with reverses in New York he rem. to California, and d. at San Francisco 4 Dec. 1859; *Ira*, b. 2 June 1815. CHARLES the f. was a farmer, and res. on the homestead; he was selectman 1826, and d. 21 Ap. 1853; his w. Eliza d. 28 or 29 Nov. 1868, a. nearly 87.

44. CHRISTOPHER, s. of Jesse (22), m. Judith, dau. of Jason Bigelow of North Brk., pub. 10 June 1811, and had *John Foster*, b. 20 Oct. 1811; *Abigail Bigelow, Nancy Bigelow, Francis Breckenridge, Mary Breckenridge*, all bap. 6 Aug. 1820; *Christopher Wesson*, bap. 26 May 1821. CHRISTOPHER the f. was a farmer, and res. about a mile and three quarters southerly from the Common, at the place marked "J. Monroe" on the R. Map. About 1821 he rem. to Prescott and owned and cultivated one of the best farms in that town; he d. 10 Sep. 1866, a. 81; his w. Judith d. 30 Dec. 1872, a. nearly 91.

45. JESSE, s. of Jesse (22), m. Mary, dau. of Foster Paige, in 1819; she d. 19 Jan. 1823, and he m. Charlotte, dau. of James Robinson of Barre, 4 Sep. 1823. His chil. were *Mary Ann*, b. 27 June 1820, m. Merritt Barnes of Bakersfield, Vt., where she res. and was mother of many children; *Rebecca Maria*, b. 28 Aug. 1822, d. unm. at Bakersfield about 1840; *Caroline Augusta*, b. 23 July 1824, m. Henry Ellsworth of Barre 2 June 1846; *Edwin Jesse*, b. 25 Feb. 1826; *Ferdinand Benjamin*, b. 10 Ap. 1828, m. Eliza J. Shepard of Barre 7 Sep. 1852; *Averana Justina*, b. 25 Aug. 1831, m. Nelson I. Tucker of Barre 29 Nov. 1855. JESSE the f. was a farmer, and inherited the homestead, which, however, he did not long retain. He res. several years in Barre, where he d. 3 Dec. 1869; his w. Charlotte d. 29 Jan. 1853; both were buried here in the new cemetery.

46. STEPHEN WEST, s. of Timothy (30), m. Lucy, dau. of Daniel Ruggles, Esq., 26 Oct. 1809, and had *Adeline*, b. 20 Mar. 1811, m. Capt. Walter Mandell 31 Jan. 1842, and d. s. p. 3 Oct. 1842; *Theodore*, b. 27 Oct. 1813, d. 21 Mar. 1814; *Lucy*, b. 30 July 1815, d. 10 June 1816; *West*, b. 23 Aug. 1817, m. Caroline Maria, dau. of Giles Warner, 13 Dec. 1848, and d. s. p. 4 Sep. 1853;

William, b. 18 Dec. 1819; *Lucy Rebecca*, b. 19 Jan. 1822, m. Elbridge Mandell 18 June 1844; *Daniel Ruggles*, b. 14 July 1829, d. 26 Aug. 1833. STEPHEN WEST the f. was a farmer, and res. on the road to Ware, at the place marked "Mr. Leonard" on the R. Map, and afterwards on the road to Gilbertville, at the place marked "L. Manly;" he was subsequently an innholder at the old "Willis Tavern," also at Princeton, Shutesbury, and Greenwich Village until 1836, when he returned to Hk., and res. on the road to Ware, at the place marked "C. Ruggles;" in 1869 he rem. to the Old Parsonage, half a mile north from the Common, marked "E. Cutler," and there closed his long life. He was captain of cavalry, 1812, representative 1843, 1844, and justice of the peace. He d. 24 Feb. 1871, a. nearly 86; his w. Lucy d. 25 Dec. 1865, a. 74.

47. TIMOTHY, s. of Timothy (30), m. Cynthia, dau. of Maj. Calvin Ammidown of Southbridge 1 Mar. 1815, and had *Cynthia Evelina*, b. 4 Dec. 1815, d. unm. 10 Nov. 1850; *Juliet Eliza*, b. 14 Ap. 1817, m. Merrick Mansfield, res. several years at Barton, Vt., and d. at Dorchester 17 June 1865; *Timothy*, b. 17 Feb. 1819, res. at Baltimore, Md., and afterwards at Chattanooga, Tenn.; *Calvin Ammidown*, b. 7 June 1820. TIMOTHY the f. taught school in Rochester 1807–8, and studied law with Samuel Eastman, Esq., of Hk., Samuel F. Dickinson, Esq., of Amherst, and Hon. Abraham Holmes of Rochester, until Oct. 1811, when he went to Georgia, and was preceptor of an academy at Waynesboro', at which place and at Augusta he also practised law. In the spring of 1814 he returned to Hk., travelling the larger portion of the way on horseback. Near the close of that year he established himself as a lawyer in Southbridge, at the organization of which town he was elected the first town clerk. He was commissioned justice of the peace 31 Jan. 1816. Besides performing creditably the various duties of his profession, he indulged his taste for general literature, and acquired a local reputation as a poet.[1] Constitutionally feeble in body, and with a very sensitive nervous organization, he was prematurely exhausted by the labors and trials of life, and died of consumption 14 Nov. 1822, before attaining half of the allotted "three-score and ten" years; his w. Cynthia d. 1 Nov. 1828, a. 35.

48. MARTIN, s. of Timothy (30), m. Mary Ann, dau. of Barnabas Billings of Chesterfield, 20 Aug. 1717, and had *Timothy*, b. at Hk. 3 Aug. 1818; *Frederick Augustus*, b. at Hk. 6 Nov. 1819; *George*, b. at Southbridge 17 Aug. 1821, a merchant in Providence, d. s. p. (drowned near Charleston, S. C.) 3 Ap. 1855; *Julia Billings*, b. at Northampton 12 Jan. 1824, d. 14 May 1825; *James*, b. at Northampton 9 Feb. 1826, d. 7 May 1826; *Henry*, b. at Lowell 5 Ap. 1829; *Martha Pomeroy*, b. at Greenfield 4 Jan. 1832, m. William Stone of Templeton 22 June 1854 (and had Frederick Paige, b. 10 Aug. 1855, Lucius Paige, b. 27 Mar. 1857, and William Sidney, b. 2 Ap. 1862); *Sarah Pomeroy*, b. at Worcester 9 Sep. 1837, d. 30 Sep. 1838. MARTIN the f. commenced active business as a clothier at the Old Furnace, and res. in the house in which his parents were married, marked "T. Elwell" on the R. Map. The erection of large manufactories of woollens in New England very soon ruined the small cloth-dressing establishments, and he, in common with many others, was obliged to abandon that business. Being, however, a very skilful dyer, he devoted himself to that art, and had the principal charge of that department in several "factories." He changed his residence frequently, as indicated by the birth-place of his children. In 1838 he rem. from Worcester to Templeton, where he res. until Dec. 1847, when he was compelled, by the failure of his health, to discontinue active labor, and rem. to Providence, R. I., where his sons were engaged in business. He d. 7 Dec. 1872, a. 81; his w. Mary Ann d. 27 Jan. 1875, a. 80.

49. LUCIUS ROBINSON, s. of Timothy (30), m. Clarinda, dau. of Ezekiel Richardson of Brk., 14 Sep. 1826; she d. 29 Aug. 1833, a. 28, and he m. Abby R., dau. of Joseph Whittemore of Charlestown, and sister of Rev. Thomas Whittemore, D. D., 5 Oct. 1834; she d. 23 Dec. 1843, a. 36, and he m. Lucy, wid. of Solomon Richardson of Brk., and dau. of Barnabas Comins of Charl-

[1] See specimen of his poetry on page 247.

ton, 22 Oct. 1845; she d. s. p. 3 Jan. 1864, a. 64, and he m. Ann Maria, wid. of Hon. David T. Brigham of Keokuk, Iowa, dau. of Robert M. Peck, and grand-daughter of Hon. Joseph Allen of Worcester, 2 Aug. 1866. His chil. were *Henry Ballou*, b. 23 Dec. 1827, d. 17 Jan. 1828; *Lucius Robinson*,[1] b. 19 Sep. 1829, a merchant in Boston, m. Ellen S. Pond of Cambridge, 15 Oct. 1851, and d. s. p. 28 Oct. 1852; *Mary Jane Pearce*, b. 8 Mar. 1832, d. unm. (of consumption, like her mother and her brother) 27 Dec. 1854; *Thomas Whittemore Robinson*, b. 17 Oct. 1837, d. 2 Ap. 1838; *Clarinda Richardson*, b. 24 Dec. 1840, d. 30 Dec. 1843. LUCIUS R. the f. was educated in the common schools of the town, and at Hopkins Academy in Hadley. He commenced preaching 1 June 1823, received the fellowship of the Southern Association of Universalists on the twelfth day of the same month, and was ordained 2 June 1825. He performed the duties of pastor nearly four years at Springfield, to 1829, about two years, to 1832, at Gloucester (now Rockport), and seven years at Cambridge, to July 1 1839, when he finally resigned all pastoral charge. He continued to preach, occasionally, about thirty years afterwards, until the precarious condition of his health compelled him to desist. During his pastorate he published "Selections from Eminent Commentators," in 1833; "Questions on Select Portions of the Gospels, designed for the Use of Sabbath Schools and Bible Classes," 1838, and a Centennial Address at Hardwick, in the same year. He subsequently wrote a "Commentary on the New Testament," in six volumes, the first of which was published in 1844, and the last in 1870. While thus engaged, as a relaxation from severer labors, he gathered materials for a "History of Cambridge," published in 1877, and for this "History of Hardwick," with a genealogy of its early families. He received the degree of A. M. from Harvard College 1850, and that of D. D. from Tufts College 1861. He was elected member of the Massachusetts Historical Society 1844, of the N. Eng. Hist. Genealogical Society 1845, of the Pennsylvania Hist. Soc. 1854, of the Phi Beta Kappa Soc. 1877, and of the American Antiquarian Soc. 1878; Hon. Member of the Worcester Soc. of Antiquity 1876, and Cor. Member of the Hist. Soc. of Wisconsin 1877. His literary labors yielding scanty returns, he devoted the business hours of the day, for many years, to the performance of secular duties. He was town clerk of Cambridge from March 1839 to Jan. 1840, and from March 1843 to May 1846; city clerk[2] from May 1846 to Oct. 1855; assessor from Mar. 1842 to Mar. 1847; treasurer of the Cambridgeport Savings Bank from April 1855 to April 1871, during the larger portion of which period he was also successively cashier and president of the Cambridge Bank. He was commissioned justice of the peace in Jan. 1843, and of the quorum in Dec. 1863; and was a representative in the General Court in 1878 and 1879. Through life he had a lively interest in Freemasonry; he was Master of Mount Zion Lodge in Hk., from Sep. 1826 to Sep. 1827, and of Amicable Lodge in Cambridge, from Jan. 1846 to Dec. 1848; Deputy Grand Master of the Grand Lodge of Mass. from Dec. 1851 to Dec. 1854; Commander of the Village Encampment of Knights Templars at Greenwich from Sep. 1826 to Sep. 1827, and Secretary[3] and permanent member of the Supreme Council of Sov.·. Gr.·. Ins.·. Gen.·. 33° of the A.·. and A.·. Rite, in the northern jurisdiction of the United States, from March 1861.

50. GARDNER, s. of Foster (31), m. Betsey Parker, 25 Ap. 1810, and had *Gardner Addison*, b. 22 Ap. 1811, m. Lydia B. Shattuck 27 May 1835; *Timothy Stillman*, b. 18 Feb. 1814, d. 16 Oct. 1817; *Betsey Maria*, b. 5 Ap. 1817, m. Samuel H. Peckham of Broome, C. E., 29 Dec. 1842, who d. s. p. in July 1844, and she m. Charles R. Parker of Lockport, N. Y., 15 Feb. 1846, and d. 7 May 1853; *Elisha Stillman*, b. 18 Mar. 1819, m. Betsey Soule of St. Albans 4 July 1857; *Mary Ann Lee*, b. 17 Feb. 1822, m. Edmund C. Knight 27 Sep. 1849, res. at St. Armand, C. E.; *Sarah Jane*, b. 27 May 1824, m. Henry Dean of Bakersfield 4 Nov. 1868. GARDNER the f. was a farmer, res. in Bakersfield, Vt., and d. 7 Nov. 1861; his w. Betsey d. 23 Feb. 1860.

[1] The original name was Lucius Emmett Clary; it was changed to Lucius Robinson, at his urgent request, by an act of the General Court.

[2] Cambridge was incorporated as a city in 1846.

[3] Secretary about two years, and member for life.

51. FOSTER, s. of Foster (31), m. Julia Soule, and had *Reed*, b. 3 Oct. 1828, d. —— 1833; *Caroline E.*, b. 6 Oct. 1830, m. Nelson Ayers of Bakersfield; *Foster A.*, b. 20 Oct. 1832, m. Clara Beals; *Julia S.*, b. 13 July 1834, m. George Clement of Dunham, C. E.; *Amittai R.*, b. 1 May 1836, m. Dr. —— Prime of Broome, C. E.; *Clarissa A.*, b. 5 July 1838; *Augustus S.*, b. 20 July 1840, m. —— Teele of Dunham; *Reed Decius*, b. 30 June 1842, grad. H. C. law school 1864, and d. in Oct. 1868; *Maria L.*, b. 1 Mar. 1845. FOSTER the f. was a farmer, res. in Bakersfield, and afterwards in St. Armand, C. E., where he died in Aug. 1865.

52. JOEL SIMONDS, s. of Moses (33), m. Jane S. Fairchild of Troy, N. Y., 1 July 1816; she d. 24 Dec. 1829, and he m. Ann Eliza Limbrick of Owego, N. Y., 18 June 1833. His chil. were *Margaretta Augustina*, b. 15 Sep. 1818, m. Hammond D. Phinney 26 May 1840, and d. 12 Jan. 1860; *Anson Fairchild* (a deaf mute),[1] b. 31 May 1822, m. Lucy Maria Sackett 8 June 1864, and was a bookbinder in Columbus, Ohio, and Springfield, Mass., d. 23 Dec. 1881; *Thomas Limbrick*, b. 31 Mar. 1834, m. Alzoa Nancy Wilbur 4 June 1862, d. 10 Dec. 1867; *Charlotte Bonner*, b. 4 Oct. 1840; *Lucy Aiken*, b. 30 Aug. 1842, m. Ransom Paige; *Mary*, b. 4 Feb. 1846. JOEL S. the f. was a physician, and res. at Owego, N. Y.; late in life he rem. to Alexander, N. Y., where he d. 10 July 1855. He pub. a Masonic address 1817. [Some of the foregoing facts are gathered from the *Winslow Memorial*, pp. 155, 156.]

53. MOSES, s. of Moses (33), m. Cordelia, widow of his brother Dr. Asa Paige, and dau. of Maj. Gardner Ruggles, 14 July 1837; and had *Asa*, b. 26 Ap. 1838, d. 20 May 1842; *Orin*, b. 16 Feb. 1840, m. Emily Moseley Root 24 Dec. 1863, a farmer in Bennington, Vt.; *Edwin*, b. 21 Mar. 1842, a farmer in Bennington, m. ——; *Lydia*, b. 16 Ap. 1844; *Cordelia*, b. 31 May 1847; a son, b. 13 Sep. 1850, d. 5 Oct. 1850. MOSES the f., after short residences elsewhere, settled in Troy, N. Y., where he was a grocer, and where he was married, and all his children, except the last two, were born. About 1846 he purchased a large farm at the foot of Mount Anthony in Bennington, and was a diligent and successful farmer during the remainder of life. He was a warden of the Episcopal Church, and d. 6 Mar. 1872.

54. JOHN KEYES, s. of Winslow (35), m. Helen Maria, dau. of Gov. Joseph C. Yates of Schenectady, N. Y., 15 Oct. 1817; she d. at Albany 29 Jan. 1829, and he m. Anna Maria, dau. of Francis Bloodgood of Albany 20 Nov. 1833. His chil. were *Joseph Christopher Yates*, b. 8 July 1819, grad. W. C. 1838, a lawyer, chamberlain of the city of Albany for several years, m. Harriet Vanderpool 1844, had three children, and d. 30 May 1876; *Anna Bloodgood*, b. 10 Dec. 1834; *John Keyes*, b. 18 Ap. 1837, d. 29 May 1838; *John Keyes*, b. ——, grad. at Union Coll. 1865; *Alonzo Winslow*, b. ——, took a partial course at U. C. 1866, and was a civil engineer; *Clara Antoinette*, b. ——; *Frances Eliza*, b. ——. JOHN KEYES the f. grad W. C. 1807; was appointed cadet in the U. S. Army 1808, lieutenant 1812, and captain 1813 of U. S. Infantry, colonel of militia 1817, admitted attorney at law 1810, district attorney 1818, clerk of the Supreme Court 1823, and regent of the University, N. Y., 1829. He res. several years in Albany, of which city he was mayor, but rem. to Schenectady, where he d. 10 Dec. 1857, a. 69.[2]

55. ALONZO CHRISTOPHER (originally Christopher Alonzo), s. of Winslow (35), m. Harriet B. Mumford 11 July 1832, and had *Benjamin M.*, b. —— 1834, d. —— 1838; *Clara Keyes*, b. —— 1836; *Harriet M.*, b. 1838, m. Douglass Campbell; *Edward Winslow*, b. ——, grad. Union Coll. 1864, and at Harvard Law School 1866; and perhaps others. ALONZO C. the f. grad. W. C. 1812, at the very early age of sixteen years, with the second honors of his class; was admitted attorney at law 1818, was district attorney 1823, member of the Assembly four years, 1827–1830, senator five years, 1836 and 1838–1841, reporter to the Court of Chancery eighteen years, 1828–1846, judge of the Su-

[1] I do not recollect to have found another deaf mute in the Paige family, here or elsewhere.

[2] The facts concerning this family, earlier than 20 Jan. 1840, were communicated to me by Col. John Keyes Paige, in a letter bearing that date; the subsequent events are gleaned from various sources.

preme Court six years, 1847–50, 1855, 1856, and member of the Constitutional Convention, 1867. He res. at Schenectady, and d. 31 Mar. 1868.[1]

56. CLARK, s. of John (36), m. Lydia, dau. of Joseph Cutler of Western (now Warren) 1 June 1813, and had *John*, b. 11 May 1814; *Lydia*, b. 8 Ap. 1816, m. Ansel Phelps, Jr., Esq., of Ware, 30 Sep. 1841, res. in Springfield, of which city her husband was mayor, and d. at Newton 26 Aug. 1876; *Joseph Cutler*, b. 18 Dec. 1818; *David*, b. 21 Dec. 1820;[2] *Frazier*, b. 16 July 1822; *Timothy*, b. 27 Mar. 1824, res. at Stockton, Cal.;[3] *Calvin*, b. 25 Oct. 1827, res. at San Francisco, Cal. CLARK the f. was a farmer, res. on the Petersham road, near the town line, at the place marked "J. Paige" on the R. Map, and afterwards bought the Gen. Warner farm, at the south end of the Common, where he d. 16 May or 6 June 1831; his w. Lydia purchased the Dr. William Cutler estate, half a mile north of the Common, where she d. 4 May 1878, a. 86.

57. CUTLER, s. of David (37), m. Hope, dau. of Dr. Arthur Rawson, 15 Ap. 1813, and had *David Cutler*, b. 25 June 1815; a child b. ——, d. 27 Feb. 1818; *Abigail*, b. 1 June 1819, m. Joseph W. Hammond of Pet., pub. 26 Ap. 1844, and res. in Cambridge; *George Rawson*, b. 29 July 1826. CUTLER the f. was a very prosperous farmer, and res. on the turnpike, nearly a mile and a half north of the Common, at the place marked "C. Paige" on the R. Map (on the farm formerly owned by Col. Stephen Rice, and still earlier by Capt. Stephen Fay); after the death of his father he rem. to the homestead, where he d. 9 Sep. 1868; his w. Hope d. 23 Sep. 1867, a. 78.

58. BENJAMIN FRANKLIN, s. of Benjamin (38), m. Pamelia W., dau. of Cyrus Danforth, 31 Dec. 1848, and had *George Danforth*, b. 25 Mar. 1850; *Mary Pamelia*, b. 8 Dec. 1852. BENJAMIN F. the f., a trader and postmaster, res. in the Old Furnace Village, at the place marked "Col. Billings" on the R. Map.

59. JOHN W., son of Benjamin (38), m. Sarah D. Williams of Barre 26 Sep. 1850, and had *Sarah Elizabeth*, b. 18 Ap. 1852; *Mary Cutler*, b. 16 Aug. 1854; *Harriet*, b. 13 Ap. 1860; *Caroline Louisa*, b. 16 Ap. 1866. JOHN W. the f., a farmer, res. on the turnpike, about half a mile north of the Common, at the place marked "J. Gorham" on the R. Map, the former residence of Dr. Convers Cutler. His w. Sarah D. d. 7 Jan. 1871, a. 44.

60. ERASTUS WARNER, s. of Luther (40), m. Lucinda, dau. of Joshua Lawrence 2 May 1833; she d. 18 Mar. 1849, and he m. Emeline M., dau. of Joseph Paige of Barre, 7 Mar. 1850. His chil. were *Delphia Mandell*, b. 19 Feb. 1834, m. Addison Spooner of Barre, pub. 24 Aug. 1858; *Joshua Lawrence*, b. 21 Feb. 1836; *Elizabeth*, b. 25 June 1838, d. unm. 19 Aug. 1857; *Sarah*, b. —— 1842, d. 29 Jan. 1843, a. 8 months; *Ellen L.*, b. 10 June 1845, d. 22 Mar. 1849. ERASTUS WARNER the f. was a farmer, selectman six years, 1841–1846; res. on the Moose Brook road, at the place marked "Wid. Lawrence" on the R. Map, and d. 29 or 30 Oct. 1850.

61. HENRY A., s. of James (41), m. Eliza W. Bigelow of Worcester, 1 Sep. 1842, and had *Henrietta*, b. 24 Dec. 1844; *Ellen*, b. 4 Sep. 1846; *Gordon Prince*, b. 7 Nov. 1849. HENRY A. the f., a merchant, res. a few years in Medford, but generally in Boston.

62. CALVIN GATES, s. of Calvin (42), m. Susan H., dau. of Dr. Nathan Keep of Boston, 3 Oct. 1854, and had *Edith*, b. 26 June 1855; *Richard Dickinson*, b. 28 Oct. 1856, and d. on the same day; *Calvin*, b. 18 Oct. 1857, d. 14 Nov. 1857; *Hollis Bowman*, b. 27 Oct. 1859; *Nathan Keep*, b. 18 Jan. 1861, d.

[1] These facts were ascertained in the manner mentioned in the previous note.

[2] His fate was tragical. After a season of prosperity in California, his wife, Sarah, and two children, *Annie* and *David*, visited Hardwick. On their return, a day or two before their arrival at San Francisco, one of the children died, but the mother kept possession of the remains. As they approached the wharf, 12 Ap. 1853, where the father was waiting to receive his family, the boiler of the steamboat exploded, and the mother and surviving child were killed. Less than one year afterwards, 8 Ap. 1854, the bereaved father himself perished in like manner, by an explosion of a steamboat boiler. A monument in the Hardwick Cemetery bears the names of this ill-fated family.

[3] His son, George W., d. at Hardwick, 22 Aug. 1857, a. one year and seven months.

21 Mar. 1864; *Fanny Bliss*, b. 3 Nov. 1864, d. 30 Nov. 1864; *Calvin Gates*, b. 9 July 1867. CALVIN GATES, the f. grad. H. C. 1852, was a physician of eminence in Boston, and d. 29 May 1869.

63. IRA, s. of Charles (43), m. Marcia Ann Brigham of Prescott, pub. 11 Ap. 1840, and had *Charles Ralph*, b. 19 Ap. 1844. IRA the f. rem. early to Acma, Mich.

64. WILLIAM, s. of Stephen West (46), m. Fanny, dau. of Lilly Manly, 26 June 1861, and had *Lucius Robinson*, b. 29 Ap. 1866. WILLIAM the f., a farmer, res. on the road to Ware, at the place marked "C. Ruggles" on the R. Map, until 1869, when he bought the Old Parsonage, formerly owned and occupied by Rev. David White, half a mile north of the Common, and marked "E. Cutler" on the R. Map.

65. CALVIN AMMIDOWN, s. of Timothy (47), m. Mercy, dau. of Harvey Dresser of Charlton, 9 May 1843; she d. 14 Sep. 1852, and he m. wid. Eleanor Jane (Scofield) Shumway 20 Feb. 1856. His chil. were *Mary Elizabeth*, b. 7 Ap. 1846, d. 2 Sep. 1848; *Calvin De Witt*, b. 20 May 1848; *Francis Skinner*, b. 18 May 1857. CALVIN A. the f., a manufacturer of cottons, res. in Southbridge, and has been much engaged in public affairs; selectman eight years, overseer of the poor six years, assessor two years, representative in 1863, and for many years notary public.

66. TIMOTHY, s. of Martin (48), m. Rebecca R. Osborn of Templeton 26 Dec. 1844, and had *George*, b. at Bridgewater, Vt., 21 Nov. 1846; *Edwin Decatur*, b. at Claremont, N. H., 3 Ap. 1849; *Mary Osborn*, b. at Cavendish, Vt., 11 May 1852; *Martha Ellen*, b. at Cavendish 6 Feb. 1863. TIMOTHY the f., a very skilful dyer, res. in Cavendish (Proctorsville), Vt.

67. FREDERICK AUGUSTUS, s. of Martin (48), m. Alice B. Joslin of Providence, R. I., 7 June 1864, and had *Harriet Robinson*, b. 10 May 1865; *Frederick Augustus*, b. 20 Sep. 1868; *Alice Dike*, b. 23 Sep. 1869. FREDERICK A. the f., a merchant, res. in Providence.

68. HENRY, s. of Martin (48), m. Caroline Maria, widow of his cousin West Paige, and dau. of Giles Warner of Hardwick, 22 Aug. 1859, and had *George Warner*, b. 2 June 1860; *Mary Staples*, b. 26 Mar. 1864; *Caroline Maria*, b. 26 Oct. 1865. HENRY the f., a merchant and partner with his brother under the firm name of F. A. Paige & Co., res. in Providence, R. I.

69. JOHN, s. of Clark (56), m. Harriet, dau. of Dr. Joseph Stone, 23 Oct. 1845, and had *Mary*, b. 13 Jan. 1847. JOHN the f., a farmer, res. on the Barre road, half a mile north of the Common, at the former residence of Dr. Stone, whose name appears on the R. Map.

70. JOSEPH CUTLER, s. of Clark (56), m. Nancy M., widow of Henry B. Gould, and dau. of Joseph D. Dexter, 2 Nov. 1865, and had *Joseph Calvin*, b. 12 Feb. 1867. JOSEPH C. the f., a farmer, res. with his mother, on the Pet. road, half a mile north of the Common, at the place marked "S. F. Cutler" on the R. Map, and inherited the homestead.

71. FRAZIER, s. of Clark (56), m. Wealthy, dau. of Theophilus Knight, 11 Mar. 1844, and had a child b. 16 May 1846, d. 18 May 1846; *Fanny*, b. 26 Nov. 1847, m. Frank J. Browning, 15 June 1876; *Timothy*, b. 16 July 1851; *Sarah A.*, b. 8 Aug. 1853, m. Charles A. Potter of West Newton, 20 Jan. 1874; *Theodotia Knight*, b. 1 Aug. 1860. FRAZIER the f., a farmer res. on the homestead of his father (the Gen. Warner farm), in the centre of the town. He was town treasurer four years, 1863–6.

72. DAVID CUTLER, s. of Cutler (57), m. Miranda Houghton of Pet., pub. 7 Mar. 1837, and had *John C.*, b. 12 Ap. 1839, d. in Berlin, Germany, 12 July 1873; *Maria L.*, b. 6 June 1842, d. 12 Dec. 1843; *David Warren*, b. 24 Jan. 1845, d. 26 Feb. 1863; *Edward H.*, b. 4 Jan. 1849; *Mary*, b. 3 July 1853; *Charles F.*, b. 25 June 1855, m. Etta L. Fisher of Worc. 5 Dec. 1876. DAVID C. the f. was a farmer and deacon of the church. He res. in Petersham, where he d. 28 July 1880, a. 65; his w. Miranda d. 5 Mar. 1880, a. 64.

73. GEORGE RAWSON, s. of Cutler (57), m. Caroline E., dau. of Bradford Spooner, 22 Jan. 1852, and had *George Cutler*, b. 20 June 1854; *Franklin*, b. 18 Mar. 1858; *David Frederick*, b. 15 May 1862; *William Arthur*, b. 23 Mar.

1864. GEORGE R. the f., a farmer, res. on the Col. Rice farm, about a mile and a half north of the Common, marked "C. Paige" on the R. Map; he d. 17 Sep. 1866; his w. Caroline E. soon afterwards rem. to Worc. with her children, and subsequently to Cambridge.

74. CALVIN DE WITT, s. of Calvin A. (65), m. Ida F., dau. of John Edwards, 21 Oct. 1873, and had *Mary Dresser*, b. 16 Nov. 1874; *John Edwards*, b. 30 Nov. 1878. CALVIN D. the f., a merchant, representative in 1878, res. in Southbridge.

75. TIMOTHY, s. of Frazier (71), m. Ellen Maria, dau. of William Browning, 11 Nov. 1874, and had *Harry Browning*, b. 6 Ap. 1876; *Frazier Knight*, b. 29 Jan. 1878; *Edith Harriet*, b. 12 Sep. 1880. TIMOTHY the f., a farmer, res. with his father on the homestead.

76. EDWARD H., s. of David Cutler (72), m. Lucy Maria, dau. of Moses Ruggles, 5 July 1876, and had *Edward Ruggles*, b. 17 Aug. 1877; *Moses Ruggles*, b. 5 Jan. 1879. EDWARD H. the f., a farmer, res. on the Col. Rice estate, formerly the res. of his grandfather, Cutler Paige, and of his uncle, George R. Paige.

PAINHEART, PETER, m. Polly Cross 2 Nov. 1783.

PARKER, SAMUEL, m. Hannah, dau. of Daniel Fay, 29 Jan. 1801, and had *Susan*, b. 5 Oct. 1801, m. Alvah Hathaway 13 Sep. 1824, res. in Boston; *Joseph*, b. 10 June 1803, m. Phebe Jane Baker, res. in Milford and afterwards in Boston; *Electa*, b. 18 June 1806, d. 28 Feb. 1807; *Electa*, b. 1 July 1809, m. George H. Francis; *Harriet A.*, b. ——, m. Lunsford B. Felton of Barre, pub. 15 Ap. 1838; *Fiske*, b. ——, drowned at sea; *Maria* (or *Ann*), b. ——, m. —— Green of Holliston. SAMUEL the f. was a shoemaker, and for many years bell-ringer. He res. in a house (since removed) at the north end of the Common, near the spot marked "P. Hammond," and afterwards at the place, a quarter of a mile northerly, marked "Wid. Parker" on the R. Map. He d. 4 Aug. 1829, a. 51; his wid. Hannah rem. to Milford, where some of her chil. had previously settled, and d. there 17 June 1869, a. 87.

2. SAMUEL D., by w. Sarah, had *Charles*, b. 7 Aug. 1816; *James*, b. 10 Ap. 1818; *Roswell*, b. 10 June 1821; *Mary H.*, b. 19 Oct. 1823; *Sarah*, b. 21 May 1825; *Orvilla*, b. 25 May 1827. SAMUEL D. the f. was a saddler, and res. at the north end of the Common. He rem. from the town with his family.

3. THOMAS, by w. Eliza, had Rosanna, b. 2 May 1868; *Thomas*, b. 9 Sep. 1870; *Mary*, b. ——, 1874; *Alfred*, b. 1 July 1878; *Joseph*, b. 1 Ap. 1881.

4. HENRY, by w. Maria, had *Leon Henry*, b. 17 Mar. 1871; *Grace Mabel*, b. 5 Jan. 1874.

JOHN A., of Roxbury, m. Fanny Warner 23 Feb. 1801. ROBERT, m. Philena Simonds, pub. 13 May 1811. JOHN, d. 28 Oct. 1813, a. 89. JENNY, w. of John, d. 19 Dec. 1811, a. 87.

PATRILL, JAMES B., m. Lovina Bosworth 30 Oct. 1836, and had *George Wilson*, b. about 1842; *Sophia M.*, b. about 1844, m. Albert Sturtevant 14 Aug. 1866; *David H.*, b. about 1845, drowned 29 May 1848, a. 3; *Ellen*, b. about 1847, m. Augustus D. Blackmer, pub. 3 May 1867, and d. at Ware 12 Feb. 1878; *Hannah Julia*, b. 20 Feb. 1849; *James Homer*, b. 29 May 1851; *Charles Elmer*, b. 15 Nov. 1854; *Joseph Warren*, b. 3 Dec. 1856, m. Emma A. Robinson of Barre 22 Aug. 1876. JAMES B. the f., a farmer, res. on the road to Enfield, on the westerly side of Muddy Brook, at or near the place marked "Mrs. Graham" on the R. Map.

2. GEORGE WILSON, s. of James B. (1), m. Diana Barber of Ware 6 Sep. 1864, and had *Effie G.*, b. 16 Sep. 1865, d. 17 Dec. 1865; and perhaps others. By second w., Lydia M., he had *Lewis W.*, b. 24 July 1878.

JOSEPH, was a soldier in the French War, 1758.

PEACOCK, JOHN, by w. ——, had *Sarah*, bap. 25 Nov. 1750; *Rebecca*, bap. 10 Dec. 1752. He had also a son *John*, b. prob. before 1740. JOHN the f. was b. in Ireland, res. on the east side of Ware River (now New Braintree), and was a soldier, 1757, in the French War. His s. *John* also served in 1756 and 1757; John Peacock, Jr., prob. the same, though described as of Greenwich, is named as adjutant in Col. Timothy Ruggles' regiment, 1757.

PECK, MILTON, m. Mary, dau. of Jedediah Dexter, pub. 13 Oct. 1823, and had *Mary*, b. about 1824, m. Ebenezer P. Staples of Taunton 11 Nov. 1845; *Jane R.*, b. about 1827, m. Francis Legate 2 June 1847; *S. E. Willard*, b. about 1832, m. Almena Austin of Hubbardston 30 Ap. 1862; *Sarah B.*, b. about 1834, m. Benjamin O. Gardner 7 Dec. 1853; a son b. — Sep. 1838, d. 16 Oct. 1838; *Luthera M.*, b. —— 1840, d. unm. 27 Dec. 1858, a. 18; *William C.*, b. about 1842; *Susan Ann*, b. 8 Nov. 1847, d. 31 July 1848; and prob. at least one other, — *Samuel Dexter*. MILTON the f. was b. in Hubbardston, where he res. at the time of his marriage, but rem. to Hk. before Oct. 1838, and res. near the Barre line, at the place marked "M. Peck" on the R. Map. He was a blacksmith, and d. 13 Ap. 1855, a. 55. His w. Mary m. —— Clark, and d. at So. Abington, 4 Feb. 1881, a. 75.

2. SAMUEL DEXTER, prob. s. of Milton (1), by w. Sarah A., had *Willie Dexter*, b. 18 Nov. 1861; a son b. 16 Ap. 1866.

3. S. E. WILLARD, s. of Milton (1), m. Almena Austin of Hubbardston 30 Ap. 1862, and had *Walter Lewis*, b. 14 May 1878, and perhaps others at an earlier date.

4. WILLIAM C., s. of Milton (1), m. Hannah Atwood 11 Mar. 1862, and had *Nellie Emily*, b. 22 Aug. 1866; *Mattie L.*, b. 6 Nov. 1871.

ANN, wid. of Robert M., and dau. of Hon. Joseph Allen of Worc., m. Samuel Hinkley 18 Mar. 1817, and d. 29 June 1828, a. 49.

PEIRCE, SETH, m. Huldah Sampson of Middleborough 9 Nov. 1769; she d. here 15 Mar. 1793, a. 43, and he m. Rebecca, dau. of Col. Timothy Paige, 22 Dec. 1793; she d. 2 Aug. 1795, a. 26, and he m. Abigail Hinkley of Brk. 19 Jan. 1797; she d. 30 Dec. 1797, a. 37, and he m. Mary McFarland of Worc. 16 Ap. 1799, who survived him, and returned to Worcester. His chil. were *Martha*, b. —— 1770, m. David Paige 23 Aug. 1792, and d. 31 July 1844; *Polly*, b. —— 1774, m. Ashbel Rice 15 Sep. 1793, and d. 7 June 1802; *Seth*, b. ——, a merchant in Boston, d. unm. ——; *Sampson*, b. —— 1778; *Betsey*, b. — Feb. 1782, m. Dr. David Billings, pub. 6 Ap. 1806, and d. 1 Feb. 1857; a child b. and d. in 1795; *Abigail*, b. —— 1797, m. —— Hotchkiss, went to England, and d. there. SETH the f. was s. of Ebenezer, and was b. in Middleborough (now Lakeville), about 1747. He rem. early to Shutesbury, and thence to Hk. before 1793. He bought, 24 Mar. 1797, the estate marked "Mr. J. Mixter" on the R. Map (previously the residence of Maj. Martin Kinsley, and afterwards of Jason Mixter, Esq.), where he died 25 Feb. 1809. "His death was occasioned by accidentally sticking a pen-knife into his knee. He was a private soldier in the company of 'minute-men' at Middleborough, commanded by Capt. Nathaniel Wood, and promptly responded at the Lexington alarm; and he afterwards commanded a company in the patriot army of the Revolution, which company was raised in the towns of Northfield, Shutesbury, Leverett, and New Salem. At the reorganization of the militia in 1781 he received the commission of captain of the local or standing company of infantry at Shutesbury. He was one of the selectmen of Shutesbury four years, and representative to the General Court from Hardwick in 1806." *Peirce Family*, p. 70. It may be added that he was a selectman in Hk. three years, 1803–5. Four head-stones, standing side by side in the old cemetery, mark the place where Capt. Peirce and three of his wives were buried.

2. SAMPSON, s. of Seth (1), m. Fanny Nichols of N. Br., and had *Mary*, b. ——, m. David Lee of Barre, and prob. others. SAMPSON the f. res. at N. Br. and d. 8 July 1843, a. 65; his w. Fanny m. David Paige, pub. 15 Aug. 1845, and d. 24 Ap. 1866, a. 84.

3. SAMUEL A., by w. Ruana, had *Mary Ann*, b. 26 July 1848.

4. ISAAC, m. Sarah A. ——; she d. 4 July 1858, a. 28, and he m. Mrs. Miranda Whitney 27 Ap. 1862. He had a son b. 24 Oct. 1851; *James Henry*, b. 13 July 1856.

5. WALDO, m. Abbie A. (or Almira) Bassett 15 Sep. 1861, andh ad *Minnie Gertrude*, b. 16 Mar. 1862, d. 31 Jan. 1864.

MARY, m. Holland Weeks, pub. 2 Feb. 1772. JAMES, m. Susanna Merrick 20 Nov. 1785. SUBMIT, m. Calvin Griffin, pub. 20 Oct. 1793. FANNY,

m. Israel Thomas of Gr., pub. 30 Nov. 1797. ELIZA, m. William Pepper of N. Br. 27 Feb. 1825. CHESTER, m. Abigail P. Marsh of Ware, pub. 17 Feb. 1831. SETH, m. Fidelia Bassett 21 Sep. 1831. GRANGER, m. Mercy Stockwell of Presc., pub. 28 Jan. 1832. TIRZAH, L., m. Stephen E. Newton 27 Dec. 1849. RUFUS J. of N. Br. m. Sarah E. Nye 16 Ap. 1860. ELLEN A., m. George D. Campbell of Ware 19 Nov. 1862.

PENNIMAN, ELIAS, s. of Lieut. Samuel of Milford, was born 1 Dec. 1748, and m. Ann, dau. of Capt. Ebenezer Jenks of Providence, 8 Dec. 1773. Their chil. were *Chiron*, b. 8 Jan. 1775; *Obadiah*, b. 1 Nov. 1776, d. in Troy, N. Y., 14 Sep. 1820; *William Comstock*, b. 12 July 1778, d. in Spencertown, N. Y., ——; *Silvanus Jenks*, b. 10 Feb. 1781, d. in Albany, N. Y., 7 Feb. 1852; *John Ritto*, b. 30 Jan. 1783, a portrait painter, d. in New York ——; *Huldah*, b. 20 Ap. 1785, d. 23 Aug. 1786; *Elias*, b. 29 May 1787, d. here 3 Sep. 1811 (the foregoing were all born in Milford); *Nancy*, b. in Providence 16 Feb. 1789; *Sally*, b. in Upton 3 Sep. 1792, m. Franklin Ruggles 21 or 22 Nov. 1812, and d. 3 Ap. 1864; *Arthur Fenner*, b. in Hk. 25 Oct. (obliterated), d. 23 Sep. 1795; *Mary*, b. in Pittsfield, Mar. — (obliterated), m. Jesse Bliss, Esq., of W. Brk., 21 Sep. 1818, and d. 28 Jan. 1837. ELIAS the f. was a physician, res. in Milford until about 1788, and after a short residence in Providence and Upton, rem. to Hk. about 1793. He res. first near the Old Furnace, at the place marked "E. Trow" on the R. Map, and afterwards on the southerly side of the turnpike, where it crosses Muddy Brook, at the place marked "C. Spooner." During many of his later years he was insane, in consequence, it is said, of a severe blow on his head, received in falling down a stairway. He was perfectly harmless; yet I remember that the children were shy of his cane with its formidable ram's-horn head. He d. 9 Feb. 1830, a. 81; his w. Ann survived him only three days, and d. 12 Feb. 1830, a. 76.

2. CHIRON, s. of Elias (1), m. Olive, dau. of Samuel Whipple, 17 Jan. 1797, at which time he res. in St. Johnsbury, Vt.; he d. before 22 Oct. 1815, at which time his wid. Olive presented for baptism, in Hk., her children, *John Ritto*, *Elias*, and *Anson Whipple*.

LAURA, an adult, bap. 25 June 1820, may possibly have been a dau. of Chiron and Olive. MARY, m. John Dean, pub. 15 Sep. 1822. SARAH F., m. Zenas H. Dexter 19 May 1831.

PEPPER, JOSEPH, was an early inhabitant, and prob. res. on the east side of the river, in what is now New Braintree, where the name long continued. He had *Sarah*, bap. 1 May 1748; *Joseph*, bap. 24 June 1753.

2. ELBRIDGE, by w. Hannah A., had *Etta M.*, b. 22 June 1861. ELBRIDGE the f. d. 23 Nov. 1863, a. 39.

3. EDWARD W., by w. Mary, had a son b. 26 Dec. 1865.

4. ASHBEL, by w. Martha M., had *Frances Maria*, b. 6 May 1867; *Lucy Jane*, b. 7 Dec. 1868.

SARAH, of Warren, m. Brigham Aiken 16 Ap. 1846, and d. s. p. 11 Nov. 1859, a. 47.

PERKINS, JAMES, m. Rhoda, dau. of George Paige, 7 Ap. 1791; she d. 8 Sep. 1835, a. 75, and he m. Hannah, dau. of Timothy Fay 23 Mar. 1837. He was a farmer, and res. about two miles north of the Common, at the place marked "J. Perkins" on the R. Map, where he d. s. p. 22 July 1845, a. 80. His w. Hannah d. 24 Mar. 1855, a. 63.

DAVID and family, and NATHAN and family, came here from Bridgewater, in 1770. JOSEPH, d. 26 Jan. 1791, a. 20. AMBROSE, d. 29 Ap. 1816, a. 69. JOSIAH, d. unm. 23 Aug. 1848, a. 81. These three were prob. brothers of James (1). ELIZABETH, of Brk., m. Thomas Stevens, pub. 15 Jan. 1748-9. ELIZABETH, of N. Br., m. Reuben Fay 11 June 1767. DEBORAH, m. Samuel Lynde 19 Mar. 1772. JOHN, m. Sarah White 23 July 1777. WILLIAM, JR., m. Anna Hilliard, 23 Mar. 1780. ABNER, m. Polly Shays 21 Jan. 1783. JESSE, m. Mary Rice 25 Ap. 1819.

PERRY, EZRA, of Sandwich, m. Elizabeth, dau. of Thomas Burge, 12 Feb. 1652. In his will, dated 16 Oct. 1689, and proved 18 Ap. 1690, he names wife Elizabeth, and chil. *Ezra* (b. 11 Feb. 1653); *Deborah* (b. 25 Nov. 1654), wife of Seth Pope; *John* (b. 1 Jan. 1657); *Samuel* (b. 15 Mar. 1667); *Benjamin* (b. 15 Jan. 1670); *Remember* (a dau., b. 1 Jan. 1676 or 1677); *Sarah*, wife of Ephraim Smith.

2. EZRA, of Sandwich, s. of Ezra (1), in his will, dated 21 Oct. 1728, and proved 10 Feb. 1729–30, names wife Rebecca, chil. *Ebenezer; Ezra; Samuel; Mary; Hannah; Rebecca*, wife of Jonathan Washburn; *Patience; Freelove;* and grandchil. Samuel and Edward Maxom. He devised land in Rochester to his son *Ebenezer*.

3. EBENEZER, s. of Ezra (2), m. Judah Savory in Rochester, where he had *Ebenezer* and *Mary*, twins, b. 21 May 1718; *Susanna*, b. 6 July 1722; *Samuel*, b. 16 Sep. 1724.

4. EBENEZER, s. of Ebenezer (3), m. Abigail Hammond at Rochester 11 Jan. 1749–50, and had *Nathan*, b. at Roch. 20 Sep. 1751. By a former wife he had *Mary*, b. ——1743, m. Capt. Daniel Egery of Dartmouth, and d. here 16 Sep. 1795, a. 52; and also a son who res. at Barre, and was grandfather of the late Dr. Marshall S. Perry. EBENEZER the f. rem. to Hk. about 1778, and prob. res. at or near the place which was afterwards the homestead of his grandson, Ebenezer Perry, Esq. He is said to have m. a third wife, who survived him, and prob. res. with his son *Nathan*, whose chil. she instructed in their youth; she is supposed to have been the Mrs. Elizabeth Perry who d. 8 Feb. 1792, a. 79.

5. NATHAN, s. of Ebenezer (4), rem. to Hk. with his father about 1778; his chil. were *Nathaniel*, b. about 1778, d. in Hk. 26 Nov. 1820, a. 42; *Stephen*, b. about 1780, rem. early from the town; *Ebenezer*, b. 10 Dec. 1782; *Nathan*, b. 27 Feb. 1784; and prob. *Abigail*, b. ——, and d. 2 Sep. 1798, a. 12 years and 5 months. NATHAN the f. d. 14 June 1815, a. 63.

6. EBENEZER, s. of Nathan (5), m. Mercy Atwood of Brewster, pub. 3 May 1807, and had *Benjamin Freeman*, b. 4 Sep. 1808, d. at San Francisco, Cal., 28 Nov. 1872; *Abigail*, b. 22 or 24 Aug. 1810, d. unm. 1 June 1832; *Jerusha*, b. 23 Aug. 1812, m. Charles Vokes 10 or 29 Oct. 1844, and d. 30 May 1877; *Anson Luce*, b. 1 May 1817, d. at Meriden, Conn., 19 Mar. 1853; *Mary*, b. 8 Nov. 1819, m. Aaron Lawrence 28 Dec. 1843; *Adeliza T.*, b. 27 Jan. 1822, a teacher, res. unm. in Worcester. EBENEZER the f. was a carpenter and schoolteacher; he possessed a strong and cultivated mind, great energy of purpose, and unswerving integrity. He was selectman four years and assessor eleven years. He res. on the Barre road, at the place marked "E. Perry" on the R. Map, where he d. 27 June 1845, a. 63; his w. Mercy d. 4 Sep. 1865, a. 81.

7. NATHAN, s. of Nathan (5), m. Sarah Hudson of Ware, pub. 22 Nov. 1807, and had *William Hudson*, b. 4 Nov. 1808, d. at Bangor, Me., 4 May 1877; *Arthur Clark*, b. 5 Feb. 1811; *Stephen*, b. 2 Dec. 1812; *Nathan*, b. 20 July 1816; *Charles*, b. 10 Feb. 1818. NATHAN the f. rem. to Bangor, Me., and d. 21 Sep. 1865.

8. THOMAS, a cordwainer, by wife Martha, had *Mary*, bap. 23 July 1738. He rem. to Rehoboth before 29 Sep. 1740.

9. CYRUS, m. Nancy Goodspeed 2 Aug. 1795, and had *Abigail*, b. —— 1798, d. 7 Jan. 1802, a. 3 years and 2 months.

10. WILLIAM A., m. Lucy A., dau. of James Browning, 18 Nov. 1850, and had *William Elmer*, b. 26 Oct. 1851; *Charles A.*, b. 22 Oct. 1855; *Harriet Elizabeth*, b. 26 Dec. 1860; *Marion*, b. 7 Mar. 1866. WILLIAM A. the f. res. on the Pet. road, a few rods north from the Common.

JOSEPH, d. 24 Sep. 1796, a. nearly 72. HANNAH, of Barre, m. John Jenney, Jr., 10 Ap. 1788. NATHANIEL, of Pittsford, Vt., m. Nabby Hammond 17 Oct. 1793. Dr. FREEMAN, of Taunton, m. Nancy Ruggles, pub. 6 May 1795.

PHELPS, ANDREW, by w. Sarah, had *William Henry*, b. 28 Feb. 1844.

E. AUGUSTA, of Ware, m. Albert E. Knight, pub. 10 Ap. 1841. ANSEL, Jr., of Ware, m. Lydia Paige 30 Sep. 1841. POLLY, m. Joseph Wright 4 Nov. 1852. WILLIAM H., of Putnam, Conn., m. Lura M. Tourtellotte 24 Dec. 1873.

PHINNEY, JOHN, s. of John of Scituate, resided successively at Plymouth, Barnstable, and Bristol, R. I. He had three wives and eight children, the eldest of whom was *John*, b. at Plymouth 24 Dec. 1638.

2. JOHN, s. of John (1), res. in Barnstable; he m. Mary Rogers 10 Aug. 1664, and had thirteen children, of whom the fourth was *Thomas*, b. — Jan. 1672.

3. THOMAS, s. of John (2), res. in Barns., m. widow Sarah Butler 25 Aug. 1698, and had *Gershom*, b. 25 Mar. 1700; *Thomas*, b. 17 Feb. 1702-3; *Abigail*, b. —— 1704; *James*, b. 15 Ap. 1706; *Mary*, b. —— 1708.[1]

4. GERSHOM, s. of Thomas (3), m. Rebecca, dau. of Stephen Griffith, 29 July 1725, and had *Gershom*, b. 7 May 1726; *Lazarus*, b. 7 Mar. 1728-9; *Sarah*, b. 28 Feb. 1730-1; *Isaac*, b. 10 May 1733; *Rebecca*, b. 17 Ap. 1736; *Temperance*, b. 9 July 1738; *Mehitable*, b. 30 Oct. 1740; *James*, b. 1 Ap. 1742; *Seth*, bap. 14 July 1745; *Rhoda*, bap. 27 Mar. 1748. GERSHOM the f. res. in that part of Harwich which is now Brewster; in his will, dated 4 Dec. 1761, and proved 7 Sep. 1762, his w. Rebecca and his ten children are named as then living.

5. GERSHOM, s. of Gershom (4), m. Thankful ——, and had *Lucy*, bap. 23 June 1751; *Zenas*, bap. 29 Oct. 1752, and born 24 Sep. 1752, according to his own family record. GERSHOM the f. res. in Harwich (Brewster), but the date of his death is not ascertained.

6. ISAAC, prob. s. of Gershom (4), early rem. to Hardwick, where he had *Heman*, b. 2 Aug. 1754; *David*, b. 28 Mar. 1756; *Mary*, b. 18 Nov. 1758; *Sarah*, b. 8 Aug. 1760; *Temperance*, b. 31 Mar. 1762 (bap. 8 May 1763); *Isaac*, b. 1 May 1764 (bap. 2 June 1765); *Nathan*, b. 14 Aug. 1766 (bap. 20 Sep. 1767). The dates of baptism indicate an error of one year in the dates of birth of the three younger children. ISAAC the f. was here as late as 9 Oct. 1770, when he bought land of Thomas Freeman; he prob. rem. soon afterwards.

7. ZENAS, s. of Gershom (5), m. Sarah, dau. of Lemuel Berry, and had, at Harwich (now Brewster), *Thankful*, b. 19 June 1781, m. Ephraim Haskell, Jr., 24 Oct. 1805, and d. 15 Nov. 1841; *Lydia*, b. 12 Feb. 1783, m. Gardner Ruggles 2 Dec. 1804, and d. 23 Sep. 1833; *Patty*, b. 12 Nov. 1784, m. David Aiken 24 Ap. 1805, and d. 16 or 17 Ap. 1877; *Sally*, b. 6 May 1787, d. 13 June 1787; *Lucy*, b. 12 Aug. 1788, m. Luke Bartlett 7 Dec. 1817; *Zenas*, b. 28 Jan. 1792, d. 17 Feb. 1792; *Sally*, b. 20 Jan. 1793, d. 7 Feb. 1793; *Zenas*, b. 10 Jan. 1794, rem. to Rhode Island. ZENAS the f. in early life was a shipmaster, and was taken prisoner by the British during the Revolution. He rem. to Hk. in Ap. 1797, and devoted himself to farming during the remainder of his patriarchal life, retaining remarkable activity both of body and of mind until extreme old age, and his perfectly erect form to the very last. He res. on the road to Gilbertville, at the place marked "Z. Phinney," where he d. 4 Mar. 1848, a. 95 years and 5 months; his w. Sarah d. 20 Dec. 1832, a. 76.

PALDIAH and family came here from Bridgewater in 1770.

PIKE, ELISHA, m. Anna Kerley 29 Nov. 1744, and had *Samuel*, b. 3 July 1745, prob. m. Nabby Snow of Sutton, 17 Dec. 1778; *Elisha*, b. 18 Ap. 1747. ELISHA the f. was a farmer, res. in the northwesterly part of the town, and d. 29 Dec. 1749; his administrator sold the farm to Nathan Sprout 6 Dec. 1756.

2. TIMOTHY, by w. Hannah, had *Sarah*, b. 29 Mar. 1756; *Simeon*, b. 7 Nov. 1759.

JABEZ, m. Rebecca Elwell 7 Mar. 1791. ABIGAIL, m. Daniel Tenney of Ware 16 Oct. 1803. POLLY, m. Chandler Woods 19 Feb. 1806. SAMUEL, m. Jane Small of Truro, pub. 8 Oct. 1810. SAMUEL, of Tolland, Conn., m. Hope C. Leonard, 3 Nov. 1831. BODICEA, m. Ansel W. Thayer 12 Dec. 1854. Mary A., of Pet., m. Sewall B. Nye, pub. 6 Ap. 1855.

POPE, RUFUS S., was pastor of the Universalist Society from April 1840 to April 1843. He was b. in Stoughton 2 Ap. 1809, m. Sarah B. Parkhurst at Milford 8 Nov. 1835, and had *George Henry*, b. in Sterling 31 Jan. 1837, d. 12 Oct. 1837; *Ellen Augusta*, b. in Sterling 14 Oct. 1838; *Charles Greenwood*, b. in Hardwick 18 Nov. 1840, grad. Tufts Coll. 1861, a successful lawyer in Cambridge, but res. in Somerville, of which city he has been a

[1] Thus far the facts concerning the Phinney family are gleaned from Freeman's *History of Cape Cod*.

representative in the General Court and President of the Common Council; he m. Josephine H. Cole of Somerville; also, in Hyannis, *Milton Granville*, b. 15 July 1845, d. unm. at Campton, N. H., 22 Aug. 1868; *Rufus Spur*, b. 23 Sep. 1847, d. unm. 12 Feb. 1868; *Elwyn Herbert*, b. 13 Oct. 1849, m. Ada M. Adsit, and res. in Traverse City, Mich.; *Sarah Hale*, b. 1 Nov. 1851, m. Francis A. Gorham 27 June 1876. RUFUS S. the f. rem. to Hyannis, where he d. 5 June 1882.

POWERS, JEREMIAH, one of the pioneers, by w. Hannah, had prob. *Jeremiah*, b. about 1732; *Eunice*, b. 14 Feb. 1734-5; *Isaac*, b. 21 Feb. 1736-7 m. Abigail Clark of Brimf., 21 July 1765; *Aaron*, b. — June 1739, m. Hannah Goodnow 10 Mar. 1768; *Esther*, b. 29 May 1741; *Elizabeth*, bap. 5 June 1743.

2. PHINEAS, another pioneer, came here from Willington, Conn., in 1734, and, by w. Martha, had *Phineas*, b. about 1729; *Martha*, b. about 1731, m. Joseph Safford 26 Oct. 1753, and d. at Woodstock, Vt., 31 Mar. 1804, a. 73; *William*, b. 15 July 1734; *Stephen*, b. 15 Mar. 1735-6; *Abraham*, b. 4 May 1738, m. Rachel Carpenter of Coventry, Conn., pub. 1 Dec. 1759, and was a soldier in the French War; *Mary*, b. 24 Mar. 1740; *Sarah*, b. 9 Aug. 1744, m. Moses Whitcomb 4 Nov. 1762; *Thomas*, b. 18 Mar. 1746-7; perhaps the same who was a prominent inhabitant of Greenwich, familiarly known as Colonel Powers; *Mercy*, b. 17 Aug. 1749, m. William Fuller of N. Br. 3 Dec. 1767.

3. JOSEPH, of Quobbin (whether brother to either or both of the foregoing I know not), m. Abigial, prob. dau. of Caleb Benjamin, 25 Dec. 1751, and had *Susanna* and *Abigail*, both bap. here 12 Sep. 1756; *Asenath*, bap. 24 Sep. 1758; *Mary*, b. 5 Oct. 1760; *Joseph*, bap. 26 June 1763.

4. JEREMIAH, prob. s. of Jeremiah (1), by w. Elizabeth, had *Dolly*, bap. 15 Aug. 1756; *Elizabeth*, bap. 3 Sep. 1758. JEREMIAH the f. prob rem. to Greenwich.

5. AARON, s. of Jeremiah (1), by w. Hannah had *Stephen*, b. 16 Sep. 1768.

6. PHINEAS, s. of Phineas (2), m. Elizabeth Allen of Ware, 15 Dec. 1751, and had *Amisa* (Amasa?); *Mary*; *Lydia*, m. Samuel Pratt 31 Jan. 1774; *Eunice*, m. Ephraim Pratt, pub. 17 June 1782; these four chil. were bap. here 7 Sep. 1760. PHINEAS the f. served in the French War, and perhaps rem. to Woodstock, Vt.

7. WILLIAM, s. of Phineas (2), m. Elizabeth Whitcomb at Rochester 16 Nov. 1758, and had *William*; *Joanna*; *Sarah*; all bap. here 24 Nov. 1771. *Joanna* prob. m. Silas Marsh of Western (Warren) 4 Aug. 1787, and *Sarah* prob. m. Zebadiah Johnson, Jr., 9 Feb. 1791. WILLIAM the f. served in the French War.

8. STEPHEN, s. of Phineas (2), m. Lydia Drew of Halifax, Mass., and had (perhaps not precisely in this order) *Lydia*, b. ——, m. Robert Paddock of Barre, Vt., and d. in 1815, a. 43; *Mary*, b. ——, m. Jason Richardson of Woodstock, Vt.; *Susanna*, b. ——, d. unm. 2 Dec. 1777, a. 17; *Stephen*, b. ——, m. Sally Perry, was father of the famous sculptor, Hiram Powers, rem. to Cincinnati in 1818, and d. there; *John Drew*, b. 16 Nov. 1769, by two wives had six sons and two daughters; he was the successor of his father as a physician in Woodstock, Vt., where he d. 26 Mar. 1855, and was succeeded, in the same profession, by his fourth son, Dr. Thomas Eleazar Powers. STEPHEN the f. studied medicine in Hardwick, commenced practice in Middleborough, Mass., where all his chil. are supposed to have been born, and thence rem. to Woodstock, Vt., in 1774, where he was the first resident physician. He d. 27 Nov. 1809; his w. Lydia d. 29 Aug. 1823, a. 88.[1]

9. LYSANDER, m. Hannah, dau. of Ichabod Dexter, pub. 21 May 1842, and had *Joel Lysander*, b. 12 Nov. 1843, m. Jennie E. Knight 1 Jan. 1866, and has been assessor for the last eight years; *Frank*, b. 19 Sep. 1846, m. Anna K. Garney of Marblehead 6 Nov. 1872 (she d. 11 Sep. 1873, a. 30); *Elmer D.*, b. 12 Dec. 1853, m. Anna W. Conant of Barre 29 June 1875. LYSANDER the f., a farmer, res. on the Dexter farm.

10. JOSEPH W., m. Harriet, dau. of Apollos Fay, 23 May 1844, and had

[1] MS. Letter from Hon. Robert S. Hale.

Sarah Harriet, b. 7 Oct. 1851; *Joseph Fay*, b. 6 Aug. 1854, d. 15 Sep. 1866; *Ella Hudson*, b. 24 Mar. 1858. JOSEPH W. the f. res. on the turnpike several years, at the place marked "A. Fay" on the R. Map, and afterwards rem. to Worcester.

SARAH, m. Nathan Carpenter 8 June 1738. ANDREW, m. Lois Emmons 27 Oct. 1740. HANNAH, of Littleton, m. Thomas Farr, pub. 5 Aug. 1758. ANNA, of Gr., m. Philip Holmes, pub. 22 Nov. 1772. EXE (Achsah ?), of Gr., m. John Thayer, pub. 5 Nov. 1780. OLIVE, m. Ephraim Ruggles 20 Mar. 1783. ANN, of Brimf., m. John Davenport Cox, pub. 17 July 1786. JEREMIAH 3d, of Gr., m. Lydia Haskell, pub. 24 Dec. 1788. EUNICE, of Gr. (dau. of Col. Thomas), m. William Walker, pub. 5 Sep. 1804. CHESTER, of Warren, m. Eunice Haskell 15 Oct. 1805, and (2d) Joanna Haskell 1 Sep. 1830. BETSEY, m. Charles Spooner of Pet. 4 June 1818. Mrs. LUCY, of Gr., m. Scotto Berry, pub. 22 May 1826, and d. 21 Nov. 1872, a. 90, lacking 21 days. LOUISA, m. Edward Dexter 6 June 1842. HIRAM, m. Urania White of Barre, pub. 4 Nov. 1843. ANGELA, m. Windsor Gleason of Pet., pub. 4 July 1850. ARATHUSA C., m. Austin Gould 16 Oct. 1851. JULIA A., m. Alfred Robinson of Fitchburg, pub. 27 July 1852. JONATHAN, d. 4 Mar. 1839, a. 73. MARY, wife of David, d. 29 June 1841, a. 53. DAVID, born at Pet., d. 17 Dec. 1866, a. 83.

PRATT, THOMAS, res. successively in Watertown, Sudbury, and Framingham, and had "these eleven children: *Thomas*, b. about 1656; *John; Ebenezer; Joseph; Philip; David; Jabez; Nathaniel; Abial* (female); *Ephraim*; and *Jonathan*; in 1682 he had land set to him at Sherborn, and d. about 1692; at least, administration that year was given to widow Susanna and son *John*. All these ten sons married and had families." Savage's *Gen. Dict.*

2. JOHN, s. of Thomas (1), by w. Ruth, had *John*, b. 27 Nov. 1691; *Susanna*, b. 12 Mar. 1693, prob. m. Obadiah Allen 17 May 1720; *Isaac*, b. 6 Aug. 1696; *Amos*, b. 26 May 1699; *Ruth*, b. 6 Feb. 1701; *Eleazar*, b. 10 Jan. 1702–3; *Hezekiah*, b. 27 Nov. 1705. JOHN the f. seems to have res. in Sherborn, and afterwards in Marlborough, prob. that part which is now Westborough. See Barry's *Hist. of Framingham.*

3. JOHN, s. of John (2), m. Bathsheba, dau. of John Fay, 4 Jan. 1715–6, and had, in Westborough, *Phinehas*, b. 8 Feb. 1716–7, d. —— 1717; *Ezekiel*, b. 4 Feb. 1718–9; *Silas*, b. 27 Feb. 1721; *Isaiah*, b. 14 Feb. 1723; *Betty*, b. 8 May 1726, m. Elisha Field of Sunderland 11 Jan. 1755; *Timothy*, b. 23 May 1731, m. Ruth Abbott, 14 Oct. 1756, and rem. to Bennington; *Samuel*, b. 18 Mar. 1733, m. Lydia Powers 31 Jan. 1774; *Ebenezer*, b. 18 Ap. 1744. JOHN the f. rem. to Hk. before 13 Oct. 1745, when he and his w. became members of the church. He subsequently removed to Bennington, where he d. 16 May 1768, a. 76. His head-stone remains in the beautiful cemetery at Bennington Centre, on which is inscribed this couplet:

"By faith in God, the sage stretches his wings,
We feel the rod, while he in glory sings."

4. ISAAC, s. of John (2), m. Eunice, dau. of John Fay, 17 Ap. 1721, and had, in Westborough, *Mary*, b. 24 Aug. 1721; *Moses*, b. 7 Oct. 1723, res. in Hk., m. Lucy Whipple of Westb. 16 Nov. 1747, and d. in Dec. 1748; *Isaac*, b. 14 Feb. 1726, res. in Hk., and was pub. to Elizabeth Rose 24 Jan. 1756, but the banns were forbidden, and she was pub. to Larkin Green three weeks afterwards. It does not appear that he made another attempt to marry, though he survived this disappointment more than half a century. He d. here 27 Nov. 1808, a. nearly 83.

5. ELEAZAR, s. of John (2), m. Ruhamah Tomlin of Westborough 15 Jan. 1729, res. in Shrewsbury, and had *Hannah*, b. — May 1730; *Ruhamah*, b. 16 Ap. 1732; *Mary*, b. 11 Dec. 1734; *Sarah*, b. 11 Oct. 1736, m. Jacob Knowlton of Hk. 21 Nov. 1759; *Rufus*, b. 2 Oct. 1738, m. Hannah Ball of Westborough 11 May 1763, and settled in Hk.; *Reuben*, b. 7 Sep. 1741; *Eleazar*, b. 20 Oct. 1743.

6. EZEKIEL, s. of John (3), by w. Mary, had *John*, bap. 6 Nov. 1743, d.

young; *Sarah*, b. 30 Mar. 1746, m. David Glazier 6 Feb. 1766; *John*, b. 25 Sep. 1748, m. Elizabeth, dau. of Nathaniel Merrick, 19 Jan. 1775; *Stephen*, b. 11 Sep. 1751; *Mary*, b. 24 Ap. 1754, m. Henry Lee of Rut. District (Barre), pub. 4 Mar. 1770. EZEKIEL the f. was an ensign in Capt. Samuel Robinson's company during the campaign of 1756 in the French War. He prob. d. before 1760, when "Widow Mary Pratt" is mentioned.

7. SILAS, s. of John (3), m. Elizabeth Chamberlin of Grafton, pub. 21 Feb. 1746–7, and had *Elizabeth*, b. 2 Ap. 1748; *Esther*, b. 24 Jan. 1749–50; *Ebenezer*, b. 1 Nov. 1751; *Moses*, b. 21 Sep. 1754; *Joshua*, b. 4 Jan. 1758. All born here. SILAS the f. rem. to Bennington about 1761.

8. ISAIAH, s. of John (3), m. Zerviah, wid. of Samuel Marsh and dau. of William Thomas (much older than himself and already the mother of nine children), 2 Mar. 1746–7, and had *Bathsheba*, b. 30 Jan. 1747–8; *Temperance*, b. 7 Aug. 1750, d. unm. 17 Dec. 1814, having been idiotic and a town pauper from her early childhood. ISAIAH the f. was a soldier in Capt. Samuel Robinson's company, 1756, and died during that campaign, prob. on the 20th of October, as his pay-roll was made up to that day. His w. Zerviah d. 18 Ap. 1798, a. 89, having been a pauper more than thirty years.

9. STEPHEN, s. of Ezekiel (6), m. Hannah, dau. of Elisha Billings, 3 Feb. 1780. He rem. to Bennington, Vt., where he d. 20 Dec. 1835. His w. Hannah d. 16 Feb. 1839.

DAVID, m. Hannah Hammond of Pet., 12 Oct. 1780. EPHRAIM, m. Eunice Powers of Gr., pub. 17 June 1782. CHARLES L., m. Susanna Nichols, pub. 9 Sep. 1816; she d. 1 Mar. 1823, a. 26.

PRESHO, SAMPSON, died here 24 Feb. 1819, a. 56 (his w. Abi m. —— Hooper, and d. 25 Oct. 1835, a. 69). No record is found of his marriage, or of the birth of his children; but he is supposed to have been the father of *Sampson*, b. ——, m. Susanna Grant, pub. 4 Nov. 1808; *Laban*, b. about 1786; *Abi*, b. ——, m. Joseph Barnard 17 Oct. 1819; *Mary*, b. about 1797, m. William P. Jordan 25 Mar. 1818, and d. 25 May 1834, a. 37; *Vincent*, b. —— 1800, d. 5 Oct. 1818, a. 18. SAMPSON the f. is understood to have been a Hessian, captured with Burgoyne's army in 1777; but if this be true, and the record of his age at the time of his death be correct, he can scarcely be regarded as a soldier at the time of the capture, being then only fourteen years old. He was employed many years as "top-man" at the Old Furnace, his duty being to cast into the huge chimney, at stated intervals, a due supply of iron-ore, oyster-shells, charcoal, and perhaps other materials.

2. LABAN, prob. s. of Sampson (1), m. Rachel Davis 18 Aug. 1816, and had an infant, b. ——, d. 5 Feb. 1817; *Laban*, b. about 1824; *John V.*, b. about 1826. LABAN the f. d. 26 Ap. 1869, a. 83; his w. Rachel d. 14 Jan. 1880, a. 87.

3. LABAN, s. of Laban (2), m. Harriet N. Vokes 17 Mar. 1853, and had *Melville Laban*, b. 18 Nov. 1856; *Mary Abbie*, b. 16 Mar. 1868.

4. JOHN V., s. of Laban (2), m. Clara B. Stone 3 Ap. 1850; she d. 1 July 1855, a. 26, and he m. Eliza A. Town of Gr., pub. 13 Jan. 1857. His chil. were *Clara Maria*, b. 8 May 1853, m. John A. Bates 7 Mar. 1873; *Clara Elizabeth*, b. 1 July 1855, m. Warren F. Rogers 7 May 1876.

PROUTY, WALTER B., by w. Susan, had *Willie Freelove*, b. 23 Aug. 1861, d. 16 Sep. 1862.

DANIEL, d. 27 June 1834, a. 35. WILLIAM E., of N. Brk., m. Adeline S. Browning 17 Oct. 1855. CLEORA D., m. Joseph N. Hamilton 16 June 1866. MARIA, m. William H. Taft of Starksboro', Vt., 22 Aug. 1866.

PURINGTON, SYLVANUS, m. Nancy Sellon, pub. 3 July 1780. MOLLY, m. William Nye 26 Dec. 1782.

PUTNAM, BENAJAH, m. Elizabeth Livermore 19 Nov. 1772. SALLY, m. James Cannon, pub. 28 Oct. 1793. STEPHEN, of Townsend, m. Deborah Egery 11 Jan. 1801. Rev. SIMEON, m. Julia Ann Bacon of Barre, pub. 22 June 1844.

RAMSDELL, SYLVANUS, m. Esther Gibbs of Gr., pub. 10 Jan. 1791, and had *Esther*, b. —— 1792, d. 6 Nov. 1802, a. 10; *Ira*, b. —— 1794, m. Clarissa

Robinson 11 May 1823, and d. 26 Ap. 1862, a. 67 years and 6 months; *Homer*, twin, b. —— 1795, d. 6 Nov. 1802, a. 7; *Anson*, twin, b. —— 1795, m. Roxana Gardner 20 Ap. 1820, and d. 28 Mar. 1875, a. 79 years and 4 months; his w. Roxana d. 13 Aug. 1872, a. 72; a child b. —— 1799, d. 2 Nov. 1802, a. 3; *Orin*, b. —— 1800. SYLVANUS the f. d. 23 Dec. 1851, a. 87; his w. Esther d. 12 Nov. 1829, a. 67.

2. ORIN, s. of Sylvanus (1), m. Sarah Terry 8 June 1823, and had *Horace S.*, b. ——; *John M.*, b. ——; *Otis A.*, b. ——; *Sarah E.*, b. about 1836, m. George H. Strickland of Ware 13 May (or June) 1858; *Orin*, b. about 1838, d. 9 Ap. 1840, a. 2; *Elizabeth*, b. about 1842, m. Darius S. Gray of Gr., 7 Ap. 1864; *Ruth Louisa*, b. 16 June 1845. ORIN the f., a farmer, d. 5 Mar. 1879, a. 78.

3. HORACE S., s. of Orin (2), m. Elizabeth H. Kilmer, pub. 10 May 1852, and had *John S. S.*, b. 2 Ap. 1853; *George W. M.*, b. 4 Nov. 1855; *Claudius Leslie*, b. 13 Jan. 1869, d. 21 Jan. 1869; *Sarah Elizabeth*, b. —— 1872, d. 19 Ap. 1872, a. 1 month and 19 days.

4. JOHN M., s. of Orin (2), m. Louisa A. Richardson, pub. 25 May 1858, and had a son b. 26 Dec. 1859; *Edith Adista*, b. 29 June 1861; *Henry Leroy*, b. 11 Jan. 1863.

JOSEPH, had dau. *Abigail*, who m. —— Bugbee, and d. at Bel. 2 Feb. 1861, a. 70. ELIZABETH, of Gr., m. Silas Dean 30 Nov. 1768. CATHERINE, m. Isaac Cummings, Jr., 11 May 1774. SARAH, m. John Terry, Jr., 26 Sep. 1782. ALANSON, m. Sarah J. Wyman 4 June 1874.

RAND, JACOB D., s. of Thomas, b. in Charlestown, 30 Mar. 1778, was a cabinet-maker, came early to Hk., and was published 12 Dec. 1801, to Esther, dau. of Dr. Lucius Doolittle. Her parents prevented the marriage, and he enlisted in the U. S. Army. After the surrender at Detroit by General Hull, in Aug. 1812, he returned to Hk. and consummated the long-delayed marriage, 21 Oct. 1813. His w. Esther d. 2 Sep. 1815, a. 30, and he m. Mrs. Selinda Fales 27 Jan. 1818. He had one child, *William Dorrill*, b. 14 June 1820. JACOB D. the f. res. between the Pet. road and the turnpike, at the place marked "J. Rand" on the R. Map, and closed his checkered earthly life 8 Oct. 1840, a. 63.

RANDALL, JOSIAH, d. 6 Mar. 1809, a. 57. HOLLAND, of Barre, m. Lydia Whipple, pub. 7 Ap. 1817. SOPHRONIA, m. Zephaniah Spooner of Springf. 8 Ap. 1841. EUNICE, m. Nehemiah H. Johnson of Illinois 21 Sep. 1841. RUTH, m. Anson F. Allen 14 June 1846, and d. 28 Aug. 1848, a. 27.

RANNEY, LA FAYETTE, by wife Adeline E., had *Julia Eliza*, b. 24 Aug. 1847, d. 15 Jan. 1850; *Ambrose L.*, b. 11 June 1849. LA FAYETTE the f. was a physician, and res. near the Common. He remained not many years, and removed to New York.

RANSOM, ELIZABETH, of Pelham, m. Philip Fraker, pub. 2 June 1776. RICHARD, of Woodstock, Vt., m. Rosamond, widow of Ezra Winslow, pub. 26 Nov. 1801. Dr. DAVID, of Carlville, N. Y., m. Harriet M. Towne 19 May 1840.

RAWSON, EDWARD, b. 16 Ap. 1615 at Gillingham, Dorsetshire, England, is understood to have come to New England in 1637; he settled in Newbury, and was representative of that town seven years. He rem. to Boston in 1650, having been that year elected secretary of the colony, which office he held until the old charter government was overturned in 1686. He m. in England "Rachel, dau. of Thomas Pirne or Perne," and had twelve chil., of whom the youngest was *Grindall*, b. 23 Jan. 1659. EDWARD the f. d. 27 Aug. 1693; his w. Rachel d. 11 Oct. 1677. See Savage's *Gen. Dict.*, and *Rawson Family*.

2. GRINDALL, s. of Edward (1), grad. H. C. 1678, m. Susanna, dau. of Rev. John Wilson of Medfield, and grand-daughter of Rev. John Wilson the first minister of Boston, and had eleven children, of whom the fifth was *Wilson*, b. 23 June 1692. GRINDALL the f. was the second minister of Mendon (ordained 7 Ap. 1684), and d. 6 Feb. 1715; his w. Susanna d. 8 July 1748, a. 83. Savage's *Gen. Dict.*

3. WILSON, s. of Grindall (2), m. Margaret Arthur, and had *Wilson*, b. 13 Aug. 1713; *Priscilla*, b. 17 Dec. 1715; *Mary*, b. 12 May 1717; *Grindall*,

b. 13 July 1719; *Edward*, b. 2 Ap. 1721; *Stephen*, b. 2 Ap. 1722 or 1723; *Paul*, b. 9 Ap. 1725; *Thomas*, b. 2 May 1733. WILSON the f. was a farmer, res. in Mendon.

4. EDWARD, s. of Wilson (3), m. Mary Morse, and had *Hooker*, b. 21 Ap. 1749; *Edward*, b. 19 June 1754, a physician in Leicester, where he d. in 1786; *Anna* (or *Nancy*), b. 22 Sep. 1756, d. unm. in 1848; *Arthur*, b. 17 Nov. 1758; *Mephibosheth*, b. 7 Aug. 1763, lived only two days. He had also *Elizabeth*, b. ——, m. Deac. Seth Chapin of Mendon 27 Oct. 1767; and *Mary*, b. ——, m. Dr. Levi Willard of Mendon 28 Ap. 1774. EDWARD the f. was deacon of the church in Mendon where his chil. were born. Late in life, he rem. to Leicester, and d. there 11 Feb. 1807. See *Rawson Family*, and Washburn's *Hist. of Leicester.*

5. ARTHUR, s. of Edward (4), m. Abigail Childs of Barre 23 June 1785, and had *George*, b. in Barre 18 Dec. 1785; and in Hk., *Edward*, twin, b. 30 July 1787; *Arthur*, twin, b. 30 July 1787, clerk in the store of Jason Mixter, rem. when young and became a merchant; *Hope*, b. 17 May 1789, m. Cutler Paige 15 Ap. 1813, and d. 23 Sep. 1867. ARTHUR the f. was a physician, res. on the road to Barre, at the place marked "Dr. Stone" on the R. Map. He was somewhat involved in the Shays Rebellion; he was probably surgeon, for when he took the oath of allegiance, he "declared he never took up arms against government, only acted as physician." *Mass. Arch.*, cxc. 168. He d. 25 Dec. 1796, at the early age of 38; his w. Abigail rem. to a house on the turnpike, half a mile north from the Common, marked "S. Weston" on the R. Map, and d. 28 Sep. 1812, a. 53.

RAYMOND, WILLIAM, by w. Deborah, had in Rochester, *William*, b. 7 Feb. 1711; *Benjamin*, b. 7 Dec. 1714; *Daniel*, b. 28 Mar. 1717; *Paul*, b. 11 Sep. 1718; *Mary*, b. 12 Mar. 1720-21; *Edward*, b. 13 June 1724; *Deborah*, b. 28 Mar. 1727; *Lemuel*, b. 11 Nov. 1729, d. 24 Ap. 1733; *Elnathan*, b. 5 Nov. 1731; *Lemuel*, b. 22 Ap. 1736. WILLIAM the f. rem. from Beverly to Rochester, prob. soon after 13 May 1712, at which date he bought a farm in that town, and the names of all his chil. are there entered on record.

2. BENJAMIN, s. of William (1), by w. Mercy, had *Benjamin*, b. 27 July 1738; *Joanna*, b. 11 May 1740, m. Asa Whitcomb 15 Mar. 1759, rem. to Barnard, Vt., and d. before 1809; *John*, bap. 12 Feb. 1743-4; *Mercy*, b. about 1746, m. William Paige 6 Oct. 1768, rem. to Ware, and d. while on a visit at Barnard 23 Jan. 1795, a. 48; *Thankful*, b. about 1748, m. James Paige 6 Oct. 1768, and d. 31 Aug. 1806, a. 58; *Mary*, prob. b. about 1751, m. James Lawton, Jr., 3 Jan. 1771; he d. 1 Jan. 1804, and she m. Maj. James Paige (whose first wife was her sister), 22 Mar. 1807; *Deborah*, b. about 1754, m. Stewart Southgate 22 July 1773, rem. to Barnard, and d. 28 Feb. 1813, a. 58. BENJAMIN the f. was a cooper; he res. in Rochester until 12 Ap. 1760, when he bought a farm in Hk. and prob. rem. at about that time, as he and his wife were admitted to church membership 6 Sep. 1761. He prob. res. on the farm which was afterwards the homestead of his son *John*, and d. 2 Oct. 1779, a. nearly 65; his w. Mercy d. 26 May 1806, a. 86.

3. JOHN, s. of Benjamin (2), m. Mercy, dau. of Dudley Jordan, 7 Mar. 1771, and had *Benjamin*, b. 9 Nov. 1771; *Asa*, b. 16 Nov. 1776. JOHN the f. was a farmer, and res. on the road to Ware, near the town line, at the place marked "Capt. Raymond" on the R. Map. He was captain of militia, and generally known by his military title. He d. 4 Oct. 1816, a. 72; his w. Mercy d. 4 (or 25) Feb. 1833, a. 87.

4. ASA, s. of John (3), m. Sybil Sumner 30 Nov. 1803, and had *John*, b. 3 Sep. 1804; *Adah Bullard*, b. 20 July 1806, d. unm. 25 Sep. 1880; *Polly Sumner*, b. 25 Nov. 1809; *James Fitch*, b. — Feb. 1814, d. 15 Ap. 1814; *Sybil*, b. 17 Oct. 1816, m. Samuel King of Barre 5 May 1840. ASA the f. was a farmer, inherited the homestead, and d. 24 Aug. 1851, a. nearly 75; his w. Sybil d. 9 June 1846, a. 64.

5. JOHN, s. of Asa (4), m. Sarah Ann, dau. of Luther Paige, 31 Mar. 1833, and had one child which died in infancy. He inherited the homestead and was a farmer, but devoted much time to the service of the public; he was cap-

tain of militia and justice of the peace; selectman seventeen years; assessor eleven years; member of the school committee eight years; representative in the General Court in 1840, and senator in 1850. He was accidentally killed by falling from a building 6 June 1854, a. nearly 50; his w. Sarah Ann d. 23 Sep. 1861, a. 48.

RECORD, DANIEL, m. Prudence, dau. of Warham Warner of N. Br., and had *Jonathan Adams*, b. 6 Oct. 1813; *Martha H.*, b. 7 Ap. 1815; *Andrew C.*, b. 15 Feb. 1817; *Samuel C.*, b. 16 Jan. 1819. DANIEL the f. res. at Barre, and d. 30 Nov. 1841, a. 56; his w. Prudence d. here, at the house of her son, *Andrew C.*, 8 Ap. 1876, a. nearly 92.

2. ANDREW C., s. of Daniel (1), m. Susan C. Thomas 23 Nov. 1852, and had *Carrie L.*, b. 2 May 1859; *Charlie A.*, b. 13 Jan. 1863; *Minnie L.*, b. 15 Jan. 1865; *Mattie G.*, b. 14 Sep. 1869. ANDREW C. the f. kept the hotel near the Common for several years, and after a temporary absence from the town returned and res. at the Furnace Village.

REED, EBENEZER, by w. Anna, had *Moses*, bap. 22 Oct. 1738.

2. JONATHAN, by w. ——, had *Abner*, bap. 10 June 1739.

3. MICAH, a descendant from William [1] and Mabel (Kendall) of Woburn, through George [2] and Elizabeth (Jennison) of Wob., William [3] and Abigail (Kendall) of Lexington, William [4] and Sarah (Poulter) of Lex., and Deac. Samuel [5] and Eunice (Stone) of Burlington, was born 28 Sep. 1746, m. Elizabeth, dau. of John Paige, of Bedford, and had *Micah*, b. 19 Oct. 1773, m. Deborah, dau. of Samuel Thurston, of Hk., pub. 3 Ap. 1797, res. near Ditch Meadow, in New Braintree, where he kept a tavern, was colonel of cavalry, and d. 3 Aug. 1825; his w. d. 30 June 1828; *Elizabeth*, b. 25 Feb. 1779; *Samuel*, b. at Hk. 11 June 1783, d. at Burlington, Vt., 5 May 1846; *Eunice*, b. 13 Jan. 1787, m. James Barr of N. Br., and (2d) Perley Granger. MICAH the f. rem. to Hk. about 1780, and prob. to N. Br. afterwards. He d. by a fall from a scaffold 1 Mar. 1804; his w. Elizabeth d. 21 Mar. 1838, a. 89.

ITHAMAR, of Pet., m. Susanna Steward 16 Jan. 1749-50. BATHSHEBA, of Rehoboth, m. Abel Walker, pub. 15 Nov. 1801. LYDIA, of Wendell, m. Obadiah Rogers, pub. 3 Ap. 1815. SALLY, m. Joshua Rogers of Gr., pub. 6 Oct. 1817. MOLLY, a pauper, d. unm. 22 Feb. 1822, a. 83. ALBERT, d. 4 Ap. 1835, a. 20.

RICE, EDMUND, was of Sudbury in 1639, rem. to Marlborough, and d. there 3 May 1663. He had eight sons and three daughters.

2. THOMAS, the third s. of Edmund (1), res. in Sudbury, and afterwards in Marlborough. By w. Mary, he had thirteen children, of whom the second was *Thomas*, b. 30 June 1654.

3. THOMAS, s. of Thomas (2), had *Thomas*, b. —— 1683, m. Mary Oakes; *Charles*, b. 7 July 1684; *Eunice*, b. 3 May 1686; *Jason*, b. 23 Feb. 1688; *Jedediah*, b. 10 June 1690, m. Dorcas Wheeler; *Abiel*, twin, b. 11 Dec. 1692, d. 27 Dec. 1692; *Anna*, twin, b. 11 Dec. 1692, d. 25 Dec. 1692, *Asher*, b. 6 July 1694, was taken prisoner by the Indians 8 Aug. 1704, and long afterward redeemed; *Adonijah*, b. 11 Aug. 1696, also taken prisoner by the Indians 8 Aug. 1704, and declined to return from his captivity; *Perez*, b. 23 July 1698; *Vashti*, b. 7 Mar. 1700, m. Daniel Hardy of Westborough 22 Dec. 1727; *Beriah*, b. 20 Aug. 1702; *Noah*, b. ——, m. Hannah Warren. THOMAS the f. res. in that part of Marlb. which afterwards became Westb., and represented Marlb. several years in the General Court. His first wife, Mary, d. 13 May 1677, and he m. his cousin Anna Rice 10 Jan. 1681, who d. 2 May 1731, a. 69. He is said to have d. about 1747, a. 94.

4. CHARLES, s. of Thomas (3), m. Rachel Wheeler at Marlb. 26 Ap. 1711, and had *Zebulon*, b. 27 Feb. 1711-12; *Solomon*, b. 1 Sep. 1713; *Adam*, b. 18 Aug. 1715; *Oliver*, b. 2 May 1717; *Elijah*, b. 26 June 1719; *Anna*, b. 6 May, 1722, m. Ebenezer Rice; *Zerviah*, b. 1 May 1724; *Adonijah*, bap. 28 May 1727; *Charles*, b. 1 Mar. 1731; *Abner*, b. 17 Sep. 1732, a soldier in the Revolutionary War. CHARLES the f. res. in that part of Marlb. which was afterwards Westb.

5. PEREZ, s. of Thomas (3), by w. Lydia, had *Phineas*, b. 4 Aug. 1724;

Jedediah, b. 29 May 1726; *Ephraim*, b. 14 Mar. 1729; *Mehetabel*, b. 3 Ap. 1731, prob. m. Joseph Willoughby, pub. 2 Aug. 1765, in Hk.; *John*, b. —— 1734; *Benjamin*, b. —— 1744; *Betsey*, b. —— 1747, m. Bartholomew Towne, Jr., 22 June 1767; *Stephen*, b. —— 1749. PEREZ the f. rem. about 1732 from Westb. to Sutton, where his w. Lydia d. — Jan. 1793, a. 92.

6. BERIAH, s. of Thomas (3), m. Mary Goodenow 6 June 1730–1, and had *Jude*, b. 3 Dec. 1731; *Asaph*, b. 9 May 1733, grad. H. C. 1752, practised medicine a few years at Brookfield, was ordained at Westminster, 16 Oct. 1765, and d. in office, after a ministry of half a century, 30 Ap. 1816; *Timothy*, b. 18 Feb. 1735; *Stephen*, b. 15 Mar. 1737; *Mary*, b. 23 Mar. 1739; *Sarah*, b. 22 Mar. 1741; *Lucy*, b. 19 Mar. 1743; *Rachel*, b. 1 May 1745; *Beriah*, bap. 16 Aug. 1747; *Benjamin*, b. 11 May 1749. BERIAH the f. res. at Westb. until about 1748, when he rem. to Annapolis, N. S.[1]

7. SOLOMON, s. of Charles (4), by w. Anna, had *Thankful*, b. prob. about 1742, m. Edward Higgins of Palmer 17 Oct. 1764; *Antipas*, b. about 1744; *Jonas*, bap. 26 Oct. 1746, m. Patty Whittemore; *Hannah*, bap. 22 May, 1748, m. Jonathan Fisk of Shelburne 18 Jan. 1770; *Moses*, twin, b. 23 Oct. 1749; *Aaron*, twin, b. 23 Oct. 1749, d. unm. 7 Aug. 1816; *Elizabeth*, b. 12 Sep. 1751, m. John Nims of Shelburne 4 Feb. 1771; *Lucy*, b. 31 Oct. 1753, m. Martin Rice of Charlemont, 6 July 1779; *Mary*, b. 24 Sep. 1755, m. Joseph Hewes of Lyme, Conn., 5 Oct. 1780; *Ruth*, b. 2 Feb. 1757, m. John Rice of Charlemont 6 Mar. 1782; *Joel*, b. 13 Ap. 1760. SOLOMON the f. rem. from Westb. to Hardwick in 1749, where the names of his chil. b. then and afterwards are recorded. He was a soldier, 1757, in the French War, and d. 11 Mar. 1802, a. 88; his w. Anna d. 9 Ap. 1802, a. 86.

8. OLIVER, s. of Charles (4), m. Hannah Barrett of Grafton 30 June 1742, and had ten children b. in Hk.; but the record is mutilated so that the names of four are lost; those which remain are *Isaac*, b. 12 Oct. 1742; *Stephen*, b. 20 Feb. 1744–5, m. Thankful Glazier 23 Oct. 1770; *Sarah*, b. 4 Feb. 1746–7; *Zerviah*, b. 16 Jan. 1748–9, m. Abner Marble of Pet. 19 Ap. 1768; *Levina*, b. 5 July 1751, m. Zachariah Harwood of Bennington, Vt., 30 Ap. 1767, and d. 6 Sep. 1808; ———, 1753; ———, 1756; ———, 11 Aug. 1757; ———, 1759; *Susan*, b. 24 June 176–, m. Stephen Watkins of Athol 6 Mar. 1789. OLIVER the f. rem. from Westb. to Hk., prob. soon after 5 Oct. 1739, at which date he bought a farm of Samuel Robinson. He served in the French War, in 1756 and 1757. Late in life he rem. to Bennington, Vt., where he died.

9. PHINEAS, s. of Perez (5), m. Hannah Cummins of Sutton in 1743, and had (all apparently born here) *Nathaniel*, b. 18 Sep. 1745, m. Elizabeth Lawrence 24 Nov. 1768; *Hannah*, b. 26 July 1747, m. John Haskell, pub. 22 July 1765; *Mary*, b. 10 Feb. 1751, m. Eli Freeman 26 Mar. 1767; *Elizabeth*, b. 6 July 1753; *Abigail*, b. 17 Ap. 1755, m. Stephen Johnson 31 May 1774; *Ruth*, b. 12 Feb. 1758; *Noah*, b. —— 1760, m. Prudence Luce 30 Aug. 1781. PHINEAS the f. rem. prob. from Sutton to Hk. before 1745, and seems to have rem. after 1760 to Rutland District, now Barre, which is described as the residence of his children at the date of their marriage.

10. JEDEDIAH, s. of Perez (5), by w. Mehetabel, had *Mehetabel*, b. 27 May 1750, m. Rand White of Spencer; *Tabitha*, b. 16 Feb. 1752; *Jedediah*, b. 26 Feb. 1754; *Anna*, b. 27 Jan. 1756. JEDEDIAH the f. was a physician, and res. on the road leading from the Mandell Farm to Ruggles Hill; he came here before 11 Ap. 1749, and d. 4 Ap. 1756, before he had quite attained the age of 30 years; his w. Mehetabel m. David Knapp of Spencer 27 Sep. 1759.

11. EPHRAIM, s. of Perez (5), seems to have res. here several years, though no trace is found of wife or children. He was a soldier in the French War, 1756, and sold to Andrew Haskell, 28 Feb. 1761, a hundred acres of land, in Hk., which he had previously bought of Aaron Thomas.

12. STEPHEN, s. of Beriah (6), m. Dorothy Woods of Marlb. 10 Nov. 1763, and had *Ashbel*, b. 27 May 1765; *Mary*, b. 18 May 1767, m. Nathan Freeman 1 Ap. 1790; *Hepzibah*, b. 12 Feb. 1771, d. unm. ——; *Lucy*, b. 12 Mar. 1773,

[1] Thus far I have relied chiefly for names and dates on Ward's *History of the Rice Family*.

d. unm. ——; *Lydia*, b. 25 Jan. 1775, d. unm. ——; *Stephen*, bap. 8 June 1777; *Thomas*, bap. 9 June 1782. The names of all these chil. are recorded as if born here; but in the deed of his farm, dated 26 Ap. 1771, STEPHEN the f. is described as of Brookfield. If this was the date of his removal, he very soon attained a prominent position in the town, being elected in 1774 selectman, assessor, a member of the committee of correspondence, delegate to the convention of committees at Worcester, and delegate to the first provincial congress at Concord, to which last-named office he was again elected in 1775, and also representative in the General Court. At the organization of the militia by the town, 22 Sep. 1774, he was elected lieutenant; he became captain before 22 May 1775, and was elected lieutenant-colonel by the General Court 10 Ap. 1776, in which capacity he marched with Col. Cushing's regiment "on the alarm to Bennington," July 1777, and served several months; he remained in office until the reorganization of the militia in 1781, after the adoption of the Constitution. He was selectman four years, assessor two years, and representative three years. He was a farmer, and res. on the turnpike, somewhat more than a mile north from the Common, at the place marked "C. Paige" on the R. Map. Though rather short in stature, he seemed to be burdened by an excess of flesh until he was about seventy years old; after which he became very thin, but retained his vigor and activity. He d. 24 Nov. 1831, a. nearly 95; his w. Dorothy, with whom he lived in wedlock almost 63 years, d. 15 Oct. 1826, a. 83. All the chil. were living 20 Ap. 1821, the date of their father's will.

13. ANTIPAS, s. of Solomon (7), m. Thankful Rider 27 Oct. 1774, and had *Seth*, b. 24 Feb. 1776, m. Polly Hammond of Hawley, pub. 9 Nov. 1800; *Solomon; Timothy; Anna*, b ——, m. Thomas Willis 16 Nov. 1800; *Mercy; Polly*. Such are the names mentioned in the will of ANTIPAS the f., dated 1 Feb. 1802, in which provision is made for the maintenance of his aged parents, both of whom, however, died within a few weeks afterwards. He d. 10 Feb. 1802.

14. ISAAC, s. of Oliver (8), m. Mehetabel Stearns of Worcester 1 Dec. 1768, and had *John*, b. 29 Mar. 1770; *Clark*, b. 4 Ap. 1772; *Charles*, b. 14 Aug. 1774; *Lucinda*, b. 7 Sep. 1776. ISAAC the f. was one of the "minute-men" who marched from Hardwick to Cambridge, on the Lexington alarm, in April 1775.

15. ASHBEL, s. of Stephen (12), m. Polly, dau. of Capt. Seth Peirce 15 Sep. 1793; she d. 7 June 1802, and he m. Sylvina, dau. of David Waite of N. Br., pub. 21 June 1807. His chil. were *Horace*, b. —— 1794; *Mary P.*, b. —— 1795, m. Horace S. Childs of Brandon, Vt., 15 Oct. 1817, and d. at Chicago about 1880; *Albert F.*, b. —— Aug. 1810; *Sylvina*, b. — Sep. 1812, d. unm. 25 Nov. 1849, a. 37. ASHBEL the f. res. on the old River road, about a mile southerly from the Furnace, at the place marked "A. Rice" on the R. Map. He was a farmer, and while at work on his farm was killed by a fall from a load of hay 17 July 1845, a. 80; his w. Sylvina d. 3 Dec. 1860, a. 84.

16. STEPHEN, s. of Stephen (12), m. Fanny, dau. of James Paige, 4 Sep. 1811, and had *Eliza Ann*, b. 13 Jan. 1814, m. John P. Robinson of Brk. 18 Feb. 1835, and rem. to Boston. STEPHEN the f. was a farmer, res. on the homestead, and was killed by a fall from a hay-cart, in front of the new cemetery, 16 Aug. 1821; his w. Fanny m. Capt. Moses Allen, pub. 7 May 1825, and d. in Boston 15 Feb. 1873, a. nearly 89.

17. THOMAS, s. of Stephen (12), grad. Y. C. 1803, studied law, and commenced practice with good prospect of success; but his passionate fondness for music predominated over his love for the law, and he abandoned the profession entirely. He was a genial companion, fond of society and its indulgences, of respectable attainments and gentlemanly deportment, but lacked the energy necessary to success. After gaining a precarious livelihood for several years, he escaped the snare, and cast off the bonds which had enslaved him. He became master of his appetites, rem. to Vermont, and devoted himself to the teaching of music, for which employment he was admirably qualified, both by taste and practice. He is reported to have been successful in obtaining a competency for the supply of his personal wants, together with the approbation of

his pupils and the respectful consideration of the community, until he d. unm. at a good old age.

18. ALBERT F., s. of Ashbel (15), m. Caroline Morse of Southbridge, pub. 13 Nov. 1835, and had *Albert W.*, b. 4 Jan. 1841; *Franklin M.*, b. 9 Feb. 1843, m. Eliza G. Howard 6 Feb. 1879, a merchant in Warren, where he d. 20 Aug. 1881. ALBERT F. the f., a farmer, res. on the homestead.

19. JOHN, perhaps the same who m. Sarah (or Polly) Woods of Pet. 10 Dec. 1789, had *Susanna* and *Perez*, bap. 29 Oct. 1799; *Willard*, bap. 29 July 1802. JOHN the f. may have been the "adult" who was bap. 2 Nov. 1806.

20. JOHN, possibly the same as John (19) above mentioned, m. Betsey Ruggles, pub. 21 Nov. 1808, and had *Betsey Ruggles*, bap. 3 Dec. 1809 (the father being then described as of Somerset, Vt.), m. Varnum Wetherbee 14 Nov. 1831.

ELIZABETH, wid. of Aaron, of Rut., m. Caleb Benjamin 18 Nov. 1760. CATHERINE, prob. dau. of Oliver (8), m. Aaron Forbush, Jr., 27 Ap. 1774. BATHSHEBA, prob. dau. of Oliver (8), m. Dudley Jordan 8 Aug. 1776. Widow SUSANNA, m. Edward Clark of Hubbardston 22 Ap. 1779. PEREZ, m. Chloe Lincoln 8 Ap. 1779. DARIUS, of Gr., m. Charity Winslow 7 Dec. 1780, and Rebecca Haskins 17 Dec. 1789. ABISHA, m. Abigail Winslow 20 Feb. 1782. ABIGAIL, m. Samuel Freeman 23 Ap. 1807. MARY, m. Jesse Perkins 25 Ap. 1819. REBECCA A., of Ware, m. Abiathar P. Ellis, pub. 24 Feb. 1844. PETER, d. 8 Jan. 1808, a. 18.

RICH, JOHN, by w. Mercy, had *Martha*, b. 26 May 1776, perhaps m. Ebenezer Titus of Gr. 30 Aug. 1792; *Bethiah*, b. 13 Ap. 1778; *John*, b. 16 May 1780; *Sabery* (*Sabra?*), called *Sylvia* in the record of baptisms, b. 8 Mar. 1782; *William*, b. — June 1784, d. 5 May 1790; *Samuel*, b. 25 Ap. 1786; *William*, b. 13 June 1792. JOHN the f. is styled captain in the records.

2. APOLLOS, perhaps brother of John (1), had *Nabby*, bap. 25 June 1780; *Alphea*, bap. 30 June 1782.

3. APOLLOS, prob. s. of Apollos (2), or John (1), by w. Bethia, had *Lyman*, b. ——, res. in Orange; *Dwight B.*, b. here, —— 1826, res. in Boston, d. at Orange Park, Fla., 22 Oct. 1882, a. 56 years and 6 months; *Charles*, bap. here 19 June 1829, d. 26 June 1829, a. 9 months; *Caroline Abigail*, bap. 26 June 1831; *Henry Alexander*, bap. 3 Nov. 1833, res. in Hyde Park; a daughter, bap. — May 1837; *Andrew J.*, b. ——, res. in Hyde Park. Either *Caroline A.* or another dau. m. Henry M. Ward of Northfield. This family had a "reunion" 26 Ap. 1882, when the four sons and Mrs. Ward were present. Six months later the circle was broken. APOLLOS the f. was a farmer, and resided near the central bridge over Ware River, at the place marked "A. Rich" on the R. Map. He was elected captain of the "Rifle Company" 29 June 1833, and lieutenant-colonel of the regiment 14 Aug. 1835. He rem. to Orange, where he d. 27 Dec. 1845, a. 47.

4. TIMOTHY, of Boston, m. Fanny, dau. of Capt. Edward Ruggles, pub. 25 Mar. 1810, and for some reason the birth of three children appears on our records: *Edward Ruggles*, b. in Medford 14 July 1810; *Timothy Smith*, b. in Boston 15 Feb. 1812; *Ann Dean*, b. 5 Nov. 1813.

EBENEZER, Jr., of Gr., m. Sarah Knowlton, pub. 14 Dec. 1786. RUTH, of Gr., m. William Wyatt Barlow, pub. 7 Feb. 1790. NABBY, of Ware, m. Sylvester Bowen 19 Aug. 1804. BARNABAS, of Enf., m. Lydia Wetherbee, pub. 26 Nov. 1827. REBECCA, of Barre, m. Moses Bolster 26 June 1836. LUCY, wife of Jonathan C., d. 4 Feb. 1841, a. 44.

RICHARDS, EDWARD, m. Susan Hunting, and d. 25 Aug. 1684; he had in Dedham five chil., of whom the fourth was *Nathaniel*, b. 25 Jan. 1648.

2. NATHANIEL, s. of Edward (1), m. Mary, dau. of Deacon John Aldis 28 Feb. 1678, and d. 15 Feb. 1726; he res. in Dedham, and had eight children, of whom the third was *James*, b. 24 Ap. 1683.

3. JAMES, s. of Nathaniel (2), m. Hannah, dau. of Deacon Jonathan Metcalf, res. in Dedham, and had eleven chil., of whom the sixth was *Ebenezer*, b. 2 Jan. 1718–19.

4. EBENEZER, s. of James (3), m. Thankful, dau. of Ebenezer Stratton of

Cambridge, and d. 27 Feb. 1799; he res. in Dedham, and had ten chil., of whom the seventh was *David*, b. 26 Jan. 1755. See *Gen. of Richards Family*.

5. DAVID, s. of Ebenezer (4), m. Chloe, dau. of Maj. Thomas Richards of Dover, and had *Thomas*, b. 16 Mar. 1782, d. at Springf. 30 Dec. 1858; *David*, b. 3 Feb. 1784; *Ebenezer*, b. 12 June 1786; *Rebecca*, b. 15 Jan. 1789, m. Aaron Johnson, Jr., 14 May 1807; *William*, b. 4 May 1791; *Whiting*, b. 11 May 1793, d. — Sep. 1854; *Leonard*, b. 10 May 1795, d. 22 Jan. 1796; *Lyman Willard*, b. 23 Feb. 1797; *Clarissa*, b. 24 Oct. 1799, m. Samuel Warner of Springf. 11 July 1820, and d. 15 Oct. 1867; *Wyatt*, b. 8 Mar. 1802; *Mary Fuller*, b. 15 Jan. 1805, m. Nathaniel R. Moseley of Springf. 9 Oct. 1823. DAVID the f. rem. to Hk. soon after his marriage, res. in the northwesterly part of the town, about a quarter of a mile northerly from the turnpike, was a farmer, and d. 29 Dec. 1817, a. nearly 63; his w. Chloe d. 24 May 1840, a. 79.

6. DAVID, s. of David (5), m. Sarah M. Mitchell at Keene, N. H. 2 Dec. 1810; she d. 2 Ap. 1814, and he m. Nancy Jackson at Hk. 20 Sep. 1821; she d. 8 Nov. 1822, and he m. Elizabeth Shackford at Boston, 22 Oct. 1826. His chil. were *Sarah Mitchell*, b. 11 Oct. 1811, d. 24 Oct. 1822; *George Osgood*, b. 18 July 1813, d. at Warren 9 Oct. 1855; *William Spencer*, b. 1 Jan. 1828; *John D.*, b. 12 Mar. 1830, d. 6 Feb. 1832; *Mary Elizabeth*, b. 14 Aug. 1832; *Sarah Mitchell*, b. 30 Sep. 1835, d. 2 Feb. 1836; *Thomas*, b. 26 July 1837. DAVID the f. was a carpenter, res. successively at Hk., Keene, N. H., Boston, and Fiskdale (Sturbridge), and is said (*Gen. Richards Fam.*) to have been living in 1860.

7. EBENEZER, s. of David (5), m. Abigail Richardson 4 Feb. 1812. No record found of children, except that an infant, aged two months, d. 14 May 1814. EBENEZER the f. res. on the homestead, and d. 27 Sep. 1833; his w. Abigail d. 24 Jan. 1868, a. 76.

8. WILLIAM, s. of David (5), m. ——; she d. here 11 Dec. 1826, a. 30, and he (then. res. in Roxbury) m. Catherine Tute 28 Feb. 1830.

9. WYATT, s. of David (5), m. Sarah P. Ruggles, 5 Ap. 1827, and had *Joseph Ruggles*, b. 18 Feb. 1828, an architect; *Sarah Eliza*, b. 19 Oct. 1829; *Martha Page*, b. 1 Nov. 1831, d. 3 Jan. 1832; *Samuel Wyatt*, b. 3 Mar. 1833, an architect; *William Whiting*, b. 1 June 1835, grad. H. C. 1855. WYATT the f. was a mason, res. in Boston, and d. 9 Feb. 1872.

10. MARSHALL, of Springf., m. Louisa R. Monroe 28 Jan. 1869, and had *Frank E.*, b. — Dec. 1869, d. 18 Nov. 1872; *Gracie*, b. 30 July 1880.

CALVIN, m. Sarah W. Gleason of Pet., pub. 10 Nov. 1832. ABIGAIL S., m. Benjamin R. Wetherbee, pub. 3 Feb. 1850. MARTHA A., of Gr., m. Charles P. Crowell, pub. 13 Nov. 1858. GIDEON, m. Adeline Dupray 12 Feb. 1865. SARAH, d. 13 June 1847, a. 19.

RICHARDSON, SILAS, m. Abigail Thayer 26 Nov. 1789, and had *Fanny*, b. 19 May 1791, m. Samuel Thayer of Dana, pub. 27 Jan. 1812; *Nabby*, b. 22 Dec. 1792, m. Ebenezer Richards 4 Feb. 1812, and d. 24 Jan. 1868; *Seth*, b. 17 Ap. 1799; *Eunice*, b. 10 Jan. 1801, m. Joel Whipple 2 Sep. 1821, and d. at N. Brk. 9 Oct. 1869; *Sarah F.*, b. 20 June 1802 (or 1805), m. James P. Coolidge 29 May 1829, and d. at N. Brk. 6 Dec. 1872; *Silas Peck*, b. 2 Jan. 1807; *Anna F.*, b. 13 Dec. 1813, m. Jonas Allen, pub. 8 Nov. 1833, and d. 9 Jan. 1864. SILAS the f. res. in the northwesterly part of the town, not far from David Richards, and d. 1 Feb. 1829, a. 67; his w. Abigail d. 23 Jan. 1867, a. 97.

2. BENJAMIN, m. Bethia ——, and had *Nancy*, b. — Aug. 1786, d. 10 July 1792, a. 5 years and 11 months; *Enoch*, b. — Sep. 1789, d. 10 July 1792, a. 2 years and 10 months. Besides the death of these two children on the same day, I find no trace of this family.

3. WYATT, perhaps brother of Silas (1), and of Benjamin (2), m. Abigail Johnson, pub. 6 May 1795, and had *Wyatt*, b. 29 Aug. 1799, m. Hannah F. Babbitt of Swanzey, N. H., pub. 5 Ap. 1824; *Nancy*, b. — Oct. 1802, m. Alvan Bassett, pub. 22 Sep. 1828; *Almira*, b. 16 Feb. 1816, m. Joseph Robinson of Amherst 31 Dec. 1840.

4. SETH, s. of Silas (1), m. Alice Johnson, pub. 3 Ap. 1820, and had *Wil-*

liam, b. about 1820, m. Louisa Lamb 4 July 1841; she d. 4 June 1842 a. 18, and he was drowned 28 Sep. 1852, a. 32; *Mary J.*, b. —— 1822, m. John King 3 Oct. 1844, and d. at Gr. 11 May 1878; *Civilla Y.*, b. about 1826, d. 2 Sep. 1849, a. 23; *Asa F.*, b. about 1832; *Rhoda*, b. — Nov. 1834, d. 14 Aug. 1835, a. 9 months. SETH the f. d. 14 or 16 June 1881; his w. Alice d. 16 Feb. 1861, a. 60.

5. SILAS P., s. of Silas (1), m. Fanny Johnson, pub. 9 June 1828; she d. 13 Aug. 1855, a. 48.

6. ERASTUS B., m. Julia ——, and had *Julia Ann*, b. 23 May 1854, m. —— Drinkwine, and d. at Athol 25 Mar. 1877.

7. SILAS O., by. w. Sarah, had *Orlando H.*, b. 9 Ap. 1856.

8. GEORGE W., m. Mary Ann Thayer in 1854, and had *George L.*, b. —— 1855, d. 11 May 1867, a. 12; *Fanny*, b. about 1857, m. Curtis C. Sleeper 8 Mar. 1873; *Susan R.*, b. about 1859, m. Albert S. Sturtevant 4 Dec. 1877; *Samuel*, b. —— 1866, drowned 24 Nov. 1872, a. 6; *James Walter*, b. 13 Nov. 1872.

9. ASA F., s. of Seth (4), m. Lydia J. Bassett 26 May 1858, and had *Leon Augustine*, b. 31 Ap. 1859; *Edgar*, twin, b. 17 Dec. 1861, d. 9 Jan. 1862; *Ednah*, twin, b. 17 Dec. 1861.

10. ALONZO, m. Martha Marsh, pub. 4 Feb. 1863, and had *William Dexter*, b. 21 July 1863; *Fanny C.*, b. 23 Nov. 1865.

11. ALFRED H., m. Lucretia Marsh 21 Nov. 1870, and had *Fanny Lucretia*, b. 11 Ap. 1873; *Milan L.*, b. — May 1878, d. 3 Sep. 1879; *Myron E.*, b. 29 Nov. 1879; *Florence Eliza*, b. 29 Mar. 1881. ALFRED H. the f. res. at Gilbertville, and was selectman in 1875.

12. HERBERT O. (s. of Orlando and Sarah), m. Mary E. Labelle 7 Oct. 1875, and had *Inez Leona*, b. 22 Feb. 1876.

CELIA, of Gr., m. Aaron Johnson 11 Sep. 1800. BETHIA, of Dana, m. Reuel Terry, pub. 26 Ap. 1807. CELIA J., m. James Sloan 16 Mar. 1837. LUCY, of Dana, m. Cyrus W. Stephens 31 Dec. 1837. ELIZABETH C., m. Joseph W. Stephens 23 Mar. 1843. FANNY, m. Hosea E. Stone, pub. 17 Oct. 1847. ESTHER G., m. Stephen King of Dana, pub. 6 Oct. 1848. BETHIA, m. Ebenezer W. Gleason, pub. 10 Mar. 1849. LOUISA A., m. John M. Ramsdell, pub. 25 May 1858. OTIS B., of Ware, m. Mary S. Smith 14 Ap. 1877.

The record of births in the Richardson Family, previous to 1854, is so imperfect that I am unable to indicate the exact relationship of its several branches, nor am I sure whether all who are here named belong to one common stock.

RICHMOND, JOSEPH, by w. Hannah, had four chil. bap. here 18 June, 1820, namely, *Benjamin Franklin*, *Elizabeth*, *Waldron*, and *Maria;* of whom *Waldron* d. (prob. unm.) 27 Dec. 1839, a. 27, and *Maria* m. Timothy P. Bruce 3 Mar. 1836. He prob. had other chil. JOSEPH the f. res. near the Barre line, at the place marked "J. Richmond" on the R. Map, and d. 22 Nov. 1839, a. 58; his w. Hannah (b. at Raynham) d. 23 Sep. 1861, a. 78. A singular mortality befell this family in 1839, when the father and two sons (perhaps three) died in the space of less than seven weeks.

2. NOAH, res. near the Barre line, at the place marked "N. Richmond" on the R. Map, and d. 16 Oct. 1846, a. 79; his w. Mercy d. 25 Sep. 1842, a. 64. They were prob. parents of *Oliver O.*, b. about 1815.

3. JOSEPH D., prob. s. of Joseph (1), m. Catherine W. Dean of Barre, pub. 14 Nov. 1835, and d. 11 Dec. 1839, a. 34; his w. Catherine W. m. Benjamin Bassett 29 June 1847. No record of children.

4. BENJAMIN F., s. of Joseph (1), m. Mary Spooner of Barre, pub. 11 Nov. 1837, and d. 10 Nov. 1839, a. 33; his w. Mary m. Timothy Fay 20 Ap. 1842, and d. 11 Aug. 1855.

5. OLIVER O., prob. s. of Noah (2), m. Mary W. Loring of Pet., pub. 19 May 1838, and d. 6 Sep. 1840, a. 25; his w. was perhaps the Mary who m. Marcus Goodman of Dana, pub. 6 Nov. 1844.

CHARLES, prob. s. of Joseph (1), or of Noah (2), d. 20 Ap. 1835, a. 15. LYDIA "Richman," of N. Br., m. Ebenezer Lawrence 18 Dec. 1763.

RIDDLE, JAMES M., m. Tryphosa F. Woodis, of W. Brk., pub. 23 Dec. 1849, and had *Eugene Leslie*, b. 25 Oct. 1850.

RIPLEY, JEPTHAH, by w. Lucinda ——, had *Lorenzo*, b. 27 Dec. 1825; *Adeline Maria*, b. 1 Dec. 1826.

RIXFORTH, HENRY (generally written Rixford), m. Sarah Stanford 22 Feb. 1781. No record of children. He served in the Revolutionary War 1775, 1776, 1777, 1778, 1780.

ROACH, MAURICE, by w. Elizabeth, had *John*, b. 16 Nov. 1866; *David*, b. 30 Sep. 1868; *Elizabeth*, b. 15 Aug. 1871; *Catherine*, b. 14 Dec. 1873; *Maurice*, b. 15 July 1876.

ROBBINS, JOSEPH, m. Ann Maria Granger, pub. 23 Nov. 1851, and had *Joseph Elmer*, b. 21 May 1853, d. 25 Oct. 1854. JOSEPH the f. d. 19 Dec. 1858, a. 31; his w. Ann Maria d. 30 June 1857, a. 29.

2. LYMAN, by w. Mary, had *Samuel*, b. 26 Mar. 1865; *Lyman*, b. 18 Aug. 1878.

EMORY, s. of Samuel and Anna, b. at Belchertown, d. unm. 9 Mar. 1877, a. 62. NANCY, m. David Thresher of N. Br., pub. 17 Sep. 1850.

ROBERTS, JOHN, m. Elizabeth Fay, in Grafton, 5 June 1746; she d. 4 Nov. 1750, and he m. Sarah Abbott 1 Ap. 1752. His chil. were *John*, b. 27 Oct. 1747; *Hannah*, b. 28 July 1749; *Elizabeth*, b. 25 Jan. 1753; *Josiah*, b. 27 Feb. 1754; *Sarah*, b. 11 Ap. 1756. JOHN the f. was a farmer, and one of the principal founders of the Separate Church. He prob. rem. about 1761, with many of that church, to Bennington, and perhaps afterwards to Morristown, Vt.

SUSANNA, of Brk., m. Joseph Foster, pub. 9 Feb. 1751-2. BENJAMIN, m. Martha Heart of Leicester, pub. 9 Oct. 1754, and (2d) Martha Abbott, 29 Feb. 1764. MALVINA, m. Almon G. Stevens, pub. — Ap. 1852. VICTOR, m. Leonora Taylor, pub. 9 Nov. 1867.

ROBINSON. As several families of this name have resided here between whom no kinship can be traced, I shall, for the sake of convenience, arrange the names in three sections.

SECTION I.

ROBINSON, WILLIAM, by w. Elizabeth, had *Elizabeth*, b. ——; *Hannah*, b. 13 July 1671, d. 5 Oct. 1672; *William*, b. 10 July, 1673; *Mercy*, b. 7 Aug. 1676; *David*, b. 23 May 1678 ("lame and helpless" in 1695); *Samuel*, b. 20 Ap. 1680; *Jonathan*, b. 20 Ap. 1682. WILLIAM the f. res. in Cambridge during most of his life; he d. in 1693, when all his chil. except *Hannah* were living.

2. SAMUEL, s. of William (1), m. Sarah, dau. of Samuel Manning of Billerica, 23 Mar. 1703-4; she d. 19 July 1709, and he m. Elizabeth, dau. of Capt. Samuel Brigham of Marlborough, 16 Oct. 1711. His chil. were *Sarah*, bap. 22 July, 1705, d. young; *Samuel*, b. 4 Ap. 1707; *Dorothy*, b. 19 Ap. 1709; *Persis*, b. 7 Sep. 1712; *Edmund*, b. 7 June 1714, d. 25 Nov. 1716; *Sarah*, b. 3 Oct. 1717. SAMUEL the f. kept a tavern in Cambridge until 13 June 1721, when he sold his house and removed to Westborough. Administration on his estate was granted to his w. Elizabeth 24 Ap. 1724, and her brother, Jedediah Brigham, was appointed guardian to the only surviving son, *Samuel*, then in his nineteenth year, 25 Feb. 1725-6. See *Hist. of Cambridge*, p. 644.

3. SAMUEL, s. of Samuel (2), m. *Mercy*, dau. of Moses Leonard and gr.-dau. of Moses Newton, 29 May 1732. At the time of their marriage they res. in Southborough, but soon rem. to Grafton. Their chil. were *Elizabeth*, b. 24 Dec. 1733 (recorded here but prob. b. in Grafton), d. young; *Leonard*, b. here 10 July 1736; *Samuel*, b. 9 Aug. 1738; *Moses*, b. 15 Mar. 1741; *Paul*, b. 17 Dec. 1743, d. —— 1754; *Silas*, b. 17 Mar. 1745-6; *Mercy*, b. 8 Oct. 1748, m. Col. Joseph Safford of Bennington, and d. 7 May 1814; *Sarah*, b.

13 Nov. 1751, m. Benjamin, s. of Capt. Stephen Fay of Ben., and (2d) Gen. Heman Swift of Cornwall, Conn.; *David*, b. 4 Nov. 1754; *Jonathan*, b. 24 Aug. 1756; *Anna*, b. 4 Oct. 1759, m. Isaac Webster of Ben. ——. SAMUEL the f. res. in Grafton a short time after his marriage, and rem. to Hk. in 1735 or 1736, where for the next quarter of a century he was one of the most active and energetic citizens; [1] selectman ten years, assessor three years, and town clerk four years. He was elected 30 Ap. 1746, deacon of the church, which office he resigned 2 Mar. 1748–9, and became deacon of the Separate Church, which was organized at or about that time. He was captain of a company in the French War during the regular campaigns, from 1755 to 1759 inclusive, with the possible exception of one year. Attracted by the beauty of what is now Bennington, which place he visited on his return from one of his campaigns, he organized a company, purchased the rights of the chartered proprietors, and commenced, in 1761, a settlement in the unbroken wilderness. Here, as well as in Hardwick, he was active and prominent; he "was the acknowledged leader in the band of pioneers in the settlement of the town, and continued to exercise almost a controlling authority in the affairs of the town the remainder of his life." [2] In the long and bitter controversy between New York and New Hampshire, concerning the territory then called the New Hampshire Grants, but which now constitutes the State of Vermont, he was actively engaged until the premature close of his life. His energy and ability were recognized by Governor Wentworth, who commissioned him, 8 Feb. 1762, justice of the peace, he thus "being the first person appointed to a judicial office within the limits" of that territory.[3] As a final resort, he was appointed to present a petition to the king for relief. He sailed from New York, 25 Dec. 1766, landed at Falmouth 30 Jan. 1767, and soon afterwards arrived at London.[4] He was partially successful in his mission, but it was left incomplete by his death, of small-pox, 27 Oct. 1767. He was buried in the cemetery connected with the church of his favorite preacher, Rev. George Whitefield, and a monument, with an elaborate inscription,[5] was erected to his memory in the cemetery

[1] While in Hardwick, he res. first in the westerly part of the town, but soon rem. to a place on the turnpike, somewhat more than a mile northerly from the Common. His farm contained nine hundred acres, and the house stood at or near the spot marked "Old House," on the R. Map. On his removal to Bennington, 15 Sep. 1761, he sold six hundred acres of this farm to Capt. Daniel Wheeler, describing it as the "easterly part of my homestead." The house was probably the same which was soon afterwards destroyed. In the *Boston Weekly News-Letter*, dated Monday, August 18, 1773, it was announced that, "On Friday last, about ten o'clock, the dwelling-house of Capt. Daniel Wheeler, of Hardwick, with the furniture, was consumed by fire; the loss is computed at upwards of £500." Thus perished what might have become a very interesting landmark.

[2] Jennings' *Memorials of a Century*, p. 204.

[3] *Ibid.* p. 206.

[4] *Early Hist. of Vermont*, p. 85. Ten days before he left New York, and apparently on his way thither, he conveyed to his son *Samuel* all his land in Massachusetts, so that, in case he should not live to return, the settlement of his estate might be more easy; it was described as, "all the land I own in the township of Hardwick and County of Worcester and Province of Massachusetts Bay, namely, one meadow lot, three acres and three quarters; also a piece of land where formerly stood a small meeting-house, containing one acre and a half; and three hundred acres or thereabouts, on the west side of the farm I formerly lived on; also one hundred and sixty acres on Greenwich River in said town, with all other lands I own in said town; with some land in the Township of Greenwich, namely, the farm Joseph Kidder formerly lived on, containing three hundred acres or thereabouts, and one hundred acres near or adjoining said Greenwich meeting-house, and also one hundred acres in the second Division, and also the west half of the original Lot 47, being about fifty acres, with all and every parcel of land or lands which I now own in said Township." Dated at New Haven 15 Dec. 1766, and acknowledged before "Roger Sherman, Assistant." The "small meeting-house" was that which had been used by the Separate Church, and stood on the easterly side of the old road, long ago discontinued, from the Common to the house marked "J. Gorham" on the R. Map, and about midway between that house and the present road to Ware. The land conveyed by this deed was more than 1,000 acres, in addition to the six hundred acres previously sold to Capt. Daniel Wheeler.

[5] The age of Capt. Robinson and of his wife is overrated by two years on their head stones; his being called 62 years instead of 60, and hers 82 years instead of 80. Such errors, especially in regard to aged persons, are frequently found on head-stones.

at Bennington Centre. His w. Mercy, who was born at Marlborough, 1 Dec. 1714, d. at Bennington, 5 June 1795.

4. LEONARD, s. of Samuel (3), m. Rebecca, dau. of Samuel Billings, 31 Aug. 1758; she d. 18 Nov. 1765, at Bennington, and he m. Mercy, wid. of Silas Newton and dau. of Deac. John Freeman, 13 Mar. 1766; not being happy in her new relation, she returned to Hardwick, and he m. Eunice Holmes of Dedham about 1768. His chil. were *Sarah*, b. 20 Ap. 1759, m. Jonah Brewster of Bennington, and d. 11 Sep. 1816; *Lydia*, b. 17 Jan. 1761, m. Moses Rice of Ben., and d. in May 1827 (these two were b. in Hk.; the fourteen following in Ben.): *Rebecca*, b. 27 Ap. 1763, m. David Cutler of Ben., and d. 3 Sep. 1827; *John*, b. 15 Feb. 1765, m. Hannah Smalley; *Samuel Leonard*, b. 23 Mar. 1767; *Joseph*, b. 22 Ap. 1769, m. Rhoda Hawks, and d. 3 Sep. 1814; *Benjamin*, b. 6 Mar. 1772, d. 18 Sep. 1775; *Elizabeth*, b. 13 Ap. 1774, d. 26 Oct. 1776; *Eunice*, b. 15 Feb. 1776, m. Martin Hopkins; *Hannah*, b. 17 Mar. 1778, m. Heman Hopkins; *Leonard*, b. 31 Mar. 1780, d. 29 May 1781; *Leonard*, b. 1 Mar. 1782, m. Sarah Atherton, and d. in 1835; *Persis*, b. 11 Feb. 1784, m. James Brown, and d. 30 July 1811; *Anna*, b. 12 Ap. 1786, m. Valentine Goodrich; *Luther*, b. 16 Feb. 1787, d. at Swanton 5 Jan. 1811; *Diantha*, b. 22 Jan. 1792, d. at Swanton 14 Ap. 1823. LEONARD the f. served in the French War, 1757, and was a member of the company commanded by his brother Samuel in the Bennington Battle. It is related by Rev. Mr. Jennings, as one of the traditions still extant, that "Leonard Robinson, whose aim was quick and deadly, declared that every time he shot he saw a man fall. 'But,' said he, 'I prayed the Lord to have mercy on his soul, and then I took care of his body.'" He was reputed to be a very pious man; but Mr. Jennings adds that "his piety would seem to have been of that kind that 'trusts God, but keeps the powder dry.'"[1] He res. in Bennington until late in life, when he rem. to Swanton, and d. 29 Sep. 1827, a. 91; his w. Eunice d. 10 Mar. 1826, a. 76.

5. SAMUEL, s. of Samuel (3), m. Hannah Clark of Barre, pub. 15 Ap. 1758; she d. 29 Nov. 1766, and he m. Esther Safford of Bennington, 6 Ap. 1767. His chil. were *Mary*, bap. here 3 Sep. 1758, d. at Bennington 28 Aug. 1761; *Persis*, b. here 22 Nov. 1759; the following ten chil. were b. at Bennington: *Hannah*, b. — Jan. 1770, m. Charles Follett, and d. 31 July 1831; *Esther*, b. 16 Dec. 1771, m. Asahel Hyde; *Samuel*, b. — Jan. 1774, m. Sarah Harwood (she compiled a genealogy of the Robinson and Harwood families, 1837, and d. 10 Sep. 1854, a. 80); *Benjamin*, b. 11 Feb. 1776, a physician, settled in Fayetteville, N. C., where he d. in 1857; *Polly*, b. 16 July 1778, d. young; *Betsey*, b. 18 Ap. 1781, m. Jared Sears; *Safford*, b. 9 May 1784; *Hiram*, b. 15 Aug. 1786; *Lucy*, b. 11 Dec. 1789, m. Erastus Montague; *Sarah*, b. 8 Oct. 1791, m. William Haswell. SAMUEL the f. inherited his father's military spirit. At the age of seventeen he was a member of the company commanded by his father in 1756, and the next year was adjutant of Col. Ruggles' regiment. He and his brother Leonard, with their families, were members of the first company which commenced the settlement of Bennington 18 June 1761. "He was an active man in the New York controversy and in the other early affairs of the town; in 1768 was chosen town committee, in place of his father, deceased; commanded one of the Bennington companies of militia in Bennington Battle; performed other important military services during the war, and rose to the rank of colonel. In 1777 and 1778 he had charge, as overseer, of the Tory prisoners; and in 1779 and 1780 represented the town in the General Assembly, and was for three years a member of the Board of War. He was the first justice of the peace appointed in town under the authority of Vermont, in 1778, and was also, during the same year, one of the judges of the Special Court for the south shire of the county, and in that capacity sat on the trial and conviction of Redding."[2] He d. 3 May 1813, a. 74; his w. Esther d. 30 Sep. 1843, a. 93.

6. MOSES, s. of Samuel (3), m. Mary, dau. of Capt. Stephen Fay, pub. 25 July 1762; she d. 12 Feb. 1801, and he m. Susanna, wid. of Maj. Artemas

[1] *Memorials of a Century*, pp. 197, 221.
[2] *Ibid.* p. 222.

Howe of N. Br., and dau. of Gen. Jonathan Warner of Hardwick. His chil., all b. in Bennington, were *Moses*, b. 16 Nov. 1763, m. Ruth Dewey, and d. 29 or 30 Jan. 1825; *Mary*, b. 3 Ap. 1765, d. — Nov. 1769; *Aaron*, b. 4 May 1767, m. Sarah Hopkins, and (2d) Mary Lyman; *Samuel*, b. 10 Feb. 1769, m. Samantha Brush, and d. 7 Jan. 1820; *Nathan*, b. 4 Mar. 1772, m. Jerusha Staniford, and d. 27 Sep. 1812 (their son John Staniford Robinson, b. 10 Nov. 1804, grad. W. C. 1824, a lawyer, representative two years, senator two years, Governor of Vermont in 1853, res. in Bennington, and d. 24 Ap. 1860 at Charleston, S. C.); *Elijah*, b. 12 Aug. 1774, d. young; *Elijah*, b. 15 Mar. 1778, d. young; *Fay*, b. —— 1783, m. Seraph Howe, and d. 2 Nov. 1816. MOSES the f. was one of the foremost citizens of Bennington and of Vermont. He was elected deacon 22 May 1789, and remained in office through life. "He was chosen town clerk at the first meeting of the town, and for nineteen years; colonel of the militia, and at the head of his regiment at Mount Independence on its evacuation by Gen. St. Clair; member of the famous Council of Safety at the time of the Battle of Bennington, and during the campaign of that year; chief justice in the Supreme Court on its first organization, and for ten years, when he was elected, 1789, to the office of governor of the State by the Legislature; in 1782 one of the agents of Vermont in the Continental Congress; and on the admission of Vermont into the Union one of the senators in "Congress" [1] in 1791. The degree of A. M. was conferred on him by Y. C. in 1789, and by D. C. in 1790. He rem. to Bennington with his father in 1761, and d. there 26 May 1813; his w. Susanna d. 2 Ap. 1844, a. nearly 77.

7. SILAS, s. of Samuel (3), m. Susanna, dau. of Thomas Weeks, 2 Oct. 1766, and had *Paul*, b. — June 1768, m. Anna Safford, and d. —— 1824; *Susanna*, b. —— 1770, m. —— Sparrow, and (2d) Wheeler Branch, and d. 2 Nov. 1806; *Silas*, b. — Mar. 1772, m. Esther Goffe. SILAS the f. rem. to Bennington with his father in 1761. Though less distinguished than his brothers in official transactions, he exhibited the family energy in the New York controversy, and was imprisoned in the Albany jail nearly a year for his participation in the "riots," so styled, but was at last liberated without trial.[2] During the Bennington Battle, while his brother Moses was performing his arduous duty at the Catamount Tavern as one of the Committee of Safety, Silas and his brothers Leonard and David were in the midst of the conflict, as members of the company commanded by their brother Samuel. After the war he is said to have rem. to St. Albans, where both he and his w. Susanna died.

8. DAVID, s. of Samuel (3), m. Sarah, dau. of Capt. Stephen Fay; she d. 25 Jan. 1801, and he m. Eunice Walbridge; she d. 25 June 1813, and he m. Nancy, wid. of George Church of Hartford. His chil. were *Sarah*, b. 27 May 1775; *David*, b. 12 July 1777, grad. W. C. 1797, a lawyer, res. in Ben , and d. 15 Mar. 1858; *Ruth*, b. 8 May 1779; *Stephen*, b. 15 Aug. 1781, a member of the Assembly and judge of the County Court, m. Sarah Hubbell, and d. 26 June 1852; *Hiram*, b. 10 Aug. 1783, d. 20 Feb. 1784; *Hiram*, b. 15 Feb. 1785, d. — Sep. 1786; *Heman*, b. 1 Feb. 1787, m. Betsey Wadsworth, had twelve chil. (of whom Judge Albert D. Robinson was one), and d. 26 Feb. 1837. DAVID the f. rem. "to Bennington with his father in 1761, being then a lad of seven years. He was in the Battle of Bennington as a private in the militia, and afterwards rose by regular promotion to the rank of major-general, which office he resigned about 1817. He was sheriff of the county for twenty two years, ending in 1811, when he was appointed United States marshal for the Vermont District, which office he held for eight years, until 1819." [3] He d. 11 or 12 Dec. 1843, a. 89; his w. Nancy d. 18 Dec. 1845, a. 82.

9. JONATHAN, s. of Samuel (3), m. Mary, dau. of John Fassett, and had *Jonathan Edwards*, b. 4 Aug. 1777, grad. W. C. 1797, was a lawyer, town clerk nine years, and judge of the County Court in 1828; *Mary*, b. 8 Sep. 1781, m. Col. Orsamus C. Merrill, and d. 1 Feb. 1831; *Henry*, b. 26 Aug. 1788; "he was successively paymaster in the army, clerk in the pension office, brigadier-general of the militia, and for ten years clerk of the County and Supreme

[1] *Memorials of a Century*, p. 234.
[2] Thompson's *Hist. Vermont*, pt. ii. p. 21.
[3] *Memorials of a Century*, p. 239.

Court;"[1] *Isaac Tichenor*, b. 17 Aug. 1790, m. Maria, dau. of Deac. Aaron Hubbell, and d. —— 1866. JONATHAN the f., like his father and his elder brothers, was distinguished for energy and intellectual vigor. "He was a lawyer, and was early in public life. He was town clerk six years; represented the town thirteen years; was chief judge of the Supreme Court from 1801 to 1807. He was then chosen senator to Congress, to fill the vacancy occasioned by the resignation of Israel Smith; and was also senator for the succeeding term of six years, which expired March 3, 1815. In October 1815 he became judge of probate and held the office for four years, and in 1818 again represented the town in the General Assembly."[2] The degree of A. M. was conferred on him by D. C. in 1790. He went to Bennington in his boyhood, and d. there 3 Nov. 1819, a. 63. His w. Mary d. 15 July 1822, a. 67.

10. SAMUEL LEONARD, s. of Leonard (4), m. Kezia, dau. of Deac. Ebenezer Willis, 20 June 1793, and had *Susanna*, b. 27 Dec. 1793, m. Thomas Elwell, 25 Ap. 1819, and d. 16 Nov. 1822; *Clarissa*, b. 27 Aug. 1795, m. Ira Ramsdell 11 May 1823; *Chloe*, b. 11 Oct. 1797, m. Benjamin Rider, Jr., of Charton, O., 17 Sep. 1827; *Marcus*, b. 3 Oct. 1799, m. Deborah Brown of Enf. 25 Mar. 1822, and d. 19 Mar. 1835 (his w. Deborah m. Alexander Bartlett of Pelh. 5 Dec. 1838); *Adeline*, b. 6 Nov. 1803, m. Thomas Elwell 19 Oct. 1823; *Ebenezer Willis*, b. ——; besides these he was probably father of *Lucinda*, b. ——, m. Warren Day of N. Sal. 30 Mar. 1829; *Samuel L.*, b. ——, m. Sally S. Moulton 19 Ap. 1835; *Kezia*, b. ——, m. Warren Billings of Amh., pub. 20 May 1843; *Mary*, b. —— 1814, d. 7 Aug. 1818, a. 4. SAMUEL LEONARD the f. was brought here by his mother when a young child, was a farmer, res. on the westerly border of the town near the southeast corner of Greenwich, at the place marked "S. Robinson" on the R. Map. Though not in public life, he exhibited many of the sterling characteristics of his race. He d. 18 Jan. 1863, a. nearly 96; his w. Kezia d. 13 July 1856, a. 80.

SECTION II.

ROBINSON, THOMAS, having lost his first w., m. Mary, wid. of John Woody and dau. of John Cogan[3] of Boston, 11 Jan. 1652–3; she d. 26 Oct. 1661, and he m. wid. Elizabeth Sherman. His chil. were *John*, b. ——, a merchant (named in his father's will 17 Mar. 1665–6, and then "supposed to be in England"); *Samuel*, b. ——, a merchant, d. unm. 16 Jan. 1661–2, a. 24; *Josiah*, b. ——, "apprentice to Mr. Joseph Rocke,"[4] d. 17 Ap. 1660; *Ephraim*, b. ——, d. 22 Sep. 1661; *Thomas*, bap. at Scituate 5 Mar. 1653–4; *James*, b. at Boston 14 Mar. 1654–5, d. — Sep. 1676; *Joseph*, bap. 8 Mar. 1656–7, m. Sarah ——, and d. — Ap. 1703; *Mary*, bap. 28 Feb. 1657–8, d. young; *Mary* bap. 6 Nov. 1659, m. Jacob Green, Jr., of Charlestown 8 Jan. 1676–7. THOMAS the f. was in Scituate as early as 1640, when he bought land of William Gillson, and represented that town in the General Court of Plymouth at its session in October 1643. He was also deacon, probably of the second church in Scituate.[5] In August and September, 1654, he bought two estates, adjoining each other, on the westerly side of Washington Street, directly opposite to the Old South Church, in Boston, bounded on the south by the lot on which the Province House was afterwards erected, and having a depth of two hundred and seventy feet. Here he prob. res. during the remainder of his life, though he seems to have retained his connection with the church at Scituate, as all his children by the second marriage, except *James*, were baptized there. There are reasons for believing that he was son of the celebrated REV. JOHN ROBINSON of Leyden, pastor of the Church of Pilgrims which came to Plymouth in 1620. Isaac Robinson, unquestionably a son of the Rev.

1 *Memorials of a Century*, p. 248.
2 *Ibid.* p. 244.
3 John Cogan (otherwise written Coggan) is said by Snow (*Hist. Boston*) to have "opened the first shop in Boston;" it was on the northeast corner of Washington and State Streets.
4 Joseph Rocke was a merchant, and married a sister of Deacon Robinson's second wife.
5 Deane's *Hist. of Scituate*, pp. 35, 275, 332, and *Plymouth Col. Rec.*, ii. 63.

John Robinson, settled at Scituate at the same time, or at very nearly the same time, that Thomas made his purchase of a homestead there; and it is not unreasonable to infer kinship. At the same time, it must be confessed that no authentic evidence of the supposed fact has yet been discovered, and that the name Thomas is not found in any known catalogue purporting to contain the names of his children. But whatever his ancestry, Deacon Robinson wrought out a good name for himself, which he left as a rich inheritance to his posterity. He d. 23 Mar. 1665-6; his w. Elizabeth d. in 1667.

2. THOMAS, s. of Thomas (1), m. Sarah, dau. of Edward Denison[1] of Roxbury, and had *Thomas*, b. 5 Nov. 1677, m. Sarah Beswick 26 June 1707, and d. s. p. 15 Feb. 1729-30; *Sarah*, bap. 28 Dec. 1679, m. John Ingoldsbury 4 May 1704, and (2d) John Perry 27 May 1707; *Joseph*, bap. 20 Nov. 1681, d. young; *Elizabeth*, b. 26 Sep. 1686, d. young; *James*, b. 15 Mar. 1689-90. THOMAS the f. inherited a part of the homestead, where he resided; he also inherited from his grandfather Cogan the house and store on the northerly corner of State and Washington streets. He was a cordwainer, and d. — June 1700; his w. Sarah d. in Roxbury 15 Nov. 1710, a. 53.

3. JAMES, s. of Thomas (2), m. Patience, dau. of Capt. Samuel Ruggles[2] of Roxbury, 3 July 1711, and had, in Boston, *James*, b. 1 Mar. 1711-12; *Thomas*, b. 15 Sep. 1713, d. young; and in Rochester, *Samuel*, b. 1 Nov. 1715; *Thomas*, b. 20 Ap. 1718; *Sarah*, b. 9 July 1720, m. Ebenezer Spooner of Rochester, pub. 3 Jan. 1745-6; *Dorothy*, b. 10 Mar. 1722-3, m. David Peckham 27 Oct. 1743, and (2d) Maj. Elnathan Haskell 26 Nov. 1749, and d. at Roch. 25 Sep. 1810; *Denison*, b. 16 July 1725; *Joseph*, b. 13 Sep. 1727; *Hannah*, b. 16 Nov. 1730, m. Benjamin Green 31 Aug. 1764.[3] JAMES the f. was a housewright; he inherited the homestead on Washington Street, Boston, which he sold 7 Feb. 1711-12, and bought a house on the southerly side of Boylston Street; this also he sold 12 April 1714, and rem. to Rochester, attracted probably by the fact that Rev. Timothy Ruggles, a brother of his wife, was there settled in the ministry. He resided in Roch. until the spring of 1757, when he exchanged his farm in Roch. for another in Hardwick, where several of his chil. had already settled. Of his eight surviving chil. Dorothy alone remained in Roch.; all the others were in Hardwick and Barre. His res. here was on the road to Ware, about two miles from the Common, at the place marked "Mr. Leonard" on the R. Map. He d. shortly before 11 Mar. 1762 (when his will was approved), a. 72; his w. Patience d. — Jan. 1768, a. 78.

[1] Edward Denison was son of William Denison, one of the earliest inhabitants of Roxbury. He had two brothers, — Daniel, the Maj.-General of the Massachusetts Colony during "Philip's War," and George, a successful and distinguished captain of Connecticut troops during the same war; both also rendered important service as legislators and magistrates. Edward manifested no taste for military affairs; but he was useful as selectman, town clerk, and representative. He m. Elizabeth, dau. of Capt. Joseph Weld, had eleven children, and d. 26 Ap. 1668; his w. Elizabeth d. 5 Feb. 1716-7, a. 91. One son and five daughters survived him; the son, *William*, grad. H. C. 1681, m. Dorothy Weld, was a teacher, selectman four years, town clerk fourteen years, and representative of Roxbury twenty years; he d. s. p. 22 Mar. 1717-18, a. 53, and the name became extinct in this branch; of the daughters, *Elizabeth* m. Jachin Rayner; *Margaret* m. Daniel Mason, and from them descended the eminent lawyer Jeremiah Mason; *Mary* m. Joseph Tompson; *Hannah* m. Ralph Bradhurst; and *Sarah* m. Thomas Robinson, as in the text.

[2] Capt. Samuel Ruggles m. Martha, dau. of Rev. John Woodbridge, by his wife Mercy, dau. of Gov. Thomas Dudley.

[3] A printed Record, preserved in the oldest branch of this family, and exhibited to me by the widow of Col. Joseph Robinson, shortly before her death, differs from the text in regard to some of the dates, which were copied from the official records of Boston and Rochester. I give it a place here: —

"I, JAMES ROBINSON, was born the 15th of March 1689-90.

PATIENCE, my wife, was born November 7th 1690.

My eldest son *James* was born February 29th 1711-12.

My second son *Thomas* was born September 13th, 1713, and dyed December 16th following.

My third son *Samuel* was born November 1st 1714.

A son, born March 11th 1716-17, and lived 12 hours.

My son *Thomas* was born April 20th 1718.

My daughter *Sarah* was born July 9th 1720.

My daughter *Dorothy* was born February 25th 1723-4.

My son *Denison* was born July 16th 1725.

My son *Joseph* was born September 13th 1727.

My daughter *Hannah* was born November 16th 1730."

4. James, s. of James (3), m. Elizabeth, dau. of Benjamin Smith, 3 July 1739, and had *James*, b. 7 Sep. 1740, d. young; *Elizabeth*, b. 14 Jan. 1742–3, m. Asahel Billings, pub. 29 Ap. 1765, and d. 13 Dec. 1826; *Joseph*, bap. 7 Ap. 1745; *Benjamin*, bap. 13 Sep. 1747; *Patience*, bap. 29 July 1750, m. Joseph Nye, pub. 24 Ap. 1771; *Hannah*, bap. 2 Aug. 1752, m. Benjamin Jenkins of Barre; *Mary*, bap. 20 Ap. 1755, m. Nathaniel Ruggles of Pomfret, Conn.; *Sarah*, bap. 7 May 1758, prob. d. young; *Susan*, bap. 20 Ap. 1760, prob. d. young. James the f. was one of the very earliest pioneers in what was then a wilderness, and res. on the River road to Barre, at or near the spot marked "Col. Robinson" on the R. Map. His farm, bounded easterly on the river and northerly on the Barre line, was included in New Braintree when that town was incorporated, and was annexed to Hardwick 10 June 1814. He was distinguished for his industry, economy, and strict honesty; and, as a natural result, he accumulated a comparatively large estate. It is related, as one of his peculiarities, that he held corn at a fixed value; that he would never sell his crop at a less nor even at a greater price; that he once rebuked a neighbor for taking what he called an extortionate price, who excused himself saying, that he could not well spare the corn, but the woman insisted on having it. "A woman!" said he; "so much the worse!" "But she offered me so much." "Then you should have beaten her down." He d. 21 May 1790, a. 78; his w. Elizabeth, who fully equalled him in industry and economy, survived him.

5. Samuel, s. of James (3), m. Elizabeth, dau. of Joseph Doty, Jr., of Rochester, 20 Oct. 1737, and had *Samuel*, b. 22 Nov. 1742; *Sarah*, b. 31 Oct. 1744, m. Aaron Hunt 24 Oct. 1765; *Isaac*, b. 20 Jan. 1746–7, a physician, settled in Chesterfield about 1771, ret. to Hk. about 1782, and after 1 Mar. 1788 rem. to Stamford, Vt.; *Joseph*, b. 29 Feb. 1752. Samuel the f. was a weaver; he rem. from Rochester to Hardwick before 13 May 1740, at which date he bought a farm on the River road to Barre, adjoining the estate of his brother James, and prob. res. there until 31 Aug. 1762, when he purchased of his sister Hannah their father's homestead on the Ware road. His death does not appear on record; but the widow of his son *Joseph* informed me, many years ago, that he d. in Mar. 1784, and that his w. Elizabeth rem. to Vermont (prob. to Stamford, where her son *Isaac* resided), and d. about 1805, a. 88.

6. Thomas, s. of James (3), m. Mary, dau. of Capt. Eleazar Warner, 23 Nov. 1744, and had *Denison*, b. 18 Sep. 1746; *Thomas*, b. 10 Feb. 1753; *Mary*, b. 3 Dec. 1758, m. Timothy Paige, Esq., 20 Jan. 1780, and d. 29 Mar. 1836. Thomas the f. came to Hardwick when a young man, and at first engaged in farming. He resided on the River road to Barre, on the farm adjoining that of his brother Samuel. Within a few years, however, he rem. to the Furnace Village, and res. at the place marked "T. Elwell" on the R. Map (now the residence of Mr. Joseph N. Lincoln). Here he kept a store and tavern, and also managed a saw-mill and grist-mill, on Moose Brook. He was prosperous in business, insomuch that only three persons in the town were assessed for a larger property than his in 1776; but of this plentiful estate he sacrificed the larger part, if not absolutely the whole, in the Revolutionary contest, in which he was actively engaged from the beginning to the end. He was one of the grand jurors who refused, 19 Ap. 1774, to be impanelled at Worcester if Peter Oliver, the chief justice, should be present. He was elected lieutenant of an "Alarm List" 9 Jan. 1775, and was afterwards styled captain. He was a selectman five years, a member of the Committee of Correspondence five years, and served on various other important committees during that troublous period. He sold his real estate, consisting of one hundred and fifty acres, in five parcels, in and near the Furnace Village, with the saw-mill and grist-mill, to Capt. Benjamin Convers 19 Oct. 1780, for £20,000, in the depreciated currency of that period, and subsequently rem. to Windsor, but returned again after a few years. About 1799, his mental faculties having become impaired, and both of his sons having left the town, he and his aged wife became inmates of their daughter's family, where he d. 4 (or 5) Jan.

1802, a. nearly 84; his w. Mary d. 7 Aug. 1812, a. 88. Her youngest and last surviving grandchild, while tracing these lines, cherishes a fresh and affectionate remembrance of her manifold kindness to him in the days of his childhood and youth.

7. DENISON, s. of James (3), m. Martha, dau. of Elijah Perry of Sandwich, 12 Oct. 1752, and had at Rochester, *Lucy*, bap. 5 Aug. 1753, d. young; and at Barre, *Lucy*, b. 1 Mar. 1755, m. Amos Parker 25 Dec. 1771; *Abigail*, b. 15 July 1756, m. Abel Haynes; *Martha*, b. 12 Jan. 1760, m. Ebenezer Haskell 26 May 1779; *Elizabeth*, b. 28 May 1761; *Denison*, b. 9 Aug. 1763; *Elijah*, b. 24 Mar. 1765; *Hannah*, b. 25 Aug. 1767, m. John Allen 18 Dec. 1788. DENISON the f. rem. to Barre about 1754, res. near the Hardwick line, and d. prob. Nov. 1803, a. 78; his w. Martha d. 28 Oct. 1807, a. 84.

8. JOSEPH, s. of James (3), m. Martha, dau. of Elisha Hedge, pub. 7 July 1753, and had *Mary*, b. 3 June 1754, m. Abijah Jennison 5 Dec. 1771; *Dorothy*, b. 23 Feb. 1756, m. Dr. Daniel Rood 27 Mar. 1777; *Lemuel*, b. 4 Jan. 1758; *Martha*, b. 23 Nov. 1759, m. Daniel Wentworth; *Samuel Hedge*, b. 25 Jan. 1761, m. Abigail Ripley 26 Nov. 1786; *Elishua*, b. 19 Jan. 1763, prob. d. young; besides these six others are named in their father's will, dated 26 Mar. 1814, namely, *Levi*, b. ——, m. Betsey Nye 20 Sep. 1798; *James*; *Joseph*; *Lydia*, wife of Benjamin Rice; *Elizabeth*, wife of Timothy Cooper; *Rebecca*. JOSEPH the f. removed early to Barre, and res. near his brother James; he d. 16 Dec. 1814, a. 87; his w. Martha was not named in his will, and had probably deceased before its date.

9. JOSEPH, s. of James (4), m. Lucy, dau. of Samuel Ruggles of Barre, 16 Feb. 1780, and had *William*, b. 24 Oct. 1781; *Sarah*, b. 25 May 1788, m. Lewis Howe, pub. 21 Aug. 1808, and (2d) Hon. John M. Niles of Hartford 17 June 1824; *James*, b. 7 Ap. 1792; *Joseph*, b. 20 June 1796; *Lucy*, b. 23 Oct. 1802, d. 25 Mar. 1803. JOSEPH the f. was a thrifty farmer, res. on the very productive homestead, and d. 23 Ap. 1836, a. 91; his w. Lucy d. 4 Aug. 1826, a. 68.

10. BENJAMIN, s. of James (4), res. in Barre; his will, dated 3 Sep. 1793, with a codicil, 3 Sep. 1799, was proved 1 Oct. 1799. In it are named wife Hannah, and chil. *Anna* Gates; *Susanna* Henry; *James*; *Benjamin*; *Hannah*, wife of Orin Trow; *Joseph*; *John*; *Josiah*; *Moses*; *Cushman*; *Ebenezer*; and *Daniel Foster*.

11. SAMUEL, s. of Samuel (5), m. Abigail, prob. dau. of Edward Doty (and sister of Zurishaddai), pub. 10 Ap. 1762, and had *James*, b. 1 Ap. 1764; *Betsey*, b. 25 July 1766, m. David Weeks 22 May 1783; *Isaac*, b. 14 July 1769; *Samuel*, b. 12 Sep. 1771.

12. JOSEPH, s. of Samuel (5), m. Sarah, dau. of Isaac Clark, 30 Sep. 1773, and had *Cinderilla*, b. 10 Feb. 1780, m. Zenas Cobb 1 Dec. 1803, and d. 9 May 1804; *Joseph*, b. 21 June 1782; *Thomas Holt*, b. — Mar. 1791, d. 13 Jan. 1792; *Arminda*, bap. 31 Mar. 1793. JOSEPH the f. was a miller, and res. on the road to Gilbertville, a few rods north of the spot marked "Wid. Howard" on the R. Map, having charge of the grist-mill at that place. He d. 6 June 1799, a. 47; his w. Sarah m. James Blair of Western (now Warren) 26 Mar. 1805; after his death she returned to Hk., res. with her son *Joseph*, and d. 16 Dec. 1844, a. 87.

13. DENISON, s. of Thomas (6), m. Millecent, dau. of Rev. Robert Cutler of Gr., pub. 10 Ap. 1769; she d. 5 July 1798, and he m. Elizabeth Hyde of Lenox about 1801. His chil. were *Mary*, b. 18 Oct. 1769, m. Alpheus Prince, and d. s. p. 11 Sep. 1829; *Alice*, b. 1 July 1771, m. Daniel Felshaw, and d. 1 Feb. 1792; *Hannah*, b. 10 June 1773, d. unm. 7 July 1796; *Josiah Quincy*, b. 31 July 1775; *Sophia*, b. 19 Aug. 1778, d. unm. 12 May 1855; *Denison*, b. 29 Dec. 1780; *Robert Cutler*, b. 12 Mar. 1785; *Thomas*, b. 20 Dec. 1787. DENISON the f. was a farmer; he was sergeant of Capt. Simeon Hazeltine's company of minute-men which marched to Cambridge on the "Lexington alarm" in April 1775, and was commissioned captain of the second company of militia in Hk. 11 June 1778; he was a member also of the important Committee of Correspondence in 1778. About 1780 he rem. to Windsor, and res. there for several

years; late in life he followed his sons to Adams, where he d. 17 Nov. 1827, a. 81; his w. Elizabeth d. about 1829.

14. THOMAS, s. of Thomas (6), m. Rebecca, dau. of John Paige, 11 Ap. 1776, and had *Prudence*, b. 4 Oct. 1778, d. unm. 20 Aug. 1832; *Mary*, b. 6 Oct. 1780, m. Giles Bronson, and d. 15 May 1842; *Thomas*, b. 23 Nov. 1782; a son b. 30 Dec. 1784, lived only one day; *John Paige*, b. 7 Jan. 1786; *Rebecca*, b. 3 Nov. 1787, m. William Cobb, and (2d) Eliphaz Case; she d. 4 July 1872; *David*, b. 7 Oct. 1790; *Alice*, b. 2 Nov. 1792, m. Giles Case, Jr., and d. 13 May 1844; *Millecent*, b. 7 Mar. 1795, d. unm. 7 Sep. 1814; *Warner*, b. 11 May 1797, a lawyer, d. unm. at Alexander, N. Y., 22 Jan. 1827; *Denison*, b. 2 June 1800. THOMAS the f. was a farmer. He was one of the "minute-men" who marched to Cambridge at the commencement of hostilities, 19 Ap. 1775, and was a sergeant in Capt. Samuel Dexter's company, at the Roxbury Camp, in Jan. 1776, and also sergeant in the company of Capt. Timothy Paige, which marched "to Bennington in an alarm," in Aug. 1777. He rem. from Hk. to Windsor about 1785, returned about 1791, and in 1799 rem. to Onondaga, N. Y., then nearly on the western frontier of civilization. He res. in that part of the town now known as Howlett Hill, on a productive farm, and in a remarkably harmonious neighborhood. His nearest neighbor was Giles Case, an emigrant from Connecticut; four children of each family intermarried with each other, and many of their posterity still remain in Onondaga and the region round about. He d. 31 Aug. 1815, a. 62; his w. Rebecca d. 3 Oct. 1828, a. nearly 71.

15. DENISON, s. of Denison (7), m. Dorcas Allen 30 Dec. 1790, and had *Hannah*, b. 28 May 1792; *Daniel*, b. 2 May 1795; *Harriet*, b. 4 Oct. 1798; *Denison Allen*, b. 17 Aug. 1800, res. in Barre, where he d. 6 Nov. 1880; *Eunice Putnam*, b. 23 Jan. 1803; *Nabby*, b. 15 July 1804; *Louisa*, b. 17 Sep. 1806. DENISON the f., a farmer, res. on the homestead in Barre, near the Hardwick line, and d. 14 Ap. 1858, a. nearly 95; his w. Dorcas d. 21 May 1838, a. 70.

16. ELIJAH, s. of Denison (7), m. Bathsheba Nye, pub. 31 May 1786, and had *Samuel Ruggles*, b. 14 Oct. 1788; *Nancy*, b. 15 Aug. 1790; *Denison*, b. 25 Jan. 1796.

17. WILLIAM, s. of Joseph (9), m. Mary, dau. of Jonathan Warner 28 Nov. 1809, and had *William*, b. 30 Sep. 1810, m. Harriet N. Bemis 7 Nov. 1839; *Mary*, b. 20 Feb. 1813, m. Harrison Harwood 22 Nov. 1832; *Sally*, b. 21 Nov. 1815, m. Samuel Smith, 17 Aug. 1841, and d. 29 Aug. 1863; *Maria*, b. 5 Dec. 1818, m. Moses Ruggles 26 May 1841, devoted a portion of her time and attention to the practice of medicine; *Lucy*, b. 27 Ap. 1822, m. Charles Bacon 31 Oct. 1844; *Hannah*, b. 10 Jan. 1827, m. Alexander W. Ellsworth 6 Ap. 1853; *James*, b. 2 Dec. 1830, d. 25 Nov. 1832; *Charles*, b. 29 July 1834, m. Mary Henry 21 May 1860. WILLIAM the f. early settled in Barre, and for several years kept a tavern on the Common. He d. 21 Aug. 1862, a. nearly 81; his w. Mary d. 13 Oct. 1866, a. about 77.

18. JOSEPH, s. of Joseph (9), m. Ann Maria, dau. of Nathan Ruggles of Hartford, Conn., 11 Dec. 1821; she d. 14 Dec. 1822, and he m. Caroline C., dau. of Capt. Seth Banister of Brookfield, 2 Feb. 1826. His chil. were *Catherine Maria*, b. 18 Nov. 1822, m. James Gallier, at Charleston, S. C., 23 June 1850; both she and her husband were lost on their passage from New York to New Orleans on board the steamer Evening Star, which foundered at sea 3 Oct. 1866; *Joseph Ruggles*, b. 16 Jan. 1827; *Seth Banister*, b. 14 Mar. 1828, m. Carrie M. Lee of New York 12 June 1860; *Lewis Howe*, b. 7 Oct. 1829, d. 7 Oct. 1848; *John Niles*, b. 29 Mar. 1833, m. Elizabeth Brown of Brimfield 17 May 1859; *Eliza A.*, b. 7 May 1842; *William A.*, b. 18 Jan. 1847, d. 27 Aug. 1848. JOSEPH the f. was a farmer, and res. on the homestead in Hk. until about 1840, when he rem. to Barre. He was a selectman 1827, 1828, and 1830, and colonel of a regiment of cavalry. He d. 10 July 1877, a. 81; his w. Caroline C. (b. 6 Jan. 1806) d. 11 July 1879.

19. JOSEPH, s. of Joseph (12), m. Rachel, dau. of Capt. Elijah Warner, 2 Ap. 1811, and had *Joseph Warner*, b. 1 Sep. 1814; *Elijah Warner*, b. 31 Jan. 1821, m. Elizabeth Eunice, dau. of Asa Clark, 23 Oct. 1855; she d. 19

Mar. 1881; *Jason Mixter*, b. 6 Oct. 1822, res. on the homestead; *Harriet Jane*, b. 6 Ap. 1831, m. William Browning 5 Ap. 1849; he d. 16 Mar. 1858, and she m. Albert E. Knight 5 Ap. 1866, and d. 16 Sep. 1869; *Sarah M.*, b. —— 1834, m. Joseph R. Robinson 20 June 1854. JOSEPH the f. was a farmer, and for several years cultivated the General Warner farm in the centre of the town (now owned by Mr. Frazier Paige), where also he kept a tavern; he afterwards bought the Jenney farm, on the road to Ware, about two miles and three quarters from the Common, marked "J. Robinson" on the R. Map, where he res. during the remainder of his life. He was a selectman three years, and d. 23 Oct. 1854, a. 72; his w. Rachel d. 6 Oct. 1863, a. 75.

20. JOSIAH QUINCY, s. of Denison (13), m. Sally Brown 23 July 1797, and had *Daniel Denison*, b. 29 Ap. 1798, a lawyer in Adams, m. Amelia Bowles, had son Josiah Quincy, and d. 14 Oct. 1827; *Benjamin Franklin*, b. 3 Dec. 1801, m. Eliza B. Whitmore, a merchant and civil magistrate, res. in Adams (now North Adams). JOSIAH QUINCY the f., born in Hardwick, was carried with the family to Windsor, and there worked on the farm until he attained manhood. He was afterwards a successful merchant and civil magistrate in Adams, and still later in North Adams, where he d. 29 Aug. 1856, a. 80; his w. Sally d. 14 Mar. 1856.

21. DENISON, s. of Denison (13), m. Lydia Jenks, and had *Robert Jenks*, b. ——, who settled in Vermont. DENISON the f. commenced business, with a fair prospect of success, but died prematurely 27 Nov. 1807, a. not quite 27 years.

22. ROBERT CUTLER, s. of Denison (13), m. Sophia, dau. of Rev. James Briggs of Cummington, and had *Albert Denison*, b. 5 Sep. 1809, m. Amy Kelley 12 Feb. 1833; *Clara Anne*, b. 10 July 1812, m. James E. Marshall, of Bradford, England, 11 Sep. 1839, res. in Sandusky, O.; *Harriet S.*, b. 17 Jan. 1820, m. Joseph P. Merriam 31 Oct. 1846; *Robert Henry*, b. 24 July 1824, m. Mary Cone 27 June 1849; *Mary Elizabeth*, b. 14 Oct. 1826, m. George P. Dickinson 27 June 1849; *George*, b. 10 June 1830, d. (drowned) 17 June 1851. ROBERT CUTLER the f. was a skilful physician in Adams, Cummington, and North Adams; he d. 10 May 1846, a. 61; his w. Sophia d. 25 Sep. 1874, a. 86.

23. THOMAS, s. of Denison (13), b. in Windsor, m. Nancy Wells 13 May 1812; she d. — Mar. 1827, and he m. Catherine McLeod — Sep. 1829. His chil. were *Millecent Cutler*, b. 12 Ap. 1813, m. F. O. Sayles, Esq., and d. 31 Jan. 1852; *Ann Eliza*, b. 29 Ap. 1815, m. Dr. Nathan Snell Babbitt; *Mary Sophia*, b. 16 May 1817, m. Jackson Mason of Richmond, Vt.; *James Thomas*, b. 6 Sep. 1822, a lawyer, a senator, clerk of the Constitutional Convention, 1853, and judge of probate for Berkshire County; received from W. C. the honorary degree of A. M. in 1855; he m. Clara Briggs, and his only surviving son, Arthur, b. 15 Mar. 1847, grad. W. C. 1870, is associated with him in the publication of the *Adams Transcript*; *Nancy W.*, b. 20 June 1826, d. 13 Oct. 1826; *Alexander McLeod*, b. 8 Sep. 1830; *Margaret Maria*, b. 14 Mar. 1833, m. Lyndon Smith of Terre Haute, Ind.; *Elizabeth Rupalee*, b. 5 Aug. 1836, m. Albert R. Smith; *John Cutler*, b. 4 Oct. 1839, a captain of volunteers in the War of the Rebellion; *Charles Henry*, b. 2 Sep. 1841; *William Denison*, b. 1 Aug. 1844. THOMAS the f. was a lawyer, and held a high rank at the Berkshire Bar; he received from W. C. the honorary degree of A. M. in 1828; he res. in Adams, and afterwards in North Adams, where he d. 3 Oct. 1867, a. nearly 80; his w. Catherine S. d. — July 1853.

24. THOMAS, s. of Thomas (14), m. Abigail, dau. of Giles Case, 28 May 1809, and had *Thomas Newton*, b. 24 May 1810, d. 7 June 1811; *Abigail Tamma*, b. 28 June 1812, m. Samuel E. Barker 25 Jan. 1832, res. in Geddes, N. Y.; *Emily Millecent*, b. 14 Ap. 1814, d. unm. 7 Sep. 1856; *Thomas*, b. 2 Sep. 1816, m. Celestia S. Howlett 5 Oct. 1841, res. in Geddes, N. Y. THOMAS the f. was a distiller and trader, res. in Onondaga, where he d. 25 June 1817, a. 34; his w. Abigail d. 20 Oct. 1854, a. 66.

25. JOHN PAIGE, s. of Thomas (14), m. Lucy Matteson 7 Sep. 1812, and

had *Lydia Louisa*, b. 5 Aug. 1813, d. 7 Sep. 1815; *John Quincy*, b. 18 Ap. 1815, m. Eliza Smiley 10 Sep. 1836; she d. 10 Jan. 1845, and he m. Philenda B. Smiley — Sep. 1845; she d. 2 July 1851, and he m. Helen Cornelia Ball — Nov. 1851; he d. in 1865, having had eight children, of whom only one survived him; *Lucy*, b. 18 July 1817; *Eunice*, b. 17 Jan. 1820, m. William C. Butler 22 Nov. 1842, res. in Syracuse; *Evelina*, b. 9 Sep. 1822, d. unm. 24 July 1844; *Denison*, b. 24 Ap. 1825, m. Sarah J. Hart 18 Nov. 1847, a farmer, res. in Onondaga. JOHN P. the f. was a farmer, res. on a part of the homestead, d. 7 Sep. 1870, a. 84.[1]

26. DAVID, s. of Thomas (14) m. Dorcas, dau. of Giles Case, 24 Nov. 1816, and had *Lurancy D.*, b. 25 Oct. 1817, m. Cephas J. Strickland, and d. 18 Dec. 1856; *Lucius David*, b. 20 Mar. 1820, m. Alzira Johnson 13 July 1852, a farmer, res. near the homestead until 1879, when he rem. to Middleport, N. Y.; *Giles Case*, b. 26 Feb. 1822, d. unm. 28 June 1863; *Cornelia L.*, b. 2 Mar. 1825, m. Philander S. White of Geddes; *Elishaba*, b. 28 Ap. 1827, m. Horace Knowles of Marcellus, N. Y.; *Rebecca Paige*, b. 15 July 1829; *Thomas*, b. 26 Mar. 1832, m. Louisa Plumb, a farmer, res. on the homestead. DAVID the f. was a farmer, res. on a part of the homestead in Onondaga, and d. 30 Oct. 1866, a. 76; his w. Dorcas d. 10 May 1874, a. nearly 83.

27. DENISON, s. of Thomas (14), m. Saviah Mason, and had a dau. b.——, d. young; *Mary Elizabeth*, b. ——, m. ——; *William*, b. ——, a lawyer in St. Louis; *Denison*, b. ——, d. young. DENISON the f. was a lawyer, res. at Port Byron, N. Y., and d. 4 May 1852.

28. JOSEPH R., s. of Joseph (18), m. Sarah M., dau. of Joseph Robinson, 20 June 1854; and had *Joseph*, b. 6 June 1858; *William Albert*, b. 4 June 1860; *Carrie Warner*, b. 16 Dec. 1862. JOSEPH R. the f. res. several years on the homestead, and afterwards at the north end of the Common.

29. WILLIAM D., s. of George W. of Barre, m. Susan S. Davis 5 Ap. 1871, and had here *Walter M.*, b. 18 Oct. 1872; *Alice Etta*, b. 8 Ap. 1878; *Alfred Edwin*, b. 3 Ap. 1880, d. 17 Sep. 1880; *Fanny E. S.*, b. 5 Aug. 1881.

SECTION III.

ROBINSON, JONATHAN, of Raynham, m. Phebe Williams of Norton, and had *Phebe*, b. about 1779, m. Stephen Haskell 27 Dec. 1801; *Jonathan*, b. 17 July 1781; *Williams*, b. about 1783, d. 15 Mar. 1811, a. 27. JONATHAN the f. d. at Raynham while yet a young man, prob. about 1787. His w. Phebe "was a woman of great energy and enterprise. Left in early life a widow with three young children, and having but small means, and the support of her family depending mainly upon her own exertions, she took her children and went to Dana, where a brother lived. While there she had an opportunity to purchase a farm in the north part of Hardwick; and by her own skilful management not only paid for it, but added much to its buildings." [2] Her house was on the road to Petersham, three miles and a quarter from the Common, at the place marked "J. Robinson" on the R. Map. She d. 19 Feb. 1831, a. 76.

2. JONATHAN, s. of Jonathan (1), m. Huldah Woodward of Pet., pub. 30 Oct. 1808, and had *John Fay*, b. 13 Feb. 1809; *Almeda*, twin, b. 6 Oct. 1810, d. 14 Mar. 1816; *Samantha*, twin, b. 6 Oct. 1810, m. Rev. William B. Stone of W. Brk.; *Phebe Williams*, b. 12 Mar. 1813, m. Rev. William B. Stone of W. Brk. 16 Feb. 1842, and d. 12 Nov. 1852; *Martha*, b. 25 Nov. 1814; *Cyrus Anson*, b. 10 Sep. 1816; *Charles*, b. 21 July 1818; *Jonathan Edwards*, b. 23 Aug. 1820, d. 18 May 1824; *William W.*, b. 26 Mar. 1822; *Alfred*, b. 26 Dec. 1824, m. Julia A. Powers, pub. 27 July 1852, res. at Fitchburg, and at Sinclair, Kan.; d. at W. Brk. 22 Aug. 1878, and was buried here. JONATHAN the f. was a farmer, and res. on his mother's homestead until 1855, when he rem. to Spencer, where he d. 10 Oct. 1858, a. 77; his w. Huldah d. at W. Brk. 24 Jan. 1870, a. 88.

[1] It is worthy of remark that John P. Robinson, his sister Rebecca, and his brother David, all born on the Green Mountain at Windsor, were the longest livers and the last survivors of their father's family.

[2] MS. letter from Rev. William B. Stone.

3. CHARLES, s. of Jonathan (2), m. Sarah Adams of W. Brk., and had two chil., both of whom d. in infancy; she d. and he m. (2d) Sara T., dau. of Myron Lawrence, Esq., of Belchertown. A brief sketch of his eventful life was published in the *Commonwealth*, at Topeka, Kansas, January 18, 1877, under the head of "Senate Directory:" "Charles Robinson of Lawrence was born in Hardwick, Massachusetts, July 21, 1818, received an academic education and passed two years at Amherst College, but left on account of ill health; studied medicine at Pittsfield Medical College, and graduated as M. D. in 1843; practised medicine at Belchertown, Springfield, and Fitchburg; went to California in 1849, was elected to the California Legislature, serving one term; returned to Fitchburg in 1851; resumed practice as a physician; in 1854 published a journal of his trip through Kansas in 1849; this led to his appointment as agent of the New England Emigrant Aid Society; removed to Kansas in 1854, and took an active and well-known part in the struggle which followed; was twice elected Governor under the Topeka Constitution of 1855; was elected first Governor of the State of Kansas under the Wyandotte Constitution; has served many years as Regent of the State University; was a member of the House in 1872; was elected to the Senate in 1874, and was reëlected in 1876."

4. DANIEL, of Monson, m. Anna Bridges 28 Ap. 1788, and had *Alvan*, b. 20 Oct. 1788, d. at Deerfield 8 Nov. 1864; a child b. — Mar. 1790, d. 3 May 1790, a. five weeks; *Arathusa*, twin, b. 13 Oct. 1794; *Minerva*, twin, b. 13 Oct. 1794, d. unm. at Deerfield 1 Mar. 1872; a child which d. 7 Aug. 1805. DANIEL the f. may have rem. to Deerfield; his name early disappears from our records.

5. NATHAN, m. Hannah Grant of Barre 16 Oct. 1804, and had *Nathan Warren*, b. 20 Mar. 1806, m. Persis Wright 5 Jan. 1853, and d. 17 Mar. 1876; *Betsey Field*, b. 12 Sep. 1807, m. Justus Allen 21 Nov. 1831, and d. 4 Dec. 1876; *Joseph Williams*, b. 25 Sep. 1809; *Lucinda*, b. 9 Aug. 1811; *Philip Rosann Grant*, b. 13 Aug. 1813. NATHAN the f. d. 18 May 1813, a. 34; his w. Hannah survived and buried an infant who d. 2 Feb. 1822, a. four months.

6. DANIEL (possibly s. of Daniel (4)), m. Rhoda Goddard, of Pet., pub. 1 Oct. 1831, and had *Daniel Lewis*, b. ——; *David Franklin*, b. 26 Feb. 1846.

7. EBENEZER W., m. Susan Bartlett of Pelh., pub. 9 Dec. 1842, and had *Lizzie Augusta*, b. 29 June 1861; and prob. others.

8. FRANK, by w. Maria, had *Emma*, b. 14 Dec. 1870.

9. WILLIAM D., of Barre, m. Susan S. Davis 5 Ap. 1871, and had, in Hk., *Walter M.*, b. 18 Oct. 1872; *Jenny M.*, b. —— 1876, d. 12 Oct. 1877; *Alice Etta*, b. 8 Ap. 1878.

HANNAH, was pub. to Isaiah Carpenter 24 Feb. 1762. MARY, m. Joseph Nye, pub. 10 Mar. 1805. JOSIAH, m. Elizabeth Walker of N. Sal., pub. 2 Nov. 1806. CHARLOTTE, m. Jesse Paige 4 Sep. 1823. JOHN P., of Brk., m. Eliza Ann, dau. of Stephen Rice, Jr., 18 Feb. 1835, and rem. to Boston, where he d. 5 Aug. 1882, a. 73. PHINEHAS L., of Bennington, m. Elizabeth Clark, pub. 30 Mar. 1836. JACOB, m. Rachel Davis 25 July 1836; she d. at Greenwich 16 Feb. 1879, a. 60. JOSEPH, of Amh., m. Almira Richardson 31 Dec. 1840. NELSON, of Norwich, Vt., m. Abigail Morton 12 Jan. 1841. SARAH, m. Alexander Bartlett of Pelh., pub. 15 Nov. 1841. ARATHUSA M., of Barre, m. Gershom P. Wright, pub. 10 Feb. 1849. ALICE A., m. Charles S. Turner 24 Nov. 1853. HARRIET A., of Barre, m. Warren W. Barnes, pub. 10 May 1854. CAROLINE, of Enfield, m. Billings Cummings, pub. 24 Dec. 1855. MELISSA, m. Billings Cummings, pub. 21 Dec. 1857. CLARA, m. Monroe Turner 4 Mar. 1858. DRUSILLA, of Barre, m. David Wyatt 9 Jan. 1873. PHILENA, of Barre, m. Edgar F. Stone 29 Jan. 1873. ELLA, m. Norman Bartlett of Orange 1 July 1873. EMMA A., of Barre, m. J. Warren Patrill 22 Aug. 1876.

ROGERS, BENJAMIN, m. Mehetabel, dau. of James Fay, 10 Sep. 1760; she d. 1761 or 1762, and he m. Temperance Phinney 5 Ap. 1763. His chil. were *John*, b. 6 Dec. 1761; *Gershom*, b. 6 May 1764; *Benjamin*, b. 26 Dec. 1766;

Naomi, bap. 26 Dec. 1768; *Rebecca*, bap. 14 Oct. 1770. BENJAMIN the f. was recommended to the church in Ashfield, 24 Jan. 1775.

2. JAMES, prob. brother of Benjamin (1), m. Hannah, dau. of James Fay, 23 Nov. 1769, and had *Martin*, b. 22 Aug. 1770; *James*, b. —— 1782, d. 27 Sep. 1796, a. 14; *Medad*, b. 25 May 1786; *John*, b. —— 1791, d. 22 Sep. 1796, a. 5; and perhaps others. JAMES the f. was a cordwainer, and rem. from Kingston to Hk. before 6 Nov. 1766, at which date he bought a farm in the northerly part of the town, at or near the place marked "Wid. Rogers" on the R. Map. He d. 7 July 1823, a. 78; his w. Hannah d. 18 Oct. 1835, a. 86.

3. MARTIN, s. of James (2), m. Elizabeth, dau. of Seth Taylor, 30 Nov. 1797, and had *James Phinney*, b. 16 July 1799; *Irena*, b. 12 Jan. 1802; *Seth Taylor*, b. 29 Aug. 1804, d. 14 Jan. 1819; *Dorus Dwight*, b. 9 June 1806; *Mary* (or *Mercy*) *Taylor*, b. 29 Aug. 1808, d. unm. 5 Dec. 1841; *Convers Cutler*, b. 24 Jan. 1811, m. Mary L. Smith 20 June 1833, and rem. to Ware; *Rhoda Taylor*, b. 15 June 1813, m. Zemira F. Shumway 11 Feb. 1835; *Arminda Spooner*, b. 25 Nov. 1815, m. Cutler Barnes 20 Dec. 1837; *Fidelia Fay*, b. 6 Mar. 1818, m. George P. Danforth of Dana, pub. 4 Ap. 1843; *Eunice Ann*, b. 23 Aug. 1820, m. Horace Terry, pub. 7 Ap. 1843. MARTIN the f. res. in the northerly part of the town, but perhaps rem. to Gr. after the death of his wife, where he was drowned in a well, 23 Feb. 1857, a. 86; his w. Elizabeth d. here 14 Nov. 1853, a. nearly 76.

4. MEDAD, s. of James (2), m. Cynthia Parkhurst 12 Nov. 1810, and had *Roxana*, b. 20 June 1811; *Charles*, b. 17 Aug. 1814, d. at Springf. 11 Aug. 1873; *Pamelia*, b. 1 Mar. 1816. MEDAD the f. res. on or near the homestead, and d. 26 Jan. 1824.

5. JAMES P., s. of Martin (3), m. Eliza Shumway 5 Mar. 1822, and had *Enos*, b. —— 1824, d. at Springf. 15 Jan. 1854, a. 29; *Warren F.*, b. about 1843. JAMES P. the f. d. 5 June 1876, a. nearly 77; his w. Eliza d. 8 Aug. 1881, a. 81.

6. DORUS DWIGHT, s. of Martin (3), m. Susanna G. Bond 1 Dec. 1831. Their s. *Joseph J.*, b. about 1838, was a soldier in the late Civil War, and was killed in the battle of the Wilderness, 6 May 1864, a. 26.

7. WARREN F., s. of James P. (5), m. Catherine E. Presho, 7 May 1876, and had *Charles Warren*, b. 30 July 1877; *Minnie E.*, b. 1 Dec. 1880.

8. SETH, m. Sally Ann Bartlett 2 May 1845, and had *Sarah A.*, b. —— 1849, d. 22 Aug. 1852, a. 3.

9. ANTHONY, b. in Canada, m. Lucy ——, and had *Lucy*, b. 27 Dec. 1862; *Julia*, b. 8 Nov. 1864; *Anthony*, b. 6 July 1866; *Ellen*, b. 10 June 1871; *Rosanna*, b. 17 Dec. 1873; *Joseph*, b. 5 July 1876; *Mary*, b. 1 May 1878; *Emma*, b. 23 Mar. 1881.

MARTHA, of Gr., m. Timothy Gilbert, pub. 13 Oct. 1771. BETSEY, m. Phineas Rollins 12 Sep. 1793. SUSANNA, m. Nathan Phinney of Williamsburg 19 Jan. 1794. SALLY, m. Dorus Dwight of Williamsburg, 29 Nov. 1798. (The before-named BETSEY, SUSANNA, and SALLY were prob. daughters of James 2.) OBADIAH, m. Lydia Reed of Wendell, pub. 3 Ap. 1815, and rem. to Tecumseh, Mich. JOSHUA, of Enf., m. Sally Reed, pub. 6 Oct. 1817. EDMUND, m. Rebecca Woodward of Ware, pub. 24 Jan. 1820. ELIZA JANE, of Barre, m. Frederick D. Ruggles 14 June 1859. FRANKLIN E., of Gr., m. Carrie E. Newland 16 Sep. 1865. Wid. SARAH d. 17 Dec. 1879, a. 81. CLARENCE, d. 23 July 1880, a. 17.

ROPES, GEORGE, of Portland, m. Charlotte, dau. of Constant Ruggles, Esq., pub. 9 July 1832.

ROSE, ELIZABETH, was pub. to Isaac Pratt 24 Jan. 1756; the banns were forbidden, and she was pub. 15 Feb. 1756, to Larkin Green, whom she married soon afterwards.

ROSS, HANNAH, m. Jonas Bridges 16 Feb. 1806. ROWENA, of Brk., m. Uriel Spooner, pub. 26 May 1816. SARAH, of Brk., m. Henry Fish, Jr., pub. 21 Sep. 1823. JEANNETTE, m. Alfred Greenwood 14 Mar. 1871. CHARLOTTE E., of Barre, m. Samuel K. Trow 5 June 1876. SAMUEL, m. Jessie Kennedy 23 Dec. 1876.

Ruggles, Thomas, m. Mary Curtis at Nazing, Essex Co., England, 1 Nov. 1620, and had *Thomas*, b. about 1623, d. in England; *John*, b. about 1625, m. Abigail, dau. of Griffin Crafts, 24 Jan. 1650-1, and had four sons, three of whom, — John, Thomas, and Samuel, — survived him; he d., or was buried 15 Sep. 1658; *Sarah*, b. about 1627, m. William Lyon of Roxbury, 17 June 1646, had six sons and one daughter, and d. 9 Feb. 1688-9; *Samuel*, b. about 1629. Thomas the f. came from England to Roxbury in 1637. He and his wife are very favorably mentioned by the "Apostle Eliot" on the Records of the Roxbury church, of which he was pastor and they were members: "Thomas Ruggles: he came to N. E. in the year 1637; he was elder brother to John Ruggles, children of a godly father; he joined to the church soon after his coming, being as well known as his brother; his first born son died in England; his second son *John* was brought over a servant by Philip Eliot; and he brought two other children with him, *Sarah* and *Samuel*. He had a great sickness the year after his coming, but the Lord recovered him in mercy." — "Mary, the wife of Thomas Ruggles: she joined to the church with her husband, and approved herself a godly Christian by a holy and blameless conversation, being converted not long before their coming from England." He res. in Roxbury seven years, and d. 15 Nov. 1644; his death is recorded by Eliot, with the following remark: "1644, 9^{m}. 15^{d}. Thomas Ruggles, a godly brother; he dyed of a consumption. These two[1] brake the knot first of the Nazing Christians; I mean they first dyed of all those Christians that came from that town in England."[2] His w. Mary was sister of the first William Curtis of Roxbury, and was bap. in Nazing — April 1589; she survived her husband, m. (2d) —— Root, and d., or was buried 14 Feb. 1674-5, a., according to the record, 88; but prob. 86 was the actual age.

2. John, brother of Thomas (1), "came to N. E. in the year 1635, and soon after his coming joined unto the church; he was a lively Christian, known to many of the church in Old England, where many of the church enjoyed society together; he brought his first-born, John Ruggles, with him to N. E., and his second son was still-born in the first month 1636, of which his first wife died." *Church Record*. He m. a second w., Margaret ——, but prob. had no chil. by her. He was representative three years, and d. 6 Oct. 1663. His son *John*, b. about 1632, m. Mary Gibson of Cambridge, 3 Ap. 1655; she d. 6 Dec. 1674, and he m. Sarah Dyer of Weymouth 15 Mar. 1675; she d. 2 May 1687, and he m. Ruth ——; she d. 11 Ap. 1710, and he d. 25 Feb. 1712-3. By his second wife he had son Benjamin, b. 11 Aug. 1676, grad. H. C. 1693, was pastor of the church in Suffield, and d. 7 Sep. 1708.

3. Samuel, s. of Thomas (1), m. Hannah, dau. of George Fowle of Charlestown, 10 Jan. 1654-5; she d. 24 Oct. 1669, and he m. Anna, dau. of Deac. Henry Bright of Watertown, 26 May 1670. His chil. were *Hannah*, b. 21 Jan. 1655-6, d. 16 Mar. 1655-6; *Mary*, b. 10 Jan. 1656-7, d. 31 Mar. 1658; *Samuel*, b. 1 June 1658; *Joseph*, b. 12 Feb. 1659-60; d. 5 Feb. 1664-5; *Hannah*, b. 11 Dec. 1661, d. 6 Nov. 1669; *Sarah*, b. 18 Nov. 1663, d. 11 Nov. 1664; *Mary*, b. 8 Dec. 1666, m. Ebenezer Pierpont 20 Oct. 1691, and (2d) Isaac Morris, 3 Nov. 1702; "an infant, newly born," buried 3 Oct. 1668; *Sarah*, b. 30 Aug. 1669, d. 17 Nov. 1669; *Thomas*, b. 10 Mar. 1670-1; *Anna*, b. 30 Sep. 1672, m. William Heath of Roxbury; *Nathaniel*, b. 22 Nov. 1674, d. — May 1674; *Elizabeth*, b. 1 May 1677, m. James Bayley; *Henry*, b. 7 July 1681, d. unm. 9 Dec. 1702; *Huldah*, b. 4 July 1684, m. Samuel Hill[3] of Guilford, Conn., 9 June 1709. Samuel the f. res. in Roxbury, kept a tavern, but was very actively engaged in public life. He was selectman fourteen years, assessor dur-

[1] "These two" were John Grave, who d. 4 Nov. 1644, and Thomas Ruggles, who d. eleven days later.

[2] Nazing is described as "a parish in the hundred of Waltham," near Epping in the county of Essex, England.

[3] Samuel Hill was "one of the most distinguished men that Guilford ever produced. He represented the town in forty-three sessions of the Legislature, was several times Speaker, was judge of our County and Probate Courts, was town clerk, and all the business of the church, society, and a large share of that of the county and of the colony for forty years seems to have centered in him." *MS. Letter from R. D. Smith, Esq., Guilford.*

ing the same period, and representative for the four critical years succeeding the Revolution of 1689. He was for several years captain of militia, and when Governor Andros and his associates were seized and imprisoned, Joseph Dudley (afterwards Governor) was committed to his special charge, while temporarily released from prison. His preservation from death by lightning on the 25th of May 1667 was so remarkable that an account of it was entered on the Church Record by Rev. Samuel Danforth: "25 (3) 1667. There was a dreadful crack of thunder. Samuel Ruggles happened at that instant to be upon the meeting-house hill, with oxen and horse, and cart loaden with corn. The horse and one ox were strucken dead with the lightning; the other had a little life in it, but it died presently. The man was singed and scorched a little on his legs, one shoe torn apieces, and the heel carried away; the man was hurled off from the cart and flung on the off side, but through mercy soon recovered himself and felt little harm. There was a chest in the cart, wherein was pewter and linen; the pewter had small holes melted in it, and the linen some of it singed and burnt." He (or his son *Samuel*) was one of the eight associates, who purchased of the Indians 27 Dec. 1686, the territory, now the town of Hardwick; and he with his son *Samuel* and four others, on the 5th of May 1686, bought of Capt. James Fitch of Norwich, Conn., a tract styled the "Mashamoquet Purchase," which afterwards became the town of Pomfret, Conn. It was many years, however, before his posterity derived much pecuniary advantage from these purchases. He d. 15 Aug. 1692, a. 63; his w. Anna d. 5 Sep. 1711, a. 67.

4. SAMUEL, s. of Samuel (3), m. Martha,[1] dau. of Rev. John Woodbridge of Newbury, and grand-daughter of Gov. Thomas Dudley, 8 July 1680, and had *Samuel*, b. 3 Dec. 1681; *Lucy*, b. 8 Sep. 1683, m. Joseph Stevens 15 Feb. 1715–16; *Timothy*, b. 3 Nov. 1685; *Hannah*, b. 10 Ap. 1688, m. William Noyes 17 Dec. 1712; *Patience*, b. 9 Nov. 1689 (or 7 Nov. 1690), m. James Robinson of Boston, 3 July 1711;[2] *Martha*, b. 1 Feb. 1691–2, m. Job Lane of Billerica, 17 Dec. 1713; *Sarah*, b. 18 June 1694, m. John Holbrook 19 Aug. 1714; *Joseph*, b. 21 July 1696, m. Joanna White 20 Oct. 1720, res. in Roxbury, and d. 9 Sep. 1742; *Mary*, b. 20 Sep. 1698, d. unm. before 1716; *Benjamin*, b. 4 July 1700. SAMUEL the f. res. in Roxbury, and was a "set-work cooper" and an innholder. He inherited his father's military spirit and succeeded him in many of his offices; he was captain of militia, 1702; assessor, 1694; representative, 1697; and selectman continuously from 1693 to 1713, except in 1701 and 1704, nineteen years. His death occurred after a very short sickness, 25 Feb. 1715–16, and his funeral is mentioned in Sewall's Diary: "Feb. 28, 1715–16. Capt. Samuel Ruggles was buried with arms. . . . He is much lamented at Roxbury."[3] His w. Martha d. —— 1738.

5. THOMAS, s. of Samuel (3), grad. at H. C. 1690, and was ordained pastor of the church in Guilford, Conn.; he m. Sarah ——; she d., and he m. Mary Hubbard of Boston 1 June 1708. His chil. were *Sarah*, b. 27 Mar. 1699, d. unm. 23 Mar. 1722; *Anne*, b. 3 May 1701, m. Charles Caldwell 3 Nov. 1724, and d. 19 May 1760; *Mary*, b. 8 Oct. 1702, d. young; *Thomas*, b. 27 Nov. 1704, grad. Y. C. 1723, succeeded his father in the ministry at Guilford, and d. 20 Nov. 1770; *Rebecca*, b. 23 May 1712, d. 11 June 1713; *Nathaniel*, b. 16 May 1713, grad. Y. C. 1732, a physician in Guilford, d. 16 Dec. 1794; *Elizabeth*, b. —— 1715, m. Jehoshaphat Starr 1 Nov. 1734, and d. 9 Sep. 1769. THOMAS the f. d. 1 June 1728; his w. Mary d. 17 Dec. 1742.

6. SAMUEL, s. of Samuel (4), grad. H. C. 1702, was ordained pastor of the church in Billerica, 19 May 1708. He m. Elizabeth, dau. of Samuel Whiting, and grand-daughter of Rev. Samuel Whiting, 19 Dec. 1710; she d. 29 July 1727, and he m. Mrs. Elizabeth Williams of Roxbury 18 Ap. 1728. His

[1] Of Mrs. Ruggles it is worthy of remark, that not only was her father a clergyman, descended from numerous clergymen on both sides (including the famous Rev. Robert Parker), but her uncle, Benjamin Woodbridge (the first graduate of Harvard College), three of her brothers, John, Benjamin, and Timothy, her husband's brother, Thomas, and three of her sons *Samuel*, *Timothy*, and *Benjamin*, also sustained the clerical office, and all held an honorable rank in the profession.

[2] See note under James Robinson (3).

[3] *Coll. Mass. Hist. Soc.*, xlvii. 75.

chil. were *Elizabeth*, b. 21 Sep. 1711, d. 21 Aug. 1713; *Samuel*, b. 29 May 1713; *Nathaniel*, b. 16 July 1715, d. 29 Dec. 1717; *Elizabeth*, b. 21 June 1717, m. Samuel Dummer, Esq., 31 May 1737, and (2d) Rev. Daniel Rogers of Littleton; *Martha*, b. 9 Dec. 1719, m. John Whiting of Littleton; *Dorothy*, b. 7 Jan. 1721-2, m. Rev. Isaac Morrill of Wilmington 4 Aug. 1743; *Lucy*, b. 9 Feb. 1723-4; *Joseph*, b. 9 Jan. 1725-6; *Nathaniel*, b. 14 June 1729, d. 14 Ap. 1730; *John*, b. 4 July 1730; *Sarah*, b. 6 Nov. 1731, m. Rev. Josiah Stearns of Epping, and d. 2 Ap. 1808 (she had three sons and three daughters; one of her sons was Rev. Samuel Stearns of Bedford, who grad. H. C. 1794, and d. 1834, and was father of Rev. Samuel H. Stearns, grad. H. C. 1823, and d. —— 1837; Rev. William A. Stearns, D. D., grad. H. C. 1827, President of Amherst College, and d. 8 June 1876; Rev. Jonathan F. Stearns, D. D., grad. H. C. 1830, res. in New Jersey; Josiah A. Stearns, Ph. D., an eminent teacher; Rev. Eben S. Stearns, D. D., Chancellor of the University in Nashville, Tenn.; and others); *William*, 30 Ap. 1733. SAMUEL the f. died in office at Billerica 1 Mar. 1748-9; his w. Elizabeth d. 25 June 1748.

7. TIMOTHY, s. of Samuel (4), grad. H. C. 1707, was ordained pastor of the church in Rochester 22 Nov. 1710. He m. Mary, dau. of Benjamin White of Brookline, 27 Sep. 1710; she d. 23 Jan. 1749, and he m. Anne Woodworth of Little Compton, pub. 26 Mar. 1750. His chil. were *Timothy*, b. 20 Oct. 1711; *Benjamin*, b. 19 May 1713; *Samuel*, b. 5 July 1715; *Joseph*, b. 13 June 1718; *Mary*, b. 1 Jan. 1719-20, m. John Hammond, Jr., 13 Nov. 1740; *Susanna*, b. 6 Jan. 1721-2, m. Paul Mandell of Dartmouth 8 Feb. 1746-7, and rem. to Hk.; *Edward*, b. 30 Aug. 1723; *Nathaniel*, b. 12 Ap. 1725; *Thomas*, b. 13 July 1727, d. 5 Dec. 1727; *Hannah*, b. 18 Oct. 1728, d. 25 Nov. 1728; *Thomas*, b. 2 Mar. 1730; *John*, b. 2 Sep. 1731 (very eccentric, perhaps partially insane, but harmless), res. several years in New Braintree, ret. to Rochester, and d. unm. about 1815. TIMOTHY the f. held a high rank in the ministry, and was preëminently a man of business. He was apparently more active and efficient than any other individual in promoting the settlement of Hardwick. Through his influence and exertions, six sons and a daughter of his own family, five sons and two daughters of his sister Patience, wife of James Robinson (also their father and mother, late in life), and many members of his parish, were among the early settlers. On behalf of the proprietors he personally visited the town several times, both arranging the financial affairs of the people and ministering to their spiritual wants. He d. in office as sole pastor of the church 26 Oct. 1768, a. nearly 83. In the epitaph on his head-stone he is described as "an Able Divine, and a Faithful Minister. Having a peculiar talent at composing Differences and healing Divisions in Churches, he was much improved in Ecclesiastical Councils."

8. BENJAMIN, s. of Samuel (4), grad. Y. C. 1721 (A. M. at Y. C., and also at H. C. 1724). He m. Dorcas, dau. of Samuel Whiting, and grand-daughter of Rev. Samuel Whiting of Billerica, 30 Dec. 1725. I have not seen his family record; but, from other sources, I learn that he had *Benjamin*, b. 18 Dec. 1726; *Whiting*, b. —— 1733; *Mary*, b. ——, m. Dr. Joel Carpenter of Hk. 9 Dec. 1755; *Dorcas*, b. ——, m. Edward Smith of Hk. 25 Aug. 1757; *Lucy*, b. —— 1740, m. Elijah Chapin of Granby —— 1801;[1] *Betsey*, b. 1745, d. unm. 29 May 1795, a. 50; and perhaps *Nancy*, who m. Dr. Freeman Perry of New Bedford, pub. 6 May 1795. BENJAMIN the f. was ordained pastor of the second church (then newly formed) in Middleborough, about 1724, where he remained until the church was organized in New Braintree 1754, of which he became the first pastor, and remained in office during the remainder of his life, having Rev. Daniel Foster as a colleague about four years. He d. suddenly 12 May 1782, a. nearly 82; his w. Dorcas d. 5 Sep. 1778, a. 75.

9. TIMOTHY, s. of Timothy (7), m. Bathsheba[2] (or Bathshua), widow of

[1] "Married at New Braintree, Mr. Elijah Chapin of Granby, aged 51, to Miss Lucy Ruggles of New Braintree, aged 61, daughter of the former minister of that place." *Mass. Spy*, Dec. 30, 1801.

[2] By her first husband, William Newcomb, who grad. H. C. 1722, and d. 8 Ap. 1736, a. 33, she had eight children: *Mercy*, b. 4 Feb. 1723-4, m. John Bassett 21 Oct. 1742; *Desire*, b. 21 July 1725, m. Dr. Elisha Tobey 12 Jan. 1746; *Peter*, b. 4 Sep. 1726, prob. d. young; *Mary*, b. 3 Sep. 1728, m.

William Newcomb, and only dau. of Hon. Melatiah Bourne of Sandwich, pub. 18 Sep. 1736, and had *Martha*, b. 10 Aug. 1737, m. John Tufts of Brk., pub. 11 Nov. 1765, d. 26 July 1813; *Timothy*, b. 7 Jan. 1738–9; *Mary*, b. 10 Feb. 1740–1, m. Dr. John Green of Worc., pub. 19 Mar. 1762, d. 16 June 1814; *John*, b. 30 Sep. 1742, was captain of the first company of militia in Hk. 1771, went to Nova Scotia with his father, and d. at Wilmot in old age; *Richard*, b. 4 Mar. 1743–4; *Bathsheba*, b. 13 Feb. 1745–6, m. Joshua Spooner of Brk., pub. 8 Jan. 1766, and was executed at Worcester 2 July 1778, having been adjudged guilty of hiring other persons to murder her husband. The known circumstances of this case, however, indicate insanity rather than moral turpitude; and confinement in a lunatic asylum would seem to have been a more appropriate result than death on the gallows, — involving, as it did, the death of her unborn child;[1] *Elizabeth*, b. 15 May 1748, m. Gardner Chandler, pub. 18 May 1772. TIMOTHY the f. grad. H. C. 1732, and was one of the most prominent citizens of Massachusetts, and indeed of New England, in both military and civil affairs. As a soldier, he raised a company for service in the West Indies, 1740, and received his commission as captain; but as the number of companies exceeded the demand, his company was disbanded, and thus escaped almost certain destruction, inasmuch as scarcely a tithe of those who embarked in this expedition lived to return. In the French War, which commenced in 1753 (though not formally declared until 1756), and continued until 1763, he rendered active and important service, first as colonel of a regiment, and afterwards as brigadier-general of the provincial troops on the northern frontier. But he was, perhaps, even more eminent in civil life. He commenced the practice of law in his native town (Rochester), rem. to Sandwich about 1737, and thence to Hardwick between 24 Ap. 1753, and 4 Mar. 1754. In his practice, before his removal to Hk., he was the dreaded rival of James Otis, senior, as he was, at a later period, of James Otis, junior, in the General Court. After his removal, he was commissioned justice of the peace and quorum 19 Ap. 1754, judge of the Court of Common Pleas 19 Ap. 1757, and chief justice of

Lemuel Pope, Jr., of Dartmouth 10 Ap. 1760; *Sarah*, b. 21 Oct. 1729, m. Benjamin Fessenden 19 Oct. 1760; *William*, b. 27 Jan. 1731, m. *Elizabeth* ——; *Hannah*, b. 4 June 1732, m. Jonathan Sturgis 14 Aug. 1768; *Thomas*, b. 17 June 1734, or 1735, prob. d. young. She must have been several years older than her second husband, General Ruggles, who was not many months more than twelve years old when her first child was born.

[1] The conduct of Mrs. Spooner, both before and after the murder, bears evident marks of insanity. It appeared on the trial, that two entire strangers, James Buchanan and William Brooks, who had been British soldiers, were invited by her into the house, and were entertained for two weeks; during which time she engaged them to kill her husband, on his return from Princeton, — provided that Ezra Ross failed to destroy his life, as he had promised. And after the murder, she not only rewarded the three murderers with money, but dressed them in her husband's clothes, in the presence of her household servants. The argument of her advocate, Hon. Levi Lincoln, Sen., although it failed, in that period of furious excitement, to convince the jury, deserves consideration. A sketch of that argument is printed in Chandler's *Criminal Trials*, ii. 26–33. Among other things, he said: "The whole evidence was that of a fool, or a distracted person. Born in a high rank of life, well educated, and accomplished, a wife and a mother, and in the enjoyment of a good estate, what object could she have in undertaking such a detestable crime? . . . Whom did she trust with the management of a villainy that so nearly affected her reputation, her safety, her life, her children, the lives of others, and the happiness of her friends? The answer was, to prostitutes, tories, regulars, deserters, strangers, and foreigners. Was a woman that is admitted to have sense so stupid, if in the exercise of her reason, as to trust all that was valuable to her and hers in the hands of such persons? . . . After the murder, she gives the murderers his watch, his buckles, waistcoat, breeches, and shirts, and even puts them on, to be worn in the eye of the world, where they were well known to be Spooner's clothes, and from their goodness and fashion might be known not to belong to the persons wearing them, being low and vulgar. Was this the conduct of a person in the exercise of reason? Would it have been less rational to have written on their foreheads, in capitals, 'the murderers of Mr. Spooner?'" Under such circumstances, a verdict of "guilty" could not be expected from a jury, at the present day; but "not guilty, by reason of insanity," would be recognized by both jury and the whole community as a righteous decision.

It may be added, that Mrs. Spooner's daughter Bathsheba, who married —— Trott, and (2d) —— Heywood, and who died at Cambridge, 1 June 1858, aged 83, was hopelessly insane many years before her death.

the same Court 21 Jan. 1762, which office he held until the Revolution. He was also appointed special justice of the Superior Court 23 Feb. 1762, "in the room of Chambers Russell, Esq., one of the standing justices of the said Court."[1] He was a representative in the General Court from Rochester in 1736, from Sandwich eight years, from 1739 to 1752, and from Hardwick fifteen years,[2] from 1754 to 1770, in all twenty-four years, and was Speaker of the House in 1762 and 1763. In 1765 he was a delegate from Massachusetts to the Congress which met in New York, and was elected President of that body; but he refused to sign the proceedings, which he deemed derogatory to the British government, and was reprimanded therefor by the House of Representatives. During the political contest which raged furiously in the succeeding years, he was the leader of the king's party in the General Court until he ceased to be a member of the House. He was elected councillor in 1764, but declined the office, thinking he could render the king more effective service on the floor of the House. On the change of the form of government in Massachusetts, he was appointed a member of the Council by Mandamus, and took the oath of office 16 Aug. 1774. After this he returned no more to Hardwick, but left Boston with the British officers and troops the next spring, retired to Nova Scotia, and died at Wilmot, near Annapolis, 4 Aug. 1795. His w. Bathsheba remained with her eldest son in Hardwick, where she died, probably, early in 1787; a notice of her death appeared in the *Worcester Magazine* for the fourth week in March. His homestead in Hardwick (where some of the traces of his agricultural skill remain visible after the lapse of more than a hundred years) was on the easterly road to Gilbertville, about three quarters of a mile from the Common, at the place marked "J. Mann" on the R. Map. The dwelling-house, which stood a few feet south of the present residence of Mr. Charles Mandell, was demolished not long ago.

10. BENJAMIN, s. of Timothy (7), m. Alice, dau. of Nathaniel Merrick of Harwich (now Brewster), 19 Oct. 1736; she d. ——, and he m. Mary Smith of Bel. 28 Dec. 1778. His chil. were *Mary*, b. 7 May 1738, m. Daniel Billings 23 Feb. 1758, and d. 8 June 1835; *Susanna*, b. 17 Ap. 1740, m. Ebenezer Chipman 4 Mar. 1762; *Benjamin*, b. 11 Dec. 1741; *Sarah*, b. 6 Feb. 1743-4, m. Abel Harwood 27 Nov. 1765, and (2d) Ezra Alden of Gr. 2 Jan. 1772; *Elizabeth*, b. 16 Ap. 1746, d. 28 Nov. 1748; *Elizabeth*, b. 31 Jan. 1748-9, m. Shearjashub Goodspeed 20 Nov. 1766; *Thomas*, bap. 24 June 1750; *Alice*, b. 23 Nov. 1754, prob. d. young; *Seth*, b. 7 Jan. 1757; *Levi*, b. 25 Oct. 1779, d. at Boston 28 Jan. 1855; *Joseph*, b. 21 Oct. 1781; *David*, b. 30 Nov. 1783, d. at Bel. 1 July 1863. BENJAMIN the f. was one of the earliest pioneers, and res. on the River road to Barre, not far from the Old Furnace. He had great vigor and energy, both physical and mental. He performed yeoman's labor on his farm, and became the father of three children after he was sixty-five years old. He faithfully served his townsmen as captain of militia, as selectman sixteen years, as assessor eleven years, and as chairman of the Committee of Correspondence in 1774 and 1775. He was also one of the most active and resolute opposers of his brother, the Brigadier, in the stormy political contest preceding the Revolution. He d. 11 Oct. 1790, a. 77; his w. Mary rem. to Bel. with her three children.

11. SAMUEL, s. of Timothy (7), m. Alice Sherman of Rochester 25 June 1738, and had at Roch. *Sarah*, b. 27 Ap. 1739; *John*, b. 6 Jan. 1741, perhaps the same who m. Mary Caldwell of Barre 20 May 1777, and d. in 1800; *Samuel*, b. 17 Mar. 1743; *Timothy*, b. 17 May 1745, res. with his grandfather Ruggles at Roch.; *Edward*, b. 31 Dec. 1746; he had also *Kezia*, bap. here 5 Oct. 1755; *Lucy*, b. 20 Dec. 1757, and bap. here five days later, m. Joseph Robinson 16 Feb. 1780, and d. 4 Aug. 1826; and prob. others between 1746 and 1755. SAMUEL the f. rem. after 1746 from Roch. to Barre, where he res. nearly or quite half a century. He d. — June 1802, a. almost 87; his w. Alice d. —— 1801, a. 79.

[1] *Council Records.*

[2] He represented this town longer than any other person, except Timothy Paige, Esq., who was elected representative for seventeen years in succession, and d. in office.

12. JOSEPH, s. of Timothy (7), m. Hannah Cushman of Plymouth 13 Jan. 1742-3, and had *Hannah*, b. 28 Aug. 1743, m. Abijah Edson of Springfield 10 June 1763; *James*, b. 30 Ap. 1746, d. 21 Oct. 1764; *Joseph*, b. 8 Ap. 1748; *Nathaniel*, b. 14 June 1750; *Lydia*, b. 10 Mar. 1753; *Ann*, b. 14 Ap. 1755, m. Jonathan Danforth 1 Oct. 1780, and d. 4 Mar. 1824. JOSEPH the f. rem. to Hk. before he was married, and res. on the turnpike about a hundred rods southeasterly from the Common, at the place marked "O. Trow" on the R. Map. He was a blacksmith, and from 1750 to 1757 an innholder; he also had a grist-mill, on Great Meadow Brook, near his house, the flume of which remained in place many years, and was used for the purpose of flowing the meadow. He was a lieutenant, and marched with his company in 1757 for the relief of Fort William Henry. He d. 28 Jan. 1791, a. 72 (wrongly inscribed 2 Jan. 1790 on his head-stone). His sons *Joseph* and *Nathaniel* prob. followed the fortunes of their uncle, the Brigadier, became refugees, and were proscribed and banished by the Act of September 1778.

13. EDWARD, s. of Timothy (7), was pub. to Ann Ferrin (Fearing?) of Wareham 16 June 1746, but some obstacle prevented their marriage; and on the 29th of December of the same year he was pub. to Lucy, dau. of Deac. Daniel Spooner, whom he m. 29 Jan. 1746-7, and had *Timothy*, bap. 25 Sep. 1748, res. in Cambridge, N. Y.; *Edward*, bap. 26 Aug. 1750; *Elizabeth*, bap. 29 Oct. 1752, m. Paul Dean 19 Sep. 1773, d. 21 Dec. 1810; *Daniel*, b. —— 1755; *Lucy*, b. 26 July 1765, d. unm. 11 May 1790; *Constant*, b. 27 Nov. 1767; *James*, b. 30 Oct. 1770, was drowned in Lake Erie; *Nathan*, b. 13 May 1774; there may have been others, born between 1755 and 1765, but no others are mentioned in the father's will, 17 July 1776. EDWARD the f. was a farmer, and ensign of militia. He res. in what is now New Braintree, somewhat more than a mile east of the river, on the road to Rutland, until about 1760, when he bought the estate on the summit of Ruggles Hill, marked "A. Ruggles" on the R. Map, where he d. 21 May 1778, a. 54; his w. Lucy remained on the homestead many years; but in her old age she res. with her son *Daniel*, and d. 2 Ap. 1821, a. 91.

14. NATHANIEL, s. of Timothy (7), m. Deliverance Barrow 5 Nov. 1752, and had *Elisha*, b. 6 Sep. 1753, d. young; *Nathaniel*, b. 4 May 1755; *Elisha*, b. 28 Sep. 1758; *Thankful*, b. 1 Mar. 1761, m. Robert Foot 19 Feb. 1784; *Timothy*, b. 27 Jan. 1763; *Mary*, b. 29 Mar. 1765, m. Aaron Foot, pub. 6 Dec. 1788; *Thomas*, b. 20 Nov. 1770, rem. to Columbia, Me., m. Ruth Clapp, pub. 14 Mar. 1797; *Benjamin*, b. 18 July 1772, rem. to Columbia, m. Azubah Clapp, pub. 26 Ap. 1798. NATHANIEL the f. res. in Rochester, was a captain, and justice of the peace; he d. 25 Dec. 1776, a. nearly 52; his w. Deliverance d. 1 Feb. 1807, a. 73.

15. THOMAS, s. of Timothy (7), m. Mary, dau. of Dr. Polycarpus Loring of Plympton, 4 Dec. 1755, and had *Hannah*, b. about 1759; *Mary*, b. about 1761, m. Zenas Bryant of Plympton; *Jacob Loring*, b. about 1763. THOMAS the f. taught school in Hk. 1747 and 1748, was a physician in his native town (Rochester), and d. in early life, before 6 May 1776, when Benjamin Cook of Kingston was appointed guardian of his children; his w. Mary d. before 7 Feb. 1780, at which date her estate was divided.

16. BENJAMIN, s. of Benjamin (8), m. Sarah Hunt of Dartmouth, pub. 21 Ap. 1750, and immediately rem. from Middleborough to Hk.; his w. Sarah d. 20 May 1772, and he m. Jerusha, wid. of John Aiken, 11 Feb. 1773, she d. 28 Oct. 1787, and he m. Hannah Hamblin of N. Br., pub. 20 July 1789. His chil. were *Samuel*, b. 9 May 1751, res. at Orange, m. Lydia Hawes of N. Br. 11 Jan. 1776, and had son Lyman, who d. at Orange 4 Dec. 1863, a. 75; *Benjamin*, b. 5 Aug. 1753; *Lemuel*, b. 26 Feb. 1755; *Ephraim*, bap. 20 Mar. 1757; *Sarah*, b. 29 Feb. 1760, m. John Aiken 10 Oct. 1782, and d. 17 Jan. 1822; *Rebecca*, b. 15 Oct. 1763, d. unm. 8 Sep. 1845; *Hannah*, b. 29 Oct. 1791, d. unm. 22 Dec. 1867. BENJAMIN the f. (ordinarily called "Bush Ben," on account of his bushy hair, and to distinguish him from three others of the same name), res. near the Furnace Village, and d. 21 Oct. 1795, a. nearly 69; his w. Hannah m. John Jones of Barre 29 May 1796, res. near the Furnace Vil-

lage, in a house which she bought three weeks before this marriage, marked "C. Jenney" on the R. Map, and survived her husband several years. She was a woman of extraordinary energy, and had she lived in the present day would have been among the foremost in the battle for "woman's rights." She d. 22 Ap. 1814, a. 60.

17. WHITING, s. of Benjamin (8), m. Wealthy Smith 20 July 1780, when he had attained the ripe age of 47 years. They seem to have had only one child, *Solomon*, bap. 25 May 1783, but prob. b. 16 Oct. 1781. WHITING the f. was a farmer, res. on the Moose Brook road, at the place marked "S. Ruggles" on the R. Map, and d. 3 Aug. 1796, a. 63; his w. Wealthy d. 26 Nov. 1840, a. 92.

18. TIMOTHY, s. of Timothy (9), m. Sarah, dau. of Col. Simeon Dwight of Western (Warren), pub. 30 July 1766, and had *Sally*, b. 2 Feb. 1768, m. Judah Hinkley 15 Dec. 1785; *Anna*, b. 8 June 1769; *Sophia*. b. 19 Jan. 1771, d. 6 Oct. 1775; *Betsey*, b. 15 Nov. 1772, d. 29 Nov. 1772; *Timothy*, b. 1 Dec. 1773, d. 19 Sep. 1775; *Timothy*, b. 7 Mar. 1776, rem. to Nova Scotia with his father, was a major of militia, justice of the peace, member of the Provincial Parliament, and d. in March 1831; *Sophia*, b. 20 Oct. 1777; *Simeon Dwight*, b. 23 Jan. 1780, was a merchant in Annapolis, N. S., where he d. — Nov. 1812; *Harriet*, b. 23 Feb. 1782; *Clarissa*, b. 3 Ap. 1784; *Israel Williams*, b. 27 Aug. 1786, was a prosperous merchant in Annapolis, where he d. 5 or 11 Jan. 1880. TIMOTHY the f. naturally favored the king's cause, in which his father was so deeply interested, and was placed under guard by vote of the town, and confined to his farm; he subsequently made his peace, however, and did not become a refugee. He was lieutenant of militia before the Revolution, but held no office afterwards while he remained here. He was a farmer, rough in manner, but manifestly a man of good natural endowments. He res. on the homestead (which had been confiscated but afterwards was released to him by the Commonwealth) until 1795, when he sold the farm, rem. to Nova Scotia, and settled in the township of Granville. Sabine says, "he was a member of the House of Assembly of Nova Scotia many years;" [1] but I suspect he mistakes the father for the son, who held that position.[2] He d. at Granville 9 Dec. 1831, a. nearly 93; his w. Sarah d. in 1842, a. 92.

19. RICHARD, s. of Timothy (9), m. Wealthy ——, and had *Bathsheba*, b. 22 Sep. 1772. RICHARD the f. was a Tory, and went to Nova Scotia at the commencement of hostilities; he settled in the township of Clements, had three sons and four daughters after his removal thither, and d. about 1834, "at an advanced age."

20. BENJAMIN, s. of Benjamin (10), m. Elizabeth Fay (perhaps dau. of Deac. James) 26 Nov. 1766, and had *Denison*, b. 9 July 1767; *Moses*, b. 20 Feb. 1771; *Benjamin*, b. 11 Mar. 1773; *John*, b. 1 Nov. 1775; *Alice*, b. 16 Dec. 1777, m. Nathan Thompson of Salem, N. Y., 21 Dec. 1797; *Betsey*, b. 9 Aug. 1780, m. Aaron Goodale of Salem, N. Y., 9 Feb. 1802; *Mary*, b. 17 Feb. 1783.

21. THOMAS, s. of Benjamin (10), m. Hannah, dau. of Thomas Winslow, 19 July 1778, and had *Miriam*, b. 23 Oct. 1778, m. Ebenezer Foster 8 June 1806; *Willard*, b. 4 Sep. 1780, m. Susan ——, and d. 3 July 1809; *Charlotte*, b. 3 Oct. 1782, d. unm. at Oakham 28 Mar. 1824; *Arathusa*, b. ——, m. Richard Howe of Poultney, Vt.; *Rhoda*, b. —— 1787, d. unm. 21 June 1809; *Phila*, b. — Aug. 1790, m. Benjamin Rice, and d. 16 Sep. 1837; *Joshua*, b. 1 Dec. 1792, m. Olive Holton, and d. 3 Sep. 1852; *Reuel*, b. 27 Mar. 1796, d. unm. 13 Dec. 1873; *Hannah*, b. 17 May 1798, m. Warner Smith, and d. 6 Jan. 1857; *Thomas*, b. 14 Dec. 1800, d. s. p. ——; *Harriet*, b. 25 June 1803, m. Richard Howe, and d. — Oct. 1861; *Seraph Howe*, b. 23 Feb. 1806, m. Norman B. Thompson 16 Aug. 1827. THOMAS the f. was a shoemaker, a soldier in the Revolutionary War, and rem. from Hardwick to Oakham before 17 May 1798,

[1] Sabine's *Loyalists of the Amer. Rev.*, ii. 246.

[2] J. W. Ruggles, Esq., says his brother Timothy "was a major in the militia, a magistrate, and representative for many years in the General Assembly;" but he does not intimate that his father performed similar service. *MS. Letter*, Oct. 4, 1839.

where he d. 12 May 1808; his w. Hannah d. 28 Mar. 1832, a. 70. (Many of these facts are gathered from the *Winslow Memorial*, i. 395, where it is stated that the last four of the chil. were b. at Oakham, and all the others at Hardwick; but I find no record of their birth here, except of the first three.)

22. SETH, s. of Benjamin (10), m. Hannah, dau. of John Amidon, 25 Nov. 1790; she d. in child-bed 26 Oct. 1791, a. 39, and he m. Hannah Bursley 22 Nov. 1792; she d. 4 Oct. 1793, a. 37, and he m. Sukey Jenks, pub. 18 May 1794. His chil. were *Seth Amidon*, b. 26 Oct. 1791; *Henry Jenks*, b. 31 Oct. 1795; *Hannah*, b. 5 Sep. 1797; *William Winthrop*, b. 1 Jan. 1800; *Samuel*, b. 3 Mar. 1802.

23. EDWARD, s. of Edward (13), m. Anna, dau. of Paul Dean, pub. 12 Jan. 1772, and had *Paul*, b. 4 Dec. 1772; *Asa*, b. 28 June 1774, drowned at sea, 19 Oct. 1798; *Abel*, b. 26 Mar. 1776, m. Lucinda Thomas 8 May 1799, res. at Carmel, Me., was a representative, and a member of the convention for framing the Constitution of Maine; he d. 18 June 1860; *Mary*, b. 18 Jan. 1778, m. Daniel Thomas 3 Sep. 1798; *Ezra*, b. 25 Jan. 1780, for several years an active citizen, a captain of militia, selectman, 1820, erected the large house on the westerly side of the Common nearest to the turnpike and marked "D. R." on the R. Map. Meeting with reverses in later life, he rem. to Maine, where he d. unmarried; *Fanny*, b. 7 Jan. 1782, m. Timothy Rich of Boston, pub. 25 Mar. 1810; *Lucy*, b. —— 1784, d. 28 Ap. 1790, a. 6; *Ira*, b. 29 Oct. 1785; *Mira*, b. 11 Dec. 1787; a child b. —— 1789, d. 2 May 1790, a. 8 months; *Lucy*, b. 20 Ap. 1791, m. Woodhull Helme of Blenheim, N. Y., 25 June 1816; *Edward*, b. 11 Ap. 1793, accidentally killed (by a cart) 30 Oct. 1810; *Spooner*, b. 4 Aug. 1795, m. —— Bennett, res. in Rockford, Ill., was a judge, and d. in March 1874; *Anna*, b. 2 Oct. 1799, m. William Barr, pub. 24 Dec. 1827. EDWARD the f., a farmer, res. on Ruggles Hill, at the place marked "H. Gould" on the R. Map; he was one of the "minute-men" who marched on the Lexington alarm in Ap. 1775, and performed a short tour of service as sergeant in 1779. He held a more conspicuous position in January and February 1787, when he was captain of a company in the defence of the government against the insurrectionary army of Shays, and shared in the perils and discomforts of that memorable march from Hadley to Petersham which resulted in the utter dispersion of the rebel army. He d. 17 Jan. 1805, a. 54; His wid. Anna m. John Amidon 14 Dec. 1809, but soon returned to her former residence, where she d. 9 Jan. 1842, a. nearly 89.

24. DANIEL, s. of Edward (13), m. Lucy, dau. of Deac. William Paige, 31 Dec. 1779, and had *Gardner*, b. 16 Feb. 1782; *Anson*, b. 17 Dec. 1783; *Franklin*, b. 21 Mar. 1786; *Mercy*, b. 26 Ap. 1788, d. 9 Oct. 1802; *Lucy*, b. 5 Ap. 1791, m. Stephen W. Paige 26 Oct. 1809, and d. 25 Dec. 1865; *Crighton*, b. 10 June 1793; *Alma*, b. 22 July 1795, m. Benjamin Smith of Rutland, Vt., 15 Sep. 1833, became insane, and d. here 24 Ap. 1857; *Luthera*, b. 4 Jan. 1798, m. Samuel F. Cutler 24 May 1819, and d. 17 Aug. 1823. DANIEL the f. was a farmer, and for seventeen years an innholder. He was lieutenant in the Revolutionary Army, 1779, a selectman four years, assessor eleven years, town treasurer six years, and justice of the peace. He res. on Ruggles Hill, at the place marked "F. Ruggles," until 1809, when he erected the spacious building near the Common, marked "Tavern" on the R. Map, and opened a public house, which he conducted until 1826, and then retired from business; soon afterwards he bought the house on the Common, built by Ezra Ruggles and marked "D. R.," where he spent a quiet old age, after a busy manhood. He d. 26 Feb. 1838, a. 83; his w. Lucy d. 3 Aug. 1840, a. 83.

25. CONSTANT, s. of Edward (13), m. Sally, wid. of —— Hudson, and dau. of —— Green, —— 1792, and had *Adin*, b. 8 Aug. 1793, m. ——, and d. 18 Nov. 1833 ("He was a manufacturer of pistols and rifles; . . . as one of his workmen was engaged in proving a new barrel, charged with a bullet, he accidentally passed in the range; the bullet struck his forehead and came out in front of the ear. . . . He left a widow and a large family of children." [1]); *Fordyce*, b. 30 Oct. 1795, m. Rebecca Bacon 8 Sep. 1822, had several children,

1 *Trumpet and Univ. Magazine*, vi. 23, Nov. 30, 1833.

res. here, and d. at Ware 29 Jan. 1828 (like his brother Adin, he was a manufacturer of fire-arms, and was destroyed by his own handiwork: a ball discharged from his pistol, in the hands of a young man who was carelessly handling it, passed through his lungs and lodged in the spine; he lingered more than a week, when death terminated his distress); *Azubah*, b. 24 Nov. 1797, m. James Abbott of W. Brk., pub. 16 Mar. 1833, and d. 18 Jan. 1871; *Eliza*, b. 3 Ap. 1800, d. 17 Dec. 1803; *Mercy*, b. 17 Sep. 1802, m. Rev. John Bisbee of Brk. 7 June 1823, and (2d) Capt. Daniel Jackson of Plymouth; left a widow a second time, she rem. to Boston, and successfully continued the practice of medicine, in which she had previously been engaged; she d. 13 Dec. 1877, having been the mother of twelve children; *Eliza*, bap. 10 Feb. 1805, m. Marcian Seavey, and d. at Greenwood, Tenn., 28 Nov. 1860; *Charlotte*, b. ——, m. George Ropes of Portland 9 July 1832, and d. while on a visit at the house of her sister at W. Brk.; *Daniel*, b. ——. CONSTANT the f. was a farmer, res. a few years on the homestead, with his mother, and elsewhere in Hk., afterwards near the meeting-house in Prescott, but returned, and for nearly a quarter of a century res. on the road to Enfield, somewhat more than a mile westerly from the Common, at the place marked with his full name on the R. Map. He long held a commission as justice of the peace. He had an uncommonly keen intellect, and his shrewd sayings are still remembered; in religious or political discussions he was especially formidable; if there was a flaw in his adversary's argument, he was sure to detect it, while his own logic was conclusive and irresistible. He d. 28 Ap. 1846, a. 78; his w. Sally d. 8 July 1855, a. 86.

26. NATHAN, s. of Edward (13), m. Catherine Shaw; she d. and he m. Harriet, dau. of Dr. William Cutler, 23 Ap. 1813. His chil. were *James*, b. ——; *Ann Maria*, b. 11 Oct. 1802, m. Joseph Robinson 11 Dec. 1821, and d. 14 Dec. 1822; *William Cutler*, b. ——, d. young; *Harriet*, b. ——, m. —— Duntree; *Julia*, b. ——, m. —— Sanborn of Greenfield. NATHAN the f. res. in Hartford, and was a manufacturer of looking-glasses and picture frames. In personal appearance he bore a striking resemblance to General Lafayette, and the brilliant Frenchman did not excel him in native gentility of manner. Late in life he rem. to New Haven, and engaged in the making of fire-works; and on the 27th of Mar. 1835, he was suddenly killed by an explosion of his own wares. It is a singular coincidence that he and his two nephews, Adin and Fordyce Ruggles, should be destroyed by the work of their own hands in the space of about seven years.

27. NATHANIEL, s. of Nathaniel (14), m. Drusilla Briggs 2 Sep. 1784, and had *Zephaniah B.*, b. 9 June 1789; *Nathaniel*, b. 27 Ap. 1791; *Mary B.*, b. 9 June 1794; *Delia*, b. 22 June 1796; *Susanna*, b. 27 Aug. 1798; *Increase S.*, b. —— 1800; *John H.*, b. 2 Nov. 1802. NATHANIEL the f. res. in Rochester, was justice of the peace, and d. 2 Mar. 1827, a. nearly 72.

28. ELISHA, s. of Nathaniel (14), m. Polly Clapp 10 July 1788, and had *Nathaniel Sprague*, b. 18 July 1789; *Micah Haskell*, b. 9 May 1791, a lawyer and member of Congress; *Henry*, b. 3 Jan. 1793; *James*, b. 28 Sep. 1795, and d. 14 Nov. 1877, a farmer and justice of the peace; *William*, b. 5 Sep. 1797. ELISHA the f. res. in Rochester, was a merchant, major of militia, and justice of the peace; he d. 20 Aug. 1830, a. nearly 72; his w. Polly d. 4 Sep. 1802, a. 38.

29. BENJAMIN, s. of Benjamin (16), m. Betsey Parks 15 Dec. 1779, and had *Parks*, b. 13 Oct. 1781; *Lucy*, b. 23 June 1784, m. William Smith 14 Feb. 1805; *Eleanor*, b. 3 Mar. 1788, perhaps m. Josiah Wilcox of N. Sal. 26 Dec. 1830; *Betsey*, b. 4 June 1790, m. John Rice, pub. 21 Nov. 1808; she m. (2d) Calvin Wetherbee, and (3d) Benjamin Skinner, 19 Jan. 1851. BENJAMIN the f. was a farmer and carpenter, res. on the Enfield road, about three miles from the Common, at the place marked "P. Ruggles" on the R. Map, and d. 22 Dec. 1820, a. 67; his w. Betsey d. 15 Mar. 1827.

30. LEMUEL, s. of Benjamin (16), m. Lydia ——, and had *Lemuel*, b. about 1780; *Lydia*, b. about 1782, m. Hatfield Gould 26 Oct. 1817, and d. 10 Mar. 1850, a. 67; *Brigham*, b. about 1784; *Sally*, b. about 1786, d. unm. 17 Feb.

1808, a. 21. LEMUEL the f. was a farmer, res. on the Moose Brook road, about a mile northerly from the Furnace Village, at the place marked "L. Ruggles" on the R. Map, and d. 22 Oct. 1806, a. 51; his w. Lydia d. 2 May 1807, a. 50.

31. EPHRAIM, s. of Benjamin (16), m. Olive Powers 20 Mar. 1783, and had *Joshua*, b. 9 Oct. 1784, d. 3 Sep. 1786; *Betsey*, b. 16 July 1786; *Polly*, b. 28 July 1788, d. 20 Dec. 1801; *Martin*, b. 13 Dec. 1790; *Olive*, b. 24 Dec. 1792, d. 28 July 1793; *Cynthia*, b. 26 Sep. 1794, m. Otis Terry 6 Mar. 1817; *Benjamin*, b. 20 Ap. 1797; *Olive*, b. 14 June 1799; *Clarissa*, b. 18 Mar. 1801, m. Martin Gardner 7 Feb. 1821; *Ephraim*, b. 10 July 1803, d. 19 Dec. 1804. EPHRAIM the f. was a farmer, and res. in the westerly part of the town, not far from the turnpike, prob. at the place marked "Mr. Ruggles" on the R. Map; he d. 21 Ap. 1836, a. 79; his w. Olive d. 3 Aug. 1858, a. 98.

32. SOLOMON, s. of Whiting (17), m. Polly Burt 8 Mar. 1803, and had *Solomon Whiting*, b. 9 Jan. 1804; *Polly Bassett*, b. 26 Ap. 1805, d. unm. 24 Aug. 1844; *Levina*, b. 25 Ap. 1807, d. 7 June 1807; *William Leonard*, b. 10 Jan. 1810; d. 24 Feb. 1810; *Harriet*, b. 28 Nov. 1815. SOLOMON the f. was a farmer, and res. on the homestead. He is remembered as a man of remarkable height, on which account, at all parades of the military company of which he was a member, whenever he was present, the right of the file was assigned to him. Late in life, he rem. to Ware, where he d. 31 Mar. 1871, a. (according to the record), 89 years, 5 months, and 15 days.

33. MOSES, s. of Benjamin (20), m. Rhoda Luce 25 Jan. 1798, and had *Anna*, b. — June 1798, d. 5 Sep. 1798.

34. JOHN, s. of Benjamin (20), m. Mrs. Sally Jenks 26 Ap. 1801, and had a child, b. — Sep. 1801, d. 8 Oct. 1801.

35. PAUL, s. of Edward (23), m. Mercy Dexter, pub. 28 Nov. 1796, and had *John Dexter*, b. 2 Dec. 1797.

36. IRA, s. of Edward (23), m. Susan, dau. of Timothy Hathaway 18 Jan. 1825, and had an infant, d. 25 Ap. 1827; *Edward*, b. ——. IRA the f. was a farmer, res. on the homestead, and d. 21 July 1832, a. 46; his w. Susan, with her surviving son, rem. to Orford, Tama Co., Iowa, and d. there.

37. GARDNER, s. of Daniel (24), m. Lydia, dau. of Capt. Zenas Phinney 2 Dec. 1804; she d. 23 Sep. 1833, and he m. ——, who survived him; his chil. were *Mercy*, b. 20 Sep. 1805, m. Willard Allen, pub. 8 Oct. 1826, res. in Westminster; *William Paige*, b. 11 Feb. 1807, m. ——, res. in Ridgeway, Wis.; *Cordelia*, b. 20 Aug. 1808, d. 5 Sep. 1810; *Daniel*, b. 31 Jan. 1810, grad. at "West Point, 1833. Entering the 5th Infantry (U. S. A.) he became 2d lieutenant, Feb. 18, 1836; 1st lieutenant, July 7, 1838; captain, June 18, 1846; served in the Florida War; was distinguished at Palo Alto and La Palma, and at the storming of Molino del Rey; brevet major and lieutenant-colonel respectively for gallantry at Contreras and Churubusco Aug. 20, and at Chapultepec Sep. 13, 1847; and resigned May 7, 1861. Made brigadier-general in the Confederate army in 1861; served in New Orleans in the winter of 1861–2, and retreated thence with the forces under Gen. M. Lovell before the surrender of the city to Flag-officer Farragut; major-general in 1863; surrendered with Lee."[1] A sad conclusion of an honorable career. It is much to be regretted that for any reason whatever he should have sacrificed his well-earned military reputation by disloyalty to the national flag. He m. ——, and res. in or near Fredericksburg, Va.; *Cordelia*, b. 25 May 1812, m. Asa Paige; he d. 19 Jan. 1836, and she m. his elder brother, Moses Paige, 14 July 1837; she res. in Troy, N. Y., and Bennington, Vt.; *Sarah Berry*, b. 25 Ap. 1814, m. Capt. Benjamin A. Cobb of Stephenson, Ill., pub. 28 Feb. 1841; *Lucy Spooner*, b. 26 Mar. 1816, a pleasant writer of prose and poetry, for many years a very successful teacher in Virginia and Kentucky, but subsequently returned to Hardwick; *Zenas Phinney*, b. 29 May 1823, m. ——, and res. in Troy, N. Y. GARDNER the f. was a farmer and a civil engineer; he surveyed many estates, and about 1833 constructed the Map of Hardwick to which reference is so frequently made in this volume. He was major of a battalion of artillery,

[1] Drake's *Dictionary of Amer. Biography*, p. 786.

and justice of the peace. Through life he was a devoted Freemason; he was Master of Mount Zion Lodge nine years, between 1823 and 1849, District Dep. G. Master for this district ten years, from 1833 to 1842, and for the last seven of those years "special agent," on behalf of the fraternity, for the whole territory west of Worcester County. After his first marriage he res. in Barre until about 1836, when he returned, and occupied a part of his father's house on the Common. He was town treasurer two years, assessor five years, representative from Barre five years, and from Hardwick in 1838 and 1839. His active and useful life had a tragical close: he was thrown from a wagon and killed 5 Aug. 1853, a. 71.

38. ANSON, s. of Daniel (24), m. Lucy, dau. of Moses Paige, 14 June 1812, and had *Dwight*, b. 31 Mar. 1816, in early life a bookseller, afterwards a physician, and surgeon in the Union army, m. ——, and res. in the city of New York; *Mary*, b. 4 Mar. 1818, m. William Mixter 7 July 1840; *Moses*, b. 3 Nov. 1819; *George*, b. 3 Sep. 1821, town clerk 1859 and 1860, d. unm. 5 Jan. 1861; *Daniel*, b. 9 Aug. 1823, m. ——, res. in Baraboo, Wis.; *Frederick D.*, b. 21 June 1835. ANSON the f. was a farmer, and res. on Ruggles Hill, upon the homestead of his grandfather. In his old age he spent several winters at the house of his son-in-law, Hon. William Mixter, near the Common, returning to the hill on the approach of warm weather. He d. 5 Dec. 1881, a. 98 years, lacking twelve days; his w. Lucy d. 29 July 1874, a. 78.

39. FRANKLIN, s. of Daniel (24), m. Sally, dau. of Dr. Elias Penniman, 21 or 22 Nov. 1812, and had *Ann J.*, b. 7 Nov. 1813, m. Dwight Billings 31 Dec. 1834, and d. 11 Jan. 1864; *James L.*, b. 12 June 1815, insane, d. unm. 11 or 12 Oct. 1851; *Henry*, b. 5 Ap. 1817, d. 6 Ap. 1825; *Charles*, b. 10 Feb. 1819, subject to occasional derangement, a farmer, res. on the homestead, d. unm. 14 May 1878; *Sarah*, b. 19 July 1820, m. Samuel Gladding of Providence 21 Jan. 1840, and d. 22 June 1851; *Mary*, b. 16 Mar. 1822, m. Rev. Franklin Whitaker of Southbridge, Mass., 1 June 1843, had five children, all of whom d. young, res. several years in Janesville, Wis., but returned to her birth-place; *Samuel F.*, b. 18 July 1824, d. 7 Feb. 1825; *Alma*, b. 9 Oct. 1826, m. Richard L. Hathaway 14 Ap. 1846, d. in the hospital at Northampton 10 Dec. 1860; *Henry*, b. 12 July 1829. FRANKLIN the f. was a farmer, and res. on the homestead. He was representative in 1850, and d. 16 Aug. 1865, a. 79; his w. Sally d. 3 Ap. 1864, a. 71.

40. CRIGHTON, s. of Daniel (24), m. Theolotia, dau. of John Lawton, 21 Nov. 1816; she d. s. p. 27 June 1817, a. 23, and he m. Rhoda, dau. of Timothy Hathaway, 30 Ap. 1820, and had *Theolotia*, b. 26 Ap. 1821, m. Ginery Twichell (a noted stage-driver, railroad president, and member of Congress), 26 Aug. 1846, and d. 9 Mar. 1876; *Luthera*, b. 3 July 1824, d. 24 Mar. 1825; *Crighton*, d. 9 Mar. 1827, m. ——, res. at Lawrence, Ill.; *Julia*, b. 17 June 1829, m. Stephen S. Seavey of Boston 15 Aug. 1855; he d. 6 Oct. 1867, and she m. Alexandre F. Leomans of Paris 28 Mar. 1878, res. at Chicago; *Cyrus, W.*, b. 10 Sep. 1831, m. ——, postmaster, res. at Brookline; *Rhoda Maria*, b. 9 Ap. 1835, m. William H. Power 28 Oct. 1867. CRIGHTON the f. was a farmer, and a captain of militia. He res. on the road to Ware, at the place marked "C. Ruggles" on the R. Map, kept the tavern near the Common from 1826 to 1832, and about 1836 rem. to Barre, where he d. 13 Aug. 1858, a. 65; his w. Rhoda d. 2 Nov. 1879, a. nearly 77.

41. PARKS, s. of Benjamin (29), m. Lucy, prob. dau. of William Smith, 29 Nov. 1804, and had *Lydia*, b. 31 Mar. 1806, m. Ransford L. Smith of Hopkinton 25 May 1839; *Mary*, b. 7 Sep. 1807; d. unm. at N. Brk. 24 Mar. 1878, a. 70; *Reed Smith*, b. 4 Sep. 1809; *Lauretta*, b. 25 Oct. 1811, m. James C. Ayres of N. Brk., pub. 9 Dec. 1838; *Almira*, b. 27 Nov. 1813, m. Henry A. Moore of Littleton 21 Aug. 1837; *Lucy*, b. 25 July 1817. PARKS the f. was a farmer, res. on the Old Greenwich road, three miles westerly from the Common, at the place marked "P. Ruggles" on the R. Map, and d. 12 Nov. 1835, a. 54; his w. Lucy d. 6 Nov. 1867, a. 87.

42. LEMUEL, s. of Lemuel (30), m. Hannah Hooker of Enf., pub. 30 Mar. 1818, and had *Elbridge*, b. 3 June 1819; *Sally*, b. 29 Mar. 1821, d. unm. 4

Ap. 1847; *Emory*, b. 5 June 1823, d. 22 Feb. 1825; *Maria*, b. 2 Nov. 1825, m. Clinton Howard of Sturbridge 20 June 1858, res. here and d. 13 May, 1877; *Jane*, b. 23 Mar. 1828, d. 3 July 1828. LEMUEL the f. was a farmer, res. on the homestead, and d. 14 Feb. 1840, a. 59; his w. Hannah d. 16 Dec. 1877, a. 85.

43. BRIGHAM, s. of Lemuel (30), m. Abigail Crain 30 Dec. 1813, and had *Albert Henry*, b. 9 Oct. 1814; "*Alucius*" *Crain*, b. 31 Dec. 1815. BRIGHAM the f. rem. to Boylston, and d. 9 Ap. 1863, a. nearly 79.

44. MARTIN, s. of Ephraim (31), m. Abigail, dau. of Eleazar Dexter, 27 Feb. 1816, and had a child, which d. 13 July 1817; *Martin Dexter*, b. 26 Oct. 1820, d. 9 Mar. 1838; *William Powers*, b. 11 Nov. 1822; *John Edwin*, b. 4 June 1826. MARTIN the f. d. 28 Sept. 1861, a. nearly 71; his w. Abigail d. 5 July 1860, a. 73.

45. SOLOMON W., s. of Solomon (32), m. Tryphena Weeks 1 Ap. 1827, and had *Benjamin Whiting*, b. 25 Mar. 1828, d. at Fitchburg 1 Oct. 1846; *John Willis*, b. 17 July 1829, d. at Fitchburg 13 July 1852. SOLOMON W. the f. rem. to Fitchburg, and d. 19 May 1863, a. 59.

46. MOSES, s. of Anson (38), m. Maria, dau. of William Robinson of Barre 26 May 1841, and had *Lucy Maria*, b. 13 Oct. 1845, m. Edward H. Paige, 5 July 1876. MOSES the f., a farmer, res. at Barre and on the homestead in Hk. for some years, and afterwards on the Mixter Farm, near the Common. He was an assessor in 1851 and 1866.

47. FREDERICK D., s. of Anson (38), m. Eliza Jane Rogers of Barre 14 June 1859, and had *Frederick Anson*, b. 19 Mar. 1861; *Anna Reed*, b. 22 Ap. 1863; *George Rawson*, b. 9 Nov. 1864; *Mary Mixter*, b. 15 Oct. 1866; *Carrie Cutler*, b. 22 May 1870; *Jennie Louisa*, b. 15 Aug. 1876; *Samuel Rogers*, b. 7 Dec. 1880. FREDERICK D. the f., a farmer, res. on the homestead.

48. HENRY, s. of Franklin (39), m. Harriette S. Geer of Norwich, Conn., 25 Oct. 1852; she d. 11 Ap. 1857, a. 26, and he m. Louise Cooke of Preston, Conn.; she d. ——, and he m. Sarah Perry of Ridgefield, Conn. His chil. were *Alice*, b. 31 Dec. 1853 or 1854, d. 17 May 1862; *William Cummings*, b. 28 Oct. 1856; *Annie Louise*, b. 18 Sep. 1863. HENRY the f. res. in Norwich, Conn. He served his country several years as consul at Barcelona, and afterwards at Malta.

49. REED S., s. of Parks (41), m. Sarah A., dau. of Rufus Sargent of N. Br., pub. 17 Ap. 1839, and had *Estes Sargent*, b. 20 Feb. 1844; *Frederick A.*, b. 14 Mar. 1848; *Mary Ann*, b. 29 May 1851, m. Edward B. Brown of Brimfield 1 Oct. 1879. REED S. the f., a farmer, res. near the central bridge over Ware River, at the place marked "A. Rich" on the R. Map. He d. 12 Oct. 1882, a. 73; his w. Sarah A. d. 27 Sep. 1876, a. 63.

50. ELBRIDGE, s. of Lemuel (42), m. Mary Aiken of Prescott, pub. 14 Dec. 1850, and had *Mary Theolotia*, b. 20 Aug. 1852; *Abbie*, b. 21 June 1854; *Frederick Elbridge*, b. 23 Sep. 1856, m. Katie E. Wesson 27 Ap. 1882; *Amory A.*, b. 26 May 1859; *Ella Frances*, b. 3 Aug. 1863; *Louis Hooker*, b. 17 Nov. 1866; *Gertrude M.*, b. 1 Feb. 1869; *Nelson Paul*, b. 29 Aug. 1871. ELBRIDGE the f., a farmer, res. on the homestead.

51. WILLIAM P., s. of Martin (44), m. Martha M., dau. of Capt. John Lawton, 22 Feb. 1846, and had *Martha Jeannette*, b. 8 Oct. 1847; *John William*, b. 9 June 1856.

52. FREDERICK A., s. of Reed S. (49), m. Carrie L. Towne 15 Jan. 1878, and had *Alice Maude*, b. 10 Oct. 1878, d. 7 Sep. 1879; *Amie L.*, b. ——, d. 12 June 1882.

53. FRANKLIN (b. in Esperance, N. Y.), by w. Julia Bell, had *Julia Bell*, b. 9 Dec. 1864.

SAMUEL, m. Mary Mace of Stafford, Conn., pub. 20 Dec. 1784. SAMUEL (perhaps the same), m. Susanna Johnson of Thompson, Conn., pub. 6 Mar. 1786. POLLY, m. Samuel French of Craftsbury, Vt., 17 July 1796. PAULINE M. (dau. of Benjamin and Mary of Otsego, N. Y.), m. John R. Fish 27 May 1855, and (2d) Isaac S. Bonney 10 Mar. 1864.

SABIN, DAVID, by w. Mary, had *Lydia*, bap. 24 Sep. 1738; *David*, bap. 19

Oct. 1740; *Chloe*, bap. — July 1743; *Lucy*, bap. 14 Sep. 1746. DAVID the f. was a comb-maker, and came here from Rehoboth. He bought a farm in Hardwick 18 Oct. 1736, and was admitted to the church here 4 Sep. 1737.

ELISHA, m. Sarah Crosby of Sturbridge 18 Feb. 1795. ABIGAIL, of Bel., m. Dr. William H. Willis, pub. 17 Sep. 1842. URSULA G., d. 5 Sep. 1856, a. 29.

SAFFORD, THOMAS, was of Ipswich as early as 1641, and by w. Elizabeth had sons *Joseph* and *John*, and four daughters. He d. in Ips. 20 Feb. 1667.

2. JOHN, s. of Thomas (1), b. about 1633, res. in Ipswich, and by w. Sarah had *Thomas, Joseph*, perhaps *John*, and five daughters.

3. THOMAS, s. of John (2), b. in Ipswich 16 Oct. 1673, m. Eleanor, wid. of Richard Shatswell and dau. of Daniel Cheney, 7 Oct. 1698, and had *Sarah, Thomas, Joseph*, b. — March 1704-5. (Thus far I have been guided by a MS. letter from Hon. Robert Safford Hale of Elizabethtown, N. Y., one of the posterity of the last-named Joseph Safford.)

4. JOSEPH, s. of Thomas (3), m. Mary Challis —— 1728, and had *Eleanor*, bap. at Ips. 29 June 1729, d. 13 Dec. 1730; *Joseph*, bap. 25 Oct. 1730; *Anna*, bap. 28 Nov. 1731, m. Israel Olmstead 25 Nov. 1756; *Challis*, bap. 9 Sep. 1733; *Philip*, b. about 1736; *Ebenezer*, b. about 1738; *Mary*, m. Azariah Wright of Westminster, Vt., 29 June 1762. JOSEPH the f. was a "joyner;" he prob. rem. from Ips. to Sutton, and thence to Hk. in 1751, and d. here before 1757, when his widow released dower in his estate; she subsequently rem. with her son *Joseph* to Woodstock, Vt.

5. JOSEPH, s. of Joseph (4), m. Martha Powers 26 Oct. 1753, and had *Jesse*, b. 9 Feb. 1755; *Eleanor*, b. 23 Oct. 1757; *Martha*, b. 11 June 1759 (bap. 24 Sep. 1758; it would seem that the date of birth should be 1758, and the date of the preceding birth 1756); *Joseph*, b. 22 June 1760; *Mary*, b. 4 Ap. 1763; *Challis*, b. 6 Feb. 1765; *Lucinda*, b. 8 Jan. 1771, d. 8 Feb. 1773. JOSEPH the f. was a housewright, and appears to have resided on the Barre road, at or near the place marked "Dr. Stone" on the R. Map. He was a partner with Deac. Joseph Allen in the hazardous enterprise of erecting, at their own risk, the spacious meeting-house which was completed in 1771. He was commissioned lieutenant of Capt. Daniel Wheeler's company of militia in 1771, and removed to Woodstock, Vt., in 1777, where he d. 19 Jan. 1798; his w. Martha d. 31 Mar. 1804, a. 73.

6. CHALLIS, s. of Joseph (4), m. Rebecca, dau. of Thomas Winslow, 10 July 1755; she d. ——, and he m. Lydia, dau. of Jonathan Warner, 8 Feb. 1760. His chil. were *Elizabeth*, b. 7 Dec. 1755; *Anna*, b. 27 Aug. 1757, d. 7 Ap. 1759; *Anna*, b. 22 Feb. 1761; *Jonas*, b. 23 July 1763; *Jonathan*, b. 27 Feb. 1766, went with his mother to Bennington in 1777, studied medicine prob. with his step-father, Dr. Jonas Fay, settled at Pawlet, Vt., in 1793, and "was a successful and popular practitioner until his death in 1821, aged 56 (55). Dr. [Jonathan] Safford raised a large family: Horace, Jonathan W., Edwin B., Annis, Eliza, Delia, and Caroline;"[1] *Robert*, b. 17 July 1768; *Challis*, b. 15 Ap. 1771, was carried to Bennington in 1777, m. Betsey Doty 1 Nov. 1796, and rem. to Enosburg, Vt., in 1800, where he was elected deacon in 1833; he was a farmer, and "won the confidence and friendship of his fellow-citizens in a remarkable degree. It was not known that he had an enemy. In politics he was a Federalist of the old school. . . . He died Aug. 22, 1841, in the 71st year of his age; and the people said 'a good man and true has gone to his rest.'"[2] CHALLIS the f., in the record of his first marriage, is described as of Rutland (prob. Rutland District, now Barre), but seems to have become an inhabitant of Hk. immediately afterwards, and res. at the north end of the Common, on or near the place marked "P. Hammond" on the R. Map. He was a physician, and during the French War served two campaigns in the regiment of Col. Ruggles, — as surgeon in 1757, and surgeon's mate in 1759. His useful life had an early close; the date of his death is not found, but the inventory of his estate was rendered 21 June 1771. His w. Lydia m. Dr. Jonas Fay of Bennington, the famous Vermont patriot and politician, 20 Nov. 1777.

[1] *Hist. of Pawlet*, p. 233.

[2] *Vermont Hist. Magazine*, ii. 156-158.

7. PHILIP, s. of Joseph (4), was a "joyner" or carpenter, and resided here as early as 1755. He subsequently rem. to Rockingham, Vt., m. —— Bigelow, and had several children. He served in the French War during five campaigns, 1755–1759, and on the roll for 1756 was described as 20 years old, and born in Ipswich. In his last campaign 1759, he held the office of lieutenant; he had previously been a drummer; and he must have been a good one, as he was the drum-major, 1757, in the regiment of Col. Ruggles, of which his brother, Dr. Challis Safford, was surgeon.

8. EBENEZER, s. of Joseph (4), m. Abiel, dau. of Elisha Higgins, 24 Nov. 1759, and had *Ebenezer*, b. 9 Dec. 1759. He served in the French War during the campaigns of 1757, 1759, and 1760, — the last year as sergeant; on the roll for 1759 he is described as 21 years old. Whether he died while attached to the army does not appear; but his w. Abiel m. Israel Johnson 29 Dec. 1761.

SAMPSON, JOHN S., by w. Lydia S., had *Alice N.*, b. 12 Feb. 1850.

2. PEREZ B., by w. Arminda R., had *Francis*, b. 16 Ap. 1861.

RACHEL, of Templeton, m. Capt. Elijah Warner 15 May 1786. OLIVE, m. Allen Cobb 1 Jan. 1795. BETSEY, m. Giles Warner 4 May 1809.

SANGER, ELEAZAR, by w. Mary, had *Eleazar* and *Abner*, twins, b. 12 Mar. 1739; *Mary*, b. 2 May 1741; *Elizabeth*, b. 6 Sep. 1743. ELEAZAR the f. was son of Nathaniel Sanger of Woodstock, formerly a part of Worcester County, but now embraced in Connecticut. He was a farmer, and rem. from Woodstock to Hk. in 1735, and apparently resided near the line of Barre. In Feb. 1746 he sold to Elisha Hedge 300 acres of land, lying on both sides of Moose Brook, and bounded north on the Barre line. He prob. soon afterwards rem. to Petersham (then called Nichewoag), where he was residing in August 1751.

2. GEORGE J., was pastor of the Union Church and Society (the old First Parish), from 1856 to 1864. His w. *Sarah E.*, d. 7 May 1858, a. 33, and he m. Susan V., dau. of Gardner Bartholomew, 31 May 1859. In the War of the Rebellion he served his country, first as lieutenant of infantry, and afterwards as chaplain, and was taken prisoner at Galveston. He rem. to Webster in 1864, and subsequently to Danvers.

SAUNDERS, ROBERT, m. Hannah Walker of Pet., pub. 30 Aug. 1768. MARY H., of Boston, m. Nathaniel Oliver 2d, pub. 18 Dec. 1846.

SEARS, RICHARD, m. Dorothy Thacher in 1632, and had *Knyvet; Paul; Silas; Deborah*, m. Zechariah Paddock. RICHARD the f. came to Plymouth in 1630, and settled in the easterly part of Yarmouth (now Dennis), where he d. in 1676, a. 86; his w. Dorothy d. in 1680.

2. SILAS, s. of Richard (1), m. ——, and had *Silas*, b. ——; *Thomas*, b. 1664; *Richard*, b. ——; *Hannah*, b. 1672, m. Thomas Snow of Eastham; *Joseph*, b. ——; *Josiah*, b. ——; *Elizabeth*, b. ——; m. John Cook; *Dorrity*. SILAS the f. was a lieutenant, res. in Yarmouth, where he d. 13 Jan. 1698, a. 60.

3. JOSEPH, s. of Silas (2), m. Hannah Hall 1700, and had *Priscilla*, b. —— 1701; *Hannah*, b. —— 1703; *Zechariah*, b. —— 1706; *Joseph*, b. —— 1708; *Stephen*, b. —— 1710; *Rowland*, b. —— 1711; *Barnabas*, b. —— 1714; *Peter*, b. —— 1716; *Bethia*, b. —— 1718; *Silas*, b. 1720, "went to Rochester;" *Thankful*, b. —— 1723. JOSEPH the f. res. in East Dennis. (Thus far, I have been guided by the *Sears Genealogy* (appended to *Pictures of the Olden Times*), Freeman's *History of Cape Cod*, and Savage's *Gen. Dictionary*.)

4. ROWLAND (generally written ROLAND), s. of Joseph (3), m. Mary, dau. of John Freeman of Rochester, pub. 11 Nov. 1738, and had in Hk. *Freeman*, b. 25 July 1740; *Barnabas*, b. 20 Nov. 1743; *Thankful*, b. 15 July 1745, m. John Cobb 19 July 1764; *Elisha*, b. 6 June 1748, m. Hannah Sears 31 Oct. 1771; *Mercy*, b. 11 Ap. 1751, m. Reuben Snow 11 May 1769; *Hannah*, b. 20 Feb. 1754, m. Ezekiel Baker, pub. 2 Oct. 1785; *Mary*, bap. 4 June 1758. ROLAND the f., in the record of his marriage at Rochester, is described as of Upton; but he seems to have rem. to Hk. before the birth of his first child, and in 1742 bought land on Moose Brook, near Barre. He was a "bloomer,"[1] or

[1] "BLOOM, a mass of iron that has passed the blomary, or undergone the first ham-

forger of iron, and his forge was prob. on the site of what has long been called "Taylor's Mills." He was lieutenant of militia, a soldier in the Revolutionary War, selectman five years, after which he rem. to Greenwich, where he res. in 1787, when he took the oath of allegiance, having been involved in the Shays Rebellion. His wife Mary was dismissed from the church in Hk. to the church in Gr. 13 Sep. 1779.

5. BARNABAS, s. of Joseph (3), m. Thankful, dau. of John Freeman, at Rochester, 25 Sep. 1732, and is said (in *Sears Gen.* p. 32) to have had two sons, *Barnabas* and *Stephen*; he had in Hk. *Mary*, b. 27 Ap. 1738, m. Capt. Jonathan Fletcher of Rut. District (Barre), 1 May 1760. BARNABAS the f. was a "bloomer," prob. an associate of his brother Roland, and had rem. from Roch. to Hk. before the birth of his dau. in 1738. He rem. to Brk., where he purchased one eighth part of certain "iron-works," 5 Jan. 1740, and did not survive quite two years; his inventory was rendered 28 Oct. 1741; his brother Roland settled the estate, and seems to have adopted the dau. *Mary*, who was bap. in Hk. 11 Sep. 1743, being styled in the record "*nephew* of Rolon Sears."

6. SILAS, perhaps s. of Joseph (3), by w. Deborah, had *Barnabas*, b. 21 Mar. 1763, possibly the Capt. Barnabas Sears who d. at Amh. 26 Feb. 1850, and was described as b. in Hardwick, and 84 years of age.

7. FREEMAN, s. of Roland (4), m. Mehetabel, dau. of Andrew Haskell, 22 Oct. 1761, and had *Roland*, b. 24 Dec. 1762, and d. at Gr. 22 Mar. 1851; *Andrew Haskell*, b. 29 Mar. 1765, m. (then res. in Gr.) Rachel Stetson, — Mar. 1787; *Melicent*, b. 20 Sep. 1767, m. —— Field, and d. in Erving 6 Mar. 1853, a. 85; *Mary*, b. 17 Feb. 1771; *Mercy*, b. 23 Jan. 1774; *Charles Doolittle*, b. 7 Oct. 1775. FREEMAN the f. prob. rem. to Gr. before 2 Feb. 1779, when his w. Mehetabel was dismissed from the church in Hk. to the church in Gr.

8. BARNABAS, s. of Roland (4), or possibly s. of Barnabas (5), m. Rachel Bullard of Rut. District (Barre) in 1764, and had *John*, b. 2 Aug. 1765; *Hannah*, b. 4 Mar. 1767; *Joseph*, b. 12 Ap. 1769; *Moses*, b. 22 Ap. 1771; *Barnabas*, b. 18 May 1773, d. 2 June 1773; *Freeman*, bap. 15 May 1774, d. 18 June 1774; *Mary*, b. 10 June 1775. BARNABAS the f. was a farmer, and res. on part of the homestead. His military service during the Revolution was abundant and conspicuous. He was sergeant of the company of "minute-men" which marched on the Lexington alarm, 19 Ap. 1775; he returned and assisted Capt. Samuel Billings in organizing a company for the regular service, of which he was commissioned lieutenant 23 May 1775, and was captain of a company in the Dorchester Camp 15 Feb. 1776. He was elected major of Col. Holman's regiment 26 June 1776, and in 1781 is mentioned as "Lieut. Colonel, Commandant," in the three months' service, when his residence was in Greenwich. In the troublous times which followed the Revolution, like many other officers and soldiers, he was concerned in the unlawful effort for relief, which is styled the Shays Rebellion or Insurrection. His offence was pardoned by the government, and he subscribed the oath of allegiance in 1787. He rem. to Greenwich, prob. before 13 Sep. 1779, when his w. Rachel was dism. from the church in Hk. to the church in Gr.

BARNABAS, d. 3 Oct. 1838, a. 67. ABIGAIL (wid. of Barnabas), d. 4 Dec. 1860, a. 80. ABIGAIL, m. Charles S. Smith of Barre 21 Sep. 1841. SARAH A., m. William A. F. Weeks of Oakham, pub. 20 Sep. 1859. NETTIE O., of Gr., m. Sylvester S. Cleveland 2 Dec. 1863. LUCIUS E., of Gr., m. Sarah E. King 10 Jan. 1865.

SEAVER, MOSES, was a soldier in the French War 1755. LUCY, m. Nathaniel Jackson of Gr., pub. 10 Jan. 1792. LUCY, m. Ezra Leonard, pub. 5 July 1807. LUTHER, m. Salome Jackson, pub. 4 Nov. 1808; she d. 13 Ap. 1809, a. 22.

SELLON, JOHN, JR., was quartermaster in the French War, 1761, and was prob. the same who bought of Isaac Abbott thirty acres of land adjoining Gr. 9 Jan. 1767, was a soldier in the Revolutionary War, 1776, and m. Martha Moseley, at Sutton, 26 Nov. 1778.

mering." "BLOMARY (or BLOOMARY), the first forge through which iron passes after it is melted from the ore." *Webster*.

NANCY, m. Sylvanus Purington, pub. 3 July 1780. SAMUEL, of Leverett, m. Abigail Moseley pub. 22 Jan. 1786. JOHN, m. Rebecca Leech (or Luch) of Bel., pub. 25 Sep. 1796.

SESSIONS, JOSIAH T., m. Sarah A., dau. of Benjamin W. Sherman, 28 Mar. 1872, and had *Anna W.*, b. — Nov. 1873; *George F.*, b. 10 Dec. 1877; *Ansel Benjamin*, b. 8 Oct. 1880.

SHAW, JESSE, m. Paulina, dau. of Joseph Crowell, 19 Dec. 1813, and had a child d. 17 Mar. 1814, a. 11 days.

2. LOREN, m. Lucy H. Totman 17 Mar. 1846, and had *Charles Henry*, b. 22 July 1850.

3. WILLIAM H., m. Lucy A. ——, and had *Abby Eliza*, b. 8 Jan. 1861; a dau. b. 1 Dec. 1863.

GINNET (JEANETTE), m. David Ayers 21 Dec. 1742. ANDREW, m. Anne Blair 17 Nov. 1749. THOMAS, m. Elizabeth Phinney of Pet. 7 June 1777. JOHN, of Brk., m. Kezia Chamberlain 12 June 1780. MEHETABEL, m. Oliver Harris, pub. 16 Ap. 1780. HANNAH, m. Thomas Reed Smith 8 Mar. 1792. LOUISA, m. Alvah Wood of Northampton 6 Ap. 1824. CHAUNCEY R., of Bel., m. Eunice M. Elwell 24 May 1831. OZIEL, of Ware, m. Levina Bassett 10 May 1836.

SHERMAN, BENJAMIN W., m. Lydia ——, and had *Elizabeth*, b. ——, d. 19 June 1842, a. 1; *Lucy*, b. 17 May 1843, d. 15 Oct. 1847; *Avery*, b. 15 Nov. 1847, d. 9 June 1849; *Anna*, b. 28 Jan. 1849; *Sarah Adeline*, b. 22 Feb. 1850, m. Josiah T. Sessions 28 Mar. 1872; a son, still-born, 28 July 1852; *George*, b. ——, d. 19 Sep. 1855, a. 3 days; *Charles W.*, b. 24 Mar. 1859, d. 24 July 1859. BENJAMIN W. the f., a farmer, res. a little more than half a mile north from the Common, at the place marked "S. Berry" on the R. Map.

2. HORACE R., m. Frances ——, and had *Clara Dustin*, b. 1 Ap. 1849, d. 15 Ap. 1850.

MARY, of Grafton, m. John Cooper 15 Mar. 1748-9. WILLIAM, of Rochester, m. Hannah Steward 11 Sep. 1766. JOHN, of Barre, m. Mrs. Sally Allen 3 Dec. 1835. MARY S., m. James H. Severance of Boston 9 Jan. 1866.

SHUGRUE, PATRICK, m. Bridget ——, and had *Abbie*, b. 11 Feb. 1858; *John*, b. about Dec. 1859, d. 1 Ap. 1860, a. 3 months. PATRICK the f., b. in Ireland, d. 9 Oct. 1879, a. 44.

2. CORNELIUS, m. Mary J. Higgins, pub. 17 Jan. 1861, and had *Mary*, b. 19 Mar. 1868; *Julia*, b. 16 Dec. 1869; *Johanna*, b. 16 Aug. 1871; *Catherine*, b. 15 Sep. 1872.

3. JOHN, m. Mary ——, and had *John*, b. 9 Mar. 1872; *Timothy*, b. 16 Aug. 1873; *Agnes*, b. 11 Jan. 1877.

JULIA, m. James Sullivan, pub. 6 Dec. 1858. JULIA, m. Florence Mahoney of Holyoke, pub. 17 Feb. 1863. PATRICK, m. Hannah Fleming 15 Jan. 1865. MICHAEL, m. Hannah Bresnihan of Ware 26 Nov. 1868. MARY, m. William Daunt, Jr., 3 Feb. 1878. JOHN, d. 29 Aug. 1880, a. 75.

SHUMWAY, PEREZ, of Pet., m. Sarah Dwight 3 Ap. 1811, and had *Relief*, bap. 2 Aug. 1812, and m. Joseph A. Gould, pub. 18 Jan. 1839, as a resident in Petersham; *Eliza Flagg*, bap. (adult) 25 June 1820, m. James P. Rogers 5 Mar. 1822, and d. 8 Aug. 1881, a. 81.

LEVIUS, of Barre, m. Mary Eliza Bolster 17 Aug. 1834. ZEMIRA F., m. Rhoda W. Rogers 11 Feb. 1835. ZEMIRA F., of Pet. (prob. the same), m. Mrs. Lucinda Dexter 1 Oct. 1856. ALFRED, d. 30 Sep. 1821, a. 14.

SHURTLEFF, JEDEDIAH, m. Lucy Newhall of Danvers 7 July 1785, and had *Otis*, b. 15 Sep. 1787, m. Lydia, dau. of Maj. Seth Hinkley, 14 Feb. 1810; *Clarissa*, b. 10 Oct. 1790; twins b. 10 May 1794, and d. 12 and 13 May 1794; *Thomas Newhall*, b. 2 Ap. 1796, d. 11 Nov. 1798; *Fairman Newhall*, b. 28 Ap. 1799. JEDEDIAH the f. was a tailor, and went from house to house to make garments. He was lame and thriftless. After a temporary absence from the town he became a pauper, and with his wife returned and received public aid for the remainder of life. He d. 26 Mar. 1845, a. 82; his w. Lucy d. 5 Ap. 1838, a. 77.

2. JONAS, m. Dolly Hawes of N. Br. 27 Mar. 1794, and had *Beriah Hawes*, b. 19 June 1795.

HEMAN, m. Sally Merrick 30 Nov. 1788.

SIBLEY, SARDIUS, had *Sardius, J.*, b. ——; and by second wife, Mary ——, had *Mary Jane*, b. 25 June 1836; *Leander*, b. 10 July 1838; *Charlotte Ellen*, b. 3 Aug. 1840; *Julia Maria*, b. 6 July 1842, m. Samuel S. Dennis 26 Nov. 1863; *Emily Louisa*, b. 22 Aug. 1844, d. 15 Feb. 1848. SARDIUS the f. d. 16 Feb. 1845, a. 41.

2. SUMNER, m. Anna G. ——, and had *Frances Jane*, b. 11 July 1843; *John Braman*, b. 8 Nov. 1847; a dau. b. 15 Sep. 1849.

3. WATERVILLE (or WALTER), of Brk., m. Hannah, dau. of Cyrus Danforth, 29 Mar. 1843, and had, in Hk., *Martha Maria*, b. 8 Jan. 1845; *Delphia Jane*, b. 15 Nov. 1846; *Ella Frances*, b. 4 Feb. 1848.

4. SARDIUS J., s. of Sardius (1), m. Augusta M. Newcomb, pub. 9 Nov. 1856, and had *Frederick*, b. 5 Feb. 1859; *Charles Sardius*, b. 5 Dec. 1862; *Minnie Augusta*, b. 4 July 1867; *Estelle* (or *Annie G.*), b. 6 Aug. 1869, d. 16 Aug. 1869. SARDIUS J., a farmer, res. on the road to Ware, at the place marked "Keyes Tyler" on the R. Map.

5. LEANDER, s. of Sardius (1), was an assessor eleven years, from 1862 to 1873, except 1868, and a member of the school committee in 1872 and 1873. He rem. to Spencer, with his mother, and was afterwards married.

SAMUEL, m. Sarah Ingersoll of Pet., pub. 29 Aug. 1773. MOLLY, m. Stephen Woodward of Pet. 13 May 1777. EUNICE, of N. Sal., m. Adonijah Dennis, pub. 1 May 1780. ELISHA, m. Elizabeth Twitchel of Athol 1 Nov. 1781. BETSEY, m. Samuel Worden of Pet. 30 June 1785. ABIJAH, m. Patty Corey 29 Sep. 1785. BRAMAN B., of Enf., m. Maria A. Utley 31 Dec. 1833. SARAH C., of Auburn, m. Constant Southworth, pub. 27 Dec. 1838. ANN MARIA, of Barre, m. Henry Wilkins, pub. 24 Oct. 1841. CAROLINE A., m. William A. Warner, Jr., 15 Nov. 1860. ISAAC (b. in Sutton), d. 5 Mar. 1853, a. 73.

SIMMONS, TAYLOR, d. 17 Nov. 1819, a. 39. SUSAN, m. John Thayer, pub. 7 Feb. 1820.

SIMONDS, ABIGAIL, m. Joseph Marsh 17 May 1750. JUDAH, m. Thankful Allis 28 May 1777. HANNAH, of Ware, m. David Aiken 15 July 1765, and d. 28 July 1837, a. 97. SARAH, of Barre, m. Frederick Henry, pub. 24 Nov. 1791. PHILENA, m. Robert Parker, pub. 13 May 1811. SARAH, m. John Towne, pub. 2 Nov. 1858.

SIMPSON, NATHANIEL, had w. Dulcinea, who d. 12 Feb. 1834, a. 41, and he m. Sarah, dau. of Samuel Spooner, 12 Mar. 1835; she d. 23 July 1846, a. 46, and he m. Harriet N. Denio, 23 Dec. 1847, and had *Homer Nathaniel*, b. 13 Aug. 1850, d. 20 Mar. 1864; *Harriet Isabel*, b. 7 Nov. 1852, d. 21 Dec. 1858. NATHANIEL the f. was b. in Wardsboro', Vt., came to Hk. about 1820, was an honest and industrious shoemaker, and res. on the turnpike about three quarters of a mile east of the Common, at the place marked "Mr. Stimpson" on the R. Map; he d. 18 Dec. 1876, a. nearly 85 years.

2. JOSEPH, m. Adeline ——, and had *Adeline*, b. 20 June 1865; *Mary Z.*, b. 21 Aug. 1867.

SLANEY, WILLIAM, m. Anna ——, and had *Sarah Gertrude*, b. 11 Sep. 1864; *Frederick James*, b. 19 Aug. 1866; *Alice Anna*, b. 25 June 1871.

MARY A., m. John H. Fay 15 Aug. 1877.

SLEEPER, SAMUEL, m. Lucy Ellen ——, and had *Emma M.*, b. about 1834, d. 27 Sep. 1848, a. 14; *Clarissa Ann*, b. 28 Nov. 1843, d. 12 June 1849; *George W. P.*, b. 1 Ap. 1846; *L. Webster*, b. 15 Mar. 1850; a dau., still-born, 15 Mar. 1852.

2. CURTIS C. (s. of Timothy and Ruth), m. Fanny, dau. of George C. Richardson, 8 Mar. 1873, and had *Mary Eliza*, b. 5 Dec. 1873; *Effie Louisa*, b. 4 May 1875; *Samuel Curtis*, b. 24 June 1877; a dau. b. 10 Ap. 1879; a dau. still-born, 29 Ap. 1880.

SLOAN, WILLARD, m. Alma, dau. of Ezra Clark, and had *Melina*, b. 27 Feb. 1822, m. Charles P. Brown of Woodstock, Conn., 24 Oct. 1849; *Julia Ann*,

b. 6 Dec. 1825; *Ezra C.*, b. 1 July 1827; *Dwight*, b. 10 Ap. 1830; *Daniel P.*, b. 1 May 1832, d. 1 Oct. 1833; *Luthera A.*, b. 10 May 1835, d. 29 May 1853, a. 18; *Elisha Winslow*, b. 18 Mar. 1837; *Elizabeth Paige*, b. 7 Jan. 1844; *Marian Louisa*, b. 28 Jan. 1846; *Elnora*, b. 10 June 1848. WILLARD the f., a farmer, res. on the road to Gr., about two miles westerly from the Common, at the place marked "W. Sloan" on the R. Map.

2. JONATHAN SHIPMAN, brother of Willard (1), had permission from the General Court to take the name of HENRY CLINTON. He m. Mary Eliza, dau. of Jacob Earl, 18 Ap. 1844, and d. s. p. (accidentally killed by the fall of a tree) 26 Mar. 1855, a. 47.

3. JAMES, m. Celia J. Richardson 16 Mar. 1837, and was, perhaps, the same who d. at Dana 1 Dec. 1875, a. 69.

SMITH, BENJAMIN, was one of the earliest and most energetic pioneers in the settlement of the town. Though not one of the original purchasers, he became a proprietor of the township by vote passed at a proprietors' meeting held in Roxbury 21 Feb. 1732–33: "Voted, that Benjamin Smith, who married one of the heirs of John Curtice, deceased, sence he has carryed on his part of the charge with us, 'tis ordered that the said Benjamin Smith shall have recorded to him the ninth part of the said John Curtises share." He was a farmer, and res. on the old River road, about a mile southerly from the Furnace, at the place marked "A. Rice" on the R. Map. When the General Court granted to the inhabitants, 1 Dec. 1736, authority to elect certain officers to manage their affairs, previous to their incorporation as a town, Mr. Smith was authorized to call the first meeting for that purpose; at which, on the 9th of Feb. 1736–7, he presided as moderator, and was elected chairman of the board of selectmen. He served on several important committees, and at the first meeting after the incorporation of the town, in 1739, was again elected to the office of selectman. He came here from Roxbury, where his first wife d., and he m. Experience, dau. of John Curtis, 21 Mar. 1716–17; she d., and he m. Hannah Phillips 23 Ap. 1724. His chil. were *Olive*, b. about 1714, m. Ezra Leonard 1 June 1737, and d. 16 Feb. 1798; *Elizabeth*, b. about 1716, m. James Robinson 3 July 1739; *Benjamin*, b. 6 Mar. 1718; *Samuel*, b. 9 Ap. 1721; *Caleb*, b. 21 Feb. 1724–5; *Hannah*, b. 24 Jan. 1727; *Mary*, b. 26 Mar. 1729. BENJAMIN the f. appears to have rem. to Rutland before 1747, and to have res. there several years; but according to a tradition related to me, nearly half a century ago, by a lady then about ninety years old, he returned and spent his last days in the family of his daughter, Olive Leonard, surviving to extreme old age. He was certainly living 16 May 1769, when he executed an imperfect will, now in possession of Mr. J. F. Morris of Hartford, one of his posterity.

2. MOSES, m. Mary ——, and had *Mary*, bap. 1 Jan. 1737–8; he prob. d. before 28 Ap. 1751, at which date *Moses*, son of "Widow Mary Smith" then residing at Ware River, was bap. here.

3. EDWARD, m. Dorcas, dau. of Rev. Benjamin Ruggles of N. Br. 25 Aug. 1757, and had *Dorcas*, bap. 9 Dec. 1759, m. Solomon Hedge 8 Mar. 1781; *Susanna*, bap. 17 Nov. 1765, m. Israel Aiken of Windsor 23 Sep. 1784; *John*, bap. 7 May 1769; *Samuel*, bap. 16 June 1771. EDWARD the f. was a cooper, and res. here as early as 10 Oct. 1750, when he bought 165 acres of land adjoining Quobbin (Greenwich), of Rev. Timothy Ruggles of Rochester. The time of his death, or removal, is not ascertained.

4. WILLIAM, m. Sarah ——, and had, prob., *William*, b. about 1771; *Elizabeth*, b. 21 Sep. 1778, m. John Walker of Gr., pub. 16 Nov. 1806; *Lucy*, b. 20 Nov. 1780, prob. m. Parks Ruggles 29 Nov. 1804; *Lydia*, b. 20 June 1783; *Mary*, b. 8 May 1785, d. unm. 8 Nov. 1809. WILLIAM the f. d. 27 Sep. 1813, a. 74; his w. Sarah d. 19 Sep. 1831, a. 88.

5. THOMAS REED, perhaps s. of William (4), m. Hannah Shaw 8 Mar. 1792, and had *Thomas*, b. 26 Aug. 1792; *Elias*, b. 24 Feb. 1796, res. long in Gr., d. in Ware 5 May 1879; *Warren*, b. 2 Aug. 1799. THOMAS REED the f. was a farmer, res. near the line of Gr., about a quarter of a mile north of the turnpike, at the place marked "T. R. Smith" on the R. Map, was selectman five years, and d. — June 1845, a. 77; his w. Hannah d. 6 Dec. 1858, a. 87.

6. WILLIAM, prob. s. of William (4), m. Lucy, dau. of Benjamin Ruggles, 14 Feb. 1805, and had *Ruggles*, b. — Mar. 1806; *William Hanson*, b. 16 June 1812, d. 4 Mar. 1846; *Sarah Reed*, b. ——. WILLIAM the f. d. 4 May 1816, a. 45; his w. Lucy d. 15 June 1867, a. nearly 83.

7. JOHN, m. Hannah, dau. of Warham Warner of N. Br., 1 Sep. 1793, and had in Hk. *Warner*, b. — 1795, d. in Barre 28 Jan. 1867, a. 71; and prob. others. JOHN the f. was a cabinet-maker, and res. generally in Barre; but he bought of James Lawton, 26 Mar. 1792, the estate near the Common, marked "W. Mandell" on the R. Map, which he sold to Elijah B. Harmon 30 July 1798, and returned to Barre.

8. OLIVER B., m. Mary ——, and had *Charles S.*, b. at N. Sal., 22 Sep. 1817; at Waitsfield, Vt., *Frances B.*, b. 13 Nov. 1819; *Mary A.*, b. 23 Aug. 1821; *Fanny R.*, b. 26 May 1823; *Horace S.*, b. 2 Ap. 1825; and after he came to Hk., *Lucy H.*, b. 7 Oct. 1827, m. Jason Cleveland 30 Jan. 1843; *Sarah M.*, b. 30 Oct. 1829; *Jane E.*, b. 9 May 1831; *Eliza Ann*, b. 5 Ap. 1833.

9. WARREN, s. of Thomas Reed (5), m. Pamela ——, and had *Caroline*, b. 14 Sep. 1830. WARREN the f. was captain of cavalry, and d. 1 Sep. 1841, a. 42.

10. MOSES, s. of Moses, and b. in Sterling, m. Adelaide, dau. of Charles Paige, 25 Dec. 1834, and had *John R.*, b. 16 Oct. 1835, d. 25 Aug. 1838; *John R.*, b. 17 Mar. 1839; *Charles Moses*, b. 8 July 1854, d. unm. 13 Feb. 1877. MOSES the f. in early life was a merchant, but was obliged to abandon active pursuits by severe chronic rheumatism. He afterwards bought, and for many years occupied, the estate on the westerly side of the Common, formerly the residence of Daniel Ruggles, Esq., and marked "D. R." on the R. Map. He d. 23 Feb. 1881, a. 79.

11. RUGGLES, s. of William (6), m. Hannah D. Bonney of Chesterfield, pub. 16 Mar. 1838, and had *Eleanor Augusta*, b. 6 Mar. 1839.

12. CHARLES S., prob. s. of Oliver B. (8), m. Abigail Sears 21 Sep. 1841, and had *Ellen Elvira*, b. 11 Oct. 1842, d. 31 July 1844; *Ellen S.*, b. 23 Aug. 1844.

13. BENTON, was ordained pastor of the Universalist church and society 2 July 1845. He m. Maria L. Sprague of Boston, pub. 26 Aug. 1845, and had *William Benton*, b. 22 July 1846. He rem. in 1849 to Shirley Village, and subsequently to So. Reading, Chatham, Waltham, and Newmarket, N. H., and returned to Waltham. He was for many years the very efficient secretary of the State Convention of Universalists in Massachusetts. His w. Maria L. d. at Waltham 5 Nov. 1882, a. 63.

14. ANDREW, m. Margaretta ——, and had *Charles Frederick*, b. 4 Aug. 1848.

15. BENJAMIN, m. Sophronia ——, and had a dau. (name not recorded), b. 26 Oct. 1849; the mother prob. d. 29 Ap. 1874, a. 61.

16. THOMAS, m. Alice H. ——, and had *Mary*, b. 26 Nov. 1851; *Alice*, b. 10 Aug. 1853; *Rosanna*, b. 1 Jan. 1856; *Margaret*, b. 1 July 1857; *Thomas*, b. 24 Sep. 1859; *William*, b. 8 Dec. 1861; *John*, b. 2 Ap. 1864.

17. JOHN, m. Elizabeth ——, and had *Mary Anna*, b. 20 June 1853; *John W.*, b. 15 Jan. 1855; and prob. *Catherine Jane*, b. 10 May 1860.

18. CONSTANTINE, m. Julia A. Thayer 3 July 1856, and had *Constantine*, b. 25 Feb. 1862.

19. ROYAL, m. Catherine ——, and had *Margaret*, b. 17 Aug. 1858.

20. JAMES M., m. Martha ——, and had *George William*, b. 4 May 1862; *Frederick Austin*, b. 26 Feb. 1875, d. 9 Nov. 1875.

21. WILLIAM, m. Agnes ——, and had *Thomas*, b. 14 Nov. 1867.

HANNAH, m. Samuel Howe of Rut. 29 May, 1739. SARAH, m. Jacob Knowlton, pub. 1 Nov. 1762. JOSEPH, m. Jane Smith of Pet. 26 Aug. 1768. MARY, of Bel., m. Capt. Benjamin Ruggles 28 Dec. 1778. KEZIA, m. John Giffin 22 July 1783. RHODA, of Pet., m. John Jameson 15 Dec. 1785. BETSEY, of Ware, m. Timothy Barlow, pub. 6 June 1791. HANNAH, m. John Baker of Pelh., pub. 15 Feb. 1794. REBECCA, m. Levi Higgins of Gr. 7 Jan. 1796. ABIGAIL, m. Obed Lain, 16 Feb. 1802. SAMUEL, m. Cynthia Mason

22 Dec. 1803. SALLY, m. Archippus Thayer of Mansfield 29 Nov. 1804. ELEANOR, m. Zenas Cobb 2 June 1805. MARY, of Gr., m. Aquila Collins 18 Oct. 1807. TRIPHENA, of Dana, m. Ephraim Hodges, Jr., pub. 25 Dec. 1815. ORREL, of Ware, m. Moses M. Warner, pub. 30 Dec. 1816. SALLY, of Pet., m. Royal Cleveland, pub. 3 Ap. 1820. NANCY M., of N. Sal., m. Samuel R. Aiken, pub. 24 Ap. 1826. AMOS K., of Wendell, m. Anna W. Dexter 12 June 1826. Dr. JAMES M., of New Haven, m. Martha Ann Paige 25 Nov. 1829. NANCY R., of Barre, m. Maj. James Danforth, pub. 11 Sep. 1830. MARY L., m. Convers C. Rogers 20 June 1833. MARTHA, m. Gamaliel Collins, 13 Oct. 1834. RANSFORD L., of Hopkinton, m. Lydia Ruggles 25 Mar. 1839. SYLVIA S., of Gr., m. Justus Johnson, pub. 28 Feb. 1840. SARAH R., m. Daniel H. Fay of Southboro' 1 Ap. 1841. MELONA, m. Elbridge Hill of Holden, pub. 19 May 1841. LUTHER, m. Elizabeth E. Grant 21 July 1847. CHARLES E., of W. Brk., m. Lucy A. Elwell 25 Dec. 1850. JONATHAN P., of Gr., m. Mary S. Earl 6 Dec. 1853. JULIA ANN, m. Francis P. Weeks 26 June 1872. Mrs. LIZZIE, m. Gardner S. Davis 23 Mar. 1874. MARY S., m. Otis B. Richardson 14 Ap. 1877.

ELEANOR, d. 14 Oct. 1823, a. 16. JOHN, d. 10 June 1829, a. 39 (he had buried two children in August 1825, names not recorded, one a. 3 years, the other a. 1 year). SALLY, w. of Minor, d. 17 Oct. 1829, a. 35. GEORGE, d. 9 Nov. 1831, a. 70. SUSAN, d. 28 June 1838, a. 14. ELIZABETH, w. of William, d. 7 Oct. 1855, a. 26. ANDREW, d. 14 Aug. 1859, a. 62. Mrs. THANKFUL, d. 22 Nov. 1872, a. 74.

I have found it impracticable to give a full account of the several families bearing the name of SMITH, who have res. here, or to show the connection, if any, between them, except in a very few cases. Many seem to have remained here only a short time; many undoubtedly neglected to register the birth of their children; and many deaths also were not recorded. I have mentioned such births, marriages, and deaths as I could ascertain, in chronological order, and regret my inability to present a more satisfactory result.

SNOW, JESSE, m. ——, and had prob. *Apollos*, b. —— 1767; prob. *Rebecca*, b. —— 1769, m. Ephraim Lane 13 Nov. 1803, d. 20 Mar. 1835, a. 65; *Jesse*, b. 29 Sep. 1771; *Mary*, b. 7 Mar. 1775, m. Abel Walker, Jr., 26 Jan. 1797; he d. ——, and she m. —— Crawford, and d. in Gr. 18 Feb. 1865, a. nearly 90. There may have been other chil. before the parents came here. JESSE the f. res. in the westerly part of the town, prob. at the place marked "B. Snow" on the R. Map, about four and a half miles from the Common; he d. in June 1825, a. 96; his w. Mary d. 5 Feb. 1813, a. 77.

2. REUBEN, m. Mercy, dau. of Roland Sears, 11 May 1769, and had *Samuel*, b. 28 May 1770; *Stephen*, b. 16 May 1772; *Barnabas*, b. 22 Aug. 1774, d. 31 Oct. 1775; *Barnabas*, b. 11 May 1778, according to the record; but prob. the date is wrong, as the date of his baptism is 8 June 1777.

3. JONATHAN, of Harwich, bought a farm here 1 May 1770, which he sold to Simeon Hazeltine 9 Dec. 1771, calling it his homestead; but no record is found of his family.

4. APOLLOS, prob. s. of Jesse (1), m. Leah Packard of Bel., pub. 14 July 1794, and had *Barnabas*, b. — Nov. 1795; *Clarissa*, b. —— 1798, m. George W. Knapp of Franklin, 21 Sep. 1823, and d. in Dana 29 May 1874, a. 75 years and 5 months; perhaps also *Hiram*, and others. APOLLOS the f. was a farmer, prob. inherited the homestead, and d. 1 Nov. 1843, a. 76. The names of his chil. and gr. chil. indicate that he was son of Reuben (2), rather than of Jesse (1); but if he was 76 years old when he d. in 1843, he must have been born as early as 1767, whereas Reuben (2) was not married until 1769.

5. BARNABAS, s. of Apollos (4), m. Eunice, dau. of Frederick Wicker, pub. 3 Feb. 1817, and had *Alanson*, b. —— 1820, d. 3 Mar. 1843, a. 23; *Reuben A.*, b. —— 1823; *Cyrus*, b. —— 1825, d. 21 Ap. 1840, a. 15; *Susan M.*, b. —— 1833, d. unm. 27 Jan. 1852, a. 18 years and 6 months. BARNABAS the f. prob. inherited the homestead; he d. in Ware 22 Dec. 1874, a. 79; his w. Eunice d. here 2 May 1869, a. 80.

6. HIRAM, perhaps s. of Apollos (4), m. Louisa F. ——, and had *Eugene*,

b. — Ap. 1845, d. 31 Aug. 1845, a. 4 months. Louisa F. the mother d. 7 June 1860, a. nearly 52.

7. Reuben A., s. of Barnabas (5), m. Persis M., dau. of Thomas Haskins, pub. 16 Nov. 1849, and had *Elmer Alanson*, b. 28 Jan. 1852; *Susan Maria*; b. 19 Sep. 1853. Reuben A. the f. d. in Dana 23 Nov. 1862, a. 39.

8. Joseph P., m. Cordelia A. Sturtevant of Gr., pub. 29 Nov. 1851, and had *Cora Nelly*, b. 28 Feb. 1857.

9. Charles L., m. Abby J. ——, and had *Samuel B.*, b. 9 Ap. 1858.

10. George F., m. Jane W. ——, and had *Frederick Henry*, b. 11 Mar. 1868.

Nabby, m. Samuel Pike 17 Dec. 1778, at Sutton. Bethany, m. Nathaniel Harriman of Chesterfield 14 Mar. 1781. Sally, m. Edward Allen of New Windsor 30 Jan. 1783. Salome, m. Nathaniel Whitcomb, Jr., of Gr., pub. 26 Ap. 1789. Almond, m. Mary S. Newton 31 Dec. 1845. Fanny M., m. Franklin B. Newland, pub. 31 Jan. 1862. Mary (a widow), d. 17 Ap. 1840, a. 85. Josephine, d. 18 Sep. 1842, a. 1 year and 6 months.

Southgate, Stewart (or Steward), m. Deborah, dau. of Benjamin Raymond, 22 July 1773, and had *Robert Scott*, b. 31 Jan. 1774; *Elizabeth*, b. 21 June 1775, d. young; *Mercy*, b. 29 May 1777, m. Samuel Danforth at Barnard 9 Mar. 1800; *Mary*, b. 22 Sep. 1778; and at Barnard, *Sally*, b. 31 Oct. 1780; *John*, b. 29 July 1783, d. 27 May 1790; *Relief*, b. 29 May 1785, d. 26 July 1795; *Deborah*, b. 27 Feb. 1787, d. 31 July 1795; *Lynde*, b. 2 Mar. 1789; *William*, b. 22 Mar. 1791, d. 3 Aug. 1795; *Joanna*, b. 4 Feb. 1793, d. 8 Aug. 1795; *Elizabeth*, b. 17 June 1795, d. 20 July 1795. Stewart the f. was b. in Leicester, 1748, being the youngest son of Stewart (or Steward), b. 1703, and grandson of Richard, who came, with wife (Elizabeth Steward) and five children, from Coombs, Suffolk County, England, in 1715, settled in Leicester three years later, and d. in 1758, a. 88.[1] He served in the Revolutionary War as a sergeant of Capt. Samuel Billings' company, 1775. He did not long remain here, but rem. to Barnard, Vt., about 1780. Fifteen years afterwards he suffered a terrible domestic affliction: five of his children died of canker-rash between 20 July and 8 Aug. 1795; less than three weeks. His w. Deborah d. at Barnard 28 Feb. 1813, a. 58.

Southworth. "Widow Alice Southworth arrived at Plymouth, 1623, in the third ship, called the Ann; and soon after was married to Governor William Bradford; she had two sons by her first husband, to wit, *Constant* and *Thomas*, who came with her or soon afterward, and were quite young, *Thomas*, not more than six years old. They both became distinguished men in the colony. *Constant* settled in Duxbury, and was one of the original proprietors of Bridgewater, and d. 1678, leaving three sons, Edward, Nathaniel, and William. . . . Nathaniel had land towards Taunton, called Freeman's land, perhaps in Middleborough. Edward, of Middleborough, perhaps s. of Nathaniel, had four sons, Constant, Edward, Lemuel, and Benjamin, who all settled early in North Bridgewater."[2]

2. Constant, s. of Edward, as above, m. Martha, dau. of Joseph Keith, and had *Betsey*, b. 19 Jan. 1735, m. Joseph Cole 8 Dec. 1757; *Nathaniel*, b. 16 Feb. 1737; *Ezekiel*, b. 10 Mar. 1739; *Martha*, twin, b. 18 Ap. 1741, d. 1 July 1741; *Mary*, twin, b. 18 Ap. 1741, d. 24 May 1741; *Desire*, b. 7 Sep. 1742, d. 28 Feb. 1747; *Jedediah*, b. 6 Jan. 1745; *Constant*, b. 29 Jan. 1747, d. young; *Sarah*, b. 9 Dec. 1749, d. unm.; *Ichabod*, b. 9 June 1751, d. 27 Jan. 1756. Constant the f. res. in Bridgewater, and d. in 1775, a. 64.

3. Nathaniel, s. of Constant (2), m. Catherine, dau. of David Howard, 27 Aug. 1762, and had *Martha*, b. —— 1764, d. young; *Simeon*, b. —— 1766; *Nathaniel*, b. —— 1769, settled in Lyme, N. H.; *David*, b. —— 1773, d. young; and by second wife (Jennet Brett) *Catherine*, b. ——, m. Ambrose Keith 20 Oct. 1796. Nathaniel the f. res. in Bridgewater, and d. in 1778, a. 41.

4. Simeon, s. of Nathaniel (3), m. Elizabeth Anderson 24 Dec. 1789; she

[1] Washburn's *Hist. of Leicester*, pp. 395, 396.

[2] Mitchell's *Hist. of Bridgewater*, pp. 304, 305. See also Kingman's *Hist. of North Bridgewater*, pp. 650–53.

d. ——, and he m. Anna ——. His chil. were *Alvah*, b. ——, d. young; *Nancy*, b. —— 1801, d. unm. 20 Jan. 1881, a. nearly 80; *Justin*, b. ——; *Sarah*, ——; *Elizabeth*, ——; *Louisa*, ——; *Alvah*, b. — 1811; *Constant*, b. —— 1814. SIMEON the f. rem. to Ward (now Auburn), and afterwards to Lyme, N. H., where his sons *Alvah* and *Constant* were born.

5. ALVAH, s. of Simeon (4), and Anna, came early to Hk., m. Fanny Hunter of Prescott, pub. 25 Mar. 1843, and d. here 19 June 1872, a. 60. No record found of children.

6. CONSTANT, s. of Simeon (4) and Anna, came here early, m. Sarah C. Sibley of Auburn, pub. 27 Dec. 1838, and had *Constant Eugene*, b. 8 Dec. 1839; *Alvah Fitzroy*, b. 11 Aug. 1843, d. unm. 10 Feb. 1869; *Oscar S.*, b. 2 Feb. 1846; *Frank Kossuth*, b. 2 Sep. 1851. CONSTANT the f. res. in the northwesterly part of the town, and owned the mills marked "Wardwell's Mills" on the R. Map, where he was largely engaged in manufacturing various kinds of lumber. He was a selectman eight years, assessor four years, member of the school committee five years, and representative in 1847 and 1857. He d. 5 Dec. 1877, a. 63.

7. CONSTANT EUGENE, s. of Constant (6), m. Lucretia L. Johnson 16 May 1865; she d. 24 Nov. 1874, a. 35, and he m. Cordelia L. Johnson of Dana 3 July 1878. His chil. were a son, b. 10 Feb. 1866 (name not recorded); *Sarah May*, b. 29 May 1867; *Constant Leroy*, b. 10 May 1870; *Cretia*, or *Lucretia A.*, b. 12 May 1879.

8. OSCAR S., s. of Constant (6), m. Fanny M. Collins 15 Ap. 1869, and had *Mary Louisa*, b. 24 July 1870.

9. FRANK KOSSUTH, s. of Constant (6), m. Hattie J. Stark 10 Dec. 1878, and had *Mabel Anna*, b. 14 Oct. 1880. Mrs. MARY W., d. 20 Feb. 1842, a. 28.

SPOONER, WILLIAM, m. Elizabeth Partridge; she d. 28 Ap. 1648, and he m. Hannah, dau. of Joshua Pratt, 18 Mar. 1652. His chil. were *John*, b.——; *Sarah*, b. 5 Oct. 1653; *Samuel*, b. 4 Jan. 1655; *Martha*, b. ——; *William*, b. ——, d. —— 1729; *Isaac*, b. ——, d. 1709; *Hannah*, b. ——; *Mercy*, b. ——; *Ebenezer*, b. — 1666, d. 5 Feb. 1718. WILLIAM the f. was in Plymouth as early as 1637, being then apparently a minor. He was sworn a freeman 6 June 1654, and res. at Plymouth until about 1660, when he rem. to that part of Dartmouth which is now Acushnet, and d. in 1684.

2. JOHN, s. of William (1), apparently by two wives, had *John*, b. 2 July 1668, d. —— 1728; *William*, b. 11 May 1680; *Jonathan*, b. 28 Aug. 1681, d. 13 Ap. 1711; *Elizabeth*, b. 19 June 1683, d. 14 July 1743; *Eleanor*, b. 1 Feb. 1685; *Phebe*, b. 11 May 1687; *Nathan*, b. 21 Sep. 1689; *Rebecca*, b. 8 Oct. 1691, d. 9 Mar. 1729; *Deborah*, b. 10 Aug. 1694; *Barnabas*, b. 6 Feb. 1699, d. —— 1734. JOHN the f. res. at Dartmouth (Acushnet), and was living 7 Feb. 1733, the date of his will.[1]

3. SAMUEL, s. of William (1), m. Experience,[2] and had *William*, b. 13 Feb. 1688–9; *Mary*, b. 4 Jan. 1690–1; *Samuel*, b. 4 Feb. 1692–3; *Daniel*, b. 28 Feb. 1693–4; *Seth*, b. 31 Jan. 1694–5; *Hannah*, b. 27 Jan. 1696–7; *Joshop*,[3] b. 13 Nov. 1698; *Anna*, b. 18 Ap. 1700; *Experience*, b. 19 June 1702; *Beulah*, b. 27 June 1705; *Wing*, b. 30 Ap. 17— (record defaced). SAMUEL the f. res. in Dartmouth (Acushnet), was a weaver, constable in 1680 and 1684, and d. in 1739, a. 84.

[1] Thus far, in my account of this family, I have relied entirely on the *Spooner Memorial*, a beautiful volume of 242 pages, published in 1871 by Hon. Thomas Spooner of Cincinnati, Ohio, one of the Vice-Presidents of the N. E. Hist. Genealogical Society. The same author has prepared for publication an exhaustive genealogy of the whole family descending from the original WILLIAM SPOONER. It is much desired that he may soon have suitable encouragement to publish the result of his arduous and long-continued labor.

[2] The author of the *Spooner Memorial* (p. 42) reasonably conjectures that her name was Experience Wing.

[3] This name is given as *Joshua* in the *Spooner Memorial*, p. 42. I think it is designed for *Jashub*, a contraction of *Shearjashub*, which name is found in the next generation. I have not seen the father's will, and know not precisely in what form the name appears there; but the Dartmouth record has it *Joshop*, as in the text.

4. JOHN, s. of John (2), m. Rosamond, dau. of Samuel and Mary (Hathaway) Hammond, 20 June 1705, and had *Jeduthun*, b. 10 Ap. 1706, m. Ruth, dau. of Lettice Jenney, and d. 1740; *Phebe*, b. 16 Ap. 1708; *John*, b. ——; *Benjamin*, b. ——; *Thomas*, b. 16 Jan. 1718; *Peter*, b. ——; *Elizabeth*, b. ——; *Rosamond*, b. 4 Jan. 1724. JOHN the f. was a farmer, res. in Dartmouth (Acushnet), and d. between 4 Mar. and 12 Ap. 1728. See *Spooner Memorial*.

5. WILLIAM, s. of John (2), m. Alice Blackwell, and had *Jemima*, b. 7 Dec. 1700; *Joanna*, twin, b. 12 May 1703, m. James Whitcomb, Jr., of Rochester 12 July 1727; *Elizabeth*, twin, b. 12 May 1703; *Micah*, b. 2 Ap. 1707; *Nathaniel*, b. 21 Ap. 1709; *Rebecca*, b. 17 Nov. 1710; *Sarah*, b. 18 Jan. 1712; *Mercy*, b. 8 Jan. 1714; *Isaac*, b. 9 Jan. 1716; *Alice*, b. 27 Mar. 1718; *William*, b. 27 Jan. 1720; *Ebenezer*, b. 29 May 1724. WILLIAM the f. was a farmer, and res. in Dartmouth (Acushnet). See *Spooner Memorial*.

6. SAMUEL, s. of Samuel (3), m. Rebecca Weston 10 Ap. 1717: she d. 26 Jan. 1728–9, and he m. Deborah, dau. of Isaac Pope, 8 Mar. 1729–30. His chil. were *Esther*, b. 26 Jan. 1717–8; *Hannah*, b. 18 Aug. 1719, m. Capt. Benjamin Willis of Dartmouth 30 Mar. 1743, rem. to Hardwick, and d. 6 Feb. 1812, a. 92; *Thomas*, b. 3 Ap. 1721; *Zephaniah*, b. 15 May 1724; *Amaziah*, b. 9 Mar. 1725–6, settled in Hk.; *Elnathan*, b. 20 Nov. 1730; *Abigail*, b. 11 Ap. 1732, m. John Jenney of Dartmouth 23 Nov. 1752, rem. to Hk., and d. 10 Dec. 1829, a. 97; *Seth*, b. 31 Jan. 1735–6. SAMUEL the f. was a farmer, res. in Dartmouth (Acushnet), and d. in 1781, a. 88.

7. DANIEL, s. of Samuel (3), m. Elizabeth Ruggles[1] at Rochester 10 Oct. 1728; she d., and he m. Mrs. Bethia Nichols of Lancaster 3 Sep. 1767; she d., and he m. Mary, widow of Paul Dean of Hk., 16 Oct. 1780. His chil. were *Lucy*, b. 29 Oct. 1729, m. Edward Ruggles of Hk. 29 Jan. 1746–7, and d. 2 Ap. 1821, a. 91; *Elizabeth*, b. 14 July 1731, m. Daniel Fay of Hk. 18 May 1749, and d. 24 Nov. 1756, a. 25; *Philip*, b. 13 Dec. 1733, m. Elizabeth, dau. of Kenelm Winslow of Hk., 25 Dec. 1755; she d. 8 Ap. 1792, and he m. Eunice, dau. of Benjamin Trow; he res. in Pet., and d. 30 Sept. 1826, a. 93; *Shearjashub*, b. 14 Aug. 1735, m. Sarah, dau. of Ebenezer Whipple of Hk., 21 May 1760, res. in Pet., was a carpenter and a soldier in the Revolutionary War; he rem. to Heath, and d. 25 Ap. 1785, a. nearly 50; *Ruggles*, b. 24 Mar. 1736–7, m. Mehetabel Nye, res. in Pet. and Dana, is said to have served in the French and Revolutionary Wars, was certainly involved in the Shays Rebellion, and through his active life almost constantly engaged in litigation, — a notable instance of which was his suit against Sarah Peckham for breach of promise of marriage, tried at Worcester, and a verdict rendered for the defendant 16 Oct. 1782. His old age was dark and dreary; he became entirely blind, lost all his property, and would not acknowledge any expectation of a future existence. He retained his mental faculties, which were naturally strong and active, until extreme old age, and, until near the close of life, often walked from Dana to Hk. He d. in 1831, a. 94; his wife Mehetabel d. 1 Sep. 1855, a. 92, or 97, according to different authorities; *Wing*, b. 29 Dec. 1738, res. in Pet., was a carpenter, a captain in the Revolutionary War, m. Eunice Stevens 27 Jan. 1763, and d. 7 Dec. 1810; *Eliakim*, b. 7 Ap. 1740; *Daniel*, b. 10 Dec. 1741, m. Abigail Munroe 18 Nov. 1766, settled in Hartland, Vt., and was selectman, representative, justice of the peace, and d. in Nov. 1828; *Hannah*, b. 25 June 1743, d. young; *Paul*, b. 20 March. 1745–6, m. Asenath Wright; she d. and he m. Mrs. Ann Post. He was a physician and an active politician. He settled early in Hartland, Vt., and "was a member of the state council four years from 1778, then Lieutenant-Governor until 1786, judge of the supreme court for nine years ending in 1788, and was an agent of the State to the Continental Congress in 1780, and again in 1782."[2] He

[1] She was prob. dau. of John and Elizabeth Ruggles, and b. at Roxbury in 1700. Her father d. early in 1712, and Capt. Samuel Ruggles was appointed guardian, who seems to have placed her in the family of his son, Rev. Timothy Ruggles of Rochester, as a safe shelter, where she remained until she was married.

[2] Hall's *History of Vermont*, p. 469.

d. 5 Sep. 1789, a. 43, while yet in the prime of life, and in the midst of his usefulness. (His second son, Paul, settled in Hardwick, Vt., was the first town clerk of that town, 1795, and also its first representative, elected in 1797, 1798, and 1799.) DANIEL the f. res. several years in Dartmouth, where he was born, and the births of all his children are recorded in that town; but a doubt is expressed in the *Spooner Memorial*, p. 96, whether all of them were born there, inasmuch as the father seems to have resided in Rhode Island about 1732. However this be, it is certain that he removed to Hardwick before 16 June 1748, when he sold a lot near the Barre line, "granted originally to Mr. Keith," and adjoining land of "Col. Willis." He did not long remain here, however, as in a deed dated 14 July 1750 he is described as of Nichewoag (Petersham); but he manifestly retained very intimate relations with the inhabitants of Hk.; five or six of his children married our sons and daughters, and in his old age he came here for his third wife. He was a "joiner" or carpenter, and was elected deacon of the church in Petersham soon after his removal into that town. The precise date of his death is not ascertained; but he is generally believed to have survived until 1797, one hundred and three years after he was born. There can be no reasonable doubt, I think, that he completed more than a century of life; and the tradition of his extreme old age is current among his descendants to the present day. His last wife, Mary, d. here 9 May 1822, a. 94; her head-stonestands in the new cemetery.

8. THOMAS, s. of John (4), m. Rebecca, dau. of Judah and Alice (Alden) Paddock, granddaughter of David Alden, and great-granddaughter of John Alden the Pilgrim, 10 June 1742, and had *Rebecca*, b. 2 Aug. 1743, m. Timothy Green of New London, Conn., 2 Jan. 1763; *John*, bap. 23 Ap. 1745, m. Lydia, dau. of John and Lydia Alden, 25 Mar. 1769, was a printer, and established the first newspaper in New Bedford; *Thomas*, b. 8 Mar. 1747, said to have lost his life in the Revolutionary Army; *Judah Paddock*, b. 5 Nov. 1748, m. Deborah Douglass 10 Sep. 1770, was a printer, settled in Westminster, Vt., and d. — Feb. 1807;[1] *Rosamond*, b. 21 Mar. 1751, m. Ezra Winslow, and rem. to Hk., where he d. 12 Aug. 1789, and she m. Richard Ransom of Woodstock, Vt., pub. 26 Nov. 1801, and d. 1829; *Alice*, b. 2 Mar. 1753, m. Paul Ingraham 28 Jan. 1770, res. in New Bedford, and d. 25 Ap. 1792; *Jeduthun*, b. 12 May 1755; *Alden*, b. 22 Aug. 1757, m. Sarah Burton of Norwich, Conn., 30 Ap. 1781, was a printer, res. in Windsor, Vt., and d. 1 May 1827;[2] *Frances*, b. 2 Mar. 1760, m. Capt. Joseph Bowman of Barnard, Vt., 26 Jan. 1786. THOMAS the f. was a carpenter or housewright, res. at Newport, R. I., and afterwards at New London, Conn.; his five sons are said to have rendered military service in the Revolutionary War, and two of them, with his son-in-law, Green, were the earliest printers in Vermont. He d. in Mar. 1767; his w. Rebecca prob. came to Hk. with her son *Jeduthun*, or her dau. *Rosamond* Winslow, m. Capt. Joseph Warner of Cummington, formerly of Hk., 12 Nov. 1781, and d. in Jan. 1812. (For much in this article I am indebted to the kindness of Hon. Thomas Spooner.)

9. EBENEZER, s. of William (5), m. Sarah, dau. of James and Patience (Ruggles) Robinson, at Rochester, pub. 3 Jan. 1745-6, and had *Micah*, bap.

[1] "The first printing-office in Vermont was established at Westminster, in the summer of 1778, by Judah Paddock Spooner and Timothy Green. At the session of the Legislature in October following, Judah P. Spooner and Alden Spooner were appointed State printers. . . . In February, 1781, was commenced at Westminster, by J. P. Spooner and Timothy Green, the publication of the first newspaper ever printed in Vermont. It was called '*The Vermont Gazette, or Green Mountain Post Boy*,' and it had for its motto the following couplet, which is truly characteristic of the inhabitants of the Green Mountain State.

'Pliant as reeds where streams of freedom glide,
Firm as the hills to stem oppression's tide.'"

Thompson's *Hist. of Vermont*, ii. 171.

[2] The printing press and types which had been used at Westminster, having been purchased by George Hough, he removed them to Windsor, and, in partnership with Alden Spooner, on the 7th of August, 1783, commenced the publication of a paper called "*The Vermont Journal and Universal Advertiser*." This was the third paper established in Vermont. Thompson's *Hist. of Vermont*, ii. 171.

25 May 1746, d. unm. in the army at Ticonderoga, 1778; *Dorothy*, bap. here 26 Feb. 1748–9, m. Samuel Miller, res. at Kent, Conn.; *Ebenezer*, b. 24 Mar. 1750–1, bap. here 5 May 1751, m. Rebecca, dau. of William and Rachel Spooner, 24 Ap. 1774, res. at Kent; *Hannah*, b. 12 Jan. 1753, bap. here 21 Jan. 1753, m. William, son of William and Rachel Spooner, 3 Sep. 1788, res. at Monkton, Vt., and d. 3 Jan. 1813; *Alice*, bap. here 15 Dec. 1754, said to have m. Hendrick Winegar; *Sarah*, b. ——, m. Isaac Dunham; *Phebe*, twin, b. 4 Sep. 1758, m. Elihu Potter 5 Ap. 1792, res. at Monkton, d. 16 Sep. 1810; *Elizabeth*, twin, b. 4 Sep. 1758, m. Benjamin Bronson, res. at Warren, Conn.; *Molly*, b. ——, m. James Sprague; *Rebecca*, b. 25 Jan. 1762, m. William Peck 22 Ap. 1784, res. at Monkton, and d. 3 Jan. 1839; *Patience*, b. 24 Feb. 1764, m. Jasper Barnes — Ap. 1790, res. at Washington, Conn., and d. 30 Nov. 1817. EBENEZER the f. rem. from Rochester to Hk. before 26 Feb. 1748–9, and res. on the east side of the River (now New Braintree). He subsequently seems to have removed to Kent, Conn., and to Monkton, Vt.; he d. — 1800; his w. Sarah d. 22 Feb. 1806, a. nearly 86.

10. AMAZIAH, s. of Samuel (6), m. Lydia, dau. of Deac. James Fay, 22 Feb. 1749–50, and had *Thomas*, b. 15 Mar. 1750–1, m. Molly Haven of Barre 7 Nov. 1777, and (2d) Martha Smith 15 Dec. 1784 (he had son Elijah, b. — Nov. 1791, d. at Gr. 12 Dec. 1872, a. 81); *Zephaniah*, b. 1 Oct. 1753; *Lucy*, b. 9 Oct. 1755, m. Eli Freeman (his second wife), 22 July 1813; *Elizabeth*, b. 28 Jan. 1758; *Lydia*, b. 12 Sep. 1760; *Samuel*, b. 20 Jan. 1763; *Charles*, b. 10 Oct. 1764, m. Charity Curtis 15 Feb. 1795; *Rebecca*, b. 17 Nov. 1767; *Hannah*, b. 11 Mar. 1771; *Seth*, b. 21 June 1773. AMAZIAH the f. was a farmer, came to Hk. from Dartmouth before he was married, res. on the north side of the turnpike, and the west side of Muddy Brook, at the place marked "C. Spooner" on the R. Map, and d. 8 July 1798, a. 72; his w. Lydia d. 10 Aug. 1817, a. 87.

11. ELIAKIM, s. of Daniel (7), m. Bathsheba, dau. of Jonathan Warner, pub. 29 July 1764, and had *Alfred*, b. 27 Nov. 1780. ELIAKIM the f. kept a tavern in Hk. 1777 and 1778, but soon afterwards rem. to Vermont. He was in military life as early as 1757, and in 1759 in the French and Indian War, and was on duty in the early part of the Revolutionary War. In early manhood he moved to Vermont, and settled at Westminster. . . . He frequently represented his town in the State Legislature, and was elected one of the Executive Council of the State from 1802 to 1807 inclusive.[1] He d. 3 Jan. 1820, a. nearly 80; his w. Bathsheba d. 29 Jan. 1831, a. 84.

12. JEDUTHUN, s. of Thomas (8), m. Hannah, dau. of Joshua Crowell, 27 Ap. 1781, and had *Harriet*, b. 20 July 1782, m. Elisha S. Sturtevant, and d. at Worcester 21 Dec. 1855; *Uriel*, b. 11 Ap. 1784, m. Rowena Ross of West Brookfield, pub. 26 May 1816; she d. 12 Sep. 1841, and he m. Hannah, dau. of Deac. Henry Fish, pub. 26 Ap. 1843; she d. at W. Brk. 10 Nov. 1857, a. 65, and he d. at the same place 8 June 1865; *Rebecca* b. 6 Mar. 1786, m. Moses Barnes Jr., of W. Brk., pub. 21 Nov. 1808, and d. 1 Sep. 1853; *Thomas*, b. 23 June 1788, settled in W. Brk., m. Beersheba McIntosh, 28 Feb. 1816, and d. 26 Jan. 1856 (*Spooner Memorial*); *Paulina*, b. 14 July 1790, d. unm. 17 Jan. 1861; *Hannah*, b. 19 Oct. 1792, m. Cephas Clapp of W. Brk. 21 Mar. 1815; *Wyman*, b. 2 July 1895, m. Elizabeth, dau. of Deac. Henry Fish, 10 Nov. 1818, was a printer in Windsor, Vt., and a prominent politician in Wisconsin,[2] where he was judge of probate and of the Circuit Court,

[1] *Spooner Memorial*, p. 93.

[2] "When about twenty-one he commenced the publication of a weekly newspaper, which he continued for about twelve years. He then began the study of law, and was admitted to its practice in 1833. . . . In 1842 he removed to Wisconsin, and in 1843 he settled in Elkhorn, Walworth County, where he has ever since resided. In 1846 he was elected judge of probate, which office he held until the probate was merged into the County Court. In 1853 he was appointed circuit judge, which position he held until the election of Judge Doolittle. He was elected to the Assembly in 1850, 1851, 1857, and 1861. In 1857 he was elected Speaker of the Assembly. He was elected State senator for the terms of 1862 and 1863. In the last session he was chosen President of the Senate, and became Lieutenant-Governor when Mr. Salomon succeeded to the executive chair. In 1863, 1865, and 1867, he was elected Lieutenant-Governor; and, by virtue of his office, he

Speaker of the House of Representatives, President of the Senate, and Lieutenant-Governor of the State; *Loring* b. 29 Ap. 1797, d. 27 or 29 Sep. 1802; *Jeduthun*, b. 5 July 1799, went early to Windsor, Vt., became a printer under the instruction of his uncle, Alden Spooner, and of his brother, Wyman Spooner, res. for a time in Burlington, m. Isabella P. Spooner, 30 Ap. 1823, and (2d) Betsey R. Ross, 3 Nov. 1826; he d. in Iowa 9 Mar. 1867. JEDUTHUN the f. came to Hk. before he was married, and was one of its most respected inhabitants during the remainder of his life. He was a saddler, and res. about fifty rods north of the Common, at the place marked "Wid. Parker" on the R. Map, until 1801, when he advertised his estate for sale, "which had been occupied as a stand for a saddler near twenty years," and bought a farm on the easterly road to Gilbertville, about two and a half miles south of the Common, marked "Wid. Marsh" on the R. Map, and devoted himself to farming; his house, which disappeared several years ago, stood a few rods from the road, and was approached by a lane, of which some vestiges still remain. He was a man of most exemplary character, and endured with Christian philosophy a severe domestic affliction, occasioned by the insanity of his wife, with tragical accompaniments. He was a selectman seven years, assessor six years, town clerk five years, and representative four years. He closed his eyes on the "lights and shadows" of mortal life 16 May 1817; his insane wife Hannah eluded the watchfulness of her friends and committed suicide 16 Dec. 1807, a. 52.

13. ZEPHANIAH, s. of Amaziah (10), m. Sally Church 5 Nov. 1789, and had *Bradford*, b. 5 Ap. 1791; *Barnabas*, b. 9 July 1793, d. 23 or 24 May 1814; *Grover*, b. 19 May 1798; *Charles C.*, b. 13 Dec. 1804. ZEPHANIAH the f. was a farmer, res. on the homestead, and d. 13 June 1810, a. 56; his w. Sally d. 30 Aug. 1833, a. 68.

14. SAMUEL, s. of Amaziah (10), m. Hannah Williams 14 Jan. 1798, and had *Sarah*, b. 12 Jan. 1800, m. Nathaniel Simpson 12 Mar. 1835, and d. 23 July 1846; *Orin*, b. 28 Nov. 1802; *Hannah*, b. 2 Oct. 1804, m. Orville Swift of Wilmington, Vt., 5 June 1832; *Samuel Brigham*, b. 17 Sep. 1806, d. at Springf. 8 May 1862; *Lydia Maria*, b. 24 July 1810, perhaps m. Julius Norton of Bennington, Vt., 29 Feb. 1836; *Zephaniah*, b. 28 Mar. 1812, res. in Springf., m. Sophronia Randall in Hk. 8 Ap. 1841. SAMUEL the f. d. 19 Ap. 1840, a. 77; his w. Hannah d. 2 June 1830, a. 53.

15. SETH, s. of Amaziah (10), m. Mehetabel Taylor 19 Feb. 1795; she d. 12 May 1812, a. 40, and he m. Mrs. Sally Gates 25 Nov. 1812. No record is is found of the birth of his children; but he had *Rhoda*, b. —— 1797, d. 21 Sep. 1811, a. 14; and perhaps *Fanny*, b. —— 1801, d. unm. 14 Dec. 1822, a. 21.

16. BRADFORD, s. of Zephaniah (13), m. Arathusa, dau. of John Earl, 30 Nov. 1821, and had *Sarah Church*, b. 18 Nov. 1822, m. Charles Wood of Barre 21 Aug. 1851; *Alden Bradford*, b. 12 Nov. 1824; *John F.*, b. —— 1826, d. unm. 26 Dec. 1873, a. 47; *Harmon C.*, bap. 11 May 1829; *Caroline E.*, b. about 1830, m. George R. Paige 22 Jan. 1852; *Henry*, b. —— 1832, d. 19 Feb. 1834, a. 1 year and 7 months; *Maria*, b. —— 1835, d. 22 May 1836, a. 1 year and three months; *Jane M.*, b. about 1839, m. A. Lyman Barr of N. Br. 1 Jan. 1862; *Henry A.*, b. 1 July 1840. BRADFORD the f. was a farmer, and res. on or near the homestead, but on the east side of Muddy Brook, at the place marked "B. Spooner" on the R. Map. He d. 1 Nov. 1872, a. 81; his wife Arethusa d. 7 Ap. 1872, a. 72.

17. GROVER, s. of Zephaniah (13), m. Ruth, dau. of Timothy Hathaway, 28 May 1829, and had *Charles*, b. ——; *Timothy Hathaway*, b. ——; *Lucius*, b. ——. GROVER the f. was a cabinet-maker, res. in Barre, and d. 19 Aug. 1858, a. 60.

18. CHARLES C., s. of Zephaniah (13), m. Anna Maria, dau. of Orin Trow, 17 Sep. 1829, and had *Hannah Robinson*, b. 30 Dec. 1830; *Barnabas Berry*, b. 30 Jan. 1833, d. 20 Mar. 1833; *Charles Grover*, b. 5 Ap. 1834, d. 27

presided over the Senate for six consecutive years. He was a member of the first board of trustees for the Deaf and Dumb at Delavan. Judge Spooner is a man of constant diligence and energy." *History of the State of Wisconsin* (1875), pp. 796, 797.

Aug. 1848; *Harrison*, b. 25 Jan. 1840; *Webster*, b. 17 Feb. 1845, res. in Boston; *George*, b. 21 Nov. 1854, d. 25 Nov. 1854. CHARLES C. the f. was for some years a farmer, and afterwards a merchant, having a store on the Common, but long ago retired from active business. He was a selectman eleven years, between 1837 and 1868.

19. ORIN, s. of Samuel (14), m. Naomi Clark 25 Feb. 1829. I have seen no record of the birth of his children; but he had *Andrew W.*, b. —— 1832, d. 6 July 1858, a. 26. ADDISON, b. —— 1835, m. Delphia M., dau. of Erastus W. Paige, pub. 24 Aug. 1858, and d. 23 Sep. 1859, a. 24; *Marion A.*, b. —— 1845, m. William H. Tucker 6 June 1877; and perhaps others. ORIN the f. res. in Barre, and d. 13 Sep. 1867, a. nearly 65; his w. Naomi d. 17 Mar. 1869, a. 60. Though resident in Barre, Mr. Spooner and his wife, with their two sons, seem to have been buried here, and their names are inscribed on a monument in the new cemetery.

20. HARMON C., s. of Bradford (16), m. Harriet E., dau. of James Browning, 14 Nov. 1855; she d. 11 July 1860, a. 25, and he m. Harriet E., dau. of William A. Warner, 16 Jan. 1862. His chil. were *James Bradford*, b. 3 Feb. 1857, d. 22 Feb. 1857; *William Bradford*, b. 8 June 1863; *Robert Billings*, b. 9 July 1868. HARMON C. the f., a cabinet-maker, was in business several years on the Common, and afterwards at Gilbertville; about 1878 he rem. to Warren.

21. ALDEN BRADFORD, s. of Bradford (16), m. Sarah A., dau. of Phinehas Morton, 26 Jan. 1858; she d. 2 (or 3) Dec. 1864, a. 29, and he m. Julia A., dau. of Capt. Pliny Alden, 7 Jan. 1873. He had *Stephen Henry*, b. 31 Mar. 1860. ALDEN B. the f., a farmer, res. on or near the homestead.

JOSHUA, of Brk., m. Bathsheba Ruggles, pub. 8 Jan. 1766; was murdered at Brk. 1 Mar. 1778. JOEL, of Northfield, m. Lydia Trow 24 Dec. 1797. ALMA, m. Daniel Hale, pub. 9 Feb. 1806. CHARLES, of Pet., m. Betsey Powers 4 June 1818. AMAZIAH, of Amh., m. Clarissa Alden 27 Ap. 1825. MARY, of Barre, m. Benjamin F. Richmond, pub. 11 Nov. 1837. MERCY J., m. Abiel B. Staples of Taunton 20 Ap. 1842. BENJAMIN A., M. D., of Southbridge, m. Mary A. Johnson, pub. 9 Feb. 1845; she d. 17 Dec. 1860, a. 34. WILLIAM J., m. Johanna Sweeney 19 Nov. 1868. EUNICE, widow of Philip Spooner and sister of Capt. Israel Trow, d. 30 May 1830, a. 86. LYDIA, d. 15 Oct. 1841, a. 78.

SPROUT, NATHANIEL, m. ——, and had *James*, b. 23 Jan. 1749; *Nathaniel*, b. about 1751; *Robert*, b. about 1754; besides these he was prob. father of *Ebenezer*, b. about 1757; *Samuel*, b. about 1760; *Nathan*, b. about 1763. NATHANIEL the f. sold land in the northeast part of the town to Walter Hastings 8 Sep. 1750, and bought fifty acres 6 Dec. 1756, near Southworth's (formerly Wardwell's) mills. He was a farmer, and a soldier in the French War, 1755 and 1759.

2. JAMES, s. of Nathaniel (1), m. ——, and had *Roxana*, b. —— 1785, m. John Barlow, pub. 12 June 1808, and d. 20 July 1876, a. 90 years and 10 months; he was prob. father also of *Abiel*, b. ——, who m. Jonas Barnes 20 Mar. 1791; and *Rachel*, b. ——, m. James McKoon 24 Feb. 1801 (both older than Roxana). JAMES the f. d. 5 Ap. 1825; his w. —— d. 15 Feb. 1825.

3. NATHANIEL, s. of Nathaniel (1), m. Azubah Cummings 28 Dec. 1775. No record found of children, nor anything further concerning him, except that he was a soldier in the Revolutionary War.

4. ROBERT, s. of Nathaniel (1), m. Betsey Lincoln 17 Sep. 1781, and had *Charles*, b. — Dec. 1782, d. 1 Oct. 1789, a. 6 years and nearly 10 months; prob. *Robert*, b. —— 1794, d. at N. Sal. 25 Feb. 1845, a. 50 years and 11 months.

5. EBENEZER, prob. s. of Nathaniel (1), m. Mary Thayer of Pet. 11 Dec. 1783; she d. 1 Nov. 1789, a. 33, and he m. Miriam Barnes 3 June 1790; she d. at Gr. 29 Feb. 1852, a. 85 years and 6 months. No record found of children.

6. NATHAN, prob. s. of Nathaniel (1), m. Lucinda Dana of Amh., pub. 10 Mar. 1795, and had *Lucinda*, b. 29 Dec. 1795; *Clarinda*, b. 28 Jan. 1798, d.

unm. at Chicopee 23 Jan. 1862; *Amariah*, b. 23 Feb. 1800; *Joseph*, b. 18 Aug. ——; *Melinda*, b. — Feb. 1807.

MERCY, m. David Ingraham of Amh. —— 1786. POLLY, of Gr., m. Joseph Cummings, pub. 19 Sep. 1812. EZRA, of Gr., m. Dency Newland 3 Dec. 1818. POLLY, m. Samuel Johnson, pub. 15 May 1825. ABIGAIL, m. Ezra Johnson of Prescott, pub. 6 Nov. 1830. CYNTHIA, d. 18 Nov. 1802, a. 7. Neglect in recording the birth of children prevents a more specific account of the Sprout family.

SQUIRES, EPHRAIM, m. Rebecca Kimball of Enfield, pub. 13 Aug. 1827.

STAPLES, MARY, of Prescott, m. Giles Warner, pub. 12 Ap. 1824. EBENEZER P., of Taunton, m. Luthera G. Dexter 26 Ap. 1841; and (2d) Mary A. Peck 11 Nov. 1845. ABIEL B., m. Mercy J. Spooner 20 Ap. 1842.

STEARNS, DANIEL, died before 23 Aug. 1758, when some of his estate in the hands of his administrator, Stephen Stearns of Cambridge, was used for the payment of a debt to John Fassett. No record found of family.

2. ASA, m. Elizabeth ——, and had *Samuel*, b. ——; *Artemas*, b. ——; *Alfred*, b. —— 1790, grad. W. C. 1812, said to have d. in 1834, a. 44; *Polly*, b. ——, d. 8 May 1791, a. 1 year and 2 months. ASA the f. res. on the road to Barre, about a mile and a half from the Common, at the place marked "S. Newton" on the R. Map, and d. 27 Jan. 1795, a. nearly 40; his w. Elizabeth m. Nathaniel Woods 17 Nov. 1795, and quitclaimed her interest in the real estate to her sons *Samuel* and *Artemas*, who, having rem. to Mendon, N. Y., sold the same to Silas Newton 21 Ap. 1819. Perhaps *Alice*, *Eliza*, and *Harriet*, named below, may have been of the same family.

BENJAMIN, of Rut., m. Mrs. Mary Warren 12 Nov. 1753. MEHETABEL, of Worc., m. Isaac Rice 1 Dec. 1768. ABIGAIL, m. Thomas Wheat, pub. 17 Jan. 1770. JOHN P., of N. Br., m. Susanna Griffin, pub. 26 July 1774. PATIENCE, of Worc., m. Isaac Clark, Jr., 6 Jan. 1774. HANNAH, m. Jesse Kenney 11 Aug. 1776. ALICE, m. Perley Williams of Hubbardston, pub. 28 Mar. 1808, and d. there 12 Sep. 1847, a. 57. ELIZA, m. John Browning of Hubbardston 5 Nov. 1810. HARRIET, m. Amherst Hastings of Pet. 29 Dec. 1811. ABIGAIL, wife of Isaac, of Monkton, Vt., d. 22 June 1809, a. 22.

STEBBINS, BENJAMIN, m. Mercy Aiken 24 Sep. 1772, and rem. to Barnard, Vt., before 1782. JOHN B., m. Martha L. Monroe 11 Ap. 1877.

STEDMAN, HARRIET, m. Elijah C. Newton 16 Nov. 1848. HANNAH, m. George S. Titus of Ware 1 May 1858. LEMUEL, d. 7 June 1874, a. 81 (b. at Sturbridge).

STEEL, SAMUEL, m. Margaret ——, and had *David*, bap. 13 Nov. 1745; *Thomas*, bap. 13 Nov. 1745; *William*, bap. 7 Oct. 1750; *Aaron*, bap. 6 Feb. 1753. SAMUEL the f. seems to have res. east of the River, now New Braintree.

STEPHENS, JACOB (otherwise written STEVENS), m. Abigail ——, and had *Sarah*, b. 23 Ap. 1741; *Tabitha*, b. 10 Aug. 1743; *Christopher*, b. 15 Feb. 1745-6; *Lucy*, bap. 21 Aug. 1748; *Jacob*, bap. 12 May 1751.

2. THOMAS, m. Elizabeth Perkins of Brk., pub. 15 Jan. 1748-9, and had *Mary*, b. 3 Oct. 1749; *Nehemiah*, b. 5 Mar. 1752; *Thomas*, b. 27 Mar. 1754; *Elizabeth*, b. 20 Nov. 1756. THOMAS the f. sold 84 acres in the west part of the town to Ephraim Cleveland 27 Mar. 1761; after which I find no trace of him.

3. DANIEL, m. Rebecca, dau. of Moses Whipple, pub. 14 Ap. 1811, and had *Lewis*, b. 11 May 1813, d. 14 Feb. 1850; *Cyrus Washburn*, b. 15 Oct. 1815, m. Lucy Richardson of Dana 31 Dec. 1837, and d. there 1 Nov. 1866; *Joseph Whipple*, b. 18 Oct. 1817; *Almon Giffin*, b. 28 July 1824, m. Malvina Roberts, pub. — Ap. 1852. DANIEL the f. d. 9 May 1864, a. 75; his w. Rebecca d. at Dana, 7 Dec. 1873, a. 83.

4. JACOB, m. Hannah Thayer, pub. 8 Nov. 1796, and had *Mary*, b. —— 1797, d. 6 Aug. 1819, a. 22; *Sarah Ann*, b. —— 1814, m. Charles N. Gibbs of Prescott, 1 Dec. 1836, and d. there 5 Ap. 1852, a. 38. JACOB the f. d. 16 Ap. 1833, a. 62; his w. Hannah d. 17 May 1830, a. 57.

5. JOSEPH WHIPPLE, s. of Daniel (3), m. Elizabeth C. Richardson 23 Mar. 1843, and had a son b. 12 Nov. 1843, and d. the next day; *Albert Augustine*,

b. 31 Dec. 1850; *Elizabeth Adella*, b. 23 Feb. 1853, d. 27 June 1856; *Eliza Jane*, b. 11 May 1856, m. William H. Giffin, 29 June 1875. JOSEPH W. the f. d. 22 Sep. 1861; his w. Elizabeth C. m. Philip Johnson 21 Aug. 1862.

ANNA, of Marlborough, m. James Woods, pub. 5 Oct. 1747. MARY, m. William Thayer 28 Nov. 1793. ROBERT, m. Abigail Davis 9 Oct. 1794. DOLLY, of Pet., m. Wilder Barnes 20 Nov. 1794. THOMAS, m. Abigail Hale of Dana, pub. 13 Nov. 1815. DEBORAH, m. Seth Whipple, pub. 22 Mar. 1819. HANNAH, m. Caleb Thayer, pub. 16 Mar. 1823. LEVI, m. Mrs. Thankful Dexter 18 Oct. 1830. MARY G., of N. Sal., m. Luther Cole, pub. 9 Mar. 1846. HATTIE R., m. Charles W. Thayer 12 Oct. 1871. PRUDENCE, w. of Thomas, d. 20 Oct. 1814, a. 68. THOMAS, d. 15 June 1819, a. 72. POLLY, d. unm. 6 Aug. 1819, a. 22. Widow DOLLY, d. 25 June 1840, a. 66. MARY E., d. 29 Sep. 1875, a. 1 year.

STETSON, ROBERT, of Scituate, historically known as "Cornet Robert," was a noted man in his day, and d. 1 Feb. 1702-3, a. 91. He had nine children, of whom the eldest was *Joseph*, b. 1639, as is stated in Deane's *Hist. of Scituate*, and Barry's *Genealogy of the Stetson Family*.

2. JOSEPH, s. of Robert (1), res. in Scituate, and had eight children, of whom the second was *Robert*, b. 9 Dec. 1670.

3. ROBERT, s. of Joseph (2), res. in Scituate, m. Mary Collamore, and had eight children, of whom the eldest was *Anthony*, b. 12 Sep. 1693.

4. ANTHONY, s. of Robert (3), res. in Scituate, m. Anna Smith 28 Mar. 1717, and had *Mary*, b. 9 Dec. 1717; *Isaac*, b. 19 Oct. 1719; *Joseph*, b. 24 Feb. 1722; *Anna*, b. 2 June 1724; *Charles*, b. 17 Oct. 1726; *Ezra*, b. 22 Sep. 1729; *Elisha*, b. 28 Jan. 1731; *Thomas*, b. 22 Ap. 1734; *Benjamin*, b. 7 July 1736; *Abiel*, b. 23 Oct. 1738, settled in Chesterfield, and m. Ruth Bonney of Hk. 24 Feb. 1767; *Martha*, b. 18 Aug. 1741.

5. EZRA, s. of Anthony (4), "m. Sarah Rider, and moved to Hardwick" (*Stetson Fam.*). His chil. were *Anthony*, b. ——, settled in Wilmington, Vt.; *Benjamin*, b. ——, m. Mercy Johnson of Hk., and settled at Sangersfield, N. Y.; *Ezra*, b. ——, settled in Springfield, N. Y.; *Sarah*, b. ——, m. Ephraim Thayer of Hk. 29 Ap. 1779; *Hannah*, b. ——, m. Solomon Hinds, Jr., of Gr. 2 Oct. 1791; *Mary*, b. ——, m. Benjamin Thayer of Hk. 22 Sep. 1793; *Anna*, b. ——, m. Thaddeus Russell of Dana 2 June 1803. EZRA the f. d. in May 1805, a. 75; he had previously m., for second wife, Susanna Gibbs of Gr., pub. 6 Ap. 1786. The Hardwick Records do not mention the birth of his children, but do mention their marriage, and his own second marriage and death. In the genealogy of the *Stetson Family*, the dau. *Hannah* is said to have m. William White of Fairhaven, and *Anna* is said to have m. Theodosius Russell of Greenwich, N. Y., but I follow the Hardwick Records.

6. ROBERT, supposed to have been of the same family, but his lineage not ascertained, by wife ——, had *Robert*, b. 29 June 1772; *Susanna*, b. 19 Dec. 1774, m. Joshua Bascom of Western (Warren), pub. 14 July 1793; *Reuben*, b. 23 Mar. 1775; *Betsey*, b. 29 Dec. 1776, m. Asa Blackmore of Pittsford, Vt., 27 Nov. 1800; *Thomas*, b. 3 Feb. 1779; *Elijah*, b. 15 June 1781; *Sally Smith*, b. 17 Feb. 1784, m. Silsbee Wetherell of Worc. 29 Nov. 1810. ROBERT the f. d. 18 Jan. 1814, a. 73.

7. DANIEL, perhaps brother of the foregoing, by wife ——, had *Susanna*, bap. 10 Ap. 1774; *Lucy*, bap. 7 May 1775; *Henry*, bap. 25 July 1779.

8. ELIJAH, s. of Robert (6), m. Dulcinea, dau. of Elijah Carpenter, 17 Ap. 1808, and had *Lydia Rich*, b. 22 Dec. 1812, d. 19 July 1816.

RACHEL, m. Andrew Sears of Gr. —— 1787. LYDIA, m. Zephaniah Hack of Gr. 4 Mar. 1790. SARAH, m. Samuel Haskins, pub. 16 Nov. 1806.

STEWART, DANIEL (otherwise written Steward and Stuart), by w. Prudence, had *Elkanah*, b. 12 Aug. 1737; *Samuel*, b. 12 Oct. 1739, a member of Capt. Samuel Robinson's company in the French War, and d. in the campaign of 1756;[1] *Hannah*, b. 20 June 1747, m. William Sherman of Rochester 11

[1] SETH STEWART (or Stuart), b. in Rochester, was a member of the same company, and lost his life in the same campaign, at the early age of 20 years.

Sep. 1766. DANIEL the f. prob. came here from Rochester, and perhaps rem. to Barnard with his son *Elkanah*.

2. ELKANAH, s. of Daniel (1), m. Lydia, prob. dau. of Elisha Cobb, 7 Sep. 1761, and had *Priscilla*, b. 3 May 1762, m. Fitch Dutton 5 Sep. 1782; *Samuel*, b. 2 Dec. 1763, m. Sarah, dau. of Capt. Daniel Egery, 22 Oct. 1789 (he then res. in Barnard, where he had Polly, b. 14 Mar. 1790); *Prudence*, b. 11 Ap. 1765, m. Timothy Banister 5 Sep. 1782; *Lydia*, b. 19 Sep. 1767, m. Asa Paige 19 Feb. 1789; *John*, b. 19 July 1769; *Moses*, b. 19 Ap. 1771. ELKANAH the f. served in the French War 1755, and rem. to Barnard, Vt., as early as 1779, where his three daughters were married. He is said to have d. of hydrophobia, being bitten by a mad wolf.

SUSANNA, m. Ithamar Reed of Pet. 16 Jan. 1749–50. PEACE, m. Samuel Atwood 30 Ap. 1753. DANIEL, perhaps the same as DANIEL (1), m. Eunice Allen 5 Sep. 1768.

STOCKWELL, CYRUS, resided here a short time only, but he left his mark. In May 1818, he established a line of mail stages from Worcester to Northampton, the first which ever passed through Hardwick, and maintained it successfully for several years. He also kept a tavern in 1822 and 1823, soon after which he removed to Worcester, where he long pursued the same business. During his residence here, his son *Stephen N.* was born, 31 Aug. 1823, who became eminent as a manager of the *Boston Journal*. In an obituary published in that paper, it is stated that "his journalistic career covers a term of nearly forty years, and with the exception of brief periods of rest, he has labored with great zeal in the field which he had chosen. From compositor in his youth to the editorial chair, he has filled nearly every intermediate position with rare ability and unsurpassed fidelity." He was also a member of the Common Council of Boston and a representative and senator in the General Court. He died in Roxbury 13 April 1881, aged 57.

2. SIMON, by wife Sophia, had *Sumner*, b. 30 Dec. 1847; *Emma Jane*, b. 8 June 1858; *Ida Josephine*, b. 26 July 1863, d. 22 June 1879.

MERCY, of Prescott, m. Granger Peirce, pub. 18 Jan. 1832.

STONE, JOSEPH, s. of Joseph, and b. in Shrewsbury 12 Nov. 1789, m. Patty Maynard of Shrewsbury, pub. 11 Mar. 1816, and had *Harriet*, b. 22 Jan. 1817, m. John Paige 23 Oct. 1845; *Mary Field*, b. 24 Sep. 1819, d. unm. 29 Sep. 1838; *Joseph*, b. 29 Sep. 1821, d. 2 Mar. 1822; *Martha*, b. 29 June 1823, m. Charles Mandell 3 Mar. 1846; *Lucretia*, b. 15 Mar. 1825; *Louisa*, b. 16 Ap. 1827, m. Charles P. Aiken 27 Sep. 1846. JOSEPH the f. was a skilful and beloved physician. He came here in the spring of 1814, immediately after the death of Dr. Beckwith, and for thirty-five years ministered relief to suffering humanity. After his marriage he resided on the Barre road, about half a mile from the Common, at the place marked "Dr. Stone" on the R. Map. His fellow citizens manifested their confidence in him by electing him to various offices of trust and honor; he was deacon of the Union Church; selectman seven years; town clerk twenty years, from 1829 to 1848 inclusive; member of the school committee eight years; delegate to the Constitutional Convention in 1820; representative in 1823; and senator in 1845 and 1846. He d. greatly lamented, 27 June 1849, a. 59.

2. CHARLES, m. Mary ——, and had *Mary E.*, b. —— 1841, d. 13 Oct. 1856, a. 15; *Sylvanus A.*, b. 6 Mar. 1844, d. 8 Aug. 1846; *William A.*, b. — Aug. 1847, d. 9 May 1854; *Sarah Louisa*, b. 25 Oct. 1853; *John Franklin*, b. 18 Sep. 1857.

3. SAMUEL, m. Elizabeth ——, and had a son, b. 20 Ap. 1844.

4. JOHN A., m. Roxana M. ——, and had *Frank Eugene*, b. 2 Jan. 1855; *Dwight Warner*, b. 25 Feb. 1857, d. 29 Mar. 1857; *Dwight*, b. 19 Jan. 1858, d. 10 Feb. 1858; *William Forest*, b. 16 Jan. 1859; *Nellie Maria*, b. 29 July 1861.

5. CHARLES E., m. Lydia ——, and had *Charles Albert*, b. 9 Jan. 1858.

6. HENRY H., m. Mrs. Huldah B. Bliss 2 June 1870, and had *Jennie Maria*, b. 4 July 1871; *Emory Mitchell* and *Emerson Almon*, twins, b. 13 Oct. 1873; *Martha Elizabeth*, b. 26 Mar. 1876.

JOHN, m. Susanna Mandell 12 May 1768 (she d. at Dana 28 July 1844, a. nearly 95). HULDAH, of Southborough, m. Azariah Bangs, pub. 2 Mar. 1769. JOHN, Jr., of Gr., m. Betsey Bryant, pub. 16 Sep. 1798. SUSANNA, of Dana, m. Thomas Haskins, pub. 25 Mar. 1818. JOHN, m. Harriet Welman of Barre, pub. 27 Ap. 1818. Dr. WILLIAM, of Enf., m. Mrs. Hannah Jenney 23 Nov. 1819. HORACE, m. Abigail Grant 14 Ap. 1822. HOSEA, m. Perna King 18 June 1824. ELIZA, m. Moses Barnes 28 May 1826. Rev. GEORGE, of Sandgate, Vt., m. Eluthera F. Lawton 10 July 1831. FIDELIA, of Pet., m. Calvin Sanford, pub. 4 Sep. 1841. Rev. WILLIAM B., of W. Brk., m. Phebe W. Robinson 16 Feb. 1842. MERCY ANN, m. Augustus Conkey of Mt. Morris, N. Y., 10 Mar. 1846. HOSEA E., m. Fanny Richardson, pub. 17 Oct. 1847. CLARA B., m. John V. Presho 3 Ap. 1850. SAMANTHA M., m. William P. Granger 28 Oct. 1852. ELLEN, of Dana, m. Elbridge Towne, pub. 24 Oct. 1857. CLARK, of Enf., m. Mrs. Hannah Danforth 30 Sep. 1858. MARY, m. Joseph Topp, pub. 30 July 1863. CAROLINE, m. Joseph St. John 10 Jan. 1869. EDGAR F., m. Philena Robinson, of Barre, 29 Jan. 1873.

STOWELL, ISAAC, m. Nabby ——, and had *Sally*, b. 9 Jan. 1783; *Jotham*, b. 15 May 1785; *Nabby*, b. 7 Feb. 1788.

ABEL, of Pet., m. Rachel Freeman, 5 July 1792. CHARLES, m. Ruth Burden of Charlton, pub. 11 Oct. 1829. AVERY W., m. Caroline S. Ingraham of Amh., pub. 14 Oct. 1845.

STRATTON, ICHABOD, a cooper, res. in Brk. 12 Feb. 1731–2. He subsequently removed to Hk. with his wife Elizabeth, who became a member of the church 13 Nov. 1737. The date of his admission does not appear; but he was manifestly a member, because he was called to account, 14 Nov. 1753, for absenting himself "from the sacrament of the Lord's Supper," but afterwards made his peace with the church. He d. 31 Oct. 1762; his wife Elizabeth d. 8 Nov. 1761. No record is found of their chil., who were prob. born in Brk.; but they are supposed to have been parents of *Francis*, *Ichabod*, and *Elizabeth*, who had a son, Judah, b. 18 July 1749, bap. 29 Ap. 1750, and who m. Thomas Elwell, pub. 25 Ap. 1762.

2. FRANCIS, prob. s. of Ichabod (1), m. Eunice Corlie (or Kerley) 29 Ap. 1740, and had *Sarah*, b. 4 Feb. 1741; *Martha*, bap. 19 June 1743; *Eunice*, b. 18 Aug. 1744.

3. ICHABOD, prob. s. of Ichabod (1), m. Abigail Church of Hadley 14 Oct. 1743; she d. 9 Ap. 1755, and he m. Hannah Goodnow 1 July 1755. His chil. were *Asa*, b. 15 July 1744 (called *David* in baptismal record 22 July 1744); *Elihu*, b. 25 Feb. 1745–6; *John*, b. 20 Ap. 1748; *Mary*, b. 2 Feb. 1749–50; *Jonathan*, b. 6 Ap. 1756; *Abigail*, b. 9 Ap. 1757; *Joel*, b. 16 Oct. 1758.

BETTY, widow of Jonathan Stratton of Marlborough, m. Elisha Hedge, pub. 4 Nov. 1765. She ret. to Marl., where she died; her son, Jonathan Stratton, was appointed administrator 11 Mar. 1794.

STURTEVANT, JAMES, b. in Duxbury, by w. Sybil, had *Sybil*, b. ——, m. James Whipple, Jr., pub. 20 Feb. 1808; *Asa*, b. in N. Br. about 1792; *Marcia*, b. —— 1796, was pub. to Lyman Thomas 19 June 1815, and m. to Adin A. Thompson 16 Dec. 1828; she d. in Phillipston 22 Feb. 1879, a. nearly 83; *James*, b. ——; *Howland*, b. in Ware about 1810; *Olive*, b. ——, living in 1852. JAMES the f. d. here 30 Sep. 1829, a. 67; his w. Sybil d. 10 Mar. 1852, a. nearly 88.

2. ASA, s. of James (1), m. Ruth Baker 1 May 1815, and had a child b. — Ap. 1819, d. 12 May 1819; *Seneca P.*, b. about 1820; *S—— R——*, b. about 1822, d. at Ware 18 Aug. 1862, a. 40; a child, b. ——, d. — June 1826; *James W.*, b. ——; *Thomas R.*, b. ——; *George Edwin*, b. — Feb. 1834, d. 23 Jan. 1835; *Asa Grafton*, b. about 1835, a soldier in the War of the Rebellion, d. at New York 28 Oct. 1862, a. 27; his head-stone is in the new cemetery. ASA is supposed to have been father also of *Prolexena*, who m. Lorenzo Newland 22 Ap. 1835; *Sybil P.*, who m. Elbridge C. Howard of Monson, pub. 23 May 1846; and perhaps *Cordelia A.*, of Gr., who m. Joseph P. Snow, pub. 29 Nov. 1851. ASA the f. d. 3 Feb. 1867, a. 74 years and 8 months; his w. Ruth d. 29 Jan. 1871, a. 78.

3. JAMES, s. of James (1), m. ——, and had *Seneca*, b. ——; *James H.*, b. ——; *Charles O.*, b. ——; *Julia*, b. —— 1826, d. 10 Dec. 1829, a. 3.

4. HOWLAND, s. of James (1), m. Mehetabel ——, and had *Evelyn*, b. about 1834, m. Alpheus S. Nye of Dana 2 Ap. 1854; *Thaddeus*, b. about 1840, d. at Dana 18 Oct. 1869, a. 29; a child b. 31 July 1843, d. 15 Aug. 1843. HOWLAND the f. was a painter, and d. 21 Sep. 1843, a. 33.

5. SENECA P., s. of Asa (2), m. Sarah ——, and had *James William*, b. 4 July 1848, d. 9 Jan. 1874; *Asa*, b. 24 Feb. 1850, d. 23 Sep. 1853; a son b. 21 Dec. 1851; *Ellen Louisa*, b. 4 Ap. 1854. SENECA P. the f. d. 11 Jan. 1855, a. 34 years and 9 months.

6. JAMES W., s. of Asa (2), m. Angeline C. Cummings 27 Nov. 1850, and had *Fred*, b. 29 Ap. 1854; *Grace*, b. 6 Feb. 1869, d. 12 Sep. 1869. JAMES W. the f., a wheelwright, res. on the road to Enfield, nearly three miles from the Common.

7. THOMAS R., s. of Asa (2), m. Frances E. Hazard of New Bedford, pub. —— 1852, and had *Mary Lilly*, b. 1 Ap. 1858.

8. SENECA, s. of James (3), m. Mary C——, and had *Albert S.*, b. about —— 1843, m. Sophia M. Patrill 14 Aug. 1866; she d. 10 Mar. 1877, a. nearly 39, and he m. Susan R. Richardson 4 Dec. 1877, and had George E., b. 25 Jan. 1881; *Mary D.*, b. about 1845, m. Charles Newton 14 Mar. 1861; *Sarah Huldah*, b. 15 Sep. 1846 (called *Huldah H.* in the record of her marriage), m. Elmer L. Barnes 8 Jan. 1864; *Charles Henry*, b. 9 July 1848, m. Lauretta Hunter of Presc., pub. 24 Dec. 1868; *Abby Eudora*, b. 7 June 1850, m. Alanson S. Bassett 13 Oct. 1874; *Flora Maria*, b. 23 Mar. 1852, d. 23 July 1854; *Flora Maria*, b. 3 Aug. 1854; *Lendall Dwight*, b. 3 May 1857, drowned 3 Aug. 1870; *Emma Angeline*, b. 30 Oct. 1861, d. 20 Dec. 1861; *Cora Emma*, b. 28 Oct. 1865.

9. JAMES H., s. of James (3), m. Maria A. Whipple, pub. 1 July 1853, and had *Cyrus Eston*, b. 11 Jan. 1854; *Eunice Celestia*, b. 12 July 1856, m. William W. Johnson 18 Aug. 1880; *Joel Rupert*, b. 30 May 1861, d. 17 Oct. 1865; *Sarah Maria*, b. 5 June 1865. JAMES H. the f., a farmer, res. in the westerly part of the town.

10. CHARLES O., s. of James (3), m. Mary Jane ——, and had *Leon Howard*, b. 5 Ap. 1867; *Amy Florence*, b. 15 July 1876; *Edgar Leroy*, b. 4 Nov. 1880.

SULLIVAN, PATRICK, by w. Bridget, had *John*, b. 28 July 1864; *Bridget*, b. 20 July 1866.

2. EUGENE, m. Mary Sullivan, pub. 13 Sep. 1868, and had *Daniel*, b. 24 Nov. 1870.

3. MICHAEL, by w. Mary, had *Mary Ellen*, b. 15 Mar. 1870; *John*, b. 18 Nov. 1871; *Cornelius*, b. 10 Mar. 1874; *Dennis*, b. 5 Nov. 1875; *Francis*, b. 2 Oct. 1877; *William*, b. 28 Sep. 1879.

SUMNER, WILLIAM, s. of Roger, b. at Bicester, Eng., in 1605, came to New Eng. in 1636, and settled at Dorchester, where he d. 9 Dec. 1688. He m. Mary West 22 Oct. 1625, and had six chil., of whom the fourth was *George*, b. —— 1634.

2. GEORGE, s. of William (1), was lieutenant, deacon, and representative. He res. at Milton, where he d. 11 Dec. 1715. He m. Mary Blake of Northampton, and had eight chil., of whom the sixth was *Edward*, b. 29 Aug. 1676.

3. EDWARD, s. of George (2), res. at Roxbury, and died there in 1763. He was one of the early proprietors of Hardwick. He m. Elizabeth Clapp 25 Sep. 1701, and had eleven chil., of whom the youngest was *Benjamin*, b. 29 Dec. 1724.

4. BENJAMIN, s. of Edward (3), res. at Ashford, Conn., was captain, representative, and deacon, and d. 4 Jan. 1803. He m. Bridget Perry 3 Oct. 1748, and had thirteen chil., of whom the eldest was *James Fitch*, b. 29 July 1749.

5. JAMES FITCH, s. of Benjamin (and cousin german to Governor Increase Sumner), m. Ada Bullard of Dedham 30 Sep. 1773 and had *Sarah*, b. 19 Oct. 1774, m. David Keyes of Eastford 30 Jan. 1793; *Drusilla*, b. 13 Ap. 1777,

m. Murray Brown of Hk., and d. 9 Aug. 1837; *William*, b. 13 Aug. 1779, d. here 7 Jan. 1837; *Sybil*, b. 29 May 1782, m. Asa Raymond 16 Oct. 1803; *Elizabeth*, twin, b. 6 June 1785, d. 22 May 1789; *Mary*, twin, b. 6 June 1785, d. unm. 25 Sep. 1809; *Benjamin*, b. 17 Feb. 1788; *Irena*, b. 15 Ap. 1793, m. Thompson Howard 25 July 1816, and d. 15 Mar. 1872; *Lucy*, b. 22 Feb. 1797, d. 13 Sep. 1803. JAMES FITCH the f. res. at Ashford, Conn., until 1801, when he came here and res. in the westerly part of the town. He was styled captain, and was "killed by a fall," 25 June 1803.

6. BENJAMIN, s. of James Fitch (5), m. Mary Osborn of Ware 10 Oct. 1816, and had *James Fitch*, b. 4 Sep. 1817; *George*, b. 30 July 1819; *Elizabeth Clark*, b. 16 Aug. 1822, d. 8 Sep. 1822; *Isaiah Clark*, b. 16 Oct. 1823; *Sarah Brown*, b. 14 May 1826, m. —— Converse, and d. 10 Ap. 1845; *William Benjamin*, b. 21 Jan. 1833, d. 27 July 1845. BENJAMIN the f. d. at Ware 21 Sep. 1855; his w. Mary d. here 29 Aug. 1850.

7. JAMES FITCH, s. of Benjamin (6), m. Martha Ann Converse of Ware —— 1843, and had *Martha Lucinda*, b. 3 Jan. 1844.

8. GEORGE, s. of Benjamin (6), m. Melina A., dau. of Jason Thayer of Amherst, 2 Oct. 1845, and had *George William*, b. 9 Nov. 1846, d. 17 Aug. 1849; *Virgil Maro*, b. 9 June 1849, d. 16 Aug. 1849. GEORGE the f. d. 16 May 1850; his w. Melina A. m. William Cummings of Ware 27 May 1856.

9. ISAIAH CLARK, s. of Benjamin (6), m. Louisa Turner of Pelham 3 Feb. 1846, and had *Benjamin Clark*, b. 30 Jan. 1849; *Mary Louisa*, b. 21 Nov. 1850, m. Walter Peirce 12 Ap. 1871; *Samuel Ambrose*, b. 12 Nov. 1853; *Charles Wyman*, b. 20 Aug. 1856; *Elizabeth Abigail*, b. 7 Oct. 1859, m. Albert Marsh 7 Oct. 1876. ISAIAH CLARK the f. d. at Ware 3 June 1882.

10. BENJAMIN CLARK, s. of Isaiah Clark (9), m. Louisa Haskins 21 Sep. 1870, and had *George*, b. 31 Aug. 1871.

Many particulars concerning this family are gathered from the *Sumner Genealogy*.

SWASEY, BETSEY, m. John Coloney 3 Aug. 1788.

SWIFT, NATHAN, of Rut. Dist. (Barre), m. Mary Willis 8 Sep. 1774. ORVILLE, of Wilmington, Vt., m. Hannah Spooner 5 June 1832. MARTIN J. Jr., of Bridgewater, m. Louisa S. Ames 11 Dec. 1845. *Mary A.*, of Bridgewater, m. Harrison F. Barnes 12 June 1861.

TAYLOR, JONATHAN, by w. ——, had *Stephen*, bap. 25 Ap. 1762; *Rebecca*, bap. 23 Sep. 1764; *David*, bap. 26 July 1767.

2. SETH, m. Mehetabel ——, and had *Mehetabel*, b. about 1772, m. Seth Spooner 19 Feb. 1795, and d. 12 May 1812, a. 40; *Sylvanus*, b. about 1774; *Seth*, b. about 1776, m. Rhoda Granger of N. Br., pub. 5 Feb. 1804, and d. 7 June 1811, a. 35. leaving an only dau. Harriet; *Betsey*, b. —— 1778, m. Martin Rogers 30 Nov. 1797, and d. 14 Nov. 1853, a. 75 years and 10 months; *Enos*, b. about 1780, m. Mary Taylor, 22 Nov. 1801, and d. 13 Nov. 1822, a. 42; *Nathan*, b. about 1782; *Olive*, b. prob. about 1784, m. Ammi Taylor of Fairlee, Vt., 14 Sep. 1800; *Rhoda*, b. about 1789, d. unm. 20 Nov. 1811, a. 22. No record is found of the birth of these children; the dates are estimated by comparison with the dates of marriages and deaths. SETH the f. was styled captain; he d. suddenly at Boston, where he was transacting some business, 5 or 7 July 1811, a. 66; his w. Mehetabel d. 22 July 1832, a. 91.

3. SYLVANUS, s. of Seth (2), m. Eunice Bridges 19 Nov. 1801; she d. 24 Jan. 1819, a. 50, and he m. Anna Dewin of Brk., pub. 30 Jan. 1820. His chil. were *Mary Mixter*, b. 8 June 1804, m. Hiram Gorham 26 Nov. 1829; *Lyman*, b. 1 Nov. 1808. SYLVANUS the f. res. near Barre, at the place marked "S. Taylor" on the R. Map, and was the proprietor of "Taylor's Mills." He d. 5 Ap. 1849, a. 75; his w. Anna d. 19 June 1841, a. 63.

4. NATHAN, s. of Seth (2), m. Susanna Gorham of Barre, pub. 27 Nov. 1806, and had five children, who were all bap. with the mother, 18 May 1820, namely, *Mehetabel*, *Fanny*, *Levina* (perhaps the same who m. Gardner Hathaway, pub. 25 Aug. 1855); *John Gorham*, b. about 1812, d. at Springf. 1 Aug. 1866, a. 54; *Nathan*, b. about 1815, m. Lucy S. Haven of Barre 7 Dec. 1853. NATHAN the f. d. 11 May 1815, a. 32.

5. LYMAN, s. of Sylvanus (3), m. Adeline M. Howland 28 Nov. 1839, and had *Mary A. G.*, b. 29 Nov. 1844, d. 27 Aug. 1848; *Sylvanus*, b. 25 Mar. 1847; *George Howland*, b. 5 Aug. 1849; *James Barnard*, b. 15 Aug. 1850.

BARTHOLOMEW, soldier in the French War, killed in battle 8 Sep. 1755. EDWARD, m. Lydia Haskell 23 Nov. 1775. SUSANNA, of Athol, m. Nathaniel Merrick 23 Oct. 1797. LEMUEL F., m. Cassandra D. Dexter 9 Ap. 1835. LEONORA, m. Victor Robert, pub. 9 Nov. 1867. HARRIET, dau. of Samuel and Lavinia, d. 16 Oct. 1803, a. 3 years and 9 months. JOHN, formerly of Wrentham, d. 27 Sep. 1811, a 65.[1]

TERRY, JOHN, JR., m. Sarah Ramsdell 26 Sep. 1782, and had prob. *John*, b. about 1783; *Sally*, b. 14 Dec. 1786, d. 18 Oct. 1795; prob. *Reuel*, b. about 1789; m. Dolly Winslow of Ware, pub. 15 Dec. 1810; *Phebe*, b. —— 1791, d. 8 Oct. 1795, a. 4; *Sylvanus*, b. —— 1793, d. 12 Oct. 1795, a. 2; prob. *Otis*, b. about 1795; a child b. —— Feb. 1799, d. 31 Oct. 1802; a child b. — May 1801, d. 24 Oct. 1802. Mrs. Sarah Terry d. 8 Aug. 1802, a. 40.

2. JOHN, prob. s. of John (1), m. Ruth Dana 17 May 1804, and had *Alvah*, b. 11 Ap. 1805; *Sarah*, b. 20 Dec. 1806, m. Oren Ramsdell 8 June 1823; *Ruth*, b. 25 Mar. 1809, m. John P. Marsh of Ware, pub. 31 Oct. 1840, and d. 30 Nov. 1878; *Horace*, b. 6 July 1811; *Alanson*, b. 24 July 1814, d. 7 May 1816; *Sylvia*, b. 25 Aug. 1818 or 1819, m. Festus Alden of Gr. 10 Sep. 1840; *Phebe*, b. 14 Mar. 1824; *William A.*, b. 12 Mar. 1830. (The last two chil. appear to have been by second wife, Esther.)

3. OTIS, prob. s. of John (1), m. Cynthia Ruggles 6 Mar. 1817, and had *Otis Lysander*, bap. 24 May 1818.

4. HORACE, m. Eunice A. Rogers, pub. 7 Ap. 1843, and had *John*, b. 11 Mar. 1844; *Eunice R.*, b. 4 Jan. 1846; *Ruth Elizabeth*, b. 17 Nov. 1851, d. 7 Dec. 1853.

PHEBE, m. David Bassett 11 Dec. 1782. LYDIA, m. Rev. Joshua Crosby of Gr. (now Enfield), 8 Feb. 1790. JOANNA, a widow, d. 6 Jan. 1814, a. 88.

THAYER, BENJAMIN, b. in Mansfield, m. Polly Stetson 22 Sep 1793, and had *Sophia*, b. about 1794, m. Jeremiah Thurston, and d. at Gr. 7 Jan. 1858, a. 64; *Relief*, b. about 1798, m. Ephraim Amsden, Jr., of Gr. 15 Oct. 1816, and d. at Ware 27 May 1868, a. 70; *Hannah*, b. about 1800, d. unm. at Dana 21 Feb. 1864, a. 63 years and 2 months; *Benjamin*, b. —— 1810, d. 11 Sep. 1813, a. 3 years. BENJAMIN the f. d. 11 Nov. 1851, a. 86.

2. JAMES, perhaps brother of Benjamin (1), m. ——, and had *Ira*, b. —— 1794, d. 3 Oct. 1813, a. 19. JAMES the f. d. 7 July 1820, a. 50.

A "widow Thayer" d. 31 Aug. 1825; age not stated.

3. SAMUEL, perhaps brother (or possibly son) of Benjamin (1), m. Fanny Richardson, pub. 27 Jan. 1812, and had *James H.*, b. about 1816; *Lendall W.*, b. about 1818, m. Clarissa C. Skinner 7 Sep. 1843, and d. 8 Ap. 1852, a. 34; *Ansel W.*, b. about 1822, m. Bodicea Pike 12 Dec. 1854, and d. 12 Aug. 1856, a. 34. SAMUEL the f. d. 11 Feb. 1873, a. 85 years and 6 months; his w. Fanny d. 3 Dec. 1869, a. 79.

4. UEL, parentage not ascertained, m. Lydia ——, and had *Augusta*, b. 2 Mar. 1800; *Thomas W.*, b. 3 Dec. 1803, d. 18 Ap. 1804; *Elbridge Gerry*, b. 21 Oct. 1805; *Nathan Wood*, b. 7 Nov. 1808.

5. HOSEA, of Dana, m. Syrena Whipple, pub. 26 Ap. 1819, and had *Joel*, b. —— 1821.

6. ERASTUS, m. Ruby Whipple 26 May 1830, and had *Elmer M.*, b. —— 1840; *Sarah*, b. 7 Dec. 1844, d. 28 Jan. 1845. ERASTUS the f. d. 16 Mar. 1848, a. 35.

7. JONAS H., s. of Samuel (4), m. Mary Ann ——; she d. 11 Jan. 1865, a. 50, and he m. Clarissa C., widow of his brother Lendall W. Thayer, 4 Nov. 1866. Some of his chil. were (prob.) *John Porter*, b. about 1837, accidentally killed near Princeton, N. J., in Sep. 1859, a. 22; *Julia Ann*, b. about 1840, m. Constantine Smith 3 July 1856, and (2d) Francis P. Weeks 26 June 1872, and d. 4 May 1874; *Scott Leroy*, b. about 1847. JONAS H. the f. d. 17 May 1871, a 55.

[1] Several members of the Taylor family were buried in a private cemetery near the Barre line.

8. Ezra, m. Julia ——, and had *Zachary Taylor*, b. 8 July 1848, d. at Dana 29 Nov. 1864.

9. Joel, s. of Hosea (5), m. Jane F. Converse 28 Nov. 1849, and had *Ida Luella*, b. here 29 May 1853, though the father is styled of Dana in the record of marriage.

10. Andrew J., m. Sylvia B. Johnson, pub. 24 Nov. 1855, and had *Philip Edwin*, b. 12 Mar. 1858; *Carrie Civilla*, b. 24 Nov. 1861; *Arthur Freeman*, b. 6 Mar. 1866.

11. Samuel E., m. Hortensia Norcutt, pub. 22 Nov. 1859, and had *Lillie Maria*, b. 18 July 1862; *Henry Alanson*, b. 30 Jan. 1866; *Emily W.*, b. 12 Mar. 1874; *Charles Mitchell*, b. 1 July 1875.

12. Elmer M., s. of Erastus (6), m. Mary Ellen Forbes 10 July 1861, and had *Jennie A.*, b. —— 1862, m. James T. Kellogg of Gr. 25 Nov. 1880.

13. Scott Leroy, s. of Jonas H. (7), m. Balarah Allen 3 Nov. 1867, and had *Abbie Florence*, b. 26 July 1868; *John Porter*, b. — Aug. 1870, d. 11 Mar. 1871; *Alice G.*, b. 15 Sep. 1872, d. 14 Oct. 1872; *Anna Lura*, b. 14 July 1875, d. 10 Sep. 1875.

14. Charles W., m. Harriet R. Stephens 12 Oct. 1871, and had *Eva May*, b. 8 Feb. 1872.

15. George W., m. Mary Ann ——, and had a son b. 4 Dec. 1876.

Grindall and wife came here from Wrentham in 1769. John, a Revolutionary soldier from 1778 to 1781, m. Exe (Achsah?) Powers of Gr., pub. 5 Nov. 1780. Ephraim, was a corporal in the army, 1777; and Samuel, was a soldier from 1778 to 1781, but no further trace of them appears. Rachel, m. Henry Butterfield of Gr. 20 Nov. 1783. Mary, of Pet., m. Ebenezer Sprout 11 Dec. 1783. Abigail, m. Silas Richardson 26 Nov. 1789. Sally, m. Moses Whipple 31 Dec. 1789. William, m. Mary Stephens 28 Nov. 1793. Hannah, m. Jacob Stephens, pub. 8 Nov. 1796, and d. 17 May 1830, a. 57. Nancy, m. John Johnson, pub. 10 Nov. 1797. Sally, m. Aaron Johnson of Gr. 4 Oct. 1798. Lina, m. George Marsh of Pet., pub. 9 Ap. 1801. Clarissa, m. John Wild of Butternuts, N. Y., pub. 15 Feb. 1819. John, m. Susan Simmons, pub. 7 Feb. 1820. Annis, m. William Kelly, pub. 25 Dec. 1820. Caleb, m. Hannah Stephens, pub. 16 Mar. 1823. Martha, m. David Whipple, pub. 26 Jan. 1827. Civilla R., m. Philip Johnson, pub. 20 Mar. 1830. Sally W., m. Solomon G. Towne of Winchendon 13 May 1834. Susan, m. Newell Bacon 31 Dec. 1839. William A., m. Sarah Ann Weaver 9 May 1850. Mary Ann, m. George W. Richardson, pub. —— 1854. Balarah, dau. of Joel, d. 21 Sep. 1810, a. 17. Melzar, s. of Joel, d. 12 Mar. 1814, a. 19.

Thomas, William, was one of the very earliest pioneers in the settlement of Hardwick, having a house here as early as 13 Dec. 1732. He res. on the old road from the Furnace Village to Gilbertville, at the place marked "C. Paige" on the R. Map.[1] His w. Patience d. 27 Oct. 1746, and he was pub. to Susanna Marble of Stow 11 Ap. 1747,[2] and d. 22 May 1747, a. prob. about 60. He was a member of the first board of selectmen after the town was incorporated in 1739, and manifestly a man of much energy.[3] His chil. who shared in the division of his comparatively large estate, 11 May 1749, were *Amos* (eldest son); *Zerviah*, b. 1709, m. Samuel Marsh, and (2d) Isaiah Pratt 2 Mar. 1746-7, and d. 18 Ap. 1798, a. 89; *Temperance*, b. ——, m. Edmund Jordan; *Hannah*, b. ——, m. Isaiah Glazier 8 Nov. 1738; *Elizabeth*, b. ——, m. Edmund Grover; *Daniel*; *Nathan*; *Aaron*, m. Elizabeth Marvile of Brk., pub. 27 Jan. 1749-50; *Israel*, b. 7 Aug. 1735. (*Mary*, b. 3 Mar. 1731-2, had prob. d. young.)

[1] He devoted a spot on his farm to the burial of the dead, which was rudely disturbed in 1871, when excavations were made for the Ware River Railroad.

[2] No record is found of the marriage; and as he lived so short a time after the intention was published, it may be doubted whether it was consummated.

[3] I once supposed this William Thomas to have been the first school-master in Hardwick, 1745; but afterwards found evidence that the school-master was of Marlborough, and father of Robert B. Thomas, the "Farmer's Almanac" maker.

2. Amos, s. of William (1), m. Abigail ——, and had *Elizabeth*, b. 4 July 1738; *William*, b. 18 Sep. 1739, d. young; *Abigail*, b. 3 Mar. 1741, m. Samuel Beals 31 July 1767; *Olive*, b. 1 Dec. 1742, prob. d. young; *William*, b. 6 Aug. 1744; *Amos*, b. 6 Ap. 1746; *Joseph*, b. 24 May 1748; *Daniel*, b. 5 May 1750; *Mercy*, b. 6 Ap. 1752, m. Luke Bonney 5 Nov. 1772; *Isaac*, b. 13 July 1754, d. 18 Dec. 1755. Amos the f. was a farmer, res. about half a mile south of his father's homestead, at the place marked "Moulton" on the R. Map, and d. 31 July 1754.

3. Nathan, s. of William (1), m. Hepzibah ——, and had *Mary*, b. 11 Jan. 1743-4; *Nathan*, b. 12 Nov. 1745; *Patience*, b. 31 Jan. 1747-8.

4. William, s. of Amos (2), was a physician, and res. in Brk.; he m. Abiel Collins 23 Aug. or Sep. 1765, and among his chil. were *Argalas* (whose name was changed, in manhood, to *Samuel Beals* Thomas), a noted keeper of a hotel, opposite to the court-house in Worcester; and *Sylvanus*, an innholder in the westerly part of West Brookfield. Dr. William the f. d. in Mar. 1805, a. 60.

5. Amos, s. of Amos (2), m. Eunice Bangs 20 Dec. 1770, and had *Isaac*, b. 11 or 13 July 1771, d. 19 Ap. 1842; *Nathaniel*, b. 13 or 21 Feb. 1773, d. 8 Dec. 1851; *Amos*, b. 24 Oct. 1774, d. 29 July 1853; *Abigail*, b. 13 Mar. 1776, d. 11 Sep. 1862; *Eunice*, b. 11 Feb. 1778, d. 8 Ap. 1852; *David*, b. 24 Oct. 1779, d. — May 1865; *Beals*, b. 29 June 1781, d. 24 Aug. 1854; *Azariah*, b. 15 Dec. 1782, d. 14 Sep. 1830; *Heman*, b. 21 June 1785, d. 9 or 29 June 1843; *Mary*, b. 9 Aug. 1786, d. 9 Nov. 1840; *Rhoda*, b. 29 Dec. 1788, d. 25 July 1789; *Rhoda*, b. 22 Dec. 1790, d. 21 Oct. 1865; *Arden*, b. 24 Sep. 1793, d. 4 Nov. 1874; *Rhoba* (Ruby?), b. 7 Aug. 1795, d. 1 Sep. 1814; *Alpheus*, b. 2 Ap. 1797, living in Athol, 1875. Amos the f. rem. soon after 1774 to N. Salem, where most of his children were born; he d. 29 Ap. 1831, a. 85; his w. Eunice d. 26 June 1830, a. 78. For most of the facts in regard to this family I am indebted to his grandson, Dr. Jason B. Thomas of Thorndike.

6. Joseph, s. of Amos (2), m. Mary, dau. of Elisha Billings, 17 Mar. 1774, and had four chil., the record of whose births is mutilated so that the several years do not appear: *Isaac*, b. 20 Dec. ——, d. 23 Feb. 1778; *Polly*, b. 9 Oct. ——; *Isaac*, b. 2 July ——, prob. m. Cynthia Washburn 27 Nov. 1805; *Sabra*, b. 29 Aug. ——. Joseph the f. prob. rem. to Hardwick, Vt., and d. 9 Mar. 1841, a. 93; his w. Mary d. 11 Sep. 1819, a. 65.

7. Daniel, s. of Amos (2), m. Mercy ——, and had *Samuel Beals*, b. 2 Feb. 1771; *Betty*, b. 9 Sep. 1772; *Perthinia*, b. 31 May 1774, m. Joseph Crowell 24 Oct. 1793; *Daniel*, b. 28 Jan. 1776; he may have been father also of *Lucinda*, b. ——, m. Abel Ruggles 8 May 1799; *Mercy*, b. ——, m. Isaac Warren 19 Oct. 1800; *Abigail*, b. about 1781, m. Gershom Cobb 2 May 1811, and (2d) David Blackmer 13 Oct. 1823, and d. 22 Mar. 1832, a. 51. Daniel the f. became (with his wife) a public charge as early as 1812, and remained so in 1819, and prob. through life; she d. in Sep. 1824, and he d. not many years later.

8. Beals, s. of Amos (5), m. Nancy Bigelow of N. Brk., pub. 16 Jan. 1815; she d. 12 May 1821, a. 29 nearly, and he m. Dolly W., dau. of Capt. Thomas Egery, 11 Ap. 1824; she d. 23 June 1836, a. 33, and he m. Sally W., dau. of Stephen Gorham, 28 Nov. 1837. His chil. were, an infant, d. 7 July 1816; *Jason B.*, b. 6 Aug. 1817; *Nancy B.*, b. 15 Dec. 1825, m. George J. Newton 8 Feb. 1855, and d. at Gloversville, N. Y., 3 or 4 June 1858; *Clara E.*, b. 21 July 1828, m. Addison A. Hunt 16 Mar. 1852; *Edwin E.*, b. 24 Jan. 1831, d. at Saratoga Springs — Jan. 1868; *Sarah J.*, b. 21 Sep. 1840, m. Franklin Wait 18 Feb. 1862, d. at Greenfield 5 Feb. 1878. Beals the f. was adopted by Maj. Samuel Beals (the husband of his aunt), and res. on his homestead on the easterly road to Gilbertville, but afterwards erected a house on the turnpike, about a hundred rods northerly from the Common; he was a farmer, and d. 23 or 24 Aug. 1854, a. 73; his w. Sally W. d. at Worc. 18 Dec. 1857, a. 54.

9. Daniel, s. of Daniel (7), m. Polly, dau. of Capt. Edward Ruggles, 3 Sep. 1798, and had *Asa R.*, b. at Penobscot 5 July 1799; *Hiram*, b. here 24 Nov. 1800, d. 6 Aug. 1803; *Elihu H.*, b. here 30 Oct. 1802.

10. Jason B., s. of Beals (8), m. Phila, dau. of Capt. Martin Mandell, 17 Ap. 1850, and had a son b. 30 Aug. 1855, d. 20 Sep. 1855; a dau. b. 21 Ap. 1860, d. 14 Aug. 1860; *Martin M.*, b. 28 June 1861. Jason B., the f., a physician, res. in Thorndike, where he d. 28 Nov. 1880.

11. Isaac, s. of Isaac of Pembroke, m. Mary, wid. of Asa Hatch of Plymouth, 12 May 1747, rem. to Hk. in 1762, was a merchant, and engaged in the manufacture of potash and ironware. His house and store were on the east road to Gilbertville, between the places marked "O. Trow" and "J. Mann" on the R. Map, which, after his death, became the property of John Rowe of Boston. He d. in 1765; his w. Mary was administratrix 22 Oct. 1765, but d. before 28 Feb. 1766.

Patience, m. Jonathan Kendall of Leominster 10 Oct. 1745. Submit, of N. Br., m. Richard Waite, pub. 20 June 1771. Anna, m. Deering Elwell of W. Hampton, pub. 20 Mar. 1791. Israel, of Gr., m. Fanny Peirce, pub. 30 Nov. 1797. Joanna, m. Jonas Barnes, pub. 24 Mar. 1806. Cynthia, m. Lawrin Mason, pub. 15 May 1813. Lyman, was pub. 19 June 1815, to Marcia Sturtevant. Israel, m. Gratia Cobb of Gr., pub. 22 Jan. 1827. Jacob, of Shutesbury, m. Nancy Burt 5 Nov. 1837.

Thompson, Adin A., m. Marcia, dau. of James Sturtevant, 16 Dec. 1828, and had *Lydia Jane*, b. 20 Nov. 1829; *Tryphosa Elizabeth*, b. 13 Dec. 1830, m. —— Moore, or —— Morse, and d. 4 Dec. 1878, at New Salem; *James Barfield*, b. 21 Mar. 1832; *Marcia Augusta*, b. — Nov. 1833, d. at N. Sal. 20 Sep. 1852; *Samuel Adin*, b. 4 May 1835; *Frances Julia*, b. 4 Aug. 1837.

2. Thomas E., m. Susan —— and had a son d. 1 Oct. 1842, a. 2 months; *Charles Henry*, b. 4 Ap. 1844.

3. Caleb, m. Josephine ——, and had *Florence Virginia*, b. 31 July 1848.

James, m. Polly Sellon 20 Aug. 1777. Eunice, m. John Wallis, Jr., of Barre 7 Feb. 1780. Nathan, of Salem, N. Y., m. Alice Ruggles 21 Dec. 1797. Irene, a widow, d. 15 Mar. 1872, a. 79.

Thresher, Hervey, s. of Timothy, and b. in N. Br., m. Aurelia Bolster 5 Dec. 1826, and had *Sylvia W.*, b. about 1828, m. Elliot B. Trow 27 Mar. 1866; *Malinda*, b. about 1830, m. William Blake of Bel. 6 Mar. 1848; *Charles H.*, b. about 1833, d. in Barre 28 June 1863, a. 30; *Elizabeth*, b. about 1835, m. William Bates of Barre, pub. 21 Oct. 1853; *Oramel S.*, b. 18 Sep. 1845. Hervey the f. d. 24 Mar. 1878, a. 75; his w. Aurelia d. at N. Br. 19 Jan. 1851, a. 42.

2. Harlow, m. Irene ——, and had *George*, b. —— 1843, d. 25 July 1847, a. 4; *Angeline*, b. 24 Feb. 1847; a daughter b. 20 Feb. 1849.

3. David, m. Nancy Robbins, pub. 17 Sep. 1850, and had *Delia E.*, b. about 1854, m. Alfred J. Graves 25 Ap. 1875; *Harrison Orcutt*, b. 12 June 1856; *Lura*, b. 3 Aug. 1858, d. 21 Oct. 1872. David the f. d. 3 Oct. 1869, a. 49; his w. Nancy d. 22 May 1869, a. 44.

4. Harrison Orcutt, s. of David (3), by w. Lizzie, had *Maud Edith*, b. 27 Oct. 1880.

5. Frederick, by w. Nancy M., had a son b. 11 June 1857; *Herbert Frederick*, b. 11 May 1859; *Effie Augusta*, b. 31 Jan. 1861.

6. Elijah C., by w. Philinda, had *Jennie Angeline*, b. 28 Aug. 1863; *Robert Orcutt*, b. 20 Dec. 1864.

Abigail, of N. Br., m. Josiah Butler 7 Feb. 1771. Lewis, of Prescott, m. Lydia Chase — Dec. 1842.

Thurston, Samuel, m. Sibbelah ——, and had *Sally*, b. about 1772, m. Abner Weston 17 Oct. 1788, and d. 13 Mar. 1836, a. 63; *Lettice*, b. about 1775, m. Stephen Gorham 6 Nov. 1798, and d. 22 Ap. 1831, a. 55; *Deborah*, b. about 1778, m. Col. Micah Reed, pub. 3 Ap. 1797, and d. 30 June 1828; *Paul*, b. 6 Aug. 1781, d. 17 Feb. 1786; *Samuel*, b. 11 Jan. 1784, d. 17 Feb. 1786. Samuel, the f. became "deranged in mind" and wandered from his home 11 Mar. 1807; his w. advertised his absence in the *Massachusetts Spy*, 1 Ap. 1807, and on the 8th or 9th of the same month he was found dead, a. 62; the church record has this remark: "Verdict of jury, that his death was accidental." His w. Sibbelah (or Sybil) m. Capt. Samuel Dexter 26 Sep.

1811, but "left his bed and board" before 19 Oct. 1812; she d. in N. Br. 13 July 1849, a. 100 years, as inscribed on her head-stone in the new cemetery in Hk., and also on the town record of N. Br., where her name is erroneously written "Isabella."

2. JEREMIAH, m. Sophia, dau. of Benjamin Thayer, and had *Mary F.*, b. about 1822, d. unm. 14 Ap. 1842, a. 20; *Martha L.*, b. about 1823, d. unm. 6 Mar. 1863, a. 40. JEREMIAH the f. d. 12 Mar. 1829, a. 34; his w. Sophia d. at Gr. 7 Jan. 1858, a. 64. All were buried in the new cemetery; but only *Martha L.* appears by the record to have died here.

TIBBETTS, FRANKLIN LA FAYETTE, m. Mary W. Hervey 12 Jan. 1853, and had *Edith M.*, b. 16 Oct. 1854; *Mary Effie*, b. 14 May 1857; *Albion B.*, b. 13 Oct. 1859.

TINNEY, ZENAS D. (otherwise written Dexter Z. Tinney), of Newburg, Me., m. Ruth Dexter 6 Nov. 1856, and had *Harriet Maria*, b. 16 Aug. 1857, d. 6 Dec. 1864. ZENAS D. the f. was a soldier in the Federal Army, and was killed in the Battle of the Wilderness, 6 May 1864, a. 33; his w. Ruth d. 25 June 1881, a. 54.

GIDEON, of Barre, m. Betsey Childs 8 Mar. 1792. DANIEL, of Ware, m. Abigail Pike 16 Oct. 1803, and d. 29 Nov. 1811, a. 63. Mrs. TINNEY, d. — June 1825, a. 70.

TISDALE, ABIJAH, m. Miriam ——, and had *Abijah*, b. 24 July 1792.

TITUS, EPHRAIM, m. Hannah Cobb 20 Dec. 1770, and had *William*, b. 19 Dec. 1771; *Seth*, b. 11 Aug. 1774.

EBENEZER, of Gr., m. Patty Rich 30 Aug. 1792. GEORGE S., of Ware, m. Hannah Stedman 1 May 1858.

TOTMAN, LUCRETIA, m. Miles Cobb, pub. 30 Dec. 1826. NANCY, m. Samuel D. Anderson of Ware 7 Aug. 1828. LYDIA, m. Laertes Evans 2 June 1833. LUCY H., m. Loren Shaw 17 Mar. 1846. L. MARIA, m. Addison A. Barber of Amh., pub. 1 Sep. 1848.

TOWNE, ELIJAH, m. Louisa ——, and had *Harriet Malvina*, b. 11 Dec. 1821, m. Dr. David Ransom of Carlville, N. Y., 19 May 1840; *Paul Allen*, b. 8 Dec. 1823; *Rosina*, b. 4 June 1825.

2. WILLIAM B., m. Elizabeth ——, and had *Carrie L.*, b. about 1860, m. Frederick A. Ruggles 15 Jan. 1878; *Ernest Eugene*, b. 8 Dec. 1864.

3. AMOS T., m. Laura M. ——, and had *Frank Elbridge*, b. 26 July 1869.

4. HENRY G., m. Mary Ann Warner 1 Jan. 1872, and had *Percie R.*, b. 22 May 1878; *George Henry*, b. 29 Jan. 1880; *William G.*, b. 17 Aug. 1881, d. 9 Sep. 1881. HENRY G. the f., a merchant and deacon, res. on the Common.

ALMIRA, m. Hosea Butterfield of Gr., 11 Ap. 1820. ELIZA A., of Gr., m. John V. Presho, pub. 13 June 1857. ELBRIDGE, m. Ella Stone of Dana, pub. 24 Oct. 1857. JOHN, m. Sarah Simonds, pub. 2 Nov. 1858. CHARLES R., d. 6 Nov. 1862, a. nearly 32. SALLY, dau. of John, b. at Dana, d. 24 Ap. 1864, a. 35.

TRASK, DANFORTH, m. Clarissa Winter of Gr., pub. 23 Nov. 1833, and had *George Danforth*, b. 15 Nov. 1834, d. 8 Mar. 1840; *Charles Edwin*, b. 26 Sep. 1836, d. 15 Mar. 1840; *Walter Scott*, b. 11 Aug. 1838, d. 12 Mar. 1840; *William Augustus*, b. 24 Feb. 1840.

2. MICHAEL, m. Milly Rawson of So. Orange, pub. 4 May 1844; she d. 13 Mar. 1847, a. 21, and he m. Martha Rawson, pub. 20 May 1848. His chil. were *Alden F.*, b. 25 Feb. 1847; *Sylvanus Michael*, b. 23 Mar. 1849; *Alpheus H.*, b. 1 Aug. 1851, d. 12 Oct. 1851.

DAVID, of Leicester, m. Pamela Cutler, pub. 21 July 1816.

TROW, BENJAMIN, m. Margaret ——, who was adm. to the church in Norton 1754. His chil. were *Solomon*, b. ——, a soldier in the French War, 1759; *Israel*, b. about 1737; *Eunice*, b. about 1744, m. Philip Spooner of Pet., and d. here 30 May 1830, a. 86; and perhaps others. BENJAMIN the f. res. in Norton, and d. 9 Sep. 1769; his w. Margaret d. in 1789, a. 86.

2. ISRAEL, s. of Benjamin (1), m. Mary Clapp 1 Jan. 1761; she d. here 13 June 1809, a. 71, and he m. Prudence Leonard of Taunton, pub. 1 Ap. 1811. His chil. were *Benjamin*, b. 18 Ap. 1763, a soldier in the Revolutionary War,

1778, settled in Buckland; *Israel*, b. 11 May 1766, m. Hannah Makepeace 28 May 1788, and d. in N. Br., 27 Aug. 1806; *Orin*, b. 9 Nov. 1769; *Lydia*, b. ——, m. Joel Spooner of Northfield 24 Dec. 1797; *Nancy*, b. ——, m. Joseph Bruce 28 Ap. 1799. ISRAEL the f. was a sergeant in the French War 1759, and a captain in the Revolutionary War, for several short campaigns; he was a member of the Committee of Correspondence four years, between 1775 and 1781; selectman four years, between 1782 and 1793; assessor six years, 1778–91; treasurer three years, 1773–75; and representative in 1784 and 1785. About 1793 he rem. from Norton to Petersham, and about two years later to Hardwick, where he res. during the remainder of his life, on the turnpike, near the Furnace, at the place marked "E. Trow" on the R. Map. He d. 17 Feb. 1825, a. 88.

3. ORIN, s. of Israel (2), came here with his father about 1795, and m. Hannah, dau. of Benjamin Robinson of Barre, pub. 26 May 1799; she d. 13 June 1817, a. 41, and he m. her niece, Lucy P., dau. of James and granddaughter of Benjamin Robinson of Barre, 14 July 1822. His chil. were *Clarissa*, b. 26 Nov. 1799, d. 8 July 1803; *Gardner*, b. 21 Sep. 1801, d. 7 July 1803; *Alma*, b. — June 1803 or 2 July 1804, m. Dan W. Lane 6 Jan. 1824, and d. in 1875; *Elliott Beckwith*, b. 10 Dec. 1805; *Orin*, b. 2 Jan. 1808; *Anna Maria*, b. 18 Sep. 1810, m. Charles C. Spooner 17 Sep. 1829; *Israel Clapp*, b. 20 Sep. 1815; a child b. 14, and d. 16 May 1817. ORIN the f. was a farmer, res. on the homestead with his father, and d. 28 Oct. 1822, a. nearly 53; his w. Lucy P. m. James Browning 26 Nov. 1829.

4. ELLIOTT B., s. of Orin (3), m. Anna P. King of Barre 27 Mar. 1831; she d. 15 Aug. 1863, a. 59, and he m. Sylvia W. Thresher 27 Mar. 1866. His chil. were *Anna Maria*, b. 7 Dec. 1831, m. George W. Reed of Hubbardston 11 Nov. 1869; *Elliott B.*, b. 25 Dec. 1833, m. Isabella Worthington of Sterling, Ill., and d. at Coloma, Ill., 12 May 1862; *Samuel King*, b. 6 June 1836, m. Charlotte E. Ross of Barre 5 June 1876; *Joseph K.*, b. 9 Aug. 1838, d. 18 or 19 Oct. 1859. ELLIOTT B. the f. was a farmer, res. on the homestead, and d. 7 or 8 Oct. 1879.

5. ORIN, s. of Orin (3), m. Eunice G. Robinson of Barre (sister of his stepmother) 31 May 1828, and had *Orin Clapp*, b. 17 Nov. 1830; *Charles Lincoln*, b. 11 Sep. 1833; *Lucian Dwight*, b. 12 Jan. 1839. ORIN the f., a farmer, res. on the turnpike, near Great Meadow Brook, at the place marked "O. Trow" on the R. Map. He was a captain of militia, a selectman six years, and representative in 1861. His w. Eunice G. d. 11 Mar. 1866, a. 51.

6. ORIN CLAPP, s. of Orin (5), m. Nina Rosalie Petri at Baltimore, Md., 3 July 1857, and had *Rosa Eunice*, b. 3 Oct. 1858. ORIN C. the f. d. at Washington, D. C., 27 Oct. 1864.

7. CHARLES LINCOLN, s. of Orin (5), m. Abbie J., dau. of Gardner Bartholomew 10 Sep. 1855, and had *Samuel B.*, b. — May 1858, d. 3 Oct. 1858. CHARLES L. the f. rem. to Richmond, Ind., where he d. 15 Feb. 1877. His w. Abbie J. m. Joseph N. Lincoln of Hardwick.

8. LUCIAN DWIGHT, s. of Orin (5), m. Rhoda Griffin of Syracuse, N. Y., 13 Sep. 1865, and had *Fannie Eunice*, b. 7 Dec. 1867; *Puella Maud*, b. 3 Aug. 1869. LUCIAN DWIGHT the f., a farmer, res. with his father on the homestead, and has long been an energetic and very useful member of the school committee.

TRUESDALE, HARVEY E., of Holden, m. Anna Fellows, pub. 29 May 1850, and had, in Hk., *Etta Cordelia*, b. 4 May 1851; *Anna Lorinda*, b. 19 May 1853; *Mary Eliza*, b. 12 Dec. 1854, m. —— Stearns, and d. at Holden 3 Jan. 1877.

TUCKER, ROBERT, with wife Martha, and children *Seth*, *Eliphaz*, *Joshua*, and *Laban*, came from Norton to Brookfield, and thence to Hardwick in 1774, and res. at first in a house of George Field. ROBERT the f. d. in 1805; his w. Martha d. 30 Nov. 1809, a. 74.

2. SETH, s. of Robert (1), m. Miriam Arvin (Marvin?) 17 Dec. 1807, and had *Robert*, b. 22 Sep. 1808, m. Elizabeth W. Tucker of N. Sal., pub. 5 Mar. 1832, and d. at Ware 30 June 1879; *Bradford*, b. 26 May 1811; *John Marvin*,

b. 26 June 1817; *Ruth A.*, b. 26 Mar. 1820, m. William S. Bassett 1 Dec. 1836; *Seth Porter*, b. 5 May 1822, d. 22 June 1836; *Sarah E.*, b. 23 July 1826. SETH the f. d. 14 May 1853, a. 89; his w. Miriam d. 28 Aug. 1858, a. 72.

3. JOSHUA, s. of Robert (1), m. Sarah Johnson of Orange, pub. 10 Mar. 1799, rem. to N. Sal., and had, perhaps, *Ebenezer*, b. about 1807, d. here 22 Ap. 1857, a. 50; *Alfred*, b. about 1808; prob. *Joshua*, b. about 1813, d. here 22 Nov. 1836, a. 23.

4. LABAN, s. of Robert (1), m. Ruth Converse of Ware, pub. 16 Oct. 1803; she d. 30 Nov. 1809, a. 27, and he m. Anna Douglass 8 Nov. 1810. His chil. were *Seneca*, b. 13 Sep. 1805; *Cynthia*, b. 12 Jan. 1807, d. unm. 7 Feb. 1865; *Laban*, b. 30 Aug. 1808; *John Estes*, b. 7 Sep. 1811, m. Adeline Gilmore 17 Mar. 1846, and d. at N. Brk. 3 May 1872; *Mary Louisa*, b. 8 Jan. 1818. LABAN the f. d. 21 Nov. 1822, a. 51.

5. ALFRED, s. of Joshua (3), m. Mary ——; she d. 21 June 1838, a. 28, and he m. ——. His chil. were *Wilcutt*, b. about 1835, d. 20 Ap. 1858, a. 23; *Addison Frederick*, b. 11 Oct. 1845. ALFRED the f. d. 26 Ap. 1866, a. 58.

6. AVERY, m. Elizabeth W. ——, and had *Lomira*, b. —— 1840, d. 29 July 1844, a. 4; *Caroline E.*, b. —— 1842, d. 2 Aug. 1844, a. 2; *Freeman Sylvester*, b. 5 July 1843; a dau. b. 11 Ap. 1848, d. 17 Ap. 1848; *Sarah Elizabeth*, b. 7 Oct. 1850, d. 11 Jan. 1851.

7. HIRAM, m. Mary E. ——, and had *George Edward*, b. 2 Nov. 1843; *Maria E.*, b. 7 Ap. 1847, d. 28 Ap. 1848; *Mary L.*, b. 19 June 1849, m. John F. Lathrop of Newtonville 16 Oct. 1872; *William H.*, b. about 1851; *Frank B.*, b. 19 Oct. 1852, d. 20 Ap. 1858; *Frederick Hermon*, b. 16 Aug. 1856.

8. CHRISTOPHER C., m. Mary S. ——, and had *Ellen Jane*, b. 14 Aug. 1853.

9. ELIJAH F., m. Abbie J. Newcomb, pub. 19 Feb. 1856, and had *Emma Augusta*, b. 25 Nov. 1858, d. — Jan. 1859; *Willie Isaiah*, b. 9 Sep. 1862.

10. WILLIAM H., s. of Hiram (7), m. Dahliette M., dau. of Adonijah Dennis, 30 Ap. 1867; she d. 12 Aug. 1874, a. 32, and he m. Marion A. Spooner of Barre 6 June 1877. His chil. were *Frank W.*, b. 7 Mar. 1868; *Ethelyn D. M.*, b. 3 Dec. 1871; *Howard H.*, b. 24 Feb. 1879.

11. EPHRAIM, parentage not ascertained, m. Abigail ——, and had *Benjamin*, b. 6 May 1780; *Ephraim*, b. — Ap. 1784.

CLARINDA, of N. Brk., m. James Vokes, pub. 16 Nov. 1784.

TUPPER, MARTYN, Rev., was the first minister of the Calvinistic Society after its separation from the original Congregational Society in Hardwick. He was born at West Stafford, Conn., 6 Jan. 1800, grad. at Nassau Hall 1826, was ordained here 16 Ap. 1828, and resigned 29 Ap. 1835; he was installed at E. Longmeadow in Oct. 1835, and dismissed in Sept. 1849; after a short pastorate at Lanesboro' he was re-installed here 23 June 1852, and remained pastor of the church until 1 Sep. 1870, when he resigned, and rem. to Waverly, Ill. He m. Persis L. Peck of W. Stafford 13 Ap. 1828, had three chil. b. here, and others in Longmeadow: *Henry Martyn*, b. 10 June 1830, grad. A. C. 1859, pastor of the church and principal of the Shaw Coll. Inst. at Ontario, Ill.; *Augusta Lomira*, b. 4 Feb. 1832, m. Theodore E. Curtis of Waverly, Ill., 22 Dec. 1868; *Emily Peck*, b. 2 Oct. 1834, m. Dr. John C. Norris of Leipsic, Del., 14 July 1863, d. at Philadelphia 24 Dec. 1866, and was buried in the family lot in the new cemetery; *James Brainard Taylor*, b. at Longmeadow 8 Nov. 1839, grad. W. C. 1861, a lawyer; *Elizabeth H.*, b. at Longmeadow 22 Oct. 1844, d. here, unm., 26 Aug. 1864. Mrs. TUPPER d. at Waverly 7 July 1871, a. 67; about a year afterwards, her bereaved husband transported her remains to Hardwick, and deposited them by the side of their children; after which he visited his friends in Stafford, and there sickened and d. 31 July 1872. He was buried here among his people, to whom he had ministered more than twenty-five years.

TURNER, BATHSHEBA, m. Luther Burgess, 24 Dec. 1797. FRANCES M., m. Alpheus Johnson, pub. 28 Ap. 1853. CHARLES S., m. Alice A. Robinson 24 Nov. 1853. MUNROE, m. Clara Robinson 4 Mar. 1858. ABIGAIL, d. 5 May 1845, a. 19.

TUTE, JAMES, m. Kezia ——, and had *John*, b. 6 July 1732, bap. here 14 Aug. 1737; *James*, bap. 21 May 1738; *Sarah*, b. 5 Mar. 1740.

Mrs. CATHERINE m. William Richards, Roxbury, 28 Feb. 1830.

TYLER, REUBEN, m. Elizabeth Billings 3 Ap. 1831, and had *Reuben Cutler*, b. 4 Dec. 1832; *Sarah Clementine*, b. 4 July 1835; *Elmira Elizabeth*, b. 15 Aug. 1838; a dau., b. 1 Nov. 1847, d. 16 Nov. 1847. REUBEN the f. d. 21 Nov. 1859, a. nearly 52.

SALLY, of Western (Warren), m. Robert Field, pub. 20 Feb. 1802.

UTLEY, JAMES, m. Mary ——, and had *Elijah*, b. about 1784, m. Abigail, dau. of Maj. Moses Mandell, 25 Sep. 1820, kept an extensive livery-stable in Hanover Street, Boston, and d. 13 May 1824, a. 40; *Oren*, b. about 1787; prob. *Susan*, b. about 1790, m. Masa Bassett 10 May 1814, and d. 17 July 1820, a. 30; prob. *Hannah*, b. ——, m. Thomas Gorham of Barre 12 Dec. 1811; *Perley*, a partner in business with his brother in Boston; *James*, b. —— 1797, d. 4 June 1800, a. 3; *Amasa Sessions* and *Mary Miller*, twins, b. 3 Mar. 1800, both d. 13 Aug. 1803. JAMES the f. was a farmer, removed here from Wilbraham 1797, and res. on the road to Enfield, about three and a half miles from the Common, at the place wrongly marked "D. Utley" on the R. Map. He d. 15 Mar. 1812, a. 56; his w. Mary m. Moses Barnes of Brk., pub. 25 May 1813, and after his death returned, and d. here 13 Feb. 1843, a. 82.

2. OREN, s. of James (1), m. Hannah Dexter of Royalton, pub. 22 Sep. 1811; she d. 19 Mar. 1829, a. 41, and he m. Susan Adams of Brk., pub. 11 Mar. 1831. Some of his chil. were *Maria A.*, b. —— 1813, m. Braman B. Sibley of Enf. 31 Dec. 1833, and d. at Ware 9 May 1853, a. nearly 40; *James Dexter*, b. about 1815, d. 2 Feb. 1818, a. 2; *Louisa V.*, b. about 1818, m. John L. Lewis of Athol 25 Sep. 1843, and d. 16 Mar. 1878, a. 60; *Mary*, b. —— 1825, d. unm. 7 Dec. 1851, a. 26; *Hannah E.*, b. —— 1832, d. unm. 7 Oct. 1850, a. 18; *Henry A.*, b. —— 1836, d. at Brk. 7 Sep. 1857, a. 21. Besides these, *John T.*, *Rebecca W.*, wife of Zelotes H. Spooner, *George D.*, and *James B.*, are mentioned, as then living, in their father's will, 28 Nov. 1850. OREN the f., a farmer, res. on the homestead, and d. 30 Nov. 1850; his w. Susan d. 22 Mar. 1866, a. 70.

VOKES, ROBERT, m. Ruth Bangs of Barre 19 July 1793, and had *Charles*, b. about 1806, and prob. others.

2. EDMUND, m. Salome, dau. of Eastman Bolster, 3 May 1832, and had *Harriet N.*, b. about 1833, m. Laban Presho, Jr., 17 Mar. 1853; a son b. —— 1835, d. 11 Dec. 1839, a. 4. SALOME the m. d. 10 Sep. 1858, a. 45.

3. CHARLES, s. of Robert (1), m. Jerusha, dau. of Ebenezer Perry, 29 Oct. 1844, and had a son b. 7 May 1851, d. 8 May 1851; *Charles Perry*, b. 8 June 1856. JERUSHA the m. d. 30 May 1887, a. nearly 65.

4. CHARLES P., s. of Charles (3), m. Harriet S. Browning of N. Br. 4 Aug. 1878, and had *Harriet*, b. 12 Sep. 1879.

WAITE, RICHARD, m. Submit Thomas of N. Br., pub. 20 June 1771, and had *Thomas*, b. 10 Ap. 1772.

2. JOSEPH E., m. Sabra A. ——, and had *Frank Augustus*, b. 26 Aug. 1855, d. unm. 12 Dec. 1878, at W. Brookfield.

DAVID, m. Bathsheba, dau. of Joshua Crowell, 23 Nov. 1769. PHINEAS, of N. Br., m. Patty Anderson, pub. 20 Sep. 1801. SYLVINA, dau. of David, m. Ashbel Rice, pub. 21 June 1807. ASA J., of Athol, m. Mary M. Richards, pub. 9 Dec. 1851. SAMUEL, d. 7 Feb. 1838, a. 60. ABIGAIL, a widow, d. 28 Dec. 1866, a. 74.

WALKER, EBENEZER, s. of Philip of Rehoboth, m. Dorothy Abell, and had, among others, *Caleb*, b. 30 Oct. 1706.

2. CALEB, s. of Ebenezer (1), m. Abigail, dau. of Dr. Ezra Dean of Taunton, and had *Caleb*, b. 14 Feb. 1728–9, m. Elizabeth Perrin, and d. 4 Mar. 1753; *Abraham*, b. 1 Nov. 1731, m. Jemima Bishop, and d. 17 Nov. 1774; *Abigail*, b. 11 Feb. 1733–4, m. Jonathan Carpenter, and d. 2 Feb. 1817; *Abel*, b. 11 May 1736; *Comfort*, b. 26 May 1739, m. Mehetabel Robinson, and d. 14 Ap. 1815. CALEB the f. res. in Rehoboth, and d. 3 Ap. 1768, a. 61; his w. Abigail was b. 10 Dec. 1704, and d. 1 Jan. 1795.

3. ABEL, s. of Caleb (2), m. Lois Read 14 Ap. 1763; she d. 24 Mar. 1801, and he m. her sister, Bathsheba Read, pub. 15 Nov. 1801. His chil. were

Cyril, b. 9 Feb. 1764, d. here unm. 30 Dec. 1849; *Lois*, b. 18 Oct. 1766, m. Lewis Baker of Pelh. — Feb. 1787, and d. 12 Aug. 1853; *Abel*, b. 27 Sep. 1770; *William*, b. 29 Oct. 1772; *Abigail*, b. 13 Aug. 1775, d. unm. at Somers, Conn., 16 Mar. 1853; *Thomas*, b. 18 Nov. 1777, a printer, m. Mary Eaton of Worc., rem. to Rome, N. Y., 1799, and was president of the Bank of Utica, and of a savings bank; *Huldah*, b. 29 Oct. 1780, m. Daniel Sexton of Somers 18 June 1812, d. 19 Nov. 1858. ABEL the f. was a Revolutionary soldier, and a farmer, rem. from Rehoboth to Hardwick in 1779, res. near Gr., and d. 17 Feb. 1819, a. nearly 83; his w. Bathsheba d. 27 Jan. 1819, a. 73.

4. ABEL, s. of Abel (3), m. Mary, dau. of Jesse Snow, 26 Jan. 1797, and had *Alvah*, b. 9 Ap. 1798, m. Vesta Whitcomb of Gr. 8 Sep. 1821, rem. to Oswego, N. Y.; *Horace*, b. 12 Oct. 1799, d. 2 Sep. 1803; *Otis*, b. 28 Dec. 1800, d. 26 Aug. 1803; *Cyril*, b. 6 Dec. 1802, d. 23 Aug. 1803; *Mary*, b. 27 Aug. 1804; *Harriet*, b. 4 Nov. 1806, m. John S. Hall, 15 Sep. 1830, rem. to Columbus, O.; *Vashti*, b. 24 Sep. 1808; *Abel*, b. 14 Dec. 1810, m. Sarah S. Allen of Brimfield 14 Oct. 1835, rem. to Elgin, Ill. ABEL the f. was killed by the fall of a rock 15 Nov. 1811; his w. Mary m. —— Crawford, and d. in Gr. 18 Feb. 1865, a. nearly 90.

5. WILLIAM, s. of Abel (3), m. Eunice, dau. of Col. Thomas Powers of Gr., pub. 4 Sep. 1804; she d. 29 May 1828, and he m. Mrs. Mercy Brown of Warren, pub. 16 Jan. 1830. His chil were *Lois Reed*, b. 9 July 1805, m. Joseph Cobb, Jr., of Boston 30 Dec. 1830; *Thomas Powers*, b. 7 Jan. 1807, m. Mary Gibbs of Gr., pub. 26 Feb. 1836; *William*, b. 9 May 1810, d. 10 May 1819; *Susan*, b. 8 Oct. 1813, m. Hammond Hunt 30 Ap. 1839, and (2d) Joshua Conkey of Rochester, N. Y., 3 Jan. 1848; *James Hervey*, b. 14 July 1818; *Eunice Elvira*, b. 1 Aug. 1820, m. John Allen of Bel. 30 Oct. 1838. WILLIAM the f. was a farmer, lieutenant of militia, and selectman three years; he res. on the turnpike near Greenwich Village, at the place marked "Lt. Walker" on the R. Map, and d. 30 Jan. 1852, a. 79.

6. JAMES H., s. of William (5), m. Sarah McClintock of Ware, pub. 2 Nov. 1852, and had *Fanny Priscilla*, b 27 Sep. 1855; *William Henry*, b. 30 Nov. 1857; *George Benjamin*, b. 9 Sep. 1862; *Mary Lois*, b. 28 Mar. 1864; *Susan Eliza*, b. 9 Sep. 1867, d. 24 May 1872. JAMES H. the f., a farmer, res. on the homestead, was selectman three years, and representative in 1882.

7. ELIAS, parentage not ascertained, by w. ——, had *Samuel*, *Leonard Robinson*, and *David Higgins*, all bap. (with others) 27 Oct. 1782; he m. (2d) Sarah, dau. of John Aiken, 27 Feb. 1772, and had *Elias*, b. 25 Mar. 1773, d. young; *Sarah*, b. 19 May 1775, bap. 27 Oct. 1782; *Susanna*, b. 12 Ap. 1778, m. Silas Guild of Lebanon, Conn., pub. 29 Aug. 1796; *Hannah*, b. 23 Sep. 1780; *Bathsheba*, b. 9 Mar. 1783; *Jerusha*, b. 17 Mar. 1785; *Elias*, b. 4 Sep. 1787; *Fanny*, b. 17 Mar. 1790; *Ruby*, b. 8 Nov. 1792.

8. ARAD, had *Mary A.*, b. at Royalton 5 Aug. 1835, m. George Warner 17 Oct. 1855, and d. 22 Nov. 1856; *James*, b. here 16 May 1839, d. 11 Ap. 1840; *Sarah Josephine*, b. here 9 Mar. 1845, d. 10 Ap. 1849.

SIMEON, m. Judith Goss 10 Oct. 1751. PATIENCE, of Pet., m. Silas Johnson 27 Nov. 1766. HANNAH, of Pet., m. Robert Saunders, pub. 30 Aug. 1768. HANNAH, m. Isaac Nye 29 Nov. 1770. ELIZABETH, of N. Sal., m. Josiah Robinson, pub. 2 Nov. 1806. JOHN, of Gr., m. Elizabeth Smith 19 Feb. 1807. MARY, of Barre, m. Job Dexter, pub. 1 Nov. 1811. HELEN C., dau. of Adam, d. 8 June 1869, a. nearly 18.

WALLACE, EDMUND (otherwise written Wallis), m. Mercy ——, and had *Sally*, b. 15 Aug. 1783.

2. JOSEPH, m. Clara J. Wallace 3 Dec. 1872, and had *Leroy*, b. 19 Sep. 1879.

NAHUM, d. 30 Aug. 1844, a. 64. MARY, m. Joseph Baker of Gardner 17 Mar. 1847. Mrs. MARY A., of Barre, m. Edwin Beeman 7 Dec. 1860. CARRIE, of Barre, m. Charles L. Warner, pub. 24 Jan. 1861.

WALTON, THOMAS, m. Betsey Haskins, pub. 19 Aug. 1810.

WARD, ALBERT B., m. Anna O. ——, and had *Charles Albert*, b. 16 Oct.

1869; *Anna Francesca*, b. 25 Feb. 1878; a dau. b. 30 Dec. 1879; *Florence M.*, b. 14 Oct. 1881.

2. WILLIAM FRANCIS, m. Mary ——, and had *William Francis*, b. 20 May 1873.

WILLIAM, of Ware, m. Melinda Bassett 10 Mar. 1831. SARAH, m. Anson Bassett 28 Nov. 1848. JOHN, d. 4 Sep. 1856, a. 56. NATHAN (b. at Athol), d. 30 Aug. 1872, a. 84.

WARDWELL, STEPHEN K., m. Balarah (or Billerah), dau. of Col. Thomas Powers of Gr., and had *Elvira*, b. — Feb. 1813, d. 16 Aug. 1814; *Catherine E.*, b. 26 Nov. 1814, m. William Edwards of Southbridge 27 Nov. 1834, and d. 23 Jan. 1876; an infant, b. ——, d. 1 Dec. 1816; *Lucia*, twin, b. 24 July 1818, m. George F. Maxwell of Philadelphia 9 Nov. 1840; *Marcia*, twin, b. 24 July 1818, m. Henry Conover of Sandusky City, O., 23 Feb. 1837; *Mary*, b. 4 Ap. 1821, m. John Blair of Philadelphia 5 Oct. 1841, and d. at Southbridge 3 Jan. 1875. STEPHEN K. the f., born at Somers, Conn., was a successful physician and a remarkably skilful surgeon; in both capacities, he had an extensive practice. He rem. here in the spring of 1814, on the death of Dr. Beckwith, and res. on the Common several years, afterwards about three quarters of a mile northerly, on the turnpike, at the place marked "Dr. Wardwell" on the R. Map. He d. 8 Oct. 1844, a. 55; his w. Balarah d. at Southbridge 8 Dec. 1873, a. 84.

WARE, SAMUEL, m. Mrs. Mary Belding, 3 Nov. 1757. By a former wife he had several children, one of whom, *Jesse*, was bap. here 9 Sep. 1750. SAMUEL the f. res. on the east side of the river, now N. Br., and was deacon of the N. Br. Church.

2. WILLIAM, by w. ——, had *Mary*, bap. 15 Mar. 1752.

WARNER, WILLIAM, came from England, and settled in Ipswich as early as 1637. He brought with him three children: *John*, b. about 1616; *Daniel*; and *Abigail*, who m. Thomas Wells, and d. in July 1671. WILLIAM the f. was living 29 Oct. 1654.

2. JOHN, s. of William (1), m. ——, who d. ——, and he m. Priscilla, dau. of Mark Symonds, about 1655; his chil. were *Samuel*, b. about 1640; *John*, b. about 1643, d. in Springf. 21 Jan. 1724; *Mark*, b. about 1646, d. in Northampton 3 May 1738, a. 92; *Nathaniel*, b. about 1650, was in Brookfield 1673, and d. in Hadley 15 Jan. 1714; *Daniel*, b. about 1653, d. in Ipswich 8 June 1659; *Joseph*, b. 15 Aug. 1657, d. 18 June 1658; *Mehetabel*, b. 16 Ap. 1659, d. in Hadley 12 June 1678; *Daniel*, b. 16 Ap. 1661, d. —— 1688; *Eleazar*, b. 13 Nov. 1662, d. in Hadley 8 May 1729; *Priscilla*, b. about 1664, m. Thomas Cummings of Dunstable, 19 Dec. 1688. JOHN the f. rem. from Ipswich to Brookfield before 1670, and was styled one of the "principal inhabitants." When that town was destroyed by the Indians in 1675, he retreated, with his younger children, to Hadley, where some of his children had already settled, and where he d. soon after 17 May 1692.

3. SAMUEL, s. of John (2), m. Mercy Swan, in Ipswich, 21 Oct. 1662; she d. in Dunstable 3 Ap. 1683, and he m. Mary Swallow 4 May, 1684. His chil. were *Priscilla*, b. 25 Sep. 1666, d. young; *Samuel*, b. 5 July 1668, settled in Pomfret, Conn.; *John*, b. 2 Aug. 1670, d. 14 July 1671; *Dorothy*, b. 2 June 1672; *Sarah*, b. 28 May 1674; *Richard*, b. 13 Aug. 1676, res. in Groton, and d. about 1767, a. 91 (his will, dated 10 June 1763, was proved 15 Oct. 1767); *Eleazar*, b. 27 Jan. 1686; *Priscilla*, b. ——. All these chil. were prob. b. in Ipswich, except the last two, who were b. in Dunstable. SAMUEL the f. res. at Brookfield (prob. without his family) in 1673, when he was one of the petitioners for the incorporation of the town, and he may have been present when the town was destroyed in 1675; he certainly testified, 26 Mar. 1678 (describing himself as about 38 years old), that he formerly owned land there. He was one of the early settlers of Dunstable, and was one of the only fourteen proprietors resident there 30 Nov. 1682, and one of the seven male members of the church, at its organization 16 Dec. 1685. He bought a farm 14 Oct. 1689, in Groton, where he prob. d. about 1703.

4. ELEAZAR, s. of Samuel (3), m. Prudence, dau. of Thomas Barnes of

Brookfield 4 Dec. 1722, and had *Mary*, b. 21 Ap. 1724, m. Thomas Robinson of Hk. 23 Nov. 1744, and d. 7 Aug. 1812; *Phineas*, b. 11 Oct. 1726, a deacon in N. Br., m. Martha Nash of Hatfield, pub. 29 Dec. 1751, and d. 25 Mar. 1795; *Patience*, b. 26 Mar. 1729, m. Beriah Hawes, pub. 15 Nov. 1750; *Warham*, b. 1 Nov. 1730; *Eleazar*, b. 26 Feb. 1733-4, a soldier in the French War, and d. in service, at Fort Massachusetts, 20 Nov. 1755; *Martin*, b. 2 Sep. 1735, settled at Norwich; *Silas*, b. 21 May 1737, a soldier in the French War, d. of wounds received in battle, 24 Aug. 1760; *Samuel*, b. 7 Oct. 1739, res. in N. Br., m. Unity Ware 19 Ap. 1769; *Noah*, b. 9 Feb. 1741-2, a soldier in the French War, killed in battle —— 1760; *Prudence*, b. 14 June 1744, m. Daniel Eldridge 10 Feb. 1767. ELEAZAR the f. devoted several years, in early life, to the service of his country. For a brief sketch of his military career, and of his single-handed deadly encounter with an Indian, see page 13 of this History. His martial spirit was inherited by his sons, seven of whom served in the French War,—three at the sacrifice of life. After his marriage, at the mature age of thirty-six years, he resided first on the westerly side of the road from N. Br. to W. Brk., and on the southerly side of the brook at the head of Ditch Meadow, then in Brk., but now included in New Braintree. About 1730 he removed to the place long known as the "Perez Cobb Farm,"[1] on the road to Rutland, about a mile east of the Furnace Village; his farm embraced a part of the Indian fort, or stronghold, at Winnimisset. After the settlement of Hk. he was one of the most active citizens, and one of the twelve men who united to form the first church; he was also selectman six years, assessor six years, and often moderator of the town meetings. He d. 28 Feb. 1776, a. 90; his w. Prudence d. 25 Feb. 1770, a. 65.

5. WARHAM, s. of Eleazar (4), m. Hannah Ware, and had *Willard*, b. 23 May 1759, d. —— 1854; *Maribel*, b. 29 Mar. 1761, d. young; *Noah*, b. 12 Sep. 1762, d. 20 Jan. 1859; *Beriah*, b. 2 Ap. 1764, d. young; *Unity*, b. 8 May 1766; m. Dr. —— Fletcher; *Lewis*, b. 22 May 1768; *Royal*, b. 30 Ap. 1770, d. 24 Sep. 1854 (two of his dau. d. here unm.: Alma, d. 2 or 3 Mar. 1869, a. 59; Mary, d. 18 or 19 Jan. 1878, a. 65); *Hannah*, b. 3 July 1772, m. John Smith 1 Sep. 1793; *Justus*, b. 11 June 1774, d. here 8 Dec. 1866 (his s. Franklin S., b. in Burlington, Vt., long a Southern planter and a colonel,[2] d. here 25 Dec. 1865, a. 66); *Susan*, b. 30 Oct. 1776, m. Thomas Paige 17 June, 1798, and d. in Compton, C. E., 8 Dec. 1863; *Samuel*, b. 22 Aug. 1778; *Sally*, b. 18 July 1781, m. Ninian Clark of Hancock, N. H.; *Prudence*, b. 27 July

[1] He sold this farm to Perez Cobb 4 May 1764, and prob. res. with his son *Warham*, during the remainder of his life.

[2] Like other Southern planters, Mr. Warner held slaves. When he returned to New England, about 1850, with shattered health, he brought with him one of the house-servants, who faithfully ministered to his wants as long as he lived. The following account, which was published in the *Barre Gazette*, Ap. 3, 1874, has reference to this subject, and is presumed to be substantially correct: "Hardwick has a real slave romance. 'Aunt Judie Warner,' as she is familiarly known, an aged negress who came to Hardwick some twenty-five years ago, with her helpless master, Colonel Frank Warner, and nursed him until his death, several years ago, when he left her eight hundred dollars, is going back to his old home in Arkansas. Within a few months she has learned that her children, sold from her when young, and whom she has mourned as dead, are living, and that one daughter is about to be married; so she is going on to the wedding. Charles P. Aiken, with whom she has been living, accompanies her on this pilgrimage."

Desiring to know the result of this matter, I addressed the Town Clerk, who ascertained for me the following particulars: Mr. Aiken left Hardwick with "Aunt Judy" April 6, 1874, and in due time she arrived at her old home in Lewisville, La Fayette Co., Arkansas. Here she found her children, but soon became homesick. She therefore "bought a home for her children, and retraced her steps to Hardwick, arriving there only a few days after Mr. Aiken, May 24, 1874, taking with her a daughter and grandson, expecting to have a home with Mr. Aiken." He could not easily accommodate so large a family; and therefore she "kept house at the Old Furnace until the next autumn, and then went back with her daughter and child to Arkansas; she lived there until the summer of 1875, when she went to Cleveland, Ohio, to the house of a brother of Colonel Warner, where she died in the autumn of 1882." Such is the conclusion of a "real slave romance," and the only one of its kind connected with the history of Hardwick.

1784, m. Daniel Record of Barre, and d. here 8 Ap. 1876. This family was remarkable for longevity; at least four of the number attained more than ninety years of age, and several others exceeded eighty. WARHAM the f. was a farmer, res. in N. Br., about half a mile from Furnace Village, and d. 4 Dec. 1817, a. 87; his w. Hannah d. at Hancock, N. H., ——, a. 90.

6. ANDREW[1] came from England as early as 1632, and settled in Cambridge; he rem. to Hartford about 1637, and thence to Hadley in 1659, where he d. 18 Dec. 1684. His chil. were *Andrew*, m. Rebecca Fletcher, and d. in Middletown, Conn., 26 Jan. 1681; *Robert*, m. Elizabeth Grant, and (2d) Mrs. Deliverance Rockwell; he d. in Middletown 10 Ap. 1690; *Jacob*, m. Rebecca ——, and (2d) Elizabeth Goodman, and d. in Hadley 29 Sept. or Nov. 1711; *Daniel*; *Isaac*, b. about 1645, m. Sarah Boltwood, res. in Northfield and in Deerfield, where he d. in 1691; *Ruth*, living in 1677; a dau. who m. John (or Daniel) Pratt; *Mary*, m. John Steele, and (2d) William Hills; *John*, res. in Middletown.

7. DANIEL, s. of Andrew (6), m. Mary ——; she d. 19 Sep. 1672, and he m. Martha, dau. of Robert Boltwood. His chil. were *Mary*, b. 24 Feb. 1663; *Sarah*, b. about 1665, m. Isaac Sheldon 25 Nov. 1685; *Daniel*, b. about 1666; *Andrew*, b. 24 June 1667; *Anna*, b. 17 Nov. 1669; m. Isaac Hubbard; *Mary*, b. 19 Sep. 1672, perhaps m. Samuel Sheldon; *Hannah*, b. 24 Jan. 1675, m. Samuel Ingram of Hatfield 14 Oct. 1696; *John*, b. — Ap. 1677, rem. to Wethersfield, Conn., and d. in 1714; *Abraham*, b. 20 Dec. 1678; *Samuel*, b. 13 Ap. 1680; *Ebenezer*, b. 5 Nov. 1681; *Mehetabel*, b. 1 Oct. 1683, m. Preserved Clapp 21 Jan. 1703; *Elizabeth*, b. ——, m. Thomas Wells of Haddam, Conn., 26 Dec. 1705; *Esther*, b. 15 Dec. 1686, m. Samuel Henry 26 June 1707; *Martha*, b. 3 Ap. 1688, d. 25 Nov. 1689; *Nathaniel*, b. 15 Oct. 1690. DANIEL the f. res. in Hatfield, and d. 30 Ap. 1692; his w. Martha d. 22 Sep. 1710. (Thus far I have been guided chiefly by Judd's *History of Dudley* in regard to the posterity of Andrew Warner.)

8. DANIEL, s. of Daniel (7), m. Mary, dau. of John Hubbard, 12 Dec. 1688, and had *Mary*, b. 31 Aug. 1689, d. 24 Feb. 1692; *Daniel*, b. 1 Mar. 1693, res. in Hatfield, and prob. m. Thankful Billings, and (2d) Elizabeth Adams of Suffield, Conn., 29 Dec. 1719; *Mary*, b. 17 Aug. 1694, m. Joseph Wait 22 Sep. 1720; *Hannah*, b. —— 1700, prob. m. Samuel Billings, rem. to Hk., and d. 5 Mar. 1767; *Jonathan*, b. about 1704; *Sarah*, b. 11 Oct. 1707; *Joseph*, b. 18 Jan. 1710. DANIEL the f. res. in Hatfield, but in his old age rem. to Hk., where some of his chil. had settled, and d. here 12 Mar. 1754, "in the 88th year of his age;" his head-stone remains in the old burial-ground. With the exception of Deac. John White, he was prob. born earlier than any other person of English descent who has ever died in Hardwick.

9. JONATHAN, s. of Daniel (8), m. Bathsheba, dau. of Ichabod Allis of Hatfield, 8 Aug. 1733, and had *Daniel*, b. 22 Dec. 1734; *Mary*, b. 23 Feb. 1736–7, m. Zurishaddai Doty 4 Dec. 1755; *Bathsheba*, b. 7 Oct. or Nov. 1738, d. 5 Dec. 1740; *Lydia*, b. 3 Nov. 1740, m. Dr. Challis Safford 8 Feb. 1760, and (2d) Hon. Jonas Fay of Bennington 20 Nov. 1777; *Sarah*, b. 1 Nov. 1742, m. Thomas Wheeler 8 Sep. 1762, and (2d) Capt. Elijah Warner 30 Dec. 1807; she d. in Gr. — Dec. 1837, a. 95; *Jonathan*, b. 14 July 1744; *Bathsheba*, b. 24 July 1746, m. Eliakim Spooner, pub. 29 July 1764, and d. 29 Jan. 1831; *Lucy*, b. 10 May 1748, m. Asa Hatch 23 Jan. 1766; *Rhoda*, b. 3 Mar. 1752, d. 15 Sep. 1753; *Rhoda*, b. 11 or 17 Nov. 1754, m. Robert McIntyre 26 Nov. 1772, and (2d) Jonathan Lynde of Pet. 26 Ap. 1778. JONATHAN the f. rem. early from Hatfield to Hk., and res. a few years in the southwest part of the town, but in 1743 bought the large farm adjoining the Common, which long remained in his family. He was an energetic, thrifty man, dealt largely in real estate, kept a store and tavern at the south end of the Common, was selectman five years, commencing in 1738, and treasurer

[1] ANDREW may have been brother of WILLIAM (1), but I have discovered no proof of the fact. It is observable that both had sons *John* and *Daniel*, and a similarity of names occurs among their later posterity.

nineteen years, from 1744 to 1762 inclusive. He d. 28 May 1763, a. 59; his w. Bathsheba m. John Burt of Springf. 4 June 1765.

10. JOSEPH, s. of Daniel (8), m. Mary, dau. of John Hubbard of Hatfield; she d. ——, and he m. Mary Whipple 14 Nov. 1764; she d. ——, and he m. Mrs. Rebecca Spooner 12 Nov. 1781. His chil. were *Elijah*, b. about 1739; prob. *Stephen*, b. ——, who m. Lois Goss 26 May 1768, and (2d, after his removal to Granby) Mrs. Damaris Church 13 Nov. 1771; *Mary*, b. 1 Nov. 1747, perhaps m. Timothy Moore 26 May 1768;[1] *Anna*, b. 2 May 1750, m. James Paige 25 Oct. 1770; *Hannah*, b. 7 Oct. 1752, m. John Bradish, Jr., 4 Mar. 1773; *John*, b. 2 Ap. 1755; *Persis*, b. 22 Oct. 1757; *Moses*, bap. 27 Ap. 1760; *Huldah*, b. 12 July 1762; *Mary*, b. —— 1771, d. unm. in Cummington 22 Dec. 1863, a. 92. JOSEPH the f. rem. from Hatfield to Hk. before 1747, was a farmer, and res. on the road to Enfield, somewhat more than a mile from the Common, at the place marked "Constant Ruggles" on the R. Map. He was captain of militia, and led his company in an expedition for the relief of Fort William Henry, in Aug. 1757, during the French War. He was selectman and assessor in 1770; but rem. and was recommended to the church in "No. 8" (now Cummington) 4 Sep. 1774.

11. DANIEL, s. of Jonathan (9), m. Mary Wright 31 May 1758, and had *Lydia*, b. 12 Aug. 1759, m. Samuel French 23 Feb. 1775; *Daniel*, b. 28 July 1761; *Jonathan*, b. 13 Sep. 1763; *Mary*, b. 19 Oct. 1765, m. Rev. Solomon Aiken of Dracut, pub. 12 Oct. 1788, and d. at Hardwick, Vt., 30 Oct. 1820; *Justus*, b. 22 May 1768; *Alpha*, b. 1 Dec. 1770, m. Lydia Cobb 14 Jan. 1796, settled in Hardwick, Vt., was colonel of militia and an innkeeper "for nearly 60 years; this house was one of the most noted in Vermont, and many a traveller would ride a little later, or go a little farther, to get to Warner's."[2] He was also a representative in the General Assembly. He rem. to Chillicothe in 1853, and d. there in Jan. 1854; *Wright*, b. 11 Sep. 1773; *Charles Lee*, b. 30 Nov. 1776; *Betsey*, bap. 23 Ap. 1780, m. Levi Whipple 21 Aug. 1803; *Patience*, b. 2 Dec. 1782. DANIEL the f. was a farmer, and res. near Gilbertville, at the place marked "Mr. May" on the R. Map. He was a soldier in the French War, and afterwards captain of militia. He was a member of the Committee of Correspondence five years, selectman six years, and assessor ten years. About the year 1807 he rem. to Ohio, and d. at Putnam in the summer of 1823, a. nearly 89.

12. JONATHAN, s. of Jonathan (9), m. *Hannah*, dau. of Paul Mandell 5 Feb. 1766, and had *Susanna*, b. 10 July 1767, m. Capt. Artemas Howe of N. Br. 16 Feb. 1786, and (2d) Gov. Moses Robinson of Bennington, Vt., where she d. 2 Ap. 1844; *Bathsheba*, b. 25 Mar. 1769, m. Luke Brown 8 June 1798, and d. at Springf. about 1855; *Hannah*, b. 20 Feb. 1771, m. Pelatiah Hitchcock 17 July 1791; *Betsey*, b. 26 Mar. 1773, d. 18 Aug. 1778; *Joseph Warren*, b. 13 July 1775, d. 9 Aug. 1777; *Fanny*, b. 14 Sep. 1778, m. John A. Parker of Roxbury 23 Feb. 1801; *Jonathan*, b. 13 June 1781; *Harriet*, b. 15 Jan. 1783, m. Alexander Holton of Westminster, Vt., 12 Oct. 1806, and was living in 1879; *Alma*, b. 15 May 1785; *Mary White*, b. 7 Mar. 1787, m. —— Bradley; *Louisa*, bap. 30 May 1790, m. Eliphaz Jones of Enf., pub. 21 Aug. 1825, d. at Springf. 2 Mar. 1872; *William Augustus*, bap. 7 June 1795, grad. H. C. 1815, a lawyer of high reputation in Boston, but d. 23 Dec. 1830, at the early age of 35. JONATHAN the f. inherited the homestead, cultivated the large farm, and managed the affairs of the store and tavern; but a large portion of his time was devoted to the public service. At the commencement of the Revolutionary contest he was lieutenant of the South Company; he was elected captain of that company 22 Sep. 1774, and captain also of the company of "minute-men" which was organized on that day. At the election of regimental officers in the next October he became colonel, and was pro-

[1] There is some confusion here; the simultaneous marriage indicates that *Mary*, who m. Timothy Moore, was sister to *Stephen*; yet another *Mary*, b. in 1771, is described in the record of her death as b. in Hk., and as the dau. of Joseph and Mary (Whipple) Warner. Perhaps Mrs. Moore d. before 1771, when the second *Mary* was born.

[2] *Vermont Hist. Magazine*, i. 334.

moted to the office of brigadier-general, 13 Feb. 1776, by the General Court. On the reorganization of the militia, in 1781, after the adoption of the Constitution, he was elected major-general, to which office he was re-commissioned 3 Ap. 1786, under a new arrangement; he faithfully performed the arduous duties of his office during the Revolutionary War and the Shays Insurrection, and was honorably discharged, on his voluntary resignation, in Dec. 1789. He was also actively engaged in civil affairs; being a member of the Committee of Correspondence three years, selectman three years, representative five years, senator nine years, and a member of the Council two years. His active and useful life was brought to a close 7 Jan. 1803, at Craftsbury, Vt., whither he had gone for the transaction of business; his w. Hannah retained her residence at the homestead until extreme old age, when she entered the family of her youngest dau. at Enf., where she d. — Aug. 1839, a. 91.

13. ELIJAH, s. of Joseph (10), m. Submit, dau. of John Wells, 14 Jan. 1762, she d. ——, and he m. Rachel Sampson of Templeton 15 May 1786; she d. 16 May 1807, and he m. Mrs. Sarah Wheeler (his cousin) 30 Dec. 1807. His chil. were *Abel*, b. 29 Ap. 1763, m. Sally Cook (at Kingston) 15 Feb. 1786; *David*, b. 10 Mar. 1765; *Elijah*, b. 10 June 1767; *Lydia*, b. 18 Aug. 1769, d. young; *Giles*, b. 3 Dec. 1771; *Lydia*, bap. 19 June 1774, m. Charles Gilbert of Chester 25 Feb. 1796; *Electa*, bap. 15 Sep. 1776, m. —— White, and d. at Phillipston 4 Mar. 1864; *Charles*, bap. 5 Feb. 1780; *Polly*, bap. 21 July 1782, prob. d. young; *Persis*, b. about 1783, m. Noah Joy of Plainfield 21 Jan. 1806, d. at Hawley 23 Oct. 1853, a. 70; *Olive*, b. ——, m. Pyam Mitchell of Cummington 27 Oct. 1807; *Patty*, b. ——; *Rachel*, b. about 1788, m. Joseph Robinson 2 Ap. 1811, d. 6 Oct. 1863, a. 75; *John Whitcomb*, bap. 2 Oct. 1791, killed at a military parade by an iron ramrod shot through his head during a sham-fight, 2 Oct. 1811 (see BENJAMIN W. CHILDS); *Submit Wells*, bap. 7 Dec. 1794, d. 9 Sep. 1828. ELIJAH the f. was a farmer, and res. on the road to Enf., three and a quarter miles from the Common, at the place marked "G. Warner" on the R. Map. He was captain of militia, selectman six years, and d. 24 Jan. 1819, a. 80. In his will, dated 2 Jan. 1810, he named thirteen chil. then living.

14. JONATHAN, s. of Daniel (11), m. Sally, dau. of John Paige, 25 Feb. 1789; she d. 11 June 1807, a. 38, and he m. Annis, wid. of Joel Marsh, 18 Oct. 1807. His chil. were *Mary*, b. 3 Dec. 1789, m. William Robinson 28 Nov. 1809, and d. at Barre 13 Oct. 1866; a child b. ——, d. 26 Mar. 1792, a. 6 days; *Moses Mandell*, b. 30 Mar. 1793; *Jonathan*, b. 28 Mar. 1795, settled in Hardwick, Vt.; *Lewis*, b. — Jan. 1797, d. 1 Ap. 1797; *Daniel*, b. 2 July 1799; *Lewis*, b. 1 June 1801; *William Augustus*, b. 8 Jan. 1804; *Levi Whipple*, b. 7 June 1806. (In these dates I follow the family record, which differs somewhat from that of the town.) JONATHAN the f. was a judicious and thrifty farmer; he inherited the homestead, but after his second marriage bought the Marsh Farm, and erected a new house on the easterly road to Gilbertville, at the place marked "A. Warner" on the R. Map. He was ensign of militia, selectman three years, and d. 1 July 1831, a. about 68; his w. Annis d. at Springf. 17 May 1859, a. nearly 94.

15. JUSTUS, s. of Daniel (11), m. Catherine Hall of N. Br. 29 Dec. 1791, and had *William Augustus*, b. — Nov. 1792, d. 26 Feb. 1793. JUSTUS the f. d. 18 May 1793, a. 25.

16. GILES, s. of Elijah (13), m. Betsey Sampson 4 May 1809; she d. 18 Jan. 1823, a. 49, and he m. Mary Staples of Pres., pub. 12 Ap. 1824. His chil. were *Rachel*, b. 14 May 1811, m. Loring Gilbert of Ware 5 May 1831; a child b. ——, d. 4 Sep. 1813, a. one month; *Mary Abigail*, b. 7 Feb. 1825, m. Charles Hathaway 24 Ap. 1845, and d. 28 Nov. 1847; *Betsey Sampson*, b. 3 Mar. 1827, d. 11 Sep. 1828; *Francis Giles*, b. 13 Ap. 1829; *Caroline Maria*, b. 9 Nov. 1832, m. West Paige 13 Dec. 1848, and (2d) Henry Paige of Providence 22 Aug. 1859; *George Elias*, b. 29 May 1834, a conductor on the Ware River Railroad; *James Loring*, b. 16 Feb. 1837, d. 18 Feb. 1874. GILES the f. was a farmer, and inherited the homestead. He d. 20 Nov. 1847, a. 76; his w. Mary d. 28 Nov. 1862, a. 66.

17. MOSES MANDELL, s. of Jonathan (14), m. Orrel Smith of Palmer, pub. 30 Dec. 1816, and had *Sarah Ann*, b. 15 Feb. 1818, d. in Dixon, Ill., 18 Feb. 1853; *Henry S.*, b. 27 July 1819, res. in Sterling, Ill.; *Clarissa S.*, b. 2 Aug. 1821; *Moses M.*, b. 1 Mar. 1824, res. in Sterling; *Orrel M.*, b. 22 Ap. 1826; *Mary L.*, b. 1 Ap. 1828, d. 4 Oct. 1830; *Mary L.*, b. 16 June 1830; *Delphia M.*, b. 20 June 1832, m. Calvin W. Mann 2 Ap. 1856; *George P.*, b. 22 July 1834. MOSES M. the f. was a farmer, and res. on the road between the roads to Gilbertville and to Ware, nearly two miles from the Common, at the place marked "Mr. Warner" on the R. Map. In 1838 he rem. to Sterling, Ill., and d. in Lyndon, Ill., 31 Jan. 1876, a. nearly 83; his w. Orrel survived, and res. with her sons at Sterling.

18. DANIEL, s. of Jonathan (14), m. Nancy, dau. of Deac. Henry Fish, 29 May 1821, and had *Henry Fish*, b. 28 Feb. 1822, d. unm. 22 Sep. 1868; twins, b. and d. in 1825; *Elizabeth Ann*, b. 6 Sep. 1826, d. unm. 19 Nov. 1850; *George*, b. 14 Ap. 1830; *Lucy Jane*, b. 15 June 1835, m. Samuel A. Howe of Barre 8 Jan. 1859. DANIEL the f. was a farmer, and res. near the central bridge over Ware River, at the place marked "D. Warner" on the R. Map; he afterwards bought the estate on the easterly road to Gilbertville, nearly two miles from the Common, marked "Mr. Bolster" on the R. Map. He d. 23 Sep. 1876, a. 77; his w. Nancy d. 2 Feb. 1775, a. 77.

19. LEWIS, s. of Jonathan (14), m. Vironia, dau. of John Anderson of N. Br., pub. 2 Ap. 1827; she d. 6 July 1853, a. 47, and he m. Susan Weeks of Oakham, pub. 21 June 1856. His chil. were *Jonathan*, b. 26 Jan. 1828; *Charles L.*, b. 27 June 1831; *Susan A.*, b. 4 Mar. 1834. LEWIS the f. was a farmer, and after a temporary absence ret. to Hk., and res. near "Taylor's Mills," at the place marked "Dea. Amidon" on the R. Map. He d. 11 Sep. 1875, a. 74.

20. WILLIAM AUGUSTUS, s. of Jonathan (14), m. Elizabeth F., dau. of Silas Billings, 24 May 1832, and had *Harriet Elizabeth*, b. 7 July 1834, m. Harmon C. Spooner 16 Jan. 1862; *William Augustus*, b. 15 Ap. 1837; *Silas Franklin*, b. 21 July 1843, d. 21 Nov. 1845; *Mary Ann*, b. 28 July 1846, m. Henry G. Towne 1 Jan. 1872; *Julia Maria*, b. 11 Jan. 1851. WILLIAM AUGUSTUS the f. inherited the homestead, and was accounted one of the best farmers in the town. He d. 30 Aug. 1878, a. 74; his w. Elizabeth F. d. 11 May 1878, a. 65.

21. LEVI WHIPPLE, s. of Jonathan (14), m. Luthera, dau. of Ezra Clark, 10 Ap. 1832, and had *William B.*, b. 10 Dec. 1832, d. 1 Jan. 1833; *Caroline Maria*, b. 12 Oct. 1835, m. Eleazar Damon of Ware 2 Aug. 1854; *Emeline Frances*, b. 3 Aug. 1837. LEVI WHIPPLE the f., a farmer, d. 28 July 1844, a. 38; his w. Luthera m. William E. Bassett 25 Dec. 1851.

22. FRANCIS G., s. of Giles (16), m. Louisa Sturtevant, pub. 20 Dec. 1851, and had *Clarence Alfred*, b. 26 Ap. 1852, d. 28 Ap. 1873; *Mary Louisa*, b. 9 July 1861. FRANCIS G. the f. was a farmer, inherited the homestead, and d. 12 Sep. 1863, a. 34.

23. GEORGE, s. of Daniel (18), m. Mary A. Walker 17 Oct. 1855; she d. 24 Nov. 1856, a. 21, and he m. Harriet, dau. of John Wheeler, 21 Oct. 1858. His chil. were *Mary Elizabeth*, b. 22 Sep. 1856; *Sarah Esther*, b. 16 Dec. 1859, d. 31 Dec. 1859; *George Franklin*, b. 11 June 1862, d. 25 Jan. 1863; *Hattie Sophia*, b. 6 Nov. 1865; *George Daniel*, b. 5 Nov. 1867. GEORGE the f., a farmer, inherited the homestead; he was assessor seven years, and has been selectman from 1876 to the present time.

24. CHARLES L., s. of Lewis (19), m. Caroline Wallace of Barre, pub. 24 Jan. 1861, and had *Lewis*, b. 13 Sep. 1865. CHARLES L. the f., a farmer and deacon, res. on the easterly road to Gilbertville, at the place marked "Dea. Fish" on the R. Map.

25. WILLIAM AUGUSTUS, s. of William Augustus (20), m. Caroline A. Sibley 15 Nov. 1860, and had *William Paige*, b. 6 Feb. 1871, d. 2 July 1872. WILLIAM AUGUSTUS the f., a farmer, has been deacon of the church, and member of the school committee many years; also a member of the Massachusetts Board of Agriculture.

26. DWIGHT, b. in Prescott, m. Mehetabel Knapp of Pet., pub. 7 Sep. 1852, and d. 7 May 1857, a. 46. By a former wife he had *Emeline L.*, b. about 1836, m. Jonas H. Allen of Worc. 3 Feb. 1858; *Livia A.*, b. about 1847, m. Henry G. Hutchinson of Worc. 6 Dec. 1865.

27. WALTER W., m. R. Alice Cleveland, pub. 2 Dec. 1852, and had a son b. 6 Aug. 1858.

28. MOSES, m. Lucy ——, and had *Joseph*, b. 7 Ap. 1864.

SAMUEL, of Springf., m. Clarissa Richards 11 July 1820. ELI, of N. Br., m. Lucia A. Cleveland 1 Ap. 1845. SARAH A., of N. Br., m. Philip Amidon, pub. 14 Nov. 1848. EMERSON, of N. Br., m. L. Angeline Cleveland, pub. 18 Jan. 1851. JOHN, d. 5 May 1844, a. 64. GILMAN E., a soldier in the Union Army, d. at Hickman Bridge 22 Sep. 1863, a. 23.

WARREN, BENJAMIN, m. Mary Maccoye 29 May 1744, and had *Benjamin*, b. 9 Sep. 1745; *Asahel*, b. 2 Nov. 1748. BENJAMIN the f. was a tailor, and d. 19 Sep. 1750; his w. Mary m. Benjamin Stearns of Rut. 12 Nov. 1753.

2. ASAHEL, s. of Benjamin (1), m. Margaret ——, and had *John*, b. 6 July 1772; *Lovisa*, b. 30 Sep. 1773; *David*, b. 7 Oct. 1775.

3. DAVID, m. Anna Boolen 17 Feb. 1791, and had *David*, b. 9 Oct. 1791; *Anna*, b. 5 Ap. 1793.

4. ISAAC, m. Mercy, dau. of Daniel Thomas, 19 Oct. 1800, and had *Minerva*, b. 6 July 1801; *Anson*, b. 20 Sep. 1802; *Cyrus*, b. —— 1804; *William*, b. 1 Nov. 1805, d. 8 Sep. 1814; *Lucinda*, b. 25 Feb. 1807; *Mary*, b. 29 Mar. 1809; *Henry*, b. 9 Mar. 1812; *Maria Emeline*, b. 4 July 1814. ISAAC the f. was a worthy mechanic, and res. near Gilbertville, but rem. to Weathersfield, Vt., about 1817.

WASHBURN, JOSEPH, b. in Bridgewater, m. Hannah Johnson, and had *Seth*, b. —— 1723; *Elijah*, b. ——; *Ebenezer*, b. —— 1734; *Abiah*, b. ——, m. Jacob Wicker —— 1747; *Sarah*, b. ——, m. Joseph Cerley; *Mary*, b. ——, m. —— Clough of Stafford, Conn. JOSEPH the f. rem. from Bridgewater to Middletown, Conn., and thence to Leicester before 1745. He d. in 1759; his w. Hannah d. in 1780, a. 87. See Washburn's *Hist. of Leicester*, pp. 412, 413.

2. JOSEPH, s. of Josiah, and a kinsman of Joseph (1), was b. in Bridgewater, 1705, m. Deliverance Orcutt, and had *Joseph*, b. —— 1729; *Jeremiah*, b. —— 1731; *Hannah*, b. —— 1733, m. Deac. Seth Pratt —— 1752; *Joanna*, b. —— 1736, m. Solomon Leonard, Jr.; *Sylvanus*, b. —— 1738; *Eliab*, b. —— 1740; *Eliphalet*, b. —— 1742; *Martha*, b. —— 1744, m. Elijah Edson —— 1766, and rem. to N. Br. JOSEPH the f. was a captain, res. at Bridgew., and d. —— 1766; his w. Deliverance m. —— Packard, and d. —— 1790, a. 88. See Mitchell's *Hist. of Bridgewater*, p. 326.

3. EBENEZER, s. of Joseph (1), m. Dorothy Newhall, and had *Artemas*, b. 16 Oct. 1767, a member of the senior class in Harvard College, d. of small-pox at Lancaster, in Dr. Atherton's Hospital, 23 Sep. 1792; *Dolly*, b. 31 Jan. 1770, d. unm. 28 Ap. 1835; *Ebenezer*, b. 25 Oct. 1772, a clergyman, d. at Racine, Wis., 29 Dec. 1857; *Cyrus*, b. 5 Nov. 1774; *Clarissa*, b. 26 May 1777, m. Thomas Egery 28 Ap. 1796; *Hannah*, b. 20 Oct. 1779, d. 15 Dec. 1781; he had also *Susanna*, b. ——, d. 12 Aug. 1771. EBENEZER the f. taught school in Leicester several years, and after his removal to Hk. was engaged in the same occupation; he was generally known as "Master Washburn." He was also the village poet, and many of his rhymes may be read on the head-stones in the old burial-ground. He was lieutenant of the famous company of "minute-men" which responded to the Lexington alarm in Ap. 1775, and was afterwards quartermaster in the army. He d. 24 Jan. 1795, a. 60; his w. Dorothy d. 29 Oct. 1807, a. 67.

4. JOSEPH, s. of Joseph (2), m. Mary Washburn, and had *Levi*, b. —— 1757; *Lavinia*, b. —— 1763; *Mary*, b. —— 1764, all b. at Bridgewater; he rem. thence to Hk., and res. not far from the Furnace, in which he seems to have had some interest.

5. SYLVANUS, s. of Joseph (2), m. Melicent Richards 7 Mar. 1765, and had a child b. ——, d. here 9 Nov. 1769; *Sylvanus*, b. 1 June 1773; *Stephen*, b. 28 Nov. 1774; *Melicent*, b. 10 May 1778, d. 14 Oct. 1778. SYLVANUS the f., a housewright, rem. from Bridgewater to Hk. as early as 1769, was town

clerk ten years, from 1778 to 1787, and assessor for the same years, except 1781. He was a man of more than ordinary intelligence, and many anecdotes of his shrewd sayings were current half a century ago. His record of the annual town-meeting in March 1787 is characteristic: "The Town met and proceeded as follows, viz. (1) Chose Gen. Jonathan Warner Moderator, and then after quarrelling the remainder of the day, voted to adjourn the meeting to Monday the second day of April next at nine o'clock in the morning." Brief, distinct, and doubtless strictly true, as this meeting occurred when the Shays excitement was at fever heat. At the adjourned meeting Mr. Washburn was reëlected clerk and assessor, but resigned both offices and removed to Barnard, Vt. The vacancies were filled 2 July 1787.

6. ELIPHALET, s. of Joseph (2), m. Anna, dau. of Caleb Benjamin, 19 Sep. 1769, and had *Naomi*, b. 24 Oct. 1770, m. Silas Newton 9 Ap. 1789; *Eliphalet*, b. 16 Aug. 1772, d. 2 Feb. 1796; *Luther*, b. 18 July 1774, m. Kate Cutter of Lancaster 25 Mar. 1799, rem. to Lanesboro' and thence to Pittsfield; "he was an able lawyer and a prominent citizen;"[1] he d. —— 1838; *Rufus*, b. 12 May 1776; *Calvin*, b. 15 May 1778; *Anna*, b. 21 May 1780, m. Benjamin W. Childs 25 Nov. 1798; *Triphena*, b. 12 May 1782, prob. d. young; *Cynthia*, b. 22 June 1784, m. Isaac Thomas 27 Nov. 1805; *Delphia*, b. 12 June 1787; *Reuel*, b. 22 June 1789, m. Mrs. Sophia Moody 13 Jan. 1817, inherited the homestead, but rem. to Ware, where he d. 22 Dec. 1869, a. 80; *Juliana*, b. 8 Oct. 1791. ELIPHALET the f. was a farmer, and res. on the road to Ware, three miles from the Common, at the place marked "T. Newcomb" on the R. Map. He d. 14 Dec. 1816, a. 74; his w. Anna d. 15 Oct. 1814, a. 68.

7. CYRUS, s. of Ebenezer (3), m. Electa Stratton of Vernon, Vt.; she d. 26 Jan. 1806, and he m. Rhoda Field of Northfield 19 Aug. 1806; she d., and he m. Lucy, dau. of Timothy Hathaway, pub. 24 Sep. 1827. His chil. b. here were *Cyrus*, b. 12 Nov. 1800, d. 28 Mar. 1802; *Electa*, bap. 5 Mar. 1803, d. 9 Mar. 1803. After his removal he had *Albert Alden*, b. ——, res. in Vernon, Vt.; *Roxana Stratton*, b. ——, m. N. F. Bryant, Esq.; *Clarasa*, b. ——, d. unm. at Vernon —— 1878. CYRUS the f. taught school and afterwards practised medicine here, residing at the north end of the Common, near the spot marked "P. Hammond" on the R. Map. "He rem. to Vernon, Vt., 1803, was president of the Vt. Med. Society several years, town clerk and superintendent of schools more than twenty years;"[2] he was justice of the peace from 1805, and probably married more couples than any other person in Vermont. He d. at Vernon 2 Mar. 1860, a. 85.

8. PHILIP, prob. s. of William of Bridgewater, b. 1743, m. Sarah, dau. of Nathan Carpenter, 8 Jan. 1767, and had *Hepzibah*, b. 28 Aug. 1768; *Marvel*, b. 17 Dec. 1770.

9. RUFUS, s. of Eliphalet (6), m. Thankful Cutter of Lancaster 25 Mar. 1799, and had *Nancy C.*, b. 7 Mar. 1801; *Lorenzo C.*, b. 3 Ap. 1806; *Lionel W.*, b. 18 June 1808; *Catherine*, b. 10 June 1810.

ELISHA and family, and WILLIAM and family, came here from Bridgewater in 1770. ELIJAH, m. Mary Winchester 1 Jan. 1778. AZUBAH, of Stafford, m. Silas Dean, Jr., pub. 23 Feb. 1783. LYDIA, m. Israel Cummings, pub. 4 Sep. 1785. RUFUS, JR., of Johnstown, N. Y., m. Laura L. Knowles 21 Feb. 1837. ELIZABETH, widow of Robert, d. 12 Sep. 1847, a. 91.

WATKINS, DARIUS, m. Rebecca Weeks of Ware, pub. 8 Nov. 1760, and had *Rhoda*, b. 5 Nov. 1761; *Bethia*, b. 15 Aug. 1762; *Stephen*, b. 18 July 1765, rem. to Wendell; *Darius*, b. 10 Sep. 1767, prob. m. Cilda Thayer of Dana, pub. 3 Sep. 1812; *David*, b. 2 June 1769, m. Polly ——, who d. 5 Dec. 1795, and he m. Hannah Garfield of Cambridge 30 May 1798.

2. GEORGE L., m. Christina Bonney 11 Mar. 1858, and had *Julia Jeanette*, b. 30 Aug. 1867; *Nellie*, b. — May 1872, d. 3 Nov. 1873.

WATSON, THANKFUL, of N. Br., m. Paul Eager, pub. 22 Oct. 1797. SUKEY, m. Royal Dennis 6 Oct. 1802. LUCINDA, of the Gore, d. 2 Oct. 1804, a. nearly 17.

WEAVER, BENJAMIN F., m. Sarah H. Russell of Ware, pub. 22 Oct. 1827;

[1] *Hist. of Pittsfield*, ii. 439.

[2] *Springfield Republican*, 1860.

she d. 14 Ap. 1854, a. 45, and he m. Mary Ann Wellman, pub. 12 Sep. 1854. He had *Sandford*, b. 18 July 1850, d. 14 Mar. 1870; *Hannah G.*, b. —— 1835, m. —— Whitman, and d. at Athol 9 May 1880, a. 45. He was perhaps father also of *George R.*, b. about 1830, m. Caroline S. Peyton 1 Feb. 1854; *Sarah Ann*, b. about 1832, m. William A. Thayer, 9 May 1850; *Dwight J.*, b. ——, m. Mary S. Bassett of Ware, pub. 8 Mar. 1853; *Mary E.*, b. ——, m. George A. Streeter of Southbridge, pub. 8 Mar. 1853. BENJAMIN F. the f. d. 16 Mar. 1862, a. 61.

HANNAH, d. 3 Dec. 1851, a. 87.

WEBB, JOHN, m. Priscilla, dau. of Thomas Winslow of Harwich, 12 Dec. 1773; she d. in child-bed 28 Mar. 1785, a. 28, and he m. Lydia Thomas 27 Ap. 1786; she d. 20 Dec. 1801, a. 46, and he m. Lydia Forbes of Barre, pub. 25 Nov. 1804. His chil. were *John*, b. at Barnstable 18 Feb. 1775, d., unm., at sea about 1805; *George Washington*, b. here 29 Sep. 1776; *Winslow*, b. 4 June 1778, m. Betsey Means of Freeport, Me., and d. at Turner, Me., in June 1843; *Elisha*, b. 14 Sep. 1780, unm., drowned at sea 24 Sep. 1805; *Betsey*, b. 5 Dec. 1782, m. Ezra Clark 17 Nov. 1803, and (2d) Capt. Benjamin Paige 6 June 1819, and d. 16 Mar. 1856; *Joshua*, b. 18 Mar. 1785, m. Betsey Lane at Freeport, Me., 7 May 1806; *Priscilla*, b. 16 Feb. 1787, m. Noah Beach 8 Jan. 1805; *Jonathan*, b. 29 July 1791; a child b. 19 Nov. 1793, d. 23 Nov. 1793; a child b. — Feb. 1795, d. 6 Mar. 1795. JOHN the f. was born in Barnstable, rem. to Hk. about 1776, res. in the westerly part of the town, and d. 5 Aug. 1828, a. 82; his w. Lydia d. 4 Dec. 1820, a. 64, or 66.

2. GEORGE WASHINGTON, s. of John (1), m. Patience, dau. of Isaac Clark, 16 Oct. 1803, and had in Hk. *Eliza*, b. 16 Mar. 1805, m. Walter Ross 5 Ap. 1824; *George Washington*, b. 27 Sep. 1808, m. Achsah Holden of Shrewsbury, Vt., — Dec. 1833; *John*, b. 15 Nov. 1810, m. Mrs. Mary G. Brown; *Sarah Ann*, b. 15 Ap. 1813, m. Reuben Holden of Shrewsbury, Vt., — Mar. 1839; *Isaac Clark*, b. 27 Sep. 1815, m. Elizabeth K. Fulkerson 2 Aug. 1843, rem. to Galesburg, Ill.; and at Shrewsbury, *Lorenzo Dow*, b. 21 Jan. 1818, m. Saloam M. Fish 21 Jan. 1848, res. at Milwaukee, Wis.; *Elbridge Gerry*, b. 19 Ap. 1820, m. Ann S. Boughton — Sep. 1845, and d. 3 Nov. 1854; *Luthera Clark*, b. 14 Nov. 1822, m. Francis B. Gibson — Mar. 1843. GEORGE W. the f. was a farmer, and rem. with his family to Shrewsbury, Vt., about 1817, where he d. 23 Mar. 1861; his w. Patience d. 8 Mar. 1857. (Thus far, I have gleaned several names and dates from the *Winslow Memorial*, pp. 302–314.)

3. JONATHAN, s. of John (1), m. Mary, dau. of David Paige 14 June 1819. He was a school-teacher and captain of militia. He rem. early and res. in two or three of the adjoining towns. I have not seen his family record; but some of his children were *Charles*, b. —— ; *Mary P.*, b. ——, m. Loring F. Wood of N. Br., pub. 5 Sep. 1839, res. in Barre; *Charlotte*, b. —— 1823, d. 29 Mar. 1828, a. 4 years and 5 months; *John*, b. ——, res. in New York city; *Elisha*, b. ——, res. in Petersham; *Charlotte A.*, b. about 1829, d. 11 Mar. 1831, a. 2; *Thomas*, b. ——, res. in N. Br.; *Jonathan T.*, b. 30 July 1834, d. 21 July 1835. JONATHAN the f. d. 23 Ap. 1871; his w. Mary d. 2 Aug. 1869, a. 69.

WEBSTER, ELIZABETH, m. John Hunt, Jr., 23 Dec. 1772. SARAH, m. Aaron Hudson 3 Nov. 1777. BETSEY, m. Moses Doty 20 Sep. 1781.

WEEKS, THOMAS, m. Catherine Clark of Rochester 3 Ap. 1743, and had *Nathaniel*, b. 8 Oct. 1744; *Joseph*, b. 6 Jan. 1746-7; *Susanna*, b. 7 Ap. 1749, m. Silas Robinson of Bennington 2 Oct. 1766; *Mary*, b. 31 Aug. 1751, m. John Giffin 7 Sep. 1769; *David*, b. 17 Jan. 1754; *Elizabeth*, bap. 9 May 1756, m. Benjamin Holmes of Bennington 10 Feb. 1780; *John*, bap. 11 Mar. 1759; *Shiverick*, bap. 5 July 1767. THOMAS the f. is supposed to have been a descendant from George of Dorchester, who was there in 1640, and had sons Ammiel, William, and Joseph. He served in the French War 1757. He rem. from Hk. to Bennington, and d. there in August 1804, a. 84; his w. Catherine d. 14 Oct. 1818, lacking three days of 96 years, though by a common mistake the head-stone bears 97 as the age.

2. JOSEPH, s. of Thomas (1), m. Hannah, dau. of Capt. Benjamin Willis, 10 May 1775; she d. 30 Jan. 1798, a. 49, and he m. Elizabeth ——; she d.

and he m. Rebecca ——, who d. 3 May 1835, a. 75. Some of his chil. were *Lemuel*, b. 30 Nov. 1777; *David*, b. —— 1800; *Shiverick*, b. —— 1801; a child b. — Feb. 1805, d. 10 Mar. 1805. JOSEPH the f., a Revolutionary soldier, res. some years on the road to Ware, about a mile from the Common. In his old age he prob. rem. to Hardwick, Vt., and d. 11 Dec. 1836, a. 90.

3. DAVID, s. of Thomas (1), m. Elizabeth Robinson 22 May 1783, rem. to Bennington, Vt., and there had *David*, b. 24 Nov. 1798, m. Harriet L. Webster; *Samuel*, b. 12 Ap. 1800, m. Ruth Dewey; and prob. others. DAVID the f. was a soldier in the Revolution, while residing here, and d. at Bennington 4 Oct. 1836, a. 82 (83 on head-stone); his w. Elizabeth d. 2 Ap. 1822, a. 55.

4. LEMUEL, s. of Joseph (2), m. Fanny, dau. of Capt. John Wheeler, 27 Dec. 1801, and had *Sally*, b. —— 1804, d. 13 Dec. 1809, a. 5; an infant, b. ——, d. 30 June 1807. LEMUEL the f. rem. to Hardwick, Vt., but both his children d. here; his w. Fanny also d. here (prob. in child-bed) 8 July 1807, a. 25. He then m. Mary ——, who survived him and d. 1 Feb. 1855, a. 80, at Hardwick, Vt., where he also d. 30 July 1853, a. 76.

5. DAVID, s. of Joseph (2), m. Anstiss Manly of Enf. 6 Mar. 1827, and had *Anna*, b. —— 1828, d. unm. 2 June 1875, a. 47; *Henry*, b. ——; *Francis P.*, b. about 1834. DAVID the f. d. 25 July 1838, a. 38; his w. Anstiss d. 20 Ap. 1874, a. 66.

6. SHIVERICK, s. of Joseph (2), m. Celia W. Hathaway 26 Nov. 1821, and had *Amelia*, b. — Jan. 1825, m. —— Mixer, and d. at Ware 27 Feb. 1857, a. 32; a son b. —— 1836, d. 19 July 1838, a. 2. SHIVERICK the f. rem. early to Ware, and d. 7 Sep. 1873, a. 72.

7. FRANCIS P., s. of David (5), m. Julia Ann, widow of Constantine Smith, and dau. of Jonas H. Thayer, 26 June 1872, and had *William F.*, b. — Ap. 1874, d. 24 Oct. 1874, a. 6 months. His w. Julia Ann d. in child-bed 4 May 1874, a. 34.

8. AMMIEL, parentage not ascertained, had w. Susanna, who d., and he m. Sarah, widow of —— Mandell, 26 Feb. 1778. He had *Artemas*, b. 9 Nov. 1769; *Ruth*, b. 13 Oct. 1773. AMMIEL the f. rem. to Leverett before 13 June 1783. He had served his country in the campaign of 1776.

9. HOLLAND, parentage not ascertained, m. Mary Peirce, pub. 2 Feb. 1772, and had *Ebenezer*, b. 30 Dec. 1772; *Mary Warner*, b. 9 Aug. 1774; *Hannah*, b. 15 Mar. 1776, m. Silas Marsh of Westborough 18 Ap. 1802.

10. JUDAH, m. Mary Clark of New Stratford, pub. 4 Dec. 1780, and rem. to Bennington, where he had *Ira*, b. 28 Sep. 1781; *Polly*, b. 11 Ap. 1783; *Judah*, b. 12 Ap. 1785; *John Clark*, b. 19 Oct. 1787; *Eunice*, b. 7 Nov. 1791.

11. DAVID, m. Abigail Bond, and had *Rich*, b. 20 Oct. 1799. In the *History of Pawlet, Vt.*, p. 253, it is said that "David Weeks from Hardwick, Mass., 1801, settled south of the village, and conducted the tanning business over fifty years; married Abigail Bond, and had *Elijah*, *Salmon*, *Rich*, *Seth B.*, *Matilda*, *Abigail*, *Eliza*, and *Nancy*."

12. SAMUEL, "from Hardwick, Mass., 1801, settled on the present homestead of Arthur Goodspead, and raised nine children: *Wheeler*, *John*, *Curtis*, *Hiram*, *Safford*, *Harvey R.*, *William P.*, *Cyrus*, and *Sarah*." *Hist. Pawlet*, p. 254.

(The two last-named were probably brothers; but the records fail to show their relationship, or that of AMMIEL, HOLLAND, and JUDAH, to THOMAS 1.)

MARGARET, w. of Nathaniel, adm. to the church 13 Nov. 1744. CONTENT, prob. sister to Thomas (1), m. Isaac Clark 29 Oct. 1742. REBECCA, of Ware, m. Darius Watkins, pub. 8 Nov. 1760. NATHAN, m. Polly Lawton 12 Ap. 1807. TRIPHENA, m. Solomon W. Ruggles 1 Ap. 1827. SUSAN, of Oakham, m. Lewis Warner, pub. 21 June 1856. WILLIAM A. F., of Oakham, m. Sarah A. Sears, pub. 20 Sep. 1859.

WELLS, JOHN, s. of John and Rachel (Marsh) Wells of Hatfield, m. Martha, dau. of Ichabod Allis, and had *John*, b. 14 Mar. 1729; *Martha*, b. 12 June 1731, m. Elisha Waite; *Mary*, b. 26 Feb. 1734, m. Jonathan Farr 5 June 1751; *Lucy*, b. 7 Mar. 1736, prob. d. young; *Lydia*, b. 16 Aug. 1738, m. Nathan Billings 24 Feb. 1757; *Submit*, b. 3 May 1742, m. Elijah Warner 14 Jan. 1762; *Elijah*, b. 1 Ap. 1744. All these births are recorded here; but the first two prob. occurred in Hatfield. JOHN the f. came here early, and seems to have res. first at Gilbertville, where he had a grist-mill, and afterwards near Enfield. He was the first treasurer of the town, and held that office four years, 1737–1740; he was also selectman four years, 1738–1741. He d. not long before 15 Feb. 1745–6, at which date his inventory was presented; his w. Martha m. Capt. Nathaniel Hammond of Swanzey, N. H., 6 Aug. 1747; he d. here, and she m. Nathaniel Kellogg of Hadley 19 July 1758, and d. 13 Sep. 1764, a. 61.

2. JOHN, s. of John (1), m. Kezia Farr 14 Dec. 1748, and had *John*, b. 27 Sep. 1749; *Lucy*, bap. 8 Mar. 1752; *Kezia*, bap. 9 June 1754; *Joshua*, bap. 3 Oct. 1756; *Oliver*, bap. 25 Mar. 1759; *Susanna*, bap. 2 Aug. 1761. JOHN the f. prob. rem. to Ware about 1752, but his chil. b. afterwards were bap. here.

WESSON, WILLIAM BRIGHAM, m. Azuba Maria Graves of Athol, pub. 11 Oct. 1807, and had *Maria Loraine*, b. 19 Nov. 1810, m. Moses F. Dickinson 27 Sep. 1831; *William Cutler*, b. 23 Dec. 1814; *Theresa Rivers*, b. 8 Ap. 1816, d. 7 May 1816; *William Brigham*, b. 21 Mar. 1820, rem. early, and res. at Detroit; *Ezekiel Lysander Bascom*, b. 5 Sep. 1823; *Alice Graves*, b. 14 Aug. 1827, d. —— 1827. WILLIAM B. the f., s. of William, was born in Hopkinton 29 May 1777, but rem. early with his parents to Athol; he grad. W. C. 1802, was ordained pastor of the first church in Hk. 30 Oct. 1805, and was dismissed, at his own request, 30 June 1824. He continued to reside here, at the place marked "Mr. Wesson" on the R. Map, being engaged for some time in mercantile business, until 9 May 1836, when he died, a. nearly 59; his w. Azuba Maria d. 13 Aug. 1863, a. about 79.

2. WILLIAM CUTLER, s. of William B. (1), m. Elizabeth Jones of Gr. 14 June 1840, and had *Maria E.*, b. 29 Mar. 1841, m. John D. Morton of Boston 7 Oct. 1862; *Sarah A.*, b. 6 Mar. 1845, m. George M. Wolcott of Holyoke 5 Nov. 1868. WILLIAM C. the f., a farmer, and for many years proprietor and driver of a mail-coach between Hk. and W. Brk., res. on the homestead.

3. EZEKIEL L. B., s. of William B. (1), m. Martha S. Dow, and had *Edwin L.*, b. 14 Aug. 1852, m. Nellie Dow 23 Sep. 1880; *George McClellan*, b. 13 Oct. 1861; *Almon Frank*, b. 4 Ap. 1864; *William Pliny*, b. 21 May 1868; *Ellen M.*, b. 31 Oct. 1870; *Elizabeth*, b. 12 Oct. 1872. EZEKIEL L. B. the f., a farmer and provision dealer, res. near the homestead, at the place marked "Mr. Tupper" on the R. Map.

WESTON ABNER, m. Sally, dau. of Samuel Thurston, 17 Oct. 1788, and had *Samuel*, b. —— 1789, bap. 2 July 1797, a shoemaker and musician, d. 20 Aug. 1838; *John Wheeler*, b. ——, bap. 2 July 1797, res. in Barre. ABNER the f. rem. to Barre, and prob. d. before 1814; his w. Sally d. 13 Mar. 1836, a. 63.

WETHERBEE, SAMPSON, m. Hannah ——, and had *Jonathan*, b. 7 Jan. 1749; *Hannah*, b. 2 May 1751.

2. CALVIN, m. Betsey, prob. wid. of John Rice and dau. of Benjamin Ruggles, and had *Benjamin Ruggles*, b. 24 June 1823; *John Stillman*, b. 1 June 1825, m. Martha M. Nims of Keene, N. H., pub. 27 Dec. 1851, and d. 31 Mar. 1854; *Samuel*, b. 17 June 1827, m. Luthera Johnson 27 Dec. 1849; *Adin Plummer*, b. 24 Aug. 1830. CALVIN the f. d. 16 Ap. 1839, a. 36; his w. Betsey m. Benjamin Skinner 19 Jan. 1851.

3. BENJAMIN R., s. of Calvin (2), m. Abigail S. Richards, pub. 3 Feb. 1850, and had *Augustus Eugene*, b. 23 Jan. 1851.

HANNAH, of Pet., m. James Wing 11 Ap. 1799. Mrs. LYDIA, m. Barnabas Rich of Enf., pub. 26 Nov. 1827. VARNUM, m. Betsey R. Rice 14 Nov. 1831. PHINEAS, d. 21 Ap. 1822, a. 52. GILBERT, d. —— Aug. 1825, a. 21. Mrs. WETHERBEE, perhaps w. of Gilbert, d. 26 Aug. 1825, a. 20.

WETHERELL, JOHN B., m. Parnell ——, and had *Laura Gertrude*, b. 25 Aug. 1847, m. Clarence E. Hitchcock of Springf. 23 May 1872; *Charlotte Elizabeth*, b. 13 Jan. 1849, m. Charles W. Wood of Worc. 13 June 1872; *John Hervey*, b. 10 Sep. 1854.

LUCINDA, m. Samuel Cook, Jr., of Pet., pub. 30 Ap. 1825.

WHEELER, THOMAS, rem. from Acton to Worcester about 1739, was elected, in 1748, deacon of the first church, and remained in Worc. until about 1764, when he rem. to Hardwick, was adm. to the church 8 Nov. 1764, and d. here

31 Jan. 1769, a. 74. In his will, dated 6 July 1764, he named sons *Daniel*, *Amos*, *Nathan*, *Thomas*, and grandson Timothy Moore.

2. DANIEL, s. of Thomas (1), m. Betty, dau. of Lieut. William Holloway of Marlborough; she d. here 7 Mar. 1774, a. 39, and he m. Mrs. Mary Cleveland of New Marlborough, pub. 2 Ap. 1775. His chil. were *John*, b. about 1757; *Mary*, b. about 1759, m. Moses Mandell 28 May 1777, and d. s. p. 20 Ap. 1782, a. 23; if others, they prob. did not live to maturity, as in his will, dated 21 Nov. 1812, the whole estate was given to the chil. of his deceased son *John*. DANIEL the f. rem. from Worc. to Hk. soon after 15 Sep. 1761, when he bought of Capt. Samuel Robinson the estate on the turnpike, a little more than a mile from the Common, marked "Old House" on the R. Map. His house was consumed by fire 15 Aug. 1773. He was a farmer, captain of militia in 1771, and d. 10 Jan. 1813, a. 84; his w. Mary d. 7 Dec. 1810, a. 76, or 77.

3. AMOS, s. of Thomas (1), res. on the homestead in Worcester, which was quitclaimed to him, 14 Ap. 1769, by his brothers, soon after the death of their father. His son *Amos* settled in Woodstock, Vt., and was father of Amos D., b. 13 Dec. 1803, grad. W. C. 1827, D. D. at Bowd. Coll. 1860, minister at Topsham, Me., and d. 28 June 1876.

4. NATHAN, s. of Thomas (1), m. Hannah, dau. of John Hunt, 1 July 1762, and probably rem. from Brk. to Hk. during the same year. He had *Persis*, b. 27 Mar. 1763; *Lemuel*, b. 30 Ap. 1764; m. Anna Ames of Barre 2 May 1793, res. several years on the road to Gilbertville, at the place marked "L. Manly," and d. s. p. 18 Feb. 1837; his w. Anna d. 4 Dec. 1846, a. 80; *Nathan*, b. 16 June 1767; *Hannah*, b. 22 Dec. 1768, m. Lewis Abbott of Oakham 2 May 1793; *Betty*, b. 4 May 1773, m. Elihu Wright of Westminster, Vt., 28 Nov. 1799; *Polly*, b. 5 Ap. 1775, m. Peter Wilder of Oakham, pub. 25 May 1794; *Artemas*, b. 10 June 1777. NATHAN the f. rem. to Stratham, N. H.

5. THOMAS, s. of Thomas (1), m. Anna, dau. of Jonathan Warner, 8 Sep. 1762, and had *Charles*, b. 13 Oct. 1763, d. unm. 11 Nov. 1805; *Thomas*, b. 3 Mar. 1767; *Moses*, b. 26 May 1769; *Daniel*, b. about 1771, d. 8 Oct. 1798; *Sally*, b. —— 1774, d. unm. 5 July 1793, a. 19. THOMAS the f. was a farmer, and res. several years on the turnpike at or near the place marked "C. Paige" on the R. Map, which he sold to Col. Stephen Rice 19 Nov. 1770, and rem. to Brk., but returned before 31 Aug. 1777, and afterwards res. on the road to Gilbertville at the place marked "L. Manly" on the R. Map. He d. very suddenly[1] 10 July 1804, a. 65; his w. Anna m. her cousin, Capt. Elijah Warner, 30 Dec. 1807, and d. in Dec. 1837, a. 95.

6. JOHN, s. of Daniel (2), m. Mary, dau. of John Paige, 18 Nov. 1779, and had *Betsey*, b. 3 June 1780, m. Isaac Davis of Rut., pub. 2 May 1825, and d. 27 July 1849; *Fanny*, b. 29 Sep. 1781, m. Lemuel Weeks 27 Dec. 1801, rem. to Hardwick, Vt., but d. here (prob. in childbed), 8 July 1807; *Daniel*, b. 7 Oct. 1783; *John*, b. 29 Aug. 1785; *Mary*, b. 16 Feb. 1788; *Holloway Taylor*, b. 29 Sep. 1790, res. in Rut., and d. 7 Ap. 1841; a child b. ——, d. 2 Dec. 1792. JOHN the f. was a farmer, and res. on the homestead with his father. He was a man of great energy, both physical and mental. He was deeply involved in the Shays Rebellion, and was an aide-de-camp to Shays himself. His contemporaries spoke of him as superior to his chief in military skill and conduct. He was arrested, tried in Hampshire County, at the April term of the Supreme Court in 1787, convicted of treason, and condemned to death. He received full pardon, however, by the Governor 30 April 1787, and on the 1st of September 1789 was commissioned captain of militia,[2] — a majority of the company doubtless approving his political opinions. But though thus sustained by his townsmen and by the government, it is said that his mind never regained its former buoyancy. Whether his mortification and chagrin tended to shorten his life is not known; but he d. 8 June 1794, at the early age of 37; his w. Mary d. 5 May 1821, a. 60.

1 "While giving directions to his hired men respecting his hay, he felt himself faint, fell into their arms, and instantly expired." *Mass. Spy*, July 18, 1804.

2 He was 1st lieut. of the same company 17 Jan. 1784, and seems to have retained the office until he was promoted in 1789.

7. THOMAS, s. of Thomas (5), m. Anna, dau. of Lieut. Job Dexter, 3 June 1790; she d. 20 Mar. 1804, a. 33, and he m. Mary, dau. of Timothy Paige, Esq., 14 Feb. 1805; she d. at Ticonderoga, N. Y., 18 Sep. 1828, a. nearly 48, and he m. twice afterwards. His chil. were *Charles*, b. 26 Mar. 1791, m. Luthera, dau. of Elijah Bangs, 2 Mar. 1814, and d. s. p. at Ticonderoga, N. Y., 30 Sep. 1818; his widow m. Joseph Adams of Shutes. 1 Ap. 1824; a child b. ——, d. 2 May 1793; *Sally*, b. 28 Ap. 1794, m. Daniel Wheeler 3 Nov. 1814; a child d. 12 Sep. 1796, aged eight days; *William Augustus*, b. 30 Mar. 1798, m. Almira W., dau. of Capt. Moses Allen, 13 Jan. 1825, was a very energetic and skilful iron-founder and manufacturer in Worcester, where he d. 17 Feb. 1876; a child b. — Nov. 1800, d. 26 Jan. 1801; a child b. ——, d. 4 July 1802; *Ann Dexter*, b. 3 Dec. 1805, d. 18 Jan. 1816; a child b. ——, d. 18 July 1807; *Thomas Alonzo*, b. 7 Nov. 1808, d. (of spotted fever) 15 Ap. 1811; *Charlotte Sophia*, b, 8 May 1811, m. William Burnett Cooper, and (2d) Ashley Cooper Bennett, had ten chil., res. in Garden Prairie, Ill., and afterwards in Rothville, Mo.; *Mary Emeline*, b. 21 June 1813, m. Thomas R. Green of Bel., and d. 20 Feb. 1843; *Rebecca Ann*, b. 6 Mar. 1816, m. Lyman Burrill, and d. at Dunkirk, N. Y., 10 June 1853; *Eliza Jane*, b. 15 Ap. 1819, m. Rev. Stephen Lovell, and d. 4 Mar. 1848; *Juliet Elvira*, b. 10 Sep. 1821, d. unm. at Greenwich 19 (or 29) June 1840. THOMAS the f. was a very ingenious blacksmith and iron-founder; he also cultivated a farm. He was long in the military service, being a captain in 1801, major in 1811, and colonel in 1813. He res. on the road to Gilbertville, at the place marked "D. Wheeler" on the R. Map, and afterwards near the New Furnace, at the place marked "M. S.," until about 1818, when he removed to Ticonderoga, N. Y.; he returned about 1830, and res. a few years at Greenwich, and afterwards at Worcester, where he d. 26 Ap. 1851, a. 84.

8. MOSES, s. of Thomas (5), m. Mehetabel Pearson of Randolph, Vt., in 1798, and had *Sophia*, b. 11 Dec. 1799, m. John Wheeler, pub. 2 May 1825; *Daniel*, b. 10 July 1801; *Amanda*, b. 6 Dec. 1802, m. Alanson Johnson, pub. 8 May 1826; *Sarah Warner*, b. 2 Dec. 1804; *Moses*, b. 2 Sep. 1806, drowned 8 June 1819; *Hitty*, b. 24 May 1808; *Henry Parsons*, b. 27 Aug. 1810, d. 15 Mar. 1816; *Harriet*, b. 24 July 1812. MOSES the f. from about 1790 to 1803 res. at Randolph, Vt., where he was m. and his first three chil. were born. He then ret. to Hk., res. on what is now the Town Farm (on the Pet. road), and d. 14 Aug. 1828, a. 59.

9. DANIEL, s. of John (6), m. Sally, dau. of Col. Thomas Wheeler, 3 Nov. 1814, and had *Sally Ann*, b. 2 Nov. 1815, d. unm. 25 Jan. 1833; *Fanny*, b. 15 Sep. 1817, m. Forester B. Aiken 10 May 1837, and d. 23 Dec. 1872; *Mary*, b. 25 Sep. 1819, m. Levi Adams of Shutes., pub. 3 May 1843; *Elizabeth*, b. 22 Aug. 1821; *Daniel Warner*, b. 15 Aug. 1823, m. Delia Jenney of Ware, pub. 28 May 1848; *Charlotte*, b. 13 Nov. 1825, m. Edwin D. McFarland of Worc. 23 Feb. 1864; *Luthera Elmira*, b. 19 June 1828, m. Edward Dean 19 June 1851; *John*, b. 17 July 1829; *Eliza Ann*, b. —— 1832, d. 7 Mar. 1833, a. 1 year; *William A.*, bap. 13 Dec. 1835. DANIEL the f. was a farmer, res. on the road to Gilbertville, at the place marked "D. Wheeler" on the R. Map, and afterwards on the Moose Brook road, near the Furnace, at the place marked "D. Billings;" late in life he rem. to Worc., where he d. 13 June 1864, a. 80; his w. Sally d. 26 June 1864, a. 70; both were buried here in the new cemetery.

10. JOHN, s. of John (6), m. ——; she d. ——, and he m. Sophia, dau. of Moses Wheeler, pub. 2 May 1825. His chil. were *Daniel*, b. 9 Ap. 1816, res. in East Boston; *John*, b. ——, m. ——, d. ——; *Mary G.*, b. 15 July 1820, m. —— Bartlett (one other child by first wife d. young); *Moses P.*, b. 2 Oct. 1828; *Harriet S.*, b. 16 Feb. 1830, m. George Warner 21 Oct. 1858; *Charles A.*, b. 31 Mar. 1832; *Sarah E.*, b. 3 July 1834, d. unm. 17 May 1866; *George F.*, b. 4 May 1836, res. in the city of New York. JOHN the f. rem. early to Rut., where all his chil. were born, except the youngest; about 1835 he returned, and for many years res. on the Gilbertville road at the place marked "D. Wheeler." He was a farmer, and d. 7 (or 27) Sep. 1865, a. 80.

11. DANIEL, s. of Moses (8), m. Mary, dau. of Barnabas Hinkley, pub. 5 Nov. 1826, and had *Mary Ann*, b. 20 Sep. 1827; *Daniel Hinkley*, b. 7 June 1829; *Susan*, b. 11 Nov. 1830. DANIEL the f. rem. to Maine about 1835.

12. MOSES P., s. of John (10), m. Anna Maria Smith of St. Louis 3 Oct. 1861, and had *Emma Louisa*, b. here 6 June 1868. MOSES P. the f. rem. to Springfield.

13. CHARLES A., s. of John (10), m. Christiana B. Howe of Barre, pub. 7 Mar. 1865, and had *Mary Louisa*, b. 26 Mar. 1869. CHARLES A. the f., a farmer and deacon, res. on the homestead.

14. EPHRAIM, parentage not ascertained, by w. Anna, had *Ephraim*, b. 8 Dec. 1764; *Anna*, b. 4 May 1767; *Persis*, b. 29 Dec. 1769; *Rhoda*, b. 31 Aug. 1772. EPHRAIM the f. came here from Braintree in 1769.

SARAH, m. Thomas Emmons 30 Ap. 1741. *Martha*, of Marlb., m. David Woods, pub. 11 Feb. 1743-4; *Rebecca*, m. Daniel Munden 8 Aug. 1771. ELIZABETH, m. Joseph Cleveland 4 May 1772. GEORGE P., of Pet., m. Almeda Aiken 13 June 1848. WILLIAM A., m. Sarah E. Howe of Shrews., pub. 9 Nov. 1857. FANNY (b. in Pet.), d. unm. 30 Ap. 1861, a. 71.

WHEELOCK, DAVID, by w. Phebe, had *Lydia*, b. 22 Sep. 1760, m. Ichabod Merritt of Ware, pub. 6 Ap. 1783.

2. CALVIN C., by w. Clarissa E., had *Hattie Maria*, b. 15 Jan. 1861, d. 24 May 1862; *Ellen M.*, b. —— 1863, d. 2 Sep. 1865, a. 2 years.

GIDEON, m. Sarah Forbush 14 Jan. 1771. SALLY, m. James Holland of Gr. 15 Nov. 1792. SARAH, m. Benjamin Merritt of Ware 8 Jan. 1797. JOHN MOORE, s. of Eli, d. 17 May 1835, a. 1 year and 9 months.

WHEET, THOMAS, and Abigail Stearns were pub. 17 Jan. 1770.

WHIPPLE, BENJAMIN, b. in Ipswich 1726, by w. Hepzibah, had *Nehemiah*, b. here 25 Mar. 1750; *Hepzibah* and *Sarah*, twins, b. 1 July 1751; *Abigail*, b. 21 June 1753; *Benjamin*, b. 16 Sep. 1755; *Prudence*, b. 27 July 1757; *David*, b. 17 Sep. 1759; and at Bennington, *Elizabeth*, b. 24 Mar. 1763; *Persis*, b. 14 Mar. 1768. BENJAMIN the f. came here from Westboro' in 1749, was a corporal in the French War, and rem. to Bennington about 1761.

2. EBENEZER, rem. to Hk. from Sutton about 1751, and by w. Prudence, had *Paul*, b. ——, d. about 1771; *Samuel*, b. 7 Dec. 1751; *John*, b. 6 Jan. 1754, perhaps the same who d. 5 July 1777; *Prudence* (posthumous), b. 17 Mar. 1756, m. George Field 13 Ap. 1775, and d. 15 Dec. 1838. EBENEZER the f. was a "joiner," a sergeant in the French War, and was killed in battle 8 Sep. 1755; his w. Prudence m. Deac. James Fay, pub. 13 Sep. 1760.

3. SAMUEL, s. of Ebenezer (2), m. Sarah, dau. of Ezra Leonard, 30 Mar. 1775, and had *Rhoda*, b. 24 Oct. 1775, m. Solomon Cutter of Rindge, N. H., 3 Jan. 1799; *Olive*, b. 6 June 1778, m. Chiron Penniman 17 Jan. 1797; *John*, b. 5 Feb. 1780; *Fanny*, b. 27 Feb. 1782; *Charles*, b. 12 Nov. 1784; *Sarah*, b. 20 Aug. 1786; *Samuel Dudley*, b. 24 June 1788; *Anson*, b. 23 Mar. 1790; *Sophia*, b. 27 Feb. 1792.

4. JAMES (a descendant from MATTHEW,[1] who d. at Ipswich 28 Sep. 1647, through JOSEPH,[2] who d. at Ips. about 1709, Deacon JAMES,[3] of Grafton, who d. 3 Nov. 1766, a. 85, and JACOB[4]), was b. at Grafton in 1732, settled in Hardwick, m. Lydia Powers 29 Nov. 1750, and had *Lydia*, b. —— 1753, and d. —— 1757; *Jacob*, b. 4 Nov. 1755; *David*, b. 12 Sep. 1759; *James*, b. —— 1765; *Moses* (posthumous), b. —— 1768. JAMES the f. d. in 1767.

5. JACOB, s. of James (4), m. Edna Forbush 30 Dec. 1777, and had *Lydia*, b. —— 1779, m. Ichabod Towne of Gr., pub. 27 Jan. 1798; *Ephraim*, b. —— 1781, d. at Dana 28 June 1862, a. 81; *Sarah*, b. —— 1782, m. Ezra Thayer; *Mercy*, b. —— 1784, d. young. (The names and dates of birth are copied from the *Whipple Genealogy*. JACOB the f. was a deacon and a preacher in the Baptist church in the north part of the town (now Dana), and d. in 1818.

6. DAVID, s. of James (4), m. Elizabeth Davis of Gr. 7 Ap. 1785; she d. 16 Sep. 1826, a. 60, and he m. Martha Thayer, pub. 26 Jan. 1827; she d. 27 May 1836, a. 71, and he m. Arathusa Estabrook 1 Dec. 1836. His chil. were *Len-*

dall, b. 14 Dec. 1795, d. unm. 21 Nov. 1817, and was the first person buried in the new cemetery (having previously assisted in building the surrounding wall); *Joel*, b. 19 July 1797; *Cyrena*, b. 28 May 1799, m. Hosea Thayer of Dana, pub. 26 Ap. 1819; *Eliza*, b. 11 Mar. 1804, m. William Johnson 15 Aug. 1822.

7. JAMES, s. of James (4), m. Electa Johnson 21 Ap. 1785, and had *James*, b. —— 1785, m. Sybil Sturtevant of Ware, pub. 20 Feb. 1808; *Cynthia*, b. —— 1788, m. Ephraim Thayer; *Bathsheba*, b. —— 1791, m. Apollos Johnson; *Seth*, b. —— 1793, m. Deborah Stephens, pub. 22 Mar. 1819, and d. at Otsego, N. Y., in 1846; *Catherine*, b. —— 1796, m. Thomas Jenkins of Otsego, and d. in 1841; *Almira*, b. —— 1778, m. Ira Haskell of Gr.; *Almond*, b. —— 1800, res. in Howell, Mich., and was clerk of the Judicial Court; *Sophronia*, b. —— 1802, m. Oliver N. Shipman of Springf., N. Y.; *Squire*, b. 1804, grad. U. C. 1830, a civil engineer in Utica, N. Y. JAMES the f. rem. in 1817 to Otsego, N. Y., and thence to Springf., N. Y. See *Gen. of Whipple Family*.

8. MOSES, s. of James (4), m. Sarah Thayer 31 Dec. 1789, and had *Rebecca*, b. 9 Oct. 1790, m. Daniel Stephens, pub. 14 Ap. 1811; *Sarah*, b. 16 Ap. 1792, m. Joel Gleason, pub. 24 June 1811; *Lydia*, b. 17 Feb. 1795, m. Holland Randall of Barre, pub. 7 Ap. 1817; *Moses*, b. 22 Sep. 1796; *Polly*, b. —— 1799, d. —— 1802; *Joseph*, b. 30 Ap. 1801; *Hannah*, b. 11 June 1803, d. unm. at Dana 17 Ap. 1858; *Susanna*, b. 9 Sep. 1805, m. Stephen N. Johnson, pub. 3 Feb. 1823; *Selinda*, b. 1 May 1809, m. Cyrus Doubleday of Dana; *Ruby*, b. 10 Nov. 1811, m. Erastus Thayer 26 May 1830. MOSES the f. d. —— 1842.

9. JOEL, s. of David (6), m. Eunice Richardson 2 Sep. 1821, and had *Charles L.*, b. about 1830, d. unm. 25 Mar. 1879, a. 48; *Eliza E.*, b. about 1840, m. Peebles Johnson 21 May 1861. JOEL the f. d. 28 or 29 Jan. 1864; his w. Eunice d. at N. Brk. 9 Oct. 1869, a. 68, and was buried here.

10. MOSES, s. of Moses (8), m. Eunice Knowles 6 Ap. 1823, and had *Harriet K.*, b. about 1824, m. S. Osborn Brown of Fitchburg 1 May 1845; *Mary Maria*, b. about 1827, m. S. Osborn Brown, then of Springf., 5 June 1850; also *Moses K.*, *Susan*, *Albert*, and *Charles*.

11. JOSEPH, s. of Moses (8), m. Deborah, dau. of George Haskell, 15 Ap. 1824, and had *Emily R.*, b. about 1825, m. John Haven, and d. at Boston 8 June 1856. JOSEPH the f. was a colonel of militia, and deacon of the church. He rem. to Springfield about 1842.

LUCY, of Westborough, m. Moses Pratt 16 Nov. 1747. MOSES, brother of James (4), m. Catherine Forbush 25 May 1758. SARAH, m. Shearjashub Spooner of Pet. 21 May 1760. MARY, m. Joseph Warner 14 Nov. 1764. LYDIA, m. Ephraim Cleveland, Jr., 15 Nov. 1770. HANNAH, m. David Leonard of "No. 5" (Cummington) 15 Feb. 1773. RACHEL, m. Joshua Johnson 12 Aug. 1798. LEVI, m. Betsey Warner 21 Aug. 1803. BETSEY of Grafton m. James W. Jenkins, pub. 1 Jan. 1804. MARIA A., m. James H. Sturtevant, pub. 1 July 1853. CHARLOTTE S., m. William E. Dart, pub. 30 Mar. 1858.

WHITAKER, FRANKLIN, a clergyman, m. Mary, dau. of Franklin Ruggles, 1 June 1843, and had *Mary*, b. here 19 Ap. 1844, d. 16 Dec. 1850; *Helen*, b. in Janesville, Wis., 2 Mar. 1848, d. 17 Aug. 1850; *Franklin*, b. in Janesville 11 Jan. 1850, d. 20 July 1857; *Willie*, b. here 19 Aug. 1851, d. 26 Nov. 1853; *Ellen*, b. in Janesville 16 Sep. 1853, d. 28 Jan. 1854.

2. IRA W., by w. ——, had *Charles Eastman*, b. 11 Aug. 1845; a son b. 7 Feb. 1848; *Lucy Maria*, b. 11 June 1850.

WHITCOMB, JAMES, s. of Robert and grandson of John, was b. at Scituate about 1668, where he m. Mary Parker in 1694, and had *James*, b. 31 Aug. 1695, d. young; *Nathaniel* and *James*, twins, b. the former on the 19th and the latter on the 21st of August 1697, as the Scituate Records distinctly show; *Mary* and *Joanna*, twins, b. 22 Mar. 1^{699}_{700} (of whom *Mary* m. —— Davis, and *Joanna* m. —— Chapman); *Robert*, b. ——, named in his father's will 22 Sep. 1727. JAMES the f. was a "set-work cooper," rem. from Scituate to Rochester, where he d. 26 June 1728, a. 60; his w. Mary d. 30 Nov. 1729, a. 62.

2. NATHANIEL, s. of James (1), m. Rosilla Coombs 21 Jan. 1722-3; she d. 8 Mar. 1737-8, and he m. Phebe Blackman 27 July 1738. His chil. were *Joanna*, b. 6 June 1725, m. Silas Dean 13 Sep. 1744; *Mary*, b. 9 Oct. 1727, m. Paul Dean 4 Dec. 1745, and (2d) Deac. Daniel Spooner 16 Oct. 1780, and d. 9 May 1822; *Dorcas*, b. 8 Mar. 1729-30, m. Solomon Aiken 8 Feb. 1749-50, and d. 10 Dec. 1803; *Nathaniel*, b. 26 May 1732; *Rosilla*, b. 19 Feb. 1733-4, m. George Paige 4 June 1752, and (2d) Capt. William Breckenridge of Ware 17 Mar. 1790, and d. 29 Oct. 1807; *Asa*, b. 29 Feb. 1735-6; *John*, b. 14 Feb. 1737-8, prob. d. young; *Lot*, b. 2 May 1739; *Content*, b. 27 Oct. 1740, m. Solomon Bush of Ware 27 Nov. 1767. NATHANIEL the f. was a cooper, rem. with his family from Rochester to Hardwick about 1742, was selectman five years between 1745 and 1759, assessor three years, and d. 18 Mar. 1772, a. 74; his head-stone remains standing in the old cemetery.

3. JAMES, s. of James (1), m. Mercy, dau. of Deac. Samuel Winslow of Roch., 15 Aug. 1721; she d. 20 Sep. 1726, a. 21, and he m. Joanna, dau. of William Spooner of Dartm., 12 July 1727; she d. ——, and he m. Mercy, dau. of Capt. Josiah Winslow of Freetown, pub. 15 Nov. 1728; she d. 20 Ap. 1729, a. 28, and he m. Sarah, widow of Thomas Lincoln and dau. of Major Edward Winslow of Roch., 31 May 1731 (three of these wives were cousins to each other). His chil., all by his last wife, were *James*, b. 3 Mar. 1731-2, a soldier in the French War, killed at Gaspereau, N. S., 24 July 1755;[1] *Thomas*, b. 2 Dec. 1733, d. at Western —— 1770; *Sarah*, b. 26 Oct. 1735; *Mercy*, b. 26 Aug. 1737; *Scottoway*, b. 1 June 1739; *Robert*, b. 1 May 1741; *Nathan*, bap. 25 Sep. 1743; also *Edward* and *Mary*, named in their father's will. JAMES the f. owned land in Hk., and seems to have res. here a short time; he rem. from Roch. to Western (now Warren) about 1743, where he d. between 30 Aug. and 16 Dec. 1763; his w. Sarah was living 28 Feb. 1771, when her dower was assigned.

4. ROBERT, s. of James (1), m. Joanna Lawrence 13 Jan. 1731-2, and had *Elizabeth*, b. 11 Nov. 1732, m. William Powers of Hk. 16 Nov. 1758; *Joshua*, b. 19 Nov. 1734; *Joanna*, b. 29 May 1737, m. Isaiah Hatch 31 Jan. 1756, and rem. to Hk.; and prob. others. ROBERT the f. res. at Rochester.

5. NATHANIEL, s. of Nathaniel (2), m. Margaret Aiken 19 June 1755; she d. ——, and he m. Mrs. Mary Freeman 17 Oct. 1779. His chil. were *Dorcas*, b. 16 June 1756, d. unm. 3 Jan. 1777; *Lucy*, b. 18 Mar. 1758; *Margaret*, bap. 8 June 1760; *Phebe*, bap. 24 Oct. 1762; *Abigail*, bap. 9 Dec. 1764. NATHANIEL the f. rem. to Gr. before 1779.

6. ASA, s. of Nathaniel (2), m. Joanna, dau. of Benjamin Raymond, 15 Mar. 1759, and had *Rhoda*, b. 22 July 1760, m. Ephraim Briggs at Barnard, Vt., 18 Ap. 1780; *John*, b. 17 Sep. 1761; *Chapman*, b. 5 Mar. 1765; *Anthony*, b. 17 June 1766; *Asa Barnard*, b. 23 Aug. 1770; *Joanna*, b. 11 July 1773; *Benjamin*, b. about 1775 (the four last named d. before 1809, and their names are inscribed together on a head-stone at Barnard); *Philocles*, b. in Barnard 27 June 1776, and the record describes him as "the first child that was born in this town." ASA the f. was a very active man, and the principal leader in the settlement of Barnard. He was the agent of the proprietors for the sale of their land, and induced a large number of his relatives and neighbors to remove thither; so many, indeed, that on the organization of that town all the principal town officers, with perhaps a single exception, were Hardwick men. He was selectman, 1778, the first justice of the peace, 1778, representative, 1779, and a leading spirit through life. He d. 31 Mar. 1812, a. 76. On his head-stone it is inscribed that "he was one of the framers of the Constitution of this State, one of the first settlers of this town, and a main pillar of its infant settlement; and during the struggle for independence was a firm supporter of the cause of his country."[2]

[1] July 25, 1755. "Lieut. Wilson came from Gaspereau; brings an account that one of Capt. Cobb's men were killed passing from the fort to the village on his horse; he and his horse were both killed; his name was Whitcum; he came from Hardwike." "Diary of Dr. John Thomas," *N. E. Gen. Reg.*, xxxiii. 390.

[2] I remember Mr. Whitcomb as a muscular man, with features indicating great energy of character. He had also a fund of humor, and sometimes expressed his

7. Lot, s. of Nathaniel (2), m. Lydia Nye of N. Br. 9 Dec. 1762, and had *Betty*, b. 28 Sep. 1763; *Mehetabel*, b. 2 Ap. 1765, d. 13 Ap. 1765; *Branch*, bap. 6 Dec. 1767; *Nathaniel*, bap. 26 July 1772; *Lot*, bap. 5 Mar. 1775; *Justus* and *Lydia*, bap. 15 Aug. 1779; *James*, bap. 9 Dec. 1781. Lot the f. rem. to Barnard, and was a member of the "Committee of Safety" (by which the first town meeting was called) in 1778. Perhaps he did not remove his family so early.

8. Moses, prob. s. of Robert (4), m. Sarah Powers 4 Nov. 1762, and had *Judith*, b. 10 Aug. 1763; *Charles*, b. 23 Sep. 1765; *Joshua*, b. 18 May 1768; *Calvin*, bap. 17 Nov. 1776; *Luther*, bap. 16 Aug. 1778; *Moses*, bap. 18 Feb. 1781.

9. Benjamin F., by w. Sarah H., had *Maria*, b. 2 Nov. 1874.

Olive, m. Rufus Carpenter of Woodstock 27 Feb. 1777. Nathaniel, Jr., of Gr., perhaps the same as Nathaniel (5), m. Salome Snow, pub. 26 Ap. 1789. Charles, recommended to the church in Rochester, Vt., 5 Feb. 1797.

White, John (s. of John who was buried at Hatfield 15 Sep. 1665, and grandson of John, who came to N. E. in 1632, res. at Cambridge, Hartford, and Hadley, was elder of the church in Hartford, and d. there between 17 Dec. 1683 and 23 Jan. 1684), was b. in Hatfield 1663, m. Hannah, dau. of Thomas Wells, 7 July 1687, and had *John*, b. 26 Sep. 1689, and d. in West Springfield 1759; *Mary*, b. 3 Jan. 1692, d. young; *Hannah*, b. 26 Mar. 1695, m. John Hastings 14 July 1720; *Mary*, b. —— 1697, prob. d. young; *Jonathan*, b. 18 Sep. 1700, d. in Hebron, Conn., 28 Mar. 1776; *Sarah*, b. ——, m. Philip Smith 11 Jan. 1722, and was m. twice afterwards; *Elizabeth*, b. ——, m. Daniel White 19 Jan. 1726, and d. 4 July 1770, a. about 65; *Martha*, b. 14 Mar. 1708, m. Joseph Olmstead of Bolton, Conn., in 1732; *David*, b. 1 July 1710. John the f. was a deacon of the church in Hatfield. In his old age he rem. here, and d. 13 Nov. 1750, a. 87. His head-stone stands by the side of that which was erected in the old cemetery in memory of his son the Rev. David White. He was born at an earlier date than any other person whose head-stone is to be found here.[1]

2. David, s. of John (1), m. Susanna, "granddaughter of the first Thomas Wells of Deerfield, and it is believed that her name was Wells; she was brought up in the family of her uncle, the second Thomas Wells of Deerfield."[2] His chil. were *Thomas Wells*, b. 12 Aug. 1739; *Sarah*, b. 29 May 1741, m. Rev. Lemuel Hedge 5 Nov. 1761, res. in Warwick, and is said to have d. in Middlebury, Vt., in 1808 (*Mem. of Elder John White, etc.*); *Susanna*, b. 30 Aug. 1743, m. Jonathan Danforth 19 Ap. 1770, and d. 14 Nov. 1779; *John*, b. 11 June 1745, grad. H. C. 1765, m. Sally, dau. of James Brown of Worc., pub. 26 Dec. 1784, rem. before 25 Mar. 1785 to Worc., was styled "major," and d. —— 1796. David the f. grad. Y. C. 1730, was ordained as the first pastor of the church in Hardwick 17 Nov. 1736, and d. in office 6 Jan. 1784, a. nearly 74; he was a thoroughly good man, but by no means brilliant. His w. Susanna d. 17 July 1783, a. 69, and her memory was blessed by all who survived her, as both brilliant and good. The parsonage, or "minister's lot," was half a mile northerly from the meeting-house, at the place marked "E. Cutler" on the R. Map; it contained two hundred acres of land, and included the farms afterwards owned by Dr. William Cutler and Mr. Timothy Hathaway. Mr. White sold this estate in 1777, and bought a house a few rods north of the Common (with 35 acres of land), at or near the place marked "P. Hammond" on the R. Map, where he died.

shrewd remarks in rhyme. For example: on one occasion when the wife of one of his friends was giving free vent to her impatience and vexation, he gravely asked his friend what he thought of Doctor Humgrum's prayer: —

"Ye Gods, ye gave to me a wife,
Out of your wonted favor,
To be the comfort of my life,
And I was glad to have her,

But if your mightiness' divine
For higher good design her,
Into your hands, at any time,
I'm ready to resign her."

To which his friend replied, "I think he spoke like a Christian and a man of sense too."

[1] For a more full account of this family, see Judd's *Hist. of Hadley*, pp. 594-596.

[2] *Memorials of Elder John White and of his Descendants.*

3. THOMAS WELLS, s. of David (2), m. Naoma Wood of Northfield, pub. 14 Oct. 1764, and had in Hardwick, *David*, b. 4 Dec. 1765; *Thomas*, b. 26 July 1767; *Theodosia*, b. 19 Aug. 1769; *Naoma*, b. 13 Sep. 1771; *Rhoda*, b. 17 Oct. 1773; *Sally*, b. 11 Feb. 1776; and in Barnard, *Susanna*, b. 28 Dec. 1780; *Hannah* and *John*, twins, b. 13 Jan. 1783; *Olcott*, b. 9 Jan. 1786; *Samuel*, b. 1 Nov. 1788. All these chil. married, and their numerous descendants are scattered through Vermont, New York, and Ohio. THOMAS WELLS the f. grad. H. C. 1759, taught school and kept a store in Hardwick, was town clerk eight years, and assessor four years, until Sep. 1777, when he resigned both offices. About this time he rem. to Barnard, Vt., and on the organization of that town, 9 Ap. 1778, he was elected its first town clerk and held that office several years. "In 1799 he removed to Ohio, and settled in Roxbury, now Waterford, Washington Co., where he lived with his son *David*, and died there 3 Sep. 1815." *Mem. of Elder John White*, etc.

4. JOHN, JR., lineage not ascertained, by w. Abigail, had *Thomas*, b. 27 Oct. 1787; *Abigail*, b. 3 Ap. 1789.

5. ELIAS, of Barre, m. Hope, dau. of Sylvanus Cobb, 2 Oct. 1789, and had (born here) *Lucy W.*, b. about 1791, m. Perley Blanchard of N. Br. 31 Dec. 1812, and d. at Brk. 19 Ap. 1875; *Betsey*, b. 15 Jan. 1793, m. Jonah Howe 21 Sep. 1812; *Noah W.*, b. 9 July 1795; *Frederick*, b. 7 May 1797; *George M.*, b. 1 May 1805, d. 19 Sep. 1833. ELIAS the f. d. 22 Aug. 1810, a. 50; his w. Hope d. 29 June 1860, a. 91.

6. NOAH W., s. of Elias (5), m. Anna Lawrence 5 Nov. 1826, and had a dau. b. 22 Sep. 1845, and prob. others. He d. at Brk. 1 July 1872, a. 77; his w. Anna d. 24 Jan. 1868, a. 65.

7. JOSIAH, m. Helen J. Granger 26 May 1863, and had *George Anson*, b. 21 May 1864; *Mary Frances*, b. 18 May 1867; *Hattie Virginia*, b. 5 Oct. 1869; *Charles William*, b. 27 Feb. 1872, d. 19 Oct. 1876.

SARAH, m. John Perkins 23 July 1777. JOHN, m. Polly Clark 19 Nov. 1795. Dr. JOSEPH, m. Beersheba Jenney of New Bedford, pub. 30 June 1799. NOAH, of Barre, m. Mivina, dau. of Sylvanus Cobb, 8 Feb. 1807; she d. at Barre, 10 Oct. 1850, a. 64. LAURISTON, m. Elizabeth O. Felton of N. Br., pub. 20 June 1855. MARY ANN, m. Charles B. Conant of Springf., 18 May 1864. CAROLINE, m. Isaac S. Bemis of Pittsford, Vt., 24 May 1866. MITCHELL m. Mary A. Laro 1 Jan. 1867. WILLIAM, m. Rose Bennett 28 Aug. 1871.

WHITING, EBENEZER, m. Abigail Bryant, pub. — Sep. 1797, and had *Isabella*, b. in Williamsburg 4 Sep. 1798, m. Southworth Jenkins Mann, pub. 19 Nov. 1827, and d. 31 May 1869; also (born here) *Lucius*, b. 18 Dec. 1800, d. unm. 1 Jan. 1833; *Calvin*, b. 28 May 1803, d. unm. 25 Feb. 1829; *Joseph Warren*, b. 24 Ap. 1805, d. unm. 1 June 1834; *Olive Packard*, b. 1 May 1807, m. Walter Mandell 30 Nov. 1837, d. s. p. 29 July 1838; *Lemuel*, b. 13 Nov. 1809, d. unm. at Buffalo, N. Y., 15 Jan. 1835. EBENEZER the f. was a bricklayer, and d. 6 July 1811, a. 42; his w. Abigail m. Jesse Paige 20 May 1812, and d. 29 July 1856, a. 79.

ABIGAIL, m. Stephen Morton 15 Ap. 1805. CALVIN, d. 24 Ap. 1803, a. 16. Widow ABIGAIL, d. 6 Feb. 1818, a. 74. These were prob. the sister, brother, and mother of EBENEZER.

WICKER, JACOB, "m. Abiah Washburn, sister of Col. Seth, 1747, and moved to Hardwick." (Washburn's *Hist. Leicester*, p. 408.) She d. here 30 June 1812, a. 86.

2. JAMES (perhaps from Leicester), by w. Martha, had *Lucinda*, b. 22 Oct. 1773; *Patty*, b. 3 Ap. 1775; *Joel*, b. 1 Oct. 1779; *Betsey*, b. 8 Ap. 1781; *Sophia*, b. 6 Ap. 1783.

3. WILLIAM, prob. s. of Jacob (1), m. Susanna Parker of Paxton, pub. 23 Feb. 1772, and had *Jacob*, b. 20 Feb. 1773; *Susanna*, b. 7 Sep. 1774, m. Seth Willis 12 Oct. 1794; *John*, b. 18 Aug. 1776; *Lavina*, b. 7 Feb. 1779, m. William Bassett, Jr., 28 Nov. 1799; *Pliny*, b. 23 Ap. 1781; *Lemuel*, b. 9 July 1783; *Ira*, b. 26 July 1785; *William*, b. 22 Ap. 1788; *Lucy*, b. 9 Oct. 1790, m. Justus Jenney 19 Feb. 1811; *Melinda*, b. 2 Aug. 1796.

4. JOHN, s. of William (3), m. Priscilla Collins 15 Nov. 1803, and had *Charles Augustus*, b. 3 Sep. 1804; *Daniel Wright*, b. 28 Feb. 1806.

5. Lemuel, s. of William (3), m. Mary P., dau. of Moses Hunt, 15 Jan. 1811; she d. 14 Oct. 1812, and he m. Sarah, dau. of George Haskell, 5 Oct. 1813. His chil. were *Mary*, bap. 12 Oct. 1812, d. 28 Oct. 1812, a. 3 months; *Cyrus Washburn*, bap. 9 Oct. 1814. Lemuel the f. rem. to Bridport, Vt., soon after 1814.

6. Ira, s. of William (3), settled at Bridport, Vt., m. Mary, dau. of George Haskell, 1 Oct. 1812, and had *Lydia Emeline*, b. ——, d. here 31 Jan. 1818, a. 1 year.

Luther, m. Catherine Johnson, pub. 19 June 1780. Mary (or Mercy), dau. of Frederick and Susan, m. Abner Giffin, pub. 20 Dec. 1813, and d. at Ware, 29 Jan. 1865, a. 80. Eunice, m. Barnabas Snow, pub. 3 Feb. 1817. Joseph, d. 10 Dec. 1795, a. 26. Widow Susanna, d. 20 Aug. 1809, a. 47.

Wiley, Albert L., m. Ellen M., dau. of Harrison G. O. Monroe, 2 June 1865, and had *Nelly* (or *Nettie*), b. —— 1866, d. 11 Nov. 1872, a. 6; *Lura Augusta*, b. 12 Ap. 1870; *Harry L.*, b. 27 May 1873, d. 6 June 1873; *Nelly Amelia*, b. 27 July 1874; *Albert L.*, b. 2 July 1877; *Edward Everett*, b. 30 Dec. 1880.

Willard, Josiah, by w. Dinah, had *Martha*, b. 22 May 1762.

Willis, Samuel, of Dartmouth, m. Mehetabel Gifford 24 Mar. 1712-13, and had *Eliakim*, b. 9 Jan. 1713-14, grad. H. C. 1735, elected pastor of the church in Malden 16 Oct. 1751, and d. in office 14 Mar. 1801, a. nearly 88; *Hannah*, b. 20 Jan. 1715-16; *Benjamin*, b. 13 May 1718; *Zerviah*, b. 23 June 1720; *Abigail*, b. 31 Jan. 1721-2, d. 8 Ap. 1722; *Jabez*, b. 12 Oct. 1723, d. 13 Jan. 1723-4; *Samuel*, b. 6 Jan. 1724-5; *Ebenezer*, b. 23 Oct. 1726; *Mehetabel*, b. 1 July 1729; *Jireh*, b. 26 Sep. 1731. Samuel the f. was a colonel and justice of the peace, and was admitted as an associate proprietor of Hardwick, 27 Dec. 1732.

2. Benjamin, s. of Samuel (1), m. Hannah, dau. of Samuel Spooner, 30 Mar. 1743; and had in Dartm. *Rebecca*, b. 20 Mar. 1743-4, m. James Wing 13 Aug. 1772, and d. 21 Oct. 1823; *Lemuel*, b. 30 Ap. 1745; *Abigail*, b. 17 July 1746, m. Ebenezer Childs of N. Sal. 26 Dec. 1769; *Hannah*, b. 29 Oct. 1748, m. Joseph Weeks 10 May 1775; also (born here) *Mehetabel*, b. 27 Nov. 1750, m. Lemuel Bryant of Wardsboro', Vt., 27 Oct. 1793, and d. here 30 July 1797; *Mary*, b. 29 Ap. 1752, m. Nathan Swift of Barre 8 Sep. 1773; *Zerviah*, b. 1 May 1754, m. John Keith 21 Oct. 1782. Benjamin the f. was a farmer and captain, rem. here from Dartm. 1748, res. near Barre, and d. about 1756; his w. Hannah d. 6 Feb. 1812, a. 92.

3. Lemuel, s. of Benjamin (2), m. Rebecca, dau. of Lemuel Berry, 27 May 1771, but had no children. He was for many years an innholder on the turnpike, three quarters of a mile northerly from the Common, at the place marked "Dr. Wardwell" on the R. Map. He was a selectman two years, assessor sixteen years, and town clerk nineteen years. In his old age he found it necessary to receive alms from the town which he had served so long and so faithfully. He d. 25 Ap. 1829, a. 84; his w. Rebecca d. 16 Ap. 1826, a. 78.

4. Ebenezer, of Middleborough, was adm. to the church there 25 July 1758; he m. Mary Jackson, who d. here 5 July 1810, a. 74, and he m. Rebecca Lane of Gr., pub. 13 May 1811. His chil. were *Ebenezer; John; Seth; Mary* (d. before 1810); *Hannah*, m. Jabez Green of Lincoln —— 1786; *Kezia*, m. Samuel L. Robinson 20 June 1793, and d. 13 July 1856, a. 80. Ebenezer the f. rem. here before 9 Sep. 1781, when he became a member of the church, and was elected deacon 12 May 1785. He res. on the road to Enfield, and d. 5 Feb. 1813, a. 78.

5. Seth, s. of Ebenezer (4), m. Susanna, dau. of William Wicker, 12 Oct. 1794, and had *John*, b. 6 Nov. 1795; *Joseph*, b. 14 Jan. 1797; *Lavina*, b. 5 July 1798; *Thomas Jefferson*, b. 11 Jan. 1800; *William Wicker*, b. ——, d. 12 May 1812, a. 9 months; an infant, d. 14 June 1815, a. 4 days. Seth the f. was deacon of the Baptist Church from 1801 to 1811, and res. with or near his father.

6. James R., parentage not ascertained, by w. Malvina, had *Leander*, b. 27 Jan. 1848.

7. JAMES M., by w. Hannah M., had *Eliza S.*, b. 28 Sep. 1849; *Frank Willard*, b. 10 Sep. 1851; *Delia Maria*, b. 31 Mar. 1853.

8. DIMMICK, JR., m. Mary E. Marsh, pub. 2 Nov. 1851, and had *Willard Francis*, b. 8 Ap. 1852. His w. Mary E. d. 15 Oct. 1860, a. 32.

EDMUND, was pub. to Mercy Fuller of Oakham 26 Feb. 1775, and again 23 Feb. 1777; recommended to the church in Woodstock, Vt., 30 July 1789. OLIVE, m. James Hawkes of Pet. 7 Mar. 1776. SILAS, JR., m. Ruth Wright of Brk., pub. 29 Nov. 1778. HANNAH, m. Atwood Aiken 9 Dec. 1779. ADAM, m. Ann Finton of N. Br. 14 Dec. 1785. BETSEY, m. Moses Hawkes of N. Br. 11 Oct. 1787. THOMAS, m. Anna Rice 16 Nov. 1800. HANNAH, m. Dr. Elliott Beckwith, pub. 2 Mar. 1812. Dr. WILLIAM H., m. Abigail A. Sabin of Bel. pub. 17 Sep. 1842.

WILSON, JOHN, by w. Lilly, had *Alexander*, b. 3 Feb. 1742–3; *Oliver*, b. 14 Jan. 1744–5; *John*, bap. 21 Dec. 1746; *Sarah*, bap. 2 Ap. 1749; *David*, bap. 24 Feb. 1754. JOHN the f. prob. res. on the east side of the river, now New Braintree.

2. ROBERT, by w. Matilda, had *Ann Maria*, b. 2 Dec. 1855.

CALEB, m. Polly Flagg 6 Oct. 1791. PATTY, m. James Lawton 12 Ap. 1804. HANNAH W., of Southbridge, m. Elder Joseph Glazier, pub. 11 Ap. 1834. MARY ANN, dau. of Charles, d. 7 Dec. 1838, a. 2.

WINCHESTER, BENJAMIN, of Grafton (perhaps previously of Roxbury), executed his will 25 Dec. 1758, proved 1 July 1762, in which he named wife Elizabeth, and chil. *Thomas*, *Benjamin*, *Joshua* (deceased), *Joseph*, *Sarah*, *Anna*, and *Mary*. The sons *Thomas* and *Benjamin* had already rem. to Hardwick.

2. THOMAS, s. of Benjamin (1), by w. Mary, had *Moses*, b. 5 Sep. 1749, m. Margery Forbush 9 Mar. 1780, d. 11 Mar. 1831; *Thomas*, b. 1 Sep. 1751, d. 24 Ap. 1753; *Mary*, b. 10 Ap. 1753, m. Elijah Washburn 1 Jan. 1778; *Prudence*, b. 10 Oct. 1755, m. Oliver Bailey of Cummington 3 June 1779; *Elizabeth*, b. 14 Mar. 1760, m. Theodorus Forbes of Wilmington 22 Jan. 1781; *Thomas*, b. 9 Dec. 1763. THOMAS the f. d. 10 Jan. 1787, a. 65; his w. Mary d. 29 Sep. 1803, a. 82.

3. BENJAMIN, s. of Benjamin (1), m. Sarah, dau. of Deac. Joseph Allen, 19 Feb. 1761, and had *Prudence*, b. 17 Oct. 1762, m. Jonas Allen (then of Sutton) 15 Feb. 1781, d. here 19 Dec. 1797; *Sarah*, b. 16 Aug. 1767, m. Jonas Allen 29 Aug. 1798, d. 10 May 1802; *Benjamin*, b. 2 Dec. 1769. BENJAMIN the f. d. suddenly, while on a journey, at the house of his brother in Grafton, 6 Jan. 1771, a. about 45.

4. JOSHUA, s. of Benjamin (1), by w. Mary, had *Sarah*, b. 17 Aug. 1753. JOSHUA the f. d. before 25 Dec. 1758.

5. THOMAS, s. of Thomas (2), m. Patience Dennis 23 Dec. 1787, and had *Anson*, b. — Nov. 1788, d. 22 Ap. 1790; *Anson*, b. 3 Dec. 1790; prob. *Thomas Elliott*, b. about 1792, and bap. (adult) 2 Ap. 1820; *David*, b. — Mar. 1795, d. 12 Nov. 1796. THOMAS the f. d. about 1812; his w. Patience d. 5 Oct. 1809, a. 40.

6. BENJAMIN, s. of Benjamin (3), m. Rebecca, dau. of James Wing, 31 May 1801, and had *Russell*, b. 25 Feb. 1802; *Hiram*, b. 8 Dec. 1803; *Benjamin Franklin*, b. 9 Mar. 1810; *Rebecca Wing*, b. 30 Jan. 1814, d. 29 Oct. 1814; *Caroline*, b. 30 Aug. 1816.

7. ANSON, s. of Thomas (5), m. Harriet, dau. of Elijah Carpenter, 2 Sep. 1812, and had *Thomas Dennis*, b. 22 July 1813; *Moses Dwight*, b. 13 Oct. 1815; *Elijah Carpenter*, b. 15 Sep. 1817; *Elliott*, b. 22 Mar. 1821; *Lewis*, b. 10 July 1823; *Lucius*, b. 14 Mar. 1826. ANSON the f. was elected deacon of the church 10 Mar. 1824, and rem. to Mendon, N. Y., about 1830.

WING, JAMES, had w. Ruth, who d. about 1771, and he m. Rebecca, dau. of Capt. Benjamin Willis, 13 Aug. 1772. His chil. were *Sarah*, b. 16 Feb. 1761, m. Elijah Carpenter 1 Feb. 1784, d. 10 Jan. 1842; *Lucy*, b. 26 Nov. 1763, m. Nathan Chandler of Rochester, Vt., pub. 16 Ap. 1786; *Kezia*, b. 19 Sep. 1765, m. Daniel Allen 20 Jan. 1791, and (2d) David Barnard of Shelburne, pub. 1 May 1815; *Nathaniel*, b. 3 Oct. 1767, prob. d. young; *Isaac*, b.

14 June 1770, prob. settled in Rochester, Vt., and m. Betsey, dau. of David Allen, 24 Jan. 1793; *James*, b. 5 July 1773, m. Hannah Wetherbee of Pet. 11 Ap. 1799; *Benjamin*, b. 22 Oct. 1774, m. Rebecca Lee of Barre, pub. 9 Feb. 1801; *Ruth*, b. 28 July 1776, d. unm. at Springf. 2 Nov. 1854; *Rebecca*, bap. 4 July 1779, m. Benjamin Winchester 31 May 1801; *Molly*, bap. 17 June 1781; *John*, bap. 29 June 1783; *Enoch* and *Lina* shared in the division of their father's estate 22 Ap. 1796. JAMES the f. res. on the turnpike, about a mile and three quarters from the Common, at the place marked "Ruth Wing" on the R. Map, where he d. 8 Jan. 1791; his w. Rebecca d. 21 Oct. 1823, a. 79, having received aid from the town for several years.

ROGER, of Williamsburg, m. Polly Dennis 24 May 1790; she d. here 17 Aug. 1790, a. 18.

WINSLOW, KENELM, s. of Edward, and brother of Governor Edward of Plymouth, was born in Droitwich, Worcestershire, England, 29 Ap. 1599, and came to New England prob. in 1629; he res. in Plymouth until about 1641, when he rem. to Marshfield. He m. Ellen, wid. of John Adams, and prob. dau. of —— Newton, — June 1634, and had *Kenelm*, b. about 1636; *Ellen*, b. about 1638, m. Samuel Baker —— 1656, and d. 27 Aug. 1676; *Nathaniel*, b. about 1639; *Job*, b. about 1641. KENELM the f. was a farmer and joiner. He represented Marshfield in the General Court eight years, and held sundry minor offices. He d. at Salem (where he had perhaps resorted for medical aid, having long been sick) 12 Sep. 1672, a. 73. His w. Ellen d. at Marshf. 5 Dec. 1681, a. 83.

2. KENELM, s. of Kenelm (1), settled in what is now Brewster, m. Mercy, dau. of Peter Warden of Yarmouth; she d. 22 Sep. 1688, "in the 48th year of her age," and he m. Damaris ——, who survived him. His chil. were *Kenelm*, b. about 1667, d. at Harwich (Brewster) 20 Mar. 1728–9, a. 61; *Josiah*, b. 7 Nov. 1669, a captain, d. at Freetown 3 Ap. 1761; *Thomas*, b. about 1672, d. 6 Ap. 1689, a. 16; *Samuel*, b. about 1674; *Mercy*, b. about 1676, m. Melatiah White of Rochester, and (2d) Thomas Jenkins of Barnstable before 22 Dec. 1715; *Nathaniel*, b. about 1678, res. in Rochester, Little Compton, and Middleborough, and rem. to Maine; *Edward*, b. 30 Jan. 1681; *Damaris*, b. ——, m. Jonathan Small of Harwich 30 July 1713; *Elizabeth*, b. ——, m. Andrew Clark of Harwich 9 Aug. 1711; *Eleanor*, b. ——, m. Shubael Hamlin of Barnstable 25 Mar. 1719; *John*, b. about 1701, a deacon of the church in Rochester, where he d. about 1755. KENELM the f. d. 11 Nov. 1715 "in the 79th year of his age," and his head-stone stands in a cemetery near his homestead, but within the easterly border of Dennis.

3. NATHANIEL, s. of Kenelm (1), m. Faith, dau. of Rev. John Miller 3 Aug. 1664, and had *Faith*, b. 19 June 1665; *Nathaniel*, b. 29 July 1667; *James*, b. 16 Aug. 1669; *Gilbert*, b. 11 July 1673; *Kenelm*, b. 22 Sep. 1675; *Eleanor*, b. 2 July 1677, m. John Jones; *Josiah*, b. 21 July 1681, buried 16 May 1682; *John*, b. 13 Jan. 1683–4. NATHANIEL the f. inherited the Marshfield homestead, was a captain, and representative in the General Court four years. He d. 1 Dec. 1719, a. 80; his w. Faith d. 9 Nov. 1729, a. 84.

4. JOB, s. of Kenelm (1), by w. Ruth, had *William*, b. ——, d. s. p. shortly before 8 Mar. 1757, when his will was proved; *Richard*, b. ——, a physician, d. 1727 or 1728; *James*, b. 9 May 1687; *Mary*, b. 1 Ap. 1689, prob. d. young; *George*, b. 2 Jan. 1690–1; *Jonathan*, b. 22 Nov. 1692; *Joseph*, b. ——; *John*, b. 20 Feb. 1694–5; *Elizabeth*, b. ——, m. John Marshall. JOB the f. settled in Swansey, where his house was burned by the Indians at the commencement of Philip's War; he then rem. to Freetown, where he was selectman in 1686, town clerk in 1690, and representative in 1686 and 1692. He was also lieutenant of militia, and d. 14 July 1720, a. about 80; his w. Ruth survived.

5. SAMUEL, s. of Kenelm (2), m. Bethia Holbrook of Scituate 26 Sep. 1700; she d. ——, and he m. Mercy King of Scituate 11 Nov. 1703; she d. 16 Feb. 1733, and he was pub. to Ruth Briggs 15 Sep. 1739. His chil. were *Mercy*, b. 16 Aug. 1705, m. James Whitcomb 15 Aug. 1721, and d. 20 Sep. 1726; *Elizabeth*, b. 29 Jan. 1706–7; *Ann*, b. 12 Feb. 1708–9, m. Roland Hammond, pub. 1 May 1731; *Thomas*, b. 7 June 1711; *Kenelm*, b. 20 Feb. 1712–13; *Judith*, b. 8

July 1716. SAMUEL the f. was early styled cordwainer, afterwards yeoman, res. in Roch., and was deacon of the church as early as 1710. He was living 18 June 1750, and prob. soon afterwards followed his sons to Hardwick.

6. EDWARD, s. of Kenelm (2), by w. Sarah, had *Edward*, b. 6 Nov. 1703, a farmer and captain, inherited the homestead, m. Hannah, dau. of his uncle Kenelm Winslow of Harwich, 14 Dec. 1728; she d. 23 Sep. 1745, and he m. Rachel, dau. of his uncle Josiah Winslow of Freetown, 1 May 1746; she d. 28 Dec. 1766, and he m. Mrs. Hannah Winslow of Dighton, pub. 9 Aug. 1767; he d. 7 May 1780 (his dau. Hannah, b. 6 May 1740, m. John Paige of Hardwick, pub. 24 Dec. 1764); *Mehetabel*, b. 6 May 1705, m. Col. Thomas Winslow, son of her uncle, Kenelm Winslow of Harwich, 12 Feb. 1722-3; *Sarah*, b. —— 1707, m. Thomas Lincoln, who d. in Rochester 15 June 1730, and she m. James Whitcomb 31 May 1731, rem. to Western (Warren), and was living there 28 Feb. 1771; *Lydia*, b. 8 Sep. 1709, m. Deac. James Foster 10 July 1729, and d. at Roch. 7 Jan. 1770 (her dau. Mary, b. 11 Ap. 1732, m. Col. Timothy Paige of Hardwick 24 Oct. 1754, and d. at N. Br. 21 July 1825, a. 93); *Mercy*, b. 1 Sep. 1712, m. Chillingsworth Foster, Esq., of Harwich (Brewster) 10 Oct. 1730, and d. 25 Jan. 1757; *Thankful*, b. 2 Ap. 1715, m. Josephus Hammond 10 Ap. 1735, and d. before 2 Oct. 1758. EDWARD the f. res. in Roch., was a farmer, and engaged in "the making and forging of iron;" he was selectman, town clerk, town treasurer, justice of the peace and of the quorum; he was also major of militia, and was generally designated by his military title. He d. 25 June 1760; his w. Sarah d. 11 Oct. 1767, a. 85.

7. THOMAS, s. of Samuel (5), m. Rebecca Ewer of Barnstable 27 June 1734, and had in Roch. *Samuel*, b. 6 Ap. 1735; *Mercy*, b. 19 Aug. 1736, prob. m. Jonathan Farr 19 Jan. 1757; *Rebecca*, b. 23 Jan. 1737-8, m. Dr. Challis Safford 10 July 1755; *Shubael*, b. 20 Sep. 1739, a soldier in the French War; *Thomas*, b. 11 July 1741; *Judith*, b. 19 Mar. 1743, m. Edward Goodspeed 19 Oct. 1764; *Nathaniel*, b. 6 Oct. 1744; *Thankful*, b. 4 May 1746, d. young; *Hannah*, b. 19 Jan. 1748, prob. m. Benjamin Fish of Gr. 15 Aug. 1770; *Kenelm*, b. 5 Ap. 1749; *Thankful*, b. 2 Sep. 1750; *Jonathan*, b. 3 May 1752; and at Hardwick, *Bethia*, bap. 18 Nov. 1753; *Lucy*, bap. 25 May 1755; *John*, bap. 15 Oct. 1758. THOMAS the f. rem. from Rochester to Hk. about 1752, and at a later period to Pomfret, Vt., where he d. 13 Mar. 1782; his w. Rebecca d. 22 Oct. 1787.

8. KENELM, s. of Samuel (5), m. Elizabeth Clapp of Roch. 21 June 1734, and had *Kenelm*, b. 19 Ap. 1735, d. young; *Elizabeth*, b. 4 May 1737, m. Philip Spooner of Pet. 25 Dec. 1755; *Ann*, b. 29 July 1739, m. —— Dalrymple; *Mary*, b. 14 Oct. 1741, m. —— Whitney; *Susanna*, b. 8 Ap. 1743, m. —— Peckham; *Kenelm*, b. 11 Dec. 1746; *Ebenezer*, b. 8 Sep. 1749; *John Clapp*, b. 27 Mar. 1752, prob. d. young; *Rhoda*, b. 25 Jan. 1754, m. —— Whitney; *Dorcas*, b. 10 May 1756, d. young; *Dorcas*, b. 7 Nov. 1758. The names of all the children, except the first, are entered on the Hardwick records; but most of them were prob. b. in Rochester, from which place KENELM the f. rem. to Hk. about 1749, and res. on the easterly road to Gilbertville between the present residence of Capt. Orin Trow and Mr. Charles Mandell. About 1758 he rem. to Pet., and was an inn-keeper many years. In his will, dated 5 Ap. 1775, and proved 5 May 1777, his wife Elizabeth and eight children, are mentioned.

9. SAMUEL, s. of Thomas (7), m. Martha Goodspeed of Barns. 12 June 1760, and had *Ebenezer*, b. 23 Ap. 1761; *Elizabeth*, b. 1 Mar. 1763. SAMUEL the f. soon afterwards rem. from Hardwick, had several more children, and d. at Pomfret, Vt., 20 Oct. 1800; his w. Martha d. 9 Mar. 1813, a. 74.

10. SETH, grandson of Nathaniel (3), and s. of James who d. at Rochester about 1733, was b. at Plymouth in 1699, m. Abigail Whittredge 23 Oct. 1729, and had at Rochester *Nathaniel*, b. 18 Aug. 1731; *Mary*, b. 18 Oct. 1733, prob. m. James Fay, Jr., 18 Mar. 1756; *Seth*, b. 20 Feb. 1735, a soldier in the French War, and also in the War of the Revolution, and perhaps the same who m. Mary Church of Gr. 23 Nov. 1775; he was living here 11 Nov. 1794, when he sold land formerly belonging to his father; *James*, b. 1 June 1740; also (born here) *Hannah*, b. 9 July 1744; *Bathsheba*, b. 20 June 1747, d. 25 Mar.

1748; *Bathsheba*, b. 6 Ap. 1749, d. 16 Ap. 1749; *Thomas*, b. 18 July 1750; *Charity*, b. 27 Ap. 1752, m. Darius Rice of Gr. 7 Dec. 1780; *Job*, bap. 11 Aug. 1754, m. Margaret Cooley of Gr. 27 July 1780; *Sarah*, b. 9 Sep. 1755, m. James Cleland of Gr. 19 Aug. 1779. SETH the f. was a brazier, came here about 1744, and res. on the road leading from Ruggles Hill to the Mandell place on the turnpike.

11. EZRA (a descendant from Job (4), through Richard of Freetown, b. about 1685, and Hezekiah of Freetown, b. 9 Dec. 1713), was b. 10 May 1751, m. Rosamond, dau. of Thomas Spooner of New London, and had *Thomas*, b. ——; *Susan*, b. ——, m. Abel Babbitt; *Alice*, bap. 16 Nov. 1777, m. Clark Dexter 16 Oct. 1796; *Joseph*, bap. 27 Aug. 1780; *Ezra*, bap. 16 Mar. 1783, a joiner, d. at Ware 27 Mar. 1857; *Rosamond*, b. —— 1785, d. 13 Sep. 1803, a. 18, reputed to have been very beautiful and amiable; *George Rex*, b. —— 1788, a blacksmith, d. at Ware 30 Oct. 1862. EZRA the f. came to Hk. about 1776, and res. between the two roads to Gilbertville, at the place marked "J. Monroe" on the R. Map. He was thrown from a horse and killed 12 Aug. 1789; his w. Rosamond m. Richard Ransom of Woodstock, Vt., pub. 26 Nov. 1801.

12. JOB, prob. brother of Ezra (11), m. Lydia Melvin (or Melville), and had *Timothy*, *Job*, *Melvin*, *Nancy* (d. 13 Ap. 1790, a. 7), and *Jane*, all bap. 30 Aug. 1789. The mother, styled a widow, rem. to Barnard, Vt., before 28 Oct. 1810.

13. JOSEPH W., by w. Sarah Jane, had *Edwin*, b. 16 Nov. 1872; *George Frederick*, b. 7 Feb. 1874, d. young; *George Frederick*, b. 24 Feb. 1875; *Alice I.*, b. 26 Dec. 1878; *Ralph Henry*, b. 2 Oct. 1880, and d. 30 Aug. 1881.

HANNAH, of Gr., m. Thomas Ruggles 19 July 1778. ABIGAIL, m. Abisha Rice of Gr. 20 Feb. 1782. JOANNA, m. Phineas Meigs of Sunderland 3 Aug. 1783. REBECCA, of Barre, m. Moses Hunt, Jr., pub. 20 Oct. 1805. DOLLY, of Ware, m. Reuel Terry, pub. 15 Dec. 1810. CLARAMOND, m. John Hathaway, pub. 10 Nov. 1823. SETH, of Barre, m. Mrs. Mary Allen, pub. 22 Oct. 1826. DAVID L., of Barre, m. Mercy H. Dexter 22 Mar. 1837.

WINTER, JAMES, of Shutesbury, m. Lucia Aiken 6 Dec. 1826. WILLIAM, m. Olive Hudson 5 June 1831. CLARISSA, m. Danforth Trask, pub. 23 Mar. 1833. MELINDA H., m. Joel Dwight Mandell, pub. 28 June 1851. OLIVE A., m. Elijah H. Marsh of Montague 24 July 1862.

WINTERBOTTOM, GEORGE, by w. Euphemia, had *Euphemia*, b. 21 Sep. 1872; *Alice*, b. 1 Sep. 1873; *John*, b. 20 Dec. 1874; *Eva*, b. 12 Jan. 1880, d. 25 Aug. 1880.

ANNIE, m. Edward Parker, Jr., 1 Nov. 1877. THOMAS, m. Mary L. C. Pelletier 6 Dec. 1881.

WISWELL, JOSEPH, by w. Emily, had *Joseph*, b. 30 Sep. 1864.

Mrs. SUSAN (dau. of Samuel Bartholomew), d. 11 Feb. 1869, a. 80, or 81.

WOOD (or WOODS), DAVID, m. Martha Wheeler of Marlb., pub. 11 Feb. 1743-4, and had *Mary*, b. 10 Nov. 1745; *Benjamin*, b. 20 Sep. 1747; *Persis*, b. 25 June 1749; *David*, bap. 6 Feb. 1753.

2. JOSEPH, by w. Tabitha, had *Moses* and *Olive*, both bap. 14 Sep. 1746.

3. JAMES, m. Anne Stephens of Marlb., pub. 5 Oct. 1747, and had *Lydia*, b. 16 Sep. 1748; *Sarah*, bap. 3 Feb. 1750-1.

4. JACOB, by w. ——, had *Josiah* and *Esther*, both bap. 14 Aug. 1749.

5. WILLIAM, m. Polly Nye 15 Nov. 1798, and had *Mary*, b. 14 Aug. 1799; *William Merrick*, b. 17 Aug. 1801.

6. HIRAM M., m. Susan A. Brimhall 18 Aug. 1840, and had *Mary Jane*, b. 13 Aug. 1843; *Abby Almira*, b. 18 July 1851.

7. LIBERTY, by w. Alice, had *Horace Taylor*, b. 5 Feb. 1848; *Mary Eliza*, b. 14 Ap. 1850.

8. CHARLES, m. Sarah C. Spooner 21 Aug. 1851, and had *John Grover*, b. 23 June 1858.

9. PATRICK, by w. Rose Ann, had *James*, b. 19 Feb. 1873.

NAOMA, of Northfield, m. Thomas Wells White, pub. 14 Oct. 1764. AARON, of Gr., m. Sarah Bridge —— 1786. LYDIA, of N. Br., m. David Allen 22

Jan. 1795. NATHANIEL, m. Mrs. Elizabeth Stearns 17 Nov. 1805. CHANDLER, m. Polly Pike 19 Feb. 1806. MARY, m. Samuel Clark of Pet. 13 Mar. 1817. PATIENCE G., m. Alfred W. Coffin of Palmer 15 Nov. 1831. LUCINDA, m. Zenas H. Dexter 28 Aug. 1837. LORING F., of N. Br., m. Mary P. Webb, pub. 5 Sep. 1839. ELIZA C., m. Aretas D. Gilbert of W. Brk., pub. 4 May 1844. SARAH F., m. Asahel B. Lamson, pub. 1 Dec. 1851. HARRIET, of Enf., m. Sumner L. F. Dart, pub. 18 Feb. 1854. GEORGE, of N. Br., m. E. Augusta Fay 6 Feb. 1862. JOSEPHINE, m. Jefferson Murphy 31 Mar. 1872. CHARLES W., of Worc., m. Charlotte E. Wetherell 13 June 1872. ANDREW, JR., m. Mary Billings 2 Feb. 1873. CARRIE E., m. Theodore Manning of Worc. 19 Jan. 1875. NABBY, w. of Nathaniel, d. 18 Sep. 1804, a. 28. ASAHEL (colored), d. 16 Dec. 1822, a. 73.

WOODBURY, MARY, m. Eleazar Packard 9 June 1769. MOLLY, dau. of Hannah, bap. 16 Sep. 1770.

WOODWARD, STEPHEN, of Pet., m. Molly Sibley 13 May 1777. SETH, of Pet., m. Ruth Ayers 25 Aug. 1778. BENJAMIN, m. Mrs. Molly Woodward 17 Jan. 1783. JOEL, of Pet., m. Nancy Comee 17 Aug. 1796. HULDAH, of Pet., m. Jonathan Robinson, pub. 30 Oct. 1808. REBECCA, of Ware, m. Edmund Rogers, pub. 24 Jan. 1820. LUCY M., m. Henry H. Granger 30 Mar. 1837. ELEANOR (a widow, prob. mother of Huldah, who m. Jonathan Robinson), d. 20 Sep. 1817, a. 74. ELIZA, of Ware, d. 10 Sep. 1831, a. 32. ANDREW A., d. 5 July 1857, a. 6.

WORDEN, ABIGAIL, of Pet., m. Joseph Goodell 15 Aug. 1780. SAMUEL, of Pet., m. Betsey Sibley 30 June 1785.

WRIGHT, JAMES, m. Mary, dau. of John Hunt, 18 June 1766, and had *Rhoda*, bap. 15 Dec. 1777. His w. Mary d. 3 Oct. 1779, a. 33.

2. THOMAS MARTIN, brother of James (1), m. Elizabeth, dau. of Timothy Newton, 19 Dec. 1776; she d. at Barnard, 22 (or 23) Sep. 1800, a. nearly 43, and he m. Sarah Black 2 Sep. 1801. His chil. were *Orpha*, b. 4 Mar. 1779; *Elizabeth*, b. 21 (or 22) Sep. 1780; and at Barnard, *Sarah*, b. 15 Feb. 1783; *James*, b. 14 Aug. 1785; *Asenath*, b. 4 Mar. 1788. THOMAS MARTIN the f. was a Revolutionary soldier, rem. to Barnard about 1782, and d. there 22 May 1839, a. 88.

3. SILAS, brother of James (1), m. Mercy Hayford 15 Feb. 1781, and had *Bathsheba*, b. 9 Aug. 1781.

4. GERSHOM P., m. Arathusa M. Robinson of Barre, pub. 10 Feb. 1849, and had *Arloa Malvina*, b. 6 Jan. 1850; *Frank Phinney*, b. 21 Sep. 1852.

MARY, m. Capt. Daniel Warner 31 May 1758. AZARIAH, of Westminster, m. Mary Safford 29 June 1762. PATIENCE, mother of James (1), m. John Hunt 25 Dec. 1765. HULDAH, sister of James (1), m. Southworth Jenkins, of Rut. Dist. (Barre), 15 Nov. 1770. ELIHU, of Westminster, Vt., m. Betsey Wheeler 28 Nov. 1799. JOSEPH, m. Polly Phelps 4 Nov. 1852. PERSIS, m. Nathan W. Robinson 5 Jan. 1853. CHARLES, d. 18 Nov. 1797, a. 67. THANKFUL, w. of Gad, d. 1 Jan. 1852, a. 82. GAD (b. at Brk.), d. 21 or 22 Sep. 1858, a. 84.

WRIN, JOHN, by w. Honora, had *Honora*, b. 25 Nov. 1858; *Johanna*, b. 22 Dec. 1859; *John*, b. 27 Dec. 1861; *Bridget*, b. 1 Feb. 1864; *Caroline*, b. 5 June 1868; *William*, b. 4 Dec. 1875.

2. HUMPHREY, m. Margaret Donahoe, pub. 11 Nov. 1859, and had *Cornelius*, b. 26 May 1862; *Patrick*, b. 29 Ap. 1865; *Johanna*, b. 8 Oct. 1866; *Michael*, b. 5 Ap. 1868.

3. JOHN, by w. Julia, had *Margaret*, b. 31 Aug. 1864.

4. JOHN, by w. Catherine, had *John*, b. 13 June 1872; *Charles*, b. 8 Feb. 1874; *Delia*, b. 4 Sep. 1877; *George Francis*, b. 1 Mar. 1880.

CORNELIUS, m. Margaret Kelly, pub. 8 Nov. 1856. BRIDGET, m. Daniel Breen, pub. 9 July 1862. HUMPHREY, m. Mary Buckley, pub. 5 Ap. 1864. HANNAH (dau. of John), d. 15 Mar. 1859, a. 4 months. CORNELIUS (b. in Ireland), d. 11 Jan. 1870, a. 50. MARY (b. Ire.), d. unm. 17 Feb. 1871, a. 56. JOHN (b. Ire.), d. 20 July 1873, a. 85.

WYATT, DAVID, m. Drusilla Robinson of Barre 9 Jan. 1873.

WYMAN, AMOS H., by w. Lucy L., had *Amos Hiram*, b. 19 Aug. 1839; *Henry Thomas*, b. 27 Feb. 1841; *Lucy Elvira*, b. 3 (or 4) Sep. 1843; *Sarah Jane*, b. 19 Ap. 1850, m. Zenas W. Tolman of Gr. 30 Sep. 1866, and prob. (2d) Alanson Ramsdell 4 June 1874. AMOS H. the f. d. 13 June 1882, a. 74.

THOMAS, d. 10 Feb. 1854, a. 78. HENRY, d. 22 Oct. 1864, a. 23.

YARRINGTON, WILLIAM N., m. Eleanor, dau. of Stephen Morton, 19 May 1836; she d. 16 May 1855, a. 47.

NOTE ON THE MIXTERS.

The early generations of the Mixter Family are displayed by Bond in his Watertown Genealogies. The name was formerly written MIXER. The line of descent to the Hardwick branch of the family, inadvertently omitted in its proper place, is here inserted:—

MIXTER (or MIXER), ISAAC, "aged 31, w. Sarah, a. 33, and son *Isaac*, aged 4 years, embarked at Ipswich, Eng., for New England, Ap. 10 1634." He was "admitted freeman, May 2 1638." His chil. were *Isaac*, b. in England, —— 1630; *Sarah*, b. ——, m. John Stearns, and d. 4 June 1656. ISAAC the f. res. in Watertown, was selectman 1651 and 1655. He "owned one quarter of the vessel Diligent, then at sea, whereof John Shepherd, under God, was master." He d. between 8 May and 19 June 1655; his w. Sarah d. 24 Nov. 1681.

2. ISAAC, s. of Isaac (1), m. Mary Coolidge 19 Sep. 1655; she d. 2 Mar. 1659–60, and he m. Rebecca Garfield 10 Jan. 1660–1; she d. 16 Mar. 1682–3, and he m. Mary, wid. of William French, Esq., —— 1687. His chil. were numerous: *Mary*, b. 18 May 1656, m. George Munnings; *Sarah*, b. 28 Oct. 1657, m. Samuel Hagar; *Rebecca*, b. 9 Mar. 1661–2, m. Samuel Kendall; *Isaac*, b. about 1663; *Elizabeth*, b. 18 June 1665, d. 19 Mar. 1665–6; *Joanna*, b. 14 Dec. 1666, m. Joseph Harrington 7 Nov. 1688; *John*, b. 5 Mar. 1668–9; *George*, b. 20 Jan. 1670–1; *Abigail*, b. — Nov. 1672, m. Samuel Howe 11 Dec. 1690; *Joseph*, b. 9 Aug. 1674; *Daniel*, b. 12 Feb. 1675–6; *Mehetabel*, b. 25 Jan. 1678, d. 22 Nov. 1678; *Benjamin*, b. 23 May 1679; *Dorothy*, b. 2 Sep. 1680, m. William Davis 12 Jan. 1710; *David*, b. 6 Aug. 1683. ISAAC the f. "was selectman many times, 1673 to 1701, and town clerk 1692." He res. in Watertown, and d. 22 Nov. 1716, a. 86; his w. Mary "was living 1735, very aged."

3. JOSEPH, s. of Isaac (2), m. Anne Jones, and had *Rebecca*, b. 22 Feb. 1704, d. 21 Mar. 1704; *Joseph*, b. 14 Dec. 1705; *Sarah*, b. 12 Mar. 1707–8, m. David Learned; *Lydia*, b. 10 June 1710, m. Thomas Warren; *David*, b. and d. in July 1713; *Mary*, b. 25 Oct. 1714, m. David Coolidge; *Josiah*, b. 16 Nov. 1716; *Anna*, b. 14 Aug. 1719, m. Isaac Rice; *Abigail*, b. 26 June 1721, m. Benjamin Bond. JOSEPH the f. res. in Watertown, was deacon of the church, and treasurer of the West Precinct.

4. JOSIAH, s. of Joseph (3), m. Mary Garfield, 7 Aug. 1740; she d. ——, and he m. Mrs. Sarah Mead 10 Ap. 1754. His chil. were *Mary*, b. 5 June 1741; *Samuel*, b. 7 Aug. 1743; *Josiah*, b. 8 Ap. 1745, d. in Lincoln 3 Dec. 1815; *Ann*, b. 8 July 1747; *Mary*, b. 18 Oct. 1749; *Sarah*, b. 16 Dec. 1754, m. Jonathan Hagar; *Persis*, b. 6 Nov. 1756, m. John Perry; *Eunice*, b. 8 Mar. 1760, m. Alpheus Bigelow; *Lois*, b. 12 Sep. 1762, m. Thomas Livermore, and (2d) Thomas Sanderson; *Elijah*, b. 9 June 1764, d. 6 Oct. 1792; *Lydia*, b. 18 Mar. 1766, m. Joel Wellington; *Daniel*, b. 26 Ap. 1769. JOSIAH the f. res. in Waltham, and was selectman three years, 1768–1770.

5. SAMUEL, s. of Josiah (4), m. Elizabeth, dau. of Jason Bigelow of Brookfield, and had *Jason*, *Samuel*, and five daughters, as already stated more particularly on page 423. Through Rebecca, wife of Isaac (2), and Mary, wife of Josiah (4), this family appears to have a double share of the GARFIELD blood, which became so illustrious in the person of the martyred President, whose ancestors were inhabitants of Watertown.

CONCLUSION.

ON examination of the foregoing Genealogical Register, it will be observed that many of the very early inhabitants of Hardwick came from widely distant towns, yet in groups of relatives and friends. The largest group, under the influence of Rev. Timothy Ruggles, came from the Old Colony, notably from Rochester, Dartmouth, Sandwich, Harwich (including Brewster), and Eastham. Another company was from Hampshire County, especially from Hatfield, with whom came the first Pastor of the Church, and the progenitors of General Warner. Another group, under the leadership of Captain Samuel Robinson, came from Grafton, Westborough, Southborough, Shrewsbury, and other towns in that section of the county, more or less connected with each other by the ties of blood and marriage. A smaller number came with Deacon Christopher Paige, from Bedford, Concord, Littleton, and other towns in that region. And, finally, a somewhat numerous and active class came with Captain Eleazar Warner from Brookfield, the only town except Rutland which was then organized in this immediate neighborhood. The names of families coming here from each town have been sufficiently designated in the Register, and need not be repeated. It may be added, that the members of these several groups generally clustered around each other in their habitations; and some of the early controversies in the town, concerning meeting-houses and other public conveniences, may have a more than merely local interpretation.

INDEX

www.ingramcontent.com/pod-product-compliance
Lightning Source LLC
Chambersburg PA
CBHW060546280326
41932CB00011B/1415